Library

EDUCATIONAL TESTING
SERVICE

BIOMETRIKA TABLES FOR STATISTICIANS

VOLUME II

BIOMETRIKA TABLES
FOR
STATISTICIANS

VOLUME II

EDITED BY

E. S. PEARSON

AND

H. O. HARTLEY

BIOMETRIKA TRUST

1976

PUBLISHED BY
BIOMETRIKA TRUST

UNIVERSITY COLLEGE LONDON
GOWER STREET WCIE 6BT
ENGLAND

ISBN. 0 904653 11 0

© Biometrika Trust 1976

First published by Cambridge University Press
for the Biometrika Trust 1972
Reprinted with corrections 1976

First printed in Great Britain at the University Printing House, Cambridge
Reprinted in Great Britain by Lowe and Brydone (Printers) Ltd, Thetford, Norfolk

LIST OF CONTENTS

vi

LIST OF TABLES WITH ASSOCIATED REFERENCES TO THE INTRODUCTION

The references under each table-heading to page numbers in the Introduction are given in two groups: (i) mathematical definition of function, (ii) description of uses of table and, where illustrated numerically, the numbers of the relevant Examples.

I. THE NORMAL PROBABILITY FUNCTION AND CERTAIN DERIVED TABLES

II. TABLES FOR PROCEDURES BASED ON THE USE OF ORDER STATISTICS

VII. TABLES FOR MULTIVARIATE ANALYSIS

VIII. GOODNESS OF FIT TESTS BASED ON THE EMPIRICAL DISTRIBUTION FUNCTION. TESTS OF UNIFORMITY

IX. ANALYSIS OF DIRECTIONS ON A CIRCLE AND SPHERE

In memory of Karl Pearson and L. J. Comrie who, without the aid of electronic computers, contributed so much to the production of mathematical tables.

PREFACE

The planning of Volume 1 of these *Tables* to supersede the first volume of Karl Pearson's *Tables for Statisticians and Biometricians* was begun in the late 1930s. A large number of the tables used had appeared in the earlier publication, their computation dating back to the period 1901–14; other tables were specially prepared under our direction. We aimed at providing what we believed to be the most essential tools of the statistician's trade. The volume was published in 1954; the later editions and reprints of 1956, 1958, 1962, 1966 and 1970 extended the scope of five tables and added nine more, all in some way related to the original tables.

The publication of the present second volume has been long delayed, partly because of other heavy commitments on both authors' time and partly because one of us moved to the U.S.A. But it is true to say that the volume which we had hoped would be published in the early 1960s could not have contained a large number of the present tables, three of which were only completed during 1970. While the choice of tables to be included in our Volume 1 presented relatively few difficulties, our problem in the case of Volume 2 was far less easy. With the advent of the electronic computer a very wide range of possibilities was open. Statistical journals appearing during the past decade are full of new tables, while others have been separately issued in university or research institute publications or, indeed, wait on the side-lines for an opportunity for reproduction.

Inevitably we have based our plan of contents on tables which have been published in *Biometrika*. Just over half of the 69 tables fall within this category, but they cover between 70 and 75 per cent of the 230 table-pages. In a number of instances such tables have been enlarged or recast. By adding several new tables and others which had been published elsewhere, we found that our selection could be shaped into groups of allied tables conveniently classified under the ten broad chapter headings shown in the List of Contents. We claim no more than that our Volume 2 is one of many possible companions to Volume 1.

It is noteworthy that about three quarters of the 69 tables were computed in North America, sometimes at *Biometrika* suggestion, a fact which shows the much greater extent to which computer facilities for the tabulation of statistical functions have been made available in recent years in that continent, compared with what has been the case in the United Kingdom.

Our original intention had been to accompany the tables with much shorter introductory comments than those given in Volume 1, merely defining the function tabled and providing references to literature containing illustration of applications. As the volume began to take shape, however, we realized that this plan was not appropriate. In the first place we had received a number of appreciative comments on the character of the Introduction to Volume 1. Generally, no doubt, the statistician will know exactly what use he wishes to make of a particular table. But there are users, not only in the student class, who value the bringing together in one place of scattered tables, accompanied with some account of the underlying theory and methods of application. With this they will often need to have a guide to interpolation and to the accuracy of approximations which can be made beyond the range of the tabling. We have tried to provide information under these headings. The need to bring things together in this way seemed to us to be particularly necessary in chapters such as those dealing with quantal assay (VI); with multivariate analysis, where the published literature suffers from a lack of unified notation (VII); and in the new subject of analysis of directions on a circle and sphere (IX).

A table may be required for a great variety of purposes. In some cases a brief inspection will make clear, for example, at what level a statistic derived in the analysis of data is significant; in other cases the value extracted is required to have the maximum possible accuracy, perhaps because it is to be used in further mathematical calculations or tabulation. To satisfy adequately this second requirement it is often essential that interpolation at intermediate arguments should be feasible and reasonably straightforward. Indeed we have tried wherever possible to arrange for a function to be tabled at argument intervals such that simple second difference interpolation will lead to errors of not more than a unit in the final figure.

To assist the use in this connection we have included a final chapter on interpolation (X). Little is said on this subject in most statistical courses and as a result we believe that where linear interpolation is inadequate, many table-users are unaware how easy it generally is to extract accurate results from a table at intermediate argument values. We have, for example, met cases where an author, comparing alternative methods of approximation to a function, has placed the procedures in the wrong order of merit because his interpolation has been at fault.

Our Volume 1 contained an eight-page table of the probability integral and a two-page table of the percentage points of χ^2; also a fourteen-page table of the percentage points of the beta distribution and an abbreviated table of percentage points of the inverted beta or F-distribution. In view of its central place in statistical theory, we think that no excuse is needed for reproducing here a large part of H. L. Harter's much fuller tables of the percentage points of χ^2, including certain entries for fractional degrees of freedom. Because we had received a number of requests to make more readily available the 1943 Merrington & Thompson five-significant-figure table of percentage points of F, we decided to include this table here, although the essential information is contained in the beta table (no. 16) of Volume 1. Through the courtesy of D. E. Amos of the Sandia Laboratories opportunity has been taken to recalculate the entire table and so detect some 300 errors in the original (all but twelve of only a unit in the final digit). Dr Amos has also provided percentage points at two further levels. It could be argued that too much space has been occupied in Chapter I with Examples based on these χ^2- and F-tables, but we felt drawn to illustrate how rich these functions are in applications, some of which we believe to be unfamiliar.

Finally we should like to think that in the chapters on univariate frequency distributions (V) and on the non-central distributions (IV) we have paid a tribute to some memorable aspects of the work of Karl Pearson and Ronald Fisher.

It seems appropriate to comment briefly on the relevance of statistical tables *vis à vis* the advent of high-speed computers. Indeed it has been argued by some that there is no need for a new volume of statistical tables since any desired numerical value of the mathematical functions involved can be readily computed with the help of fast subroutines loaded into a high-speed computer. Tables, it is argued, will in due course be superseded by a library of algorithms for mathematical functions.

Whilst we do not wish to underrate the growing importance of the latter, we believe the need for printed tables will be with us for a good time to come, both in the area of (*a*) data analysis and (*b*) research in statistical methodology. With regard to (*a*) there is a real danger that automated, stereotype 'processing' of data may discourage intelligent examination of observations for unexpected features which may suggest new results and interpretations. Such intelligent inspection, besides being often assisted by graphical means, will generally be accompanied by the computation of test criteria, the need to apply which evolves in the course of the examination of the observations; this process will require the use of appropriate pre-tabled functions. Moreover, the immediate access to a high-speed computer permitting the permanent storage of computer codes for all statistical criteria is not likely to be universal for some time longer.

With regard to (*b*), research in statistical methodology, there is no doubt that systematic evaluations of the properties of new statistical functions are today being performed to an increasing extent with the help of special algorithms implemented as computer subroutines. However, the efficient planning of such computations invariably requires pilot studies for which pre-worked numerical values are invaluable. Indeed it is an essential feature of research that new ideas should be tested in small pilot computations which will provide feed-backs to the researcher leading to modifications and improvements in method. It would clearly be foolish to invest in large systematic computations before a reasonable chance of success is indicated by such pilot studies.

On a more personal level, those of us who have learnt to get the 'feel' of our data or gain fresh sidelights on our research by work done at home at the end of the day or at weekends, or even on vacation, find it hard to believe that there is not still a place for the desk computer and appropriate books of printed tables. There is surely something lost if a new generation of students is taught to think that the proper thing is to hand everything over to computerized subroutines.

We have mentioned the help provided by visual presentation; the process of plotting can often, of course, be mechanized but in many instances such a procedure is hardly called for. Some illustrations of very simple plotting procedures have been given in the chapter on order statistics (II) by way of introduction to a subject far larger than we could attempt to cover and one which is receiving much more thorough treatment elsewhere.

Originally it had been intended to include in this volume a section giving tables for computing bivariate normal probabilities. Here two forms of table were available. (*a*) The table of triple entry giving quadrant probabilities in the form $F(d|h, k, \rho)$ as presented in Tables VIII and IX of Karl Pearson's *Tables for Statisticians and Biometricians*, Part 2, now long out of print. The scope of these tables has been considerably extended by computations made since the War in the National Bureau of Standards, Washington, D.C. (*b*) A table of double entry in the form $T(h, a)$, for which see D. B. Owen's (1962) *Handbook of Statistical Tables*, pp. 184–201. Dr Owen had indeed kindly prepared for us a table of this type in slightly different form. Unfortunately we were forced to the conclusion that the amount of space involved in providing really adequate tables of his kind in our Volume 2 was prohibitive. Were there sufficient demand for tables of multivariate normal probabilities, these might of course be issued in a separate publication.

A study of the following pages will at once make clear that a number of persons have been concerned in the computation of these *Tables*. In addition we have received much help from the table-authors themselves and from other statisticians in shaping the relevant sections of the Introduction. In particular we should like to mention the following names: over Chapter II on order statistics, H. A. David and B. G. Greenberg; over Chapter IV on non-central distributions, N. L. Johnson in connection with χ', and D. B. Owen and B. L. Welch over t'; over Chapter V on univariate frequency distributions, N. L. Johnson; over Chapter VI on quantal response, Joseph Berkson whose contributions have previously, perhaps, been too scattered for justice to be done to them; over Chapter VII on multivariate analysis, T. W. Anderson, M. S. Bartlett, N. L. Johnson, A. M. Kshirsagar, K. C. S. Pillai and Martin Schatzoff; over Chapters VIII and IX on goodness of fit tests, etc., and on the analysis of directions on a circle and sphere, M. A. Stephens.

For suggestions and criticisms received from these statisticians we are exceedingly grateful. We do not of course wish to imply that our introductory sections have been presented in the way which our friends would have chosen themselves nor that they have verified our algebra or numerical examples. But the warmth of encouragement we have received from them on various aspects of the work suggests that the heavy labour involved in putting the material together has been worth while. We are also indebted to D. R. Cox, M. G. Kendall and Alan Stuart for helpful suggestions made at an early stage on the proposed contents of the volume and to those other table-makers H. L. Harter, D. B. Owen and D. E. Amos for help in various ways. The production would also, of course, have been impossible without the support and encouragement of the Biometrika Trustees, particularly of L. H. C. Tippett, their Chairman since 1962.

Miss Sheila Burrough of the University College Mathematics Department gave much help in computing some of the smaller tables and in modifying some larger tables to make them more easily interpolable. She has been responsible also for checking many of the tables at the proof stage. The whole of the typing, and in parts retyping, of the Introduction has been the work of Mrs Janet Abrahams. Finally, we were delighted to be able to make use of Dr Shirley Hitchcock's considerable experience in going through the typescript, looking for errors both in algebra and numerical examples, and in sharing the proof-reading of the Introduction and Appendices.

Appendix II, pp. 148–9 below, summarizes the origin of the 69 tables. Apart from cases where we have arranged the computation personally, permission to reproduce has been obtained from the authors concerned. We should like also to thank the editors of the following journals for freely given permissions: *Annals of the Institute of Statistical Mathematics, Annals of Mathematical Statistics, Biometrics, Journal of the American Statistical Association, Journal of the Royal Statistical Society, The Japanese Union of Scientists and Engineers, Technometrics* and also the Director of the Nautical Almanac Office.

It is now just over 70 years since the Cambridge University Press was first associated with *Biometrika* and its allied publications. It gives us great pleasure to record the help and skill which the Press has again provided over yet another publication.

E. S. PEARSON
University College London

H. O. HARTLEY
Institute of Statistics
Texas A & M University

December 1971

COMMENTS ON NOTATION

1. In general we have used the same notation in this volume as in Volume 1. An obvious abbreviation has been to denote by *B.T.S.* **1** and *B.T.S.* **2**, Volumes 1 and 2, respectively of *Biometrika Tables for Statisticians*. We have also used the rather more commonly adopted $E(x)$ in place of $\mathscr{E}(x)$ for the expectation of a random variable x.

2. As before, if x is a random variable distributed continuously in the interval (a_1, a_2) and if $f(x|\theta_1, \theta_2, \ldots)$ stands for the probability density function (p.d.f.) of x, dependent on parameters $\theta_1, \theta_2, \ldots$, we write

$$P(x|\theta_1, \theta_2, \ldots) = \int_{a_1}^{x} f(u|\theta_1, \theta_2, \ldots)\, du$$

and

$$Q(x|\theta_1, \theta_2, \ldots) = \int_{x}^{a_2} f(u|\theta_1, \theta_2, \ldots)\, du = 1 - P(x|\theta_1, \theta_2, \ldots).$$

We also express certain probability statements involving inequalities in the shortened form

$$\Pr\{x \leqslant X|\theta_1, \theta_2, \ldots\} = \alpha, \text{ say.}$$

$F(x|\theta_1, \theta_2, \ldots)$ is sometimes used instead of $P(x|\theta_1, \theta_2, \ldots)$ to denote the cumulative distribution function (c.d.f.) of x, while $F^{-1}(P) = x$ is the value of x for which its c.d.f. equals P.

3. When a random variable can assume only integral values, e.g. $i = 0, 1, 2, \ldots$ as for the binomial distribution, $f(c)$ has been used to denote the probability that $i = c$.

4. In dealing with tests of significance, the risk of rejecting the hypothesis tested, or null hypothesis, when it is true may be calculated (*a*) from the lower tail of the p.d.f. of the test criterion, i.e. correspond to P, (*b*) from the upper tail, corresponding to Q or (*c*) by summing integrals from both tails. To avoid confusion it is useful to have a separate notation to denote this risk or level of significance; as before we have used the letter α for this purpose. The term *significance level* is reserved for a probability whilst we denote by *percentage points* the critical value or values of the test criterion associated with this level. α has also been used in connection with the determination of *confidence intervals* in problems of estimation.

5. Complete consistency in the use of statistical notation is unattainable unless certain long-established practices are discarded. In general, Greek letters have been used for population parameters for which corresponding Roman letters denote the sample estimators. However, we have not hesitated to use χ^2 as a random variable nor $p = 1 - q$ for the probability of an event in binomial sampling. For this reason we have, as before, a, b for the two parameters in the incomplete beta function ratio, i.e. we take $I_x(a, b)$ for the traditional $I_x(p, q)$.

6. Occasionally it has seemed necessary to use the same letter in different parts of the volume to indicate two, or even more, different statistics or test criteria. An extreme example of this occurs over the surprisingly popular letter W ! (i) In Chapter II, § 7.1, W is the Shapiro–Wilk statistic used in a test for departure from normality. (ii) In Chapter III, § 9.1, it is used for the criterion in the Wilcoxon two-sample rank-sum test. (iii) Later in that chapter, in § 12, it is briefly referred to as Kendall's concordance coefficient. (iv) In Chapter VII, 26.2, W is used for Wilks' likelihood ratio criterion in multivariate analysis. (v) Finally in Chapter VIII, § 30.1, W^2 is the Cramer–von Mises criterion which can be used in goodness-of-fit tests. Clearly in three

of these cases the letter W had been adopted because of the initial letter of the surname of the author of the test. Possibly in the remaining cases the original writer believed he had found a letter not so far associated with another test in common use. W, however, seems to represent an extreme case and even here we think that no confusion need arise.

7. In Chapter VII concerned with multivariate analysis, but not elsewhere, we have freely used the standard matrix notation which has become familiar in this field.

8. The notation for the differences of a tabled function used throughout the volume is not perhaps completely standard but we hope that it is adequately defined in Chapter X.

9. Throughout, 'log' denotes a natural logarithm.

NOTE ON THE SECOND IMPRESSION

The only substantial changes are that Table 34 has been completely re-set and Table 35 corrected and enlarged, following N. L. Johnson (*Biometrika*, 1974, **61,** 203–5). The opportunity has been taken of correcting a few minor errors that have come to light.

January 1976.

INTRODUCTION

I. THE NORMAL PROBABILITY FUNCTION AND CERTAIN DERIVED TABLES

The tables collected under this heading to some extent supplement similar tables which appeared in *B.T.S.* **1**, either by giving the values tabled to additional decimal places, by increasing the range of the arguments, or by providing probability integrals where before we had only given percentage points. Tables 3, 4 and 5, for example, extend the earlier tables of percentage points of χ^2 and of the variance ratio, F. The uses of these two statistics were illustrated fully in our Volume 1, but a number of further applications are given in the following sections as well as in later chapters of this volume.

1. TABLE OF X AND Z AS FUNCTIONS OF THE PROBABILITY, P (TABLE 1)

1.1 *Definitions and notation*

The equation of the normal or Gaussian frequency function may be written in the standardized form

$$Z(X) = f(X) = \frac{1}{\sqrt{(2\pi)}} e^{-\frac{1}{2}X^2} \tag{1}$$

and the associated probability integral as

$$P(X) = \int_{-\infty}^{X} Z(u)\, du, \tag{2}$$

with $Q(X) = 1 - P(X)$. Inverting the functional relation (2) yields the standardized normal variable X as a function of the probability integral P, used as a tabular argument. The resulting function $X(P)$ is therefore defined by

$$P = \int_{-\infty}^{X(P)} Z(u)\, du, \tag{3}$$

whilst substituting $X(P)$ in (1) yields the frequency ordinate Z as the function $Z\{X(P)\}$ of P.

Table 1 gives $X(P)$ and $Z\{X(P)\}$ to ten decimals for $P = 0\cdot500(0\cdot001)0\cdot9990(0\cdot0001)0\cdot9999$. The original ten figure table, which also included values of the ratios P/Z, Q/Z, Z/P and Z/Q, was computed by Kondo & Elderton (1931), but it was recently found that these authors had not always carried the expansions used to an adequate number of terms. As a result the table was recomputed for us by Professor J. S. White of the School of Mechanical Engineering, University of Minnesota. We have, however, decided that for reasons of space we cannot include here the values of the ratios. On rare occasions when required on a large scale they can either be obtained with generally sufficient accuracy from the original 1931 *Biometrika* paper or may be calculated from the table of $Z(P)$ given here. A copy of Professor White's corrected table can be obtained on request from Biometrika. Dr Arthur Greenwood independently recalculated the 1931 table, giving a perfect check on Professor White's work.

While it can be used for various purposes referred to later in this volume, we regard Table 1 as providing a basic record to high decimal accuracy; its main purpose is to supply foundation values for the preparation of shorter tables, 'custom-made' for specific purposes.

A second, allied table which might have been included is one giving the same ratios P/Z, Q/Z, Z/P and Z/Q against argument X. This table appeared in *Biometrika* (1955), following a paper by R. F. Tate; it was partly computed by Z. W. Birnbaum and partly in the University College Department of Statistics. For reasons of space, this table also has been omitted.

1.2 *Interpolation*

Bessel's formula (314) based on differences may be used (see §36.1 below). The necessary coefficients are given in Table 66 and a guide to the number of differences which are required to obtain a specified degree of accuracy is provided by the inequalities (317). If the full ten decimal place accuracy is necessary, the number of terms which must be taken in (314) will depend very much on the part of the table entered. If, for example, P is in the neighbourhood of 0·5, the B_2 and B_3 terms are required when interpolating for X (i.e. (320) must be used), while for Z formula (319), only involving the B_2 term, will be adequate. On the other hand, towards the end of the table, as $P \to 1$, accurate interpolation to ten decimals becomes increasingly difficult.

A typical example would be to find X ($P = 0.833421$). From Table 1 we find:

P	X	δ^2	δ^3	δ^4
0·833	0·96608 82971	1 54363		31
			1847	
0·834	0·97009 32766	1 56210		30

and from Table 66:

$$1 - \theta = 0.579, \quad \theta = 0.421, \quad B_2 = -0.060940, \quad B_3 = 0.00321, \quad B_4 = 0.0114.$$

It follows that

$$X\,(P = 0.833421) = 0.96777\,43935 - 18926 + 6 + 1 = 0.96777\,25016.$$

2. Table of derivatives of the normal ordinate, $D^n Z(X)$ (Table 2)

2.1 *Definitions*

The derivatives of the normal ordinate $Z(X)$ defined by equation (1) are here denoted by

$$D^n Z(X) = \frac{d^n}{dX^n} Z(X). \tag{4}$$

Table 2 gives, for $X = 0(0.02)4.00(0.05)6.20$

to six decimals,
$$\begin{cases} D^{-1}Z(X) = \int_0^X Z(u)\,du = P(X) - 0.5, \\ D^0 Z(X) = Z(X) \quad \text{and} \quad D^n Z(X) \quad (n = 1, 2); \end{cases}$$

to five decimals, $D^n Z(X) \quad (n = 3, 4)$;

to four decimals, $D^n Z(X) \quad (n = 5, 6)$;

to three decimals, $D^7 Z(X)$;   to two decimals, $D^8 Z(X)$;   to one decimal, $D^9 Z(X)$.

In deciding on this reduction in the number of significant figures we have had in mind the use of the following Taylor expansion for interpolation in the table:

$$D^n Z(X + h) = D^n Z(X) + h D^{n+1} Z(X) + \frac{h^2}{2!} D^{n+2} Z(X) + \dots. \tag{5}$$

2

If X is the tabular argument nearest to that at which the functions are required, then $h \leqslant 0.01$ for $X \leqslant 4.00$, and $h \leqslant 0.025$ for $X > 4.00$. This means for example that for four decimal place accuracy in $D^6Z(X)$, progressive reduction in the number of figures in the higher differentials is permissible. Taking $X = 1.50$, $h = 0.01$

$$D^6Z(1.51) = 2.8109 - 0.01 \times 7.058 - \tfrac{1}{2}0.0001 \times 9.09 + \tfrac{1}{6}0.000001 \times 70.1$$

$$= 2.8109 - 0.07058 - 0.00045 + 0.00001 = 2.7399.$$

These functions are related to the Hermite polynomials, $h_n(X)$, by the relations

$$h_n(X) = (-1)^n D^n Z(X)/Z(X), \tag{6}$$

so that

$$h_0 = 1, \quad h_1 = X, \quad h_2 = X^2 - 1, \quad h_3 = X^3 - 3X, \quad h_4 = X^4 - 6X^2 + 3, \text{ etc.}$$

Accordingly they represent a complete orthogonal system of functions over the range $-\infty < X < \infty$. Whilst they have been used as a basis for expanding functions in various areas of applied mathematics, this possibility in statistical applications has been almost exclusively confined to the expansion of frequency ordinates and probability integrals of distribution functions with doubly infinite range, giving rise to the so-called Gram–Charlier type A and Edgeworth expansions discussed in §2.2 below.

2.2 *Applications*: *Gram–Charlier Type* A *and Edgeworth expansions*

Both the Gram–Charlier and Edgeworth expansions of a frequency ordinate, $f(X)$, of a variate in standardized form with doubly infinite range, $-\infty < X < \infty$, can be given in the operational form

$$\exp\left\{ \sum_{n=3}^{\infty} (-1)^n \kappa_n D^n/n! \right\} Z(X) \equiv f(X), \tag{7}$$

where $E(X) = 0$, $\mathrm{var}\, X = 1$ and κ_n ($n = 3, 4, \ldots$) are the standardized cumulants of $f(X)$. With the Gram–Charlier series this expansion is truncated by taking all terms up to and including the term containing D^n. For example, taking terms up to D^8, the expansion (7) becomes

$$f(X) = \sum_{n=0}^{8} (-1)^n c_n D^n Z(X) \doteqdot \sum_{n=0}^{8} c_n h_n(X) Z(X), \tag{8}$$

where

$$\left.\begin{aligned}
&c_0 = 1, \quad c_1 = c_2 = 0, \quad c_3 = \kappa_3/6, \quad c_4 = \kappa_4/24, \\
&c_5 = \kappa_5/120, \quad c_6 = (\kappa_6 + 10\kappa_3^2)/720, \\
&c_7 = (\kappa_7 + 35\kappa_4\kappa_3)/5040, \quad c_8 = (\kappa_8 + 56\kappa_5\kappa_3 + 35\kappa_4^2)/40320.
\end{aligned}\right\} \tag{9}$$

On the other hand with the Edgeworth series it is assumed that $\kappa_s = O(N^{1-\frac{1}{2}s})$, where N is the sample size and the expansion (7) is truncated at a given order (say order T) of N^{-T}. We shall here confine ourselves to the use of the Gram–Charlier expansion. In the evaluation of (8) with the help of Table 2 we must recognize that the interval in X is rather wide, requiring interpolation for all $D^n Z(X)$ involved. However, by using the Taylor expansion (5) the terms involved in the interpolation can be merged with the Gram–Charlier A series terms. Denote the argument for which (8) is to be evaluated by $X + h$ (where X is the nearest tabular argument); then using terms up to $n = 6$ in (8) we may write it in the form

$$f(X+h) = \sum_{n=0}^{6} D^n(X) \frac{h^n}{n!} + \sum_{n=3}^{6} (-1)^n c_n \left\{ \sum_{t=0}^{6-n} D^{n+t}(X) \frac{h^t}{t!} \right\}, \tag{10}$$

3

which may be set out for convenience of computation in the triangular table shown below, where we have omitted the D^5 and D^6 terms in the top line since these will usually be negligible.

c_n	$D^0(X)$	$D^1(X)$	$D^2(X)$	$D^3(X)$	$D^4(X)$	$D^5(X)$	$D^6(X)$
$c_0 = 1$	1	h	$h/2$	$h^3/6$	$h^4/24$	.	.
$c_1 = 0$	.	.	.	.	.	.	.
$c_2 = 0$	.	.	.	.	.	.	.
$-c_3$	.	.	.	1	h	$h^2/2$	$h^3/6$
c_4	.	.	.	.	1	h	$h^2/2$
$-c_5$	.	.	.	.	.	1	h
c_6	.	.	.	.	.	.	1

$$(11)$$

On a desk computer the first row ($n = 0$) can be evaluated by the continued multiplication

$$[\{(D^4(X)\tfrac{1}{4}h + D^3(X))\tfrac{1}{3}h + D^2(X)\}\tfrac{1}{2}h + D^1(X)]\,h + D^0(X). \qquad (12)$$

Similarly the lines for $n = 3, 4$ and 5 can be evaluated and recorded, and finally the sum of products with the c_n formed in accordance with (11).

Example 1. Evaluate $f(X + h)$ for $X + h = 1\cdot250$ (i.e. $X = 1\cdot24$ and $h = 0\cdot01$) and $c_3 = 0\cdot4$, $c_4 = 0\cdot06$, $c_5 = 0\cdot02$, $c_6 = 0\cdot002$. We take the following entries from Table 2:

$$D^6 = 4\cdot1359, \quad D^5 = -0\cdot4559, \quad D^4 = -0\cdot71411, \quad D^3 = 0\cdot33536,$$

$$D^2 = 0\cdot099422, \quad D^1 = -0\cdot229322, \quad D^0 = 0\cdot184937.$$

Hence for the line $n = 0$ we have

$$\left[\left\{\left((-0\cdot71411)\frac{0\cdot01}{4} + 0\cdot33536\right)\frac{0\cdot01}{3} + 0\cdot099422\right\}\frac{0\cdot01}{2} - 0\cdot229322\right]0\cdot01 + 0\cdot184937 = 0\cdot18265.$$

Likewise for the lines $n = 3, 4$ and 5

$$\left[\left\{(4\cdot1359)\frac{0\cdot01}{3} - 0\cdot4559\right\}\frac{0\cdot01}{2} - 0\cdot71411\right]0\cdot01 + 0\cdot33536 = 0\cdot32820,$$

$$\left\{(4\cdot1359)\frac{0\cdot01}{2} - 0\cdot4559\right\}0\cdot01 - 0\cdot71411 \qquad\qquad = -0\cdot71846,$$

$$(4\cdot1359)0\cdot01 - 0\cdot4559 \qquad\qquad\qquad\qquad = -0\cdot41454.$$

Finally we obtain from (10) the sum of products

$$f(1\cdot250) = 0\cdot18265 - c_3(0\cdot32820) + c_4(-0\cdot71846) - c_5(-0\cdot41454) + c_6(4\cdot1359) = 0\cdot0248.$$

The table can, of course, also be used for the evaluation of the c.d.f. $\int_{-\infty}^{X} f(u)\,du$. Since

$$\int_{-\infty}^{X} D^n Z(u) = D^{n-1} Z(X),$$

equation (10) and Table 2 are directly applied with $D^n Z(X)$ replaced by $D^{n-1} Z(X)$ throughout. To this end $D^{-1} Z(X) = P(X)$ is provided in Table 2 in the form $P(X) - 0\cdot5$.

4

2.3 *Application to correlation in a four-fold table*

Let the standardized bivariate normal distribution

$$f(X, Y) = \frac{1}{2\pi(1-\rho^2)^{\frac{1}{2}}} \exp\left\{-\frac{1}{2(1-\rho^2)}(X^2 - 2\rho XY + Y^2)\right\} \tag{13}$$

be divided into four quadrants by lines at $X = h$, $Y = k$, where the fractions of the total in these quadrants are α, β, γ and δ as shown in the left-hand diagram below.

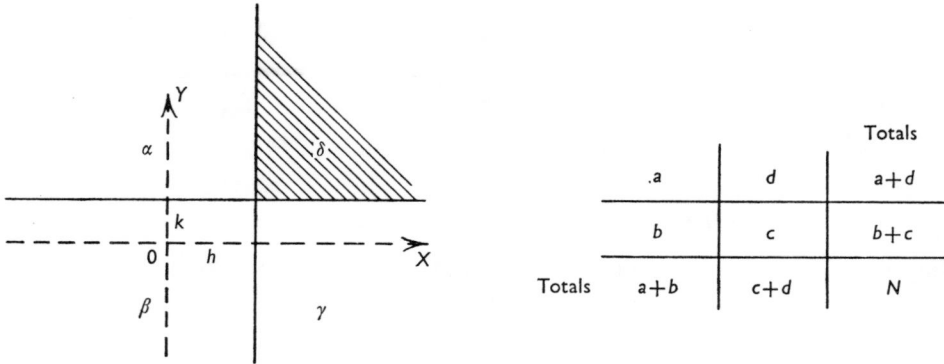

Then if $h, k \geqslant 0$, it is known that

$$\delta = Q(h)\,Q(k) + \sum_{j=1}^{\infty} \{D^{j-1}Z(h)\,D^{j-1}Z(k)\,\rho^j/j\,!\} = f(\rho, h, k). \tag{14}$$

Tables of δ as a function of ρ, h and k appeared in *Biometrika* between 1915 and 1930 and were reproduced in Part 2 of Karl Pearson's (1931) *Tables for Statisticians and Biometricians*; a rather more extensive table in this form has been computed by the National Bureau of Standards, Washington, D.C. Because of the space involved we have not felt able to include such a table in the present volume, but it is evident that the formula (14) together with Table 2 could be used to calculate δ with a reasonable degree of accuracy.

If only a sample of N observations are available, giving frequencies a, b, c, d in a four-fold table as shown on the right of the diagram, it is possible to use a certain number of terms in the expansion (14) to obtain an estimate, r_t, of ρ. First we estimate h and k from the marginal frequencies using Table 1, i.e.

$$h = X\{(a+b)/N\}, \quad k = X\{(b+c)/N\}.$$

We then estimate δ by d/N and truncating the series, say, at $j = 4$ would have a quartic $d/N = f(r_t, h, k)$ to solve for r_t.

The quantity r_t has been termed a tetrachoric coefficient of correlation derivable from a four-fold table. It is clearly a meaningful estimate of ρ if the data have been sampled from a bivariate normal population with dichotomies at $X = h$, $Y = k$. Also r_t has often been used as a coefficient of association when the existence of two underlying continuously distributed variables is more doubtful.

To solve the quartic equation $d/N = f(r_t, h, k)$ we first compute the products

$$\begin{aligned}
t_j &= D^j Z(h) \cdot D^j Z(k) \quad (j = 0, 1, ..., 4), \\
t_{-1} &= (0{\cdot}5 - D^{-1}Z(h))\,(0{\cdot}5 - D^{-1}Z(k)),
\end{aligned} \right\} \tag{15}$$

and then for a trial value r_t evaluate

$$f(r_t) = \left[\left\{\left(\left(t_4\frac{r_t}{5}+t_3\right)\frac{r_t}{4}+t_2\right)\frac{r_t}{3}+t_1\right\}\frac{r_t}{2}+t_0\right]r_t+t_{-1},$$

$$\frac{df(r_t)}{dr_t} = \left[\left\{\left(t_4\frac{r_t}{4}+t_3\right)\frac{r_t}{3}+t_2\right\}\frac{r_t}{2}+t_1\right]r_t+t_0,$$

$$\tag{16}$$

and hence find

$$r_t' \doteq r_t+\frac{d/N-f(r_t)}{df(r_t)/dr_t}. \tag{17}$$

If the first trial value, r_t, has been a bad guess, (16) and (17) must be repeated.

Example 2. Estimation of δ given ρ, h and k. We shall illustrate the use of equation (14) by determining the value of δ when $\rho = 0\cdot5, h = 1\cdot4, k = 1\cdot0$. The first term (with $j = 0$) represents the value of δ when $\rho = 0$; the probabilities $Q(h), Q(k)$ can be obtained from the second column in Table 2, by noting that

$$Q(h) = 1-P(h) = 0\cdot5-\{P(X = h)-0\cdot5\}.$$

We could proceed to compute δ sequentially as in (16), but to show the degree of convergence give the separate terms in (14) up to and including that with $j = 9$. We have

$$\begin{array}{cccccc} j & 0 & 1 & 2 & 3 & 4 & 5 \\ \delta= & 0\cdot01281+ & 0\cdot01811+ & 0\cdot00634+ & 0 & +0\cdot00027+ & 0\cdot00009 \end{array}$$

$$\begin{array}{cccc} 6 & 7 & 8 & 9 \\ -0\cdot00001+ & 0\cdot00002- & 0\cdot00000+ & 0\cdot00000 = 0\cdot03763 \end{array}$$

The correct value taken from K. Pearson (1931, p. 93) is $0\cdot037651$. The series does not converge uniformly, in fact may diverge for larger values of ρ. In the present example, however, it will be seen that going only as far as $j = 4$ we get a reasonably accurate value of $\delta = 0\cdot03753$.

3. Percentage points of the χ^2-distribution for integral and fractional degrees of freedom (Table 3)

3.1 *Definitions*

The χ^2 integral, the incomplete gamma function, the probability integral of Pearson's Type III distribution and the cumulative sum of terms of the Poisson distribution are all different forms of the same mathematical function. We shall first define this function in terms of the χ^2-integral. If $X_1, X_2, ..., X_\nu$ are ν independent normal variates each with expectation zero and unit variance, then

$$\chi^2 = \sum_{i=1}^{\nu} X_i^2 \tag{18}$$

has for its probability integral

$$P(\chi^2|\nu) = 2^{-\frac{1}{2}\nu}\{\Gamma(\tfrac{1}{2}\nu)\}^{-1}\int_0^{\chi^2} e^{-\frac{1}{2}x}x^{\frac{1}{2}\nu-1}\,dx, \tag{19}$$

where ν are the degrees of freedom of χ^2. We define the upper 'tail area' of this distribution by

$$Q(\chi^2|\nu) = 1-P(\chi^2|\nu).$$

For many applications we require the moments or cumulants of the p.d.f. of χ^2. They are

$$\left.\begin{array}{l} \kappa_r = \nu 2^{r-1}(r-1)!, \quad \kappa_1 = \nu, \\[4pt] \mu_2 = 2\nu, \quad \mu_3 = 8\nu, \quad \mu_4 = 48\nu+12\nu^2, \\[4pt] \beta_1 = \mu_3^2/\mu_2^3 = 8/\nu, \quad \beta_2 = \mu_4/\mu_2^2 = 3+12/\nu. \end{array}\right\} \tag{20}$$

and hence

6

By changing the scale and origin in (19) we obtain the general form of the probability integral of Pearson's Type III distribution, namely

$$P(x|m, a, p) = \frac{1}{a\Gamma(p)} \int_m^x \left(\frac{v-m}{a}\right)^{p-1} \exp\{-(v-m)/a\}\, dv, \left.\right\}$$

where
$$\nu = 2p, \quad \chi^2 = 2(x-m)/a. \qquad (21)$$

Finally we have the following relation between the cumulative sum of the Poisson distribution and $Q(\chi^2|\nu)$:

$$Q(\chi^2|\nu) = \sum_{j=0}^{c-1} e^{-m} m^j/j!, \left.\right\}$$

where
$$m = \tfrac{1}{2}\chi^2, \quad c = \tfrac{1}{2}\nu. \qquad (22)$$

The *Tables of the Incomplete Gamma Function* (K. Pearson, 1922) uses the notation $I(u, p)$ for our $P(\chi^2|\nu)$, where

$$p = \tfrac{1}{2}\nu - 1, \quad u = \tfrac{1}{2}\chi^2/\sqrt{(p+1)} = \chi^2/\sqrt{(2\nu)}.$$

The most extensive table of the probability integral is that of Khamis & Rudert (1965) which gives results to ten decimal places, using arguments $N = \tfrac{1}{2}\nu$, $X = \tfrac{1}{2}\chi^2$, with fractional entries. Two forms of the table were given in *B.T.S.* **1**:

Table 7, which gave values of $Q(\chi^2|\nu)$ for arguments χ^2 and ν (the latter for integer values only):

Table 8, which gave to six significant figures the so-called percentage points of χ^2, $\chi^2(Q|\nu)$ for the range of arguments

$$\nu = 1(1)30(10)100,$$

$$Q = 0\cdot995,\ 0\cdot990,\ 0\cdot975,\ 0\cdot95,\ 0\cdot90,\ 0\cdot75,\ 0\cdot50,\ 0\cdot25,\ 0\cdot10,\ 0\cdot05,\ 0\cdot025,\ 0\cdot010,\ 0\cdot005,\ 0\cdot001.$$

The present Table 3 due to Harter (1964 b, c) which is entered with ν and P, rather than Q, is more comprehensive than Table 8 of *B.T.S.* **1** in the following respects:

(*a*) It includes additional entries for P.

(*b*) It contains a number of entries for small, fractional values of ν.

We have not included all Harter's columns in the present table, but take

$$\nu = 0\cdot1(0\cdot1)3\cdot0(0\cdot2)10\cdot0(1)100.$$

The great advantage of including results for fractional ν is that interpolation is made easier in applications where the χ^2 distribution is used as an approximating function with parameters determined either on the basis of making moments agree or by other means. We illustrate some applications of this kind in §§ 3.5, 3.6 below.

Note that beyond the range of Table 3, i.e. for $\nu > 100$, we may take

$$\chi^2(Q|\nu) = \nu\left\{1 - \frac{2}{9\nu} + X(P)\sqrt{\frac{2}{9\nu}}\right\}^3, \left.\right\}$$

or
$$\chi^2(Q|\nu) = \tfrac{1}{2}\{X(P) + \sqrt{(2\nu-1)}\}^2, \qquad (23)$$

according to the degree of accuracy required. $X(P)$ is the standardized normal deviate corresponding to $P = 1 - Q$, obtainable from Table 1.

3.2   *Applications discussed elsewhere*

Most of the applications of χ^2 are well known; we list below those which have been illustrated in *B.T.S.* **1** or which will be described in later chapters of the present volume. Afterwards, in §§ 3.3–3.6, we describe and illustrate in more detail four further applications, two involving integral and two fractional degrees of freedom.

(*a*)   The χ^2 test of goodness of fit of a theoretical distribution to observational data (*B.T.S.* **1**, §§ 3·2, 3.4).

(*b*)   Confidence limits for a population variance, σ^2, derived from a sample estimate of variance, s^2 (*B.T.S.* **1**, §§ 4.3, 4.4).

(*c*)   Confidence limits for the expectation in a Poisson distribution, based on a single observation (*B.T.S.* **1**, § 22.2).

(*d*)   Bartlett's approximation in the M-test for homogeneity of variance among a number of univariate distributions (*B.T.S.* **1**, § 16.1).

(*e*)   Approximation to H in the Kruskal–Wallis test (*B.T.S.* **2**, § 11.1, pp. 49–50).

(*f*)   Friedman's approximation to the distribution of Kendall's coefficient of concordance, W (*B.T.S.* **1**, § 25.2 (*c*); *B.T.S.* **2**, § 12, p. 52).

(*g*)   The combination of evidence contained in k independent test statistics T_i, through

$$\chi^2 = -2 \sum_i \log Q_i(T_i), \quad \nu = 2k$$

(this volume, *B.T.S.* **2**, § 4.8, pp. 20–1; § 5.2, p. 25; § 5.3, p. 27; § 7.4, p. 39; § 18.3, p. 86).

(*h*)   The Wilks' criterion for the equality of mean vectors in bivariate populations (this volume, *B.T.S.* **2**, § 26.5, p. 101).

(*i*)   Test for the equality of covariance matrices in k multi-variate normal populations. The Bartlett–Box χ^2 approximation (this volume, *B.T.S.* **2**, § 27.1, p. 108).

(*j*)   Test for the hypothesis that a population covariance matrix $\Sigma = \Sigma_0$. The Bartlett–Box approximation (this volume, *B.T.S.* **2**, § 28.1, p. 111).

3.3   *Confidence limits for the expectation of a Poisson distribution, given several observations*

In (*c*) above reference is made to the case of a single observation. A more general problem is one in which we observe n values, $x_1, x_2, \ldots, x_n$ all believed subject to the same Poisson law, and wish to obtain confidence limits for the common expectation, m. In this case we know that $c = \sum_i x_i$ follows a Poisson distribution with expectation $M = nm$. Further, since

$$\sum_{j=0}^{c-1} \frac{e^{-M} M^j}{j!} = Q(\chi^2 | \nu = 2c) \tag{24}$$

it follows that the symmetrical two-sided confidence limits for m, namely $m_A < m_B$, are given by

$$m_A = \tfrac{1}{2}\chi^2(\alpha | \nu = 2c)/n, \quad m_B = \tfrac{1}{2}\chi^2(1-\alpha | \nu = 2c+2)/n, \tag{25}$$

where the P of Table 3 equals α. We can then associate the statement $m_A \leqslant m \leqslant m_B$ with a confidence coefficient $\geqslant 1 - 2\alpha$.

Example 3.   In Example 29 on p. 41 below we are given the intervals in hours between successive failures of the air conditioning system on a Boeing 720 aircraft (Proschan, 1963). Suppose that the only records kept were the numbers of failures per consecutive two-day periods and that these were available for twenty days or ten two-day periods. The record would then be as follows:

no. of failures per period (x_i)	0	1	2	3
no. of times x_i observed (f_i)	6	2	1	1

Here $n = 10$, $c = \sum_i (f_i x_i) = 7$; hence from (25) for $\alpha = 0.025$, we have

$$m_A = \tfrac{1}{2}\chi^2(0.025\,|\,14)/10 = 0.28, \quad m_B = \tfrac{1}{2}\chi^2(0.975\,|\,16)/10 = 1.44,$$

and finally we say that $0.28 \leqslant m \leqslant 1.44$, with a confidence coefficient $\geqslant 0.95$. For the twenty-eight failures of the complete table, the mean interval was 76.81, giving the estimated expectation per forty-eight hours as $48/76.81 = 0.62$.

Example 4. We take Bortkewitsch's classical example of the deaths of Prussian soldiers from kicks from a horse, recorded during twenty years in 10 Army Corps:

annual deaths (x_i)	0	1	2	3	4	Total
frequency observed (f_i)	109	65	22	3	1	200

Here $n = 200$, $c = \Sigma f_i x_i = 122$. Since the degrees of freedom involved are $2c = 244$ and $2c + 2 = 246$, we use the second of the two approximations (Fisher's) given in (23). If we ask for a 99 per cent confidence interval for m, we find

$$\chi^2(0.995\,|\,244) = 189.97, \quad \chi^2(0.005\,|\,246) = 305.89$$

and hence from (25)

$$m_A = 0.475, \quad m_B = 0.765.$$

3.4 *Sub-tabulation of $x = \tfrac{1}{2}\chi^2$, with P as argument*

Example 5. Suppose that we are considering the incomplete gamma distribution in the form

$$P(x) = \frac{1}{\Gamma(p)} \int_0^x u^{p-1} e^{-x}\,dx,$$

and for some special purpose wish to form a small table giving $x(P)$ as a function of P for $P = 0.01(0.01)0.10$. Take the particular case $p = 2$. The results can be obtained by interpolating between the unequally spaced percentage levels in Table 3 using the appropriate Lagrangian formulae (330) of §37.2 for which the coefficients L_i are given in Table 69. We note that $\chi^2 = 2x$, $\nu = 2p = 4$. The appropriate interpolation formulae will be those associated with 'Grid 3', using the 0.5, 1.0, 2.5, 5.0 and 10.0 per cent points of χ^2 for $\nu = 4$. The working for $P = 0.02$ is as follows:

From Table 3 $\begin{cases} P_i \\ (P_i \| \nu = 4) \end{cases}$	0.005	0.01	0.025	0.05	0.10
	0.206989	0.297109	0.484418	0.710723	1.063623†
From Table 69 $L_i(0.02)$	-0.031146	0.199495	0.988448	-0.183001	0.026203

$\chi^2(0.02\,|\,4) = \sum\limits_i L_i \chi^2(P_i\,|\,4) = 0.429454$. Hence $x = 0.2147$.

Proceeding in this way for the other values of P, we compute the small table:

P	$x(P)$	P	$x(P)$	P	$x(P)$
0.01	0.1486	0.05	0.3554	0.08	0.4658
0.02	0.2147	0.06	0.3942	0.09	0.4994
0.03	0.2675	0.07	0.4309	0.10	0.5318
0.04	0.3135				

† The seventh digit is taken from *B.T.S.* **1**, Table 8.

These values can be checked by noting that for $p = 2$

$$P(x) = 1 - e^{-x}(1+x).$$

On examination, it is found that certain of the x values are a unit in error in the fourth decimal place.

3.5 *Approximation to the percentage points of non-central χ^2*

A number of applications arise when we use the χ^2-distribution to approximate to the sampling distribution of a statistic for which the moments are known, but the distribution itself is not amenable to simple treatment. In this connection we need to know the moments μ_r, or the cumulants κ_r of χ^2 given by the relations (20). It will then generally be found that the degrees of freedom involved will be fractional. Table 3 with entries for certain fractional ν eases the necessary interpolation. The following approximations illustrate the procedure.

Using the notation, χ'^2, for non-central χ^2, we have

$$\chi'^2 = \sum_{i=1}^{\nu} (a_i + X_i)^2, \tag{26}$$

where the X_i are ν independent $N(0, 1)$ variates and

$$\lambda = \sum_i a_i^2 \tag{27}$$

is termed the non-centrality parameter. The first three cumulants of χ'^2 are known to be

$$\kappa_1 = \nu + \lambda, \quad \kappa_2 = 2(\nu + 2\lambda), \quad \kappa_3 = 8(\nu + 3\lambda). \tag{28}$$

Patnaik (1949) suggested that we take

$$\chi'^2 \simeq c\chi^2(\nu') \tag{29}$$

where c and ν' are determined so that the first two moments of χ'^2 and a central χ^2 having ν' degrees of freedom are made to agree. This means that

$$\nu + \lambda = c\nu', \quad 2(\nu + 2\lambda) = 2c^2\nu'$$

whence

$$c = (\nu + 2\lambda)/(\nu + \lambda), \quad \nu' = (\nu + \lambda)^2/(\nu + 2\lambda). \tag{30}$$

In general a rather better approximation is obtained by making the first three moments of the two distributions agree and not tying down the start of the approximating χ^2 distribution.

Pearson (1959) showed that this latter procedure involved taking

$$\chi'^2 \simeq \frac{\nu + 3\lambda}{\nu + 2\lambda}\chi^2(\nu') - \frac{\lambda^2}{\nu + 3\lambda}, \quad \nu' = \frac{(\nu + 2\lambda)^3}{(\nu + 3\lambda)^2}. \tag{31}$$

Example 6. Find the lower and upper 1 per cent points of a non-central χ^2 with $\nu = 5$, $\lambda = 4$. These points are given in Table 24 as

$$(1 \cdot 090)^2 = 1 \cdot 188 \quad \text{and} \quad (4 \cdot 946)^2 = 24 \cdot 463.$$

What values do we obtain from the two-moment and three-moment approximations?

Using the Patnaik approximation, the relations (30) give

$$c = 1 \cdot 4444, \quad \nu' = 6 \cdot 2308$$

so that we must interpolate for $\chi^2(\nu')$ in Table 3 between entries at $6 \cdot 2$ and $6 \cdot 4$. If four decimal place accuracy were required we must use the simple second difference formula (319) for the lower 1 per cent point, but linear interpolation is adequate for the upper 1 per cent point. The resulting values for χ'^2 from (29) are shown in the table below.

Using the three moment approximation of (31) we find

$$\nu' = 7 \cdot 6021 \quad \text{and} \quad \chi'^2 \simeq 1 \cdot 3077 \chi^2(\nu') - 0 \cdot 9412.$$

Interpolating in Table 3 between $\nu = 7 \cdot 6$ and $7 \cdot 8$ we obtain the values shown below:

	Lower 1 %	Upper 1 %
True	1·188	24·46
Patnaik approx.	1·376	24·84
3-moment approx.	0·994	24·50

Because the distribution of χ'^2 is in this case rather skew with $\beta_1 = 1 \cdot 05$, the position of the lower terminal has some importance and the first approximation gives a slightly better result than the second: at the upper 1 per cent point the three-moment approximation, however, has considerable advantages. As ν' increases the second approximation is in general better at both terminals. Its use beyond the range of the exact table (Table 24) is advocated in §13.3 below where some further examination of its accuracy is made.

3.6 *Approximation to the weighted sum of several χ^2 statistics*

Another situation in which approximation will lead to a fractional value of ν is one arising when it is necessary to consider a weighted sum of χ^2 statistics of the form

$$S = \sum_{i=1}^{k} c_i \chi^2(\nu_i), \tag{32}$$

with $c_i > 0$. Attempting an approximation of the form $S \sim c\chi^2(\nu)$ and equating the first two moments leads to the equations

$$\nu = (\Sigma c_i \nu_i)^2 / (\Sigma c_i^2 \nu_i) \tag{33}$$

and

$$c = \Sigma c_i^2 \nu_i / (\Sigma c_i \nu_i). \tag{34}$$

The accuracy of this approximation has been tested in a number of special cases (see e.g. Welch, 1937).

Example 7. Recently Johnson & Kotz (1967) have evaluated the exact probability integral of S for the special cases $\sum_i \nu_i = 5$, $k \leqslant 5$, for various sets of c_i. We have used their tables to evaluate the exact probability associated with the upper 5 per cent points obtained from the above approximation, for the three cases shown in the table below, with $\nu_i = 1$ throughout:

c_1	c_2	c_3	c_4	c_5	c	ν	Approx. 5 % point $S_{0 \cdot 05}$	Exact probability $\Pr\{S \geqslant S_{0 \cdot 05}\}$
1·1	1·1	1·1	0·9	0·8	1·016	4·92	11·122	0·0500
2·0	1·5	0·8	0·4	0·3	1·428	3·50	12·374	0·0501
3·0	0·5	0·5	0·5	0·5	2·000	2·50	13·856	0·0492

Although the above examples cannot claim to be more than illustrations, they are indicative of a general experience that for positive c_i the approximation is of fair accuracy.

11

4. Percentage points of the F-distribution for integral and fractional degrees of freedom

4.1 *Definitions, interpolation and relation to other distributions*

Consider two independent χ^2 values, χ_1^2 and χ_2^2 based respectively on ν_1 and ν_2 degrees of freedom; the variance ratio F is defined by

$$F = \frac{\chi_1^2}{\nu_1} \bigg/ \frac{\chi_2^2}{\nu_2} \tag{35}$$

and has for its frequency function

$$f(F|\nu_1, \nu_2) = \frac{\Gamma(\tfrac{1}{2}\nu_1 + \tfrac{1}{2}\nu_2)}{\Gamma(\tfrac{1}{2}\nu_1)\,\Gamma(\tfrac{1}{2}\nu_2)}\, \nu_1^{\frac{1}{2}\nu_1} \nu_2^{\frac{1}{2}\nu_2} F^{\frac{1}{2}\nu_1 - 1}(\nu_2 + \nu_1 F)^{-\frac{1}{2}(\nu_1 + \nu_2)}. \tag{36}$$

It is useful to note that

$$E(F) = \frac{\nu_2}{\nu_2 - 2} \text{ for } \nu_2 > 2, \quad \sigma^2(F) = \frac{\nu_2^2}{(\nu_2 - 2)^2} \cdot \frac{2(\nu_1 + \nu_2 - 2)}{\nu_1(\nu_2 - 4)} \text{ for } \nu_2 > 4, \tag{37a}$$

$$\beta_1 = \frac{8(\nu_2 - 4)(2\nu_1 + \nu_2 - 2)^2}{\nu_1(\nu_2 - 6)^2(\nu_1 + \nu_2 - 2)}, \quad \beta_2 = \frac{3}{\nu_2 - 8}\{\nu_2 - 4 + \tfrac{1}{2}(\nu_2 - 6)\beta_1\} \tag{37b}$$

for $\nu_2 > 6$ and $\nu_2 > 8$, respectively.

Table 5 gives eight upper percentage points and the median value of F, that is to say it gives the roots $F(Q|\nu_1, \nu_2)$ of the equation

$$Q = \int_{F(Q|\nu_1, \nu_2)}^{\infty} f(F|\nu_1, \nu_2)\, dF \tag{38}$$

to five significant figures for $Q = 0\cdot001,\ 0\cdot0025,\ 0\cdot005,\ 0\cdot01,\ 0\cdot025,\ 0\cdot05,\ 0\cdot10,\ 0\cdot25,\ 0\cdot50$; $\nu_1 = 1(1)10,\ 12,\ 15,\ 20,\ 24,\ 30,\ 40,\ 60,\ 120,\ \infty$; $\nu_2 = 1(1)30,\ 40,\ 60,\ 120,\ \infty$. Clearly we have

$$F(1 - Q|\nu_1, \nu_2) = 1/F(Q|\nu_2, \nu_1). \tag{39}$$

We note the following relations which hold for the entries in the marginal columns and rows:

for $\nu_2 = \infty$, $F(Q|\nu_1, \nu_2) = \nu_1^{-1}\chi^2(Q|\nu_1)$;

for $\nu_1 = \infty$, $F(Q|\nu_1, \nu_2) = \nu_2/\chi^2(Q|\nu_2)$;

for $\nu_1 = 1$, $F(Q|1, \nu_2) = t^2(\tfrac{1}{2}Q|\nu_2)$ where $t(\alpha|\nu)$ is the upper 100α per cent point of Student's t.

As a result, for these limiting cases some additional percentage points for F can be obtained from Table 3 of this volume and, in a few instances, from Table 12 of *B.T.S.* **1** for t.

Interpolation

Table 5 was primarily designed for use with integral values of ν_1 and ν_2. For $\nu_1 > 10$ and $\nu_2 > 30$ the function is tabled at harmonic intervals of the degrees of freedom and the arguments should here be taken as $60/\nu$ or $120/\nu$ as appropriate. Throughout the greater part of the tables interpolation in a single row or column, accurate to five significant figures, can be obtained using the simple Bessel formula of equation (319), involving second differences only. The 7-point Lagrangian coefficients given in Table 68, and described on p. 138 below, were obtained by Comrie & Hartley (1941) to provide more accurate values when this simple 4-point Bessel formula is inadequate.

12

Interpolation may become impossible, however, in the bottom right-hand corner of the second of each pair of facing pages, e.g. when ν_1 and $\nu_2 \geqslant 60$. Various approximations have been suggested for use in this region, generally in terms of the beta variate x, rather than of $F = \nu_2(1-x)/(\nu_1 x)$. An approximation due to Carter (1947) was described and illustrated in §8.5 of *B.T.S.* **1**.

The values of the function also change very rapidly as ν_1 and ν_2 approach zero. This does not matter in so far as integral values of ν_1 and ν_2 are concerned since the percentage points are tabled for all integers ν_1, $\nu_2 \leqslant 10$. To deal with low fractional degrees of freedom Table 4 described separately in §4.2 will be found useful; it forms, however, only a small part of a much fuller table planned by K. V. Mardia.

The F-distribution is a special case of Pearson's Type VI curve, given by

$$y = y_0(x'-a)^{q_2}x'^{-q_1}, \quad a \leqslant x' < \infty, \tag{40}$$

so that the table provides upper 100α percentage points for the distribution of x', i.e. we have

$$\left.\begin{aligned} x'(\alpha|q_1, q_2, a) &= a(1+\nu_1 F/\nu_2), \\ \nu_1 = 2(q_2+1), \quad \nu_2 &= 2(q_1-q_2-1). \end{aligned}\right\} \tag{41}$$

Many useful F-approximations to multivariate test criteria have been obtained through this variate transformation (see e.g. Box, 1949); some of these are discussed below.

An equivalent form of the variance ratio F can be obtained by expressing one of the two χ^2 variates in (35) as a fraction of their sum. Thus writing

$$\left.\begin{aligned} x &= \frac{\chi_2^2}{\chi_1^2 + \chi_2^2} = \frac{\nu_2}{\nu_2 + \nu_1 F} \\ 1 - x &= \frac{\chi_1^2}{\chi_1^2 + \chi_2^2} = \frac{\nu_1 F}{\nu_2 + \nu_1 F}, \end{aligned}\right\} \tag{42}$$

or

we find for the frequency function of x, the beta distribution

$$f(x) = \{B(a,b)\}^{-1} x^{a-1}(1-x)^{b-1}, \tag{43a}$$

with $a = \tfrac{1}{2}\nu_2$, $b = \tfrac{1}{2}\nu_1$ and $B(a,b) = \Gamma(a)\,\Gamma(b)/\Gamma(a+b)$. The resulting probability integral for x is the incomplete beta function ratio defined by

$$I_x(a,b) = \int_0^x f(u)\,du. \tag{43b}$$

Accordingly, Tables 4 and 5 giving *upper* percentage points $F(Q|\nu_1, \nu_2)$ can be used to yield *lower* 100α percentage points, $x(\alpha|a,b)$, using the transformation (42), i.e. from

$$\left.\begin{aligned} x(\alpha|a,b) &= \nu_2/\{\nu_2 + \nu_1 F(\alpha|\nu_1, \nu_2)\}, \\ a = \tfrac{1}{2}\nu_2, \quad b &= \tfrac{1}{2}\nu_1. \end{aligned}\right\} \tag{44}$$

where

The mean and variance of the beta variable are given, respectively, by

$$\mu = E(x) = \frac{a}{a+b}, \quad \sigma^2(x) = \frac{ab}{(a+b)^2(a+b+1)}, \tag{45}$$

and these equations may be inverted for the moment estimation of the parameters, a, b, yielding

$$a = \mu(\mu - \sigma^2 - \mu^2)/\sigma^2, \quad b = (1-\mu)(\mu - \sigma^2 - \mu^2)/\sigma^2. \tag{46}$$

Just as the F-distribution is a special case of Pearson's Type VI curve, so the beta distribution is a special case of his Type I, given by

$$u = y_0 \left(1 + \frac{x'}{a_1}\right)^{m_1} \left(1 - \frac{x'}{a_2}\right)^{m_2}, \quad -a_1 \leqslant x' \leqslant a_2. \tag{47}$$

The lower percentage points of x' can therefore be obtained from the upper percentage points of F through

$$x'(\alpha | a_1, a_2, m_1, m_2) = (a_1 + a_2) \nu_2 / \{\nu_2 + \nu_1 F(\alpha | \nu_1, \nu_2)\} - a_1, \tag{48}$$

where $m_1 = \frac{1}{2}\nu_2 - 1$, $m_2 = \frac{1}{2}\nu_1 - 1$.

Finally, the relation to the tail area of the binomial distribution is given by

$$\sum_{i=c}^{n} \binom{n}{i} p^i (1-p)^{n-i} = \sum_{i=c}^{n} f(i | n, p) = I_p(c, n - c + 1). \tag{49}$$

If c successes are observed in a binomial sample of n observations, then confidence limits for p can be derived in terms of F, using relations (44) and (49), as illustrated in §4.7 below.

Note on the comparison of the x and F tables

The parallel character of these two fundamental distributions appeared at an early stage in the development of statistical theory in the relation between the Type I (beta) and Type VI (inverted beta) distributions of Karl Pearson's system of frequency curves. From the point of view of tabulation, the probability integral or percentage points of one distribution are immediately obtainable from that of the other, through the relation (44). For the probability integral it is necessary to turn to the *Tables of the Incomplete Beta Function* (Karl Pearson, 1934; 1968), but for percentage points we have a choice of the two forms. For some purposes the x-table is the more convenient to use; for others, that of F. For example, the x-form arises most naturally when dealing with the percentage points of order statistics (§4.9) while in the field of analysis of variance it is the F-form which is preferable. Ease of interpolation is also a factor which may need to be taken into account.

The first really extensive table of percentage points of F was derived by Merrington & Thompson (1943) from the table of Thompson (1941) giving the percentage points of x to five significant figures. In publishing *B.T.S.* **1** it was decided to give the most complete table in terms of x (Table 16) and only a reduced table for F (Table 18). A number of reasons, however, have prompted us to include a more complete table for F in the present volume: (*a*) in many areas of the α, ν_1, ν_2 range, interpolation is easier for F than for x; this may be important in cases where high accuracy is needed. (*b*) Table 18 of *B.T.S.* **1** did not include for F a table of the 50 per cent point, nor of the 0·25 and 0·10 per cent points, which were added for x in the 1966 edition of *B.T.S.* **1**. (*c*) There have been found to be a certain number of errors, by far the most of only a unit in the last place, in the Merrington & Thompson (1943) table (see Amos & Pearson, 1970).

We therefore asked Dr D. E. Amos whether he would recompute *ab initio* a five-significant-figure table of percentage points of F, adding the 0·25 and 0·10 per cent points, as he had done for x. This he kindly agreed to do and it is this corrected and expanded table which appears as Table 5 in the present volume.

4.2 *Fractional degrees of freedom for the F-distribution: Table 4*

In using the beta or F-distributions as approximating functions, it is likely to be necessary to extract values having one or both degrees of freedom fractional. For low degrees of freedom, however, interpolation between the entries in Table 5 is not possible. Vogler & Norton (1970) have completed a table of percentage points of F for fractional ν_2, but only integral ν_1.

More recently Dr K. V. Mardia has developed a computer program which generates the percentage points of the F-distribution for degrees of freedom both fractional and integral. He has been preparing an extensive table and has given us permission to incorporate a small part of this work in Table 4, covering the arguments

$$100\alpha = 5\cdot0,\ 2\cdot5,\ 1\cdot0,\ 0\cdot5,\ 0\cdot1$$

and $$\nu_1 = 0\cdot1(0\cdot1)1\cdot0(0\cdot2)2\cdot0(0\cdot5)4\cdot5; \quad \nu_2 = 0\cdot5(0\cdot1)1\cdot0(0\cdot2)3\cdot0(0\cdot5)7\cdot0.$$

He also gave us the values for $\nu_2 = 0\cdot1(0\cdot1)0\cdot4$ corresponding to these α and ν_1. From these values, we found that interpolation for very low ν_2 seems impossible. Hence for $\nu_2 < 0\cdot5$ we recommend the use of the beta variable x in the following approximation. If P is the probability integral of the distribution (43a), writing x_α for the $100\alpha = 100P$ per cent point, we have the binomial expansion

$$
\begin{aligned}
B(a,b)\,P &= \int_0^{x_\alpha} x^{a-1} \sum_{i=0}^{\infty} \binom{b-1}{i}(-x)^i\,dx \\
&= \sum_{i=0}^{\infty} \binom{b-1}{i}(-1)^i\,x_\alpha^{a+i}/(a+i) \\
&= \frac{x_\alpha^a}{a}\left\{1 + \frac{a(1-b)}{a+1}x_\alpha + \dots\right\}.
\end{aligned}
\tag{50}
$$

If a and b are small, the second term within brackets on the right-hand side of (50) approximates to ax_α and for $\alpha \leqslant 0\cdot05$ will be small compared to unity. Thus approximately

$$x_\alpha \sim \{aPB(a,b)\}^{1/a}.$$

Taking logarithms and writing $a = \tfrac{1}{2}\nu_2$, $b = \tfrac{1}{2}\nu_1$, we have

$$
\log_{10} x_\alpha = \frac{2}{\nu_2}\{\log_{10}\Gamma(1+\tfrac{1}{2}\nu_1) + \log_{10}\Gamma(1+\tfrac{1}{2}\nu_2) - \log_{10}\Gamma[1+\tfrac{1}{2}(\nu_1+\nu_2)]
$$
$$
+ \log_{10}(\nu_1+\nu_2) - \log_{10}\nu_1 + \log_{10}\alpha\}. \tag{51}
$$

For $\nu_1 + \nu_2 \leqslant 2$, the values of $\log_{10}\Gamma(1+p)$ can be derived from *B.T.S.* **1**, Table 52, which gives $\log_{10}\Gamma(1+p)$ to seven decimal places for $p = 0\cdot00(0\cdot01)1\cdot00$. Beyond this range, a simple reduction formula to bring $\Gamma(r+p)$ to $\Gamma(1+p)$ will be needed.

Having determined x_α from (51), the upper 100α per cent points for F are found from

$$F_\alpha = \nu_2(1-x_\alpha)/(\nu_1 x_\alpha), \tag{52}$$

which, for very small x, is approximately $\nu_2/(\nu_1 x)$. Since x_α decreases with α and ν_1 and increases with ν_2, the effect of neglecting the second term in the expansion (50) will (for values given in Table 4) be most serious when $\alpha = 0\cdot05$, $\nu_2 = 0\cdot5$, $\nu_1 = 0\cdot1$. Below are given some comparisons between true F_α values found by Mardia and the approximations found using (51) and (52). This table shows clearly where and to what extent the accuracy of approximation falls off.

15

α	ν_1	ν_2	F_α True	F_α Approx.
0·05	0·1	0·5	659·4	655·6
	0·2	0·5	3039·8	3038
	0·5	0·5	13539	13538
	1·0	0·5	27079	27082
0·05	0·1	0·4	4391·2	4388
0·025	0·1	0·5	10568	10564

It will be noted that if we proceed in reverse, i.e. know x or F and wish to find $P = \alpha$, when a and b are small, there will be no difficulty in including the second term in the expansion (50). The use of this expansion was suggested by Comrie & Hartley (1941, p. 158) in their note accompanying Catherine Thompson's table of percentage points of x.

4.3 *Applications discussed elsewhere*

As in the case of χ^2, the applications of the F-distribution are widespread and largely well known. It will be useful, however, to list those which have been illustrated in $B.T.S.$ **1** or which will be described in later sections of this volume.

(a) The use in comparing two independent estimates of a population σ^2 in the analysis of variance was illustrated by a single example in $B.T.S.$ **1**, § 9.2.

(b) Distribution of the multiple correlation coefficient, R, in samples of n from uncorrelated normally distributed material. Significance points for R^2 can be derived through the transformation (42), since

$$R^2 = S_1/(S_1 + S_2) = \chi_1^2/(\chi_1^2 + \chi_2^2), \tag{53}$$

where S_1 is the sum of squares component of y due to its multilinear regression on variables $x_1, x_2, \ldots, x_{\nu_1}$ and S_2 is the residual sum of squares about this regression based on $\nu_2 = n - \nu_1 - 1$ degrees of freedom ($B.T.S.$ **1**, § 8.4). See also § 29.2 below.

(c) The F-approximation to multivariate likelihood criteria. In summarizing some of the applications of the χ^2 distribution (§ 3.2 i,j) we referred to the Bartlett–Box approximation which is applicable to certain distributions in multivariate analysis. Box (1949) derived an even more accurate approximation using the F-distribution. As only one of the degrees of freedom, ν_1, is integral, the other being in general a fraction, the approximation is less easy to apply than that based on χ^2. Illustrations of the comparative accuracy of the χ^2 and F-approximations are given in §§ 27.2 and 28.1 below.

(d) The F-approximation of Kruskal–Wallis in the analysis of variance, using ranks; this volume, $B.T.S.$ **2**, § 11.2, pp. 50–1. Further applications of Table 4 are described and illustrated in more detail below in the following §§ 4.4–4.9.

4.4 *Confidence intervals for σ_1^2/σ_2^2*

Denote by s_1^2 and s_2^2 two 'mean squares' of normal variates based respectively on ν_1 and ν_2 degrees of freedom, with expectations

$$E(s_1^2) = \sigma_1^2, \quad E(s_2^2) = \sigma_2^2.$$

Then
$$F = \frac{s_1^2}{s_2^2} \bigg/ \frac{\sigma_1^2}{\sigma_2^2} \tag{54}$$

follows the F-distribution for ν_1, ν_2 degrees of freedom. Accordingly for any pair of upper tail probabilities, $Q_1 \geqslant Q_2$, the statement

$$F(Q_1|\nu_1, \nu_2) \leqslant \frac{s_1^2}{s_2^2}\bigg/\frac{\sigma_1^2}{\sigma_2^2} \leqslant F(Q_2|\nu_1, \nu_2) \tag{55}$$

is correct with probability $Q_1 - Q_2$. This inequality may be used for computing:

(a) A single-tail upper $100(1-\alpha)$ per cent confidence limit for σ_1^2/σ_2^2 from

$$\frac{\sigma_1^2}{\sigma_2^2} \leqslant \frac{s_1^2}{s_2^2}\bigg/ F(1-\alpha|\nu_1, \nu_2) = \frac{s_1^2}{s_2^2}F(\alpha|\nu_2, \nu_1). \tag{56a}$$

(b) A single-tail lower $100(1-\alpha)$ per cent limit for σ_1^2/σ_2^2 from

$$\frac{s_1^2}{s_2^2}\bigg/ F(\alpha|\nu_1, \nu_2) \leqslant \frac{\sigma_1^2}{\sigma_2^2}. \tag{56b}$$

(c) A symmetrical double-tail $100(1-\alpha)$ per cent confidence interval from

$$\frac{s_1^2}{s_2^2}\bigg/ F(\tfrac{1}{2}\alpha|\nu_1, \nu_2) \leqslant \frac{\sigma_1^2}{\sigma_2^2} \leqslant \frac{s_1^2}{s_2^2}F(\tfrac{1}{2}\alpha|\nu_2, \nu_1). \tag{56c}$$

Example 8. A case of some interest arises in the estimation of components of variance from a single classification of $n \times k$ observations into k groups (random model), in which

$$\sigma_2^2 = \sigma_e^2 \text{ (error variance)}, \quad \sigma_1^2 = \sigma_e^2 + n\sigma_B^2,$$

with σ_B^2 representing the superimposed component of variance contributed by the 'group variables'. In this case it may be of interest to set confidence limits for the ratio σ_B^2/σ_e^2. We shall have confidence limits derivable directly from (56).

Suppose we have an experiment in which the observations fall into $k = 25$ groups of $n = 8$. Then $\nu_1 = 24$, $\nu_2 = 175$. As a first step we need to find $F(\tfrac{1}{2}\alpha|24, 175)$ and $F(\tfrac{1}{2}\alpha|175, 24)$. For ν_1 or $\nu_2 = 175$ interpolation must be in the end panel. Suppose we take $\alpha = 0\cdot01$; we find:

	(a) For $F(0\cdot005|24, 175)$				(b) For $F(0\cdot005|175, 24)$			
ν_2	$120/\nu_2$	F	δ^2	δ^3	ν_1	$120/\nu_1$	F	δ^2	δ^3
∞	0	1·8983	**90**		∞	0	2·4276	-81	**16**
120	1	2·0890	101	11	120	1	2·5463	-65	12
60	2	2·2898	114	13	60	2	2·6585	-53	9
40	3	2·5020	130	16	40	3	2·7654	-44	
30	4	2·7272			30	4	2·8679		

Following the suggestion made in §36.2 on pp. 135–6 below, it seems reasonable to add third differences of 11 and 16 at the head of the δ^3 columns in (a) and (b) respectively, and hence to add second differences of 90 and -81. These additions are printed in bold type. We may now apply the Bessel interpolation formula (319), using as arguments (a) $120/\nu_2$ and (b) $120/\nu_1$. Since $120/175 = 0\cdot68571$ and $B_2 = -0\cdot0539$ (from Table 66), we have

$$F(0\cdot005|24, 175) = 0\cdot31429 \times 1\cdot8983 + 0\cdot68571 \times 2\cdot0890 - 0\cdot0539 \times 0\cdot0191 = 2\cdot0280,$$

$$F(0\cdot005|175, 24) = 0\cdot31429 \times 2\cdot4276 + 0\cdot68571 \times 2\cdot5463 + 0\cdot0539 \times 0\cdot0146 = 2\cdot5098.$$

Finally, using the inequality (56c), we have for the 99 per cent two-sided confidence statement

$$\frac{s_1^2}{s_2^2}\bigg/ 2\cdot0280 \leqslant \frac{\sigma_e^2 + 8\sigma_B^2}{\sigma_e^2} \leqslant \frac{s_1^2}{s_2^2}2\cdot5098.$$

If, for simplicity we suppose that $s_1^2 = 30$, $s_2^2 = 10$, we have

$$1 \cdot 479 - 1 \leqslant 8\sigma_B^2/\sigma_e^2 \leqslant 7 \cdot 529 - 1$$

or

$$0 \cdot 060 \leqslant \sigma_B^2/\sigma_e^2 \leqslant 0 \cdot 816.$$

4.5 *Power of the F-test (random model)*

The relation (54) provides a straightforward method of computing the power of the F-test (when applied at a significance level α) to detect a given departure in the ratio σ_1^2/σ_2^2 from unity.

Example 9. Davies (1947, p. 74) has described an experiment concerned with assessing the variation in quality of a Naphthalene Black dyestuff; in this, yields were measured for each of $n = 5$ preparations made from $k = 6$ H-acid 'samples'. With the notation of the previous section, what is the chance of establishing significance at the 5 per cent level, if $\sigma_B^2/\sigma_e^2 = 2$? This probability is

$$\Pr\{F(\nu_1, \nu_2)(1 + n\sigma_B^2/\sigma_e^2) \geqslant F(0 \cdot 05 | \nu_1, \nu_2)\}$$

where $\nu_1 = k - 1 = 5$, $\nu_2 = k(n-1) = 24$. Thus we have

$$\Pr\{F(5, 24)(1 + 5 \times 2) \geqslant F(0 \cdot 05 | 5, 24)\}$$

$$= \Pr\{F(5, 24) \geqslant 2 \cdot 6207/11\} = \Pr\left\{F(5, 24) \geqslant \frac{1}{4 \cdot 197}\right\}$$

$$= 1 - \Pr\{F(24, 5) \geqslant 4 \cdot 197\}.$$

From Table 5 we extract the following values of α and F:

α	$\log_{10}(10^3\alpha)$	δ	$F(\alpha | 24, 5)$
0·10	2·000		3·1905
0·05	1·699	− 0·301	4·5272
0·025	1·398	− 0·301	6·2780
0·010			9·4665
0·005			12·780

We need to interpolate backwards for α at $F(\alpha | 24, 5) = 4 \cdot 197$. A rough plot of $F(\alpha | 24, 5)$ against $\log_{10}(10^3\alpha)$ suggests that the required value of α is about $0 \cdot 058$, giving a power of $1 - 0 \cdot 058 = 0 \cdot 942$. If for any reason greater accuracy were required we could use Table 69, Grid 3 to determine the following intermediate F-values:

α	$F(\alpha | 24, 5)$	δ^2	
0·050	4·527	.	From these we find that
0·055	4·321	25	$F(0 \cdot 05835 | 24, 5) = 4 \cdot 197$
0·060	4·140	20	giving a power of $0 \cdot 9416$
0·065	3·979	.	

4.6 *The ratio of means in samples from two exponential populations*

If $x_1, x_2, \ldots, x_{n_1}$ and $y_1, y_2, \ldots, y_{n_2}$ are independent random samples from negative exponential populations

$$f(x) = \mu_1^{-1}\exp(-x/\mu_1), \quad f(y) = \mu_2^{-1}\exp(-y/\mu_2), \tag{57}$$

then $2x/\mu_1$ and $2y/\mu_2$ are distributed as χ^2 with two degrees of freedom, while $2\Sigma x_i/\mu_1$ and $2\Sigma y_i/\mu_2$ are distributed as χ^2's with $\nu_1 = 2n_1$ and $\nu_2 = 2n_2$ degrees of freedom, respectively. It follows that if $\mu_1 = \mu_2$, and $\bar{x}, \bar{y}$ are the means of the two samples, then

$$\bar{x}/\bar{y} = F(\nu_1 = 2n_1, \nu_2 = 2n_2). \tag{58}$$

18

A test for significance of the hypothesis $\mu_1 = \mu_2$ follows at once. It is also possible to obtain confidence limits for μ_1/μ_2.

Example 10. The following illustration is taken from Maguire *et al.* (1952). A district in a coal mine had been working for over 2 years and there had been 63 compensatable accidents. The mean time interval between accidents was 13·7 days. It became necessary to transfer a group of men to a new district, replacing the experienced men by new face-workers. Immediately after the change there were five accidents with a mean interval of 1·8 days. Assuming, as seems to be the case, that the intervals between successive accidents of this kind among a group of workers follows the exponential distribution, is this reduction in mean interval significant?

We have $F = 13\cdot7/1\cdot8 = 7\cdot6$ and $\nu_1 = 124$, $\nu_2 = 8$ (the number of intervals being one less than the number of accidents). Reference to Table 5 shows that the 0·25 per cent point of F for these degrees of freedom is at about 7·39, so that there is a highly significant increase in the expectation of accidents among the new workers.

4.7 *Confidence limits for p in binomial sampling*

We here make use of the relation (49), from which it follows that from an observed proportion of 'successes', c/n, in a sample of n we may obtain lower and upper confidence limits for p from the percentage points of the incomplete beta function. However, using the transformation (44) we may also derive these limits in terms of F from Table 5. Writing the limits as p_A and $p_B > p_A$, we wish to make the statement

$$p_A(c|n, \tfrac{1}{2}\alpha) \leqslant p \leqslant p_B(c|n, \tfrac{1}{2}\alpha) \tag{59}$$

with a probability $\geqslant 1 - \alpha$, in the sense of confidence interval theory. To do this we proceed as follows, putting

$$\left. \begin{array}{l} \tfrac{1}{2}\alpha = \sum\limits_{i=c}^{n} f(i|n, p_A) = I_{p_A}(c, n-c+1) \\[2mm] \text{and} \qquad \tfrac{1}{2}\alpha = \sum\limits_{i=0}^{c} f(i|n, p_B) = 1 - I_{p_B}(c+1, n-c) = I_{1-p_B}(n-c, c+1). \end{array} \right\} \tag{60}$$

Then using (44) we have

$$\left. \begin{array}{l} p_A = x(\tfrac{1}{2}\alpha|c, n-c+1) = \nu_2/\{\nu_2 + \nu_1 F(\tfrac{1}{2}\alpha|\nu_1, \nu_2)\} \\[1mm] \qquad \text{with} \quad \nu_1 = 2(n-c+1), \quad \nu_2 = 2c; \\[2mm] p_B = 1 - x(\tfrac{1}{2}\alpha|n-c, c+1) = 1 - \nu_2'/\{\nu_2' + \nu_1' F(\tfrac{1}{2}\alpha|\nu_1', \nu_2')\} \\[1mm] \qquad \text{with} \quad \nu_1' = 2(c+1), \quad \nu_2' = 2(n-c). \end{array} \right\} \tag{61}$$

The limits defined by (61) were discussed in *B.T.S.* **1**, § 22.3 and used to derive the charts of Table 41 in that volume.

Example 11. Suppose that $c = 4$ 'successes' are observed in a sample of $n = 10$ observations. Find the symmetrical limits for the unknown p associated with a confidence coefficient of $1 - \alpha = 0\cdot95$. Here

$$\nu_1 = 14, \quad \nu_2 = 8; \quad \nu_1' = 10, \quad \nu_2' = 12.$$

For the upper limit p_B, $F(0\cdot025|10, 12)$ can be read directly from Table 5 as 3·3736, so that (61) gives $p_B = 1 - 12/\{12 + 10 \times 3\cdot3736\} = 0\cdot7376$. To obtain $F(0\cdot025|14, 8)$ interpolation in Table 5 is required. In practice it would be sufficient to take the value on inspection as 4·13, but as an illustration of making full use of the table we proceed as follows, extracting four values of F on the line $\nu_2 = 8$.

ν_1	$60/\nu_1$	F	δ^2
10	6	4·2951	.
12	5	4·1997	-31
15	4	4·1012	-32
20	3	3·9995	.

Since $60/14 = 4·2857$, we use the second difference Bessel formula (319) and Table 66, so finding

$$F(0·025\,|\,14, 8) = 4·1012 \times 0·7143 + 4·1997 \times 0·2857 + 0·0511 \times 0·0063 = 4·1297.$$

It follows that $p_A = 8/\{8 + 14 \times 4·1297\} = 0·1216$. Finally we associate the statement

$$0·122 \leqslant p \leqslant 0·738$$

with a confidence coefficient of at least 0·95.

Inspection shows that these limits could have been read roughly from the chart in Table 41 of *B.T.S.* **1**. However, limits for only two confidence coefficients, 0·95 and 0·99, are given there; with the present Tables 4 and 5 or Table 16 of *B.T.S.* **1** many more limits can be determined.

4.8 *Combination of evidence contained in k independent F-ratios*

R. A. Fisher (1932, § 21.1) suggested a method of combining the evidence contained in a number, k, of independent test criteria all providing partial support for the same inference. Consider the special case of k independent variance ratios $F_i = F(\nu_{1i}, \nu_{2i})$ based respectively on ν_{1i}, ν_{2i} degrees of freedom. The product of the associated tail areas Q_i computed as in equation (38) is then defined as

$$Q = \prod_{i=1}^{k} Q_i = \prod_{i=1}^{k} \int_{F_i}^{\infty} f(F\,|\,\nu_{1i}, \nu_{2i})\,dF. \qquad (62)$$

The hypothesis tested is that in none of the k comparisons is there a real effect; if this is true the Q_i form a sample of k independent observations from a rectangular distribution

$$0 \leqslant Q_i \leqslant 1, \quad \text{so that} \quad -2\log Q_i = \chi^2(\nu = 2)$$

and

$$-2\log Q = -2 \sum_{i=1}^{k} \log Q_i = \chi^2(\nu = 2k), \qquad (63)$$

i.e. follows a χ^2 distribution having $\nu = 2k$ degrees of freedom. A significant value for χ^2 suggests that some, at least, of the effects are real.

Example 12. Suppose we have three F-ratios

$$F_1(4, 20) = 2·43, \quad F_2(6, 30) = 2·58. \quad F_3(4, 24) = 3·01.$$

Since only moderate accuracy is likely to be required in a test of significance, it may be possible to reach a conclusion from a rapid examination of the entries in Table 5. We note that $F(0·10\,|\,4, 20) = 2·25$, $F(0·05\,|\,4, 20) = 2·87$ and therefore $0·05 < Q_1 < 0·10$. Similarly

$$0·025 < Q_2 < 0·05 \quad \text{and} \quad 0·025 < Q_3 < 0·05.$$

Using for conservative testing the upper limits, we obtain

$$\chi^2(\nu = 6) \geqslant -2\{\log 0·10 + 2\log 0·05\}$$
$$= 2\{2.30 + 2 \times 3·00\} = 16·60.$$

With $\nu = 6$, Table 3 shows that the test criterion is certainly significant at the 2·5 per cent level.

For a more accurate result, inverse interpolation in Table 5 is needed. This can be done more readily at this part of the table if we regard $\log Q$ as the argument, a fact which is most convenient as conversion to $\log Q$ is in any case required by formula (63). We then have the following workings:

Q	$-\log Q$	δ	$F(Q\|4,20)$	δ	$F(Q\|6,30)$	δ	$F(Q\|4,24)$	δ
0·025	3·689		3·51		2·87		3·38	
0·05	2·996	−0·693	2·87	−0·64	2·42	−0·45	2·78	−0·60
0·10	2·303	−0·693	2·25	−0·62	1·98	−0·44	2·19	−0·59

It is clear from the first differences, δ, that in these cases at any rate inverse linear interpolation is justified. We get
$$-\log Q_1 = 2\cdot303 + 0\cdot693 \times 18/62 = 2\cdot504$$

and similarly
$$-\log Q_2 = 3\cdot242, \quad -\log Q_3 = 3\cdot262,$$

so that
$$\chi^2 = 2\{2\cdot504 + 3\cdot242 + 3\cdot262\} = 18\cdot016,$$

a result, for $\nu = 6$, significant at the 1 per cent level. Higher accuracy in interpolation is rarely required for the present purpose but in case it is, the linear inverse interpolate may be used to obtain by direct Lagrangian interpolation (using Table 69) intermediate values of $F(Q|\nu_1, \nu_2)$; these can then be used for repeated inverse interpolation at a finer interval.

It should be noted finally that this procedure of combining the evidence from k independent test criteria is, of course, not confined to F-ratios in that the tail areas Q_i – or in some cases the P_i – of any set of test criteria can be entered in (63). The appropriate tail areas to be chosen are those for which a small area supports the likely alternative to the null hypothesis under test.

4.9 *Percentage points of order statistics*

Denote by
$$x_{(1)} \leqslant x_{(2)} \leqslant \ldots \leqslant x_{(n)}$$

a random sample of n observations, arranged in ascending order of magnitude, drawn from a population having cumulative distribution function

$$\Phi(X) = \Pr\{x \leqslant X\}. \tag{64}$$

$x_{(i)}$ is termed the ith order statistic in the sample. Then it is well known that

$$\Pr\{x_{(i)} \leqslant X\} = I_{\Phi(X)}(i, n-i+1), \tag{65}$$

where $I_y(a,b)$ is the incomplete beta function defined in (43a,b). The equations (64) and (65) relate the c.d.f. of any order statistic to the c.d.f. of the parent distribution. This important link may be used, for example:

(a) To determine the probability that $x_{(i)}$ will fall below a given percentage point, say X_α, of the population.

(b) To derive specific significance levels for $x_{(i)}$.

(c) To obtain from the order statistic in the sample, confidence limits for a quantile in the population.

The property involved in (65) is clearly most easily utilized by reference to tables of the incomplete beta function, whether the table is that of the c.d.f. of the beta function or of its percentage points. However, the same results can be derived using Table 5, through the transformation (44), with $\nu_1 = 2b = 2(n-i+1)$, $\nu_2 = 2a = 2i$. As the procedure was not illustrated in *B.T.S.* **1**, we take the opportunity of illustrating it here with a number of examples.

Example 13. Find the lower 5 per cent point of the largest individual, $x_{(n)}$, in a sample of $n = 10$ from a standardized normal distribution. If we use the table of percentage points of F, it will follow from (65) on introducing the transformation (45), that

$$\Phi(X) = \frac{\nu_2}{\nu_2 + \nu_1 F(0 \cdot 05 | \nu_1, \nu_2)} = \frac{20}{20 + 2F(0 \cdot 05 | 2, 20)} = \frac{10}{10 + 3 \cdot 4928} = 0 \cdot 7411.$$

Now referring to Table 1 of the normal function, we find that when $P(X) = \Phi(X) = 0 \cdot 7411$, $X = 0 \cdot 647$, which agrees with the value given in *B.T.S.* **1**, Table 24.

Example 14. Find the upper 1 per cent point of the $i = $ sixth order statistic in a sample of $n = 20$ χ^2-values, all based on $\nu = 10$ degrees of freedom. We have

$$F(0 \cdot 99 | \nu_1, \nu_2) = F(0 \cdot 99 | 30, 12) = 1/F(0 \cdot 01 | 12, 30) = 1/2 \cdot 843$$

and
$$\Phi(X) = 12/\{12 + 30/2 \cdot 843\} = 0 \cdot 532.$$

Table 7 of *B.T.S.* **1** gives values of $Q(\chi^2 | \nu)$. We need therefore to find χ^2 for which $Q(\chi^2 | 10) = 0 \cdot 468$. Inspection of the differences at this point of the table shows that inverse linear interpolation is appropriate and, in fact, $\chi^2 = 9 \cdot 69$.

Example 15. Find the lower and upper 2·5 per cent points of the median observation, $x_{(8)}$, in samples of $n = 15$ from a Weibull distribution with c.d.f.

$$\Phi(x) = 1 - \exp\left[-\{(x - a)/b\}^m\right] \quad (x \geqslant a), \tag{66}$$

and $m = 2 \cdot 0$. Writing $X = (x - a)/b$ we have $\Phi(X) = 1 - \exp[-X^2]$. We need the value of $F(0 \cdot 025 | 16, 16)$ and using harmonic arguments $60/\nu_1$ and the Bessel formula (319) find it to be $2 \cdot 761$. Hence for the lower and upper 2·5 per cent limits X_1 and X_2 we have

$$\Phi(X_1) = 16/\{16 + 16F(0 \cdot 025 | 16, 16)\} = 1/3 \cdot 761 = 0 \cdot 2659,$$

$$\Phi(X_2) = 16/\{16 + 16/F(0 \cdot 025 | 16, 16)\} = 2 \cdot 761/3 \cdot 761 = 0 \cdot 7341.$$

Since for the population distribution

$$X = \sqrt{\{-\log[1 - \Phi(X)]\}},$$

we find
$$X_1 = 0 \cdot 556, \quad X_2 = 1 \cdot 151.$$

Given the values of the parameters a and b in (66), the limits in terms of $x = a + bX$ follow at once.

Example 16. To find confidence limits for the population median, X_m, based on the use of two order statistics in a sample of n observations. In this case $\Phi(X_m) = 0 \cdot 50$ and we have to find the integers i and j such that

$$\left.\begin{aligned} \Pr\{x_{(i|n)} \leqslant X_m\} &= I_{0 \cdot 5}(i, n - i + 1) \leqslant 1 - \tfrac{1}{2}\alpha, \\ \Pr\{x_{(j|n)} \leqslant X_m\} &= I_{0 \cdot 5}(j, n - j + 1) \leqslant \tfrac{1}{2}\alpha. \end{aligned}\right\} \tag{67}$$

The solution is obtained most readily by an inspection of the *Tables of the Incomplete Beta Function* (Karl Pearson, 1934, 1968).

Suppose we take $n = 40$, $\alpha = 0 \cdot 10$. Inspection of these tables shows that

p	q	$I_{0 \cdot 50}(p, q)$
25	16	0·0769
26	15	0·0403

It follows that we should take the twenty-sixth and fifteenth order statistics in the samples of forty and have a coefficient of $1 - 2\alpha \geqslant 0.90$ for the interval

$$x_{(15|40)} \leqslant X_m \leqslant x_{(26|40)}.$$

An alternative procedure would be to use the charts of Table 17 of *B.T.S.* **1**, with the scales contained in the pocket at the end of that volume. In this case $a = p$, $b = q$. We know that $a + b = 41$ and have to find the appropriate a and $b = 41 - a$ so that $x = 0.50$ on the scale gives a P just below but as near to $P = \alpha = 0.05$ as possible. We place the scale, (A, B, or C) successively on top of a vertical marked b, with the arrow → on top of the curve associated with $a = 41 - b$, making trials until the value of P read off opposite $x = 0.50$ on the scale comes against a curve as near as possible below that labelled $P = 0.05$.

In the present example with $a + b = 41$, putting the B-scale along the vertical $b = 15$ and the arrow as near as possible to what we judge to be a curve for $a = 26$, we find that 0.50 on the x-scale falls a little below the $P = 0.05$ curve. Then using the C-scale and placing it as near as we can to the vertical at $b = 16$, with the arrow on the curve $a = 25$, we find that 0.50 on the x-scale clearly gives $P > 0.05$. It follows that the fifteenth and twenty-sixth order statistics are the appropriate ones to take, giving an interval for the median associated with a confidence coefficient of $1 - 2\alpha > 0.90$.

Very recently Van der Parren (1970) has given a table of confidence limits of this kind for the median, for arguments $n = 1(1)100$, $1 - 2\alpha = 0.70$, 0.80, 0.90, 0.95, 0.98, 0.99. Besides giving the above answer in the example selected it shows, e.g. that 99 per cent confidence limits would in this case be the twelfth and twenty-ninth observations.

A similar procedure could of course be used to determine confidence limits based on order statistics for other population quantiles.

Example 17. The quality specification for a particular electronic component, for which the distribution of life follows a negative exponential, specifies that the mean life should be 200 hours. Samples of $n = 20$ components from each batch are taken and tested until $i = 12$ have failed. It is required to compute the upper 10 per cent limit, $X_{0.90}$, for the duration of such a test procedure.

From the 10 per cent point section in Table 5 we find

$$F(0.90 | 18, 24) = 1/F(0.10 | 24, 18) = 1/1.810.$$

Hence
$$\Phi(X_{0.90}) = 24 \times 1.810/(24 \times 1.810 + 18) = 0.707.$$

But for the parent exponential

$$\Phi(X) = \frac{1}{200} \int_0^X \exp(-u/200) \, du = 1 - \exp(-X/200).$$

Hence $X_{0.90} = 200\{-\log(0.293)\} = 200 \times 1.228 = 246$ hours.

Example 18. A new specification has laid down that an endurance test be applied to five specimens from each batch of an industrial product and that if more than one specimen breaks down within thirty-eight days, the batch be rejected. A manufacturer wishes to know how his product stands with regard to this test. In the past he has accumulated a considerable number of endurance records of his standard output (which appears under control) and from the resulting frequency distribution has found that:

$$\text{mean} = 60.4 \text{ days}, \quad \text{s.d.} = 14.5 \text{ days}$$

$$\sqrt{\beta_1} \sim 0.4, \quad \beta_2 \sim 3.6.$$

If he assumes that the distribution can be roughly represented by a Pearson curve (of Type VI) he can find the fraction of this distribution falling below thirty-eight by (a) calculating the standardized deviate $X = (38 - 60 \cdot 4)/14 \cdot 5 = -1 \cdot 54$, (b) inspecting Table 32.

It is seen that for $\sqrt{\beta_1} = 0 \cdot 4$, $\beta_2 = 3 \cdot 6$, the lower 5 per cent point has a standardized deviate of $-1 \cdot 531$. Hence $\Phi(X)$ is slightly less than $0 \cdot 05$. Then $\Pr\{x_{(2|5)} \leqslant 38\} \sim I_{0 \cdot 05}(2, 4)$. It is a little troublesome to find this probability from Table 5, but examination of the *Tables of the Incomplete Beta Function* shows that

$$I_{0 \cdot 05}(2, 4) = 1 - I_{0 \cdot 95}(4, 2) = 1 - 0 \cdot 977 = 0 \cdot 023.$$

This suggests that in a little less than one in forty applications the test may reject the product because $x_{(2|5)}$ will be less than thirty-eight days. Steps to improve quality are therefore probably desirable.

5. The probability integrals of the extreme values in normal samples and of the mean deviation

In *B.T.S.* **1** we included tables of the percentage points of the ratios $X_n = (x_{(n)} - \mu)/\sigma$ (Table 24), $u_n = (x_{(n)} - \bar{x})/\sigma$ (Table 25) and of

$$m = \sum_i |x_i - \bar{x}|/\sigma$$

(Table 21), where $x_{(1)}, x_{(2)}, \ldots, x_{(n)}$ is an ordered random sample of n observations from a $N(\mu, \sigma)$ population and m is the standardized mean deviation from the sample mean. These percentage point tables were only given for limited sizes of sample, but are adequate for most purposes of data testing and analysis. However, occasionally the need for the complete probability integral of these standardized statistics will arise; a particular case of this need occurs if we wish to combine the evidence derived from, say, k independent samples by taking the product of the tail probabilities Q_i in the form

$$\chi^2(\nu = 2k) = -2 \sum_{i=1}^{k} \log Q_i. \tag{63 bis}$$

The three probability integral tables for X_n, u_n and m included here as Tables 6, 7 and 8, respectively, make the use of this overall test straight-forward. Its application has already been discussed in §4.8 above in connection with the combination of a series of F-values.

5.1 *The extreme standardized deviate from the population mean* (*Table* 6)

It is sometimes of interest to use as test criteria one or other of the standardized outliers

$$X_n = (x_{(n)} - \mu)/\sigma, \quad X_1 = -(x_{(1)} - \mu)/\sigma. \tag{68}$$

These criteria require, of course, a knowledge or specification of both parameters μ and σ for their evaluation. The c.d.f. of X_n (or X_1) is given by

$$\Pr\{X_n \leqslant X\} = P(X)^n, \tag{69}$$

where $P(X)$ is the normal c.d.f. defined by equation (2). Table 6 gives the c.d.f. of X_n to seven decimals for $n = 3(1)25(5)60, 100(100)1000$. It is based partly on a table of Tippett's (1926) to which fresh calculations for the lower sample sizes have been added.

5.2   *The extreme standardized deviate from the sample mean (Table 7)*

It is sometimes relevant to eliminate the (unknown) value of μ from X_n or X_1 and to use the criteria

$$u_n = (x_{(n)} - \bar{x})/\sigma, \quad u_1 = -(x_{(1)} - \bar{x})/\sigma, \tag{70}$$

where $\bar{x}$ is the sample mean; the population standard deviation σ must still be known or specified. The c.d.f. of u_n (or u_1) is given (see Nair, 1948 equation (20)) by

$$\Pr\{u_n \leqslant u\} = P(u|n) = 1 - Q(u|n) = n^{\frac{1}{2}}(2\pi)^{-\frac{1}{2}(n-1)} G_{n-1}(nu), \tag{71}$$

where the G-functions (Godwin, 1945) are defined by the recurrence relation

$$G_r(x) = \int_0^x \exp\left\{-\frac{t^2}{2r(r+1)}\right\} G_{r-1}(t)\, dt, \quad G_0(x) = 1. \tag{72}$$

Table 7 gives $P(u|n)$ to six decimal places for $n = 3(1)9$ and to five decimals for $n = 10(1)25$; the former section is due to Nair (1948) and the latter to Grubbs (1950).

It should be noted that the present table places on record the G-functions defined by the recurrence relations (72) and it has been observed (see e.g. Nair, 1948) that there are numerous criteria depending on contrasts of normal order statistics whose c.d.f. can be evaluated with the help of these functions. Indeed, one such criterion is the sample mean deviation discussed in § 5.3. It seemed therefore of interest to have a basic table available for *pilot* computations of such probability integrals. However, it is unlikely that the table would be useful for systematic computations on high-speed computers since the G-functions are the solutions of a system of first order linear differential equations arising from the differentiation of (72), viz.

$$\left.\begin{array}{l} \dfrac{dG_r(x)}{dx} = \exp\left\{-\dfrac{1}{2}\dfrac{x^2}{r(r+1)}\right\} G_{r-1}(x) \quad (r = 1, 2, \ldots), \\[3mm] G_0(x) = 1, \quad G_r(0) = 0, \end{array}\right\} \tag{73}$$

which are readily solved by (say) Runge–Kutta type algorithms usually available on high-speed computers.

An application

In the following example we suggest how Tables 6 or 7 could be used to provide an overall monitoring test based on the results of a number of small samples.

Example 19. In quality testing of batches of a chemical product it is suspected that a particular cause of breakdown may sometimes operate, resulting in a few isolated batches dropping in quality. In addition there may be long-term trends in the average quality level μ. Samples of $n = 6$ batches are tested periodically and in order to monitor the cause of breakdown, the outlier criterion $u_1 = -(x_{(1)} - \bar{x})/\sigma$ is computed for each sample, where σ is the standard deviation specified for the quality control process. The following table shows the value of u_1 for each of $k = 4$ samples of $n = 6$ batches. In the third column we have

$$Q(u_1|6) = 1 - P(u_1|6),$$

derived from Table 7 and in the last column the values of the natural logarithms of the Q_i. None of the individual criteria is significant at the 5 per cent level, but when they are combined in the form of (63 bis) they give $-2\sum_i \log Q_i = 18{\cdot}224$, which as a χ^2 with $\nu = 2k = 8$ degrees of

25

freedom is seen from Table 3 to be significant at the 2·5 per cent level. This suggests that the breakdown cause is operative.

Sample no.	u_1	$Q(u_1|6)$	$-\log Q(u_1|6)$
1	2·0	0·0847	2·469
2	1·9	0·1110	2·198
3	1·7	0·1834	1·696
4	2·1	0·0640	2·749
Total			9·112

5.3 *Probability integral of the mean deviation (Table 8)*

If x_i, $i = 1, 2, ..., n$ is a random sample of n observations from $N(\mu, \sigma)$ it is sometimes appropriate to use as a measure of dispersion the mean deviation about the sample mean defined by

$$m = n^{-1} \sum_{i=1}^{n} |x_i - \bar{x}|, \tag{74}$$

where $\bar{x}$ is the arithmetic mean of the x_i. If σ is taken as unity, the p.d.f. of m has been given by Godwin (1945) as

$$f(m) = n^{\frac{3}{2}} 2^{-\frac{1}{2}(n+1)} \pi^{-\frac{1}{2}(n-1)} \sum_{t=1}^{n-1} \binom{n}{t} \exp\left\{\frac{-m^2 n^3}{8t(n-t)}\right\} G_{t-1}(\tfrac{1}{2}mn) G_{n-t-1}(\tfrac{1}{2}mn). \tag{75}$$

Table 8 gives the probability integral of m, i.e. of

$$P(m|n) = \int_0^m f(m') \, dm' \tag{76}$$

to five decimals for $m = 0(0\cdot01)3\cdot00$ and $n = 2(1)10$.

Expectations and variances of m (Helmert, 1876; Fisher, 1920) are given by

$$\left. \begin{aligned} E(m) &= \sigma \left\{\frac{2(n-1)}{n\pi}\right\}^{\frac{1}{2}}, \\ \operatorname{var}(m) &= \sigma^2 \frac{2(n-1)}{n^2\pi} \left\{\tfrac{1}{2}\pi + [n(n-2)]^{\frac{1}{2}} - n + \sin^{-1}\frac{1}{n-1}\right\}. \end{aligned} \right\} \tag{77}$$

Means, variances and the β_1, β_2 coefficients of m for $n = 2(1)20, 30, 60$ are given in Table 20 and upper and lower percentage points for $n = 2(1)10$ in Table 21 of *B.T.S.* **1**.

Applications of the mean deviation

The mean deviation is sometimes used as an alternative measure of dispersion and it is involved in certain quality control specifications in place of range and standard deviation. Undoubtedly the attractive graphical representation of m and its ready assessment by direct measurement has contributed to these usages. Since all quality control procedures involve the use of a large number of small samples we must face the question of combining the information contained in a number, k, of mean deviations, m_t ($t = 1, ..., k$), for the purpose of (a) obtaining a point estimate of σ, (b) monitoring the data for variability in excess of the specified σ. Whilst for the sample mean squares both purposes (a) and (b) are answered by 'pooling the sums of squares', and for range the distribution of mean range has been developed, the corresponding problem for m requires attention. Problems (a) and (b) can be treated approximately by using the arithmetic mean $\bar{m} = \Sigma m_t/k$ and the associated formulae:

$$E(\bar{m}) = E(m), \quad \operatorname{var} \bar{m} = \operatorname{var} m/k, \quad \beta_1(\bar{m}) = \beta_1(m)/k, \quad \beta_2(\bar{m}) - 3 = \{\beta_2(m) - 3\}/k$$

26

and by referring to Table 32 to obtain approximate significance limits for $\bar{m}$ from the corresponding Pearson curve. Problem (b) is, however, amenable to a distributionally exact treatment by using the present Table 8 of $P(m/\sigma|n) = 1 - Q(m/\sigma|n)$ and again using the χ^2 test (63 bis) for combining tail-area probabilities.

Example 20. Consider the following $k = 5$ values of m_t all computed from samples of size $n = 6$, and monitor these against a value of $\sigma = 20$ units.

t	m_t	$m_t/20$	$P(m_t/20|6)$	$-\log Q_t$
1	18	0·9	0·7690	1·465
2	22	1·1	0·9262	2·606
3	14	0·7	0·4830	0·660
4	16	0·8	0·6392	1·019
5	20	1·0	0·8640	1·995
Total				7·745

The entries $P(m_t/20|6)$ are read from Table 8; hence we find from the last column that

$$-2\sum_t \log Q_t = 15\cdot49$$

which is not significant as a χ^2 having $\nu = 2k = 10$ degrees of freedom.

It should be noted that this analysis may be applied to mean deviations based on samples of varying sizes.

II. TABLES FOR PROCEDURES BASED ON THE USE OF ORDER STATISTICS

If a random sample of n independent observations, $x_1, x_2, \ldots, x_n$, is drawn from a population having probability density function $f(x)$, then the observations arranged in ascending order of magnitude will be denoted by $\{x_{(i)}\}$ where

$$x_{(1)} \leqslant x_{(2)} \leqslant \ldots \leqslant x_{(n)}.$$

The $x_{(i)}$ are termed order statistics and are often scaled to their standardized form, $X_{(i)} = (x_{(i)} - \mu)/\sigma$, where $\mu = E(x_i)$, $\sigma^2 = \mathrm{var}\, x_i$. The thirteen tables in the present group are concerned with certain properties of order statistics for samples from the normal, the so-called 'half-normal', the negative exponential and five other gamma distributions. A very full account of properties and uses has been given in Sarhan & Greenberg (1962) and more recently by H. A. David (1970); besides dealing with the theory the former book includes a considerable number of tables and illustrations of their use. The tables included in the present volume have been taken from a number of sources, referred to below. We shall only mention a few of the uses to which they may be put. Tables 9, 19 and 20 have recently been reproduced in Harter (1970, **2**).

6. Normal order statistics

6.1 *Expected values, variances and covariances* (*Tables* 9 *and* 10)

If $f(X)$ represents the standardized normal density function defined in equation (1), then Tables 9 and 10, give values in random samples of size n, for

$$E(X_{(i)}) = \xi(i|n), \quad \mathrm{var}\, X_{(i)} = E(X_{(i)}^2) - \{E(X_{(i)})\}^2, \quad \mathrm{cov}\, X_{(i)} X_{(j)} = E(X_{(i)} X_{(j)}) - E(X_{(i)}) \times E(X_{(j)}).$$

27

A table of $E(X_{(i)})$, denoted there by $\xi(i|n)$, was given in *B.T.S.* **1**, Table 28, for the following range of arguments:

$$n = 2(1)20 \text{ to three decimals,}$$

$$n = 21(1)26(2)50 \text{ to two decimals,}$$

and the more elementary applications were also discussed there. We include here as Table 9 a much fuller five-decimal place table due to Harter (1961), covering the range

$$n = 2(1)100(25)200.$$

Harter also tabled values for $n = 100(25)250(50)400$,† but for samples of between 100 and 400 observations he suggested the use of a very accurate empirical formula based on a suggestion of Blom's. We take

$$E(X_{(i)}) = X\{P = (i-\alpha_n)/(n-2\alpha_n+1)\}, \tag{78}$$

where $X(P)$ has been defined in equation (3) and α_n has two values:

$$\begin{aligned}
&\text{(i)} \quad \text{for} \quad i = 1, \quad \alpha_{1,n} = 0\cdot315065 + 0\cdot057974u - 0\cdot009776u^2, \\
&\text{(ii)} \quad \text{for} \quad i \neq 1, \quad \alpha_{2,n} = 0\cdot327511 + 0\cdot058212u - 0\cdot007909u^2,
\end{aligned} \tag{79}$$

with $u = \log_{10} n$. Formulae (79) were suggested by Harter (1961), p. 155.

As an illustration, we find the expected value of the third-order statistic $E(X_{(3)})$, when $n = 300$. It follows from (79) that $u = 2\cdot47712$, $\alpha_{2,n} = 0\cdot4232$, and hence from (78), $E(X_{(3)}) = X(P = 0\cdot008585)$. Interpolating in Table 1, for $P = 1 - 0\cdot008585 = 0\cdot991415$, we find that $E(X_{(3)}) = -2\cdot3830$. The true value given in Harter's (1961) fuller table is $-2\cdot38365$, so that the approximation is in error by a unit in the third decimal place, which is indicative of the precision of (78) when used for $n > 100$.

Values of the variances and covariances have as far as we know only been published for $n \leqslant 20$, although Ruben (1956) has referred to an ambitious programme involving the calculations of first order moments, variances and covariances up to $n = 100$. Table 10 contains six-decimal place values derived from Sarhan & Greenberg's (1962) ten-decimal place table, itself based on raw moments calculated by D. Teichroew.

As far as we are aware, for $n > 20$, the best approximations to $\mathrm{var}\, X_{(i)}$ and $\mathrm{cov}\, X_{(i)} X_{(j)}$ are those obtained from expansions in inverse powers of $(n+2)$ given by David & Johnson (1954). Writing

$$P_i = 1 - Q_i = \frac{i}{n+1}, \quad X_i = F^{-1}(P_i), \quad Z_i = \frac{1}{\sqrt{(2\pi)}} \exp -\tfrac{1}{2}X_i^2$$

and

$$a_i = P_i/Z_i, \quad b_i = Q_i/Z_i,$$

then

$$E(X_{(i)}) = X_i + \frac{a_i b_i X_i}{2(n+2)} + \frac{a_i b_i}{(n+2)^2}\{\tfrac{1}{3}(b_i - a_i)(1 + 2X_i^2) + \tfrac{1}{8}a_i b_i X_i(7 + 6X_i^2)\} + \dots, \tag{80}$$

$$\mathrm{var}\, X_{(i)} = \frac{a_i b_i}{n+2} + \frac{a_i b_i}{(n+2)^2}\{2(b_i - a_i)X_i + a_i b_i(1 + \tfrac{5}{2}X_i^2)\} + \dots, \tag{81}$$

$$\begin{aligned}
\mathrm{cov}\, X_{(i)} X_{(j)} = \frac{a_i b_j}{n+2} + \frac{a_i b_j}{(n+2)^2}\{(b_i - a_i)X_i + (b_j - a_j)X_j + \tfrac{1}{2}a_i b_i(1 + 2X_i^2) \\
+ \tfrac{1}{2}a_j b_j(1 + 2X_j^2) + \tfrac{1}{2}a_i b_j X_i X_j\} + \dots, \quad (82)
\end{aligned}$$

where $i \leqslant j$. The quantities a_i, b_i are obtainable by entering Table 1 with $P_i = i/(n+1)$ and finding Z_i. The following table gives some idea of the accuracy of these approximations at $n = 20$, where a comparison with the true values is possible.

† This table has recently been reproduced in even greater detail in Harter (1970, Table C 1).

	Means			Variances	
i	True	Approx.		True	Approx.
20	1·8675	1·8699		0·2757	0·2689
19	1·4076	1·4076		0·1596	0·1575
18	1·1309	1·1308		0·1228	0·1217
11	0·06200	0·06199		0·0769	0·0766

		Covariances	
j	i	True	Approx.
20	19	0·1345	0·1331
	18	0·0913	0·0908
	11	0·02966	0·02966
19	18	0·1088	0·1079
	11	0·03556	0·03548
18	11	0·04035	0·04022

The greatest error occurs in the variance of the first, or last, order statistic, where the accuracy only improves slowly as n increases. Using Table 12, we obtain the following comparison for var $X_{(1)}$:

n	True	Approx.
30	0·2458	0·2406
49	0·2168	0·2124

The approximations for the covariances are rather closer.

David & Johnson also gave the terms of order $(n+2)^{-3}$, but the expressions involved are very lengthy. While the terms given in equations (80)–(82) involve considerable computation, there may be occasions when the formulae are useful for exploratory purposes. Moreover they may be used on a high-speed computer in conjunction with a suitable algorithm for $X(P)$.*

6.2 *Illustrative examples (Tables 9 and 10)*

Example 21. As in the case of other distributions, the expected values of normal order statistics may be used in a graphical plot as a rapid check on the assumption of normal variation. If the observed values of the order statistics $x_{(i)}$ are plotted as ordinates against the corresponding $\xi(i|n)$ as abscissae, the points, except for chance sampling fluctuations, should, on the normal hypothesis, lie close to a straight line. The disadvantage of this type of examination is, of course, that it provides no means of judging the significance of departure from linearity. However, the calculations based on Tables 15 and 16 to be described in §7 provide an objective test of non-normality, whose form was originally suggested by the graphical approach.

The table below gives the results of rotating bend fatigue tests, applied to fifteen specimens, the variable, x, being the endurance at a stress level of forty tons per square inch, expressed in terms of 10^6 cycles to breaking (data from Rolls Royce Ltd). The second column shows the ordered observations $x_{(i)}$, the third column $1 + \log_{10} x_{(i)}$. Both these variables are plotted against $\xi(i|15)$ in Fig. 1. It is at once clear that $\log x$ is more nearly normally distributed than x; there are physical reasons for expecting that this would be so. The factors $a_{i,n}$ in the final column are defined in §7.1 below.

Example 22. Provided that $n \leqslant 20$, Tables 9 and 10 may be used to compare the accuracy of alternative estimators of the population mean and standard deviation, based on order statistics. Such estimators may be applied to censored samples. Suppose, for example, that the

* Note for 2nd impression. Mr. B. N. Vincent working at McGill University under Professor Ruben has now completed values for variances and covariances up to $n = 50$, and has work for higher n-values in progress.

Specimen (ordered)	$x_{(i)}$	$1 + \log_{10} x_{(i)}$	$\xi(i \mid 15)$	Factors $a_{i,n}$
1	0·200	0·301	−1·736	0·5150
2	0·330	0·519	−1·248	0·3306
3	0·450	0·653	−0·948	0·2495
4	0·490	0·690	−0·715	0·1878
5	0·780	0·892	−0·516	0·1353
6	0·920	0·964	−0·335	0·0880
7	0·950	0·978	−0·165	0·0433
8	0·970	0·987	0·000	0·0000
9	1·040	1·017	0·165	
10	1·710	1·233	0·335	
11	2·220	1·346	0·516	
12	2·275	1·357	0·715	
13	3·650	1·562	0·948	
14	7·000	1·845	1·248	
15	8·800	1·944	1·736	

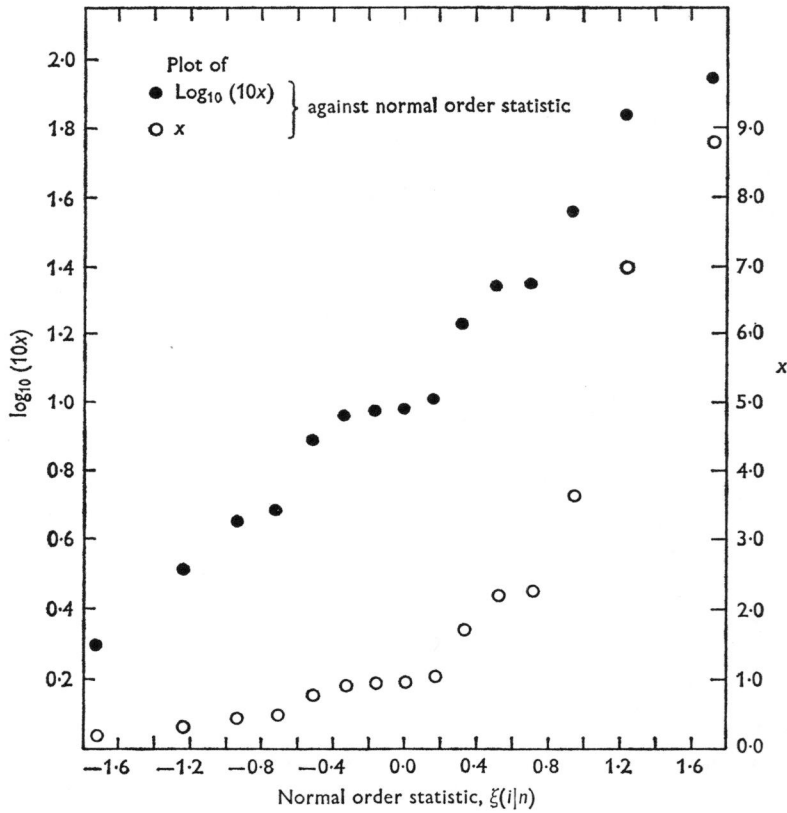

Fig. 1. Rotating bend fatigue data. Graphical test for normality.

highest five observations in a sample of $n = 15$ are missing. Would the population standard deviation, σ, be estimated more accurately from

$$s_1 = \frac{x_{(9)} + x_{(10)} - x_{(1)} - x_{(2)}}{\xi(9|15) + \xi(10|15) - \xi(1|15) - \xi(2|15)}$$

or from

$$s_2 = \frac{x_{(9)} + x_{(10)} - x_{(6)} - x_{(7)}}{\xi(9|15) + \xi(10|15) - \xi(6|15) - \xi(7|15)}?$$

Since $E(x_{(i)}) = \mu + \xi(i|n)\sigma$, it follows that $E(s_1) = \sigma = E(s_2)$ and

$$\operatorname{var} x_{(i)} = \sigma^2 \operatorname{var} X_{(i)}, \quad \operatorname{cov} x_{(i)} x_{(j)} = \sigma^2 \operatorname{cov} X_{(i)} X_{(j)}.$$

Hence $\operatorname{var} s_1$ and $\operatorname{var} s_2$ can be found using the appropriate expectations, variances and covariances of the standardized normal order statistics $X_{(i)}$ given in Tables 9 and 10. On calculation, it is found that $\operatorname{var} s_1 = 0 \cdot 07206\sigma^2$, $\operatorname{var} s_2 = 0 \cdot 21373\sigma^2$.

It follows that the estimator based on four order statistics having the maximum spread is a good deal more accurate than the symmetrical estimator, s_2. It is possible, however, that s_2 would be more robust than s_1, in respect of departures from parental normality.

6.3 Sums of squares of scores, $\xi(i|n)$, associated with rankings (Table 13)

If the integers $u_1, u_2, ..., u_n$ represent the rankings of a set of n individuals in respect of a character not quantitatively measurable, the normal order statistics $\xi(i|n)$ can be used as scores to replace the rankings. Fisher & Yates (1938, pp. 12–14) suggested that various standard statistical techniques might now be applied to these scores, and they provided a table of sums of squares of the $\xi(i|n)$ to help in such analyses. The present Table 13, giving $c_n^2 = \sum_{i=1}^{n} \xi^2(i|n)$ for $n = 2(1)100$ has been computed from Harter's normal order statistics given in Table 9.

Example 23. As a particular case, we may obtain a measure of correlation between n pairs of associated rankings $u_1, u_2, ..., u_n$ and $v_1, v_2, ..., v_n$. The integers u_i may be taken in ascending order as $1, 2, ..., n$ and the v_i will then be a permutation of these integers. The measure of correlation may then be written

$$r_F = \sum_{i=1}^{n} \xi(i|n)\,\xi(v_i|n) \Big/ \sum_{i=1}^{n} \xi^2(i|n). \tag{83}$$

We may take as a numerical example the case of the ten boys ranked for mathematics and music, for which Spearman's coefficient r_s was determined in *B.T.S.* 1, §25.1. The necessary figures are as follows:

Boy ...	I	F	C	B	J	E	A	H	G	D
Mathematics										
Rank, u_i	1	2	3	4	5	6	7	8	9	10
Score	$-1\cdot54$	$-1\cdot00$	$-0\cdot66$	$-0\cdot38$	$-0\cdot12$	$0\cdot12$	$0\cdot38$	$0\cdot66$	$1\cdot00$	$1\cdot54$
Music										
Rank, v_i	8	9	3	7	4	1	5	2	6	10
Score	$0\cdot66$	$1\cdot00$	$-0\cdot66$	$0\cdot38$	$-0\cdot38$	$-1\cdot54$	$-0\cdot12$	$-1\cdot00$	$0\cdot12$	$1\cdot54$

$$\sum_{i=1}^{10} \xi(i|10)\xi(v_i|10) = -0\cdot0784; \quad c_{10}^2 = \sum_{i=1}^{10} \xi^2(i|10) = 7\cdot914, \text{ from Table 13}; \quad r_F = -0\cdot010.$$

The correlation of scores, $r_F = -0 \cdot 010$ is certainly not significant. The Spearman rank correlation was previously found to be $r_s = -0 \cdot 103$, also not significant.

In situations where (a) u_i, v_i are generated as indices of two continuous variates x_i, y_i, (b) the monotonic transformations of the x and y scales to normality transform the joint distribution into a bivariate normal one, r_F is an estimator of the product moment correlation between the transformed variates. For a discussion of the position see Fieller *et al.* (1957) and Fieller & Pearson (1961).

6.4 *Estimation of the mean and standard deviation using linear functions of k order statistics (Table 11)*

The series of tables from which the present Table 11 has been taken were prepared to meet the following situation (Eisenberger & Posner, 1965). It is often possible to take a large number of observations on a spacecraft and to compute quantiles of the sample which can be transmitted to Earth. What quantiles and how many, it was asked, should be recorded so that, for example, accurate estimates of the mean and standard deviation of an assumed normal distribution of observations could be made? The coefficients tabled involve the use of an even number of quantiles, $k = 2, 4, 6, \ldots$. They depend only on the quantiles selected which have the population quantiles as asymptotic expectations; further the linear estimators, $\breve{\mu}$ and $\breve{\sigma}$, given within their class, have minimum variances.

Although primarily designed for use with samples of considerable size, where the ranking is effected on a computer, the authors believe that if $n \geqslant 50$, the estimators $\breve{\sigma}$ of σ will be nearly unbiased ($\breve{\mu}$ is necessarily unbiased for a symmetrical population distribution) and the measures of efficiency quoted still roughly applicable.

Definitions

If $x_{(i)}$ $(i = 1, 2, \ldots, n)$ are as before the ordered observations, then

$$z(p) = x_{([np]+1)},$$

where $[np]$ is the greatest integer $\leqslant np$. For example, if $n = 250$ and a table entry is $z(0 \cdot 1068)$, the ordered observation to be used is $x_{([26 \cdot 7]+1)} = x_{(27)}$. The efficiencies given in the last columns of Table 11 are the ratios of asymptotic variances, i.e.

$$\text{eff}(\breve{\mu}) = \frac{\sigma^2}{n \, \text{var}(\breve{\mu}|k)}, \quad \text{eff}(\breve{\sigma}) = \frac{\sigma^2}{2n \, \text{var}(\breve{\sigma}|k)},$$

where the variances in the denominators are those of the corresponding minimum variance linear unbiased estimator, based on k symmetrically placed quantiles. The solutions were derived using a digital computer.

It will be seen that for both $\breve{\mu}$ and $\breve{\sigma}$, three separate tables are included:

Tables 11 (*a*) *and* (*d*); the estimators have minimum variance for $\breve{\mu}$ and $\breve{\sigma}$, respectively. The quantiles to be used differ in the two cases.

Tables 11 (*b*) *and* (*e*); here the quantiles are the same in both cases and have been chosen by the authors to minimize expressions of the type

$$\text{var}(\breve{\mu}) + c^2 \, \text{var}(\breve{\sigma}) = \text{var}(\breve{\mu} + c\breve{\sigma})$$

because $\text{cov}(\breve{\mu}\breve{\sigma}) = 0$. We confine our table to the case $c = 1$. The gain in using common quantiles is counterbalanced by some loss in efficiency.

Tables 11 (*c*) *and* (*f*); for increasing k, the two optimum extreme quantiles, those of order p_1 and p_k, move further out into the tails of the distribution. There may be two objections to

32

this: (1) the asymptotic theory has assumed that the sampling distribution of each quantile is normal; departure from normality will be most pronounced in the tails; (2) departure from normality in the parent distribution is likely to have most effect on the extreme quantiles.

For these reasons, Eisenberger & Posner derived sub-optimum estimators in which $p_1 = 1 - p_k$ was restricted to be not less than (i) 0·025, (ii) 0·010. We give estimators with the former limitation in Tables 11 (c) and (f). They are, of course, theoretically somewhat less efficient than the preceding estimators. It will be noticed that for $\breve{\mu}$, the p_1 of Table 11 (a) is already greater than 0·025 for $k = 2, 4, 6, 8$; the same holds in Table 11 (d) when $k = 2$.

The authors' tables are extended up to $k = 20$, but the gain in efficiency is not very marked for $k > 12$. They have also tabled appropriate coefficients when

$$\text{(i)} \quad \operatorname{var} \breve{\mu} + 2 \operatorname{var} \breve{\sigma}, \qquad \text{(ii)} \quad \operatorname{var} \breve{\mu} + 3 \operatorname{var} \breve{\sigma}$$

are minimized. Later sections of their paper deal with tests of goodness of fit based on four quantiles, in particular, a test with high power against bimodal parent distributions.

Length of life of lamps in hours

Sample no. (t)	Life	Rank (j)	s_t^2	Sample no. (t)	Life	Rank (j)	s_t^2	Sample no. (t)	Life
1	1717	29	81635	6	1663	26	199266	11	761
	1591	24			2397	48			2278
	1677	27			**1182**	9			1175
	2037	42			1528	19			**694**
	2271	46			1816	31			1427
2	1551	20	51371	7	2050	43	52979	12	**617**
	1497	16			1929	39			1373
	1016	2			**1448**	15			928
	1561	23			1911	37			946
	1398	13			1794	30			847
3	1947	40	192778	8	1852	33	241569	13	725
	2014	41			**1069**	5			1378
	1011	1			2307	47			**347**
	1857	34			2140	45			815
	2082	44			1560	22			581
4	1348	12	101919	9	1150	7	101329	14	1666
	1020	3			1559	21			1054
	1308	10			1501	17			**527**
	1312	11			1821	32			1085
	1897	35			**1038**	4			2021
5	**1515**	18	32151	10	1155	8	500102	15	**262**
	1707	28			2608	50			536
	1609	25			**1123**	6			1103
	1924	38			1438	14			1500
	1902	36			2398	49			1535

The lives in bold type are the shortest in each sample of $n = 5$.

Example 24. As indicated in § 7.4 below, the first ten samples of five observations given in the table above showing length of life of electric lamps may be regarded as coming from a single normal population. The third column of the table gives the order of the observations, $j = 1, 2, \ldots, 50$. If we take the minimum variance estimator with $k = 2$ from Table 11 (a), we need

$$z(0·2709) = x_{(14)} = 1438, \quad z(0·7291) = x_{(37)} = 1911,$$

giving $\mathring{\mu} = 0\cdot5(1438 + 1911) = 1674\cdot5$ hours. If we choose to take $k = 6$ quantiles from the same table, we need

$$z(0\cdot0540) = x_{(3)} = 1020, \quad z(0\cdot1915) = x_{(10)} = 1308, \quad z(0\cdot3898) = x_{(20)} = 1551$$

and also
$$x_{(48)} = 2397, \quad x_{(41)} = 2014, \quad x_{(31)} = 1816,$$

giving $\mathring{\mu} = 1680\cdot3$ hours. Similarly, using Table 11d with $k = 2$ and 6, we find $\mathring{\sigma} = 428\cdot2$ hours and $415\cdot0$ hours, respectively. For the complete fifty observations

$$\text{mean} = \bar{x} = \hat{\mu} = 1664\cdot1 \text{ hours}, \quad \text{s.d.} = s = \hat{\sigma} = 399\cdot4 \text{ hours}.$$

It is inevitable that with only fifty observations the estimators of μ and σ obtained by various methods will differ considerably, but the differences are within their standard errors.

6.5 *Moments of $x_{(1)}$ or $x_{(n)}$, the extreme members in a sample of n (Table 12)*

This table due to Ruben (1954) gives for $n = 1(1)50$, the second, third and fourth central moments, the ratios $\beta_1 = \mu_3^2/\mu_2^3$ and $\beta_2 = \mu_4/\mu_2^2$ as well as the standard deviation of $x_{(1)}$ and $x_{(n)}$. The skewness is positive for $x_{(n)}$, negative for $x_{(1)}$.

Example 25. Suppose that in the life tests to which the last example refers, the five lamps in a sample were only kept alight until the first lamp failed. Then the data available would consist in the fifteen figures shown in bold type. If satisfactory performance was represented by a normal distribution of life with mean, $\mu = 1650$ hours and standard deviation, $\sigma = 450$ hours, then a control chart for the shortest life in samples of $n = 5$ could be derived as follows:

(a) From Table 9, $\qquad$ mean $x_{(1)} = 1650 - 1\cdot1630 \times 450 = 1127.$

(b) From Table 12, $\qquad \sigma(x_{(1)}) = 0\cdot6690 \times 450 = 301,$

$$\sqrt{\beta_1} = -\sqrt{(0\cdot091549)} = -0\cdot303, \quad \beta_2 = 3\cdot201.$$

(c) We may now assume that the distribution of $x_{(1)}$ is represented approximately by a Pearson curve, having $\sqrt{\beta_1} = -0\cdot30$, $\beta_2 = 3\cdot20$.

Table 32 then gives appropriate standardized upper and lower 5 and 1 per cent points. Converting these to appropriate units we have:

Upper	1% point	$1127 + 2\cdot122 \times 301 =$	1766 hours	(1766)
	5% point	$1127 + 1\cdot556 \times 301 =$	1595 hours	(1594)
Lower	5% point	$1127 - 1\cdot722 \times 301 =$	609 hours	(606)
	1% point	$1127 - 2\cdot555 \times 301 =$	358 hours	(355)

The figures in parentheses are those obtained using the exact percentage points of $(x_{(1)} - \mu)/\sigma$ given in *B.T.S.* **1**, Table 24. The Pearson curve approximation is a little in error at the lower tail of the distribution of $x_{(1)}$.

The control chart is shown in Fig. 2. It seems clear that the mean length of life is falling from the eleventh sample onwards. If records for complete samples of five were available, smaller changes than this would certainly be detected in a control chart for means, but there may be circumstances where time or expense favours working in terms of the weakest unit of a sample only. Up to its limit, at $n = 30$, the use of Table 24 of *B.T.S.* **1**, is more expeditious. It will be noted that the table of the probability integral of $x_{(1)}$ (Table 6 in this volume) is also available, and could be used on the lines illustrated in Example 19, p. 25.

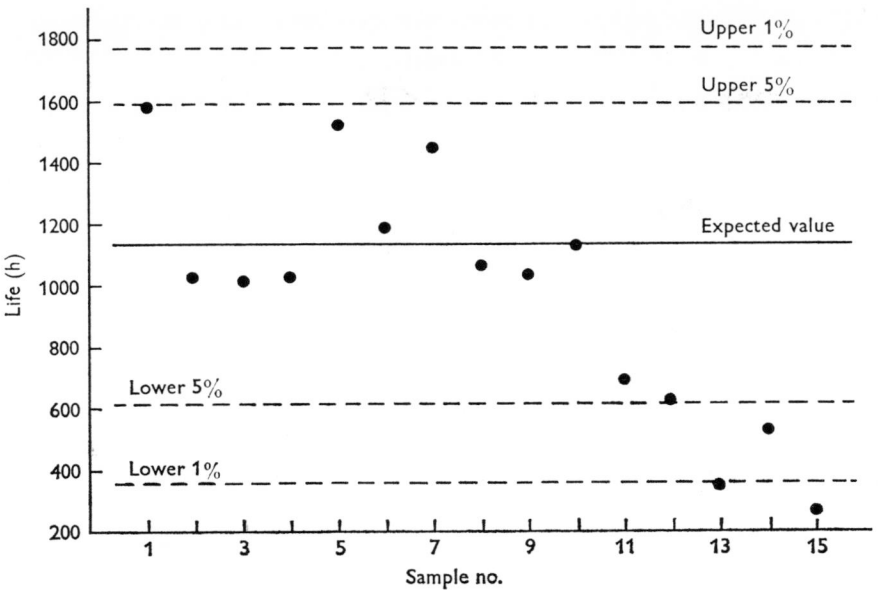

Fig. 2. Control chart for shortest life in samples of 5 electric lamps.

6.6 *Best linear unbiased estimate of σ (Tables 14 and 15)*

Section 6.4 has dealt with the estimation of a population standard deviation, using a linear function of a limited number of the order statistics, $x_{(i)}$. If all the n order statistics are used, we have what has been termed the best linear unbiased estimator of σ, in the form

$$\check{\sigma} = \sum_{i=1}^{h} b_{i,\,n}(x_{(n-i+1)} - x_{(i)}); \qquad (84)$$

$h = \frac{1}{2}n$ or $\frac{1}{2}(n-1)$ according to whether n is even or odd. The factors $b_{i,\,n}$, $n = 2(1)10$, were first given by Gupta (1952, Table 4) and the range has been extended to $n = 20$ by Sarhan & Greenberg (1962, Table 10 C 1). Gupta also gave the factors to use with singly censored samples and Sarhan & Greenberg those to use with doubly censored samples. These authors also tabled the variance of the estimators.

If the complete sample is available, the coefficients $b_{i,\,n}$ for $n = 2(1)50$ may be derived from the $a_{i,\,n}$ given in our Table 15, using the appropriate multiplying factor g_n given in Table 14, where

$$\check{\sigma} = g_n \sum_{i=1}^{h} a_{i,\,n}(x_{(n-i+1)} - x_{(i)}). \qquad (85)$$

Up to $n = 20$, the factors should be exact; beyond this a certain empirical element entered into the determination of Shapiro & Wilk's $a_{i,\,n}$ of Table 15. This will be referred to again in § 7 p. 36 below. Remember that $a_{n-i+1} = -a_{i,\,n}$.

Example 26. Take the rotating bend fatigue tests of Example 21 and assume that the variable $y = \log_{10}x$ is normally distributed. The appropriate factors $a_{i,\,15}$ are given in the last column of the table on p. 30, while Table 14 gives $g_{15} = 0 \cdot 2803$. It follows that

$$\check{\sigma} = 0 \cdot 2803 \times 1 \cdot 723 = 0 \cdot 483.$$

For the root-mean-square estimate based on fourteen degrees of freedom

$$\sum_{i=1}^{15} (y_i - \bar{y})^2 = 3 \cdot 062, \quad \hat{s}^2 = 0 \cdot 2187, \quad \hat{s} = 0 \cdot 468.$$

3-2

7. TESTS FOR DEPARTURE FROM NORMALITY

7.1 *The Shapiro–Wilk test* (*Tables* 15–18)

In *B.T.S.* **1**, § 17, three tests were described involving the use of the statistics

$$\sqrt{b_1} = m_3/m_2^{\frac{3}{2}}, \quad b_2 = m_4/m_2^2 \quad \text{and} \quad a = \sum_i |x_i - \bar{x}|/\{n\sum_i (x_i - \bar{x})^2\}^{\frac{1}{2}}.$$

It was also suggested there in § 14.6 that the range/standard deviation ratio

$$u = (x_{(n)} - x_{(1)})/s$$

might pick out large departures from normality. Tables 34 B, C, A and 29c, respectively gave certain percentage points of the sampling distributions of these four statistics under the hypothesis of normal variation for the x_i. Entries were carried down to samples as small as 25 for $\sqrt{b_1}$, 50 for b_2, 11 for a and 3 for u.

Shapiro & Wilk (1965) proposed another test based on the use of all the order statistics $x_{(i)}$, $i = 1, 2, \ldots, n$. They have said that their form of solution was suggested, in part, by an attempt to summarize formally certain features observed in plots such as those shown in our Fig. 1 above. If the observed order statistics, $x_{(i)}$, are plotted against the corresponding expected normal order statistics, $\xi(i|n)$, defined in § 6.1, then the best linear unbiased estimate of the slope of this regression is, apart from a normalizing constant, the estimate $\hat{\sigma}$ of the population σ given in equation (85). The test statistic, W, which they proposed is in fact proportional to the ratio of the square of an estimate based on this slope to the usual mean square estimate; thus

$$W = \left(\sum_{i=1}^n a_{i,n} x_{(i)} \right)^2 \bigg/ \sum_{i=1}^n (x_i - \bar{x})^2. \tag{86}$$

The coefficients $a_{i,n}$ given in Table 15 are the normalized coefficients $b_{i,n}$ of equation (84), i.e.

$$\sum_i a_{i,n}^2 = 1,$$

and the g_n of Table 14 is given by

$$g_n^2 = \sum_i b_{i,n}^2.$$

Note that $a_{n-i+1,n} = -a_{i,n}$, so that the numerator of the W-ratio can be written

$$A^2 = \left\{ \sum_{i=1}^h a_{i,n}(x_{(n-i+1)} - x_{(i)}) \right\}^2, \tag{87}$$

where $h = \frac{1}{2}n$ if n is even and $\frac{1}{2}(n-1)$ if n is odd. If two observations have a common value, i.e. if $x_{(i)} = x_{(i+1)}$, the authors have suggested multiplying both by $\frac{1}{2}(a_{i,n} + a_{i+1,n})$. Presumably this procedure could be extended to cover ties of more than two.

For $n > 20$, the true variances and covariances of the normal order statistics are not yet available; the empirical method used in determining the $a_{i,n}$ in these cases is described in Shapiro & Wilk (1965). The same paper indicates the part theoretical, part empirical method used in deriving the sampling distribution of W under the null hypothesis of normality.

For non-normal populations the two variance estimators in (86) will not in general be estimating the same thing. Heuristic considerations augmented by extensive Monte Carlo sampling from populations with a wide range of $\sqrt{\beta_1}$, β_2 values have shown that the mean W for non-null distributions tends to shift to the left, while var W increases. As a net result, it is small values of W which indicate significance.

Table 16 gives a median value for W and also lower and upper 1, 2, 5 and 10 per cent points. Since $W = 1$ if $x_{(i)} = ca_{i,n}$ and since the $a_{i,n}$ are essentially proportional to the $\xi(i|n)$ (see

36

Shapiro & Wilk 1965, p. 596), a large value of W close to unity is indicative of sample order statistics falling very close to the expected values of normal order statistics. It appears that such an event is most unlikely to occur for non-normal samples, so that no population seems likely to give values of W exceeding the upper per cent points more often than the normal population.

7.2 An illustration of applying the W-test

Example 27. We use the data of Example 21. Here $n = 15$ and the values of $a_{i,15}$ taken from Table 15 are shown in the last column.

Taking x as variable,

$$\sum_i (x_i - \bar{x})^2 = 90{\cdot}41, \quad A = 8{\cdot}036, \quad W(x) = 0{\cdot}714.$$

Taking $y = \log_{10} x$ as variable,

$$\sum_i (y_i - \bar{y})^2 = 3{\cdot}062, \quad A = 1{\cdot}723, \quad W(y) = 0{\cdot}970.$$

Table 16 shows that for $n = 15$ the lower 1 per cent point is at $0{\cdot}835$ while the median (50 per cent) value is $0{\cdot}950$. We should clearly reject the hypothesis that x is normally distributed, while seeing no reason to doubt the normality of $\log_{10} x$ on the data available. The test therefore confirms the conclusions drawn visually from Fig. 1.

7.3 Comparison of the power of alternative tests†

While $\sqrt{b_1}$ and b_2 are ratios of symmetric functions of the observations, W and u involve in their numerators linear functions of the differences between symmetrically placed order statistics. In the same way Geary's $a = (\text{mean deviation})/s$ would, if sample mean was at sample median, be an unweighted sum of these differences. It is likely in fact, that the numerical values of the weighting coefficients in the expression for A in (87) could be adjusted to increase the power of the resulting test statistic in regard to particular classes of alternative population distributions.

Shapiro *et al.* (1968) have carried out a very interesting and extensive Monte Carlo experiment. In this, tests based on W, $\sqrt{b_1}$, b_2 and u (but not Geary's a) were applied to sets of 500 samples of size 10, 15, 20, 35 and 50 drawn from a great variety of symmetrical and skew populations.

In these comparisons the two-tail tests for $\sqrt{b_1}$, b_2 and u were compared with the single-tail test for W; e.g. if a lower 5 per cent significance level for W is taken, the comparable critical region for b_2 was that falling beyond the upper and lower $2{\cdot}5$ per cent points. This was done because W itself cannot distinguish between flat-toppedness and long-tailedness in a distribution, nor between positive and negative skewness. On this basis of comparison, we believe that the following is a fair summary of Shapiro & Wilk's results. We confine attention to alternatives which have continuous probability density functions, though the authors have dealt with a number of discontinuous distributions, e.g. the Poisson and binomial.

Symmetric alternatives

(a) In the case of the uniform distribution ($\beta_2 = 1{\cdot}8$), u provides greatest power of detection, then b_2, then W. As β_2 is increased towards $3{\cdot}0$ (the normal), the power of b_2 begins to surpass that of u, W remaining in third place.

† Since this Introduction was completed for Press R. B. D'Agostino has put forward another 'omnibus' test with percentage points for $n \geqslant 50$ (*Biometrika*, 1971, **58**, 341–8). Later D'Agostino & G. L. Tietjen (*loc. cit.* 669–72) have given a table of percentage points of b_2 for $7 \leqslant n \leqslant 50$, based on Monte Carlo sampling.

(b) For long-tailed distributions with $\beta_2 > 3\cdot0$, e.g. for the logistic and the t distributions, u drops out while b_2 remains slightly ahead or equal in power to W. Owing to the fact that in small samples from long-tailed populations, one or two extreme observations on one side of the mean may lead to a larger value of $\sqrt{b_1}$, this test has some power.

Skew alternatives

W and $\sqrt{b_1}$ now provide the most powerful of the four tests here considered, with W somewhat in the lead. It must of course be remembered that there are circumstances in which the statistician will have prior reasons for expecting that if the population is not normal, it will be (i) flat-topped, or (ii) long-tailed, or again (iii) positively or (iv) negatively skewed. In these cases the appropriate single-tailed test would be used, i.e. one using a lower or an upper 5 per cent level for b_2 or for $\sqrt{b_1}$, not the two-tailed tests with their 2·5 per cent levels. It is then likely that the b_2 or $\sqrt{b_1}$ tests will become considerably more powerful than the W test.

Finally, it should be emphasized that:

(a) Limits for the W test, even if somewhat approximate, have been tabled down to samples of the smallest size, whereas our tables for $\sqrt{b_1}$ and b_2 go down to $n = 25$ and 50 only.† This facility is essential in tackling the problem discussed in the next section. However it seems probable, as described in § 7.5 below, that for $n < 25$ a good approximation to the distribution of $\sqrt{b_1}$ can be obtained by using either the distribution of Student's t or of Johnson's S_U.

(b) On the other hand, the W-test is at present limited in application to samples with $n \leqslant 50$. There is no such restriction with $\sqrt{b_1}$ and b_2.

(c) Whereas $\sqrt{b_1}$ and b_2 are separately tailored for different classes of alternative, the W-test appears to work well in all circumstances.

7.4   *The joint assessment of normality using several independent samples*
(*Tables* 17 *and* 18)

Suppose that k independent samples of size n_t drawn randomly from populations which may have different means and variances, provide the values W_t $(t = 1, 2, ..., k)$ of the W-statistic. Shapiro & Wilk (1968a, b) have suggested two related overall tests of the hypothesis that the sampled populations are normal. In so far as the distribution functions $F(W|n)$ are known or can be approximated, we can determine for each W_t a normal equivalent deviate G_t through the relation

$$\int_{-\infty}^{G_t} (2\pi)^{-\frac{1}{2}} e^{-\frac{1}{2}u^2} du = \alpha_t = F(W_t|n). \tag{88a}$$

Then, on the hypothesis tested, $G_{(1)} \leqslant G_{(2)} \leqslant ... \leqslant G_{(k)}$ will form a set of ordered normal variates. Their behaviour may either be studied by plotting against the corresponding expected normal order statistics $\xi(t|k)$; or, alternatively we get an overall test by referring the normalized mean

$$G = \sum_{t=1}^{k} G_t/\sqrt{k} \tag{88b}$$

to a standard table of the normal probability integral.

As an alternative test Shapiro & Wilk have suggested finding the C_t given by

$$\alpha_t = \int_{C_t}^{\infty} \tfrac{1}{2} e^{-\frac{1}{2}v} dv. \tag{89a}$$

† In making their comparisons, Shapiro & Wilk obtained significance levels for these two statistics from Monte Carlo sampling of a normal population.

Then $C_t = -2\log\alpha_t$ is an equivalent 'two degrees of freedom' χ^2 variable. Again, the C_t can be ranked and plotted against the corresponding expected order statistics of the negative exponential, $\eta(t|n)$, which are given in Table 19. As an overall test

$$C = \sum_{t=1}^{k} C_t \qquad (89b)$$

may be referred to the χ^2 distribution with $\nu = 2k$ degrees of freedom. The authors of the procedure have found that the plots may provide useful clues to the type of heterogeneity present which may be less clear if only the summary statistics G and C are calculated.

The possibility of using these tests depends, of course, on having a good approximation to the cumulative distribution function $F(W|n)$. Shapiro & Wilk (1965) gave reasons for believing that the p.d.f. of W could be well represented by a Johnson S_B curve, which at once opens the way to the determination of G, given W, from the following relation

$$G_t = \gamma(n) + \delta(n)\log\frac{W_t - \epsilon(n)}{1 - W_t}. \qquad (90)$$

The coefficients γ, δ and ϵ, as functions of n, are given in Table 17 for $n = 7(1)50$. For $n = 3(1)6$ rather more special treatment is needed and Table 18 gives G_t for such samples in terms of a transformed function, $v_t = \log[\{W_t - \epsilon(n)\}/(1 - W_t)]$.

It must be remembered that unlike $\sqrt{b_1}$, b_2, a and u, the W criterion is significantly low for *any* considerable departure from normality. This feature is beneficial for accumulating evidence of non-normality of any shape or form. But it is disadvantageous if the two tails of one of the former test criteria provide information on different types of non-normality which are separately of interest.

Example 28. Taking the first ten samples used in Example 24, we have $k = 10$ samples of $n_t = n = 5$. Using the coefficients $a_{i,5}$ from Table 15, we obtain first ten values of W_t, hence ten values of v_t and by interpolation in Table 18, we get ten values of G_t, as follows:

W_t	0·8890	0·7752	0·7288	0·8611	0·9123	0·9649	0·8834	0·9592	0·9456	0·8278
v_t	1·1102	−0·0076	−0·4285	0·7997	1·4127	2·4647	1·0441	2·3004	1·9786	0·4706
G_t	−0·39	−1·62	−2·03	−0·74	−0·05	0·97	−0·46	0·83	0·54	−1·11

From the last row of figures we find $G = \Sigma G_t/\sqrt{10} = -1\cdot28$, a value which, though on the low side, cannot be regarded as significant. In this case a plot of $G_{(t)}$ against $\xi(t|n)$ is not particularly revealing.

The G_t will also provide the α_t of equation (88a) from which the C_t could be found.

7.5 *Joint assessment of normality based on $\sqrt{b_1}$, using several independent samples*

Although the test is not based on order statistics it seems appropriate to mention here that some recent Monte Carlo sampling by D'Agostino (1970) leads to the conclusion that $\sqrt{b_1}$ may also be used to provide an overall test of normality based on a number of quite small independent samples. As pointed out by one of us (Pearson, 1963, 1965), when the population is normal, the unknown true distribution of $\sqrt{b_1}$ may be represented approximately either by Student's t or Johnson's S_U distribution having the correct first four moments. Since this null distribution is necessarily symmetrical about $\sqrt{b_1} = 0$, this suggests that the approximating distribution should be given the correct variance and β_2-ratio, which may be derived from the work of Fisher (1930).

When completing the table of percentage points of $\sqrt{b_1}$ for *B.T.S.* **1** (Table 34 B, 1966 edition) we did not cover samples with $n < 25$ because the t and S_U solutions, which had agreed closely for higher values of n, appeared now to diverge and no simple method was then available to help decide which was the better approximation. D'Agostino's more recent Monte Carlo investigation suggests, however, that the S_U solution may well hold good for samples as small as $n = 8$. The transformation involved can be written

$$X = \delta \sinh^{-1}(\sqrt{b_1}/\lambda), \tag{91}$$

where X is a unit normal deviate.

The γ and ξ of equations (170) and (178) below vanish for the symmetrical case and the parameters δ and λ are functions of the sample size n, which can be computed either from expressions given by D'Agostino or by Johnson (1949, 1965). The table below gives freshly computed values of δ and $1/\lambda$ for $n = 8(1)25$. Assuming normality in the parent distribution, the relation (91) can be used to derive approximations to the percentage points of $\sqrt{b_1}$ or to the tail probabilities P and Q, where $P = 1 - Q = \Pr\{\sqrt{b_1} \leqslant$ an observed value$\}$.

Table to normalize $\sqrt{b_1}$

n	δ	$1/\lambda$	n	δ	$1/\lambda$	n	δ	$1/\lambda$
8	5·563	0·3030	14	3·069	0·6423	20	2·890	0·7779
9	4·260	·4080	15	3·010	·6753	21	2·884	·7934
10	3·734	·4794	16	2·968	·7001	22	2·882	·8078
11	3·447	·5339	17	2·937	·7224	23	2·882	·8211
12	3·270	·5782	18	2·915	·7426	24	2·884	·8336
13	3·151	·6153	19	2·900	·7610	25	2·889	·8452

$X = \delta \log(\sqrt{b_1}/\lambda)$ is approximately a unit normal deviate (log to base e).

If then we have independent samples of n_i observations ($i = 1, 2, ..., k$) from k populations and have prior reasons for expecting that if the populations are not normal, they will (i) all be positively skewed or (ii) all be negatively skewed, we can then find (i) Q_i or (ii) P_i by referring the X_i of (91) to a table of the normal probability integral and then test significance by referring (i) $-2 \sum_i \log Q_i$ or (ii) $-2 \sum_i \log P_i$ to the χ^2 distribution with $\nu = 2k$. These are overall single-tailed tests of departure from normality which may, under the assumption made be more powerful than the corresponding test using the Shapiro–Wilk criterion discussed in § 7.4.

If however it is not considered justifiable to confine alternatives to normality to distributions having a single specified direction of skewness as under (i) or (ii), it is still possible (iii) to use a two-tailed overall alternative test, as suggested by E. S. Pearson (1938, p. 137). This consists in referring $-2 \sum_i \log R_i$ to the χ^2 distribution with $\nu = 2k$, where for the ith sample

$$\begin{aligned} R_i &= 2Q_i \quad \text{if} \quad \sqrt{b_1} \geqslant 0, \\ &= 2P_i \quad \text{if} \quad \sqrt{b_1} < 0. \end{aligned} \tag{92}$$

This test is probably somewhat less powerful than the overall Shapiro–Wilk test, but no comparative investigation has so far been carried out.

8. Expected values of order statistics in samples from certain gamma distributions

8.1 The negative exponential; χ^2 with $\nu = 2$ (Table 19)

The population distribution is taken in the form

$$f(X) = e^{-X} \quad (0 \leqslant X \leqslant \infty). \tag{93}$$

$X_{(i)}$ $(i = 1, 2, ..., n)$ are then the order statistics in a random sample of n observations drawn from (93). We write

$$EX_{(i)} = \eta(i|n).$$

Table 19 is based on a table of Harter (1964; 1970, Table C 2) which gives $\eta(i|n)$ to five decimal places for $n = 1(1)120$. We give results to only two decimal places for $n = 1(1)59$; these will be adequate for plotting purposes. More accurate values can, however, be derived if needed from the column of five-decimal-place entries at $n = 60$, by noting that for $n < 60$

$$\eta(i|n) = \eta(60-n+i|60) - \eta(60-n|60). \tag{94}$$

The table may be used to provide a rough graphical test of whether a set of observations can be regarded as a sample from an exponential distribution. This will provide a quick check if there are mechanical means of plotting the observed order statistics against the corresponding $\eta(i|n)$. This is a procedure suggested by Shapiro & Wilk in testing normality from several independent samples, using the equivalent exponential variates C_t defined in equation (89a). (See § 7.4.)

Example 29. We take as another form of illustration the data given in the following table by Proschan (1963, p. 376). These represent the twenty-seven intervals, in hours, between twenty-eight successive failures of the air conditioning system fitted on one member of a fleet of Boeing 720s. If the expectation of failure per unit time was constant, the distribution of intervals between failures should follow a negative exponential. In Fig. 3 the intervals, ranked in ascending order of magnitude, $x_{(i)}$, have been plotted against $\eta(i|27)$. The straight line has a slope based on the mean of the observations, i.e. is the line $x = 76 \cdot 81\eta$. The plot seems to be closely linear, though we would be prepared to find the longest interval considerably greater than the 216 hours observed. This conclusion drawn from the visual examination is confirmed more objectively in Example 62, p. 121. Similar data from a number of aircraft plotted mechanically on the same sheet would provide a quick means of examining for linearity and comparing slopes (i.e. the mean failure times).

Intervals between air conditioning system failures

Interval no.	Length (h)	Interval no.	Length (h)	Interval no.	Length (h)	Interval no.	Length (h)
1	97	8	68	15	82	22	63
2	51	9	77	16	54	23	18
3	11	10	80	17	31	24	191
4	4	11	1	18	216	25	18
5	141	12	16	19	46	26	163
6	18	13	106	20	111	27	24
7	142	14	206	21	39	Mean	76·81

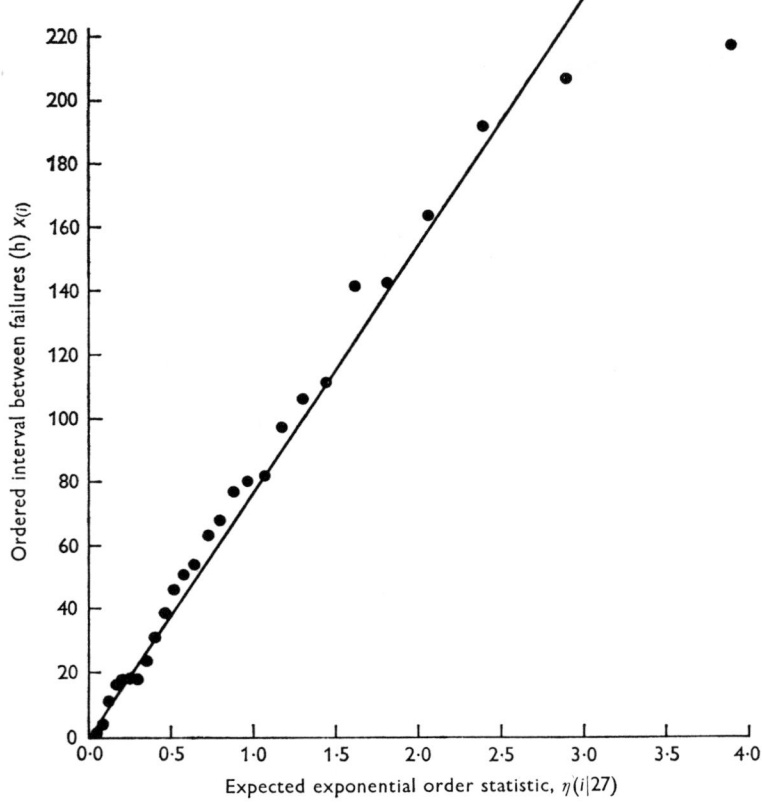

Fig. 3. Intervals in hours between 28 failures of air conditioning system on one aircraft of the Boeing fleet of 720s

8.2 *Other gamma distributions*; χ^2 *with* $\nu = 1, 3, 4, 5, 7$ (*Table* 20)

If the population probability density function is taken in the standard form

$$f(X) = X^{m-1}e^{-X}/\Gamma(m) \quad (0 \leqslant X \leqslant \infty), \tag{95}$$

then $2X$ is distributed as χ^2 with $\nu = 2m$ degrees of freedom. If $X_{(i)}$ $(i = 1, 2, ..., n)$ are the order statistics in a random sample of n observations from this population, we write

$$EX_{(i)} = \eta(i|n; m).$$

The case $m = 1$ has been discussed in the preceding section. In the publications already referred to, Harter (1964; 1970, Table C 4) has given a table of $\eta(i|n; m)$ to five decimal places, for arguments
$$n = 1(1)40; \quad m = 0.5(0.5)4.0.$$

Table 20 of the present volume is a considerably shortened version of Harter's table, giving the $\eta(i|n; m)$ to three decimal places, for $n = 1(1)20$; $m = 0.5, 1.5, 2.0, 2.5, 3.5$.

As suggested by Harter, the table will provide a graphical test of homogeneity of variance where a number (in our case $k = n \leqslant 20$) of small samples of equal size $\nu + 1 = 2m + 1$ from assumed normal populations are available. If the variances s_t^2 $(t = 1, 2, ..., k)$ are ranked as $s_{(t)}^2$, then these may be plotted as ordinates against $\eta(t|k; \frac{1}{2}\nu)$. Using Table 20, this can be done with up to twenty samples, each containing 2, 4, 5, 6 or 8 observations. For samples of size 3, with $\nu = 2$, the expected order statistics are those of Table 19.

42

For sample sizes greater than twenty, the expectations may be found approximately using a device similar to that suggested by Blom and Harter in the case of normal order statistics (see §6.1, p. 28). We take

$$EX_{(i)} = F^{-1}\left(\frac{i+\alpha_\nu}{n+1+\beta_\nu}\right) = F^{-1}(P),\tag{96}$$

where $P = F_\nu(\chi^2)$ is the distribution function of χ^2 based on $\nu = 2m$ degrees of freedom. The five values of α_ν, β_ν given in the following table were determined empirically, using Harter's table of $EX_{(i)}$ for the case $n = 20$. The same numerical values were found to apply with surprising accuracy at $n = 30$ and 40. It can be assumed that they will hold for intermediate values of n and it is likely that they could be used for extrapolation some way beyond $n = 40$, the last sample size for which Harter calculated the expected order statistics.

Factors for use in equation (96)

m	ν	α_ν	β_ν
0·5	1	$+0\cdot404$	$-0\cdot039$
1·5	3	$-0\cdot119$	$-0\cdot550$
2·0	4	$-0\cdot178$	$-0\cdot606$
2·5	5	$-0\cdot213$	$-0\cdot638$
3·5	7	$-0\cdot256$	$-0\cdot674$

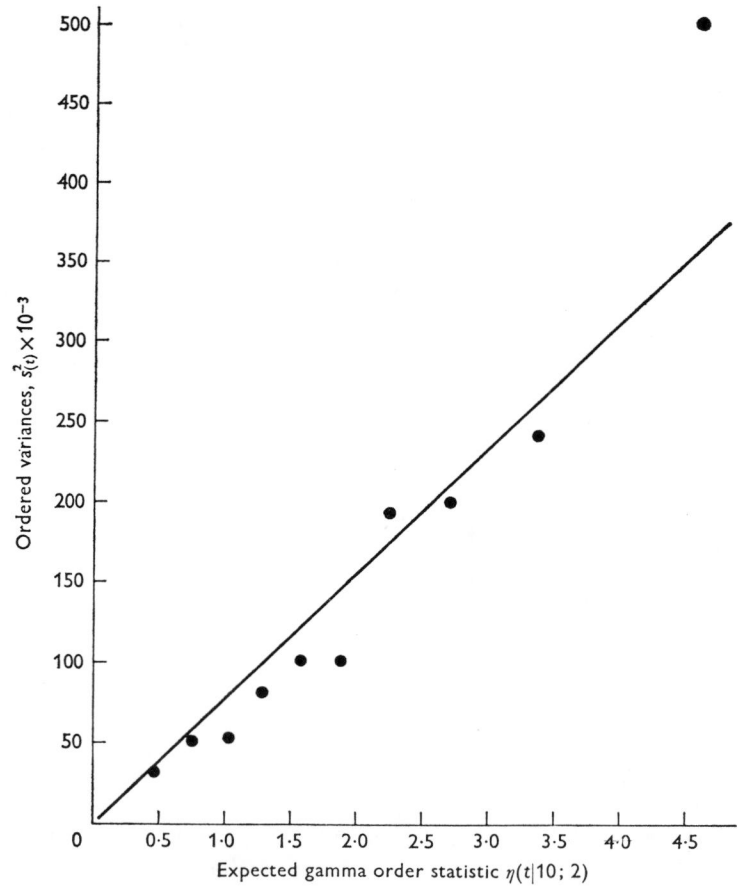

Fig. 4. Variance in length of life in 10 samples of 5 lamps.

43

A disadvantage of this procedure is that there is no table giving χ^2 values against the probability integral, P, as argument, and therefore inverse interpolation is necessary in a table showing P, or $Q = 1 - P$, for given χ^2, e.g. Table 7, $B.T.S.$ **1**.

Example 30. In Fig. 4 the ten variance estimates, s_t^2, of lamp life from Example 24, have been plotted after ordering, against the expected order statistics $\eta(t|10; 2)$, appropriate for samples of five from a gamma or χ^2 distribution having $\nu = \frac{1}{2}m = 4$. Since s^2 should be distributed as $\chi^2\sigma^2/\nu = 2X\sigma^2/4 = \frac{1}{2}X\sigma^2$, if there is variance homogeneity, the plotted points should be distributed about the line $s^2 = \frac{1}{2}\sigma^2\eta$. The line in the diagram has been drawn using the within-sample estimate of σ^2, namely $s^2 = 155 \cdot 5 \times 10^3$. The trend of points appears linear, though a visual inspection hardly tells us whether the large variance in the last sample is exceptional.

If we apply the overall M-test ($B.T.S.$ **1**, Table 32a), we find $M = 12 \cdot 73$, well below the 10 per cent significance level. Since an application of the F-test shows there to be no significant variation among the sample means, and as we have found (Example 28) no clear evidence of departure from normality, the use of the pooled data in Example 24 to illustrate Eisenberger & Posner's method of estimating a standard deviation, would seem justified.

Example 31. Find the expectations $EX_{(i)} = \eta(i|35; 2)$ of the first, twentieth and thirty-fifth order statistics in a random sample of $n = 35$ χ^2-variates, each having $\nu = 2m = 4$ degrees of freedom. Using the appropriate α_4, β_4 of the table on p. 43, we first find the values of

$$P = (i - 0 \cdot 178)/(36 - 0 \cdot 606) = (i - 0 \cdot 178)/35 \cdot 394$$

and use these to determine values of χ^2 by backward linear interpolation in the row $\nu = 4$ of Table 7, $B.T.S.$ **1**. The procedure is summarized in the table below, and is seen to give in this case remarkably accurate results, considering the approximate nature of the procedure.

i	$P = (i - 0 \cdot 178)/35 \cdot 394$	$Q = 1 - P$	$\frac{1}{2}\chi^2(Q)$	True $EX_{(i)}$ (Harter)
1	0·0232	0·9768	0·2317	0·2314
20	0·5600	0·4400	1·878	1·882
35	0·9838	0·0162	6·089	6·085

8.3 *The half-normal distribution; χ with $\nu = 1$ (Table 21)*

We define the half-normal distribution by

$$f(X) = \sqrt{(2/\pi)}\, e^{-\frac{1}{2}X^2} \quad (0 \leqslant X \leqslant \infty). \tag{97}$$

If $X_{(i)}$ are the order statistics in a random sample of n observations from this population, we write

$$EX_{(i)} = \zeta(i|n).$$

Table 21 gives to four decimal places values of $\zeta(i|n)$ for $n = 1(1)30$. It has been derived from a six-decimal-place table of Govindarajulu & Eisenstat (1964), computed for $n = 1(1)20(10)100$. Values for $n = 21(1)29$ were obtained from those for $n = 30$ using the well known reduction equation for any parent, namely:

$$\zeta(i|n-1) = \{i\zeta(i+1|n) + (n-i)\,\zeta(i|n)\}/n. \tag{98}$$

For $n > 30$ the expectations may be found with reasonable accuracy from the expected values of normal order statistics, $\xi(i|n)$, given in Table 9, by noting that

$$\zeta(j|n) = \xi(n+1-j|2n+1). \tag{99}$$

44

On comparison with Govindarajulu & Eisenstat's fuller table, it is found that the maximum error (true − approx.) is − 0·004 when $n = 30$, − 0·003 when $n = 40$ and may be expected to decrease as n increases.

Example 32. Federer (1955, pp. 183–6) describes an educational experiment involving three factors, coded A, B, C, and arranged as a 2^3 factorial with six experimental units per treatment combination. None of the effects is significant. For a half-normal plot we obtain the following square roots of single degree of freedom mean squares:

	$\sqrt{A}$	$\sqrt{B}$	$\sqrt{C}$	$\sqrt{(AB)}$	$\sqrt{(AC)}$	$\sqrt{(BC)}$	$\sqrt{(ABC)}$
	0·70	9·81	16·2	13·1	8·05	4·71	4·05
Rank	1	5	7	6	4	3	2

Plotting the ranked square roots $x_{(i)}$ of the seven ranked mean squares against the appropriate $\zeta(i \mid 7)$ from Table 21 gives the plot in Fig. 5, indicating virtually no departure from a straight line. Moreover since a mean effect, $\sqrt{A}$, is actually the lowest half-normal and an interaction the second highest, the impression of completely random normal data can hardly be discounted.

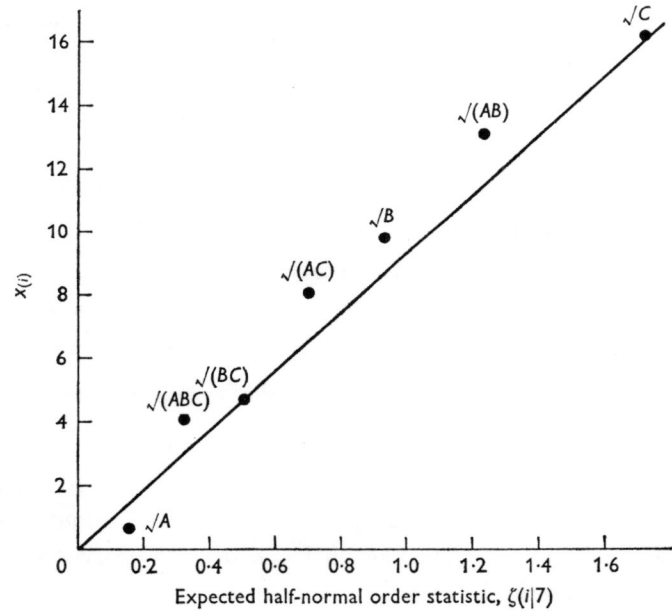

Fig. 5 Half-normal plots of square roots of seven single degrees of freedom mean squares, $x_{(i)}$.

The sloping line inserted in the figure has equation

$$\hat{x}_{(i)} = 9 \cdot 3 \zeta(i \mid 7),$$

where 9·3 is the estimate of the within-treatment standard deviation given by Federer. A graphical estimate of slope derived from the seven plotted points might be slightly higher than 9·3, but the excess would hardly be of importance.

III. MEAN SLIPPAGE TESTS BASED ON RANKS

The tests in this group are the rank equivalents to some of the well-known tests of analysis of variance theory as applied to measurements on a continuous scale. There are two main reasons for the use of rank-based analysis of variance criteria:

(a) For the N experimental units entering into the analysis no response measurements are available, but it is possible to place the units into an order of merit, $1, 2, ..., N$.

(b) Although response measurements *are* available it is feared that the normality-based test criteria used in the analysis of variance may be misleading.

The four basic analysis of variance situations covered by rank-based analogues may be set out as follows:

	Comparison of	
	$k = 2$ groups	$k > 2$ groups
Units in groups are unrelated	Wilcoxon 2-sample test, Table 22 (see §9)	Kruskal–Wallis test (see §11)
Units in equal sized groups are logically related	Wilcoxon paired rank test, Table 23 (see §10)	Friedman rank test and Kendall's concordance coefficient (see §12)

9. The two-sample Wilcoxon (1945) or Mann–Whitney (1947) tests

9.1 *Definition of test and illustration of Table* 22

The total number of N experimental units is arranged in *two* experimental groups of m and n, respectively, with $m \leqslant n$. The N units are now ranked in ascending order of magnitude, i.e. the numbers $1, 2, ..., N$ are attached to them. The following test criterion is then found:

$$W = \text{sum of rank numbers in the smaller group of } m \text{ units.} \tag{100}$$

The null hypothesis is that the N rank numbers are divided purely at random into one group of m and another of $n = N - m$, and the observed W is referred to the distribution which would result from such a random partition. As in the case, for example, of Student's 2-sample t-test we use a lower tail, an upper tail or a two-tail test according to the alternative to the null hypothesis which we are anxious not to overlook.

The lower and upper limits for W occur when one set of sample values is wholly below the other. These limits are seen to be $\frac{1}{2}m(m+1)$ and $\frac{1}{2}m(N+n+1)$, respectively. The null distribution is symmetrical about the mean

$$\overline{W} = \tfrac{1}{2}m(N+1), \tag{101}$$

and if $W_l(\alpha|m, n)$ is the lower 100α per cent value, then the upper 100α per cent value is

$$W_u(\alpha|m, n) = m(N+1) - W_l(\alpha|m, n) = 2\overline{W} - W_l(\alpha|m, n). \tag{102}$$

Table 22 due to Verdooren (1963) gives the lower percentage points for all combinations of $m = 1(1)25$, $n = m(1)25$, $\alpha = 0 \cdot 001, 0 \cdot 005, 0 \cdot 01, 0 \cdot 025, 0 \cdot 05, 0 \cdot 10$. Values of $2\overline{W}$ are included in the last column of each section of the table to facilitate calculation of upper percentage points.

To illustrate the use of the table, suppose that $m = 2$, $n = 18$, $N = 20$. Then we find that the lower 5 per cent point is

$$W_l(0 \cdot 05|2, 18) = 7,$$

while the upper 5 per cent point is

$$W_u(0.05|2, 18) = 2\overline{W} - 7 = 42 - 7 = 35.$$

For the single-tail test, therefore, W is significantly small at the 5 per cent level if $W \leqslant 7$.

Owing to the discrete character of the distribution, the significance levels are chosen to be 'conservative', i.e. the true probability that $W \leqslant W_l(\alpha|m, n)$ is $\leqslant \alpha$. To illustrate this we note that there are nine out of $\binom{N}{m} = \binom{20}{2} = 190$ possible selections of $m = 2$ rank numbers which give a total $W \leqslant 7$, as shown below:

	Pair of rank numbers selected for smaller group								
	1,2	1,3	1,4	2,3	1,5	2,4	1,6	2,5	3,4
Rank sum, W	3	4	5	5	6	6	7	7	7

Thus the exact probability $\Pr\{W \leqslant 7\} = 9/190 = 0.047 < 0.05$. Suppose now that we wish to apply a two-tail test at the 5 per cent level in the same situation where $m = 2, n = 18$. We find

$$W_l(0.025|2, 18) = 5, \quad W_u(0.025|2, 18) = 42 - 5 = 37.$$

Hence we would reject the null hypothesis for any pair of samples of two and eighteen for which $W \leqslant 5$ or $\geqslant 37$.

9.2 *Case where m and/or n > 25*

For many purposes an adequate approximation is obtained by taking W as normally distributed, with

$$E(W) = \tfrac{1}{2}m(N+1), \quad \sigma^2(W) = \tfrac{1}{12}mn(N+1), \tag{103}$$

and using a correction for continuity, i.e. by referring the ratio

$$X = (W + 0.5 - E(W))/\sigma(W) \tag{104}$$

to a table of $X(P)$ (e.g. to Table 1).

Fix & Hodges (1955) have suggested that a better approximation is obtained by introducing a term of the Edgeworth series, giving

$$\Pr\{W \leqslant W_l\} \sim P(X) + \frac{m^2 + n^2 + mn + m + n}{20mn(m+n+1)} D^3Z(X), \tag{105}$$

where X is given by (104) and $D^3Z(X)$ can be found from Table 2.

Example 33. Table 22 shows that for $m = 5, n = 25, W_l(0.005|5, 25) = 32$. What results do we obtain using (a) the simple normal approximation based on (104), (b) the second approximation (105)? The exact probability $\Pr\{W \leqslant 32\} = 0.0044 < 0.005$.

Equation (103) gives $E(W) = 77.5, \sigma(W) = 17.970$; whence from (104), $X = -2.504$ and $P(X) = 0.0061$. For the second approximation we have, using Table 2,

$$\Pr\{W \leqslant 32\} \sim 0.0061 + \tfrac{805}{77500} \times (-0.142)$$

$$= 0.0061 - 0.0015 = 0.0046.$$

Clearly in this case, where we are dealing with a rather extreme percentage point the second approximation (0.0046) is a good deal better than the first (0.0061). Verdooren (1963, p. 184) tables a number of comparisons.

Example 34. For $m = 20, n = 39$ we have observed a rank sum of 420; does this indicate a significant difference between the average ranks of the two groups? We have

$$E(W) = \tfrac{1}{2}20 \times 60 = 600, \quad \sigma^2(W) = \tfrac{1}{12} 20 \times 39 \times 60 = 3900, \quad \sigma(W) = 62.45$$

$$X = (420 + 0.5 - 600)/62.45 = -2.87,$$

clearly indicating a significant difference in the sense that the m units have the lower rank numbers, although no prior knowledge was available for the difference going in either direction. In a case of this kind there is obviously no need to use the second approximation.

9.3 *Additional notes*

(a) *Ties*. When the number of these is not large we can still use Table 22, assigning average ranks to the tied observations; the true significance level will be rather smaller than that given in the table. For $m, n > 25$ we may use the normal approximation, noting that $E(W)$ is unchanged but $\sigma(W)$ is reduced, namely

$$\sigma^2(W \text{ with ties}) = \sigma^2(W) - \frac{mn}{12N(N-1)}\left\{\sum_{i=1}^{r} t_i^3 - \sum_{i=1}^{r} t_i\right\}, \tag{106}$$

where t_i = size of tie i and r = number of ties.

(b) *The Mann–Whitney* (1947) test criterion U is given by

$$U = W - \tfrac{1}{2}m(m+1). \tag{107}$$

(c) *Test for variability based on ranks*. The Wilcoxon two-sample test criterion has also been used for the comparison of the variability in two samples (see Siegel & Tukey, 1960; 1961).

10. The Wilcoxon paired rank test

10.1 *Definition of test and illustration of Table* 23

The test is likely to be of value in situations coming under heading (b) of p. 46, where we are doubtful of the validity of applying the paired t-test. The procedure is best explained in terms of an example.

Example 35. Below are shown the blood glucose uptakes (in units of mg/g. tissue) by $N = 9$ rats of two compounds, A and B (data based on table in Wilcoxon & Wilcox, 1964). The Wilcoxon signed rank test uses the total, T^- of the (say) negatively signed ranks as a test criterion. In our example $T^- = 3 + 5 + 9 = 17$.

i ...	1	2	3	4	5	6	7	8	9
Compound A, x_{1i}	9·4	8·5	4·7	3·9	4·6	5·3	10·2	3·3	7·0
Compound B, x_{2i}	8·4	8·8	4·1	3·5	5·1	5·2	10·0	4·6	6·1
Diff. $x_{1i} - x_{2i}$	1·0	−0·3	0·6	0·4	−0·5	0·1	0·2	−1·3	0·9
Rank of $|x_{1i} - x_{2i}|$	8	3	6	4	5	1	2	9	7
Sign of $x_{1i} - x_{2i}$	+	−	+	+	−	+	+	−	+

To test significance for sample sizes $5 \leqslant N \leqslant 50$, the right-hand side of Table 23 may be used giving lower single-tail percentage points $T_l(\alpha|N)$ for $\alpha = 0.05, 0.025, 0.01, 0.005$; these are at the same time the lower two-tail percentage points for $2\alpha = 0.10, 0.05, 0.02, 0.01$. To obtain corresponding upper percentage points, compute

$$T_u(\alpha|N) = \tfrac{1}{2}N(N+1) - T_l(\alpha|N), \tag{108}$$

with the value of $\tfrac{1}{2}N(N+1)$ shown in the right hand margin.

If we apply a two-tailed test at the 5 per cent level to the data of our example, with $N = 9$, we find from Table 23

$$T_l(0.025|9) = 6, \quad T_u(0.025|9) = 45 - 6 = 39.$$

The observed $T^- = 17$ falls between these two values, so that no significant differences are indicated.

For $N \leqslant 15$ the left-hand side of Table 23 shows the complete lower tail probability integral of T^-, $P(T^-|N)$. Because of symmetry, the upper tail is given by

$$Q[\{\tfrac{1}{2}N(N+1) - T^-\}|N] = P(T^-|N). \tag{109}$$

For example, with $N = 9$, we have

$$Q(28|9) = Q([45-17]|9) = P(17|9) = 0\cdot285.$$

10.2 *Case where $N > 50$*

Here, as in the case of the Wilcoxon two-sample test, we can use the normal approximation; since

$$E(T^-) = \tfrac{1}{4}N(N+1), \quad \sigma^2(T^-) = \tfrac{1}{24}N(N+1)(2N+1), \tag{110}$$

we take the standardized deviate

$$X = \{T^- - E(T^-)\}/\sigma(T^-)$$

and obtain an approximation to the tail area probability from a table of $X(P)$. With $N > 50$, any correction for continuity seems unnecessary.

As an illustration of the accuracy of the approximation, suppose $T^- = 466$, $N = 50$. We have from (110),

$$E(T^-) = \tfrac{1}{4} \times 50 \times 51 = 637\cdot5, \quad \sigma^2(T^-) = \tfrac{1}{24} \times 50 \times 51 \times 101 = 10731\cdot25,$$

$$X = (466 - 637\cdot5)/103\cdot59 = -1\cdot656, \quad P(X) = 0\cdot049.$$

Since the entry in Table 23 for the 5 per cent point is 466, the agreement in this case is close.

11. THE KRUSKAL–WALLIS TEST

This represents the k-sample generalization of the Wilcoxon two-sample test and may be described as the rank analogue of the single-classification analysis of variance test. It applies to both situations (*a*) and (*b*) of p. 46. Again, the procedure involved is most easily explained by an example.

11.1 *Illustration and definition*

Example 36. This is taken from Kruskal & Wallis (1952), where it is referred to as based on artificial data. The table below gives the daily production of bottle-caps produced using three different ways of operating an automatic machine; these are described as standard and modifications 1 and 2. The figures in parentheses are the rank numbers for the $N = 12$ days of production, (1) representing the lowest output of 330 caps and (12) the highest output of 355 caps. In this table R_i are the rank sums and n_i the number of observations (i.e. in this case the number of day records) in the ith column. The Kruskal–Wallis criterion is now simply a standardized 'between groups' sum of squares based on the rank numbers. If we write $\bar{r}_i = R_i/n_i$, $\bar{r} =$ mean rank $= \tfrac{1}{2}(N+1)$, the test statistic is

$$H = \sum_{i=1}^{k} n_i(\bar{r}_i - \bar{r})^2/\{\tfrac{1}{12}N(N+1)\} \tag{111a}$$

$$= \frac{12}{N(N+1)} \sum_i \frac{R_i^2}{n_i} - 3(N+1). \tag{111b}$$

The divisor on the right in the first form is the total mean square of the rank numbers, 1 to N, given by

$$\frac{1}{N-1} \sum_{i=1}^{N} (i - \bar{\imath})^2 = \frac{N(N^2-1)}{12(N-1)} = \frac{N(N+1)}{12}.$$

Method	Standard	Mod. 1	Mod. 2	
i	1	2	3	
	340 (5)	339 (4)	347 (10)	
	345 (9)	333 (2)	343 (7)	
	330 (1)	344 (8)	349 (11)	
	342 (6)	.	355 (12)	
	338 (3)	.		
R_i	24	14	40	$\Sigma R_i = 78$
n_i	5	3	4	$N = \Sigma n_i = 12$

Equation (111 a) in terms of the mean ranks, $\bar{r}_i, \bar{r}$ is given to show the structure of the criterion, but (111 b) is clearly the form to be used in computation.

The first approximation to the null distribution of H is to take H as a χ^2 variable having $\nu = k-1$ degrees of freedom.

Continuing with the example, we have

$$H = \frac{12}{12 \times 13} \left\{ \frac{24^2}{5} + \frac{14^2}{3} + \frac{40^2}{4} \right\} - 3 \times 13 = 5 \cdot 656,$$

which, on reference to Table 3, is seen to be a value just below

$$\chi^2(0 \cdot 95 | 2) = 5 \cdot 991.$$

11.2   *A more accurate approximation to the distribution of H. Interpolation in the F-table*

As in similar problems, Kruskal & Wallis (1952, p. 609) suggest that an improvement on the χ^2 approximation may be obtained by using a beta distribution with correct terminals, mean and variance. In this case they find that

$$\left. \begin{aligned} E(H) &= k-1, \\ \text{var } H = V &= 2(k-1) - \frac{2\{3k^2 - 6k + N(2k^2 - 6k + 1)\}}{5N(N+1)} - \frac{6}{5} \sum_{i=1}^{k} \frac{1}{n_i}, \\ \text{max. } H = M &= \frac{N^3 - \sum_i n_i^3}{N(N+1)}. \end{aligned} \right\} \tag{112}$$

We take min. $H = 0$ as for the χ^2 approximation, although owing to the discontinuity of the distribution this value is unlikely to be exactly attained.

Equations (46) give us the a, b values of the beta distribution for $x = H/M$. Since it is the upper tail of this distribution in which we shall be interested for significance, we are concerned with $I_{x'}(b, a)$, where $x' = 1 - H/M$. We now make the transformation to the F-distribution using equation (42) and find

$$F(\nu_1, \nu_2) = \frac{H(M-k+1)}{(k-1)(M-H)}, \tag{113}$$

where

$$\left. \begin{aligned} \nu_1 &= (k-1) \frac{(k-1)(M-k+1)-V}{\frac{1}{2}MV}, \\ \nu_2 &= \frac{M-k+1}{k-1} \nu_1. \end{aligned} \right\} \tag{114}$$

50

Example 37. As an illustration of the use of this second approximation we shall derive the 5 per cent point of H for $k = 3$, $n_1 = 5$, $n_2 = 3$, $n_3 = 4$, $N = 12$, as in Example 36. Using the relations (112) and (114), we find

$$\text{var}\, H = V = 3 \cdot 0062, \quad \max. H = M = 9 \cdot 6923,$$

$$\nu_1 = 1 \cdot 699, \quad \nu_2 = 6 \cdot 536.$$

Inspection of Table 5 shows that $F(0 \cdot 05 | 1 \cdot 699, 6 \cdot 536)$ is in a region where accurate interpolation is almost impossible. As an alternative, providing easier interpolation, we can use Table 4 with its fractional ν_1, ν_2 arguments. If we use only double linear interpolation, we need the four table entries shown on the left below. The factors in the tabular scheme (*b*) of p. 137 are shown on the right.

ν_2 \ ν_1	1·6	1·8
6·5	5·170	5·034
7·0	4·988	4·853

	0·072	
[0·0356]		[0·0364]
	0·495	0·505
[0·4594]	0·928	[0·4686]

Using equation (326) we obtain

$$F(0 \cdot 05 | 1 \cdot 699, 6 \cdot 536) = 5 \cdot 170 \times 0 \cdot 4686 + 5 \cdot 034 \times 0 \cdot 4594 + 4 \cdot 853 \times 0 \cdot 0356 + 4 \cdot 988 \times 0 \cdot 0364$$

$$= 5 \cdot 090.$$

However, linear interpolation will not be accurate to three decimal places as the following difference table shows. We are just on the border of this table as far as ν_2 is concerned, and if greater accuracy were needed, the end-panel Everett formula (322) could be used to interpolate in the four columns for argument $\nu_2 = 6 \cdot 536$. Since the δ^4 terms are below twelve in the last two figures, this second difference formula should give a result accurate to within a unit in the last place. We have $\theta_0 = 0 \cdot 928$, $\theta_1 = 0 \cdot 072$, $\frac{1}{6}\theta_0\theta_1 = 0 \cdot 01114$. The resulting values of $F(0 \cdot 05 | \nu_1, 6 \cdot 536)$ are shown at the bottom of the table below. The differences ν_1-wise shown on the right clearly allow the use of the simple second difference Bessel formula (319) in the final stage, with

$$\theta = 0 \cdot 495, \quad 1 - \theta = 0 \cdot 505, \quad B_2 = -0 \cdot 0625$$

giving $F(0 \cdot 05 | 1 \cdot 699, 6 \cdot 536) = 5 \cdot 088$.

ν_2 \ ν_1	1·4		δ^2	1·6	δ^2	1·8	δ^2	2·0	δ^2	ν_1	$F(\nu_1, 6 \cdot 536)$	δ^2
5·5	f_{-2}	5·829	79	5·670	80	5·537	81	5·424	81	1·4	5·319	
6·0	f_{-1}	5·552	56	5·392	56	5·257	57	5·143	58	1·6	5·158	25
6·5	f_0	5·331	40	5·170	40	5·034	42	4·920	40	1·8	5·022	22
7·0	f_1	5·150		4·988		4·853		4·737		2·0	4·908	
$F(\nu_1, 6 \cdot 536)$		5·319		5·158		5·022		4·908				

If we invert the relation (113) using this value for F we find that $H = 5 \cdot 520$. In a table at the end of their paper for the situation where $k = 3$ and all $n_i \leqslant 5$, Kruskal & Wallis give the true 5 per cent point for H as $5 \cdot 631$. We have seen that the χ^2 approximation gives the 5 per cent point at $5 \cdot 991$. The F-approximation is an improvement on this last value, but not in this case altogether satisfactory. The value of H calculated from the data was $5 \cdot 656$, just beyond the true 5 per cent value.

12. The Friedman rank test and Kendall's concordance coefficient

This test (Friedman, 1937) represents the rank analogue to a 2-way analysis of variance and in this form usually arises under category (b) of p. 46 above, that is in a situation in which responses in a 2-way table *are* available, but rank analysis is conducted either as a non-parametric precaution or as a short-cut procedure. On the other hand, Kendall & Babbington Smith's (1939) concordance coefficient, W, whose relation to the Friedman coefficient is given in (116) below was designed to deal with situations where only rankings are possible.

Example 38. To illustrate the analysis of variance approach, consider the data from a randomized block experiment (Federer, 1955, p. 118) in which $n = 5$ fertilizer treatments were applied to plots of soya beans in each of $m = 6$ blocks, with yields given below (the beans were cultured in pots).

Yields per plot in grams

i \ j	Block					
	1	2	3	4	5	6
1	8·8	12·9	11·7	31·2	22·0	9·9
2	23·5	26·3	21·6	15·6	24·4	23·3
3	41·2	22·5	21·8	46·3	15·6	22·6
4	28·4	48·4	16·4	44·5	38·8	43·6
5	67·4	33·2	39·5	49·8	57·1	36·6

In the Friedman test the treatments are ranked *separately* for each block (highest yield 1, lowest yield 5) with results as follows:

i \ j	Block						Total R_i	$R_i - \bar{R}$
	1	2	3	4	5	6		
1	5	5	5	4	4	5	28	10
2	4	3	3	5	3	3	21	3
3	2	4	2	2	5	4	19	1
4	3	1	4	3	2	1	14	−4
5	1	2	1	1	1	2	8	−10
Total	15	15	15	15	15	15	90	0

We give also the totals of the rank number in each row, R_i, and the differences $R_i - \bar{R}$. The test statistic is again, as for Kruskal–Wallis, in the form of a standardized between-treatment sum of squares, namely

$$K = \frac{1}{m} \sum_{i=1}^{n} (R_i - \bar{R})^2 / \{\tfrac{1}{12} n(n+1)\}, \tag{115}$$

which under the null hypothesis is distributed approximately as a χ^2 having $\nu = n - 1$ degrees of freedom.

For the example, $K = \tfrac{1}{6} \times 226 / \{\tfrac{1}{12} \times 5 \times 6\} = 15·1$. Referring to Table 3, with $\nu = 4$, we find a tail area of a little less than 0·005. It is of interest to note that when the F-test is applied to the original yield data, Federer finds $F(\nu_1 = 4, \nu_2 = 20) = 1078·6/119·0 = 9·03$. This, as shown by Table 5, has a significance level below 0·001 indicating that in this example, at any rate, the use of the rank-based test results in some loss of power.

If it was desired to test differences between blocks by the Friedman test, the blocks would now be ranked separately for each treatment, $1, 2, \ldots, m$ and the test applied with n and m reversed.

Friedman's criterion (115) is directly connected with Kendall's concordance coefficient, W, through the relation

$$W = 12 \sum_i (R_i - \bar{R})^2 / \{m^2(n^3 - n)\} = K / \{m(n-1)\}. \tag{116}$$

With this latter coefficient the 'blocks' would be interpreted as 'judges', each ranking the 'treatments' in order of merit and a significantly high value of W is evidence of 'concordance' or consistency among the judges. A very small table of the exact probability integral for $n = 3$, $m = 3(1)10$; $n = 4$, $m = 3(1)6$; $n = 5$, $m = 3$ was given in $B.T.S.$ **1**, Table 46. Also the use of the χ^2 approximation and two approximations based on the beta distribution were suggested in § 25.2 (c) of the Introduction to that volume.

IV. TABLES AND CHARTS OF NON-CENTRAL DISTRIBUTIONS

The term 'non-central' has been applied to the distributions of χ^2 and Student's t in the case where the several normal variables (whose squares are summed in χ^2) and the single normal variable (forming the numerator in the t-ratio) no longer have zero expectations. The term has also been applied to the variance ratio, F, where the χ^2 in the numerator is non-central, though there may be some ambiguity in this case as the denominator χ^2, or both χ^2's, may now be non-central. Since a common application of these distributions is in connection with the power functions of the standard χ^2, t and F-tests, many available tables or charts have been planned for this special purpose. The non-central distributions can however be turned to other uses, for example to studies of robustness of central tests to non-centralities. For this reason we have provided tables of percentage points for both non-central t and χ^2, as well as tables and charts for use in the determination of power; we also discuss certain approximations to the distributions and give their sampling moments.

13. THE DISTRIBUTION OF NON-CENTRAL χ^2 (Tables 24, 25, 29)

13.1 *Percentage points of χ'; definition and description of Table* 24

If $X_1, X_2, \ldots, X_\nu$ are ν independent normally distributed variables each having zero mean and unit standard deviation, and if $a_1, a_2, \ldots, a_\nu$ are constants with

$$\lambda = \sum_{i=1}^{\nu} a_i^2, \tag{117}$$

then

$$\chi'^2 = \sum_{i=1}^{\nu} (X_i + a_i)^2 \tag{118}$$

is termed a non-central chi-squared having ν degrees of freedom and non-centrality parameter λ. The probability density distribution of χ'^2 was first given by Fisher (1928, p. 663, equation B) and may be written

$$f(\chi'^2) = \frac{\exp\{-\tfrac{1}{2}(\chi'^2 + \lambda)\}}{2^{\frac{1}{2}\nu}} \sum_{j=0}^{\infty} \frac{(\chi'^2)^{\frac{1}{2}\nu + j - 1} \lambda^j}{\Gamma(\tfrac{1}{2}\nu + j)\, 2^{2j} j!}. \tag{119}$$

An extensive table of the probability integral of the distribution (119) was computed at the Case Institute of Technology, but so far has not been published (Hayman *et al.* 1962). A table

53

giving seventeen percentage points of the distribution of χ'^2 for $\sqrt{\lambda} = 0.2(0.2)6.0$ and $\nu = 1(1)12, 15, 20$ has been computed by Johnson (1968), and this forms the basis of the more restricted Table 24 of the present volume, which is reproduced from Johnson & Pearson (1969).

Fisher's paper of 1928 contained a table of upper 5 per cent points of $B = \chi'$ calculated by A. J. Page for arguments

$$n_1 = \nu = 1(1)7, \quad \beta = \sqrt{\lambda} = 0.0(0.2)5.0.$$

Lower 5 per cent points for the same argument were calculated by Garwood (1933), but have never been reproduced in print. From a study of Page's table, it was clear that interpolation would be easier if the new table was expressed in terms of $\sqrt{\lambda}$ and χ' rather than λ and χ'^2. Table 24 therefore gives, to three decimal places, the upper and lower 5, 2·5, 1 and 0·5 per cent points of χ' for arguments

$$\nu = 1(1)12, 15, 20; \quad \sqrt{\lambda} = 0.0(0.2)6.0.$$

In Table 29, we have used the three-moment approximation discussed in § 13.3 below to extend Table 24 so as to include entries for $\sqrt{\lambda} = 8.0$ and 10.0, giving values of χ' to only two decimal places.

The method of computation used to derive Johnson's (1968) table was described in his Report and also by Johnson & Pearson (1969). In calculating the square roots to form our Table 24, use was made of Johnson's original six-figure machine output and it is believed that the four-figure values of χ' which we give should not be in error by more than a unit in the last place.

13.2 Interpolation in Table 24

Linear interpolation between values of $\sqrt{\lambda}$ is possible over a large part of the table, the second differences being less than 4 in the fourth significant figure. Elsewhere, accurate interpolation may nearly always be obtained using the simple Bessel second difference formula (319). For interpolation between $\sqrt{\lambda} = 0$ and 0.2 the end-panel interpolation procedures described in §§ 36.2, 36.3 below may be used.

The final entries for degrees of freedom are $\nu = 12, 15$ and 20. Linear interpolation will often be adequate to fill the gaps, but if not a scheme of four-point Lagrangian interpolation can be used, the coefficients for which are given in Table 67 C, and the procedure described in § 37.1.

13.3 The moments of χ'^2. Approximate methods for use beyond the range of Table 24

The first four cumulants of χ'^2 are:

$$\left. \begin{array}{ll} \kappa_1 = \nu + \lambda, & \kappa_2 = 2(\nu + 2\lambda), \\ \kappa_3 = 8(\nu + 3\lambda), & \kappa_4 = 48(\nu + 4\lambda), \end{array} \right\} \tag{120}$$

giving the two moment ratios

$$\beta_1 = \left(\frac{\kappa_3}{\sigma^3} \right)^2 = \frac{8(\nu + 3\lambda)^2}{(\nu + 2\lambda)^3}; \quad \beta_2 = 3 + \frac{\kappa_4}{\sigma^4} = 3 + \frac{12(\nu + 4\lambda)}{(\nu + 2\lambda)^2}. \tag{121}$$

In the (β_1, β_2)-plane, a point with co-ordinates defined by (121) falls in a wedge-shaped region lying between the two lines

$$\beta_2 - 3 = \tfrac{4}{3}\beta_1 \quad \text{and} \quad \beta_2 - 3 = \tfrac{3}{2}\beta_1,$$

the latter being the Pearson Type III or gamma line. An approximation suggested by one of

54

us (Pearson, 1959) involves the use of a central χ^2 distribution having the correct first three moments. This involves taking

$$\chi'^2(\nu) \simeq \frac{\nu + 3\lambda}{\nu + 2\lambda} \chi^2_{\nu'} - \frac{\lambda^2}{\nu + 3\lambda}, \tag{122}$$

where $\nu' = (\nu + 2\lambda)^3/(\nu + 3\lambda)^2$ and $\chi^2_{\nu'}$ is distributed as a central χ^2 with fractional degrees of freedom, ν'. Percentage points of χ'^2 can then be obtained by interpolating for ν' in any standard table of percentage points for χ^2 (e.g. in $B.T.S.$ **1**, Table 8, or Table 3 of this volume) or the probability integral may be approximated by interpolating in a table of the probability integral of χ^2 (e.g. $B.T.S.$ **1**, Table 7 or Khamis & Rudert, 1965).

We give below some comparisons showing the accuracy of this approximation at the boundaries, $\nu = 20$ and $\sqrt{\lambda} = 6 \cdot 0$, of Table 24. The greatest errors occur at the lower terminal, due to the fact that the three-moment fit does not hold down the start of the approximating distribution at $\chi'^2 = 0$. The fit is, however, in general much better than that suggested by Patnaik (1949), based on the first two moments and correct start. A comparison of the two approximations in a single case was given in Example 6, pp. 10–11.

Accuracy of three-moment approximation at $\nu = 20$

$\sqrt{\lambda}$	1·0		3·0		5·0		6·0	
P	True χ'	Error	True χ'	Error	True χ'	Error	True χ'	Error
0·005	2·795	−0·001	3·353	−0·012	4·443	−0·015	5·139	−0·013
·01	2·946	·000	3·528	− ·007	4·647	− ·009	5·354	− ·008
·05	3·376	·000	4·025	·000	5·216	− ·001	5·948	·000
·95	5·742	·000	6·679	− ·001	8·117	·000	8·933	− ·001
·99	6·278	·000	7·266	·002	8·740	·003	9·567	·002
·995	6·478	·000	7·484	·003	8·970	·004	9·800	·005

Accuracy of (a) three-moment and (b) four-moment approximations at $\sqrt{\lambda} = 6 \cdot 0$

ν	1			6			15		20		
		Error			Error			Error		Error	
P	True χ'	(a)	(b)	True χ'	(a)	(b)	True χ'	(a)	True χ'	(a)	(b)
0·005	3·424	−0·038	−0·003	3·939	−0·028	0·001	4·741	−0·017	5·139	−0·013	0·001
·01	3·674	− ·023	·000	4·174	− ·016	·003	4·961	− ·010	5·354	− ·008	·001
·05	4·355	− ·001	·003	4·822	− ·001	·003	5·570	·000	5·948	·000	·001
·95	7·645	− ·002	·001	8·005	− ·001	·001	8·614	− ·001	8·933	− ·001	·000
·99	8·326	·005	·000	8·672	·004	·000	9·258	·003	9·567	·002	·000
·995	8·576	·008	− ·001	8·916	·007	− ·002	9·495	·005	9·800	·005	·000

It is, however, possible to obtain an even closer approximation by using a Pearson curve, which will be of Type I or beta form, with the correct first *four* moments. To effect this, values of $\sqrt{\beta_1}$ and β_2 are first calculated from equation (121) and the required standardized percentage points found by bi-linear interpolation in Table 32, i.e. using formula (326). The corresponding approximate percentage points of χ'^2 are then obtained, using the correct mean and standard deviation given in (120). The calculations take a little longer than those based on the three-moment approximation because Table 32 requires double-entry interpolation.

55

Some results of using this approximation are shown above in the columns (b); the improvement over the three-moment approximation, particularly at the lower tail, is striking. While it is true that the Pearson Type I distributions used have a finite upper terminal, whereas the upper limit for χ'^2 is infinite, this is of little importance. For instance in the most extreme case of the comparisons made, where $\nu = 1$, $\sqrt{\lambda} = 6$ and $\sqrt{\beta_1} = 0 \cdot 49$, $\beta_2 = 3 \cdot 33$, the upper terminal of the approximating distribution falls at over twelve times the standard deviation from the mean.

On the evidence available it was considered justifiable to use this four-moment approximation to obtain the percentage points given in Table 29 for $\sqrt{\lambda} = 8 \cdot 0$ and $10 \cdot 0$. The necessary interpolation in Table 32 was carried out on the McGill University computer under Dr M. A. Stephens' directions.

13.4   *The power function of the χ^2 test (Table 25)*

We define the power as

$$\beta(\alpha, \nu, \lambda) = \int_{\chi_\alpha^2}^{\infty} f(\chi'^2 | \nu, \lambda) \, d\chi'^2, \tag{123}$$

where χ_α^2 is the upper 100α per cent point of the central χ^2 distribution based on ν degrees of freedom. The earliest table of this function is that of Fix (1949). More recently extensive calculations have been carried out by Haynam *et al.* (1962), who present their results in three forms: (*a*) values of β against arguments α, ν and λ; (*b*) values of λ against arguments α, ν and β; (*c*) values of ν against arguments α, λ and β. In Table 25 we present results in form (*b*), for

$$\alpha = 0 \cdot 05, 0 \cdot 01; \quad \nu = 1(1)30(2)50(5)100;$$

$$\beta = 0 \cdot 25, \ 0 \cdot 50, \ 0 \cdot 60, \ 0 \cdot 70(0 \cdot 05)0 \cdot 95, \ 0 \cdot 97, \ 0 \cdot 99.$$

These results are taken directly from Haynam *et al.*, Table II (see also Harter & Owen, 1970, pp. 45–78) except that the values for $\beta = 0 \cdot 25$, were obtained by four-point Lagrangian interpolation, using these authors' values for

$$\beta = 0 \cdot 22, \ 0 \cdot 24, \ 0 \cdot 26, \ 0 \cdot 28.$$

It is also possible to obtain λ for given α, β and ν from Tables 24 and 29, within the limits of the probability levels there provided. Table 25, however, provides a more informative presentation.

Example 39. Suppose that $\nu = 6$ and we ask how large must λ be to provide a probability of $0 \cdot 99$ of obtaining a value of χ^2 significant at the 5 per cent level. Entering Table 25 with $\alpha = 0 \cdot 05$, $\beta = 0 \cdot 99$ and $\nu = 6$ we find at once that $\lambda = 28 \cdot 046$. If Table 24 is used, it is necessary to determine for $\nu = 6$, the value of $\sqrt{\lambda}$ for which the lower 1 per cent point of χ' equals the upper 5 per cent point of a central χ.

We see that when $\lambda = 0$, the upper 5 per cent point is at $3 \cdot 548$. We then extract the following $\sqrt{\lambda}$, χ' values for lower 1 per cent points:

$\sqrt{\lambda}$	5·0	5·2	5·4	5·6
χ'	3·293	3·465	3·640	3·816

Backward linear interpolation between the two central values gives $\sqrt{\lambda} = 5 \cdot 295$ or $\lambda = 28 \cdot 04$, when $\chi' = 3 \cdot 548$.

13.5 Confidence limits for λ, given a single value $x = \chi'(\nu, \lambda)$

Example 40. A symmetrical $100(1-\alpha)$ per cent confidence interval for the non-centrality parameter may be obtained by backward interpolation for $\underline{\lambda}(x)$ and $\bar{\lambda}(x)$ in the appropriate rows of the upper and lower $\frac{1}{2}\alpha$ probability level sections of Tables 24 or 29. Suppose that with $\nu = 9$ an observed value of $\chi'^2 = 21{\cdot}7$ has been obtained and we choose $\alpha = 0{\cdot}05$. Then $\chi' = \sqrt{21{\cdot}7} = 4{\cdot}658$ and we obtain from Table 24:

Lower 2·5 per cent points			Upper 2·5 per cent points		
$\sqrt{\lambda}$	χ' (for $\nu = 9$)	δ	$\sqrt{\lambda}$	χ' (for $\nu = 9$)	δ^2
5·6	4·446		0·8	4·510	
5·8	4·617	0·171	1·0	4·589	0·013
6·0	4·789	0·172	1·2	4·681	0·013
			1·4	4·786	

Inverse linear interpolation in the first case gives, for $\chi' = 4{\cdot}658$, a value $\sqrt{\bar{\lambda}} = 5{\cdot}848$, $\bar{\lambda} = 34{\cdot}20$.

In the second case, where the second differences are not negligible, we have $\theta = (\sqrt{\lambda} - 1{\cdot}0)/0{\cdot}2$ as a solution of the quadratic

$$4{\cdot}658 = 4{\cdot}589 + 0{\cdot}092\theta - \tfrac{1}{2}\,0{\cdot}013\theta(1-\theta),$$

leading to $\sqrt{\underline{\lambda}} = 1{\cdot}153$, $\underline{\lambda} = 1{\cdot}329$. This means that in the confidence theory sense there is a probability of $0{\cdot}95$ that the interval $(1{\cdot}33, 34{\cdot}20)$ includes the unknown λ.

It must be remembered that the X_i of equation (118) have unit variances; when this is not the case, $\lambda = \Sigma a_i^2/\sigma_x^2$.

13.6 Approximation to the distribution of the multiple correlation coefficient

Example 41. Suppose we have a sample of N observations from a $(k+1)$-variate normal population and that R is the sample coefficient of multiple correlation of one variate, say y, on the remaining k variates $x_1, x_2, \ldots, x_k$. Let the corresponding coefficient in the population sampled, supposed infinite, be $\mathbf{R}$. Fisher (1928, p. 660, distribution A) gave the probability density function of R, which is a function of $\mathbf{R}$ and of the two degrees of freedom

$$\nu_1 = k, \quad \nu_2 = N - k - 1.$$

He also suggested that an approximation to this distribution could be obtained from that of non-central χ by taking

$$R = \tanh(\chi'_\nu/\sqrt{\nu_2}) \tag{124}$$

with

$$\nu = \nu_1, \quad \sqrt{\lambda} = \sqrt{\nu_2}\,\tanh^{-1}\mathbf{R}. \tag{125}$$

It is possible to compare the lower and upper 5 and 1 per cent points calculated in this way with the true values obtained by Kramer (1970) given in Table 52. We have selected the case $\nu_2 = 50$, i.e. the largest value comprised in Table 52 and have taken three values of the population $\mathbf{R}$: 0·3, 0·5 and 0·8 and three values of ν_1: 2, 10 and 20. It is impossible to draw any general conclusions about the accuracy of Fisher's approximation without far more extensive comparisons than those given in the table below, but it will be noted that for $\nu_1 = k = 2$ the error is relatively small, nearly constant and always in the same direction. However, a more accurate approximation is possibly that of Khatri described in § 29.3 below.

R	Per cent point	$v_1 = 2$ True R	$v_1 = 2$ Error	$v_1 = 10$ True R	$v_1 = 10$ Error	$v_1 = 20$ True R	$v_1 = 20$ Error
0·3	Lower 1%	0·066	− 0·002	0·276	0·000	0·414	0·012
	5%	·133	− ·003	·336	·000	·466	·013
	Upper 5%	·517	− ·005	·621	− ·001	·699	·007
	1%	·584	− ·006	·673	− ·003	·739	·005
0·5	Lower 1%	0·247	− 0·004	0·401	− 0·011	0·513	− 0·005
	5%	·333	− ·005	·465	− ·010	·565	− ·003
	Upper 5%	·667	− ·005	·725	− ·005	·774	− ·001
	1%	·718	− ·005	·766	− ·005	·807	− ·002
0·8	Lower 1%	0·658	− 0·005	0·716	− 0·018	0·765	− 0·023
	5%	·710	− ·005	·757	− ·015	·798	− ·019
	Upper 5%	·874	− ·003	·892	− ·006	·908	− ·007
	1%	·896	− ·003	·910	− ·005	·923	− ·006

14. The distribution of non-central t

14.1 *Definition and scope of Tables* 26, 27, 28 *and* 30, *chart* 1

If (a) X is a $N(0, 1)$ variable, and (b) χ^2, independent of X, has the standard central χ^2-distribution defined in equation (19) above, based on ν degrees of freedom, then a non-central t, or t', is defined as

$$t' = \frac{X + \Delta}{\sqrt{(\chi^2/\nu)}}, \tag{126}$$

where Δ is the non-centrality parameter. The probability density function of t' may be written in the form

$$f(t'|\nu, \Delta) = \frac{\Gamma(\nu+1)}{2^{\frac{1}{2}(\nu-1)}\Gamma(\frac{1}{2}\nu)\sqrt{(\pi\nu)}} \left(1 + \frac{t'^2}{\nu}\right)^{-\frac{1}{2}(\nu+1)} \exp\left\{-\frac{1}{2}\frac{\nu\Delta^2}{(\nu+t'^2)}\right\} Hh_\nu\left\{\frac{-t'\Delta}{\sqrt{(\nu+t'^2)}}\right\}, \tag{127}$$

where

$$Hh_\nu(x) = \int_0^\infty \frac{v^\nu}{\nu!} \exp\left\{-\frac{1}{2}(v+x)^2\right\} dv \tag{128}$$

is an Hh function as defined by Fisher (1931).

This general distribution may be applied in a number of statistical situations, some of which are described in §§ 14.4 and 14.5 below. The probability integral of non-central t demands a table of triple entry since the probability that t' exceeds t'_0, say, depends on ν, Δ and t'_0. A complete table would demand a prohibitive allocation of space but, following the original presentation of Johnson & Welch (1939) we have adopted two forms of less ambitious tabulation, providing:

(a) in Table 26, at seven upper percentage levels, a table of an auxiliary factor l *for determining t'_0 given ν and Δ*, such that

$$\Pr\{t' \geqslant t'_0|\nu, \Delta\} = \alpha; \tag{129}$$

(b) in Table 27, for four values of α, a table of the same auxiliary factor l, *for determining Δ given ν and t'_0*, such that the inequality (129) also holds.

In both cases a simple change of signs makes it possible to determine results for the corresponding lower 100α per cent points. The form of procedure, introducing the factor l, may at first seem a little cumbersome, but it does make it possible to cover in compact form a very wide range of values for the parameters ν and Δ, at the same time permitting relatively simple interpolation at intermediate values. The factors tabled have been largely taken directly from Owen's (1963) detailed *Tables*, which in turn had extended considerably the original tabulation of Johnson & Welch (1939).

Two other tables concerning non-central t belong to this group: Table 28 giving factors to facilitate the calculation of the first four moments of the distribution (127), and Table 30, chart 1, from which the power function of Student's t-test can be read off. They are described in §§ 14.5 and 14.6 below.

14.2   *Rules to follow in using Tables 26 and 27*

The basis of the procedure involving the use of the factor l has been described by Johnson & Welch and we shall not repeat the discussion here. For use of the tables it is only necessary to note the following instructions repeated below the left of each pair of facing table pages.

Table 26. Given ν, Δ and α, to determine t'_0 such that $\Pr\{t' \geqslant t'_0 | \nu, \Delta\} = \alpha$.

(i)   Calculate

$$u = \frac{\Delta}{\sqrt{(2\nu)}}\left(1 + \frac{\Delta^2}{2\nu}\right)^{-\frac{1}{2}}. \tag{130}$$

(ii)   Interpolate for l in the appropriate α-section of the table.

(iii)   Determine $t'_0 = t'_0(\alpha | \nu, \Delta)$ from

$$t'_0 = \frac{\Delta + l\{1 + \Delta^2/(2\nu) - l^2/(2\nu)\}^{\frac{1}{2}}}{1 - l^2/(2\nu)}. \tag{131}$$

A lower percentage point is obtained following the same procedure, substituting $-\Delta$ for Δ in (130) and (131), and finally giving a negative sign to the resulting expression on the right-hand side of (131); i.e. $t'_0(1 - \alpha | \nu, \Delta) = -t'_0(\alpha | \nu, -\Delta)$.

The separate tables make it possible to find the 50 per cent and the upper and lower 25, 10, 5, 2·5, 1 and 0·5 per cent points for t'.

Table 27. Given ν, t'_0 and α, to determine a lower confidence limit, $\underline{\Delta}$, such that

$$\Pr\{t' \geqslant t'_0 | \nu, \Delta\} = \alpha.$$

(i)   Calculate

$$y = \frac{t'_0}{\sqrt{(2\nu)}}\left(1 + \frac{t'^2_0}{2\nu}\right)^{-\frac{1}{2}}. \tag{132}$$

(ii)   Interpolate for l in the appropriate α-section of the table.

(iii)   Determine $\underline{\Delta} = \underline{\Delta}(\alpha | \nu, t'_0)$ from

$$\underline{\Delta} = t'_0 - l\left(1 + \frac{t'^2_0}{2\nu}\right)^{\frac{1}{2}}. \tag{133}$$

An upper confidence limit, $\bar{\Delta}$, is obtained following the same procedure, substituting $-t'_0$ for t'_0 in (132) and (133), and finally giving a negative sign to the resulting expression on the right-hand side of (133); $\bar{\Delta}(1 - \alpha | \nu, t'_0) = -\underline{\Delta}(\alpha | \nu, -t'_0)$.

The values of α given make it possible to determine either lower or upper 5, 2·5, 1 and 0·5 per cent confidence limits for Δ. Alternatively, using both ends, we can find the limits of the central 90, 95, 98 and 99 per cent confidence intervals. Note that if Δ replaces $\underline{\Delta}$ on the left-hand side of (133), it is seen after the necessary manipulation that the relations (131) and (133) are identical.

14.3 *Derivation of Tables* 26 *and* 27; *interpolation*

The whole of Table 26 and the central portions of Table 27 were taken directly from Owen's (1963) five decimal place tables of η and l.† Whenever these tables gave a 5 in the last figure, the entry has been *reduced* in cutting it down to four decimal places, e.g. 2·57715 becomes 2·5771. Without recalculation, which did not seem justified, it was impossible to determine whether the figure in the fourth decimal place should be raised or lowered. Owen's Table 5 uses an argument interval of 0·01 for u. His Table 6 uses an interval of 0·1 for y, except that for $\alpha = 0.05$ the interval is 0·05. Also when $|y| \geqslant 0.60$ (following Johnson & Welch) entry must be made with argument $\{1 + t_0'^2/(2\nu)\}^{-\frac{1}{2}}$ rather than with y. To give a common argument, y, throughout, this region of our Table 27 was recomputed by an appropriate interpolation in Owen's Table 5.

Interpolation for u and y

The argument intervals have been chosen so that when linear interpolation is not adequate, use of the simple Bessel second difference formula (319) will nearly always give answers which are not in error by more than a unit in the fourth decimal place. To achieve this result a reduction in the argument interval from 0·1 to 0·05 has been made in the upper rows of Table 26 and the lower rows of Table 27.

Interpolation for ν

To extend the range of the tables beyond $\nu = 9$ towards infinity, we follow the previous authors in giving columns for $\nu = 16, 36$ and 144, while the infinity value for all u and y, corresponding to the standardized normal percentage point, is shown at the top of each table. Since for the sequence $\nu = 9, 16, 36, 144, \infty$ we have $12/\sqrt{\nu} = 4, 3, 2, 1, 0$, interpolation for intermediate ν-values may be simply effected by considering l as tabled at equal intervals of $12/\sqrt{\nu}$. For three decimal place accuracy linear interpolation will generally be adequate, while to obtain the full four decimal place accuracy the second difference equation (319) should be used.

14.4 *The distribution of the coefficient of variation in normal samples*

Let μ and σ^2 be the mean and variance of a variable, x, in an infinite population, and $\bar{x}$ and s^2 the usual unbiased estimators derived from a random sample of n observations. Then

$$V = \sigma/\mu \quad \text{and} \quad v = s/\bar{x}$$

are defined as the coefficients of variation in the population and sample, respectively. These coefficients seem only likely to be useful as measures of relative variability in situations where the whole distribution of x is far removed from the origin, e.g. we may determine the coefficient of variation for stature in a population of adult human males, or that of breaking strength among test specimens of steel wire. While strictly speaking a $N(\mu, \sigma)$ distribution always allows the possibility of a negative value of x, this possibility becomes negligible if σ is no more than 20 or 25 per cent of μ. A meaningful coefficient of variation can therefore, under these conditions be associated with a near-normal distribution of x. It is then seen that

$$\frac{\sqrt{n}}{v} = \frac{\sqrt{n}\,\bar{x}}{s} = \left\{ \frac{(\bar{x} - \mu)\sqrt{n}}{\sigma} + \frac{\mu\sqrt{n}}{\sigma} \right\} \div \frac{s}{\sigma} \tag{134}$$

† Owen uses λ for our l. His η is our u and our y he calls y'. This was also the notation of Johnson & Welch.

will be distributed as non-central t with $\nu = n-1$, $\Delta = \mu\sqrt{n}/\sigma = \sqrt{n}/V$. Table 26 may therefore be used to find control limits for v, given V, and Table 27 to find confidence limits for V, given v.

It should be remembered, of course, that confidence limits for μ can be computed from the central t-distribution (see *B.T.S.* **1**, §5.5).

Example 42. A random sample of $n = 12$ observations, from a population assumed approximately normal, yields a coefficient of variation, $v = 0.0623$; to determine upper and lower 2.5 per cent confidence limits for V.

We have

$$t_0' = \frac{\sqrt{12}}{0.0623} = 55.60, \quad \nu = 11.$$

Since great accuracy in estimation would not here be justified, we shall extract values of l from Table 27 to two decimal places only. Using equation (132) it is found that $y = 0.996$ and straight-forward interpolation gives $l = 1.93$. It follows from equation (133) that

$$\Delta = 55.60 - 1.93 \times 11.90 = 32.63,$$

whence $\overline{V} = \sqrt{12/32.63} = 0.106$.

For $\overline{\Delta}$ and $\underline{V}$, we change the sign of t_0' in (132) and have $y = -0.996$; again $l = 1.93$, to two decimals. Equation (133) with appropriate reversals of signs gives

$$\overline{\Delta} = -\{-55.60 - 1.93 \times 11.90\} = 78.57,$$

consequently $\underline{V} = \sqrt{12/78.57} = 0.044$. The 95 per cent central confidence interval for V is therefore given by the inequality

$$0.044 \leqslant V \leqslant 0.106.$$

If we extract the values of l to three decimal places, using second difference interpolation, we find the limits to be 0.0441 and 0.1061, but clearly such additional accuracy is unnecessary.

14.5 *Computation of the power of Student's t-test*

Although the relationship between Δ and β is displayed more clearly in Table 30, chart 1 (see §14.7 below), Table 27 may be used to determine how large the value of the non-centrality parameter must be to provide a probability of at least β of establishing significance at the 100α per cent level of central t. As in the case of non-central χ', for a given ν we have to determine the value of Δ which places the lower $(1-\beta)$ point of t' at the upper α point of t.

In the case of a single sample of n observations, where $t = (\bar{x} - \mu_0)\sqrt{n}/s$, we have

$$\Delta = (\mu - \mu_0)\sqrt{n}/\sigma_x.$$

For the case of two samples of size n_1, n_2 from two populations, where

$$t = (\bar{x}_1 - \bar{x}_2)\bigg/\bigg\{s\left(\frac{1}{n_1} + \frac{1}{n_2}\right)^{\frac{1}{2}}\bigg\},$$

s^2 being the pooled estimate of an assumed common variance, σ_x^2, we have

$$\Delta = (\mu_1 - \mu_2)\bigg/\bigg\{\sigma_x\left(\frac{1}{n_1} + \frac{1}{n_2}\right)^{\frac{1}{2}}\bigg\}.$$

We cannot, of course, obtain the value of the non-central displacement, $\mu_1 - \mu_2$, corresponding to a given β, only of the ratio, $(\mu_1 - \mu_2)/\sigma_x$.

Example 43. Using the two-tailed t-test with $\alpha = 0.05$, what is the smallest standardized difference $|\mu_1 - \mu_2|/\sigma_x$ which there is a 95 per cent chance of detecting, using a sample of $n = 9$ from each of the populations?

Here $\nu = 16$, $t(\alpha|\nu) = t(0{\cdot}025|16) = 2{\cdot}120$. We want to find from Table 27 the value of Δ for which the *lower* 5 per cent point of t' falls at $2{\cdot}120$. Substituting in equation (132) with $t'_0 = -2{\cdot}120$ we find $y = -0{\cdot}3509$. The relevant entries in the 5 per cent section of Table 27 are:

y	l	δ^2
$-0{\cdot}3$	$1{\cdot}6187$	7
$-0{\cdot}4$	$1{\cdot}6109$	10

The interpolation fraction is $\theta = 0{\cdot}509$ while $B_2 = -0{\cdot}0625$ so that the second difference interpolation equation (319) gives

$$l_y = 0{\cdot}491 \times 1{\cdot}6187 + 0{\cdot}509 \times 1{\cdot}6109 - 0{\cdot}0625 \times 0{\cdot}0017 = 1{\cdot}6146.$$

It follows from (133) that $\underline{\Delta}$ is given by

$$\underline{\Delta} = -\{-2{\cdot}120 - 1{\cdot}6146 \times 1{\cdot}0679\} = 3{\cdot}844,$$

and that
$$(\mu_1 - \mu_2)/\sigma_x = 3{\cdot}844 \times \sqrt{2/3} = 1{\cdot}812.$$

Essentially the same result is obtained in the following section, using chart 1 of Table 30. Thus if only two samples of nine observations are available the difference between the population means must be at least $1{\cdot}81 \times \sigma_x$ if the probability is to be $0{\cdot}95$ or more of establishing a significant difference, using a two-tailed t-test at the 5 per cent level.

14.6 *Tolerance limits in industrial quality control*

Suppose that x is a $N(\mu, \sigma)$ variable and L_P is some limiting value for x such that

$$\Pr\{x \leqslant L_P\} = P.$$

P may be determined from L_P by entering a table of the normal probability integral with

$$K_P = (L_P - \mu)/\sigma. \tag{135}$$

If a random sample of n observations from the population is available having mean $\bar{x}$ and variance s^2,
$$k = (L_P - \bar{x})/s \tag{136}$$

is an estimator for K_P. Further, it is seen that

$$k\sqrt{n} = -\left\{ \frac{(\bar{x} - \mu)\sqrt{n}}{\sigma} + \frac{(\mu - L_P)\sqrt{n}}{\sigma} \right\} \div \frac{s}{\sigma}$$

will be distributed as t' with $\nu = n - 1$, $\Delta = K_P \sqrt{n}$.

If then in a manufacturing process it is important to keep at less than $100(1 - P)$ per cent, the percentage of items for which a characteristic x exceeds L_P, the non-central t-distribution can be used to provide an upper control limit for the ratio k, determined from successive samples of n. Alternatively, Table 27 may be used to determine a one-sided confidence limit for K_P, and hence for P, given an observed sample value of k.

Various aspects of this problem have been found to be of sufficient importance in industrial quality control to justify the preparation of extensive tables, presented in the most appropriate form in terms of k and K_P (e.g. Resnikoff & Liebermann, 1957; Owen, 1963). It is however possible, with a little additional labour, to obtain the answers required from Tables 26 and 27, although without the fuller choice of probability levels given in the specialized tables.

An allied problem, although not based on the non-central t-distribution, is to determine from the mean $\bar{x}$ and standard deviation s in a sample of n observations, tolerance limits, say

$\bar{x} - h(\tfrac{1}{2}\alpha, P, n) s$ and $\bar{x} + h(\tfrac{1}{2}\alpha, P, n) s$, which will include with a probability $1 - \alpha$ a fraction of at least P of the assumed normal population. An extensive table of $h(\alpha, P, n)$ was given by Eisenhart *et al.* (1947, Table 2.1); Owen (1962) has also given a table of somewhat wider application (his Table 5.4). The result which involves some approximation for small samples was first established by Wald & Wolfowitz (1946).

Example 44. To find an upper 2·5 per cent control limit for k when samples of size ten are being drawn from bulk materials, assumed approximately normal, the situation being such that although μ and σ may vary a little from time to time it is important that no more than 10 per cent of items should exceed $L_{0 \cdot 90} = 120$ units.

Here $K_{0 \cdot 90} = 1 \cdot 2816$, $\Delta = \sqrt{10} \times 1 \cdot 2816 = 4 \cdot 0528$. In the situation posed it is expected that $k = (120 - \bar{x})/s$ will be positive but we do not want its value to fall too low; consequently it is necessary to extract the *lower* 2·5 per cent point of $t' = t'(0 \cdot 025 | 9, 4 \cdot 0528)$ from Table 26. From equation (130) we find $u = -0 \cdot 6907$ and have therefore to interpolate among the following values:

u	l	δ^2
$-0 \cdot 60$	$1 \cdot 9290$	$\cdot$
$-0 \cdot 65$	$1 \cdot 9209$	9
$-0 \cdot 70$	$1 \cdot 9137$	15
$-0 \cdot 75$	$1 \cdot 9080$	$\cdot$

$$\theta = \frac{0 \cdot 407}{0 \cdot 500} = 0 \cdot 814, \qquad B_2 = -0 \cdot 03785.$$

Using the interpolation equation (319), we find that for $u = -0 \cdot 6907$, $l = 1 \cdot 9149$.

Remembering that we are finding a lower percentage point, equation (131) gives

$$t'_0 = -\left\{ \frac{-4 \cdot 0528 + 1 \cdot 9149 \, (1 \cdot 7088)^{\frac{1}{2}}}{1 - 0 \cdot 2037} \right\} = 1 \cdot 946.$$

Therefore $k = 1 \cdot 946/\sqrt{10} = 0 \cdot 6154$, and using this control limit the rule would be:

'take action if $\bar{x} + 0 \cdot 6154s > 120$'.

If Owen's detailed *Tables* (1963) are available, we find directly without need for computation that $k = 0 \cdot 615$ (see his Table 2.11, p. 88).

An alternative procedure is to use the Pearson Type IV curve in the approximation mentioned on p. 66 below. This involves the use of Table 28 giving the moments of t' (§ 14.6) and then deriving a standardized percentage point with the resulting $\sqrt{\beta_1}$, β_2 values from Table 32. We proceed by the following steps:

(a) For $\nu = 9$, $\Delta = 4 \cdot 0528$ we find from Table 28 and the equations (139):

$$\mu_1'(t') = 4 \cdot 4347, \quad \mu_2(t') = 2 \cdot 7369, \quad \sigma(t') = 1 \cdot 6543, \quad \mu_3(t') = 5 \cdot 5888,$$

$$\mu_4(t') = 50 \cdot 4988, \quad \sqrt{\beta_1}(t') = 1 \cdot 2344, \quad \beta_2(t') = 6 \cdot 7416.$$

(b) Now determine the lower 2·5 per cent point of a Pearson curve with these values, using bilinear interpolation in Table 32, with interpolation fractions $\theta = 0 \cdot 344$, $\phi = 0 \cdot 708$. Taking out the four required table entries:

	$\sqrt{\beta_1}$	
β_2	$1 \cdot 2$	$1 \cdot 3$
$6 \cdot 6$	$-1 \cdot 522$	$-1 \cdot 442$
$6 \cdot 8$	$-1 \cdot 537$	$-1 \cdot 460$

and applying either procedure suggested below equations (326 a, b) we find the standardized lower 2·5 per cent point to lie at $-1 \cdot 506$.

(c) Hence, for non-central t,

$$t'_{0\cdot025} \simeq 4\cdot4347 - 1\cdot506 \times 1\cdot6543 = 1\cdot943.$$

This compares with the correct value of $1\cdot946$ derived above from Table 26. The use of Table 26, though not altogether straightforward, is probably rather quicker and, of course, more accurate than using the approximation based on Tables 28 and 32. It will be noticed that the point $\beta_1(t') = 1\cdot523$, $\beta_2(t') = 6\cdot742$ lies outside the diagram of Fig. 6, p. 65.

14.7   *The power function of the t-test, using Table 30, chart 1*

This chart was included as Table 10 in $B.T.S.$ **1**, but is reproduced again here because it forms the first of a series of ten charts of the power function for analysis of variance tests. If we write

$$t' = (x+\Delta)/s_x = (X+\Delta/\sigma_x) \div s_x/\sigma_x,$$

where $X = x/\sigma_x$ is a $N(0,1)$ variate and s_x^2 is the usual unbiased estimator of σ_x^2 based on ν degrees of freedom, then the curves in chart 1 represent the power of the two-tail test, having significance level α. The ordinates are the sum of the two integrals

$$\int_{-\infty}^{-t_{\frac{1}{2}\alpha}} f(t'|\nu, \Delta/\sigma_x)\,dt' + \int_{t_{\frac{1}{2}\alpha}}^{\infty} f(t'|\nu, \Delta/\sigma_x)\,dt'$$

and these are plotted on a logarithmic scale against abscissae, $\phi = (\Delta/\sigma_x) \times 1/\sqrt{2}$ for $\alpha = 0\cdot05$ and $0\cdot01$. Since the first of the two integrals becomes rapidly negligible as Δ/σ_x increases above zero (and similarly for the second integral as Δ/σ_x decreases below zero), the chart can also be used to give the power function of the single-tail test for significance levels $\alpha = 0\cdot025$ and $0\cdot005$.

Taking again Example 43 of the preceding section, we have

$$\phi = \frac{\mu_1 - \mu_2}{\sigma_x \sqrt{(2/9)}} \times \frac{1}{\sqrt{2}} = \tfrac{3}{2}(\mu_1 - \mu_2)/\sigma_x.$$

Interpolating between the curves for $\nu = 15$ and 20, in the family with $\alpha = 0\cdot05$, we find that the horizontal rule for power $\beta = 0\cdot95$ is associated with $\phi = 2\cdot72$. This means that

$$(\mu_1 - \mu_2)/\sigma_x = \tfrac{2}{3} \times 2\cdot72 = 1\cdot81,$$

agreeing with the result obtained by using Table 27.

14.8   *The moments of $f(t'|\nu, \Delta)$; Table 28*

For the mean and variance of t' we have

$$\mu_1' = (\tfrac{1}{2}\nu)^{\frac{1}{2}} \frac{\Gamma\{\tfrac{1}{2}(\nu-1)\}}{\Gamma(\tfrac{1}{2}\nu)} \Delta = \frac{\nu}{\nu-1} \Delta E\left(\frac{\chi_\nu}{\sqrt{\nu}}\right), \tag{137}$$

$$\mu_2 = \frac{\nu}{\nu-2}(1+\Delta^2) - (\mu_1')^2. \tag{138}$$

Hogben *et al.* (1961) have provided a table of coefficients, reproduced here as Table 28, with the help of which the mean and the central moments μ_2, μ_3 and μ_4 can be readily calculated. If we write

$$\left.\begin{array}{ll} \mu_1' = c_{11}\Delta, & \mu_2 = c_{22}\Delta^2 + c_{20}, \\ \mu_3 = c_{33}\Delta^3 + c_{31}\Delta, & \mu_4 = c_{44}\Delta^4 + c_{42}\Delta^2 + c_{40}, \end{array}\right\} \tag{139}$$

then the table gives the coefficients, c_{ij}, to six significant figures, for

$$\nu = 2(1)25(5)50, \ 60, \ 70, \ 75, \ 80, \ 90, \ 100, \ 150, \ 200(100)1000.$$

64

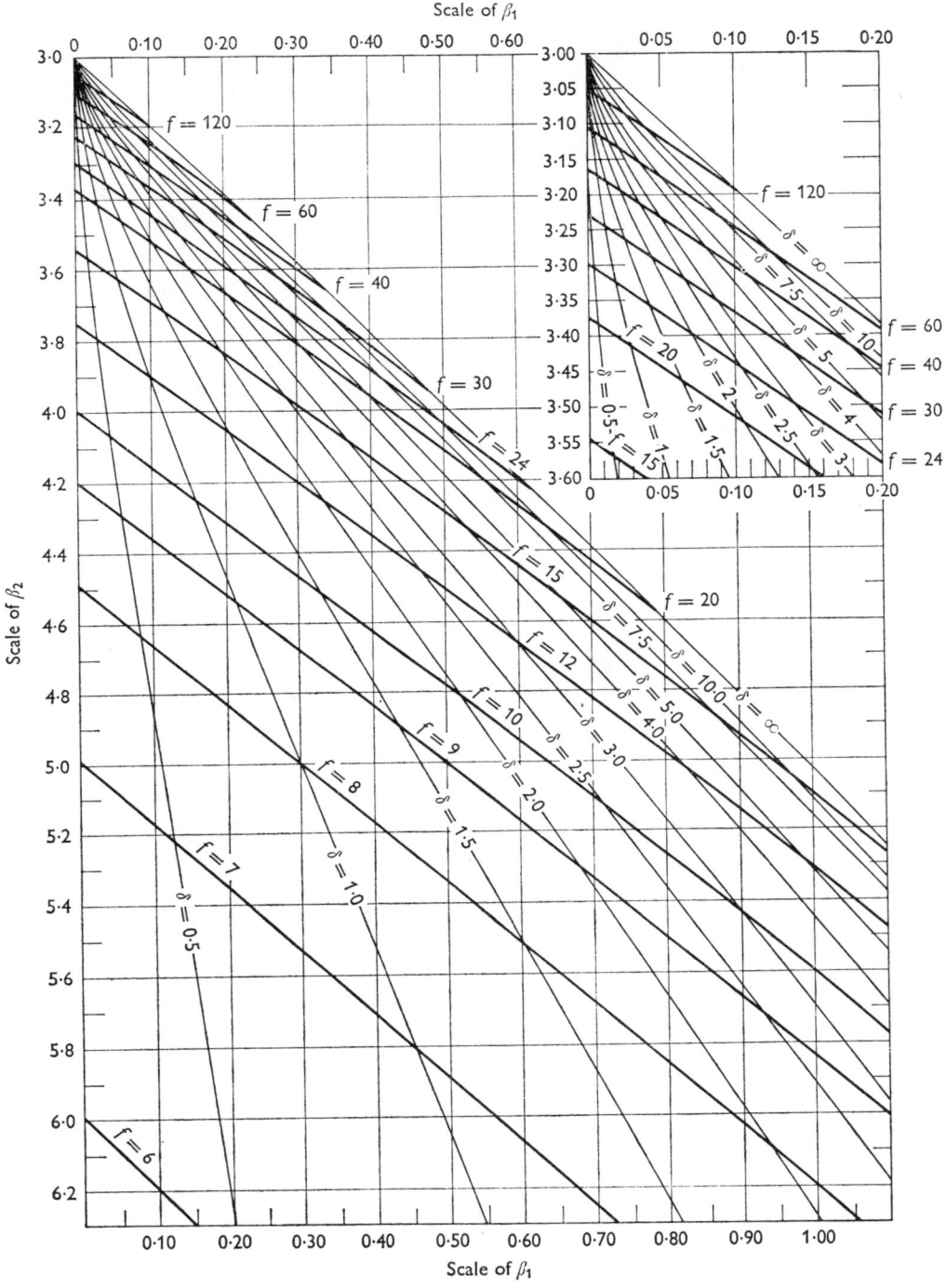

Fig. 6. Distribution of non-central t: contours of constant f and δ in β_1, β_2 plane (where $f = \nu$, $\delta = \Delta$).

The non-central t-distribution can assume very varied shapes according to the values of ν and Δ. In Fig. 6 (taken from Merrington & Pearson, 1958) we reproduce a diagram showing the contours of constant $f(=\nu)$ and $\delta(=\Delta)$, in the plane having co-ordinates $\beta_1 = (\mu_3/\sigma^3)^2$, $\beta_2 = \mu_4/\sigma^4$. The central t-distribution is represented by points on the line $\beta_1 = 0$ while the other boundary of the area is a curve on which $\Delta = \infty$ and t'/Δ is distributed as $\sqrt{\nu}/\chi_\nu$. This curve lies a little below, but very close to the upper boundary for Type IV distributions in the Pearson system – i.e. to the Pearson Type V line.

It has been shown (Merrington & Pearson, 1958; Pearson, 1963) that the agreement between Type IV and non-central t-distributions having the same first four moments is remarkably close. Indeed, were no tables of percentage points of t' available, these could be found approximately by entering Table 32 with values of $\sqrt{\beta_1}(t)$, $\beta_2(t)$ calculated with the help of Table 28. The agreement between these two distributions and Johnson's S_U distribution (see §16 below) is also good, but not quite so close.

An illustration of the use of Tables 28 and 32 to derive an approximate percentage point of t' has been given in Example 44, p. 63.

15. The distribution of non-central F

15.1 Definitions and an approximation

If $\chi_1'^2$ is a value of non-central χ^2 having ν_1 degrees of freedom and χ_2^2 a central χ^2 with ν_2 degrees of freedom independent of $\chi_1'^2$, then we may write

$$F' = \frac{\chi_1'^2}{\nu_1}\bigg/\frac{\chi_2^2}{\nu_2} = \frac{\nu_2 \sum\limits_{i=1}^{\nu_1} (X_i + a_i)^2}{\nu_1 \sum\limits_{i=\nu_1+1}^{\nu_1+\nu_2} X_i^2} \qquad (140)$$

where all the X_i $(i = 1, 2, \ldots, \nu_1 + \nu_2)$ are independent normal variates having unit variance and zero mean. F' may be termed a non-central variance ratio. The probability density distribution of F' is known to be

$$f(F' | \nu_1, \nu_2, \lambda) = \sum_{j=0}^{\infty} \left\{ \frac{e^{-\frac{1}{2}\lambda}(\frac{1}{2}\lambda)^j}{j!\, B(\frac{1}{2}\nu_1 + j, \frac{1}{2}\nu_2)} \left(\frac{\nu_1}{\nu_2}\right)^{\frac{1}{2}\nu_1 + j} F'^{\frac{1}{2}\nu_1 - 1 + j} \left(1 + \frac{\nu_1}{\nu_2}F'\right)^{-\frac{1}{2}(\nu_1+\nu_2)-j} \right\}, \qquad (141)$$

where $\lambda = \sum\limits_{i=1}^{\nu_1} a_i^2$ as in equation (117). The distribution is immediately derivable from the form given by Fisher (1928, p. 671, distribution C), who took as variable

$$R^2 = \chi_1'^2/(\chi_1'^2 + \chi_2^2) \quad \text{so that} \quad \frac{\nu_2 R^2}{\nu_1(1-R^2)} = F'.$$

Any general tabulation of the probability integral of (140) would involve very extensive computation as three parameters ν_1, ν_2 and λ are involved. The first four moments of F' about zero were given by Patnaik (1949), but they cannot be put into quite as simple forms as was possible for χ'^2. We give only the mean and second moment:

$$\left.\begin{aligned} \mu_1' &= \frac{\nu_2(\nu_1 + \lambda)}{(\nu_2 - 2)\nu_1}, \\[2mm] \mu_2' &= \frac{\nu_2^2}{(\nu_2 - 2)(\nu_2 - 4)\nu_1^2}\{(\nu_1 + \lambda)^2 + 2(\nu_1 + 2\lambda)\}. \end{aligned}\right\} \qquad (142)$$

66

For the third and fourth moments see Pearson & Tiku (1970). The $\sqrt{\beta_1}$, β_2 values for F' will usually fall outside the region covered by Table 32, so that four-moment approximation for percentage points using a Pearson curve would not be straightforward. Patnaik (1949) suggested and tested an approximation by a central F-distribution, such that

$$F'(\nu_1, \nu_2, \lambda) \doteq kF(\nu, \nu_2), \qquad (143)$$

where k and ν are determined so that the first two moments of the approximating distribution have the correct values given by equation (142). Thus he found

$$k = \frac{\nu_1 + \lambda}{\nu_1}, \quad \nu = \frac{(\nu_1 + \lambda)^2}{\nu_1 + 2\lambda}. \qquad (144)$$

Tiku (1965, 1966) has compared a number of approximations and has reached the conclusion that the best of these is one in which F' is represented by a central F having the correct first three moments but not the correct start. In fact he makes $F'(\nu_1, \nu_2, \lambda) \sim hF(\nu_1', \nu_2) - c$. This gives the approximation in the following form

$$\Pr\{F' \geqslant F_0'(\nu_1, \nu_2, \lambda)\} \simeq I_{y_0}(\tfrac{1}{2}\nu_2, \tfrac{1}{2}\nu_1'), \qquad (145)$$

where $I_x(a, b)$ is the incomplete beta function and the quantities y_0, ν_1', h and c are related to F_0', ν_1, ν_2 and λ as follows:

$$\left.\begin{aligned}
y_0 &= 1/\{1 + (\nu_1'/\nu_2)(F_0' + c)/h\}, \\
\nu_1' &= \tfrac{1}{2}(\nu_2 - 2)\left\{\sqrt{\left(\frac{E}{E-4}\right)} - 1\right\}, \\
h &= \left(\frac{\nu_1'}{\nu_1}\right)\frac{1}{(2\nu_1' + \nu_2 - 2)}\frac{H}{K}, \\
c &= \frac{\nu_2}{\nu_2 - 2}\left\{h - \frac{\nu_1 + \lambda}{\nu_1}\right\},
\end{aligned}\right\} \qquad (146)$$

where

$$\left.\begin{aligned}
H &= 2(\nu_1 + \lambda)^3 + 3(\nu_1 + \lambda)(\nu_1 + 2\lambda)(\nu_2 - 2) + (\nu_1 + 3\lambda)(\nu_2 - 2)^2, \\
K &= (\nu_1 + \lambda)^2 + (\nu_2 - 2)(\nu_1 + 2\lambda), \quad E = H^2/K^3.
\end{aligned}\right\} \qquad (147)$$

It will be found that when $\lambda = 0$, then $\nu_1' = \nu_1, h = 1, c = 0$ so that $y_0 = \nu_2/(\nu_2 + \nu_1 F_0)$, giving the correct central distribution.

This approximation requires considerable labour to carry out, but it gives surprisingly accurate results. Tiku made 138 comparisons between the true power, $\beta = \Pr\{F'(\nu_1, \nu_2, \lambda) \geqslant F_\alpha(\nu_1, \nu_2)\}$ and the result given by (145), (146) and (147), taking $\alpha = 0.01$ and 0.05 for the significance levels of F and several different values of ν_1, ν_2 and λ. In 110 of these cases the error in the *fourth* decimal place was 0 or 1. The largest errors, never reaching 2 in the *third* decimal place, occurred with $\alpha = 0.01$ and $\nu_1 = 3$ (the smallest value used in the comparisons). A later investigation into the reasons for the accuracy of the approximation was carried out by Pearson & Tiku (1970).

15.2 *Charts of the power function of the F-test (Table 30)*

The application of the non-central F-distribution considered here is in connection with the analysis of variance and is based on what has been described as the fixed effects model. If in a comparison of two variance estimates the underlying variables in the numerator sum of squares are non-central, then the chance of establishing significance for a given non-centrality can be determined from the probability integral of the distribution (141). Thus

$$\int_{F_\alpha}^{\infty} f(F') \, dF' = \beta(\lambda \,|\, \alpha, \nu_1, \nu_2), \qquad (148)$$

where F_α is the upper 100α per cent significance level of the ordinary variance ratio test, gives the probability of establishing significance at the 100α per cent level for a given value of λ. In other words $\beta(\lambda|\alpha, \nu_1, \nu_2)$ regarded as a function of λ, is the power function of the F-test.

In contrast, the so called random model is one in which the numerator sum of squares remains 'central' but is multiplied by a scale factor of the form $(1 + n\sigma_B^2/\sigma_e^2)$; this has been discussed in §4.4 above.

In the 10 charts of Table 30, the β of (148) is plotted against a non-centrality parameter ϕ, where

$$\phi = \sqrt{\{\lambda/(\nu_1+1)\}} = \left\{ \sum_{i=1}^{\nu_1} a_i^2/(\nu_1+1) \right\}^{\frac{1}{2}}. \tag{149}$$

The reason for the choice of ϕ, originally made by Tang (1938), rather than λ or $\sqrt{\lambda}$ will be made clear in what follows.

The ten charts correspond to the ten values $\nu_1 = 1(1)8, 12, 24$. Each chart gives two families of power curves corresponding to $\alpha = 0.05$ and 0.01. The curves are drawn for

$$\nu_2 = 6(1)10, 12, 15, 30, 60, \infty$$

and rough interpolation by eye between them is not difficult. It should be noted that the β-scale is logarithmic, thereby expanding the scale in the important region of high power, $0.80 \leqslant \beta \leqslant 0.99$, whilst at the same time straightening the curves and facilitating interpolation. In many applications the charts are used to obtain the power β, corresponding to given values of α, ν_1, ν_2 and ϕ, but often β is specified and it is required to find ν_2 or ϕ. For such problems where inverse and multivariate interpolation is required, a graphical presentation has advantages over tabulation, particularly as high accuracy is unnecessary. The first eight of the charts of Table 30 were published by Pearson & Hartley (1951) and the discussion and illustrations in §§ 15.3, 15.4, 15.5 are taken from that paper. The last two charts with $\nu_1 = 12, 24$ are new, and we are indebted to M. L. Tiku for data on which the curves were based.

Tang (1938) gave the first tables of β with ϕ, ν_1 and ν_2 as arguments. Very recently Tiku (1967) has provided some extensive tables which give values of $1 - \beta$ to four decimal places, for arguments

$$\phi = 0.5, 1.0(0.2)2.2(0.4)3.0; \quad \nu_1 = 1(1)10, 12; \quad \nu_2 = 2(2)30, 40, 60, 120, \infty.$$

Fox (1956) gave a series of charts of the power function in an alternative form to ours.

15.3   *Formal application of the theory to the analysis of variance*

To bring the distribution (141) into play, the mathematical structure which we must regard as appropriate to the experimental data is one in which the random variation is due to a normally distributed error element, superimposed upon a number of additive constant terms. In the most general form, x_i is defined by

$$x_i = \xi_i + z_i \quad (i = 1, 2, ..., N), \tag{150}$$

where

(i) $\xi_i = c_{i1}\theta_1 + c_{i2}\theta_2 + ... + c_{is}\theta_s \quad (i = 1, 2, ..., N),$ (151)

(ii) the z_i are N independent normal deviates each having expectation zero and a common variance σ_z^2.

The θ's are s parameters whose values are generally unknown, while the c's are known constants, usually equalling 1 or 0. The null hypothesis specifies the values of, say, r of the θ's, e.g. $\theta_j = \theta_j^0$ $(j = 1, 2, ..., r)$. The power function of the test measures the probability of establishing significance when $\theta_j - \theta_j^0 \neq 0$ $(j = 1, 2, ..., r)$, the non-centrality parameter ϕ being a function of these differences and of σ_z.

It is well known that this mathematical model cannot always be regarded as appropriate; for example, the differences $\theta_j - \theta_j^0$, if they are not zero, may be more reasonably regarded as random variables rather than constants. Again, in many applications of analysis of variance the residuals z_i cannot be assumed independent. The model however implied by equations (150) and (151) is applicable to a considerable number of problems.

Starting with this model, Kolodziejczyk (1935) showed how it was possible to determine in a systematic way the two appropriate sums of squares to compare in a test of any hypothesis concerning the values of the θ's. He described the general procedure as the test of a linear hypothesis. It is usually unnecessary, however, to determine from first principles which are the appropriate sums of squares to compare, as they are known from the well-recognized character of the experimental arrangement. We shall therefore suppose that the two sums of squares appropriate for a given comparison are known, and that they do in fact arise from use of the likelihood ratio principle. They may be termed the 'treatment' sum of squares S_1 based on ν_1 degrees of freedom and the 'error' sum of squares S_2 based on ν_2 degrees of freedom. All that is necessary for use of the charts is to determine the ϕ of equation (149). The procedure is simple:

(a) We must define the assumed algebraic set-up of equations (150) and (151) and note which are the parameters $\theta_1, \theta_2, ..., \theta_r$, whose values are specified by the null hypothesis.

(b) S_1 will be expressible as a sum of squares of linear functions of the x_i. $\lambda\sigma_z^2$ is then the value of S_1 obtained by substituting into this sum of squares $\sum_{j=1}^{r} c_{ij}\theta_j$ in place of $x_i (i = 1, 2, ..., N)$. Since the form of S_1 is such that the remaining θ_j $(j = r+1, r+2, ..., s)$ cancel out on substitution for x_i, the procedure is equivalent to making the z_i in equation (150) zero and substituting ξ_i for x_i.

(c) Finally we have
$$\phi = \sqrt{\{\lambda/(\nu_1+1)\}}.$$

The procedure can be made clear by applying the rule to particular forms of analysis. To put the notation in more familiar form the general θ's will be replaced by the more suggestive parameters μ, α, β, etc.

15.4 *Application to selected problems*

(15.4.1) *The one-way classification into k groups with n observations in each*

The set-up assumed may be written
$$x_{ti} = \mu + \alpha_t + z_{ti} \quad (t = 1, ..., k; \; i = 1, ..., n). \tag{152}$$

Here we shall take the customary restriction $\Sigma_t \alpha_t = 0$, representing the average level by μ. The null hypothesis is that
$$\alpha_t = 0 \quad (t = 1, ..., k-1). \tag{153}$$

Note that since $\Sigma \alpha_t = 0$ there are only k independent parameters in (152) and the hypothesis specifies values for $k-1$ of them. For the analysis
$$S_1 = n\sum_t (\bar{x}_t. - \bar{x}..)^2, \quad \nu_1 = k-1; \quad S_2 = \sum_t \sum_i (x_{ti} - \bar{x}_t.)^2, \quad \nu_2 = N-k,$$

where $\bar{x}_t.$ is the mean for the observations in the tth group, $\bar{x}..$ the grand mean and $N = kn$. Since
$$\bar{x}_t. = \mu + \alpha_t + \bar{z}_t., \quad \bar{x}.. = \mu + \bar{z}..,$$

it is seen from rules (b) and (c) in § 15.3 that

$$\lambda \sigma_z^2 = n \sum_t \alpha_t^2$$

and
$$\phi = \frac{1}{\sigma_z} \sqrt{\left\{ \frac{n}{k} \sum_t \alpha_t^2 \right\}} = \sqrt{\left\{ \frac{1}{k} \sum_t \alpha_t^2 \right\}} \div \frac{\sigma_z}{\sqrt{n}}. \tag{154}$$

From the second form of (154) it is seen that ϕ is the ratio of the standard deviation of the k values of α_t to the standard error of $\bar{z}_t$. If the number of observations in each group is not the same then $\lambda \sigma_z^2 = \sum_t n_t \alpha_t^2$.

In the special case of two groups ($\nu_1 = 1$, $k = 2$) we have $\alpha_1 = -\alpha_2$ so that the non-centrality ϕ is related to the distance apart, $\Delta = 2|\alpha_1|$, of the two group means α_1 and α_2. We find that $\phi = \frac{1}{2}\Delta \sqrt{n}/\sigma_z$. In this case the use of the chart has already been discussed and illustrated in connection with Student's t-test (§ 14.7 above).

(15.4.2) *The double classification without interaction and with one observation in each cell*

The set-up is now
$$x_{st} = \mu + \alpha_s + \beta_t + z_{st} \quad (s = 1, ..., h; \, t = 1, ..., k). \tag{155}$$

Again we shall take $\sum_s \alpha_s = 0 = \sum_t \beta_t$. If we are testing whether an α-effect exists, the null hypothesis is that
$$\alpha_s = 0 \quad (s = 1, ..., h-1).$$

For the analysis
$$S_1 = k \sum_s (\bar{x}_{s\cdot} - \bar{x}_{\cdot\cdot})^2, \quad \nu_1 = h-1; \quad S_2 = \sum_s \sum_t (x_{st} - \bar{x}_{s\cdot} - \bar{x}_{\cdot t} + \bar{x}_{\cdot\cdot})^2, \quad \nu_2 = (h-1)(k-1).$$

We find at once that $\bar{x}_{s\cdot} - \bar{x}_{\cdot\cdot} = \alpha_s + \bar{z}_{s\cdot} - \bar{z}_{\cdot\cdot}$, so that $\lambda \sigma_z^2 = k \sum_s \alpha_s^2$ and
$$\phi = \frac{1}{\sigma_z} \sqrt{\left\{ \frac{k}{h} \sum_s \alpha_s^2 \right\}} = \sqrt{\left\{ \frac{1}{h} \sum_s \alpha_s^2 \right\}} \div \frac{\sigma_z}{\sqrt{k}}. \tag{156}$$

(15.4.3) *The double classification with interaction and n observations in each cell*

In this case it is possible to examine the data for the presence of interaction and the set-up may be written†
$$x_{sti} = \mu + \alpha_s + \beta_t + \gamma_{st} + z_{sti} \quad (s = 1, ..., h; \, t = 1, ..., k; \, i = 1, ..., n). \tag{157}$$

Again we shall take $\sum_s \alpha_s = 0 = \sum_t \beta_t = 0$ and also
$$\sum_s \gamma_{st} = 0 \quad (t = 1, ..., k) \quad \text{and} \quad \sum_t \gamma_{st} = 0 \quad (s = 1, ..., h).$$

If we test for the presence of a main effect, say whether $\alpha_s = 0$ ($s = 1, ..., h-1$), we find that
$$S_1 = kn \sum_s (\bar{x}_{s\cdot\cdot} - \bar{x}_{\cdot\cdot\cdot})^2, \quad \phi = \frac{1}{\sigma_z} \sqrt{\left\{ \frac{kn}{h} \sum_s \alpha_s^2 \right\}} = \sqrt{\left\{ \frac{1}{h} \sum_s \alpha_s^2 \right\}} \div \frac{\sigma_z}{\sqrt{(kn)}}. \tag{158}$$

If we test for the presence of interaction, the null hypothesis is that $\gamma_{st} = 0$ for all combinations of s and t where, in view of the relations above, only $(h-1)(k-1)$ are independent. For the analysis
$$S_1 = n \sum_s \sum_t (\bar{x}_{st\cdot} - \bar{x}_{s\cdot\cdot} - \bar{x}_{\cdot t\cdot} + \bar{x}_{\cdot\cdot\cdot})^2, \quad \nu_1 = (h-1)(k-1);$$
$$S_2 = \sum_s \sum_t \sum_i (x_{sti} - \bar{x}_{st\cdot})^2, \quad \nu_2 = hk(n-1).$$

† We are here concerned with systematic main effects, α_s, β_t and interactions γ_{st}. Often it is more appropriate to regard one of the main effects (e.g. 'blocks') and the interactions as random variables, and in this case the appropriate test procedure is different.

It is found that $\lambda\sigma_z^2 = n\sum_s\sum_t \gamma_{st}^2$ so that

$$\phi = \frac{1}{\sigma_z}\sqrt{\left\{\frac{n}{(h-1)(k-1)+1}\sum_s\sum_t \gamma_{st}^2\right\}}. \tag{159}$$

Since there are now $h \times k$ different γ_{st}, ϕ has not now the simple interpretation of a ratio of two standard deviations which it had in previous cases.

(15.4.4) *The Latin square*

Here, we have a $k \times k$ square, and assume the additive model,

$$x_{rst} = \mu + \alpha_r + \beta_s + \gamma_t + z_{rst} \quad (r = 1, \ldots, k; \; s = 1, \ldots, k; \; t = 1, \ldots, k).$$

Let α_r and β_s represent the row and column terms and γ_t the possible treatment effects. We assume

$$\sum_r \alpha_r = \sum_s \beta_s = \sum_t \gamma_t = 0$$

and the null hypothesis is that

$$\gamma_t = 0 \quad (t = 1, \ldots, k-1).$$

For the analysis

$$S_1 = k\sum_t (\bar{x}_{..t} - \bar{x}_{...})^2, \quad \nu_1 = k-1$$

$$S_2 = \sum_r\sum_s (x_{rst} - \bar{x}_{r..} - \bar{x}_{.s.} - \bar{x}_{..t} + 2\bar{x}_{...})^2, \quad \nu_2 = (k-1)(k-2).$$

We find $\lambda\sigma_z^2 = k\sum_t \gamma_t^2$ and

$$\phi = \frac{1}{\sigma_z}\sqrt{\sum_t \gamma_t^2} = \sqrt{\left\{\frac{1}{k}\Sigma\gamma_t^2\right\}} \div \frac{\sigma_z}{\sqrt{k}}. \tag{160}$$

15.5   *Illustrative examples*

Example 45. Effect of machine variation on the standard deviation of the manufactured bulk. In a machine shop six machines contribute equal shares to the total output of mass-produced parts for which a dimension, x, is subject to tolerances. It is suspected that the average dimension of the parts produced by the six machines may differ from machine to machine, thereby increasing the standard deviation of x for the bulk. It is further feared that if such an increase should exceed 20 per cent of the standard deviation of x for parts from a single machine previously employed, difficulties would arise in meeting the tolerances.

In order to have advance warning of machine differences of such a magnitude, it is planned to measure nine parts for each of the six machines and test for machine differences in an analysis of variance, using the 1 per cent level of significance. What is the chance of detecting machine differences of such a magnitude by this test?

It would seem reasonable to adopt the set-up of §15.4.1. Let $\mu + \alpha_t$ denote the average dimension of parts produced by the tth machine, x_{ti} the dimension of the ith part measured for the tth machine and σ the standard deviation of dimensions of parts from the same machine. Then it is desired to detect by the test the presence of differences among the α_t such that

$$\sqrt{\left\{\tfrac{1}{6}\sum_t \alpha_t^2 + \sigma^2\right\}}/\sigma \geqslant 1\cdot2 \quad \text{(increase of 20 per cent for the mixture of distributions)}$$

or that

$$\sqrt{\left\{\tfrac{1}{6}\Sigma\alpha_t^2\right\}}/\sigma \geqslant \sqrt{(1\cdot2^2 - 1)} = \sqrt{0\cdot44} = 0\cdot663.$$

Hence $\phi = 0\cdot663\sqrt{9} = 1\cdot99$ is the critical value.

Entering the chart for $\nu_1 = 6 - 1 = 5$ and the section for $\alpha = 0.01$ (1 per cent level of significance), we find for $\phi = 1.99$ and $\nu_2 = 6(9-1) = 48$ the value of the power of 0.86. This means that, following the procedure described, our chance of detecting machine differences of the above magnitude is 0.86, i.e. the odds are about 6 to 1 on detection. Should these not be considered sufficient, we must make provision for more parts to be measured, until a satisfactory value of the power is reached.

Whilst the planning of the present experiment was concerned with the value of the root mean square of the group means α_t, situations may of course arise in which the values of individual α_t are of interest.

Example 46. *The effect of personal factors introduced by test operators in certain routine tests.* Davies (1947, p. 90) has described an investigation into the possible influence of personal factors on the results of a standard procedure of testing the compressive strength of samples of Portland cement. Two classes of men are employed in the test: the 'gauger' who works up the mixture of cement and water from which the test cubes are moulded, and the assistant who operates the testing machine, who is described as a 'breaker'. Let us suppose, as in the case of the data given, that there were three assistants regularly employed on the testing and three labourers who were used for the gauging. To investigate the possible effects of personal factors among the men, we may plan a simple 3×3 experiment in which n cubes are tested for each of the nine combinations of gauger and breaker. If we were concerned with six specified men who were to be employed on this work in a routine way, it would seen reasonable to adopt the set-up of (15.4.3) above. α_1, α_2 and α_3 will represent the possible gauger effects and β_1, β_2 and β_3 the breaker effects. In testing for the presence of either of these we shall have

$$\nu_1 = 2, \quad \nu_2 = 9(n-1),$$

while from (158), since $h = k = 3$,

$$\phi_\alpha = \sqrt{\{n \Sigma \alpha_s^2\}}/\sigma_z$$

and similarly for ϕ_β. If we were to decide to take $n = 4$, so that $\nu_2 = 27$, we can derive, for example, the following information from the chart for $\nu_1 = 2$:

(*a*) The probability will be at least 0.90 of establishing significance for a gauger (or breaker) effect at the 5 per cent level of F if

$$\phi \geqslant 2.16 \quad \text{or if} \quad \sqrt{\{\tfrac{1}{3} \sum_s \alpha_s^2\}} \geqslant \frac{2.16}{\sqrt{12}} \sigma_z = 0.62\sigma_z.$$

(*b*) To have the same probability, using the 1 per cent significance level, we must have

$$\phi \geqslant 2.63 \quad \text{or} \quad \sqrt{\{\tfrac{1}{3} \sum_s \alpha_s^2\}} \geqslant 0.76\sigma_z.$$

(*c*) If, however, the values of the men's averages were less scattered, i.e. only such that

$$\sqrt{\{\tfrac{1}{3} \sum_s \alpha_s^2\}} = 0.5\sigma_z \quad \text{or} \quad \phi = \sqrt{(12)}\,0.5 = 1.73,$$

then there would be probabilities of only (i) 0.72 and (ii) 0.45 of establishing significance at (i) the 5 per cent and (ii) the 1 per cent level.

(*d*) Were the number of tests for each gauger–breaker combination increased from $n = 4$ to $n = 8$, so that ν_2 becomes 63, then, still using the same chart, we find that $\sqrt{\{\tfrac{1}{3} \sum_s \alpha_s^2\}}$ need only be (i) $0.43\sigma_z$ and (ii) $0.51\sigma_z$, to give a probability of 0.90 of establishing significance at (i) the 5 per cent and (ii) the 1 per cent level.

This example brings out two points needing further consideration. In the first place the root mean square of the group-means α_t is expressed in terms of σ_z, the standard deviation of the normal residuals. It will often happen that this is roughly known in advance of the experiment. For example, it might have been known in advance from past experience that if a breaker tests a series of cement cubes made from the same mix, the standard deviation of his results would be about $500\,\mathrm{lb/in^2}$. Having this information, rough numerical figures could be assigned to the critical values for $\sqrt{\{\frac{1}{3}\Sigma\alpha_s^2\}}$ quoted above. Thus for case (a) we have

$$\sqrt{\{\tfrac{1}{3}\Sigma\alpha_s^2\}} = 0 \cdot 62 \times 500 = 310\,\mathrm{lb/in^2}.$$

The second point is this. How far does the root mean square of the α_s provide the kind of information needed in a preliminary survey? To generalize for the purpose of the present discussion, we write the relevant factors $\alpha_s, \beta_t, \ldots$, as δ_j ($j = 1, 2, \ldots, k$), where

$$\sum_j \delta_j = 0, \quad \sum_j \delta_j^2 = c^2\phi^2\sigma_z^2,\dagger \qquad (161)$$

the constant, c, depending on the experimental design. Thus we have for the arrangements of §15.4:

Para.	Equation	c value	Para.	Equation	c value
15.4.1	(154)	$\sqrt{(k/n)}$	15.4.3	$\begin{cases}(158)\\(159)\end{cases}$	$\begin{array}{l}\{h/(kn)\}^{\frac{1}{2}}\\ \{(h-1)(k-1)+1\}^{\frac{1}{2}}/\sqrt{n}\end{array}$
15.4.2	(156)	$\sqrt{(h/k)}$	15.4.4	(160)	1

For a given value of the non-centrality parameter, whether expressed as λ, ϕ or $\Sigma\delta_j^2$, there will be an infinite set of possible combinations of the δ_j. Can we pick out some characteristics of this set to which we can attach particular meaning? This question was discussed in some detail by Pearson & Hartley (1951, pp. 127–9) who considered that the range or spread, W, of the δ_j was possibly the characteristic of most interest. Denote by $W(\mathrm{max.})$ and $W(\mathrm{min.})$ the upper and lower bounds of the ranges of the combination of δ's satisfying (161) for fixed ϕ and σ_z. Then it can be shown that

$$W(\mathrm{max.}) = c\phi\sigma_z \times \sqrt{2}, \qquad (162)$$

$$W(\mathrm{min.}) = \begin{cases} c\phi\sigma_z \times 2/\sqrt{k} & k \text{ even,} \\ c\phi\sigma_z \times 2\sqrt{\{k/(k^2-1)\}} & k \text{ odd.} \end{cases} \qquad (163)$$

The maximum range occurs when the extreme δ_j are $\pm c\phi\sigma_z/\sqrt{2}$ and the remaining $k-2$ zero. The minimum range occurs, (i) if k is even, when $\frac{1}{2}k$ of the δ_j equal $+c\phi\sigma_z/\sqrt{k}$ and the remaining $\frac{1}{2}k$ of the δ_j equal $-c\phi\sigma_z/\sqrt{k}$; (ii) if $k = 2p+1$ is odd, when $p+1$ of the δ_j equal

$$\pm c\phi\sigma_z[(k-1)/\{(k+1)k\}]^{\frac{1}{2}},$$

and the remaining p equal $\qquad \mp c\phi\sigma_z[(k+1)/\{(k-1)k\}]^{\frac{1}{2}}.$

The interpretation is as follows. For given values of ϕ and σ_z, the range of the δ_j, i.e. the spread in the expectations of the x's resulting from treatment differences, must be at least $W(\mathrm{min.})$ but cannot exceed $W(\mathrm{max.})$. Alternatively, given W and σ_z, we can invert the relations (162) and (163) to obtain lower and upper bounds for ϕ and therefore for the power of the test.

† This form of relation between the δ's and ϕ is appropriate for all the arrangements considered in §15.4, but it will not always be so in tests of the general linear hypothesis. For example, if there are unequal frequencies in subgroups, the weighted sum of squares of the δ's is involved.

Kastenbaum *et al.* (1970 a, b) have recently provided tables giving values of $W(\text{max.})/\sigma_z$ for the designs associated with equations (154) and (158), entered with arguments: the significance level α, the power β, n, h and k.

Example 47. Some of these points may be illustrated on the data used in Example 46. Here, the differences between the gaugers,

$$\sum_{s=1}^{3} \alpha_s^2 = \frac{1}{n} \phi^2 \sigma_z^2$$

or the c of equation (161) is $1/\sqrt{n}$ as $h = k = 3$. Suppose that having regard to the general programme of routine testing and the conclusions to be based upon it, it was considered that the maximum spread of what may be termed the gauger bias should not be more than $W = 250\,\text{lb/in}^2$. Further, suppose again that our rough estimate of σ_z is $500\,\text{lb/in}^2$.

(*a*) We might first ask if there is any prospect of establishing significance at the 5 per cent level when $W = 250\,\text{lb/in}^2$ if a 3×3 experimental arrangement were used with only $n = 4$ replications. $k = 3$ and is odd, so from (163) we see that

$$\phi(\text{max.}) = \frac{W}{2\sigma_z} \sqrt{\left\{\frac{n(k^2-1)}{k}\right\}}$$

$$= \frac{250}{2 \times 500} \sqrt{\frac{4 \times 8}{3}} = \sqrt{\frac{2}{3}} = 0\cdot816. \tag{164}$$

Turning to the chart for $\nu_1 = 2$, with $\nu_2 = 27$, it is clear that the value of ϕ is outside the range of both charts. Extrapolation suggests that there is a probability of only about 0·25 of establishing significance at the 5 per cent level. Thus four replications would be quite inadequate to detect a spread of $250\,\text{lb/in}^2$.

(*b*) As indicated under (*a*) in Example 46, for the probability of establishing significance at the 5 per cent level to be 0·90 or more, we must have $\phi \geqslant 2\cdot16$. Taking $W = 250$, $\sigma_z = 500\,\text{lb/in}^2$ as before, we have from (162)

$$\phi(\text{min.}) = \frac{W}{\sigma_z} \sqrt{(\tfrac{1}{2}n)} = \tfrac{1}{2}\sqrt{(\tfrac{1}{2}n)}. \tag{165}$$

If this expression is to be $\geqslant 2\cdot16$, we must have $n \geqslant 37\cdot3$ or 38 replications would be needed.

(*c*) Suppose now that we were content with a reasonable chance of establishing significance if the spread in gauger bias were $W = 500\,\text{lb/in}^2$. From (164) and (165) we have

$$\phi(\text{max.}) = 0\cdot816\sqrt{n}, \quad \phi(\text{min.}) = 0\cdot707\sqrt{n}.$$

Taking $n = 4$ and examining the chart with $\nu_1 = 2$ again, we find that the probability of establishing significance at the 5 per cent level lies between 0·66 and 0·52. The former will result if, say, $\alpha_1 = \alpha_2 = 167\,\text{lb/in}^2$ and $\alpha_3 = -333\,\text{lb/in}^2$; and the latter if $\alpha_1 = -\alpha_3 = 250\,\text{lb/in}^2$, $\alpha_2 = 0$.

(*d*) Keeping $\sigma_z = 500 = W(\text{max.})$, for the probability to be at least 0·90 the number of replications must satisfy the inequality

$$n \geqslant (2\cdot16/0\cdot707)^2 = 9\cdot3,$$

or ten replications would suffice.

Finally we should note that while for small k the upper and lower bounds $W(\text{max.})$ and $W(\text{min.})$ are not too far apart and may be used informatively as in Example 47, their increasing divergence for larger k may make such an interpretation less useful. In such cases it may be possible to interpret the practical significance of a value of ϕ directly, as in Example 46 or to make some additional assumptions on the distribution of the δ_j.

V. SYSTEMS OF UNIVARIATE FREQUENCY DISTRIBUTIONS

16. COMPARISON OF DISTRIBUTIONS HAVING THE SAME FIRST FOUR MOMENTS

There are three important applications of systems of non-normal univariate frequency curves: (*a*) to graduate observational data; (*b*) to approximate to the sampling distributions of statistics whose moments are known, but whose exact probability density functions are unknown or difficult to handle; (*c*) to use in studies of robustness. It was the application (*a*) which was in the minds of Pearson, Gram-Charlier and Edgeworth when they developed their systems of curves some 60–80 years ago. But with the later advances in statistical sampling theory it has been found that application (*b*) is certainly of equal importance.

In connection with investigations of this latter type, it has been found (see, for example, Pearson, 1963; Pearson & Tukey, 1965) that there is often a remarkable similarity in shape between distributions of different functional forms, whose probability density functions are given identical first four moments. While from the strictly mathematical point of view the correspondence cannot be regarded as exact, for many practical purposes the agreement may be satisfactory and in so far as there is agreement the choice of function can be based on practical convenience.

If the variate is standardized as $X = (x - \mu)/\sigma$, then comparable distributions may be indexed in terms of the two moment ratios

$$\sqrt{\beta_1} = \gamma_1 = \mu_3/\sigma^3, \quad \beta_2 = \gamma_2 + 3 = \mu_4/\sigma^4.$$

As an illustration of the extent of correspondence, we choose the following four groups of skew distributions, all having a β_1 (or $\sqrt{\beta_1}$) value a little below unity. The values of the moment ratios are shown at the head of the table; below are given six lower and six upper standardized percentage points for the Pearson curves and the differences from these for the other curves.

Distributions compared

(i) Pearson Type I (beta distribution), a Johnson S_B distribution (see §§ 18.1, 18.3 below) and a Weibull distribution with $m = 1.6$, where the latter may be expressed in simplest form as

$$f(x) = mx^{m-1} \exp(-x^m), \quad x \geqslant 0. \tag{166}$$

The probability integral of (166) assumes the simple form

$$\Pr\{x < x_0\} = 1 - \exp(-x_0^m). \tag{167}$$

A table of the moment coefficients of (166) has been given by Harter (1967), for $m = 1.1(0.1)10.0$.

(ii) Pearson Type I (beta) and a non-central χ^2-distribution with $\nu = 1$, $\lambda = 9$ (see § 13.1 above).

(iii) Pearson Type VI (inverted beta or F-distribution) and a log–normal distribution with $\omega = 1.1035$ (see § 18.1, equations (172), (173)).

(iv) Pearson Type IV, non-central t with $\nu = 8.27$, $\Delta = 1.95$ (see § 14.1) and a Johnson S_U distribution with $\omega = 1.3$, $\Omega = 0.5$ (see §§ 18.1, 18.2 below).

The table gives the standardized percentage points for the Pearson distribution (derived by interpolation in Table 32) and the differences between these points and those for the distributions under comparison. For example, the lower 5 per cent point for the Type I in the first comparison is at -1.294 while that for the Weibull is at -1.290, hence the difference $W - I$ is 0.004. The following are some of the points which stand out on examination of the table.

Standardized percentage points and their differences among distributions having the same β_1, β_2 values

$\sqrt{\beta_1}$	0.962			0.956		0.998		0.906		
β_1	0.925			0.914		0.997		0.822		
β_2	4.044			4.230		4.823		5.781		
P	I	$W-$I	S_B-I	I	χ'^2-I	VI	$LN-$VI	IV	$t'-$IV	S_U-IV
0·005	−1·548	0·049	−0·065	−1·644	0·054	−1·783	−0·007	−2·175	0·003	−0·072
0·01	−1·502	·038	− ·042	−1·575	·027	−1·679	− ·003	−1·960	·003	− ·039
0·025	−1·405	·017	− ·017	−1·451	·004	−1·508	− ·001	−1·661	·003	− ·006
0·05	−1·294	·004	− ·001	−1·319	−0·005	−1·343	·001	−1·415	·002	·010
0·10	−1·129	− ·007	·010	−1·135	− ·008	−1·130	·001	−1·135	·000	·016
0·25	−0·754	− ·009	·012	−0·740	− ·005	−0·715	·001	−0·666	− ·001	·012
0·75	0·569	0·006	−0·005	0·564	0·004	0·549	−0·001	0·543	0·000	−0·013
0·90	1·373	·000	·004	1·352	− ·001	1·316	·000	1·254	·001	− ·006
0·95	1·904	− ·006	·014	1·882	− ·005	1·849	·001	1·765	·001	·007
0·975	2·390	− ·012	·021	2·376	− ·008	2·364	·001	2·280	− ·001	·020
0·99	2·977	− ·013	·021	2·987	− ·007	3·029	·003	2·982	− ·001	·038
0·995	3·387	− ·008	·014	3·425	− ·004	3·529	·003	3·542	− ·002	·045

I, VI and IV are Pearson curves, i.e. beta, inverted beta or F, and Type IV; W is Weibull; χ'^2 is non-central χ^2; LN is log–normal; t' is non-central t; S_B and S_U are Johnson's bounded and unbounded curves.

(1) For the cases taken, the similarity between the Pearson curve and the log–normal and non-central t-distributions is striking. For a further illustration of an approximation to the latter distribution, see Example 44, pp. 63–4.

(2) Towards the lower tails, where the curves come down rather steeply to the start, the agreement between the beta (Type I) and the Weibull and non-central χ^2-distributions is not so good. Correspondence at the lower tail could probably be improved if the beta distribution were given the correct start, and the first three moments only made to agree; but agreement may then become worse elsewhere.

(3) In the upper, drawn out tail, except for the cases of S_B and S_U, the differences are rarely more than 1 per cent of the standard deviation and often much less.

(4) In these comparisons, the differences for both upper and lower 5 per cent points are only in one case out of twelve greater than 1 per cent of the standard deviation.

These and a number of other comparisons of distributions with $\sqrt{\beta_1}$, β_2 values spread out over a wide field, pointed to the value of making available an extensive table of standardized percentage points for distributions of the Pearson system. This table (Table 32 with extensions in Tables 31 and 33) provides a useful standard against which other systems may be compared and also gives a means of approximating to the percentage points of sampling distributions for which moments only are readily available. (A much fuller table due to Amos & Daniel (1971) has just been issued as we go to Press.)

17. STANDARDIZED PERCENTAGE POINTS OF PEARSON CURVES

17.1 *Definitions and explanation of Table 32*

A smaller table appeared as Table 42 of *B.T.S.* **1**. The present Table 32 published first by Johnson *et al.* (1963) is far more extensive in that it gives:

(*a*) Four-decimal-places throughout. The original table gave only three decimals for Types IV and VII; we owe the extension and complete re-checking to D. E. Amos of the Sandia Laboratories.

(b) the standardized values for the terminal or terminals (0 and 100 per cent points), when the curve is of finite range;

(c) seven additional percentage points;

(d) a much more extensive range of $\sqrt{\beta_1}$, β_2 values.

Tables 31 and 33, based on D. E. Amos's unpublished computations, extend information into the J-curve area (see Fig. 7) of the Type I or beta distributions. These two tables will be referred to later in §19 in comparison with the Johnson S_B curves having $\sqrt{\beta_1}$, β_2 values in this area.

The earlier table took β_1 as argument but it was realized that for interpolation purposes it was better to use $\sqrt{\beta_1}$.

The curves of Karl Pearson's system are all derived as solutions of the differential equation

$$\frac{1}{y}\frac{dy}{dx} = \frac{-(c_1+x)}{c_0+c_1x+c_2x^2}, \tag{168}$$

where the origin is at the mean and the parameters c_0, c_1 and c_2 are functions of $\sqrt{\mu_2} = \sigma$, β_1 and β_2. Using a standard notation (see Elderton & Johnson, 1969) the main curves of the system may be expressed as follows:

Type	Equation	Origin for x	Limits for x
I	$y = y_0 x^{m_1}\left(1-\dfrac{x}{a}\right)^{m_2}$	At start	$0 \leqslant x \leqslant a$
II	$y = y_0\left(1-\dfrac{x^2}{a^2}\right)^m$	Mean (= mode)	$-a \leqslant x \leqslant a$
III	$y = y_0 x^m e^{-x/a}$	At start	$0 \leqslant x \leqslant \infty$
IV	$y = y_0\left(1+\dfrac{x^2}{a^2}\right)^{-m} e^{-b\tan^{-1}(x/a)}$	Mean $+d*$	$-\infty < x < \infty$
V	$y = y_0 x^{-m} e^{-a/x}$	At start	$0 \leqslant x < \infty$
VI	$y = y_0 x^{m_2}\left(1+\dfrac{x}{a}\right)^{-m_1}$	At start	$0 \leqslant x < \infty$
VII	$y = y_0\left(1+\dfrac{x^2}{a^2}\right)^{-m}$	Mean (= mode)	$-\infty < x < \infty$

$* \quad d = \frac{1}{2}ab/(m-1).$

The regions and their boundaries in the β_1, β_2 field with which the different types of solution are associated have been illustrated in Fig. 7. Because all types derive from the solution of (168), their shapes may be described as changing continuously across the boundaries of the regions, although the mathematical forms differ.

17.2 *Illustrations of use of Table* 32

To derive the full benefit from Table 32, it will generally be necessary to use second difference interpolation formulae for both $\sqrt{\beta_1}$ and β_2; the procedure needed lends itself readily to a computer routine. In one example below we illustrate, however, the steps needed in computing with a desk calculator.

Example 48 (taken from Johnson *et al.* 1963, pp. 464–5). Stephens (1963) derived the first four moments of the distribution of G. S. Watson's goodness of fit statistic, U_N^2. For the case of a sample of size $N = 10$, the following results are derived from his expressions (equation (4)):

$$\text{mean} = 0\cdot08333, \quad \text{s.d.} = 0\cdot05000, \quad \sqrt{\beta_1} = 1\cdot6190, \quad \beta_2 = 6\cdot7905.$$

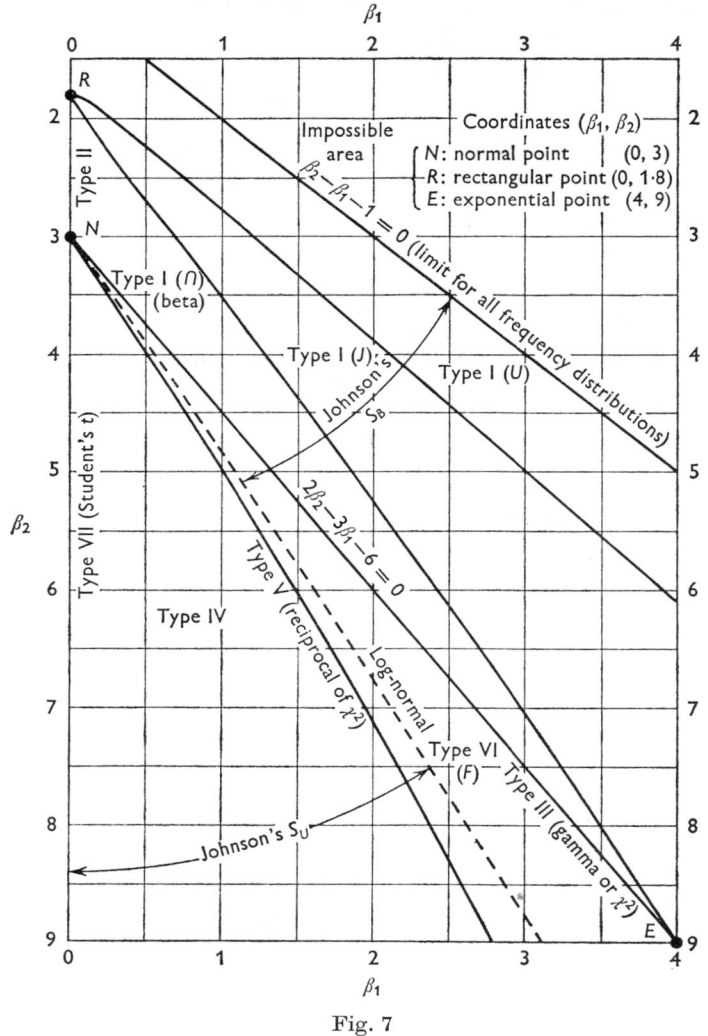

Fig. 7

The following work illustrates the use of the present table in deriving an upper 1 per cent point for a Pearson curve having the correct first four moments. We first extract the following entries from Table 32:

β_2 \ $\sqrt{\beta_1}$	1·5	δ^2	1·6	δ^2	1·7	δ^2	1·8	δ^2
6·4	3·3297		3·4016		3·4748		3·5435	
6·6	3·3239	−4	3·3960	−10	3·4710	−21	3·5452	−44
6·8	3·3177	−3	3·3894	−5	3·4651	−12	3·5425	−28
7·0	3·3112		3·3823		3·4580		3·5370	

Interpolating in each column at $\beta_2 = 6 \cdot 7905$, using the simple Bessel formula (319), we find:

$\sqrt{\beta_1}$	X	δ^2
1·5	3·3180	
1·6	3·3897	40
1·7	3·4654	16
1·8	3·5427	

78

Interpolating in the same way in this last table at $\sqrt{\beta_1} = 1 \cdot 6190$, we obtain finally for the standardized upper 1 per cent point at the correct $(\sqrt{\beta_1}, \beta_2)$, $X_{0 \cdot 01} = 3 \cdot 4039$. This gives a 1 per cent point for U_{10}^2 at

$$0 \cdot 08333 + 0 \cdot 05000 \times 3 \cdot 4039 = 0 \cdot 2535.$$

The true point is unknown but Stephens carried out a Monte Carlo experiment consisting of over 19,000 samples of ten, for which the upper 1 per cent point fell at $0 \cdot 251$. Stephens (1963, Table 6) shows that other approximate percentage points derived in the same way are in striking agreement with the Monte Carlo values at the upper tail. Since agreement was also good at $N = \infty$, where the true asymptotic distribution of U_N^2 is known, this encouraged him to make further use of Table 32 in deriving approximate percentage points of this statistic at intermediate values of N. The agreement at the lower percentage points is less satisfactory, but here the curve rises very steeply and the four-moment approximation does not start at the correct point.

It is of interest to note that while in this example the correct $\sqrt{\beta_1}, \beta_2$ point falls within the region of bell-shaped Type I (Ω) curves, of the sixteen distributions used in the interpolation, seven are Type I (J), four are Type I (Ω) and five are Type VI. In spite of this diversity, the differences among the standardized deviates are seen not to have got out of hand.

Example 49. It is noted below in connection with Table 51, §28.2, that the 10, 2·5 and 0·5 per cent points for the statistic C could be derived with fair accuracy, given the 5 and 1 per cent points. This was because the ratios

$$(C_{0 \cdot 05} - C_{0 \cdot 10})/d, \quad (C_{0 \cdot 025} - C_{0 \cdot 05})/d \quad \text{and} \quad (C_{0 \cdot 005} - C_{0 \cdot 01})/d, \tag{169}$$

where $d = C_{0 \cdot 01} - C_{0 \cdot 05}$, remained remarkably constant throughout the range of distributions covered by the table. The entries in Table 32 may be used to examine how far this stability in inter-percentage-point ratios is widespread.

Inter-percentage-point ratios for certain Pearson curves

			Ratios		
	$\sqrt{\beta_1}$	β_2	$(x_{0 \cdot 05} - x_{0 \cdot 10})/d*$	$(x_{0 \cdot 025} - x_{0 \cdot 05})/d$	$(x_{0 \cdot 005} - x_{0 \cdot 01})/d$
1st line	0	2·4	0·66	0·50	0·29
	0·8	3·4	0·53	0·47	0·35
	1·2	4·6	0·50	0·45	0·38
	1·5	5·8	0·48	0·45	0·39
2nd line	0	3·0	0·53	0·46	0·37
	0·8	4·0	0·48	0·44	0·40
	1·2	5·2	0·46	0·44	0·41
	1·5	6·4	0·45	0·44	0·42
3rd line	0	3·6	0·48	0·44	0·41
	0·8	4·6	0·45	0·43	0·43
	1·2	5·8	0·44	0·43	0·44
	1·5	7·0	0·43	0·43	0·44
4th line	0	4·2	0·46	0·43	0·43
	0·8	5·2	0·43	0·43	0·45
	1·2	6·4	0·42	0·42	0·46
	1·5	7·6	0·42	0·42	0·46

$* \; d = x_{0 \cdot 01} - x_{0 \cdot 05}.$

We shall take a broad 'panel' running diagonally across the field, and find the ratios, (169), at each of four points, lying on four diagonal lines, as shown in the accompanying table. It is evident that the ratios do change in value, but the panel chosen covers a very considerable area in the $\sqrt{\beta_1}, \beta_2$ plane. It is quite possible that the $\sqrt{\beta_1}, \beta_2$ values for the distributions holding in a particular table might be confined to a relatively small area of the field, so that the ratios throughout the table would remain approximately constant.

In the case of the table of the upper percentage points, C_α of a Wishart matrix (Table 51), the three average ratios which emerged were 0·50, 0·45 and 0·39, respectively. From among the soundings included in our table, these correspond most nearly to those with co-ordinates (0·8, 4·0) and (1·2, 4·6). We do not at present know the true moment ratios for C.

These results apply to percentage points in the upper tail of a positively skew distribution; the corresponding ratios in the lower tail are a good deal less stable.

Johnson *et al.* (1963) gave three other examples in section 4 of their paper. One of these involved the use of divided differences to fit a Pearson Type IV curve to a frequency distribution of barometric heights.

17.3 *Fitting with three moments and a fixed start*

If the position of one terminal of the distribution to be fitted is sharply defined, the fit at this end of the distribution will sometimes be improved by making the fitted curve start at this point, giving it in addition the correct mean, standard deviation and $\sqrt{\beta_1}$, while dispensing with agreement in β_2. The procedure involved, using a desk calculator, is inevitably tedious as it requires the following steps:

(*a*) Finding the standardized distance, say X_0, from mean to start of the distribution or data to be graduated.

(*b*) Interpolating inversely for β_2, using as argument the unequally spaced values in the 0·0 columns of Table 32. (This can be done employing the divided difference formula (325).)

(*c*) Then, having found the β_2, which with the $\sqrt{\beta_1}$ of the data gives the correct X_0, proceeding as before to use these two moment ratios to determine any desired percentage points, preferably first checking directly that they provide the correct X_0.

It has been found that a difficulty in following this procedure is that in any one column, the standardized 0·0 per cent values have an accelerating increase as β_2 increases which may make interpolation using differences rather inaccurate.

18. The Johnson S_U and S_B, and the log–normal distributions

18.1 *Definitions*

Any system of distributions which can be easily transformed into a standardized normal distribution has certain obvious practical advantages. Using what Edgeworth termed the method of translation, Johnson (1949) derived the properties of two systems of curves, defined as follows:

The S_U distributions, of unlimited range in either direction. These are defined by the relation

$$X = \gamma + \delta \sinh^{-1} y \quad (-\infty < y < \infty), \tag{170}$$

where X is an $N(0, 1)$ variate.

The S_B distributions, for which the variate is bounded in both directions. These are defined by

$$X = \gamma + \delta \log \{y/(1-y)\} \quad (0 \leqslant y \leqslant 1), \tag{171}$$

where again X is an $N(0, 1)$ variate. Note that for S_B the term multiplying δ is the logit, l, defined in equation (200) and given in Table 41 for $y = P = 0.000(0.001)0.500$. The β_1, β_2 points of the curves belonging to these two systems lie in non-overlapping regions of the β_1, β_2 plane, one above and one below what may be termed the log–normal line (see Fig. 7). The log–normal distribution is defined as

$$X = \gamma + \delta \log y \quad (0 \leqslant y < \infty), \tag{172}$$

where X is again an $N(0, 1)$ variate. The beta points of this dividing line are given by the parametric equations

$$\left.\begin{aligned} \beta_1 &= (\omega - 1)(\omega + 2)^2 \quad (\sqrt{\beta_1} > 0), \\ \beta_2 &= \omega^4 + 2\omega^3 + 3\omega^2 - 3, \end{aligned}\right\} \tag{173}$$

where

$$\omega = \exp(\delta^{-2}). \tag{174}$$

Tables 34, 35 and 36 have been prepared by Johnson to make it possible to determine the parameters of an S_U or S_B distribution, given the moment ratios $\sqrt{\beta_1}$ and β_2.

18.2 *Tables to facilitate the fitting of S_U frequency curves (Tables 34 and 35)**

When expressed in the simple form of equation (170) the mean and variance of y may be expressed as

$$E(y) = -\omega^{\frac{1}{2}} \sinh \Omega, \tag{175}$$

$$\operatorname{var} y = \sigma^2(y) = \tfrac{1}{2}(\omega - 1)\{\omega \cosh(2\Omega) + 1\}, \tag{176}$$

where

$$\omega = \exp(\delta^{-2}), \quad \Omega = \gamma/\delta \quad (\text{for symmetry}, \Omega = 0). \tag{177}$$

Since it is not possible, as it is for distributions of the Pearson system, to express γ and δ (or ω and Ω) as explicit functions of $\sqrt{\beta_1}$ and β_2, Johnson (1965) computed two tables giving $-\gamma$ and δ against arguments $\sqrt{\beta_1}$ and β_2. These tables are reproduced as Tables 34 and 35. Note that γ has the opposite sign to μ_3 and $\sqrt{\beta_1}$.

For a large section of these Tables, linear interpolation is adequate, and Johnson has given the following guide rules for interpolation.

For $-\gamma$ (linear interpolation possible to four decimal places):

with respect to $\begin{cases} \beta_2 \text{ (for given } \sqrt{\beta_1}), \text{ if } \beta_2 > (\text{least tabled } \beta_2) + 2.3, \\ \sqrt{\beta_1} \text{ (for given } \beta_2), \text{ if } \sqrt{\beta_1} < (\text{greatest tabled } \sqrt{\beta_1}) - 0.8. \end{cases}$

For δ (linear interpolation possible to three decimal places):

with respect to $\begin{cases} \beta_2 \text{ (for given } \sqrt{\beta_1}), \text{ if } \beta_2 > (\text{least tabled } \beta_2) + 1.5, \\ \sqrt{\beta_1} \text{ (for given } \beta_2), \text{ if } \sqrt{\beta_1} < (\text{greatest tabled } \sqrt{\beta_1}) - 0.5. \end{cases}$

Above and to the right of these limits second difference interpolation will be needed, until the $\sqrt{\beta_1}, \beta_2$ values become so near to those appropriate to a log–normal distribution that ordinary difference interpolation breaks down. In such cases a value of δ obtained roughly from the table may be used as an initial value for the iterative process described by Johnson (1965, pp. 548–9).

In judging the accuracy required in γ and δ it is useful to bear in mind that the accuracy of estimated frequencies is directly related to that of the value of X. Since X is a linear function of γ and δ it is easy to assess the effect on X of errors in γ and δ.

The simple form of equation (170) in terms of y, does not of course permit any adjustment in location and scale. In practice if x is the variate with whose distribution we are concerned, then we write

$$y = (x - \xi)/\lambda, \tag{178}$$

* For the 2nd impression, Table 34 has been entirely re-set and Table 35 corrected and enlarged, following N. L. Johnson (*Biometrika*, 1974, **61**, 203–5).

from which it follows that, if the first two moments of the S_U distribution are to be identical with those of x, then
$$\lambda = \sigma(x)/\sigma(y), \quad \xi = E(x) - \lambda E(y), \tag{179}$$
where $E(y)$ and $\sigma(y)$ are expressible in terms of γ and δ through equations (175), (176) and (177).

Example 50. As an illustration, we show how to determine the standardized percentage points of the S_U distribution having $\sqrt{\beta_1} = 0\cdot9064$, $\beta_2 = 5\cdot7813$ used in the last comparison of the table on p. 76. It is here necessary to use the simple Bessel interpolation formula, based on second differences. Further, we are at the point in Table 34 where only three significant figures in γ are obtainable.

We find
$$\gamma = -0\cdot976, \quad \delta = 1\cdot952.$$

Next using (177) we have
$$\omega = 1\cdot300, \quad \Omega = -0\cdot500$$

and hence from (175) and (176)
$$E(y) = 0\cdot5941, \quad \sigma(y) = 0\cdot6715.$$

Since we are seeking percentage points in the standardized distribution, $E(x) = 0$, $\sigma(x) = 1$, so that (179) gives
$$\lambda = 1\cdot4892, \quad \xi = -0\cdot8848.$$

It follows from (170) and (178) that
$$X = -0\cdot976 + 1\cdot952 \sinh^{-1}\{(x + 0\cdot8848)/1\cdot4892\}$$

is an $N(0, 1)$ variable. Inverting this equation, we have
$$x = -0\cdot8848 + 1\cdot4892 \sinh\{(X + 0\cdot976)/1\cdot952\}. \tag{180}$$

To obtain, say, the standardized (*a*) upper 5 per cent and (*b*) lower 0·5 per cent points of x we insert (*a*) $X = 1\cdot6449$ and (*b*) $X = -2\cdot5758$ into equation (180) and finally obtain
$$(a) \ x_{0\cdot95} = 1\cdot772, \quad (b) \ x_{0\cdot005} = -2\cdot247.$$

These are the values derivable from the last section of the table on p. 76 namely $1\cdot765 + 0\cdot007$ and $-2\cdot175 - 0\cdot072$.

18.3 *Table to facilitate the fitting of S_B frequency curves (Table 36)*

The determination of the parameters of an S_B distribution, given the moments, is less straightforward than for S_U. This is because the inversion of the expressions giving the moments in terms of the parameters cannot be carried out explicitly; we cannot, for example, provide expressions for the expectation and variance of y in terms of γ and δ, as in the S_U equations (175) and (176). The computational method employed to solve the problem has been described in an Appendix by J. O. Kitchen to Johnson (1970). Table 36 of this volume is a slightly curtailed version of that provided in Johnson's Report, in that information is not included for S_B distributions which are bimodal,† except for the six specially selected $\sqrt{\beta_1}$ values listed on page 87.

The table is in different form from Tables 34 and 35, providing the four entries, γ, δ, $\mu_1'(y)$ and $\sigma(y)$ for each combination of argument values $\sqrt{\beta_1} = 0\cdot00(0\cdot05)2\cdot00$, and β_2 intervals of $0\cdot1$.

† Owing to the format of the table this statement is not exactly correct, but see §19 below.

If x is the true variable, then $\xi < x \leqslant \xi + \lambda$, and the full transformation is

$$X = \gamma + \delta \log \{y/(1-y)\} = \gamma + \delta \log \{(x-\xi)/(\xi + \lambda - x)\}, \qquad (181)$$

where
$$\lambda = \sigma(x)/\sigma(y), \qquad \left.\begin{array}{l}\\\\\end{array}\right\} \qquad (182)$$
$$\xi = \mu_1'(x) - \lambda\mu_1'(y),$$

X being a standardized $N(0, 1)$ variable.

If $\sqrt{\beta_1}$ is negative γ should be replaced by $-\gamma$ and μ_1' by $1 - \mu_1'$; the values of δ and σ remain unchanged.

Note that Tables 41 and 42 giving logits and anti-logits may be found useful in dealing with this distribution.

Interpolation

It will usually be necessary to interpolate with respect to both $\sqrt{\beta_1}$ and β_2. Except near the log–normal line (i.e. for the highest values of β_2 for given $\sqrt{\beta_1}$), repeated univariate interpolation using one of the Bessel formulae of § 36.1 can be used in a two-stage procedure as illustrated in Example 48, p. 78 in the case of Table 32. The use of a computer routine based on sixteen entries from the table, i.e. a bivariate interpolation assuming that differences beyond the second are negligible will, of course, save a great amount of time. For values of $\sqrt{\beta_1}$ greater than one, linear interpolation will often be adequate. When γ and/or δ are large (say greater than one) it is advantageous to interpolate for $\gamma\delta^{-1}$ and δ^{-2} rather than for γ and δ directly. Interpolation with respect to $\delta\sigma$ rather than σ, may also be helpful.

Example 51. The table on page 76 has included the standardized percentage points of an S_B distribution having the same first four moments as the Weibull distribution of equation (166), with $m = 1.6$, namely (see Harter, 1967)

$$\text{mean} = 0.8966, \quad \text{S.D.} = 0.5737, \quad \sqrt{\beta_1} = 0.96196, \quad \beta_2 = 4.04396.$$

If the interpolation in Table 36 has to be carried out with a desk calculator, the necessary entries for determining γ may be set out as follows:

β_2 \ $\sqrt{\beta_1}$	0.90	δ^2	δ^4	0.95	δ^2	1.00	δ^2	1.05	δ^2
3.9	2.396	105	.	2.032	.	1.779	.	1.592	.
4.0	2.824	165	63	2.315	81	1.982	45	1.746	28
4.1	3.417	288	174	2.679	119	2.230	62	1.928	35
4.2	4.298	585	.	3.162	.	2.540	.	2.145	.
$\gamma(4.044, \sqrt{\beta_1})$	3.060	.	.	2.463	.	2.084	.	1.822	.

When $\sqrt{\beta_1} = 0.90$ the differences become very large as the log–normal boundary for S_B curves is approached. As a result, when interpolating for β_2 in this column, third and fourth differences need to be used. The coefficients required for the Bessel formula (314), taken from Table 66, are

$$1 - \theta = 0.5604, \quad \theta = 0.4396, \quad B_2 = -0.0616, \quad B_3 = 0.0025, \quad B_4 = 0.0115.$$

Consequently

$$\gamma(\sqrt{\beta_1} = 0.9, \beta_2 = 4.04396) = 3.085 - 0.028 + 0.000 + 0.003 = 3.060.$$

We obtain the other three values in the last row of the table using the simple Bessel formula (319). Next, we have to interpolate for $\sqrt{\beta_1} = 0.96196$ in the table, as follows:

83

$\sqrt{\beta_1}$	γ	δ^2	δ^3
0·90	3·060		
0·95	2·463	218	
1·00	2·084	117	-101
1·05	1·822		

Assuming that we need only go as far as the B_3 term, we use formula (320) which gives

$$\gamma(0\cdot96196, 4\cdot04396) = 2\cdot372 - 0\cdot015 - 0\cdot001 = 2\cdot356.$$

As a check, the interpolation was carried out in reverse order, i.e. first interpolating for $\sqrt{\beta_1}$ given β_2. The results were identical to three decimal places.

A similar procedure was used to find δ, $\mu_1'(y)$ and $\sigma(y)$; in all cases the differences were smaller so that the simple Bessel formula (319) was adequate. As a result we have

$$\gamma = 2\cdot356, \quad \delta = 1\cdot576, \quad \mu_1'(y) = 0\cdot2005, \quad \sigma(y) = 0\cdot0983.$$

Hence, using equations (182), with the Weibull mean x and $\sigma(x)$ quoted above, we find

$$\lambda = 5\cdot836, \quad \xi = -0\cdot2735, \quad \xi + \lambda = 5\cdot562.$$

The inversion of (181) gives

$$x = [-0\cdot2735 + 5\cdot562 \exp\{(X - \gamma)/\delta\}]/[1 + \exp\{(X - \gamma)/\delta\}] \tag{183}$$

with γ and δ as above. Inserting the standardized normal percentage points for X, we obtain x from (183), and then standardize these values, using the mean $x = 0\cdot8966$, $\sigma(x) = 0\cdot5737$. The resulting lower and upper standardized S_B points form the basis of the figures in the fourth column of the table on page 76. For example, for the lower 5 per cent point $X = -1\cdot6449$; inserting this value in (183) we obtain $x_{0\cdot05} = 0\cdot15367$. Hence the standardized value is $(0\cdot1537 - 0\cdot8966)/0\cdot5737 = -1\cdot295$, whereas the Pearson curve value (second column in table) was $-1\cdot294$.

Example 52. The following example illustrates the value in certain situations of being able to transform a skew distribution to a standardized normal one. Pearson & Welch (1937) discuss some of the uses which might be made in quality control from a distribution of 1000 tests of warp strength made on strips of a duck cloth which had been described by A. W. Bayes in the preceding paper. The accompanying table shows, first, the observed frequency distribution and next the theoretical frequencies obtained by Pearson & Welch from the following Type I (beta) distribution which they fitted to the data, using the first four moments

$$f(x) = 21\cdot966(x - 370\cdot02)^{5\cdot1218}(495\cdot59 - x)^{1\cdot9805}. \tag{184}$$

Taking the moments quoted by Pearson & Welch, namely

$$\text{mean } x = 454\cdot09 \text{ lb}, \quad \text{s.d.} = 17\cdot358, \quad \sqrt{b_1} = -0\cdot421, \quad b_2 = 2\cdot75,$$

we have used Table 36 to estimate the parameters of an S_B curve, and find

$$\gamma = -0\cdot979, \quad \delta = 1\cdot526, \quad 1 - \mu_1'(y) = 0\cdot6423, \quad \sigma(y) = 0\cdot1390.$$

From these we find $\quad \lambda = 124\cdot88, \quad \xi = 373\cdot88, \quad \xi + \lambda = 498\cdot76.$

It will be seen that the S_B terminals agree closely with those of the beta distribution (184). The resulting transformation becomes

$$X = -0\cdot979 + 1\cdot526 \log\{(x - 373\cdot88)/(498\cdot76 - x)\}. \tag{185}$$

84

Warp strength in strips of duck cloth; observed and fitted frequencies

Strength (lb, central values)	Frequency Observed	Type I	S_B	Strength (lb, central values)	Frequency Observed	Type I	S_B
400 or less	2	2·6	2·3	455	113	106·6	106·7
405	4	3·8	3·8	460	125	109·5	110·3
410	4	7·4	7·6	465	105	105·5	106·7
415	17	13·0	13·2	470	97	93·6	94·4
420	27	20·7	21·1	475	73	74·2	73·9
425	27	30·8	30·7	480	38	49·2	47·7
430	50	43·1	43·2	485	19	23·1	22·1
435	49	57·0	56·7	490	10	4·2	5·2
440	68	71·7	71·1	495	1	0·0	0·2
445	76	85·9	85·1				
450	95	98·1	98·0	Total	1000	1000·0	1000·0

Inserting the group boundaries of the observed x-distribution into (185) and referring the resulting X-values to a table of the normal probability integral, we find, on differencing, the expected S_B frequencies shown in the fourth columns of the table.

It is clear that the beta and S_B distributions are in this case remarkably similar and that the only considerable discrepancy with observation is at the steep upper tail. Applying the χ^2-test of goodness-of-fit, grouping together frequencies for $x < 407\cdot5$ lb and for $x > 487\cdot5$ lb, we obtain, with eighteen groups:

$$\text{for Type I,} \quad \chi^2 = 25\cdot86; \qquad \text{for } S_B, \quad \chi^2 = 18\cdot87.$$

Assuming that the fitting by moments is reasonably efficient we refer to a table of the χ^2 integral, e.g. *B.T.S.* **1**, Table 7, and find P-values of $0\cdot018$ and $0\cdot127$, respectively for $\nu = 18 - 5 = 13$ degrees of freedom. The fit of S_B is very slightly the better for almost every group, but the main difference is concentrated in the last group (with $x > 487\cdot5$) where the frequencies are: observation, 11; Type I, $4\cdot2$; S_B, $5\cdot4$.

Suppose now that this distribution of 1000 test results could be taken as based on standard, approved output and used to monitor quality in smaller samples drawn from future production. By using the transformation (185) a variety of 'normal theory' tests, applicable directly to the X's, become available, e.g. could be used to form a control chart for the range in samples of n values of X. In particular we might monitor results by computing X from the lowest values $x_{(1)}$ in successive samples of n and referring these $X_{(1)}$ to the probability integral of the extreme standardized deviate from the assumed population mean (§5.1, and Table 6).

Data for test on weakest strips of duck cloth in eight samples of $n = 5$

Sample	$x_{(1)}$	$X_{(1)}$	P^*	$-\log P$
1	421	$-1\cdot743$	$0\cdot188$	$1\cdot67$
2	434	$-1\cdot092$	$0\cdot522$	$0\cdot65$
3	419	$-1\cdot848$	$0\cdot152$	$1\cdot88$
4	416	$-2\cdot010$	$0\cdot106$	$2\cdot24$
5	423	$-1\cdot640$	$0\cdot229$	$1\cdot47$
6	406	$-2\cdot597$	$0\cdot0233$	$3\cdot76$
7	412	$-2\cdot234$	$0\cdot0625$	$2\cdot77$
8	400	$-3\cdot008$	$0\cdot00658$	$5\cdot02$
			Total	$\dot{1}9\cdot46$

* P = probability that lowest X in sample of five is less than observed $X_{(1)}$.

The table on p. 85 shows in column 2, $k = 8$ successive values $x_{(1)}$ of the weakest strip in a sample of $n = 5$. The third column gives the values of $X_{(1)}$ calculated from equation (185) and the fourth column the probabilities P, extracted from Table 6, that the lowest X in a sample of five from an $N(0, 1)$ population is less than the observed $X_{(1)}$. Finally the fifth column gives $-\log P$. The combined test of the null hypothesis that the population is represented by the fitted S_B distribution consists in referring $-2\Sigma \log P = 38 \cdot 92$ to the χ^2 distribution having sixteen degrees of freedom. Since the 0·5 and 0·1 per cent points of this distribution are at 34·27 and 39·25 respectively, the sample results undoubtedly point to a falling off in warp strength, although taken sample by sample only the eighth sample with $x_{(1)} = 400\,\mathrm{lb}$ could be regarded as really exceptional.

19. J- AND U-CURVES OF PEARSON AND JOHNSON S_B SYSTEMS (Tables 31 and 33)

For the Type I or beta distribution,

$$f(x) = B^{-1}(a, b)\, x^{a-1}(1-x)^{b-1}. \tag{186}$$

This leads to a J-curve with infinite ordinate at $x = 0$ or 1 if a or $b < 1$, and a U-curve with infinite ordinates at both terminals if a and $b < 1$. The limiting boundary curves in the β_1, β_2 plane which are defined by the conditions a or $b = 1$ and $a = b = 1$ are shown in Fig. 7. In Table 32 the entries are almost entirely confined to percentage points for bell-shaped (Ω) curves, having β_1, β_2 co-ordinates below the Ω–J line, but to aid interpolation a few entries are for curves across the boundary (see last column on the right-hand pages). The decision to restrict the table in this way was based on the fact that in fitting a J-curve it seemed likely that there would be at least one terminal known and for a U-curve both terminals, so that β_2 and possibly also $\sqrt{\beta_1}$ would not be used in the fitting process.

D. E. Amos had, however, determined the fifteen standardized percentage points used in Table 32 for J- and U-curves having β_1, β_2 values right up to the limiting line, $\beta_2 - \beta_1 - 1 = 0$, and we now put some of these results on record in Table 33. They are mainly for J-curves but a few U-curve values are included to aid interpolation. The Table 33 includes the exponents a, b of equation (186), but the lower 0·5 and 0·25 per cent points have been omitted since their values, to five decimal places, are identical with those of the lower 1 per cent point.

In Table 31 we give the a, b values for the J- and U-curves already included in Table 32.

When both terminals are clearly defined the first and second moments of the distribution to be graduated may be used in equation (46), p. 14, to determine values for the a and b in (186). Since both these values are likely to be small, Table 4 with its lower and upper 0·5, 1·0, 2·5 and 5·0 per cent points for F, convertible to those for x through equation (42) may well prove helpful.

When we come to Johnson's S_B curves, the position is rather different, since the probability density function of the y in equation (181) has zero ordinates at $y = 0$ and 1 and also high contact with the base line (see Johnson, 1949, p. 158). The system therefore provides no true J- or U-distributions although for a greater part of the range $0 \leqslant y \leqslant 1$ may give a very good representation of a true J- or U-curve. Johnson (1949, p. 159) has given a series of diagrams illustrating how S_B changes shape with the parameters γ and δ.

The S_B distribution is bimodal in a region of the plane where

$$|\gamma| < \delta^{-1}\sqrt{(1 - 2\delta^2)} - 2\delta \tanh^{-1}\sqrt{(1 - 2\delta^2)}. \tag{187}$$

The lower boundary of this region (in the sense of Fig. 7) lies very close to the boundary between J- and U-Type I Pearson curves, a point illustrated by Draper (1952, Fig. 2). With the exceptions referred to in the next sentence, the entries in Table 36 are roughly cut off at this boundary because, as in the case of the Pearson curves, it seems probable that any fitting of bimodal distributions would involve the use of the terminals. However, to aid in possible exploration, the parameters for bimodal distributions have been included for $\sqrt{\beta_1} = 0{\cdot}00, 0{\cdot}05, 0{\cdot}10$ (p. 296) and $0{\cdot}90, 0{\cdot}95, 1{\cdot}00$ (p. 298). Johnson (1970, p. 8) has reported that he is computing a table giving γ and δ against $\mu_1'(y)$ and $\sigma(y)$, which may be used when the terminals are clearly known.

In the case of J- or pseudo-J-curves it is interesting to note the difference between Type I (beta) and S_B. For example, take the case where $\sqrt{\beta_1} = 1{\cdot}0$, $\beta_2 = 2{\cdot}8$. Table 33 shows that this gives a beta distribution with $a = 0{\cdot}3661$, $b = 1{\cdot}0457$, so that the ordinate rises to an infinite value at $x = 0$. On the other hand the S_B distribution has, as Table 36 shows, $\gamma = 0{\cdot}7807$, $\delta = 0{\cdot}4710$, $\mu_1'(y) = 0{\cdot}2726$, $\sigma(y) = 0{\cdot}2785$. We can find the ordinates of $f(y)$ from

$$f(y) = \delta Z(X)/\{y(1-y)\}, \tag{188}$$

where X is computed from (181) and $Z(X)$ from equation (1). Taking values of y near zero, we find

y	0	0·0005	0·001	0·005	0·01	0·05	0·10
$f(y)$	0	7·48	8·86	8·72	7·29	3·29	2·02

Clearly, if we divided the distribution into, say, 100 frequency groups with class intervals for y of

$$0{\cdot}00 - 0{\cdot}01,\ 0{\cdot}01 - 0{\cdot}02,\ 0{\cdot}02 - 0{\cdot}03,\ \ldots$$

the maximum frequency would fall in the first group, but the distribution would not be strictly J-shaped.

This distinction is of some interest because the distributions to be fitted, whether observational or theoretical, may be of either form but from the practical view-point both curves may give a satisfactory fit for most of the range. For example, going a little further with the comparison of Type I and S_B for $\sqrt{\beta_1} = 1{\cdot}0$, $\beta_2 = 2{\cdot}8$, we obtain the following table of standardized distances from the mean to eleven percentage points.

Lower % points	Type I	S_B	Upper % points	Type I	S_B
0 (start)	−0·919	−0·979	25	0·630	0·615
1	− ·919	− ·974	10	1·671	1·690
5	− ·918	− ·958	5	2·110	2·117
10	− ·913	− ·934	1	2·510	2·482
25	− ·843	− ·823	0·5	2·565	2·534
50	− ·413	− ·404	0 (end)	2·625	2·612

Except for the two first entries, the maximum difference between the points of the two distributions is four-hundredths of the standard deviation. In the range shown the curves have three cross-overs, and the differences increase towards the terminals, particularly the lower one.

20. MAXIMUM LIKELIHOOD ESTIMATION OF THE PARAMETERS IN A TYPE III (GAMMA) DISTRIBUTION (Tables 37 and 38)

In the preceding sections of this chapter we have been largely concerned with illustrating the uses of Tables 31–36 in approximating to mathematical probability distributions on the basis of their moments. In one case however, Example 52, we fitted two curves to a frequency distribution consisting of 1000 test observations, again using moments. It is generally accepted, however, that in the second type of problem 'better' estimates to the parameters of the sampled population can be obtained if the method of maximum likelihood is used. In most cases the solution of the maximum likelihood equations can only be reached by iteration, perhaps using the moment solution as a first approximation, and if the latter appears adequate, as was the case in Example 52, the statistician may feel satisfied without going further.

There is, however, one situation where the maximum likelihood estimation of parameters of a Pearson curve is straightforward. This is the case of fitting to data a Type III (gamma) distribution whose finite terminal is known. If this is the case, we can take the origin at the terminal and write $f(x)$ in the form

$$f(x) = \left(\frac{p}{b}\right)^p \frac{1}{\Gamma(p)} x^{p-1} e^{-px/b} \quad (0 \leqslant x < \infty). \tag{189}$$

If the data consist of N observations $x_1, x_2, \ldots, x_N$ then it is easy to show that the equations giving the maximum likelihood estimators $\hat{b}$ and $\hat{p}$ of the population parameters are

$$\hat{b} = \sum_i x_i/N = \bar{x}, \tag{190}$$

$$\log \hat{p} - \frac{d}{dp} \log \Gamma(\hat{p}) = \log \bar{x} - \sum_i (\log x_i)/N. \tag{191}$$

If we denote by v the expression on the right-hand side of (191) it will be seen that it is the logarithm of the ratio of the arithmetic to the geometric mean of the N observations. Table 37 is based on a table computed by Greenwood & Durand (1960) and makes it easy to compute $\hat{p}$, given v. The second differences of $v\hat{p}$ change very slowly so that the Bessel formula (319) may always be used for interpolation; often linear interpolation will be adequate.

In the form of parameterization used, b is directly estimated by $\bar{x}$, whose sampling properties are well known. Further, to order N^{-1}, $\bar{x}$ and $\hat{p}$ are uncorrelated. It is, however, important to have some idea of the bias and sampling variance of $\hat{p}$. Its asymptotic variance was first given by Fisher (1922) as

$$\text{var } \hat{p} = \frac{1}{N} \frac{p}{p\psi' - 1}, \tag{192}$$

where $\psi' = d^2 \log \Gamma(p)/dp^2$. Masuyama & Kuroiwa (1951) have tabled the function $p/(p\psi' - 1)$. However, recent investigation has shown, see e.g. Bowman & Shenton (1968), that very large samples indeed must be taken before equation (192) can be accepted as accurate and also that there is considerable bias in the estimate $\hat{p}$ unless N is large. Bowman & Shenton have derived expansions for $E\hat{p}$ and var $\hat{p}$ (as well as for higher moments) in the form

$$E(\hat{p} - p)/p = a_0 N^{-1}(1 + a_1/N + a_2/N^2 + \ldots), \tag{193}$$

$$\text{var } \hat{p}/p = b_0 N^{-1}(1 + b_1/N + b_2/N^2 + \ldots), \tag{194}$$

and have tabled the coefficients a_i, b_i up to the terms of order N^{-6}. We include in Table 38 the values of these coefficients to a reduced number of figures, up to N^{-5}, for $p = 0\cdot1(0\cdot1)1\cdot0, 2, 5,$ 10, 25, 50. Coefficients for intermediate values of p can be determined with sufficient accuracy by graphical interpolation, bearing in mind the fact that when fitting a curve to observational data, $\hat{p}$ will have to be substituted for the unknown p when entering Table 38. In a second paper, Bowman & Shenton (1970) give considerably more detailed theoretical and numerical results.

If the start of the population gamma distribution is at $x = m$ and m is unknown, the p.d.f. may then be written in the form

$$f(x) = \frac{p^p}{c\Gamma(p)} \left(\frac{x-d+c}{c}\right)^{p-1} \exp\{-p(x-d+c)/c\}, \, d = m+c. \tag{195}$$

The maximum likelihood estimator of d is $\hat{d} = \bar{x}$, but the equations for determining $\hat{p}$ and $\hat{c}$ are much less tractable, because they contain the sums of (a) the logarithms and (b) the reciprocals of $(x_i - \bar{x} + c)$. Further as Bowman & Shenton (in a recent unpublished communication) have shown numerically the expansions in terms of N^{-1} of bias, variances and covariances converge a good deal less rapidly than in the two-parameter case.

VI. TABLES FOR USE IN APPLYING TECHNIQUES OF QUANTAL ASSAY

21. General discussion and definitions

Methods of quantal assay are applied in situations where the individuals in a population require a varying amount of 'stimulus' to produce a characteristic 'quantal response'. The stimulus may be a dose of a drug and the response may be survival or death. Or again the stimulus may be the shock wave from the detonation of an explosive and the response may be the shattering or survival of a target. Let x_t represent a particular value of the stimulus or of an appropriate function of it, such as its logarithm. If then r_t individuals respond out of n_t to whom the stimulus has been applied,

$$p_t = r_t/n_t$$

will be an estimate of the probability of response, P_t, in the population sampled. This probability can be identified with the probability that the 'critical dose', x, of an individual is $\leqslant x_t$, and the statistical problem concerns the estimation of the parameters of the distribution of these critical doses, or what may be often appropriately termed the susceptibility, among the individuals of the population. Two different probability models have been most commonly used to represent this distribution, the normal and the logistic. These lead to alternative forms of relationship between p and x, namely:

For the normal model

$$P = 1 - Q = \frac{1}{\sqrt{(2\pi)}} \int_{-\infty}^{X} e^{-\frac{1}{2}u^2} \, du, \tag{196}$$

where

$$X = \frac{x-\mu}{\sigma} = \alpha + \beta x, \tag{197}$$

and μ, σ are the mean and standard deviation of the hypothesized normal distribution of critical doses whose parameters μ and σ are to be estimated. The mathematical treatment also uses

$$\frac{dP}{dX} = Z(X) = \frac{1}{\sqrt{(2\pi)}} e^{-\frac{1}{2}X^2}. \tag{198}$$

For the logistic model

$$P = 1 - Q = \frac{1}{1 + e^{-l}}, \tag{199}$$

where

$$l = \log\frac{P}{1-P} = \alpha + \beta x. \tag{200}$$

For other critical dose distributions see, for example, Finney (1952).

Sometimes there may be biological or physical reasons supporting the use of one model rather than the other, but when this is not the case the observations themselves will rarely be sufficient to discriminate clearly between them. This is because the cumulative distributions or, alternatively, the probability density functions are not very different in shape. Both are symmetrical about the point $x = -\alpha/\beta$, while the p.d.f. of the logistic, namely

$$f(l) = \frac{e^{-l}}{(1+e^{-l})^2},$$ (201)

is only moderately leptokurtic; its variance is $\frac{1}{3}\pi^2$ and its standardized fourth moment is $\beta_2 = \mu_4/\sigma^4 = 4\cdot2$, against the normal value of $3\cdot0$. Comparisons have been made from time to time between the fits to sample data of the normal and logistic models (e.g. Berkson, 1944, p. 364); two such comparisons are made in the following sections. Judged by the χ^2-test, there has generally been little to choose between them.

It seems therefore that the decision to use equation (196) or (199) may depend to a large extent on the ease with which the data can be analysed. Here, we are at once brought up against a further choice, that between two alternative methods of procedure – to fit by the method of maximum likelihood as advocated by Bliss, Fisher and Finney, or by Berkson's method of weighted least squares, which essentially involves minimizing an appropriate χ^2. This choice between methods has involved much controversy which it is not proposed to enter into here. We shall only remark that:

(a) Tables are available to assist in the computation involved in applying either method, using either model.

(b) Asymptotically both methods of fitting are equivalent.

(c) Except in the case of fitting the logistic in the special case where the number of individuals, n_t ($t = 1, 2, ..., k$) treated at each level of x is the same (where Berkson has provided appropriate nomograms for $k = 3(1)6$), the solution commonly recommended using maximum likelihood involves a process of iteration. This may involve rather tedious calculations and unless strict rules are adhered to, the answers provided by different computers may not be identical.

(d) On the other hand, accepting the principle as a workmanlike one, the minimum χ^2 procedure leads in one step to a unique solution.

(e) Berkson (1957b) described a fairly extensive sampling investigation which he had carried out, comparing the biases and mean square errors of the estimates of the parameters α and β obtained by applying the two methods to the normal model. Under the experimental conditions which he adopted, the mean square errors associated with his 'minimum normit χ^2' procedure were always somewhat less than those associated with the maximum likelihood procedure.

In the Introduction to our Volume 1 (§2 and Table 6) we described and illustrated the standard method of obtaining a maximum likelihood fit, using the normal model. In that case we worked in terms of the *probit*

$$Y = X + 5.$$

where X is the normal equivalent deviate defined in equations (196) to (198) above. In the present instance we shall work in terms of X, which in this particular quantal assay problem following Berkson, we shall term a *normit*. Similarly, for the logistic model, we term the l of equations (199) and (200) a *logit*.

Tables 39–46, all due to Berkson (1953, 1957 a, b, 1960) and published previously in a number of journals, are planned to simplify the following procedures.

For the normal model. The minimum normit χ^2 solution. (§ 22 and Tables 39 and 40.)

For the logistic model

(a) The minimum logit χ^2 solution. (§ 23 and Table 41 of logits, Table 42 of anti-logits and Table 43 of logistic weights.)

(b) The maximum likelihood solution, *without iteration*, which involves the use of nomograms and is available when the number of observations at each of three to six levels is the same, i.e. $n_t = n$ and the x_t are equally spaced. (§ 24 and nomograms 1–8 of Table 44; also Table 45 for estimated standard errors.)

(c) The maximum likelihood solution with iteration. (Since the anti-logits have already been given in Table 42, the only additional table needed is one of the appropriate weights; see § 25 and Table 46.)

In describing these procedures we have drawn freely, with his permission, on Berkson's papers (1944, 1953, 1957 a, b, 1960).

Before proceeding to the detailed techniques we should point out that all the above theories relate to what may be termed 'within single assay methods'. The distribution theory underlying them and the inference procedures resulting from them only apply to the *particular* assay considered and cannot claim 'reproducibility' (within the calculated statistical tolerances) when the assay is repeated with a different batch of animals or other experimental units. Indeed, much experience with repeated assays has shown that the 'between assay errors' are usually an order of magnitude larger than the 'within assay errors'. From this point of view strenuous efforts in statistical efficiency in the minimization of 'within assay errors' are usually wasted in the face of the large 'between assay errors'. Thus simple or short-cut methods may become very acceptable.

The need for awareness of the pitfalls here involved is of course present throughout the whole field of applied statistics, but it is perhaps particularly important to keep the difference between these 'within' and 'between' errors in mind in animal experimentation.

22. The normal model: minimimum normit χ^2 solution

22.1 *Definitions and procedure*

The data consist of values of r_t, n_t and x_t ($t = 1, 2, ..., k$). We then obtain the normit values X_t by entering a table of the cumulative normal probability function (e.g. Table 4 of *B.T.S.* **1** or Table 1 of *B.T.S.* **2**) with $p_t = r_t/n_t$ substituted for P in equation (196). If the model is appropriate, the X_t when plotted as ordinates against the corresponding x_t as abscissae will only diverge through sampling fluctuations in the observed r_t from the population line, say

$$\tilde{X} = \alpha + \beta x.$$

The problem is to obtain estimates, a and b, of α and β. This is effected by minimizing

$$\chi^2 \text{(normit)} = \sum_{t=1}^{k} n_t w_t (X_t - a - bx_t)^2 \tag{202}$$

with regard to a and b, where $\quad\quad w_t = Z_t^2/(p_t q_t), \tag{203}$

Z_t being given by equation (198) with $X = X_t$ determined from the observed $p_t = 1 - q_t$ as described above. The minimization leads to the usual equations

$$b = \frac{\Sigma(nwXx) - \Sigma(nwX)\,\Sigma(nwx)/\Sigma(nw)}{\Sigma(nwx^2) - \{\Sigma(nwx)\}^2/\Sigma(nw)}, \qquad (204)$$

$$a = \bar{X} - b\bar{x} = \frac{\Sigma(nwX) - b\Sigma(nwx)}{\Sigma(nw)}. \qquad (205)$$

The estimate of the so called median (or mean) lethal dose is

$$ED(x_{50}) = -a/b. \qquad (206)$$

To facilitate calculations Table 39, entered with r_t and n_t, gives w_t and $w_t X_t$ for $2 \leqslant n_t \leqslant 50$; for $n_t > 50$ Table 40 must be entered with $P = p_t$. When $p_t = 0$ or $p_t = 1$, X is negatively or positively infinite and wX is zero. In such cases Berkson (1957b, pp. 412, 421) suggests the use of working values $1/(2n)$ and $1 - 1/(2n)$ respectively.

For large samples the following asymptotic formulae for estimates of the error variances of a, b and $-a/b$ are available:

$$\left. \begin{aligned} s^2(b) &= 1/\{\Sigma nw(x - \bar{x})^2\}, \\ s^2(a) &= 1/\Sigma(nw) + \bar{x}^2 s^2(b), \end{aligned} \right\} \qquad (207)$$

$$s^2(x_{50}) = \frac{1}{b^2}\left\{ \frac{1}{\Sigma(nw)} + (x_{50} - \bar{x})^2\, s^2(b) \right\}, \qquad (208)$$

where
$$\bar{x} = \Sigma(nwx)/\Sigma(nw).$$

The equations (204), (205), (207) and (208) are of the same form as those used in the maximum likelihood solution (see e.g. $B.T.S.$ $\mathbf{1}$, §§ 2.1, 2.2), but where in following the minimum normit χ^2 procedure the weights, w_t, are based directly on the observed frequencies, under the maximum likelihood procedure a process of iteration is called for, so that the weights $w_t = \hat{Z}_t^2/(\hat{P}_t \hat{Q}_t)$ are based on the maximum likelihood estimates.

Subject to the usual limitation when any of the expected frequencies are very small, goodness of fit may be tested by calculating

$$\chi^2 = \sum_{t=1}^{k} (r_t - n_t P_t)^2/(n_t P_t Q_t), \qquad (209)$$

where the P_t and $Q_t = 1 - P_t$ are obtained from a table of the normal integral entered with X_t derived from the estimated normit regression line

$$X_t = a + bx_t.$$

Tables of the χ^2 integral or of its percentage points are then entered with degree of freedom $\nu = k - 2$.

22.2 *Illustration of the use of Table 39*

Example 53. We take the example used to illustrate the fit of the normal model by maximum likelihood in $B.T.S.$ $\mathbf{1}$, § 2.2. In the experiment, a fixed weight of explosive was detonated sixteen times at each of five different distances from a standard disk of cardboard, and a record made of the number of times, r_t, when the disk was perforated. Thus, $k = 5$ and $n_t = n = 16$ for all t. A summary of the calculations which are made simpler because the values of n_t vanish from equations (204) and (205) is given below. As $n < 50$, Table 39 gives w and wX directly.

When $r = 0$ and 16, the entries in the Table are based on 'working values' for p, namely $\frac{1}{32}$ and $\frac{31}{32}$, respectively.

ft	x_t Working scale	r_t	w_t	$w_t X_t$	$w_t x_t$	$w_t X_t x_t$	$w_t x_t^2$
53	0	0	0·16345	− 0·30458	0	0	0
49	1	9	·63092	·09925	0·63092	0·09925	0·63092
45	2	9	·63092	·09925	1·26184	0·19850	2·52368
41	3	12	·53857	·36326	1·61571	1·08978	4·84713
37	4	16	·16345	·30458	0·65380	1·21832	2·61520
Sum			2·12731	0·56176	4·16227	2·60585	10·61693

Carrying out the straightforward calculations involved in equations (204) to (208), we obtain the following estimates for β, α and $-\alpha/\beta = ED(x_{50})$, with their large-sample estimated standard errors:

$$b = 0·609 \pm 0·159, \quad a = -0·928 \pm 0·355, \quad -a/b = 1·52 \pm 0·30.$$

The maximum likelihood solution carried out in $B.T.S.$ **1** in Example 2, gave at the fifth iteration:
$$\hat{b} = 0·76, \quad \hat{a} = -1·23, \quad -\hat{a}/\hat{b} = 1·62 \pm 0·23.$$

The estimates differ by a fair amount, but having regard to the large standard errors associated with such a limited quantity of data, it is impossible to attach any significant meaning to this. In any case the validity of the asymptotic formulae for the standard errors must be in doubt.

We may now examine the goodness of fit, using the χ^2-test. The following table shows: values of X_t calculated from

$$X_t = a + b x_t = -0·9280 + 0·6092 x_t$$

(using a fourth decimal place figure in a and b not quoted above); values of P_t obtained from tables of the normal integral; and the resulting expected values, $16P_t$. Using equation (209) we find
$$\chi^2 = 7·60, \quad \nu = 5 - 2 = 3.$$

The last two columns in the table show the expected values $16P_t$ of (a) the maximum likelihood solution for the normal model taken from $B.T.S.$ **1**, § 2.2; for this fit, χ^2 was 8·37; (b) the minimum logit χ^2 solution (see § 23.1 below) for the logistic model which gives a goodness of fit χ^2 of 8·36 and an estimate of ED (50) of 1·41. Thus, judged by the χ^2-test, the minimum normit χ^2 analysis has given a slightly better fit than that of the maximum likelihood solution (M.L.) for the normal model, but the difference is of no significance. Both χ^2 values lie not far from the 5 per cent level. The fit to the logistic is also of the same nature.

				Estimates of $16P_t$		
				Normal model		Logistic model
x_t	X_t	P_t	r_t	Min. χ^2	M.L.	min. χ^2
0	− 0·9280	0·1767	0	2·83	1·76	3·61
1	− ·3187	·3750	9	6·00	5·12	6·58
2	·2905	·6143	9	9·83	9·81	10·01
3	·8998	·8158	12	13·05	13·63	12·80
4	1·5090	·9344	16	14·95	15·43	14·49

23. The logistic model: minimum logit χ^2 solution

23.1 Definitions and procedure

We use the same notation for the data as in the preceding sections. The values of the logits

$$l_t = \log p_t/q_t, \quad \text{where} \quad q_t = 1 - p_t,$$

are determined from Table 41 entered with $P = p_t$. If the model is appropriate, the points (l_t, x_t) will only diverge from the population regression line, say

$$l = \alpha + \beta x,$$

through sampling fluctuations in the r_t, assumed to have the binomial variance $n_t P_t Q_t$. Estimates a, b of α, β are obtained by minimizing

$$\chi^2 \text{(logit)} = \sum_{t=1}^{k} n_t p_t q_t (l_t - a - b x_t)^2. \tag{210}$$

The procedure involves a least squares fit, with $n_t p_t q_t$ taken as the weight of l_t. Writing

$$w_t = p_t q_t \tag{211}$$

the estimates, b and a, may be calculated from

$$b = \frac{\Sigma(nwlx) - \Sigma(nwl)\,\Sigma(nwx)/\Sigma(nw)}{\Sigma(nwx^2) - \{\Sigma(nwx)\}^2/\Sigma(nw)}, \tag{212}$$

$$a = \bar{l} - b\bar{x} = \frac{\Sigma(nwl) - b\Sigma(nwx)}{\Sigma(nw)}. \tag{213}$$

The estimate of the median lethal dose will again be

$$ED(x_{50}) = -a/b. \tag{214}$$

Table 43, entered with $P = p_t$, gives the values of $w_t = p_t q_t$ and $w_t l_t$. The estimates of the asymptotic standard errors of b, a and x_{50} are of identical form to those given in equations (207) and (208), with w_t given by (211) instead of (203).

As in the normit analysis, when r_t is 0 or n_t, Berkson suggests the use of working values for p_t of $1/(2n_t)$ and $1 - 1/(2n_t)$ respectively.

For goodness of fit, χ^2 is determined as in equation (209), the values of P_t being found by entering Table 42 of anti-logits with l_t calculated from the estimated logit regression line

$$l_t = a + b x_t.$$

The degrees of freedom will again be $\nu = k - 2$.

23.2 Illustration of the use of Tables 41, 42 and 43

Example 54. We take an example which has been used by Irwin & Cheeseman (1939) and Garwood (1941) to illustrate the maximum likelihood fit for the normal model. It concerns the result of applying antipneumococcus serum in different strengths to five groups, each of forty mice. In the present case we shall use Berkson's minimum *logit* χ^2 procedure, also quoting results of a minimum *normit* χ^2 analysis and comparing these with Garwood's results.

The data and computations are shown below. The working unit x is related to the dose (in cm³) as follows:

$$x = 2 + \{\log_{10} (\text{dose}) + 2\}/\log_{10} 2.$$

We define r as the *survivals* out of $n = n_t = 40$, not the deaths. The values of w_t and $w_t l_t$ can in this case be obtained directly, without need for interpolation, from Table 43. Since n_t is constant it does not have to be introduced into the summations. The estimates of β, α and $ED(50)$ follow at once by inserting the appropriate sums into equations (212)–(214) and the estimates of their asymptotic standard errors follow from (207) and (208).

x_t	r_t	$P_t = r_t/40$	w_t	$w_t l_t$	$w_t x_t$	$w_t l_t x_t$	$w_t x_t^2$
-2	7	0·175	0·1444	$-0·2239$	$-0·2888$	0·4478	0·5776
-1	18	·450	·2475	$-$ ·0497	$-$ ·2475	·0497	·2475
0	32	·800	·1600	·2218	0	0	0
1	35	·875	·1094	·2128	·1094	·2128	·1094
2	38	·950	·0475	·1399	·0950	·2798	·1900
	Sum		0·7088	0·3009	$-0·3319$	0·9901	1·1245

Thus we have

$$b = 1·167 \pm 0·161, \quad a = 0·971 \pm 0·202, \quad -a/b = -0·832 \pm 0·169.$$

Converting back to units of dose from working units, it is found that $ED(50) = 0·00140\,\mathrm{cm}^3$.

To apply the χ^2-test we calculate values of l_t from the estimated regression line,

$$l_t = 0·9710 + 1·167 x_t,$$

determine the associated estimates of P from the anti-logit Table 42 and proceed on similar lines to those used in Example 53. The result is shown in the table below. Also added are the results from using the *normal* model, with (i) the minimum normit χ^2 solution as described in §22.1 and (ii) the maximum likelihood solution as worked out by Garwood (1941). More data are available in this example than in Example 53 and the results are remarkably alike among themselves.

Serum dose (cm³)	Working scale x_t	r_t	Estimates of $40P_t$		
			Min. logit χ^2	Min. normit χ^2	M.L. (Garwood)
0·000625	-2	7	8·1	8·6	8·5
·00125	-1	18	18·0	18·0	18·1
·0025	0	32	29·0	28·3	28·4
·005	1	35	35·8	35·5	35·6
·01	2	38	38·6	38·8	38·9
χ^2			1·73	2·66	2·70
$ED(50)$ cm³			0·00140	0·00142	0·00142

24. THE LOGISTIC MODEL: A SIMPLE MAXIMUM LIKELIHOOD SOLUTION WHEN GROUP SIZES ARE EQUAL

24.1 *Specification of conditions and outline of procedure*

As was the case in Examples 53 and 54, it may often be possible, particularly when carrying out routine analyses, to arrange that (*a*) the number of observations at each level of the stimulus, which we shall term the 'dosage', are the same, i.e. $n_t = n$ ($t = 1, 2, ..., k$); (*b*) the 'dosages' are equally spaced. Under these conditions and for $k = 3, 4, 5$ and 6 the nomograms of Table 44, due to Berkson (1960), provide a rapid maximum likelihood solution. This is

95

because the estimates $\hat{a}$ and $\hat{b}$ of α and β are now functions of the sufficient statistics Σp_t and $\Sigma p_t x_t$ and also do not involve the differences in spacing between the x_t.

For each value of k, nomograms are provided for the estimators $\hat{g}$ and $\hat{b}$ of $\gamma = -\alpha/\beta$ and β. For the most efficient spacing in the construction of the nomograms the dosages are coded with $x = 0$ at the centre of the range, but for computation it is probably easier to scale the dosages as $0, 1, 2, \ldots, (k-1)$. The dosage on the computing scale will be referred to as x', that on the nomographic scale as x. For the use of the nomograms, one therefore computes Σp and $\Sigma px'$ from the data recorded as dosages x' and then, for consulting the nomogram takes

$$\Sigma px = \Sigma px' - \tfrac{1}{2}(k-1)\Sigma p. \tag{215}$$

The estimate of ED(50) is provided by the nomogram in terms of the computing scale x'. However, to increase the sensitivity within the space available on the chart, the nomogram has been designed to give a direct estimate, $\hat{g}$, only when $ED(50)$ is *positive in terms of x*. In this case Σp ($\leqslant \tfrac{1}{2}k$) will be located on the left-hand scale. When the estimate of $ED(50)$ is *negative in terms of x*, Σp ($\geqslant \tfrac{1}{2}k$) will be found on the right-hand scale. In the latter case the value read from the nomogram in terms of x' as $\hat{g}$, must be converted to the correct value by taking

$$\hat{g}' = k - 1 - \hat{g}. \tag{216}$$

Values of $\hat{g}$ are provided over the entire, or almost entire, range of doses, $0 \leqslant x' \leqslant k-1$. In a well-designed experiment, the $ED(50)$ should fall near the centre of the range; if it falls far from this position the error of estimation may be large and the experiment may need to be extended. Values of $\hat{b}$ have been given over a range which should cover most practical work.

The 'large sample' estimates of the error variance of $\hat{g}$ and $\hat{b}$ are of the same form as those given in equations (207) and (208) except that the weights, w_t, are now equal to $\hat{P}_t \hat{Q}_t$, these probabilities being obtained from the estimated regression line

$$\hat{P}_t = 1 - \hat{Q}_t = \hat{b}(x'_t - \hat{g}).$$

Since for any specified, equally spaced number of doses, $\hat{P}$, $\hat{Q}$ and $\bar{x} = \Sigma(\hat{P}\hat{Q}x)/\Sigma(\hat{P}\hat{Q})$ are determined solely by $\hat{g}$ and $\hat{b}$, it is possible to determine the estimated variances as functions of $\hat{g}$, $\hat{b}$ and n. In Table 45 the standard error of each estimate, multiplied by $\sqrt{n}$ is given for $k = 3, 4, 5, 6$. The entries are to two significant figures, which are enough for most practical purposes. The tables are entered with the values, $\gamma = \hat{g}$ and $\beta = \hat{b}$ read from the appropriate nomograms; when $\Sigma p > \tfrac{1}{2}k$ we use $\hat{g}'$ of (216), not $\hat{g}$.

The standard errors change slowly with the estimated parameters which are tabled as arguments with sufficient refinement only to determine the standard errors unequivocally.

24.2 *Illustration of the use of the nomograms and tables (Tables 44 and 45)*

Example 55 (Berkson 1960, p. 123): k = 4 doses

x'	x	n	r	p	
0	$-1\cdot5$	30	1	0·0333	
1	$-0\cdot5$	30	8	·2667	$\Sigma p = 1\cdot5667$
2	$0\cdot5$	30	15	·5000	$\Sigma px' = 3\cdot5667$
3	$1\cdot5$	30	23	·7667	$\Sigma px = \Sigma px' - \tfrac{3}{2}\Sigma p = 1\cdot2167.$

Since $\Sigma p < \tfrac{1}{2}k = 2$, we locate 1·567 on the left-hand ordinate scale for Σp_j and 1·217 on the lower or upper abscissal Σpx scale. A straight edge, preferably thin and transparent, should be used as an aid in locating the position of the co-ordinate values. The estimates $\hat{g}$, $\hat{b}$ can generally be read exactly to two significant figures with the third significant figure estimated by visual interpolation. In some sections of the nomograms it is even possible to estimate an additional place. In the present case we find

$$\hat{g} = 2 \cdot 008, \quad \hat{b} = 1 \cdot 30.$$

The values obtained by an iterative maximum likelihood computation were

$$\hat{g} = 2 \cdot 0030, \quad \hat{b} = 1 \cdot 2992.$$

From Table 45 we find

$$s(\hat{g}) = 0 \cdot 98/\sqrt{30} = 0 \cdot 18, \quad s(\hat{b}) = 1 \cdot 3/\sqrt{30} = 0 \cdot 24,$$

so that finally
$$\hat{g} = 2 \cdot 01 \pm 0 \cdot 18, \quad \hat{b} = 1 \cdot 30 \pm 0 \cdot 24.$$

Example 56. We shall now take the data used in Example 54. Here $k = 5$ and since the values of x_t quoted have an origin at the centre of the range, they correspond to x, not x', in the present notation. We find
$$\Sigma p = 3 \cdot 25, \quad \Sigma px = 1 \cdot 975.$$

Since $\Sigma p > \frac{1}{2}k = 2 \cdot 5$, we use for Σp the right-hand scales of the two nomograms and obtain $\hat{g}$ from equation (216). The readings made give

$$\hat{g} = 2 \cdot 847, \quad \hat{g}' = 5 - 1 - \hat{g} = 1 \cdot 153 \text{ in terms of } x'$$
$$= -2 \cdot 0 + 1 \cdot 153 = -0 \cdot 847 \text{ in terms of } x,$$
$$\hat{b} = 1 \cdot 19.$$

Entering Table 45, for $k = 5$, with $\gamma = 2 \cdot 847$, $\beta = 1 \cdot 19$ we find

$$s(\hat{g}) = 1 \cdot 0\sqrt{40} = 0 \cdot 16, \quad s(\hat{b}) = 1 \cdot 1/\sqrt{40} = 0 \cdot 17,$$

giving finally
$$\hat{g}' = -0 \cdot 85 \pm 0 \cdot 16, \quad \hat{b} = 1 \cdot 19 \pm 0 \cdot 17.$$

These results may be compared with those derived in §23.2, using the minimum logit χ^2 solution, namely
$$-a/b = -0 \cdot 83 \pm 0 \cdot 15, \quad b = 1 \cdot 17 \pm 0 \cdot 16.$$

It is clear that if the design of the experiment is appropriate, i.e. with constant $n_t = n$, equal spacing of the x_t and $k = 3, 4, 5$ or 6, the maximum likelihood solution using the nomograms will be quicker to carry out than the minimum normit χ^2 solution and very much quicker than the maximum likelihood solution with iteration. Some care, however, must be taken in making the readings and following the directions with regard to x, x', etc.

25. The logistic model: maximum likelihood solution
with iteration

When the conditions required for the nomographic solution are not satisfied and the statistician wishes to employ the method of maximum likelihood rather than that of minimum logit χ^2, the solution can be carried out starting with initial provisional estimates of α and β and proceeding by iteration. In addition to the anti-logits given in Table 42 all that is needed is a table of weights $w = pq$, entered with l instead of P (as in Table 43). These weights are given in Table 46, and a method of iteration using these two tables has been described and illustrated by Berkson (1957a).

VII. TABLES FOR MULTIVARIATE ANALYSIS

In the following sections we are concerned with the distributions of a variety of statistics, useful in the analysis of multivariate data. A number of other tables might have been included, but this would have occupied more space than could be allowed to the subject and we have therefore, largely, concentrated on tables or modifications of tables which have already been published in *Biometrika*. Since these tables generally involve entry with three parameters, a good deal of attention has been given to the choice of appropriate argument intervals in order to compress some of the original tables. To provide concise definitions, matrix notation has necessarily been introduced. For brevity we shall describe what is strictly a variance–covariance matrix as a covariance matrix.

It should be emphasized that while the tests on mean vectors are likely to be fairly robust, those involving comparisons of covariance matrices may well be rather sensitive to departure from multivariate normality in the populations sampled. (See for example Box (1953) on the univariate case.)

26. MULTIVARIATE ANALYSIS OF VARIANCE: TESTS REGARDING VECTOR MEAN VALUES

26.1 *Historical summary*

The first comprehensive survey of some of the problems needing to be dealt with was given by Wilks (1932). On the assumption that random samples have been drawn from one or more p-variate normal populations, he drew attention to a number of problems of which three were of particular interest.

Problem 1. To test the equality of the p-dimensional mean vectors of, say, k p-variate populations which have common covariance matrices.

Problem 2. To test the independence of a p_1-set and a p_2-set of variates in a $p = (p_1 + p_2)$-variate population.

Problem 3. To test the equality of the covariance matrices among k p-variate populations.

The above Problems 1 and 2 can be regarded as special cases of a more general formulation of Problem 2 in a 'generalized regression problem', comprising a multivariate normally distributed vector of dependent variables (Bartlett, 1934, p. 337). However, the tables here offered address themselves specifically to the special cases. The tests which Wilks suggested for Problems 1 and 3 were analogous to those already used in the univariate case. The appropriate statistics could be derived from an application of the Neyman–Pearson likelihood ratio principle, although in the case of Problem 3 the weights came out as sample sizes, not the degrees of freedom as used today.† In the simplest cases Wilks found that the probability density distribution of the test statistic could be expressed in relatively straightforward explicit form; in other cases he derived expressions for the sampling moments. A first suggestion (e.g. by Pearson & Wilks, 1933) was that the distribution of a power of the likelihood ratio should be approximated by a beta distribution, having terminals at 0 and 1, and the correct mean and variance. Later Bartlett (1937, 1938), Wald & Brookner (1941), Rao (1948) and Box (1949) suggested approximations which were simpler to apply.

† If the Wishart distribution of sample sums of squares and products is taken as a starting point for the likelihood ratio derivation, the weights are in fact, degrees of freedom.

Subsequent theoretical work has shown that Wilks' criteria and others that have since been suggested are all functions, generally symmetric functions, of the characteristic roots of appropriate determinantal equations, the joint probability density distribution of these roots (on the null hypothesis) having been derived independently in 1939 by Fisher, Girshick, Hsu and Roy. The subsequent development of methodology has been closely bound up with the sampling behaviour of the roots. For a detailed treatment of the theory and some discussion of its applications, see for example Anderson (1958), Kendall & Stuart (particularly **3**, 1966), Roy (1958); for some historical notes, see Bartlett (1967).

26.2 *Test of the general linear hypothesis. Treatment of Wilks' Problem* 1

Basically, as in the simpler problems of analysis of variance, the procedure consists in obtaining from the sample data two independent estimates,

$$\mathbf{A}/\nu_1 \quad \text{and} \quad \mathbf{B}/\nu_2$$

depending on ν_1 and ν_2 degrees of freedom, of what on the null hypothesis, is the same dispersion matrix. The formal model is one in which $\mathbf{X}_{p \times n}$ ($n \geqslant p$) and $\mathbf{Y}_{p \times q}$ are a pair of random matrices whose elements have a joint probability density function

$$(2\pi)^{-\frac{1}{2}p(n+q)} |\boldsymbol{\Sigma}|^{-\frac{1}{2}(n+q)} \exp\left[-\tfrac{1}{2}\operatorname{tr}\boldsymbol{\Sigma}^{-1}\{\mathbf{XX}' + (\mathbf{Y}-\boldsymbol{\mu})(\mathbf{Y}-\boldsymbol{\mu})'\}\right], \tag{217}$$

where $\boldsymbol{\Sigma}_{p \times p}$ is positive definite. In our particular problem, p is the number of variates, while

$$\mathbf{A} = \mathbf{XX}', \quad \mathbf{B} = \mathbf{YY}' \tag{218}$$

are the sums of squares and products matrices for 'error' and 'hypothesis' respectively, having ν_1 and ν_2 degrees of freedom. The null hypothesis to be tested is that $\boldsymbol{\mu} = 0$.

If our problem is to test whether the mean vectors $\boldsymbol{\mu}_t$ ($t = 1, 2, \ldots, k$) in k populations are the same, assuming that these populations have common covariance matrices, then we may define x_{tui} as the ith observation of the uth variate in a sample from the tth population,

$$i = 1, 2, \ldots, n_t; \quad u = 1, 2, \ldots, p; \quad t = 1, 2, \ldots, k.$$

Using an obvious notation for sample mean values, we may write

$$a_{uv} = \sum_{t=1}^{k} \sum_{i=1}^{n_t} (x_{tui} - \overline{x}_{tu.})(x_{tvi} - \overline{x}_{tv.}), \tag{219}$$

$$b_{uv} = \sum_{t=1}^{k} n_t (\overline{x}_{tu.} - \overline{x}_{.u.})(\overline{x}_{tv.} - \overline{x}_{.v.}). \tag{220}$$

Then the matrices $\mathbf{A}$ and $\mathbf{B}$ of (218) become

$$\mathbf{A} = (a_{uv}), \quad \mathbf{B} = (b_{uv}), \tag{221}$$

with

$$\nu_1 = \Sigma n_t - k = N - k, \quad \nu_2 = k - 1 \tag{222}$$

and the likelihood ratio statistic for testing the hypothesis of common population mean vectors is

$$W = \frac{\det(\mathbf{A})}{\det(\mathbf{A}+\mathbf{B})} = \frac{|\mathbf{A}|}{|\mathbf{A}+\mathbf{B}|}, \tag{223}$$

or, more strictly, $W^{\frac{1}{2}N}$.

Table 47, whose meaning and use will be illustrated in §§ (26.5) and (26.7) below, gives values of a factor, C, relating $-\log W$ to a χ^2 distribution having $p\nu_2$ degrees of freedom.

7-2

26.3 *The relation of test criteria to the characteristic roots of a determinantal equation*

The determinantal equation required may be expressed in several forms, e.g.

$$|\mathbf{B} - g\mathbf{A}| = 0, \tag{224}$$

or

$$|\mathbf{B} - t(\mathbf{A} + \mathbf{B})| = 0, \tag{225}$$

where

$$t = g/(1+g). \tag{226}$$

The joint distribution of the p roots of (225) has a density function

$$K(p, m, n) \prod_{i=1}^{p} t_i^m (1-t_i)^n \prod_{i>j} (t_i - t_j) \quad (0 \leqslant t_1 \leqslant \dots \leqslant t_p \leqslant 1), \tag{227}$$

where K is a ratio of products of Γ-functions depending only on p, m and n, with

$$m = \tfrac{1}{2}(|\nu_2 - p| - 1), \quad n = \tfrac{1}{2}(\nu_1 - p - 1). \tag{228}$$

It may be shown that the Wilks' statistic W of equation (223) is a symmetric function of the roots of (224) or (225), namely

$$W = \prod_{i=1}^{p} (1 - t_i) = \prod_{i=1}^{p} \frac{1}{1 + g_i}. \tag{229}$$

The nearer the t_i are to unity, or the larger the g_i, the smaller is W, and the less acceptable the hypothesis tested.

Other tests of the hypothesis of equal mean vectors have been suggested, all expressible in terms of the roots of equations (224) or (225). Here we shall only mention:

(a) the maximum root of (224), $g_{\text{max.}}$, or alternatively $t_{\text{max.}}$ of (225) introduced by Roy (1953);

(b) the sum of the roots suggested by Lawley (1938) and Hotelling (1951), namely

$$\sum_i g_i = \text{tr} (\mathbf{BA}^{-1}); \tag{230}$$

(c) the function

$$\sum_i g_i/(1 + g_i) = \text{tr} [\mathbf{B}(\mathbf{A} + \mathbf{B})^{-1}] \tag{231}$$

introduced by Pillai (1955).

Anderson (1958, p. 221) has shown that the roots of (224) or (225) are the only invariants of the sufficient statistics associated with the problem.

If the null hypothesis of the equality of the k mean vectors $\boldsymbol{\mu}_t$ is not true, $\mathbf{B}$ has a non-central Wishart distribution (James, 1964) and this involves the roots of the non-centrality matrix $\boldsymbol{\Sigma}^{-1}\beta$, where

$$\left.\begin{aligned} \beta &= \sum_{t=1}^{k} n_t (\boldsymbol{\mu}_t - \boldsymbol{\mu}) (\boldsymbol{\mu}_t - \boldsymbol{\mu})', \\ \boldsymbol{\mu} &= \sum_{t=1}^{k} n_t \boldsymbol{\mu}_t/N. \end{aligned}\right\} \tag{232}$$

The distribution of the roots of (224) also depends on the eigenvalues of this $\boldsymbol{\Sigma}^{-1}\beta$, when the null hypothesis is not true.

26.4 *The choice between alternative test statistics*

There is at present no adequate theory to guide the choice of test likely to give greatest power against specified alternatives to the null hypothesis. An interesting investigation was carried out recently by Schatzoff (1966a) involving Monte Carlo sampling. In this he took as his criterion for comparing test statistics not the power, but the 'expected significance level' (ESL)

100

previously developed and illustrated by Dempster & Schatzoff (1965). He explored the behaviour of the ESL for several different structures of the $\boldsymbol{\mu}_i$ of the alternative hypothesis, for various values of p, ν_1 and ν_2 and, within the limits permissible, of the rank of the non-centrality matrix.

His conclusions based on the behaviour of the ESL, may be summarized as follows:

(i) The only situations in which the max. g_i appeared to advantage were those in which the non-centrality matrix was of rank 1. In practice, since exact collinearity is unlikely, this will happen if the mean vectors $\boldsymbol{\mu}_i$ are approximately collinear in the p-dimensional space. A particular case of this would arise if the mean points fell into two compact groups or, indeed, if $k-1$ of them fell close together and a single point was divergent. The sample discriminant functions for discriminating among the k populations are $\mathbf{l'x}$, where $\mathbf{x}$ is the column vector of the p variables and the column vector $\mathbf{l}$ satisfies

$$[\mathbf{A} - t(\mathbf{A} + \mathbf{B})]\mathbf{l} = 0,$$

corresponding to (225). The adequate number of discriminant functions will depend on the dimensionality of the space in which the means of the k populations lie and so is the number of non-zero eigenvalues of the non-centrality matrix $\boldsymbol{\Sigma}^{-1}\beta$.

(ii) Apart from this case, there appeared no clear advantage in favour of any one of the three statistics defined in equations (229), (230) and (231).

Interesting studies involving comparisons of power have also been made by Pillai & Jayachandran (1967, 1968). As far as they go, these results seem to confirm our decision to include only tables of percentage points for W (Table 47) and for the maximum root (Tables 48 and 49).

26.5 *The Wilks test; explanation and illustration of Table* 47

Table 47 reproduces in modified form the tables of Schatzoff (1966b), to which Pillai & Gupta (1969) made some substantial additions. Originally Schatzoff had computed values of percentage points of W of equation (223), but at M. S. Bartlett's suggestion the form was modified and a conversion factor C was tabled, which made use of the fact that under the null hypothesis $-\{\nu_1 - \frac{1}{2}(p - \nu_2 + 1)\}\log W$ is distributed asymptotically as $C\chi^2$, the χ^2 having $p\nu_2$ degrees of freedom. As a consequence, if $-\{\nu_1 - \frac{1}{2}(p - \nu_2 + 1)\}\log W$ is calculated from the data, and divided by $C(\nu_1, \nu_2, M = \nu_1 - p + 1)$, the statistical significance of the departure from hypothesis can be judged by referring the result to a table of the percentage points of χ^2, with $\nu = p\nu_2$ degrees of freedom. As will be seen, the factor C tends steadily to unity as ν_1 and therefore M increases. We repeat here equation (222),

$$\nu_1 = \Sigma n_t - k = N - k, \quad \nu_2 = k - 1. \tag{222 bis}$$

By using the concept of total available degrees of freedom

$$n' = N - 1 = \nu_1 + \nu_2,$$

regarding the p variables as a first set of $p = p_1$ variables and the $k-1$ contrasts between the group means as a second set of $p_2 = k - 1 = \nu_2$ variables, the χ^2 criterion can be written in the symmetrical form

$$-\{n' - \tfrac{1}{2}(p_1 + p_2 + 1)\}\log W \quad \text{for} \quad \nu = p_1 p_2 \text{ degrees of freedom.}$$

This is the form preferred by Bartlett and is indeed the form in which Table 47 is used to answer Problem 2 (see § 26.8 below), indicating how both problems may be regarded as special cases of the generalized regression problem (Bartlett, 1934).

101

When the means of k populations are collinear, Wilks' likelihood ratio criterion can be factorized into what has been termed a direction factor and a collinearity factor, corresponding to a hypothetical discriminant function. This possibility provides some more exact tests (see Bartlett, 1951; Williams, 1967).

To economize in space, the original Schatzoff–Pillai & Gupta tables have been modified in two respects:

(a) The higher entries for M, instead of following the harmonic series $20, 24, \ldots, 120, \infty$ have been taken at $10, 12, \ldots, 60, \infty$. The entries at 14, 16, 18, 24, 40 and 120 have thus been omitted and considerable space saved. The entries for $M = 15$ were found by interpolation in the original tables. Adequately accurate interpolation for C when $n > 10$ can then be carried out using $60/n$ as argument.

(b) The original tables gave factors for the 100α per cent point with $\alpha = 0.10, 0.05, 0.025, 0.01, 0.005$. We give only values for $\alpha = 0.05$ and 0.01. If we write

$$d = C_{0.01} - C_{0.05}$$

it is found that, with sufficient accuracy, if $M \geqslant 2$

$$C_{0.10} = C_{0.05} - 0.47d, \quad C_{0.025} = C_{0.01} - 0.56d, \quad C_{0.005} = C_{0.01} + 0.40d.$$

To illustrate this, take the case where $p = 6$, $v_2 = 10$; we have

				From proposed formulae:		
M	$C_{0.05}$	$C_{0.01}$	d	$C_{0.10}$	$C_{0.025}$	$C_{0.005}$
2	1·307	1·348	0·041	1·288	1·325	1·364+
5	1·120	1·131	0·011	1·115	1·125	1·135
10	1·051	1·055	0·004	1·049	1·053	1·057−

Reference back to Schatzoff's original tables (1966) will show that the interpolated values are correct, except that the first and third figures in the last column should be 1·365 and 1·056 respectively. Clearly for computing purposes, we may use the formulae

$$C_{0.10} = 1.47C_{0.05} - 0.47C_{0.01}, \quad C_{0.025} = 0.56C_{0.05} + 0.44C_{0.01}, \quad C_{0.005} = -0.40C_{0.05} + 1.40C_{0.01}.$$

The factors 0·47, 0·56 and 0·40 were obtained by determining the ratios of inter-percentage-point differences for seventeen different combinations of p, v_2. As the results were surprisingly constant with no very clear trend, the ratios were averaged for $M = 1, 2, 3$ and 4 and this led to the factors quoted.

It should be noted that results are given for the number of variables $p = 2(1)10$, while the v_2 values are only for even integers. Many of the missing panels in the table may be filled by noting that

$$C(p, v_2, M = v_1 - p + 1) = C(v_2, p, M),$$

where M in the second expression retains its original value. For example, if we wish to find $C_{0.01}$ for $p = 4$, $v_2 = 3$, $v_1 = 18$, we have

$$C_{0.01}(4, 3, 15) = C_{0.01}(3, 4, 15) = 1.009.$$

The structure of the table is based on Schatzoff's method of derivation, in which it was necessary for either p or v_2 to be even. This limitation was removed in Pillai & Gupta's approach. However, there is every reason for expecting that when both p and v_2 are odd, a satisfactory value of C can be found by interpolation.

Case where p (or v_2) = 2

Values of C for this case were not tabulated by Schatzoff because the exact percentage points of W can here be obtained from tables of percentage points of either the beta distribution (*B.T.S.* **1**, Table 16) or of the F-distribution (Table 5 above) as follows:

Write $x^2 = W(2, v_1, v_2)$, then

$$f(x) = \frac{\Gamma(v_1 + v_2 - 1)}{\Gamma(v_1 - 1)\,\Gamma(v_2)}\, x^{v_1 - 2}(1 - x)^{v_2 - 1}. \tag{233}$$

Alternatively, if
$$F = \frac{1 - \sqrt{W}}{\sqrt{W}}\,\frac{v_1 - 1}{v_2} \tag{234}$$

the F-table, using equation (52), may be entered with

degrees of freedom $(1) = 2v_2$,   degrees of freedom $(2) = 2(v_1 - 1)$.

Low values of x and high values of F will be significant. To complete Table 47 and make interpolation at the boundary easier, panels with $v_2 = 2$ (remembering the reversibility of p and v_2) were added to the Schatzoff–Pillai results.

26.6   The maximum root test; explanation of Tables 48 and 49

Although these tables to some extent overlap, it was decided to include both because each provides certain results not given in the other. Both give upper percentage points for the maximum root, $t_{\max.}$, of the solution of the determinantal equation (225).

(*a*) *Table* 49. This was computed by Foster & Rees (1957), and Foster (1957, 1958) and gave to four decimal places the five 100α percentage points for

$$\alpha = 0.20,\ 0.15,\ 0.10,\ 0.05,\ 0.01$$

for $p = 2, 3,$ and 4 and certain values of v_1 and v_2. Because of the form of the distribution of the greatest root, which can be derived from equation (227), Foster & Rees described it as a 'generalized Beta distribution', $I_x(p; m+1, n+1)$. The original tables covered twenty-three pages but are here cut down to nine pages by omitting a large number of entries with high values of v_1. The values retained have been chosen at harmonic intervals, so that interpolation is possible using the simple Bessel second difference formula (319). The scheme will be seen to be as follows:

(i) $p = 2$, $v_2 = 2, 3(2)21$;

   $v_1 = 5(2)41, 51, 54\cdot3,\dagger$ $61(10)101, 121, 161$.

It will be seen that the sequence $v_1 = 33, 41, 54\cdot3, 81, 161, \infty$ (where the percentage points all approach zero), turns into the sequence 5, 4, 3, 2, 1, 0 if the argument is taken as $160/(v_1 - 1)$.

(ii) $p = 3$; $v_2 = 3(1)10$; $v_1 = 4(2)46(4)70, 98, 194$. Again, the sequence 50, 66, 98, 194, ∞ turns into the sequence 4, 3, 2, 1, 0 on taking the argument as $192/(v_1 - 2)$.

(iii) $p = 4$; $v_2 = 4(1)11$; $v_1 = 5(2)47(4)71, 99, 195$. The sequence 51, 67, 99, 195, ∞ becomes the sequence 4, 3, 2, 1, 0 on taking as argument $192/(v_1 - 3)$.

The use of harmonic intervals for very high values of v_1 was suggested by Foster & Rees, but we have found it possible to extend their use for medium values and so to reduce the total table pages by fourteen. The user who wishes easier interpolation to the full four decimal places can refer back to the original tables published in *Biometrika*.

† The artificial values required to give the harmonic sequence were derived from the basic table by interpolation.

(b) *Table* 48. This was computed by Pillai and a number of collaborators, starting with Pillai (1956). References to the original sources of publication of tables covering values of p from 2 to 20 are given in Pillai (1967). Complete tables up to $p = 20$ have been given by Pillai in mimeographed form (Reports No. 51 (1965) and No. 72 (1966) of the Department of Statistics, Purdue University). All these tables contain only 5 and 1 per cent points of the maximum root, $t_{\max}$. In the present Table 48 we give these percentage points to four decimal places, adjusting the entries for large n so as to make interpolation possible using the argument $240/n$. The range $p = 2(1)10$ only is covered.

Two points should be recorded: (a) Where, as in most cases, the Pillai table give a result to five decimal places and the last digit is a 5, we have *reduced* the entry in cutting down to four decimals, e.g. $0 \cdot 84775$ becomes $0 \cdot 8477$. (b) Pillai's entries for the argument n were 5(5)30, 40, 60, 80, 100, 130, 160, 200, 300, 500, 1000. To make interpolation easier we have added entries at 35, 45 and 50 and changed the higher entries to 48, 60, 80, 120, 240, ∞, making interpolation with argument $240/n$ straightforward. The new entries were obtained by interpolation in Pillai's table; for high values of n this was done by taking as argument the reciprocal of n and using Lagrangian interpolation, with unequal argument intervals. To find that the range between $n = 120$ and ∞ could be spanned with the help of a single entry at $n = 240$ was unexpected, but conforms with what was found in the case of Table 49. Some comments on interpolation for argument m are given in § 37.1 below.

We have followed Pillai's notation, using the parameters m and n of the fundamental equation (227). In the problem of testing the equality of the k p-dimensional mean vectors,

$$
\begin{aligned}
m &= \tfrac{1}{2}(|\nu_2 - p| - 1), & n &= \tfrac{1}{2}(\nu_1 - p - 1), \\
&= \tfrac{1}{2}(|k - p - 1| - 1) & &= \tfrac{1}{2}(N - k - p - 1).
\end{aligned}
\right\}
\tag{235}
$$

26.7 *An illustrative example*

Example 57. We take as an illustration the two dimensional example ($p = 2$) first used by Pearson & Wilks (1938, pp. 356, 369–72) and developed further by Kendall & Stuart (1966, **3**, pp. 272–3, Ex. 42.2). Five samples were available, each containing twelve specimens of aluminium die-castings on which two measurements of (i) tensile strength, x (in $1000\,\text{lb/in}^2$) and (ii) hardness, y (in one half Rockwell's E) were taken. Thus

$$
p = 2, \quad k = 5, \quad N = 60, \quad n_t = 12.
$$

The problem is to test the hypothesis that the mean x and mean y in the five populations are the same. As there is found to be no evidence that the covariance matrices in the populations differ (see Example 58 below), it will be assumed that in testing for mean values, we may use common estimates of $\mathrm{var}\,x$, $\mathrm{var}\,y$ and $\mathrm{cov}\,xy$.

The basic data required are as follows:

t	Mean x	Mean y	Sums of squares about means x	Sums of squares about means y	Sums of products about means
1	33·399	68·49	78·948	1247·18	214·18
2	28·216	68·02	223·695	2519·31	657·62
3	30·313	66·57	57·448	1241·78	190·63
4	33·150	76·12	187·618	1473·44	375·91
5	34·269	69·92	88·456	1171·73	259·18
Totals	159·347	349·12	636·165	7653·44	1697·52

From this we find:†

Source of variation	Degrees of freedom	Sums of squares, x	Sums of squares, y	Sums of products, xy
Between samples	$\nu_2 = 4$	306·089	663·26	214·89
Within samples	$\nu_1 = 55$	636·165	7653·44	1697·52
Total	59	942·254	8316·70	1912·41

Hence

$$|\mathbf{A}| = \begin{vmatrix} 636\cdot165 & 1697\cdot52 \\ 1697\cdot52 & 7653\cdot44 \end{vmatrix} = 1,987,277,$$

$$|\mathbf{A}+\mathbf{B}| = \begin{vmatrix} 942\cdot254 & 1912\cdot41 \\ 1912\cdot41 & 8316\cdot70 \end{vmatrix} = 4,179,132,$$

$$W = |\mathbf{A}|/|\mathbf{A}+\mathbf{B}| = 0\cdot4755.$$

To enter Table 47 we have $M = \nu_1 - p + 1 = 54$ and

$$C(p, \nu_2, M) = C(2, 4, 54) = C(4, 2, 54).$$

Clearly the factor C may be taken as unity, and consequently

$$-\{\nu_1 - \tfrac{1}{2}(p - \nu_2 + 1)\} \log 0\cdot4755 = 40\cdot52$$

may be referred to the χ^2 distribution with degrees of freedom $p\nu_2 = 8$. Table 3 shows that the upper 0·01 per cent point of χ_8^2 is 31·83 so that there is no doubt whatever about the significance of the differences among the means.

To apply the maximum root test we must solve the determinantal equation (225), or $|\mathbf{B} - t(\mathbf{A}+\mathbf{B})| = 0$, where the elements of $|\mathbf{B}|$ are given in the top row of the last table. The solution gives

$$t_1 = 0\cdot07739, \quad t_2 = 0\cdot48454.$$

As a check we find that $W = (1 - t_1)(1 - t_2) = 0\cdot4756$. We can now enter Table 49 with $\nu_1 = 55, \nu_2 = 4$, or Table 48 with $m = \tfrac{1}{2}(|\nu_2 - p| - 1) = 0\cdot5, n = \tfrac{1}{2}(\nu_1 - p - 1) = 26$. It is clear that $t_{\max.} = 0\cdot4845$ falls far beyond the 1 per cent point, confirming the result of applying the W-test.

Since $p = 2$ it is possible and perhaps instructive to use these data in Fig. 8 to illustrate the assumptions and conclusions. For convenience in the diagram we have taken one half unit of Rockwell's E as the unit of y. It follows that common estimates of the within population variances and correlation are:

$$s_x^2 = \frac{636\cdot165}{55} = 11\cdot5666, \quad s_y^2 = \frac{7653\cdot44}{55 \times 4} = 34\cdot788, \quad r_{xy} = \frac{1697\cdot52}{110 s_x s_y} = 0\cdot7693,$$

$$s_x = 3\cdot401, \qquad s_y = 5\cdot898,$$

$$\bar{x} = 31\cdot869, \qquad \bar{y} = 34\cdot912.$$

To transform to principal axes through the sample mean point $\bar{x}, \bar{y}$ we must rotate through an angle θ given by

$$\theta = \tfrac{1}{2} \tan^{-1} \frac{2 r s_x s_y}{s_x^2 - s_y^2} = -26° 31'.$$

† The numerical results below differ to an unimportant extent from those quoted by Pearson & Wilks; it is possible that an additional figure in y was used in the original calculations.

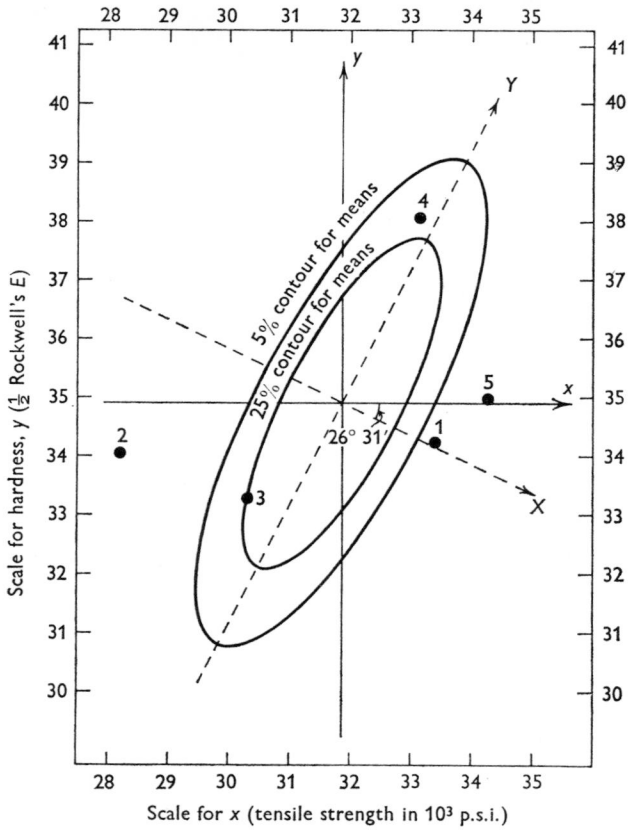

Fig. 8. Tests on samples of aluminium die castings. $k = 5$, $n = 12$.

The transformed variates are:

$$X = (x - \bar{x}) \cos \theta + (y - \bar{y}) \sin \theta = 0 \cdot 8948(x - \bar{x}) - 0 \cdot 4465(y - \bar{y}),$$

$$Y = -(x - \bar{x}) \sin \theta + (y - \bar{y}) \cos \theta = 0 \cdot 4465(x - \bar{x}) + 0 \cdot 8948(y - \bar{y}),$$

$$S_X^2 = 3 \cdot 8665, \quad S_Y^2 = 42 \cdot 4932, \quad r_{XY} = 0.$$

If the hypothesis of equal mean vectors were true, the means $\bar{X}$, $\bar{Y}$ of samples of twelve observations should be distributed independently about the grand mean with variances which may be estimated as

$$S_X^2/12 = 0 \cdot 3222, \quad S_Y^2/12 = 3 \cdot 5411.$$

The diagram shows the transformed axes, the plots of the five group means $\bar{X}_t$, $\bar{Y}_t$ and the estimated elliptic contours within which, on the hypothesis tested, there is a probability of (a) 0·25, (b) 0·05 that a group mean should lie.

The departure from hypothesis clearly lies in the direction of the transformed X variate axis, and it is this that the significant root of $|\mathbf{B} - t(\mathbf{A} + \mathbf{B})| = 0$, or $t_2 = t_{\max.} = 0 \cdot 4845$ is picking out.

26.8 *Tests of independence of two sets of variates. Treatment of Wilks' Problem* 2

In this case the independence property may be examined as follows. Let $x_1, x_2, ..., x_{p_1}$ and $y_1, y_2, ..., y_{p_2}$ be $p = p_1 + p_2$ correlated, normally distributed variables, with $p_1 \leqslant p_2$. The

106

hypothesis that the variation among the x set is independent of that among the y set is equivalent to the hypothesis that, in the linear regression equations

$$E(x_s) = \sum_{i=1}^{p_2} \beta_{is} y_i \quad (s = 1, 2, ..., p_1), \tag{236}$$

the regression coefficients β_{is} are all zero. If this is true we may obtain two independent estimates of the population dispersion matrix of the $x_1, x_2, ..., x_{p_1}$ variables, namely

(a) the sum of squares and products matrix for the x's due to the fitted regression functions, namely

$$\mathbf{B} = \mathbf{S}_{12} \mathbf{S}_{22}^{-1} \mathbf{S}_{12}', \tag{237}$$

which is based on $\nu_2 = p_2$ degrees of freedom;

(b) the sum of squares and products matrix of the x's due to departure from the fitted regressions, or the 'error' matrix

$$\mathbf{A} = \mathbf{S}_{11} - \mathbf{B}, \tag{238}$$

which is based on $\nu_1 = N - p_2 - 1$ degrees of freedom, N being the number of observations.

Here, $\mathbf{S}_{11}$ and $\mathbf{S}_{22}$ are the sum of squares and products matrices of the p_1 sample x's and p_2 sample y's, respectively; $\mathbf{S}_{12}$ is the sum of products matrix between the p_1 set of x's and p_2 set of y's; $\mathbf{S}_{12}'$ is the transpose of $\mathbf{S}_{12}$ and $\mathbf{S}_{22}^{-1}$ the inverse of $\mathbf{S}_{22}$. For the underlying theory see, for example, Anderson (1958, pp. 241–3).

It follows that as in the problem of § 26.2 above, the likelihood ratio with which to test the hypothesis of independence is

$$W = \frac{|\mathbf{A}|}{|\mathbf{A} + \mathbf{B}|} = \frac{\mathbf{S}_{11} - \mathbf{S}_{12} \mathbf{S}_{22}^{-1} \mathbf{S}_{12}'}{\mathbf{S}_{11}} = \prod_{i=1}^{p_1} (1 - t_i). \tag{239}$$

This means that we can use Table 47 with

$$\nu_1 = N - p_2 - 1, \quad \nu_2 = p_2.$$

If the largest root, $t_{\max.}$, is found then Table 49 may be used with these degrees of freedom, or Table 48 with

$$m = \tfrac{1}{2}(p_2 - p_1 - 1), \quad n = \tfrac{1}{2}(N - p_1 - p_2 - 2).$$

Illustrations of the application of this test have been given by Foster & Rees (1957, pp. 240–2) and Pillai (1960, pp. 5–6).

27. TESTS OF THE EQUALITY OF COVARIANCE MATRICES IN k POPULATIONS

27.1 *General statement of the problem and approximations*

This is Wilks' Problem 3. We suppose that the sample from the tth p-variate normal population contains n_t observations; write

$$a_{uvt} = \sum_{i=1}^{n_t} (x_{cui} - \bar{x}_{tu.}) (x_{tvi} - \bar{x}_{tv.}). \tag{240}$$

Then $s_{uvt} = a_{uvt}/\nu_t$, where $\nu_t = n_t - 1$, is the unbiased estimate of the covariance of the uth and vth characters in the tth population ($t = 1, 2, ..., k$). Further, we shall write

$$a_{uv} = \sum_t a_{uvt} \quad \text{and} \quad s_{uv} = \sum_t \nu_t s_{uvt}/N = \sum_t a_{uvt}/N, \tag{241}$$

where

$$N = \sum_t \nu_t.$$

107

Then the likelihood ratio criterion for testing the hypothesis of equal population covariance matrices may be taken in the form

$$V = \frac{\prod\limits_{t=1}^{k} |s_{uvt}|^{\frac{1}{2}\nu_t}}{|s_{uv}|^{\frac{1}{2}N}} = \frac{\prod\limits_{t=1}^{k} |\mathbf{A}_t|^{\frac{1}{2}\nu_t}}{|\mathbf{A}|^{\frac{1}{2}N}} \times \frac{N^{\frac{1}{2}pN}}{\prod\limits_{t} \nu_t^{\frac{1}{2}p\nu_t}}. \tag{242}$$

The first form of expression for V was that derived by Wilks (1932, p. 489, equation (42)), except that his sums of squares and products were divided by $n_t = \nu_t + 1$, and similarly n_t was used in the powers of the determinants.

There are no tables of significance points for V in the general case, but, as will appear below, Korin (1968) has computed a table of approximate upper 5 per cent points in the case where the ν_t are all equal. The best approximations in the general case appear to be those suggested by Box (1949). He took as his test statistic

$$M = -2 \log V = N \log |s_{uv}| - \sum_{t=1}^{k} (\nu_t \log |s_{uvt}|). \tag{243}$$

He then derived the following χ^2 and F-approximations to the distribution of M:

(a) χ^2 approximation

$$M \sim \chi^2_{f_1}/(1 - D_1), \tag{244}$$

where

$$f_1 = \tfrac{1}{2}p(p+1)(k-1), \tag{245}$$

$$D_1 = \frac{2p^2 + 3p - 1}{6(p+1)(k-1)} \left\{ \sum_{t=1}^{k} \frac{1}{\nu_t} - \frac{1}{N} \right\}, \tag{246}$$

$$= \frac{(2p^2 + 3p - 1)(k+1)}{6(p+1)k\nu_0} \quad \text{if} \quad \nu_t = \nu_0 \quad (t = 1, 2, ..., k). \tag{247}$$

Note that the factor 2 in front of p^2 was omitted in Box's equation (69) but not in his (68).

(b) F-approximation

$$M \sim bF_{f_1, f_2}, \tag{248}$$

where f_1 and D_1 required in the following equations are given by (245) and (246),

$$f_2 = \frac{f_1 + 2}{D_2 - D_1^2}, \tag{249}$$

$$D_2 = \frac{(p-1)(p+2)}{6(k-1)} \left\{ \sum_{t=1}^{k} \frac{1}{\nu_t^2} - \frac{1}{N^2} \right\}, \tag{250}$$

$$= \frac{(p-1)(p+2)(k^2 + k + 1)}{6k^2\nu_0^2} \quad \text{if} \quad \nu_t = \nu_0 \quad (t = 1, 2, ..., k), \tag{251}$$

$$b = \frac{f_1}{1 - D_1 - f_1/f_2}. \tag{252}$$

In the case where the k degrees of freedom are all equal, the χ^2 approximation is very easy to apply, f_1 being always an integer and D_1 easily determined from equation (247). The more accurate approximation, using the variance ratio F, requires more computation as it may be necessary to interpolate for both f_2 and f_1, if the latter is large. Some comparisons of the accuracy of the approximations are made in §27.2 below.

27.2 *The case of equal degrees of freedom* (*Table* 50)

The table, due to Korin (1969), gives approximations to the upper 5 per cent significance points of the M of equation (243), when $\nu_1 = \nu_2 = \ldots = \nu_k = \nu_0$. The computations were carried out using a series expansion in terms of gamma functions and exponential series due to Box (1949, pp. 320–3). The number of terms in the expansions taken was considered by Korin to be more than adequate for the accuracy of the table.

It is probable that Box's χ^2 and F-approximations, for given p and k, will increase in accuracy as ν_0 increases. The following comparisons were therefore made by Pearson (1969) at the highest values of ν_0 given in Table 50.

Accuracy of Box's approximations illustrated on the 5 per cent points of M at the highest values of ν_0 given in Korin's table

p, ν_0 ...	2, 10					3, 13		
k ...	2	4	6	8	10	2	6	10
Series	8·76	18·61	27·33	35·61	43·64	14·43	48·66	79·72
χ^2 approx.	8·76	18·60	27·30	35·56	43·58	14·39	48·49	79·43
F-approx.	—	—	—	—	43·64	14·43	48·63	79·69

p, ν_0 ...	4, 15			5, 16		6, 20	
k ...	2	6	10	2	7	2	5
Series	21·47	76·38	127·1	30·21	130·6	39·11	122·7
χ^2 approx.	21·37	75·97	126·4	29·99	129·6	38·84	121·9
F-approx.	21·45	76·32	127·2	30·17	130·7	39·06	122·8

It is clear that the F-approximation is remarkably accurate. However, the simpler χ^2 approximation will usually be adequate for practical purposes. Both Box and Korin made some additional comparisons. According to Box's results the errors in approximating to the 1 per cent points are, proportionally, only a little greater than those for the 5 per cent points. When the ν_t are unequal, little information is available, but Box made a few comparisons in his Table 9. His tentative conclusion was that if p and k were not greater than five and all ν_t were nine or more, the F-approximation should be fairly satisfactory. Of course, in a planned experiment it is likely that the ν_t will be equal.

Example 58. We take the data for the aluminium die castings used in Example 57. Here $p = 2$, $k = 5$, $\nu_t = \nu_0 = 11$. From the last three columns of the table on p. 104 above we compute the 2×2 determinants $|s_{uvt}| = \frac{1}{121}|a_{uvt}|$, find their logarithms and sum:

t	$|s_{uvt}|$	$\log_{10} s_{uvt}$
1	434·62	2·63811
2	1083·41	3·03479
3	289·24	2·46126
4	1116·82	3·04798
5	301·42	2·47917
Sum		13·66131

Further, from (241)

$$s_{uv} = \tfrac{1}{55} \sum_t a_{uvt}$$

and hence

$$|s_{uv}| = \begin{vmatrix} 11·567 & 30·864 \\ 30·864 & 139·153 \end{vmatrix} = 657·00.$$

It follows from equation (243) that

$$M = 2·30259\{55 \log_{10} 657·00 - 11 \times 13·66131\} = 10·80.$$

Table 50 does not give a 5 per cent significance level for $p = 2$, $k = 5$, $\nu_0 = 11$, but a rough extrapolation suggests that $M_{0.05}$ is at $22 \cdot 85$, so that the differences between sample variance–covariance matrices are far from significant.

If we use Box's χ^2 approximation, we find from (245) and (247) that

$$f_1 = 12, \quad D_1 = 0 \cdot 07879, \quad M \sim \chi_{12}^2 \times 1 \cdot 086,$$

giving $22 \cdot 82$ as an estimate of the 5 per cent significance level. It was clearly reasonable to assume in Example 57, when testing for the difference in mean vectors, that the five populations had a common covariance matrix.

27.3 *The case of testing equality of covariance matrices in $k = 2$ populations*

This special case is of some interest, and here three different test criteria have been suggested. In the first place we have the likelihood ratio statistic, V, given by equation (242) with $k = 2$. Box's approximations to the distribution of $M = -2 \log V$ may again be used. Having now only two independent estimates, $\mathbf{A}_1/\nu_1$ and $\mathbf{A}_2/\nu_2$ of the population covariance matrices, assumed the same on the hypothesis tested, we may relate V to the roots of

$$|\mathbf{A}_2 - g\mathbf{A}_1| = 0 \tag{224 bis}$$

or of

$$|\mathbf{A}_2 - t(\mathbf{A}_1 + \mathbf{A}_2)| = 0. \tag{225 bis}$$

Anderson has shown (1958, pp. 258–9) that the statistic

$$V_1 = \frac{|\mathbf{A}_1|^{\frac{1}{2}\nu_1}|\mathbf{A}_2|^{\frac{1}{2}\nu_2}}{|\mathbf{A}_1 + \mathbf{A}_2|^{\frac{1}{2}(\nu_1 + \nu_2)}} = \prod_{i=1}^{p} \frac{g_i^{\frac{1}{2}\nu_2}}{(1 + g_i)^{\frac{1}{2}(\nu_1 + \nu_2)}} \tag{253}$$

$$= \prod_{i=1}^{p} t_i^{\frac{1}{2}\nu_2}(1 - t_i)^{\frac{1}{2}\nu_1}, \tag{254}$$

where g_i and $t_i = g_i/(1 + g_i)$ are as before the characteristic roots of (224) and (225). Here $V_1 = cV$, where $c = \{\nu_1^{\nu_1} \nu_2^{\nu_2}/(\nu_1 + \nu_2)^{\nu_1 + \nu_2}\}^{\frac{1}{2}p}$, and it follows that the hypothesis tested becomes less likely as V_1 decreases, which will happen when one or more of the roots, t_i, approach zero *or* unity.

On the other hand it has been pointed out by Pillai & Gupta (1969) and Pillai & Jayachandran (1968) that

$$U = \frac{|\mathbf{A}_1|}{|\mathbf{A}_1 + \mathbf{A}_2|} = \prod_{i=1}^{p} (1 - t_i) \tag{255}$$

will have the same distribution, under the null hypothesis, as Wilks' statistic, W, considered in §§ 26.2 and 26.3 above. Hence lower significance levels for U may be obtained by entering Table 47 with ν_1, ν_2 and $M = \nu_1 - p + 1$. U is however *not* in this case the likelihood ratio statistic as may be seen by comparing equations (254) and (255); it will only detect significance when one or more of the t_i are large.

Consider the case where the samples have the same number of observations so that $\nu_1 = \nu_2$. The correspondence between $\mathbf{A}_1$ and $\mathbf{A}_2$ will be close when all the roots g_i are near $1 \cdot 0$ and all the t_i near $0 \cdot 5$. Departure of the t_i from $0 \cdot 5$ in *either* direction will reduce the values of V and V_1. But this effect may not be detected by U, which will not pick up the presence of one or more small values of t_i. To discover these it may be necessary to reverse the $\mathbf{A}$'s in equation (225 bis). Roy's maximum root test may of course also be used in conjunction with Tables 48 and 49.

The situation is somewhat analogous to that which holds when $p = 1$, the likelihood ratio test cutting off unequal areas from the two tails of the F-distribution, whereas the standard procedure for a two-tailed test would base the rejection region on two equal tail areas. However, when $p > 2$, it is not easy to grasp the physical significance of the roots g_i or t_i, and therefore it is hard to be clear what differences in the variance–covariance structure of the two populations are likely to be detected by the U or maximum root test.

28. Tests involving the roots of a single p-variate matrix

28.1 *Definitions; the likelihood ratio criterion and approximations to its distribution (Table 53)*

Suppose that a random sample of N observations, x_{ui}, is taken from a p-variate normal population having covariance matrix $\mathbf{\Sigma}$. Write

$$a_{uv} = \sum_{i=1}^{N} (x_{ui} - \bar{x}_{u\cdot})(x_{vi} - \bar{x}_{v\cdot}) \quad (u, v = 1, 2, \ldots, p; \ i = 1, 2, \ldots, N). \tag{256}$$

The sample covariance matrix is $\mathbf{S} = \nu^{-1}(a_{uv})$, where $\nu = N - 1$. Then the distribution of $\mathbf{A} = \nu\mathbf{S}$ is the well-known Wishart distribution $W(\mathbf{\Sigma}, \nu)$.

Denote the characteristic roots of

$$|\mathbf{A}\mathbf{\Sigma}^{-1} - c\mathbf{I}| = 0 \tag{257}$$

by $0 < c_1 \leqslant c_2 \leqslant \ldots \leqslant c_p$. Then the joint distribution of the roots has a density function

$$K(p, m) \prod_{i=1}^{p} c_i^m \exp\left(-\tfrac{1}{2} \sum_{i=1}^{p} c_i\right) \prod_{i>j} (c_i - c_j), \tag{258}$$

where $m = \tfrac{1}{2}(\nu - p - 1)$ and K depends on p and ν only.

As pointed out by Anderson (1958, pp. 264–6), the modified likelihood ratio statistic for testing the hypothesis that the population covariance matrix is $\mathbf{\Sigma} = \mathbf{\Sigma}_0$ may be expressed in the form

$$U = \left\{\frac{|\mathbf{S}|}{|\mathbf{\Sigma}_0|}\right\}^{\frac{1}{2}\nu} \exp\left(\tfrac{1}{2}\nu p - \tfrac{1}{2}\nu \operatorname{tr} \mathbf{S}\mathbf{\Sigma}_0^{-1}\right) \tag{259}$$

$$= \left(\frac{e}{\nu}\right)^{\frac{1}{2}p\nu} \prod_{i=1}^{p} (c_i^{\frac{1}{2}\nu}) \exp\left(-\tfrac{1}{2}\sum_i c_i\right), \tag{260}$$

where the c_i are the roots of equation (257).

Writing
$$L = -2 \log U = \nu \log |\mathbf{\Sigma}_0| - \nu p - \nu \log |\mathbf{S}| + \nu \operatorname{tr}(\mathbf{S}\mathbf{\Sigma}_0^{-1}) \tag{261}$$

Korin (1968) has used the technique of Box (1949) to express the distribution of L under the null hypothesis in the form of an asymptotic series of central χ^2 distributions. By this means he has derived the upper 5 and 1 per cent points of L shown in Table 53 for a limited range of values of p and ν. Some additional values from his thesis have been added to those given in the published paper. As in the case of the test for equality of covariance matrices (§ 27.1 above) Korin used the Box technique to derive χ^2 and F-approximations to the distribution of L.

(a) *χ^2 approximation*
$$L \sim \chi^2_{f_1}/(1 - D_1), \tag{262}$$

where
$$f_1 = \tfrac{1}{2}p(p + 1), \tag{263}$$

$$D_1 = \{2p + 1 - 2/(p + 1)\}/(6\nu). \tag{264}$$

(b) *F-approximation*
$$L \sim bF_{f_1, f_2}, \tag{265}$$

where f_1 and D_1 required in the following equations have been given by (263) and (264),

$$f_2 = \frac{f_1 + 2}{D_2 - D_1^2}, \tag{266}$$

$$D_2 = (p-1)(p+2)/(6\nu^2), \tag{267}$$

$$b = \frac{f_1}{1 - D_1 - f_1/f_2}. \tag{268}$$

Apart from the different expressions for D_1 and D_2, these equations correspond to equations (244)–(252). Korin made a number of comparisons between the series values (representing the true values) and those obtained from (262) and (265). Below, we select a few comparisons from his extensive Table 2. For given p, the approximations improve as ν increases and for most purposes the χ^2 approximation should be adequate when ν exceeds the values given in Table 53.

Significance points and probabilities for L from the χ^2 series and the approximations

		$p = 2, \nu = 6$		$p = 5, \nu = 20$		$p = 8, \nu = 40$	
5%	Series	8·94	0·0500	27·60	0·0500	55·03	0·0500
	χ^2	8·88	·0511	27·43	·0520	54·83	·0518
	F	8·93	·0502	27·6	·0512	55·0	·0494
1%	Series	13·00	0·0100	33·79	0·0100	63·28	0·0100
	χ^2	12·90	·0104	33·56	·0107	63·03	·0106
	F	13·00	·6100	33·80	·0103	63·2	·0102

28.2 Tests based on the largest and smallest roots of the Wishart matrix (Table 51)

If we write $C = C_{\max.}$ and $c = c_{\min.}$ as the largest and smallest roots, respectively, of the determinantal equation (257), approximate values of certain upper percentage points of C and lower percentage points of c were derived by Hanumara & Thompson (1968), using some earlier results of Nanda and Pillai. The first authors gave 100α per cent points for both C and c, to four significant figures and the following range of arguments.

$$\alpha = 0·05, 0·025, 0·010, 0·005; \quad p = 2(1)10;$$
$$\nu = 2(1)10(5)30(10)100.$$

At the same time Pillai & Chang (1968, 1970) were completing a similar table for the upper percentage points of C. The quantity they tabled was C/ν and the scope of their table was somewhat wider than that of Hanumara & Thompson in that they added results for $\alpha = 0·10$, gave five significant figures for the three outer per cent points and covered the argument range:

$$p = 2(1)20; \quad \nu = 2(1)20(2)30(5)50(10)100(20)160, 200.$$

Both pairs of authors gave some examination to the accuracy of the approximations involved and concluded that their tabulations should not be in error by more than a unit in the last digit.

Table 51 is based on a combination of the two tables referred to. Compression has been carried out in two respects:

(a) by taking as argument for ν the values

$$2(1)12, 15(5)30(10)100(20)200,$$

the figures in certain rows being obtained by appropriate interpolation;

(b) by giving only 5 and 1 per cent points. As when presenting Table 47 (see § 26.5) a remarkable constancy was noticed in the ratios of inter-percentage-point differences. Writing

$$d = C_{0 \cdot 01} - C_{0 \cdot 05}$$

it was found that for $\nu \geqslant 20$, the 10, 2·5 and 0·5 per cent points could be found with sufficient accuracy for most purposes, from

$$
\begin{aligned}
C_{0 \cdot 10} &= C_{0 \cdot 05} - 0 \cdot 50d & C_{0 \cdot 025} &= C_{0 \cdot 01} - 0 \cdot 55d & C_{0 \cdot 005} &= C_{0 \cdot 01} + 0 \cdot 39d \\
&= 1 \cdot 50 C_{0 \cdot 05} - 0 \cdot 50 C_{0 \cdot 01}; & &= 0 \cdot 55 C_{0 \cdot 05} + 0 \cdot 45 C_{0 \cdot 01}; & &= 1 \cdot 39 C_{0 \cdot 01} - 0 \cdot 39 C_{0 \cdot 05}.
\end{aligned}
$$

These factors were almost independent of p.

For the smallest root, where no 10 per cent point results are available, the factors β and γ in the expressions

$$c_{0 \cdot 025} = c_{0 \cdot 01} - \beta d, \quad c_{0 \cdot 005} = c_{0 \cdot 01} + \gamma d$$

are slightly more dependent on ν as the following table shows:

ν	β	γ
20	0·51	0·32
30	·52	·33
60	·53	·35
100	·53	·36

It will be found that these factors are very similar to those holding for the upper and lower inter-percentage-point differences of a χ^2 having ν degrees of freedom.

We have followed Hanumara & Thompson in tabling limits for C and c rather than the limits divided by ν because interpolation with this argument is easier, although Pillai & Chang's C/ν and c/ν may be more meaningful. It will be seen that, following Hanumara & Thompson, and also to save space, we omit rows for c when $\nu < p$. If needed, the missing values can be obtained by noting that $c(p, \nu) = c(\nu, p)$, a result seen to hold in the table of percentage points of C.

A possible application of the table is to determine limits within which, given $\boldsymbol{\Sigma} = \boldsymbol{\Sigma}_0$, all the roots of equation (257) will lie, with a specified probability.

Writing $P\{C \leqslant u_1\} = 1 - \alpha$ and $P\{c \geqslant l\} = 1 - \alpha$ for a fixed l, u may be determined so that

$$P\{l \leqslant c \leqslant C \leqslant u\} = 1 - 2\alpha, \tag{269}$$

where u_1 and l are the upper and lower 100α per cent points of C and c respectively. Hanumara & Thompson point out that a separate table for u is not needed as exact results for $p = 2$ and theoretical investigations for $p \geqslant 3$ suggest that u and u_1 are approximately equal for $\alpha \leqslant 0 \cdot 05$.

28.3 Anderson's bounds for the roots

Approaching the problem from another angle, Anderson (1965) has obtained optimal confidence bounds for all the roots of the determinantal equation

$$|\boldsymbol{\Sigma} - c\mathbf{I}| = 0. \tag{270}$$

These bounds are optimal in the sense of being the shortest within a large class of bounds depending only on the characteristic roots of $\mathbf{S}$. Writing $c(\mathbf{S})$ and $C(\mathbf{S})$ as the minimum and maximum roots of the sample covariance matrix $\mathbf{S}$, he shows that the confidence bounds for the roots of $\boldsymbol{\Sigma}$, denoted by $\mathrm{ch}\,(\boldsymbol{\Sigma})$, are given by

$$c(\mathbf{S})/u \leqslant \mathrm{ch}\,(\boldsymbol{\Sigma}) \leqslant C(\mathbf{S})/l, \tag{271}$$

113

where
$$\Pr\{\chi_\nu^2 \geqslant \nu l\} \times \Pr\{\chi_{\nu-p+1}^2 \leqslant \nu u\} = 1 - \epsilon, \qquad (272)$$

χ_m^2 denoting a random variable having a χ^2 distribution with m degrees of freedom. The confidence coefficient associated with the statement (271) is *at least* $1 - \epsilon$.

Taking the case of two variates, $p = 2$, with $\nu = 20$ and cutting off equal tail areas of $0\cdot025$ from the two χ^2 distributions, we have the lower $2\cdot5$ per cent point of χ_{20}^2 and upper $2\cdot5$ per cent point of χ_{19}^2 as $9\cdot591$ and $32\cdot852$, respectively. Hence

$$l = 9\cdot591/20 = 0\cdot480, \quad u = 32\cdot852/20 = 1\cdot643, \quad 1 - \epsilon = 0\cdot9506.$$

Anderson compares these factors with those obtainable from Table 51, i.e. $c_{0\cdot025}/20 = 0\cdot358$ and $C_{0\cdot025}/20 = 1\cdot985$. The former limits will be seen to be the narrower.

29. Distribution of the Multiple Correlation Coefficient

29.1 *Definitions*

Let $x_1, x_2, \ldots, x_p$ be p correlated variates forming a multivariate normal population. Then we may write
$$E(x_1 | x_2, \ldots, x_p) \quad \text{and} \quad \sigma_{1|2,\ldots,p}^2 = E\{x_1 - E(x_1 | x_2, \ldots, x_p)\}^2 \qquad (273)$$

for the expectation and variance of x_1, given $x_2, \ldots, x_p$. We define the multiple correlation coefficient between x_1 and $x_2, \ldots, x_p$ as $\mathbf{R} = \mathbf{R}_{1(2,\ldots,p)}$† given by

$$1 - \mathbf{R}^2 = \sigma_{1|2,\ldots,p}^2 / \sigma_1^2, \qquad (274)$$

where σ_1^2 is the total variance of x_1. $\mathbf{R}$, defined as the positive square root of $\mathbf{R}^2$, is also the ordinary product moment correlation coefficient between x_1 and the conditional expectation $E(x_1 | x_2, \ldots, x_p)$.

If $x_{1i}, x_{2i}, \ldots, x_{pi}$, $i = 1, 2, \ldots, N$ is a random sample of N p-variate observations from the population, then we may derive from it a multiple correlation coefficient R^2 defined by

$$1 - R^2 = s_{1|2,\ldots,p}^2 / s_1^2, \qquad (275)$$

where the denominator is the sample estimate of the variance of x_1, based on $N-1$ degrees of freedom, and the numerator is the mean square deviation of the x_{1i} from the regression plane of x_1 on $x_2, \ldots, x_p$ fitted to the observations.

29.2 *The conditional distribution of R^2, when $x_2, \ldots, x_p$ are fixed*

If in the population x_1 is independent of the other variates so that the multiple regression coefficients in the equation to the regression plane are all zero, then $s_1^2 - s_{1|2,\ldots,p}^2$ and $s_{1|2,\ldots,p}^2$ are two independent estimators of σ_1^2 based on $p-1$ and $N-p$ degrees of freedom, respectively. Consequently the p.d.f. of R^2 has the beta distribution

$$f(R^2 | p, N) = \{B(p-1, N-p)\}^{-1} (R^2)^{\frac{1}{2}(p-3)} (1 - R^2)^{\frac{1}{2}(N-p-2)}. \qquad (276)$$

Alternatively, using the transformation (52),

$$F = \frac{R^2(N-p)}{(1-R^2)(p-1)} \qquad (277)$$

is distributed as the variance ratio F with $\nu_1 = p-1$, $\nu_2 = N-p$ degrees of freedom (see §4.1). A test of significance can therefore be applied using tables of the percentage points of either the beta distribution or that of F.

† Following Kendall & Stuart (1961, **2**, §27.23) we shall use a bold-face $\mathbf{R}$ for the population coefficient and an ordinary R for the sample coefficient. For a full account of the theory underlying §§ 29.1–29.3, Kendall & Stuart's Chapter 27 may be consulted.

If the hypothesis of independence is not true, then the F of equation (277) has the non-central F-distribution of equation (141) with $\nu_1 = p-1$, $\nu_2 = N-p$ and the non-centrality parameter $\lambda = N\mathbf{R}^2$. The properties of this distribution discussed in §§ 15.1, 15.2 are then applicable.

29.3   *The unconditional distribution of R^2 (Table 52)*

In this case the values of $x_2, ..., x_p$ as well as those of x_1 will vary from sample to sample in a multi-normal distribution. In the case where x_1 is independent of the other variates and $\mathbf{R}^2 = 0$, the sampling distribution of R^2 still has the beta form (276) since the conditional distribution is independent of the particular set of fixed $x_2, ..., x_p$. For $\mathbf{R}^2 \neq 0$ the position is, however, changed and the distribution of R^2 is that derived by Fisher (1928, p. 660 (A)), namely

$$f(R^2|N, p, \mathbf{R}^2) = \frac{(R^2)^{\frac{1}{2}(p-3)}(1-R^2)^{\frac{1}{2}(N-p-2)}}{B\{\frac{1}{2}(p-1), \frac{1}{2}(N-p)\}} (1-\mathbf{R}^2)^{\frac{1}{2}(N-1)} F[\tfrac{1}{2}(N-1), \tfrac{1}{2}(N-1), \tfrac{1}{2}(p-1); \mathbf{R}^2 R^2],$$

(278)

where $F[a, b, c; x]$ is the hypergeometric function.

As Fisher pointed out, when $N \to \infty$ the conditional and unconditional distributions of R^2 both tend to that of a non-central χ^2, with

$$\chi'^2 = NR^2, \quad \nu = p-1, \quad \lambda = N\mathbf{R}^2.$$

Table 52, computed by K. H. Kramer[†] from a terminating series derived by Fisher (1928, p. 667) from (278) when $N-p$ is even gives to three decimal places the lower and upper 5 and 1 per cent points of R for $\mathbf{R} = 0 \cdot 1(0 \cdot 1)0 \cdot 9$, $\nu_1 = p-1 = 2(2)12(4)24$, 30, 34, 40 and $\nu_2 = N-p = 10(10)50$.

It is not easy to give any general rules for interpolation in a table of triple entry of this kind. Interpolating for a single argument can usually be carried out using the simple second difference Bessel formula (319), and for two arguments the procedure described in § 36.6 may be used. If it is necessary to interpolate for all three arguments the procedure will be troublesome. However, for many purposes a much rougher interpolation may be adequate, sometimes helped by graphical plots.

The computational procedure used by Kramer becomes very laborious as ν_2 increases and for this reason the calculations were stopped at $\nu_2 = 50$.[‡] This means that it is important to have a method of approximation to the distribution of R^2 for larger values of ν_2. In § 13.6 we have given the approximation suggested by Fisher (1928, p. 665) involving the use of the non-central χ^2 distribution. This consists in taking

$$R = \tanh(\chi'_{\nu_1}/\sqrt{\nu_2}),$$

(279)

where χ'_{ν_1} is a non-central χ having degrees of freedom $\nu_1 = p-1$ and non-centrality parameter $\sqrt{\lambda} = \sqrt{\nu_2} \tanh^{-1} \mathbf{R}$. As an example, we made some limited investigation into the accuracy of the approximation.

In a recent paper Khatri (1966) has suggested two other approximations involving the transformation

$$u = gR^2/(1-R^2)$$

or its inverse

$$R^2 = u/(u+g).$$

(280)

† A smaller table of the upper 5 per cent points of R was published earlier by Kramer (1963).

‡ Since this volume went to Press a table of upper 5 and 1 per cent points of R has been completed by Dr Y-S. Lee and will be published shortly in *Biometrika*. It uses $\nu = 60/\sqrt{\nu_2}$ as argument instead of ν_2, making possible interpolation for larger ν_2 values.

Khatri's Approximation A

Here the distribution of u is approximated by that of a non-central F with degrees of freedom $\nu_1 = p-1$, $\nu_2 = N-p$ and the non-centrality parameter, as well as g, a function of N, p and $\mathbf{R}$. While this approximation may well be as or more accurate than Approximation B, it suffers from the disadvantage that there are no tables of either the probability integral or the percentage points of non-central F.

Khatri's Approximation B

This takes the u of (280) to be distributed as a central F having degrees of freedom ν and $N-p$, where

$$\nu = \{p-1+(N-p)\,\mathbf{R}^2\}^2/\{p-1+(N-p)\,\mathbf{R}^2(2-\mathbf{R}^2)\} \qquad (281)$$

and

$$g = (N-p)\,(1-\mathbf{R}^2)/\{p-1+(N-p)\,\mathbf{R}^2\}. \qquad (282)$$

As for the Box approximations to multivariate test criteria described in §§ 27.1 and 28.1, one of the degrees of freedom, ν, will in general be fractional and the other, $N-p$, though integral, may not correspond to a table entry. However, if sufficiently accurate, the procedure is clearly an acceptable one.

We have only made a very limited examination of its accuracy in the case when $\nu_2 = N-p = 50$. Below we show the results obtained and repeat the corresponding results derived from the Fisher approximation (279) already given in Example 41, pp. 57–8.

Percentage points of R in case $\nu_1 = p-1 = 10$, $\nu_2 = N-p = 50$

	$\mathbf{R} = 0.5$				$\mathbf{R} = 0.8$			
	Lower 1 %	Lower 5 %	Upper 5 %	Upper 1 %	Lower 1 %	Lower 5 %	Upper 5 %	Upper 1 %
True	0·401	0·465	0·725	0·766	0·716	0·757	0·892	0·910
Khatri B	·409	·469	·726	·767	·719	·758	·892	·910
Fisher	·389	·455	·720	·761	·698	·742	·886	·905

It is clear that in these two cases Khatri's Approximation B is the more accurate, but it would not be justifiable to draw any general conclusions without a fuller investigation than we have felt able to undertake.

Example 59: determination of confidence limits for $\mathbf{R}$. Suppose that in a sample of $N = 50$ values from a 5-variate multi-normal population the multiple correlation coefficient of x_1 on x_2, x_3, x_4, x_5 is found to be $R = 0.63$. Find a central 90 per cent confidence interval for the population $\mathbf{R}$. We have

$$\nu_1 = p-1 = 4, \quad \nu_2 = N-p = 45.$$

The method we suggest for obtaining the confidence limits involves in part interpolation (since $\nu_2 = 45$ is not a table entry) and in part a graphical procedure. Writing $R(P|\nu_1, \nu_2, \mathbf{R})$ for a quantile of R extracted from Table 52, the following shows the procedure needed to obtain lower and upper 5 per cent points for R at $\nu_1 = 4$, $\nu_2 = 45$, $\mathbf{R} = 0.3$. We have to interpolate at $\nu_2 = 45$, i.e. with interpolation fraction $\theta = 0.5$. For the lower 5 per cent point we interpolate linearly and get 0·206. For the upper 5 per cent point we can use Newton's forward difference formula which when $\theta = 0.5$ becomes

$$y_{0.5} = y_0 + \tfrac{1}{2}\delta_{0.5} - \tfrac{1}{8}\delta_1^2 = 0.562.$$

116

ν_2	$R(0.05\|4, \nu_2, 0.3)$	δ	δ^2	$R(0.95\|4, \nu_2, 0.3)$	δ	δ^2
50	0·204			0·549		
40	·208	4	4	·578	29	13
30	·216	8		·620	42	

Proceeding in this way for $\mathbf{R} = 0.3(0.1)0.8$ and generally finding that linear interpolation is adequate, we obtain the following results:

$\mathbf{R}$	0·3	0·4	0·5	0·6	0·7	0·8
$R(0.05\|4, 45, \mathbf{R})$	0·206	0·278	0·370	0·476	0·594	0·720
$R(0.95\|4, 45, \mathbf{R})$	0·562	0·627	0·693	0·758	0·821	0·883

We now plot the points (i) $\mathbf{R}$, $R(0.05|4, 45, \mathbf{R})$, and $\mathbf{R}$, $R(0.95|4, 45, \mathbf{R})$, draw two smooth curves through them and find the intercepts with the line $R = 0.63$ to fall at about (i) 0·405, (ii) 0·730. It follows that the inequality $0.405 \leqslant \mathbf{R} \leqslant 0.730$ for the unknown population $\mathbf{R}$ can be associated with a confidence coefficient of 0·90.

VIII. GOODNESS OF FIT TESTS BASED ON THE EMPIRICAL DISTRIBUTION FUNCTION. TESTS OF UNIFORMITY

30. The single sample case (tests of Kolmogorov–Smirnov; Cramér–von Mises; Kuiper; Watson; Anderson–Darling) (Table 54)

30.1 *Description of tests*

Several goodness of fit tests are based on a comparison of the hypothesized cumulative distribution function $F(x)$ with the empirical distribution function $F_n(x)$ obtained from a random sample of n observations
$$x_{(1)} \leqslant x_{(2)} \leqslant \ldots \leqslant x_{(n)}.$$

Tests are given below in this section, based on five statistics usually associated with the names of Kolmogorov–Smirnov (the statistic D), Cramér–von Mises (W^2), Kuiper (V), Watson (U^2) and Anderson–Darling (A). In many problems it has been found that the tests give very similar answers, but because the procedure involved in their application has been put into the simple form devised by M. A. Stephens, set out in the single page of Table 54, we shall describe and illustrate the use of all five statistics.

The tests will be defined for three cases, depending on what is known of $F(x)$:

Case 1. $F(x)$ is completely specified and we write $z_{(i)} = F(x_{(i)})$.

Case 2. $F(x)$ is the *normal distribution* function, $N(\mu, \sigma)$, with μ and σ unspecified. Here we shall write $\Phi(X)$ for the standardized function and set
$$z_{(i)} = \Phi\{(x_{(i)} - \bar{x})/s\}, \tag{283}$$
where $\bar{x}$ is the sample mean and $s^2 = \sum_i (x_i - \bar{x})^2/(n-1)$.

Case 3. $F(x)$ is the *negative exponential* distribution function which we write as
$$F(x) = 1 - \exp(-ax),$$
$(x > 0)$, and a is unknown. We now set
$$z_{(i)} = 1 - \exp(-x_{(i)}/\bar{x}). \tag{284}$$

The test statistics defined in equations (285)–(289) below are all expressed in terms of the $z_{(i)}$, which will be in ascending order of magnitude. The asymptotic distributions of the statistics are known, but Stephens has been able to show that appropriate modifications of the finite-sample statistics, defined in the second column of Table 54, may be referred without serious error to their asymptotic distributions, five of the upper percentage points of which are contained in the last column of the table. The basis of this ingenious empirical procedure, based on part theoretical and part Monte Carlo investigation, has been described in the references given below.

(a) The Kolmogorov–Smirnov statistics D^+, D^- and D

Define
$$D^+ = \max_{1 \leqslant i \leqslant n} [i/n - z_{(i)}], \quad D^- = \max_{1 \leqslant i \leqslant n} [z_{(i)} - (i-1)/n], \quad D = \max [D^+, D^-]. \tag{285}$$

Proceed by calculating the modified statistic, $T(D)$, shown in the second column of Table 54, using the formula appropriate to Case 1, 2 or 3. Finally compare $T(D)$ with the significance points shown in the last column of the table. For example, if in the test for normality (Case 2) we had $n = 25$ observations and from (285) found $D = 0.186$, then

$$T(D) = 0.186(5 - 0.01 + 0.85/5) = 0.960.$$

This result is seen to be just significant at the 2·5 per cent level.

For Case 1 a modification is given also for the one-sided statistics D^+, D^-; this is the same in both cases as also are the percentage points.

(b) The Cramér–von Mises statistic, W^2

Calculate
$$W^2 = \sum_{i=1}^{n} \{z_{(i)} - (2i-1)/(2n)\}^2 + \frac{1}{12n}. \tag{286}$$

Modify to $T(W^2)$ and refer to the appropriate significance level.

(c) The Kuiper statistic, V

Calculate D^+, D^- as in (285); then
$$V = D^+ + D^-. \tag{287}$$
Proceed as in the other cases.

(d) The Watson statistic, U^2

Calculate
$$U^2 = W^2 - n(\bar{z} - 0.5)^2, \tag{288}$$

where W^2 is defined in (286) and $\bar{z}$ is the sample mean of the $z_{(i)}$. Modify and test as before.

(e) The Anderson–Darling statistic, A

Calculate
$$A = \left(-\left[\sum_{i=1}^{n} (2i-1)\{\log z_{(i)} + \log (1 - z_{(n+1-i)})\}\right] \Big/ n\right) - n. \tag{289}$$

Modify and test as before.

The following are references to the papers deriving the modified statistics T and discussing their accuracy: for Case 1, where $F(x)$ is completely known, Stephens (1970*b*); for Case 2, tests of normality, Stephens (1969*c*); for Case 3, tests of exponentiality, Stephens (1970*c*). Small modifications to the asymptotic per cent points given in the last two references will be published shortly by Stephens. They have been included in Table 54.

30.2 *Comparative properties of the tests*

The following comments are based largely on extensive Monte Carlo studies carried out by Stephens.

(*a*) In Case 1, when $F(x)$ is completely specified, D and V tend to detect the presence of one or possibly more outlying observations from an otherwise good fit. W^2 and U^2 are more likely to detect a slight but steady departure from hypothesis. D and W^2 are powerful for alternatives with a shift from $F(x)$ in mean; V and U^2 for alternatives involving a change in variance. A appears to be effective in detecting deviations in the tails of the distribution.

(*b*) In Case 1, D^+, D^- detect only one-sided departures from $F(x)$, D^+ when the observations tend to be lower than under the null hypothesis, D^- when they are higher. If there are prior grounds for suspecting one of the alternatives, then the appropriate one-sided test will be more powerful than D.

(*c*) In Case 1, with observations on a circle any origin may be chosen, but only V and U^2 may be used; D and W^2 are dependent on choice of origin.

(*d*) In Cases 2 and 3, A appears to be the most powerful statistic for detecting deviations in the tails and after that, W^2.

30.3 *Another test for uniformity*

Many problems reduce, after transformation, to a test of the null hypothesis that a sample of n ordered values, $z_{(i)}$, comes from a uniform distribution, limits 0, 1, which may be written $U(0, 1)$. The test statistics defined in § 30.1 above for Case 1 provide tests of this hypothesis, for if the x values come from $F(x)$, then the derived z will be $U(0, 1)$. This is not so for Cases 2 and 3.

Other statistics have been suggested for Case 1, including the C statistics defined as follows:

$$C^+ = \max_{1 \leqslant i \leqslant n} [i/(n+1) - z_{(i)}], \quad C^- = \max_{1 \leqslant i \leqslant n} [z_{(i)} - i/(n+1)], \quad C = \max. [C^+, C^-]. \qquad (290)$$

In this case the suggested modified statistic is given by the empirical formula

$$T(C) = (C + 0.4/n)(\sqrt{n} + 0.2 + 0.68/\sqrt{n}), \qquad (291)$$

the same transformation being applicable to C^+, C^- and C. The percentage points with which to compare these modified statistics are the same as those given in Table 54 for $T(D^+)$, $T(D^-)$ and $T(D)$ respectively. As far as can be judged from Stephens' Monte Carlo studies, the power properties of the C-statistics are very similar to those of the corresponding D-statistics.†

30.4 *Illustrative examples*

Example 60. The table below contains a record of the time of twenty successive warp breaks, t_i, which occurred during a period of $\tau = 1520$ hours running of an experimental loom. The data, from the Shirley Institute, Manchester, were used by E. S. Pearson (1963). The hypothesis to be tested is that the breaks occur randomly in time and under this assumption $z_{(i)} = t_{(i)}/\tau$ $(i = 1, 2, ..., 20)$ come from a uniform $U(0, 1)$ distribution. The problem falls under Case 1 and we can use the $z_{(i)}$ shown in the third column of the table to derive any one of the

† In a paper to be published shortly H. O. Hartley & R. C. Pfaffenberger have studied the properties of another criterion based on the $z_{(i)}$, which is closely related to that suggested by M. Greenwood in *J. R. Statist. Soc.* (1946), **109**, 85–110.

test criteria defined in equations (285)–(289). Values of $z_{(i)} - (i-1)/n$ are given in the fourth column. From these we pick out directly $D^- = 0.3559$. If we change the sign of these differences and add $1/n = 0.05$ to each we obtain the values of $i/n - z_{(i)}$ and pick out $D^+ = 0.0816$. Hence $D = \max(D^+, D^-) = D^- = 0.356$. Using Table 54, we find that the modified test statistics are

$$T(D) = T(D^-) = 0.356(\sqrt{20} + 0.12 + 0.11/\sqrt{20}) = 0.356 \times 4.62 = 1.64.$$

It follows that D is just significant at the 1 per cent level (1.63) and D^- is even more significant, indicating that the warp-break rate is increasing with time.

Warp-break data

i	$t_{(i)}$	$z_{(i)} = t_{(i)}/\tau$	$z_{(i)} - (i-1)/20$	i	$t_{(i)}$	$z_{(i)}$	$z_{(i)} - (i-1)/20$
1	30	0.0197	0.0197	11	1208	0.7947	0.2947
2	36	·0236	− ·0264	12	1240	·8158	·2658
3	104	·0684	− ·0316	13	1277	·8401	·2401
4	286	·1882	·0382	14	1282	·8434	·1934
5	291	·1914	− ·0086	15	1363	·8967	·1967
6	658	0.4329	0.1829	16	1384	0.9105	0.1605
7	893	·5875	·2875	17	1421	·9349	·1349
8	955	·6283	·2783	18	1477	·9717	·1217
9	1149	·7559	·3559	19	1504	·9895	·0895
10	1195	·7862	·3362	20	1510	·9934	·0434

$$\tau = 1520. \qquad \bar{z} = 0.6336.$$

To obtain W^2 we note that

$$\Sigma\{z_{(i)} - (2i-1)/(2n)\}^2 = \Sigma\{z_{(i)} - (i-1)/n\}^2 - \Sigma\{z_{(i)} - (i-1)/n\}/n + 1/(4n)$$
$$= 0.7968 - 0.1586 + 0.0125 = 0.6507,$$

by computing the sum and sum of squares of the differences in the fourth column of the table of data. Hence from equation (286)

$$W^2 = 0.6507 + 1/240 = 0.6549 \quad \text{and} \quad T(W^2) = 0.668,$$

a value which Table 54 shows to be significant at the 2.5 per cent, but not at the 1 per cent level.

Finally, $U^2 = W^2 - n(\bar{z} - 0.5)^2 = 0.298$ and $T(U^2) = 0.305$, a value which Table 54 shows to be significant at the 1 per cent level.

Rotating bend fatigue data. Values of log (*endurance*)

i	$y_{(i)}$	$(y_{(i)} - \bar{y})/s$	$z_{(i)}$	$z_{(i)} - (2i-1)/30$
1	0.301	−1.678	0.0467	0.0134
2	·519	−1.212	·1127	·0127
3	·653	−0.926	·1772	·0105
4	·690	− ·847	·1985	− ·0348
5	·892	− ·415	·3391	·0391
6	·964	− ·261	·3970	·0303
7	·978	− ·231	·4087	− ·0246
8	·987	− ·212	·4161	− ·0839
9	1.017	−0.148	0.4412	−0.1255
10	1.233	·314	·6232	− ·0101
11	1.346	·556	·7108	·0108
12	1.357	·579	·7187	− ·0480
13	1.562	1.018	·8456	·0123
14	1.845	1.623	·9477	·0477
15	1.944	1.835	·9667	·0000

$$\bar{y} = 1.0859, \quad \bar{z} = 0.4900.$$

Example 61. We now take a Case 2 problem using the fifteen values of, say, $y_{(i)} = \log_{10}(10x_{(i)})$ given in Example 21, pp. 29–30, for the rotating bend test data. Testing for normality, we find

$$\bar{y} = 1 \cdot 0859, \quad s^2 = 0 \cdot 2187, \quad s = 0 \cdot 4677.$$

The values of $(y_{(i)} - \bar{y})/s$, of $z_{(i)} = \Phi\{(y_{(i)} - \bar{y})/s\}$ (derived from Table 1 of *B.T.S.* **1**) and of $z_{(i)} - (2i - 1)/30$ are shown above. Squaring and summing the figures in the fifth column, we find

$$\sum_i (z_{(i)} - (2i - 1)/30)^2 = 0 \cdot 03245 \quad \text{so that} \quad W^2 = 0 \cdot 03801,$$
$$T(W^2) = 0 \cdot 03801(1 + 0 \cdot 5/15) = 0 \cdot 0393.$$

Reference to Table 54 shows that W^2 is therefore far from significant, the 15 per cent level for $T(W^2)$ falling at $0 \cdot 091$. From the table we also find that $D^+ = 9/15 - z_{(9)} = 0 \cdot 1588$ and $D^- = z_{(14)} - \frac{13}{15} = 0 \cdot 0810$, so that $D = 0 \cdot 1588$ and $T(D) = 0 \cdot 1588(\sqrt{15} - 0 \cdot 01 + 0 \cdot 85/\sqrt{15}) = 0 \cdot 648$. Again, reference to Table 54 shows that this value is not significant at the 15 per cent level.

These results confirm that obtained in §7.2, p. 37 above, when we applied the Shapiro–Wilk test for departure from normality to the $\log x_{(i)}$.

Example 62. To illustrate Case 3, the test of exponentiality, we take the data of Example 29, p. 41, i.e. the intervals in days between twenty-eight air-conditioning system failures on a Boeing 720 aircraft. In this case $z_{(i)} = 1 - \exp(x_{(i)}/\bar{x})$ and the table below shows the elements needed to determine W^2. The $z_{(i)}$ are obtained from tables of the negative exponential function and, if these are adequate, can be read at sight.

Intervals between failures in air-conditioning system

i	$x_{(i)}$	$x_{(i)}/\bar{x}$	$z_{(i)}$	$z_{(i)} - \dfrac{2i-1}{54}$	i	$x_{(i)}$	$x_{(i)}/\bar{x}$	$z_{(i)}$	$z_{(i)} - \dfrac{2i-1}{54}$
1	1	0·013	0·013	− 0·006	16	77	1·002	0·633	0·059
2	4	·052	·051	− ·005	17	80	1·041	·647	·036
3	11	·143	·133	·040	18	82	1·067	·656	·008
4	16	·208	·188	·058	19	97	1·263	·717	·032
5	18	·234	·209	·042	20	106	1·380	·748	·026
6	18	0·234	0·209	0·005	21	111	1·445	0·764	0·005
7	18	·234	·209	− ·032	22	141	1·836	·841	·045
8	24	·312	·268	− ·010	23	142	1·849	·843	·010
9	31	·404	·332	·017	24	163	2·122	·880	·010
10	39	·508	·298	·046	25	191	2·486	·917	·010
11	46	0·599	0·451	0·062	26	206	2·682	0·932	− 0·012
12	51	·664	·485	·059	27	216	2·812	·940	− ·042
13	54	·703	·505	·042					
14	63	·820	·560	·060					
15	68	·885	·587	·050					

$$\bar{x} = 2074/27 = 76 \cdot 815. \qquad \bar{z} = 14 \cdot 116/27 = 0 \cdot 5228.$$

We find $\qquad W^2 = 0 \cdot 0394, \quad T(W^2) = 0 \cdot 0394(1 + 0 \cdot 16/27) = 0 \cdot 0396.$

Reference to Table 54, Case 3, shows that this value is far from significant.

Again, since

$$D^- = \max. (z_{(i)} - (2i - 1)/54) + \tfrac{1}{54} \quad D^+ = \max. ((2i - 1)/54 - z_{(i)}) + \tfrac{1}{54}$$
$$= 0 \cdot 080, \qquad\qquad\qquad = 0 \cdot 060,$$
$$D = 0 \cdot 080, \quad T(D) = (D - 0 \cdot 2/27)(\sqrt{27} + 0 \cdot 26 + 0 \cdot 5/\sqrt{27})$$
$$= 0 \cdot 405$$

and this is clearly not significant.

There is therefore no evidence to suggest that the air-conditioning system failures do not occur at random. This was the view gained visually from the much more rapidly derived plot of the $x_{(i)}$ against the expected exponential order statistics, made in Example 29, Fig. 3, p. 42 above.

31. The Kolmogorov two-sample test, based on $D_{m,n}$ (Table 55)

Suppose that two independent samples, $x_1, x_2, ..., x_m$ and $y_1, y_2, ..., y_n$ with $m \leqslant n$ are drawn randomly from populations with continuous distribution functions $F(x)$, $G(y)$. We define

$$F_m(t) = (\text{number of } x_i \leqslant t)/m, \quad G_n(t) = (\text{number of } y_i \leqslant t)/n. \tag{292}$$

The hypothesis to be tested is that the two distribution functions $F(x)$ and $G(y)$ are identical. The test statistic is

$$D_{m, n} = \max_{t} \{|F_m(t) - G_n(t)|\}. \tag{293}$$

A very full table of the distribution function of $D_{m, n}$ under the null hypothesis has been computed by Kim & Jennrich (1970). The present Table 55 of 100α per cent points for $m = 1(1)25$, $n = m(1)25$ and $\alpha = 0.10, 0.05, 0.025, 0.01, 0.005, 0.001$ was derived by Kim from this basic table and appeared in somewhat different form in Harter & Owen (1970, pp. 129–31). The quantities tabled are denoted by c, where

$$\Pr\left\{D_{m, n} \geqslant \frac{c}{mn}\right\} \leqslant \alpha. \tag{294}$$

The entries are the smallest value of c for which the exact probability is $\leqslant \alpha$. A blank space in a column indicates that with this particular combination m, n no value of the statistic is significant at that level. Owing to the discontinuous nature of the distribution, cases occur where the same value of c corresponds to two α-levels. For example, with $m = 2$, $n = 12$, $D_{2, 12} = 24/(2 \times 12) = 1.0$ is significant at the 2.5 per cent level; we cannot find a lower value of $D_{2, 12}$ just significant at the 5 per cent level. The figure 24 is therefore repeated within parentheses in the column headed 0.050.

Example 63. In Example 29, pp. 41–2 above, results (say y_i, $i = 1, 2, ..., 15$) were given for rotating bend fatigue tests applied to fifteen specimens of an industrial product manufactured for the aircraft industry. Suppose that in a further sample of ten tests, results, x_i ($i = 1, 2, ..., 10$) were obtained. The distributions are clearly not normal and we shall use the $D_{m, n}$ test with $m = 10$, $n = 15$ to obtain a check on whether any change in material or conditions of test seems to have occurred between the two experiments.

To determine $D_{m, n}$ we arrange the observations in ascending order of magnitude, in the following scheme:

$x_{(i)}$	0·071	0·165		0·201	0·239		0·392	0·426	
$y_{(i)}$			0·200			0·330			0·450
$F_m(t) - G_n(t)$	0·100	0·200	0·133	0·233	0·333	0·267	0·367	0·467	0·400

$x_{(i)}$ (cont.)		0·605	0·618						
$y_{(i)}$ (cont.)	0·490			0·780	0·920	0·950	0·970	1·040	1·710
$F_m(t) - G_n(t)$ (cont.)	0·333	0·433	0·533	0·467	0·400	0·333	0·267	0·200	0·133

$x_{(i)}$ (cont.)				3·825	6·404			
$y_{(i)}$ (cont.)	2·220	2·275	3·650			7·000	8·800	
$F_m(t) - G_n(t)$ (cont.)	0·067	0·000	−0·067	0·033	0·133	0·067	0·000	

We note that each additional observation, $x_{(i)}$, adds an amount 0·100 to $F_m(t)$ and each additional $y_{(i)}$ adds $1/15 = 0.067$ to $G_n(t)$. The figures in the third row of the scheme give the cumulative differences, $F_m(t) - G_n(t)$. It is seen that $\max_{t} |F_m(t) - G_n(t)| = 0.533$, so that

$$mnD_{m,n} = 150 \times 0.533 = 80.0.$$

Examination of Table 55 shows that for $m = 10$, $n = 15$ the 5 per cent point is at $c = 80$, so that there will be some doubt whether the distributions are the same.

It may be noted that if we apply the Wilcoxon test to the sum of the ranks of the pooled data associated with the $y_{(i)}$, we find

$$W = 1 + 2 + 4 + 5 + 7 + 8 + 11 + 12 + 22 + 23 = 95.$$

Reference to Table 22 with $m = 10$, $n = 15$ gives $W_{0.05} = 99$, $W_{0.025} = 94$. This second test is therefore rather more sensitive to a possible change between the two experiments, and this will often be the case. Examination of the $D_{m,n}$ table shows, indeed, that for $m, n \leqslant 25$ very large differences in the observed cumulative distribution functions are needed to detect significance.

For larger samples, approximations to the distribution of $D_{m,n}$ have been discussed, for example, by Kim (1969).

IX. ANALYSIS OF DIRECTIONS ON A CIRCLE AND SPHERE

There is now an extensive literature on this subject starting from the papers of Fisher (1953), Gumbel, Greenwood & Durand (1953), Watson (1956), and Watson & Williams (1956). The rounding off of the theory so as to make possible the computation of suitable tables owes much to the initiative of M. A. Stephens. We are indebted to him for the summary he provided of his work and that of others, and for picking out the most important tables to reproduce in the present volume. This summary formed the essential basis for the preparation of the introductory comments which follow.

32. Definitions and general considerations associated with the von Mises and Fisher distributions

In connection with the procedures described in Chapter VIII it was stated that Watson's U_N^2 and Kuiper's V_N criteria could be used to test for uniformity in the distribution of points on a circle. A fresh series of problems arises when we are concerned with (a) the scatter of points on a sphere, (b) the formulation of an alternative hypothesis to uniformity. In this wider context it is convenient to think of the problems as 'directional' ones. A direction in two or three dimensions may be recorded as a unit vector OP from the origin O to a point P on the surface of a circle or sphere of unit radius. The position of P is defined by the single polar co-ordinate θ for the circle or by spherical polars θ, ϕ for the three-dimensional sphere.

Where the probability density for P is not uniform over circle or sphere, it is believed that for many situations met in practice simple approximating functions for this density may be taken as follows:

For the circle,
$$f(\theta) = \frac{1}{2\pi I_0(\kappa)} e^{\kappa \cos \theta} \quad (-\pi \leqslant \theta \leqslant \pi), \tag{295}$$

where $I_0(\kappa)$ is the imaginary Bessel function of the first kind.

For the sphere,

$$f(\theta, \phi) = \frac{\kappa \sin \theta}{4 \sinh \kappa} e^{\kappa \cos \theta} \quad (0 \leqslant \theta \leqslant \pi, \, 0 \leqslant \phi \leqslant 2\pi). \tag{296}$$

Distribution (295) was suggested by von Mises (1918) and distribution (296) by Fisher (1953). In both cases κ is a positive constant, measuring the degree of concentration; if $\kappa = 0$, the distribution is uniform over circle or sphere. Otherwise the distributions are unimodal with mode along $\theta = 0$ (the modal vector $\mathbf{A}$) and with symmetry about $\mathbf{A}$. A rotation of co-ordinates may be used to place $\mathbf{A}$ along any vector through 0.

Just as in the case of the normal distribution, we can envisage a number of procedures associated with the distributions (295) and (296).

For a single sample, a test for the position of $\mathbf{A}$ and for the value of κ; also problems of estimation and the determination of confidence limits.

For two or more samples, tests of whether the dispersion parameters κ_t or the modal vectors $\mathbf{A}_t$ in the populations can be regarded as identical.

Again we may need to consider as alternatives not only uniform and polar concentration, but also equatorial or bimodal concentration. Distributions of these last types are discussed in § 35.

In the sections below a number of procedures, associated with Tables 56–65 will be described. It will be seen that they have an affinity to the well established procedures used in the analysis of normally distributed data. Before proceeding in detail some properties and notation connected with the distributions (295) and (296) will be set out.

Suppose that we have a sample of N unit vectors defined by the angles θ_i or (θ_i, ϕ_i), $i = 1, 2, ..., N$. Then $\mathbf{R}$ is defined as the resultant vector sum for this sample; the length of $\mathbf{R}$ we term R. For the component X of $\mathbf{R}$ on the modal vector $\mathbf{A}$, when this is known or hypothesized, we write

$$X = \sum_{i=1}^{N} \cos \alpha_i \tag{297}$$

where α_i is the angle between the ith vector and $\mathbf{A}$. The statistics R and X play a leading part in the procedures to be described. If there are two or more samples, then the notation is extended to $\theta_{ti}, \phi_{ti}, \mathbf{R}_t, R_t, X_t$ for $t = 1, 2, \ldots$.

It is clear that when the position of the modal vector is known so that the α_i can be determined from the N observed vectors, the probability density of the sample is a function of X only and X is a sufficient statistic for κ. The maximum likelihood equations for determining κ are then

$$\frac{I_0'(\hat{\kappa})}{I_0(\hat{\kappa})} = \frac{X}{N} \quad \text{for circle,} \tag{298}$$

$$\coth \hat{\kappa} - \frac{1}{\hat{\kappa}} = \frac{X}{N} \quad \text{for sphere.} \tag{299}$$

When the polar vector is not known, the maximum likelihood estimator of its direction is that of the vector resultant $\mathbf{R}$ of the N unit vectors, while the maximum likelihood equations for estimating κ are the equations (298) and (299), respectively, with X replaced by R.

33. Problems in two dimensions, using the von Mises distribution

33.1 Tests and estimation for κ (Table 56; Stephens, 1969a)

Table 56 entered with arguments κ and N, gives upper and lower 5 and 1 per cent points for R/N. It can be used to test the hypothesis that $\kappa = \kappa_0$ when the modal vector is unknown. The procedure simply involves the calculation of R.

The table may also be used to derive confidence limits for an unknown κ, given an observed $R = R_0$. This is most easily done graphically by (a) plotting the appropriate upper and lower 100α per cent limits as ordinates against κ as abscissa, (b) drawing a smooth curve through them, (c) finding where on the κ-scale a horizontal line drawn at $R/N = R_0/N$ cuts the two curves.

The lowest line in the table, for $N = \infty$, gives the roots of equation (298), with R substituted for X. For given R/N it provides the maximum likelihood estimate of κ. If the position of the modal vector is known, so that X can be determined from the data, the values of X/N would be used rather than R/N. Interpolation for $\hat{\kappa}$, given R/N or X/N, can be done graphically but to ease the process Table 62 has been provided giving for argument $a = R/N$ or X/N, taken at equal intervals of a. It will usually be adequate to employ linear interpolation for N, taking $1/\sqrt{N}$ as argument.

The maximum likelihood estimator is likely to be somewhat biased. As $R \to N$, $\hat{\kappa} \to \frac{1}{2}N/(N-R)$ and bias is probably reduced by putting $\hat{\kappa} = \frac{1}{2}(N-1)/(N-R)$.

Extension beyond the range of Table 56

Stephens (1969a) has shown that for $\kappa \geqslant 4$ a very good approximation to the probability integral of R, given N and κ, may be obtained from the probability integral of χ^2. Thus

$$2\gamma\{N - R(P|N, \kappa)\} \sim \chi^2(1 - P|\nu = N - 1), \tag{300}$$

where

$$\frac{1}{\gamma} = \frac{1}{\kappa} + \frac{3}{8\kappa^2}. \tag{301}$$

For example, if $N = 20$, $\kappa = 5.0$ then $1/\gamma = 0.215$. Hence (300) gives

$$R(P|20, 5)/20 = 1 - 0.005375\chi^2(1 - P|19).$$

Taking $P = 0.99, 0.95, 0.05$ and 0.01 we find $\chi^2(1 - P|19)$ from Table 3 as $7.633, 10.117, 30.143$ and 36.191, respectively. Inserting these values into the last equation we get precisely the four values $R(P|20, 5)$, namely $0.959, 0.946, 0.838$ and 0.805 given in the last column of Table 56. These are the upper 1 per cent, upper 5 per cent, lower 5 per cent and lower 1 per cent points, respectively, of R. For $2 \leqslant \kappa \leqslant 4$ the approximation (300), (301) is still reasonably accurate.

Test for randomness, i.e. that $\kappa = 0$

We here use the upper 5 and 1 per cent points for R/N given in the $\kappa = 0$ column of Table 56. For $N \geqslant 20$, and with increasing accuracy as N increases, it is found that $2R^2/N$ is approximately distributed under the null hypothesis as a χ^2 having two degrees of freedom. If for the alternative to randomness, the modal vector is known, a more powerful test can be made using X (Stephens, 1969a).

125

33.2 *The position of the modal vector (Table 57, charts* A *and* B; *Stephens,* 1962 a)

Since X is a sufficient statistic for κ when the position of the modal vector is known, the conditional distribution of R, given X, is independent of κ. The charts of Table 57 plot the upper 5 per cent and 1 per cent points of R against X, for $N = 4(1)16, 18, 20, 25, 30$. The uses of these charts can be illustrated with the help of a diagram. In Fig. 9 we have taken the case where $N = 20$. Suppose OX points in the direction of the modal vector **A** and let OY be the axis at right angles. For every sample with resultant **R**, we can calculate $Y = \pm \sqrt{(R^2 - X^2)}$ and set $C \equiv (X, Y)$. **OC** is the resultant **R**, and C, which must lie inside the circle, centre O, radius 20, represents the sample.

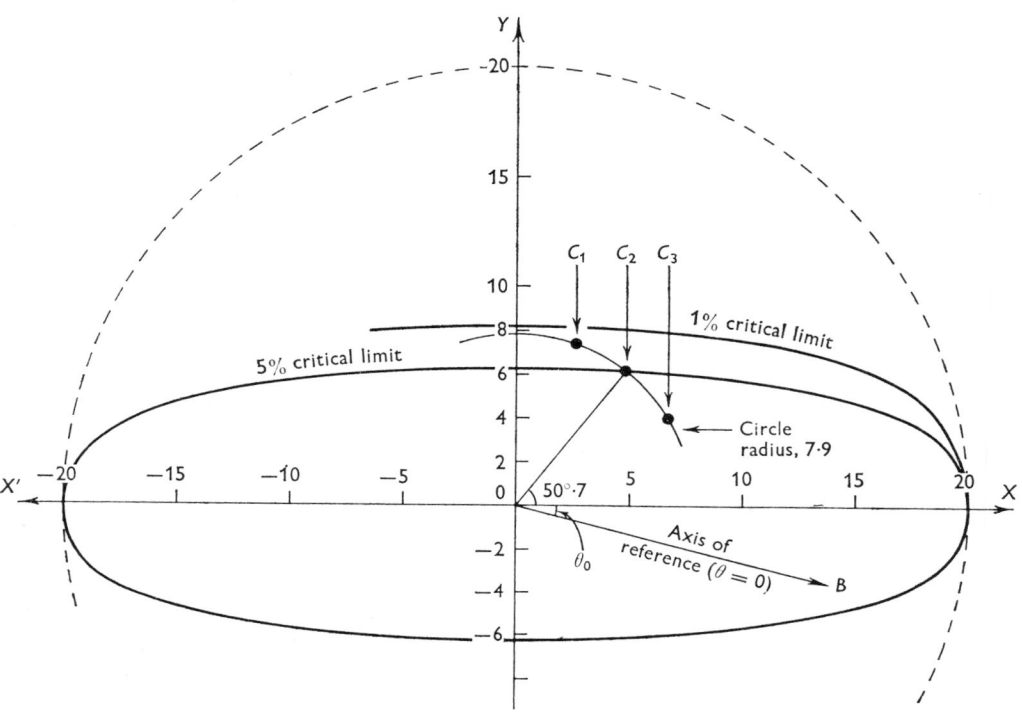

Fig. 9. Illustrating tests regarding the direction, $\theta = \theta_c$, of the modal vector.

Let R_0 be the critical value of R for given X, at the 5 per cent level given by the chart of Table 57 A, and draw the curve $Y^2 = R_0^2 - X^2$; call this the 5 per cent *critical limit*. This is shown in the illustration and also part of the 1 per cent critical limit obtained from the 1 per cent level for R given in the chart of Table 57 B. These curves are symmetrical about OY as well as OX. Since for every X the probability of C falling outside the curve is 0·05, with Y either positive or negative, the probability of falling *above the upper curve* is 0·025, and of falling *below the lower curve* is also 0·025, whatever be the value of κ.

Suppose now that OX, with co-ordinate θ_0 measured anti-clockwise from an initial line OB has been wrongly hypothesized as the modal vector; if the true modal vector were along a line with angle $\theta_1 > \theta_0$, more than 2·5 per cent of sample points C would fall above the upper 2·5 per cent curve. In the same way, if $\theta_1 < \theta_0$, an excess of sample points will lie below the lower 2·5 per cent critical boundary. As a result, a test of the hypothesis, H_0, that the direction of the polar vector is $\theta_c = \theta_0$ against the one-sided alternative that $\theta_c > \theta_0$ consists in (a) calculating X and R from the sample, (b) finding from the charts whether the observed R, given X, is $> R(0{\cdot}05)$ (or $> R(0{\cdot}01)$), the critical value of R for given N and X and (c) if so rejecting H_0 at the 2·5 (or 0·5) per cent level. There will be a corresponding one-sided test of H_0 against the alternative $\theta_c < \theta_0$.

If the alternative is simply $\theta_c \neq \theta_0$, then the steps (a) and (b) are followed but H_0 is rejected, if R is too large, at the 5 per cent (or 1 per cent) level.

For N, X not given in the charts, Stephens (1962a) has put forward the following approximations for the upper 100α per cent points, R_α of R:

(i) for $N \geqslant 15$, $X < \tfrac{1}{3}N$:

$$R_\alpha^2 \sim X^2 + \tfrac{1}{2}N\chi_\alpha^2(\nu = 1);$$

(ii) for $N > 3$, $\tfrac{1}{2}N < X < \tfrac{3}{4}N$:

$$\frac{R_\alpha - X}{N - R_\alpha} \sim \frac{F_\alpha(2, 2N-2)}{N-1};$$

$\qquad\qquad\qquad\qquad\qquad\qquad\qquad\qquad\qquad\qquad\qquad\qquad$ (302)

(iii) for $N > 3$, $\tfrac{5}{6}N < X$:

$$\frac{R_\alpha - X}{N - R_\alpha} \sim \frac{F_\alpha(1, N-1)}{N-1};$$

where $R(\alpha)$, $\chi_\alpha^2(\nu)$ and $F_\alpha(\nu_1\nu_2)$ are the upper 100α per cent points of the corresponding distributions, so that in Table 3, $P = 1 - \alpha$.

For $N \geqslant 3$, $\tfrac{1}{3}N < X < \tfrac{1}{2}N$, Stephens suggests that the average of the $R(\alpha)$ values obtained from the formulae (302 i) and (302 iii) should be taken. If $\tfrac{3}{4}N < X \leqslant \tfrac{5}{6}N$, then take the average of (302 ii) and (302 iii).

Note that if κ is not too small the sample X will almost always be positive, but for small κ this will not be so. Consequently there will then be a risk of accepting the hypothesis that OX points in the direction of the modal vector **A** when in fact the true direction is OX', or $\theta_0 + \pi$. Thus the test is strictly not one of *direction* but of the *axis* along which the modal vector lies. The probability of X being negative depends on the value of κ. Stephens (1969a) has given a table of percentage points of X, given N and κ. From this the following probabilities may be roughly inferred:

N	10	10	20	20	40	40
$p = \Pr\{X > 0 \mid N, \kappa\}$	0·95	0·99	0·95	0·99	0·95	0·99
Approximate κ	0·74	1·08	0·53	0·74	0·37	0·53

Thus for $\kappa > 1$, the risk of mistaking the direction along the axis of the modal vector will be very small.

Confidence limits for θ_c

Suppose that the true modal vector has direction $\theta_c = \theta_0$, but that we are unaware of this and must estimate θ_c from the direction of the sample vector resultant. Fig. 9 shows three possible resultants OC_1, OC_2 and OC_3 at angles θ_1, θ_2 and θ_3 respectively, all of the same length $R = 7{\cdot}90$. We find from Table 57 A that for $N = 20$ the corresponding abscissa is $X \sim 5{\cdot}0$ and note that

$$\phi = \cos^{-1}(X/R) = \cos^{-1}(5{\cdot}0/7{\cdot}90) = \cos^{-1}(0{\cdot}6329) = 50°{\cdot}7.$$

Suppose that the procedure for finding a lower confidence limit for θ_c is to subtract ϕ from the angle of **R**. For the three examples shown we should get lower confidence values (a) $\theta_1 - 50°{\cdot}7$ (b) $\theta_2 - 50°{\cdot}7$, (c) $\theta_3 - 50°{\cdot}7$. In case (a) the limit does not include the true modal vector, and this is clearly because C_1 lies above the 5 per cent boundary. In case (c) the limit includes the modal vector, because C_3 is below the 5 per cent boundary. Since 2·5 per cent of points representing the sample will, like C_1, lie above the boundary and 97·5 per cent of points will lie below it, it follows that the procedure gives a lower 97·5 per cent confidence limit for θ_c. Similarly, if we add $\phi = 50°\!\cdot\!7$ to the angle of the sample resultant vector we shall have an upper 97·5 per cent confidence limit for θ_c.

These two limits will define a central 95 per cent confidence interval for θ_c. The width of the interval will of course depend on the value of R. Similar, wider, limits associated with 99 per cent confidence may be found using the second chart of Table 57.

As in the case of testing the hypothesis that $\theta_c = \theta_0$, it is strictly only correct to claim that the confidence angle includes the *axis* along which the modal vector lies. However, unless κ is small, the probability p will be very large that the angle derived from the observations in the way described will include the *true, positive direction*.

33.3 *Two-sample tests (assuming that the populations have von Mises distributions)*

Let the sample sizes be N_1, N_2, the modal vectors be $\mathbf{R}_1$, $\mathbf{R}_2$ and their lengths R_1, R_2.

To test the hypothesis that the dispersion parameters are equal, i.e. that $\kappa_1 = \kappa_2$

In this case, provided κ is not too small, use can be made of the χ^2 approximation (300). If the two populations have a common value of κ the parameters γ of (301) will also be identical, so that under the null hypothesis

$$U = \frac{N_1 - R_1}{N_1 - 1} \bigg/ \frac{N_2 - R_2}{N_2 - 1} \sim \frac{\chi_1^2}{\nu_1} \bigg/ \frac{\chi_2^2}{\nu_2} = F(\nu_1 = N_1 - 1, \nu_2 = N_2 - 1). \tag{303}$$

If we label the samples 1 and 2 so that U is greater than unity, we should reject the hypothesis, $\kappa_1 = \kappa_2$ at the 100α per cent level if $U > F(\tfrac{1}{2}\alpha | N_1 - 1, N_2 - 1)$.

Test that the two populations have the same modal vector, assuming that $\kappa_1 = \kappa_2$ (Tables 58 A and B; Stephens 1969c)

Write $\mathbf{R} = \mathbf{R}_1 + \mathbf{R}_2$, $N = N_1 + N_2$ and R for the length of $\mathbf{R}$. Having determined from the data R_1, R_2 and R, set

$$W = R/N, \quad Z = (R_1 + R_2)/N. \tag{304}$$

For given W, the larger Z is, the less likely it is that the directions of the modal vectors are the same. Tables 58 A, B give 1, 2·5, 5 and 10 per cent critical values of Z for given W. If Z exceeds a critical value, the hypothesis of a common modal vector may be rejected at that level.

It will be seen that Table 58 A deals with the case $N_1 = N_2 = \tfrac{1}{2}N$ while Table 58 B gives critical values for $N_2 = \tfrac{1}{2}N_1$ and $N_2 = \tfrac{1}{4}N_1$. For values of $r = N_1/N_2$ intermediate between 1, 2 and 4 a graph of critical values of Z plotted against r, for the same values of $N = N_1 + N_2$ and W can be used for interpolation. For $W > 0·4$ the critical values for Z are the same for $r = 2, 4$ as for $r = 1$ and are not therefore repeated in Table 58 B.

Extension beyond the limits of Table 58

If in Table 58 A, $W > 0·6$, critical values of Z may be found from the approximation

$$Z = (W + H)/(1 + H),$$

where

$$H = F(\alpha | 1, N - 2)/(N - 2). \tag{305}$$

Other approximate tests and multi-sample tests have been discussed by Stephens (1969c).

128

33.4 *An illustrative example*

Example 64. The following data due to Kiersch (1950) give the directions of slope of lamination surfaces of sandstone rocks in two samples, the first containing $N_1 = 44$, the second $N_2 = 34$ measurements. The angles, θ_{ti}, $i = 1, 2, \ldots, N_t$, $t = 1, 2$ are in degrees measured from a specified direction:

Sample 1

0,	0,	0,	15,	45,	68,	100,	110,	113,	135,	135,	140,
140,	155,	165,	165,	169,	180,	180,	180,	180,	180,	180,	180,
189,	206,	209,	210,	214,	215,	225,	226,	230,	235,	245,	250,
255,	255,	260,	260,	260,	260,	270,	270.				

Sample 2

90,	100,	115,	115,	130,	135,	145,	160,	165,	170,	180,	190,
190,	196,	200,	205,	210,	225,	230,	245,	250,	250,	253,	254,
254,	255,	256,	261,	270,	277,	280,	290,	290,	305.		

We shall derive confidence limits for κ and for the position of the polar vector, θ_c, in the population from which the first sample has been drawn and then test the hypothesis that the two populations have the same κ and θ_c values.

We first find that

$$X_1 = \sum_i \cos \theta_{1i} = -19 \cdot 499, \quad Y_1 = \sum_i \sin \theta_{1i} = -6 \cdot 870,$$

$$X_2 = \sum_i \cos \theta_{2i} = -15 \cdot 127, \quad Y_2 = \sum_i \sin \theta_{2i} = -11 \cdot 008.$$

Hence
$$R_1 = (X_1^2 + Y_1^2)^{\frac{1}{2}} = 20 \cdot 67, \quad R_2 = (X_2^2 + Y_2^2)^{\frac{1}{2}} = 18 \cdot 71,$$

$$\theta_{1c} = 180° + \tan^{-1}(0 \cdot 3523) = 199° \cdot 41, \quad \theta_{2c} = 180° + \tan^{-1}(0 \cdot 7277) = 216° \cdot 04.$$

(33.4.1) 90 *per cent confidence limits for* κ_1

$R_1/N_1 = 0 \cdot 4698$; we now turn to Table 56 and inspection suggests that we need to find the 5 per cent critical values of R/N at $N = 44$ and $\kappa = 0 \cdot 5, 1 \cdot 0, 1 \cdot 5$. Take first the case of the upper 5 per cent limit for R/N at $\kappa = 0 \cdot 5$. Using $1/\sqrt{N}$ as argument, we have the following small table:

N	$1/\sqrt{N}$	5 % limit	$\triangle$	$\triangle^2$	
30	0·1826	0·466			
40	·1581	·434	1·306	0·561	Also, $1/\sqrt{44} = 0 \cdot 1508$.
60	·1291	·397	1·276		

If we now use the first three terms of the divided difference formula (325) we have for the critical value of R/N at $N = 44$:

$$0 \cdot 397 + (0 \cdot 1508 - 0 \cdot 1291) \times 1 \cdot 276 + (0 \cdot 1508 - 0 \cdot 1291)(0 \cdot 1508 - 0 \cdot 1581)$$

$$\times 0 \cdot 561 = 0 \cdot 397 + 0 \cdot 028 - 0 \cdot 000(1) = 0 \cdot 425.$$

The second difference term is here negligible and this is true at the other five points needed; this means, as suggested in § 33.1, that we can interpolate linearly between two entries, using $1/\sqrt{N}$ as argument. We find (with possible errors of one unit in the last decimal place):

κ	0·5	1·0	1·5
Upper 5 % critical value	0·425	0·599	0·721
Lower 5 % critical value	·111	·309	·477

129

Plotting these values against κ, and drawing rough curves through them we find that the horizontal line at $R_1/N_1 = 0\cdot470$ cuts the upper curve at about $\kappa = 0\cdot61$ and the lower curve at $\kappa = 1\cdot47$, leading to a 90 per cent central confidence interval, $0\cdot61 \leqslant \kappa_1 \leqslant 1\cdot47$. If we interpolate in Table 62, with $a = 0\cdot470$ we find that the single-valued maximum likelihood estimate is $\hat{\kappa} = 1\cdot07$.

(33.4.2)   90 *per cent confidence interval for θ_c from first sample*

With $N_1 = 44$ we are beyond the range of the charts in Table 57. It is likely that $\tfrac{1}{3}N < X < \tfrac{1}{2}N$ and therefore we are not well placed in regard to the approximations (302). Taking (302, case (i)) we have

$$X^2 = R^2 - \tfrac{1}{2}N\chi^2(0\cdot95|1) = (20\cdot67)^2 - 22 \times 3\cdot841 = 342\cdot75, \ X = 18\cdot51.$$

Taking (302, case (ii)) we have

$$X = R - F(0\cdot05|2, 86)\,(N-R)/(N-1) = 20\cdot67 - 3\cdot10 \times 23\cdot33/43 = 18\cdot99.$$

Following Stephens' advice (1962a, p. 467) we take X as the average of these two values, namely $18\cdot75$. Then $\cos^{-1}(X/R) = \cos^{-1}(0\cdot9071) = 24°\cdot9$, so that the 90 per cent confidence limits for θ_{1c} are at $199°\cdot4 \pm 24°\cdot9$.

(33.4.3)   *Tests of the hypothesis that the two samples come from a common population*

With $\kappa < 2\cdot0$, the test based on the F-approximation of formula (303) will not be very accurate. However, if we use it we find that $33(44 - 20\cdot67)/\{43(34 - 18\cdot71)\} = 1\cdot17$ should, on the null hypothesis, be distributed as $F(43, 33)$. Since Table 5 shows that the 25 per cent point of $F(43, 33)$ is at about $1\cdot26$, it seems clear that there are no grounds for rejecting the hypothesis of equal dispersions.

To compare the directions of the modal vectors, we need to find the resultant vector $\mathbf{R} = \mathbf{R}_1 + \mathbf{R}_2$. The X and Y components are

$$X = X_1 + X_2 = -34\cdot626, \quad Y = Y_1 + Y_2 = -17\cdot878.$$

Hence
$$R = \sqrt{(X^2 + Y^2)} = 38\cdot97, \quad N = N_1 + N_2 = 78.$$

Using (304),
$$W = 38\cdot97/78 = 0\cdot500, \quad Z = (20\cdot67 + 18\cdot71)/78 = 0\cdot505.$$

We now refer to Table 58; as $W > 0\cdot40$ the critical values for $N_1/N_2 > 1$ can be read from Table 58 A. Using as argument $120/N$, we interpolate linearly at $120/78 = 1\cdot54$ in the column headed $W = 0\cdot50$, between the entries at $N = 60$ and 120, and find that the 10 per cent point for $N = 78$ is at $0\cdot511 + 0\cdot54 \times 0\cdot009 = 0\cdot516$. The observed value of $Z = 0\cdot505$ is therefore not significant at the 10 per cent point.

We conclude that there is no evidence that the samples have come from different populations. The best estimate of the common modal vector, using $\mathbf{R}$, is then along $\theta = 207°\cdot3$, i.e. $\tan^{-1}(X/Y)$.

34. Analogous problems in three dimensions, using Fisher's distribution

The procedures available for the Fisher distribution on a sphere correspond closely to those described in § 33 for the circle, although separate tables are required. It will suffice to refer to them briefly.

34.1 *Single sample case (Tables 59, 60 and 63; Stephens, 1962b, 1967)*

When dealing with the dispersion parameter κ, Tables 59 and 63 replace Tables 56 and 62. The maximum likelihood estimator $\hat{\kappa}$ derived from Table 63 will be somewhat biased. For R/N approaching unity, $\hat{\kappa} \sim N/(N-R)$ and the bias will be reduced by substituting $N-1$ in the numerator. For $\kappa \geqslant 5$, but with decreasing accuracy as κ falls below this value, the probability integral of R may be obtained approximately from the probability integral of χ^2, as follows (Watson, 1956), remembering that in the notation of Table 3, $\chi^2(1-P)$ is the upper $100P$ percent point:

$$2\kappa\{N - R(P|N,\kappa)\} \sim \chi^2(1-P|\nu = 2N-2). \tag{306}$$

For example, taking $N = 10$, $\kappa = 4$, (306) gives

$$R(0\cdot05|10,4)/N \sim 1 - \chi^2(0\cdot95|18)/80 = 1 - 28\cdot87/80 = 0\cdot639.$$

Table 59 gives a value of $0\cdot642$ as the lower 5 per cent point of R.

In the case of the position of the modal vector, Table 60 with its two charts replaces Table 57. For N and X not given in the charts, Stephens (1962b) suggests the following approximations to the upper 100α per cent points R_α of R; these are similar but not identical with the formulae (302):

(i) for $N > 6$, $X < \frac{1}{4}N$: $R_\alpha^2 \sim X^2 + \frac{1}{3}N\chi_\alpha^2(\nu = 2)$;

(ii) for $3 < N < 8$, $X > \frac{1}{2}N$ or for $N > 8$, $X > \frac{3}{5}N$:

$$\frac{R_\alpha - X}{N - R_\alpha} \sim F_\alpha(2, 2N-2)/(N-1);$$

(iii) for $\frac{1}{4}N < X < \frac{3}{5}N$ take the mean R_α from (i) and (ii).

$$\tag{307}$$

Here $\chi_\alpha^2(\nu)$ and $F_\alpha(\nu_1, \nu_2)$ are the upper 100α per cent points of the χ^2 and F-distributions given in Tables 3 and 5, so that in the former case entry is made at $P = 1 - \alpha$.

The argument underlying the determination of confidence limits follows the same lines as in the circular case. Both in testing whether $\theta_c = \theta_0$ and in finding confidence limits for θ_c, the procedures strictly apply only to the *axis* along which the modal vector lies. However, if κ is not too small, X will almost certainly be positive so that the sample modal vector will determine the *direction* of **A**. As for the two-dimensional case, we can obtain the following approximate results from Stephens (1967):

N	10	10	20	20	40	40
$p = \mathrm{Pr}\{X < 0|N,\kappa\}$	0·95	0·99	0·95	0·99	0·95	0·99
Approximate κ	0·91	1·30	0·64	0·91	0·45	0·64

Example 65. Fisher (1953) has quoted data of J. Hospers, recording the directions in terms of declination and inclination or dip of the remanent magnetism in $N = 9$ specimens of a recent Icelandic lava flow. He gives the direction cosines of R as $0\cdot9449$, $0\cdot2984$ and $0\cdot1346$, while $R = 8\cdot77203$. As R so nearly equals 9, it is clear that there is great concentration of the unit vectors about the pole. Examination of Table 60 shows that with $N = 9$, $R = 8\cdot77$, the corresponding 5 per cent value of X cannot be read with sufficient accuracy to justify calculation of $\theta = \cos^{-1}(X/R)$. We turn therefore to the approximation (307, case (ii)) and find

$$X = R - 0\cdot228F_{0\cdot05}(2, 16)/8 = 8\cdot669.$$

This gives a critical 5 per cent angle of $\theta = \cos^{-1}(X/R) = \cos^{-1}(0.9882) = 8°.8$. That is to say possible directions more than $8°.8$ away from the direction of the observed polar vector R can be excluded with a confidence coefficient of 0.95.

To obtain a central 95 per cent confidence interval for κ we insert the observed $R = 8.772$ into the approximation (306) with lower and upper 2.5 per cent limits for a χ^2 having sixteen degrees of freedom. As a result we find

$$15.1 \leqslant \kappa \leqslant 63.3.$$

The maximum likelihood estimate, obtained from (299) in the form $1 - 1/\hat{\kappa} = R/N$ (since with this magnitude $\coth \hat{\kappa} \simeq 1$) gives $\hat{\kappa} = 39.5$. Use of $\kappa = (N-1)/(N-R)$ as suggested on p. 131 leads to $\kappa = 35.1$, as given by Fisher.

34.2 Two-sample case (Tables 61 A and B; Stephens, 1972)

Here, Tables 61 A and B replace Tables 58 A and B. For $W > 0.30$ the limits for the case $N_1/N_2 = r = 2, 4$ are the same as those in Table 61 A for $r = 1$. For $W > 0.6$ critical values of Z may be found from the approximation

$$Z = (W+H)/(1+H),$$
$$H = F_\alpha(2, 2N-4)/(N-2). \qquad (308)$$

where

For testing the hypothesis that $\kappa_1 = \kappa_2$ we make use of the χ^2 approximation (306) and derive a test in terms of the variance ratio F as follows:

$$U = (N_2-1)(N_1-R_1)/\{(N_1-1)(N_2-R_2)\} \sim F(\nu_1 = 2N_1-2, \nu_2 = 2N_2-2). \qquad (309)$$

If the samples are labelled 1 and 2 so as to make $U > 1$, then we should reject the null hypothesis at the 100α per cent level if $U > F_{\frac{1}{2}\alpha}(2N_1-2, 2N_2-2)$. This test is certainly applicable if $R_t/N_t > 0.65$ ($t = 1, 2$) but will provide an approximate test for lower R/N ratios. For other approximate tests and multi-sample tests see Stephens (1967, 1969b).

35. Tests for uniformity against the alternatives of equatorial and bimodal distributions

35.1 Bimodal distributions on the circle and sphere

A possible distribution for the circle, symmetrical with regard to the two opposite poles, is one in which the density is proportional to $\exp\{\lambda \cos(2\theta)\}$. For statistical analysis, the angles for a set C of vectors may then be doubled and the vectors with the new angles will form a set C^*. If $\mathbf{A}$ is hypothesized along $\theta = \theta_0$, $\mathbf{A}^*$ is defined along $\theta = 2\theta_0$. Then R and X (the component of $\mathbf{R}$ along $\mathbf{A}^*$) are calculated for the new set C^* and the tests described above in § 33 may all be used as for the unimodal von Mises distribution of equation (295), λ replacing κ. In the particular case of testing for uniformity, the resultant R/N of the set C^* is referred to the $\kappa = 0$ column of Table 56. Unfortunately no corresponding modification exists for the three-dimensional case.

Another way to treat bimodal or axial data, in two or three dimensions, is to assume a population of two von Mises or Fisher distributions, with opposite modes, superimposed. Techniques of analysis which make use of the tables given here for the unimodal distributions are described by Stephens (1970a).

35.2 Test for uniformity on the sphere against equatorial distributions
(Tables 64 and 65; Stephens, 1965; Anderson & Stephens, 1971)

A distribution suitable for populations of points P concentrated around a great circle of a sphere has been treated by Watson (1965). He represents this by the law

$$f(\theta, \phi) = C(\kappa) \exp(-\kappa \cos^2 \theta),$$

where

$$\{C(\kappa)\}^{-1} = 4\pi \int_0^1 \exp(-\kappa t^2)\, dt. \qquad (310)$$

There are antimodes along $\theta = 0$ (the vector $\mathbf{A}$) and $\theta = \pi$, and the density is concentrated around $\theta = \frac{1}{2}\pi$. Watson gives approximate tests.

A test of uniformity ($\kappa = 0$) against an alternative of this type in which $\mathbf{A}$ is known to lie at $\theta = 0$ can be conducted using the statistic

$$S = \sum_{i=1}^N \cos^2 \theta_i / N, \qquad (311)$$

and referring it to the lower tail of its distribution under the null hypothesis (Table 64). In the more realistic case where $\mathbf{A}$ is unknown, the appropriate statistic to use is the minimum value of S obtained as $\mathbf{A}$ is varied. Let this be $S_{\text{min.}}$; it may be found as follows. Let the N points P have spherical co-ordinates θ_i, ϕ_i referred to any fixed set of axes and define for each vector the direction cosines:

$$l_i = \sin \theta_i \cos \phi_i, \quad m_i = \sin \theta_i \sin \phi_i, \quad n_i = \cos \theta_i.$$

Form the matrix (312) and let its latent roots in ascending order be μ_1, μ_2, μ_3.

$$
M = \begin{vmatrix}
\sum_i l_i^2 & \sum_i l_i m_i & \sum_i l_i n_i \\
\sum_i l_i m_i & \sum_i m_i^2 & \sum_i m_i n_i \\
\sum_i l_i n_i & \sum_i m_i n_i & \sum_i n_i^2
\end{vmatrix}. \qquad (312)
$$

Then Watson shows that

$$S_{\text{min.}} = \mu_1 / N.$$

Uniformity is rejected if $S_{\text{min.}}$ is too small. Four lower-tail percentage points are given in Table 65.

35.3 Test for uniformity on the sphere against bimodal distributions
(Tables 64 and 65)

A distribution of P with density per unit area proportional to $\exp(\lambda \cos^2 \theta)$ ($\lambda \geqslant 0$) gives a bimodal density concentrated around $\theta = 0$ (the vector $\mathbf{A}$). When $\mathbf{A}$ is known, a test of the hypothesis that $\lambda = 0$ against this alternative will again use the statistic S of (311), judging significance by a shift into the upper tail of the distribution, for which five significance points are given in Table 64.

When $\mathbf{A}$ is not known, the appropriate statistic is $S_{\text{max.}} = \mu_3 / N$, where μ_3 is the largest latent root of the matrix M defined by (312) and the right-hand half of Table 65 is used.

133

X. TABLES TO AID INTERPOLATION

In this chapter we assemble a number of formulae which will aid in interpolation in the various tables of both *B.T.S.* **1** and *B.T.S.* **2**. The coefficients to be used with the more important of these formulae are contained in Tables 66–9. For numerical examples illustrating the use of formulae and tables, reference should be made to the applications sections of various earlier chapters of the present volume.

36. INTERPOLATION BASED ON DIFFERENCES

36.1 *Bessel's interpolation formula*

We use a central difference notation, assuming equidistant argument steps of unity, as shown in the difference table below:

Argument x	Function f_x	Differences 1st δ_x	2nd δ_x^2	3rd δ_x^3	4th δ_x^4	5th δ_x^5	6th δ_x^6	
-3	f_{-3}							
-2	f_{-2}	$\delta_{-2\frac{1}{2}}$	δ_{-2}^2					
-1	f_{-1}	$\delta_{-1\frac{1}{2}}$	δ_{-1}^2	$\delta_{-1\frac{1}{2}}^3$	δ_{-1}^4			
0	f_0	$\delta_{-\frac{1}{2}}$	δ_0^2	$\delta_{-\frac{1}{2}}^3$	δ_0^4	$\delta_{-\frac{1}{2}}^5$	δ_0^6	(313)
1	f_1	$\delta_{\frac{1}{2}}$	δ_1^2	$\delta_{\frac{1}{2}}^3$	δ_1^4	$\delta_{\frac{1}{2}}^5$	δ_1^6	
2	f_2	$\delta_{1\frac{1}{2}}$	δ_2^2	$\delta_{1\frac{1}{2}}^3$	δ_2^4	$\delta_{1\frac{1}{2}}^5$		
3	f_3	$\delta_{2\frac{1}{2}}$	δ_3^2	$\delta_{2\frac{1}{2}}^3$				
4	f_4	$\delta_{3\frac{1}{2}}$						

Using the above notation, the interpolate f_θ for $0 \leqslant \theta \leqslant 1$ is given (apart from a truncation error) by Bessel's formula:

$$f_\theta = f_0 + \theta\delta_{\frac{1}{2}} + B_2(\delta_0^2 + \delta_1^2) + B_3\delta_{\frac{1}{2}}^3 + B_4(\delta_0^4 + \delta_1^4) + B_5\delta_{\frac{1}{2}}^5 + \ldots, \qquad (314)$$

where the Bessel coefficients, B_i, are given by

$$\left. \begin{aligned} B_2 &= \tfrac{1}{4}\theta(\theta - 1), \quad B_3 = \tfrac{1}{6}\theta(\theta - 1)(\theta - \tfrac{1}{2}), \\ B_4 &= \tfrac{1}{48}(\theta + 1)\theta(\theta - 1)(\theta - 2), \\ B_5 &= \tfrac{1}{120}(\theta + 1)\theta(\theta - 1)(\theta - 2)(\theta - \tfrac{1}{2}), \end{aligned} \right\} \qquad (315)$$

or in general by

$$B_{2i} = \frac{1}{2}\binom{\theta + i - 1}{2i}, \quad B_{2i+1} = (\theta - \tfrac{1}{2})\binom{\theta + i - 1}{2i + 1} \bigg/ (\theta - i - 1). \qquad (316)$$

Table 66 taken with permission from *Interpolation and Allied Tables* (H.M. Nautical Almanac Office, 1956) gives values of B_2, B_3 and B_4 to six, five and four decimals, respectively, for $\theta = 0.000(0.001)1.000$. For intermediate values of θ, B_3 and B_4 can be obtained 'by sight'; this is also possible for five-decimal accuracy in B_2 which is normally adequate. However, in this case first differences are shown to help if needed in obtaining intermediate values.

The use of Bessel's or any other difference formula requires the formation of a small difference table of the δ_x^{2i}, δ_x^{2i+1}. Although this entails some additional labour, the differences may be used to monitor the accuracy of the formula, or in other words to show at what term the formula may be truncated to provide a given accuracy. Specifically, the terms involving

$B_2, B_3, \ldots$ are negligible if in units of the last decimal digit required in f_θ, the differences are numerically smaller than the upper limits shown below:

Term involving $\rightarrow$	B_2	B_3	B_4	B_5	B_6
is negligible if	$\|\delta^2\| \leqslant 4$	$\|\delta^3\| \leqslant 60$	$\|\delta^4\| \leqslant 20$	$\|\delta^5\| \leqslant 500$	$\|\delta^6\| \leqslant 100$

$$(317)$$

We here use 'negligible' in the sense that the products

$$\left| B_{2i}(\delta_0^{2i} + \delta_1^{2i}) \right| \leqslant 0{\cdot}5, \quad \left| B_{2i+1}\delta_1^{2i+1} \right| \leqslant 0{\cdot}5$$

in units of the last decimal required in f_θ. It is usually adequate to check whether the above inequalities (317) are satisfied for two consecutive differences δ^{2i}, δ^{2i+1}.

The use of linear interpolation assumes that to the number of decimal places required $|\delta^2| \leqslant 4$ (in this case almost invariably $|\delta^3| \leqslant 60$). To avoid optimistically retaining more figures than are justified it will generally be worth while examining the value of the second differences. If a desk machine is available we can obtain δ^2 in one operation from

$$\delta^2 f_0 = f_{-1} - 2f_0 + f_1.$$

Linear interpolation means, of course, the reduction of formula (314) to

$$f_\theta = (1-\theta)f_0 + \theta f_1. \tag{318}$$

In very many of the tables in this volume the argument interval has been chosen so that

$$|\delta^3| \leqslant 60, \quad |\delta^4| \leqslant 20, \ldots.$$

In this case we have the simple interpolation formula

$$f_\theta = (1-\theta)f_0 + \theta f_1 + B_2(\delta_0^2 + \delta_1^2) \tag{319}$$

for which only two second differences need to be formed. For an example, see Example 11, p. 20. However, if $|\delta_{\frac{1}{2}}^3| > 60$, but $|\delta^4| \leqslant 20$, the fuller formula

$$f_\theta = (1-\theta)f_0 + \theta f_1 + B_2(\delta_0^2 + \delta_1^2) + B_3\delta_{\frac{1}{2}}^3 \tag{320}$$

must be used. For an application when the B_4 term is needed, see §1.2, p. 2.

36.2 *Interpolation in an end panel*

It will sometimes be necessary to interpolate within the first or last panel of a table. If the differential coefficients near the terminal are large, so that the forward or backward differences into the table do not converge, difference interpolation may be only possible after using an appropriate transformation. However, it will often happen that the successive terminal differences do decrease. In this situation a relatively simple procedure using the Bessel formula will often meet the case.

For example, if f_1 is the last entry in the table, differencing as below may show that to the number of places required, δ^3 can be taken as constant. We then set $\delta_{\frac{1}{2}}^3 = \delta_{-\frac{1}{2}}^3$ and complete the difference table by the entries below in bold type. Formula (320) is now applied, using the entries $f_0, f_1, \delta_0^2, \boldsymbol{\delta_1^2}, \boldsymbol{\delta_{\frac{1}{2}}^3}$. It is equivalent to the Lagrangian four-point formula for the last panel, based on the table entries f_{-2}, f_{-1}, f_0 and f_1. For an example, see Example 8, p. 17.

$$
\begin{array}{cccc}
f_{-3} & & & \\
 & \delta_{-2\frac{1}{2}} & & \\
f_{-2} & & \delta_{-2}^2 & \\
 & \delta_{-1\frac{1}{2}} & & \delta_{-1\frac{1}{2}}^3 \\
f_{-1} & & \delta_{-1}^2 & \\
 & \delta_{-\frac{1}{2}} & & \delta_{-\frac{1}{2}}^3 \\
f_0 & & \delta_0^2 & \\
 & \delta_{\frac{1}{2}} & & \boldsymbol{\delta_{\frac{1}{2}}^3} = \delta_{-\frac{1}{2}}^3 \\
f_1 & & \boldsymbol{\delta_1^2} & \\
\end{array}
$$

135

Similar extensions, taking a constant highest order difference may be used for higher order Bessel formulae. The principle employed is simply this: the table is differenced using entries f_x for negative x (or increasing positive x if we are in the first panel) until a higher difference which may be regarded as constant is found. This is then added forward (or backward) to extend the next lower difference column, and so on. The method may take longer than the use of a special end-panel formula, but it serves to determine the order of the Bessel formula required. However, where the argument for the interpolate required is a multiple of one-tenth of the tabular argument interval (as for example in Table 51) the brief Table 67 B of four-point Lagrangian coefficients will be found useful.

36.3   *Everett central difference interpolation formula*

We quote this formula here because (*a*) the coefficients have been very fully tabled by A. J. Thompson (1943), (*b*) it is expressed in terms of the even central differences only, and these can be obtained rapidly using a desk calculator, without any need to formulate the odd differences. We have in symmetrical form

$$f_\theta = \theta_0 f_0 + \theta_1 f_1 - \tfrac{1}{6}\theta_0\theta_1\{(1+\theta_0)\,\delta_0^2 + (1+\theta_1)\,\delta_1^2\}$$
$$+ \tfrac{1}{120}\theta_0\theta_1(1+\theta_0)(1+\theta_1)\{(2+\theta_0)\,\delta_0^4 + (2+\theta_1)\,\delta_1^4\} + \dots, \qquad (321)$$

where $\theta_0 = 1-\theta_1 = 1-\theta$ in notation of § 36.1. The δ^2 term involves the use of four table entries and includes the $\delta_{\frac{3}{2}}^3$ term of the Bessel formula; in the same way the δ^4 term, using six table entries, f_{-2} to f_3, includes the $\delta_{\frac{5}{2}}^5$ term of the Bessel formula (314). As for Bessel, we may truncate (321) after the δ^2 term if $|\delta^4| \leqslant 20$ and after the $|\delta^4|$ term if $|\delta^6| \leqslant 100$ in units of the last figure required. Formula (321) reduces to the form (319) if $|\delta^3| \leqslant 60$, $|\delta^4| \leqslant 20$.

For end-panel interpolation, when the fourth differences term can be neglected, which is likely to be so if $|\delta_1^4| < 12$ in units of the last figure, we have

$$f_\theta = \theta_0 f_0 + \theta_1 f_1 - \tfrac{1}{6}\theta_0\theta_1\{(4+\theta_1)\,\delta_0^2 - (1+\theta_1)\,\delta_{-1}^2\}. \qquad (322)$$

This simplifies to
$$f_\theta = \theta_0 f_0 + \theta_1 f_1 - \tfrac{1}{4}\theta_0\theta_1(\delta_0^2 + \delta_{-1}^2) \qquad (323)$$

if $|\delta^3| \leqslant 4$. An illustration of using (322) is given in Example 37, p. 51.

36.4   *Divided difference interpolation formula*

If a function $f(x)$ is tabled at unequal intervals of the argument x, it is sometimes easiest to carry out an interpolation using Newton's divided difference formula. Writing f_a for $f(x_a)$, etc., we have the difference scheme

$$
\begin{array}{llllll}
x_a & f_a & & & & \\
 & & \triangle f_a & & & \\
x_b & f_b & & \triangle^2 f_a & & \\
 & & \triangle f_b & & \triangle^3 f_a & \\
x_c & f_c & & \triangle^2 f_b & & \\
 & & \triangle f_c & & & \\
x_d & f_d & & & &
\end{array}
$$

where
$$\triangle f_a = \frac{f_b - f_a}{x_b - x_a}, \quad \triangle^2 f_a = \frac{\triangle f_b - \triangle f_a}{x_c - x_a}, \left.\begin{array}{c} \\ \\ \\ \\ \end{array}\right\}$$
$$\triangle^3 f_a = \frac{\triangle^2 f_b - \triangle^2 f_a}{x_d - x_a}, \quad \dots, \text{etc.} \qquad (324)$$

Then Newton's formula can be expressed as follows:

$$f(x) = f_a + (x-x_a)\,\triangle f_a + (x-x_a)(x-x_b)\,\triangle^2 f_a + (x-x_a)(x-x_b)(x-x_c)\,\triangle^3 f_a + \dots. \qquad (325)$$

136

If we neglect terms containing fourth and higher divided differences, equation (325) represents the cubic which passes through the four points with co-ordinates $(x_a, f_a), ..., (x_d, f_d)$. In general the remainder term, using the cubic is likely to be least when x_a is defined so that x falls in the central panel between x_b and x_c.

An illustration of the use of this formula is given in Example 64, p. 129.

36.5 *Harmonic interpolation*

A number of tables in this volume and in *B.T.S.* 1 use 'harmonic arguments' of the form $120/i$ (e.g. Table 5), sometimes $240/i$ (e.g. Table 48) or $60/i$ (i.e. Table 47). In such cases i is used as the argument for interpolation rather than $120/i$, etc. Even when the series of argument values includes $240/i$, having regard to the convergence of successive differences it may pay in *part* of the range to use a double harmonic interval corresponding to the series $240/(2i) = \infty, 120, 60, 40, 30, 24, 20$ rather than $240/i = \infty, 240, 120, 80, 60, 48, 40$. Table 68 is discussed on p. 138 below.

In the case of Tables 26 and 27 the highest arguments are $\nu = 9, 16, 36, 144, \infty$ making interpolation easy with an argument $12/\sqrt{\nu} = 4, 3, 2, 1, 0$.

36.6 *Double-entry interpolation. Use of Table* 68

Many tables in both *B.T.S.* 1 and *B.T.S.* 2 are double-entry tables for a function $f(x, y)$ depending on two arguments x and y. Assuming that both x and y progress at equidistant argument steps of unity, the simplest case is one in which it is permissible to use double-linear interpolation, based on the four nearest table entries only.

If θ, ϕ are the interpolation fractions ($0 \leqslant \theta \leqslant 1$, $0 \leqslant \phi \leqslant 1$) for x and y, then $f_{\theta, \phi}$ is given by

$$f_{\theta, \phi} = (1 - \theta - \phi + \theta\phi)f_{0,0} + (\theta - \theta\phi)f_{1,0} + (\phi - \theta\phi)f_{0,1} + \theta\phi f_{1,1} \qquad (326\,a)$$

$$= (1 - \theta)(1 - \phi)f_{0,0} + \theta(1 - \phi)f_{1,0} + \theta\phi f_{1,1} + (1 - \theta)\phi f_{0,1}. \qquad (326\,b)$$

The form (326 *a*) is useful for an occasional interpolation since only $\theta\phi$ need be pre-worked and the terms within the parentheses can be applied sequentially. The second form (326 *b*) is useful since it sometimes happens that we wish to make more than one interpolation at θ, ϕ, e.g. to determine more than one percentage point of $F(\alpha | \nu_1, \nu_2)$, and it may be found helpful to pre-work the numerical values of the coefficients and to use the tabular scheme shown below. It is seen that we have to multiply each table entry by the fractional factor shown in brackets in the *diagonally opposite quadrant* of the square.

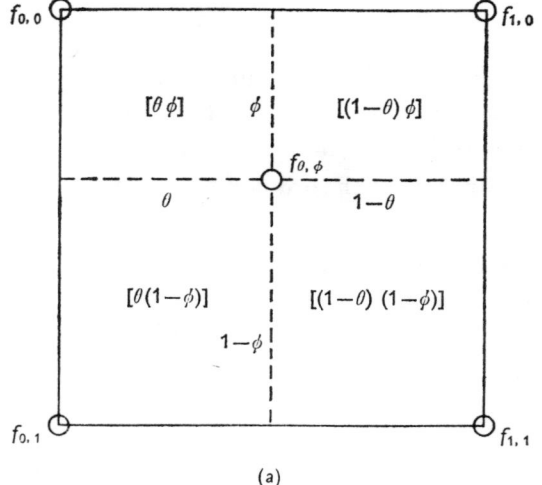

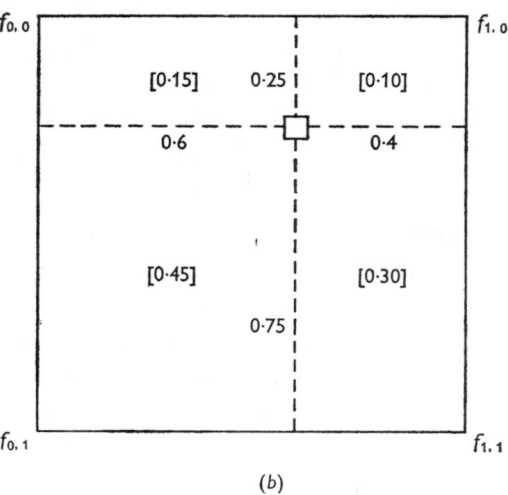

(a)   (b)

For example, if $\theta = 0.6$, $\phi = 0.25$ we get the scheme (b) and going round in cyclic order have

$$f_{0.60,\,0.25} = 0.30f_{0,\,0} + 0.45f_{1,\,0} + 0.15f_{1,\,1} + 0.10f_{0,\,1}.$$

The procedure is illustrated in Example 37, p. 51.

When double-linear interpolation is not sufficiently accurate, then it is necessary to proceed in two stages. Suppose a study of the differences shows that four-point interpolation, using formula (319) is adequate x-wise, but that the δ^3 term is not negligible y-wise (or indeed that the δ^4 term must be used). Then we should start by interpolating for x at four (or if necessary six) appropriately chosen table entries for y, and taking the four (or six) resulting figures with correct x, proceed to a single interpolation y-wise, using formula (320) (or if necessary incorporating the B_4 term in (314)). The procedure is illustrated in Examples 48, p. 77 and 51, p. 83.

If double interpolation to a high order is required for *both* arguments x and y, the number of differences to be formed may become excessive, and the above procedure should if possible only be used if at most one of the four-point formulae (319) or (320) is needed for the first stage interpolation. In rare cases, when higher precision is required one of the seven-point Lagrangian formulae given in Table 68 (Comrie & Hartley, 1941) may be found helpful. These were primarily devised for use with the harmonic arguments of the tables of percentage points of the beta distribution (Table 16, *B.T.S.* **1**) and the F-distribution (Table 5, *B.T.S.* **2**), but they can of course be used with any function which can be adequately represented by a polynomial in $1/x$ and for which the function has been tabled at seven values of x in harmonic progression.

To explain the use of the table consider the case of a single entry interpolation for $F(\alpha|\nu_1, \nu_2)$, where ν_1 corresponds to a tabular value but ν_2 does not. Then if full accuracy is called for, $F(\alpha|\nu_1, \nu_2)$ may need to be obtained by interpolation between seven tabular values $F(\alpha|\nu_1, \nu_2(i))$, $i = 1, 2, ..., 7$. The argument ν_2 of the required interpolate is shown as a row heading while the seven column headings are the arguments $\nu_2(i)$ of the tabular values to be used in the Lagrangian formula

$$F(\alpha|\nu_1, \nu_2) = \sum_{i=1}^{7} L(\nu_2, \nu_2(i))\, F(\alpha|\nu_1, \nu_2(i)). \tag{327}$$

The Lagrangian coefficients, $L(\nu_2, \nu_2(i))$ are shown in the body of the table.

For double-entry interpolation to high accuracy for both ν_1 and ν_2, the formula (327) is first applied ν_2-wise seven times for each of the tabular $\nu_1(j)$ which are needed for the second stage, ν_1-wise interpolation.

Two further points should be noted:

(a) In the early part of the table with the tabular values in the column headings $\leqslant 30$, ordinary Lagrangian coefficients based on equal, not harmonic intervals have been given. This means that for the row entries 16, 17, 18 and 19 two formulae are available. In the case of the percentage points of the beta distribution it is likely that the ordinary formula will here be the more accurate.

(b) The table may be used not only for the progression 10, 12, 15, 20, 24, 30, 40, 60, 120, ∞ but also for sub-multiple progressions. The most important of these is 10, 12, 15, 20, 30, 60, ∞. For this, the arguments for the interpolate and tabular values are halved, as shown in parentheses in the margins. It can also be used for the progression 40, 48, 60, 80, 120, 240, ∞ (as in Table 48) but in this case only even arguments of the interpolate are catered for.

37. Lagrangian interpolation

37.1 *Specialized tables of coefficients* (*Tables* 67 A, B, C *and* D)

While for most purposes the Bessel formula (314), using the differences of the tabled function with their monitoring property, seems to provide the quickest and most reliable interpolation procedure, there are circumstances where a simple Lagrangian formula will prove useful. These occur, for example, when:

(*a*) The function has been tabled for values of the argument which are neither equally spaced nor in harmonic progression.

(*b*) The interpolate is required at integer values of the argument, but in part of the range covered has only been tabled at every tenth or even every twentieth integer.

To meet these needs we give in Tables 67 A–D coefficients of the four-point Lagrangian

$$f_x = L_{-1}f_{-1} + L_0 f_0 + L_1 f_1 + L_2 f_2 \tag{328}$$

appropriate to use in certain tables included in this volume and in *B.T.S.* **1**.

Case A. Here we use the ordinary four-point Lagrangian formula appropriate for application to four equally spaced table entries, f_{-1}, f_0, f_1, f_2, namely:

$$\left. \begin{aligned} f_\theta &= \frac{(\theta+1)\,\theta(\theta-1)\,(\theta-2)}{6} \left\{ -\frac{f_1}{\theta+1} + \frac{3f_0}{\theta} - \frac{3f_1}{\theta-1} + \frac{f_2}{\theta-2} \right\} \\ &= L_{-1}f_{-1} + L_0 f_0 + L_1 f_1 + L_2 f_2. \end{aligned} \right\} \tag{329}$$

The table provides the coefficients for $\theta = 0\cdot05(0\cdot05)0\cdot95$. The coefficients are given as integral multipliers with a common integral divisor.

Case B. This table may be used for end-panel interpolation between f_1 and f_2, using formula (329). It gives coefficients for $\theta = 1\cdot1(0\cdot1)1\cdot9$.

Case C. Table 24 (for non-central χ) and Table 51 (dealing with the largest and smallest roots of a matrix) give, for values of the argument $\nu \geqslant 12$, values of the function only at $\nu = 15$ and 20. Table 67 C provides the coefficients L, by which to multiply f_{-1}, f_0, f_1 and f_2, where in the case of Table 24

$$f_{-1} = \chi'(\alpha | \nu = 11), \quad f_0 = \chi'(\alpha | 12), \quad f_1 = \chi'(\alpha | 15), \quad f_2 = \chi'(\alpha | 20).$$

In this way we find $\chi'(\alpha | \nu)$ at $\nu = 13, 14, 16, 17, 18$ and 19. These coefficients are again given in the form of an integral multiplier and a common integral divisor.

Case D. In Table 48 (for Roy's maximum root criterion $t_{\max.}$) the function is given for values of one of the arguments (*m*) at 0(1)5, 7, 10, 15. We give in Table 68 B:

(i) coefficients to determine $t_{\max.}$ at $m = 6$ from its values at $m = 4, 5, 7$ and 10;

(ii) coefficients to determine $t_{\max.}$ at $m = 8, 9, 11, 12, 13$ and 14 from values at $m = 5, 7, 10$ and 15.

37.2 *Lagrangian coefficients for interpolation between percentage points or quantiles* (*Table* 69)

If other things were equal, an easily interpolable table of the probability integral of a function, $f(x)$, would have more general value than a table of a limited number of percentage points or quantiles. But the increasing need to deal with functions not only of single but of double and sometimes triple entry has made the publication, if not always the computation, of finely graduated probability integrals prohibitive. R. A. Fisher's memorable first edition of

Statistical Methods for Research Workers, published in 1925, contained tables using percentage levels as arguments for the χ^2, t, r and z distributions, the last for a 5 per cent level only. While there are now tables, e.g. Table 3, giving as many as twenty-three quantiles, the majority are less ambitious. Writing

$$P = \int_{\infty}^{x(P)} f(u)\,du = 1 - Q,$$

we find in this volume, as elsewhere, that values of $x(P_i)$ are tabled at certain standard or conventional levels generally included in the series

$$P \text{ (or } Q) = 0{\cdot}001,\ 0{\cdot}0025,\ 0{\cdot}005,\ 0{\cdot}01,\ 0{\cdot}025,\ 0{\cdot}05,\ 0{\cdot}10,\ 0{\cdot}25,\ 0{\cdot}50,$$

with values at $0{\cdot}20$, $0{\cdot}30$, $0{\cdot}40$ sometimes added.

While we should like to be able to use such tables both to find x for an intermediate P or to find P for an intermediate x, the former is the easier problem. If we can break down an interval sufficiently, linear interpolation either way may then become possible. The need for this gap-filling may arise:

(a) If for some special and perhaps limited purpose, it is desired to form an easily interpolable table of x_P at equal intervals of the argument P. This has of course been done with great accuracy for the normal function, but a similar, rougher table might be needed for the gamma function or, within some limited range of arguments, for the beta function.

(b) If an experiment has given one or more specific values of $P(x)$ we might wish to determine the corresponding value or values of $x(P)$ with reasonable accuracy. To do this it may be helpful to compute some additional value of $x(P)$ for P-values falling between the conventional tabled entries.

Table 69 contains the coefficients for a series of five-point Lagrangian interpolation formulae which may be used in this way to break down the gaps between the standard quantiles $x(P)$. Several 'grids', each based on a group of five P-values are of course needed to cover the full range of P (or Q), needed, but apart from this necessary shifting of grids a difficulty arises because published tables vary considerably in the standard quantiles which they record. The method of determining the coefficients in Table 69, based on the logit transformation $l_P = \log\{P/(1-P)\}$ has been described by Pearson (1968). Coefficients to use with eight different grids are provided, the grids being defined in the following table:

Levels used for grids in Table 69

Grid no.	Standard P-values for which x_P is assumed known				
1	0·001	0·0025	0·005	0·01	0·025
1A	·001	·005	·01	·025	·05
2	·0025	·005	·01	·025	·05
3	·005	·01	·025	·05	·10
4	·05	·10	·20	·30	·40
4A	·025	·05	·10	·25	·50
5	·20	·30	·40	·50	·60
5A	·10	·25	·50	·75	·90

The desired $x(P)$ is determined from the five-point formula

$$x(P) = L_1 x(P_1) + L_2 x(P_2) + L_3 x(P_3) + L_4 x(P_4) + L_5 x(P_5), \tag{330}$$

where the L_i are given to six decimals in Table 69 and the $x(P_i)$ are the percentage points or quantiles for the five pivotal levels of the chosen percentage grid, given to us in the particular table we are using.

As an example, we could find the lower 2 per cent point of χ^2, when $\nu = 30$, using Grid 3, by taking the $\chi^2(P_i)$ from Table 3 and proceeding as follows:

P_i	0·005	0·01	0·025	0·05	0·10
L_i	-0.031146	0·199495	0·988448	-0.183001	0·026203
$\chi^2(P_i)$	13·7867	14·9535	16·7908	18·4927	20·5992

Summing the products $L_i \chi^2(P_i)$ we find $\chi^2(0.02 | 30) = 16.3062$. The value given in Table IV of Fisher & Yates (1963) is 16·306.

Pearson (1968) examined the accuracy of these interpolation formulae by applying them to several distributions some of which differed very considerably from the logistic, for which interpolation would be exact. The following table summarizes his published results. The comparisons were made at a large number of P-values taken roughly in the middle of panels of a grid, where errors would be greatest. Maximum errors found are expressed in units of $10^5 \times$ population σ, e.g. for the negative exponential, with $\sigma = 1.0$, a maximum error recorded as 12 is one of 0·00012. For the two symmetrical populations, only half the number of comparisons were made. Where there is complete freedom of choice, the grids nos. 1, 2, 3, 4 and 5 will give the best results, using one or other of the two central panels in each case. However, at the lower end of the P-scale it may be necessary to use Grid 1 A because of the absence of a quantile at $P = 0.0025$ in many tables. Again the Grids 4 A and 5 A may be needed if the only quantile tabled between 0·10 and 0·50 is at 0·25. For many purposes, however, even an error of 0·005 would be tolerable. As Pearson points out, improved results might be obtained by basing the Lagrangian on different transforms of P, according to the shape of $f(x)$, but his object was to provide a single series of Lagrangian coefficients to be used over a very wide field of distributions. Illustrations of the use of the table have been given in Example 5, p. 9, and in Example 9, p. 18.

			Maximum errors (numerical values) in units of $10^5 \times$ S.D. (no. of comparisons given in parentheses)						
			Grids 1–5		Grid 1A		Grid 4A		Grid 5A	
Distribution	$\sqrt{\beta_1}$	β_2	Max.	(No.)	Max.	(No.)	Max.	(No.)	Max.	(No.)
Rectangle	0·0	1·80	60	(15)	120	(3)	700	(4)	1600	(3)
Symmetrical S_U	0·0	8·02	1	(15)	2	(3)	20	(4)	70	(3)
Log-normal	0·78	4·10	12	(30)	16	(6)	90	(8)	500	(6)
Skew S_U	1·65	9·00	5	(30)	22	(6)	60	(8)	70	(6)
Neg. exponential	2·00	9·00	12	(30)	50	(6)	140	(8)	190	(6)

APPENDIX I

LIST OF REFERENCES

D'AGOSTINO, R. B. (1970). Transformation to normality of the null distribution of g_1. *Biometrika* **57**, 679–81.

AMOS, D. E. & DANIEL, S. L. (1971). *Tables of Percentage Points of Standardized Pearson Distributions.* Sandia Research Report, S.C.–RR–0348.

AMOS, D. E. & PEARSON, E. S. (1970). Corrections and additions to a table of the percentage points of the variance ratio F. *Biometrika* **57**, 211–2.

ANDERSON, T. W. (1958). *An Introduction to Multivariate Statistical Analysis.* New York: John Wiley and Sons.

ANDERSON, T. W. (1965). Some optimum confidence bounds for roots of determinantal equations. *Ann. Math. Statist.* **36**, 468–88.

ANDERSON, T. W. & STEPHENS, M. A. (1971). Tests for randomness of directions against equatorial and bimodal distributions. Stanford Univ. Dept. of Statistics, Tech. Report no 181.

BARTLETT, M. S. (1934). The vector representation of a sample. *Proc. Camb. Phil. Soc.* **30**, 327–40.

BARTLETT, M. S. (1937). Properties of sufficiency and statistical tests. *Proc. Roy. Soc.* A **160**, 268–82.

BARTLETT, M. S. (1938). Further aspects of the theory of multiple regression. *Proc. Cam. Phil. Soc.* **34**, 33–40.

BARTLETT, M. S. (1951). The goodness of fit of a hypothetical discriminant function. *Ann. Eugen.* **16**, 199–214.

BARTLETT, M. S. (1967). Contribution to discussion following paper by E. J. Williams. *J. R. Statist. Soc.* B **29**, 231–2.

BERKSON, J. (1944). Application of the logistic function to bio-assay. *J. Amer. Statist. Ass.* **39**, 357–65.

BERKSON, J. (1953). A statistically precise and relatively simple method of estimating the bio-assay with quantal response, based on the logistic function. *J. Amer. Statist. Ass.* **48**, 565–99.

BERKSON, J. (1957*a*). Tables for the maximum likelihood estimate of the logistic function. *Biometrics* **13**, 28–34.

BERKSON, J. (1957*b*). Tables for use in estimating the normal distribution function by normit analysis. *Biometrika* **44**, 411–35.

BERKSON, J. (1960). Nomograms for fitting the logistic function by maximum likelihood. *Biometrika* **47**, 121–41.

BOWMAN, K. O. & SHENTON, L. R. (1968). Properties of estimators for the Gamma distribution. *Union Carbide Corporation Report CTC*-1, Oak Ridge, Tennessee.

BOWMAN, K. O. & SHENTON, L. R. (1970). Small sample properties of estimators for the Gamma distribution. *Union Carbide Corporation Report CTC*-28, Oak Ridge, Tennessee.

BOX, G. E. P. (1949). A general distribution theory for a class of likelihood criteria. *Biometrika* **36**, 317–46.

BOX, G. E. P. (1953). Non-normality and tests on variances. *Biometrika* **40**, 318–35.

CARTER, A. H. (1947). Approximation to percentage points of the z-distribution. *Biometrika* **34**, 352–8.

COMRIE, L. J. & HARTLEY, H. O. (1941). Table of Lagrangian coefficients for harmonic interpolation in certain tables of percentage points. *Biometrika* **32**, 183–6.

DAVID, F. N. & JOHNSON, N. L. (1954). Statistical treatment of censored data. I. Fundamental formulae. *Biometrika* **41**, 228–40.

DAVID, H. A. (1970). *Order Statistics.* New York: John Wiley and Sons.

DAVIES, O. L. (1947). *Statistical Methods in Research and Production.* Edinburgh: Oliver and Boyd.

DEMPSTER, A. P. & SCHATZOFF, M. (1965). Expected significance level as a sensitivity index for test statistics. *J. Amer. Statist. Ass.* **60**, 420–36.

DRAPER, J. (1952). Properties of distributions resulting from certain simple transformations of the normal distribution. *Biometrika* **39**, 290–301.

EISENBERGER, I. & POSNER, E. C. (1965). Systematic statistics used for data compression in space telemetry. *J. Amer. Statist. Ass.* **60**, 97–133.

EISENHART, C., HASTAY, M. W. & WALLIS, W. A. (1947). *Selected Techniques of Statistical Analysis.* New York: McGraw-Hill Book Co.

ELDERTON, W. P. & JOHNSON, N. L. (1969). *Systems of Frequency Curves.* Cambridge University Press.

FEDEREE, W. T. (1955). *Experimental Design.* New York and London: The Macmillan Co.

FIELLER, E. C., HARTLEY, H. O. & PEARSON, E. S. (1957). Tests for rank correlation coefficients. I. *Biometrika* **44**, 470–81.

142

FIELLER, E. C. & PEARSON, E. S. (1961). Tests for rank correlation coefficients. II. *Biometrika* **48**. 29–40.

FINNEY, D. J. (1952). *Statistical Methods in Biological Assay.* London: Chas. Griffin and Co.

FISHER, R. A. (1920). A mathematical examination of the methods of determining the accuracy of an observation by the mean error, and by the mean square error. *Mon. Not. Roy. Astro. Soc.* **80**, 758–70.

FISHER, R. A. (1922). On the mathematical foundations of theoretical statistics. *Phil. Trans.* A **222**, 309–68.

FISHER, R. A. (1928). The general sampling distribution of the multiple correlation coefficient. *Proc. Roy. Soc.* A, **121**, 654–73.

FISHER, R. A. (1929). The moments of the distribution for normal samples of measures of departure from normality. *Lond. Math. Soc.* **30**, 199–238.

FISHER, R. A. (1931). Properties of *Hh* functions. Introduction to *British Association Mathematical Tables* **1**, xxvi.

FISHER, R. A. (1932). *Statistical Methods for Research Workers*, 4th Ed. Edinburgh: Oliver and Boyd.

FISHER, R. A. (1939). The sampling distribution of some statistics obtained from non-linear equations. *Ann. Eugen.* **9**, 238–49.

FISHER, R. A. (1953). Dispersion on a sphere. *Proc. Roy. Soc.* A **217**, 295–305.

FISHER, R. A. & YATES, F. (1938). *Statistical Tables for Biological, Agricultural and Medical Research.* Edinburgh: Oliver and Boyd.

FIX, EVELYN (1949). Tables of non-central χ^2. *University of California Publications in Statistics* **1**, No. 2, 15–19.

FIX, EVELYN & HODGES, J. L. (1955). Significance probabilities of the Wilcoxon test. *Ann. Math. Statist.* **26**, 301–12.

FOSTER, F. G. (1957, 1958). Upper percentage points of the generalized beta distribution. II. *Biometrika* **44**, 441–53; III, **45**, 492–503.

FOSTER, F. G. & REES, D. H. (1957). Upper percentage points of the generalised beta distribution. I. *Biometrika* **44**, 237–47.

FOX, M. (1956). Charts of the power function of the *F*-test. *Ann. Math. Statist.* **27**, 484–97.

FRIEDMAN, M. (1937). The use of ranks to avoid the assumption of normality implicit in the analysis of variance. *J. Amer. Statist. Ass.* **32**, 675–701.

GARWOOD, F. (1933). Unpublished Ph.D. Thesis, University of London.

GARWOOD, F. (1941). The application of maximum likelihood to dosage mortality curves. *Biometrika* **32**, 46–58.

GIRSHICK, M. A. (1939). On the sampling theory of the roots of determinantal equations. *Ann. Math. Statist.* **10**, 203–24.

GODWIN, H. J. (1945). On the distribution of the estimate of mean deviation obtained from samples from a normal population. *Biometrika* **33**, 254–6.

GOVINDARAJULU, Z. & EISENSTAT, S. (1964). Best estimates of location and scale parameters of a chi (i.d.f.) distribution, using ordered observations. *Case Institute of Technology Statistical Laboratory Report* No. 206. Re-issued (1965) in *Reports of Statistical Application Research* (Japanese Union of Scientists and Engineers) **12**, 149–64.

GREENWOOD, J. A. & DURAND, D. (1960). Aids for fitting the gamma distribution by maximum likelihood. *Technometrics* **2**, 55–65.

GRUBBS, F. E. (1950). Sample criteria for testing outlying observations. *Ann. Math. Statist.* **21**, 27–58.

GUMBEL, E. J., GREENWOOD, J. A. & DURAND, D. (1953). The circular normal distribution: theory and tables. *J. Amer. Statist. Ass.* **48**, 131–52.

GUPTA, A. K. (1952). Estimation of the mean and standard deviation of a normal population from a censored sample. *Biometrika* **39**, 260–73.

HANUMARA, R. C. & THOMPSON, W. A. (1968). Percentage points of the extreme roots of a Wishart matrix. *Biometrika* **55**, 505–12.

HARTER, H. L. (1961). Expected values of normal order statistics. *Biometrika* **48**, 151–65.

HARTER, H. L. (1964 a). *Expected Values of Exponential, Weibull and Gamma Order Statistics.* Aerospace Research Laboratories Report **64–31**, Wright Patterson Air Force Base, Ohio.

HARTER, H. L. (1964 b). A new table of percentage points of the chi-square distribution. *Biometrika* **51**, 231–9.

HARTER, H. L. (1964 c). *More Tables of the Incomplete Gamma-Function Ratio and of the Percentage Points of the Chi-square Distribution.* Aerospace Research Laboratories Report **64–123**, Wright Patterson Air Force Base, Ohio.

HARTER, H. L. (1967). *Theory and Tables for Tests of Hypotheses concerning the Mean and the Variance of a Weibull Distribution.* Aerospace Research Laboratories Report **67–0059**, Wright Patterson Air Force Base, Ohio.

HARTER, H. L. (1970). *Order Statistics and their Use in Testing and Estimation* **1**, **2**. Aerospace Research Laboratories, Wright Patterson Air Force Base, Ohio.

HARTER, H. L. & OWEN, D. B. (1970). *Selected Tables in Mathematical Statistics*. Sponsored by the Institute of Mathematical Statistics. Chicago: Markham Publishing Co.

HAYNAM, G. E., GOVINDARAJULU, Z. & LEONE, F. C. (1962). Unpublished Report of Case Institute of Technology.

HELMERT, R. F. (1876). Die Genauigkeit der Formel von Peters zur Berechnung des wahrscheinlichen Beobachtungsfehlers direkter Beobachtungen gleicher Genauigkeit. *Astr. Nachr.* **88**, no. 2096.

H.M. NAUTICAL ALMANAC OFFICE (1956). *Interpolation and Allied Tables*. London: H.M. Stationery Office.

HOGBEN, D., PINKHAM, R. S. & WILK, M. B. (1961). The moments of the non-central t-distribution. *Biometrika* **48**, 465–8.

HOTELLING, H. (1951). A generalized T test and a measure of multivariate dispersion. *Proc. 2nd Berkeley Symp. Math. Statist. and Prob., Univ. of California Press*, 23–42.

HSU, D. L. (1939). On the distribution of roots of certain determinantal equations. *Ann. Eugen.* **9**, 250–8.

IRWIN, J. O. & CHEESMAN, E. A. (1939). On the maximum-likelihood method of determining dosage–response curves and approximations to the median-effective dose, in cases of quantal response. *J. R. Statist. Soc.* Suppl. **6**, 174–85.

JAMES, A. T. (1964). Distribution of matrix variates and latent roots derived from normal samples. *Ann. Math. Statist.* **35**, 475–501.

JOHNSON, N. L. (1949). Systems of frequency curves generated by methods of translation. *Biometrika* **36**, 149–76.

JOHNSON, N. L. (1965). Tables to facilitate fitting S_U frequency curves. *Biometrika* **52**, 547–58.

JOHNSON, N. L. (1968). Tables of Percentile Points of the Non-central Chi-square Distribution. Univ. of N. Carolina, Institute of Statistics, Mimeo Series no. 568.

JOHNSON, N. L. (1970). *Tables to facilitate fitting S_B curves*. With an Appendix by J. O. Kitchen. Univ. of N. Carolina, Institute of Statistics. Mimeo Series no. 683.

JOHNSON, N. L. & KOTZ, S. (1967). *Tables of Distributions of Quadratic Forms in Central Normal Variables*. II. Univ. of N. Carolina, Institute of Statistics, Mimeo Series no. 557.

JOHNSON, N. L., NIXON, E., AMOS, D. E. & PEARSON, E. S. (1963). Table of percentage points of Pearson curves, for given $\sqrt{\beta_1}$ and β_2, expressed in standard measure. *Biometrika* **50**, 459–98.

JOHNSON, N. L. & PEARSON, E. S. (1969). Tables of percentage points of non-central χ. *Biometrika* **56**, 255–72.

JOHNSON, N. L. & WELCH, B. L. (1939). Applications of the non-central t-distribution. *Biometrika* **31**, 362–89.

KASTENBAUM, M. A., HOEL, D. G. & BOWMAN, K. O. (1970*a, b*). Sample size requirements (*a*) One way analysis of variance. (*b*) Randomized block designs. *Biometrika* **57**, (*a*) 421–30; (*b*) 573–7.

KENDALL, M. G. & BABINGTON SMITH, B. (1939). The problem of m rankings. *Ann. Math. Statist.* **10**, 275–87.

KENDALL, M. G. & STUART, A. (1961). *The Advanced Theory of Statistics* **2**, London: Charles Griffin and Co.

KENDALL, M. G. & STUART, A. (1966). *The Advanced Theory of Statistics*, **3**. London: Charles Griffin and Co.

KHAMIS, S. H. & RUDERT, W. (1965). *Tables of the Incomplete Gamma Function Ratio*. Darmstadt: Justus von Leibig.

KHATRI, C. G. (1966). A note on a large sample distribution of a transformed multiple correlation coefficient. *Ann. Inst. Statist. Maths.* **18**, 375–80.

KIERSCH, G. A. (1950). Small scale structures and other features of Navajo sandstone, northern part of Rafael Swell, Utah. *Am. Assoc. Pet. Geol.* **34**, 923–42.

KIM, P. J. (1969). On the exact and approximate sampling distribution of the two sample Kolmogorov–Smirnov criterion, $D_{m,n}$, $m \leqslant n$. *J. Amer. Statist. Ass.* **64**, 1625–37.

KIM, P. J. & JENNRICH, R. I. (1970). *Selected Tables in Mathematical Statistics* I. Edited by H. L. Harter and D. B. Owen. Chicago: Markham Publishing Co. for the Institute of Mathematical Statistics.

KOLODZIETCZYK, S. (1935). On an important class of statistical hypotheses. *Biometrika* **27**, 161–90.

KONDO, T. & ELDERTON, E. M. (1931). Table of normal curve functions to each permille of frequency. *Biometrika* **22**, 368–76.

KORIN, B. P. (1968). On the distribution of a statistic used for testing a covariance matrix. *Biometrika* **55**, 171–8.

KORIN, B. P. (1969). On testing the equality of k covariance matrices. *Biometrika* **56**, 216–18.

KRAMER, K. H. (1963). Tables for constructing confidence limits on the multiple correlation coefficient. *J. Amer. Statist. Ass.* **58**, 1082–5.

KRUSKAL, W. H. & WALLIS, W. A. (1952). The use of ranks in one-criterion variance analysis. *J. Amer. Statist. Ass.* **47**, 583–621.

LAWLEY, D. N. (1938). A generalization of Fisher's z-test. *Biometrika* **30**, 180–7.

MAGUIRE, B. A., PEARSON, E. S. & WYNN, A. H. A. (1952). The time intervals between industrial accidents. *Biometrika* **39**, 168–80.

MANN, H. B. & WHITNEY, D. R. (1947). On a test of whether one of two random variables is stochastically larger than the other. *Ann. Math. Statist.* **18**, 50–60.

MARSHALL, A. W. (1958). Small sample distribution of nw_n^2. *Ann. Math. Statist.* **29**, 307–9.

MASUYAMA, M. & KUROIWA, Y. (1951). Table of the likelihood solutions of gamma distribution and its medical applications. *Rep. Statist. Appl. Res. Un. Jap. Sci. Engrs* **1**, 18–23.

MERRINGTON, MAXINE & PEARSON, E. S. (1958). An approximation to the distribution of non-central *t*. *Biometrika* **45**, 484–91.

MERRINGTON, MAXINE & THOMPSON, CATHERINE M. (1943). Tables of percentage points of the inverted beta (*F*) distribution. *Biometrika* **33**, 74–88.

NAIR, K. R. (1948). The distribution of the extreme deviate from the sample mean and its studentized form. *Biometrika* **35**, 118–44.

OWEN, D. B. (1962). *Handbook of Statistical Tables*. Reading, Massachusetts: Addison-Wesley Publishing Co.

OWEN, D. B. (1963). *Factors for One-sided Tolerance Limits and for Variables Sampling Plans*. Sandia Corporation Monograph, no. 607.

PATNAIK, P. B. (1949). The non-central χ^2 and *F*-distributions and their applications. *Biometrika* **36**, 202–32.

PEARSON, E. S. (1938). The probability integral transformation for testing goodness of fit and combining independent tests of significance. *Biometrika* **30**, 134–48.

PEARSON, E. S. (1959). Note on an approximation to the distribution of non-central χ^2. *Biometrika* **46**, 364.

PEARSON, E. S. (1963*a*). Some problems arising in approximating to probability distributions, using moments. *Biometrika* **50**, 95–112.

PEARSON, E. S. (1963*b*). Comparison of tests for randomness of points on a line. *Biometrika* **50**, 315–23.

PEARSON, E. S. (1965). Percentage points of $\sqrt{b_1}$ and b_2 in normal samples; a rounding off. *Biometrika* **52**, 282–5.

PEARSON, E. S. (1968). Lagrangian coefficients for interpolation between tabled percentage points. *Biometrika* **55**, 19–28.

PEARSON, E. S. (1969). Some comments on the accuracy of Box's approximations to the distribution of *M*. *Biometrika* **56**, 219–20.

PEARSON, E. S. & HARTLEY, H. O. (1951). Charts of the power function for analysis of variance tests, derived from the non-central *F*-distribution. *Biometrika* **38**, 112–30.

PEARSON, E. S. & TIKU, M. L. (1970). Some notes on the relationship between the distributions of central and non-central *F*. *Biometrika* **57**, 175–9.

PEARSON, E. S. & TUKEY, J. W. (1965). Approximate means and standard deviations based on distances between percentage points of frequency curves. *Biometrika* **52**, 533–46.

PEARSON, E. S. & WELCH, B. L. (1937). Notes on some statistical problems raised by Mr Bayes's paper. *J. R. Statist. Soc. Suppl.* **4**, 94–101.

PEARSON, E. S. & WILKS, S. S. (1933). Methods of statistical analysis appropriate for *k* samples of two variables. *Biometrika* **25**, 353–78.

PEARSON, K. (1922). *Tables of the Incomplete Γ-function*. Cambridge University Press.

PEARSON, K. (1931). *Tables for Statisticians and Biometricians*. Part 2. Cambridge University Press.

PEARSON, K. (1934). *Tables of the Incomplete Beta Function*; (1968) 2nd Edition with new Introduction by Pearson, E. S. & Johnson, N. L. Cambridge University Press.

PILLAI, K. C. S. (1955). Some new test criteria in multivariate analysis. *Ann. Math. Statist.* **26**, 117–21.

PILLAI, K. C. S. (1956). On the distribution of the largest or the smallest root of a matrix in multivariate analysis. *Biometrika* **43**, 122–7.

PILLAI, K. C. S. (1960). *Statistical Tables for Tests of Multivariate Hypotheses*. Manila: The Statistical Center, University of the Philippines.

PILLAI, K. C. S. (1967). Upper percentage points of the largest root of a matrix in multivariate analysis. *Biometrika* **54**, 189–94.

PILLAI, K. C. S. & CHANG, T. C. (1968, 1970). An approximation to the C.D.F. of the largest root of a covariance matrix. First published (1968) with tables for $p = 2(1)20$ in *Purdue Dept. Statist. Mimeo Series* no. 184. Re-issued (1970) with tables for $p = 11(1)20$ in *Ann. Inst. Statist. Math.* Suppl. 6, 115–24.

PILLAI, K. C. S. & GUPTA, A. K. (1969). On the exact distribution of Wilks' criterion. *Biometrika* **56**, 109–18.

PILLAI, K. C. S. & JAYACHANDRAN, K. (1967). Power comparisons of tests of two multivariate hypotheses based on four criteria. *Biometrika* **54**, 195–210.

PILLAI, K. C. S. & JAYACHANDRAN, K. (1968). Power comparisons of tests of equality of two covariance matrices based on four criteria. *Biometrika* **55**, 335–42.

PROSCHAN, F. (1963). Theoretical explanation of observed decreasing failure rate. *Technometrics* **5**, 376.

RAO, C. R. (1948). Tests of significance in multivariate analysis. *Biometrika* **35**, 58–79.

RESNIKOFF, G. J. & LIEBERMAN, G. J. (1957). *Tables of the Non-central t-distribution.* Stanford University Press.

ROY, S. N. (1939). *p*-Statistics or some generalisations in analysis of variance appropriate to multivariate problems. *Sankhyā*, **4**, 381–96.

ROY, S. N. (1953). On a heuristic method of test construction and its use in multivariate analysis. *Ann. Math. Statist.* **24**, 220–38.

ROY, S. N. (1958). *Some Aspects of Multivariate Analysis.* New York: John Wiley and Sons.

RUBEN, H. (1954). On the moments of order statistics in samples from normal populations. *Biometrika* **41**, 200–7.

RUBEN, H. (1956). On the moments of the range and product moments of extreme order statistics in normal samples. *Biometrika* **43**, 458–60.

SARHAN, A. E. & GREENBERG, B. G. (1956). Estimation of location and scale parameters by order statistics from singly and doubly censored samples. *Ann. Math. Statist.* **27**, 427–51.

SARHAN, A. E. & GREENBERG, B. G. Editors. (1962). *Contributions to Order Statistics.* New York: John Wiley and Sons.

SCHATZOFF, M. (1966a). Sensitivity comparisons among tests of the general linear hypothesis. *J. Amer. Statist. Ass.* **61**, 415–35.

SCHATZOFF, M. (1966b). Exact distributions of Wilks's likelihood ratio criterion. *Biometrika* **53**, 347–58.

SHAPIRO, S. S. & WILK, M. B. (1965). An analysis of variance test for normality (complete samples). *Biometrika* **52**, 591–611.

SHAPIRO, S. S. & WILK, M. B. (1968). Approximations to the null distribution of the W statistic. *Technometrics* **10**, 861–6.

SHAPIRO, S. S., WILK, M. B. & CHEN, H. J. (1968). A comparative study of various tests for normality. *J. Amer. Statist. Ass.* **63**, 1343–72.

SIEGEL, S. & TUKEY, J. W. (1960). A non-parametric sum of ranks procedure for relative spread in unpaired samples. *J. Amer. Statist. Ass.* **55**, 429–45. Corrigenda: *J. Amer. Statist. Ass.* **56**, 1005.

STEPHENS, M. A. (1962a, b). Exact and approximate tests for directions. I. *Biometrika* **49**, 463–77; II. *Biometrika* **49**, 547–52.

STEPHENS, M. A. (1963). The distribution of the goodness-of-fit statistic, U_N^2. I. *Biometrika* **50**, 303–13.

STEPHENS, M. A. (1965). Appendix to G. S. Watson's Equatorial distributions on a sphere. *Biometrika* **52**, 200–1.

STEPHENS, M. A. (1967). Tests for the dispersion and for the modal vector of a distribution on a sphere. *Biometrika* **54**, 211–23.

STEPHENS, M. A. (1969a). Tests for the von Mises distribution. *Biometrika* **56**, 149–60.

STEPHENS, M. A. (1969b). Multi-sample test for the Fisher distribution for directions. *Biometrika* **56**, 169–83.

STEPHENS, M. A. (1969c). Tests for normality. *Stanford Univ. Dept. of Statistics Tech. Report* no. 152.

STEPHENS, M. A. (1970a). Techniques for directional data. *Stanford Univ. Dept. of Statistics Tech. Report* no. 150.

STEPHENS, M. A. (1970b). Use of the Kolmogorov–Smirnov, Cramér–von Mises and related statistics without extensive tables. *J. R. Statist. Soc.* B **32**, 115–22.

STEPHENS, M. A. (1970c). Kolmogorov-type tests for exponentiality when the scale parameter is unknown. *Stanford Univ. Dept. of Statistics Tech. Report* no. 154.

STEPHENS, M. A. (1972). Multi-sample tests for the von Mises distribution. *J. Amer. Statist. Ass.* **67**. (To appear in March issue.)

TANG, P. C. (1938). The power function of the analysis of variance tests with tables and illustrations. *Statist. Res. Mem.* **2**, 126–57.

TATE, R. F. (1955). The theory of correlation between two continuous variables when one is dichotomized. *Biometrika* **42**, 205–22.

THOMPSON, A. J. (1943). *Table of the Coefficients of Everett's Central Difference Interpolation Formula,* 2nd ed. Cambridge University Press, Tracts for Computers, no. v.

THOMPSON, CATHERINE M. (1941). Tables of percentage points of the incomplete beta-function. *Biometrika* **32**, 168–91.

TIKU, M. L. (1965). Laguerre series forms of non-central χ^2 and F-distributions. *Biometrika* **52**, 415–27.

TIKU, M. L. (1966). A note on approximating to the non-central F distribution. *Biometrika* **53**, 606–10.

TIKU, M. L. (1967). Tables of the power of the F-test. *J. Amer. Statist. Ass.* **62**, 525–39.

TIPPETT, L. H. C. (1925). On the extreme individuals and the range of samples taken from a normal population. *Biometrika* **17**, 364–87.

VAN DER PARREN, J. L. (1970). Tables for distribution-free confidence limits for the median. *Biometrika* **57**, 613–17.

VERDOOREN, L. R. (1963). Extended tables of critical values for Wilcoxon's test statistic. *Biometrika* **50**, 177–86.

VOGLER, L. E. & NORTON, K. A. (1970). *Table of Percentage Points of the F Distribution*. Unpublished Report.

VON MISES, R. (1918). Über die 'Ganzzahligkeit' der Atomgewichte und verwandte Fragen. *Physikal. Zeitschr.* **19**, 490–500.

WALD, A. & BROOKNER, R. J. (1941). On the distribution of Wilks' statistic for testing the independence of several groups of variates. *Ann. Math. Statist.* **12**, 137–52.

WALD, A. & WOLFOWITZ, J. (1946). Tolerance limits for a normal distribution. *Ann. Math. Statist.* **17**, 208–15.

WATSON, G. S. (1956). Analysis of dispersion on a sphere. *Mon. Not. R. Astr. Soc.* Geophys. Suppl. **7**, 153–9.

WATSON, G. S. (1965). Equatorial distribution on a sphere. *Biometrika* **52**, 193–201.

WATSON, G. S. & WILLIAMS, E. J. (1956). On the construction of significance tests on the circle and the sphere. *Biometrika* **43**, 344–52.

WELCH, B. L. (1937). The significance of the difference between two means when the population variances are unequal. *Biometrika* **29**, 350–62.

WILCOXON, F. (1945). Individual comparisons by ranking methods. *Biometrics Bulletin* (later *Biometrics*) **1**, 80–7.

WILCOXON, F. & WILCOX, ROBERTA A. (1964). *Some Rapid Approximate Statistical Procedures*. Lederle Laboratories, Pearl River, New York.

WILK, M. B. & SHAPIRO, S. S. (1968). The joint assessment of normality of several independent samples. *Technometrics* **10**, 825–39.

WILKS, S. S. (1932). Certain generalizations in the analysis of variance. *Biometrika* **24**, 471–94.

WILLIAMS, E. J. (1967). The analysis of association among many variates. *J. R. Statist. Soc.* B. **29**, 199–228.

APPENDIX II

ORIGIN OF INDIVIDUAL TABLES

The following list shows the sources from which each of the tables in the present Volume has been taken, as well as the names of the persons primarily responsible for the production. In a few instances the name of the computer or programmer working under the 'table author's' direction has been added. Full titles of the papers or Reports including the tables can be found using Table Contents List (pp. vii–xi) and the list of References (pp. 142–7).

We again take this opportunity of thanking the table authors for allowing the reproduction of their work.

	SOURCE	AUTHORS RESPONSIBLE FOR THE COMPUTATION
1	*Biometrika* (1931), **22**, 368–76	T. Kondo and E. M. Elderton
	Recomputed and errors corrected, 1969	J. S. White, Dept. of Engineering, Univ. of Minnesota
2	Freshly computed	Michael H. Kutner, Institute of Statistics, Texas A & M University
3	*Biometrika* (1964), **51**, 234–9	H. L. Harter
	Aerospace Research Labs. A.R.L. **64**, 83–123	
4	Freshly computed	K. V. Mardia, Dept. of Statistics, Hull Univ.
5	*Biometrika* (1943), **33**, 74–87	Maxine Merrington and Catherine M. Thompson
	Recomputed and enlarged; errors corrected	D. E. Amos, Sandia Laboratories
6	*Biometrika* (1925), **17**, 385	L. H. C. Tippett
	Additional values freshly computed	Sheila M. Burrough, Univ. Coll. Lond.
7	*Biometrika* (1948), **35**, 131–40	K. R. Nair
	Ann. Math. Statist. (1950), **21**, 33–7	F. E. Grubbs
8	*Biometrika* (1945), **33**, 260–4	M. Sumner, Scientific Computing Service Ltd
9	*Biometrika* (1961), **48**, 158–63	H. L. Harter
10	*Ann. Math. Statist.* (1956), **27**, 428–33	A. E. Sarhan and B. G. Greenberg
11	*J. Amer. Statist. Ass.* (1965) **60**, 104–7	I. Eisenberger and E. C. Posner
12	*Biometrika* (1954), **41**, 226	H. Ruben
13	Freshly computed from Table 9	Sheila M. Burrough, Univ. Coll. London
14	Freshly computed from Table 15	E. S. Pearson
15	*Biometrika* (1965), **52**, 603–4	
16	*Biometrika* (1965), **52**, 605	S. S. Shapiro and M. B. Wilk
17	*Technometrics* (1968), **10**, 863	
18	*Technometrics* (1968), **10**, 828	S. S. Shapiro and M. B. Wilk (smoothed by E.S.P.)
19	Aerospace Research Labs. A.R.L. **64**-31, 22–9	H. L. Harter
20	Aerospace Research Labs. A.R.L. **64**-31, 82–102	H. L. Harter
21	Case Inst. Tech. *Statist. Lab. Report*, 1964, 206	Z. Govindarajulu and S. Eisenstat
22	*Biometrika* (1963), **50**, 179–82	L. R. Verdooren
23	Report (1964) of Lederer Labs., New York	F. Wilcoxon and Roberta A. Wilcox
	A Non-parametric Introduction to Statistics. Macmillan, London & New York (1968) 221–3	C. H. Kraft and Constance van Eeden
24	*Biometrika* (1969), **56**, 262–9	N. L. Johnson and Carol Newman
25	Case Inst. Tech., *Statist. Lab. Report* 1962, no. 104. Reproduced in Harter & Owen (1970), 51–4, 63–6	G. E. Haynam, Z. Govindarajulu and F. C. Leone
26 27	Sandia Corp. Monograph S.C.R. 1963–607	Table 5 D. B. Owen (With slight modification by E.S.P.) Table 6 D. B. Owen
28	*Biometrika* (1961), **48**, 467	D. Hogben, R. S. Pinkham and M. B. Wilk
29	*Biometrika* (1969), **56**, 270	E. S. Pearson and M. A. Stephens
30	*Biometrika* (1951), **38**, 115–22, with additions	E. S. Pearson and H. O. Hartley
31	Freshly published	D. E. Amos, Sandia Laboratories

SOURCE	AUTHORS RESPONSIBLE FOR THE COMPUTATION
32 *Biometrika* (1963), **50**, 473–97.	N. L. Johnson, E. Nixon, D. E. Amos and E. S. Pearson
33 Freshly published	D. E. Amos, Sandia Laboratories
34 *Biometrika* (1965), **52**, 551–4	} N. L. Johnson and K. Yelverton
35 *Biometrika* (1965), **52**, 555–8	
36 Univ. of N. Carolina, *Dept. of Statistics Report* 683 (1968)	N. L. Johnson and J. O. Kitchen
37 *Technometrics* (1960), **2**, 57–8	J. A. Greenwood and D. Durand
38 Union Carbide Corp. *Report* 1968-*CTC* 1	K. O. Bowman and L. R. Shenton
39 *Biometrika* (1957), **44**, 414–17	} J. Berkson
40 *Biometrika* (1957), **44**, 418–19	
41 *J. Amer. Statist. Ass.* (1953), **48**, 568–9	} J. Berkson
42 *J. Amer. Statist. Ass.* (1953), **48**, 570	
43 *J. Amer. Statist. Ass.* (1953), **48**, 571–2	
44 *Biometrika* (1960), **47**, 134–41	} J. Berkson
45 *Biometrika* (1960), **47**, 124–31	
46 *Biometrics* (1957), **13**, 33–4	J. Berkson
47 { *Biometrika* (1966), **53**, 353–8	M. Schatzoff
{ *Biometrika* (1969), **56**, 113–17	K. C. S. Pillai and A. K. Gupta (combined with some modifications by E.S.P.)
48 *Biometrika* (1967), **54**, 193–4 (giving references to several publications)	K. C. S. Pillai *et al.* (with some modifications by E.S.P.)
49 *Biometrika* (1957), **44**, 245–7; 444–53; **45**, 494–503	F. G. Foster and D. H. Rees (with some modifications by E.S.P.)
50 *Biometrika* (1969), **56**, 218	B. P. Korin
51 { *Biometrika* (1968), **55**, 507–9	R. C. Hanumara and W. A. Thompson
{ *Ann. Inst. Statist. Math.* (1968), Suppl. 6, 120–3	K. C. S. Pillai and T. C. Chang
52 Freshly computed	K. H. Kramer, United Steel Corporation
53 *Biometrika* (1968), **55**, 177 and author's Thesis	B. P. Korin (adjusted by E.S.P.)
54 *J. R. Statist. Soc.* B (1970), **32**, 118	M. A. Stephens
55 Freshly computed	P. J. Kim (see also Harter & Owen, 1970, 129–70)
56 *Biometrika* (1969), **56**, 153	} M. A. Stephens
57 *Biometrika* (1962), **49**, 465	
58 *J. Amer. Statist. Ass.* (1972)	
59 *Biometrika* (1967), **54**, 214	
60 *Biometrika* (1962), **49**, 548	
61 *Biometrika* (1969), **56**, 171–2	
62 *J. Amer. Statist. Ass.* (1953), **48**, 140	E. J. Gumbel, J. A. Greenwood and D. Durand
63 Thesis for Univ. of Toronto (1962)	M. A. Stephens
64 *Biometrika* (1965), **52**, 200	M. A. Stephens
65 Stanford Univ. Dept. Statistics, Tech. Report no. 181	T. W. Anderson and M. A. Stephens
66 *Interpolation and Allied Tables* (1956), 37–41	Prepared by H.M. Nautical Almanac Office
67 Freshly computed	E. S. Pearson
68 *Biometrika* (1941), **32**, 183–5	L. J. Comrie and H. O. Hartley
69 *Biometrika* (1968), **55**, 24–7	Sheila Burrough and E. S. Pearson

TABLES

Table 1. *The Normal probability function. Values of X and Z in terms of P*

P	X(P)	Z(P)	P	X(P)	Z(P)	P	X(P)	Z(P)
0·500	0·00000 00000	0·39894 22804	0·560	0·15096 92155	0·39442 17995	0·620	0·30548 07881	0·38075 55202
·501	·00250 66309	·39894 10271	·561	·15350 50604	·39426 95624	·621	·30810 82024	·38044 87259
·502	·00501 32775	·39893 72671	·562	·15604 18928	·39411 47890	·622	·31073 77455	·38013 93031
·503	·00751 99557	·39893 10005	·563	·15857 97298	·39395 74783	·623	·31336 94389	·37982 72496
·504	·01002 66811	·39892 22272	·564	·16111 85885	·39379 76292	·624	·31600 33044	·37951 25635
0·505	0·01253 34695	0·39891 09471	0·565	0·16365 84862	0·39363 52408	0·625	0·31863 93640	0·37919 52423
·506	·01504 03367	·39888 71602	·566	·16619 94402	·39347 03119	·626	·32127 76395	·37887 52840
·507	·01754 72984	·39888 08664	·567	·16874 14676	·39330 28416	·627	·32391 81533	·37855 26863
·508	·02005 43704	·39886 20656	·568	·17128 45859	·39313 28286	·628	·32656 09274	·37822 74469
·509	·02256 15684	·39884 07577	·569	·17382 88125	·39296 02720	·629	·32920 59843	·37789 95637
0·510	0·02506 89083	0·39881 69424	0·570	0·17637 41648	0·39278 51706	0·630	0·33185 33464	0·37756 90342
·511	·02757 64057	·39879 06198	·571	·17892 06603	·39260 75233	·631	·33450 30364	·37723 58562
·512	·03008 40766	·39876 17896	·572	·18146 83165	·39242 73289	·632	·33715 50770	·37690 00273
·513	·03259 19367	·39873 04516	·573	·18401 71512	·39224 45863	·633	·33980 94910	·37656 15453
·514	·03510 00018	·39869 66056	·574	·18656 71818	·39205 92942	·634	·34246 63015	·37622 04076
0·515	0·03760 82877	0·39866 02515	0·575	0·18911 84263	0·39187 14515	0·635	0·34512 55315	0·37587 66118
·516	·04011 68102	·39862 13890	·576	·19167 09022	·39168 10570	·636	·34778 72043	·37553 01557
·517	·04262 55852	·39858 00178	·577	·19422 46276	·39148 81093	·637	·35045 13433	·37518 10366
·518	·04513 46285	·39853 61377	·578	·19677 96202	·39129 26073	·638	·35311 79720	·37482 92522
·519	·04764 39560	·39848 97484	·579	·19933 58981	·39109 45496	·639	·35578 71140	·37447 47998
0·520	0·05015 35835	0·39844 08497	0·580	0·20189 34791	0·39089 39350	0·640	0·35845 87933	0·37411 76771
·521	·05266 35269	·39838 94412	·581	·20445 23815	·39069 07622	·641	·36113 30336	·37375 78814
·522	·05517 38021	·39833 55225	·582	·20701 26234	·39048 50298	·642	·36380 98590	·37339 54102
·523	·05768 44251	·39827 90934	·583	·20957 42229	·39027 67365	·643	·36648 92939	·37303 02608
·524	·06019 54117	·39822 01536	·584	·21213 71983	·39006 58809	·644	·36917 13625	·37266 24307
0·525	0·06270 67779	0·39815 87025	0·585	0·21470 15680	0·38985 24617	0·645	0·37185 60894	0·37229 19172
·526	·06521 85397	·39809 47399	·586	·21726 73503	·38963 64773	·646	·37454 34992	·37191 87176
·527	·06773 07130	·39802 82653	·587	·21983 45638	·38941 79265	·647	·37723 36168	·37154 28293
·528	·07024 33138	·39795 92783	·588	·22240 32269	·38919 68077	·648	·37992 64670	·37116 42495
·529	·07275 63582	·39788 77785	·589	·22497 33583	·38897 31195	·649	·38262 20752	·37078 29754
0·530	0·07526 98621	0·39781 37654	0·590	0·22754 49766	0·38874 68605	0·650	0·38532 04664	0·37039 90044
·531	·07778 38416	·39773 72386	·591	·23011 81007	·38851 80291	·651	·38802 16662	·37001 23336
·532	·08029 83129	·39765 81976	·592	·23269 27492	·38828 66238	·652	·39072 57002	·36962 29601
·533	·08281 32919	·39757 66418	·593	·23526 89411	·38805 26431	·653	·39343 25941	·36923 08812
·534	·08532 87949	·39749 25708	·594	·23784 66954	·38781 60854	·654	·39614 23739	·36883 60940
0·535	0·08784 48379	0·39740 59840	0·595	0·24042 60311	0·38757 69492	0·655	0·39885 50656	0·36843 85955
·536	·09036 14371	·39731 68810	·596	·24300 69674	·38733 52328	·656	·40157 06956	·36803 83829
·537	·09287 86088	·39722 52610	·597	·24558 95234	·38709 09347	·657	·40428 92903	·36763 54531
·538	·09539 63691	·39713 11235	·598	·24817 37185	·38684 40532	·658	·40701 08763	·36722 98033
·539	·09791 47342	·39703 44680	·599	·25075 95719	·38659 45867	·659	·40973 54803	·36682 14304
0·540	0·10043 37205	0·39693 52939	0·600	0·25334 71031	0·38634 25335	0·660	0·41246 31294	0·36641 03313
·541	·10295 33443	·39683 36004	·601	·25593 63317	·38608 78919	·661	·41519 38508	·36599 65031
·542	·10547 36218	·39672 93870	·602	·25852 72773	·38583 06603	·662	·41792 76717	·36557 99426
·543	·10799 45694	·39662 26529	·603	·26111 99595	·38557 08368	·663	·42066 46196	·36516 06467
·544	·11051 62036	·39651 33976	·604	·26371 43982	·38530 84198	·664	·42340 47224	·36473 86123
0·545	0·11303 85406	0·39640 16203	·605	0·26631 06132	0·38504 34074	0·665	0·42614 80078	0·36431 38362
·546	·11556 15971	·39628 73203	·606	·26890 86245	·38477 57979	·666	·42889 45041	·36388 63152
·547	·11808 53894	·39617 04968	·607	·27150 84520	·38450 55895	·667	·43164 42394	·36345 60461
·548	·12060 99341	·39605 11492	·608	·27411 01160	·38423 27804	·668	·43439 72423	·36302 30256
·549	·12313 52477	·39592 92767	·609	·27671 36367	·38395 73687	·669	·43715 35414	·36258 72505
0·550	0·12566 13469	0·39580 48785	0·610	0·27931 90344	0·38367 93525	0·670	0·43991 31657	0·36214 87174
·551	·12818 82481	·39567 79538	·611	·28192 63296	·38339 87300	·671	·44267 61442	·36170 74231
·552	·13071 59681	·39554 85017	·612	·28453 55427	·38311 54992	·672	·44544 25063	·36126 33640
·553	·13324 45236	·39541 65215	·613	·28714 66943	·38282 96583	·673	·44821 22815	·36081 65369
·554	·13577 39313	·39528 20124	·614	·28975 98052	·38254 12052	·674	·45098 54994	·36036 69383
0·555	0·13830 42080	0·39514 49734	0·615	0·29237 48962	0·38225 01380	0·675	0·45376 21902	0·35991 45648
·556	·14083 53704	·39500 54037	·616	·29499 19882	·38195 64547	·676	·45654 23838	·35945 94128
·557	·14336 74355	·39486 33023	·617	·29761 11022	·38166 01533	·677	·45932 61108	·35900 14788
·558	·14590 04200	·39471 86685	·618	·30023 22594	·38136 12318	·678	·46211 34018	·35854 07594
·559	·14843 43411	·39457 15012	·619	·30285 54809	·38105 96881	·679	·46490 42875	·35807 72508

Table 1 (*continued*). *The Normal probability function*

P	X(P)	Z(P)	P	X(P)	Z(P)	P	X(P)	Z(P)
0·680	0·46769 87991	0·35761 09496	**0·740**	0·64334 54054	0·32436 52159	**0·800**	0·84162 12336	0·27996 19204
·681	·47049 69679	·35714 18520	·741	·64643 14163	·32372 03280	·801	·84519 85353	·27911 85114
·682	·47329 88254	·35666 99544	·742	·64952 35958	·32307 23510	·802	·84878 66859	·27827 15197
·683	·47610 44035	·35619 52531	·743	·65262 19983	·32242 12787	·803	·85238 57980	·27742 09344
·684	·47891 37341	·35571 77443	·744	·65572 66788	·32176 71049	·804	·85599 59855	·27656 67444
0·685	0·48172 68496	0·35523 74244	**0·745**	0·65883 76927	0·32110 98232	**0·805**	0·85961 73642	0·27570 89387
·686	·48454 37824	·35475 42894	·746	·66195 50963	·32044 94274	·806	·86325 00516	·27484 75059
·687	·48736 45655	·35426 83355	·747	·66507 89462	·31978 59109	·807	·86689 41666	·27398 24348
·688	·49018 92317	·35377 95589	·748	·66820 92997	·31911 92673	·808	·87054 98302	·27311 37138
·689	·49301 78145	·35328 79558	·749	·67134 62149	·31844 94901	·809	·87421 71649	·27224 13312
0·690	0·49585 03473	0·35279 35220	**0·750**	0·67448 97502	0·31777 65727	**0·810**	0·87789 62951	0·27136 52755
·691	·49868 68641	·35229 62537	·751	·67763 99649	·31710 05084	·811	·88158 73470	·27048 55347
·692	·50152 73990	·35179 61469	·752	·68079 69188	·31642 12905	·812	·88529 04488	·26960 20968
·693	·50437 19862	·35129 31976	·753	·68396 06724	·31573 89123	·813	·88900 57306	·26871 49497
·694	·50722 06606	·35078 74016	·754	·68713 12868	·31505 33669	·814	·89273 33243	·26782 40812
0·695	0·51007 34570	0·35027 87549	**0·755**	0·69030 88239	0·31436 46474	**0·815**	0·89647 33640	0·26692 94789
·696	·51293 04106	·34976 72533	·756	·69349 33463	·31367 27469	·816	·90022 59857	·26603 11303
·697	·51579 15570	·34925 28927	·757	·69668 49171	·31297 76584	·817	·90399 13276	·26512 90227
·698	·51865 69321	·34873 56688	·758	·69988 36002	·31227 93747	·818	·90776 95299	·26422 31434
·699	·52152 65718	·34821 55774	·759	·70308 94603	·31157 78888	·819	·91156 07351	·26331 34793
0·700	0·52440 05127	0·34769 26142	**0·760**	0·70630 25628	0·31087 31934	**0·820**	0·91536 50878	0·26240 00175
·701	·52727 87914	·34716 67749	·761	·70952 29738	·31016 52812	·821	·91918 27351	·26148 27447
·702	·53016 14451	·34663 80552	·762	·71275 07602	·30945 41450	·822	·92301 38263	·26056 16475
·703	·53304 85109	·34610 64506	·763	·71598 59896	·30873 97772	·823	·92685 85128	·25963 67125
·704	·53594 00266	·34557 19567	·764	·71922 87304	·30802 21705	·824	·93071 69489	·25870 79259
0·705	0·53883 60303	0·34503 45690	**0·765**	0·72247 90519	0·30730 13172	**0·825**	0·93458 92911	0·25777 52740
·706	·54173 65601	·34449 42831	·766	·72573 70241	·30657 72098	·826	·93847 56984	·25683 87427
·707	·54464 16548	·34395 10944	·767	·72900 27178	·30584 98406	·827	·94237 63326	·25589 83178
·708	·54755 13533	·34340 49982	·768	·73227 62047	·30511 92018	·828	·94629 13580	·25495 39852
·709	·55046 56950	·34285 59901	·769	·73555 75574	·30438 52856	·829	·95022 09415	·25400 57303
0·710	0·55338 47196	0·34230 40653	**0·770**	0·73884 68492	0·30364 80840	**0·830**	0·95416 52531	0·25305 35384
·711	·55630 84670	·34174 92191	·771	·74214 41544	·30290 75892	·831	·95812 44654	·25209 73948
·712	·55923 69776	·34119 14468	·772	·64544 95482	·30216 37930	·832	·96209 87539	·25113 72845
·713	·56217 02923	·34063 07435	·773	·74876 31066	·30141 66874	·833	·96608 82971	·25017 31922
·714	·56510 84520	·34006 71046	·774	·75208 49067	·30066 62641	·834	·97009 32766	·24920 51027
0·715	0·56805 14983	0·33950 05250	**0·775**	0·75541 50264	0·29991 25148	**0·835**	0·97411 38771	0·24823 30004
·716	·57099 94731	·33893 09999	·776	·75875 35445	·29915 54312	·836	·97815 02863	·24725 68697
·717	·57395 24186	·33835 85244	·777	·76210 05410	·29839 50049	·837	·98220 26953	·24627 66945
·718	·57691 03772	·33778 30934	·778	·76545 60967	·29763 12273	·838	·98627 12987	·24529 24589
·719	;57987 33924	·33720 47020	·779	·76882 02935	·29686 40898	·839	·99035 62942	·24430 41465
0·720	0·58284 15073	0·33662 33449	**0·780**	0·77219 32142	0·29609 35838	**0·840**	0·99445 78832	0·24331 17408
·721	·58581 47657	·33603 90172	·781	·77557 49428	·29531 97004	·841	·99857 62706	·24231 52251
·722	·58879 32119	·33545 17137	·782	·77896 55643	·29454 24309	·842	1·00271 16650	·24131 45826
·723	·59177 68906	·33486 14291	·783	·78236 51649	·29376 17663	·843	1·00686 42788	·24030 97960
·724	·59476 58468	·33426 81581	·784	·78577 38315	·29297 76976	·844	1·01103 43281	·23930 08482
0·725	0·59776 01260	0·33367 18956	**0·785**	0·78919 16527	0·29219 02156	**0·845**	1·01522 20332	0·23828 77215
·726	·60075 97742	·33307 26361	·786	·79261 87177	·29139 93112	·846	1·01942 76182	·23727 03982
·727	·60376 48378	·33247 03742	·787	·79605 51173	·29060 49751	·847	1·02365 13116	·23624 88602
·728	·60677 53635	·33186 51046	·788	·79950 09431	·28980 71978	·848	1·02789 33458	·23522 30894
·729	·60979 13987	·33125 68217	·789	·80295 62883	·28900 59700	·849	1·03215 39580	·23419 30673
0·730	0·61281 29910	0·33064 55199	**0·790**	0·80642 12470	0·28820 12820	**0·850**	1·03643 33895	0·23315 87753
·731	·61584 01887	·33003 11938	·791	·80989 59147	·28739 31243	·851	1·04073 18865	·23212 01942
·732	·61887 30405	·32941 38377	·792	·81338 03882	·28658 14869	·852	1·04504 96997	·23107 73050
·733	·62191 15956	·32879 34458	·793	·81687 47655	·28576 63602	·853	1·04938 70847	·23003 00883
·734	·62495 59035	·32817 00126	·794	·82037 91460	·28494 77341	·854	1·05374 43021	·22897 85243
0·735	0·62800 60144	0·32754 35321	**0·795**	0·82389 36303	0·28412 55985	**0·855**	1·05812 16177	0·22792 25930
·736	·63106 19791	·32691 39986	·796	·82741 83207	·28329 99434	·856	1·06251 93023	·22686 22742
·737	·63412 38485	·32628 14062	·797	·83095 33206	·28247 07584	·857	1·06693 76322	·22579 75475
·738	·63719 16745	·32564 57489	·798	·83449 87348	·28163 80333	·858	1·07137 68893	·22472 83920
·739	·64026 55092	·32500 70208	·799	·83805 46699	·28080 17575	·859	1·07583 73610	·22365 47867

Table 1 (*continued*)

P	X(P)	Z(P)	P	X(P)	Z(P)	P	X(P)	Z(P)
0·860	1·08031 93408	0·22257 67101	0·910	1·34075 50337	0·16239 06278	0·960	1·75068 60713	0·08617 37740
·861	1·08482 31279	·22149 41407	·911	1·34693 86261	·16104 67853	·961	1·76241 02979	·08441 72460
·862	1·08934 90279	·22040 70565	·912	1·35317 41545	·15969 67333	·962	1·77438 19103	·08264 88710
·863	1·09389 73526	·21931 54352	·913	1·35946 27454	·15834 04193	·963	1·78661 33655	·08086 83955
·864	1·09846 84203	·21821 92542	·914	1·36580 55626	·15697 77897	·964	1·79911 81068	·07907 55532
0·865	1·10306 25562	0·21711 84906	0·915	1·37220 38090	0·15560 87897	0·965	1·81191 06730	0·07727 00634
·866	1·10768 00921	·21601 31213	·916	1·37865 87286	·15423 33632	·966	1·82500 68211	·07545 16306
·867	1·11232 13672	·21490 31225	·917	1·38517 16082	·15285 14529	·967	1·83842 36692	·07361 99429
·868	1·11698 67279	·21378 84705	·918	1·39174 37794	·15146 30002	·968	1·85217 98588	·07177 46702
·869	1·12167 65279	·21266 91409	·919	1·39837 66208	·15006 79451	·969	1·86629 57435	·06991 54633
0·870	1·12639 11290	0·21154 51092	0·920	1·40507 15603	0·14866 62263	0·970	1·88079 36082	0·06804 19514
·871	1·13113 09008	·21041 63503	·921	1·41183 00775	·14725 77808	·971	1·89569 79240	·06615 37406
·872	1·13589 62212	·20928 28389	·922	1·41865 37062	·14584 25444	·972	1·91103 56475	·06425 04111
·873	1·14068 74763	·20814 45492	·923	1·42554 40017	·14442 04512	·973	1·92683 65733	·06233 15149
·874	1·14550 50614	·20700 14551	·924	1·43250 27208	·14299 14335	·974	1·94313 37511	·06039 65726
0·875	1·15034 93804	0·20585 35302	0·925	1·43953 14709	0·14155 54224	0·975	1·95996 39845	0·05844 50698
·876	1·15522 08466	·20470 07473	·926	1·44663 20672	·14011 23467	·976	1·97736 84282	·05647 64533
·877	1·16011 98830	·20354 30793	·927	1·45380 63589	·13866 21337	·977	1·99539 33102	·05449 01262
·878	1·16504 69223	·20238 04982	·928	1·46105 62692	·13720 47087	·978	2·01409 08120	·05248 54425
·879	1·17000 24075	·20121 29760	·929	1·46838 37982	·13573 99953	·979	2·03352 01493	·05046 17007
0·880	1·17498 67921	0·20004 04838	0·930	1·47579 10282	0·13426 79146	0·980	2·05374 89106	0·04841 81359
·881	1·18000 05403	·19886 29926	·931	1·48328 01273	·13278 83859	·981	2·07485 47344	·04635 39107
·882	1·18504 41279	·19768 04728	·932	1·49085 33552	·13130 13263	·982	2·09692 74292	·04426 81043
·883	1·19011 80419	·19649 28942	·933	1·49851 30679	·12980 66504	·983	2·12007 16897	·04215 96988
·884	1·19522 27814	·19530 02264	·934	1·50626 17233	·12830 42705	·984	2·14441 06209	·04002 75629
0·885	1·20035 88580	0·19410 24382	0·935	1·51410 18876	0·12679 40964	0·985	2·17009 03776	0·03787 04310
·886	1·20552 67960	·19289 94981	·936	1·52203 62417	·12527 60353	·986	2·19728 63766	·03568 68772
·887	1·21072 71328	·19169 13738	·937	1·53006 75881	·12374 99916	·987	2·22621 17693	·03347 52823
·888	1·21596 04197	·19047 80328	·938	1·53819 88586	·12221 58668	·988	2·25712 92445	·03123 37903
·889	1·22122 72221	·18925 94418	·939	1·54643 31223	·12067 35596	·989	2·29036 78779	·02896 02511
0·890	1·22652 81200	0·18803 55670	0·940	1·55477 35946	0·11912 29652	0·990	2·32634 78740	0·02665 21422
·891	1·23186 37087	·18680 63740	·941	1·56322 36469	·11756 39758	·991	2·36561 81269	·02430 64606
·892	1·23723 45992	·18557 18278	·942	1·57178 68165	·11599 64802	·992	2·40891 55458	·02191 95667
·893	1·24264 14186	·18433 18928	·943	1·58046 68184	·11442 03633	·993	2·45726 33902	·01948 69510
·894	1·24808 48111	·18308 65328	·944	1·58926 75571	·11283 55063	·994	2·51214 43279	·01700 28705
0·895	1·25356 54385	0·18183 57108	0·945	1·59819 31399	0·11124 17865	0·995	2·57582 93035	0·01445 97430
·896	1·25908 39804	·18057 93893	·946	1·60724 78919	·10963 90770	·996	2·65206 98079	·01184 70585
·897	1·26464 11357	·17931 75300	·947	1·61643 63711	·10802 72462	·997	2·74778 13854	·00914 91911
·898	1·27023 76224	·17805 00939	·948	1·62576 33862	·10640 61581	·998	2·87816 17391	·00634 01932
·899	1·27587 41791	·17677 70414	·949	1·63523 40154	·10477 56715	·999	3·09023 23062	·00336 70901
0·900	1·28155 15655	0·17549 83319	0·950	1·64485 36270	0·10313 56404	0·9991	3·12138 915	0·00305 6534
·901	1·28727 05631	·17421 39244	·951	1·65462 79024	·10148 59127	·9992	3·15590 676	·00274 2700
·902	1·29303 19761	·17292 37767	·952	1·66456 28612	·09982 63310	·9993	3·19465 105	·00242 5212
·903	1·29883 66326	·17162 78460	·953	1·67466 48890	·09815 67313	·9994	3·23888 012	·00210 3588
·904	1·30468 53852	·17032 60887	·954	1·68494 07679	·09647 69433			
						0·9995	3·29052 673	0·00177 7190
0·905	1·31057 91122	0·16901 84602	0·955	1·69539 77103	0·09478 67895	·9996	3·35279 478	·00144 5132
·906	1·31651 87184	·16770 49152	·956	1·70604 33969	·09308 60850	·9997	3·43161 440	·00110 6086
·907	1·32250 51367	·16638 54072	·957	1·71688 60184	·09137 46370	·9998	3·54008 380	·00075 7842
·908	1·32853 93289	·16505 98890	·958	1·72793 43224	·08965 22444	·9999	3·71901 648	·00039 5848
·909	1·33462 22867	·16372 83123	·959	1·73919 76653	·08791 86967			

X	$P(X)-0.5$	$Z(X)$	$D^1Z(X)$	$D^2Z(X)$	$D^3Z(X)$	$D^4Z(X)$	$D^5Z(X)$	$D^6Z(X)$	$D^7Z(X)$	$D^8Z(X)$	$D^9Z(X)$
0.00	0.000000	0.398942	0.000000	−0.398942	0.00000	1.19683	0.0000	−5.9841	0.000	41.89	0.0
·02	·007978	·398863	− ·007977	− ·398703	·02393	1.19563	− ·1196	−5.9758	·837	41.81	−7.5
·04	·015953	·398623	− ·015945	− ·397985	·04781	1.19204	− ·2389	−5.9507	1.672	41.59	−15.0
·06	·023922	·398225	− ·023893	− ·396791	·07159	1.18608	− ·3575	−5.9089	2.500	41.21	−22.5
·08	·031881	·397668	− ·031813	− ·395123	·09524	1.17775	− ·4752	−5.8507	3.319	40.69	−29.8
0.10	·039828	·396953	−0.039695	−0.392983	·11869	1.16708	−0.5915	−5.7763	4.126	40.02	−37.0
·12	·047758	·396080	− ·047530	− ·390377	·14190	1.15410	− ·7061	−5.6858	4.919	39.21	−44.1
·14	·055670	·395052	− ·055307	− ·387309	·16484	1.13885	− ·8188	−5.5796	5.694	38.26	−50.9
·16	·063560	·393868	− ·063019	− ·383785	·18744	1.12137	− ·9292	−5.4582	6.448	37.18	−57.5
·18	·071424	·392531	− ·070656	− ·379813	·20968	1.10170	−1.0370	−5.3218	7.180	35.96	−63.9
0.20	·079260	0.391043	−0.078209	−0.375401	·23150	1.07990	−1.1420	−5.1711	7.886	34.62	−70.0
·22	·087064	·389404	− ·085669	− ·370557	·25286	1.05604	−1.2438	−5.0066	8.564	33.16	−75.8
·24	·094835	·387617	− ·093028	− ·365290	·27373	1.03018	−1.3421	−4.8288	9.212	31.59	−81.3
·26	·102568	·385683	− ·100278	− ·359611	·29405	1.00238	−1.4368	−4.6383	9.827	29.91	−86.4
·28	·110261	·383606	− ·107410	− ·353532	·31381	0.97273	−1.5276	−4.4359	10.408	28.14	−91.1
0.30	0.117911	0.381388	−0.114416	−0.347063	·33295	0.94130	−1.6142	−4.2223	10.952	26.27	−95.5
·32	·125516	·379031	− ·121290	− ·340218	·35145	·90819	−1.6964	−3.9981	11.458	24.32	−99.2
·34	·133072	·376537	− ·128023	− ·333009	·36927	·87348	−1.7741	−3.7642	11.924	22.30	−103.0
·36	·140576	·373911	− ·134608	− ·325452	·38638	·83726	−1.8469	−3.5214	12.349	20.20	−106.1
·38	·148027	·371154	− ·141038	− ·317559	·40275	·79963	−1.9149	−3.2705	12.732	18.06	−108.7
0.40	0.155422	0.368270	−0.147308	−0.309347	·41835	0.76070	−1.9777	−3.0124	13.071	15.86	−110.9
·42	·162757	·365263	− ·153410	− ·300830	·43317	·72056	−2.0353	−2.7480	13.366	13.62	−112.5
·44	·170031	·362135	− ·159339	− ·292026	·44717	·67932	−2.0876	−2.4781	13.616	11.36	−113.9
·46	·177242	·358890	− ·165090	− ·282949	·46034	·63709	−2.1344	−2.2036	13.820	9.07	−114.7
·48	·184386	·355533	− ·170656	− ·273618	·47265	·59398	−2.1757	−1.9256	13.978	6.77	−115.1
0.50	0.191463	0.352065	−0.176033	−0.264049	·48409	0.55010	−2.2114	−1.6448	14.091	4.47	−115.0
·52	·198468	·348493	− ·181216	− ·254260	·49465	·50556	−2.2415	−1.3622	14.157	2.17	−114.4
·54	·205402	·344818	− ·186202	− ·244269	·50431	·46048	−2.2659	−1.0788	14.178	−0.10	−113.4
·56	·212260	·341046	− ·190986	− ·234094	·51306	·41497	−2.2846	−0.7954	14.153	−2.36	−111.9
·58	·219043	·337180	− ·195564	− ·223753	·52091	·36913	−2.2977	− ·5130	14.084	−4.58	−110.0
0.60	0.225747	0.333225	−0.199935	−0.213264	·52783	0.32309	−2.3052	−0.2324	13.970	−6.76	−107.7
·62	·232371	·329184	− ·204094	− ·202646	·53383	·27696	−2.3070	·0455	13.814	−8.88	−105.0
·64	·238914	·325062	− ·208040	− ·191917	·53891	·23085	−2.3034	·3199	13.615	−10.95	−101.9
·66	·245373	·320864	− ·211770	− ·181096	·54306	·18486	−2.2943	·5899	13.376	−12.96	−98.5
·68	·251748	·316593	− ·215283	− ·170200	·54630	·13912	−2.2798	·8547	13.098	−14.89	−94.7
0.70	0.258036	0.312254	−0.218578	−0.159250	·54863	0.09371	−2.2601	1.1135	12.781	−16.74	−90.5
·72	·264238	·307851	− ·221653	− ·148261	·55005	·04874	−2.2353	1.3657	12.429	−18.51	−86.1
·74	·270350	·303389	− ·224508	− ·137253	·55058	·00433	−2.2055	1.6105	12.041	−20.18	−81.4
·76	·276373	·298872	− ·227143	− ·126244	·55023	− ·03944	−2.1709	1.8471	11.622	−21.76	−76.4
·78	·282305	·294305	− ·229558	− ·115250	·54901	− ·08248	−2.1317	2.0751	11.172	−23.24	−71.2
0.80	0.288145	0.289692	−0.231753	−0.104289	·54694	−0.12468	−2.0880	2.2938	10.693	−24.61	−65.9
·82	·293892	·285036	− ·233730	− ·093378	·54403	− ·16597	−2.0400	2.5027	10.188	−25.87	−60.3
·84	·299546	·280344	− ·235489	− ·082533	·54031	− ·20626	−1.9880	2.7012	9.659	−27.02	−54.6
·86	·305106	·275618	− ·237032	− ·071771	·53579	− ·24546	−1.9320	2.8889	9.108	−28.05	−48.7
·88	·310570	·270864	− ·238360	− ·061107	·53049	− ·28351	−1.8725	3.0654	8.537	−28.97	−42.8
0.90	0.315940	0.266085	−0.239477	−0.050556	·52445	−0.32034	−1.8095	3.2303	7.950	−29.77	−36.8
·92	·321214	·261286	− ·240383	− ·040134	·51769	− ·35587	−1.7434	3.3833	7.348	−30.44	−30.8
·94	·326391	·256471	− ·241083	− ·029853	·51023	− ·39005	−1.6743	3.5241	6.733	−31.00	−24.7
·96	·331472	·251644	− ·241579	− ·019729	·50210	− ·42283	−1.6025	3.6525	6.108	−31.43	−18.7
·98	·336457	·246810	− ·241873	− ·009774	·49332	− ·45414	−1.5282	3.7684	5.476	−31.75	−12.7
1.00	0.341345	0.241971	−0.241971	0.000000	·48394	−0.48394	−1.4518	3.8715	4.839	−31.94	−6.8
1.02	·346136	·237132	− ·241875	·009580	·47398	− ·51220	−1.3735	3.9619	4.200	−32.02	−0.9
1.04	·350830	·232297	− ·241589	·018955	·46346	− ·53887	−1.2934	4.0395	3.560	−31.98	4.8
1.06	·355428	·227470	− ·241118	·028115	·45243	− ·56393	−1.2120	4.1043	2.921	−31.83	10.4
1.08	·359929	·222654	− ·240466	·037050	·44092	− ·58734	−1.1293	4.1564	2.287	−31.56	15.8
1.10	0.364334	0.217852	−0.239637	0.045749	·42895	−0.60909	−1.0458	4.1958	1.659	−31.20	21.0
1.12	·368643	·213069	− ·238637	·054205	·41657	− ·62917	−0.9616	4.2228	1.040	−30.72	26.1
1.14	·372857	·208308	− ·237471	·062409	·40380	− ·64755	− ·8770	4.2375	0.431	−30.15	30.9
1.16	·376976	·203571	− ·236143	·070354	·39067	− ·66425	− ·7922	4.2401	− ·166	−29.49	35.5
1.18	·381000	·198863	− ·234658	·078034	·37724	− ·67924	− ·7074	4.2310	− ·748	−28.73	39.9
1.20	0.384930	0.194186	−0.233023	0.085442	·36352	−0.69255	−0.6230	4.2103	−1.314	−27.90	44.0
1.22	·388768	·189543	− ·231243	·092573	·34955	− ·70417	− ·5391	4.1785	−1.863	−26.98	47.8
1.24	·392512	·184937	− ·229322	·099422	·33536	− ·71411	− ·4559	4.1359	−2.393	−25.98	51.4
1.26	·396165	·180371	− ·227268	·105986	·32099	− ·72241	− ·3737	4.0830	−2.902	−24.92	54.6
1.28	·399727	·175847	− ·225085	·112261	·30648	− ·72907	− ·2927	4.0200	−3.389	−23.80	57.6

Table 2 (*continued*)

X	P(X)−0·5	Z(X)	D¹Z(X)	D²Z(X)	D³Z(X)	D⁴Z(X)	D⁵Z(X)	D⁶Z(X)	D⁷Z(X)	D⁸Z(X)	D⁹Z(X)
1·30	0·403200	0·171369	−0·222779	0·118244	0·29184	−0·73413	−0·2130	3·9475	−3·854	−22·62	60·2
1·32	·406583	·166937	− ·220357	·123934	·27712	− ·73760	− ·1348	3·8660	−4·294	−21·39	62·6
1·34	·409877	·162555	− ·217824	·129329	·26235	− ·73953	− ·0584	3·7759	−4·709	−20·12	64·6
1·36	·413085	·158225	− ·215186	·134428	·24755	− ·73995	·0161	3·6778	−5·099	−18·81	66·4
1·38	·416207	·153948	− ·212449	·139231	·23276	− ·73890	·0886	3·5722	−5·461	−17·47	67·8
1·40	0·419243	0·149727	−0·209618	0·143738	0·21800	−0·73642	0·1590	3·4595	−5·797	−16·10	68·9
1·42	·422196	·145564	− ·206701	·147951	·20331	− ·73256	·2270	3·3405	−6·105	−14·71	69·7
1·44	·425066	·141460	− ·203702	·151871	·18871	− ·72736	·2926	3·2155	−6·386	−13·31	70·3
1·46	·427855	·137417	− ·200628	·155501	·17423	− ·72087	·3556	3·0852	−6·638	−11·91	70·5
1·48	·430563	·133435	− ·197484	·158841	·15988	− ·71315	·4159	2·9502	−6·862	−10·50	70·4
1·50	0·433193	0·129518	−0·194276	0·161897	0·14571	−0·70425	0·4735	2·8109	−7·058	−9·09	70·1
1·52	·435745	·125665	− ·191010	·164671	·13172	− ·69423	·5283	2·6681	−7·226	−7·69	69·5
1·54	·438220	·121878	− ·187691	·167167	·11795	− ·68314	·5803	2·5221	−7·366	−6·31	68·6
1·56	·440620	·118157	− ·184325	·169390	·10440	− ·67104	·6292	2·3736	−7·478	−4·95	67·5
1·58	·442947	·114505	− ·180918	·171345	·09111	− ·65799	·6752	2·2232	−7·564	−3·61	66·2
1·60	0·445201	0·110921	−0·177473	0·173037	0·07809	− ·64405	0·7181	2·0712	−7·623	−2·30	64·7
1·62	·447384	·107406	− ·173998	·174470	·06535	− ·62928	·7580	1·9184	−7·656	−1·03	62·9
1·64	·449497	·103961	− ·170496	·175653	·05292	− ·61375	·7949	1·7652	−7·664	0·21	61·0
1·66	·451543	·100586	− ·166973	·176589	·04081	− ·59751	·8286	1·6120	−7·648	1·41	58·8
1·68	·453521	·097282	− ·163434	·177287	·02903	− ·58063	·8593	1·4594	−7·608	2·57	56·6
1·70	0·455435	0·094049	−0·159883	0·177753	0·01759	−0·56316	0·8870	1·3079	−7·545	3·67	54·1
1·72	·457284	·090887	− ·156326	·177993	·00650	− ·54516	·9117	1·1577	−7·461	4·73	51·6
1·74	·459071	·087796	− ·152765	·178015	− ·00422	− ·52671	·9333	1·0095	−7·357	5·73	48·9
1·76	·460796	·084776	− ·149206	·177827	− ·01456	− ·50785	·9521	·8636	−7·232	6·68	46·1
1·78	·462462	·081828	− ·145653	·177435	− ·02453	− ·48865	·9679	·7204	−7·090	7·58	43·2
1·80	0·464070	0·078950	−0·142110	0·176848	−0·03411	−0·46915	0·9809	0·5801	−6·930	8·41	40·3
1·82	·465621	·076143	− ·138581	·176074	− ·04329	− ·44943	·9911	·4433	−6·754	9·19	37·3
1·84	·467116	·073407	− ·135069	·175119	− ·05208	− ·42953	·9987	·3101	−6·563	9·90	34·3
1·86	·468557	·070740	− ·131577	·173993	− ·06047	− ·40950	1·0036	·1809	−6·358	10·56	31·2
1·88	·469946	·068144	− ·128110	·172703	− ·06846	− ·38940	1·0059	·0559	−6·141	11·15	28·2
1·90	0·471283	0·065616	−0·124670	0·171257	−0·07605	−0·36928	1·0058	−0·0647	−5·912	11·69	25·1
1·92	·472571	·063157	− ·121261	·169664	− ·08323	− ·34918	1·0034	− ·1805	−5·674	12·16	22·0
1·94	·473810	·060765	− ·117884	·167931	− ·09002	− ·32916	·9986	− ·2916	−5·426	12·57	19·0
1·96	·475002	·058441	− ·114544	·166066	− ·09640	− ·30925	·9917	− ·3975	−5·171	12·92	16·0
1·98	·476148	·056183	− ·111243	·164077	− ·10239	− ·28950	·9828	− ·4984	−4·910	13·21	13·1
2·00	0·477250	0·053991	−0·107982	0·161973	−0·10798	−0·26995	0·9718	−0·5939	−4·643	13·44	10·3
2·02	·478308	·051864	− ·104764	·159761	− ·11319	− ·25064	·9590	− ·6841	−4·372	13·62	7·5
2·04	·479325	·049800	− ·101592	·157448	− ·11801	− ·23160	·9445	− ·7688	−4·099	13·74	4·8
2·06	·480301	·047800	− ·098467	·155043	− ·12245	− ·21287	·9283	− ·8480	−3·823	13·81	2·1
2·08	·481237	·045861	− ·095391	·152552	− ·12653	− ·19448	·9106	− ·9217	−3·547	13·83	−0·4
2·10	0·482136	0·043984	−0·092366	0·149984	−0·13024	−0·17646	0·8915	−0·9899	−3·270	13·80	−2·8
2·12	·482997	·042166	− ·089392	·147345	− ·13359	− ·15883	·8711	−1·0525	−2·995	13·72	−5·1
2·14	·483823	·040408	− ·086472	·144643	− ·13659	− ·14162	·8494	−1·1097	−2·722	13·59	−7·3
2·16	·484614	·038707	− ·083607	·141884	− ·13926	− ·12486	·8267	−1·1614	−2·452	13·43	−9·4
2·18	·485371	·037063	− ·080797	·139075	− ·14159	− ·10856	·8030	−1·2078	−2·185	13·22	−11·3
2·20	0·486097	0·035475	−0·078044	0·136222	−0·14360	−0·09274	0·7784	−1·2489	−1·923	12·97	−13·2
2·22	·486791	·033941	− ·075349	·133333	− ·14530	− ·07743	·7531	−1·2847	−1·666	12·69	−14·8
2·24	·487455	·032460	− ·072711	·130412	− ·14670	− ·06263	·7271	−1·3155	−1·416	12·38	−16·4
2·26	·488089	·031032	− ·070132	·127467	− ·14781	− ·04835	·7005	−1·3414	−1·171	12·04	−17·8
2·28	·488696	·029655	− ·067612	·124502	− ·14864	− ·03461	·6735	−1·3625	−0·934	11·67	−19·1
2·30	0·489276	0·028327	−0·065152	0·121523	−0·14920	−0·02141	0·6460	−1·3788	−0·705	11·27	−20·3
2·32	·489830	·027048	− ·062752	·118536	− ·14950	− ·00877	·6183	−1·3907	− ·484	10·86	−21·3
2·34	·490358	·025817	− ·060411	·115545	− ·14955	·00332	·5904	−1·3982	− ·271	10·42	−22·2
2·36	·490863	·024631	− ·058130	·112555	− ·14937	·01485	·5624	−1·4016	− ·067	9·97	−23·0
2·38	·491344	·023491	− ·055909	·109571	− ·14896	·02582	·5344	−1·4010	·128	9·50	−23·6
2·40	0·491803	0·022395	−0·053747	0·106598	−0·14834	0·03623	0·5064	−1·3965	0·313	9·02	−24·2
2·42	·492240	·021341	− ·051645	·103639	− ·14752	·04608	·4786	−1·3885	·489	8·54	−24·6
2·44	·492656	·020328	− ·049601	·100699	− ·14650	·05537	·4509	−1·3771	·655	8·04	−24·9
2·46	·493053	·019356	− ·047616	·097780	− ·14531	·06411	·4235	−1·3624	·810	7·54	−25·0
2·48	·493431	·018423	− ·045690	·094887	− ·14394	·07231	·3964	−1·3447	·956	7·04	−25·1
2·50	0·493790	0·017528	−0·043821	0·092024	−0·14242	0·07997	0·3697	−1·3242	1·092	6·54	−25·1
2·52	·494132	·016670	− ·042009	·089192	− ·14075	·08710	·3435	−1·3011	1·218	6·04	−25·0
2·54	·494457	·015848	− ·040253	·086395	− ·13894	·09372	·3177	−1·2756	1·334	5·54	−24·7
2·56	·494766	·015060	− ·038553	·083635	− ·13700	·09982	·2925	−1·2478	1·440	5·05	−24·4
2·58	·495060	·014305	− ·036907	·080915	− ·13495	·10542	·2678	−1·2180	1·536	4·56	−24·1

Table 2 (*continued*). *The Normal probability function. Differential coefficients* $D^n Z(X)$

X	$P(X)-0.5$	$Z(X)$	$D^1Z(X)$	$D^2Z(X)$	$D^3Z(X)$	$D^4Z(X)$	$D^5Z(X)$	$D^6Z(X)$	$D^7Z(X)$	$D^8Z(X)$	$D^9Z(X)$
2·60	0·495339	0·013583	−0·035316	0·078238	−0·13279	0·11053	0·2438	−1·1864	1·622	4·09	−23·6
2·62	·495604	·012892	− ·033777	·075605	− ·13053	·11517	·2204	−1·1532	1·699	3·62	−23·1
2·64	·495855	·012232	− ·032291	·073017	− ·12818	·11935	·1976	−1·1185	1·767	3·16	−22·5
2·66	·496093	·011600	− ·030856	·070478	− ·12576	·12308	·1756	−1·0826	1·826	2·72	−21·8
2·68	·496319	·010997	− ·029472	·067987	− ·12326	·12638	·1543	−1·0456	1·876	2·29	−21·1
2·70	0·496533	0·010421	−0·028137	0·065548	−0·12071	0·12926	0·1338	−1·0076	1·918	1·88	−20·4
2·72	·496736	·009871	− ·026850	·063160	− ·11810	·13174	·1140	− ·9689	1·951	1·48	−19·6
2·74	·496928	·009347	− ·025610	·060824	− ·11544	·13383	·0951	− ·9296	1·977	1·09	−18·8
2·76	·497110	·008846	− ·024416	·058542	− ·11274	·13555	·0769	− ·8899	1·995	0·72	−18·0
2·78	·497282	·008370	− ·023268	·056315	− ·11002	·13691	·0595	− ·8499	2·006	·37	−17·1
2·80	0·497445	0·007915	−0·022163	0·054142	−0·10727	0·13793	0·0429	−0·8097	2·010	0·04	−16·2
2·82	·497599	·007483	− ·021102	·052024	− ·10450	·13863	·0271	− ·7695	2·008	− ·27	−15·3
2·84	·497744	·007071	− ·020082	·049962	− ·10173	·13902	·0121	− ·7294	1·999	− ·57	−14·4
2·86	·497882	·006679	− ·019103	·047955	− ·09895	·13912	− ·0021	− ·6896	1·985	− ·85	−13·4
2·88	·498012	·006307	− ·018163	·046004	− ·09616	·13894	− ·0155	− ·6501	1·965	−1·11	−12·5
2·90	0·498134	0·005953	−0·017262	0·044108	−0·09339	0·13850	−0·0281	−0·6110	1·941	−1·35	−11·6
2·92	·498250	·005616	− ·016399	·042268	− ·09063	·13782	− ·0399	− ·5725	1·911	−1·57	−10·7
2·94	·498359	·005296	− ·015571	·040483	− ·08788	·13691	− ·0510	− ·5346	1·878	−1·78	−9·8
2·96	·498462	·004993	− ·014779	·038753	− ·08515	·13579	− ·0613	− ·4974	1·840	−1·97	−8·9
2·98	·498559	·004705	− ·014021	·037077	− ·08245	·13446	− ·0709	− ·4610	1·799	−2·13	−8·0
3·00	0·498650	0·004432	−0·013296	0·035455	−0·07977	0·13296	−0·0798	−0·4255	1·755	−2·29	−7·2
3·02	·498736	·004173	− ·012602	·033886	− ·07713	·13128	− ·0879	− ·3908	1·708	−2·42	−6·3
3·04	·498817	·003928	− ·011940	·032369	− ·07452	·12944	− ·0954	− ·3572	1·658	−2·54	−5·5
3·06	·498893	·003695	− ·011307	·030905	− ·07195	·12747	− ·1022	− ·3245	1·606	−2·64	−4·8
3·08	·498965	·003475	− ·010703	·029491	− ·06943	·12536	− ·1084	− ·2929	1·553	−2·73	−4·0
3·10	0·499032	0·003267	−0·010127	0·028127	−0·06694	0·12313	−0·1140	−0·2624	1·497	−2·80	−3·3
3·12	·499096	·003070	− ·009578	·026813	− ·06450	·12080	− ·1189	− ·2330	1·441	−2·86	−2·6
3·14	·499155	·002884	− ·009054	·025547	− ·06211	·11838	− ·1233	− ·2048	1·383	−2·91	−1·9
3·16	·499211	·002707	− ·008556	·024328	− ·05977	·11588	− ·1271	− ·1777	1·324	−2·94	−1·3
3·18	·499264	·002541	− ·008081	·023156	− ·05747	·11330	− ·1304	− ·1518	1·265	−2·96	−0·7
3·20	0·499313	0·002384	−0·007629	0·022029	−0·05523	0·11066	−0·1332	−0·1271	1·206	−2·97	−0·1
3·22	·499359	·002236	− ·007199	·020946	− ·05305	·10798	− ·1355	− ·1036	1·147	−2·97	·4
3·24	·499402	·002096	− ·006791	·019907	− ·05092	·10525	− ·1373	− ·0813	1·087	−2·95	·9
3·26	·499443	·001964	− ·006403	·018909	− ·04884	·10249	− ·1387	− ·0601	1·028	−2·93	1·3
3·28	·499481	·001840	− ·006034	·017953	− ·04682	·09970	− ·1397	− ·0401	0·970	−2·90	1·8
3·30	0·499517	0·001723	−0·005684	0·017036	−0·04485	0·09690	−0·1404	−0·0213	0·912	−2·86	2·1
3·32	·499550	·001612	− ·005353	·016158	− ·04294	·09409	− ·1406	− ·0036	·856	−2·82	2·5
3·34	·499581	·001508	− ·005038	·015318	− ·04109	·09128	− ·1405	·0129	·800	−2·76	2·8
3·36	·499610	·001411	− ·004740	·014515	− ·03929	·08847	− ·1401	·0284	·745	−2·70	3·1
3·38	·499638	·001319	− ·004457	·013746	− ·03755	·08567	− ·1394	·0428	·692	−2·64	3·4
3·40	0·499663	0·001232	−0·004190	0·013012	−0·03586	0·08290	−0·1384	0·0561	0·640	−2·57	3·6
3·42	·499687	·001151	− ·003936	·012311	− ·03423	·08014	− ·1371	·0684	·589	−2·49	3·8
3·44	·499709	·001075	− ·003697	·011643	− ·03266	·07741	− ·1357	·0796	·540	−2·42	4·0
3·46	·499730	·001003	− ·003470	·011005	− ·03114	·07471	− ·1340	·0900	·493	−2·33	4·1
3·48	·499749	·000936	− ·003256	·010397	− ·02967	·07205	− ·1321	·0994	·447	−2·25	4·3
3·50	0·499767	0·000873	−0·003054	0·009818	−0·02825	0·06943	−0·1300	0·1078	0·403	−2·16	4·4
3·52	·499784	·000814	− ·002864	·009266	− ·02689	·06685	− ·1278	·1155	·360	−2·08	4·4
3·54	·499800	·000758	− ·002684	·008742	− ·02558	·06432	− ·1254	·1223	·320	−1·99	4·5
3·56	·499815	·000706	− ·002514	·008243	− ·02432	·06184	− ·1229	·1283	·281	−1·90	4·5
3·58	·499828	·000657	− ·002354	·007769	− ·02310	·05941	− ·1203	·1335	·244	−1·81	4·5
3·60	0·499841	0·000612	−0·002203	0·007318	−0·02194	0·05703	−0·1175	0·1380	0·208	−1·72	4·5
3·62	·499853	·000569	− ·002061	·006891	− ·02082	·05471	− ·1147	·1419	·175	−1·63	4·5
3·64	·499864	·000529	− ·001927	·006485	− ·01975	·05244	− ·1119	·1450	·143	−1·54	4·4
3·66	·499874	·000492	− ·001801	·006100	− ·01873	·05023	− ·1090	·1476	·113	−1·45	4·4
3·68	·499883	·000457	− ·001683	·005736	− ·01774	·04808	− ·1060	·1496	·085	−1·36	4·3
3·70	0·499892	0·000425	−0·001572	0·005390	−0·01680	0·04599	−0·1030	0·1510	0·059	−1·28	4·2
3·72	·499900	·000394	− ·001467	·005063	− ·01590	·04396	− ·0999	·1520	·034	−1·19	4·2
3·74	·499908	·000366	− ·001369	·004754	− ·01504	·04200	− ·0969	·1524	·011	−1·11	4·1
3·76	·499915	·000340	− ·001277	·004462	− ·01422	·04009	− ·0938	·1524	− ·010	−1·03	4·0
3·78	·499922	·000315	− ·001190	·004185	− ·01344	·03824	− ·0908	·1520	− ·030	−0·95	3·8
3·80	0·499928	0·000292	−0·001109	0·003924	−0·01269	0·03646	−0·0878	0·1512	−0·048	−0·88	3·7
3·82	·499933	·000271	− ·001033	·003677	− ·01198	·03473	− ·0848	·1501	− ·065	− ·80	3·6
3·84	·499939	·000251	− ·000962	·003444	− ·01130	·03307	− ·0818	·1487	− ·080	− ·73	3·5
3·86	·499943	·000232	− ·000896	·003225	− ·01066	·03146	− ·0788	·1469	− ·094	− ·66	3·3
3·88	·499948	·000215	− ·000833	·003018	− ·01004	·02991	− ·0759	·1449	− ·107	− ·60	3·2

Table 2 (*continued*)

X	$P(X)-0.5$	$Z(X)$	$D^1Z(X)$	$D^2Z(X)$	$D^3Z(X)$	$D^4Z(X)$	$D^5Z(X)$	$D^6Z(X)$	$D^7Z(X)$	$D^8Z(X)$	$D^9Z(X)$
3·90	0·499952	0·000199	− 0·000775	0·002823	− 0·00946	0·02842	− 0·0730	0·1426	− 0·118	− 0·54	3·0
3·92	·499956	·000184	− ·000720	·002639	− ·00891	·02699	− ·0702	·1402	− ·128	− ·48	2·9
3·94	·499959	·000170	− ·000669	·002466	− ·00838	·02562	− ·0674	·1375	− ·137	− ·42	2·8
3·96	·499963	·000157	− ·000621	·002304	− ·00788	·02430	− ·0647	·1347	− ·145	− ·37	2·6
3·98	·499966	·000145	− ·000577	·002151	− ·00741	·02303	− ·0620	·1317	− ·152	− ·32	2·5
4·00	0·499968	0·000134	− 0·000535	0·002007	− 0·00696	0·02181	− 0·0594	0·1286	− 0·158	− 0·27	2·3
4·05	·499974	·000109	− ·000443	·001686	− ·00594	·01900	− ·0532	·1204	− ·169	− ·16	2·0
4·10	·499979	·000089	− ·000366	·001411	− ·00505	·01649	− ·0474	·1118	− ·174	− ·07	1·7
4·15	·499983	·000073	− ·000301	·001178	− ·00429	·01425	− ·0420	·1031	− ·176	·01	1·4
4·20	·499987	·000059	− ·000248	·000981	− ·00362	01228	− ·0371	·0943	− ·174	·07	1·1
4·25	0·499989	0·000048	− 0·000203	0·000814	− 0·00305	0·01054	− 0·0326	0·0857	− 0·169	0·12	0·9
4·30	·499992	·000039	− ·000166	·000674	− ·00257	·00901	− ·0285	·0775	− ·162	·15	·6
4·35	·499993	·000031	− ·000135	·000556	− ·00215	·00768	− ·0248	·0696	− ·154	·18	·4
4·40	·499995	·000025	− ·000110	·000458	− ·00180	·00653	− ·0215	·0621	− ·144	·20	·3
4·45	·499996	·000020	− ·000089	·000376	− ·00149	·00552	− ·0186	·0552	− ·134	·21	·1
4·50	0·499997	0·000016	− 0·000072	0·000308	− 0·00124	0·00466	− 0·0160	0·0487	− 0·123	0·21	0·0
4·55	·499997	·000013	− ·000058	·000251	− ·00103	·00392	− ·0137	·0428	− ·113	·21	− ·1
4·60	·499998	·000010	− ·000047	·000204	− ·00085	·00328	− ·0117	·0375	− ·102	·21	− ·1
4·65	·499998	·000008	− ·000037	·000166	− ·00070	·00274	− ·0100	·0326	− ·092	·20	− ·2
4·70	·499999	·000006	− ·000030	·000134	− ·00057	·00228	− ·0084	·0283	− ·082	·19	− ·2
4·75	0·499999	0·000005	− 0·000024	0·000108	− 0·00047	0·00189	− 0·0071	0·0244	− 0·073	0·18	− 0·3
4·80	·499999	·000004	− ·000019	·000087	− ·00038	·00157	− ·0060	·0210	− ·065	·16	− ·3
4·85	·499999	·000003	− ·000015	·000070	− ·00031	·00129	− ·0050	·0179	− ·057	·15	− ·3
4·90	·500000	·000002	− ·000012	·000056	− ·00025	·00106	− ·0042	·0153	− ·050	·14	− ·3
4·95	·500000	·000002	− ·000009	·000045	− ·00020	·00087	− ·0035	·0130	− ·043	·12	− ·3
5·00	0·500000	0·000001	− 0·000007	0·000036	− 0·00016	0·00071	− 0·0029	0·0109	− 0·037	0·11	− 0·3
5·05	·500000	·000001	− ·000006	·000028	− ·00013	·00058	− ·0024	·0092	− ·032	·10	− ·2
5·10	·500000	·000001	− ·000005	·000022	− ·00011	·00047	− ·0020	·0077	− .028	·09	− ·2
5·15	·500000	·000001	− ·000004	·000018	− ·00008	·00038	− ·0016	·0064	− ·023	·08	− ·2
5·20	·500000	·000001	− ·000003	·000014	− ·00007	·00031	− ·0013	·0054	− ·020	·07	− ·2
5·25	0·500000	0·000000	− 0·000002	0·000011	− 0·00005	0·00025	− 0·0011	0·0044	− 0·017	0·06	− 0·2
5·30	·500000	—	− ·000002	·000009	− ·00004	·00020	− ·0009	·0037	− ·014	·05	− ·1
5·35	·500000	—	− ·000001	·000007	− ·00003	·00016	− ·0007	·0030	− ·012	·04	− ·1
5·40	·500000	—	− ·000001	·000005	− ·00003	·00013	− ·0006	·0025	− ·010	·04	− ·1
5·45	·500000	—	− ·000001	·000004	− ·00002	·00010	− ·0005	·0020	− ·008	·03	− ·1
5·50	0·500000	—	− 0·000001	0·000003	− 0·00002	0·00008	− 0·0004	0·0016	− 0·007	0·03	− 0·1
5·55	·500000	—	− ·000000	·000002	− ·00001	·00006	− ·0003	·0013	− ·006	·02	− ·1
5·60	·500000	—	—	·000002	− ·00001	·00005	− ·0002	·0011	− ·005	·02	− ·1
5·65	·500000	—	—	·000001	− ·00001	·00004	− ·0002	·0009	− ·004	·02	− ·1
5·70	·500000	—	—	·000001	− ·00001	·00003	− ·0001	·0007	− ·003	·01	− ·0
5·75	0·500000	—	—	0·000001	− 0·00000	0·00002	− 0·0001	0·0006	− 0·003	0·01	—
5·80	·500000	—	—	·000001	—	·00002	− ·0001	·0004	− ·002	·01	—
5·85	·500000	—	—	·000000	—	·00001	− ·0001	·0004	− ·002	·01	—
5·90	·500000	—	—	—	—	·00001	− ·0001	·0003	− ·001	·01	—
5·95	·500000	—	—	—	—	·00001	− ·0000	·0002	− ·001	·00	—
6·00	0·500000	—	—	—	—	0·00001	—	0·0002	− 0·001	—	—
6·05	·500000	—	—	—	—	·00001	—	·0001	− ·001	—	—
6·10	·500000	—	—	—	—	·00000	—	·0001	− ·001	—	—
6·15	·500000	—	—	—	—	—	—	·0001	− ·000	—	—
6·20	·500000	—	—	—	—	—	—	·0001	—	—	—

Table 3. *Percentage points of the χ^2 distribution for integral and fractional degrees of freedom*

P \\ ν	0·1	0·2	0·3	0·4	0·5	0·6
0·0001	$0.0^{79}116893$	$0.0^{39}121461$	$0.0^{26}271457$	$0.0^{19}130510$	$0.0^{15}134994$	$0.0^{13}647288$
·0005	$.0^{65}111478$	$.0^{32}118614$	$.0^{21}124023$	$.0^{16}407843$	$.0^{13}843712$	$.0^{10}138356$
·001	$.0^{59}116893$	$.0^{29}121461$	$.0^{19}125999$	$.0^{14}130510$	$.0^{11}134994$	$.0^{9}139454$
·005	$.0^{45}111478$	$.0^{22}118614$	$.0^{15}575663$	$.0^{11}407843$	$.0^{9}843712$	$.0^{7}298079$
·010	$.0^{39}116893$	$.0^{19}121461$	$.0^{13}584837$	$.0^{9}130510$	$.0^{7}134994$	$.0^{6}300445$
·025	$.0^{31}106313$	$.0^{15}115834$	$.0^{10}263007$	$.0^{7}127451$	$.0^{6}527320$	$.0^{5}637136$
·050	$.0^{25}111478$	$.0^{12}118614$	$.0^{8}267199$	$.0^{6}407843$	$.0^{5}843715$	$.0^{4}642207$
0·10	$0.0^{19}116893$	$0.0^{9}121461$	$0.0^{6}271457$	$0.0^{4}130510$	$0.0^{3}135001$	$0.0^{3}647449$
·20	$.0^{13}122571$	$.0^{6}124376$	$.0^{4}275787$	$.0^{3}417703$	$.0^{2}216177$	$.0^{2}654068$
·30	$.0^{10}407579$	$.0^{5}717217$	$.0^{3}411706$	$.0^{2}317558$	·0109826	·0254533
·40	$.0^{7}128525$	$.0^{3}127368$	$.0^{2}280520$	·0134391	·0350448	·0674796
·50	$.0^{5}111478$	$.0^{2}118678$	·0124696	·0414927	·0873476	·146262
·60	$.0^{4}427387$	$.0^{2}736890$	·0425976	·106021	·188412	·282505
·70	$.0^{3}933127$	·0348556	·123216	·242075	·374696	·513130
·80	·0135640	·138780	·326574	·527087	·726170	·920148
·90	·152634	·532309	·889597	1·20980	1·50078	1·76962
0·950	0·531865	1·16087	1·65117	2·06105	2·42023	2·74470
·975	1·13435	1·95581	2·54506	3·02221	3·43324	3·80053
·990	2·17525	3·17696	3·86119	4·40461	4·86777	5·27882
·995	3·08925	4·18912	4·92727	5·50939	6·00362	6·44114
·999	5·47292	6·72735	7·55521	8·20393	8·75289	9·23787
·9995	6·57533	7·87676	8·73335	9·40409	9·97154	10·4728
·9999	9·24820	10·6325	11·5418	12·2539	12·8566	13·3893

P \\ ν	0·7	0·8	0·9	1·0	1·1	1·2	1·3
0·0001	$0.0^{11}536368$	$0.0^{9}148307$	$0.0^{8}197223$	$0.0^{7}157080$	$0.0^{7}861549$	$0.0^{6}357163$	$0.0^{5}119364$
·0005	$.0^{9}532746$	$.0^{8}829062$	$.0^{7}705058$	$.0^{6}392699$	$.0^{5}160744$	$.0^{5}522177$	$.0^{4}141976$
·001	$.0^{8}386016$	$.0^{7}468988$	$.0^{6}328988$	$.0^{5}157080$	$.0^{5}566843$	$.0^{4}165781$	$.0^{4}412422$
·005	$.0^{6}383410$	$.0^{5}262173$	$.0^{4}117611$	$.0^{4}392704$	$.0^{3}105762$	$.0^{3}242391$	$.0^{3}490613$
·010	$.0^{5}277811$	$.0^{4}148308$	$.0^{4}548796$	$.0^{3}157088$	$.0^{3}372989$	$.0^{3}769670$	$.0^{2}142556$
·025	$.0^{4}380826$	$.0^{3}146566$	$.0^{3}420510$	$.0^{3}982069$	$.0^{2}197446$	$.0^{2}354744$	$.0^{2}584496$
·050	$.0^{3}275963$	$.0^{3}829307$	$.0^{2}196319$	$.0^{2}393214$	$.0^{2}697388$	·0112897	·0170363
0·10	$0.0^{2}200084$	$0.0^{2}469775$	$0.0^{2}918331$	0·0157908	0·0247335	0·0361209	0·0499825
·20	·0145652	·0267845	·0433564	·0641848	·0890340	·117607	·149589
·30	·0469482	·0750838	·109174	·148472	·192278	·239978	·291046
·40	·109267	·158724	·214367	·274996	·339667	·407645	·478359
·50	·214739	·290156	·370657	·454936	·542073	·631404	·722448
·60	·383777	·489505	·598032	·708326	·819731	·931818	1·04430
·70	·653661	·794514	·934828	1·07419	1·21244	1·34950	1·48538
·80	1·10838	1·29114	1·46896	1·64237	1·81190	1·97798	2·14100
·90	2·02139	2·25969	2·48710	2·70554	2·91647	3·12101	3·32003
0·950	3·04392	3·32392	3·58881	3·84146	4·08400	4·31802	4·54478
·975	4·13667	4·44943	4·74398	5·02389	5·29176	5·54955	5·79874
·990	5·65317	6·00019	6·32602	6·63490	6·92986	7·21318	7·48660
·995	6·83889	7·20709	7·55241	7·87944	8·19147	8·49097	8·77980
·999	9·67813	10·0852	10·4666	10·8276	11·1717	11·5017	11·8198
·9995	10·9278	11·3485	11·7427	12·1157	12·4712	12·8122	13·1408
·9999	13·8731	14·3205	14·7399	15·1367	15·5151	15·8780	16·2277

The table gives the values of χ^2 for which $P(\chi^2|\nu) = 2^{-\frac{1}{2}\nu}\{\Gamma(\tfrac{1}{2}\nu)\}^{-1} \int_0^{\chi^2} x^{\frac{1}{2}\nu-1} e^{-\frac{1}{2}x} dx$.

Table 3 (*continued*)

P \ ν	1·4	1·5	1·6	1·7	1·8	1·9	2·0
0·0001	$0.0^5336747$	$0.0^5829515$	$0.0^4182997$	$0.0^4368620$	$0.0^4688306$	$0.0^3120566$	$0.0^3200010$
·0005	$·0^4335611$	$·0^4709238$	$·0^3136826$	$·0^3244862$	$·0^3411580$	$·0^3656211$	$·0^2100025$
·001	$·0^4903413$	$·0^3178722$	$·0^3325447$	$·0^3553490$	$·0^3889173$	$·0^2136143$	$·0^2200100$
·005	$·0^3900572$	$·0^2152864$	$·0^2243471$	$·0^2367955$	$·0^2532263$	$·0^2742041$	·0100251
·010	$·0^2242525$	$·0^2385450$	$·0^2579615$	$·0^2832707$	·0115163	·0154238	·0201007
·025	$·0^2899664$	·0131130	·0182839	·0245789	·0320486	·0407274	·0506356
·050	·0243264	·0332328	·0437951	·0560263	·0699189	·0854503	·102587
0·10	0·0662910	0·0849810	0·105964	0·129137	0·154393	0·181624	0·210721
·20	·184677	·222586	·263057	·305858	·350783	·397647	·446287
·30	·345040	·401589	·460384	·521161	·583702	·647818	·713350
·40	·551360	·626292	·702871	·780867	·860094	·940398	1·02165
·50	·814847	·908334	1·00270	1·09779	1·19349	1·28968	1·38629
·60	1·15700	1·26978	1·38254	1·49524	1·60783	1·72028	1·83258
·70	1·62013	1·75379	1·88643	2·01811	2·14888	2·27881	2·40795
·80	2·30129	2·45912	2·61474	2·76836	2·92015	3·07028	3·21888
·90	3·51426	3·70426	3·89052	4·07343	4·25332	4·43049	4·60517
0·950	4·76524	4·98020	5·19029	5·39605	5·59792	5·79629	5·99146
·975	6·04051	6·27581	6·50539	6·72989	6·94983	7·16566	7·37776
·990	7·75148	8·00890	8·25976	8·50477	8·74454	8·97959	9·21034
·995	9·05943	9·33102	9·59554	9·85375	10·1063	10·3538	10·5966
·999	12·1275	12·4262	12·7169	13·0005	13·2778	13·5492	13·8155
·9995	13·4587	13·7672	14·0675	14·3604	14·6466	14·9269	15·2018
·9999	16·5660	16·8944	17·2139	17·5255	17·8301	18·1283	18·4207

P \ ν	2·1	2·2	2·3	2·4	2·5	2·6	2·7
0·0001	$0.0^3316675$	$0.0^3481566$	$0.0^3707046$	$0.0^2100666$	$0.0^2139492$	$0.0^2188710$	$0.0^2249901$
·0005	$·0^2146697$	$·0^2208089$	$·0^2286725$	$·0^2385157$	$·0^2505917$	$·0^2651481$	$·0^2824242$
·001	$·0^2283963$	$·0^2390932$	$·0^2524169$	$·0^2686743$	$·0^2881588$	·0111147	·0137896
·005	·0131838	·0169385	·0213252	·0263750	·0321134	·0385615	·0457355
·010	·0255888	·0319216	·0391249	·0472174	·0562121	·0661161	·0769326
·025	·0617817	·0741649	·0877765	·102602	·118623	·135816	·154157
·050	·121286	·141504	·163188	·186290	·210758	·236541	·263589
0·10	0·241582	0·274109	0·308210	0·343797	0·380789	0·419112	0·458695
·20	·496559	·548335	·601500	·655952	·711599	·768361	·826162
·30	·780160	·848131	·917160	·987156	1·05804	1·12975	1·20221
·40	1·10375	1·18660	1·27012	1·35425	1·43894	1·52413	1·60979
·50	1·48327	1·58055	1·67810	1·77587	1·87385	1·97200	2·07030
·60	1·94471	2·05667	2·16846	2·28007	2·39150	2·50277	2·61386
·70	2·53634	2·66403	2·79107	2·91749	3·04333	3·16862	3·29340
·80	3·36606	3·51195	3·65662	3·80018	3·94268	4·08420	4·22481
·90	4·77758	4·94791	5·11630	5·28292	5·44788	5·61130	5·77327
0·950	6·18373	6·37333	6·56047	6·74533	6·92808	7·10886	7·28780
·975	7·58645	7·79202	7·99471	8·19474	8·39230	8·58755	8·78067
·990	9·43718	9·66042	9·88035	10·0972	10·3112	10·5226	10·7315
·995	10·8352	11·0700	11·3011	11·5290	11·7538	11·9757	12·1949
·999	14·0770	14·3341	14·5871	14·8364	15·0822	15·3247	15·5642
·9995	15·4717	15·7370	15·9981	16·2553	16·5089	16·7591	17·0061
·9999	18·7077	18·9899	19·2675	19·5409	19·8104	20·0763	20·3387

Table 3 (*continued*). *Percentage points of the χ^2 distribution*

P \ ν	2·8	2·9	3·0	3·2	3·4	3·6	3·8
0·0001	$0.0^2324678$	$0.0^2414666$	$0.0^2521483$	$0.0^2791963$	0·0114840	0·0160220	0·0216365
·0005	·0102648	·0126036	·0152790	·0217126	·0296973	·0393405	·0507273
·001	·0168644	·0203605	·0242976	·0335617	·0447717	·0580128	·0733444
·005	·0536482	·0623083	·0717218	·0928181	·116934	·144039	·174079
·010	·0886606	·101296	·114832	·144568	·177777	·214351	·254170
·025	·173619	·194175	·215795	·262116	·312355	·366289	·423710
·050	·291853	·321287	·351846	·416168	·484495	·556536	·632025
0·10	0·499473	0·541385	0·584374	0·673381	0·766116	0·862253	0·961505
·20	·884938	·944626	1·00517	1·12865	1·25502	1·38399	1·51531
·30	1·27539	1·34921	1·42365	1·57422	1·72681	1·88121	2·03722
·40	1·69587	1·78234	1·86917	2·04382	2·21964	2·39650	2·57426
·50	2·16874	2·26730	2·36597	2·56359	2·76152	2·95971	3·15811
·60	2·72479	2·83556	2·94617	3·16694	3·38713	3·60679	3·82595
·70	3·41768	3·54150	3·66487	3·91038	4·15437	4·39696	4·63828
·80	4·36455	4·50347	4·64163	4·91580	5·18735	5·45653	5·72356
·90	5·93389	6·09324	6·25139	6·56437	6·87329	7·17856	7·48052
0·950	7·46503	7·64064	7·81473	8·15868	8·49749	8·83165	9·16161
·975	8·97176	9·16097	9·34840	9·71832	10·0822	10·4407	10·7942
·990	10·9381	11·1425	11·3449	11·7439	12·1359	12·5217	12·9018
·995	12·4116	12·6260	12·8382	13·2563	13·6669	14·0707	14·4683
·999	15·8009	16·0348	16·2662	16·7220	17·1692	17·6086	18·0410
·9995	17·2502	17·4914	17·7300	18·1998	18·6607	19·1134	19·5588
·9999	20·5979	20·8542	21·1075	21·6063	22·0954	22·5756	23·0479

P \ ν	4·0	4·2	4·4	4·6	4·8	5·0	5·2
0·0001	0·0284185	0·0364463	0·0457865	0·0564938	0·0686126	0·0821774	0·0972142
·0005	·0639220	·0789712	·0959054	·114742	·135487	·158138	·182683
·001	·0908040	·110410	·132168	·156067	·182091	·210213	·240402
·005	·206989	·242691	·281104	·322141	·365716	·411742	·460133
·010	·297109	·343044	·391849	·443403	·497590	·554298	·613420
·025	·484419	·548228	·614967	·684475	·756602	·831212	·908176
·050	·710723	·792415	·876904	·964015	1·05359	1·14548	1·23955
0·10	1·06362	1·16839	1·27560	1·38509	1·49671	1·61031	1·72577
·20	1·64878	1·78420	1·92141	2·06029	2·20070	2·34253	2·48570
·30	2·19470	2·35350	2·51352	2·67465	2·83680	2·99991	3·16389
·40	2·75284	2·93216	3·11213	3·29272	3·47385	3·65550	3·83762
·50	3·35669	3·55542	3·75428	3·95325	4·15231	4·35146	4·55068
·60	4·04463	4·26286	4·48068	4·69811	4·91516	5·13187	5·34824
·70	4·87843	5·11750	5·35557	5·59271	5·82897	6·06443	6·29912
·80	5·98862	6·25186	6·51343	6·77346	7·03204	7·28928	7·54526
·90	7·77944	8·07559	8·36917	8·66038	8·94940	9·23636	9·52140
0·950	9·48773	9·81032	10·1297	10·4460	10·7596	11·0705	11·3790
·975	11·1433	11·4882	11·8293	12·1669	12·5012	12·8325	13·1609
·990	13·2767	13·6468	14·0125	14·3741	14·7320	15·0863	15·4373
·995	14·8603	15·2470	15·6290	16·0066	16·3800	16·7496	17·1156
·999	18·4668	18·8867	19·3011	19·7104	20·1149	20·5150	20·9109
·9995	19·9974	20·4297	20·8563	21·2775	21·6937	22·1053	22·5126
·9999	23·5127	23·9709	24·4227	24·8687	25·3093	25·7448	26·1756

The table gives the values of χ^2 for which $P(\chi^2|\nu) = 2^{-\frac{1}{2}\nu}\{\Gamma(\frac{1}{2}\nu)\}^{-1} \int_0^{\chi^2} x^{\frac{1}{2}\nu-1} e^{-\frac{1}{2}x} dx.$

Table 3 (*continued*)

P \ ν	5·4	5·6	5·8	6·0	6·2	6·4	6·6
0·0001	0·113741	0·131770	0·151307	0·172352	0·194902	0·218950	0·244486
·0005	·209106	·237385	·267495	·299408	·333091	·368514	·405641
·001	·272622	·306834	·342997	·381067	·421001	·462755	·506284
·005	·510807	·563682	·618681	·675727	·734749	·795677	·858446
·010	·674853	·738503	·804277	·872090	·941861	1·01351	1·08697
·025	·987377	1·06870	1·15206	1·23734	1·32447	1·41336	1·50394
·050	1·33568	1·43376	1·53370	1·63538	1·73874	1·84369	1·95015
0·10	1·84298	1·96184	2·08225	2·20413	2·32741	2·45200	2·57786
·20	2·63012	2·77570	2·92238	3·07009	3·21878	3·36839	3·51888
·30	3·32870	3·49428	3·66058	3·82755	3·99516	4·16338	4·33216
·40	4·02016	4·20313	4·38646	4·57015	4·75418	4·93851	5·12315
·50	4·74996	4·94930	5·14869	5·34812	5·54759	5·74710	5·94664
·60	5·56430	5·78006	5·99555	6·21076	6·42571	6·64043	6·85491
·70	6·53310	6·76641	6·99907	7·23114	7·46263	7·69358	7·92401
·80	7·80006	8·05375	8·30640	8·55806	8·80878	9·05862	9·30762
·90	9·80465	10·0862	10·3662	10·6446	10·9217	11·1974	11·4718
0·950	11·6852	11·9893	12·2914	12·5916	12·8900	13·1866	13·4816
·975	13·4867	13·8099	14·1308	14·4494	14·7659	15·0804	15·3930
·990	15·7851	16·1301	16·4723	16·8119	17·1490	17·4838	17·8164
·995	17·4782	17·8376	18·1940	18·5476	18·8985	19·2468	19·5927
·999	21·3030	21·6913	22·0762	22·4577	22·8362	23·2117	23·5844
·9995	22·9157	23·3150	23·7106	24·1028	24·4917	24·8775	25·2604
·9999	26·6019	27·0240	27·4420	27·8563	28·2671	28·6744	29·0785

P \ ν	6·8	7·0	7·2	7·4	7·6	7·8	8·0
0·0001	0·271496	0·299967	0·329881	0·361220	0·393965	0·428097	0·463594
·0005	·444440	·484875	·526911	·570514	·615649	·662282	·710379
·001	·551545	·598494	·647089	·697287	·749049	·802335	·857105
·005	·922992	·989256	1·05718	1·12671	1·19779	1·27037	1·34441
·010	1·16217	1·23904	1·31753	1·39757	1·47911	1·56211	1·64650
·025	1·59613	1·68987	1·78509	1·88174	1·97977	2·07911	2·17973
·050	2·05806	2·16735	2·27797	2·38986	2·50296	2·61724	2·73264
0·10	2·70491	2·83311	2·96239	3·09272	3·22405	3·35633	3·48954
·20	3·67021	3·82232	3·97519	4·12878	4·28306	4·43800	4·59357
·30	4·50149	4·67133	4·84166	5·01245	5·18369	5·35535	5·52742
·40	5·30806	5·49324	5·67866	5·86433	6·05022	6·23633	6·42264
·50	6·14621	6·34581	6·54543	6·74508	6·94474	7·14442	7·34412
·60	7·06916	7·28321	7·49705	7·71069	7·92415	8·13742	8·35053
·70	8·15396	8·38343	8·61246	8·84106	9·06925	9·29704	9·52446
·80	9·55582	9·80325	10·0500	10·2960	10·5413	10·7860	11·0301
·90	11·7450	12·0170	12·2880	12·5578	12·8267	13·0946	13·3616
0·950	13·7751	14·0671	14·3577	14·6470	14·9350	15·2217	15·5073
·975	15·7037	16·0128	16·3201	16·6260	16·9303	17·2331	17·5345
·990	18·1469	18·4753	18·8018	19·1265	19·4494	19·7706	20·0902
·995	19·9363	20·2777	20·6170	20·9544	21·2897	21·6232	21·9550
·999	23·9544	24·3219	24·6869	25·0496	25·4100	25·7683	26·1245
·9995	25·6404	26·0178	26·3925	26·7649	27·1348	27·5025	27·8680
·9999	29·4795	29·8775	30·2727	30·6652	31·0552	31·4426	31·8276

Table 3 (*continued*). *Percentage points of the χ^2 distribution*

P \ ν	8·2	8·4	8·6	8·8	9·0	9·2	9·4
0·0001	0·500435	0·538599	0·578064	0·618808	0·660809	0·704046	0·748497
·0005	·759908	·810835	·863130	·916762	·971699	1·02791	1·08538
·001	·913322	·970950	1·02995	1·09030	1·15195	1·21488	1·27905
·005	1·41986	1·49668	1·57482	1·65425	1·73493	1·81682	1·89989
·010	1·73224	1·81930	1·90762	1·99716	2·08790	2·17979	2·27280
·025	2·28157	2·38460	2·48877	2·59405	2·70039	2·80777	2·91614
·050	2·84912	2·96664	3·08518	3·20468	3·32511	3·44645	3·56867
0·10	3·62363	3·75856	3·89432	4·03086	4·16816	4·30619	4·44494
·20	4·74975	4·90651	5·06382	5·22168	5·38005	5·53893	5·69828
·30	5·69988	5·87271	6·04590	6·21944	6·39331	6·56749	6·74199
·40	6·60916	6·79586	6·98275	7·16981	7·35703	7·54442	7·73197
·50	7·54384	7·74357	7·94331	8·14307	8·34283	8·54261	8·74240
·60	8·56346	8·77623	8·98885	9·20132	9·41364	9·62582	9·83787
·70	9·75151	9·97822	10·2046	10·4306	10·6564	10·8818	11·1069
·80	11·2736	11·5165	11·7589	12·0008	12·2421	12·4830	12·7234
·90	13·6276	13·8929	14·1572	14·4208	14·6837	14·9457	15·2071
0·950	15·7917	16·0751	16·3574	16·6387	16·9190	17·1983	17·4768
·975	17·8347	18·1335	18·4311	18·7275	19·0228	19·3169	19·6100
·990	20·4083	20·7248	21·0399	21·3536	21·6660	21·9771	22·2869
·995	22·2850	22·6134	22·9402	23·2655	23·5893	23·9118	24·2328
·999	26·4787	26·8310	27·1815	27·5302	27·8772	28·2225	28·5662
·9995	28·2315	28·5929	28·9524	29·3100	29·6658	30·0199	30·3723
·9999	32·2104	32·5909	32·9693	33·3456	33·7199	34·0924	34·4629

P \ ν	9·6	9·8	10·0	11·0	12·0	13·0	14·0
0·0001	0·794140	0·840955	0·888920	1·14529	1·42749	1·73332	2·06080
·0005	1·14406	1·20394	1·26498	1·58685	1·93438	2·30506	2·69673
·001	1·34443	1·41101	1·47874	1·83385	2·21421	2·61722	3·04067
·005	1·98411	2·06944	2·15586	2·60322	3·07382	3·56503	4·07467
·010	2·36689	2·46204	2·55821	3·05348	3·57057	4·10692	4·66042
·025	3·02549	3·13577	3·24697	3·81575	4·40379	5·00875	5·62873
·050	3·69174	3·81562	3·94030	4·57481	5·22603	5·89186	6·57063
0·10	4·58436	4·72445	4·86518	5·57778	6·30380	7·04150	7·78953
·20	5·85810	6·01837	6·17908	6·98867	7·80733	8·63386	9·46733
·30	6·91678	7·09186	7·26722	8·14787	9·03428	9·92568	10·8215
·40	7·91966	8·10750	8·29547	9·23729	10·1820	11·1291	12·0785
·50	8·94220	9·14200	9·34182	10·3410	11·3403	12·3398	13·3393
·60	10·0498	10·2616	10·4732	11·5298	12·5838	13·6356	14·6853
·70	11·3318	11·5564	11·7807	12·8987	14·0111	15·1187	16·2221
·80	12·9634	13·2029	13·4420	14·6314	15·8120	16·9848	18·1508
·90	15·4678	15·7278	15·9872	17·2750	18·5493	19·8119	21·0641
0·950	17·7544	18·0311	18·3070	19·6751	21·0261	22·3620	23·6848
·975	19·9020	20·1931	20·4832	21·9201	23·3367	24·7356	26·1189
·990	22·5955	22·9029	23·2093	24·7250	26·2170	27·6882	29·1412
·995	24·5525	24·8710	25·1882	26·7568	28·2995	29·8195	31·3193
·999	28·9084	29·2491	29·5883	31·2641	32·9095	34·5282	36·1233
·9995	30·7230	31·0722	31·4198	33·1366	34·8213	36·4778	38·1094
·9999	34·8317	35·1987	35·5640	37·3670	39·1344	40·8706	42·5793

The table gives the values of χ^2 for which $P(\chi^2|\nu) = 2^{-\frac{1}{2}\nu}\{\Gamma(\tfrac{1}{2}\nu)\}^{-1}\displaystyle\int_0^{\chi^2} x^{\frac{1}{2}\nu-1}e^{-\frac{1}{2}x}dx.$

Table 3 (*continued*)

P \ ν	15	16	17	18	19	20	21	22
0·0001	2·40819	2·77394	3·15667	3·55516	3·96832	4·39516	4·83481	5·28646
·0005	3·10752	3·53581	3·98018	4·43939	4·91234	5·39807	5·89570	6·40447
·0010	3·48268	3·94163	4·41609	4·90485	5·40682	5·92104	6·44668	6·98297
·0050	4·60092	5·14221	5·69722	6·26480	6·84397	7·43384	8·03365	8·64272
·0100	5·22935	5·81221	6·40776	7·01491	7·63273	8·26040	8·89720	9·54249
·0250	6·26214	6·90766	7·56419	8·23075	8·90652	9·59078	10·2829	10·9823
·0500	7·26094	7·96165	8·67176	9·39045	10·1170	10·8508	11·5913	12·3380
0·1000	8·54676	9·31224	10·0852	10·8649	11·6509	12·4426	13·2396	14·0415
·2000	10·3070	11·1521	12·0023	12·8569	13·7158	14·5784	15·4446	16·3140
·3000	11·7212	12·6244	13·5307	14·4399	15·3517	16·2659	17·1823	18·1007
·4000	13·0297	13·9827	14·9373	15·8932	16·8504	17·8088	18·7683	19·7288
·5000	14·3389	15·3385	16·3382	17·3379	18·3376	19·3374	20·3372	21·3370
·6000	15·7332	16·7795	17·8244	18·8679	19·9102	20·9514	21·9915	23·0307
·7000	17·3217	18·4179	19·5110	20·6014	21·6891	22·7745	23·8578	24·9390
·8000	19·3107	20·4651	21·6146	22·7595	23·9004	25·0375	26·1711	27·3015
·9000	22·3071	23·5418	24·7690	25·9894	27·2036	28·4120	29·6151	30·8133
0·9500	24·9958	26·2962	27·5871	28·8693	30·1435	31·4104	32·6706	33·9244
·9750	27·4884	28·8453	30·1910	31·5264	32·8523	34·1696	35·4789	36·7807
·9900	30·5779	31·9999	33·4087	34·8053	36·1909	37·5662	38·9322	40·2894
·9950	32·8013	34·2672	35·7185	37·1565	38·5822	39·9968	41·4011	42·7956
·9990	37·6973	39·2524	40·7902	42·3124	43·8202	45·3147	46·7970	48·2679
·9995	39·7188	41·3081	42·8792	44·4338	45·9731	47·4984	49·0108	50·5111
·9999	44·2632	45·9249	47·5663	49·1894	50·7955	52·3860	53·9620	55·5246

P \ ν	23	24	25	26	27	28	29	30
0·0001	5·74941	6·22300	6·70663	7·19978	7·70193	8·21264	8·73149	9·25809
·0005	6·92367	7·45269	7·99096	8·53795	9·09320	9·65627	10·2268	10·8044
·0010	7·52924	8·08488	8·64934	9·22213	9·80278	10·3909	10·9861	11·5880
·0050	9·26042	9·88623	10·5197	11·1602	11·8076	12·4613	13·1211	13·7867
·0100	10·1957	10·8564	11·5240	12·1981	12·8785	13·5647	14·2565	14·9535
·0250	11·6886	12·4012	13·1197	13·8439	14·5734	15·3079	16·0471	16·7908
·0500	13·0905	13·8484	14·6114	15·3792	16·1514	16·9279	17·7084	18·4927
0·1000	14·8480	15·6587	16·4734	17·2919	18·1139	18·9392	19·7677	20·5992
·2000	17·1865	18·0618	18·9398	19·8202	20·7030	21·5880	22·4750	23·3641
·3000	19·0211	19·9432	20·8670	21·7924	22·7192	23·6475	24·5770	25·5078
·4000	20·6902	21·6525	22·6156	23·5794	24·5440	25·5092	26·4751	27·4416
·5000	22·3369	23·3367	24·3366	25·3365	26·3363	27·3362	28·3361	29·3360
·6000	24·0689	25·1063	26·1430	27·1789	28·2141	29·2486	30·2825	31·3159
·7000	26·0184	27·0960	28·1719	29·2463	30·3193	31·3909	32·4612	33·5302
·8000	28·4288	29·5533	30·6752	31·7946	32·9117	34·0266	35·1394	36·2502
·9000	32·0069	33·1962	34·3816	35·5632	36·7412	37·9159	39·0875	40·2560
0·9500	35·1725	36·4150	37·6525	38·8851	40·1133	41·3371	42·5570	43·7730
·9750	38·0756	39·3641	40·6465	41·9232	43·1945	44·4608	45·7223	46·9792
·9900	41·6384	42·9798	44·3141	45·6417	46·9630	48·2782	49·5879	50·8922
·9950	44·1813	45·5585	46·9279	48·2899	49·6449	50·9934	52·3356	53·6720
·9990	49·7282	51·1786	52·6179	54·0520	55·4760	56·8923	58·3012	59·7030
·9995	52·0002	53·4788	54·9475	56·4069	57·8576	59·3000	60·7346	62·1619
·9999	57·0746	58·6130	60·1403	61·6573	63·1645	64·6624	66·1517	67·6326

Table 3 (*continued*). *Percentage points of the χ^2 distribution*

P \ ν	31	32	33	34	35	36	37	38
0·0001	9·79209	10·3331	10·8810	11·4352	11·9957	12·5622	13·1343	13·7120
·0005	11·3887	11·9794	12·5763	13·1791	13·7875	14·4012	15·0202	15·6441
·0010	12·1963	12·8107	13·4309	14·0567	14·6878	15·3241	15·9653	16·6112
·0050	14·4578	15·1340	15·8153	16·5013	17·1918	17·8867	18·5858	19·2889
·0100	15·6555	16·3622	17·0735	17·7891	18·5089	19·2327	19·9602	20·6914
·0250	17·5387	18·2908	19·0467	19·8063	20·5694	21·3359	22·1056	22·8785
·0500	19·2806	20·0719	20·8665	21·6643	22·4650	23·2686	24·0749	24·8839
0·1000	21·4336	22·2706	23·1102	23·9523	24·7967	25·6433	26·4921	27·3429
·2000	24·2551	25·1478	26·0422	26·9383	27·8359	28·7350	29·6355	30·5373
·3000	26·4397	27·3728	28·3069	29·2421	30·1782	31·1152	32·0532	32·9919
·4000	28·4087	29·3763	30·3444	31·3130	32·2821	33·2517	34·2216	35·1920
·5000	30·3359	31·3359	32·3358	33·3357	34·3356	35·3356	36·3355	37·3354
·6000	32·3486	33·3809	34·4126	35·4438	36·4746	37·5049	38·5348	39·5644
·7000	34·5981	35·6649	36·7307	37·7954	38·8591	39·9220	40·9839	42·0451
·8000	37·3591	38·4663	39·5718	40·6757	41·7780	42·8788	43·9782	45·0763
·9000	41·4217	42·5848	43·7452	44·9032	46·0588	47·2122	48·3634	49·5126
0·9500	44·9853	46·1943	47·3999	48·6024	49·8018	50·9985	52·1923	53·3835
·9750	48·2319	49·4804	50·7251	51·9660	53·2033	54·4373	55·6680	56·8955
·9900	52·1914	53·4858	54·7755	56·0609	57·3421	58·6192	59·8925	61·1621
·9950	55·0027	56·3281	57·6485	58·9639	60·2748	61·5812	62·8833	64·1814
·9990	61·0983	62·4872	63·8701	65·2472	66·6188	67·9851	69·3465	70·7029
·9995	63·5820	64·9955	66·4025	67·8035	69·1986	70·5881	71·9722	73·3512
·9999	69·1057	70·5712	72·0296	73·4812	74·9262	76·3650	77·7977	79·2247

P \ ν	39	40	41	42	43	44	45	46
0·0001	14·2950	14·8831	15·4761	16·0738	16·6762	17·2829	17·8940	18·5093
·0005	16·2729	16·9062	17·5440	18·1861	18·8323	19·4825	20·1366	20·7945
·0010	17·2616	17·9164	18·5754	19·2385	19·9055	20·5763	21·2507	21·9287
·0050	19·9959	20·7065	21·4208	22·1385	22·8595	23·5837	24·3110	25·0413
·0100	21·4262	22·1643	22·9056	23·6501	24·3976	25·1480	25·9013	26·6572
·0250	23·6543	24·4330	25·2145	25·9987	26·7854	27·5746	28·3662	29·1601
·0500	25·6954	26·5093	27·3256	28·1440	28·9647	29·7875	30·6123	31·4390
0·1000	28·1958	29·0505	29·9071	30·7654	31·6254	32·4871	33·3504	34·2152
·2000	31·4405	32·3450	33·2506	34·1574	35·0653	35·9744	36·8844	37·7955
·3000	33·9315	34·8719	35·8131	36·7550	37·6975	38·6408	39·5847	40·5292
·4000	36·1628	37·1340	38·1055	39·0774	40·0496	41·0222	41·9950	42·9682
·5000	38·3354	39·3353	40·3353	41·3352	42·3352	43·3352	44·3351	45·3351
·6000	40·5935	41·6222	42·6506	43·6786	44·7063	45·7336	46·7607	47·7874
·7000	43·1054	44·1649	45·2236	46·2817	47·3390	48·3957	49·4517	50·5071
·8000	46·1730	47·2685	48·3628	49·4560	50·5480	51·6389	52·7288	53·8177
·9000	50·6598	51·8051	52·9485	54·0902	55·2302	56·3685	57·5053	58·6405
0·9500	54·5722	55·7585	56·9424	58·1240	59·3035	60·4809	61·6562	62·8296
·9750	58·1201	59·3417	60·5606	61·7767	62·9904	64·2014	65·4102	66·6165
·9900	62·4281	63·6907	64·9501	66·2062	67·4593	68·7095	69·9568	71·2014
·9950	65·4756	66·7660	68·0527	69·3360	70·6159	71·8925	73·1661	74·4365
·9990	72·0547	73·4019	74·7449	76·0838	77·4186	78·7495	80·0767	81·4003
·9995	74·7253	76·0946	77·4593	78·8197	80·1757	81·5277	82·8757	84·2198
·9999	80·6462	82·0623	83·4733	84·8793	86·2806	87·6773	89·0694	90·4574

The table gives the values of χ^2 for which $P(\chi^2|\nu) = 2^{-\frac{1}{2}\nu}\{\Gamma(\frac{1}{2}\nu)\}^{-1}\int_0^{\chi^2} x^{\frac{1}{2}\nu-1}e^{-\frac{1}{2}x}dx$.

Table 3 (continued)

P \ ν	47	48	49	50	51	52	53	54	55
0·0001	19·1285	19·7517	20·3787	21·0093	21·6435	22·2812	22·9223	23·5666	24·2141
·0005	21·4559	22·1209	22·7893	23·4610	24·1359	24·8139	25·4949	26·1789	26·8658
·0010	22·6101	23·2949	23·9828	24·6739	25·3680	26·0651	26·7650	27·4677	28·1731
·0050	25·7746	26·5106	27·2493	27·9907	28·7347	29·4812	30·2300	30·9813	31·7348
·0100	27·4158	28·1770	28·9406	29·7067	30·4750	31·2457	32·0185	32·7934	33·5705
·0250	29·9562	30·7545	31·5549	32·3574	33·1618	33·9681	34·7763	35·5863	36·3981
·0500	32·2676	33·0981	33·9303	34·7643	35·5999	36·4371	37·2759	38·1162	38·9580
0·1000	35·0814	35·9491	36·8182	37·6886	38·5604	39·4334	40·3076	41·1830	42·0596
·2000	38·7075	39·6205	40·5344	41·4492	42·3649	43·2814	44·1987	45·1167	46·0356
·3000	41·4744	42·4201	43·3664	44·3133	45·2607	46·2086	47·1571	48·1060	49·0554
·4000	43·9417	44·9154	45·8895	46·8638	47·8383	48·8132	49·7882	50·7635	51·7391
·5000	46·3350	47·3350	48·3350	49·3349	50·3349	51·3349	52·3348	53·3348	54·3348
·6000	48·8139	49·8401	50·8660	51·8916	52·9170	53·9421	54·9670	55·9916	57·0160
·7000	51·5619	52·6161	53·6697	54·7228	55·7753	56·8274	57·8789	58·9299	59·9805
·8000	54·9056	55·9926	57·0786	58·1638	59·2481	60·3316	61·4142	62·4961	63·5772
·9000	59·7743	60·9066	62·0375	63·1671	64·2954	65·4224	66·5482	67·6728	68·7962
0·9500	64·0011	65·1708	66·3387	67·5048	68·6693	69·8321	70·9935	72·1532	73·3115
·9750	67·8207	69·0226	70·2224	71·4202	72·6160	73·8098	75·0019	76·1920	77·3805
·9900	72·4433	73·6826	74·9195	76·1539	77·3860	78·6157	79·8433	81·0688	82·2921
·9950	75·7041	76·9688	78·2307	79·4900	80·7467	82·0008	83·2525	84·5019	85·7489
·9990	82·7204	84·0371	85·3506	86·6608	87·9679	89·2721	90·5734	91·8718	93·1675
·9995	85·5603	86·8971	88·2305	89·5605	90·8872	92·2108	93·5312	94·8487	96·1632
·9999	91·8412	93·2209	94·5967	95·9688	97·3371	98·7019	100·063	101·421	102·776

P \ ν	56	57	58	59	60	61	62	63	64
0·0001	24·8648	25·5185	26·1751	26·8346	27·4969	28·1619	28·8297	29·5000	30·1729
·0005	27·5554	28·2478	28·9428	29·6404	30·3405	31·0430	31·7480	32·4553	33·1648
·0010	28·8812	29·5918	30·3049	31·0204	31·7383	32·4586	33·1811	33·9058	34·6326
·0050	32·4905	33·2484	34·0084	34·7704	35·5345	36·3005	37·0684	37·8382	38·6098
·0100	34·3495	35·1305	35·9135	36·6982	37·4849	38·2732	39·0633	39·8551	40·6486
·0250	37·2116	38·0267	38·8435	39·6619	40·4817	41·3031	42·1260	42·9503	43·7760
·0500	39·8013	40·6459	41·4920	42·3393	43·1880	44·0379	44·8890	45·7414	46·5949
0·1000	42·9373	43·8162	44·6960	45·5770	46·4589	47·3418	48·2257	49·1105	49·9963
·2000	46·9552	47·8755	48·7965	49·7182	50·6406	51·5637	52·4873	53·4116	54·3365
·3000	50·0053	50·9556	51·9063	52·8575	53·8091	54·7611	55·7135	56·6663	57·6195
·4000	52·7148	53·6908	54·6670	55·6434	56·6200	57·5968	58·5738	59·5510	60·5283
·5000	55·3348	56·3347	57·3347	58·3347	59·3347	60·3346	61·3346	62·3346	63·3346
·6000	58·0402	59·0642	60·0879	61·1115	62·1348	63·1580	64·1810	65·2037	66·2263
·7000	61·0305	62·0802	63·1294	64·1782	65·2265	66·2745	67·3220	68·3692	69·4160
·8000	64·6576	65·7373	66·8162	67·8945	68·9721	70·0490	71·1253	72·2010	73·2761
·9000	69·9185	71·0397	72·1598	73·2789	74·3970	75·5141	76·6302	77·7454	78·8597
0·9500	74·4683	75·6238	76·7778	77·9305	79·0819	80·2321	81·3810	82·5287	83·6753
·9750	78·5671	79·7522	80·9356	82·1174	83·2977	84·4764	85·6537	86·8296	88·0040
·9900	83·5134	84·7328	85·9502	87·1657	88·3794	89·5913	90·8015	92·0100	93·2168
·9950	86·9937	88·2363	89·4768	90·7153	91·9517	93·1861	94·4186	95·6493	96·8781
·9990	94·4605	95·7510	97·0388	98·3242	99·6073	100·888	102·166	103·442	104·716
·9995	97·4749	98·7838	100·090	101·394	102·695	103·993	105·289	106·583	107·875
·9999	104·127	105·476	106·821	108·163	109·503	110·840	112·174	113·505	114·834

Table 3 (*continued*). *Percentage points of the χ² distribution*

P \ ν	65	66	67	68	69	70	71	72	73
0·0001	30·8483	31·5261	32·2063	32·8888	33·5736	34·2607	34·9499	35·6413	36·3348
·0005	33·8767	34·5906	35·3068	36·0250	36·7452	37·4674	38·1916	38·9177	39·6457
·0010	35·3616	36·0926	36·8257	37·5606	38·2976	39·0364	39·7770	40·5195	41·2637
·0050	39·3831	40·1582	40·9350	41·7135	42·4935	43·2752	44·0584	44·8431	45·6293
·0100	41·4436	42·2402	43·0384	43·8380	44·6392	45·4417	46·2457	47·0510	47·8577
·0250	44·6030	45·4314	46·2610	47·0920	47·9242	48·7576	49·5922	50·4279	51·2648
·0500	47·4496	48·3054	49·1623	50·0202	50·8792	51·7393	52·6003	53·4623	54·3253
0·1000	50·8829	51·7705	52·6588	53·5480	54·4381	55·3289	56·2205	57·1129	58·0061
·2000	55·2620	56·1881	57·1147	58·0419	58·9696	59·8978	60·8266	61·7558	62·6856
·3000	58·5731	59·5270	60·4812	61·4358	62·3908	63·3460	64·3016	65·2575	66·2137
·4000	61·5059	62·4836	63·4615	64·4395	65·4177	66·3961	67·3746	68·3533	69·3322
·5000	64·3346	65·3345	66·3345	67·3345	68·3345	69·3345	70·3345	71·3344	72·3344
·6000	67·2488	68·2710	69·2931	70·3150	71·3368	72·3583	73·3798	74·4011	75·4222
·7000	70·4624	71·5085	72·5542	73·5995	74·6446	75·6893	76·7337	77·7777	78·8215
·8000	74·3506	75·4245	76·4979	77·5707	78·6429	79·7147	80·7859	81·8566	82·9268
·9000	79·9730	81·0855	82·1971	83·3079	84·4179	85·5270	86·6354	87·7431	88·8499
0·9500	84·8206	85·9649	87·1081	88·2502	89·3912	90·5312	91·6702	92·8083	93·9453
·9750	89·1771	90·3489	91·5194	92·6885	93·8565	95·0232	96·1887	97·3531	98·5162
·9900	94·4221	95·6257	96·8278	98·0284	99·2275	100·425	101·621	102·816	104·010
·9950	98·1052	99·3304	100·554	101·776	102·996	104·215	105·432	106·648	107·862
·9990	105·988	107·258	108·526	109·791	111·055	112·317	113·577	114·835	116·092
·9995	109·164	110·451	111·736	113·018	114·299	115·578	116·854	118·129	119·402
·9999	116·160	117·484	118·805	120·124	121·440	122·755	124·067	125·377	126·684

P \ ν	74	75	76	77	78	79	80	81	82
0·0001	37·0303	37·7279	38·4274	39·1288	39·8322	40·5374	41·2445	41·9533	42·6639
·0005	40·3755	41·1072	41·8405	42·5757	43·3125	44·0509	44·7910	45·5328	46·2760
·0010	42·0097	42·7573	43·5066	44·2576	45·0101	45·7642	46·5199	47·2770	48·0357
·0050	46·4170	47·2060	47·9965	48·7884	49·5816	50·3761	51·1719	51·9690	52·7673
·0100	48·6657	49·4750	50·2856	51·0974	51·9104	52·7247	53·5401	54·3566	55·1743
·0250	52·1028	52·9419	53·7821	54·6234	55·4656	56·3089	57·1532	57·9984	58·8446
·0500	55·1892	56·0541	56·9198	57·7864	58·6539	59·5223	60·3915	61·2615	62·1323
0·1000	58·9000	59·7946	60·6898	61·5858	62·4825	63·3799	64·2778	65·1765	66·0757
·2000	63·6158	64·5466	65·4777	66·4094	67·3415	68·2740	69·2069	70·1403	71·0741
·3000	67·1702	68·1271	69·0841	70·0415	70·9992	71·9571	72·9153	73·8738	74·8325
·4000	70·3111	71·2903	72·2695	73·2489	74·2285	75·2081	76·1879	77·1679	78·1479
·5000	73·3344	74·3344	75·3344	76·3344	77·3344	78·3343	79·3343	80·3343	81·3343
·6000	76·4432	77·4640	78·4848	79·5053	80·5258	81·5461	82·5663	83·5863	84·6062
·7000	79·8650	80·9081	81·9510	82·9936	84·0359	85·0779	86·1197	87·1612	88·2025
·8000	82·9965	85·0658	86·1346	87·2030	88·2709	89·3383	90·4054	91·4720	92·5382
·9000	89·9561	91·0615	92·1662	93·2702	94·3735	95·4761	96·5782	97·6796	98·7803
0·9500	95·0815	96·2167	97·3510	98·4844	99·6169	100·749	101·879	103·010	104·139
·9750	99·6784	100·839	101·999	103·158	104·316	105·473	106·629	107·783	108·937
·9900	105·202	106·393	107·582	108·771	109·958	111·144	112·329	113·512	114·695
·9950	109·074	110·286	111·495	112·704	113·911	115·117	116·321	117·524	118·726
·9990	117·346	118·599	119·850	121·100	122·348	123·594	124·839	126·082	127·324
·9995	120·673	121·942	123·209	124·475	125·739	127·001	128·261	129·520	130·778
·9999	127·990	129·294	130·595	131·895	133·193	134·489	135·783	137·075	138·365

The table gives the values of χ^2 for which $P(\chi^2|\nu) = 2^{-\frac{1}{2}\nu}\{\Gamma(\frac{1}{2}\nu)\}^{-1}\int_0^{\chi^2} x^{\frac{1}{2}\nu-1}e^{-\frac{1}{2}x}dx.$

Table 3 (continued)

P \ ν	83	84	85	86	87	88	89	90	91
0·0001	43·3763	44·0903	44·8060	45·5234	46·2424	46·9629	47·6851	48·4087	49·1339
·0005	47·0209	47·7672	48·5151	49·2644	50·0151	50·7673	51·5209	52·2758	53·0321
·0010	48·7958	49·5573	50·3203	51·0846	51·8503	52·6173	53·3856	54·1552	54·9261
·0050	53·5669	54·3677	55·1696	55·9727	56·7769	57·5823	58·3888	59·1963	60·0049
·0100	55·9931	56·8130	57·6339	58·4559	59·2790	60·1030	60·9281	61·7541	62·5811
·0250	59·6918	60·5398	61·3888	62·2386	63·0894	63·9409	64·7934	65·6466	66·5007
·0500	63·0039	63·8763	64·7494	65·6233	66·4979	67·3732	68·2493	69·1260	70·0035
0·1000	66·9756	67·8761	68·7772	69·6788	70·5810	71·4838	72·3872	73·2911	74·1955
·2000	72·0083	72·9429	73·8779	74·8132	75·7490	76·6851	77·6216	78·5584	79·4956
·3000	75·7915	76·7507	77·7102	78·6699	79·6299	80·5901	81·5505	82·5111	83·4719
·4000	79·1281	80·1084	81·0888	82·0693	83·0500	84·0307	85·0116	85·9925	86·9736
·5000	82·3343	83·3343	84·3343	85·3343	86·3342	87·3342	88·3342	89·3342	90·3342
·6000	85·6260	86·6457	87·6653	88·6847	89·7041	90·7233	91·7424	92·7614	93·7803
·7000	89·2435	90·2842	91·3247	92·3650	93·4050	94·4448	95·4844	96·5238	97·5629
·8000	93·6040	94·6693	95·7343	96·7990	97·8632	98·9271	99·9906	101·054	102·117
·9000	99·8805	100·980	102·079	103·177	104·275	105·372	106·469	107·565	108·661
0·9500	105·267	106·395	107·522	108·648	109·773	110·898	112·022	113·145	114·268
·9750	110·090	111·242	112·393	113·544	114·693	115·841	116·989	118·136	119·282
·9900	115·876	117·057	118·236	119·414	120·591	121·767	122·942	124·116	125·289
·9950	119·927	121·126	122·325	123·522	124·718	125·913	127·106	128·299	129·491
·9990	128·565	129·804	131·041	132·277	133·512	134·745	135·978	137·208	138·438
·9995	132·033	133·288	134·540	135·792	137·041	138·290	139·537	140·782	142·027
·9999	139·654	140·941	142·226	143·509	144·791	146·071	147·350	148·627	149·903

P \ ν	92	93	94	95	96	97	98	99	100
0·0001	49·8606	50·5887	51·3182	52·0492	52·7816	53·5153	54·2504	54·9869	55·7246
·0005	53·7896	54·5485	55·3087	56·0702	56·8329	57·5968	58·3619	59·1282	59·8957
·0010	55·6983	56·4716	57·2462	58·0219	58·7989	59·5770	60·3562	61·1365	61·9179
·0050	60·8146	61·6253	62·4370	63·2496	64·0633	64·8780	65·6936	66·5101	67·3276
·0100	63·4090	64·2379	65·0677	65·8984	66·7299	67·5624	68·3957	69·2299	70·0649
·0250	67·3556	68·2113	69·0677	69·9249	70·7828	71·6415	72·5009	73·3611	74·2219
·0500	70·8816	71·7603	72·6398	73·5198	74·4005	75·2819	76·1638	77·0463	77·9295
0·1000	75·1005	76·0060	76·9120	77·8184	78·7254	79·6329	80·5408	81·4492	82·3581
·2000	80·4332	81·3711	82·3093	83·2478	84·1867	85·1259	86·0654	87·0052	87·9453
·3000	84·4330	85·3943	86·3558	87·3175	88·2794	89·2415	90·2038	91·1663	92·1289
·4000	87·9548	88·9361	89·9175	90·8990	91·8806	92·8622	93·8440	94·8259	95·8078
·5000	91·3342	92·3342	93·3342	94·3342	95·3342	96·3341	97·3341	98·3341	99·3341
·6000	94·7991	95·8178	96·8364	97·8549	98·8733	99·8916	100·910	101·928	102·946
·7000	98·6018	99·6405	100·679	101·717	102·755	103·793	104·831	105·868	106·906
·8000	103·179	104·241	105·303	106·364	107·425	108·486	109·547	110·607	111·667
·9000	109·756	110·850	111·944	113·038	114·131	115·223	116·315	117·407	118·498
0·9500	115·390	116·511	117·632	118·752	119·871	120·990	122·108	123·225	124·342
·9750	120·427	121·571	122·715	123·858	125·000	126·141	127·282	128·422	129·561
·9900	126·462	127·633	128·803	129·973	131·141	132·309	133·476	134·642	135·807
·9950	130·681	131·871	133·059	134·247	135·433	136·619	137·803	138·987	140·169
·9990	139·666	140·893	142·119	143·344	144·567	145·789	147·010	148·230	149·449
·9995	143·269	144·511	145·751	146·990	148·228	149·465	150·700	151·934	153·167
·9999	151·177	152·450	153·721	154·991	156·259	157·526	158·791	160·056	161·319

Table 4. *Percentage points of the F-distribution for certain fractional degrees of freedom*
Upper 5·0 per cent points

ν_2 \ ν_1	0·1	0·2	0·3	0·4	0·5	0·6	0·7	0·8	0·9	1·0
0·5	659·39	3039·8	6388·2	10009	13539	16825	19814	22505	24918	27079
0·6	210·51	727·97	1343·8	1957·1	2528·0	3044·2	3505·1	3914·9	4278·9	4602·9
0·7	100·28	280·15	467·29	641·65	797·86	935·75	1056·9	1163·4	1257·3	1340·4
0·8	60·190	143·15	220·30	288·29	347·25	398·24	442·42	480·89	514·55	544·19
0·9	41·655	87·590	126·35	158·90	186·34	209·64	229·59	246·81	261·78	274·90
1·0	31·615	60·425	82·705	100·63	115·36	127·67	138·09	147·01	154·72	161·45
1·2	21·565	36·018	45·582	52·702	58·291	62·822	66·579	69·748	72·458	74·802
1·4	16·781	25·670	30·769	34·293	36·938	39·019	40·708	42·112	43·298	44·316
1·6	14·070	20·261	23·360	25·339	26·752	27·826	28·677	29·371	29·950	30·440
1·8	12·352	17·032	19·080	20·276	21·078	21·661	22·107	22·461	22·750	22·991
2·0	11·176	14·921	16·352	17·102	17·564	17·877	18·102	18·272	18·406	18·513
2·2	10·326	13·448	14·486	14·961	15·216	15·366	15·460	15·522	15·564	15·592
2·4	9·6853	12·368	13·141	13·434	13·554	13·600	13·611	13·604	13·588	13·568
2·6	9·1860	11·545	12·131	12·298	12·326	12·302	12·257	12·204	12·150	12·098
2·8	8·7868	10·900	11·348	11·423	11·387	11·313	11·229	11·144	11·064	10·989
3·0	8·4607	10·382	10·724	10·732	10·647	10·537	10·425	10·318	10·219	10·128
3·5	7·8593	9·4462	9·6132	9·5114	9·3505	9·1845	9·0286	8·8867	8·7589	8·6441
4·0	7·4488	8·8231	8·8846	8·7192	8·5156	8·3186	8·1392	7·9788	7·8360	7·7086
4·5	7·1514	8·3796	8·3720	8·1662	7·9361	7·7204	7·5271	7·3558	7·2043	7·0698
5·0	6·9262	8·0486	7·9926	7·7594	7·5118	7·2840	7·0817	6·9036	6·7467	6·6079
5·5	6·7500	7·7922	7·7008	7·4481	7·1883	6·9521	6·7439	6·5614	6·4010	6·2593
6·0	6·6084	7·5880	7·4697	7·2024	6·9338	6·6917	6·4794	6·2937	6·1309	5·9874
6·5	6·4921	7·4216	7·2822	7·0038	6·7285	6·4821	6·2668	6·0789	5·9145	5·7696
7·0	6·3950	7·2835	7·1271	6·8400	6·5595	6·3099	6·0923	5·9029	5·7372	5·5914

ν_2 \ ν_1	1·2	1·4	1·6	1·8	2·0	2·5	3·0	3·5	4·0	4·5
0·5	30760	33752	36214	38267	40000	43327	45696	47463	48828	49913
0·6	5151·0	5594·0	5957·3	6259·5	6514·3	7002·9	7350·6	7609·8	7810·1	7969·2
0·7	1480·1	1592·5	1684·3	1760·6	1824·8	1947·8	2035·2	2100·4	2150·7	2190·8
0·8	593·78	633·46	665·80	692·60	715·14	758·27	788·90	811·73	829·36	843·39
0·9	296·74	314·14	328·28	339·98	349·81	368·59	381·92	391·85	399·52	405·62
1·0	172·60	181·44	188·61	194·53	199·50	208·98	215·71	220·71	224·58	227·66
1·2	78·653	81·682	84·125	86·135	87·817	91·019	93·286	94·972	96·274	97·309
1·4	45·971	47·261	48·295	49·142	49·849	51·190	52·136	52·839	53·381	53·812
1·6	31·228	31·835	32·317	32·710	33·036	33·651	34·083	34·403	34·649	34·845
1·8	23·370	23·656	23·880	24·061	24·209	24·486	24·678	24·820	24·928	25·014
2·0	18·674	18·790	18·877	18·945	19·000	19·098	19·164	19·211	19·247	19·274
2·2	15·627	15·644	15·652	15·655	15·655	15·650	15·643	15·636	15·629	15·623
2·4	13·523	13·479	13·438	13·400	13·367	13·298	13·246	13·205	13·172	13·145
2·6	12·001	11·916	11·842	11·779	11·724	11·613	11·531	11·468	11·418	11·377
2·8	10·856	10·744	10·649	10·567	10·497	10·358	10·256	10·177	10·115	10·065
3·0	9·9696	9·8377	9·7269	9·6328	9·5521	9·3933	9·2766	9·1875	9·1172	9·0603
3·5	8·4477	8·2867	8·1528	8·0399	7·9436	7·7549	7·6169	7·5117	7·4288	7·3618
4·0	7·4925	7·3167	7·1711	7·0486	6·9443	6·7403	6·5914	6·4778	6·3882	6·3158
4·5	6·8425	6·6583	6·5062	6·3784	6·2696	6·0571	5·9019	5·7834	5·6900	5·6144
5·0	6·3739	6·1846	6·0285	5·8976	5·7861	5·5685	5·4095	5·2880	5·1922	5·1145
5·5	6·0210	5·8286	5·6701	5·5371	5·4240	5·2031	5·0416	4·9182	4·8207	4·7417
6·0	5·7462	5·5518	5·3917	5·2575	5·1433	4·9202	4·7571	4·6323	4·5337	4·4537
6·5	5·5266	5·3308	5·1696	5·0345	4·9196	4·6951	4·5308	4·4051	4·3056	4·2249
7·0	5·3471	5·1503	4·9885	4·8528	4·7374	4·5119	4·3468	4·2204	4·1203	4·0390

Table 4 (*continued*)
Upper 2·5 per cent points

ν_1 / ν_2	0·1	0·2	0·3	0·4	0·5	0·6	0·7	0·8	0·9	1·0
0·5	10568	48648	1·0222 (5)	1·6015 (5)	2·1664 (5)	2·6920 (5)	3·1703 (5)	3·6009 (5)	3·9869 (5)	4·3327 (5)
0·6	2136·4	7345·8	13551	19731	25485	30688	35334	39463	43132	46397
0·7	739·33	2037·2	3391·3	4653·7	5785·0	6783·7	7661·4	8433·0	9113·1	9715·0
0·8	352·11	816·40	1251·1	1634·8	1967·8	2255·9	2505·6	2723·0	2913·3	3080·8
0·9	205·22	414·89	594·08	745·13	872·67	981·06	1073·9	1154·0	1223·8	1284·9
1·0	136·74	247·59	335·12	406·00	464·44	513·34	554·78	590·28	620·99	647·79
1·2	77·947	119·86	148·72	170·54	187·81	201·88	213·58	223·47	231·94	239·27
1·4	54·107	74·363	86·652	95·384	102·04	107·33	111·65	115·26	118·32	120·95
1·6	41·998	53·285	59·268	63·240	66·145	68·392	70·194	71·676	72·921	73·981
1·8	34·909	41·759	44·836	46·699	47·984	48·938	49·681	50·279	50·772	51·187
2·0	30·338	34·709	36·258	37·051	37·532	37·855	38·087	38·261	38·397	38·506
2·2	27·181	30·037	30·704	30·898	30·938	30·921	30·880	30·830	30·779	30·728
2·4	24·886	26·752	26·872	26·705	26·486	26·270	26·073	25·896	25·738	25·597
2·6	23·150	24·335	24·096	23·699	23·318	22·981	22·688	22·434	22·213	22·018
2·8	21·796	22·493	22·006	21·457	20·970	20·555	20·202	19·900	19·639	19·411
3·0	20·712	21·046	20·385	19·730	19·172	18·705	18·312	17·979	17·692	17·443
3·5	18·766	18·517	17·592	16·786	16·130	15·594	15·149	14·776	14·457	14·182
4·0	17·479	16·894	15·831	14·952	14·251	13·686	13·221	12·832	12·502	12·218
4·5	16·567	15·770	14·627	13·710	12·988	12·409	11·936	11·542	11·208	10·921
5·0	15·888	14·947	13·756	12·817	12·084	11·500	11·024	10·629	10·294	10·007
5·5	15·364	14·320	13·097	12·145	11·408	10·822	10·346	9·9510	9·6173	9·3314
6·0	14·948	13·828	12·583	11·624	10·884	10·298	9·8233	9·4296	9·0974	8·8131
6·5	14·609	13·431	12·170	11·207	10·467	9·8821	9·4087	9·0167	8·6864	8·4037
7·0	14·328	13·104	11·832	10·866	10·127	9·5438	9·0722	8·6821	8·3536	8·0727

ν_1 / ν_2	1·2	1·4	1·6	1·8	2·0	2·5	3·0	3·5	4·0	4·5
0·5	4·9217 (5)	5·4004 (5)	5·7943 (5)	6·1228 (5)	6·4000 (5)	6·9324 (5)	7·3115 (5)	7·5941 (5)	7·8125 (5)	7·9861 (5)
0·6	51927	56387	60048	63095	65663	70588	74092	76705	78723	80327
0·7	10727	11541	12207	12759	13224	14115	14749	15221	15586	15876
0·8	3361·2	3585·5	3768·3	3919·9	4047·3	4291·2	4464·4	4593·5	4693·2	4772·5
0·9	1386·6	1467·7	1533·6	1588·1	1633·9	1721·4	1783·6	1829·9	1865·6	1894·1
1·0	692·22	727·48	756·07	779·69	799·50	837·33	864·16	884·15	899·58	911·86
1·2	251·34	260·84	268·51	274·82	280·11	290·18	297·31	302·61	306·71	309·97
1·4	125·25	128·61	131·31	133·52	135·37	138·88	141·36	143·21	144·63	145·77
1·6	75·697	77·026	78·087	78·954	79·676	81·042	82·005	82·719	83·270	83·708
1·8	51·848	52·352	52·750	53·072	53·339	53·840	54·190	54·449	54·648	54·806
2·0	38·670	38·788	38·876	38·945	39·000	39·099	39·165	39·213	39·248	39·276
2·2	30·633	30·551	30·479	30·417	30·364	30·257	30·177	30·116	30·068	30·029
2·4	25·358	25·164	25·004	24·869	24·756	24·535	24·375	24·254	24·159	24·083
2·6	21·694	21·434	21·222	21·046	20·897	20·610	20·403	20·247	20·126	20·028
2·8	19·034	18·734	18·491	18·289	18·119	17·792	17·557	17·380	17·242	17·131
3·0	17·033	16·708	16·445	16·227	16·044	15·692	15·439	15·249	15·101	14·982
3·5	13·731	13·377	13·090	12·853	12·655	12·273	12·000	11·794	11·634	11·505
4·0	11·753	11·389	11·095	10·853	10·649	10·259	9·9792	9·7688	9·6045	9·4727
4·5	10·453	10·086	9·7909	9·5476	9·3434	8·9516	8·6710	8·4596	8·2944	8·1618
5·0	9·5394	9·1739	8·8796	8·6371	8·4336	8·0434	7·7636	7·5527	7·3879	7·2553
5·5	8·8661	8·5027	8·2102	7·9693	7·7672	7·3795	7·1014	6·8916	6·7275	6·5955
6·0	8·3507	7·9898	7·6995	7·4604	7·2599	6·8750	6·5988	6·3904	6·2272	6·0957
6·5	7·9445	7·5861	7·2980	7·0608	6·8617	6·4797	6·2054	5·9983	5·8361	5·7053
7·0	7·6164	7·2606	6·9746	6·7391	6·5415	6·1622	5·8898	5·6840	5·5226	5·3925

The number in brackets indicates the power of ten by which the number preceding is to be multiplied.

Upper 1·0 per cent points

ν_2 \ ν_1	0·1	0·2	0·3	0·4	0·5	0·6	0·7	0·8	0·9	1·0
0·5	4·1287 (5)	1·9003 (6)	3·9930 (6)	6·2557 (6)	8·4624 (6)	1·0516 (7)	1·2384 (7)	1·4066 (7)	1·5574 (7)	1·6925 (7)
0·6	45337	1·5580 (5)	2·8737 (5)	4·1844 (5)	5·4045 (5)	6·5079 (5)	7·4931 (5)	8·3688 (5)	9·1468 (5)	9·8393 (5)
0·7	10161	27940	46498	63802	79308	92998	1·0503 (5)	1·1560 (5)	1·2493 (5)	1·3318 (5)
0·8	3502·3	8080·5	12373	16163	19453	22299	24766	26914	28794	30450
0·9	1592·8	3190·0	4559·8	5715·5	6691·7	7521·5	8232·3	8846·1	9380·0	9847·9
1·0	873·59	1557·9	2102·0	2543·6	2908·0	3213·1	3471·6	3693·2	3884·9	4052·2
1·2	375·96	561·32	691·57	790·75	869·48	933·72	987·21	1032·5	1071·2	1104·8
1·4	216·16	284·06	327·06	358·12	382·00	401·07	416·71	429·80	440·92	450·49
1·6	147·05	175·83	192·24	203·51	211·90	218·47	223·77	228·17	231·87	235·04
1·8	111·07	123·62	129·82	133·78	136·62	138·77	140·48	141·87	143·03	144·02
2·0	89·834	94·583	96·203	97·020	97·513	97·842	98·077	98·254	98·392	98·503
2·2	76·151	76·731	76·061	75·363	74·756	74·244	73·810	73·439	73·119	72·841
2·4	66·739	64·912	63·004	61·519	60·358	59·428	58·667	58·033	57·494	57·032
2·6	59·935	56·633	54·018	52·103	50·648	49·503	48·576	47·809	47·163	46·610
2·8	54·821	50·573	47·537	45·380	43·766	42·508	41·496	40·663	39·964	39·367
3·0	50·856	45·978	42·686	40·390	38·690	37·374	36·321	35·456	34·732	34·116
3·5	44·035	38·308	34·724	32·295	30·526	29·171	28·095	27·217	26·485	25·864
4·0	39·734	33·641	29·977	27·536	25·775	24·436	23·378	22·518	21·803	21·198
4·5	36·795	30·532	26·863	24·446	22·715	21·405	20·373	19·537	18·843	18·257
5·0	34·666	28·326	24·678	22·296	20·599	19·319	18·314	17·500	16·827	16·258
5·5	33·057	26·685	23·068	20·721	19·056	17·804	16·823	16·030	15·375	14·822
6·0	31·799	25·419	21·836	19·522	17·887	16·659	15·699	14·924	14·284	13·745
6·5	30·791	24·414	20·864	18·581	16·971	15·766	14·824	14·065	13·438	12·911
7·0	29·964	23·598	20·078	17·823	16·237	15·051	14·125	13·379	12·764	12·246

ν_2 \ ν_1	1·2	1·4	1·6	1·8	2·0	2·5	3·0	3·5	4·0	4·5
0·5	1·9225 (7)	2·1095 (7)	2·2634 (7)	2·3917 (7)	2·5000 (7)	2·7080 (7)	2·8560 (7)	2·9665 (7)	3·0518 (7)	3·1196 (7)
0·6	1·1011 (6)	1·1958 (6)	1·2734 (6)	1·3380 (6)	1·3925 (6)	1·4969 (6)	1·5712 (6)	1·6266 (6)	1·6694 (6)	1·7035 (6)
0·7	1·4705 (5)	1·5821 (5)	1·6733 (5)	1·7491 (5)	1·8128 (5)	1·9350 (5)	2·0218 (5)	2·0865 (5)	2·1365 (5)	2·1763 (5)
0·8	33220	35436	37243	38740	40000	42409	44121	45396	46382	47165
0·9	10627	11248	11753	12170	12521	13191	13667	14022	14296	14514
1·0	4329·6	4549·7	4728·3	4875·8	4999·5	5235·8	5403·4	5528·2	5624·6	5701·3
1·2	1160·1	1203·7	1238·8	1267·8	1292·1	1338·3	1371·0	1395·4	1414·2	1429·1
1·4	466·14	478·39	488·24	496·32	503·08	515·93	525·02	531·78	537·00	541·15
1·6	240·18	244·18	247·38	250·00	252·18	256·33	259·25	261·42	263·10	264·44
1·8	145·60	146·82	147·79	148·57	149·23	150·47	151·34	151·98	152·48	152·87
2·0	98·668	98·787	98·875	98·945	99·000	99·100	99·166	99·214	99·249	99·277
2·2	72·382	72·018	71·722	71·478	71·273	70·879	70·597	70·386	70·222	70·091
2·4	56·278	55·688	55·214	54·825	54·499	53·878	53·436	53·106	52·850	52·646
2·6	45·714	45·016	44·457	43·999	43·616	42·888	42·371	41·986	41·687	41·448
2·8	38·403	37·654	37·056	36·566	36·158	35·381	34·830	34·419	34·101	33·847
3·0	33·122	32·352	31·738	31·235	30·817	30·021	29·457	29·036	28·710	28·450
3·5	24·866	24·096	23·484	22·983	22·566	21·775	21·215	20·797	20·473	20·214
4·0	20·227	19·481	18·887	18·403	18·000	17·236	16·694	16·290	15·977	15·727
4·5	17·319	16·598	16·026	15·559	15·171	14·435	13·914	13·524	13·222	12·981
5·0	15·349	14·652	14·099	13·649	13·274	12·563	12·060	11·684	11·392	11·158
5·5	13·939	13·263	12·726	12·289	11·926	11·237	10·749	10·384	10·101	9·8741
6·0	12·884	12·226	11·703	11·278	10·925	10·254	9·7795	9·4244	9·1483	8·9272
6·5	12·069	11·425	10·915	10·500	10·155	9·5005	9·0367	8·6897	8·4198	8·2035
7·0	11·422	10·791	10·291	9·8846	9·5466	8·9056	8·4513	8·1113	7·8466	7·6345

The number in brackets indicates the power of ten by which the number preceding is to be multiplied.

Table 4 (*continued*)

Upper 0·5 per cent points

ν_2 \ ν_1	0·1	0·2	0·3	0·4	0·5	0·6	0·7	0·8	0·9	1·0
0·5	6·6059 (6)	3·0405 (7)	6·3888 (7)	1·0009 (8)	1·3540 (8)	1·6825 (8)	1·9814 (8)	2·2505 (8)	2·4918 (8)	2·7080 (8)
0·6	4·5698 (5)	1·5703 (6)	2·8966 (6)	4·2176 (6)	5·4474 (6)	6·5595 (6)	7·5525 (6)	8·4352 (6)	9·2194 (6)	9·9174 (6)
0·7	73637	2·0246 (5)	3·3692 (5)	4·6230 (5)	5·7466 (5)	6·7385 (5)	7·6102 (5)	8·3765 (5)	9·0520 (5)	9·6498 (5)
0·8	19824	45717	69995	91435	1·1005 (5)	1·2614 (5)	1·4010 (5)	1·5225 (5)	1·6289 (5)	1·7225 (5)
0·9	7443·4	14891	21281	26673	31227	35099	38416	41279	43770	45954
1·0	3505·3	6237·7	8412·5	10178	11635	12855	13889	14775	15542	16211
1·2	1204·1	1787·8	2199·7	2513·7	2763·2	2966·8	3136·4	3279·9	3402·9	3509·4
1·4	592·15	770·17	884·32	967·13	1030·9	1081·9	1123·8	1158·8	1188·6	1214·3
1·6	359·91	423·65	461·09	487·08	506·55	521·85	534·24	544·51	553·18	560·61
1·8	249·98	272·43	284·23	291·99	297·63	301·96	305·41	308·25	310·62	312·63
2·0	189·67	194·54	196·18	197·01	197·51	197·84	198·07	198·25	198·39	198·50
2·2	152·95	149·44	146·59	144·47	142·84	141·55	140·50	139·62	138·88	138·25
2·4	128·81	121·00	116·00	112·55	109·98	108·00	106·41	105·10	104·00	103·06
2·6	112·01	101·85	95·797	91·720	88·747	86·464	84·647	83·160	81·919	80·865
2·8	99·769	88·285	81·715	77·362	74·219	71·823	69·924	68·377	67·089	65·998
3·0	90·523	78·289	71·474	67·016	63·822	61·399	59·487	57·934	56·643	55·552
3·5	75·160	62·207	55·299	50·875	47·750	45·401	43·561	42·073	40·843	39·806
4·0	65·861	52·839	46·081	41·814	38·827	36·597	34·858	33·458	32·304	31·333
4·5	59·691	46·797	40·232	36·129	33·276	31·157	29·510	28·188	27·099	26·186
5·0	55·324	42·613	36·232	32·276	29·538	27·512	25·942	24·685	23·651	22·785
5·5	52·081	39·559	33·342	29·511	26·871	24·923	23·416	22·211	21·223	20·395
6·0	49·584	37·240	31·166	27·441	24·882	22·998	21·544	20·383	19·431	18·635
6·5	47·604	35·424	29·472	25·837	23·348	21·518	20·108	18·983	18·062	17·292
7·0	45·999	33·964	28·120	24·562	22·131	20·347	18·974	17·879	16·984	16·236

ν_2 \ ν_1	1·2	1·4	1·6	1·8	2·0	2·5	3·0	3·5	4·0	4·5
0·5	3·0761 (8)	3·3752 (8)	3·6214 (8)	3·8267 (8)	4·0000 (8)	4·3327 (8)	4·5697 (8)	4·7463 (8)	4·8828 (8)	4·9913 (8)
0·6	1·1098 (7)	1·2053 (7)	1·2835 (7)	1·3486 (7)	1·4035 (7)	1·5088 (7)	1·5837 (7)	1·6395 (7)	1·6827 (7)	1·7170 (7)
0·7	1·0655 (6)	1·1464 (6)	1·2125 (6)	1·2673 (6)	1·3135 (6)	1·4020 (6)	1·4649 (6)	1·5118 (6)	1·5481 (6)	1·5769 (6)
0·8	1·8792 (5)	2·0046 (5)	2·1068 (5)	2·1915 (5)	2·2627 (5)	2·3990 (5)	2·4959 (5)	2·5680 (5)	2·6238 (5)	2·6681 (5)
0·9	49589	52486	54841	56790	58426	61555	63775	65430	66708	67724
1·0	17320	18201	18915	19505	20000	20944	21615	22114	22500	22806
1·2	3684·8	3823·0	3934·5	4026·4	4103·3	4249·9	4353·8	4431·1	4490·8	4538·3
1·4	1256·3	1289·1	1315·5	1337·2	1355·4	1389·9	1414·3	1432·4	1446·4	1457·6
1·6	572·67	582·07	589·59	595·76	600·90	610·66	617·55	622·67	626·62	629·77
1·8	315·88	318·40	320·40	322·04	323·40	325·97	327·78	329·13	330·17	330·99
2·0	198·67	198·79	198·88	198·94	199·00	199·10	199·17	199·21	199·25	199·28
2·2	137·22	136·42	135·78	135·25	134·81	133·97	133·37	132·93	132·58	132·31
2·4	101·55	100·38	99·446	98·681	98·044	96·836	95·981	95·345	94·852	94·460
2·6	79·168	77·858	76·814	75·963	75·254	73·910	72·961	72·255	71·708	71·273
2·8	64·245	62·896	61·822	60·948	60·220	58·842	57·870	57·146	56·586	56·141
3·0	53·803	52·459	51·391	50·522	49·799	48·432	47·467	46·750	46·195	45·752
3·5	38·150	36·882	35·878	35·062	34·384	33·102	32·199	31·528	31·008	30·594
4·0	29·786	28·606	27·672	26·913	26·284	25·096	24·259	23·636	23·155	22·770
4·5	24·734	23·627	22·753	22·044	21·456	20·346	19·565	18·983	18·533	18·173
5·0	21·410	20·364	19·538	18·869	18·314	17·267	16·530	15·981	15·556	15·217
5·5	19·082	18·085	17·298	16·661	16·133	15·137	14·435	13·913	13·508	13·185
6·0	17·374	16·416	15·662	15·050	14·544	13·589	12·917	12·416	12·028	11·717
6·5	16·073	15·148	14·420	13·830	13·342	12·421	11·772	11·289	10·914	10·615
7·0	15·052	14·155	13·449	12·877	12·404	11·511	10·882	10·414	10·050	9·7599

The number in brackets indicates the power of ten by which the number preceeding is to be multiplied.

ν_2 \ ν_1	0·1	0·2	0·3	0·4	0·5	0·6	0·7	0·8	0·9	1·0
0·5	4·1287(9)	1·9003(10)	3·9930(10)	6·2557(10)	8·4624(10)	1·0516(11)	1·2384(11)	1·4066(11)	1·5574(11)	1·6925(11)
0·6	9·7679(7)	3·3566(8)	6·1913(8)	9·0150(8)	1·1644(9)	1·4021(9)	1·6143(9)	1·8030(9)	1·97·6(9)	2·1198(9)
0·7	7·3142(6)	2·0109(7)	3·3465(7)	4·5918(7)	5·7078(7)	6·6930(7)	7·5588(7)	8·3200(7)	8·9909(7)	9·5846(7)
0·8	1·1083(6)	2·5557(6)	3·9129(6)	5·1114(6)	6·1518(6)	7·0517(6)	7·8318(6)	8·5110(6)	9·1057(6)	9·6291(6)
0·9	2·6620(5)	5·3241(5)	7·6082(5)	9·5356(5)	1·1164(6)	1·2548(6)	1·3734(6)	1·4757(6)	1·5648(6)	1·6428(6)
1·0	87721	1·5599(5)	2·1035(5)	2·5448(5)	2·9090(5)	3·2139(5)	3·4724(5)	3·6939(5)	3·8856(5)	4·0528(5)
1·2	17671	26173	32185	36771	40416	43391	45868	47965	49762	51319
1·4	5956·6	7705·1	8834·2	9655·2	10288	10795	11211	11559	11856	12111
1·6	2739·5	3193·3	3465·7	3656·1	3799·5	3912·3	4003·8	4079·8	4144·0	4199·0
1·8	1538·9	1652·3	1715·9	1758·8	1790·4	1814·8	1834·5	1850·7	1864·3	1875·8
2·0	989·53	994·51	996·17	997·00	997·50	997·83	998·07	998·25	998·39	998·50
2·2	699·62	666·12	647·56	635·25	626·33	619·49	614·05	609·60	605·88	602·73
2·4	529·81	482·33	457·26	441·02	429·41	420·60	413·65	407·99	403·28	399·29
2·6	422·23	370·21	343·57	326·60	314·58	305·53	298·42	292·66	287·89	283·86
2·8	349·79	297·10	270·74	254·16	242·52	233·81	226·99	221·49	216·94	213·11
3·0	298·61	246·83	221·42	205·61	194·59	186·39	179·99	174·84	170·60	167·03
3·5	220·74	173·06	150·50	136·76	127·31	120·34	114·95	110·64	107·10	104·14
4·0	178·26	134·54	114·38	102·28	94·046	88·017	83·379	79·684	76·662	74·137
4·5	152·15	111·62	93·284	82·396	75·046	69·693	65·593	62·338	59·681	57·468
5·0	134·72	96·689	79·739	69·760	63·062	58·205	54·497	51·561	49·170	47·181
5·5	122·35	86·310	70·430	61·144	54·941	50·458	47·045	44·347	42·155	40·333
6·0	113·18	78·730	63·696	54·953	49·134	44·941	41·755	39·241	37·201	35·507
6·5	106·12	72·981	58·627	50·317	44·805	40·841	37·835	35·467	33·546	31·954
7·0	100·55	68·485	54·689	46·733	41·469	37·691	34·830	32·579	30·756	29·245

ν_2 \ ν_1	1·2	1·4	1·6	1·8	2·0	2·5	3·0	3·5	4·0	4·5
0·5	1·9225(11)	2·1095(11)	2·2634(11)	2·3917(11)	2·5000(11)	2·7080(11)	2·8560(11)	2·9665(11)	3·0518(11)	3·1196(11)
0·6	2·3722(9)	2·5762(9)	2·7435(9)	2·8827(9)	3·0000(9)	3·2250(9)	3·3851(9)	3·5045(9)	3·5967(9)	3·6700(9)
0·7	1·0583(8)	1·1386(8)	1·2043(8)	1·2588(8)	1·3047(8)	1·3926(8)	1·4551(8)	1·5016(8)	1·5376(8)	1·5662(8)
0·8	1·0505(7)	1·1206(7)	1·1777(7)	1·2251(7)	1·2649(7)	1·3411(7)	1·3952(7)	1·4356(7)	1·4667(7)	1·4915(7)
0·9	1·7728(6)	1·8764(6)	1·9605(6)	2·0302(6)	2·0887(6)	2·2005(6)	2·2799(6)	2·3391(6)	2·3848(6)	2·4211(6)
1·0	4·3302(5)	4·5503(5)	4·7288(5)	4·8763(5)	5·0000(5)	5·2362(5)	5·4038(5)	5·5286(5)	5·6250(5)	5·7017(5)
1·2	53882	55901	57532	58875	59999	62142	63660	64790	65663	66357
1·4	12528	12855	13118	13334	13514	13857	14100	14281	14420	14531
1·6	4288·5	4358·1	4414·0	4459·7	4497·9	4570·4	4621·7	4659·7	4689·1	4712·5
1·8	1894·6	1909·1	1920·7	1930·2	1938·1	1953·1	1963·6	1971·5	1977·5	1982·3
2·0	998·67	998·79	998·88	998·94	999·00	999·10	999·17	999·21	999·25	999·28
2·2	597·65	593·72	590·60	588·06	585·94	581·93	579·10	577·00	575·37	574·08
2·4	392·90	387·99	384·09	380·91	378·27	373·28	369·77	367·16	365·15	363·54
2·6	277·41	272·47	268·55	265·36	262·72	257·73	254·21	251·61	249·60	248·00
2·8	207·00	202·32	198·63	195·62	193·13	188·43	185·13	182·67	180·78	179·28
3·0	161·35	157·01	153·58	150·80	148·50	144·16	141·11	138·85	137·10	135·71
3·5	99·438	95·866	93·053	90·775	88·891	85·345	82·858	81·015	79·592	78·460
4·0	70·147	67·126	64·751	62·831	61·246	58·265	56·177	54·630	53·436	52·486
4·5	53·978	51·341	49·273	47·603	46·225	43·637	41·826	40·484	39·449	38·625
5·0	44·051	41·691	39·842	38·352	37·122	34·816	33·202	32·007	31·085	30·351
5·5	37·471	35·317	33·631	32·273	31·153	29·055	27·587	26·500	25·661	24·994
6·0	32·851	30·854	29·293	28·036	27·000	25·060	23·703	22·699	21·924	21·306
6·5	29·459	27·585	26·122	24·944	23·975	22·158	20·889	19·949	19·223	18·645
7·0	26·880	25·105	23·720	22·606	21·689	19·972	18·772	17·884	17·198	16·652

The number in brackets indicates the power of ten by which the number preceding is to be multiplied.

Table 5. *Percentage points of the F-distribution (variance ratio). Integral degrees of freedom only*
50 per cent points

ν_2 \ ν_1	1	2	3	4	5	6	7	8	9
1	1·0000	1·5000	1·7092	1·8227	1·8937	1·9422	1·9774	2·0041	2·0250
2	0·66667	1·0000	1·1349	1·2071	1·2519	1·2824	1·3046	1·3213	1·3344
3	·58506	0·88110	1·0000	1·0632	1·1024	1·1289	1·1482	1·1627	1·1741
4	·54863	·82843	0·94053	1·0000	1·0367	1·0617	1·0797	1·0933	1·1040
5	0·52807	0·79877	0·90715	0·96456	1·0000	1·0240	1·0414	1·0545	1·0648
6	·51489	·77976	·88578	·94191	0·97654	1·0000	1·0169	1·0298	1·0398
7	·50572	·76655	·87094	·92619	·96026	0·98334	1·0000	1·0126	1·0224
8	·49898	·75683	·86004	·91465	·94831	·97111	0·98757	1·0000	1·0097
9	·49382	·74938	·85168	·90580	·93916	·96175	·97805	0·99037	1·0000
10	0·48974	0·74349	0·84508	0·89882	0·93193	0·95436	0·97054	0·98276	0·99232
11	·48643	·73872	·83973	·89316	·92608	·94837	·96445	·97660	·98610
12	·48370	·73477	·83531	·88848	·92124	·94342	·95943	·97152	·98097
13	·48140	·73145	·83159	·88455	·91718	·93927	·95520	·96724	·97665
14	·47944	·72863	·82842	·88119	·91371	·93572	·95160	·96360	·97298
15	0·47775	0·72619	0·82568	0·87830	0·91072	0·93267	0·94850	0·96046	0·96981
16	·47628	·72406	·82330	·87579	·90812	·93001	·94580	·95772	·96705
17	·47499	·72219	·82121	·87357	·90583	·92767	·94342	·95532	·96462
18	·47384	·72054	·81935	·87161	·90381	·92560	·94132	·95319	·96247
19	·47282	·71906	·81770	·86986	·90200	·92375	·93944	·95129	·96056
20	0·47191	0·71773	0·81621	0·86829	0·90038	0·92209	0·93776	0·94959	0·95884
21	·47108	·71654	·81487	·86688	·89891	·92060	·93624	·94805	·95728
22	·47033	·71545	·81365	·86559	·89758	·91924	·93486	·94665	·95588
23	·46964	·71446	·81255	·86442	·89637	·91800	·93360	·94538	·95459
24	·46902	·71356	·81153	·86335	·89526	·91687	·93245	·94422	·95342
25	0·46844	0·71273	0·81060	0·86236	0·89425	0·91583	0·93140	0·94315	0·95234
26	·46791	·71196	·80974	·86145	·89331	·91487	·93042	·94217	·95135
27	·46743	·71125	·80895	·86061	·89244	·91398	·92952	·94126	·95043
28	·46697	·71059	·80821	·85984	·89164	·91316	·92869	·94041	·94958
29	·46655	·70998	·80753	·85911	·89089	·91240	·92791	·93963	·94879
30	0·46616	0·70941	0·80689	0·85844	0·89019	0·91169	0·92719	0·93890	0·94805
40	·46332	·70530	·80228	·85357	·88516	·90654	·92197	·93361	·94272
60	·46050	·70122	·79770	·84873	·88017	·90144	·91679	·92837	·93743
120	·45771	·69717	·79316	·84393	·87521	·89638	·91165	·92318	·93219
∞	·45494	·69315	·78866	·83917	·87029	·89135	·90654	·91802	·92698

ν_2 \ ν_1	10	12	15	20	24	30	40	60	120	∞
1	2·0419	2·0674	2·0931	2·1191	2·1321	2·1452	2·1584	2·1716	2·1848	2·1981
2	1·3450	1·3610	1·3771	1·3933	1·4014	1·4096	1·4178	1·4261	1·4344	1·4427
3	1·1833	1·1972	1·2111	1·2252	1·2322	1·2393	1·2465	1·2536	1·2608	1·2680
4	1·1126	1·1255	1·1386	1·1517	1·1583	1·1649	1·1716	1·1782	1·1849	1·1916
5	1·0730	1·0855	1·0980	1·1106	1·1170	1·1234	1·1297	1·1361	1·1426	1·1490
6	1·0478	1·0600	1·0722	1·0845	1·0907	1·0969	1·1031	1·1093	1·1156	1·1219
7	1·0304	1·0423	1·0543	1·0664	1·0724	1·0785	1·0846	1·0908	1·0969	1·1031
8	1·0175	1·0293	1·0412	1·0531	1·0591	1·0651	1·0711	1·0772	1·0832	1·0893
9	1·0077	1·0194	1·0311	1·0429	1·0489	1·0548	1·0608	1·0667	1·0727	1·0788
10	1·0000	1·0116	1·0232	1·0349	1·0408	1·0467	1·0526	1·0585	1·0645	1·0705
11	0·99374	1·0052	1·0168	1·0284	1·0343	1·0401	1·0460	1·0519	1·0578	1·0637
12	·98856	1·0000	1·0115	1·0231	1·0289	1·0347	1·0405	1·0464	1·0523	1·0582
13	·98421	0·99560	1·0071	1·0186	1·0243	1·0301	1·0360	1·0418	1·0476	1·0535
14	·98051	·99186	1·0033	1·0147	1·0205	1·0263	1·0321	1·0379	1·0437	1·0495
15	0·97732	0·98863	1·0000	1·0114	1·0172	1·0229	1·0287	1·0345	1·0403	1·0461
16	·97454	·98582	0·99716	1·0086	1·0143	1·0200	1·0258	1·0315	1·0373	1·0431
17	·97209	·98335	·99466	1·0060	1·0117	1·0175	1·0232	1·0289	1·0347	1·0405
18	·96993	·98116	·99244	1·0038	1·0095	1·0152	1·0209	1·0267	1·0324	1·0382
19	·96800	·97920	·99047	1·0018	1·0075	1·0132	1·0189	1·0246	1·0304	1·0361
20	0·96626	0·97745	0·98870	1·0000	1·0057	1·0114	1·0171	1·0228	1·0285	1·0343
21	·96470	·97587	·98710	0·99838	1·0040	1·0097	1·0154	1·0211	1·0268	1·0326
22	·96328	·97444	·98565	·99692	1·0026	1·0082	1·0139	1·0196	1·0253	1·0311
23	·96199	·97313	·98433	·99558	1·0012	1·0069	1·0126	1·0183	1·0240	1·0297
24	·96081	·97194	·98312	·99436	1·0000	1·0057	1·0113	1·0170	1·0227	1·0284
25	0·95972	0·97084	0·98201	0·99324	0·99887	1·0045	1·0102	1·0159	1·0215	1·0273
26	·95872	·96983	·98099	·99220	·99783	1·0035	1·0091	1·0148	1·0205	1·0262
27	·95780	·96889	·98004	·99125	·99687	1·0025	1·0082	1·0138	1·0195	1·0252
28	·95694	·96802	·97917	·99036	·99598	1·0016	1·0073	1·0129	1·0186	1·0243
29	·95614	·96722	·97835	·98954	·99515	1·0008	1·0064	1·0121	1·0177	1·0234
30	0·95540	0·96647	0·97759	0·98877	0·99438	1·0000	1·0056	1·0113	1·0170	1·0226
40	·95003	·96104	·97211	·98323	·98880	0·99440	1·0000	1·0056	1·0112	1·0169
60	·94471	·95566	·96667	·97773	·98328	·98884	0·99441	1·0000	1·0056	1·0112
120	·93942	·95032	·96128	·97228	·97780	·98333	·98888	0·99443	1·0000	1·0056
∞	·93418	·94503	·95592	·96687	·97236	·97787	·98338	·98891	0·99445	1·0000

$F = \dfrac{s_1^2}{s_2^2} = \dfrac{S_1}{\nu_1} \Big/ \dfrac{S_2}{\nu_2}$, where $s_1^2 = S_1/\nu_1$ and $s_2^2 = S_2/\nu_2$ are independent mean square estimators of a common variance σ^2, based on ν_1 and ν_2 degrees of freedom, respectively.

Table 5 (continued). Percentage points of the F-distribution
Upper 25 per cent points

ν_2 \ ν_1	1	2	3	4	5	6	7	8	9
1	5·8284	7·5000	8·1999	8·5809	8·8198	8·9833	9·1021	9·1923	9·2631
2	2·5714	3·0000	3·1534	3·2321	3·2799	3·3121	3·3352	3·3526	3·3661
3	2·0239	2·2798	2·3556	2·3901	2·4095	2·4218	2·4302	2·4364	2·4410
4	1·8074	2·0000	2·0467	2·0642	2·0723	2·0766	2·0790	2·0805	2·0814
5	1·6925	1·8528	1·8843	1·8927	1·8947	1·8945	1·8935	1·8923	1·8911
6	1·6214	1·7622	1·7844	1·7872	1·7852	1·7821	1·7789	1·7760	1·7733
7	1·5732	1·7010	1·7169	1·7157	1·7111	1·7059	1·7011	1·6969	1·6931
8	1·5384	1·6569	1·6683	1·6642	1·6575	1·6508	1·6448	1·6396	1·6350
9	1·5121	1·6236	1·6315	1·6253	1·6170	1·6091	1·6022	1·5961	1·5909
10	1·4915	1·5975	1·6028	1·5949	1·5853	1·5765	1·5688	1·5621	1·5563
11	1·4749	1·5767	1·5798	1·5704	1·5598	1·5502	1·5418	1·5346	1·5284
12	1·4613	1·5595	1·5609	1·5504	1·5389	1·5286	1·5197	1·5120	1·5054
13	1·4500	1·5452	1·5451	1·5336	1·5214	1·5105	1·5011	1·4931	1·4861
14	1·4403	1·5331	1·5317	1·5194	1·5066	1·4952	1·4854	1·4770	1·4697
15	1·4321	1·5227	1·5202	1·5071	1·4938	1·4820	1·4718	1·4631	1·4556
16	1·4249	1·5137	1·5103	1·4965	1·4827	1·4705	1·4601	1·4511	1·4433
17	1·4186	1·5057	1·5015	1·4872	1·4730	1·4605	1·4497	1·4405	1·4325
18	1·4130	1·4988	1·4938	1·4790	1·4644	1·4516	1·4406	1·4311	1·4230
19	1·4081	1·4925	1·4870	1·4717	1·4568	1·4437	1·4325	1·4228	1·4145
20	1·4037	1·4870	1·4808	1·4652	1·4500	1·4366	1·4252	1·4153	1·4069
21	1·3997	1·4820	1·4753	1·4593	1·4438	1·4302	1·4186	1·4086	1·4000
22	1·3961	1·4774	1·4703	1·4540	1·4382	1·4244	1·4126	1·4025	1·3937
23	1·3928	1·4733	1·4657	1·4491	1·4331	1·4191	1·4072	1·3969	1·3880
24	1·3898	1·4695	1·4615	1·4447	1·4285	1·4143	1·4022	1·3918	1·3828
25	1·3870	1·4661	1·4577	1·4406	1·4242	1·4099	1·3977	1·3871	1·3781
26	1·3845	1·4629	1·4542	1·4369	1·4203	1·4058	1·3935	1·3828	1·3736
27	1·3821	1·4600	1·4510	1·4334	1·4166	1·4021	1·3896	1·3788	1·3696
28	1·3800	1·4573	1·4480	1·4302	1·4133	1·3986	1·3860	1·3752	1·3658
29	1·3780	1·4547	1·4452	1·4272	1·4102	1·3953	1·3826	1·3717	1·3623
30	1·3761	1·4524	1·4426	1·4244	1·4073	1·3923	1·3795	1·3685	1·3590
40	1·3626	1·4355	1·4239	1·4045	1·3863	1·3706	1·3571	1·3455	1·3354
60	1·3493	1·4188	1·4055	1·3848	1·3657	1·3491	1·3348	1·3226	1·3119
120	1·3362	1·4024	1·3873	1·3654	1·3453	1·3278	1·3128	1·2999	1·2886
∞	1·3233	1·3863	1·3694	1·3463	1·3251	1·3068	1·2910	1·2774	1·2654

ν_2 \ ν_1	10	12	15	20	24	30	40	60	120	∞
1	9·3201	9·4064	9·4934	9·5813	9·6254	9·6698	9·7144	9·7592	9·8041	9·8492
2	3·3770	3·3934	3·4098	3·4263	3·4346	3·4428	3·4511	3·4594	3·4677	3·4761
3	2·4447	2·4500	2·4552	2·4602	2·4626	2·4650	2·4674	2·4697	2·4719	2·4742
4	2·0820	2·0826	2·0829	2·0828	2·0827	2·0825	2·0821	2·0817	2·0812	2·0806
5	1·8899	1·8877	1·8851	1·8820	1·8802	1·8784	1·8763	1·8742	1·8719	1·8694
6	1·7708	1·7668	1·7621	1·7569	1·7540	1·7509	1·7477	1·7443	1·7407	1·7368
7	1·6898	1·6843	1·6781	1·6712	1·6675	1·6635	1·6593	1·6548	1·6501	1·6452
8	1·6310	1·6244	1·6170	1·6088	1·6043	1·5996	1·5945	1·5893	1·5836	1·5777
9	1·5863	1·5788	1·5705	1·5611	1·5560	1·5506	1·5449	1·5389	1·5325	1·5257
10	1·5513	1·5430	1·5338	1·5235	1·5179	1·5119	1·5056	1·4990	1·4919	1·4843
11	1·5229	1·5140	1·5041	1·4930	1·4869	1·4805	1·4737	1·4664	1·4587	1·4504
12	1·4996	1·4902	1·4796	1·4678	1·4613	1·4544	1·4471	1·4393	1·4310	1·4221
13	1·4801	1·4701	1·4590	1·4465	1·4397	1·4324	1·4247	1·4164	1·4075	1·3980
14	1·4634	1·4530	1·4414	1·4284	1·4212	1·4136	1·4055	1·3967	1·3874	1·3772
15	1·4491	1·4383	1·4263	1·4127	1·4052	1·3973	1·3888	1·3796	1·3698	1·3591
16	1·4366	1·4255	1·4131	1·3990	1·3913	1·3830	1·3742	1·3646	1·3543	1·3432
17	1·4256	1·4142	1·4014	1·3869	1·3790	1·3704	1·3613	1·3514	1·3406	1·3290
18	1·4159	1·4042	1·3911	1·3762	1·3680	1·3592	1·3497	1·3395	1·3284	1·3162
19	1·4073	1·3953	1·3819	1·3666	1·3582	1·3492	1·3394	1·3289	1·3174	1·3048
20	1·3995	1·3873	1·3736	1·3580	1·3494	1·3401	1·3301	1·3193	1·3074	1·2943
21	1·3925	1·3801	1·3661	1·3502	1·3414	1·3319	1·3217	1·3105	1·2983	1·2848
22	1·3861	1·3735	1·3593	1·3431	1·3341	1·3245	1·3140	1·3026	1·2900	1·2761
23	1·3803	1·3675	1·3531	1·3366	1·3275	1·3176	1·3069	1·2952	1·2824	1·2681
24	1·3750	1·3621	1·3474	1·3307	1·3214	1·3113	1·3004	1·2885	1·2754	1·2607
25	1·3701	1·3570	1·3422	1·3252	1·3158	1·3056	1·2945	1·2823	1·2688	1·2538
26	1·3656	1·3524	1·3374	1·3202	1·3106	1·3002	1·2889	1·2765	1·2628	1·2474
27	1·3615	1·3481	1·3329	1·3155	1·3058	1·2953	1·2838	1·2712	1·2572	1·2414
28	1·3576	1·3441	1·3288	1·3112	1·3013	1·2906	1·2790	1·2662	1·2519	1·2358
29	1·3541	1·3404	1·3249	1·3071	1·2971	1·2863	1·2745	1·2615	1·2470	1·2306
30	1·3507	1·3369	1·3213	1·3033	1·2933	1·2823	1·2703	1·2571	1·2424	1·2256
40	1·3266	1·3119	1·2952	1·2758	1·2649	1·2529	1·2397	1·2249	1·2080	1·1883
60	1·3026	1·2870	1·2690	1·2481	1·2361	1·2229	1·2081	1·1912	1·1715	1·1474
120	1·2787	1·2621	1·2428	1·2200	1·2068	1·1921	1·1752	1·1555	1·1314	1·0987
∞	1·2549	1·2371	1·2163	1·1914	1·1767	1·1600	1·1404	1·1164	1·0838	1·0000

$F = \dfrac{s_1^2}{s_2^2} = \dfrac{S_1}{\nu_1} \Big/ \dfrac{S_2}{\nu_2}$, where $s_1^2 = S_1/\nu_1$ and $s_2^2 = S_2/\nu_2$ are independent mean square estimators of a common variance σ^2, based on ν_1 and ν_2 degrees of freedom, respectively.

Table 5 (*continued*)

Upper 10 per cent points

ν_2 \ ν_1	1	2	3	4	5	6	7	8	9
1	39·863	49·500	53·593	55·833	57·240	58·204	58·906	59·439	59·858
2	8·5263	9·0000	9·1618	9·2434	9·2926	9·3255	9·3491	9·3668	9·3805
3	5·5383	5·4624	5·3908	5·3426	5·3092	5·2847	5·2662	5·2517	5·2400
4	4·5448	4·3246	4·1909	4·1072	4·0506	4·0097	3·9790	3·9549	3·9357
5	4·0604	3·7797	3·6195	3·5202	3·4530	3·4045	3·3679	3·3393	3·3163
6	3·7759	3·4633	3·2888	3·1808	3·1075	3·0546	3·0145	2·9830	2·9577
7	3·5894	3·2574	3·0741	2·9605	2·8833	2·8274	2·7849	2·7516	2·7247
8	3·4579	3·1131	2·9238	2·8064	2·7264	2·6683	2·6241	2·5893	2·5612
9	3·3603	3·0065	2·8129	2·6927	2·6106	2·5509	2·5053	2·4694	2·4403
10	3·2850	2·9245	2·7277	2·6053	2·5216	2·4606	2·4140	2·3772	2·3473
11	3·2252	2·8595	2·6602	2·5362	2·4512	2·3891	2·3416	2·3040	2·2735
12	3·1765	2·8068	2·6055	2·4801	2·3940	2·3310	2·2828	2·2446	2·2135
13	3·1362	2·7632	2·5603	2·4337	2·3467	2·2830	2·2341	2·1953	2·1638
14	3·1022	2·7265	2·5222	2·3947	2·3069	2·2426	2·1931	2·1539	2·1220
15	3·0732	2·6952	2·4898	2·3614	2·2730	2·2081	2·1582	2·1185	2·0862
16	3·0481	2·6682	2·4618	2·3327	2·2438	2·1783	2·1280	2·0880	2·0553
17	3·0262	2·6446	2·4374	2·3077	2·2183	2·1524	2·1017	2·0613	2·0284
18	3·0070	2·6239	2·4160	2·2858	2·1958	2·1296	2·0785	2·0379	2·0047
19	2·9899	2·6056	2·3970	2·2663	2·1760	2·1094	2·0580	2·0171	1·9836
20	2·9747	2·5893	2·3801	2·2489	2·1582	2·0913	2·0397	1·9985	1·9649
21	2·9610	2·5746	2·3649	2·2333	2·1423	2·0751	2·0233	1·9819	1·9480
22	2·9486	2·5613	2·3512	2·2193	2·1279	2·0605	2·0084	1·9668	1·9327
23	2·9374	2·5493	2·3387	2·2065	2·1149	2·0472	1·9949	1·9531	1·9189
24	2·9271	2·5383	2·3274	2·1949	2·1030	2·0351	1·9826	1·9407	1·9063
25	2·9177	2·5283	2·3170	2·1842	2·0922	2·0241	1·9714	1·9292	1·8947
26	2·9091	2·5191	2·3075	2·1745	2·0822	2·0139	1·9610	1·9188	1·8841
27	2·9012	2·5106	2·2987	2·1655	2·0730	2·0045	1·9515	1·9091	1·8743
28	2·8938	2·5028	2·2906	2·1571	2·0645	1·9959	1·9427	1·9001	1·8652
29	2·8870	2·4955	2·2831	2·1494	2·0566	1·9878	1·9345	1·8918	1·8568
30	2·8807	2·4887	2·2761	2·1422	2·0492	1·9803	1·9269	1·8841	1·8490
40	2·8354	2·4404	2·2261	2·0909	1·9968	1·9269	1·8725	1·8289	1·7929
60	2·7911	2·3933	2·1774	2·0410	1·9457	1·8747	1·8194	1·7748	1·7380
120	2·7478	2·3473	2·1300	1·9923	1·8959	1·8238	1·7675	1·7220	1·6842
∞	2·7055	2·3026	2·0838	1·9449	1·8473	1·7741	1·7167	1·6702	1·6315

ν_2 \ ν_1	10	12	15	20	24	30	40	60	120	∞
1	60·195	60·705	61·220	61·740	62·002	62·265	62·529	62·794	63·061	63·328
2	9·3916	9·4081	9·4247	9·4413	9·4496	9·4579	9·4662	9·4746	9·4829	9·4912
3	5·2304	5·2156	5·2003	5·1845	5·1764	5·1681	5·1597	5·1512	5·1425	5·1337
4	3·9199	3·8955	3·8704	3·8443	3·8310	3·8174	3·8036	3·7896	3·7753	3·7607
5	3·2974	3·2682	3·2380	3·2067	3·1905	3·1741	3·1573	3·1402	3·1228	3·1050
6	2·9369	2·9047	2·8712	2·8363	2·8183	2·8000	2·7812	2·7620	2·7423	2·7222
7	2·7025	2·6681	2·6322	2·5947	2·5753	2·5555	2·5351	2·5142	2·4928	2·4708
8	2·5380	2·5020	2·4642	2·4246	2·4041	2·3830	2·3614	2·3391	2·3162	2·2926
9	2·4163	2·3789	2·3396	2·2983	2·2768	2·2547	2·2320	2·2085	2·1843	2·1592
10	2·3226	2·2841	2·2435	2·2007	2·1784	2·1554	2·1317	2·1072	2·0818	2·0554
11	2·2482	2·2087	2·1671	2·1230	2·1000	2·0762	2·0516	2·0261	1·9997	1·9721
12	2·1878	2·1474	2·1049	2·0597	2·0360	2·0115	1·9861	1·9597	1·9323	1·9036
13	2·1376	2·0966	2·0532	2·0070	1·9827	1·9576	1·9315	1·9043	1·8759	1·8462
14	2·0954	2·0537	2·0095	1·9625	1·9377	1·9119	1·8852	1·8572	1·8280	1·7973
15	2·0593	2·0171	1·9722	1·9243	1·8990	1·8728	1·8454	1·8168	1·7867	1·7551
16	2·0281	1·9854	1·9399	1·8913	1·8656	1·8388	1·8108	1·7816	1·7507	1·7182
17	2·0009	1·9577	1·9117	1·8624	1·8362	1·8090	1·7805	1·7506	1·7191	1·6856
18	1·9770	1·9333	1·8868	1·8368	1·8103	1·7827	1·7537	1·7232	1·6910	1·6567
19	1·9557	1·9117	1·8647	1·8142	1·7873	1·7592	1·7298	1·6988	1·6659	1·6308
20	1·9367	1·8924	1·8449	1·7938	1·7667	1·7382	1·7083	1·6768	1·6433	1·6074
21	1·9197	1·8750	1·8271	1·7756	1·7481	1·7193	1·6890	1·6569	1·6228	1·5862
22	1·9043	1·8593	1·8111	1·7590	1·7312	1·7021	1·6714	1·6389	1·6041	1·5668
23	1·8903	1·8450	1·7964	1·7439	1·7159	1·6864	1·6554	1·6224	1·5871	1·5490
24	1·8775	1·8319	1·7831	1·7302	1·7019	1·6721	1·6407	1·6073	1·5715	1·5327
25	1·8658	1·8200	1·7708	1·7175	1·6890	1·6589	1·6272	1·5934	1·5570	1·5176
26	1·8550	1·8090	1·7596	1·7059	1·6771	1·6468	1·6147	1·5805	1·5437	1·5036
27	1·8451	1·7989	1·7492	1·6951	1·6662	1·6356	1·6032	1·5686	1·5313	1·4906
28	1·8359	1·7895	1·7395	1·6852	1·6560	1·6252	1·5925	1·5575	1·5198	1·4784
29	1·8274	1·7808	1·7306	1·6759	1·6465	1·6155	1·5825	1·5472	1·5090	1·4670
30	1·8195	1·7727	1·7223	1·6673	1·6377	1·6065	1·5732	1·5376	1·4989	1·4564
40	1·7627	1·7146	1·6624	1·6052	1·5741	1·5411	1·5056	1·4672	1·4248	1·3769
60	1·7070	1·6574	1·6034	1·5435	1·5107	1·4755	1·4373	1·3952	1·3476	1·2915
120	1·6524	1·6012	1·5450	1·4821	1·4472	1·4094	1·3676	1·3203	1·2646	1·1926
∞	1·5987	1·5458	1·4871	1·4206	1·3832	1·3419	1·2951	1·2400	1·1686	1·0000

ν_2 \ ν_1	1	2	3	4	5	6	7	8	9
1	161·45	199·50	215·71	224·58	230·16	233·99	236·77	238·88	240·54
2	18·513	19·000	19·164	19·247	19·296	19·330	19·353	19·371	19·385
3	10·128	9·5521	9·2766	9·1172	9·0135	8·9406	8·8867	8·8452	8·8123
4	7·7086	6·9443	6·5914	6·3882	6·2561	6·1631	6·0942	6·0410	5·9988
5	6·6079	5·7861	5·4095	5·1922	5·0503	4·9503	4·8759	4·8183	4·7725
6	5·9874	5·1433	4·7571	4·5337	4·3874	4·2839	4·2067	4·1468	4·0990
7	5·5914	4·7374	4·3468	4·1203	3·9715	3·8660	3·7870	3·7257	3·6767
8	5·3177	4·4590	4·0662	3·8379	3·6875	3·5806	3·5005	3·4381	3·3881
9	5·1174	4·2565	3·8625	3·6331	3·4817	3·3738	3·2927	3·2296	3·1789
10	4·9646	4·1028	3·7083	3·4780	3·3258	3·2172	3·1355	3·0717	3·0204
11	4·8443	3·9823	3·5874	3·3567	3·2039	3·0946	3·0123	2·9480	2·8962
12	4·7472	3·8853	3·4903	3·2592	3·1059	2·9961	2·9134	2·8486	2·7964
13	4·6672	3·8056	3·4105	3·1791	3·0254	2·9153	2·8321	2·7669	2·7144
14	4·6001	3·7389	3·3439	3·1122	2·9582	2·8477	2·7642	2·6987	2·6458
15	4·5431	3·6823	3·2874	3·0556	2·9013	2·7905	2·7066	2·6408	2·5876
16	4·4940	3·6337	3·2389	3·0069	2·8524	2·7413	2·6572	2·5911	2·5377
17	4·4513	3·5915	3·1968	2·9647	2·8100	2·6987	2·6143	2·5480	2·4943
18	4·4139	3·5546	3·1599	2·9277	2·7729	2·6613	2·5767	2·5102	2·4563
19	4·3807	3·5219	3·1274	2·8951	2·7401	2·6283	2·5435	2·4768	2·4227
20	4·3512	3·4928	3·0984	2·8661	2·7109	2·5990	2·5140	2·4471	2·3928
21	4·3248	3·4668	3·0725	2·8401	2·6848	2·5727	2·4876	2·4205	2·3660
22	4·3009	3·4434	3·0491	2·8167	2·6613	2·5491	2·4638	2·3965	2·3419
23	4·2793	3·4221	3·0280	2·7955	2·6400	2·5277	2·4422	2·3748	2·3201
24	4·2597	3·4028	3·0088	2·7763	2·6207	2·5082	2·4226	2·3551	2·3002
25	4·2417	3·3852	2·9912	2·7587	2·6030	2·4904	2·4047	2·3371	2·2821
26	4·2252	3·3690	2·9752	2·7426	2·5868	2·4741	2·3883	2·3205	2·2655
27	4·2100	3·3541	2·9604	2·7278	2·5719	2·4591	2·3732	2·3053	2·2501
28	4·1960	3·3404	2·9467	2·7141	2·5581	2·4453	2·3593	2·2913	2·2360
29	4·1830	3·3277	2·9340	2·7014	2·5454	2·4324	2·3463	2·2783	2·2229
30	4·1709	3·3158	2·9223	2·6896	2·5336	2·4205	2·3343	2·2662	2·2107
40	4·0847	3·2317	2·8387	2·6060	2·4495	2·3359	2·2490	2·1802	2·1240
60	4·0012	3·1504	2·7581	2·5252	2·3683	2·2541	2·1665	2·0970	2·0401
120	3·9201	3·0718	2·6802	2·4472	2·2899	2·1750	2·0868	2·0164	1·9588
∞	3·8415	2·9957	2·6049	2·3719	2·2141	2·0986	2·0096	1·9384	1·8799

ν_2 \ ν_1	10	12	15	20	24	30	40	60	120	∞
1	241·88	243·91	245·95	248·01	249·05	250·10	251·14	252·20	253·25	254·31
2	19·396	19·413	19·429	19·446	19·454	19·462	19·471	19·479	19·487	19·496
3	8·7855	8·7446	8·7029	8·6602	8·6385	8·6166	8·5944	8·5720	8·5494	8·5264
4	5·9644	5·9117	5·8578	5·8025	5·7744	5·7459	5·7170	5·6877	5·6581	5·6281
5	4·7351	4·6777	4·6188	4·5581	4·5272	4·4957	4·4638	4·4314	4·3985	4·3650
6	4·0600	3·9999	3·9381	3·8742	3·8415	3·8082	3·7743	3·7398	3·7047	3·6689
7	3·6365	3·5747	3·5107	3·4445	3·4105	3·3758	3·3404	3·3043	3·2674	3·2298
8	3·3472	3·2839	3·2184	3·1503	3·1152	3·0794	3·0428	3·0053	2·9669	2·9276
9	3·1373	3·0729	3·0061	2·9365	2·9005	2·8637	2·8259	2·7872	2·7475	2·7067
10	2·9782	2·9130	2·8450	2·7740	2·7372	2·6996	2·6609	2·6211	2·5801	2·5379
11	2·8536	2·7876	2·7186	2·6464	2·6090	2·5705	2·5309	2·4901	2·4480	2·4045
12	2·7534	2·6866	2·6169	2·5436	2·5055	2·4663	2·4259	2·3842	2·3410	2·2962
13	2·6710	2·6037	2·5331	2·4589	2·4202	2·3803	2·3392	2·2966	2·2524	2·2064
14	2·6022	2·5342	2·4630	2·3879	2·3487	2·3082	2·2664	2·2229	2·1778	2·1307
15	2·5437	2·4753	2·4034	2·3275	2·2878	2·2468	2·2043	2·1601	2·1141	2·0658
16	2·4935	2·4247	2·3522	2·2756	2·2354	2·1938	2·1507	2·1058	2·0589	2·0096
17	2·4499	2·3807	2·3077	2·2304	2·1898	2·1477	2·1040	2·0584	2·0107	1·9604
18	2·4117	2·3421	2·2686	2·1906	2·1497	2·1071	2·0629	2·0166	1·9681	1·9168
19	2·3779	2·3080	2·2341	2·1555	2·1141	2·0712	2·0264	1·9795	1·9302	1·8780
20	2·3479	2·2776	2·2033	2·1242	2·0825	2·0391	1·9938	1·9464	1·8963	1·8432
21	2·3210	2·2504	2·1757	2·0960	2·0540	2·0102	1·9645	1·9165	1·8657	1·8117
22	2·2967	2·2258	2·1508	2·0707	2·0283	1·9842	1·9380	1·8894	1·8380	1·7831
23	2·2747	2·2036	2·1282	2·0476	2·0050	1·9605	1·9139	1·8648	1·8128	1·7570
24	2·2547	2·1834	2·1077	2·0267	1·9838	1·9390	1·8920	1·8424	1·7896	1·7330
25	2·2365	2·1649	2·0889	2·0075	1·9643	1·9192	1·8718	1·8217	1·7684	1·7110
26	2·2197	2·1479	2·0716	1·9898	1·9464	1·9010	1·8533	1·8027	1·7488	1·6906
27	2·2043	2·1323	2·0558	1·9736	1·9299	1·8842	1·8361	1·7851	1·7306	1·6717
28	2·1900	2·1179	2·0411	1·9586	1·9147	1·8687	1·8203	1·7689	1·7138	1·6541
29	2·1768	2·1045	2·0275	1·9446	1·9005	1·8543	1·8055	1·7537	1·6981	1·6376
30	2·1646	2·0921	2·0148	1·9317	1·8874	1·8409	1·7918	1·7396	1·6835	1·6223
40	2·0772	2·0035	1·9245	1·8389	1·7929	1·7444	1·6928	1·6373	1·5766	1·5089
60	1·9926	1·9174	1·8364	1·7480	1·7001	1·6491	1·5943	1·5343	1·4673	1·3893
120	1·9105	1·8337	1·7505	1·6587	1·6084	1·5543	1·4952	1·4290	1·3519	1·2539
∞	1·8307	1·7522	1·6664	1·5705	1·5173	1·4591	1·3940	1·3180	1·2214	1·0000

$F = \dfrac{s_1^2}{s_2^2} = \dfrac{S_1}{\nu_1}\Big/\dfrac{S_2}{\nu_2}$, where $s_1^2 = S_1/\nu_1$ and $s_2^2 = S_2/\nu_2$ are independent mean square estimators of a common variance σ^2, based on ν_1 and ν_2 degrees of freedom, respectively.

Table 5 (*continued*)
Upper 2·5 per cent points

ν_1 ν_2	1	2	3	4	5	6	7	8	9
1	647·79	799·50	864·16	899·58	921·85	937·11	948·22	956·66	963·28
2	38·506	39·000	39·165	39·248	39·298	39·331	39·355	39·373	39·387
3	17·443	16·044	15·439	15·101	14·885	14·735	14·624	14·540	14·473
4	12·218	10·649	9·9792	9·6045	9·3645	9·1973	9·0741	8·9796	8·9047
5	10·007	8·4336	7·7636	7·3879	7·1464	6·9777	6·8531	6·7572	6·6811
6	8·8131	7·2599	6·5988	6·2272	5·9876	5·8198	5·6955	5·5996	5·5234
7	8·0727	6·5415	5·8898	5·5226	5·2852	5·1186	4·9949	4·8993	4·8232
8	7·5709	6·0595	5·4160	5·0526	4·8173	4·6517	4·5286	4·4333	4·3572
9	7·2093	5·7147	5·0781	4·7181	4·4844	4·3197	4·1970	4·1020	4·0260
10	6·9367	5·4564	4·8256	4·4683	4·2361	4·0721	3·9498	3·8549	3·7790
11	6·7241	5·2559	4·6300	4·2751	4·0440	3·8807	3·7586	3·6638	3·5879
12	6·5538	5·0959	4·4742	4·1212	3·8911	3·7283	3·6065	3·5118	3·4358
13	6·4143	4·9653	4·3472	3·9959	3·7667	3·6043	3·4827	3·3880	3·3120
14	6·2979	4·8567	4·2417	3·8919	3·6634	3·5014	3·3799	3·2853	3·2093
15	6·1995	4·7650	4·1528	3·8043	3·5764	3·4147	3·2934	3·1987	3·1227
16	6·1151	4·6867	4·0768	3·7294	3·5021	3·3406	3·2194	3·1248	3·0488
17	6·0420	4·6189	4·0112	3·6648	3·4379	3·2767	3·1556	3·0610	2·9849
18	5·9781	4·5597	3·9539	3·6083	3·3820	3·2209	3·0999	3·0053	2·9291
19	5·9216	4·5075	3·9034	3·5587	3·3327	3·1718	3·0509	2·9563	2·8801
20	5·8715	4·4613	3·8587	3·5147	3·2891	3·1283	3·0074	2·9128	2·8365
21	5·8266	4·4199	3·8188	3·4754	3·2501	3·0895	2·9686	2·8740	2·7977
22	5·7863	4·3828	3·7829	3·4401	3·2151	3·0546	2·9338	2·8392	2·7628
23	5·7498	4·3492	3·7505	3·4083	3·1835	3·0232	2·9023	2·8077	2·7313
24	5·7166	4·3187	3·7211	3·3794	3·1548	2·9946	2·8738	2·7791	2·7027
25	5·6864	4·2909	3·6943	3·3530	3·1287	2·9685	2·8478	2·7531	2·6766
26	5·6586	4·2655	3·6697	3·3289	3·1048	2·9447	2·8240	2·7293	2·6528
27	5·6331	4·2421	3·6472	3·3067	3·0828	2·9228	2·8021	2·7074	2·6309
28	5·6096	4·2205	3·6264	3·2863	3·0626	2·9027	2·7820	2·6872	2·6106
29	5·5878	4·2006	3·6072	3·2674	3·0438	2·8840	2·7633	2·6686	2·5919
30	5·5675	4·1821	3·5894	3·2499	3·0265	2·8667	2·7460	2·6513	2·5746
40	5·4239	4·0510	3·4633	3·1261	2·9037	2·7444	2·6238	2·5289	2·4519
60	5·2856	3·9253	3·3425	3·0077	2·7863	2·6274	2·5068	2·4117	2·3344
120	5·1523	3·8046	3·2269	2·8943	2·6740	2·5154	2·3948	2·2994	2·2217
∞	5·0239	3·6889	3·1161	2·7858	2·5665	2·4082	2·2875	2·1918	2·1136

ν_1 ν_2	10	12	15	20	24	30	40	60	120	∞
1	968·63	976·71	984·87	993·10	997·25	1001·4	1005·6	1009·8	1014·0	1018·3
2	39·398	39·415	39·431	39·448	39·456	39·465	39·473	39·481	39·490	39·498
3	14·419	14·337	14·253	14·167	14·124	14·081	14·037	13·992	13·947	13·902
4	8·8439	8·7512	8·6565	8·5599	8·5109	8·4613	8·4111	8·3604	8·3092	8·2573
5	6·6192	6·5245	6·4277	6·3286	6·2780	6·2269	6·1750	6·1225	6·0693	6·0153
6	5·4613	5·3662	5·2687	5·1684	5·1172	5·0652	5·0125	4·9589	4·9044	4·8491
7	4·7611	4·6658	4·5678	4·4667	4·4150	4·3624	4·3089	4·2544	4·1989	4·1423
8	4·2951	4·1997	4·1012	3·9995	3·9472	3·8940	3·8398	3·7844	3·7279	3·6702
9	3·9639	3·8682	3·7694	3·6669	3·6142	3·5604	3·5055	3·4493	3·3918	3·3329
10	3·7168	3·6209	3·5217	3·4185	3·3654	3·3110	3·2554	3·1984	3·1399	3·0798
11	3·5257	3·4296	3·3299	3·2261	3·1725	3·1176	3·0613	3·0035	2·9441	2·8828
12	3·3736	3·2773	3·1772	3·0728	3·0187	2·9633	2·9063	2·8478	2·7874	2·7249
13	3·2497	3·1532	3·0527	2·9477	2·8932	2·8372	2·7797	2·7204	2·6590	2·5955
14	3·1469	3·0502	2·9493	2·8437	2·7888	2·7324	2·6742	2·6142	2·5519	2·4872
15	3·0602	2·9633	2·8621	2·7559	2·7006	2·6437	2·5850	2·5242	2·4611	2·3953
16	2·9862	2·8890	2·7875	2·6808	2·6252	2·5678	2·5085	2·4471	2·3831	2·3163
17	2·9222	2·8249	2·7230	2·6158	2·5598	2·5020	2·4422	2·3801	2·3153	2·2474
18	2·8664	2·7689	2·6667	2·5590	2·5027	2·4445	2·3842	2·3214	2·2558	2·1869
19	2·8172	2·7196	2·6171	2·5089	2·4523	2·3937	2·3329	2·2696	2·2032	2·1333
20	2·7737	2·6758	2·5731	2·4645	2·4076	2·3486	2·2873	2·2234	2·1562	2·0853
21	2·7348	2·6368	2·5338	2·4247	2·3675	2·3082	2·2465	2·1819	2·1141	2·0422
22	2·6998	2·6017	2·4984	2·3890	2·3315	2·2718	2·2097	2·1446	2·0760	2·0032
23	2·6682	2·5699	2·4665	2·3567	2·2989	2·2389	2·1763	2·1107	2·0415	1·9677
24	2·6396	2·5411	2·4374	2·3273	2·2693	2·2090	2·1460	2·0799	2·0099	1·9353
25	2·6135	2·5149	2·4110	2·3005	2·2422	2·1816	2·1183	2·0516	1·9811	1·9055
26	2·5896	2·4908	2·3867	2·2759	2·2174	2·1565	2·0928	2·0257	1·9545	1·8781
27	2·5676	2·4688	2·3644	2·2533	2·1946	2·1334	2·0693	2·0018	1·9299	1·8527
28	2·5473	2·4484	2·3438	2·2324	2·1735	2·1121	2·0477	1·9797	1·9072	1·8291
29	2·5286	2·4295	2·3248	2·2131	2·1540	2·0923	2·0276	1·9591	1·8861	1·8072
30	2·5112	2·4120	2·3072	2·1952	2·1359	2·0739	2·0089	1·9400	1·8664	1·7867
40	2·3882	2·2882	2·1819	2·0677	2·0069	1·9429	1·8752	1·8028	1·7242	1·6371
60	2·2702	2·1692	2·0613	1·9445	1·8817	1·8152	1·7440	1·6668	1·5810	1·4821
120	2·1570	2·0548	1·9450	1·8249	1·7597	1·6899	1·6141	1·5299	1·4327	1·3104
∞	2·0483	1·9447	1·8326	1·7085	1·6402	1·5660	1·4835	1·3883	1·2684	1·0000

ν_2 \ ν_1	1	2	3	4	5	6	7	8	9
1	4052·2	4999·5	5403·4	5624·6	5763·6	5859·0	5928·4	5981·1	6022·5
2	98·503	99·000	99·166	99·249	99·299	99·333	99·356	99·374	99·388
3	34·116	30·817	29·457	28·710	28·237	27·911	27·672	27·489	27·345
4	21·198	18·000	16·694	15·977	15·522	15·207	14·976	14·799	14·659
5	16·258	13·274	12·060	11·392	10·967	10·672	10·456	10·289	10·158
6	13·745	10·925	9·7795	9·1483	8·7459	8·4661	8·2600	8·1017	7·9761
7	12·246	9·5466	8·4513	7·8466	7·4604	7·1914	6·9928	6·8400	6·7188
8	11·259	8·6491	7·5910	7·0061	6·6318	6·3707	6·1776	6·0289	5·9106
9	10·561	8·0215	6·9919	6·4221	6·0569	5·8018	5·6129	5·4671	5·3511
10	10·044	7·5594	6·5523	5·9943	5·6363	5·3858	5·2001	5·0567	4·9424
11	9·6460	7·2057	6·2167	5·6683	5·3160	5·0692	4·8861	4·7445	4·6315
12	9·3302	6·9266	5·9525	5·4120	5·0643	4·8206	4·6395	4·4994	4·3875
13	9·0738	6·7010	5·7394	5·2053	4·8616	4·6204	4·4410	4·3021	4·1911
14	8·8616	6·5149	5·5639	5·0354	4·6950	4·4558	4·2779	4·1399	4·0297
15	8·6831	6·3589	5·4170	4·8932	4·5556	4·3183	4·1415	4·0045	3·8948
16	8·5310	6·2262	5·2922	4·7726	4·4374	4·2016	4·0259	3·8896	3·7804
17	8·3997	6·1121	5·1850	4·6690	4·3359	4·1015	3·9267	3·7910	3·6822
18	8·2854	6·0129	5·0919	4·5790	4·2479	4·0146	3·8406	3·7054	3·5971
19	8·1849	5·9259	5·0103	4·5003	4·1708	3·9386	3·7653	3·6305	3·5225
20	8·0960	5·8489	4·9382	4·4307	4·1027	3·8714	3·6987	3·5644	3·4567
21	8·0166	5·7804	4·8740	4·3688	4·0421	3·8117	3·6396	3·5056	3·3981
22	7·9454	5·7190	4·8166	4·3134	3·9880	3·7583	3·5867	3·4530	3·3458
23	7·8811	5·6637	4·7649	4·2636	3·9392	3·7102	3·5390	3·4057	3·2986
24	7·8229	5·6136	4·7181	4·2184	3·8951	3·6667	3·4959	3·3629	3·2560
25	7·7698	5·5680	4·6755	4·1774	3·8550	3·6272	3·4568	3·3239	3·2172
26	7·7213	5·5263	4·6366	4·1400	3·8183	3·5911	3·4210	3·2884	3·1818
27	7·6767	5·4881	4·6009	4·1056	3·7848	3·5580	3·3882	3·2558	3·1494
28	7·6356	5·4529	4·5681	4·0740	3·7539	3·5276	3·3581	3·2259	3·1195
29	7·5977	5·4204	4·5378	4·0449	3·7254	3·4995	3·3303	3·1982	3·0920
30	7·5625	5·3903	4·5097	4·0179	3·6990	3·4735	3·3045	3·1726	3·0665
40	7·3141	5·1785	4·3126	3·8283	3·5138	3·2910	3·1238	2·9930	2·8876
60	7·0771	4·9774	4·1259	3·6490	3·3389	3·1187	2·9530	2·8233	2·7185
120	6·8509	4·7865	3·9491	3·4795	3·1735	2·9559	2·7918	2·6629	2·5586
∞	6·6349	4·6052	3·7816	3·3192	3·0173	2·8020	2·6393	2·5113	2·4073

ν_2 \ ν_1	10	12	15	20	24	30	40	60	120	∞
1	6055·8	6106·3	6157·3	6208·7	6234·6	6260·6	6286·8	6313·0	6339·4	6365·9
2	99·399	99·416	99·433	99·449	99·458	99·466	99·474	99·482	99·491	99·499
3	27·229	27·052	26·872	26·690	26·598	26·505	26·411	26·316	26·221	26·125
4	14·546	14·374	14·198	14·020	13·929	13·838	13·745	13·652	13·558	13·463
5	10·051	9·8883	9·7222	9·5526	9·4665	9·3793	9·2912	9·2020	9·1118	9·0204
6	7·8741	7·7183	7·5590	7·3958	7·3127	7·2285	7·1432	7·0567	6·9690	6·8800
7	6·6201	6·4691	6·3143	6·1554	6·0743	5·9920	5·9084	5·8236	5·7373	5·6495
8	5·8143	5·6667	5·5151	5·3591	5·2793	5·1981	5·1156	5·0316	4·9461	4·8588
9	5·2565	5·1114	4·9621	4·8080	4·7290	4·6486	4·5666	4·4831	4·3978	4·3105
10	4·8491	4·7059	4·5581	4·4054	4·3269	4·2469	4·1653	4·0819	3·9965	3·9090
11	4·5393	4·3974	4·2509	4·0990	4·0209	3·9411	3·8596	3·7761	3·6904	3·6024
12	4·2961	4·1553	4·0096	3·8584	3·7805	3·7008	3·6192	3·5355	3·4494	3·3608
13	4·1003	3·9603	3·8154	3·6646	3·5868	3·5070	3·4253	3·3413	3·2548	3·1654
14	3·9394	3·8001	3·6557	3·5052	3·4274	3·3476	3·2656	3·1813	3·0942	3·0040
15	3·8049	3·6662	3·5222	3·3719	3·2940	3·2141	3·1319	3·0471	2·9595	2·8684
16	3·6909	3·5527	3·4089	3·2587	3·1808	3·1007	3·0182	2·9330	2·8447	2·7528
17	3·5931	3·4552	3·3117	3·1615	3·0835	3·0032	2·9205	2·8348	2·7459	2·6530
18	3·5082	3·3706	3·2273	3·0771	2·9990	2·9185	2·8354	2·7493	2·6597	2·5660
19	3·4338	3·2965	3·1533	3·0031	2·9249	2·8442	2·7608	2·6742	2·5839	2·4893
20	3·3682	3·2311	3·0880	2·9377	2·8594	2·7785	2·6947	2·6077	2·5168	2·4212
21	3·3098	3·1730	3·0300	2·8796	2·8010	2·7200	2·6359	2·5484	2·4568	2·3603
22	3·2576	3·1209	2·9779	2·8274	2·7488	2·6675	2·5831	2·4951	2·4029	2·3055
23	3·2106	3·0740	2·9311	2·7805	2·7017	2·6202	2·5355	2·4471	2·3542	2·2558
24	3·1681	3·0316	2·8887	2·7380	2·6591	2·5773	2·4923	2·4035	2·3100	2·2107
25	3·1294	2·9931	2·8502	2·6993	2·6203	2·5383	2·4530	2·3637	2·2696	2·1694
26	3·0941	2·9578	2·8150	2·6640	2·5848	2·5026	2·4170	2·3273	2·2325	2·1315
27	3·0618	2·9256	2·7827	2·6316	2·5522	2·4699	2·3840	2·2938	2·1985	2·0965
28	3·0320	2·8959	2·7530	2·6017	2·5223	2·4397	2·3535	2·2629	2·1670	2·0642
29	3·0045	2·8685	2·7256	2·5742	2·4946	2·4118	2·3253	2·2344	2·1379	2·0342
30	2·9791	2·8431	2·7002	2·5487	2·4689	2·3860	2·2992	2·2079	2·1108	2·0062
40	2·8005	2·6648	2·5216	2·3689	2·2880	2·2034	2·1142	2·0194	1·9172	1·8047
60	2·6318	2·4961	2·3523	2·1978	2·1154	2·0285	1·9360	1·8363	1·7263	1·6006
120	2·4721	2·3363	2·1915	2·0346	1·9500	1·8600	1·7628	1·6557	1·5330	1·3805
∞	2·3209	2·1847	2·0385	1·8783	1·7908	1·6964	1·5923	1·4730	1·3246	1·0000

$F = \dfrac{s_1^2}{s_2^2} = \dfrac{S_1}{\nu_1} \bigg/ \dfrac{S_2}{\nu_2}$, where $s_1^2 = S_1/\nu_1$ and $s_2^2 = S_2/\nu_2$ are independent mean square estimators of a common variance σ^2, based on ν_1 and ν_2 degrees of freedom, respectively.

Table 5 (*continued*)

Upper 0·5 per cent points

ν_2 \ ν_1	1	2	3	4	5	6	7	8	9
1	16211	20000	21615	22500	23056	23437	23715	23925	24091
2	198·50	199·00	199·17	199·25	199·30	199·33	199·36	199·37	199·39
3	55·552	49·799	47·467	46·195	45·392	44·838	44·434	44·126	43·882
4	31·333	26·284	24·259	23·155	22·456	21·975	21·622	21·352	21·139
5	22·785	18·314	16·530	15·556	14·940	14·513	14·200	13·961	13·772
6	18·635	14·544	12·917	12·028	11·464	11·073	10·786	10·566	10·391
7	16·236	12·404	10·882	10·050	9·5221	9·1553	8·8854	8·6781	8·5138
8	14·688	11·042	9·5965	8·8051	8·3018	7·9520	7·6941	7·4959	7·3386
9	13·614	10·107	8·7171	7·9559	7·4712	7·1339	6·8849	6·6933	6·5411
10	12·826	9·4270	8·0807	7·3428	6·8724	6·5446	6·3025	6·1159	5·9676
11	12·226	8·9122	7·6004	6·8809	6·4217	6·1016	5·8648	5·6821	5·5368
12	11·754	8·5096	7·2258	6·5211	6·0711	5·7570	5·5245	5·3451	5·2021
13	11·374	8·1865	6·9258	6·2335	5·7910	5·4819	5·2529	5·0761	4·9351
14	11·060	7·9216	6·6804	5·9984	5·5623	5·2574	5·0313	4·8566	4·7173
15	10·798	7·7008	6·4760	5·8029	5·3721	5·0708	4·8473	4·6744	4·5364
16	10·575	7·5138	6·3034	5·6378	5·2117	4·9134	4·6920	4·5207	4·3838
17	10·384	7·3536	6·1556	5·4967	5·0746	4·7789	4·5594	4·3894	4·2535
18	10·218	7·2148	6·0278	5·3746	4·9560	4·6627	4·4448	4·2759	4·1410
19	10·073	7·0935	5·9161	5·2681	4·8526	4·5614	4·3448	4·1770	4·0428
20	9·9439	6·9865	5·8177	5·1743	4·7616	4·4721	4·2569	4·0900	3·9564
21	9·8295	6·8914	5·7304	5·0911	4·6809	4·3931	4·1789	4·0128	3·8799
22	9·7271	6·8064	5·6524	5·0168	4·6088	4·3225	4·1094	3·9440	3·8116
23	9·6348	6·7300	5·5823	4·9500	4·5441	4·2591	4·0469	3·8822	3·7502
24	9·5513	6·6609	5·5190	4·8898	4·4857	4·2019	3·9905	3·8264	3·6949
25	9·4753	6·5982	5·4615	4·8351	4·4327	4·1500	3·9394	3·7758	3·6447
26	9·4059	6·5409	5·4091	4·7852	4·3844	4·1027	3·8928	3·7297	3·5989
27	9·3423	6·4885	5·3611	4·7396	4·3402	4·0594	3·8501	3·6875	3·5571
28	9·2838	6·4403	5·3170	4·6977	4·2996	4·0197	3·8110	3·6487	3·5186
29	9·2297	6·3958	5·2764	4·6591	4·2622	3·9831	3·7749	3·6131	3·4832
30	9·1797	6·3547	5·2388	4·6234	4·2276	3·9492	3·7416	3·5801	3·4505
40	8·8279	6·0664	4·9758	4·3738	3·9860	3·7129	3·5088	3·3498	3·2220
60	8·4946	5·7950	4·7290	4·1399	3·7599	3·4918	3·2911	3·1344	3·0083
120	8·1788	5·5393	4·4972	3·9207	3·5482	3·2849	3·0874	2·9330	2·8083
∞	7·8794	5·2983	4·2794	3·7151	3·3499	3·0913	2·8968	2·7444	2·6210

ν_2 \ ν_1	10	12	15	20	24	30	40	60	120	∞
1	24224	24426	24630	24836	24940	25044	25148	25253	25359	25464
2	199·40	199·42	199·43	199·45	199·46	199·47	199·47	199·48	199·49	199·50
3	43·686	43·387	43·085	42·778	42·622	42·466	42·308	42·149	41·989	41·828
4	20·967	20·705	20·438	20·167	20·030	19·892	19·752	19·611	19·468	19·325
5	13·618	13·384	13·146	12·903	12·780	12·656	12·530	12·402	12·274	12·144
6	10·250	10·034	9·8140	9·5888	9·4742	9·3582	9·2408	9·1219	9·0015	8·8793
7	8·3803	8·1764	7·9678	7·7540	7·6450	7·5345	7·4224	7·3088	7·1933	7·0760
8	7·2106	7·0149	6·8143	6·6082	6·5029	6·3961	6·2875	6·1772	6·0649	5·9506
9	6·4172	6·2274	6·0325	5·8318	5·7292	5·6248	5·5186	5·4104	5·3001	5·1875
10	5·8467	5·6613	5·4707	5·2740	5·1732	5·0706	4·9659	4·8592	4·7501	4·6385
11	5·4183	5·2363	5·0489	4·8552	4·7557	4·6543	4·5508	4·4450	4·3367	4·2255
12	5·0855	4·9062	4·7213	4·5299	4·4314	4·3309	4·2282	4·1229	4·0149	3·9039
13	4·8199	4·6429	4·4600	4·2703	4·1726	4·0727	3·9704	3·8655	3·7577	3·6465
14	4·6034	4·4281	4·2468	4·0585	3·9614	3·8619	3·7600	3·6552	3·5473	3·4359
15	4·4235	4·2497	4·0698	3·8826	3·7859	3·6867	3·5850	3·4803	3·3722	3·2602
16	4·2719	4·0994	3·9205	3·7342	3·6378	3·5389	3·4372	3·3324	3·2240	3·1115
17	4·1424	3·9709	3·7929	3·6073	3·5112	3·4124	3·3108	3·2058	3·0971	2·9839
18	4·0305	3·8599	3·6827	3·4977	3·4017	3·3030	3·2014	3·0962	2·9871	2·8732
19	3·9329	3·7631	3·5866	3·4020	3·3062	3·2075	3·1058	3·0004	2·8908	2·7762
20	3·8470	3·6779	3·5020	3·3178	3·2220	3·1234	3·0215	2·9159	2·8058	2·6904
21	3·7709	3·6024	3·4270	3·2431	3·1474	3·0488	2·9467	2·8408	2·7302	2·6140
22	3·7030	3·5350	3·3600	3·1764	3·0807	2·9821	2·8799	2·7736	2·6625	2·5455
23	3·6420	3·4745	3·2999	3·1165	3·0208	2·9221	2·8197	2·7132	2·6015	2·4837
24	3·5870	3·4199	3·2456	3·0624	2·9667	2·8679	2·7654	2·6585	2·5463	2·4276
25	3·5370	3·3704	3·1963	3·0133	2·9176	2·8187	2·7160	2·6088	2·4961	2·3765
26	3·4916	3·3252	3·1515	2·9685	2·8728	2·7738	2·6709	2·5633	2·4501	2·3297
27	3·4499	3·2839	3·1104	2·9275	2·8318	2·7327	2·6296	2·5217	2·4079	2·2867
28	3·4117	3·2460	3·0727	2·8899	2·7941	2·6949	2·5916	2·4834	2·3690	2·2470
29	3·3765	3·2110	3·0379	2·8551	2·7594	2·6600	2·5565	2·4479	2·3331	2·2102
30	3·3440	3·1787	3·0057	2·8230	2·7272	2·6278	2·5241	2·4151	2·2998	2·1760
40	3·1167	2·9531	2·7811	2·5984	2·5020	2·4015	2·2958	2·1838	2·0636	1·9318
60	2·9042	2·7419	2·5705	2·3872	2·2898	2·1874	2·0789	1·9622	1·8341	1·6885
120	2·7052	2·5439	2·3727	2·1881	2·0890	1·9840	1·8709	1·7469	1·6055	1·4311
∞	2·5188	2·3583	2·1868	1·9998	1·8983	1·7891	1·6691	1·5325	1·3637	1·0000

Table 5 (*continued*). *Percentage points of the F-distribution*

Upper 0·25 per cent points

ν_2 \ ν_1	1	2	3	4	5	6	7	8	9
1	64845	80000	86460	90000	92224	93750	94859	95703	96365
2	398·50	399·00	399·17	399·25	399·30	399·33	399·36	399·37	399·39
3	89·584	79·933	76·056	73·948	72·621	71·708	71·041	70·532	70·132
4	45·674	38·000	34·956	33·303	32·261	31·543	31·018	30·617	30·300
5	31·407	24·964	22·426	21·048	20·178	19·578	19·138	18·802	18·537
6	24·807	19·104	16·867	15·652	14·884	14·354	13·964	13·666	13·431
7	21·111	15·887	13·843	12·733	12·031	11·545	11·188	10·914	10·698
8	18·780	13·889	11·979	10·941	10·283	9·8280	9·4930	9·2358	9·0320
9	17·188	12·539	10·726	9·7411	9·1164	8·6830	8·3639	8·1188	7·9243
10	16·036	11·572	9·8334	8·8876	8·2875	7·8709	7·5638	7·3276	7·1401
11	15·167	10·848	9·1668	8·2521	7·6712	7·2675	6·9698	6·7406	6·5584
12	14·490	10·287	8·6517	7·7618	7·1963	6·8031	6·5127	6·2891	6·1112
13	13·947	9·8392	8·2424	7·3728	6·8200	6·4352	6·1509	5·9318	5·7575
14	13·503	9·4748	7·9097	7·0572	6·5148	6·1371	5·8579	5·6425	5·4710
15	13·133	9·1726	7·6343	6·7961	6·2626	5·8909	5·6159	5·4037	5·2346
16	12·820	8·9179	7·4027	6·5768	6·0509	5·6843	5·4129	5·2034	5·0364
17	12·552	8·7006	7·2053	6·3901	5·8708	5·5085	5·2403	5·0331	4·8679
18	12·321	8·5130	7·0351	6·2293	5·7157	5·3573	5·0918	4·8866	4·7229
19	12·118	8·3494	6·8870	6·0893	5·5808	5·2258	4·9627	4·7593	4·5969
20	11·940	8·2056	6·7569	5·9665	5·4625	5·1105	4·8495	4·6477	4·4865
21	11·782	8·0782	6·6417	5·8579	5·3579	5·0086	4·7495	4·5490	4·3889
22	11·640	7·9646	6·5391	5·7611	5·2648	4·9178	4·6605	4·4612	4·3021
23	11·513	7·8626	6·4470	5·6744	5·1813	4·8366	4·5807	4·3826	4·2243
24	11·398	7·7706	6·3640	5·5963	5·1061	4·7634	4·5089	4·3118	4·1543
25	11·294	7·6871	6·2889	5·5255	5·0380	4·6971	4·4439	4·2477	4·0909
26	11·199	7·6111	6·2204	5·4611	4·9761	4·6368	4·3848	4·1894	4·0332
27	11·112	7·5416	6·1578	5·4022	4·9195	4·5817	4·3308	4·1362	3·9806
28	11·031	7·4778	6·1004	5·3482	4·8676	4·5312	4·2812	4·0874	3·9323
29	10·958	7·4190	6·0476	5·2985	4·8199	4·4848	4·2357	4·0425	3·8879
30	10·889	7·3646	5·9987	5·2526	4·7758	4·4419	4·1936	4·0011	3·8469
40	10·411	6·9857	5·6589	4·9336	4·4695	4·1441	3·9017	3·7135	3·5625
60	9·9616	6·6317	5·3425	4·6373	4·1854	3·8681	3·6314	3·4472	3·2992
120	9·5387	6·3008	5·0479	4·3619	3·9218	3·6122	3·3809	3·2005	3·0553
∞	9·1406	5·9915	4·7734	4·1060	3·6771	3·3749	3·1486	2·9718	2·8292

ν_2 \ ν_1	10	12	15	20	24	30	40	60	120	∞
1	96899	97707	98522	99345	99759	100180	100590	101010	101440	101860
2	399·40	399·42	399·43	399·45	399·46	399·47	399·47	399·48	399·49	399·50
3	69·808	69·317	68·819	68·313	68·058	67·801	67·542	67·281	67·018	66·754
4	30·044	29·655	29·260	28·859	28·655	28·450	28·243	28·035	27·824	27·612
5	18·322	17·994	17·661	17·321	17·149	16·975	16·800	16·622	16·443	16·261
6	13·239	12·948	12·651	12·348	12·193	12·038	11·880	11·720	11·558	11·395
7	10·522	10·253	9·9789	9·6982	9·5553	9·4105	9·2638	9·1150	8·9641	8·8109
8	8·8665	8·6135	8·3546	8·0891	7·9536	7·8162	7·6768	7·5351	7·3912	7·2447
9	7·7661	7·5242	7·2762	7·0214	6·8912	6·7589	6·6245	6·4877	6·3483	6·2063
10	6·9875	6·7538	6·5139	6·2669	6·1405	6·0119	5·8810	5·7476	5·6114	5·4723
11	6·4101	6·1828	5·9490	5·7080	5·5844	5·4585	5·3302	5·1992	5·0652	4·9280
12	5·9663	5·7440	5·5151	5·2786	5·1572	5·0334	4·9070	4·7777	4·6452	4·5093
13	5·6153	5·3970	5·1719	4·9391	4·8194	4·6971	4·5722	4·4442	4·3128	4·1775
14	5·3311	5·1161	4·8942	4·6643	4·5459	4·4249	4·3010	4·1739	4·0432	3·9084
15	5·0966	4·8844	4·6651	4·4376	4·3203	4·2002	4·0772	3·9507	3·8205	3·6857
16	4·9000	4·6901	4·4730	4·2475	4·1310	4·0118	3·8893	3·7633	3·6333	3·4985
17	4·7328	4·5249	4·3097	4·0849	3·9701	3·8514	3·7295	3·6038	3·4738	3·3388
18	4·5891	4·3829	4·1693	3·9468	3·8316	3·7135	3·5919	3·4664	3·3363	3·2009
19	4·4641	4·2595	4·0473	3·8259	3·7113	3·5935	3·4721	3·3467	3·2166	3·0807
20	4·3546	4·1513	3·9403	3·7200	3·6057	3·4882	3·3671	3·2417	3·1113	2·9749
21	4·2579	4·0557	3·8457	3·6263	3·5124	3·3951	3·2741	3·1487	3·0180	2·8811
22	4·1717	3·9706	3·7616	3·5429	3·4293	3·3122	3·1913	3·0658	2·9348	2·7972
23	4·0946	3·8944	3·6862	3·4682	3·3548	3·2379	3·1170	2·9914	2·8601	2·7218
24	4·0252	3·8258	3·6183	3·4009	3·2877	3·1710	3·0501	2·9243	2·7926	2·6536
25	3·9623	3·7637	3·5569	3·3400	3·2270	3·1103	2·9894	2·8634	2·7314	2·5917
26	3·9052	3·7072	3·5010	3·2846	3·1717	3·0551	2·9341	2·8080	2·6755	2·5351
27	3·8530	3·6557	3·4500	3·2339	3·1212	3·0046	2·8836	2·7572	2·6243	2·4831
28	3·8051	3·6084	3·4032	3·1875	3·0748	2·9583	2·8372	2·7106	2·5773	2·4353
29	3·7611	3·5649	3·3601	3·1448	3·0322	2·9157	2·7945	2·6677	2·5339	2·3912
30	3·7205	3·5247	3·3204	3·1053	2·9928	2·8763	2·7550	2·6280	2·4938	2·3502
40	3·4385	3·2460	3·0444	2·8310	2·7188	2·6019	2·4795	2·3500	2·2114	2·0600
60	3·1774	2·9879	2·7885	2·5761	2·4636	2·3456	2·2209	2·0872	1·9410	1·7756
120	2·9355	2·7486	2·5509	2·3386	2·2251	2·1051	1·9764	1·8356	1·6760	1·4802
∞	2·7112	2·5265	2·3300	2·1168	2·0014	1·8777	1·7425	1·5891	1·4007	1·0000

$F = \dfrac{s_1^2}{s_2^2} = \dfrac{S_1}{\nu_1} \bigg/ \dfrac{S_2}{\nu_2}$, where $s_1^2 = S_1/\nu_1$ and $s_2^2 = S_2/\nu_2$ are independent mean square estimators of a common variance σ^2, based on ν_1 and ν_2 degrees of freedom, respectively.

Table 5 (*continued*)

Upper 0·10 per cent points

ν_2 \ ν_1	1	2	3	4	5	6	7	8	9
1	405280	500000	540380	562500	576400	585940	592870	598140	602280
2	998·50	999·00	999·17	999·25	999·30	999·33	999·36	999·37	999·39
3	167·03	148·50	141·11	137·10	134·58	132·85	131·58	130·62	129·86
4	74·137	61·246	56·177	53·436	51·712	50·525	49·658	48·996	48·475
5	47·181	37·122	33·202	31·085	29·752	28·834	28·163	27·649	27·244
6	35·507	27·000	23·703	21·924	20·803	20·030	19·463	19·030	18·688
7	29·245	21·689	18·772	17·198	16·206	15·521	15·019	14·634	14·330
8	25·415	18·494	15·829	14·392	13·485	12·858	12·398	12·046	11·767
9	22·857	16·387	13·902	12·560	11·714	11·128	10·698	10·368	10·107
10	21·040	14·905	12·553	11·283	10·481	9·9256	9·5175	9·2041	8·9558
11	19·687	13·812	11·561	10·346	9·5784	9·0466	8·6553	8·3548	8·1163
12	18·643	12·974	10·804	9·6327	8·8921	8·3788	8·0009	7·7104	7·4797
13	17·815	12·313	10·209	9·0727	8·3541	7·8557	7·4886	7·2061	6·9818
14	17·143	11·779	9·7294	8·6223	7·9218	7·4358	7·0775	6·8017	6·5826
15	16·587	11·339	9·3353	8·2527	7·5674	7·0917	6·7408	6·4707	6·2559
16	16·120	10·971	9·0059	7·9442	7·2719	6·8049	6·4604	6·1950	5·9839
17	15·722	10·658	8·7269	7·6831	7·0219	6·5625	6·2234	5·9620	5·7541
18	15·379	10·390	8·4875	7·4593	6·8078	6·3550	6·0206	5·7628	5·5575
19	15·081	10·157	8·2799	7·2655	6·6225	6·1754	5·8452	5·5904	5·3876
20	14·819	9·9526	8·0984	7·0960	6·4606	6·0186	5·6920	5·4400	5·2392
21	14·587	9·7723	7·9383	6·9467	6·3179	5·8805	5·5571	5·3076	5·1087
22	14·380	9·6120	7·7960	6·8142	6·1914	5·7580	5·4376	5·1901	4·9929
23	14·195	9·4685	7·6688	6·6957	6·0783	5·6486	5·3308	5·0853	4·8896
24	14·028	9·3394	7·5545	6·5892	5·9768	5·5504	5·2349	4·9912	4·7968
25	13·877	9·2225	7·4511	6·4931	5·8851	5·4617	5·1484	4·9063	4·7131
26	13·739	9·1163	7·3572	6·4057	5·8018	5·3812	5·0698	4·8292	4·6372
27	13·613	9·0194	7·2715	6·3261	5·7259	5·3078	4·9983	4·7590	4·5680
28	13·498	8·9305	7·1931	6·2532	5·6565	5·2407	4·9328	4·6947	4·5047
29	13·391	8·8488	7·1210	6·1863	5·5927	5·1791	4·8727	4·6358	4·4466
30	13·293	8·7734	7·0545	6·1245	5·5339	5·1223	4·8173	4·5814	4·3930
40	12·609	8·2508	6·5945	5·6981	5·1283	4·7306	4·4355	4·2070	4·0243
60	11·973	7·7678	6·1712	5·3067	4·7565	4·3721	4·0864	3·8648	3·6873
120	11·380	7·3211	5·7814	4·9472	4·4157	4·0437	3·7670	3·5519	3·3792
∞	10·828	6·9078	5·4221	4·6167	4·1030	3·7430	3·4746	3·2656	3·0975

ν_2 \ ν_1	10	12	15	20	24	30	40	60	120	∞
1	605620	610670	615760	620910	623500	626100	628710	631340	633970	636620
2	999·40	999·42	999·43	999·45	999·46	999·47	999·47	999·48	999·49	999·50
3	129·25	128·32	127·37	126·42	125·93	125·45	124·96	124·47	123·97	123·47
4	48·053	47·412	46·761	46·100	45·766	45·429	45·089	44·746	44·400	44·051
5	26·917	26·418	25·911	25·395	25·133	24·869	24·602	24·333	24·060	23·785
6	18·411	17·989	17·559	17·120	16·897	16·672	16·445	16·214	15·981	15·745
7	14·083	13·707	13·324	12·932	12·732	12·530	12·326	12·119	11·909	11·696
8	11·540	11·194	10·841	10·480	10·295	10·109	9·9194	9·7272	9·5321	9·3337
9	9·8943	9·5700	9·2381	8·8976	8·7239	8·5476	8·3685	8·1865	8·0014	7·8128
10	8·7539	8·4452	8·1288	7·8037	7·6376	7·4688	7·2971	7·1224	6·9443	6·7625
11	7·9224	7·6256	7·3210	7·0076	6·8471	6·6839	6·5178	6·3483	6·1753	5·9983
12	7·2920	7·0046	6·7092	6·4048	6·2488	6·0898	5·9278	5·7623	5·5931	5·4195
13	6·7992	6·5192	6·2312	5·9340	5·7814	5·6258	5·4670	5·3046	5·1381	4·9671
14	6·4041	6·1302	5·8483	5·5568	5·4070	5·2542	5·0979	4·9378	4·7735	4·6042
15	6·0808	5·8121	5·5351	5·2484	5·1009	4·9502	4·7959	4·6377	4·4750	4·3070
16	5·8117	5·5473	5·2745	4·9918	4·8462	4·6972	4·5446	4·3878	4·2263	4·0592
17	5·5844	5·3237	5·0544	4·7751	4·6311	4·4836	4·3323	4·1767	4·0160	3·8496
18	5·3900	5·1324	4·8663	4·5899	4·4471	4·3009	4·1507	3·9960	3·8360	3·6698
19	5·2219	4·9672	4·7037	4·4297	4·2881	4·1429	3·9936	3·8396	3·6801	3·5141
20	5·0752	4·8229	4·5618	4·2900	4·1493	4·0050	3·8564	3·7030	3·5438	3·3778
21	4·9462	4·6960	4·4369	4·1670	4·0272	3·8836	3·7357	3·5827	3·4237	3·2575
22	4·8317	4·5835	4·3262	4·0579	3·9189	3·7759	3·6285	3·4759	3·3170	3·1505
23	4·7296	4·4831	4·2274	3·9606	3·8222	3·6798	3·5328	3·3804	3·2216	3·0548
24	4·6379	4·3929	4·1387	3·8732	3·7354	3·5935	3·4468	3·2946	3·1357	2·9685
25	4·5551	4·3116	4·0587	3·7944	3·6570	3·5155	3·3692	3·2171	3·0581	2·8904
26	4·4801	4·2378	3·9861	3·7228	3·5859	3·4448	3·2987	3·1467	2·9875	2·8193
27	4·4117	4·1706	3·9200	3·6576	3·5211	3·3803	3·2344	3·0825	2·9231	2·7543
28	4·3491	4·1091	3·8595	3·5980	3·4618	3·3213	3·1755	3·0236	2·8640	2·6947
29	4·2917	4·0526	3·8039	3·5432	3·4074	3·2671	3·1215	2·9695	2·8097	2·6397
30	4·2388	4·0006	3·7527	3·4928	3·3572	3·2171	3·0716	2·9196	2·7595	2·5889
40	3·8744	3·6425	3·4003	3·1450	3·0111	2·8721	2·7268	2·5737	2·4103	2·2326
60	3·5415	3·3153	3·0781	2·8266	2·6938	2·5549	2·4086	2·2523	2·0821	1·8905
120	3·2372	3·0162	2·7833	2·5344	2·4019	2·2621	2·1128	1·9502	1·7667	1·5433
∞	2·9588	2·7425	2·5132	2·2657	2·1324	1·9901	1·8350	1·6601	1·4468	1·0000

Table 6. *Probability integral of the extreme standardized deviate from the population mean,*
$$X_n = (x_{(n)} - \mu)/\sigma \text{ or } X_1 = (\mu - x_{(1)})/\sigma$$

X_n \ n	3	4	5	6	7	8	9	10
−2·6	0·00000 01							
−2·4	·00000 06							
−2·2	·00000 27	0·00000 00						
−2·0	·00001 18	·00000 03	0·00000 00					
−1·8	·00004 64	·00000 17	·00000 01					
−1·6	·00016 46	·00000 90	·00000 05	0·00000 00				
−1·4	·00052 67	·00004 25	·00000 34	·00000 03	0·00000 00			
−1·2	·00152 36	·00017 53	·00002 02	·00000 23	·00000 03	0·00000 00	0·00000 00	
−1·0	0·00399 36	0·00063 36	0·00010 05	0·00001 59	0·00000 25	0·00000 04	0·00000 01	0·00000 00
−0·8	·00950 86	·00201 45	·00042 68	·00009 04	·00001 92	·00000 41	·00000 09	·00000 02
−0·6	·02062 79	·00565 73	·00155 15	·00042 55	·00011 67	·00003 20	·00000 88	·00000 24
−0·4	·04091 32	·01409 78	·00485 78	·00167 39	·00057 68	·00019 87	·00006 85	·00002 36
−0·2	·07448 05	·03133 69	·01318 47	·00554 73	·00233 40	·00098 20	·00041 32	·00017 38
0·0	·12500 00	·06250 00	·03125 00	·01562 50	·00781 25	·00390 62	·00195 31	·00097 66
0·1	0·15731 34	0·08492 22	0·04584 34	0·02474 75	0·01335 94	0·00721 18	0·00389 31	0·00210 16
0·2	·19436 59	·11258 83	·06521 79	·03777 81	·02188 33	·01267 61	·00734 28	·00425 34
0·3	·23592 76	·14578 23	·09008 06	·05566 18	·03439 41	·02125 25	·01313 22	·00811 45
0·4	·28155 45	·18453 70	·12094 95	·07927 30	·05195 72	·03405 39	·02231 97	·01462 88
0·5	·33060 23	·22859 91	·15806 77	·10929 79	·07557 54	·05225 75	·03613 41	·02498 54
0·6	0·38225 71	0·27742 19	0·20133 81	0·14612 05	0·10604 65	0·07696 29	0·05585 56	0·04053 70
0·7	·43558 22	·33018 71	·25029 38	·18973 18	·14382 36	·10902 35	·08264 38	·06264 70
0·8	·48957 33	·38585 45	·30410 92	·23968 20	·18890 41	·14888 37	·11734 19	·09248 24
0·9	·54321 84	·44323 36	·36165 19	·29508 62	·24077 26	·19645 60	·16029 63	·13079 21
1·0	·59555 51	·50106 72	·42157 02	·35468 59	·29841 31	·25106 83	·21123 50	·17772 15
1·1	0·64572 07	0·55811 83	0·48240 06	0·41695 52	0·36038 85	0·31149 60	0·26923 66	0·23271 03
1·2	·69299 04	·61324 83	·54268 20	·48023 57	·42497 52	·37607 34	·33279 88	·29450 37
1·3	·73680 25	·66547 97	·60106 09	·54287 79	·49032 71	·44286 32	·39999 38	·36127 42
1·4	·77676 83	·71403 91	·65637 57	·60336 89	·55464 29	·50985 18	·46867 79	·43082 90
1·5	·81266 98	·75837 76	·70771 25	·66043 23	·61631 06	·57513 66	·53671 34	·50085 70
1·6	0·84444 65	0·79817 14	0·75443 22	0·71308 98	0·67401 30	0·63707 76	0·60216 62	0·56916 79
1·7	·87217 33	·83330 45	·79616 79	·76068 63	·72678 60	·69439 64	·66345 03	·63388 34
1·8	·89603 56	·86384 08	·83280 27	·80287 98	·77403 21	·74622 09	·71940 89	·69356 03
1·9	·91630 06	·88998 76	·86443 02	·83960 67	·81549 61	·79207 79	·76933 21	·74723 95
2·0	·93329 05	·91205 81	·89130 86	·87103 12	·85121 51	·83184 99	·81292 52	·79443 10
2·1	0·94735 84	0·93043 44	0·91381 28	0·89748 80	0·88145 49	0·86570 82	0·85024 29	0·83505 38
2·2	·95886 69	·94553 53	·93238 91	·91942 57	·90664 25	·89403 71	·88160 69	·86934 95
2·3	·96817 15	·95778 87	·94751 72	·93735 60	·92730 37	·91735 92	·90752 13	·89778 89
2·4	·97560 84	·96761 09	·95967 88	·95181 18	·94400 93	·93627 08	·92859 57	·92098 35
2·5	·98148 64	·97539 17	·96933 49	·96331 56	·95733 38	·95138 91	·94548 12	·93961 01
2·6	0·98608 15	0·98148 52	0·97691 03	0·97235 68	0·96782 44	0·96331 32	0·95882 30	0·95435 38
2·7	·98963 51	·98620 41	·98278 49	·97937 76	·97598 21	·97259 84	·96922 65	·96586 62
2·8	·99235 42	·98981 86	·98728 95	·98476 68	·98225 06	·97974 08	·97723 75	·97474 05
2·9	·99441 30	·99255 76	·99070 57	·98885 72	·98701 22	·98517 06	·98333 25	·98149 77
3·0	·99595 58	·99461 13	·99326 87	·99192 79	·99058 89	·98925 17	·98791 63	·98658 27
3·1	0·99710 00	0·99613 52	0·99517 13	0·99420 84	0·99324 64	0·99228 53	0·99132 52	0·99036 60
3·2	·99794 00	·99725 43	·99656 90	·99588 42	·99519 99	·99451 61	·99383 27	·99314 98
3·3	·99855 04	·99806 77	·99758 52	·99710 30	·99662 09	·99613 91	·99565 76	·99517 63
3·4	·99898 96	·99865 30	·99831 65	·99798 01	·99764 39	·99730 77	·99697 17	·99663 58
3·5	·99930 23	·99906 98	·99883 74	·99860 50	·99837 27	·99814 05	·99790 83	·99767 61
3·6	0·99952 28	0·99936 37	0·99920 47	0·99904 57	0·99888 68	0·99872 78	0·99856 89	0·99841 01
3·7	·99967 66	·99956 89	·99946 11	·99935 34	·99924 56	·99913 79	·99903 02	·99892 25
3·8	·99978 30	·99971 06	·99963 83	·99956 60	·99949 37	·99942 14	·99934 91	·99927 68
3·9	·99985 57	·99980 76	·99975 95	·99971 15	·99966 34	·99961 53	·99956 72	·99951 91
4·0	·99990 50	·99987 33	·99984 17	·99981 00	·99977 83	·99974 67	·99971 50	·99968 33
4·2	0·99996 00	0·99994 66	0·99993 33	0·99991 99	0·99990 66	0·99989 32	0·99987 99	0·99986 66
4·4	·99998 38	·99997 83	·99997 29	·99996 75	·99996 21	·99995 67	·99995 13	·99994 59
4·6	·99999 37	·99999 15	·99998 94	·99998 73	·99998 52	·99998 31	·99998 10	·99997 89
4·8	·99999 76	·99999 68	·99999 60	·99999 52	·99999 44	·99999 37	·99999 29	·99999 21
5·0	·99999 91	·99999 89	·99999 86	·99999 83	·99999 80	·99999 77	·99999 74	·99999 71
5·2	0·99999 97	0·99999 96	0·99999 95	0·99999 94	0·99999 93	0·99999 92	0·99999 91	0·99999 90
5·4	·99999 99	·99999 99	·99999 98	·99999 98	·99999 98	·99999 97	·99999 97	·99999 97
5·6	1·00000 00	1·00000 00	·99999 99	·99999 99	·99999 99	·99999 99	·99999 99	·99999 99

Table 6 (*continued*)

X_n \ n	11	12	13	14	15	16	17
−0·7	0·00000 02	0·00000 00					
−0·6	·00000 07	·00000 02	0·00000 00	0·00000 00			
−0·5	·00000 24	·00000 07	·00000 02	·00000 01	0·00000 00		
−0·4	·00000 81	·00000 28	·00000 10	·00000 03	·00000 01	0·00000 00	0·00000 00
−0·3	·00002 53	·00000 97	·00000 37	·00000 14	·00000 05	·00000 02	·00000 01
−0·2	·00007 31	·00003 08	·00001 29	·00000 54	·00000 23	·00000 10	·00000 04
−0·1	·00019 59	·00009 02	·00004 15	·00001 91	·00000 88	·00000 40	·00000 19
0·0	·00048 83	·00024 41	·00012 21	·00006 10	·00003 05	·00001 53	·00000 76
0·1	0·00113 45	0·00061 24	0·00033 06	0·00017 85	0·00009 63	0·00005 20	0·00002 81
0·2	·00246 38	·00142 72	·00082 67	·00047 89	·00027 74	·00016 07	·00009 31
0·3	·00501 40	·00309 82	·00191 44	·00118 30	·00073 10	·00045 17	·00027 91
0·4	·00958 80	·00628 42	·00411 88	·00269 96	·00176 93	·00115 97	·00076 01
0·5	·01727 65	·01194 60	·00826 02	·00571 16	·00394 94	·00273 08	·00188 83
0·6	0·02941 96	0·02135 12	0·01549 56	0·01124 59	0·00816 16	0·00592 33	0·00429 88
0·7	·04748 87	·03599 82	·02728 79	·02068 52	·01568 02	·01188 61	·00901 01
0·8	·07288 95	·05744 75	·04527 69	·03568 48	·02812 47	·02216 64	·01747 03
0·9	·10671 85	·08707 59	·07104 87	·05797 15	·04730 12	·03859 50	·03149 12
1·0	·14952 50	·12580 21	·10584 29	·08905 04	·07492 21	·06303 53	·05303 44
1·1	0·20113 94	0·17385 16	0·15026 59	0·12987 99	0·11225 96	0·09702 98	0·08386 61
1·2	·26061 53	·23062 64	·20408 83	·18060 39	·15982 19	·14143 12	·12515 68
1·3	·32630 27	·29471 64	·26618 77	·24042 06	·21714 78	·19612 78	·17714 25
1·4	·39603 67	·36405 41	·33465 43	·30762 87	·28278 57	·25994 88	·23895 62
1·5	·46739 62	·43617 08	·40703 14	·37983 88	·35446 28	·33078 21	·30868 35
1·6	0·53797 79	0·50849 71	0·48063 18	0·45429 35	0·42939 86	0·40586 78	0·38362 65
1·7	·60563 41	·57864 37	·55285 62	·52821 79	·50467 76	·48218 64	·46069 76
1·8	·66864 05	·64461 60	·62145 48	·59912 57	·57759 89	·55684 56	·53683 80
1·9	·72578 14	·70493 94	·68469 60	·66503 39	·64593 64	·62738 73	·60937 09
2·0	·77635 76	·75869 54	·74143 50	·72456 72	·70808 32	·69197 42	·67623 17
2·1	0·82013 60	0·80548 48	0·79109 52	0·77696 28	0·76308 28	0·74945 08	0·73606 23
2·2	·85726 25	·84534 36	·83359 04	·82200 07	·81057 20	·79930 23	·78818 92
2·3	·88816 09	·87863 62	·86921 36	·85989 21	·85067 05	·84154 78	·83252 30
2·4	·91343 37	·90594 58	·89851 92	·89115 36	·88384 83	·87660 29	·86941 70
2·5	·93377 55	·92797 70	·92221 46	·91648 80	·91079 69	·90514 11	·89952 05
2·6	0·94990 53	0·94547 77	0·94107 06	0·93668 41	0·93231 80	0·92797 23	0·92364 69
2·7	·96251 76	·95918 05	·95585 51	·95254 12	·94923 87	·94594 77	·94266 82
2·8	·97224 99	·96976 57	·96728 78	·96481 63	·96235 10	·95989 21	·95743 94
2·9	·97966 65	·97783 86	·97601 41	·97419 31	·97237 54	·97056 11	·96875 02
3·0	·98525 09	·98392 10	·98259 28	·98126 64	·97994 17	·97861 89	·97729 79
3·1	0·98940 77	0·98845 04	0·98749 39	0·98653 84	0·98558 38	0·98463 02	0·98367 75
3·2	·99246 74	·99178 54	·99110 39	·99042 29	·98974 24	·98906 23	·98838 26
3·3	·99469 52	·99421 43	·99373 37	·99325 33	·99277 31	·99229 32	·99181 35
3·4	·99630 00	·99596 43	·99562 88	·99529 33	·99495 80	·99462 27	·99428 76
3·5	·99744 41	·99721 20	·99698 00	·99674 81	·99651 62	·99628 44	·99605 27
3·6	0·99825 12	0·99809 24	0·99793 36	0·99777 48	0·99761 60	0·99745 73	0·99729 86
3·7	·99881 48	·99870 72	·99859 95	·99849 19	·99838 42	·99827 66	·99816 90
3·8	·99920 45	·99913 22	·99905 99	·99898 76	·99891 53	·99884 31	·99877 08
3·9	·99947 11	·99942 30	·99937 49	·99939 69	·99927 88	·99923 07	·99918 27
4·0	·99965 17	·99962 00	·99958 84	·99955 67	·99952 50	·99949 34	·99946 17
4·1	0·99977 28	0·99975 21	0·99973 15	0·99971 08	0·99969 02	0·99966 95	0·99964 89
4·2	·99985 32	·99983 99	·99982 65	·99981 32	·99979 98	·99978 65	·99977 31
4·3	·99990 61	·99989 75	·99988 90	·99988 04	·99987 19	·99986 34	·99985 48
4·4	·99994 05	·99994 51	·99992 96	·99992 42	·99991 88	·99991 34	·99990 80
4·5	·99996 26	·99995 92	·99995 58	·99995 24	·99994 90	·99994 56	·99994 22
4·6	0·99997 68	0·99997 47	0·99997 25	0·99997 04	0·99996 83	0·99996 62	0·99906 41
4·7	·99998 57	·99998 44	·99998 31	·99998 18	·99998 05	·99997 92	·99997 79
4·8	·99999 13	·99999 05	·99998 97	·99998 89	·99998 81	·99998 73	·99998 65
4·9	·99999 47	·99999 42	·99999 38	·99999 33	·99999 28	·99999 23	·99999 19
5·0	·99999 68	·99999 66	·99999 63	·99999 60	·99999 57	·99999 54	·99999 51
5·2	0·99999 89	0·99999 88	0·99999 87	0·99999 86	0·99999 85	0·99999 84	0·99999 83
5·4	·99999 96	·99999 96	·99999 96	·99999 95	·99999 95	·99999 95	·99999 94
5·6	·99999 99	·99999 99	·99999 99	·99999 98	·99999 98	·99999 98	·99999 98
5·8	1·00000 00	1·00000 00	1·00000 00	1·00000 00	1·00000 00	·99999 99	·99999 99

Table 6 (*continued*). *Probability integral of the extreme standardized deviate from the population mean,*

$$X_n = (x_{(n)} - \mu)/\sigma \text{ or } X_1 = (\mu - x_{(1)})/\sigma$$

X_n $\backslash$ n	18	19	20	21	22	23	24	25
−0·2	0·00000 02	0·00000 01	0·00000 00	0·00000 00				
−0·1	·00000 09	·00000 04	·00000 02	·00000 01	0·00000 00	0·00000 00	0·00000 00	
0·0	·00000 38	·00000 19	·00000 10	·00000 05	·00000 02	·00000 01	·00000 01	0·00000 00
0·1	0·00001 52	0·00000 82	0·00000 44	0·00000 24	0·00000 13	0·00000 07	0·00000 04	0·00000 02
0·2	·00005 39	·00003 12	·00001 81	·00001 05	·00000 61	·00000 35	·00000 20	·00000 12
0·3	·00017 25	·00010 66	·00006 58	·00004 07	·00002 51	·00001 55	·00000 96	·00000 59
0·4	·00049 82	·00032 65	·00021 40	·00014 03	·00009 19	·00006 03	·00003 95	·00002 59
0·5	·00130 57	·00090 28	·00062 43	·00043 17	·00029 85	·00020 64	·00014 27	·00009 87
0·6	0·00311 98	0·00226 42	0·00164 32	0·00119 26	0·00086 55	0·00062 81	0·00045 59	0·00033 08
0·7	·00683 00	·00517 74	·00392 46	·00297 50	·00225 52	·00170 95	·00129 59	·00098 23
0·8	·01376 91	·01085 21	·00855 30	·00674 10	·00531 29	·00418 73	·00330 02	·00260 10
0·9	·02569 49	·02096 55	·01710 66	·01395 79	·01138 88	·00929 26	·00758 22	·00618 66
1·0	·04462 02	·03754 10	·03158 49	·02657 38	·02235 77	·01881 06	·01582 62	·01331 53
1·1	0·07248 83	0·06265 41	0·05415 41	0·04680 72	0·04045 71	0·03496 84	0·03022 44	0·02612 40
1·2	·11075 50	·09801 05	·08673 24	·07675 22	·06792 03	·06010 48	·05318 85	·04706 81
1·3	·15999 50	·14450 74	·13051 91	·11788 47	·10647 34	·09616 68	·08685 78	·07844 99
1·4	·21965 89	·20192 00	·18561 36	·17062 41	·15684 51	·14417 88	·13253 54	·12183 23
1·5	·28806 12	·26881 67	·25085 78	·23409 87	·21845 92	·20386 45	·19024 49	·17753 52
1·6	0·36260 41	0·34273 36	0·32395 21	0·30619 97	0·28942 02	0·27356 02	0·25856 93	0·24439 99
1·7	·44016 64	·42055 01	·40180 81	·38390 14	·36679 26	·35044 63	·33482 85	·31990 68
1·8	·51754 92	·49895 35	·48102 59	·46374 25	·44708 01	·43101 64	·41552 98	·40059 97
1·9	·59187 19	·57487 54	·55836 69	·54233 26	·52675 86	·51163 19	·49693 96	·48266 92
2·0	·66084 74	·64581 30	·63112 07	·61676 26	·60273 12	·58901 90	·57561 87	·56252 33
2·1	0·72291 29	0·70999 85	0·69731 48	0·68485 77	0·67262 31	0·66060 71	0·64880 57	0·63721 52
2·2	·77723 07	·76642 45	·75576 85	·74526 08	·73489 91	·72468 14	·71460 59	·70467 04
2·3	·82359 49	·81476 26	·80602 50	·79738 11	·78882 99	·78037 04	·77200 16	·76372 26
2·4	·86228 99	·85522 12	·84821 05	·84125 73	·83436 11	·82752 14	·82073 77	·81400 97
2·5	·89393 48	·88838 37	·88286 72	·87738 49	·87193 66	·86652 22	·86114 14	·85579 40
2·6	0·91934 16	0·91505 64	0·91079 11	0·90654 57	0·90232 02	0·89811 43	0·89392 80	0·88976 12
2·7	·93940 00	·93614 31	·93289 75	·92966 32	·92644 00	·92322 81	·92002 73	·91683 76
2·8	·95499 31	·95255 29	·95011 90	·94769 14	·94526 99	·94285 46	·94044 55	·93804 25
2·9	·96694 27	·96513 86	·96333 78	·96154 04	·95974 64	·95795 57	·95616 83	·95438 43
3·0	·97597 86	·97466 12	·97334 55	·97203 16	·97071 94	·96940 90	·96810 04	·96679 36
3·1	0·98272 57	0·98177 48	0·98082 48	0·97987 57	0·97892 76	0·97798 04	0·97703 41	0·97608 87
3·2	·98770 35	·98702 48	·98634 66	·98566 88	·98499 15	·98431 47	·98363 84	·98296 25
3·3	·99133 40	·99085 48	·99037 58	·98989 70	·98941 85	·98894 02	·98846 21	·98798 42
3·4	·99395 26	·99361 77	·99328 29	·99294 83	·99261 37	·99227 93	·99194 50	·99161 07
3·5	·99582 09	·99558 93	·99535 77	·99512 61	·99489 46	·99466 32	·99443 18	·99420 05
3·6	0·99713 99	0·99698 13	0·99682 26	0·99666 40	0·99650 55	0·99634 69	0·99618 84	0·99602 99
3·7	·99806 14	·99795 38	·99784 62	·99773 86	·99763 11	·99752 35	·99741 60	·99730 85
3·8	·99869 85	·99862 63	·99855 40	·99848 18	·99840 96	·99833 73	·99826 51	·99819 29
3·9	·99913 46	·99908 66	·99903 85	·99899 05	·99894 24	·99889 44	·99884 63	·99879 83
4·0	·99943 01	·99939 84	·99936 68	·99933 51	·99930 35	·99927 18	·99924 02	·99920 85
4·1	0·99962 82	0·99960 76	0·99958 69	0·99956 63	0·99954 56	0·99952 50	0·99950 43	0·99948 37
4·2	·99975 98	·99974 65	·99973 31	·99971 98	·99970 64	·99969 31	·99967 98	·99966 64
4·3	·99984 63	·99983 78	·99982 92	·99982 07	·99981 21	·99980 36	·99979 51	·99978 65
4·4	·99990 26	·99989 72	·99989 18	·99988 63	·99988 09	·99987 55	·99987 01	·99986 47
4·5	·99993 88	·99993 54	·99993 20	·99992 87	·99992 53	·99992 19	·99991 85	·99991 51
4·6	0·99996 20	0·99995 99	0·99995 78	0·99995 56	0·99995 35	0·99995 14	0·99994 93	0·99994 72
4·7	·99997 66	·99997 53	·99997 40	·99997 27	·99997 14	·99997 01	·99996 88	·99996 75
4·8	·99998 57	·99998 49	·99998 41	·99998 33	·99998 25	·99998 18	·99998 10	·99998 02
4·9	·99999 14	·99999 09	·99999 04	·99998 99	·99998 95	·99998 90	·99998 85	·99998 80
5·0	·99999 48	·99999 46	·99999 43	·99999 40	·99999 37	·99999 34	·99999 31	·99999 28
5·1	0·99999 69	0·99999 68	0·99999 66	0·99999 64	0·99999 63	0·99999 61	0·99999 59	0·99999 58
5·2	·99999 82	·99999 81	·99999 80	·99999 79	·99999 78	·99999 77	·99999 76	·99999 75
5·3	·99999 90	·99999 89	·99999 88	·99999 88	·99999 87	·99999 87	·99999 86	·99999 86
5·4	·99999 94	·99999 94	·99999 93	·99999 93	·99999 93	·99999 92	·99999 92	·99999 92
5·5	·99999 97	·99999 96	·99999 96	·99999 96	·99999 96	·99999 96	·99999 95	·99999 95
5·6	0·99999 98	0·99999 98	0·99999 98	0·99999 98	0·99999 98	0·99999 98	0·99999 97	0·99999 97
5·7	·99999 99	·99999 99	·99999 99	·99999 99	·99999 99	·99999 99	·99999 99	·99999 99
5·8	·99999 99	·99999 99	·99999 99	·99999 99	·99999 99	·99999 99	·99999 99	·99999 99
5·9	1·00000 00	1·00000 00	1·00000 00	1·00000 00	1·00000 00	1·00000 00	1·00000 00	1·00000 00

Table 6 (*continued*)

X_n n	30	35	40	45	50	55	60	100
0·2	0·00000 01							
0·3	·00000 05	0·00000 00						
0·4	·00000 31	·00000 04	0·00000 00	0·00000 00				
0·5	·00001 56	·00000 25	·00000 04	·00000 01	0·00000 00			
0·6	0·00006 66	0·00001 34	0·00000 27	0·00000 05	0·00000 01	0·00000 00	0·00000 00	
0·7	·00024 59	·00006 15	·00001 54	·00000 39	·00000 10	·00000 02	·00000 01	
0·8	·00079 10	·00024 06	·00007 32	·00002 22	·00000 68	·00000 21	·00000 06	
0·9	·00223 74	·00080 92	·00029 26	·00010 58	·00003 83	·00001 38	·00000 50	
1·0	·00561 33	·00236 64	·00099 76	·00042 06	·00017 73	·00007 47	·00003 15	0·00000 00
1·1	0·01260 22	0·00607 93	0·00293 27	0·00141 47	0·00068 25	0·00032 92	0·00015 88	0·00000 05
1·2	·02554 30	·01386 17	·00752 25	·00408 23	·00221 54	·00120 23	·00065 24	·00000 49
1·3	·04715 32	·02834 19	·01703 52	·01023 92	·00615 44	·00369 92	·00222 34	·00003 79
1·4	·07996 77	·05248 89	·03445 24	·02261 37	·01484 31	·00974 26	·00639 48	·00022 03
1·5	·12564 39	·08891 98	·06292 96	·04453 61	·03151 87	·02230 62	·01578 64	·00099 34
1·6	0·18438 31	0·13910 46	0·10494 49	0·07917 38	0·05973 13	0·04506 32	0·03399 71	0·00356 78
1·7	·25469 95	·20278 36	·16144 98	·12854 11	·10234 03	·08148 01	·06487 18	·01047 35
1·8	·33362 05	·27784 01	·23138 60	·19269 88	·16048 01	·13364 83	·11130 26	·02575 39
1·9	·41723 38	·36066 95	·31177 36	·26950 65	·23296 96	·20138 59	·17408 41	·05427 48
2·0	·50138 19	·44688 60	·39831 33	·35502 01	·31643 25	·28203 90	·25138 38	·10012 95
2·1	0·58229 54	0·53210 89	0·48624 79	0·44433 96	0·40604 32	0·37104 74	0·33906 79	0·16487 11
2·2	·65702 70	·61260 48	·57118 61	·53256 77	·49656 03	·46298 75	·43168 45	·24657 22
2·3	·72364 03	·68566 17	·64967 63	·61557 95	·58327 22	·55266 04	·52365 53	·34020 64
2·4	·78118 79	·74968 95	·71946 11	·69045 16	·66261 18	·63589 45	·61025 45	·43905 44
2·5	·82955 09	·80411 27	·77945 45	·75555 24	·73238 33	·70992 47	·68815 48	·53638 50
2·6	0·86921 69	0·84914 70	0·82954 04	0·81038 66	0·79167 50	0·77339 55	0·75553 81	0·62674 94
2·7	·90105 41	·88554 24	·87029 77	·85531 55	·84059 12	·82612 03	·81189 86	·70659 35
2·8	·92611 95	·91434 80	·90272 62	·89125 20	·87992 38	·86873 95	·85769 73	·77426 58
2·9	·94551 39	·93672 60	·92801 98	·91939 45	·91084 93	·90238 36	·89399 65	·82964 65
3·0	·96028 58	·95382 19	·94740 14	·94102 42	·93468 99	·92839 82	·92214 89	·87364 51
3·1	0·97137 55	0·96668 51	0·96201 73	0·95737 20	0·95274 92	0·94814 87	0·94357 04	0·90773 10
3·2	·97958 99	·97622 90	·97287 96	·96954 17	·96621 52	·96290 01	·95959 64	·9335 718
3·3	·98559 85	·98321 85	·98084 42	·97847 57	·97611 29	·97375 58	·97140 44	·95279 63
3·4	·98994 13	·98827 48	·98661 10	·98495 00	·98329 19	·98163 65	·97998 39	·96686 29
3·5	·99304 46	·99189 01	·99073 69	·98958 51	·98843 46	·98728 54	·98613 76	·97700 29
3·6	0·99523 77	0·99444 62	0·99365 54	0·99286 51	0·99207 55	0·99128 65	0·99049 82	0·98421 38
3·7	·99677 11	·99623 39	·99569 71	·99516 05	·99462 42	·99408 82	·99355 25	·98927 73
3·8	·99783 18	·99747 09	·99711 02	·99674 95	·99638 90	·99602 86	·99566 84	·99279 10
3·9	·99855 81	·99831 80	·99807 79	·99783 80	·99759 80	·99735 81	·99711 83	·99520 18
4·0	·99905 03	·99889 21	·99873 39	·99857 58	·99841 77	·99825 96	·99810 15	·99683 78
4·1	0·99938 05	0·99927 72	0·99917 40	0·99907 08	0·99896 76	0·99886 45	0·99876 13	0·99793 64
4·2	·99959 97	·99953 30	·99946 63	·99939 96	·99933 29	·99926 62	·99919 96	·99866 63
4·3	·99974 38	·99970 11	·99965 85	·99961 58	·99957 31	·99953 04	·99948 77	·99914 64
4·4	·99983 76	·99981 06	·99978 35	·99975 65	·99972 94	·99970 24	·99967 53	·99945 89
4·5	·99989 81	·99988 11	·99986 41	·99984 71	·99983 01	·99981 31	·99979 62	·99966 03
4·6	0·99993 66	0·99992 61	0·99991 55	0·99990 49	0·99989 44	0·99988 38	0·99987 33	0·99978 88
4·7	·99996 10	·99995 45	·99994 80	·99994 15	·99993 50	·99992 85	·99992 20	·99986 99
4·8	·99997 62	·99997 22	·99996 83	·99996 43	·99996 03	·99995 64	·99995 24	·99992 07
4·9	·99998 56	·99998 32	·99998 08	·99997 84	·99997 60	·99997 36	·99997 13	·99995 21
5·0	·99999 14	·99999 00	·99998 85	·99998 71	·99998 57	·99998 42	·99998 28	·99997 13
5·1	0·99999 49	0·99999 41	0·99999 32	0·99999 24	0·99999 15	0·99999 07	0·99998 98	0·99998 30
5·2	·99999 70	·99999 65	·99999 60	·99999 50	·99999 50	·99999 45	·99999 40	·99999 00
5·3	·99999 83	·99999 80	·99999 77	·99999 74	·99999 71	·99999 68	·99999 65	·99999 42
5·4	·99999 90	·99999 88	·99999 87	·99999 85	·99999 83	·99999 82	·99999 80	·99999 67
5·5	·99999 94	·99999 93	·99999 92	·99999 91	·99999 91	·99999 90	·99999 89	·99999 81
5·6	0·99999 97	0·99999 96	0·99999 96	0·99999 95	0·99999 95	0·99999 94	0·99999 94	0·99999 89
5·7	·99999 98	·99999 98	·99999 98	·99999 97	·99999 97	·99999 97	·99999 97	·99999 94
5·8	·99999 99	·99999 99	·99999 99	·99999 99	·99999 99	·99999 98	·99999 98	·99999 97
5·9	·99999 99	·99999 99	·99999 99	·99999 99	·99999 99	·99999 99	·99999 99	·99999 98
6·0	1·00000 00	1·00000 00	1·00000 00	1·00000 00	1·00000 00	·99999 99	·99999 99	·99999 99
6·1						1·00000 00	1·00000 00	·99999 99

Table 6 (*continued*). *Probability integral of the extreme standardized deviate from the population mean,*
$$X_n = (x_{(n)} - \mu)/\sigma \text{ or } X_1 = (\mu - x_{(1)})/\sigma$$

X_n \ n	200	300	400	500	600	700	800	900	1000
1·4	0·00000 00								
1·5	·00000 10								
1·6	0·00001 27	0·00000 00							
1·7	·00010 97	·00000 11	0·00000 00						
1·8	·00066 33	·00001 71	·00000 04	0·00000 00					
1·9	·00294 58	·00015 99	·00000 87	·00000 05	0·00000 00	0·00000 00			
2·0	·01002 59	·00100 39	·00010 05	·00001 01	·00000 10	·00000 01	0·00000 00	0·00000 00	
2·1	0·02718 25	0·00448 16	0·00073 88	0·00012 18	0·00002 01	0·00000 33	0·00000 05	0·00000 01	0·00000 00
2·2	·06079 78	·01499 11	·00369 64	·00091 14	·00022 47	·00005 54	·00001 37	·00000 34	·00000 08
2·3	·11574 04	·03937 56	·01339 58	·00455 74	·00155 04	·00052 75	·00017 94	·00006 10	·00002 08
2·4	·19276 87	·08463 60	·03715 98	·01631 52	·00716 32	·00314 51	·00138 08	·00060 63	·00026 61
2·5	·28770 89	·15432 27	·08277 66	·04440 01	·02381 56	·01277 43	·00685 20	·00367 53	·00197 14
2·6	0·39281 48	0·24619 64	0·15430 35	0·09670 96	0·06061 27	0·03798 90	0·02380 96	0·01492 26	0·00935 27
2·7	·49927 43	·35278 40	·24927 49	·17613 60	·12445 66	·08794 02	·06213 81	·04390 63	·03102 39
2·8	·59948 76	·46416 27	·35938 53	·27825 98	·21544 71	·16681 33	·12915 78	·10000 25	·07742 85
2·9	·68831 33	·57105 67	·47377 51	·39306 59	·32610 57	·27055 25	·22446 29	·18622 48	·15450 08
3·0	·76325 58	·66681 48	·58255 95	·50895 03	·44464 19	·38845 93	·33937 55	·29649 38	·25903 00
3·1	0·82397 56	0·74794 82	0·67893 58	0·61629 11	0·55942 66	0·50780 89	0·46095 38	0·41842 21	0·37981 48
3·2	·87155 63	·81366 04	·75961 04	·70915 08	·66204 32	·61806 49	·57700 79	·53867 83	·50289 49
3·3	·90782 09	·86496 84	·82413 87	·78523 64	·74817 03	·71285 40	·67920 46	·64714 37	·61659 60
3·4	·93482 38	·90384 64	·87389 55	·84493 72	·81693 84	·78986 74	·76369 34	·73838 68	·71391 22
3·5	·95453 48	·93258 33	·91113 66	·89018 31	·86971 15	·84971 07	·83016 99	·81107 84	·79242 60
3·6	0·96867 68	0·95338 51	0·93833 48	0·92352 20	0·90894 31	0·89459 44	0·88047 22	0·86657 28	0·85289 29
3·7	·97866 44	·96817 57	·95779 43	·94752 42	·93736 43	·92731 33	·91737 00	·90753 33	·89780 22
3·8	·98563 41	·97852 87	·97147 45	·96447 12	·95751 83	·95061 57	·94376 27	·93695 92	·93020 46
3·9	·99042 66	·98567 44	·98094 49	·97623 81	·97155 39	·96689 22	·96225 29	·95763 58	·95304 09
4·0	·99368 57	·99054 35	·98741 12	·98428 88	·98117 64	·97807 37	·97498 09	·97189 79	·96882 45
4·1	0·99587 70	0·99382 18	0·99177 10	0·98972 43	0·98768 19	0·98564 36	0·98360 96	0·98157 98	0·97955 42
4·2	·99733 44	·99600 43	·99467 59	·99334 93	·99202 45	·99070 14	·98938 01	·98806 06	·98674 28
4·3	·99829 35	·99744 13	·99658 99	·99573 91	·99488 91	·99403 99	·99319 13	·99234 35	·99149 64
4·4	·99891 81	·99837 75	·99783 73	·99729 74	·99675 78	·99621 84	·99567 93	·99514 05	·99460 21
4·5	·99932 07	·99898 12	·99864 19	·99830 26	·99796 35	·99762 45	·99728 56	·99694 68	·99660 81
4·6	0·99957 76	0·99936 65	0·99915 54	0·99894 43	0·99873 33	0·99852 24	0·99831 15	0·99810 06	0·99788 98
4·7	·99973 99	·99960 98	·99947 98	·99934 97	·99921 98	·99908 98	·99895 99	·99883 00	·99870 00
4·8	·99984 13	·99976 20	·99968 27	·99960 34	·99952 41	·99944 48	·99936 55	·99928 62	·99920 70
4·9	·99990 42	·99985 63	·99980 83	·99976 04	·99971 25	·99966 46	·99961 67	·99956 88	·99952 09
5·0	·99994 27	·99991 40	·99988 53	·99985 67	·99982 80	·99979 94	·99977 07	·99974 21	·99971 34
5·1	0·99996 60	0·99994 91	0·99993 21	0·99991 51	0·99989 81	0·99988 11	0·99986 42	0·99984 72	0·99983 02
5·2	·99998 01	·99997 01	·99996 01	·99995 02	·99994 02	·99993 03	·99992 03	·99991 03	·99990 04
5·3	·99998 84	·99998 26	·99997 67	·99997 11	·99996 53	·99995 95	·99995 37	·99994 79	·99994 21
5·4	·99999 33	·99999 00	·99998 67	·99998 33	·99998 00	·99997 67	·99997 33	·99997 00	·99996 67
5·5	·99999 62	·99999 43	·99999 24	·99999 05	·99998 86	·99998 68	·99998 48	·99998 29	·99998 10
5·6	0·99999 79	0·99999 68	0·99999 57	0·99999 46	0·99999 36	0·99999 25	0·99999 14	0·99999 03	0·99998 93
5·7	·99999 88	·99999 82	·99999 76	·99999 70	·99999 64	·99999 58	·99999 52	·99999 46	·99999 40
5·8	·99999 93	·99999 90	·99999 87	·99999 83	·99999 80	·99999 77	·99999 74	·99999 70	·99999 67
5·9	·99999 96	·99999 95	·99999 93	·99999 91	·99999 89	·99999 87	·99999 85	·99999 84	·99999 82
6·0	·99999 98	·99999 97	·99999 96	·99999 96	·99999 94	·99999 93	·99999 92	·99999 91	·99999 90
6·1	0·99999 99	0·99999 99	0·99999 98	0·99999 98	0·99999 97	0·99999 96	0·99999 96	0·99999 95	0·99999 95
6·2	1·00000 00	·99999 99	·99999 99	·99999 99	·99999 98	·99999 98	·99999 98	·99999 98	·99999 98
6·3		1·00000 00	·99999 99	·99999 99	·99999 99	·99999 99	·99999 99	·99999 99	·99999 99
6·4			1·00000 00	1·00000 00	1·00000 00	1·00000 00	·99999 99	·99999 99	·99999 99
6·5							1·00000 00	1·00000 00	1·00000 00

Table 7. *Probability integral of the extreme standardized deviate from the sample mean,*

$$u_n = (x_{(n)} - \bar{x})/\sigma \text{ or } u_1 = (\bar{x} - x_{(1)})/\sigma$$

u_n \ n	3	4	5	6	7	8	9
0·00							
·01	0·000 124						
·02	496	0·000 010					
·03	1 115	36					
·04	1 982	87	0·000 003				
0·05	0·003 095	0·000 169	0·000 009				
·06	4 453	293	19	0·000 001			
·07	6 056	464	35	2			
·08	7 901	690	59	5	0·000 001		
·09	9 987	979	95	9	1		
0·10	0·012 312	0·001 338	0·000 145	0·000 016	0·000 002		
·11	14 874	1 777	212	25	3		
·12	17 671	2 301	299	39	5	0·000 001	
·13	20 701	2 917	410	57	8	1	
·14	23 960	3 631	549	83	13	2	
0·15	0·027 446	0·004 451	0·000 720	0·000 116	0·000 019	0·000 003	
·16	31 156	5 382	927	159	28	5	
·17	35 086	6 430	1 175	214	39	7	0·000 001
·18	39 234	7 601	1 468	283	55	10	2
·19	43 595	8 901	1 812	368	75	15	3
0·20	0·048 166	0·010 334	0·002 210	0·000 472	0·000 101	0·000 021	0·000 005
·21	52 943	11 906	2 669	597	134	29	7
·22	57 922	13 621	3 192	747	175	41	10
·23	63 099	15 483	3 786	924	225	55	13
·24	68 469	17 495	4 455	1 132	288	73	18
0·25	0·074 028	0·019 663	0·005 204	0·001 375	0·000 363	0·000 096	0·000 025
·26	79 772	21 988	6 039	1 656	453	124	34
·27	85 696	24 474	6 964	1 978	561	159	45
·28	91 794	27 124	7 985	2 346	689	202	59
·29	98 063	29 939	9 106	2 765	838	254	77
0·30	0·104 497	0·032 922	0·010 333	0·003 237	0·001 013	0·000 317	0·000 099
·31	·111 091	36 075	11 670	3 768	1 215	392	126
·32	·117 840	39 398	13 121	4 361	1 448	480	159
·33	·124 738	42 893	14 691	5 021	1 715	585	200
·34	·131 781	46 560	16 384	5 754	2 018	707	248
0·35	0·138 963	0·050 400	0·018 205	0·006 562	0·002 363	0·000 850	0·000 306
·36	·146 279	54 412	20 157	7 451	2 752	1 015	375
·37	·153 723	58 597	22 244	8 426	3 188	1 205	456
·38	·161 290	62 954	24 469	9 490	3 677	1 423	551
·39	·168 975	67 481	26 835	10 649	4 221	1 672	662
0·40	0·176 771	0·072 179	0·029 346	0·011 906	0·004 825	0·001 954	0·000 791
·41	·184 674	77 045	32 004	13 266	5 493	2 273	940
·42	·192 677	82 079	34 813	14 734	6 228	2 631	1 111
·43	·200 777	87 277	37 773	16 313	7 036	3 033	1 307
·44	·208 966	92 638	40 887	18 007	7 921	3 482	1 530
0·45	0·217 239	0·098 159	0·044 157	0·019 821	0·008 886	0·003 981	0·001 783
·46	·225 591	·103 838	47 584	21 758	9 936	4 535	2 069
·47	·234 017	·109 672	51 169	23 822	11 076	5 147	2 390
·48	·242 512	·115 658	54 913	26 015	12 309	5 820	2 751
·49	·251 069	·121 793	58 816	28 342	13 640	6 560	3 154
0·50	0·259 684	0·128 073	0·062 880	0·030 805	0·015 073	0·007 370	0·003 602

Table 7 (*continued*). *Probability integral of the extreme standardized deviate from the sample mean*

u_n \ n	3	4	5	6	7	8	9
0·50	0·259 684	0·128 073	0·062 880	0·030 805	0·015 073	0·007 370	0·003 602
·51	·268 351	·134 495	67 103	33 407	16 611	8 254	4 099
·52	·277 066	·141 054	71 487	36 151	18 259	9 216	4 649
·53	·285 823	·147 748	76 029	39 039	20 021	10 260	5 255
·54	·294 616	·154 572	80 730	42 073	21 899	11 391	5 922
0·55	0·303 442	0·161 522	0·085 589	0·045 255	0·023 899	0·012 612	0·006 652
·56	·312 295	·168 594	90 604	48 587	26 023	13 928	7 450
·57	·321 170	·175 782	95 774	52 069	28 275	15 343	8 321
·58	·330 063	·183 084	·101 097	55 705	30 657	16 860	9 267
·59	·338 969	·190 494	·106 572	59 493	33 173	18 484	10 294
0·60	0·347 883	0·198 008	0·112 195	0·063 436	0·035 825	0·020 218	0·011 404
·61	·356 801	·205 621	·117 965	67 534	38 616	22 066	12 602
·62	·365 720	·213 328	·123 879	71 786	41 549	24 032	13 893
·63	·374 633	·221 124	·129 935	76 193	44 625	26 118	15 279
·64	·383 538	·229 006	·136 129	80 754	47 846	28 329	16 766
0·65	0·392 430	0·236 967	0·142 459	0·085 468	0·051 214	0·030 668	0·018 356
·66	·401 305	·245 003	·148 921	90 334	54 730	33 137	20 054
·67	·410 159	·253 110	·155 511	95 352	58 396	35 740	21 863
·68	·418 989	·261 283	·162 227	·100 521	62 213	38 478	23 787
·69	·427 791	·269 516	·169 064	·105 838	66 180	41 355	25 830
0·70	0·436 562	0·277 805	0·176 019	0·111 302	0·070 300	0·044 373	0·027 995
·71	·445 298	·286 145	·183 088	·116 912	74 572	47 534	30 285
·72	·453 996	·294 532	·190 266	·122 666	78 996	50 839	32 703
·73	·462 652	·302 960	·197 550	·128 560	83 571	54 290	35 253
·74	·471 264	·311 425	·204 935	·134 593	88 298	57 889	37 936
0·75	0·479 829	0·319 923	0·212 417	0·140 761	0·093 176	0·061 637	0·040 756
·76	·488 344	·328 448	·219 992	·147 062	98 203	65 535	43 715
·77	·496 805	·336 997	·227 655	·153 493	·103 380	69 583	46 814
·78	·505 211	·345 564	·235 402	·160 050	·108 703	73 781	50 057
·79	·513 559	·354 147	·243 228	·166 731	·114 172	78 131	53 444
0·80	0·521 847	0·362 739	0·251 129	0·173 531	0·119 785	0·082 632	0·056 978
·81	·530 072	·371 337	·259 100	·180 447	·125 540	87 284	60 660
·82	·538 232	·379 938	·267 137	·187 476	·131 434	92 086	64 490
·83	·546 325	·388 536	·275 235	·194 613	·137 466	97 038	68 471
·84	·554 349	·397 129	·283 390	·201 855	·143 632	·102 138	72 601
0·85	0·562 303	0·405 711	0·291 597	0·209 197	0·149 930	0·107 386	0·076 883
·86	·570 184	·414 280	·299 851	·216 636	·156 357	·112 780	81 315
·87	·577 991	·422 831	·308 149	·224 167	·162 910	·118 319	85 899
·88	·585 722	·431 362	·316 484	·231 786	·169 585	·124 000	90 633
·89	·593 376	·439 868	·324 854	·239 488	·176 380	·129 822	95 517
0·90	0·600 951	0·448 346	0·333 254	0·247 270	0·183 290	0·135 783	0·100 550
·91	·608 446	·456 793	·341 679	·255 127	·190 313	·141 880	·105 732
·92	·615 860	·465 206	·350 125	·263 054	·197 444	·148 111	·111 061
·93	·623 192	·473 581	·358 588	·271 047	·204 680	·154 472	·116 536
·94	·630 441	·481 917	·367 063	·279 102	·212 016	·160 961	·122 154
0·95	0·637 606	0·490 210	0·375 547	0·287 214	0·219 449	0·167 575	0·127 913
·96	·644 686	·498 457	·384 035	·295 379	·226 974	·174 310	·133 811
·97	·651 680	·506 656	·392 523	·303 591	·234 587	·181 164	·139 848
·98	·658 588	·514 803	·401 008	·311 848	·242 285	·188 132	·146 021
·99	·665 408	·522 895	·409 486	·320 143	·250 062	·195 211	·152 329
1·00	0·672 142	0·530 930	0·417 952	0·328 474	0·257 914	0·202 397	0·158 771

Table 7 (*continued*)

u_n \ n	3	4	5	6	7	8	9
1·00	0·672 142	0·530 930	0·417 952	0·328 474	0·257 914	0·202 397	0·158 771
1·01	·678 787	·538 909	·426 404	·336 835	·265 838	·209 687	·165 335
1·02	·685 344	·546 827	·434 838	·345 222	·273 827	·217 076	·172 023
1·03	·691 812	·554 683	·443 250	·353 632	·281 879	·224 561	·178 832
1·04	·698 191	·562 474	·451 636	·362 059	·289 989	·232 136	·185 758
1·05	0·704 481	0·570 199	0·459 994	0·370 499	0·298 151	0·239 799	0·192 798
1·06	·710 682	·577 856	·468 321	·378 949	·306 362	·247 544	·199 947
1·07	·716 793	·585 443	·476 613	·387 405	·314 618	·255 368	·207 203
1·08	·722 815	·592 959	·484 867	·395 861	·322 913	·263 266	·214 561
1·09	·728 748	·600 402	·493 080	·404 316	·331 244	·271 234	·222 018
1·10	0·734 592	0·607 770	0·501 250	0·412 764	0·339 606	0·279 267	0·229 568
1·11	·740 346	·615 064	·509 374	·421 202	·347 995	·287 360	·237 209
1·12	·746 011	·622 280	·517 449	·429 626	·356 406	·295 510	·244 935
1·13	·751 588	·629 418	·525 472	·438 032	·364 835	·303 712	·252 743
1·14	·757 077	·636 478	·533 442	·446 418	·373 278	·311 961	·260 627
1·15	0·762 477	0·643 458	0·541 356	0·454 780	0·381 732	0·320 253	0·268 585
1·16	·767 790	·650 356	·549 212	·463 114	·390 191	·328 583	·276 610
1·17	·773 015	·657 173	·557 007	·471 417	·398 652	·336 948	·284 700
1·18	·778 154	·663 908	·564 740	·479 686	·407 110	·345 342	·292 848
1·19	·783 206	·670 559	·572 408	·487 918	·415 563	·353 761	·301 052
1·20	0·788 172	0·677 127	0·580 010	0·496 110	0·424 006	0·362 202	0·309 305
1·21	·793 053	·683 611	·587 545	·504 259	·432 435	·370 659	·317 604
1·22	·797 849	·690 010	·595 009	·512 363	·440 847	·379 128	·325 945
1·23	·802 561	·696 324	·602 403	·520 419	·449 239	·387 606	·334 322
1·24	·807 190	·702 552	·609 724	·528 423	·457 606	·396 088	·342 731
1·25	0·811 735	0·708 695	0·616 971	0·536 375	0·465 946	0·404 570	0·351 169
1·26	·816 199	·714 752	·624 143	·544 271	·474 255	·413 049	·359 629
1·27	·820 581	·720 723	·631 238	·552 109	·482 530	·421 520	·368 109
1·28	·824 882	·726 608	·638 256	·559 887	·490 767	·429 979	·376 604
1·29	·829 104	·732 407	·645 195	·567 603	·498 965	·438 424	·385 109
1·30	0·833 246	0·738 120	0·652 055	0·575 255	0·507 120	0·446 849	0·393 621
1·31	·837 309	·743 746	·658 834	·582 841	·515 229	·455 252	·402 135
1·32	·841 295	·749 287	·665 531	·590 359	·523 290	·463 629	·410 647
1·33	·845 205	·754 743	·672 147	·597 808	·531 300	·471 978	·419 153
1·34	·849 038	·760 112	·678 680	·605 185	·539 256	·480 293	·427 650
1·35	0·852 796	0·765 397	0·685 131	0·612 491	0·547 156	0·488 573	0·436 133
1·36	·856 479	·770 596	·691 497	·619 722	·554 998	·496 814	·444 599
1·37	·860 090	·775 711	·697 779	·626 878	·562 780	·505 014	·453 044
1·38	·863 628	·780 742	·703 977	·633 958	·570 499	·513 168	·461 465
1·39	·867 094	·785 688	·710 089	·640 960	·578 154	·521 276	·469 858
1·40	0·870 489	0·790 552	0·716 117	0·647 884	0·585 742	0·529 333	0·478 219
4·41	·873 814	·795 333	·722 059	·654 727	·593 262	·537 337	·486 546
1·42	·877 071	·800 031	·727 916	·661 490	·600 712	·545 286	·494 835
1·43	·880 259	·804 647	·733 688	·668 172	·608 090	·553 178	·503 084
1·44	·883 381	·809 183	·739 374	·674 771	·615 396	·561 010	·511 288
1·45	0·886 436	0·813 637	0·744 975	0·681 288	0·622 627	0·568 779	0·519 446
1·46	·889 425	·818 012	·750 490	·687 722	·629 782	·576 485	·527 554
1·47	·892 351	·822 307	·755 920	·694 071	·636 859	·584 124	·535 610
1·48	·895 213	·826 524	·761 265	·700 336	·643 859	·591 695	·543 611
1·49	·898 012	·830 663	·766 525	·706 516	·650 779	·599 197	·551 556
1·50	0·900 750	0·834 724	0·771 701	0·712 611	0·657 619	0·606 627	0·559 440

Table 7 (*continued*). *Probability integral of the extreme standardized deviate from the sample mean*

n u_n	3	4	5	6	7	8	9
1·50	0·900 750	0·834 724	0·771 701	0·712 611	0·657 619	0·606 627	0·559 440
1·51	·903 428	·838 710	·776 792	·718 621	·664 377	·613 983	·567 262
1·52	·906 045	·842 619	·781 800	·724 545	·671 053	·621 265	·575 021
1·53	·908 604	·846 453	·786 724	·730 383	·677 647	·628 471	·582 713
1·54	·911 105	·850 214	·791 565	·736 136	·684 156	·635 600	·590 337
1·55	0·913 550	0·853 901	0·796 324	0·741 803	0·690 582	0·642 650	0·597 892
1·56	·915 938	·857 515	·801 000	·747 384	·696 923	·649 620	·605 374
1·57	·918 271	·861 058	·805 595	·752 879	·703 179	·656 509	·612 783
1·58	·920 550	·864 531	·810 109	·758 289	·709 349	·663 317	·620 117
1·59	·922 775	·867 933	·814 543	·763 613	·715 433	·670 042	·627 375
1·60	0·924 949	0·871 266	0·818 897	0·768 852	0·721 431	0·676 684	0·634 555
1·61	·927 071	·874 531	·823 172	·774 007	·727 343	·683 241	·641 656
1·62	·929 142	·877 728	·827 368	·779 076	·733 169	·689 714	·648 677
1·63	·931 164	·880 859	·831 487	·784 062	·738 908	·696 101	·655 616
1·64	·933 137	·883 924	·835 529	·788 964	·744 560	·702 402	·662 473
1·65	0·935 062	0·886 925	0·839 494	0·793 783	0·750 126	0·708 617	0·669 246
1·66	·936 940	·889 862	·843 384	·798 518	·755 605	·714 745	·675 935
1·67	·938 772	·892 737	·847 199	·803 172	·760 999	·720 786	·682 540
1·68	·940 559	·895 549	·850 941	·807 743	·766 306	·726 740	·689 058
1·69	·942 301	·898 300	·854 609	·812 233	·771 527	·732 607	·695 491
1·70	0·944 000	0·900 991	0·858 205	0·816 643	0·776 663	0·738 387	0·701 837
1·71	·945 656	·903 623	·861 729	·820 973	·781 714	·744 078	·708 095
1·72	947 270	·906 197	·865 182	·825 223	·786 680	·749 683	·714 266
1·73	·948 843	·908 713	·868 566	·829 395	·791 561	·755 200	·720 349
1·74	·950 376	·911 172	·871 881	·833 488	·796 359	·760 630	·726 344
1·75	0·951 870	0·913 577	0·875 128	0·837 505	0·801 073	0·765 973	0·732 251
1·76	·953 324	·915 926	·878 308	·841 445	·805 704	·771 229	·738 069
1·77	·954 741	·918 222	·881 421	·845 309	·810 253	·776 398	·743 799
1·78	·956 121	·920 465	·884 469	·849 099	·814 720	·781 482	·749 440
1·79	·957 464	·922 656	·887 453	·852 814	·819 106	·786 479	·754 993
1·80	0·958 772	0·924 795	0·890 373	0·856 456	0·823 411	0·791 391	0·760 458
1·81	·960 045	·926 885	·893 230	·860 025	·827 637	·796 219	·765 834
1·82	·961 284	·928 925	·896 026	·863 523	·831 783	·800 961	·771 123
1·83	·962 489	·930 917	·898 760	·866 950	·835 851	·805 620	·776 324
1·84	·963 662	·932 861	·901 435	·870 308	·839 842	·810 196	·781 438
1·85	0·964 803	0·934 759	0·904 051	0·873 596	0·843 756	0·814 689	0·786 466
1·86	·965 913	·936 610	·906 608	·876 816	·847 593	·819 099	·791 407
1·87	·966 992	·938 417	·909 109	·879 969	·851 356	·823 429	·796 261
1·88	·968 042	·940 180	·911 553	·883 056	·855 044	·827 677	·801 031
1·89	·969 062	·941 899	·913 942	·886 077	·858 658	·831 846	·805 715
1·90	0·970 054	0·943 576	0·916 276	0·889 034	0·862 200	0·835 935	0·810 315
1·91	·971 018	·945 211	·918 557	·891 927	·865 670	·839 945	·814 832
1·92	·971 954	·946 805	·920 785	·894 747	·869 068	·843 878	·819 265
1·93	·972 864	·948 359	·922 962	·897 526	·872 397	·847 734	·823 616
1·94	·973 748	·949 874	·925 087	·900 234	·875 657	·851 514	·827 885
1·95	0·974 607	0·951 350	0·927 163	0·902 882	0·878 848	0·855 219	0·832 073
1·96	·975 441	·952 789	·929 189	·905 471	·881 972	·858 849	·836 181
1·97	·976 251	·954 190	·931 168	·908 002	·885 029	·862 405	·840 209
1·98	·977 037	·955 556	·933 099	·910 476	·888 021	·865 889	·844 159
1·99	·977 800	·956 886	·934 983	·912 894	·890 949	·869 301	·848 031
2·00	0·978 541	0·958 181	0·936 822	0·915 257	0·893 813	0·872 642	0·851 826

Table 7 (*continued*)

u_n \ n	3	4	5	6	7	8	9
2·00	0·978 541	0·958 181	0·936 822	0·915 257	0·893 813	0·872 642	0·851 826
2·01	·979 260	·959 442	·938 616	·917 566	·896 614	·875 913	·855 544
2·02	·979 958	·960 670	·940 366	·919 821	·899 353	·879 116	·859 188
2·03	·980 635	·961 866	·942 073	·922 023	·902 032	·882 250	·862 757
2·04	·981 291	·963 030	·943 738	·924 174	·904 650	·885 317	·866 252
2·05	0·981 928	0·964 162	0·945 362	0·926 274	0·907 210	0·888 318	0·869 675
2·06	·982 545	·965 265	·946 945	·928 325	·909 712	·891 253	·873 027
2·07	·983 144	·966 337	·948 488	·930 326	·912 157	·894 124	·876 307
2·08	·983 724	·967 380	·949 992	·932 280	·914 545	·896 932	·879 518
2·09	·984 286	·968 395	·951 458	·934 187	·916 879	·899 678	·882 661
2·10	0·984 832	0·969 382	0·952 886	0·936 047	0·919 158	0·902 362	0·885 735
2·11	·985 360	·970 342	·954 278	·937 862	·921 384	·904 986	·888 742
2·12	·985 872	·971 275	·955 633	·939 632	·923 558	·907 550	·891 684
2·13	·986 367	·972 182	·956 954	·941 359	·925 680	·910 056	·894 561
2·14	·986 847	·973 064	·958 240	·943 043	·927 752	·912 504	·897 373
2·15	0·987 312	0·973 921	0·959 493	0·944 685	0·929 775	0·914 896	0·900 123
2·16	·987 763	·974 754	·960 712	·946 286	·931 748	·917 232	·902 811
2·17	·988 198	·975 563	·961 899	·947 846	·933 674	·919 514	·905 438
2·18	·988 620	·976 349	·963 055	·949 367	·935 553	·921 741	·908 005
2·19	·989 029	·977 113	·964 180	·950 850	·937 386	·923 916	·910 513
2·20	0·989 424	0·977 855	0·965 274	0·952 294	0·939 173	0·926 040	0·912 963
2·21	·989 806	·978 575	·966 339	·953 701	·940 917	·928 112	·915 355
2·22	·990 176	·979 275	·967 375	·955 072	·942 617	·930 134	·917 692
2·23	·990 534	·979 954	·968 383	·956 407	·944 274	·932 107	·919 974
2·24	·990 880	·980 613	·969 364	·957 708	·945 890	·934 032	·922 201
2·25	0·991 214	0·981 253	0·970 317	0·958 974	0·947 465	0·935 910	0·924 375
2·26	·991 538	·981 874	·971 244	·960 207	·949 000	·937 742	·926 498
2·27	·991 851	·982 476	·972 145	·961 407	·950 496	·939 528	·928 568
2·28	·992 153	·983 061	·973 022	·962 575	·951 953	·941 270	·930 589
2·29	·992 445	·983 628	·973 873	·963 712	·953 373	·942 968	·932 560
2·30	0·992 727	0·984 178	0·974 701	0·964 819	0·954 756	0·944 623	0·934 483
2·31	·992 999	·984 711	·975 505	·965 896	·956 102	·946 236	·936 358
2·32	·993 263	·985 228	·976 287	·966 943	·957 414	·947 808	·938 187
2·33	·993 517	·985 730	·977 046	·967 962	·958 691	·949 340	·939 970
2·34	·993 763	·986 216	·977 784	·968 953	·959 934	·950 832	·941 708
2·35	0·994 000	0·986 687	0·978 500	0·969 916	0·961 144	0·952 286	0·943 402
2·36	·994 229	·987 144	·979 196	·970 853	·962 322	·953 702	·945 053
2·37	·994 450	·987 587	·979 871	·971 765	·963 468	·955 081	·946 662
2·38	·994 663	·988 015	·980 527	·972 650	·964 583	·956 424	·948 230
2·39	·994 869	·988 431	·981 164	·973 511	·965 668	·957 732	·949 758
2·40	0·995 067	0·988 833	0·981 782	0·974 348	0·966 723	0·959 005	0·951 245
2·41	·995 259	·989 223	·982 381	·975 161	·967 750	·960 243	·952 694
2·42	·995 443	·989 600	·982 963	·975 951	·968 748	·961 449	·954 105
2·43	·995 621	·989 966	·983 528	·976 718	·969 719	·962 622	·955 479
2·44	·995 793	·990 320	·984 075	·977 464	·970 663	·963 764	·956 817
2·45	0·995 959	0·990 662	0·984 607	0·978 188	0·971 581	0·964 875	0·958 119
2·46	·996 118	·990 993	·985 122	·978 891	·972 473	·965 955	·959 386
2·47	·996 272	·991 314	·985 622	·979 574	·973 340	·967 006	·960 620
2·48	·996 420	·991 625	·986 106	·980 237	·974 183	·968 028	·961 820
2·49	·996 563	·991 925	·986 576	·980 881	·975 001	·969 021	·962 987
2·50	0·996 701	0·992 215	0·987 031	0·981 505	0·975 797	0·969 987	0·964 123

u_n \ n	3	4	5	6	7	8	9
2·50	0·996 701	0·992 215	0·987 031	0·981 505	0·975 797	0·969 987	0·964 123
2·51	·996 833	·992 496	·987 473	·982 112	·976 569	·970 926	·965 228
2·52	·996 961	·992 768	·987 901	·982 700	·977 320	·971 839	·966 303
2·53	·997 084	·993 031	·988 315	·983 271	·978 049	·972 726	·967 347
2·54	·997 202	·993 285	·988 717	·983 825	·978 757	·973 588	·968 363
2·55	0·997 316	0·993 530	0·989 106	0·984 362	0·979 444	0·974 426	0·969 351
2·56	·997 425	·993 768	·989 483	·984 883	·980 111	·975 240	·970 311
2·57	·997 531	·993 997	·989 848	·985 389	·980 759	·976 030	·971 244
2·58	·997 632	·994 219	·990 201	·985 879	·981 387	·976 798	·972 151
2·59	·997 730	·994 433	·990 544	·986 354	·981 998	·977 544	·973 032
2·60	0·997 824	0·994 640	0·990 875	0·986 815	0·982 590	0·978 268	0·973 889
2·61	·997 914	·994 840	·991 196	·987 261	·983 164	·978 971	·974 720
2·62	·998 001	·995 033	·991 506	·987 694	·983 721	·979 653	·975 528
2·63	·998 084	·995 219	·991 807	·988 113	·984 262	·980 316	·976 313
2·64	·998 165	·995 399	·992 098	·988 520	·984 786	·980 959	·977 074
2·65	0·998 242	0·995 573	0·992 379	0·988 914	0·985 294	0·981 583	0·977 814
2·66	·998 316	·995 740	·992 651	·989 295	·985 787	·982 188	·978 533
2·67	·998 387	·995 902	·992 915	·989 665	·986 265	·982 776	·979 230
2·68	·998 456	·996 058	·993 169	·990 022	·986 728	·983 346	·979 907
2·69	·998 521	·996 209	·993 416	·990 369	·987 178	·983 898	·980 563
2·70	0·998 585	0·996 355	0·993 654	0·990 705	0·987 613	0·984 434	0·981 201
2·71	·998 645	·996 495	·993 884	·991 029	·988 035	·984 954	·981 819
2·72	·998 703	·996 630	·994 107	·991 344	·988 443	·985 458	·982 419
2·73	·998 759	·996 761	·994 322	·991 648	·988 839	·985 947	·983 001
2·74	·998 813	·996 886	·994 530	·991 943	·989 223	·986 421	·983 566
2·75	0·998 865	0·997 008	0·994 731	0·992 228	0·989 594	0·986 880	0·984 113
2·76	·998 914	·997 125	·994 925	·992 504	·989 954	·987 325	·984 644
2·77	·998 961	·997 237	·995 112	·992 771	·990 303	·987 756	·985 159
2·78	·999 007	·997 346	·995 293	·993 029	·990 640	·988 174	·985 658
2·79	·999 050	·997 451	·995 468	·993 279	·990 967	·988 579	·986 141
2·80	0·999 092	0·997 551	0·995 637	0·993 520	0·991 283	0·988 971	0·986 610
2·81	·999 132	·997 649	·995 800	·993 754	·991 589	·989 351	·987 064
2·82	·999 171	·997 742	·995 958	·993 979	·991 885	·989 719	·987 505
2·83	·999 208	·997 832	·996 110	·994 198	·992 172	·990 075	·987 931
2·84	·999 243	·997 919	·996 257	·994 408	·992 449	·990 420	·988 344
2·85	0·999 277	0·998 003	0·996 399	0·994 612	0·992 717	0·990 754	0·988 745
2·86	·999 309	·998 083	·996 535	·994 809	·992 977	·991 077	·989 132
2·87	·999 340	·998 161	·996 667	·995 000	·993 228	·991 390	·989 508
2·88	·999 370	·998 235	·996 795	·995 184	·993 471	·991 693	·989 871
2·89	·999 399	·998 307	·996 917	·995 361	·993 705	·991 986	·990 223
2·90	0·999 426	0·998 376	0·997 036	0·995 533	0·993 932	0·992 269	0·990 564
2·91	·999 452	·998 442	·997 150	·995 699	·994 152	·992 543	·990 894
2·92	·999 477	·998 506	·997 260	·995 859	·994 364	·992 809	·991 213
2·93	·999 501	·998 568	·997 366	·996 014	·994 569	·993 065	·991 522
2·94	·999 524	·998 627	·997 469	·996 163	·994 767	·993 314	·991 821
2·95	0·999 546	0·998 683	0·997 567	0·996 307	0·994 959	0·993 554	0·992 111
2·96	·999 567	·998 738	·997 663	·996 446	·995 143	·993 786	·992 390
2·97	·999 587	·998 790	·997 754	·996 580	·995 322	·994 010	·992 661
2·98	·999 606	·998 841	·997 842	·996 710	·995 495	·994 227	·992 923
2·99	·999 625	·998 889	·997 928	·996 835	·995 662	·994 437	·993 176
3·00	0·999 642	0·998 936	0·998 010	0·996 955	0·995 823	0·994 639	0·993 421

Table 7 (continued)

n u_n	3	4	5	6	7	8	9
3·00	0·999 642	0·998 936	0·998 010	0·996 955	0·995 823	0·994 639	0·993 421
3·01	·999 659	·998 981	·998 088	·997 072	·995 978	·994 835	·993 658
3·02	·999 675	·999 024	·998 164	·997 184	·996 128	·995 024	·993 887
3·03	·999 690	·999 065	·998 238	·997 292	·996 273	·995 207	·994 108
3·04	·999 705	·999 105	·998 308	·997 396	·996 413	·995 383	·994 322
3·05	0·999 719	0·999 143	0·998 376	0·997 497	0·996 548	0·995 554	0·994 528
3·06	·999 732	·999 179	·998 441	·997 594	·996 678	·995 718	·994 728
3·07	·999 745	·999 215	·998 504	·997 687	·996 804	·995 877	·994 921
3·08	·999 757	·999 248	·998 565	·997 777	·996 925	·996 031	·995 107
3·09	·999 769	·999 281	·998 623	·997 864	·997 043	·996 179	·995 287
3·10	0·999 780	0·999 312	0·998 679	0·997 948	0·997 155	0·996 322	0·995 461
3·11	·999 791	·999 341	·998 733	·998 029	·997 264	·996 460	·995 629
3·12	·999 801	·999 370	·998 785	·998 106	·997 369	·996 594	·995 792
3·13	·999 810	·999 397	·998 834	·998 181	·997 471	·996 722	·995 948
3·14	·999 820	·999 424	·998 882	·998 253	·997 568	·996 846	·996 099
3·15	0·999 829	0·999 449	0·998 929	0·998 322	0·997 662	0·996 966	0·996 245
3·16	·999 837	·999 473	·998 973	·998 389	·997 753	·997 082	·996 386
3·17	·999 845	·999 496	·999 015	·998 454	·997 840	·997 193	·996 522
3·18	·999 853	·999 519	·999 056	·998 515	·997 925	·997 301	·996 653
3·19	·999 860	·999 540	·999 096	·998 575	·998 006	·997 404	·996 780
3·20	0·999 867	0·999 560	0·999 134	0·998 632	0·998 084	0·997 504	0·996 902
3·21	·999 873	·999 580	·999 170	·998 688	·998 159	·997 600	·997 020
3·22	·999 880	·999 599	·999 205	·998 741	·998 232	·997 693	·997 133
3·23	·999 886	·999 617	·999 238	·998 792	·998 302	·997 783	·997 243
3·24	·999 891	·999 634	·999 270	·998 841	·998 369	·997 869	·997 349
3·25	0·999 897	0·999 650	0·999 301	0·998 888	0·998 434	0·997 952	0·997 451
3·26	·999 902	·999 666	·999 331	·998 934	·998 497	·998 032	·997 549
3·27	·999 907	·999 681	·999 359	·998 978	·998 557	·998 109	·997 644
3·28	·999 912	·999 696	·999 387	·999 020	·998 615	·998 184	·997 735
3·29	·999 916	·999 709	·999 413	·999 060	·998 670	·998 255	·997 823
3·30	0·999 920	0·999 723	0·999 438	0·999 099	0·998 724	0·998 324	0·997 908
3·31	·999 924	·999 735	·999 462	·999 136	·998 775	·998 391	·997 989
3·32	·999 928	·999 747	·999 486	·999 172	·998 825	·998 455	·998 068
3·33	·999 932	·999 759	·999 508	·999 207	·998 873	·998 516	·998 144
3·34	·999 935	·999 770	·999 529	·999 240	·998 919	·998 575	·998 217
3·35	0·999 939	0·999 781	0·999 550	0·999 272	0·998 963	0·998 633	0·998 287
3·36	·999 942	·999 791	·999 569	·999 302	·999 005	·998 687	·998 355
3·37	·999 945	·999 801	·999 588	·999 332	·999 046	·998 740	·998 420
3·38	·999 948	·999 810	·999 606	·999 360	·999 085	·998 791	·998 483
3·39	·999 951	·999 819	·999 624	·999 387	·999 123	·998 840	·998 544
3·40	0·999 953	0·999 827	0·999 640	0·999 413	0·999 159	0·998 887	0·998 602
3·41	·999 956	·999 835	·999 656	·999 438	·999 194	·998 932	·998 658
3·42	·999 958	·999 843	·999 671	·999 462	·999 228	·998 976	·998 712
3·43	·999 960	·999 850	·999 686	·999 485	·999 260	·999 018	·998 764
3·44	·999 962	·999 857	·999 700	·999 507	·999 291	·999 058	·998 813
3·45	0·999 964	0·999 864	0·999 713	0·999 528	0·999 320	0·999 097	0·998 862
3·46	·999 966	·999 871	·999 726	·999 549	·999 349	·999 134	·998 908
3·47	·999 968	·999 877	·999 738	·999 568	·999 376	·999 169	·998 952
3·48	·999 970	·999 883	·999 750	·999 587	·999 403	·999 204	·998 995
3·49	·999 971	·999 888	·999 761	·999 605	·999 428	·999 237	·999 036
3·50	0·999 973	0·999 894	0·999 772	0·999 622	0·999 452	0·999 269	0·999 076

u_n \ n	3	4	5	6	7	8	9
3·50	0·999 973	0·999 894	0·999 772	0·999 622	0·999 452	0·999 269	0·999 076
3·55	·999 979	·999 917	·999 820	·999 698	·999 560	·999 410	·999 251
3·60	·999 985	·999 935	·999 858	·999 759	·999 647	·999 525	·999 395
3·65	·999 988	·999 950	·999 888	·999 809	·999 718	·999 618	·999 513
3·70	·999 991	·999 961	·999 912	·999 848	·999 775	·999 694	·999 609
3·75	0·999 994	0·999 970	0·999 931	0·999 880	0·999 821	0·999 756	0·999 686
3·80	·999 995	·999 977	·999 946	·999 906	·999 858	·999 806	·999 749
3·85	·999 996	·999 982	·999 958	·999 926	·999 888	·999 846	·999 800
3·90	·999 997	·999 987	·999 968	·999 942	·999 912	·999 878	·999 841
3·95	·999 998	·999 990	·999 975	·999 955	·999 931	·999 903	·999 874
4·00	0·999 999	0·999 992	0·999 981	0·999 965	0·999 946	0·999 924	0·999 900
4·05	·999 999	·999 994	·999 985	·999 973	·999 958	·999 940	·999 921
4·10	·999 999	·999 996	·999 989	·999 979	·999 967	·999 953	·999 938
4·15	1·000 000	·999 997	·999 991	·999 984	·999 975	·999 963	·999 951
4·20		·999 997	·999 993	·999 987	·999 980	·999 971	·999 962
4·25		0·999 998	0·999 995	0·999 990	0·999 985	0·999 978	0·999 970
4·30		·999 999	·999 996	·999 993	·999 988	·999 983	·999 977
4·35		·999 999	·999 997	·999 994	·999·991	·999 987	999 982
4·40		·999 999	·999 998	·999 996	·999 993	·999 990	·999 986
4·45		·999 999	·999 998	·999 997	·999 995	·999 992	·999 989
4·50		0·999 999	0·999 999	0·999 998	0·999 996	0·999 994	0·999 992
4·55		1·000 000	·999 999	·999 998	·999 997	·999 995	·999 993
4·60			1·000 000	·999 999	·999 998	·999 996	·999 995
4·65				·999 999	·999 999	·999 997	·999 996
4·70				·999 999	·999 999	·999 998	·999 997

u_n \ n	10	11	12	13	14	15	16	17
0·25	0·00001	0·00000						
·30	·00003	·00001	0·00000	0·00000				
·35	·00011	·00004	·00001	·00001	0·00000			
·40	·00032	·00013	·00005	·00002	·00001	0·00000	0·00000	
·45	·00080	·00036	·00016	·00007	·00003	·00001	·00001	0·00000
0·50	0·00176	0·00086	0·00042	0·00021	0·00010	0·00005	0·00002	0·00001
·55	·00351	·00185	·00098	·00051	·00027	·00014	·00008	·00004
·60	·00643	·00363	·00204	·00115	·00065	·00037	·00021	·00012
·65	·01098	·00657	·00393	·00235	·00141	·00084	·00050	·00030
·70	·01766	·01113	·00702	·00443	·00279	·00176	·00111	·00070
0·75	0·02694	0·01780	0·01177	0·00777	0·00514	0·00339	0·00224	0·00148
·80	·03928	·02707	·01865	·01285	·00886	·00610	·00420	·00289
·85	·05503	·03938	·02818	·02016	·01442	·01031	·00738	·00527
·90	·07444	·05510	·04077	·03017	·02232	·01652	·01222	·00904
·95	·09761	·07448	·05682	·04334	·03305	·02521	·01922	·01466
1·00	0·12452	0·09763	0·07655	0·06000	0·04703	0·03687	0·02889	0·02265
1·05	·15497	·12454	·10008	·08041	·06460	·05190	·04169	·03348
1·10	·18867	·15503	·12737	·10464	·08595	·07060	·05799	·04762
1·15	·22520	·18879	·15825	·13263	·11116	·09315	·07806	·06541
1·20	·26407	·22542	·19240	·16420	·14013	·11957	·10203	·08706

Table 7 (*continued*)

u_n \ n	10	11	12	13	14	15	16	17
1·25	0·30475	0·26442	0·22941	0·19901	0·17263	0·14973	0·12987	0·11264
1·30	·34666	·30525	·26876	·23662	·20830	·18336	·16140	·14207
1·35	·38924	·34734	·30992	·27650	·24667	·22005	·19629	·17509
1·40	·43196	·39011	·35229	·31810	·28721	·25931	·23411	·21135
1·45	·47430	·43302	·39529	·36082	·32934	·30058	·27433	·25036
1·50	0·51583	0·47555	0·43838	0·40408	0·37244	0·34327	0·31636	0·29156
1·55	·55615	·51726	·48104	·44733	·41595	·38676	·35960	·33434
1·60	·59495	·55774	·52282	·49004	·45930	·43046	·40342	·37807
1·65	·63196	·59668	·56332	·53178	·50199	·47384	·44726	·42216
1·70	·66699	·63380	·60221	·57216	·54358	·51641	·49058	·46602
1·75	0·69991	0·66892	0·63925	0·61086	0·58370	0·55773	0·53289	0·50915
1·80	·73063	·70189	·67424	·64763	·62204	·59744	·57380	·55108
1·85	·75912	·73264	·70704	·68229	·65838	·63528	·61297	·59144
1·90	·78538	·76113	·73758	·71472	·69254	·67102	·65016	·62992
1·95	·80945	·78737	·76584	·74486	·72443	·70453	·68516	·66630
2·00	0·83141	0·81140	0·79183	0·77269	0·75399	0·73571	0·71786	0·70042
2·05	·85133	·83330	·81560	·79824	·78121	·76453	·74819	·73218
2·10	·86932	·85314	·83721	·82155	·80614	·79101	·77614	·76153
2·15	·88550	·87105	·85678	·84271	·82885	·81519	·80174	·78849
2·20	·89998	·88713	·87440	·86183	·84941	·83715	·82505	·81311
2·25	0·91290	0·90151	0·89021	0·87902	0·86795	0·85699	0·84616	0·83545
2·30	·92437	·91431	·90432	·89441	·88458	·87484	·86518	·85563
2·35	·93453	·92568	·91688	·90812	·89943	·89081	·88224	·87375
2·40	·94348	·93572	·92799	·92030	·91264	·90504	·89748	·88997
2·45	·95134	·94457	·93781	·93106	·92435	·91766	·91101	·90440
2·50	0·95823	0·95233	0·94644	0·94055	0·93468	0·92883	0·92300	0·91720
2·55	·96424	·95912	·95400	·94887	·94376	·93866	·93357	·92850
2·60	·96948	·96504	·96060	·95616	·95172	·94728	·94285	·93844
2·65	·97401	·97019	·96635	·96251	·95866	·95482	·95098	·94715
2·70	·97793	·97464	·97134	·96802	·96471	·96139	·95807	·95475
2·75	0·98131	0·97849	0·97565	0·97280	0·96995	0·96709	0·96423	0·96137
2·80	·98422	·98180	·97937	·97693	·97448	·97203	·96957	·96712
2·85	·98671	·98464	·98257	·98048	·97839	·97629	·97418	·97208
2·90	·98883	·98708	·98531	·98353	·98174	·97995	·97816	·97636
2·95	·99064	·98915	·98765	·98614	·98462	·98309	·98156	·98003
3·00	0·99218	0·99092	0·98965	0·98837	0·98708	0·98578	0·98448	0·98318
3·05	·99348	·99242	·99134	·99026	·98917	·98807	·98697	·98587
3·10	·99458	·99369	·99278	·99187	·99095	·99002	·98909	·98816
3·15	·99551	·99476	·99400	·99323	·99245	·99167	·99089	·99010
3·20	·99628	·99566	·99502	·99437	·99372	·99307	·99241	·99175
3·25	0·99694	0·99641	0·99588	0·99534	0·99479	0·99424	0·99369	0·99314
3·30	·99748	·99704	·99660	·99615	·99569	·99523	·99477	·99431
3·35	·99793	·99757	·99720	·99682	·99644	·99606	·99568	·99529
3·40	·99831	·99801	·99770	·99739	·99707	·99676	·99644	·99611
3·45	·99862	·99837	·99812	·99786	·99760	·99733	·99707	·99680
3·50	0·99888	0·99867	0·99846	0·99825	0·99803	0·99781	0·99759	0·99737
3·55	·99909	·99892	·99875	·99857	·99839	·99821	·99803	·99785
3·60	·99926	·99912	·99898	·99884	·99869	·99854	·99839	·99824
3·65	·99940	·99929	·99917	·99906	·99894	·99881	·99869	·99857
3·70	·99952	·99943	·99933	·99924	·99914	·99904	·99894	·99883
3·75	0·99961	0·99954	0·99946	0·99938	0·99930	0·99922	0·99914	0·99905
3·80	·99969	·99963	·99957	·99950	·99944	·99937	·99930	·99923
3·85	·99975	·99970	·99965	·99960	·99955	·99949	·99944	·99938
3·90	·99980	·99976	·99972	·99968	·99964	·99959	·99955	·99950
3·95	·99984	·99981	·99978	·99974	·99971	·99967	·99964	·99960

Table 7 (*continued*). *Probability integral of the extreme standardized deviate from the sample mean*

u_n \\ n	10	11	12	13	14	15	16	17
4·00	0·99988	0·99985	0·99982	0·99980	0·99977	0·99974	0·99971	0·99968
4·05	·99990	·99988	·99986	·99984	·99982	·99979	·99977	·99974
4·10	·99992	·99991	·99989	·99987	·99985	·99983	·99981	·99979
4·15	·99994	·99993	·99991	·99990	·99988	·99987	·99985	·99984
4·20	·99995	·99994	·99993	·99992	·99991	·99990	·99988	·99987
4·25	0·99996	0·99995	0·99995	0·99994	0·99993	0·99992	0·99991	0·99990
4·30	·99997	·99996	·99996	·99995	·99994	·99993	·99993	·99992
4·35	·99998	·99997	·99997	·99996	·99996	·99995	·99994	·99993
4·40	·99998	·99998	·99997	·99997	·99996	·99996	·99995	·99995
4·45	·99999	·99998	·99998	·99998	·99997	·99997	·99996	·99996
4·50	0·99999	0·99999	0·99998	0·99998	0·99998	0·99998	0·99997	0·99997
4·55	·99999	·99999	·99999	·99999	·99998	·99998	·99998	·99997
4·60	·99999	·99999	·99999	·99999	·99999	·99998	·99998	·99998
4·65	1·00000	·99999	·99999	·99999	·99999	·99999	·99999	·99998
4·70		1·00000	·99999	·99999	·99999	·99999	·99999	·99999
4·75			1·00000	1·00000	0·99999	0·99999	0·99999	0·99999
4·80					1·00000	·99999	·99999	·99999
4·85						1·00000	1·00000	1·00000

u_n \\ n	18	19	20	21	22	23	24	25
0·50	0·00001	0·00000						
·55	·00002	·00001						
·60	·00007	·00004	0·0000					
·65	·00018	·00011	·0001	0·0000	0·0000			
·70	·00044	·00028	·0002	·0001	·0001	0·0000	0·0000	0·0000
0·75	0·00098	0·00065	0·0004	0·0003	0·0002	0·0001	0·0001	0·0001
·80	·00199	·00137	·0009	·0007	·0004	·0003	·0002	·0001
·85	·00377	·00270	·0019	·0014	·0010	·0007	·0005	·0004
·90	·00669	·00494	·0037	·0027	·0020	·0015	·0011	·0008
·95	·01118	·00853	·0065	·0049	·0038	·0029	·0022	·0017
1·00	0·01775	0·01391	0·0109	0·0085	0·0067	0·0052	0·0041	0·0032
1·05	·02690	·02161	·0174	·0139	·0112	·0090	·0072	·0058
1·10	·03911	·03212	·0264	·0217	·0178	·0146	·0120	·0099
1·15	·05481	·04592	·0385	·0322	·0270	·0226	·0190	·0159
1·20	·07428	·06338	·0541	·0461	·0394	·0336	·0287	·0244
1·25	0·09769	0·08472	0·0735	0·0637	0·0553	0·0479	0·0416	0·0360
1·30	·12504	·11005	·0969	·0853	·0750	·0660	·0581	·0512
1·35	·15618	·13930	·1242	·1108	·0988	·0882	·0786	·0701
1·40	·19080	·17225	·1555	·1404	·1267	·1144	·1033	·0932
1·45	·22848	·20851	·1903	·1736	·1585	·1446	·1320	·1204
1·50	0·26869	0·24761	0·2282	0·2103	0·1938	0·1786	0·1646	0·1516
1·55	·31084	·28899	·2687	·2498	·2322	·2159	·2007	·1866
1·60	·35430	·33202	·3111	·2916	·2732	·2560	·2399	·2248
1·65	·39845	·37607	·3549	·3349	·3162	·2984	·2816	·2658
1·70	·44269	·42052	·3994	·3794	·3604	·3424	·3252	·3089
1·75	0·48645	0·46476	0·4440	0·4242	0·4053	0·3872	0·3699	0·3534
1·80	·52924	·50827	·4881	·4687	·4502	·4323	·4152	·3987
1·85	·57065	·55058	·5312	·5125	·4945	·4771	·4603	·4441
1·90	·61031	·59130	·5729	·5549	·5377	·5209	·5047	·4890
1·95	·64796	·63011	·6127	·5958	·5794	·5634	·5479	·5328

Table 7 (*continued*)

n / u_n	18	19	20	21	22	23	24	25
2·00	0·68340	0·66678	0·6506	0·6348	0·6193	0·6042	0·5895	0·5752
2·05	·71650	·70114	·6861	·6714	·6570	·6429	·6291	·6156
2·10	·74719	·73311	·7193	·7058	·6924	·6793	·6665	·6540
2·15	·77545	·76262	·7500	·7375	·7254	·7133	·7015	·6899
2·20	·80132	·78971	·7782	·7670	·7558	·7448	·7340	·7234
2·25	0·82486	0·81440	0·8041	0·7938	0·7838	0·7738	0·7640	0·7543
2·30	·84616	·83679	·8275	·8184	·8093	·8003	·7914	·7827
2·35	·86533	·85699	·8487	·8405	·8324	·8244	·8164	·8085
2·40	·88251	·87511	·8678	·8605	·8533	·8461	·8390	·8319
2·45	·89783	·89129	·8848	·8784	·8720	·8656	·8593	·8530
2·50	0·91142	0·90568	0·9000	0·8943	0·8887	0·8831	0·8775	0·8719
2·55	·92345	·91842	·9134	·9084	·9035	·8985	·8936	·8888
2·60	·93404	·92965	·9253	·9209	·9166	·9123	·9080	·9037
2·65	·94332	·93951	·9357	·9319	·9282	·9244	·9207	·9169
2·70	·95144	·94814	·9448	·9416	·9382	·9351	·9318	·9286
2·75	0·95852	0·95567	0·9528	0·9500	0·9472	0·9444	0·9415	0·9387
2·80	·96466	·96220	·9598	·9573	·9549	·9524	·9500	·9476
2·85	·96997	·96787	·9658	·9637	·9616	·9595	·9574	·9553
2·90	·97456	·97275	·9710	·9692	·9674	·9656	·9638	·9620
2·95	·97850	·97696	·9754	·9739	·9724	·9709	·9693	·9678
3·00	0·98187	0·98057	0·9793	0·9780	0·9767	0·9753	0·9741	0·9728
3·05	·98476	·98365	·9825	·9814	·9803	·9793	·9781	·9771
3·10	·98722	·98629	·9853	·9844	·9835	·9826	·9816	·9807
3·15	·98931	·98852	·9877	·9869	·9862	·9853	·9846	·9838
3·20	·99108	·99042	·9898	·9891	·9884	·9878	·9871	·9865
3·25	0·99258	0·99202	0·9915	0·9909	0·9904	0·9898	0·9893	0·9887
3·30	·99384	·99337	·9929	·9924	·9920	·9915	·9911	·9906
3·35	·99490	·99451	·9941	·9937	·9933	·9930	·9926	·9922
3·40	·99579	·99546	·9951	·9948	·9945	·9942	·9939	·9936
3·45	·99653	·99626	·9960	·9957	·9955	·9952	·9949	·9947
3·50	0·99715	0·99693	0·9967	0·9965	0·9963	0·9961	0·9958	0·9956
3·55	·99766	·99748	·9973	·9971	·9969	·9968	·9966	·9964
3·60	·99809	·99794	·9978	·9976	·9975	·9973	·9972	·9971
3·65	·99844	·99832	·9982	·9981	·9979	·9978	·9977	·9976
3·70	·99873	·99863	·9985	·9984	·9983	·9982	·9982	·9981
3·75	0·99897	0·99889	0·9988	0·9987	0·9986	0·9986	0·9985	0·9984
3·80	·99917	·99910	·9990	·9990	·9989	·9988	·9988	·9988
3·85	·99933	·99927	·9992	·9992	·9991	·9991	·9990	·9990
3·90	·99946	·99941	·9994	·9993	·9993	·9993	·9992	·9992
3·95	·99956	·99953	·9995	·9995	·9994	·9994	·9994	·9994
4·00	0·99965	0·99962	0·9996	0·9996	0·9995	0·9995	0·9995	0·9995
4·05	·99972	·99969	·9997	·9996	·9996	·9996	·9996	·9996
4·10	·99977	·99975	·9997	·9997	·9997	·9997	·9997	·9997
4·15	·99982	·99980	·9998	·9998	·9998	·9998	·9998	·9998
4·20	·99986	·99984	·9998	·9998	·9998	·9998	·9998	·9998
4·25	0·99989	·99987	0·9999	0·9999	0·9999	0·9999	0·9999	0·9999
4·30	·99991	·99990	·9999	·9999	·9999	·9999	·9999	·9999
4·35	·99993	·99992	·9999	·9999	·9999	·9999	·9999	·9999
4·40	·99994	·99994	·9999	·9999	·9999	·9999	·9999	·9999
4·45	·99995	·99995	1·0000	·9999	·9999	·9999	·9999	·9999
4·50	0·99996	0·99996		1·0000	1·0000	1·0000	0·9999	0·9999
4·55	·99997	·99997					1·0000	1·0000
4·60	·99998	·99997						
4·65	·99998	·99998						
4·70	·99998	·99998						
4·75	0·99999	0·99998						
4·80	·99999	·99999						
4·85	·99999	·99999						
4·90	1·00000	1·00000						

Table 8. *Probability integral of the mean deviation, m, from the sample mean*

m \ n	2	3	4	5	6	7	8	9	10
0·00	0·00000	0·00000							
·01	·01128	·00019	0·00000						
·02	·02256	·00074	·00003	0·00000					
·03	·03384	·00167	·00009	·00001					
·04	·04511	·00297	·00022	·00002					
0·05	0·05637	0·00464	0·00042	0·00004	0·00000				
·06	·06762	·00668	·00073	·00009	·00001				
·07	·07886	·00908	·00115	·00016	·00002	0·00000			
·08	·09008	·01184	·00172	·00027	·00004	·00001			
·09	·10128	·01496	·00244	·00042	·00007	·00001			
0·10	0·11246	0·01843	0·00333	0·00064	0·00012	0·00002	0·00000		
·11	·12362	·02226	·00442	·00093	·00019	·00004	·00001		
·12	·13476	·02644	·00571	·00130	·00030	·00007	·00002	0·00000	
·13	·14587	·03095	·00723	·00178	·00044	·00011	·00003	·00001	
·14	·15695	·03581	·00899	·00237	·00064	·00017	·00005	·00001	0·00000
0·15	0·16800	0·04100	0·01101	0·00310	0·00089	0·00026	0·00008	0·00002	0·00001
·16	·17901	·04651	·01329	·00398	·00122	·00037	·00012	·00004	·00001
·17	·18999	·05234	·01585	·00503	·00163	·00053	·00018	·00006	·00002
·18	·20094	·05849	·01871	·00626	·00214	·00074	·00026	·00009	·00003
·19	·21184	·06495	·02187	·00770	·00277	·00101	·00038	·00014	·00005
0·20	0·22270	0·07171	0·02534	0·00936	0·00354	0·00135	0·00053	0·00021	0·00008
·21	·23352	·07876	·02914	·01126	·00445	·00179	·00073	·00030	·00012
·22	·24430	·08610	·03327	·01342	·00554	·00232	·00099	·00042	·00018
·23	·25502	·09371	·03773	·01585	·00682	·00297	·00132	·00059	·00026
·24	·26570	·10160	·04254	·01858	·00830	·00377	·00173	·00080	·00037
0·25	0·27633	0·10974	0·04769	0·02161	0·01002	0·00472	0·00225	0·00108	0·00052
·26	·28690	·11814	·05320	·02497	·01199	·00585	·00289	·00143	·00072
·27	·29742	·12679	·05907	·02867	·01423	·00717	·00366	·00188	·00097
·28	·30788	·13567	·06528	·03271	·01677	·00873	·00459	·00244	·00130
·29	·31828	·14478	·07186	·03713	·01962	·01052	·00571	·00312	·00172
0·30	0·32863	0·15410	0·07879	0·04192	0·02280	0·01259	0·00703	0·00395	0·00224
·31	·33891	·16364	·08608	·04709	·02634	·01495	·00858	·00496	·00289
·32	·34913	·17337	·09372	·05266	·03025	·01763	·01039	·00616	·00368
·33	·35928	·18330	·10171	·05864	·03455	·02065	·01248	·00759	·00465
·34	·36936	·19340	·11005	·06503	·03926	·02404	·01488	·00928	·00582
0·35	0·37938	0·20367	0·11872	0·07183	0·04439	0·02783	0·01762	0·01124	0·00722
·36	·38933	·21410	·12773	·07905	·04996	·03202	·02073	·01352	·00887
·37	·39921	·22469	·13706	·08670	·05598	·03666	·02424	·01615	·01082
·38	·40901	·23541	·14671	·09476	·06247	·04175	·02817	·01915	·01309
·39	·41874	·24626	·15667	·10325	·06942	·04731	·03256	·02257	·01573
0·40	0·42839	0·25724	0·16693	0·11215	0·07686	0·05338	0·03742	0·02643	0·01877
·41	·43797	·26832	·17748	·12147	·08478	·05995	·04279	·03076	·02224
·42	·44747	·27951	·18831	·13120	·09319	·06705	·04869	·03560	·02618
·43	·45689	·29079	·19941	·14133	·10209	·07468	·05513	·04099	·03063
·44	·46623	·30215	·21075	·15186	·11148	·08286	·06215	·04693	·03563
0·45	0·47548	0·31358	0·22234	0·16277	0·12136	0·09160	0·06975	0·05347	0·04121
·46	·48466	·32507	·23416	·17405	·13172	·10089	·07796	·06063	·04741
·47	·49375	·33661	·24620	·18569	·14255	·11074	·08677	·06843	·05425
·48	·50275	·34820	·25843	·19768	·15386	·12115	·09621	·07689	·06177
·49	·51167	·35982	·27086	·21001	·16562	·13212	·10627	·08602	·06998
0·50	0·52050	0·37146	0·28345	0·22265	0·17783	0·14364	0·11697	0·09584	0·07892

Table 8 (*continued*)

m \ n	2	3	4	5	6	7	8	9	10
0·50	0·52050	0·37146	0·28345	0·22265	0·17783	0·14364	0·11697	0·09584	0·07892
·51	·52924	·38313	·29620	·23559	·19047	·15569	·12829	·10635	·08860
·52	·53790	·39479	·30909	·24881	·20352	·16828	·14023	·11756	·09903
·53	·54646	·40646	·32211	·26230	·21697	·18137	·15279	·12947	·11022
·54	·55494	·41811	·33525	·27604	·23079	·19497	·16595	·14207	·12218
0·55	0·56332	0·42975	0·34847	0·28999	0·24497	0·20904	0·17970	0·15536	0·13491
·56	·57162	·44135	·36178	·30416	·25948	·22357	·19402	·16931	·14840
·57	·57982	·45293	·37516	·31851	·27430	·23852	·20889	·18392	·16264
·58	·58792	·46446	·38858	·33302	·28941	·25389	·22427	·19916	·17761
·59	·59594	·47593	·40204	·34768	·30477	·26963	·24016	·21501	·19329
0·60	0·60386	0·48735	0·41552	0·36245	0·32037	0·28572	0·25650	0·23144	0·20965
·61	·61168	·49871	·42901	·37733	·33617	·30213	·27328	·24840	·22667
·62	·61941	·50999	·44249	·39228	·35215	·31882	·29046	·26588	·24431
·63	·62705	·52120	·45594	·40729	·36827	·33576	·30799	·28383	·26252
·64	·63459	·53232	·46936	·42233	·38452	·35293	·32585	·30220	·28127
0·65	0·64203	0·54335	0·48273	0·43739	0·40087	0·37027	0·34398	0·32095	0·30050
·66	·64938	·55428	·49603	·45244	·41727	·38777	·36235	·34004	·32016
·67	·65663	·56511	·50926	·46746	·43372	·40537	·38092	·35941	·34021
·68	·66378	·57583	·52240	·48244	·45017	·42306	·39965	·37902	·36058
·69	·67084	·58644	·53544	·49734	·46661	·44078	·41848	·39882	·38122
0·70	0·67780	0·59693	0·54836	0·51217	0·48300	0·45852	0·43739	0·41875	0·40206
·71	·68467	·60729	·56117	·52689	·49932	·47623	·45632	·43877	·42306
·72	·69143	·61753	·57384	·54148	·51555	·49388	·47523	·45882	·44414
·73	·69810	·62764	·58637	·55594	·53166	·51143	·49409	·47886	·46525
·74	·70468	·63762	·59874	·57025	·54762	·52886	·51284	·49883	·48634
0·75	0·71116	0·64745	0·61096	0·58439	0·56342	0·54614	0·53147	0·51868	0·50735
·76	·71754	·65714	·62300	·59834	·57903	·56324	·54992	·53838	·52821
·77	·72382	·66669	·63487	·61210	·59443	·58012	·56816	·55788	·54888
·78	·73001	·67609	·64655	·62564	·60961	·59677	·58616	·57713	·56930
·79	·73610	·68534	·65804	·63897	·62454	·61316	·60388	·59609	·58943
0·80	0·74210	0·69443	0·66934	0·65206	0·63922	0·62926	0·62130	0·61474	0·60922
·81	·74800	·70337	·68043	·66492	·65362	·64506	·63839	·63303	·62864
·82	·75381	·71215	·69131	·67752	·66773	·66054	·65512	·65092	·64763
·83	·75952	·72078	·70198	·68986	·68154	·67567	·67147	·66840	·66617
·84	·76514	·72924	·71243	·70193	·69503	·69045	·68742	·68544	·68422
0·85	0·77067	0·73754	0·72266	0·71373	0·70821	0·70486	0·70295	0·70201	0·70175
·86	·77610	·74568	·73266	·72525	·72105	·71888	·71805	·71810	·71875
·87	·78144	·75366	·74244	·73649	·73355	·73252	·73270	·73368	·73519
·88	·78669	·76147	·75199	·74744	·74571	·74575	·74689	·74874	·75105
·89	·79184	·76912	·76132	·75810	·75752	·75857	·76061	·76327	·76632
0·90	0·79691	0·77660	0·77040	0·76847	0·76898	0·77097	0·77386	0·77727	0·78099
·91	·80188	·78392	·77926	·77854	·78008	·78296	·78663	·79072	·79505
·92	·80677	·79107	·78789	·78832	·79082	·79453	·79891	·80363	·80851
·93	·81156	·79806	·79628	·79780	·80120	·80567	·81071	·81599	·82135
·94	·81627	·80489	·80444	·80698	·81122	·81640	·82202	·82780	·83359
0·95	0·82089	0·81155	0·81237	0·81587	0·82089	0·82671	0·83286	0·83907	0·84522
·96	·82542	·81805	·82007	·82447	·83021	·83660	·84321	·84981	·85626
·97	·82987	·82439	·82754	·83277	·83917	·84608	·85310	·86001	·86671
·98	·83423	·83057	·83478	·84079	·84778	·85515	·86252	·86970	·87659
·99	·83851	·83659	·84180	·84852	·85605	·86382	·87149	·87887	·88591
1·00	0·84270	0·84245	0·84860	0·85597	0·86398	0·87210	0·88001	0·88755	0·89468

Table 8 (continued). *Probability integral of the mean deviation, m, from the sample mean*

m \ n	2	3	4	5	6	7	8	9	10
1·00	0·84270	0·84245	0·84860	0·85597	0·86398	0·87210	0·88001	0·88755	0·89468
·01	·84681	·84816	·85518	·86315	·87158	·87999	·88809	·89574	·90292
·02	·85084	·85371	·86154	·87005	·87885	·88751	·89575	·90347	·91065
·03	·85478	·85911	·86768	·87668	·88581	·89465	·90299	·91074	·91788
·04	·85865	·86436	·87362	·88305	·89245	·90144	·90984	·91756	·92464
1·05	0·86244	0·86946	0·87935	0·88916	0·89878	0·90788	0·91629	0·92397	0·93095
·06	·86614	·87442	·88487	·89502	·90482	·91398	·92237	·92997	·93681
·07	·86977	·87922	·89020	·90063	·91057	·91976	·92809	·93557	·94227
·08	·87333	·88389	·89533	·90600	·91604	·92521	·93346	·94081	·94733
·09	·87680	·88841	·90027	·91114	·92123	·93037	·93850	·94568	·95202
1·10	0·88020	0·89280	0·90502	0·91605	0·92616	0·93523	0·94322	0·95022	0·95635
·11	·88353	·89705	·90959	·92074	·93084	·93980	·94764	·95444	·96034
·12	·88679	·90117	·91398	·92521	·93527	·94411	·95176	·95835	·96403
·13	·88997	·90516	·91820	·92947	·93947	·94815	·95561	·96198	·96741
·14	·89308	·90901	·92224	·93353	·94344	·95195	·95920	·96533	·97052
1·15	0·89612	0·91275	0·92613	0·93740	0·94718	0·95551	0·96253	0·96843	0·97337
·16	·89910	·91635	·92985	·94108	·95072	·95885	·96564	·97128	·97598
·17	·90200	·91984	·93341	·94458	·95406	·96197	·96851	·97391	·97836
·18	·90484	·92321	·93682	·94790	·95720	·96488	·97118	·97633	·98054
·19	·90761	·92647	·94009	·95105	·96016	·96760	·97365	·97855	·98252
1·20	0·91031	0·92961	0·94321	0·95404	0·96294	0·97014	0·97594	0·98058	0·98432
·21	·91296	·93264	·94620	·95687	·96555	·97250	·97805	·98245	·98595
·22	·91553	·93556	·94905	·95955	·96800	·97470	·97999	·98415	·98743
·23	·91805	·93838	·95177	·96209	·97030	·97675	·98178	·98571	·98877
·24	·92051	·94109	·95437	·96449	·97246	·97865	·98343	·98713	·98998
1·25	0·92290	0·94371	0·95685	0·96676	0·97448	0·98041	0·98495	0·98842	0·99107
·26	·92524	·94623	·95921	·96890	·97637	·98204	·98634	·98959	·99206
·27	·92751	·94865	·96146	·97092	·97813	·98355	·98761	·99066	·99294
·28	·92973	·95098	·96360	·97283	·97978	·98495	·98878	·99162	·99373
·29	·93190	·95322	·96564	·97462	·98132	·98624	·98985	·99250	·99445
1·30	0·93401	0·95538	0·96758	0·97631	0·98275	0·98743	0·99082	0·99329	0·99508
·31	·93606	·95745	·96942	·97790	·98408	·98852	·99172	·99401	·99566
·32	·93807	·95944	·97117	·97940	·98533	·98953	·99253	·99465	·99616
·33	·94002	·96135	·97283	·98081	·98648	·99046	·99327	·99523	·99662
·34	·94191	·96318	·97441	·98213	·98755	·99132	·99394	·99576	·99702
1·35	0·94376	0·96494	0·97591	0·98337	0·98855	0·99210	0·99455	0·99623	0·99738
·36	·94556	·96662	·97733	·98453	·98947	·99282	·99510	·99665	·99770
·37	·94731	·96824	·97867	·98562	·99033	·99348	·99560	·99703	·99798
·38	·94902	·96979	·97995	·98664	·99112	·99409	·99606	·99736	·99823
·39	·95067	·97127	·98115	·98759	·99186	·99464	·99647	·99767	·99845
1·40	0·95229	0·97269	0·98229	0·98849	0·99254	0·99515	0·99684	0·99794	0·99865
·41	·95385	·97405	·98337	·98932	·99316	·99561	·99717	·99818	·99882
·42	·95538	·97534	·98439	·99010	·99374	·99603	·99748	·99839	·99897
·43	·95686	·97659	·98535	·99083	·99427	·99641	·99775	·99858	·99910
·44	·95830	·97777	·98626	·99151	·99477	·99676	·99799	·99875	·99922
1·45	0·95970	0·97891	0·98712	0·99215	0·99522	0·99708	0·99821	0·99890	0·99932
·46	·96105	·97999	·98793	·99274	·99564	·99737	·99841	·99904	·99941
·47	·96237	·98103	·98869	·99329	·99602	·99763	·99859	·99915	·99949
·48	·96365	·98201	·98941	·99380	·99637	·99786	·99874	·99926	·99956
·49	·96490	·98296	·99009	·99427	·99669	·99808	·99889	·99935	·99962
1·50	0·96611	0·98385	0·99073	0·99472	0·99699	0·99828	0·99901	0·99943	0·99967

Table 8 (continued)

n / m	2	3	4	5	6	7	8	9	10
1·50	0·96611	0·98385	0·99073	0·99472	0·99699	0·99828	0·99901	0·99943	0·99967
·51	·96728	·98471	·99133	·99513	·99726	·99845	·99913	·99950	·99972
·52	·96841	·98552	·99190	·99551	·99751	·99861	·99923	·99957	·99976
·53	·96952	·98630	·99243	·99586	·99774	·99875	·99932	·99962	·99979
·54	·97059	·98704	·99293	·99619	·99795	·99888	·99940	·99967	·99982
1·55	0·97162	0·98774	0·99340	0·99650	0·99814	0·99900	0·99947	0·99971	0·99984
·56	·97263	·98841	·99384	·99678	·99831	·99911	·99953	·99975	·99987
·57	·97360	·98905	·99425	·99704	·99847	·99920	·99959	·99978	·99989
·58	·97455	·98966	·99464	·99728	·99861	·99929	·99964	·99981	·99990
·59	·97546	·99023	·99500	·99750	·99875	·99936	·99968	·99984	·99992
1·60	0·97635	0·99078	0·99534	0·99771	0·99887	0·99943	0·99972	0·99986	0·99993
·61	·97721	·99130	·99566	·99790	·99898	·99949	·99975	·99988	·99994
·62	·97804	·99179	·99596	·99808	·99908	·99955	·99978	·99990	·99995
·63	·97884	·99226	·99624	·99824	·99917	·99960	·99981	·99991	·99996
·64	·97962	·99270	·99650	·99839	·99925	·99964	·99983	·99992	·99996
1·65	0·98038	0·99312	0·99675	0·99852	0·99932	0·99968	0·99986	0·99993	0·99997
·66	·98110	·99352	·99698	·99865	·99939	·99972	·99987	·99994	·99997
·67	·98181	·99390	·99719	·99877	·99945	·99975	·99989	·99995	·99998
·68	·98249	·99425	·99739	·99887	·99951	·99978	·99990	·99996	·99998
·69	·98315	·99459	·99758	·99897	·99956	·99980	·99992	·99996	·99998
1·70	0·98379	0·99491	0·99775	0·99906	0·99960	0·99983	0·99993	0·99997	0·99999
·71	·98441	·99521	·99791	·99915	·99964	·99985	·99994	·99997	·99999
·72	·98500	·99550	·99806	·99922	·99968	·99986	·99994	·99998	·99999
·73	·98558	·99577	·99820	·99929	·99971	·99988	·99995	·99998	·99999
·74	·98614	·99603	·99834	·99936	·99974	·99989	·99996	·99998	·99999
1·75	0·98667	0·99627	0·99846	0·99941	0·99977	0·99991	0·99996	0·99999	0·99999
·76	·98719	·99650	·99857	·99947	·99979	·99992	·99997	·99999	·99999
·77	·98769	·99671	·99868	·99952	·99982	·99993	·99997	·99999	·99999
·78	·98817	·99691	·99878	·99956	·99983	·99993	·99998	·99999	1·00000
·79	·98864	·99710	·99887	·99960	·99985	·99994	·99998	·99999	
1·80	0·98909	0·99729	0·99895	0·99964	0·99987	0·99995	0·99998	0·99999	
·81	·98952	·99746	·99903	·99967	·99988	·99995	·99998	·99999	
·82	·98994	·99762	·99911	·99970	·99990	·99996	·99999	1·00000	
·83	·99035	·99777	·99917	·99973	·99991	·99996	·99999		
·84	·99074	·99791	·99924	·99976	·99992	·99997	·99999		
1·85	0·99111	0·99804	0·99930	0·99978	0·99993	0·99997	0·99999		
·86	·99147	·99817	·99935	·99980	·99993	·99997	·99999		
·87	·99182	·99829	·99940	·99982	·99994	·99998	·99999		
·88	·99216	·99840	·99945	·99984	·99995	·99998	·99999		
·89	·99248	·99850	·99949	·99986	·99995	·99998	1·00000		
1·90	0·99279	0·99860	0·99953	0·99987	0·99996	0·99998			
·91	·99309	·99869	·99957	·99988	·99996	·99999			
·92	·99338	·99878	·99960	·99989	·99997	·99999			
·93	·99366	·99886	·99963	·99990	·99997	·99999			
·94	·99392	·99894	·99966	·99991	·99998	·99999			
1·95	0·99418	0·99901	0·99969	0·99992	0·99998	0·99999			
·96	·99443	·99907	·99972	·99993	·99998	·99999			
·97	·99466	·99914	·99974	·99993	·99998	1·00000			
·98	·99489	·99920	·99976	·99994	·99998				
·99	·99511	·99925	·99978	·99994	·99999				
2·00	0·99532	0·99930	0·99980	0·99995	0·99999				

n \ m	2	3	4	5	6		n \ m	2	3
2·00	0·99532	0·99930	0·99980	0·99995	0·99999		2·50	0·99959	0·99999
·01	·99552	·99935	·99981	·99995	·99999		·51	·99961	·99999
·02	·99572	·99940	·99983	·99996	·99999		·52	·99964	·99999
·03	·99591	·99944	·99984	·99996	·99999		·53	·99965	·99999
·04	·99609	·99948	·99986	·99997	·99999		·54	·99967	·99999
2·05	0·99626	0·99951	0·99987	0·99997	0·99999		2·55	0·99969	0·99999
·06	·99642	·99955	·99988	·99998	·99999		·56	·99971	·99999
·07	·99658	·99958	·99989	·99998	1·00000		·57	·99972	·99999
·08	··99673	·99961	·99990	·99998			·58	·99974	·99999
·09	·99688	·99964	·99991	·99998			·59	·99975	·99999
2·10	0·99702	0·99966	0·99992	0·99998			2·60	0·99976	0·99999
·11	·99716	·99969	·99992	·99999			·61	·99978	·99999
·12	·99728	·99971	·99993	·99999			·62	·99979	1·00000
·13	·99741	·99973	·99994	·99999			·63	·99980	
·14	·99753	·99975	·99994	·99999			·64	·99981	
2·15	0·99764	0·99977	0·99995	0·99999			2·65	0·99982	
·16	·99775	·99979	·99995	·99999			·66	·99983	
·17	·99785	·99980	·99996	·99999			·67	·99984	
·18	·99795	·99982	·99996	·99999			·68	·99985	
·19	·99805	·99983	·99996	·99999			·69	·99986	
2·20	0·99814	0·99984	0·99997	0·99999			2·70	0·99987	
·21	·99822	·99985	·99997	1·00000			·71	·99987	
·21	·99831	·99987	·99997				·72	·99988	
·23	·99839	·99988	·99997				·73	·99989	
·24	·99846	·99989	·99998				·74	·99989	
2·25	0·99854	0·99989	0·99998				2·75	0·99990	
·26	·99861	·99990	·99998				·76	·99991	
·27	·99867	·99991	·99998				·77	·99991	
·28	·99874	·99992	·99998				·78	·99992	
·29	·99880	·99992	·99999				·79	·99992	
2·30	0·99886	0·99993	0·99999				2·80	0·99992	
·31	·99891	·99993	·99999				·81	·99993	
·32	·99897	·99994	·99999				·82	·99993	
·33	·99902	·99994	·99999				·83	·99994	
·34	·99906	·99995	·99999				·84	·99994	
2·35	0·99911	0·99995	0·99999				2·85	0·99994	
·36	·99916	·99996	·99999				·86	·99995	
·37	·99920	·99996	·99999				·87	·99995	
·38	·99924	·99996	·99999				·88	·99995	
·39	·99928	·99997	·99999				·89	·99996	
2·40	0·99931	0·99997	1·00000				2·90	0·99996	
·41	·99935	·99997					·91	·99996	
·42	·99938	·99997					·92	·99996	
·43	·99941	·99998					·93	·99997	
·44	·99944	·99998					·94	·99997	
2·45	0·99947	0·99998					2·95	0·99997	
·46	·99950	·99998					·96	·99997	
·47	·99952	·99998					·97	·99997	
·48	·99955	·99998					·98	·99998	
·49	·99957	·99999					·99	·99998	
2·50	0·99959	0·99999					3·00	0·99998*	

* 0·99999 is reached for $m = 3·07$; 1·00000 is reached for $m = 3·23$.

Table 9. *Expected values of normal order statistics, $\xi(i|n)$*

k \ n	2	3	4	5	6	7	8	9
1	0·56419	0·84628	1·02938	1·16296	1·26721	1·35218	1·42360	1·48501
2	—	·00000	0·29701	0·49502	0·64176	0·75737	0·85222	0·93230
3	—	—	—	·00000	·20155	·35271	·47282	·57197
4	—	—	—	—	—	·00000	·15251	·27453
5	—	—	—	—	—	—	—	·00000

k \ n	10	11	12	13	14	15	16	17	18	19
1	1·53875	1·58644	1·62923	1·66799	1·70338	1·73591	1·76599	1·79394	1·82003	1·84448
2	1·00136	1·06192	1·11573	1·16408	1·20790	1·24794	1·28474	1·31878	1·35041	1·37994
3	0·65606	0·72884	0·79284	0·84983	0·90113	0·94769	0·99027	1·02946	1·06573	1·09945
4	·37576	·46198	·53684	·60285	·66176	·71488	·76317	0·80738	0·84812	0·88586
5	·12267	·22489	·31225	·38833	·45557	·51570	·57001	·61946	·66479	·70661
6	—	0·00000	0·10259	0·19052	0·26730	0·33530	0·39622	0·45133	0·50158	0·54771
7	—	—	—	·00000	0·08816	·16530	·23375	·29519	·35084	·40164
8	—	—	—	—	—	·00000	·07729	·14599	·20774	·26374
9	—	—	—	—	—	—	—	·00000	·06880	·13072
10	—	—	—	—	—	—	—	—	—	·00000

k \ n	20	21	22	23	24	25	26	27	28	29
1	1·86748	1·88917	1·90969	1·92916	1·94767	1·96531	1·98216	1·99827	2·01371	2·02852
2	1·40760	1·43362	1·45816	1·48137	1·50338	1·52430	1·54423	1·56326	1·58145	1·59888
3	1·13095	1·16047	1·18824	1·21445	1·23924	1·26275	1·28511	1·30641	1·32674	1·34619
4	0·92098	0·95380	0·98459	1·01356	1·04091	1·06679	1·09135	1·11471	1·13697	1·15822
5	·74538	·78150	·81527	0·84697	0·87682	0·90501	0·93171	0·95705	0·98115	1·00414
6	0·59030	0·62982	0·66667	0·70115	0·73354	0·76405	0·79289	0·82021	0·84615	0·87084
7	·44833	·49148	·53157	·56896	·60399	·63690	·66794	·69727	·72508	·75150
8	·31493	·36203	·40559	·44609	·48391	·51935	·55267	·58411	·61385	·64205
9	·18696	·23841	·28579	·32965	·37047	·40860	·44436	·47801	·50977	·53982
10	·06200	·11836	·16997	·21755	·26163	·30268	·34105	·37706	·41096	·44298
11	—	0·00000	0·05642	0·10813	0·15583	0·20006	0·24128	0·27983	0·31603	0·35013
12	—	—	—	·00000	·05176	·09953	·14387	·18520	·22389	·26023
13	—	—	—	—	—	·00000	·04781	·09220	·13361	·17240
14	—	—	—	—	—	—	—	·00000	·04442	·08588
15	—	—	—	—	—	—	—	—	—	·00000

k \ n	30	31	32	33	34	35	36	37	38	39
1	2·04276	2·05646	2·06967	2·08241	2·09471	2·10661	2·11812	2·12928	2·14009	2·15059
2	1·61560	1·63166	1·64712	1·66200	1·67636	1·69023	1·70362	1;71659	1·72914	1·74131
3	1·36481	1·38268	1·39985	1·41637	1·43228	1·44762	1·46244	1·47676	1·49061	1·50402
4	1·17855	1·19803	1·21672	1·23468	1·25196	1·26860	1·28466	1·30016	1·31514	1·32964
5	1·02609	1·04709	1·06721	1·08652	1·10509	1·12295	1·14016	1·15677	1·17280	1·18830
6	0·89439	0·91688	0·93841	0·95905	0·97886	0·99790	1·01624	1·03390	1·05095	1·06741
7	·77666	·80066	·82359	·84555	·86660	·88681	0·90625	0·92496	0·94300	0·96041
8	·66885	·69438	·71875	·74204	·76435	·78574	·80629	·82605	·84508	·86343
9	·56834	·59545	·62129	·64596	·66954	·69214	·71382	·73465	·75468	·77398
10	·47329	·50206	·52943	·55552	·58043	·60427	·62710	·64902	·67009	·69035
11	0·38235	0·41287	0·44185	0·46942	0·49572	0·52084	0·54488	0·56793	0·59005	0·61131
12	·29449	·32686	·35755	·38669	·41444	·44091	·46620	·49042	·51363	·53592
13	·20885	·24322	·27573	·30654	·33582	·36371	·39032	·41576	·44012	·46348
14	·12473	·16126	·19572	·22832	·25924	·28863	·31663	·34336	·36892	·39340
15	·04148	·08037	·11695	·15147	·18415	·21515	·24463	·27272	·29954	·32520
16	—	0·00000	0·03890	0·07552	0·11009	0·14282	0·17388	0·20342	0·23159	0·25849
17	—	—	—	·00000	·03663	·07123	·10399	·13509	·16469	·19292
18	—	—	—	—	—	·00000	·03461	·06739	·09853	·12817
19	—	—	—	—	—	—	—	·00000	·03280	·06395
20	—	—	—	—	—	—	—	—	—	·00000

Table 9 (*continued*). *Expected values of normal order statistics,* ξ(i|n)

k \ n	40	41	42	43	44	45	46	47	48	49
1	2·16078	2·17068	2·18032	2·18969	2·19882	2·20772	2·21639	2·22486	2·23312	2·24119
2	1·75312	1·76458	1·77571	1·78654	1·79707	1·80733	1·81732	1·82706	1·83655	1·84582
3	1·51702	1·52964	1·54188	1·55377	1·56533	1·57658	1·58754	1·59820	1·60860	1·61874
4	1·34368	1·35728	1·37048	1·38329	1·39574	1·40784	1·41962	1·43108	1·44224	1·45312
5	1·20330	1·21782	1·23190	1·24556	1·25881	1·27170	1·28422	1·29641	1·30827	1·31983
6	1·08332	1·09872	1·11364	1·12810	1·14213	1·15576	1·16899	1·18186	1·19439	1·20658
7	0·97722	0·99348	1·00922	1·02446	1·03924	1·05358	1·06751	1·08104	1·09420	1·10701
8	·88114	·89825	0·91480	0·93082	0·94634	0·96139	0·97599	0·99018	1·00396	1·01737
9	·79259	·81056	·82792	·84472	·86097	·87673	·89201	·90684	0·92125	0·93525
10	·70988	·72871	·74690	·76448	·78148	·79795	·81391	·82939	·84442	·85902
11	0·63177	0·65149	0·67052	0·68889	0·70666	0·72385	0·74049	0·75663	0·77228	0·78748
12	·55736	·57799	·59788	·61707	·63561	·65353	·67088	·68768	·70397	·71978
13	·48591	·50749	·52827	·54830	·56763	·58631	·60438	·62186	·63881	·65523
14	·41688	·43944	·46114	·48204	·50220	·52166	·54046	·55865	·57625	·59331
15	·34978	·37337	·39604	·41784	·43885	·45912	·47868	·49759	·51588	·53360
16	0·28423	0·30890	0·33257	0·35533	0·37723	0·39833	0·41868	0·43834	0·45734	0·47573
17	·21988	·24569	·27043	·29418	·31701	·33898	·36016	·38060	·40034	·41942
18	·15644	·18345	·20931	·23411	·25792	·28081	·30285	·32410	·34460	·36441
19	·09362	·12192	·14897	·17488	·19972	·22358	·24652	·26862	·28992	·31049
20	·03117	·06085	·08917	·11625	·14219	·16707	·19097	·21396	·23610	·25746
21	—	0·00000	0·02969	0·05803	0·08513	0·11109	0·13600	0·15993	0·18296	0·20514
22	—	—	—	·00000	·02835	·05546	·08144	·10637	·13033	·15338
23	—	—	—	—	—	·00000	·02712	·05311	·07805	·10203
24	—	—	—	—	—	—	—	·00000	·02599	·05095
25	—	—	—	—	—	—	—	—	—	·00000

k \ n	50	51	52	53	54	55	56	57	58	59
1	2·24907	2·25678	2·26432	2·27169	2·27891	2·28598	2·29291	2·29970	2·30635	2·31288
2	1·85487	1·86371	1·87235	1·88080	1·88906	1·89715	1·90506	1·91282	1·92041	1·92786
3	1·62863	1·63829	1·64773	1·65695	1·66596	1·67478	1·68340	1·69185	1·70012	1·70822
4	1·46374	1·47409	1·48420	1·49407	1·50372	1·51315	1·52237	1·53140	1·54024	1·54889
5	1·33109	1·34207	1·35279	1·36326	1·37348	1·38346	1·39323	1·40278	1·41212	1·42127
6	1·21846	1·23003	1·24132	1·25234	1·26310	1·27361	1·28387	1·29391	1·30373	1·31334
7	1·11948	1·13162	1·14347	1·15502	1·16629	1·17729	1·18804	1·19855	1·20882	1·21886
8	1·03042	1·04312	1·05550	1·06757	1·07934	1·09083	1·10205	1·11300	1·12371	1·13419
9	0·94887	0·96213	0·97504	0·98762	0·99988	1·01185	1·02352	1·03493	1·04607	1·05695
10	·87321	·88701	·90045	·91354	·92629	0·93873	0·95086	0·96271	0·97427	0·98557
11	0·80225	0·81661	0·83058	0·84417	0·85742	0·87033	0·88292	0·89520	0·90719	0·91890
12	·73513	·75004	·76455	·77866	·79240	·80578	·81883	·83155	·84397	·85609
13	·67117	·68666	·70170	·71633	·73057	·74444	·75794	·77111	·78396	·79649
14	·60986	·62592	·64152	·65668	·67143	·68578	·69976	·71337	·72665	·73960
15	·55077	·56742	·58358	·59928	·61455	·62940	·64385	·65793	·67164	·68502
16	0·49354	0·51080	0·52755	0·54380	0·55960	0·57495	0·58989	0·60444	0·61860	0·63241
17	·43789	·45578	·47312	·48995	·50629	·52217	·53761	·55263	·56725	·58150
18	·38357	·40211	·42007	·43749	·45439	·47080	·48675	·50226	·51736	·53205
19	·33036	·34957	·36818	·38621	·40369	·42065	·43713	·45314	·46872	·48388
20	·27807	·29799	·31726	·33592	·35400	·37154	·38856	·40510	·42117	·43681
21	0·22653	0·24719	0·26716	0·28648	0·30518	0·32331	0·34090	0·35797	0·37456	0·39068
22	·17559	·19702	·21772	·23772	·25708	·27583	·29400	·31163	·32875	·34538
23	·12511	·14735	·16880	·18953	·20957	·22896	·24774	·26595	·28362	·30078
24	·07494	·09803	·12029	·14177	·16252	·18259	·20201	·22082	·23906	·25677
25	·02496	·04896	·07206	·09434	·11584	·13661	·15669	·17614	·19498	·21325
26	—	0·00000	0·02400	0·04712	0·06940	0·09091	0·11170	0·13180	0·15127	0·17013
27	—	—	—	·00000	·02312	·04541	·06693	·08773	·10785	·12733
28	—	—	—	—	—	·00000	·02229	·04382	·06463	·08476
29	—	—	—	—	—	—	—	·00000	·02153	·04234
30	—	—	—	—	—	—	—	—	—	·00000

Table 9 (*continued*)

n / k	60	61	62	63	64	65	66	67	68	69
1	2·31928	2·32556	2·33173	2·33778	2·34373	2·34958	2·35532	2·36097	2·36652	2·37199
2	1·93516	1·94232	1·94934	1·95624	1·96301	1·96965	1·97618	1·98260	1·98891	1·99510
3	1·71616	1·72394	1·73158	1·73906	1·74641	1·75363	1·76071	1·76767	1·77451	1·78122
4	1·55736	1·56567	1·57381	1·58180	1·58963	1·59732	1·60487	1·61228	1·61955	1·62670
5	1·43023	1·43900	1·44760	1·45603	1·46430	1·47241	1·48036	1·48817	1·49584	1·50338
6	1·32274	1·33195	1·34097	1·34982	1·35848	1·36698	1·37532	1·38351	1·39154	1·39942
7	1·22869	1·23832	1·24774	1·25698	1·26603	1·27490	1·28360	1·29213	1·30051	1·30873
8	1·14443	1·15445	1·16427	1·17388	1·18329	1·19252	1·20157	1·21044	1·21915	1·22769
9	1·06760	1·07802	1·08821	1·09819	1·10797	1·11754	1·12693	1·13613	1·14516	1·15401
10	0·99662	1·00742	1·01799	1·02833	1·03846	1·04838	1·05810	1·06762	1·07696	1·08612
11	0·93034	0·94153	0·95247	0·96317	0·97365	0·98391	0·99395	1·00380	1·01345	1·02291
12	·86793	·87950	·89081	·90187	·91270	·92329	·93367	·94383	·95379	·96355
13	·80873	·82068	·83237	·84379	·85496	·86590	·87660	·88708	·89735	·90741
14	·75224	·76459	·77665	·78843	·79996	·81123	·82226	·83306	·84364	·85400
15	·69807	·71081	·72324	·73540	·74727	·75889	·77025	·78138	·79226	·80293
16	0·64587	0·65901	0·67183	0·68436	0·69659	0·70856	0·72025	0·73170	0·74290	0·75387
17	·59538	·60893	·62214	·63504	·64764	·65996	·67200	·68377	·69529	·70657
18	·54637	·56033	·57395	·58723	·60020	·61288	·62526	·63737	·64921	·66080
19	·49864	·51303	·52705	·54073	·55408	·56712	·57985	·59230	·60447	·61638
20	·45202	·46685	·48129	·49537	·50911	·52252	·53561	·54841	·56091	·57314
21	0·40637	0·42164	0·43652	0·45101	0·46515	0·47894	0·49240	0·50555	0·51839	0·53095
22	·36155	·37729	·39260	·40752	·42207	·43625	·45009	·46360	·47680	·48969
23	·31745	·33366	·34944	·36480	·37976	·39435	·40857	·42245	·43601	·44925
24	·27396	·29066	·30691	·32272	·33812	·35312	·36775	·38201	·39594	·40953
25	·23098	·24820	·26494	·28122	·29706	·31249	·32753	·34219	·35649	·37045
26	0·18842	0·20618	0·22343	0·24019	0·25650	0·27237	0·28784	0·30290	0·31759	0·33192
27	·14621	·16452	·18230	·19957	·21636	·23269	·24859	·26408	·27917	·29389
28	·10425	·12315	·14148	·15927	·17656	·19337	·20973	·22565	·24116	·25627
29	·06248	·08198	·10089	·11923	·13704	·15435	·17118	·18755	·20349	·21902
30	·02081	·04096	·06047	·07938	·09774	·11556	·13288	·14972	·16611	·18207
31	—	0·00000	0·02014	0·03966	0·05858	0·07694	0·09478	0·11211	0·12896	0·14536
32	—	—	—	·00000	·01952	·03844	·05681	·07465	·09199	·10885
33	—	—	—	—	—	·00000	·01893	·03730	·05514	·07249
34	—	—	—	—	—	—	—	·00000	·01837	·03622
35	—	—	—	—	—	—	—	—	—	·00000

n / k	70	71	72	73	74	75	76	77	78	79
1	2·37736	2·38265	2·38785	2·39298	2·39802	2·40299	2·40789	2·41271	2·41747	2·42215
2	2·00120	2·00720	2·01310	2·01890	2·02462	2·03024	2·03578	2·04124	2·04662	2·05191
3	1·78783	1·79432	1·80071	1·80699	1·81317	1·81926	1·82525	1·83115	1·83696	1·84268
4	1·63373	1·64063	1·64742	1·65410	1·66067	1·66714	1·67350	1·67976	1·68592	1·69200
5	1·51078	1·51805	1·52520	1·53223	1·53914	1·54594	1·55263	1·55921	1·56569	1·57207
6	1·40717	1·41478	1·42226	1·42961	1·43684	1·44395	1·45094	1·45782	1·46459	1·47125
7	1·31680	1·32473	1·33252	1·34017	1·34770	1·35510	1·36237	1·36953	1·37657	1·38350
8	1·23608	1·24431	1·25240	1·26034	1·26815	1·27583	1·28338	1·29080	1·29810	1·30529
9	1·16270	1·17123	1·17961	1·18784	1·19592	1·20387	1·21168	1·21936	1·22691	1·23434
10	1·09511	1·10393	1·11259	1·12110	1·12945	1·13766	1·14572	1·15365	1·16145	1·16912
11	1·03220	1·04130	1·05024	1·05902	1·06764	1·07610	1·08442	1·09260	1·10063	1·10854
12	0·97313	0·98252	0·99173	1·00078	1·00966	1·01838	1·02695	1·03537	1·04364	1·05178
13	·91728	·92695	·93644	0·94576	0·95490	0·96387	0·97269	0·98135	0·98986	0·99822
14	·86416	·87412	·88388	·89346	·90286	·91209	·92115	·93005	·93880	·94739
15	·81338	·82362	·83366	·84351	·85317	·86265	·87196	·88110	·89008	·89890
16	0·76462	0·77514	0·78546	0·79558	0·80550	0·81524	0·82480	0·83418	0·84339	0·85244
17	·71761	·72843	·73903	·74942	·75960	·76960	·77940	·78903	·79848	·80776
18	·67214	·68325	·69413	·70480	·71526	·72551	·73557	·74544	·75512	·76463
19	·62803	·63943	·65060	·66155	·67227	·68279	·69310	·70322	·71314	·72289
20	·58510	·59681	·60827	·61950	·63050	·64128	·65185	·66222	·67239	·68237
21	0·54323	0·55525	0·56701	0·57852	0·58980	0·60085	0·61168	0·62230	0·63272	0·64294
22	·50230	·51463	·52669	·53850	·55006	·56138	·57248	·58336	·59403	·60449
23	·46219	·47484	·48721	·49932	·51117	·52277	·53414	·54528	·55621	·56692
24	·42281	·43579	·44848	·46089	·47304	·48493	·49657	·50798	·51917	·53013
25	·38404	·39739	·41041	·42313	·43558	·44777	·45970	·47138	·48283	·49404

Table 9 (*continued*). Expected values of normal order statistics, $\xi(i|n)$

k \ n	70	71	72	73	74	75	76	77	78	79
26	0·34591	0·35958	0·37292	0·38597	0·39873	0·41122	0·42343	0·43540	0·44711	0·45859
27	·30825	·32227	·33596	·34934	·36242	·37521	·38772	·39997	·41196	·42371
28	·27102	·28540	·29945	·31317	·32657	·33968	·35250	·36504	·37731	·38934
29	·23416	·24893	·26333	·27740	·29114	·30457	·31770	·33055	·34311	·35542
30	·19762	·21277	·22756	·24199	·25608	·26984	·28329	·29645	·30931	·32190
31	0·16134	0·17690	0·19208	0·20688	0·22133	0·23543	0·24922	0·26269	0·27586	0·28875
32	·12527	·14125	·15683	·17202	·18684	·20130	·21543	·22923	·24272	·25591
33	·08936	·10579	·12178	·13737	·15257	·16740	·18188	·19602	·20983	·22334
34	·05357	·07045	·08688	·10289	·11848	·13370	·14854	·16303	·17718	·19101
35	·01785	·03520	·05209	·06852	·08453	·10014	·11536	·13021	·14471	·15888
36	—	0·00000	0·01736	0·03424	0·05068	0·06670	0·08231	0·09754	0·11240	0·12691
37	—	—	—	·00000	·01689	·03333	·04935	·06497	·08020	·09507
38	—	—	—	—	—	·00000	·01644	·03247	·04809	·06333
39	—	—	—	—	—	—	—	·00000	·01602	·03165
40	—	—	—	—	—	—	—	—	—	·00000

k \ n	80	81	82	83	84	85	86	87	88	89
1	2·42677	2·43133	2·43582	2·44026	2·44463	2·44894	2·45320	2·45741	2·46156	2·46565
2	2·05714	2·06228	2·06735	2·07236	2·07729	2·08216	2·08696	2·09170	2·09637	2·10099
3	1·84832	1·85387	1·85935	1·86475	1·87007	1·87532	1·88049	1·88560	1·89064	1·89561
4	1·69798	1·70387	1·70968	1·71540	1·72104	1·72660	1·73209	1·73750	1·74283	1·74810
5	1·57836	1·58455	1·59065	1·59665	1·60258	1·60841	1·61417	1·61984	1·62544	1·63096
6	1·47781	1·48428	1·49064	1·49691	1·50309	1·50918	1·51518	1·52110	1·52693	1·53269
7	1·39032	1·39704	1·40366	1·41017	1·41659	1·42292	1·42915	1·43529	1·44135	1·44732
8	1·31236	1·31932	1·32617	1·33292	1·33957	1·34611	1·35257	1·35893	1·36520	1·37138
9	1·24165	1·24884	1·25593	1·26290	1·26977	1·27653	1·28320	1·28976	1·29624	1·30262
10	1·17666	1·18409	1·19139	1·19859	1·20567	1·21264	1·21951	1·22628	1·23295	1·23952
11	1·11631	1·12396	1·13148	1·13889	1·14618	1·15336	1·16043	1·16740	1·17426	1·18102
12	1·05978	1·06764	1·07539	1·08300	1·09050	1·09788	1·10515	1·11231	1·11936	1·12631
13	1·00644	1·01453	1·02249	1·03031	1·03802	1·04560	1·05306	1·06041	1·06765	1·07478
14	0·95584	0·96414	0·97231	0·98034	0·98825	0·99603	1·00369	1·01122	1·01865	1·02596
15	·90757	·91609	·92447	·93271	·94082	·94880	0·95665	0·96437	0·97198	0·97948
16	0·86134	0·87007	0·87867	0·88711	0·89542	0·90360	0·91164	0·91956	0·92735	0·93502
17	·81687	·82583	·83464	·84329	·85180	·86017	·86841	·87651	·88449	·89234
18	·77398	·78315	·79217	·80103	·80975	·81832	·82675	·83504	·84320	·85123
19	·73246	·74186	·75109	·76016	·76908	·77785	·78647	·79496	·80330	·81152
20	·69217	·70179	·71124	·72053	·72965	·73862	·74744	·75611	·76465	·77304
21	0·65297	0·66282	0·67249	0·68199	0·69133	0·70050	0·70952	0·71838	0·72710	0·73568
22	·61476	·62484	·63473	·64445	·65399	·66337	·67259	·68165	·69056	·69932
23	·57742	·58773	·59785	·60779	·61755	·62714	·63656	·64581	·65492	·66387
24	·54088	·55143	·56178	·57193	·58191	·59171	·60133	·61079	·62009	·62923
25	·50504	·51583	·52641	·53680	·54700	·55701	·56684	·57650	·58600	·59533
26	0·46985	0·48088	0·49170	0·50232	0·51274	0·52297	0·53301	0·54288	0·55258	0·56210
27	·43522	·44651	·45757	·46842	·47907	·48952	·49979	·50986	·51976	·52949
28	·40111	·41265	·42397	·43506	·44594	·45662	·46710	·47739	·48750	·49743
29	·36747	·37927	·39084	·40218	·41330	·42421	·43491	·44542	·45574	·46587
30	·33423	·34630	·35813	·36972	·38108	·39223	·40316	·41389	·42443	·43477
31	0·30136	0·31371	0·32580	0·33765	0·34926	0·36065	0·37182	0·38278	0·39353	0·40409
32	·26881	·28144	·29381	·30592	·31779	·32943	·34084	·35203	·36300	·37378
33	·23655	·24947	·26212	·27450	·28664	·29852	·31018	·32161	·33281	·34381
34	·20453	·21775	·23069	·24335	·25576	·26790	·27981	·29148	·30292	·31415
35	·17272	·18625	·19949	·21244	·22512	·23753	·24970	·26162	·27330	·28476
36	0·14108	0·15493	0·16848	0·18172	0·19469	0·20738	0·21981	0·23199	0·24392	0·25562
37	·10959	·12377	·13763	·15118	·16444	·17741	·19012	·20256	·21475	·22669
38	·07820	·09272	·10691	·12078	·13434	·14761	·16059	·17330	·18576	·19796
39	·04689	·06177	·07629	·09049	·10436	·11793	·13121	·14420	·15692	·16938
40	·01562	·03087	·04575	·06028	·07448	·08836	·10193	·11521	·12821	·14094
41	—	0·00000	0·01524	0·03013	0·04466	0·05886	0·07275	0·08633	0·09961	0·11262
42	—	—	—	·00000	0·01488	·02942	·04362	·05751	·07110	·08439
43	—	—	—	—	—	·00000	·01454	·02874	·04263	·05622
44	—	—	—	—	—	—	—	·00000	·01421	·02810
45	—	—	—	—	—	—	—	—	—	·00000

Table 9 (continued)

k \ n	90	91	92	93	94	95	96	97	98	99
1	2·46970	2·47370	2·47764	2·48154	2·48540	2·48920	2·49297	2·49669	2·50036	2·50400
2	2·10554	2·11004	2·11448	2·11887	2·12321	2·12749	2·13172	2·13590	2·14003	2·14411
3	1·90052	1·90536	1·91015	1·91487	1·91953	1·92414	1·92869	1·93318	1·93763	1·94201
4	1·75329	1·75842	1·76348	1·76848	1·77341	1·77828	1·78309	1·78784	1·79254	1·79718
5	1·63641	1·64178	1·64709	1·65232	1·65749	1·66259	1·66763	1·67261	1·67752	1·68238
6	1·53836	1·54396	1·54949	1·55494	1·56033	1·56564	1·57089	1·57607	1·58118	1·58624
7	1·45321	1·45903	1·46476	1·47042	1·47600	1·48151	1·48695	1·49232	1·49762	1·50286
8	1·37747	1·38348	1·38941	1·39526	1·40103	1·40673	1·41235	1·41790	1·42338	1·42879
9	1·30891	1·31511	1·32123	1·32726	1·33321	1·33909	1·34489	1·35061	1·35626	1·36183
10	1·24600	1·25239	1·25869	1·26491	1·27104	1·27708	1·28305	1·28894	1·29475	1·30049
11	1·18769	1·19426	1·20073	1·20712	1·21342	1·21964	1·22577	1·23182	1·23779	1·24368
12	1·13316	1·13990	1·14656	1·15311	1·15958	1·16596	1·17226	1·17847	1·18459	1·19064
13	1·08181	1·08873	1·09555	1·10228	1·10891	1·11546	1·12191	1·12827	1·13455	1·14075
14	1·03316	1·04026	1·04726	1·05415	1·06095	1·06765	1·07426	1·08078	1·08721	1·09356
15	0·98686	0·99413	1·00129	1·00835	1·01531	1·02217	1·02894	1·03561	1·04219	1·04868
16	0·94258	0·95002	0·95735	0·96458	0·97170	0·97872	0·98564	0·99246	0·99919	1·00583
17	·90007	·90769	·91519	·92258	·92986	·93704	·94411	·95109	·95797	0·96475
18	·85914	·86693	·87460	·88215	·88959	·89693	·90416	·91129	·91831	·92524
19	·81960	·82756	·83540	·84312	·85072	·85822	·86560	·87288	·88006	·88713
20	·78131	·78944	·79745	·80533	·81310	·82075	·82829	·83572	·84305	·85027
21	0·74412	0·75243	0·76061	0·76866	0·77659	0·78441	0·79210	0·79968	0·80716	0·81452
22	·70795	·71643	·72478	·73300	·74110	·74907	·75692	·76466	·77228	·77980
23	·67267	·68134	·68986	·69825	·70651	·71464	·72266	·73055	·73832	·74598
24	·63822	·64706	·65576	·66432	·67275	·68105	·68922	·69727	·70519	·71301
25	·60451	·61353	·62241	·63115	·63974	·64821	·65654	·66474	·67282	·68079
26	0·57147	0·58068	0·58974	0·59865	0·60742	0·61605	0·62454	0·63291	0·64115	0·64926
27	·53905	·54845	·55769	·56678	·57572	·58452	·59318	·60170	·61010	·61837
28	·50718	·51677	·52620	·53547	·54459	·55356	·56239	·57108	·57963	·58805
29	·47582	·48561	·49522	·50468	·51398	·52312	·53212	·54097	·54969	·55827
30	·44493	·45491	·46472	·47436	·48384	·49316	·50233	·51136	·52024	·52898
31	0·41445	0·42463	0·43464	0·44447	0·45414	0·46364	0·47299	0·48218	0·49123	0·50013
32	·38436	·39474	·40495	·41498	·42483	·43452	·44404	·45341	·46263	·47170
33	·35461	·36520	·37561	·38584	·39588	·40576	·41547	·42501	·43440	·44364
34	·32517	·33598	·34660	·35702	·36727	·37733	·38722	·39695	·40652	·41593
35	·29601	·30704	·31787	·32850	·33895	·34921	·35929	·36920	·37895	·38853
36	0·26710	0·27835	0·28940	0·30025	0·31090	0·32136	0·33163	0·34173	0·35166	0·36142
37	·23841	·24990	·26117	·27223	·28309	·29375	·30423	·31452	·32464	·33458
38	·20991	·22164	·23314	·24443	·25550	·26637	·27705	·28754	·29785	·30797
39	·18159	·19356	·20530	·21681	·22810	·23919	·25008	·26077	·27127	·28159
40	·15341	·16563	·17761	·18936	·20088	·21219	·22328	·23418	·24488	·25539
41	0·12536	0·13783	0·15006	0·16205	0·17380	0·18533	0·19665	0·20776	0·21866	0·22937
42	·09740	·11014	·12262	·13486	·14685	·15861	·17015	·18148	·19259	·20351
43	·06952	·08253	·09528	·10777	·12001	·13201	·14378	·15533	·16666	·17778
44	·04169	·05499	·06801	·08076	·09325	·10550	·11750	·12928	·14083	·15217
45	·01389	·02748	·04078	·05381	·06656	·07906	·09131	·10332	·11510	·12666
46	—	0·00000	0·01359	0·02689	0·03992	0·05267	0·06518	0·07743	0·08944	0·10123
47	—	—	—	·00000	·01330	·02633	·03909	·05159	·06385	·07586
48	—	—	—	—	—	·00000	·01303	·02579	·03829	·05055
49	—	—	—	—	—	—	—	·00000	·01276	·02527
50	—	—	—	—	—	—	—	—	—	·00000

i \ n	100	125	150	175	200	i \ n	125	150	175	200
1	2·50759	2·58634	2·64925	2·70148	2·74604	51	0·24258	0·42094	0·55682	0·66585
2	2·14814	2·23630	2·30638	2·36434	2·41365	52	·22201	·40278	·54019	·65030
3	1·94635	2·04090	2·11578	2·17755	2·22999	53	·20154	·38475	·52371	·63490
4	1·80176	1·90146	1·98019	2·04500	2·09991	54	·18115	·36684	·50737	·61966
5	1·68718	1·79137	1·87341	1·94081	1·99783	55	·16084	·34904	·49116	·60456
6	1·59123	1·69947	1·78448	1·85419	1·91308	56	0·14059	0·33136	0·47508	0·58959
7	1·50803	1·62002	1·70777	1·77959	1·84019	57	·12040	·31378	·45913	·57476
8	1·43414	1·54966	1·63997	1·71376	1·77594	58	·10026	·29630	·44329	·56005
9	1·36734	1·48623	1·57896	1·65462	1·71828	59	·08016	·27891	·42756	·54546
10	1·30615	1·42828	1·52333	1·60075	1·66583	60	·06009	·26160	·41193	·53099
11	1·24950	1·37477	1·47206	1·55118	1·61760	61	0·04005	0·24437	0·39641	0·51663
12	1·19661	1·32493	1·42438	1·50514	1·57287	62	·02002	·22721	·38098	·50237
13	1·14687	1·27819	1·37975	1·46210	1·53109	63	·00000	·21012	·36564	·48822
14	1·09982	1·23409	1·33771	1·42161	1·49182	64	—	·19309	·35039	·47416
15	1·05509	1·19226	1·29791	1·38333	1·45472	65	—	·17612	·33521	·46020
16	1·01238	1·15243	1·26007	1·34697	1·41953	66	—	0·15919	0·32012	0·44632
17	0·97145	1·11435	1·22396	1·31232	1·38602	67	—	·14232	·30510	·43253
18	·93208	1·07783	1·18937	1·27917	1·35399	68	—	·12548	·29014	·41882
19	·89411	1·04268	1·15616	1·24738	1·32330	69	—	·10868	·27525	·40519
20	·85739	1·00879	1·12417	1·21680	1·29381	70	—	·09191	·26042	·39164
21	0·82179	0·97601	1·09330	1·18731	1·26540	71	—	0·07516	0·24565	0·37816
22	·78720	·94426	1·06344	1·15883	1·23798	72	—	·05844	·23093	·36474
23	·75353	·91342	1·03449	1·13126	1·21146	73	—	·04173	·21626	·35139
24	·72070	·88344	1·00639	1·10452	1·18577	74	—	·02503	·20164	·33811
25	·68863	·85423	0·97907	1·07855	1·16084	75	—	·00834	·18706	·32488
26	0·65725	0·82573	0·95245	1·05329	1·13661	76	—	—	0·17252	0·31171
27	·62651	·79789	·92650	1·02868	1·11303	77	—	—	·15802	·29859
28	·59635	·77065	·90115	1·00469	1·09005	78	—	—	·14355	·28553
29	·56672	·74398	·87638	0·98125	1·06763	79	—	—	·12911	·27251
30	·53758	·71782	·85212	·95835	1·04574	80	—	—	·11470	·25954
31	0·50890	0·69215	0·82836	0·93594	1·02434	81	—	—	0·10031	0·24661
32	·48062	·66692	·80506	·91399	1·00340	82	—	—	·08594	·23373
33	·45273	·64212	·78219	·89247	0·98290	83	—	—	·07159	·22088
34	·42518	·61770	·75973	·87135	·96279	84	—	—	·05725	·20807
35	·39796	·59365	·73764	·85062	·94307	85	—	—	·04293	·19529
36	0·37102	0·56993	0·71590	0·83025	0·92371	86	—	—	0·02862	0·18254
37	·34436	·54653	·69450	·81022	·90469	87	—	—	·01431	·16983
38	·31793	·52343	·67341	·79051	·88599	88	—	—	·00000	·15714
39	·29173	·50061	·65261	·77110	·86760	89	—	—	—	·14448
40	·26572	·47804	·63210	·75197	·84950	90	—	—	—	·13184
41	0·23990	0·45571	0·61185	0·73312	0·83167	91	—	—	—	0·11922
42	·21423	·43361	·59184	·71453	·81410	92	—	—	—	·10662
43	·18870	·41172	·57208	·69618	·79678	93	—	—	—	·09404
44	·16330	·39002	·55253	·67806	·77969	94	—	—	—	·08147
45	·13800	·36851	·53319	·66016	·76283	95	—	—	—	·06891
46	0·11279	0·34717	0·51405	0·64247	0·74619	96	—	—	—	0·05637
47	·08765	·32598	·49509	·62498	·72975	97	—	—	—	·04383
48	·06257	·30494	·47632	·60768	·71350	98	—	—	—	·03130
49	·03753	·28403	·45770	·59056	·69744	99	—	—	—	·01878
50	·01251	·26325	·43925	·57361	·68156	100	—	—	—	·00626

Table 10. *Variances and covariances of normal order statistics*

n	i	j		n	i	j		n	i	j		n	i	j		n	i	j	
2	1	1	0·681690	8	1	1	0·372897	10	1	9	0·034041	11	5	6	0·116745	13	1	11	0·026854
		2	·318310			2	·186307			10	·026699			7	·099194			12	·022886
	2	2	0·681690			3	·125966		2	2	0·214524		6	6	0·137162			13	·018435
						4	·094723			3	·146623						2	2	0·190413
3	1	1	0·559467			5	·074765			4	·111702	12	1	1	0·323636			3	·130206
		2	·275664			6	·060208			5	·089743			2	·160237			4	·099726
		3	·164868			7	·048299			6	·074200			3	·108931			5	·080879
	2	2	0·448671			8	·036835			7	·062228			4	·083069			6	·067815
					2	2	0·239401			8	·052307			5	·067088			7	·058046
4	1	1	0·491715			3	·163196			9	·043371			6	·055993			8	·050317
		2	·245593			4	·123263		3	3	0·175003			7	·047662			9	·043910
		3	·158008			5	·097565			4	·133802			8	·041021			10	·038360
		4	·104684			6	·078722			5	·107745			9	·035444			11	·033315
	2	2	0·360455			7	·063247			6	·089225			10	·030501			12	·028402
		3	·235944		3	3	0·200769			7	·074918			11	·025795		3	3	0·151392
						4	·152358			8	·063033			12	·020622			4	·116270
5	1	1	0·447534			5	·120964		4	4	0·157939		2	2	0·197265			5	·094457
		2	·224331			6	·097817			5	·127509			3	·134902			6	·079292
		3	·148148		4	4	0·187186			6	·105786			4	·103196			7	·067928
		4	·105772			5	·149175			7	·088946			5	·083505			8	·058922
		5	·074215						5	5	0·151054			6	·069786			9	·051446
	2	2	0·311519	9	1	1	0·357353			6	·125599			7	·059459			10	·044964
		3	·208435			2	·178143							8	·051211			11	·039064
		4	·149943			3	·120745	11	1	1	0·333247			9	·044275		4	4	0·133011
	3	3	0·286834			4	·091307			2	·165365			10	·038119			5	·108251
						5	·072742			3	·112358			11	·032251			6	·090986
6	1	1	0·415927			6	·059483			4	·085517		3	3	0·157979			7	·078017
		2	·208503			7	·049076			5	·068848			4	·121206			8	·067722
		3	·139435			8	·040094			6	·057201			5	·098261			9	·059163
		4	·102429			9	·031055			7	·048375			6	·082223			10	·051733
		5	·077364		2	2	0·225697			8	·041242			7	·070121		5	5	0·123250
		6	·056341			3	·154116			9	·035110			8	·060438			6	·103737
	2	2	0·279578			4	·117006			10	·029420			9	·052283			7	·089043
		3	·188986			5	·093448			11	·023315			10	·045036			8	·077355
		4	·139664			6	·076546		2	2	0·205198		4	4	0·139811			9	·067623
		5	·105905			7	·063235			3	·140310			5	·113569		6	6	0·118318
	3	3	0·246213			8	·051715			4	·107149			6	·095165			7	·101682
		4	·183273		3	3	0·186383			5	·086443			7	·081242			8	·088419
7	1	1	0·391918			4	·142078			6	·071931			8	·070080		7	7	0·116799
		2	·196199			5	·113768			7	·060887			9	·060662	14	1	1	0·307730
		3	·132116			6	·093363			8	·051950		5	5	0·130614			2	·151720
		4	·098487			7	·077235			9	·044255			6	·109621			3	·103172
		5	·076560		4	4	0·170559			10	·037103			7	·093695			4	·078872
		6	·059919			5	·136991		3	3	0·165724			8	·080897			5	·063966
		7	·044802			6	·112667			4	·126967		6	6	0·126638			6	·053706
	2	2	0·256733		5	5	0·166101			5	·102641			7	·108395			7	·046090
		3	·174483							6	·085518							8	·040114
		4	·130730	10	1	1	0·344344			7	·072474	13	1	1	0·315205			9	·035214
		5	·101955			2	·171263			8	·061887			2	·155727			10	·031037
		6	·079981			3	·116259			9	·052755			3	·105891			11	·027336
	3	3	0·219722			4	·088249		4	4	0·147955			4	·080865			12	·023906
		4	·165560			5	·070741			5	·119875			5	·065463			13	·020508
		5	·129605			6	·058399			6	·100035			6	·054822			14	·016628
	4	4	0·210447			7	·048921			7	·084877			7	·046883		2	2	0·184420
						8	·041084			8	·072545			8	·040613			3	·126079
									5	5	0·139641			9	·035423			4	·096652
														10	·030932				

N.B. If $i = j$, we have var $X_{(i)}$; also cov $X_{(i)} X_{(j)} =$ cov $X_{(n-j+1)} X_{(n-i+1)}$.

Table 10 (continued). Variances and covariances of normal order statistics

n	i	j		n	i	j		n	i	j		n	i	j		n	i	j	
14	2	5	0.078520	15	2	4	0·093907	16	1	11	0·027535	16	7	8	0·085618	17	4	11	0·042926
						5	·076391			12	·024648			9	·076002			12	·038694
		6	·066003							13	·021996			10	·067893			13	·034862
		7	·056690			6	·064339			14	·019459		8	8	0·095721			14	·031288
		8	·049371			7	·055407			15	·016871			9	·085029				
		9	·043362			8	·048424												
		10	·038234			9	·042729			16	·013829						5	5	0·103400
						10	·037918												
		11	·033686						2	2	0·174394	17	1	1	0·289533			6	·087573
		12	·029468							3	·119141			2	·141942			7	·075853
		13	·025286			11	·033715			4	·091436			3	·096475			8	·066720
	3	3	0·145705			12	·029915			5	·074459			4	·073885			9	·059319
		4	·111982			13	·026330							5	·060127			10	·053126
		5	·091118			14	·022721			6	·062809								
		6	·076675							7	·054203			6	·050733			11	·047799
		7	·065908		3	3	0·140732			8	·047501			7	·043824			12	·043097
		8	·057434			4	·108214			9	·042064			8	·038467			13	·038838
		9	·050468			5	·088161			10	·037502			9	·034144				
		10	·044517											10	·030539		6	6	0·096882
		11	·039235			6	·074327			11	·033557							7	·083981
		12	·034332			7	·064056			12	·030046			11	·027447			8	·073913
	4	4	0·127227			8	·056014			13	·026819			12	·024724			9	·065744
		5	·103693			9	·049449			14	·023730			13	·022262			10	·058903
						10	·043896			15	·020579			14	·019969				
		6	·087356											15	·017748			11	·053014
		7	·075152			11	·039043		3	3	0·136339							12	·047812
		8	·065531			12	·034651			4	·104871			16	·015455				
		9	·057612			13	·030506			5	·085519			17	·012726		7	7	0·092903
		10	·050840															8	·081819
					4	4	0·122233			6	·072208		2	2	0·170143			9	·072815
		11	·044824			5	·099732			7	·062357			3	·116187			10	·065267
										8	·054675			4	·089198				
	5	5	0·117101			6	·084171			9	·048437			5	·072697			11	·058763
						7	·072595			10	·043198								
		6	·098775			8	·063518							6	·061400		8	8	0·090736
		7	·085054			9	·056099			11	·038665			7	·053076			9	·080800
		8	·074218			10	·049819			12	·034628			8	·046614			10	·072460
		9	·065287							13	·030915			9	·041393				
		10	·057640			11	·044325			14	·027360			10	·037035		9	9	0·090047
						12	·039350												
	6	6	0·111532						4	4	0·117866			11	·033294				
		7	·096141		5	5	0·111870			5	·096251			12	·029998	18	1	1	0·284530
		8	·083962											13	·027017			2	·139250
		9	·073907			6	·094521			6	·081348			14	·024239			3	·094617
						7	·081589			7	·070300			15	·021546			4	·072485
	7	7	0·109027			8	·071433			8	·061673							5	·059030
		8	·095309			9	·063122			9	·054660			16	·018766				
						10	·056080			10	·048765							6	·049860
													3	3	0·132421			7	·043130
						11	·049913			11	·043661			4	·101879			8	·037926
15	1	1	0·301042							12	·039111			5	·083142			9	·033739
		2	·148130							13	·034925							10	·030261
		3	·100722		6	6	0·105867							6	·070285				
		4	·077059			7	·091468		5	5	0·107352			7	·060796			11	·027294
		5	·062585			8	·080141							8	·053421			12	·024700
						9	·070858			6	·090823			9	·047456			13	·022380
		6	·052653			10	·062982			7	·078548			10	·042473			14	·020254
		7	·045308							8	·068949							15	·018249
		8	·039574		7	7	0·102692			9	·061136			11	·038193				
		9	·034904			8	·090050			10	·054564			12	·034419			16	·016285
		10	·030961			9	·079674							13	·031005			17	·014237
										11	·048868			14	·027821			18	·011772
		11	·027521		8	8	0·101695			12	·043788			15	·024734				
		12	·024413	16	1	1	0·295010		6	6	0·101046		4	4	0·114007				
		13	·021482			2	·144888			7	·087463			5	·093162		2	2	0·166293
		14	·018533			3	·098501			8	·076824							3	·113506
		15	·015114			4	·075404			9	·068155			6	·078827			4	·087160
						5	·061309			10	·060853			7	·068230			5	·071083
	2	2	0·179122											8	·059983				
		3	·122418			6	·051662			11	·054521			9	·053306			6	·060098
						7	·044550							10	·047724			7	·052022
						8	·039019		7	7	0·097403							8	·045768
						9	·034538											9	·040732
						10	·030781											10	·036545

Table 10 (*continued*)

n	i	j		n	i	j		n	i	j		n	i	j		n	i	j	
18	2	11	0·032970	18	7	11	0·056850	19	3	13	0·030722	19	10	10	0·080791	20	4	5	·085644
		12	·029844			12	·051520			14	·027984								
		13	·027046							15	·025442	20	1	1	0·275697			6	·072632
		14	·024481		8	8	0·086496							2	·134494			7	·063073
		15	·022061			9	·077176			16	·023020			3	·091323			8	·055686
						10	·069389			17	·020621			4	·069988			9	·049754
		16	·019689						4	4	0·107474			5	·057057			10	·044846
		17	·017215			11	·062712			5	·087905							11	·040681
														6	·048270			12	·037071
	3	3	0·128900		9	9	0·085313			6	·074503			7	·041844			13	·033879
		4	·099183			10	·076744			7	·064641			8	·036894			14	·031005
		5	·080990							8	·057003			9	·032930			15	·028365
				19	1	1	0·279936			9	·050857			10	·029656				
		6	·068532			2	·136777			10	·045758							16	·025890
		7	·059360			3	·092906							11	·026884			17	·023507
		8	·052249			4	·071190			11	·041417			12	·024484				
		9	·046516			5	·058009			12	·037637			13	·022365		5	5	0·093996
		10	·041747							13	·034277			14	·020458				
						6	·049041			14	·031226			15	·018710			6	·079777
		11	·037673			7	·042471			15	·028394							7	·069318
		12	·034108			8	·037401							16	·017071			8	·061225
		13	·030916			9	·033332			16	·025694			17	·015495			9	·054722
		14	·027988			10	·029963							18	·013923			10	·049337
		15	·025224						5	5	0·096794			19	·012253				
						11	·027101							20	·010205			11	·044766
		16	·022516			12	·024613			6	·082106							12	·040801
						13	·022404			7	·071280		2	2	0·159573			13	·037295
	4	4	0·110566			14	·020401			8	·062887			3	·108814			14	·034135
		5	·090397			15	·018543			9	·056127			4	·083576			15	·031233
										10	·050514			5	·068225				
		6	·076558			16	0·016773											16	·028511
		7	·066352			17	·015022			11	·045733			6	·057770				
		8	·058431			18	·013179			12	·041568			7	·050111		6	6	0·087151
		9	·052039			19	·010938			13	·037864			8	·044204			7	·075770
		10	·046718							14	·034500			9	·039469			8	·066956
					2	2	0·162786			15	·031375			10	·035557			9	·059866
		11	·042169			3	·111059											10	·053991
		12	·038187			4	·085293		6	6	0·090022			11	·032241				
		13	·034619			5	·069597			7	·078203			12	·029368			11	·049001
		14	·031345							8	·069029			13	·026832			12	·044670
		15	·028255			6	·058891			9	·061634			14	·024548			13	·040839
						7	·051035			10	·055488			15	·022453			14	·037385
	5	5	0·099908			8	·044965							16	·020489			15	·034211
						9	·040089			11	·050249			17	·018599				
		6	·084688			10	·036049			12	·045683			18	·016714		7	7	0·082612
		7	·073446							13	·041620			19	·014711			8	·073038
		8	·064710			11	·032614			14	·037929							9	·065331
		9	·057654			12	·029626						3	3	0·122813			10	·058939
		10	·051776			13	·026972		7	7	0·085617			4	·094505				
						14	·024564			8	·075615			5	·077236			11	·053506
		11	·046747			15	·022331			9	·067543							12	·048788
		12	·042342							10	·060830			6	·065451			13	·044612
		13	·038393			16	·020202							7	·056806			14	·040846
		14	·034768			17	·018095			11	·055103			8	·050131				
						18	·015877			12	·050109			9	·044776		8	8	0·079631
	6	6	0·093241							13	·045662			10	·040348			9	·071259
		7	·080920		3	3	0·125714											10	·064310
		8	·071334			4	·096737		8	8	0·082834			11	·036593				
		9	·063583			5	·079030			9	·074027			12	·033340			11	·058400
		10	·057120							10	·066696			13	·030465			12	·053264
						6	·066927							14	·027876			13	·048716
		11	·051587			7	·058034			11	·060437			15	·025499				
		12	·046737			8	·051154			12	·054975						9	9	0·077812
		13	·042388			9	·045623							16	·023272			10	·070253
						10	·041037		9	9	0·081288			17	·021128				
	7	7	0·089017							10	·073270			18	·018987			11	·063818
		8	·078518			11	·037135											12	·058223
		9	·070020			12	·033739			11	·066420		4	4	0·104677				
		10	·062927														10	10	0·076947
																		11	·069927

N.B. If $i = j$, we have var $X_{(i)}$; also cov $X_{(i)} X_{(j)} = $ cov $X_{(n-j+1)} X_{(n-i+1)}$.

Table 11. *Coefficients for estimating mean and standard deviation as linear functions of k normal order statistics*

Estimators of mean, $\breve{\mu}$

Table 11a. *With minimum variance $\sigma^2(\breve{\mu})$*

k		Efficiency
2	$0 \cdot 5[z(0 \cdot 2709) + z(0 \cdot 7291)]$	$0 \cdot 8098$
4	$0 \cdot 1918[z(0 \cdot 1068) + z(0 \cdot 8932)] + 0 \cdot 3082[z(0 \cdot 3512) + z(0 \cdot 6488)]$	$0 \cdot 9201$
6	$0 \cdot 0968[z(0 \cdot 0540) + z(0 \cdot 9460)] + 0 \cdot 1787[z(0 \cdot 1915) + z(0 \cdot 8085)]$ $+ 0 \cdot 2245[z(0 \cdot 3898) + z(0 \cdot 6102)]$	$0 \cdot 9560$
8	$0 \cdot 0559[z(0 \cdot 0310) + z(0 \cdot 9690)] + 0 \cdot 1119[z(0 \cdot 1154) + z(0 \cdot 8846)]$ $+ 0 \cdot 1550[z(0 \cdot 2481) + z(0 \cdot 7519)] + 0 \cdot 1772[z(0 \cdot 4126) + z(0 \cdot 5874)]$	$0 \cdot 9722$
10	$0 \cdot 0366[z(0 \cdot 0203) + z(0 \cdot 9797)] + 0 \cdot 0751[z(0 \cdot 0768) + z(0 \cdot 9232)]$ $+ 0 \cdot 1086[z(0 \cdot 1684) + z(0 \cdot 8316)] + 0 \cdot 1334[z(0 \cdot 2887) + z(0 \cdot 7113)]$ $+ 0 \cdot 1463[z(0 \cdot 4274) + z(0 \cdot 5726)]$	$0 \cdot 9808$
12	$0 \cdot 0246[z(0 \cdot 0135) + z(0 \cdot 9865)] + 0 \cdot 0522[z(0 \cdot 0525) + z(0 \cdot 9475)]$ $+ 0 \cdot 0786[z(0 \cdot 1178) + z(0 \cdot 8822)] + 0 \cdot 1012[z(0 \cdot 2075) + z(0 \cdot 7925)]$ $+ 0 \cdot 1174[z(0 \cdot 3163) + z(0 \cdot 6837)] + 0 \cdot 1260[z(0 \cdot 4373) + z(0 \cdot 5627)]$	$0 \cdot 9859$

Table 11b. *With minimum $\sigma^2(\breve{\mu}) + \sigma^2(\breve{\sigma})$*

k		Efficiency
2	$0 \cdot 5[z(0 \cdot 1525) + z(0 \cdot 8475)]$	$0 \cdot 7289$
4	$0 \cdot 1414[z(0 \cdot 0668) + z(0 \cdot 9332)] + 0 \cdot 3586[z(0 \cdot 2912) + z(0 \cdot 7088)]$	$0 \cdot 9083$
6	$0 \cdot 0497[z(0 \cdot 0231) + z(0 \cdot 9769)] + 0 \cdot 1550[z(0 \cdot 1180) + z(0 \cdot 8820)]$ $+ 0 \cdot 2953[z(0 \cdot 3369) + z(0 \cdot 6631)]$	$0 \cdot 9459$
8	$0 \cdot 0249[z(0 \cdot 0119) + z(0 \cdot 9881)] + 0 \cdot 0764[z(0 \cdot 0604) + z(0 \cdot 9396)]$ $+ 0 \cdot 1568[z(0 \cdot 1721) + z(0 \cdot 8279)] + 0 \cdot 2419[z(0 \cdot 3711) + z(0 \cdot 6289)]$	$0 \cdot 9659$
10	$0 \cdot 0147[z(0 \cdot 00718) + z(0 \cdot 99282)] + 0 \cdot 0443[z(0 \cdot 0358) + z(0 \cdot 9642)]$ $+ 0 \cdot 0897[z(0 \cdot 1008) + z(0 \cdot 8992)] + 0 \cdot 1490[z(0 \cdot 2172) + z(0 \cdot 7828)]$ $+ 0 \cdot 2023[z(0 \cdot 3942) + z(0 \cdot 6058)]$	$0 \cdot 9767$
12	$0 \cdot 0094[z(0 \cdot 00463) + z(0 \cdot 99537)] + 0 \cdot 0280[z(0 \cdot 0230) + z(0 \cdot 9770)]$ $+ 0 \cdot 0562[z(0 \cdot 0642) + z(0 \cdot 9358)] + 0 \cdot 0940[z(0 \cdot 1377) + z(0 \cdot 8623)]$ $+ 0 \cdot 1384[z(0 \cdot 2524) + z(0 \cdot 7476)] + 0 \cdot 1740[z(0 \cdot 4102) + z(0 \cdot 5898)]$	$0 \cdot 9830$

Table 11c.† *With minimum variance and $p_1 \geqslant 0 \cdot 025$*

k		Efficiency
10	$0 \cdot 0426[z(0 \cdot 025) + z(0 \cdot 975)] + 0 \cdot 0768[z(0 \cdot 0839) + z(0 \cdot 9161)]$ $+ 0 \cdot 1084[z(0 \cdot 1764) + z(0 \cdot 8236)] + 0 \cdot 1304[z(0 \cdot 2949) + z(0 \cdot 7051)]$ $+ 0 \cdot 1418[z(0 \cdot 4297) + z(0 \cdot 5703)]$	$0 \cdot 9806$
12	$0 \cdot 387[z(0 \cdot 025) + z(0 \cdot 975)] + 0 \cdot 0566[z(0 \cdot 0698) + z(0 \cdot 9302)]$ $+ 0 \cdot 0786[z(0 \cdot 1371) + z(0 \cdot 8629)] + 0 \cdot 0972[z(0 \cdot 2243) + z(0 \cdot 7757)]$ $+ 0 \cdot 1109[z(0 \cdot 3278) + z(0 \cdot 6722)] + 0 \cdot 1180[z(0 \cdot 4415) + z(0 \cdot 5585)]$	$0 \cdot 9851$
14	$0 \cdot 0352[z(0 \cdot 025) + z(0 \cdot 975)] + 0 \cdot 0414[z(0 \cdot 0583) + z(0 \cdot 9417)]$ $+ 0 \cdot 0581[z(0 \cdot 1077) + z(0 \cdot 8923)] + 0 \cdot 0740[z(0 \cdot 1735) + z(0 \cdot 8265)]$ $+ 0 \cdot 0882[z(0 \cdot 2537) + z(0 \cdot 7463)] + 0 \cdot 0987[z(0 \cdot 3473) + z(0 \cdot 6527)]$ $+ 0 \cdot 1044[z(0 \cdot 4476) + z(0 \cdot 5524)]$	$0 \cdot 9876$

† The coefficients for $k = 2, 4, 6, 8$ are the same as those in Table 11a.

Table 11 (*continued*)

Estimators of standard deviation, $\check{\sigma}$

Table 11*d*. *With minimum variance* $\sigma^2(\check{\sigma})$

k		Efficiency
2	$0{\cdot}3374[z(0{\cdot}9306) - z(0{\cdot}0694)]$	0·6522
4	$0{\cdot}116[z(0{\cdot}9770) - z(0{\cdot}0230)] + 0{\cdot}236[z(0{\cdot}8729) - z(0{\cdot}1271)]$	0·8244
6	$0{\cdot}0549[z(0{\cdot}9896) - z(0{\cdot}0104)] + 0{\cdot}1244[z(0{\cdot}9452) - z(0{\cdot}0548)]$ $+ 0{\cdot}1825[z(0{\cdot}8304) - z(0{\cdot}1696)]$	0·8943
8	$0{\cdot}0307[z(0{\cdot}99451) - z(0{\cdot}00549)] + 0{\cdot}0730[z(0{\cdot}9714) - z(0{\cdot}0286)]$ $0{\cdot}1168[z(0{\cdot}9149) - z(0{\cdot}0851)] + 0{\cdot}1477[z(0{\cdot}7983) - z(0{\cdot}2017)]$	0·9294
10	$0{\cdot}0192[z(0{\cdot}99669) - z(0{\cdot}00331)] + 0{\cdot}0467[z(0{\cdot}9830) - z(0{\cdot}0170)]$ $+ 0{\cdot}0776[z(0{\cdot}9505) - z(0{\cdot}0495)] + 0{\cdot}1063[z(0{\cdot}8876) - z(0{\cdot}1124)]$ $+ 0{\cdot}1228[z(0{\cdot}7727) - z(0{\cdot}2273)]$	0·9496
12	$0{\cdot}0133[z(0{\cdot}99776) - z(0{\cdot}00224)] + 0{\cdot}0323[z(0{\cdot}9888) - z(0{\cdot}0112)]$ $+ 0{\cdot}0544[z(0{\cdot}9680) - z(0{\cdot}0320)] + 0{\cdot}0767[z(0{\cdot}9290) - z(0{\cdot}0710)]$ $+ 0{\cdot}0955[z(0{\cdot}8628) - z(0{\cdot}1372)] + 0{\cdot}1041[z(0{\cdot}7512) - z(0{\cdot}2488)]$	0·9622

Table 11*e*. *With minimum* $\sigma^2(\check{u}) + \sigma^2(\check{\sigma})$

k		Efficiency
2	$0{\cdot}4875[z(0{\cdot}8475) - z(0{\cdot}1525)]$	0·5516
4	$0{\cdot}2581[z(0{\cdot}9332) - z(0{\cdot}0668)] + 0{\cdot}2051[z(0{\cdot}7088) - z(0{\cdot}2912)]$	0·7352
6	$0{\cdot}1088[z(0{\cdot}9769) - z(0{\cdot}0231)] + 0{\cdot}1951[z(0{\cdot}8820) - z(0{\cdot}1180)]$ $+ 0{\cdot}1228[z(0{\cdot}6631) - z(0{\cdot}3369)]$	0·8541
8	$0{\cdot}0600[z(0{\cdot}9881) - z(0{\cdot}0119)] + 0{\cdot}1249[z(0{\cdot}9396) - z(0{\cdot}0604)]$ $+ 0{\cdot}1528[z(0{\cdot}8279) - z(0{\cdot}1721)] + 0{\cdot}0789[z(0{\cdot}6289) - z(0{\cdot}3711)]$	0·9050
10	$0{\cdot}0379[z(0{\cdot}99282) - z(0{\cdot}00718)] + 0{\cdot}0829[z(0{\cdot}9642) - z(0{\cdot}0358)]$ $+ 0{\cdot}1181[z(0{\cdot}8992) - z(0{\cdot}1008)] + 0{\cdot}1184[z(0{\cdot}7828) - z(0{\cdot}2172)]$ $+ 0{\cdot}0540[z(0{\cdot}6058) - z(0{\cdot}3942)]$	0·9328
12	$0{\cdot}0255[z(0{\cdot}99537) - z(0{\cdot}00463)] + 0{\cdot}00576[z(0{\cdot}9770) - z(0{\cdot}0230)]$ $+ 0{\cdot}0877[z(0{\cdot}9358) - z(0{\cdot}0642)] + 0{\cdot}1047[z(0{\cdot}8623) - z(0{\cdot}1377)]$ $+ 0{\cdot}0933[z(0{\cdot}7476) - z(0{\cdot}2524)] + 0{\cdot}0394[z(0{\cdot}5898) - z(0{\cdot}4102)]$	0·9501

Table 11*f*.† *With minimum variance and* $p_1 \geqslant 0{\cdot}025$

k		Efficiency
4	$0{\cdot}1208[z(0{\cdot}975) - z(0{\cdot}025)] + 0{\cdot}2341[z(0{\cdot}8696) - z(0{\cdot}1304)]$	0·8241
6	$0{\cdot}0953[z(0{\cdot}975) - z(0{\cdot}025)] + 0{\cdot}1249[z(0{\cdot}9203) - z(0{\cdot}0797)]$ $+ 0{\cdot}1609[z(0{\cdot}8036) - z(0{\cdot}1964)]$	0·8777
8	$0{\cdot}0842[z(0{\cdot}975) - z(0{\cdot}025)] + 0{\cdot}0825[z(0{\cdot}9389) - z(0{\cdot}0611)]$ $+ 0{\cdot}1070[z(0{\cdot}8741) - z(0{\cdot}1259)] + 0{\cdot}1198[z(0{\cdot}7609) - z(0{\cdot}2391)]$	0·8965
10	$0{\cdot}0779[z(0{\cdot}975) - z(0{\cdot}025)] + 0{\cdot}0606[z(0{\cdot}9483) - z(0{\cdot}0517)]$ $+ 0{\cdot}0772[z(0{\cdot}9052) - z(0{\cdot}0948)] + 0{\cdot}0903[z(0{\cdot}8380) - z(0{\cdot}1620)]$ $+ 0{\cdot}0945[z(0{\cdot}7316) - z(0{\cdot}2684)]$	0·9051
12	$0{\cdot}0741[z(0{\cdot}975) - z(0{\cdot}025)] + 0{\cdot}0484[z(0{\cdot}9535) - z(0{\cdot}0465)]$ $+ 0{\cdot}0600[z(0{\cdot}9213) - z(0{\cdot}0787)] + 0{\cdot}0701[z(0{\cdot}8744) - z(0{\cdot}1256)]$ $+ 0{\cdot}0767[z(0{\cdot}8073) - z(0{\cdot}1927)] + 0{\cdot}0764[z(0{\cdot}7069) - z(0{\cdot}2931)]$	0·9098

† The coefficients for $k = 2$ are the same as those in Table 11*d*.

Table 12. *Moments and moment ratios of the extreme values, $x_{(1)}$ and $x_{(n)}$, in normal samples*

n	μ_2	μ_3	μ_4	β_1	$\beta_2 - 3$	$\sqrt{\mu_2}$
1	1·00000 000	0	3·00000 00	0	0	1·00000 00
2	0·68169 011	0·07707 945	1·42279 69	0·01875 50	0·06174 43	0·82564 53
3	0·55946 720	0·08919 934	0·97955 22	0·04543 59	0·12952 43	0·74797 54
4	0·49171 524	0·09120 683	0·76459 74	0·06997 03	0·16231 77	0·70122 41
5	0·44753 407	0·09058 710	0·64107 54	0·09154 92	0·20078 82	0·66897 99
6	0·41592 711	0·08917 023	0·55943 20	0·11050 66	0·23379 78	0·64492 41
7	0·39191 778	0·08753 521	0·50113 26	0·12728 60	0·26259 20	0·62603 34
8	0·37289 714	0·08588 990	0·45721 20	0·14227 12	0·28805 84	0·61065 30
9	0·35735 333	0·08431 165	0·42279 90	0·15576 92	0·31084 08	0·59779 04
10	0·34434 382	0·08282 697	0·39501 52	0·16802 22	0·33141 89	0·58680 82
11	0·33324 744	0·08144 141	0·37204 79	0·17922 15	0·35015 75	0·57727 59
12	0·32363 639	0·08015 182	0·35269 69	0·18951 99	0·36733 95	0·56889 05
13	0·31520 538	0·07895 167	0·33613 48	0·19904 06	0·38318 91	0·56143 15
14	0·30773 010	0·07783 336	0·32177 24	0·20788 42	0·39788 63	0·55473 43
15	0·30104 157	0·07678 934	0·30917 77	0·21613 37	0·41157 72	0·54867 26
16	0·29500 981	0·07581 253	0·29802 68	0·22385 80	0·42438 30	0·54314 81
17	0·28953 300	0·07489 647	0·28807 16	0·23111 52	0·43640 41	0·53808 27
18	0·28453 013	0·07403 540	0·27911 89	0·23795 45	0·44772 53	0·53341 37
19	0·27993 580	0·07322 415	0·27101 57	0·24441 81	0·45841 87	0·52908 96
20	0·27569 662	0·07245 817	0·26363 94	0·25054 19	0·46854 62	0·52506 82
21	0·27176 844	0·07173 345	0·25689 02	0·25635 77	0·47816 00	0·52131 41
22	0·26811 447	0·07104 635	0·25068 64	0·26189 23	0·48730 80	0·51779 77
23	0·26470 377	0·07039 370	0·24496 01	0·26716 97	0·49603 01	0·51449 37
24	0·26151 002	0·06977 268	0·23965 45	0·27221 11	0·50436 15	0·51138 05
25	0·25851 078	0·06918 079	0·23472 16	0·27703 53	0·51233 28	0·50843 96
26	0·25568 671	0·06861 576	0·23012 06	0·28165 88	0·51997 21	0·50565 47
27	0·25302 107	0·06807 556	0·22581 68	0·28609 63	0·52730 46	0·50301 20
28	0·25049 931	0·06755 837	0·22178 02	0·29036 13	0·53435 19	0·50049 91
29	0·24810 866	0·06706 255	0·21798 48	0·29446 55	0·54113 42	0·49810 51
30	0·24583 790	0·06658 663	0·21440 79	0·29841 97	0·54766 97	0·49582 04
31	0·24367 711	0·06612 926	0·21102 97	0·30223 38	0·55397 34	0·49363 66
32	0·24161 750	0·06568 923	0·20783 28	0·30591 67	0·56006 08	0·49154 60
33	0·23965 122	0·06526 541	0·20480 20	0·30947 61	0·56594 66	0·48954 19
34	0·23777 127	0·06485 680	0·20192 34	0·31291 97	0·57164 13	0·48761 80
35	0·23597 135	0·06446 249	0·19918 49	0·31625 42	0·57715 59	0·48576 88
36	0·23424 579	0·06408 161	0·19657 59	0·31948 58	0·58250 37	0·48398 95
37	0·23258 948	0·06371 339	0·19408 62	0·32262 00	0·58768 62	0·48227 53
38	0·23099 780	0·06335 710	0·19170 75	0·32566 20	0·59272 11	0·48062 23
39	0·22946 652	0·06301 212	0·18943 18	0·32861 71	0·59761 04	0·47902 66
40	0·22799 182	0·06267 778	0·18725 20	0·33148 92	0·60236 66	0·47748 49
41	0·22657 020	0·06235 357	0·18516 15	0·33428 30	0·60699 15	0·47599 39
42	0·22519 846	0·06203 894	0·18315 46	0·33700 20	0·61149 41	0·47455 08
43	0·22387 366	0·06173 341	0·18122 58	0·33964 99	0·61587 96	0·47315 29
44	0·22259 311	0·06143 652	0·17937 03	0·34222 99	0·62015 48	0·47179 77
45	0·22135 432	0·06114 786	0·17758 36	0·34474 54	0·62432 34	0·47048 31
46	0·22015 501	0·06086 702	0·17586 17	0·34719 89	0·62839 06	0·46920 68
47	0·21899 305	0·06059 368	0·17420 05	0·34959 37	0·63235 93	0·46796 69
48	0·21786 649	0·06032 745	0·17259 69	0·35193 19	0·63623 67	0·46676 17
49	0·21677 350	0·06006 804	0·17104 75	0·35421 62	0·64002 38	0·46558 94
50	0·21571 241	0·05981 512	0·16954 94	0·35644 83	0·64372 80	0·46444 85

μ_3 is positive for $x_{(n)}$, negative for $x_{(1)}$.

Table 13. *Sums of squares of expected values of normal order statistics*

n	c_n^2	n	c_n^2	n	c_n^2	n	c_n^2	n	c_n^2
		21	18·66307	41	38·47266	61	58·37282	81	79·30663
2	0·63662	22	19·64882	42	39·46643	62	59·36892	82	79·30394
3	1·43238	23	20·63536	43	40·46024	63	60·36505	83	80·30114
4	2·29568	24	21·62261	44	41·45417	64	61·36130	84	81·29856
5	3·19504	25	22·61039	45	42·44851	65	62·35771	85	82·29580
6	4·11660	26	23·59895	46	43·44282	66	63·35398	86	83·29324
7	5·05281	27	24·58796	47	44·43736	67	64·35050	87	84·29061
8	5·99947	28	25·57742	48	54·43191	68	65·34703	88	85·28809
9	6·95391	29	26·56739	49	46·42676	69	66·34349	89	86·28551
10	7·91426	30	27·55780	50	47·42170	70	67·34027	90	87·28304
11	8·87935	31	28·54851	51	48·41662	71	68·33691	91	88·28057
12	9·84812	32	29·53975	52	49·41192	72	69·33362	92	89·27820
13	10·82002	33	30·53118	53	50·40718	73	70·33052	93	90·27579
14	11·79451	34	31·52295	54	51·40255	74	71·32729	94	91·27355
15	12·77121	35	32·51500	55	52·39806	75	72·32427	95	92·27122
16	13·74971	36	33·50732	56	53·39352	76	73·32121	96	93·26903
17	14·72986	37	34·50004	57	54·38934	77	74·31825	97	94·26673
18	15·71142	38	35·49279	58	55·38502	78	75·31524	98	95·26441
19	16·69425	39	36·48592	59	56·38092	79	76·31228	99	96·26222
20	17·67819	40	37·47921	60	57·37675	80	77·30951	100	97·25999

$$c_n^2 = \sum_{i=1}^{n} \{\xi(i|n)\}^2.$$

Table 14. *Conversion factors to be applied to Table 15 to derive a best linear estimate of* σ

n	g_n	n	g_n	n	g_n	n	g_n	n	g_n
		11	0·3362	21	0·230	31	0·189	41	0·165
2	1·2533	12	·3193	22	·224	32	·186	42	·163
3	0·8355	13	·3046	23	·220	33	·184	43	·161
4	·6606	14	·2917	24	·215	34	·181	44	·159
5	·5602	15	·2803	25	·211	35	·178	45	·157
6	0·4937	16	0·2701	26	0·207	36	0·176	46	0·155
7	·4457	17	·2609	27	·203	37	·173	47	·154
8	·4091	18	·2527	28	·199	38	·171	48	·152
9	·3800	19	·2451	29	·196	39	·169	49	·151
10	·3562	20	·2382	30	·192	40	·167	50	·149

Values of g_n for $n \leqslant 20$ should be exact, for $n > 20$ they have been based on
Shapiro & Wilk's approximations.

Table 15. *Test for departure from normality: coefficients $a_{i,n}$ to use in the W-test*

i \ n	2	3	4	5	6	7	8	9	10
1	0·7071	0·7071	0·6872	0·6646	0·6431	0·6233	0·6052	0·5888	0·5739
2	—	·0000	·1667	·2413	·2806	·3031	·3164	·3244	·3291
3	—	—	—	·0000	·0875	·1401	·1743	·1976	·2141
4	—	—	—	—	—	·0000	·0561	·0947	·1224
5	—	—	—	—	—	—	—	·0000	·0399

i \ n	11	12	13	14	15	16	17	18	19	20
1	0·5601	0·5475	0·5359	0·5251	0·5150	0·5056	0·4968	0·4886	0·4808	0·4734
2	·3315	·3325	·3325	·3318	·3306	·3290	·3273	·3253	·3232	·3211
3	·2260	·2347	·2412	·2460	·2495	·2521	·2540	·2553	·2561	·2565
4	·1429	·1586	·1707	·1802	·1878	·1939	·1988	·2027	·2059	·2085
5	·0695	·0922	·1099	·1240	·1353	·1447	·1524	·1587	·1641	·1686
6	0·0000	0·0303	0·0539	0·0727	0·0880	0·1005	0·1109	0·1197	0·1271	0·1334
7	—	—	·0000	·0240	·0433	·0593	·0725	·0837	·0932	·1013
8	—	—	—	—	·0000	·0196	·0359	·0496	·0612	·0711
9	—	—	—	—	—	—	·0000	·0163	·0303	·0422
10	—	—	—	—	—	—	—	—	·0000	·0140

i \ n	21	22	23	24	25	26	27	28	29	30
1	0·4643	0·4590	0·4542	0·4493	0·4450	0·4407	0·4366	0·4328	0·4291	0·4254
2	·3185	·3156	·3126	·3098	·3069	·3043	·3018	·2992	·2968	·2944
3	·2578	·2571	·2563	·2554	·2543	·2533	·2522	·2510	·2499	·2487
4	·2119	·2131	·2139	·2145	·2148	·2151	·2152	·2151	·2150	·2148
5	·1736	·1764	·1787	·1807	·1822	·1836	·1848	·1857	·1864	·1870
6	0·1399	0·1443	0·1480	0·1512	0·1539	0·1563	0·1584	0·1601	0·1616	0·1630
7	·1092	·1150	·1201	·1245	·1283	·1316	·1346	·1372	·1395	·1415
8	·0804	·0878	·0941	·0997	·1046	·1089	·1128	·1162	·1192	·1219
9	·0530	·0618	·0696	·0764	·0823	·0876	·0923	·0965	·1002	·1036
10	·0263	·0368	·0459	·0539	·0610	·0672	·0728	·0778	·0822	·0862
11	0·0000	0·0122	0·0228	0·0321	0·0403	0·0476	0·0540	0·0598	0·0650	0·0697
12	—	—	·0000	·0107	·0200	·0284	·0358	·0424	·0483	·0537
13	—	—	—	—	·0000	·0094	·0178	·0253	·0320	·0381
14	—	—	—	—	—	—	·0000	·0084	·0159	·0227
15	—	—	—	—	—	—	—	—	·0000	·0076

Table 15 (*continued*)

i \ n	31	32	33	34	35	36	37	38	39	40
1	0·4220	0·4188	0·4156	0·4127	0·4096	0·4068	0·4040	0·4015	0·3989	0·3964
2	·2921	·2898	·2876	·2854	·2834	·2813	·2794	·2774	·2755	·2737
3	·2475	·2463	·2451	·2439	·2427	·2415	·2403	·2391	·2380	·2368
4	·2145	·2141	·2137	·2132	·2127	·2121	·2116	·2110	·2104	·2098
5	·1874	·1878	·1880	·1882	·1883	·1883	·1883	·1881	·1880	·1878
6	0·1641	0·1651	0·1660	0·1667	0·1673	0·1678	0·1683	0·1686	0·1689	0·1691
7	·1433	·1449	·1463	·1475	·1487	·1496	·1505	·1513	·1520	·1526
8	·1243	·1265	·1284	·1301	·1317	·1331	·1344	·1356	·1366	·1376
9	·1066	·1093	·1118	·1140	·1160	·1179	·1196	·1211	·1225	·1237
10	·0899	·0931	·0961	·0988	·1013	·1036	·1056	·1075	·1092	·1108
11	0·0739	0·0777	0·0812	0·0844	0·0873	0·0900	0·0924	0·0947	0·0967	0·0986
12	·0585	·0629	·0669	·0706	·0739	·0770	·0798	·0824	·0848	·0870
13	·0435	·0485	·0530	·0572	·0610	·0645	·0677	·0706	·0733	·0759
14	·0289	·0344	·0395	·0441	·0484	·0523	·0559	·0592	·0622	·0651
15	·0144	·0206	·0262	·0314	·0361	·0404	·0444	·0481	·0515	·0546
16	0·0000	0·0068	0·0131	0·0187	0·0239	0·0287	0·0331	0·0372	0·0409	0·0444
17	—	—	·0000	·0062	·0119	·0172	·0220	·0264	·0305	·0343
18	—	—	—	—	·0000	·0057	·0110	·0158	·0203	·0244
19	—	—	—	—	—	—	·0000	·0053	·0101	·0146
20	—	—	—	—	—	—	—	—	·0000	·0049

i \ n	41	42	43	44	45	46	47	48	49	50
1	0·3940	0·3917	0·3894	0·3872	0·3850	0·3830	0·3808	0·3789	0·3770	0·3751
2	·2719	·2701	·2684	·2667	·2651	·2635	·2620	·2604	·2589	·2574
3	·2357	·2345	·2334	·2323	·2313	·2302	·2291	·2281	·2271	·2260
4	·2091	·2085	·2078	·2072	·2065	·2058	·2052	·2045	·2038	·2032
5	·1876	·1874	·1871	·1868	·1865	·1862	·1859	·1855	·1851	·1847
6	0·1693	0·1694	0·1695	0·1695	0·1695	0·1695	0·1695	0·1693	0·1692	0·1691
7	·1531	·1535	·1539	·1542	·1545	·1548	·1550	·1551	·1553	·1554
8	·1384	·1392	·1398	·1405	·1410	·1415	·1420	·1423	·1427	·1430
9	·1249	·1259	·1269	·1278	·1286	·1293	·1300	·1306	·1312	·1317
10	·1123	·1136	·1149	·1160	·1170	·1180	·1189	·1197	·1205	·1212
11	0·1004	0·1020	0·1035	0·1049	0·1062	0·1073	0·1085	0·1095	0·1105	0·1113
12	·0891	·0909	·0927	·0943	·0959	·0972	·0986	·0998	·1010	·1020
13	·0782	·0804	·0824	·0842	·0860	·0876	·0892	·0906	·0919	·0932
14	·0677	·0701	·0724	·0745	·0765	·0783	·0801	·0817	·0832	·0846
15	·0575	·0602	·0628	·0651	·0673	·0694	·0713	·0731	·0748	·0764
16	0·0476	0·0506	0·0534	0·0560	0·0584	0·0607	0·0628	0·0648	0·0667	0·0685
17	·0379	·0411	·0442	·0471	·0497	·0522	·0546	·0568	·0588	·0608
18	·0283	·0318	·0352	·0383	·0412	·0439	·0465	·0489	·0511	·0532
19	·0188	·0227	·0263	·0296	·0328	·0357	·0385	·0411	·0436	·0459
20	·0094	·0136	·0175	·0211	·0245	·0277	·0307	·0335	·0361	·0386
21	0·0000	0·0045	0·0087	0·0126	0·0163	0·0197	0·0229	0·0259	0·0288	0·0314
22		—	·0000	·0042	·0081	·0118	·0153	·0185	·0215	·0244
23	—	—	—	—	·0000	·0039	·0076	·0111	·0143	·0174
24	—	—	—	—	—	—	·0000	·0037	·0071	·0104
25	—	—	—	—	—	—	—	—	·0000	·0035

Table 16. *Test for departure from normality: percentage points of W*

					Level				
n	0·01	0·02	0·05	0·10	0·50	0·90	0·95	0·98	0·99
3	0·753	0·756	0·767	0·789	0·959	0·998	0·999	1·000	1·000
4	·687	·707	·748	·792	·935	·987	·992	·996	·997
5	·686	·715	·762	·806	·927	·979	·986	·991	·993
6	0·713	0·743	0·788	0·826	0·927	0·974	0·981	0·986	0·989
7	·730	·760	·803	·838	·928	·972	·979	·985	·988
8	·749	·778	·818	·851	·932	·972	·978	·984	·987
9	·764	·791	·829	·859	·935	·972	·978	·984	·986
10	·781	·806	·842	·869	·938	·972	·978	·983	·986
11	0·792	0·817	0·850	0·876	0·940	0·973	0·979	0·984	0·986
12	·805	·828	·859	·883	·943	·973	·979	·984	·986
13	·814	·837	·866	·889	·945	·974	·979	·984	·986
14	·825	·846	·874	·895	·947	·975	·980	·984	·986
15	·835	·855	·881	·901	·950	·975	·980	·984	·987
16	0·844	0·863	0·887	0·906	0·952	0·976	0·981	0·985	0·987
17	·851	·869	·892	·910	·954	·977	·981	·985	·987
18	·858	·874	·897	·914	·956	·978	·982	·986	·988
19	·863	·879	·901	·917	·957	·978	·982	·986	·988
20	·868	·884	·905	·920	·959	·979	·983	·986	·988
21	0·873	0·888	0·908	0·923	0·960	0·980	0·983	0·987	0·989
22	·878	·892	·911	·926	·961	·980	·984	·987	·989
23	·881	·895	·914	·928	·962	·981	·984	·987	·989
24	·884	·898	·916	·930	·963	·981	·984	·987	·989
25	·888	·901	·918	·931	·964	·981	·985	·988	·989
26	0·891	0·904	0·920	0·933	0·965	0·982	0·985	0·988	0·989
27	·894	·906	·923	·935	·965	·982	·985	·988	·990
28	·896	·908	·924	·936	·966	·982	·985	·988	·990
29	·898	·910	·926	·937	·966	·982	·985	·988	·990
30	·900	·912	·927	·939	·967	·983	·985	·988	·900
31	0·902	0·914	0·929	0·940	0·967	0·983	0·986	0·988	0·990
32	·904	·915	·930	·941	·968	·983	·986	·988	·990
33	·906	·917	·931	·942	·968	·983	·986	·989	·990
34	·908	·919	·933	·943	·969	·983	·986	·989	·990
35	·910	·920	·934	·944	·969	·984	·986	·989	·990
36	0·912	0·922	0·935	0·945	0·970	0·984	0·986	0·989	0·990
37	·914	·924	·936	·946	·970	·984	·987	·989	·990
38	·916	·925	·938	·947	·971	·984	·987	·989	·990
39	·917	·927	·939	·948	·971	·984	·987	·989	·991
40	·919	·928	·940	·949	·972	·985	·987	·989	·991
41	0·920	0·929	0·941	0·950	0·972	0·985	0·987	0·989	0·991
42	·922	·930	·942	·951	·972	·985	·987	·989	·991
43	·923	·932	·943	·951	·973	·985	·987	·990	·991
44	·924	·933	·944	·952	·973	·985	·987	·990	·991
45	·926	·934	·945	·953	·973	·985	·988	·990	·991
46	0·927	0·935	0·945	0·953	0·974	0·985	0·988	0·990	0·991
47	·928	·936	·946	·954	·974	·985	·988	·990	·991
48	·929	·937	·947	·954	·974	·985	·988	·990	·991
49	·929	·937	·947	·955	·974	·985	·988	·990	·991
50	·930	·938	·947	·955	·974	·985	·988	·990	·991

Low values of *W* indicate significance.

Table 17. *Test for departure from normality: coefficients for converting W to a standardized normal variate, n = 7(1)50*

n	$\gamma(n)$	$\delta(n)$	$\epsilon(n)$	n	$\gamma(n)$	$\delta(n)$	$\epsilon(n)$
7	−2·356	1·245	0·4533	29	−6·074	1·934	0·1907
8	−2·696	1·333	·4186	30	−6·150	1·949	·1872
9	−2·968	1·400	·3900				
10	−3·262	1·471	·3660	31	−6·248	1·965	0·1840
				32	−6·324	1·976	·1811
11	−3·485	1·515	0·3451	33	−6·402	1·988	·1781
12	−3·731	1·571	·3270	34	−6·480	2·000	·1755
13	−3·936	1·613	·3111	35	−6·559	2·012	·1727
14	−4·155	1·655	·2969				
15	−4·373	1·695	·2842	36	−6·640	2·024	0·1702
				37	−6·721	2·037	·1677
16	−4·567	1·724	0·2727	38	−6·803	2·049	·1656
17	−4·713	1·739	·2622	39	−6·887	2·062	·1633
18	−4·885	1·770	·2528	40	−6·961	2·075	·1612
19	−5·018	1·786	·2440				
20	−5·153	1·802	·2359	41	−7·035	2·088	0·1591
				42	−7·111	2·101	·1572
21	−5·291	1·818	0·2264	43	−7·188	2·114	·1552
22	−5·413	1·835	·2207	44	−7·266	2·128	·1534
23	−5·508	1·848	·2157	45	−7·345	2·141	·1516
24	−5·605	1·862	·2106				
25	−5·704	1·876	·2063	46	−7·414	2·155	0·1499
				47	−7·484	2·169	·1482
26	−5·803	1·890	0·2020	48	−7·555	2·183	·1466
27	−5·905	1·905	·1980	49	−7·615	2·198	·1451
28	−5·988	1·919	·1943	50	−7·677	2·212	·1436

$G_t = \gamma(n) + \delta(n)\log\{(W_t - \epsilon(n))/(1 - W_t)\}$ is approximately $N(0, 1)$.

Table 18. *Test for departure from normality: values of G for argument v, for normal conversion of W, n = 3(1)6*

v \ n	3 (0·7500)	4 (0·6297)	5 (0·5521)	6 (0·4963)	v \ n	3 (0·7500)	4 (0·6297)	5 (0·5521)	6 (0·4963)
−7·0	−3·29	—	—	—	2·2	0·52	0·74	0·75	0·64
−5·4	−2·81	—	—	—	2·6	0·67	1·00	1·09	1·06
−5·0	−2·68	—	—	—	3·0	0·81	1·23	1·40	1·45
−4·6	−2·54	—	—	—	3·4	0·95	1·44	1·67	1·83
−4·2	−2·40	—	—	—	3·8	1·07	1·65	1·91	2·17
−3·8	−2·25	−3·50	—	—	4·2	1·19	1·85	2·15	2·50
−3·4	−2·10	−3·27	—	—	4·6	1·31	2·03	2·47	2·77
−3·0	−1·94	−3·05	−4·01	—	5·0	1·42	2·19	2·85	3·09
−2·6	−1·77	−2·84	−3·70	—	5·4	1·52	2·34	3·24	3·54
−2·2	−1·59	−2·64	−3·38	—	5·8	1·62	2·48	3·64	—
−1·8	−1·40	−2·44	−3·11	—	6·2	1·72	2·62	—	—
−1·4	−1·21	−2·22	−2·87	—	6·6	1·81	2·75	—	—
−1·0	−1·01	−1·96	−2·56	−3·72	7·0	1·90	2·87	—	—
−0·6	−0·80	−1·66	−2·20	−2·88	7·4	1·98	2·97	—	—
−0·2	−0·60	−1·31	−1·81	−2·27	7·8	2·07	3·08	—	—
0·2	−0·39	−0·94	−1·41	−1·85	8·2	2·15	3·22	—	—
0·6	−0·19	−0·57	−0·97	−1·38	8·6	2·23	3·36	—	—
1·0	−0·00	−0·19	−0·51	−0·84	9·0	2·31	—	—	—
1·4	0·18	0·15	−0·06	−0·33	9·4	2·38	—	—	—
1·8	0·35	0·45	0·37	0·18	9·8	2·45	—	—	—

$v_t = \log\{(W_t - \epsilon)/(1 - W_t)\}$, where the value of ϵ is given in parentheses at the head of column.

Table 19. *Expected values of negative exponential order statistics,* $\eta(i|n)$

	1	2	3	4	5	6	7	8	9	10	11	12	13	14	n / i
	1·00	0·50	0·33	0·25	0·20	0·17	0·14	0·12	0·11	0·10	0·09	0·08	0·08	0·07	1
	——	1·50	·83	·58	·45	·37	·31	·27	·24	·21	·19	·17	·16	·15	2
60	4·67987	——	1·83	1·08	·78	·62	·51	·43	·38	·34	·30	·27	·25	·23	3
59	3·67987	4·66	——	2·08	1·28	·95	·76	·63	·55	·48	·43	·39	·35	·32	4
58	3·17987	3·66	4·65	——	2·28	1·45	1·09	·88	·75	·65	·57	·51	·46	·42	5
57	2·84654	3·16	3·65	4·63	——	2·45	1·59	1·22	1·00	·85	·74	·65	·59	·53	6
56	2·59654	2·83	3·15	3·63	4·61	——	2·59	1·72	1·33	1·10	·94	·82	·73	·66	7
55	2·39654	2·58	2·81	3·13	3·61	4·59	——	2·72	1·83	1·43	1·19	1·02	·90	·80	8
54	2·22987	2·38	2·56	2·80	3·11	3·59	4·58	——	2·83	1·93	1·52	1·27	1·10	·97	9
53	2·08701	2·21	2·36	2·55	2·78	3·09	3·58	4·56	——	2·93	2·02	1·60	1·35	1·17	10
52	1·96201	2·07	2·20	2·35	2·53	2·76	3·08	3·56	4·54	——	3·02	2·10	1·68	1·42	11
51	1·85090	1·95	2·05	2·18	2·33	2·51	2·74	3·06	3·54	4·52	——	3·10	2·18	1·75	12
50	1·75090	1·83	1·93	2·04	2·16	2·31	2·49	2·72	3·04	3·52	4·50	——	3·18	2·25	13
49	1·65999	1·73	1·82	1·91	2·02	2·14	2·29	2·47	2·70	3·02	3·50	4·48	——	3·25	14
48	1·57666	1·64	1·72	1·80	1·89	2·00	2·13	2·27	2·45	2·69	3·00	3·48	4·46	——	
47	1·49974	1·56	1·63	1·70	1·78	1·88	1·98	2·11	2·25	2·44	2·67	2·98	3·46	4·44	
46	1·42831	1·48	1·54	1·61	1·68	1·76	1·86	1·96	2·09	2·24	2·42	2·65	2·96	3·44	
45	1·36164	1·41	1·47	1·53	1·59	1·66	1·75	1·84	1·95	2·07	2·22	2·40	2·63	2·94	
44	1·29914	1·34	1·39	1·45	1·51	1·57	1·65	1·73	1·82	1·93	2·05	2·20	2·38	2·60	
43	1·24032	1·28	1·33	1·38	1·43	1·49	1·56	1·63	1·71	1·80	1·91	2·03	2·18	2·35	
42	1·18476	1·22	1·27	1·31	1·36	1·41	1·47	1·54	1·61	1·69	1·78	1·89	2·01	2·15	
41	1·13213	1·17	1·21	1·25	1·29	1·34	1·40	1·45	1·52	1·59	1·67	1·76	1·87	1·99	
40	1·08213	1·12	1·15	1·19	1·23	1·28	1·32	1·38	1·43	1·50	1·57	1·65	1·74	1·85	
39	1·03451	1·07	1·10	1·13	1·17	1·21	1·26	1·31	1·36	1·42	1·48	1·55	1·63	1·72	
38	0·98906	1·02	1·05	1·08	1·12	1·15	1·19	1·24	1·29	1·34	1·40	1·46	1·53	1·61	
37	·94558	0·97	1·00	1·03	1·06	1·10	1·14	1·18	1·22	1·27	1·32	1·38	1·44	1·51	
36	·90391	·93	0·96	0·98	1·01	1·05	1·08	1·12	1·16	1·20	1·25	1·30	1·36	1·42	
35	·86391	·89	·91	·94	0·97	1·00	1·03	1·06	1·10	1·14	1·18	1·23	1·28	1·33	
34	·82545	·85	·87	·89	·92	0·95	0·98	1·01	1·04	1·08	1·12	1·16	1·21	1·26	
33	·78841	·81	·83	·85	·88	·90	·93	0·96	0·99	1·02	1·06	1·10	1·14	1·19	
32	·75270	·77	·79	·81	·84	·86	·88	·91	·94	0·97	1·00	1·04	1·08	1·12	
31	·71822	·74	·75	·77	·80	·82	·84	·87	·89	·92	0·95	0·98	1·02	1·06	
30	0·68488	0·70	0·72	0·74	0·76	0·78	0·80	·82	0·85	0·87	0·90	0·93	0·96	1·00	
29	·65263	·67	·68	·70	·72	·74	·76	·78	·80	·83	·85	·88	·91	0·94	
28	·62138	·64	·65	·67	·68	·70	·72	·74	·76	·78	·81	·83	·86	·89	
27	·59107	·60	·62	·63	·65	·67	·68	·70	·72	·74	·76	·79	·81	·84	
26	·56166	·57	·59	·60	·62	·63	·65	·67	·68	·70	·72	·74	·77	·79	
25	·53309	·54	·56	·57	·58	·60	·61	·63	·65	·66	·68	·70	·72	·75	
24	·50531	·52	·53	·54	·55	·57	·58	·60	·61	·63	·64	·66	·68	·70	
23	·47828	·49	·50	·51	·52	·54	·55	·56	·58	·59	·61	·62	·64	·66	
22	·45197	·46	·47	·48	·49	·50	·52	·53	·54	·56	·57	·59	·60	·62	
21	·42633	·44	·44	·45	·46	·48	·49	·50	·51	·52	·54	·55	·57	·58	
20	0·40133	0·41	·042	0·43	0·44	0·45	0·46	0·47	0·48	0·49	0·50	0·52	0·53	0·55	
19	·37694	·38	·39	·40	·41	·42	·43	·44	·45	·46	·47	·48	·50	·51	
18	·35313	·36	·37	·38	·38	·39	·40	·41	·42	·43	·44	·45	·46	·48	
17	·32987	·34	·34	·35	·36	·37	·37	·38	·39	·40	·41	·42	·43	·44	
16	·30714	·31	·32	·33	·33	·34	·35	·36	·36	·37	·38	·39	·40	·41	
15	·28492	·29	·30	·30	·31	·32	·32	·33	·34	·34	·35	·36	·37	·38	
14	·26318	·27	·27	·28	·28	·29	·30	·30	·31	·32	·32	·33	·34	·35	
13	·24191	·25	·25	·26	·26	·27	·27	·28	·28	·29	·30	·30	·31	·32	
12	·22107	·23	·23	·23	·24	·24	·25	·25	·26	·27	·27	·28	·28	·29	
11	·20067	·20	·21	·21	·22	·22	·23	·23	·24	·24	·25	·25	·26	·26	
10	0·18067	0·18	0·19	0·19	0·19	0·20	0·20	0·21	0·21	0·22	0·22	0·23	0·23	0·24	
9	·16106	·16	·17	·17	·17	·18	·18	·18	·19	·19	·20	·20	·21	·21	
8	·14183	·14	·15	·15	·15	·16	·16	·16	·17	·17	·17	·18	·18	·18	
7	·12296	·13	·13	·13	·13	·13	·14	·14	·14	·15	·15	·15	·16	·16	
6	·10444	·11	·11	·11	·11	·11	·12	·12	·12	·12	·13	·13	·13	·14	
5	·08626	·09	·09	·09	·09	·09	·10	·10	·10	·10	·10	·11	·11	·11	
4	·06840	·07	·07	·07	·07	·07	·08	·08	·08	·08	·08	·08	·09	·09	
3	·05086	·05	·05	·05	·05	·06	·06	·06	·06	·06	·06	·06	·06	·07	
2	·03362	·03	·03	·04	·04	·04	·04	·04	·04	·04	·04	·04	·04	·04	
1	·01667	·02	·02	·02	·02	·02	·02	·02	·02	·02	·02	·02	·02	·02	
i / n	60	59	58	57	56	55	54	53	52	51	50	49	48	47	

The negative exponential is taken in standard form, $f(X) = e^{-X}$. For five decimal place accuracy and $n < 60$, take
$$\eta(i|n) = \eta(60-n+i|60) - \eta(60-n|60).$$

Table 19 (*continued*)

	15	16	17	18	19	20	21	22	23	24	25	26	27	28	29	30	*n* / *i*
	0·07	0·06	0·06	0·06	0·05	0·05	0·05	0·05	0·04	0·04	0·04	0·04	0·04	0·04	0·03	0·03	1
	·14	·13	·12	·11	·11	·10	·10	·09	·09	·09	·08	·08	·08	·07	·07	·07	2
	·22	·20	·19	·18	·17	·16	·15	·14	·14*	·13	·13	·12	·12	·11	·11	·10	3
	·30	·28	·26	·24	·23	·22	·21	·20	·19	·18	·17	·16	·16	·15	·15	·14	4
	·39	·36	·34	·31	·30	·28	·26	·25	·24	·23	·22	·21	·20	·19	·19	·18	5
	·49	·45	·42	·39	·37	·35	·33	·31	·29	·28	·27	·26	·25	·24	·23	·22	6
	·60	·55	·51	·48	·44	·42	·39	·37	·35	·34	·32	·31	·29	·28	·27	·26	7
	·73	·66	·61	·57	·53	·49	·47	·44	·42	·40	·38	·36	·34	·33	·32	·30	8
	·87	·79	·72	·67	·62	·58	·54	·51	·48	·46	·44	·41	·40	·38	·36	·35	9
	1·03	·93	·85	·78	·72	·67	·63	·59	·55	·52	·50	·47	·45	·43	·41	·40	10
	1·23	1·10	0·99	0·90	0·83	0·77	0·72	0·67	0·63	0·60	0·56	0·54	0·51	0·49	0·47	0·45	11
	1·48	1·30	1·16	1·05	·95	·88	·82	·76	·71	·67	·64	·60	·57	·55	·52	·50	12
	1·82	1·55	1·36	1·21	1·10	1·00	·93	·86	·81	·76	·71	·67	·64	·61	·58	·56	13
	2·32	1·88	1·61	1·41	1·26	1·15	1·05	·97	·91	·85	·80	·75	·71	·68	·64	·61	14
	3·32	2·38	1·94	1·66	1·46	1·31	1·20	1·10	1·02	·95	·89	·83	·79	·75	·71	·68	15
	—	3·38	2·44	2·00	1·71	1·51	1·36	1·24	1·14	1·06	·99	·93	·87	·82	·78	·74	16
46	4·42	—	3·44	2·50	2·05	1·76	1·56	1·41	1·28	1·18	1·10	1·03	·96	·91	·86	·81	17
45	3·42	4·39	—	3·50	2·55	2·10	1·81	1·61	1·45	1·33	1·22	1·14	1·06	1·00	·94	·89	18
44	2·92	3·39	4·37	—	3·55	2·60	2·15	1·86	1·65	1·49	1·37	1·26	1·17	1·10	1·03	·98	19
43	2·58	2·89	3·37	4·35	—	3·60	2·65	2·19	1·90	1·69	1·53	1·40	1·30	1·21	1·13	1·07	20
42	2·33	2·56	2·87	3·35	4·33	—	3·65	2·69	2·23	1·94	1·73	1·57	1·44	1·33	1·24	1·17	21
41	2·13	2·31	2·54	2·85	3·33	4·30	—	3·69	2·73	2·28	1·98	1·77	1·61	1·48	1·37	1·28	22
40	1·97	2·11	2·29	2·52	2·83	3·30	4·28	—	3·73	2·78	2·32	2·02	1·81	1·64	1·51	1·40	23
39	1·82	1·94	2·09	2·27	2·49	2·80	3·28	4·25	—	3·78	2·82	2·35	2·06	1·84	1·68	1·54	24
38	1·70	1·80	1·92	2·07	2·24	2·47	2·78	3·25	4·23	—	3·82	2·85	2·39	2·09	1·88	1·71	25
37	1·59	1·68	1·78	1·90	2·04	2·22	2·45	2·75	3·23	4·20	—	3·85	2·89	2·43	2·13	1·91	26
36	1·49	1·57	1·65	1·76	1·88	2·02	2·20	2·42	2·73	3·20	4·17	—	3·89	2·93	2·46	2·16	27
35	1·40	1·47	1·54	1·63	1·73	1·85	2·00	2·17	2·39	2·70	3·17	4·15	—	3·93	2·96	2·49	28
34	1·31	1·38	1·44	1·52	1·61	1·71	1·83	1·97	2·14	2·37	2·67	3·15	4·12	—	3·96	2·99	29
33	1·24	1·29	1·35	1·42	1·50	1·59	1·69	1·80	1·94	2·12	2·34	2·65	3·12	4·09	—	3·99	30
32	1·17	1·21	1·27	1·33	1·40	1·47	1·56	1·66	1·78	1·92	2·09	2·31	2·62	3·09	4·06	—	
31	1·10	1·14	1·19	1·25	1·31	1·37	1·45	1·54	1·64	1·75	1·89	2·06	2·28	2·59	3·06	4·03	
30	1·04	1·08	1·12	1·17	1·22	1·28	1·35	1·42	1·51	1·61	1·72	1·86	2·03	2·26	2·56	3·03	
29	0·98	1·01	1·05	1·10	1·15	1·20	1·26	1·32	1·40	1·48	1·58	1·70	1·83	2·01	2·23	2·53	
28	·92	·96	·99	1·03	1·08	1·12	1·18	1·23	1·30	1·40	1·48	1·55	1·67	1·81	1·98	2·19	
27	·87	·90	·93	·97	1·01	1·05	1·10	1·15	1·21	1·27	1·35	1·43	1·53	1·64	1·78	1·94	
26	·82	·85	·88	·91	0·95	0·98	1·03	1·07	1·12	1·18	1·25	1·32	1·40	1·50	1·61	1·74	
25	·77	·80	·82	·85	·89	·92	·96	1·00	1·05	1·10	1·15	1·22	1·29	1·37	1·47	1·58	
24	·73	·75	·77	·80	·83	·86	·90	·94	·98	1·02	1·07	1·13	1·19	1·26	1·34	1·43	
23	·68	·70	·73	·75	·78	·81	·84	·87	·91	·95	0·99	1·04	1·10	1·16	1·23	1·31	
22	·64	·66	·68	·70	·73	·76	·78	·81	·85	·88	·92	·97	1·01	1·07	1·13	1·20	
21	·60	·62	·64	·66	·68	·71	·73	·76	·79	·82	·86	·90	·94	·99	1·04	1·10	
20	0·56	0·58	0·60	0·62	0·64	0·66	0·68	0·71	0·73	0·76	0·79	0·83	0·87	0·91	0·96	1·01	
19	·53	·54	·56	·57	·59	·61	·63	·66	·68	·71	·74	·77	·80	·84	·88	0·92	
18	·49	·50	·52	·53	·55	·57	·59	·61	·63	·65	·68	·71	·74	·77	·81	·85	
17	·46	·47	·48	·50	·51	·53	·54	·56	·58	·60	·63	·65	·68	·71	·74	·78	
16	·42	·43	·45	·46	·47	·49	·50	·52	·54	·56	·58	·60	·62	·65	·68	·71	
15	·39	·40	·41	·42	·44	·45	·46	·48	·49	·51	·53	·55	·57	·59	·62	·65	
14	·36	·37	·38	·39	·40	·41	·42	·44	·45	·47	·48	·50	·52	·54	·56	·59	
13	·33	·34	·35	·36	·37	·38	·39	·40	·41	·43	·44	·46	·47	·49	·51	·53	
12	·30	·31	·31	·32	·33	·34	·35	·36	·37	·39	·40	·41	·43	·44	·46	·48	
11	·27	·28	·28	·29	·30	·31	·32	·33	·34	·35	·36	·37	·38	·40	·41	·43	
10	0·24	0·25	0·25	0·26	0·27	0·28	0·28	0·29	0·30	0·31	0·32	0·33	0·34	0·35	0·37	0·38	
9	·22	·22	·23	·23	·24	·24	·25	·26	·27	·27	·28	·29	·30	·31	·32	·34	
8	·19	·19	·20	·20	·21	·21	·22	·23	·23	·24	·25	·26	·26	·27	·28	·29	
7	·16	·17	·17	·18	·18	·18	·19	·20	·20	·21	·21	·22	·23	·23	·24	·25	
6	·14	·14	·14	·15	·15	·16	·16	·16	·17	·17	·18	·19	·19	·20	·20	·21	
5	·11	·12	·12	·12	·13	·13	·13	·14	·14	·14	·15	·15	·16	·16	·17	·17	
4	·09	·09	·09	·10	·10	·10	·10	·11	·11	·11	·12	·12	·12	·13	·13	·14	
3	·07	·07	·07	·07	·07	·08	·08	·08	·08	·08	·09	·09	·09	·09	·10	·10	
2	·04	·04	·05	·05	·05	·05	·05	·05	·05	·05	·06	·06	·06	·06	·06	·07	
1	·02	·02	·02	·02	·02	·02	·02	·03	·03	·03	·03	·03	·03	·03	·03	·03	
i / *n*	46	45	44	43	42	41	40	39	38	37	36	35	34	33	32	31	

Table 20. *Expected values of order statistics,* $\eta(i|n, m)$, *in samples from certain gamma distributions*

n	i	m = 0·5	m = 1·5	m = 2·0	m = 2·5	m = 3·5	n	i	m = 0·5	m = 1·5	m = 2·0	m = 2·5	m = 3·5
1	1	0·500	1·500	2·000	2·500	3·500	10	6	0·330	1·368	1·890	2·410	3·445⁺
2	1	0·182	0·863	1·250	1·651	2·481		7	·485⁺	1·685⁻	2·260	2·825⁺	3·939
	2	·818	2·137	2·750	3·349	4·519		8	·713	2·091	2·725⁻	3·341	4·540
3	1	0·096	0·632	0·963	1·316	2·062		9	1·086	2·679	3·384	4·062	5·367
	2	·352	1·327	1·824	2·322	3·320		10	1·900	3·810	4·623	5·394	6·858
	3	1·051	2·541	3·213	3·862	5·118	11	1	0·010	0·242	0·441	0·674	1·210
4	1	0·060	0·508	0·805⁻	1·126	1·819		2	·032	·431	·715⁻	1·027	1·705⁺
	2	·205⁻	1·002	1·438	1·883	2·790		3	·066	·613	·960	1·328	2·103
	3	·500	1·652	2·210	2·762	3·851		4	·114	·801	1·201	1·616	2·472
	4	1·235⁺	2·838	3·547	4·229	5·540		5	·179	1·003	1·452	1·909	2·837
5	1	0·042	0·430	0·702	1·002	1·656		6	0·266	1·227	1·723	2·221	3·218
	2	·136	·820	1·215⁺	1·625⁺	2·472		7	·383	1·486	2·029	2·568	3·634
	3	·308	1·275⁺	1·772	2·270	3·267		8	·544	1·798	2·391	2·973	4·112
	4	·628	1·903	2·503	3·090	4·239		9	·777	2·201	2·850⁺	3·479	4·701
	5	1·387	3·072	3·808	4·514	5·865⁺		10	1·154	2·785⁺	3·503	4·192	5·515⁻
6	1	0·030	0·376	0·629	0·912	1·536		11	1·974	3·913	4·735⁻	5·514	6·992
	2	·097	·701	1·067	1·451	2·254	12	1	0·009	0·227	0·420	0·646	1·170
	3	·213	1·057	1·512	1·973	2·909		2	·027	·403	·677	·980	1·643
	4	·403	1·494	2·032	2·566	3·626		3	·056	·570	·904	1·261	2·018
	5	·740	2·108	2·738	3·352	4·546		4	·096	·741	1·126	1·527	2·360
	6	1·516	3·264	4·022	4·746	6·129		5	·150⁻	·921	1·352	1·793	2·694
7	1	0·023	0·336	0·574	0·843	1·443		6	0·220	1·117	1·592	2·071	3·036
	2	·073	·617	·960	1·324	2·092		7	·312	1·337	1·855⁻	2·371	3·400
	3	·157	·912	1·335⁻	1·769	2·659		8	·434	1·592	2·154	2·708	3·802
	4	·287	1·251	1·747	2·245⁻	3·242		9	·599	1·901	2·510	3·105⁻	4·268
	5	·491	1·676	2·246	2·807	3·913		10	·836	2·301	2·963	3·604	4·845⁺
	6	0·840	2·280	2·935⁻	3·569	4·799		11	1·218	2·882	3·611	4·309	5·649
	7	1·629	3·428	4·204	4·942	6·351		12	2·043	4·007	4·837	5·624	7·115⁻
8	1	0·018	0·304	0·531	0·789	1·369	13	1	0·008	0·215⁻	0·401	0·622	1·135⁺
	2	·057	·554	·878	1·226	1·965⁺		2	·023	·379	·644	·940	1·588
	3	·121	·807	1·205⁺	1·619	2·472		3	·048	·534	·857	1·204	1·944
	4	·216	1·087	1·551	2·021	2·972		4	·082	·691	1·062	1·452	2·265⁻
	5	·357	1·415⁺	1·943	2·469	3·513		5	·127	·854	1·269	1·696	2·574
	6	0·571	1·832	2·427	3·011	4·154		6	0·186	1·029	1·485⁻	1·948	2·886
	7	·930	2·430	3·104	3·755⁺	5·014		7	·261	1·221	1·717	2·214	3·211
	8	1·729	3·571	4·361	5·112	6·541		8	·357	1·437	1·973	2·505⁺	3·561
9	1	0·015⁻	0·280	0·495⁺	0·744	1·307		9	·482	1·689	2·267	2·835⁻	3·952
	2	·046	·504	·813	1·147	1·863		10	·651	1·995⁺	2·618	3·225⁻	4·408
	3	·096	·727	1·106	1·501	2·324		11	0·892	2·392	3·067	3·718	4·976
	4	·170	·967	1·405⁺	1·854	2·767		12	1·277	2·972	3·710	4·417	5·771
	5	·274	1·237	1·733	2·230	3·228		13	2·107	4·093	4·931	5·724	7·227
	6	0·423	1·558	2·112	2·659	3·741	14	1	0·007	0·204	0·384	0·600	1·104
	7	·645⁻	1·969	2·585⁺	3·186	4·360		2	·020	·358	·616	·904	1·540
	8	1·011	2·561	3·252	3·918	5·201		3	·042	·503	·816	1·155⁻	1·879
	9	1·818	3·697	4·499	5·261	6·709		4	·071	·648	1·007	1·387	2·182
10	1	0·012	0·259	0·466	0·706	1·255⁻		5	·110	·797	1·198	1·614	2·472
	2	·038	·464	·759	1·082	1·778		6	0·159	0·956	1·395⁺	1·845⁻	2·760
	3	·079	·664	1·026	1·406	2·204		7	·221	1·126	1·604	2·085⁺	3·055⁺
	4	·138	·874	1·292	1·722	2·604		8	·300	1·315⁺	1·829	2·343	3·368
	5	·219	1·105⁻	1·575⁺	2·051	3·010		9	·399	1·529	2·081	2·627	3·707
								10	·528	1·778	2·370	2·950⁺	4·088
								11	0·700	2·082	2·717	3·335⁻	4·536
								12	·944	2·477	3·162	3·822	5·097

The gamma distribution is in the form $f(X|m) = X^{m-1} e^{-X}/\Gamma(m)$, so that $2X$ is distributed as a χ^2 variate, having $\nu = 2m$ degrees of freedom; for case $m = 1$, see Table 19.

Table 20 (*continued*)

n	i	m = 0.5	m = 1.5	m = 2.0	m = 2.5	m = 3.5	n	i	m = 0.5	m = 1.5	m = 2.0	m = 2.5	m = 3.5
14	13	1·333	3·054	3·802	4·516	5·883	18	4	0·044	0·526	0·848	1·195⁺	1·934
	14	2·166	4·173	5·018	5·817	7·330		5	·066	·639	·997	1·376	2·170
15	1	0·006	0·194	0·370	0·581	1·076		6	0·095⁺	0·755⁻	1·146	1·553	2·397
	2	·018	·340	·590	·872	1·497		7	·130	·876	1·298	1·732	2·621
	3	·036	·476	·780	1·111	1·821		8	·172	1·003	1·455⁺	1·915⁻	2·848
	4	·062	·611	·960	1·330	2·109		9	·223	1·139	1·620	2·105⁻	3·081
	5	·095⁺	·749	1·138	1·543	2·382		10	·283	1·286	1·796	2·306	3·324
	6	0·138	0·894	1·319	1·756	2·651		11	0·356	1·447	1·987	2·522	3·583
	7	·191	1·048	1·509	1·977	2·923		12	·445⁻	1·628	2·197	2·759	3·864
	8	·256	1·216	1·712	2·209	3·206		13	·554	1·834	2·435⁺	3·024	4·176
	9	·338	1·402	1·933	2·460	3·509		14	·692	2·076	2·712	3·331	4·533
	10	·440	1·613	2·180	2·738	3·839		15	·873	2·374	3·048	3·699	4·957
	11	0·572	1·861	2·465⁺	3·056	4·213		16	1·126	2·762	3·482	4·171	5·496
	12	·746	2·162	2·809	3·436	4·653		17	1·526	3·333	4·110	4·849	6·259
	13	·993	2·555⁺	3·250⁺	3·919	5·207		18	2·371	4·444	5·312	6·131	7·678
	14	1·385⁺	3·131	3·887	4·608	5·987	19	1	0·004	0·164	0·324	0·520	0·987
	15	2·222	4·247	5·099	5·904	7·426		2	·011	·285⁺	·512	·773	1·360
16	1	0·005⁺	0·185⁺	0·357	0·563	1·051		3	·023	·396	·671	·976	1·642
	2	·016	·324	·568	·844	1·458		4	·039	·503	·818	1·159	1·887
	3	·032	·452	·748	1·072	1·770		5	·060	·610	·960	1·331	2·113
	4	·055⁻	·579	·918	1·280	2·045⁻		6	0·085⁺	0·719	1·101	1·500⁺	2·330
	5	·084	·708	1·085⁺	1·480	2·303		7	·116	·832	1·244	1·669	2·543
	6	0·121	0·841	1·254	1·680	2·556		8	·154	·950⁺	1·390	1·840	2·756
	7	·166	·982	1·429	1·884	2·809		9	·198	1·075⁺	1·543	2·017	2·974
	8	·222	1·133	1·613	2·096	3·070		10	·250⁺	1·209	1·705⁻	2·202	3·200
	9	·291	1·299	1·811	2·322	3·343		11	0·313	1·355⁻	1·878	2·399	3·437
	10	·375⁻	1·482	2·027	2·567	3·637		12	·388	1·514	2·066	2·611	3·690
	11	0·480	1·692	2·271	2·841	3·960		13	·478	1·694	2·274	2·845⁻	3·966
	12	·614	1·937	2·553	3·154	4·328		14	·589	1·899	2·510	3·107	4·273
	13	·791	2·237	2·894	3·530	4·762		15	·729	2·140	2·785⁻	3·410	4·626
	14	1·040	2·629	3·332	4·009	5·310		16	0·912	2·436	3·118	3·776	5·046
	15	1·435⁻	3·202	3·966	4·694	6·084		17	1·167	2·824	3·550⁻	4·245⁺	5·580
	16	2·275⁻	4·317	5·174	5·984	7·515⁺		18	1·568	3·393	4·176	4·920	6·339
17	1	0·005⁻	0·177	0·345⁻	0·547	1·028		19	2·416	4·502	5·375⁺	6·198	7·523
	2	·014	·310	0·547	0·818	1·422	20	1	0·003	0·158	0·315⁻	0·507	0·968
	3	·029	·431	·720	1·037	1·723		2	·010	·275⁻	·497	·753	1·333
	4	·049	·551	·881	1·235⁺	1·987		3	·021	·380	·650⁺	·950⁻	1·607
	5	·074	·671	1·039	1·425⁺	2·233		4	·035⁺	·483	·791	1·126	1·843
	6	0·107	0·795⁺	1·197	1·613	2·472		5	·054	·584	·927	1·291	2·061
	7	·146	·925⁺	1·359	1·803	2·709		6	0·077	0·687	1·061	1·452	2·269
	8	·195⁻	1·063	1·528	1·999	2·951		7	·105⁻	·793	1·196	1·612	2·472
	9	·253	1·212	1·708	2·205⁺	3·203		8	·138	·904	1·333	1·774	2·674
	10	·324	1·375⁺	1·902	2·426	3·468		9	·177	1·020	1·476	1·940	2·879
	11	0·410	1·557	2·115⁺	2·667	3·755⁺		10	·223	1·143	1·626	2·112	3·090
	12	·518	1·765⁺	2·356	2·936	4·072		11	0·278	1·275⁺	1·784	2·293	3·309
	13	·654	2·009	2·635⁺	3·245⁺	4·434		12	·342	1·419	1·954	2·486	3·541
	14	·833	2·308	2·973	3·617	4·863		13	·418	1·578	2·140	2·695⁻	3·790
	15	1·084	2·698	3·409	4·093	5·406		14	·510	1·756	2·346	2·925⁺	4·061
	16	1·481	3·270	4·040	4·774	6·174		15	·623	1·960	2·580	3·185⁻	4·364
	17	2·324	4·382	5·245⁺	6·060	7·599		16	0·764	2·200	2·853	3·486	4·713
18	1	0·004	0·170	0·334	0·533	1·006		17	·949	2·495⁺	3·185⁻	3·849	5·129
	2	·013	·297	·529	·794	1·390		18	1·205⁺	2·882	3·614	4·315⁺	5·660
	3	·026	·413	·694	1·005⁺	1·681		19	1·608	3·450⁻	4·238	4·987	6·414
								20	2·458	4·558	5·435⁻	6·262	7·823

Table 21. Expected values of order statistics in samples from a half-normal distribution, $\zeta(j\mid n)$

Top column headings give j for the rows $n \le 15$; bottom column headings give j for the rows $n \ge 16$.

n	15	14	13	12	11	10	9	8	7	6	5	4	3	2	1
30	0·7074	·7612	·8173	·8760	·9381	1·0039	1·0746	1·1511	1·2349	1·3286	1·4357	1·5625	1·7209	1·9394	2·3229
29	0·7361	·7930	·8525	·9153	·9820	1·0534	1·1307	1·2154	1·3098	1·4179	1·5456	1·7050	1·9248	2·3101	
28	0·7675	·8279	·8915	·9590	1·0312	1·1094	1·1949	1·2903	1·3993	1·5280	1·6885	1·9097	2·2968		
27	0·8020	·8665	·9349	1·0080	1·0870	1·1735	1·2699	1·3798	1·5096	1·6713	1·8939	2·2830			
26	0·8402	·9096	·9836	1·0636	1·1511	1·2485	1·3594	1·4904	1·6534	1·8774	2·2686				
25	0·8829	·9580	1·0390	1·1276	1·2260	1·3381	1·4702	1·6345	1·8602	2·2535					
24	0·9310	1·0131	1·1028	1·2024	1·3157	1·4491	1·6148	1·8421	2·2378						
23	0·9857	1·0766	1·1775	1·2921	1·4269	1·5941	1·8232	2·2213							
22	1·0489	1·1512	1·2672	1·4034	1·5723	1·8032	2·2040								
21	1·1233	1·2408	1·3786	1·5493	1·7823	2·1858									
20	1·2128	1·3524	1·5249	1·7601	2·1666										
19	1·3245	1·4990	1·7365	2·1462											
18	1·4715	1·7115	2·1247												
17	1·6849	2·1017													
16	2·0772														
15	2·0509	1·6256	1·3763	1·1914	1·0404	·9102	·7941	·6879	·5893	·4962	·4075	·3221	·2393	·1583	0·0787
14		2·0225	1·5923	1·3393	1·1512	·9970	·8637	·7445	·6353	·5334	·4371	·3449	·2559	·1691	0·0841
13			1·9918	1·5562	1·2990	1·1071	·9494	·8127	·6899	·5771	·4715	·3712	·2749	·1815	0·0901
12				1·9583	1·5166	1·2547	1·0586	·8968	·7560	·6292	·5121	·4021	·2972	·1959	0·0972
11					1·9215	1·4730	1·2057	1·0047	·8381	·6926	·5609	·4388	·3234	·2128	0·1054
10						1·8807	1·4244	1·1509	·9441	·7720	·6207	·4832	·3549	·2329	0·1152
9							1·8351	1·3697	1·0888	·8753	·6964	·5382	·3933	·2573	0·1269
8								1·7834	1·3073	1·0176	·7958	·6085	·4416	·2875	0·1414
7									1·7239	1·2349	·9344	·7021	·5042	·3260	0·1597
6										1·6540	1·1490	·8349	·5890	·3769	0·1834
5											1·5698	1·0443	·7119	·4476	0·2157
4												1·4647	·9114	·5534	0·2621
3													1·3264	·7324	0·3349
2														1·1284	0·4674
1															0·7979

j (for $n \ge 16$):	16	17	18	19	20	21	22	23	24	25	26	27	28	29	30

For $n > 30$, $\zeta(j\mid n) \sim \xi(n-j-1\mid 2n+1)$, where the ξ's are read from Table 9 of expected normal order statistics. The maximum error involved is 0·004 when $n = 30$ and this appears to decrease as n increases.

Table 22. *Lower tail critical values, W_l, for the Wilcoxon two-sample rank-sum test*

| | m = 1 | | | | | | | m = 2 | | | | | | | |
n	0.001	0.005	0.010	0.025	0.05	0.10	$2\overline{W}$	0.001	0.005	0.010	0.025	0.05	0.10	$2\overline{W}$	n
2							4						—	10	2
3							5						3	12	3
4							6					—	3	14	4
5							7					3	4	16	5
6							8					3	4	18	6
7							9				—	3	4	20	7
8						—	10				3	4	5	22	8
9						1	11				3	4	5	24	9
10						1	12				3	4	6	26	10
11						1	13				3	4	6	28	11
12						1	14			—	4	5	7	30	12
13						1	15			3	4	5	7	32	13
14						1	16			3	4	6	8	34	14
15						1	17			3	4	6	8	36	15
16						1	18			3	4	6	8	38	16
17						1	19			3	5	6	9	40	17
18					—	1	20		—	3	5	7	9	42	18
19					1	2	21		3	4	5	7	10	44	19
20					1	2	22		3	4	5	7	10	46	20
21					1	2	23		3	4	6	8	11	48	21
22					1	2	24		3	4	6	8	11	50	22
23					1	2	25		3	4	6	8	12	52	23
24					1	2	26		3	4	6	9	12	54	24
25	—	—	—	—	1	2	27	—	3	4	6	9	12	56	25

| | m = 3 | | | | | | | m = 4 | | | | | | | |
n	0.001	0.005	0.010	0.025	0.05	0.10	$2\overline{W}$	0.001	0.005	0.010	0.025	0.05	0.10	$2\overline{W}$	n
3					6	7	21								
4				—	6	7	24			—	10	11	13	36	4
5				6	7	8	27		—	10	11	12	14	40	5
6			—	7	8	9	30		10	11	12	13	15	44	6
7			6	7	8	10	33		10	11	13	14	16	48	7
8		—	6	8	9	11	36		11	12	14	15	17	52	8
9		6	7	8	10	11	39	—	11	13	14	16	19	56	9
10		6	7	9	10	12	42	10	12	13	15	17	20	60	10
11		6	7	9	11	13	45	10	12	14	16	18	21	64	11
12		7	8	10	11	14	48	10	13	15	17	19	22	68	12
13		7	8	10	12	15	51	11	13	15	18	20	23	72	13
14		7	8	11	13	16	54	11	14	16	19	21	25	76	14
15		8	9	11	13	16	57	11	15	17	20	22	26	80	15
16	—	8	9	12	14	17	60	12	15	17	21	24	27	84	16
17	6	8	10	12	15	18	63	12	16	18	21	25	28	88	17
18	6	8	10	13	15	19	66	13	16	19	22	26	30	92	18
19	6	9	10	13	16	20	69	13	17	19	23	27	31	96	19
20	6	9	11	14	17	21	72	13	18	20	24	28	32	100	20
21	7	9	11	14	17	21	75	14	18	21	25	29	33	104	21
22	7	10	12	15	18	22	78	14	19	21	26	30	35	108	22
23	7	10	12	15	19	23	81	14	19	22	27	31	36	112	23
24	7	10	12	16	19	24	84	15	20	23	27	32	38	116	24
25	7	11	13	16	20	25	87	15	20	23	28	33	38	120	25

The tables show (i) values W_l which are just significant at the probability level quoted at the head of column, (ii) twice $E(\mathbf{W}) = 2\overline{W}$. A blank space indicates that no value is significant at that level. The upper critical value is $W_u = 2\overline{W} - W_l$. The lower critical value for U is $U_l = W_l - \frac{1}{2}m(m+1)$. For treatment of ties, see para. (a), p. 48.

Table 22 (continued). Wilcoxon two-sample rank-sum test

n	m = 5 0.001	0.005	0.010	0.025	0.05	0.10	$2\overline{W}$	m = 6 0.001	0.005	0.010	0.025	0.05	0.10	$2\overline{W}$	n
5		15	16	17	19	20	55								
6	—	16	17	18	20	22	60	—	23	24	26	28	30	78	6
7	—	16	18	20	21	23	65	21	24	25	27	29	32	84	7
8	15	17	19	21	23	25	70	22	25	27	29	31	34	90	8
9	16	18	20	22	24	27	75	23	26	28	31	33	36	96	9
10	16	19	21	23	26	28	80	24	27	29	32	35	38	102	10
11	17	20	22	24	27	30	85	25	28	30	34	37	40	108	11
12	17	21	23	26	28	32	90	25	30	32	35	38	42	114	12
13	18	22	24	27	30	33	95	26	31	33	37	40	44	120	13
14	18	22	25	28	31	35	100	27	32	34	38	42	46	126	14
15	19	23	26	29	33	37	105	28	33	36	40	44	48	132	15
16	20	24	27	30	34	38	110	29	34	37	42	46	50	138	16
17	20	25	28	32	35	40	115	30	36	39	43	47	52	144	17
18	21	26	29	33	37	42	120	31	37	40	45	49	55	150	18
19	22	27	30	34	38	43	125	32	38	41	46	51	57	156	19
20	22	28	31	35	40	45	130	33	39	43	48	53	59	162	20
21	23	29	32	37	41	47	135	33	40	44	50	55	61	168	21
22	23	29	33	38	43	48	140	34	42	45	51	57	63	174	22
23	24	30	34	39	44	50	145	35	43	47	53	58	65	180	23
24	25	31	35	40	45	51	150	36	44	48	54	60	67	186	24
25	25	32	36	42	47	53	155	37	45	50	56	62	69	192	25

n	m = 7 0.001	0.005	0.010	0.025	0.05	0.10	$2\overline{W}$	m = 8 0.001	0.005	0.010	0.025	0.05	0.10	$2\overline{W}$	n
7	29	32	34	36	39	41	105								
8	30	34	35	38	41	44	112	40	43	45	49	51	55	136	8
9	31	35	37	40	43	46	119	41	45	47	51	54	58	144	9
10	33	37	39	42	45	49	126	42	47	49	53	56	60	152	10
11	34	38	40	44	47	51	133	44	49	51	55	59	63	160	11
12	35	40	42	46	49	54	140	45	51	53	58	62	66	168	12
13	36	41	44	48	52	56	147	47	53	56	60	64	69	176	13
14	37	43	45	50	54	59	154	48	54	58	62	67	72	184	14
15	38	44	47	52	56	61	161	50	56	60	65	69	75	192	15
16	39	46	49	54	58	64	168	51	58	62	67	72	78	200	16
17	41	47	51	56	61	66	175	53	60	64	70	75	81	208	17
18	42	49	52	58	63	69	182	54	62	66	72	77	84	216	18
19	43	50	54	60	65	71	189	56	64	68	74	80	87	224	19
20	44	52	56	62	67	74	196	57	66	70	77	83	90	232	20
21	46	53	58	64	69	76	203	59	68	72	79	85	92	240	21
22	47	55	59	66	72	79	210	60	70	74	81	88	95	248	22
23	48	57	61	68	74	81	217	62	71	76	84	90	98	256	23
24	49	58	63	70	76	84	224	64	73	78	86	93	101	264	24
25	50	60	64	72	78	86	231	65	75	81	89	96	104	272	25

n	m = 9 0.001	0.005	0.010	0.025	0.05	0.10	$2\overline{W}$	m = 10 0.001	0.005	0.010	0.025	0.05	0.10	$2\overline{W}$	n
9	52	56	59	62	66	70	171								
10	53	58	61	65	69	73	180	65	71	74	78	82	87	210	10
11	55	61	63	68	72	76	189	67	73	77	81	86	91	220	11
12	57	63	66	71	75	80	198	69	76	79	84	89	94	230	12
13	59	65	68	73	78	83	207	72	79	82	88	92	98	240	13
14	60	67	71	76	81	86	216	74	81	85	91	96	102	250	14
15	62	69	73	79	84	90	225	76	84	88	94	99	106	260	15
16	64	72	76	82	87	93	234	78	86	91	97	103	109	270	16
17	66	74	78	84	90	97	243	80	89	93	100	106	113	280	17
18	68	76	81	87	93	100	252	82	92	96	103	110	117	290	18
19	70	78	83	90	96	103	261	84	94	99	107	113	121	300	19
20	71	81	85	93	99	107	270	87	97	102	110	117	125	310	20
21	73	83	88	95	102	110	279	89	99	105	113	120	128	320	21
22	75	85	90	98	105	113	288	91	102	108	116	123	132	330	22
23	77	88	93	101	108	117	297	93	105	110	119	127	136	340	23
24	79	90	95	104	111	120	306	95	107	113	122	130	140	350	24
25	81	92	98	107	114	123	315	98	110	116	126	134	144	360	25

The tables show (i) values W_l which are just significant at the probability level quoted at the head of column, (ii) twice $E(\mathbf{W}) = 2\overline{W}$. A blank space indicates that no value is significant at that level. The upper critical value is $W_u = 2\overline{W} - W_l$. The lower critical value for $\mathbf{U}$ is $U_l = W_l - \frac{1}{2}m(m+1)$. For treatment of ties, see para. (a), p. 48.

Table 22 (*continued*)

			m = 11								m = 12				
n	0·001	0·005	0·010	0·025	0·05	0·10	$2\overline{W}$	0·001	0·005	0·010	0·025	0·05	0·10	$2\overline{W}$	n
11	81	87	91	96	100	106	253								
12	83	90	94	99	104	110	264	98	105	109	115	120	127	300	12
13	86	93	97	103	108	114	275	101	109	113	119	125	131	312	13
14	88	96	100	106	112	118	286	103	112	116	123	129	136	324	14
15	90	99	103	110	116	123	297	106	115	120	127	133	141	336	15
16	93	102	107	113	120	127	308	109	119	124	131	138	145	348	16
17	95	105	110	117	123	131	319	112	122	127	135	142	150	360	17
18	98	108	113	121	127	135	330	115	125	131	139	146	155	372	18
19	100	111	116	124	131	139	341	118	129	134	143	150	159	384	19
20	103	114	119	128	135	144	352	120	132	138	147	155	164	396	20
21	106	117	123	131	139	148	363	123	136	142	151	159	169	408	21
22	108	120	126	135	143	152	374	126	139	145	155	163	173	420	22
23	111	123	129	139	147	156	385	129	142	149	159	168	178	432	23
24	113	126	132	142	151	161	396	132	146	153	163	172	183	444	24
25	116	129	136	146	155	165	407	135	149	156	167	176	187	456	25

			m = 13								m = 14				
n	0·001	0·005	0·010	0·025	0·05	0·10	$2\overline{W}$	0·001	0·005	0·010	0·025	0·05	0·10	$2\overline{W}$	n
13	117	125	130	136	142	149	351								
14	120	129	134	141	147	154	364	137	147	152	160	166	174	406	14
15	123	133	138	145	152	159	377	141	151	156	164	171	179	420	15
16	126	136	142	150	156	165	390	144	155	161	169	176	185	434	16
17	129	140	146	154	161	170	403	148	159	165	174	182	190	448	17
18	133	144	150	158	166	175	416	151	163	170	179	187	196	462	18
19	136	148	154	163	171	180	429	155	168	174	183	192	202	476	19
20	139	151	158	167	175	185	442	159	172	178	188	197	207	490	20
21	142	155	162	171	180	190	455	162	176	183	193	202	213	504	21
22	145	159	166	176	185	195	468	166	180	187	198	207	218	518	22
23	149	163	170	180	189	200	481	169	184	192	203	212	224	532	23
24	152	166	174	185	194	205	494	173	188	196	207	218	229	546	24
25	155	170	178	189	199	211	507	177	192	200	212	223	235	560	25

			m = 15								m = 16				
n	0·001	0·005	0·010	0·025	0·05	0·10	$2\overline{W}$	0·001	0·005	0·010	0·025	0·05	0·10	$2\overline{W}$	n
15	160	171	176	184	192	200	465								
16	163	175	181	190	197	206	480	184	196	202	211	219	229	528	16
17	167	180	186	195	203	212	495	188	201	207	217	225	235	544	17
18	171	184	190	200	208	218	510	192	206	212	222	231	242	560	18
19	175	189	195	205	214	224	525	196	210	218	228	237	248	576	19
20	179	193	200	210	220	230	540	201	215	223	234	243	255	592	20
21	183	198	205	216	225	236	555	205	220	228	239	249	261	608	21
22	187	202	210	221	231	242	570	209	225	233	245	255	267	624	22
23	191	207	214	226	236	248	585	214	230	238	251	261	274	640	23
24	195	211	219	231	242	254	600	218	235	244	256	267	280	656	24
25	199	216	224	237	248	260	615	222	240	249	262	273	287	672	25

			m = 17								m = 18				
n	0·001	0·005	0·010	0·025	0·05	0·10	$2\overline{W}$	0·001	0·005	0·010	0·025	0·05	0·10	$2\overline{W}$	n
17	210	223	230	240	249	259	595								
18	214	228	235	246	255	266	612	237	252	259	270	280	291	666	18
19	219	234	241	252	262	273	629	242	258	265	277	287	299	684	19
20	223	239	246	258	268	280	646	247	263	271	283	294	306	702	20
21	228	244	252	264	274	287	663	252	269	277	290	301	313	720	21
22	233	249	258	270	281	294	680	257	275	283	296	307	321	738	22
23	238	255	263	276	287	300	697	262	280	289	303	314	328	756	23
24	242	260	269	282	294	307	714	267	286	295	309	321	335	774	24
25	247	265	275	288	300	314	731	273	292	301	316	328	343	792	25

Table 22 (*continued*). *Wilcoxon two-sample rank-sum test*

			$m = 19$								$m = 20$					
n	0·001	0·005	0·010	0·025	0·05	0·10	$2\overline{W}$	0·001	0·005	0·010	0·025	0·05	0·10	$2\overline{W}$	n
19	267	283	291	303	313	325	741								
20	272	289	297	309	320	333	760	298	315	324	337	348	361	820	20
21	277	295	303	316	328	341	779	304	322	331	344	356	370	840	21
22	283	301	310	323	335	349	798	309	328	337	351	364	378	860	22
23	288	307	316	330	342	357	817	315	335	344	359	371	386	880	23
24	294	313	323	337	350	364	836	321	341	351	366	379	394	900	24
25	299	319	329	344	357	372	855	327	348	358	373	387	403	920	25

			$m = 21$								$m = 22$					
n	0·001	0·005	0·010	0·025	0·05	0·10	$2\overline{W}$	0·001	0·005	0·010	0·025	0·05	0·10	$2\overline{W}$	n
21	331	349	359	373	385	399	903								
22	337	356	366	381	393	408	924	365	386	396	411	424	439	990	22
23	343	363	373	388	401	417	945	372	393	403	419	432	448	1012	23
24	349	370	381	396	410	425	966	379	400	411	427	441	457	1034	24
25	356	377	388	404	418	434	987	385	408	419	435	450	467	1056	25

			$m = 23$								$m = 24$					
n	0·001	0·005	0·010	0·025	0·05	0·10	$2\overline{W}$	0·001	0·005	0·010	0·025	0·05	0·10	$2\overline{W}$	n
23	402	424	434	451	465	481	1081								
24	409	431	443	459	474	491	1104	440	464	475	492	507	525	1176	24
25	416	439	451	468	483	500	1127	448	472	484	501	517	535	1200	25

			$m = 25$				
n	0·001	0·005	0·010	0·025	0·05	0·10	$2\overline{W}$
25	480	505	517	536	552	570	1275

Table 23. *The Wilcoxon paired rank test*

A. Probability integral, $P(T|N)$ for $3 \leqslant N \leqslant 15$

T^-	15	14	13	12	11	10	9	N
0					0.000	0.001	0.002	
1				0.000	·001	·002	·004	
2			0.000	·001	·001	·003	·006	
3			·001	·001	·002	·005	·010	
4		0.000	·001	·002	·003	·007	·014	
5		·001	·001	·002	·005	·010	·020	
6	0.000	0.001	0.002	0.003	·0007	0.014	0.027	
7	·001	·001	·002	·005	·009	·019	·037	
8	·001	·002	·003	·006	·012	·024	·049	
9	·001	·002	·004	·008	·016	·032	·064	
10	·001	·003	·005	·010	·021	·042	·082	
11	0.002	0.003	0.007	0.013	0.027	0.053	0.102	
12	·002	·004	·009	·017	·034	·065	·125	
13	·003	·005	·011	·021	·042	·080	·150	
14	·003	·007	·013	·026	·051	·097	·180	
15	·004	·008	·016	·032	·062	·116	·213	
16	0.005	0.010	0.020	0.039	0.074	0.138	0.248	
17	·006	·012	·024	·046	·087	·161	·285	
18	·008	·015	·029	·055	·103	·188	·326	
19	·009	·018	·034	·065	·120	·216	·367	
20	·011	·021	·040	·076	·139	·246	·410	
21	0.013	0.025	0.047	0.088	0.160	0.278	0.455	
22	·015	·029	·055	·102	·183	·312	·500	
23	·018	·034	·064	·117	·207	·348		
24	·021	·039	·073	·133	·232	·385		
25	·024	·045	·084	·151	·260	·423		
26	0.028	0.052	0.095	0.170	0.289	0.461		
27	·032	·059	·108	·190	·319	·500		
28	·036	·068	·122	·212	·350			
29	·042	·077	·137	·235	·382			
30	·047	·086	·153	·259	·416			
31	0.053	0.097	0.170	0.285	0.449			
32	·060	·108	·188	·311	·483			
33	·068	·121	·207	·339	·517			
34	·076	·134	·227	·367				
35	·084	·148	·249	·396				
36	0.094	0.163	0.271	0.425				
37	·104	·179	·294	·455				
38	·115	·196	·318	·485				
39	·126	·213	·342	·515				
40	·138	·232	·368					
41	0.151	0.251	0.393					
42	·165	·271	·420				0.527	18
43	·180	·292	·446				·473	17
44	·195	·313	·473				·422	16
45	·211	·335	·500				0.371	15
46	0.227	0.357				0.531	·320	14
47	·244	·380				·469	·273	13
48	·262	·404				·406	·230	12
49	·281	·428				·344	·191	11
50	·300	·452			0.500	0.289	0.156	10
51	0.319	0.476			·422	·234	·125	9
52	·339	·500			·344	·188	·098	8
53	·360			0.500	·281	·148	·074	7
54	·381			·406	·219	·109	·055	6
55	·402		0.562	0.312	·156	0.078	0.039	5
56	0.423		·438	·219	·109	·055	·027	4
57	·445	0.625	·312	·156	·078	·039	·020	3
58	·467	·375	·188	·094	·047	·023	·012	2
59	·489	·250	·125	·062	·031	·016	·008	1
60	·511	·125	·062	·031	·016	·008	·004	0

(lower-section column headings, read against the right-hand T^- index: col 14 = N 3, col 13 = N 4, col 12 = N 5, col 11 = N 6, col 10 = N 7, col 9 = N 8*)*

B. Lower percentage points, $T_l(\alpha|N)$ for $5 \leqslant N \leqslant 50$

Single-tail: ·05	·025	·01	·005	N	$\tfrac{1}{2}N(N+1)$
Double-tail: ·10	·05	·02	·01		
1				5	15
2	1			6	21
4	2	0		7	28
6	4	2	0	8	36
8	6	3	2	9	45
11	8	5	3	10	55
14	11	7	5	11	66
17	14	10	7	12	78
21	17	13	10	13	91
26	21	16	13	14	105
30	25	20	16	15	120
36	30	24	19	16	136
41	35	28	23	17	153
47	40	33	28	18	171
54	46	38	32	19	190
60	52	43	37	20	210
68	59	49	43	21	231
75	66	56	49	22	253
83	73	62	55	23	276
92	81	69	61	24	300
101	90	77	68	25	325
110	98	85	76	26	351
120	107	93	84	27	378
130	117	102	92	28	406
141	127	111	100	29	435
152	137	120	109	30	465
163	148	130	118	31	496
175	159	141	128	32	528
188	171	151	138	33	561
201	183	162	149	34	595
214	195	174	160	35	630
228	208	186	171	36	666
242	222	198	183	37	703
256	235	211	195	38	741
271	250	224	208	39	780
287	264	238	221	40	820
303	279	252	234	41	861
319	295	267	248	42	903
336	311	281	262	43	946
353	327	297	277	44	990
371	344	313	292	45	1035
389	361	329	307	46	1081
408	379	345	323	47	1128
427	397	362	339	48	1176
446	415	380	356	49	1225
466	434	398	373	50	1275

Table 24. *Percentage points of the non-central χ distribution*
Lower 5% points

ν \\ $\sqrt{\lambda}$	0·0	0·2	0·4	0·6	0·8	1·0	1·2	1·4	1·6	1·8
1	0·06271	0·06397	0·06793	0·07507	0·08634	0·1033	0·1286	0·1662	0·2225+	0·3061
2	·3203	·3235+	·3333	·3504	·3756	·4104	·4567	·5169	·5935+	·6888
3	·5932	·5971	·6092	·6297	·6593	·6991	0·7501	0·8135−	0·8906	0·9821
4	0·8430	0·8473	0·8600	0·8816	0·9125+	0·9533	1·005−	1·067	1·142	1·229
5	1·070	1·075−	1·087	1·109	1·140	1·181	1·231	1·292	1·364	1·447
6	1·279	1·283	1·296	1·318	1·348	1·388	1·437	1·496	1·566	1·645+
7	1·472	1·476	1·489	1·510	1·540	1·579	1·627	1·685−	1·752	1·828
8	1·653	1·657	1·670	1·690	1·720	1·758	1·805−	1·860	1·925+	1·999
9	1·823	1·828	1·840	1·860	1·889	1·926	1·971	2·026	2·088	2·160
10	1·985+	1·989	2·001	2·021	2·049	2·085+	2·129	2·182	2·243	2·313
11	2·139	2·143	2·154	2·174	2·201	2·237	2·280	2·331	2·391	2·458
12	2·286	2·290	2·301	2·320	2·347	2·382	2·424	2·474	2·532	2·598
15	2·695−	2·698	2·709	2·727	2·752	2·785−	2·824	2·871	2·925+	2·987
20	3·294	3·297	3·307	3·324	3·347	3·376	3·413	3·455+	3·505−	3·560

ν \\ $\sqrt{\lambda}$	2·0	2·2	2·4	2·6	2·8	3·0	3·2	3·4	3·6	3·8
1	0·4252	0·5809	0·7627	0·9570	1·156	1·355+	1·555+	1·755+	1·955+	2·155+
2	0·8035+	0·9367	1·085+	1·246	1·415−	1·590	1·769	1·952	2·138	2·325+
3	1·088	1·208	1·341	1·485−	1·637	1·797	1·963	2·133	2·307	2·485−
4	1·329	1·440	1·562	1·695+	1·836	1·985+	2·140	2·301	2·466	2·635+
5	1·541	1·646	1·761	1·886	2·019	2·159	2·306	2·459	2·617	2·779
6	1·735+	1·835−	1·944	2·062	2·188	2·322	2·462	2·608	2·760	2·916
7	1·914	2·010	2·114	2·227	2·348	2·476	2·610	2·751	2·897	3·048
8	2·082	2·174	2·274	2·382	2·498	2·622	2·751	2·887	3·028	3·174
9	2·240	2·329	2·425+	2·530	2·642	2·761	2·887	3·018	3·155−	3·297
10	2·390	2·476	2·570	2·671	2·780	2·895−	3·017	3·144	3·277	3·415+
11	2·534	2·617	2·708	2·806	2·912	3·024	3·142	3·266	3·396	3·530
12	2·671	2·752	2·841	2·937	3·039	3·148	3·263	3·384	3·511	3·642
15	3·055+	3·131	3·213	3·302	3·397	3·499	3·606	3·719	3·838	3·961
20	3·623	3·691	3·766	3·846	3·933	4·025+	4·123	4·226	4·335−	4·448

ν \\ $\sqrt{\lambda}$	4·0	4·2	4·4	4·6	4·8	5·0	5·2	5·4	5·6	5·8	6·0
1	2·355+	2·555+	2·755+	2·955+	3·155+	3·355+	3·555+	3·755+	3·955+	4·155+	4·355+
2	2·514	2·705−	2·896	3·089	3·282	3·476	3·670	3·865+	4·060	4·256	4·452
3	2·665−	2·847	3·031	3·217	3·404	3·592	3·782	3·972	4·163	4·355−	4·547
4	2·808	2·983	3·161	3·341	3·522	3·706	3·891	4·076	4·264	4·452	4·640
5	2·945−	3·114	3·286	3·461	3·637	3·816	3·996	4·178	4·362	4·546	4·732
6	3·076	3·240	3·407	3·577	3·749	3·923	4·100	4·278	4·458	4·639	4·822
7	3·203	3·362	3·524	3·689	3·858	4·028	4·201	4·376	4·552	4·731	4·910
8	3·325−	3·480	3·638	3·799	3·964	4·131	4·300	4·472	4·645+	4·820	4·997
9	3·443	3·594	3·748	3·906	4·067	4·231	4·397	4·565+	4·736	4·909	5·083
10	3·558	3·705+	3·856	4·010	4·168	4·329	4·492	4·657	4·825+	4·995+	5·167
11	3·670	3·814	3·961	4·112	4·267	4·425−	4·585−	4·748	4·913	5·081	5·250−
12	3·779	3·919	4·064	4·212	4·364	4·519	4·676	4·837	5·000	5·165−	5·332
15	4·089	4·222	4·359	4·499	4·643	4·791	4·941	5·095−	5·251	5·409	5·570
20	4·566	4·688	4·814	4·944	5·078	5·216	5·356	5·500+	5·647	5·796	5·948

ν = degrees of freedom; λ = non-central parameter. For interpolation when $\nu > 12$, see pp. 54,139. For an extension to $\sqrt{\lambda} = 8$, 10, obtained by approximation, see Table 29.

Table 24 (*continued*)
Upper 5% points

$\sqrt{\lambda}$ ν	0·0	0·2	0·4	0·6	0·8	1·0	1·2	1·4	1·6	1·8
1	1·960	1·999	2·107	2·265$^+$	2·450$^+$	2·646	2·845$^-$	3·045$^-$	3·245$^-$	3·445$^-$
2	2·448	2·472	2·542	2·650$^-$	2·785$^+$	2·940	3·106	3·280	3·458	3·641
3	2·795$^+$	2·814	2·868	2·953	3·064	3·194	3·339	3·493	3·656	3·825$^-$
4	3·080	3·096	3·141	3·212	3·308	3·422	3·551	3·691	3·841	3·998
5	3·327	3·340	3·380	3·443	3·527	3·629	3·746	3·876	4·015$^-$	4·162
6	3·548	3·560	3·595$^+$	3·652	3·728	3·821	3·929	4·049	4·179	4·318
7	3·751	3·761	3·793	3·845$^-$	3·914	4·000	4·101	4·213	4·336	4·468
8	3·938	3·948	3·977	4·025$^-$	4·089	4·170	4·264	4·370	4·486	4·612
9	4·113	4·122	4·149	4·194	4·254	4·330	4·419	4·519	4·630	4·750$^+$
10	4·279	4·287	4·313	4·355$^-$	4·411	4·483	4·567	4·662	4·768	4·884
11	4·436	4·444	4·468	4·507	4·561	4·629	4·709	4·800	4·902	5·013
12	4·585$^+$	4·593	4·616	4·653	4·705$^-$	4·769	4·846	4·933	5·031	5·138
15	5·000	5·006	5·026	5·059	5·104	5·161	5·229	5·308	5·396	5·493
20	5·604	5·610	5·627	5·655$^-$	5·693	5·742	5·800	5·868	5·944	6·029

$\sqrt{\lambda}$ ν	2·0	2·2	2·4	2·6	2·8	3·0	3·2	3·4	3·6	3·8
1	3·645$^-$	3·845$^-$	4·045$^-$	4·245$^-$	4·445$^-$	4·645$^-$	4·845$^-$	5·045$^-$	5·245$^-$	5·445$^-$
2	3·826	4·014	4·203	4·393	4·585$^-$	4·777	4·970	5·164	5·359	5·554
3	3·998	4·174	4·354	4·536	4·720	4·906	5·093	5·281	5·470	5·661
4	4·160	4·328	4·499	4·673	4·851	5·030	5·211	5·395$^-$	5·579	5·765$^+$
5	4·316	4·475$^+$	4·639	4·806	4·977	5·151	5·327	5·506	5·686	5·867
6	4·464	4·617	4·774	4·935$^+$	5·101	5·269	5·440	5·614	5·790	5·968
7	4·607	4·753	4·904	5·060	5·220	5·384	5·551	5·720	5·892	6·067
8	4·745$^+$	4·885$^+$	5·031	5·182	5·337	5·496	5·659	5·824	5·993	6·163
9	4·878	5·013	5·154	5·300	5·451	5·606	5·765$^-$	5·926	6·091	6·259
10	5·007	5·137	5·273	5·415$^+$	5·562	5·713	5·868	6·026	6·188	6·352
11	5·131	5·257	5·390	5·528	5·671	5·818	5·970	6·125$^-$	6·283	6·444
12	5·253	5·375$^-$	5·503	5·637	5·777	5·921	6·069	6·221	6·376	6·535$^-$
15	5·597	5·709	5·828	5·953	6·083	6·218	6·357	6·501	6·648	6·799
20	6·121	6·221	6·327	6·439	6·556	6·679	6·807	6·939	7·075$^-$	7·215$^-$

$\sqrt{\lambda}$ ν	4·0	4·2	4·4	4·6	4·8	5·0	5·2	5·4	5·6	5·8	6·0
1	5·645$^-$	5·845$^-$	6·045$^-$	6·245$^-$	6·445$^-$	6·645$^-$	6·845$^-$	7·045$^-$	7·245$^-$	7·445$^-$	7·645$^-$
2	5·749	5·945$^+$	6·141	6·338	6·534	6·731	6·928	7·126	7·323	7·521	7·718
3	5·852	6·043	6·236	6·429	6·622	6·816	7·011	7·205$^+$	7·400	7·596	7·791
4	5·952	6·140	6·329	6·519	6·709	6·900	7·092	7·284	7·477	7·670	7·863
5	6·051	6·235$^+$	6·421	6·607	6·795$^-$	6·983	7·172	7·362	7·552	7·743	7·935$^-$
6	6·147	6·328	6·511	6·694	6·879	7·065$^-$	7·251	7·439	7·627	7·816	8·005$^+$
7	6·243	6·420	6·600	6·781	6·963	7·146	7·330	7·515$^+$	7·701	7·888	8·075$^+$
8	6·336	6·511	6·687	6·865$^+$	7·045$^-$	7·225$^+$	7·407	7·590	7·774	7·959	8·145$^-$
9	6·428	6·600	6·774	6·949	7·126	7·304	7·484	7·665$^-$	7·847	8·030	8·213
10	6·519	6·688	6·859	7·032	7·206	7·382	7·560	7·739	7·919	8·100	8·282
11	6·608	6·774	6·943	7·113	7·285$^+$	7·459	7·635$^-$	7·812	7·990	8·169	8·349
12	6·696	6·860	7·026	7·194	7·364	7·536	7·709	7·884	8·060	8·237	8·416
15	6·952	7·109	7·268	7·430	7·594	7·759	7·927	8·096	8·267	8·440	8·614
20	7·358	7·504	7·654	7·806	7·960	8·117	8·277	8·438	8·601	8·766	8·933

Table 24 (*continued*). *Percentage points of the non-central χ distribution*
Lower 2·5% points

$\sqrt{\lambda}$ ν	0·0	0·2	0·4	0·6	0·8	1·0	1·2	1·4	1·6	1·8
1	0·03134	0·03197	0·03395⁻	0·03752	0·04315⁺	0·05166	0·06435⁺	0·08339	0·1123	0·1569
2	·2250⁺	·2273	·2342	·2462	·2640	·2886	·3217	·3652	·4217	·4939
3	·4645⁺	·4676	·4771	·4932	·5165⁺	·5480	·5886	·6396	·7025⁺	0·7787
4	·6960	·6995⁻	·7100	·7279	·7535⁺	0·7875⁺	0·8306	0·8836	0·9474	1·023
5	·9117	·9154	·9264	·9450⁻	·9715⁻	1·006	1·050⁻	1·103	1·166	1·239
6	1·112	1·116	1·127	1·146	1·173	1·208	1·251	1·303	1·365⁺	1·437
7	1·300	1·304	1·315⁻	1·334	1·360	1·395⁻	1·438	1·489	1·549	1·619
8	1·476	1·480	1·491	1·510	1·536	1·570	1·612	1·663	1·722	1·789
9	1·643	1·647	1·658	1·676	1·702	1·736	1·777	1·827	1·884	1·950⁻
10	1·802	1·806	1·816	1·835⁻	1·860	1·893	1·934	1·982	2·038	2·102
11	1·953	1·957	1·968	1·985⁺	2·011	2·043	2·083	2·130	2·185⁺	2·248
12	2·099	2·102	2·113	2·130	2·155⁻	2·187	2·226	2·272	2·326	2·387
15	2·502	2·506	2·516	2·532	2·556	2·586	2·623	2·667	2·718	2·775⁺
20	3·097	3·100	3·109	3·125⁻	3·146	3·174	3·209	3·249	3·296	3·348

$\sqrt{\lambda}$ ν	2·0	2·2	2·4	2·6	2·8	3·0	3·2	3·4	3·6	3·8
1	0·2258	0·3295⁺	0·4736	0·6498	0·8423	1·040	1·240	1·440	1·640	1·840
2	·5847	·6954	0·8255⁻	0·9721	1·131	1·300	1·474	1·654	1·837	2·022
3	0·8690	0·9741	1·093	1·225⁺	1·368	1·521	1·680	1·846	2·016	2·190
4	1·110	1·210	1·321	1·444	1·576	1·718	1·867	2·022	2·183	2·348
5	1·324	1·419	1·524	1·640	1·765⁻	1·898	2·039	2·186	2·340	2·498
6	1·518	1·609	1·710	1·820	1·939	2·066	2·200	2·341	2·488	2·640
7	1·698	1·785⁺	1·882	1·988	2·102	2·223	2·352	2·488	2·629	2·775⁺
8	1·866	1·950⁺	2·044	2·146	2·255⁺	2·373	2·497	2·627	2·764	2·906
9	2·024	2·106	2·197	2·295⁺	2·401	2·515⁻	2·635⁻	2·761	2·894	3·031
10	2·175⁻	2·255⁻	2·342	2·438	2·541	2·651	2·767	2·890	3·019	3·153
11	2·318	2·396	2·482	2·575⁻	2·675⁻	2·781	2·895⁻	3·014	3·139	3·270
12	2·456	2·532	2·615⁺	2·706	2·803	2·907	3·018	3·134	3·257	3·384
15	2·840	2·911	2·989	3·074	3·165⁻	3·262	3·365⁺	3·474	3·589	3·708
20	3·407	3·473	3·544	3·621	3·704	3·793	3·887	3·987	4·091	4·201

$\sqrt{\lambda}$ ν	4·0	4·2	4·4	4·6	4·8	5·0	5·2	5·4	5·6	5·8	6·0
1	2·040	2·240	2·440	2·640	2·840	3·040	3·240	3·440	3·640	3·840	4·040
2	2·209	2·398	2·589	2·780	2·973	3·166	3·360	3·554	3·749	3·945⁻	4·140
3	2·368	2·548	2·730	2·915⁻	3·100	3·288	3·476	3·665⁺	3·856	4·047	4·239
4	2·518	2·690	2·866	3·044	3·224	3·405⁺	3·589	3·774	3·960	4·147	4·335⁻
5	2·660	2·826	2·996	3·168	3·343	3·520	3·698	3·879	4·061	4·245⁻	4·429
6	2·796	2·957	3·121	3·288	3·458	3·630	3·805⁺	3·982	4·160	4·340	4·522
7	2·927	3·082	3·242	3·404	3·570	3·738	3·909	4·082	4·257	4·434	4·613
8	3·052	3·203	3·359	3·517	3·679	3·844	4·011	4·181	4·352	4·526	4·702
9	3·174	3·321	3·472	3·627	3·785⁺	3·946	4·110	4·277	4·446	4·617	4·789
10	3·291	3·435⁻	3·582	3·734	3·889	4·047	4·208	4·371	4·537	4·705⁺	4·876
11	3·406	3·546	3·690	3·838	3·990	4·145⁺	4·303	4·464	4·627	4·793	4·960
12	3·516	3·654	3·795⁻	3·940	4·089	4·241	4·397	4·555⁻	4·715⁺	4·879	5·044
15	3·833	3·962	4·095⁺	4·233	4·374	4·519	4·667	4·818	4·972	5·128	5·287
20	4·315⁺	4·434	4·558	4·685⁻	4·816	4·951	5·089	5·230	5·375⁻	5·522	5·672

ν = degrees of freedom; λ = non-central parameter. For interpolation when $\nu > 12$, see pp. 54, 139.
For an extension to $\sqrt{\lambda} = 8, 10$, obtained by approximation, see Table 29.

Table 24 (*continued*)

Upper 2·5% points

$\sqrt{\lambda}$ / ν	0·0	0·2	0·4	0·6	0·8	1·0	1·2	1·4	1·6	1·8
1	2·241	2·285+	2·405−	2·573	2·763	2·961	3·160	3·360	3·560	3·760
2	2·716	2·743	2·819	2·935−	3·077	3·236	3·406	3·582	3·763	3·947
3	3·058	3·078	3·136	3·227	3·344	3·480	3·628	3·787	3·952	4·123
4	3·338	3·355−	3·403	3·480	3·580	3·699	3·833	3·977	4·131	4·290
5	3·582	3·597	3·638	3·705+	3·794	3·901	4·023	4·156	4·299	4·449
6	3·801	3·814	3·851	3·911	3·991	4·089	4·201	4·325+	4·459	4·602
7	4·002	4·013	4·047	4·101	4·175−	4·265−	4·369	4·486	4·612	4·747
8	4·187	4·198	4·229	4·279	4·347	4·431	4·529	4·639	4·759	4·888
9	4·362	4·371	4·400	4·447	4·510	4·589	4·681	4·786	4·900	5·023
10	4·526	4·535−	4·562	4·606	4·665+	4·740	4·827	4·927	5·036	5·154
11	4·682	4·690	4·716	4·757	4·814	4·884	4·968	5·062	5·167	5·281
12	4·831	4·839	4·863	4·902	4·956	5·023	5·103	5·194	5·295−	5·404
15	5·243	5·250−	5·271	5·305+	5·352	5·412	5·482	5·564	5·655−	5·754
20	5·845+	5·851	5·869	5·898	5·938	5·988	6·049	6·119	6·198	6·285−

$\sqrt{\lambda}$ / ν	2·0	2·2	2·4	2·6	2·8	3·0	3·2	3·4	3·6	3·8
1	3·960	4·160	4·360	4·560	4·760	4·960	5·160	5·360	5·560	5·760
2	4·133	4·322	4·512	4·703	4·895−	5·088	5·281	5·476	5·671	5·866
3	4·298	4·476	4·657	4·840	5·025+	5·212	5·400	5·589	5·779	5·970
4	4·455+	4·625−	4·798	4·974	5·152	5·333	5·515+	5·699	5·885−	6·071
5	4·606	4·768	4·933	5·103	5·275+	5·451	5·628	5·807	5·988	6·171
6	4·750+	4·905+	5·065−	5·228	5·395+	5·565+	5·738	5·913	6·090	6·269
7	4·890	5·038	5·192	5·350+	5·512	5·677	5·846	6·017	6·190	6·365+
8	5·024	5·167	5·315+	5·469	5·626	5·787	5·951	6·118	6·288	6·460
9	5·154	5·292	5·436	5·584	5·737	5·894	6·055−	6·218	6·385−	6·553
10	5·281	5·414	5·553	5·697	5·846	5·999	6·156	6·316	6·479	6·645−
11	5·403	5·532	5·667	5·807	5·953	6·102	6·256	6·412	6·572	6·735+
12	5·522	5·647	5·778	5·915+	6·057	6·203	6·353	6·507	6·664	6·824
15	5·862	5·977	6·098	6·225+	6·357	6·495−	6·636	6·782	6·931	7·083
20	6·380	6·482	6·590	6·705−	6·824	6·950−	7·079	7·213	7·351	7·493

$\sqrt{\lambda}$ / ν	4·0	4·2	4·4	4·6	4·8	5·0	5·2	5·4	5·6	5·8	6·0
1	5·960	6·160	6·360	6·560	6·760	6·960	7·160	7·360	7·560	7·760	7·960
2	6·061	6·257	6·454	6·650+	6·847	7·044	7·241	7·439	7·636	7·834	8·032
3	6·161	6·353	6·546	6·739	6·933	7·127	7·322	7·517	7·712	7·908	8·103
4	6·259	6·447	6·637	6·827	7·018	7·209	7·401	7·594	7·787	7·980	8·174
5	6·355+	6·540	6·726	6·914	7·102	7·290	7·480	7·670	7·861	8·052	8·244
6	6·450−	6·631	6·815−	6·999	7·184	7·371	7·558	7·746	7·934	8·123	8·313
7	6·543	6·721	6·902	7·083	7·266	7·450−	7·635−	7·820	8·007	8·194	8·382
8	6·634	6·810	6·987	7·166	7·346	7·528	7·710	7·894	8·079	8·264	8·450+
9	6·724	6·897	7·072	7·248	7·426	7·605+	7·786	7·967	8·150−	8·333	8·518
10	6·813	6·983	7·155+	7·329	7·505−	7·682	7·860	8·040	8·220	8·402	8·585−
11	6·901	7·068	7·238	7·409	7·583	7·757	7·934	8·111	8·290	8·470	8·651
12	6·987	7·152	7·319	7·488	7·659	7·832	8·007	8·182	8·359	8·538	8·717
15	7·239	7·397	7·557	7·720	7·885+	8·052	8·221	8·391	8·563	8·737	8·911
20	7·638	7·786	7·937	8·090	8·246	8·405−	8·565+	8·728	8·892	9·058	9·225+

Table 24 (*continued*). *Percentage points of the non-central χ distribution*
Lower 1% points

$\sqrt{\lambda}$ \ ν	0·0	0·2	0·4	0·6	0·8	1·0	1·2	1·4	1·6	1·8
1	0·01253	0·01279	0·01358	0·01500+	0·01726	0·02066	0·02575−	0·03339	0·04505+	0·06324
2	·1418	·1432	·1476	·1551	·1664	·1820	·2030	·2309	·2676	·3155+
3	·3389	·3411	·3480	·3598	·3769	·4000	·4300	·4681	·5155−	·5739
4	·5451	·5478	·5561	·5701	·5903	·6171	·6513	·6936	·7451	·8067
5	·7445+	·7475−	·7565+	·7717	·7934	·8221	·8582	·9023	·9552	1·017
6	0·9339	0·9370	0·9464	0·9622	0·9847	1·014	1·051	1·096	1·149	1·211
7	1·113	1·116	1·126	1·142	1·165−	1·195−	1·232	1·276	1·329	1·390
8	1·283	1·286	1·296	1·312	1·335+	1·365−	1·402	1·446	1·499	1·559
9	1·445−	1·448	1·458	1·474	1·497	1·527	1·563	1·607	1·659	1·718
10	1·599	1·603	1·612	1·628	1·651	1·681	1·717	1·760	1·811	1·869
11	1·747	1·751	1·760	1·776	1·799	1·828	1·864	1·906	1·956	2·013
12	1·890	1·893	1·902	1·918	1·940	1·969	2·005−	2·047	2·096	2·152
15	2·287	2·290	2·299	2·314	2·336	2·363	2·397	2·438	2·485−	2·538
20	2·874	2·877	2·886	2·900	2·920	2·946	2·978	3·016	3·059	3·109

$\sqrt{\lambda}$ \ ν	2·0	2·2	2·4	2·6	2·8	3·0	3·2	3·4	3·6	3·8
1	0·09222	0·1392	0·2153	0·3325+	0·4919	0·6780	0·8745+	1·074	1·274	1·474
2	·3779	·4579	·5581	·6792	·8192	·9740	1·139	1·312	1·491	1·673
3	·6448	·7297	·8294	·9438	1·072	1·212	1·362	1·520	1·684	1·853
4	·8793	·9638	1·060	1·169	1·289	1·419	1·559	1·706	1·861	2·020
5	1·090	1·172	1·266	1·369	1·483	1·607	1·739	1·878	2·025−	2·177
6	1·282	1·362	1·453	1·553	1·662	1·779	1·905+	2·039	2·179	2·325−
7	1·460	1·539	1·626	1·723	1·828	1·941	2·062	2·190	2·325−	2·466
8	1·627	1·704	1·789	1·882	1·984	2·093	2·210	2·334	2·464	2·600
9	1·785−	1·860	1·942	2·033	2·132	2·238	2·351	2·471	2·597	2·729
10	1·935−	2·008	2·089	2·177	2·273	2·376	2·486	2·602	2·725+	2·853
11	2·078	2·149	2·228	2·315−	2·408	2·508	2·615+	2·729	2·848	2·974
12	2·215−	2·285+	2·362	2·447	2·538	2·636	2·740	2·851	2·968	3·090
15	2·598	2·664	2·737	2·816	2·902	2·994	3·092	3·196	3·305+	3·420
20	3·164	3·225+	3·292	3·365+	3·444	3·528	3·618	3·714	3·814	3·919

$\sqrt{\lambda}$ \ ν	4·0	4·2	4·4	4·6	4·8	5·0	5·2	5·4	5·6	5·8	6·0
1	1·674	1·874	2·074	2·274	2·474	2·674	2·874	3·074	3·274	3·474	3·674
2	1·857	2·044	2·233	2·423	2·615−	2·807	3·000	3·194	3·388	3·583	3·779
3	2·027	2·204	2·383	2·565+	2·749	2·935+	3·122	3·310	3·500−	3·690	3·881
4	2·185+	2·354	2·526	2·701	2·879	3·058	3·240	3·423	3·608	3·794	3·981
5	2·334	2·496	2·662	2·831	3·003	3·177	3·354	3·533	3·713	3·895+	4·079
6	2·476	2·632	2·792	2·956	3·123	3·293	3·465+	3·640	3·816	3·994	4·174
7	2·612	2·762	2·918	3·077	3·239	3·405−	3·573	3·744	3·917	4·091	4·268
8	2·742	2·888	3·039	3·193	3·352	3·514	3·678	3·845+	4·015−	4·187	4·360
9	2·867	3·009	3·156	3·307	3·461	3·620	3·781	3·945−	4·111	4·280	4·450+
10	2·987	3·126	3·269	3·417	3·568	3·723	3·881	4·042	4·205+	4·371	4·539
11	3·104	3·240	3·380	3·524	3·672	3·824	3·979	4·137	4·298	4·461	4·626
12	3·218	3·350+	3·487	3·628	3·774	3·923	4·075−	4·230	4·388	4·549	4·712
15	3·540	3·665−	3·794	3·928	4·065+	4·207	4·352	4·500−	4·651	4·805−	4·961
20	4·030	4·145−	4·264	4·388	4·515+	4·647	4·782	4·920	5·062	5·206	5·354

ν = degrees of freedom; λ = non-central parameter. For interpolation when $\nu > 12$, see pp. 54, 139.
For an extension to $\sqrt{\lambda} = 8, 10$, obtained by approximation, see Table 29.

Table 24 (*continued*)

Upper 1% points

√λ ∖ ν	0·0	0·2	0·4	0·6	0·8	1·0	1·2	1·4	1·6	1·8
1	2·576	2·626	2·757	2·934	3·128	3·327	3·526	3·726	3·926	4·126
2	3·035−	3·065−	3·148	3·272	3·421	3·584	3·757	3·936	4·118	4·304
3	3·368	3·390	3·454	3·552	3·675−	3·816	3·969	4·131	4·299	4·472
4	3·644	3·662	3·714	3·796	3·903	4·027	4·165+	4·314	4·470	4·633
5	3·884	3·900	3·945−	4·016	4·110	4·223	4·349	4·487	4·633	4·787
6	4·100	4·114	4·154	4·218	4·303	4·405+	4·522	4·650+	4·788	4·934
7	4·298	4·310	4·347	4·405−	4·482	4·577	4·686	4·807	4·937	5·076
8	4·482	4·493	4·526	4·580	4·652	4·740	4·842	4·956	5·080	5·212
9	4·655−	4·665−	4·696	4·745+	4·812	4·895+	4·991	5·100	5·218	5·345−
10	4·818	4·827	4·856	4·902	4·965+	5·043	5·135−	5·238	5·351	5·473
11	4·972	4·981	5·008	5·052	5·112	5·186	5·273	5·371	5·480	5·597
12	5·120	5·129	5·154	5·196	5·252	5·323	5·406	5·500+	5·605−	5·718
15	5·530	5·537	5·559	5·595+	5·645−	5·707	5·781	5·865+	5·959	6·062
20	6·129	6·135+	6·154	6·184	6·225+	6·278	6·341	6·414	6·495+	6·586

√λ ∖ ν	2·0	2·2	2·4	2·6	2·8	3·0	3·2	3·4	3·6	3·8
1	4·326	4·526	4·726	4·926	5·126	5·326	5·526	5·726	5·926	6·126
2	4·492	4·681	4·871	5·063	5·256	5·449	5·643	5·838	6·033	6·229
3	4·649	4·829	5·011	5·196	5·382	5·569	5·758	5·947	6·138	6·329
4	4·800	4·972	5·147	5·324	5·504	5·686	5·869	6·054	6·241	6·428
5	4·946	5·110	5·278	5·449	5·623	5·800	5·979	6·159	6·341	6·525+
6	5·086	5·243	5·405	5·571	5·740	5·911	6·086	6·262	6·440	6·620
7	5·221	5·372	5·529	5·689	5·853	6·020	6·191	6·363	6·538	6·714
8	5·352	5·498	5·649	5·805−	5·964	6·127	6·293	6·462	6·633	6·807
9	5·479	5·620	5·766	5·917	6·073	6·232	6·394	6·559	6·727	6·897
10	5·602	5·738	5·880	6·027	6·179	6·334	6·493	6·655+	6·820	6·987
11	5·722	5·854	5·992	6·135+	6·283	6·435−	6·590	6·749	6·911	7·075+
12	5·839	5·967	6·101	6·241	6·385−	6·533	6·686	6·842	7·001	7·162
15	6·173	6·291	6·415−	6·545−	6·680	6·819	6·963	7·111	7·262	7·416
20	6·683	6·788	6·899	7·016	7·139	7·266	7·399	7·535−	7·675−	7·819

√λ ∖ ν	4·0	4·2	4·4	4·6	4·8	5·0	5·2	5·4	5·6	5·8	6·0
1	6·326	6·526	6·726	6·926	7·126	7·326	7·526	7·726	7·926	8·126	8·326
2	6·425−	6·621	6·817	7·014	7·211	7·408	7·606	7·803	8·001	8·199	8·397
3	6·521	6·714	6·907	7·101	7·295−	7·489	7·684	7·879	8·075−	8·270	8·466
4	6·616	6·806	6·995+	7·186	7·377	7·569	7·762	7·955−	8·148	8·341	8·535+
5	6·710	6·896	7·083	7·270	7·459	7·648	7·838	8·029	8·220	8·412	8·604
6	6·802	6·985−	7·169	7·354	7·540	7·727	7·914	8·103	8·292	8·482	8·672
7	6·892	7·072	7·253	7·436	7·619	7·804	7·989	8·176	8·363	8·551	8·739
8	6·982	7·159	7·337	7·517	7·698	7·880	8·064	8·248	8·433	8·619	8·806
9	7·070	7·244	7·420	7·597	7·776	7·956	8·137	8·320	8·503	8·687	8·872
10	7·157	7·328	7·501	7·676	7·853	8·031	8·210	8·390	8·572	8·754	8·938
11	7·242	7·411	7·582	7·755−	7·929	8·105−	8·282	8·461	8·640	8·821	9·003
12	7·327	7·493	7·662	7·832	8·004	8·178	8·354	8·530	8·708	8·887	9·067
15	7·573	7·733	7·895+	8·060	8·226	8·394	8·564	8·735+	8·908	9·083	9·258
20	7·965+	8·115+	8·268	8·423	8·581	8·740	8·902	9·066	9·231	9·399	9·567

$\sqrt{\lambda}$ ν	0·0	0·2	0·4	0·6	0·8	1·0	1·2	1·4	1·6	1·8
1	$0.0^2 6267$	$0.0^2 6393$	$0.0^2 6789$	$0.0^2 7502$	$0.0^2 8630$	0·01033	0·01287	0·01670	0·02254	0·03165+
2	·1001	·1011	·1042	·1096	·1175−	·1285+	·1434	·1632	·1894	·2239
3	·2678	·2696	·2750+	·2844	·2979	·3162	·3401	·3704	·4085−	·4557
4	·4550−	·4572	·4641	·4759	·4927	·5152	·5439	·5796	·6233	·6758
5	·6417	·6442	·6520	·6651	·6839	·7087	·7400	·7784	·8246	·8793
6	0·8220	0·8248	0·8330	0·8470	0·8668	0·8929	0·9255+	0·9653	1·013	1·068
7	0·9946	0·9975−	1·006	1·020	1·041	1·068	1·101	1·141	1·189	1·244
8	1·159	1·162	1·171	1·186	1·207	1·234	1·267	1·308	1·355+	1·410
9	1·317	1·320	1·329	1·344	1·365−	1·392	1·425+	1·466	1·513	1·568
10	1·468	1·471	1·480	1·495−	1·516	1·543	1·576	1·616	1·663	1·717
11	1·613	1·616	1·625+	1·640	1·661	1·688	1·721	1·761	1·807	1·860
12	1·753	1·756	1·765−	1·780	1·800	1·827	1·860	1·899	1·945+	1·998
15	2·145−	2·148	2·156	2·171	2·191	2·217	2·249	2·287	2·331	2·382
20	2·727	2·729	2·737	2·751	2·770	2·795−	2·825+	2·861	2·903	2·950−

$\sqrt{\lambda}$ ν	2·0	2·2	2·4	2·6	2·8	3·0	3·2	3·4	3·6	3·8
1	0·04625+	0·07025+	0·1106	0·1786	0·2883	0·4435+	0·6286	0·8250+	1·024	1·224
2	·2694	·3292	·4067	·5050+	·6251	0·7647	0·9198	1·086	1·259	1·438
3	·5138	·5845−	·6693	·7692	0·8840	1·013	1·154	1·304	1·463	1·628
4	·7384	0·8120	0·8974	0·9950+	1·105−	1·226	1·358	1·498	1·647	1·802
5	·9433	1·017	1·101	1·196	1·302	1·417	1·542	1·675+	1·816	1·964
6	1·132	1·205+	1·288	1·380	1·482	1·593	1·712	1·839	1·974	2·115+
7	1·308	1·380	1·461	1·551	1·649	1·756	1·871	1·994	2·123	2·259
8	1·473	1·544	1·623	1·711	1·806	1·910	2·021	2·140	2·265−	2·397
9	1·630	1·699	1·777	1·862	1·955+	2·056	2·164	2·279	2·400	2·528
10	1·778	1·847	1·923	2·006	2·097	2·195−	2·300	2·412	2·530	2·654
11	1·921	1·988	2·062	2·144	2·233	2·328	2·431	2·540	2·655+	2·776
12	2·057	2·123	2·196	2·276	2·363	2·457	2·557	2·663	2·776	2·894
15	2·438	2·501	2·571	2·646	2·728	2·816	2·910	3·011	3·116	3·228
20	3·003	3·061	3·126	3·196	3·271	3·353	3·439	3·532	3·629	3·731

$\sqrt{\lambda}$ ν	4·0	4·2	4·4	4·6	4·8	5·0	5·2	5·4	5·6	5·8	6·0
1	1·424	1·624	1·824	2·024	2·224	2·424	2·624	2·824	3·024	3·224	3·424
2	1·620	1·805+	1·992	2·181	2·372	2·563	2·756	2·949	3·143	3·337	3·532
3	1·798	1·972	2·149	2·329	2·512	2·696	2·882	3·069	3·258	3·447	3·638
4	1·963	2·128	2·297	2·470	2·646	2·824	3·004	3·186	3·369	3·554	3·741
5	2·117	2·275+	2·438	2·604	2·774	2·946	3·121	3·299	3·478	3·659	3·841
6	2·263	2·415−	2·572	2·733	2·897	3·065−	3·235+	3·408	3·583	3·760	3·939
7	2·401	2·549	2·701	2·857	3·017	3·180	3·346	3·515−	3·686	3·860	4·035+
8	2·534	2·677	2·824	2·976	3·132	3·291	3·454	3·619	3·787	3·957	4·129
9	2·662	2·800	2·944	3·092	3·244	3·399	3·558	3·720	3·885−	4·052	4·221
10	2·784	2·920	3·060	3·204	3·353	3·505−	3·661	3·819	3·981	4·145+	4·312
11	2·903	3·035+	3·172	3·313	3·459	3·608	3·760	3·916	4·075+	4·237	4·400
12	3·018	3·147	3·281	3·419	3·562	3·708	3·858	4·011	4·167	4·326	4·488
15	3·344	3·466	3·592	3·723	3·858	3·997	4·139	4·285+	4·434	4·586	4·741
20	3·839	3·951	4·067	4·188	4·314	4·443	4·575+	4·711	4·851	4·994	5·139

ν = degrees of freedom; λ = non-central parameter. For interpolation when $\nu > 12$, see pp. 54, 139.

For an extension to $\sqrt{\lambda} = 8, 10$, obtained by approximation, see Table 29.

Table 24 (*continued*)
Upper 0·5% *points*

$\sqrt{\lambda}$ ν	0·0	0·2	0·4	0·6	0·8	1·0	1·2	1·4	1·6	1·8
1	2·807	2·861	3·000	3·181	3·377	3·576	3·776	3·976	4·176	4·376
2	3·255+	3·287	3·375+	3·504	3·656	3·823	3·998	4·178	4·361	4·548
3	3·583	3·607	3·674	3·776	3·903	4·047	4·203	4·367	4·537	4·711
4	3·855−	3·874	3·929	4·015−	4·125−	4·253	4·394	4·545−	4·703	4·868
5	4·093	4·109	4·156	4·231	4·328	4·444	4·573	4·713	4·862	5·018
6	4·307	4·321	4·363	4·430	4·518	4·623	4·743	4·874	5·014	5·162
7	4·503	4·516	4·554	4·614	4·695−	4·792	4·904	5·027	5·160	5·301
8	4·686	4·697	4·732	4·787	4·862	4·953	5·058	5·174	5·301	5·435+
9	4·857	4·868	4·900	4·951	5·021	5·106	5·205−	5·316	5·436	5·565+
10	5·019	5·029	5·059	5·107	5·172	5·252	5·346	5·452	5·567	5·692
11	5·173	5·182	5·210	5·255+	5·317	5·393	5·483	5·584	5·695−	5·814
12	5·320	5·328	5·355−	5·398	5·456	5·529	5·614	5·711	5·818	5·933
15	5·727	5·735−	5·758	5·795+	5·846	5·910	5·986	6·072	6·169	6·274
20	6·324	6·331	6·349	6·381	6·423	6·478	6·542	6·617	6·700	6·792

$\sqrt{\lambda}$ ν	2·0	2·2	2·4	2·6	2·8	3·0	3·2	3·4	3·6	3·8
1	4·576	4·776	4·976	5·176	5·376	5·576	5·776	5·976	6·176	6·376
2	4·736	4·926	5·117	5·309	5·502	5·696	5·890	6·085+	6·280	6·476
3	4·889	5·070	5·253	5·438	5·625−	5·813	6·002	6·192	6·383	6·575−
4	5·037	5·210	5·385+	5·564	5·745−	5·927	6·111	6·297	6·484	6·671
5	5·179	5·344	5·514	5·686	5·861	6·039	6·218	6·400	6·582	6·767
6	5·316	5·475−	5·638	5·805+	5·975+	6·148	6·323	6·501	6·680	6·860
7	5·448	5·602	5·759	5·921	6·087	6·255+	6·426	6·600	6·775+	6·952
8	5·577	5·725−	5·877	6·035−	6·196	6·360	6·527	6·697	6·869	7·043
9	5·702	5·845−	5·993	6·145+	6·302	6·463	6·626	6·793	6·962	7·133
10	5·823	5·961	6·105+	6·254	6·407	6·563	6·724	6·887	7·053	7·221
11	5·941	6·075+	6·215+	6·360	6·509	6·662	6·819	6·979	7·142	7·308
12	6·057	6·187	6·323	6·464	6·610	6·760	6·913	7·071	7·231	7·394
15	6·386	6·506	6·632	6·764	6·901	7·042	7·187	7·336	7·489	7·644
20	6·892	6·998	7·112	7·230	7·355−	7·484	7·617	7·755+	7·897	8·042

$\sqrt{\lambda}$ ν	4·0	4·2	4·4	4·6	4·8	5·0	5·2	5·4	5·6	5·8	6·0
1	6·576	6·776	6·976	7·176	7·376	7·576	7·776	7·976	8·176	8·376	8·576
2	6·672	6·869	7·065+	7·262	7·459	7·656	7·854	8·051	8·249	8·447	8·645+
3	6·767	6·960	7·153	7·347	7·541	7·736	7·931	8·126	8·322	8·518	8·714
4	6·860	7·050−	7·240	7·431	7·623	7·815−	8·007	8·200	8·394	8·588	8·782
5	6·952	7·138	7·326	7·514	7·703	7·892	8·083	8·274	8·465+	8·657	8·849
6	7·042	7·226	7·410	7·596	7·782	7·969	8·157	8·346	8·536	8·726	8·916
7	7·131	7·312	7·494	7·677	7·861	8·046	8·231	8·418	8·606	8·794	8·983
8	7·219	7·397	7·576	7·756	7·938	8·121	8·305−	8·489	8·675−	8·861	9·048
9	7·306	7·481	7·657	7·835+	8·015−	8·195+	8·377	8·560	8·744	8·928	9·114
10	7·391	7·564	7·738	7·913	8·091	8·269	8·449	8·630	8·812	8·995−	9·178
11	7·476	7·645+	7·817	7·991	8·166	8·342	8·520	8·699	8·879	9·061	9·243
12	7·559	7·726	7·896	8·067	8·240	8·415−	8·591	8·768	8·946	9·126	9·307
15	7·802	7·963	8·126	8·291	8·459	8·628	8·798	8·970	9·144	9·319	9·495+
20	8·190	8·341	8·494	8·651	8·809	8·970	9·133	9·297	9·463	9·631	9·800

Table 25. *Non-central χ^2. Values of the non-central parameter, λ, for given degrees of freedom, ν, and power, β, with $\alpha = 0.05$*

ν \ β	0·25	0·50	0·60	0·70	0·75	0·80	0·85	0·90	0·95	0·97	0·99
1	1·647	3·841	4·899	6·172	6·940	7·849	8·978	10·507	12·995	14·751	18·372
2	2·256	4·957	6·213	7·702	8·591	9·635	10·923	12·654	15·443	17·398	21·396
3	2·705	5·760	7·154	8·792	9·765	10·903	12·301	14·171	17·170	19·262	23·521
4	3·078	6·419	7·924	9·682	10·722	11·935	13·422	15·405	18·572	20·774	25·243
5	3·403	6·991	8·591	10·453	11·550	12·828	14·391	16·469	19·780	22·076	26·726
6	3·696	7·503	9·187	11·141	12·289	13·624	15·255	17·419	20·857	23·237	28·046
7	3·965	7·971	9·732	11·768	12·963	14·351	16·042	18·284	21·838	24·294	29·247
8	4·214	8·405	10·236	12·349	13·587	15·022	16·770	19·083	22·744	25·270	30·356
9	4·448	8·810	10·708	12·892	14·170	15·650	17·450	19·829	23·589	26·180	31·391
10	4·669	9·193	11·153	13·404	14·720	16·241	18·090	20·532	24·386	27·037	32·365
11	4·879	9·556	11·575	13·890	15·240	16·802	18·697	21·198	25·140	27·849	33·286
12	5·080	9·903	11·977	14·353	15·737	17·336	19·276	21·833	25·858	28·623	34·164
13	5·273	10·235	12·363	14·796	16·212	17·847	19·829	22·439	26·545	29·362	35·003
14	5·458	10·554	12·733	15·221	16·669	18·338	20·361	23·022	27·204	30·071	35·808
15	5·637	10·861	13·090	15·631	17·108	18·811	20·873	23·583	27·839	30·754	36·583
16	5·809	11·159	13·434	16·027	17·533	19·268	21·367	24·125	28·452	31·414	37·331
17	5·977	11·446	13·768	16·411	17·944	19·710	21·845	24·650	29·045	32·052	38·054
18	6·139	11·726	14·092	16·783	18·343	20·139	22·309	25·158	29·620	32·670	38·755
19	6·297	11·997	14·407	17·144	18·731	20·555	22·760	25·652	30·178	33·270	39·436
20	6·451	12·262	14·713	17·496	19·108	20·961	23·199	26·132	30·721	33·855	40·098
21	6·601	12·519	15·012	17·839	19·475	21·356	23·626	26·600	31·250	34·424	40·743
22	6·748	12·771	15·304	18·174	19·834	21·741	24·043	27·057	31·767	34·979	41·372
23	6·892	13·017	15·588	18·501	20·184	22·118	29·450	27·503	32·271	35·521	41·986
24	7·032	13·257	15·867	18·820	20·527	22·486	24·848	27·939	32·763	36·050	42·586
25	7·170	13·493	16·140	19·133	20 862	22·847	25·238	28·366	33·246	36·569	43·173
26	7·304	13·723	16·407	19·440	21·191	23·200	25·620	28·784	33·718	37·076	43·748
27	7·437	13·950	16·669	19·741	21·513	23·546	25·994	29·194	34·181	37·574	44·312
28	7·566	14·172	16·926	20·036	21·829	23·885	26·361	29·596	34·635	38·062	44·865
29	7·694	14·390	17·179	20·325	22·139	24·219	26·722	29·991	35·081	38·541	45·407
30	7·819	14·604	17·427	20·610	22·444	24·547	27·076	30·379	35·519	39·012	45·940
32	8·063	15·023	17·911	21·165	23·039	25·186	27·767	31·135	36·372	39·930	46·979
34	8·300	15·428	18·381	21·703	23·615	25·804	28·436	31·867	37·199	40·818	47·985
36	8·531	15·821	18·836	22·225	24·174	26·405	29·085	32·578	38·001	41·680	48·960
38	8·755	16·204	19·279	22·733	24·718	26·989	29·716	33·268	38·780	42·517	49·908
40	8·973	16·576	19·710	23·227	25·247	27·557	30·330	33·940	39·539	43·332	50·830
42	9·186	16·939	20·130	23·709	25·763	28·111	30·929	34·595	40·278	44·126	51·729
44	9·394	17·294	20·540	24·179	26·267	28·652	31·513	35·235	41·000	44·901	52·605
46	9·597	17·641	20·941	24·639	26·759	29·181	32·084	35·860	41·704	45·658	53·462
48	9·796	17·980	21·334	25·088	27·240	29·698	32·642	26·470	42·394	46·398	54·299
50	9·991	18·312	21·718	25·528	27·712	30·204	33·189	37·069	43·068	47·123	55·119
55	10·462	19·115	22·646	26·591	28·850	31·426	24·509	38·513	44·697	48·872	57·097
60	10·911	19·881	23·533	27·607	29·937	32·593	35·770	39·891	46·251	50·542	58·984
65	11·344	20·617	24·383	28·580	30·979	33·711	36·978	41·213	47·741	52·142	60·793
70	11·759	21·324	25·201	29·517	31·981	34·787	38·140	42·483	49·174	53·680	62·531
75	12·160	22·006	25·990	30·420	32·948	35·825	39·261	43·709	50·555	55·163	64·207
80	12·547	22·666	26·753	31·294	33·883	36·829	40·345	44·893	51·890	56·596	65·827
85	12·924	23·306	27·492	32·140	34·789	37·801	41·394	46·041	53·184	57·984	67·395
90	13·289	23·927	28·210	32·962	35·669	38·745	42·414	47·155	54·439	59·332	68·918
95	13·644	24·532	28·908	33·761	36·524	39·663	43·404	48·238	55·659	60·642	70·397
100	13·990	25·120	29·588	34·539	37·357	40·556	44·369	49·293	56·848	61·917	71·838

Table 25 (*continued*), *with* $\alpha = 0.01$

ν \ β	0·25	0·50	0·60	0·70	0·75	0·80	0·85	0·90	0·95	0·97	0·99
1	3·615	6·635	8·004	9·611	10·565	11·679	13·048	14·879	17·814	19·861	24·031
2	4·699	8·190	9·752	11·567	12·636	13·881	15·403	17·427	20·650	22·886	27·415
3	5·437	9·310	11·008	12·970	14·121	15·458	17·087	19·247	22·674	25·043	29·826
4	6·072	10·232	12·040	14·121	15·339	16·749	18·466	20·737	24·329	26·806	31·794
5	6·625	11·033	12·935	15·119	16·395	17·869	19·661	22·028	25·762	28·333	33·498
6	7·123	11·751	13·738	16·014	17·340	18·872	20·731	23·182	27·043	29·697	35·020
7	7·578	12·408	14·472	16·831	18·204	19·787	21·707	24·235	28·212	30·941	36·408
8	8·002	13·017	15·153	17·588	19·003	20·635	22·611	25·211	29·294	32·092	37·692
9	8·399	13·588	15·790	18·297	19·752	21·429	23·457	26·123	30·305	33·168	38·891
10	8·775	14·126	16·390	18·965	20·458	22·177	24·254	26·982	31·258	34·182	40·021
11	9·132	14·638	16·961	19·599	21·128	22·886	25·011	27·798	32·161	35·143	41·092
12	9·473	15·126	17·505	20·204	21·767	23·563	25·732	28·575	33·022	36·059	42·112
13	9·799	15·593	18·027	20·784	22·378	24·211	26·422	29·319	33·846	36·936	43·088
14	10·114	16·043	18·528	21·341	22·966	24·833	27·085	30·033	34·638	37·777	44·026
15	10·417	16·476	19·011	21·877	23·533	25·433	27·724	30·722	35·400	38·588	44·928
16	10·711	16·985	19·478	22·396	24·080	26·013	28·341	31·387	36·136	39·371	45·800
17	10·995	17·301	19·930	22·898	24·610	26·574	28·939	32·031	36·849	40·128	46·643
18	11·271	17·695	20·369	23·385	25·124	27·118	29·519	32·655	37·540	40·863	47·460
19	11·540	18·078	20·795	23·859	25·624	27·647	30·082	33·262	38·211	41·577	48·255
20	11·801	18·451	21·211	24·320	26·110	28·162	30·631	33·852	38·865	42·271	49·027
21	12·056	18·814	21·616	24·769	26·585	28·664	31·165	34·427	39·501	42·948	49·780
22	12·305	19·169	22·011	25·208	27·047	29·154	31·686	34·989	40·122	43·608	50·514
23	12·549	19·516	22·397	25·636	27·500	29·632	32·195	35·537	40·729	44·253	51·231
24	12·788	19·856	22·775	26·055	27·942	30·100	32·693	36·073	41·322	44·883	51·932
25	13·021	20·188	23·145	26·466	28·375	30·558	33·181	36·598	41·903	45·500	52·619
26	13·250	20·514	23·507	26·868	28·799	31·007	33·659	37·113	42·471	46·104	53·290
27	13·474	20·833	23·863	27·262	29·215	31·447	34·127	37·617	43·029	46·697	53·949
28	13·695	21·146	24·211	27·649	29·623	31·879	34·587	38·111	43·576	47·278	54·595
29	13·912	21·454	24·554	28·029	30·024	32·303	35·038	38·597	44·113	47·848	55·230
30	14·124	21·757	24·891	28·403	30·418	32·720	35·482	39·074	44·641	48·409	55·853
32	14·540	22·347	25·548	29·131	31·186	33·533	36·346	40·005	45·669	49·502	57·067
34	14·943	22·920	26·184	29·837	31·930	34·320	37·184	40·906	46·666	50·560	58·243
36	15·335	23·475	26·802	30·522	32·653	35·084	37·997	41·781	47·632	51·587	59·384
38	15·715	24·015	27·403	31·188	33·355	35·827	38·787	42·631	48·572	52·585	60·493
40	16·086	24·542	27·988	31·837	34·039	36·550	39·557	43·459	49·486	53·556	61·572
42	16·448	25·055	28·559	32·469	34·706	37·256	40·307	44·266	50·378	54·502	62·623
44	16·801	25·556	29·116	33·086	35·356	37·944	41·039	45·053	51·248	55·426	63·649
46	17·146	26·045	29·660	33·690	35·993	38·617	41·754	45·822	52·098	56·329	64·652
48	17·484	26·525	30·193	34·280	36·615	39·275	42·454	46·575	52·929	57·211	65·632
50	17·816	26·994	30·715	34·858	37·224	39·919	43·139	47·312	53·743	58·075	66·591
55	18·616	28·128	31·975	36·254	38·696	41·475	44·794	49·091	55·707	60·161	68·907
60	19·381	29·211	33·178	37·587	40·101	42·960	46·374	50·790	57·583	62·152	71·118
65	20·115	30·250	34·333	38·866	41·448	44·385	47·888	52·418	59·381	64·061	73·236
70	20·821	31·249	35·443	40·096	42·745	45·755	49·345	53·984	61·109	65·895	75·272
75	21·502	32·214	36·515	41·282	43·995	47·077	50·750	55·494	62·776	67·664	77·235
80	22·162	33·147	37·551	42·430	45·204	48·355	52·109	56·954	64·388	69·375	79·132
85	22·802	34·051	38·556	43·542	46·376	49·593	53·425	58·369	65·949	71·031	80·970
90	23·423	34·929	39·531	44·621	47·513	50·796	54·703	59·742	67·464	72·639	82·753
95	24·026	35·782	40·479	45·671	48·620	51·965	55·945	61·078	68·937	74·202	84·487
100	24·615	36·614	41·403	46·693	49·697	53·103	57·155	62·378	70·372	75·724	86·175

Table 26. *Non-central t. Factors, l, for determination of percentage points of t'*

$\Pr\{t' \geqslant t_0'|\Delta\} = \alpha = 0.50$. For $\nu = \infty$, all values of l are zero.

u \ ν	2	3	4	5	6	7	8	9	16	36	144
−1·00	− 0·3349	− 0·2742	− 0·2374	− 0·2122	− 0·1936	− 0·1791	− 0·1675	− 0·1578	− 0·1182	− 0·0787	− 0·0393
−0·95	− ·3149	− ·2567	− ·2217	− ·1979	− ·1804	− ·1668	− ·1558	− ·1468	− ·1097	− ·0730	− ·0364
− ·90	− ·2943	− ·2391	− ·2062	− ·1839	− ·1675	− ·1548	− ·1446	− ·1361	− ·1017	− ·0675	− ·0337
− ·85	− ·2734	− ·2218	− ·1911	− ·1702	− ·1550	− ·1431	− ·1337	− ·1258	− ·0939	− ·0624	− ·0311
− ·80	− ·2526	− ·2047	− ·1763	− ·1570	− ·1429	− ·1319	− ·1232	− ·1160	− ·0865	− ·0574	− ·0286
−0·7	− ·2124	− 0·1722	− 0·1482	− 0·1320	− 0·1201	− 0·1109	− 0·1035	− 0·0974	− 0·0726	− 0·0482	− 0·0240
− ·6	− ·1750	− ·1420	− ·1223	− ·1089	− ·0991	− ·0915	− ·0854	− ·0804	− ·0599	− ·0398	− ·0198
− ·5	− ·1407	− ·1142	− ·0984	− ·0877	− ·0798	− ·0737	− ·0688	− ·0648	− ·0483	− ·0320	− ·0160
− ·4	− ·1090	− ·0886	− ·0764	− ·0681	− ·0620	− ·0573	− ·0535	− ·0503	− ·0375	− ·0249	− ·0124
−0·3	− 0·0797	− 0·0649	− 0·0559	− 0·0499	− 0·0454	− 0·0420	− 0·0392	− 0·0369	− 0·0275	− 0·0183	− 0·0091
− ·2	− ·0521	− ·0425	− ·0366	− ·0327	− ·0298	− ·0275	− ·0257	− ·0242	− ·0180	− ·0120	− ·0060
− ·1	− ·0258	− ·0210	− ·0181	− ·0162	− ·0147	− ·0136	− ·0127	− ·0120	− ·0089	− ·0059	− ·0030
0·0	·0000	·0000	·0000	·0000	·0000	·0000	·0000	·0000	·0000	·0000	·0000

For u positive the values of l are the same but with positive sign.

$\Pr\{t' \geqslant t_0'|\Delta\} = \alpha = 0.25$. For $\nu = \infty$, all values of $l = 0.67449$.

u \ ν	2	3	4	5	6	7	8	9	16	36	144
−1·00	0·3548	0·4170	0·4534	0·4780	0·4959	0·5097	0·5208	0·5299	0·5671	0·6036	0·6393
−0·95	·3830	·4390	·4718	·4940	·5103	·5228	·5329	·5412	·5752	·6086	·6417
− ·90	·4121	·4611	·4902	·5099	·5245	·5357	·5448	·5523	·5830	·6136	·6441
− ·85	·4415	·4830	·5082	·5255	·5383	·5482	·5563	·5630	·5906	·6183	·6463
− ·80	·4705	·5045	·5257	·5406	·5517	·5604	·5674	·5733	·5979	·6229	·6484
−0·7	0·5247	0·5447	0·5587	0·5689	0·5769	0·5832	0·5884	0·5928	0·6117	0·6316	0·6525
− ·6	·5722	·5808	·5885	·5947	·5998	·6041	·6077	·6107	·6244	·6397	·6564
− ·5	·6133	·6126	·6151	·6180	·6206	·6231	·6252	·6271	·6362	·6472	·6599
− ·4	·6490	·6409	·6391	·6390	·6396	·6404	·6413	·6421	·6471	·6542	·6633
−0·3	0·6803	0·6663	0·6608	0·6582	0·6570	0·6564	0·6561	0·6561	0·6573	0·6608	0·6666
− ·2	·7082	·6893	·6807	·6760	·6731	·6712	·6700	·6691	·6669	·6672	·6697
− ·1	·7332	·7105	·6992	·6925	·6883	·6853	·6831	·6814	·6762	·6732	·6727
0·0	·7559	·7301	·7165	·7082	·7026	·6986	·6956	·6933	·6850	·6792	·6757
0·1	0·7766	0·7485	0·7330	0·7232	0·7164	0·7115	0·7077	0·7047	0·6937	0·6850	0·6786
·2	·7957	·7659	·7487	·7376	·7298	·7240	·7195	·7159	·7023	·6908	·6815
·3	·8134	·7824	·7639	·7516	·7429	·7363	·7311	·7269	·7108	·6967	·6845
·4	·8302	·7984	·7787	·7654	·7557	·7484	·7426	·7379	·7194	·7026	·6876
·5	·8464	·8139	·7932	·7790	·7685	·7605	·7541	·7489	·7281	·7086	·6907
0·6	0·8623	0·8293	0·8077	0·7926	0·7814	0·7727	0·7658	0·7601	0·7370	0·7149	0·6940
·7	·8784	·8448	·8223	·8064	·7944	·7851	·7776	·7714	·7461	·7213	·6974
·8	·8948	·8605	·8371	·8204	·8078	·7979	·7898	·7831	·7555	·7281	·7011
·9	·9114	·8764	·8522	·8348	·8215	·8110	·8024	·7953	·7654	·7352	·7049
1·0	·9273	·8922	·8675	·8494	·8356	·8245	·8155	·8079	·7758	·7428	·7090

To determine an upper 100α per cent point, $t'(\alpha|\nu, \Delta)$:

(1) calculate $u = \dfrac{\Delta}{\sqrt{(2\nu)}}\left(1 + \dfrac{\Delta^2}{2\nu}\right)^{-\frac{1}{2}}$;

(2) interpolate for l in the appropriate α-table;

(3) determine $t_0' = t'(\alpha, \nu, \Delta)$ from $t_0' = \dfrac{\Delta + l(1 + (\Delta^2/2\nu) - (l^2/2\nu))^{\frac{1}{2}}}{1 - (l^2/2\nu)}$.

A lower percentage point is obtained by the same procedure, noting that $t'(1-\alpha|\nu, \Delta) = -t'(\alpha|\nu, -\Delta)$.

Table 26 (*continued*)

$\Pr\{t' \geqslant t'_0|\delta\} = \alpha = 0.10$. For $\nu = \infty$, all values of $l = 1.28155^+$.

u	ν 2	3	4	5	6	7	8	9	16	36	144
−1·00	1·0348	1·0864	1·1160	1·1357	1·1499	1·1608	1·1694	1·1765	1·2049	1·2319	1·2575
−0·95	1·0549	1·1001	1·1265	1·1442	1·1572	1·1672	1·1751	1·1817	1·2082	1·2337	1·2583
− ·90	1·0797	1·1165	1·1389	1·1544	1·1658	1·1747	1·1818	1·1878	1·2120	1·2358	1·2591
− ·85	1·1081	1·1351	1·1530	1·1658	1·1755	1·1831	1·1894	1·1946	1·2163	1·2382	1·2601
− ·80	1·1386	1·1551	1·1681	1·1781	1·1859	1·1923	1·1975	1·2020	1·2209	1·2408	1·2611
−0·7	1·1993	1·1962	1·1997	1·2040	1·2081	1·2117	1·2149	1·2178	1·2310	1·2464	1·2634
− ·6	1·2535	1·2354	1·2307	1·2299	1·2304	1·2315	1·2328	1·2341	1·2418	1·2526	1·2660
− ·5	1·2977	1·2702	1·2593	1·2543	1·2519	1·2508	1·2504	1·2503	1·2527	1·2590	1·2688
− ·4	1·3304	1·2995	1·2846	1·2765	1·2718	1·2689	1·2670	1·2657	1·2634	1·2656	1·2718
−0·3	1·3523	1·3228	1·3060	1·2960	1·2897	1·2853	1·2823	1·2801	1·2738	1·2721	1·2748
− ·2	1·3650	1·3405	1·3236	1·3126	1·3052	1·3000	1·2961	1·2931	1·2835	1·2784	1·2778
− ·1	1·3709	1·3531	1·3374	1·3264	1·3185	1·3127	1·3082	1·3048	1·2926	1·2845	1·2808
0·0	1·3720	1·3615	1·3479	1·3374	1·3295	1·3235	1·3187	1·3149	1·3009	1·2903	1·2838
0·1	1·3701	1·3665	1·3555	1·3460	1·3384	1·3324	1·3276	1·3236	1·3084	1·2957	1·2866
·2	1·3666	1·3692	1·3608	1·3524	1·3454	1·3396	1·3349	1·3309	1·3150	1·3007	1·2894
·3	1·3625	1·3701	1·3642	1·3571	1·3507	1·3453	1·3408	1·3369	1·3207	1·3053	1·2919
·4	1·3583	1·3699	1·3662	1·3604	1·3547	1·3498	1·3455	1·3417	1·3256	1·3093	1·2943
·5	1·3546	1·3691	1·3673	1·3626	1·3576	1·3531	1·3491	1·3456	1·3297	1·3129	1·2965
0·6	1·3516	1·3682	1·3678	1·3640	1·3597	1·3556	1·3518	1·3485	1·3331	1·3159	1·2984
·7	1·3498	1·3674	1·3681	1·3650	1·3612	1·3574	1·3539	1·3508	1·3358	1·3185	1·3002
·8	1·3491	1·3672	1·3684	1·3658	1·3623	1·3588	1·3556	1·3526	1·3380	1·3207	1·3016
·9	1·3496	1·3675	1·3690	1·3666	1·3634	1·3601	1·3569	1·3540	1·3398	1·3224	1·3028
1·0	1·3508	1·3684	1·3699	1·3677	1·3645	1·3613	1·3582	1·3554	1·3412	1·3238	1·3038

$\Pr\{t' \geqslant t'_0|\delta\} = \alpha = 0.05$. For $\nu = \infty$, all values of $l = 1.64485^+$.

u	ν 2	3	4	5	6	7	8	9	16	36	144
−1·00	1·4616	1·5039	1·5277	1·5431	1·5542	1·5625	1·5691	1·5744	1·5952	1·6141	1·6307
−0·95	1·4648	1·5037	1·5262	1·5411	1·5519	1·5601	1·5666	1·5720	1·5930	1·6124	1·6298
− ·90	1·4798	1·5108	1·5302	1·5435	1·5534	1·5610	1·5671	1·5721	1·5924	1·6116	1·6293
− ·85	1·5047	1·5242	1·5388	1·5497	1·5580	1·5646	1·5700	1·5745	1·5931	1·6115	1·6290
− ·80	1·5362	1·5422	1·5511	1·5588	1·5651	1·5704	1·5749	1·5786	1·5951	1·6121	1·6290
−0·75	1·5707	1·5631	1·5658	1·5700	1·5742	1·5779	1·5813	1·5843	1·5980	1·6133	1·6293
− ·70	1·6049	1·5853	1·5819	1·5826	1·5845	1·5867	1·5889	1·5910	1·6017	1·6149	1·6297
− ·65	1·6364	1·6075	1·5986	1·5960	1·5957	1·5963	1·5973	1·5985	1·6060	1·6170	1·6304
− ·60	1·6631	1·6285	1·6152	1·6096	1·6072	1·6063	1·6062	1·6065	1·6108	1·6194	1·6312
−0·5	1·6984	1·6641	1·6456	1·6357	1·6300	1·6265	1·6244	1·6230	1·6213	1·6251	1·6333
− ·4	1·7101	1·6888	1·6701	1·6582	1·6505	1·6453	1·6417	1·6390	1·6322	1·6313	1·6359
− ·3	1·7045	1·7023	1·6874	1·6758	1·6675	1·6614	1·6569	1·6535	1·6427	1·6378	1·6387
− ·2	1·6892	1·7065	1·6979	1·6883	1·6805	1·6744	1·6696	1·6658	1·6525	1·6442	1·6417
− ·1	1·6700	1·7040	1·7025	1·6959	1·6894	1·6839	1·6793	1·6755	1·6611	1·6503	1·6447
0·0	1·6501	1·6970	1·7024	1·6994	1·6947	1·6902	1·6862	1·6828	1·6682	1·6558	1·6477
0·1	1·6312	1·6876	1·6991	1·6995	1·6969	1·6937	1·6905	1·6875	1·6739	1·6607	1·6504
·2	1·6141	1·6769	1·6934	1·6970	1·6965	1·6947	1·6924	1·6901	1·6780	1·6647	1·6529
·3	1·5990	1·6660	1·6864	1·6927	1·6941	1·6936	1·6923	1·6907	1·6807	1·6678	1·6551
·4	1·5861	1·6553	1·6785	1·6872	1·6902	1·6909	1·6906	1·6897	1·6819	1·6699	1·6568
·5	1·5751	1·6452	1·6705	1·6808	1·6853	1·6870	1·6875	1·6873	1·6818	1·6711	1·6581
0·6	1·5661	1·6361	1·6625	1·6741	1·6796	1·6823	1·6834	1·6838	1·6805	1·6714	1·6588
·7	1·5590	1·6280	1·6549	1·6673	1·6736	1·6769	1·6786	1·6795	1·6782	1·6707	1·6590
·8	1·5536	1·6210	1·6479	1·6607	1·6674	1·6712	1·6734	1·6746	1·6750	1·6692	1·6586
·9	1·5497	1·6153	1·6416	1·6544	1·6613	1·6654	1·6678	1·6693	1·6710	1·6667	1·6576
1·0	1·5470	1·6106	1·6362	1·6487	1·6556	1·6597	1·6622	1·6638	1·6664	1·6635	1·6560

For $\nu > 9$, interpolate using argument $12/\sqrt{\nu}$. The arguments $\nu = 9, 16, 36, 144, \infty$ then become $12/\sqrt{\nu} = 4, 3, 2, 1, 0$.

Table 26 (continued). Non-central t. Factors, l, for determination of percentage points of t'

$\Pr\{t' \geqslant t'_0|\Delta\} = \alpha = 0\cdot025$. For $\nu = \infty$, all values of $l = 1\cdot95996$.

u \ ν	2	3	4	5	6	7	8	9	16	36	144
−1·00	1·8413	1·8745	1·8924	1·9038	1·9116	1·9174	1·9219	1·9255	1·9386	1·9490	1·9563
−0·95	1·8204	1·8553	1·8751	1·8880	1·8971	1·9040	1·9093	1·9135	1·9298	1·9433	1·9536
− ·90	1·8229	1·8509	1·8687	1·8809	1·8898	1·8967	1·9021	1·9066	1·9239	1·9392	1·9515
− ·85	1·8450	1·8587	1·8713	1·8810	1·8887	1·8947	1·8997	1·9038	1·9206	1·9364	1·9499
− ·80	1·8804	1·8757	1·8809	1·8869	1·8924	1·8971	1·9011	1·9045	1·9195	1·9348	1·9487
− ·75	1·9213	1·8985	1·8955	1·8971	1·8999	1·9028	1·9055	1·9080	1·9203	1·9342	1·9480
−0·70	1·9599	1·9237	1·9130	1·9101	1·9100	1·9109	1·9122	1·9137	1·9226	1·9346	1·9477
− ·65	1·9900	1·9484	1·9316	1·9246	1·9217	1·9206	1·9205	1·9209	1·9260	1·9357	1·9477
− ·60	2·0080	1·9704	1·9497	1·9394	1·9341	1·9313	1·9298	1·9290	1·9304	1·9375	1·9481
− ·55	2·0132	1·9879	1·9661	1·9537	1·9465	1·9421	1·9394	1·9377	1·9354	1·9397	1·9487
− ·50	2·0073	2·0003	1·9801	1·9668	1·9583	1·9527	1·9490	1·9464	1·9408	1·9424	1·9495
− ·45	1·9933	2·0074	1·9912	1·9781	1·9690	1·9627	1·9582	1·9550	1·9464	1·9453	1·9505
−0·4	1·9742	2·0098	1·9992	1·9874	1·9783	1·9716	1·9667	1·9630	1·9520	1·9485	1·9517
− ·3	1·9297	2·0030	2·0064	1·9996	1·9922	1·9860	1·9809	1·9769	1·9628	1·9551	1·9544
− ·2	1·8857	1·9861	2·0040	2·0038	1·9997	1·9951	1·9908	1·9871	1·9722	1·9615	1·9574
− ·1	1·8467	1·9643	1·9947	2·0016	2·0015	1·9992	1·9963	1·9934	1·9797	1·9675	1·9604
0·0	1·8136	1·9411	1·9814	1·9947	1·9986	1·9989	1·9978	1·9961	1·9851	1·9725	1·9633
0·1	1·7861	1·9183	1·9658	1·9845	1·9922	1·9951	1·9959	1·9956	1·9882	1·9765	1·9659
·2	1·7633	1·8970	1·9494	1·9724	1·9833	1·9886	1·9912	1·9923	1·9892	1·9792	1·9681
·3	1·7444	1·8775	1·9330	1·9592	1·9727	1·9801	1·9843	1·9867	1·9881	1·9806	1·9697
·4	1·7289	1·8600	1·9171	1·9456	1·9612	1·9703	1·9759	1·9795	1·9852	1·9806	1·9707
·5	1·7160	1·8444	1·9021	1·9320	1·9491	1·9596	1·9663	1·9709	1·9806	1·9792	1·9710
0·6	1·7055	1·8307	1·8882	1·9188	1·9368	1·9483	1·9560	1·9613	1·9746	1·9765	1·9704
·7	1·6971	1·8188	1·8753	1·9061	1·9247	1·9368	1·9451	1·9511	1·9674	1·9724	1·9690
·8	1·6906	1·8085	1·8637	1·8942	1·9129	1·9254	1·9341	1·9404	1·9591	1·9671	1·9667
·9	1·6855	1·7998	1·8533	1·8831	1·9017	1·9141	1·9230	1·9296	1·9499	1·9606	1·9634
1·0	1·6818	1·7925	1·8441	1·8729	1·8910	1·9032	1·9121	1·9187	1·9400	1·9529	1·9592

$\Pr\{t' \geqslant t'_0|\Delta\} = \alpha = 0\cdot01$. For $\nu = \infty$, all values of $l = 2\cdot32635^{-}$.

u \ ν	2	3	4	5	6	7	8	9	16	36	144
−1·00	2·2919	2·3139	2·3246	2·3307	2·3345	2·3370	2·3388	2·3401	2·3431	2·3424	2·3371
−0·95	2·2305	2·2635	2·2815	2·2928	2·3004	2·3059	2·3101	2·3133	2·3242	2·3307	2·3318
− ·90	2·2152	2·2417	2·2593	2·2713	2·2799	2·2864	2·2915	2·2956	2·3105	2·3216	2·3274
− ·85	2·2380	2·2432	2·2540	2·2632	2·2707	2·2766	2·2815	2·2855	2·3014	2·3149	2·3239
− ·80	2·2844	2·2617	2·2617	2·2658	2·2704	2·2746	2·2784	2·2817	2·2962	2·3102	2·3212
− ·75	2·3338	2·2899	2·2782	2·2759	2·2768	2·2786	2·2807	2·2828	2·2942	2·3073	2·3191
−0·70	2·3654	2·3200	2·2990	2·2908	2·2876	2·2868	2·2870	2·2877	2·2948	2·3060	2·3177
− ·65	2·3675	2·3454	2·3204	2·3075	2·3009	2·2975	2·2958	2·2951	2·2974	2·3059	2·3169
− ·60	2·3420	2·3617	2·3392	2·3240	2·3150	2·3095	2·3061	2·3040	2·3015	2·3069	2·3165
− ·55	2·2986	2·3673	2·3533	2·3385	2·3282	2·3214	2·3167	2·3135	2·3066	2·3087	2·3166
− ·50	2·2476	2·3629	2·3618	2·3499	2·3398	2·3323	2·3269	2·3229	2·3123	2·3111	2·3171
−0·45	2·1963	2·3504	2·3646	2·3576	2·3490	2·3417	2·3360	2·3316	2·3182	2·3140	2·3178
− ·40	2·1482	2·3322	2·3622	2·3616	2·3555	2·3492	2·3437	2·3393	2·3241	2·3172	2·3189
− ·35	2·1050	2·3104	2·3556	2·3620	2·3592	2·3544	2·3497	2·3456	2·3297	2·3206	2·3201
− ·30	2·0670	2·2869	2·3456	2·3593	2·3603	2·3576	2·3540	2·3504	2·3348	2·3240	2·3214

To determine an upper 100α per cent point, $t'(\alpha|\nu, \Delta)$:

(1) calculate $u = \dfrac{\Delta}{\sqrt{(2\nu)}}\left(1 + \dfrac{\Delta^2}{2\nu}\right)^{-\frac{1}{2}}$;

(2) interpolate for l in the appropriate α-table;

(3) determine $t'_0 = t'(\alpha|\nu, \Delta)$ from $t'_0 = \dfrac{\Delta + l(1 + (\Delta^2/2\nu) - (l^2/2\nu))^{\frac{1}{2}}}{1 - (l^2/2\nu)}$.

A lower per cent point is obtained by the same procedure, noting that $t'(1 - \alpha|\nu, \Delta) = -t'(\alpha|\nu, -\Delta)$.

Table 26 (*continued*)

$\Pr\{t' \geqslant t'_0|\Delta\} = \alpha = 0.01$ (continued). For $\nu = \infty$, all values of $l = 2.32635^-$.

u \ ν	2	3	4	5	6	7	8	9	16	36	144
−0·3	2·0670	2·2869	2·3456	2·3593	2·3603	2·3576	2·3540	2·3504	2·3348	2·3240	2·3214
− ·2	2·0050	2·2393	2·3191	2·3465	2·3556	2·3578	2·3572	2·3555	2·3430	2·3304	2·3244
− ·1	1·9581	2·1950	2·2886	2·3272	2·3439	2·3512	2·3541	2·3549	2·3481	2·3360	2·3274
0·0	1·9223	2·1558	2·2575	2·3044	2·3276	2·3396	2·3460	2·3494	2·3500	2·3401	2·3302
0·1	1·8945	2·1220	2·2277	2·2803	2·3086	2·3246	2·3342	2·3401	2·3487	2·3425	2·3326
·2	1·8727	2·0930	2·2000	2·2563	2·2883	2·3076	2·3199	2·3280	2·3446	2·3431	2·3343
·3	1·8553	2·0681	2·1748	2·2332	2·2677	2·2895	2·3039	2·3139	2·3379	2·3418	2·3351
·4	1·8413	2·0469	2·1520	2·2112	2·2474	2·2710	2·2870	2·2985	2·3291	2·3385	2·3350
·5	1·8299	2·0287	2·1315	2·1907	2·2277	2·2524	2·2697	2·2823	2·3185	2·3335	2·3338
0·6	1·8208	2·0130	2·1131	2·1716	2·2089	2·2342	2·2522	2·2656	2·3063	2·3267	2·3315
·7	1·8134	1·9996	2·0967	2·1540	2·1910	2·2165	2·2349	2·2488	2·2930	2·3181	2·3279
·8	1·8075	1·9882	2·0820	2·1378	2·1741	2·1994	2·2179	2·2320	2·2786	2·3080	2·3230
·9	1·8030	1·9784	2·0690	2·1229	2·1582	2·1830	2·2014	2·2154	2·2633	2·2964	2·3166
1·0	1·7995	1·9703	2·0576	2·1094	2·1434	2·1675	2·1853	2·1992	2·2474	2·2832	2·3089

$\Pr\{t' \geqslant t'_0|\Delta\} = \alpha = 0.005$. For $\nu = \infty$, all values of $l = 2.57583$.

u \ ν	2	3	4	5	6	7	8	9	16	36	144
−1·00	2·6036	2·6177	2·6232	2·6256	2·6265	2·6267	2·6265	2·6260	2·6217	2·6126	2·5977
−0·95	2·5060	2·5398	2·5576	2·5684	2·5755	2·5804	2·5839	2·5866	2·5942	2·5959	2·5903
− ·90	2·4781	2·5043	2·5226	2·5352	2·5441	2·5508	2·5560	2·5600	2·5742	2·5828	2·5841
− ·85	2·5063	2·5028	2·5121	2·5212	2·5288	2·5350	2·5401	2·5442	2·5604	2·5730	2·5791
− ·80	2·5641	2·5251	2·5199	2·5222	2·5261	2·5302	2·5339	2·5372	2·5520	2·5659	2·5751
− ·75	2·6095	2·5588	2·5394	2·5336	2·5326	2·5335	2·5352	2·5370	2·5481	2·5612	2·5720
−0·70	2·6068	2·5904	2·5634	2·5506	2·5449	2·5425	2·5417	2·5418	2·5476	2·5586	2·5698
− ·65	2·5535	2·6094	2·5857	2·5693	2·5599	2·5545	2·5515	2·5498	2·5498	2·5577	2·5683
− ·60	2·4725	2·6110	2·6018	2·5861	2·5749	2·5675	2·5627	2·5595	2·5539	2·5581	2·5674
− ·55	2·3863	2·5963	2·6094	2·5987	2·5880	2·5799	2·5740	2·5697	2·5593	2·5597	2·5671
− ·50	2·3071	2·5695	2·6083	2·6060	2·5979	2·5903	2·5841	2·5794	2·5653	2·5621	2·5673
−0·45	2·2389	2·5354	2·5994	2·6078	2·6040	2·5980	2·5925	2·5877	2·5715	2·5650	2·5679
− ·40	2·1818	2·4981	2·5845	2·6044	2·6061	2·6028	2·5985	2·5944	2·5775	2·5683	2·5688
− ·35	2·1344	2·4604	2·5655	2·5967	2·6045	2·6046	2·6021	2·5990	2·5830	2·5717	2·5700
− ·30	2·0951	2·4240	2·5438	2·5855	2·5996	2·6034	2·6033	2·6015	2·5877	2·5752	2·5713
− ·25	2·0624	2·3900	2·5208	2·5718	2·5921	2·5998	2·6021	2·6021	2·5915	2·5785	2·5728
−0·20	2·0350	2·3586	2·4975	2·5564	2·5823	2·5939	2·5989	2·6007	2·5943	2·5816	2·5743
− ·15	2·0118	2·3299	2·4744	2·5399	2·5709	2·5863	2·5939	2·5976	2·5961	2·5843	2·5758
− ·10	1·9921	2·3039	2·4519	2·5228	2·5584	2·5771	2·5873	2·5929	2·5968	2·5866	2·5773
− ·05	1·9752	2·2803	2·4304	2·5055	2·5450	2·5669	2·5795	2·5870	2·5965	2·5884	2·5787
0·00	1·9606	2·2589	2·4100	2·4883	2·5311	2·5558	2·5707	2·5799	2·5953	2·5897	2·5801
0·1	1·9368	2·2220	2·3725	2·4550	2·5028	2·5321	2·5508	2·5633	2·5899	2·5907	2·5822
·2	1·9184	2·1915	2·3395	2·4238	2·4749	2·5074	2·5292	2·5442	2·5814	2·5894	2·5834
·3	1·9040	2·1662	2·3105	2·3951	2·4479	2·4827	2·5067	2·5238	2·5702	2·5858	2·5836
·4	1·8925	2·1450	2·2851	2·3689	2·4224	2·4586	2·4841	2·5027	2·5568	2·5799	2·5826
·5	1·8832	2·1271	2·2628	2·3451	2·3985	2·4353	2·4617	2·4814	2·5416	2·5719	2·5803
0·6	1·8758	2·1118	2·2431	2·3234	2·3762	2·4131	2·4399	2·4602	2·5251	2·5620	2·5765
·7	1·8698	2·0989	2·2258	2·3037	2·3554	2·3919	2·4188	2·4394	2·5074	2·5501	2·5712
·8	1·8650	2·0879	2·2104	2·2858	2·3361	2·3719	2·3985	2·4190	2·4889	2·5365	2·5642
·9	1·8613	2·0786	2·1969	2·2695	2·3182	2·3529	2·3789	2·3991	2·4697	2·5211	2·5557
1·0	1·8584	2·0707	2·1850	2·2548	2·3016	2·3351	2·3602	2·3799	2·4499	2·5042	2·5453

For $\nu > 9$, interpolate using argument $12/\sqrt{\nu}$. The arguments 9, 16, 36, 144, ∞ then become 4, 3, 2, 1, 0.

Table 27. *Non-central t. Factors, l, for determination of confidence limits for the non-central parameter,* Δ

$\Pr\{t' \geqslant t'_0 | \Delta\} = \alpha = 0\cdot05$. For $\nu = \infty$, all values of $l = 1\cdot64485^{+}$.

y \\ ν	2	3	4	5	6	7	8	9	16	36	144
$-1\cdot0$	1·4616	1·5039	1·5277	1·5431	1·5542	1·5625	1·5691	1·5744	1·5952	1·6141	1·6307
$-0\cdot9$	1·4625	1·5030	1·5260	1·5411	1·5519	1·5601	1·5666	1·5719	1·5927	1·6120	1·6294
$-\cdot8$	1·4691	1·5070	1·5287	1·5430	1·5533	1·5611	1·5673	1·5724	1·5926	1·6115	1·6290
$-\cdot7$	1·4815	1·5157	1·5354	1·5486	1·5580	1·5653	1·5711	1·5758	1·5946	1·6125	1·6293
$-\cdot6$	1·4990	1·5285	1·5458	1·5574	1·5658	1·5722	1·5774	1·5816	1·5986	1·6148	1·6303
$-0\cdot5$	1·5204	1·5447	1·5591	1·5689	1·5760	1·5815	1·5859	1·5895	1·6041	1·6183	1·6319
$-\cdot4$	1·5445	1·5633	1·5746	1·5824	1·5881	1·5925	1·5961	1·5990	1·6109	1·6226	1·6339
$-\cdot3$	1·5700	1·5834	1·5917	1·5974	1·6016	1·6049	1·6075	1·6097	1·6187	1·6276	1·6363
$-\cdot2$	1·5958	1·6042	1·6095	1·6132	1·6159	1·6181	1·6198	1·6212	1·6272	1·6331	1·6390
$-\cdot1$	1·6211	1·6249	1·6274	1·6292	1·6305	1·6315	1·6324	1·6331	1·6360	1·6390	1·6419
$0\cdot0$	1·6449	1·6449	1·6449	1·6449	1·6449	1·6449	1·6449	1·6449	1·6449	1·6449	1·6449
$\cdot1$	1·6663	1·6632	1·6612	1·6596	1·6585	1·6575	1·6568	1·6561	1·6534	1·6506	1·6478
$\cdot2$	1·6845	1·6794	1·6757	1·6730	1·6709	1·6691	1·6677	1·6665	1·6614	1·6561	1·6505
$\cdot3$	1·6986	1·6925	1·6878	1·6843	1·6815	1·6792	1·6773	1·6756	1·6686	1·6610	1·6531
$\cdot4$	1·7075	1·7018	1·6969	1·6930	1·6898	1·6871	1·6849	1·6830	1·6745	1·6652	1·6553
$0\cdot5$	1·7100	1·7063	1·7021	1·6983	1·6952	1·6925	1·6901	1·6881	1·6789	1·6685	1·6571
$\cdot6$	1·7045	1·7049	1·7025	1·6997	1·6970	1·6946	1·6925	1·6906	1·6815	1·6707	1·6584
$\cdot7$	1·6889	1·6961	1·6971	1·6962	1·6947	1·6930	1·6914	1·6899	1·6819	1·6714	1·6590
$\cdot75$	1·6763	1·6885	1·6918	1·6923	1·6916	1·6906	1·6894	1·6881	1·6811	1·6712	1·6590
$0\cdot80$	1·6599	1·6783	1·6847	1·6868	1·6872	1·6869	1·6862	1·6854	1·6797	1·6706	1·6589
$\cdot85$	1·6389	1·6652	1·6754	1·6797	1·6814	1·6820	1·6820	1·6816	1·6775	1·6696	1·6585
$\cdot90$	1·6124	1·6490	1·6639	1·6708	1·6741	1·6758	1·6765	1·6768	1·6746	1·6680	1·6579
$\cdot95$	1·5797	1·6300	1·6505	1·6603	1·6654	1·6683	1·6699	1·6708	1·6709	1·6660	1·6571
$1\cdot00$	1·5470	1·6106	1·6362	1·6487	1·6556	1·6597	1·6622	1·6638	1·6664	1·6635	1·6560

$\Pr\{t' \geqslant t'_0 | \Delta\} = \alpha = 0\cdot025$. For $\nu = \infty$, all values of $l = 1\cdot95996$.

y \\ ν	2	3	4	5	6	7	8	9	16	36	144
$-1\cdot0$	1·8413	1·8745	1·8924	1·9038	1·9116	1·9174	1·9219	1·9255	1·9386	1·9490	1·9563
$-0\cdot9$	1·8267	1·8601	1·8786	1·8905	1·8988	1·9051	1·9100	1·9139	1·9288	1·9417	1·9522
$-\cdot8$	1·8195	1·8523	1·8707	1·8826	1·8911	1·8976	1·9026	1·9067	1·9227	1·9370	1·9495
$-\cdot7$	1·8201	1·8510	1·8686	1·8801	1·8884	1·8947	1·8997	1·9038	1·9198	1·9346	1·9481
$-\cdot6$	1·8281	1·8559	1·8720	1·8827	1·8904	1·8963	1·9009	1·9048	1·9200	1·9343	1·9477
$-0\cdot5$	1·8427	1·8664	1·8803	1·8896	1·8964	1·9016	1·9057	1·9091	1·9228	1·9359	1·9483
$-\cdot4$	1·8625	1·8813	1·8925	1·9001	1·9057	1·9100	1·9135	1·9163	1·9278	1·9390	1·9497
$-\cdot3$	1·8858	1·8994	1·9077	1·9134	1·9176	1·9209	1·9235	1·9257	1·9345	1·9432	1·9517
$-\cdot2$	1·9108	1·9194	1·9247	1·9284	1·9312	1·9333	1·9351	1·9365	1·9425	1·9484	1·9542
$-\cdot1$	1·9361	1·9400	1·9425	1·9443	1·9456	1·9466	1·9475	1·9482	1·9511	1·9541	1·9570
$0\cdot0$	1·9600	1·9600	1·9600	1·9600	1·9600	1·9600	1·9600	1·9600	1·9600	1·9600	1·9600
$0\cdot1$	1·9811	1·9781	1·9761	1·9746	1·9735	1·9725	1·9718	1·9712	1·9685	1·9657	1·9629
$\cdot2$	1·9980	1·9933	1·9898	1·9873	1·9852	1·9836	1·9822	1·9811	1·9762	1·9710	1·9656
$\cdot3$	2·0093	2·0042	2·0001	1·9970	1·9944	1·9923	1·9906	1·9891	1·9825	1·9754	1·9679
$\cdot4$	2·0132	2·0095	2·0059	2·0027	2·0001	1·9979	1·9960	1·9944	1·9870	1·9787	1·9697
$\cdot5$	2·0079	2·0077	2·0057	2·0035	2·0014	1·9995	1·9978	1·9963	1·9891	1·9805	1·9707
$0\cdot55$	2·0011	2·0037	2·0030	2·0016	2·0000	1·9984	1·9970	1·9957	1·9890	1·9807	1·9710
$\cdot60$	1·9910	1·9970	1·9983	1·9979	1·9970	1·9960	1·9949	1·9939	1·9882	1·9804	1·9709
$\cdot65$	1·9771	1·9876	1·9912	1·9923	1·9924	1·9920	1·9914	1·9907	1·9864	1·9796	1·9706
$\cdot70$	1·9589	1·9749	1·9815	1·9844	1·9857	1·9862	1·9863	1·9862	1·9836	1·9781	1·9701
$\cdot75$	1·9355	1·9585	1·9688	1·9741	1·9769	1·9785	1·9795	1·9800	1·9797	1·9759	1·9692
$0\cdot80$	1·9059	1·9376	1·9527	1·9609	1·9657	1·9687	1·9707	1·9720	1·9746	1·9730	1·9679
$\cdot85$	1·8686	1·9116	1·9327	1·9445	1·9518	1·9565	1·9597	1·9621	1·9682	1·9693	1·9664
$\cdot90$	1·8211	1·8791	1·9081	1·9246	1·9348	1·9416	1·9464	1·9500	1·9603	1·9648	1·9644
$\cdot95$	1·7593	1·8390	1·8784	1·9006	1·9145	1·9239	1·9306	1·9355	1·9510	1·9593	1·9620
$1\cdot00$	1·6818	1·7925	1·8441	1·8729	1·8910	1·9032	1·9121	1·9187	1·9400	1·9529	1·9592

To determine a lower confidence limit, $\underline{\Delta}(\alpha|\nu, t'_0)$

(1) calculate $y = \dfrac{t'_0}{\surd(2\nu)}\left(1 + \dfrac{t'^2_0}{2\nu}\right)^{-\frac{1}{2}}$;　(2) interpolate for l in the appropriate α-table;

(3) determine $\underline{\Delta} = \underline{\Delta}(\alpha|\nu, t'_0)$ from $\underline{\Delta} = t'_0 - l\left(1 + \dfrac{t'^2_0}{2\nu}\right)^{\frac{1}{2}}$.

The upper confidence limit, $\bar{\Delta}$, is obtained by the same procedure, noting that $(\bar{\Delta}(1-\alpha|\nu, t'_0) = -\underline{\Delta}(\alpha|\nu, -t'_0))$.

Table 27 (*continued*)

$\Pr\{t' \geqslant t|\Delta\} = \alpha = 0.01$. For $\nu = \infty$, all values of $l = 2.32635^-$.

y \ ν	2	3	4	5	6	7	8	9	16	36	144
−1·0	2·2919	2·3139	2·3246	2·3307	2·3345	2·3370	2·3388	2·3401	2·3431	2·3424	2·3371
−0·9	2·2583	2·2826	2·2953	2·3030	2·3081	2·3118	2·3146	2·3167	2·3239	2·3282	2·3292
− ·8	2·2339	2·2597	2·2737	2·2825	2·2886	2·2931	2·2966	2·2994	2·3096	2·3177	2·3234
− ·7	2·2193	2·2455	2·2600	2·2694	2·2760	2·2810	2·2849	2·2881	2·3001	2·3107	2·3195
− ·6	2·2148	2·2399	2·2541	2·2635	2·2701	2·2752	2·2792	2·2824	2·2952	2·3068	2·3173
−0·5	2·2201	2·2426	2·2555	2·2641	2·2703	2·2751	2·2789	2·2819	2·2942	2·3058	2·3165
− ·4	2·2337	2·2522	2·2631	2·2704	2·2758	2·2799	2·2832	2·2859	2·2967	2·3071	2·3170
− ·3	2·2536	2·2673	2·2756	2·2812	2·2854	2·2886	2·2912	2·2933	2·3019	2·3103	2·3185
− ·2	2·2773	2·2860	2·2914	2·2951	2·2979	2·3000	2·3018	2·3032	2·3091	2·3150	2·3207
− ·1	2·3023	2·3063	2·3088	2·3106	2·3120	2·3130	2·3139	2·3146	2·3175	2·3205	2·3234
0·0	2·3263	2·3263	2·3263	2·3263	2·3263	2·3263	2·3263	2·3263	2·3263	2·3263	2·3263
0·1	2·3471	2·3442	2·3423	2·3408	2·3397	2·3388	2·3380	2·3374	2·3348	2·3320	2·3292
·2	2·3623	2·3581	2·3550	2·3526	2·3507	2·3491	2·3479	2·3468	2·3421	2·3371	2·3318
·3	2·3699	2·3661	2·3629	2·3602	2·3580	2·3562	2·3546	2·3533	2·3474	2·3409	2·3338
·4	2·3675	2·3663	2·3642	2·3621	2·3602	2·3586	2·3572	2·3559	2·3499	2·3429	2·3350
·5	2·3522	2·3564	2·3571	2·3567	2·3559	2·3550	2·3542	2·3533	2·3488	2·3427	2·3351
0·55	2·3387	2·3468	2·3496	2·3506	2·3507	2·3505	2·3502	2·3497	2·3466	2·3415	2·3347
·60	2·3206	2·3335	2·3391	2·3418	2·3432	2·3439	2·3442	2·3442	2·3431	2·3395	2·3338
·65	2·2972	2·3161	2·3251	2·3301	2·3330	2·3348	2·3360	2·3368	2·3381	2·3366	2·3326
·70	2·2675	2·2938	2·3071	2·3149	2·3197	2·3230	2·3253	2·3270	2·3316	2·3328	2·3309
·75	2·2302	2·2657	2·2845	2·2957	2·3030	2·3081	2·3118	2·3146	2·3233	2·3279	2·3287
0·80	2·1838	2·2308	2·2563	2·2719	2·2823	2·2897	2·2951	2·2993	2·3131	2·3218	2·3260
·85	2·1256	2·1872	2·2215	2·2427	2·2570	2·2672	2·2747	2·2806	2·3006	2·3144	2·3227
·90	2·0508	2·1324	2·1783	2·2069	2·2261	2·2398	2·2501	2·2581	2·2857	2·3056	2·3188
·95	1·9503	2·0620	2·1244	2·1629	2·1886	2·2069	2·2206	2·2311	2·2681	2·2953	2·3142
1·00	1·7995	1·9703	2·0576	2·1094	1·1434	2·1675	2·1853	2·1992	2·2474	2·2832	2·3089

$\Pr\{t' \geqslant t'_0|\Delta\} = \alpha = 0.005$. For $\nu = \infty$, all values of $l = 2.57583$.

y \ ν	2	3	4	5	6	7	8	9	16	36	144
−1·0	2·6036	2·6177	2·6232	2·6256	2·6265	2·6267	2·6265	2·6260	2·6217	2·6126	2·5977
−0·9	2·5565	2·5743	2·5827	2·5874	2·5902	2·5920	2·5931	2·5939	2·5953	2·5931	2·5869
− ·8	2·5197	2·5404	2·5511	2·5576	2·5620	2·5650	2·5673	2·5691	2·5749	2·5783	2·5787
− ·7	2·4942	2·5167	2·5289	2·5366	2·5420	2·5459	2·5490	2·5514	2·5604	2·5677	2·5729
− ·6	2·4806	2·5033	2·5160	2·5243	2·5301	2·5345	2·5380	2·5408	2·5515	2·5611	2·5692
−0·5	2·4787	2·4999	2·5121	2·5201	2·5259	2·5302	2·5337	2·5365	2·5477	2·5580	2·5674
− ·4	2·4874	2·5055	2·5160	2·5231	2·5282	2·5322	2·5353	2·5379	2·5482	2·5580	2·5672
− ·3	2·5044	2·5181	2·5263	2·5319	2·5360	2·5392	2·5417	2·5438	2·5522	2·5604	2·5683
− ·2	2·5269	2·5357	2·5411	2·5448	2·5476	2·5498	2·5515	2·5529	2·5588	2·5646	2·5703
− ·1	2·5517	2·5558	2·5583	2·5601	2·5615	2·5625	2·5634	2·5641	2·5670	2·5700	2·5729
0·0	2·5758	2·5758	2·5758	2·5758	2·5758	2·5758	2·5758	2·5758	2·5758	2·5758	2·5758
0·1	2·5963	2·5935	2·5916	2·5901	2·5890	2·5882	2·5874	2·5868	2·5842	2·5815	2·5787
·2	2·6103	2·6065	2·6035	2·6013	2·5995	2·5980	2·5968	2·5957	2·5912	2·5863	2·5812
·3	2·6153	2·6124	2·6096	2·6073	2·6054	2·6037	2·6023	2·6011	2·5957	2·5896	2·5830
·4	2·6081	2·6087	2·6077	2·6063	2·6050	2·6038	2·6026	2·6016	2·5967	2·5907	2·5837
·5	2·5856	2·5927	2·5953	2·5962	2·5964	2·5963	2·5960	2·5957	2·5931	2·5889	2·5830
0·55	2·5672	2·5790	2·5843	2·5869	2·5884	2·5891	2·5896	2·5898	2·5892	2·5866	2·5821
·60	2·5432	2·5608	2·5694	2·5743	2·5773	2·5792	2·5806	2·5815	2·5837	2·5833	2·5806
·65	2·5128	2·5374	2·5502	2·5579	2·5629	2·5663	2·5688	2·5706	2·5763	2·5789	2·5786
·70	2·4747	2·5079	2·5260	2·5371	2·5446	2·5499	2·5538	2·5568	2·5669	2·5732	2·5761
·75	2·4274	2·4712	2·4957	2·5112	2·5217	2·5294	2·5351	2·5396	2·5551	2·5661	2·5729
0·80	2·3688	2·4257	2·4583	2·4793	2·4937	2·5042	2·5122	2·5185	2·5408	2·5575	2·5690
·85	2·2953	2·3690	2·4121	2·4400	2·4594	2·4736	2·4844	2·4929	2·5236	2·5472	2·5644
·90	2·2007	2·2973	2·3544	2·3916	2·4174	2·4362	2·4507	2·4620	2·5031	2·5351	2·5589
·95	2·0717	2·2031	2·2810	2·3311	2·3656	2·3907	2·4098	2·4248	2·4787	2·5208	2·5526
1·00	1·8584	2·0707	2·1850	2·2548	2·3016	2·3351	2·3602	2·3799	2·4499	2·5042	2·5453

For $\nu > 9$, interpolate using argument $12/\sqrt{\nu}$. The arguments $\nu = 9, 16, 36, 144, \infty$ then become $12/\sqrt{\nu} = 4, 3, 2, 1, 0$.

Table 28. *Coefficients to assist the determination of the moments of non-central t*

f	c_{11}	c_{22}	c_{20}	c_{33}	c_{31}	c_{44}	c_{42}	c_{40}
2	1·77245	—	—	—	—	—	—	—
3	1·38198	1·090141	3·00000	—	—	—	—	—
4	1·25331	0·429204	2·00000	1·430774	7·51988	—	—	—
5	1·18942	·251956	1·66667	0·391819	2·97354	2·32912	21·7058	25·0000
6	1·15124	·174641	1·50000	·173514	1·72686	0·555627	7·11961	13·5000
7	1·12587	·132419	1·40000	·0958806	1·18216	·220997	3·62848	9·80000
8	1·10778	·106149	1·33333	·0602294	0·886227	·112216	2·25553	8·00000
9	1·09424	·0883494	1·28571	·0411291	·703441	·0658634	1·56996	6·94286
10	1·08372	·0755460	1·25000	·0297802	·580566	·0425458	1·17491	6·25000
11	1·07532	·0659193	1·22222	·0225163	·492853	·0294140	0·924366	5·76190
12	1·06844	·0584307	1·20000	·0175994	·427377	·0213878	·754190	5·40000
13	1·06272	·0524464	1·18182	·0141225	·376782	·0161682	·632497	5·12121
14	1·05788	·0475588	1·16667	·0115764	·336598	·0126046	·541926	4·90000
15	1·05373	·0434943	1·15385	·00965776	·303961	·0100748	·472333	4·72028
16	1·05014	·0400628	1·14286	·00817696	·276960	·00822029	·417451	4·57413
17	1·04700	·0371282	1·13333	·00701076	·254271	·00682400	·373228	4·44615
18	1·04423	·0345905	1·12500	·00607629	·234951	·00574860	·336939	4·33929
19	1·04176	·0323749	1·11765	·00531620	·218311	·00490411	·306697	4·24706
20	1·03956	·0304241	1·11111	·00468978	·203835	·00422971	·281155	4·16667
21	1·03758	·0286935	1·10526	·00416752	·191133	·00368316	·259332	4·09598
22	1·03579	·0271480	1·10000	·00372761	·179900	·00323446	·240493	4·03333
23	1·03416	·0257595	1·09524	·00335365	·169897	·00286183	·224085	3·97744
24	1·03267	·0245054	1·09091	·00303312	·160935	·00254919	·209678	3·92727
25	1·03130	·0233672	1·08696	·00275632	·152861	·00228444	·196937	3·88199
30	1·02590	·0189588	1·07143	·00181055	·122131	·00141976	·150530	3·70879
35	1·02209	·0159462	1·06061	·00127910	·101628	·0³964543	·121426	3·59238
40	1·01925	·0137581	1·05263	·0³951236	·0869916	·0³696724	·101573	3·50877
45	1·01706	·0120972	1·04651	·0³734909	·0760262	·0³526289	·0872081	3·44583
50	1·01532	·0107936	1·04167	·0³584744	·0675079	·0³411303	·0763532	3·39674
60	1·01272	·00887919	1·03448	·0³395412	·0551391	·0³270773	·0610691	3·32512
70	1·01088	·00754117	1·02941	·0³285075	·0465944	·0³191529	·0508439	3·27540
75	1·01014	·00701270	1·02740	·0³246471	·0432423	·0³164338	·0469076	3·25584
80	1·00950	·00655342	1·02564	·0³215207	·0403396	·0³142542	·0435333	3·23887
90	1·00843	·00579435	1·02273	·0³168194	·0355638	·0³110177	·0380512	3·21089
100	1·00758	·00519282	1·02041	·0³135056	·0317982	·0⁴876917	·0337901	3·18878
150	1·00503	·00341823	1·01351	·0⁴584851	·0207881	·0⁴369838	·0216437	3·12384
200	1·00377	·00254753	1·01010	·0⁴324755	·0154402	·0⁴202676	·0159134	3·09215
300	1·00251	·00168769	1·00671	·0⁴142490	·0101943	·0⁵877648	·0104011	3·06095
400	1·00188	·00126180	1·00503	·0⁵796378	·00760893	·0⁵487310	·00772428	3·04553
500	1·00150	·00100754	1·00402	·0⁵507727	·00606957	·0⁵309461	·00614302	3·03634
600	1·00125	·0³838566	1·00334	·0⁵351686	·00504825	·0⁵213793	·00509909	3·03024
700	1·00107	·0³718127	1·00287	·0⁵257910	·00432113	·0⁵156492	·00435839	3·02589
800	1·00094	·0³627940	1·00251	·0⁵197192	·00377709	·0⁵119482	·00380557	3·02263
900	1·00083	·0³557878	1·00223	·0⁵155640	·00335473	·0⁶942025	·00337720	3·02010
1000	1·00075	·0³501880	1·00200	·0⁵125961	·00301732	·0⁶761727	·00303550	3·01808

Note: $0^6761727$ should be read $0·000000761727$, etc.

Table 29. *Percentage points of non-central χ. Extension of Table 24 for $\sqrt{\lambda} = 8, 10$*

ν	$\sqrt{\lambda}$	Lower % points of χ'				Upper % points of χ'			
		0·5	1·0	2·5	5·0	5·0	2·5	1·0	0·5
1	6	3·42	3·67	4·04	4·36	7·64	7·96	8·33	8·58
	8	5·42	5·67	6·04	6·36	9·65⁻	9·96	10·33	10·58
	10	7·42	7·67	8·04	8·36	11·65⁻	11·96	12·33	12·58
2	6	3·53	3·78	4·14	4·45⁺	7·72	8·03	8·40	8·65⁻
	8	5·50⁻	5·75⁻	6·11	6·43	9·70	10·02	10·38	10·63
	10	7·48	7·73	8·10	8·41	11·69	12·01	12·37	12·62
3	6	3·64	3·88	4·24	4·55⁻	7·79	8·10	8·47	8·71
	8	5·57	5·82	6·18	6·49	9·76	10·07	10·44	10·68
	10	7·54	7·79	8·15⁺	8·46	11·74	12·05⁺	12·42	12·66
4	6	3·74	3·98	4·33	4·64	7·86	8·17	8·54	8·78
	8	5·65⁻	5·89	6·25⁺	6·56	9·81	10·13	10·49	10·74
	10	7·60	7·84	8·21	8·52	11·78	12·10	12·46	12·71
5	6	3·84	4·08	4·43	4·73	7·93	8·24	8·60	8·85⁻
	8	5·72	5·96	6·32	6·63	9·87	10·18	10·54	10·79
	10	7·65⁺	7·90	8·26	8·57	11·83	12·14	12·51	12·75⁺
6	6	3·94	4·17	4·52	4·82	8·01	8·31	8·67	8·92
	8	5·79	6·03	6·39	6·70	9·93	10·24	10·60	10·84
	10	7·71	7·95⁺	8·31	8·63	11·87	12·19	12·55⁻	12·80
7	6	4·04	4·27	4·61	4·91	8·08	8·38	8·74	8·98
	8	5·86	6·10	6·46	6·76	9·98	10·29	10·65⁺	10·90
	10	7·76	8·01	8·37	8·68	11·92	12·23	12·59	12·84
8	6	4·13	4·36	4·70	5·00⁻	8·14	8·45⁺	8·81	9·05⁻
	8	5·93	6·17	6·53	6·83	10·04	10·34	10·70	10·95⁻
	10	7·82	8·06	8·42	8·73	11·96	12·28	12·64	12·88
9	6	4·22	4·45⁺	4·79	5·08	8·21	8·52	8·87	9·11
	8	6·00	6·24	6·59	6·90	10·09	10·40	10·76	11·00
	10	7·87	8·12	8·48	8·78	12·01	12·32	12·68	12·93
10	6	4·31	4·54	4·88	5·17	8·28	8·58	8·94	9·18
	8	6·07	6·31	6·66	6·96	10·14	10·45⁺	10·81	11·05⁺
	10	7·93	8·17	8·53	8·83	12·05⁺	12·36	12·72	12·97
11	6	4·40	4·63	4·96	5·25⁻	8·35⁻	8·65⁺	9·00	9·24
	8	6·14	6·37	6·72	7·02	10·20	10·50⁺	10·86	11·10
	10	7·98	8·22	8·58	8·89	12·10	12·41	12·77	13·01
12	6	4·49	4·71	5·04	5·33	8·42	8·72	9·07	9·31
	8	6·20	6·44	6·79	7·09	10·25⁺	10·56	10·91	11·16
	10	8·04	8·28	8·63	8·94	12·14	12·45⁺	12·81	13·06
15	6	4·74	4·96	5·29	5·57	8·61	8·91	9·26	9·50⁻
	8	6·40	6·64	6·98	7·28	10·41	10·71	11·07	11·31
	10	8·20	8·44	8·79	9·09	12·28	12·58	12·94	13·18
20	6	5·14	5·35⁺	5·67	5·95⁻	8·93	9·23	9·57	9·80
	8	6·72	6·95⁻	7·29	7·58	10·67	10·97	11·32	11·56
	10	8·46	8·69	9·04	9·34	12·49	12·80	13·15⁺	13·39

Table 30. *Charts for determining the power of the t and F tests: fixed effects model*

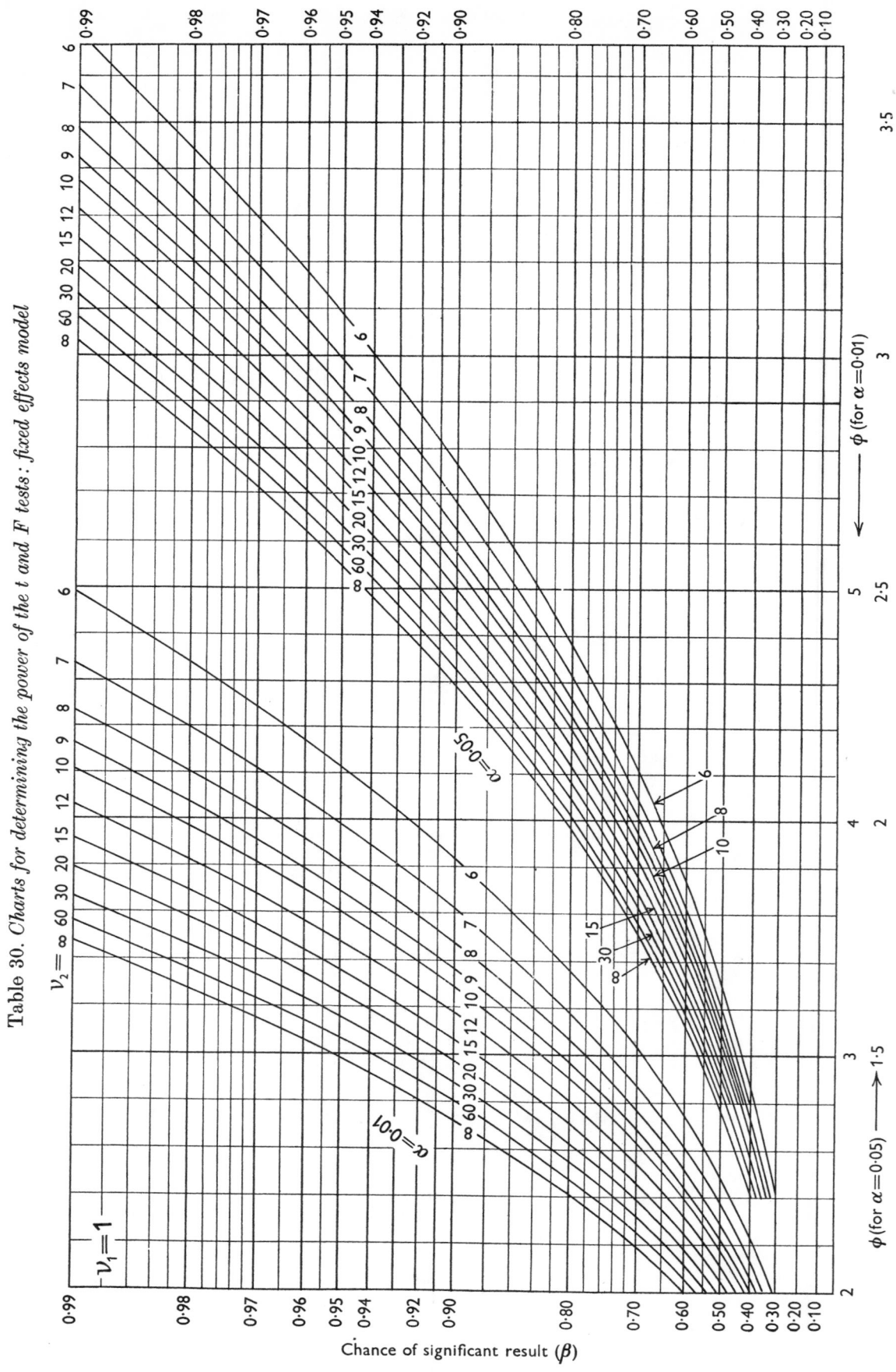

Chance of significant result (β)

250

Table 30 (continued)

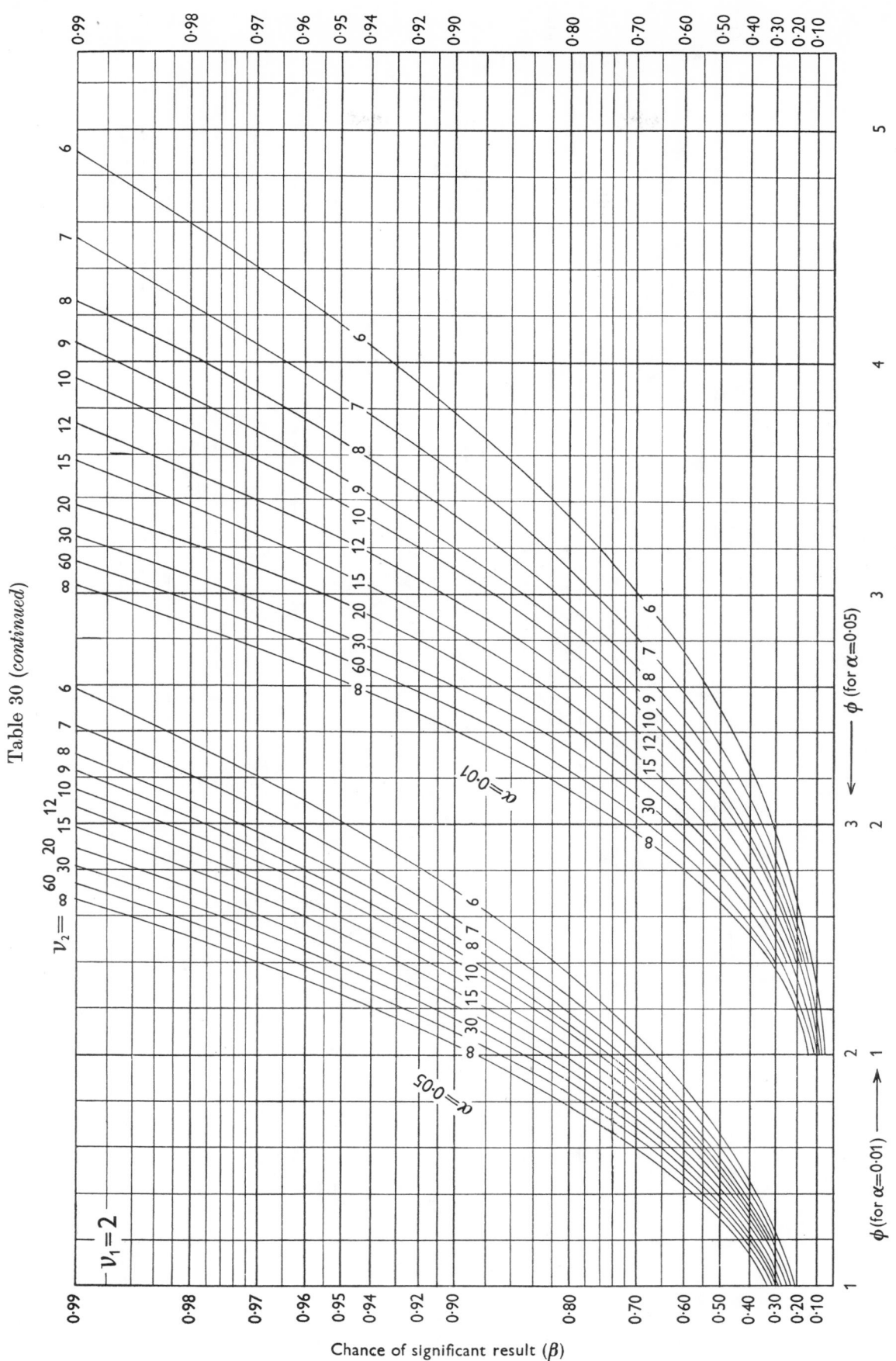

Chance of significant result (β)

251

Table 30 (continued). Charts for determining the power of the t and F tests: fixed effects model

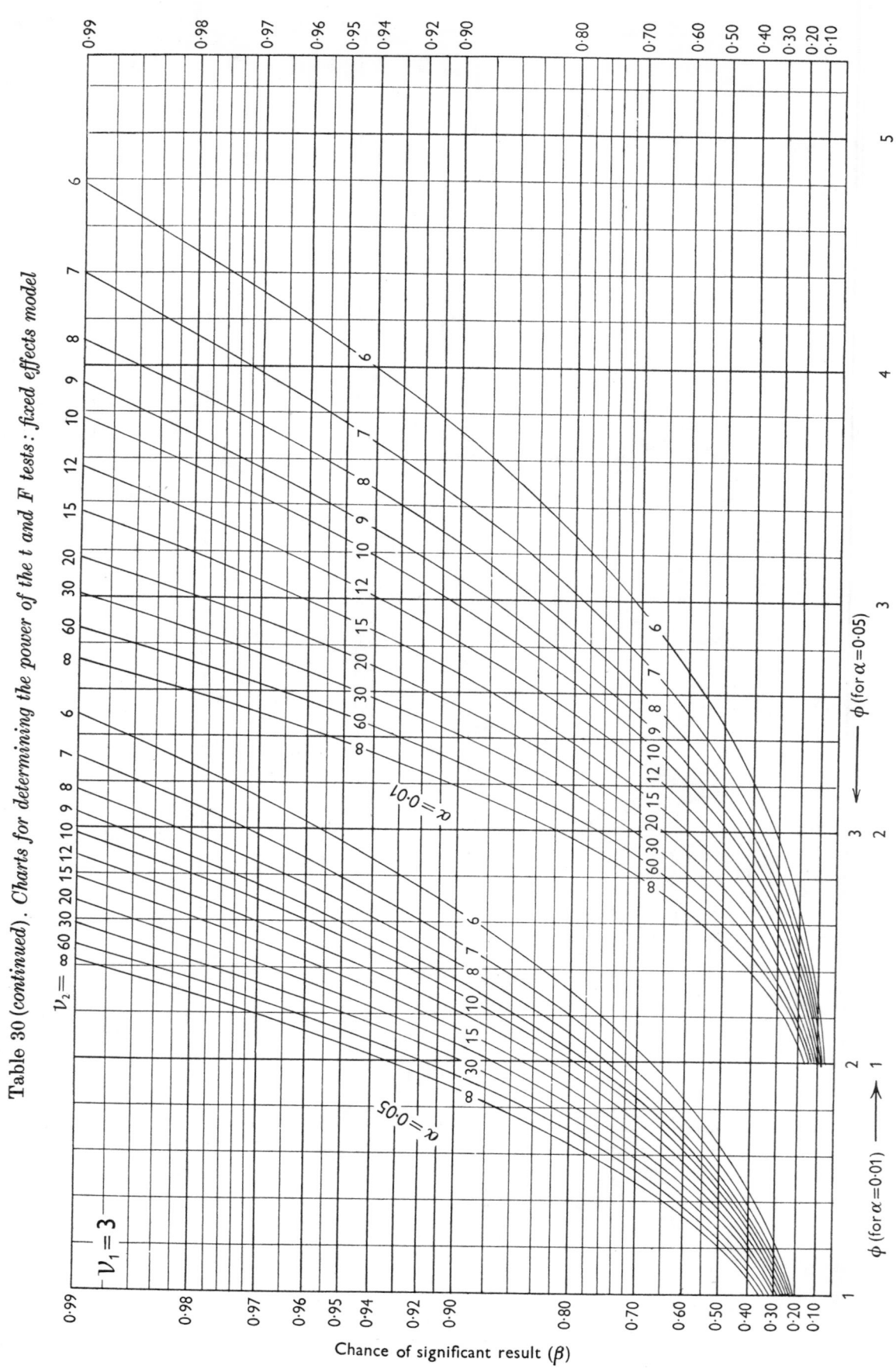

$\nu_1 = 3$

Chance of significant result (β)

Table 30 (*continued*)

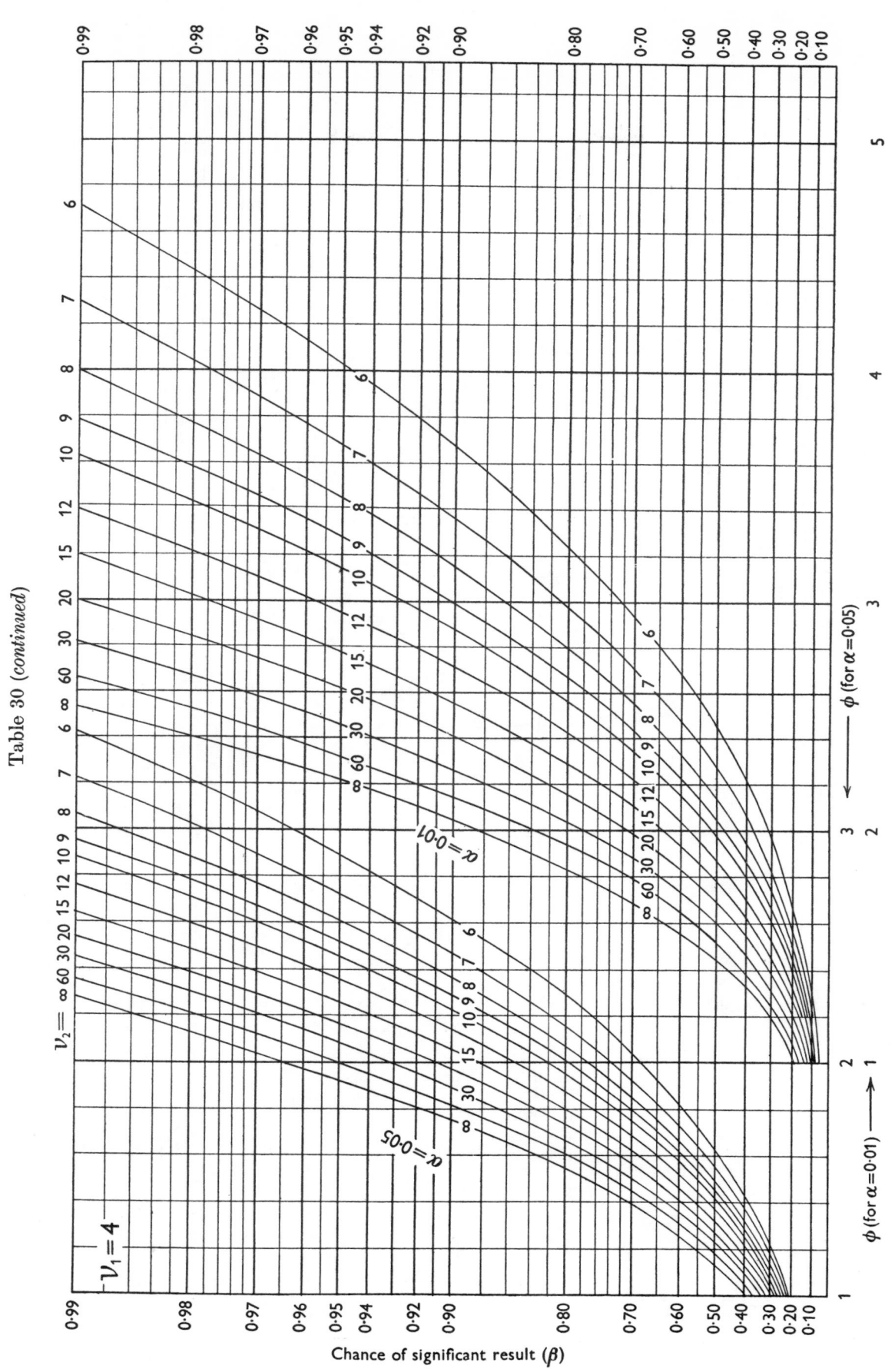

Table 30 (continued). Charts for determining the power of the t and F tests; fixed effects model

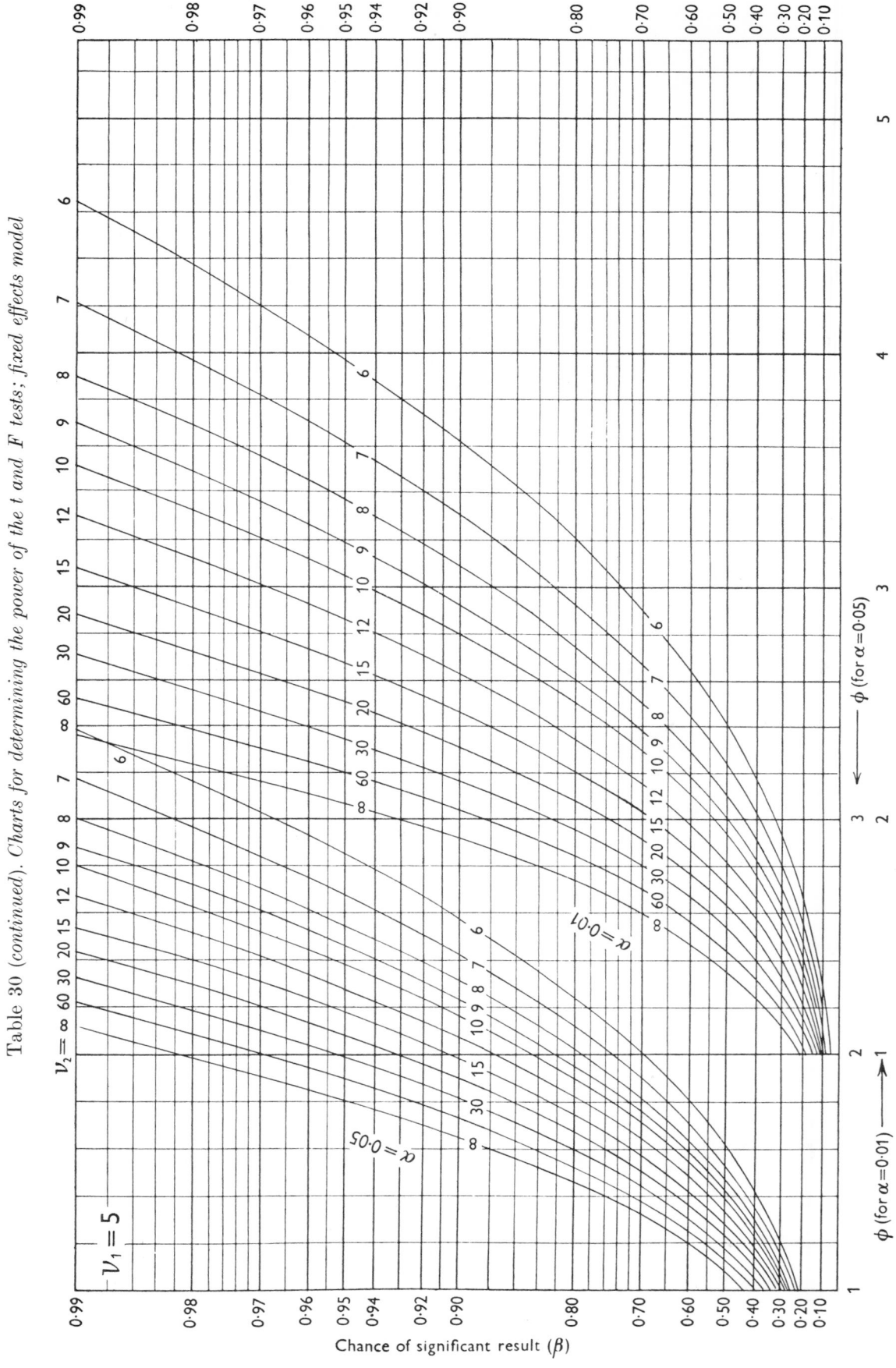

$\nu_1 = 5$

Chance of significant result (β)

Table 30 (*continued*)

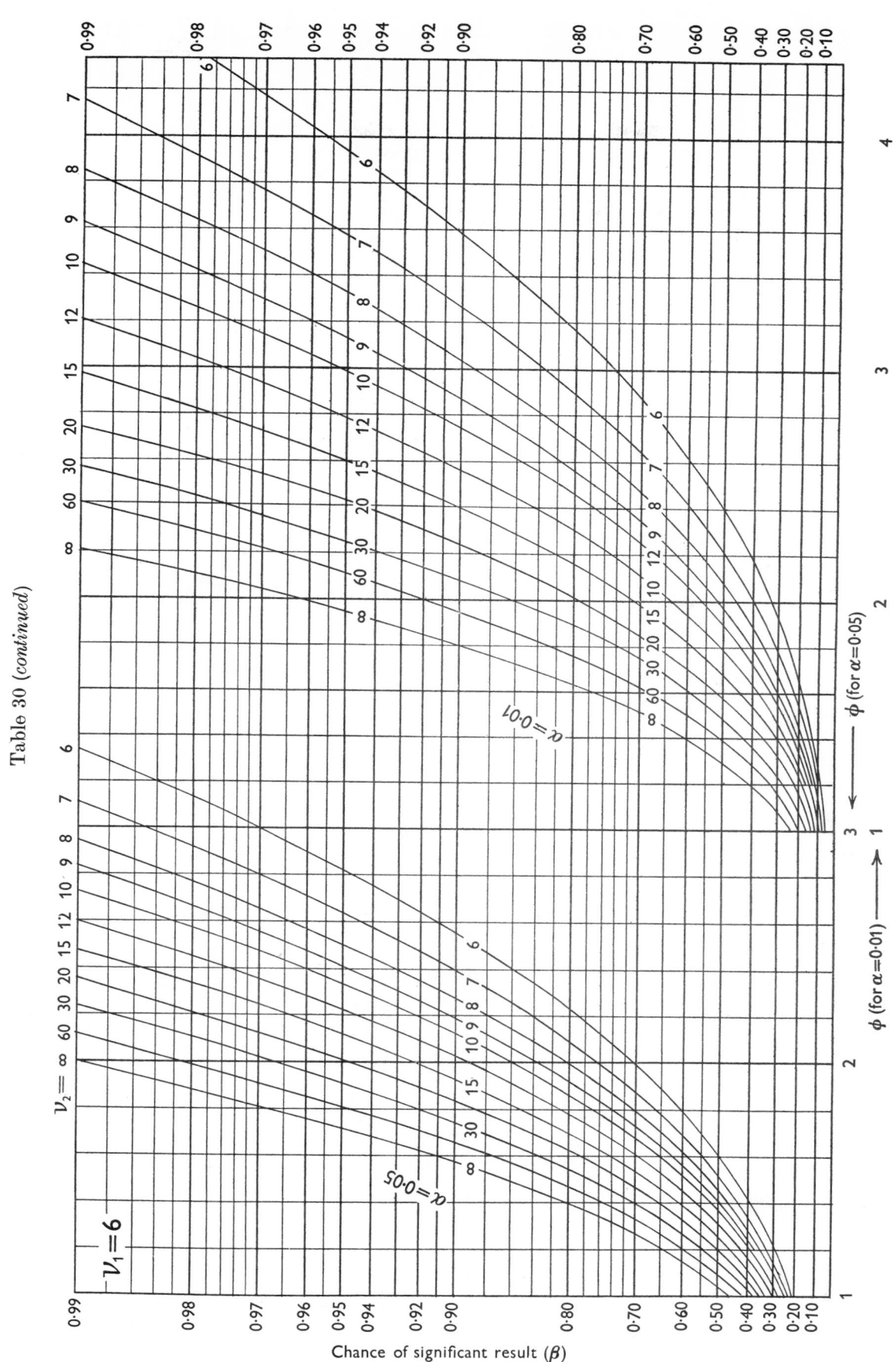

Table 30 (continued). Charts for determining the power of the t and F tests; fixed effects model

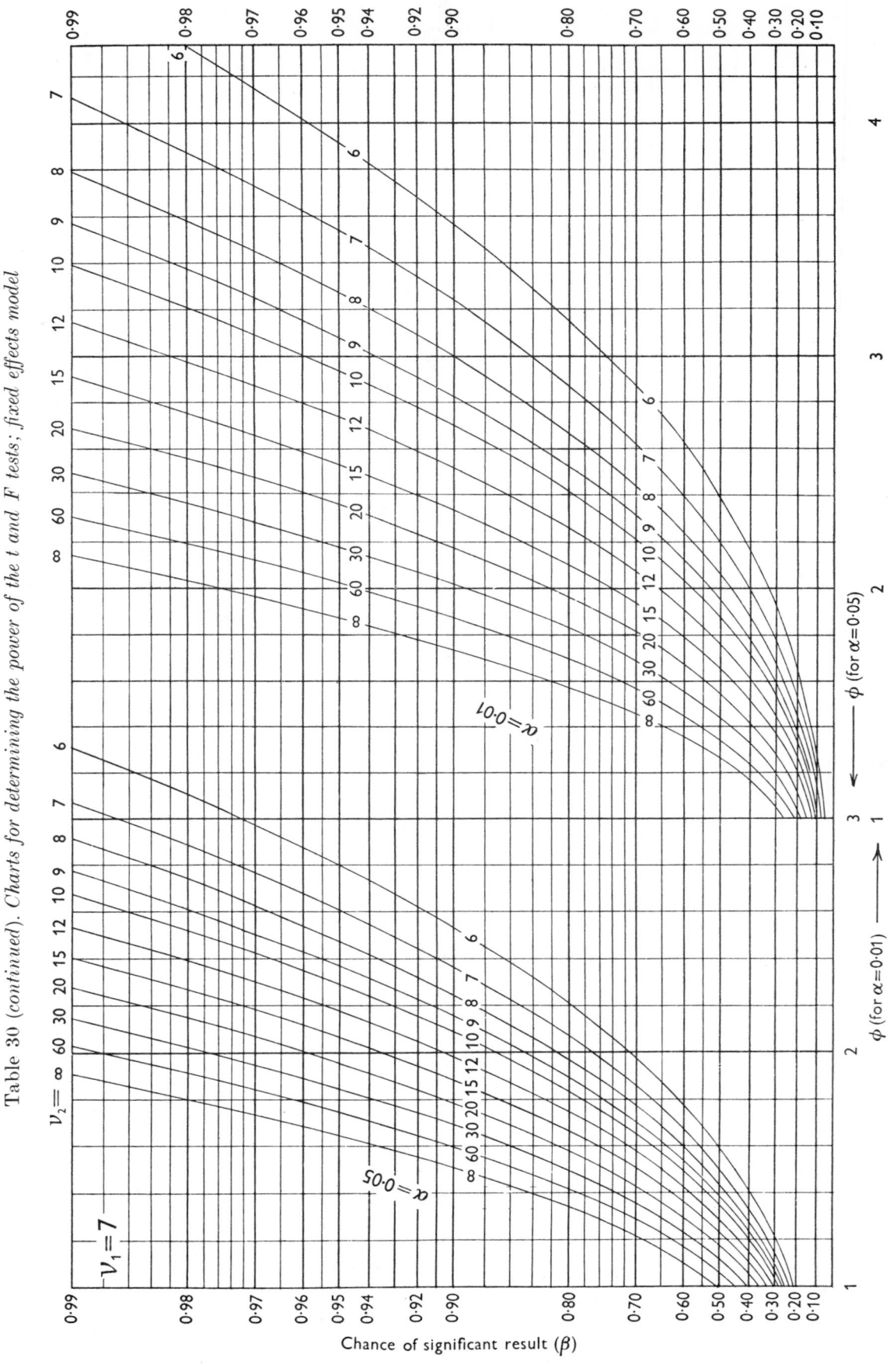

Chance of significant result (β)

Table 30 (*continued*)

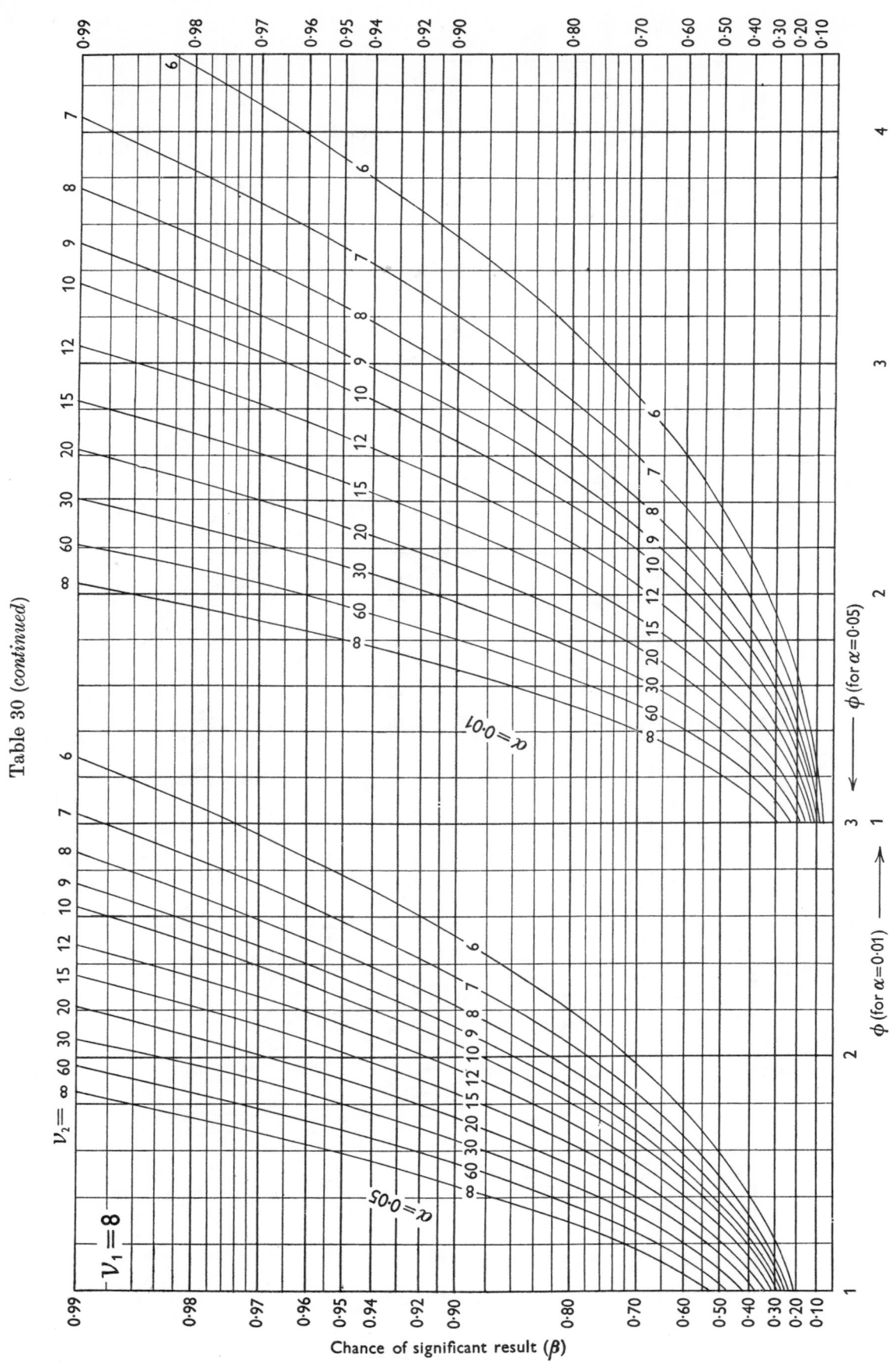

$V_1 = 8$

Chance of significant result (β)

257

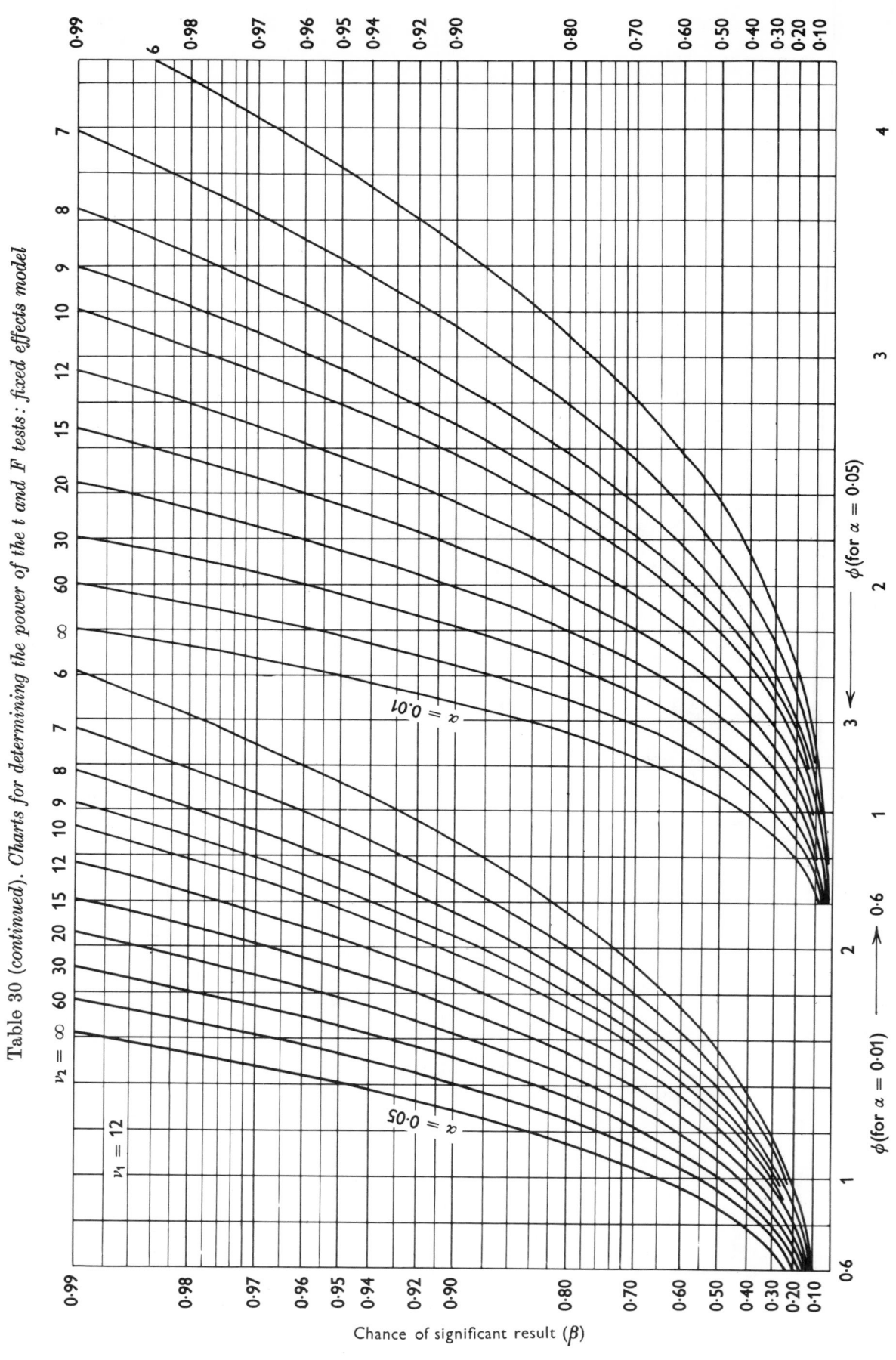

Table 30 (continued). Charts for determining the power of the t and F tests: fixed effects model

Chance of significant result (β)

258

Table 30 (continued)

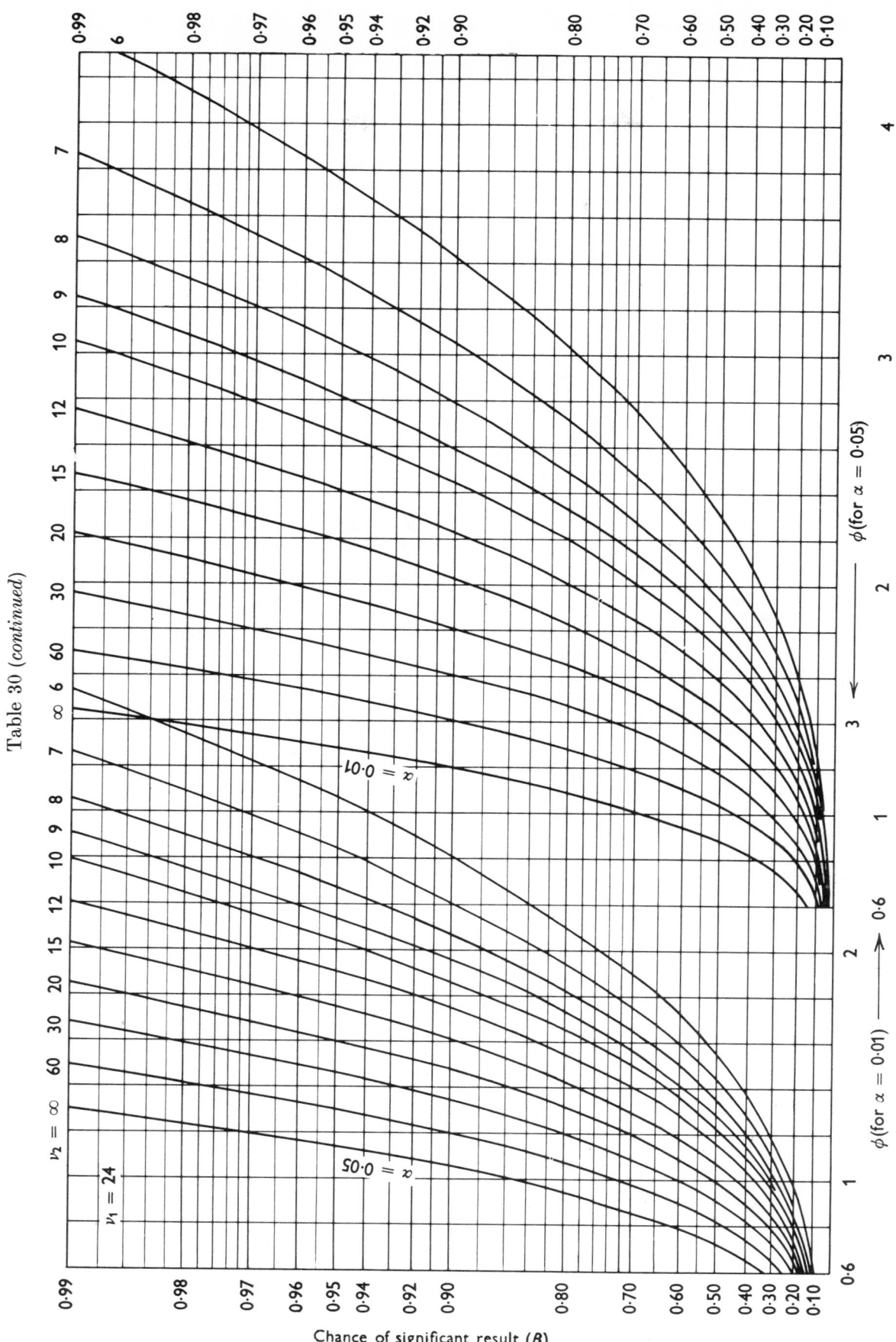

Table 31. *Pearson curves: parameters a and b against $\sqrt{\beta_1}$, β_2 for J and U Type I distributions included in Table 32*

$\sqrt{\beta_1}$	β_2	a	b	$\sqrt{\beta_1}$	β_2	a	b	$\sqrt{\beta_1}$	β_2	a	b
0·0	1·6	0·6429	0·6429	1·2	3·6	0·4720	1·7588	1·7	5·8	0·4742	3·2587
0·1	1·6	0·5916	0·6593		3·8	·6000	2·4000		6·0	·5522	4·1894
	1·8	·9193	1·0313		4·0	·7505	3·2839		6·2	·6384	5·4673
0·2	1·8	·8026	1·0069		4·2	·9303	4·5697		6·4	·7344	7·3190
0·3	1·8	·6661	0·9295	1·3	4·0	0·4894	2·0709		6·6	·8420	10·2192
	2·0	·9907	1·4146		4·2	·6082	2·7850		6·8	·9635	15·3543
0·4	2·0	0·7869	1·2454		4·4	·7464	3·7735	1·8	6·4	0·4904	3·9479
0·5	2·0	·5976	1·0387		4·6	·9090	5·2193		6·6	·5323	5·0567
	2·2	·8655	1·5601	1·4	4·4	0·4867	2·3185		6·8	·6412	6·6041
0·6	2·2	·6353	1·2453		4·6	·5940	3·0776		7·0	·7281	8·8998
	2·4	·8963	1·8405		4·8	·7171	4·1250		7·2	·8245	12·6301
0·7	2·4	0·6381	1·4068		5·0	·8597	5·6510		7·4	·9320	19·6767
	2·6	·8814	2·0525	1·5	4·8	0·4685	2·4839	1·9	7·0	0·4909	4·5762
0·8	2·6	·6113	1·5064		5·0	·5632	3·2549		7·2	·5558	5·8393
	2·8	·8292	2·1708		5·2	·6704	4·3083		7·4	·6264	7·6199
0·9	2·8	0·5624	1·5365		5·4	·7926	5·8228		7·6	·7034	10·3028
	3·0	·7514	2·1869		5·6	·9334	8·1634		7·8	·7878	14·7732
	3·2	·9869	3·1215	1·6	5·2	0·4393	2·5607		8·0	·8808	23·6252
1·0	3·0	·5000	1·5000		5·4	·5217	3·3117		8·2	·9839	49·1092
	3·2	·6600	2·1092		5·6	·6135	4·3220	2·0	7·6	0·4791	5·0924
	3·4	·8545	2·9636		5·8	·7166	5·7449		7·8	·5367	6·4633
1·1	3·2	0·4313	1·4077		6·0	·8333	7·8810		8·0	·5989	8·4011
	3·4	·5646	1·9583		6·2	·9666	11·4084		8·2	·6660	11·3340
	3·6	·7230	2·7091						8·4	·7388	16·2612
	3·8	·9142	3·7853						8·6	·8181	26·1819
									8·8	·9047	56·0953

The Type I distribution is taken in the form $f(x|a, b) = \Gamma(a+b)/\{\Gamma(a)\,\Gamma(b)\}x^{a-1}(1-x)^{b-1}$.

If a and b are both < 1, the distribution is U-shaped; if $a < 1$ and $b > 1$, the distribution is J-shaped with maximum to the left.

Table 32. *Pearson curves: percentage points for given $\sqrt{\beta_1}$, β_2 expressed in standard measure*

Table A. *Lower and upper standardized percentage points*

Percent	50·0	25·0	10·0	5·0	2·5	1·0	0·5	0·25	0·0	Type
β_2					$\sqrt{\beta_1} = 0{\cdot}0$					
1·6	0·0000	0·9480	1·3717	1·4639	1·4955	1·5079	1·5105	1·5114	1·5119	II (U)
·8	·0000	·8660	1·3856	1·5588	1·6454	1·6974	1·7147	1·7234	1·7321	Rectangle
2·0	0·0000	0·8079	1·3741	1·6108	1·7567	1·8687	1·9175	1·9481	2·0000	
·2	·0000	·7658	1·3545	1·6361	1·8333	2·0097	2·1006	2·1664	2·3452	
·4	·0000	·7342	1·3339	1·6467	1·8848	2·1207	2·2562	2·3643	2·8284	II (Ω)
·6	·0000	·7097	1·3144	1·6495	1·9196	2·2068	2·3846	2·5363	3·6056	
·8	·0000	·6903	1·2970	1·6482	1·9435	2·2737	2·4897	2·6829	5·2915	
3·0	0·0000	0·6745	1·2816	1·6449	1·9600	2·3263	2·5758	2·8070	∞†	Normal
·2	·0000	·6614	1·2679	1·6404	1·9716	2·3683	2·6469	2·9123		VII
·4	·0000	·6504	1·2559	1·6356	1·9798	2·4021	2·7062	3·0020		
·6	·0000	·6411	1·2453	1·6307	1·9857	2·4298	2·7560	3·0790		↓
·8	·0000	·6330	1·2358	1·6258	1·9899	2·4528	2·7984	3·1455		
4·0	0·0000	0·6259	1·2273	1·6211	1·9929	2·4720	2·8347	3·2033		
·2	·0000	·6197	1·2197	1·6167	1·9950	2·4883	2·8661	3·2540		
·4	·0000	·6143	1·2129	1·6124	1·9965	2·5022	2·8935	3·2987		
·6	·0000	·6094	1·2066	1·6085	1·9975	2·5142	2·9175	3·3383		
·8	·0000	·6050	1·2010	1·6047	1·9981	2·5246	2·9387	3·3737		
5·0	0·0000	0·6010	1·1958	1·6012	1·9985	2·5337	2·9576	3·4054		
·2	·0000	·5974	1·1911	1·5979	1·9986	2·5418	2·9745	3·4340		
·4	·0000	·5942	1·1867	1·5948	1·9986	2·5489	2·9897	3·4599		
·6	·0000	·5912	1·1827	1·5919	1·9984	2·5552	3·0034	3·4835		
·8	·0000	·5884	1·1790	1·5892	1·9982	2·5609	3·0158	3·5050		
6·0	0·0000	0·5859	1·1756	1·5866	1·9979	2·5660	3·0271	3·5247		
·2	·0000	·5835	1·1723	1·5842	1·9975	2·5706	3·0374	3·5428		
·4	·0000	·5814	1·1694	1·5819	1·9971	2·5748	3·0469	3·5595		
·6	·0000	·5793	1·1666	1·5797	1·9967	2·5786	3·0557	3·5749		
·8	·0000	·5775	1·1639	1·5777	1·9963	2·5820	3·0637	3·5892		
7·0	0·0000	0·5757	1·1615	1·5757	1·9958	2·5852	3·0712	3·6026		
·2	·0000	·5741	1·1592	1·5739	1·9953	2·5881	3·0781	3·6150		
·4	·0000	·5725	1·1570	1·5721	1·9948	2·5908	3·0845	3·6266		
·6	·0000	·5711	1·1549	1·5705	1·9944	2·5933	3·0905	3·6374		
·8	·0000	·5697	1·1530	1·5689	1·9939	2·5956	3·0961	3·6476		
8·0	0·0000	0·5684	1·1511	1·5674	1·9934	2·5977	3·1014	3·6571		
·2	·0000	·5672	1·1494	1·5660	1·9930	2·5997	3·1063	3·6661		
·4	·0000	·5660	1·1477	1·5646	1·9925	2·6016	3·1109	3·6746		
·6	·0000	·5649	1·1461	1·5633	1·9920	2·6033	3·1153	3·6826		
·8	·0000	·5639	1·1446	1·5620	1·9916	2·6049	3·1194	3·6902		
9·0	0·0000	0·5629	1·1432	1·5608	1·9912	2·6065	3·1233	3·6974		

† Here, and below, in the columns indicating the lower and upper terminals, headed 0·0, the symbol ∞ has been omitted after its first appearance. All Types IV and VII distributions have unlimited range in both directions and Type VI (if $\sqrt{\beta_1} > 0$) has unlimited range in the positive direction.

Table 32 (*continued*). *Pearson curves*

Table A (*cont.*). *Lower standardized percentage points (all signs negative)*

Percent	0·0	0·25	0·5	1·0	2·5	5·0	10·0	25·0	50·0
β_2					$\sqrt{\beta_1}=0·1$				
1·6	1·4212	1·4210	1·4206	1·4192	1·4115	1·3899	1·3205	0·9602	0·0527
·8	1·6218	1·6169	1·6113	1·5996	1·5615	1·4936	1·3491	·8810	·0392
2·0	1·8621	1·8281	1·8057	1·7685	1·6785	1·5556	1·3475	0·8226	0·0313
·2	2·1655	2·0387	1·9864	1·9121	1·7625	1·5893	1·3342	·7794	·0263
·4	2·5785	2·2340	2·1437	2·0279	1·8210	1·6064	1·3176	·7466	·0228
·6	3·2134	2·4068	2·2758	2·1194	1·8617	1·6141	1·3009	·7212	·0202
·8	4·4667	2·5561	2·3852	2·1915	1·8904	1·6166	1·2854	·7009	·0183
3·0	12·3383	2·6838	2·4757	2·2488	1·9109	1·6161	1·2714	0·6844	0·0168
·2	∞	2·7928	2·5510	2·2948	1·9258	1·6139	1·2588	·6707	·0155
·4	—	2·8863	2·6141	2·3322	1·9368	1·6110	1·2476	·6592	·0146
·6	—	2·9668	2·6674	2·3630	1·9450	1·6076	1·2376	·6494	·0137
·8	—	3·0365	2·7129	2·3887	1·9512	1·6040	1·2287	·6409	·0130
4·0	—	3·0974	2·7520	2·4104	1·9560	1·6004	1·2206	0·6335	0·0124
·2	—	3·1509	2·7860	2·4288	1·9596	1·5969	1·2134	·6271	·0119
·4	—	3·1981	2·8156	2·4447	1·9624	1·5935	1·2069	·6213	·0114
·6	—	3·2401	2·8417	2·4584	1·9645	1·5902	1·2009	·6162	·0110
·8	—	3·2776	2·8648	2·4703	1·9662	1·5871	1·1955	·6116	·0107
5·0	—	3·3114	2·8854	2·4808	1·9675	1·5842	1·1906	0·6075	0·0104
·2	—	3·3418	2·9039	2·4901	1·9684	1·5814	1·1860	·6037	·0101
·4	—	3·3694	2·9205	2·4984	1·9692	1·5787	1·1818	·6003	·0098
·6	—	3·3945	2·9355	2·5058	1·9697	1·5762	1·1779	·5972	·0096
·8	—	3·4175	2·9492	2·5124	1·9701	1·5739	1·1744	·5943	·0094
6·0	—	3·4385	2·9616	2·5184	1·9703	1·5716	1·1710	0·5916	0·0092
·2	—	3·4579	2·9730	2·5238	1·9705	1·5695	1·1679	·5892	·0090
·4	—	3·4758	2·9835	2·5288	1·9706	1·5675	1·1650	·5869	·0089
·6	—	3·4923	2·9931	2·5333	1·9706	1·5656	1·1623	·5848	·0087
·8	—	3·5077	3·0020	2·5374	1·9706	1·5638	1·1598	·5828	·0086
7·0	—	3·5220	3·0102	2·5412	1·9705	1·5621	1·1574	0·5810	0·0084
·2	—	3·5353	3·0179	2·5447	1·9704	1·5604	1·1551	·5793	·0083
·4	—	3·5477	3·0250	2·5480	1·9703	1·5589	1·1530	·5776	·0082
·6	—	3·5594	3·0317	2·5509	1·9701	1·5574	1·1510	·5761	·0081
·8	—	3·5703	3·0379	2·5537	1·9699	1·5560	1·1491	·5747	·0080
8·0	—	3·5806	3·0438	2·5563	1·9697	1·5547	1·1474	0·5733	0·0079
·2	—	3·5903	3·0493	2·5587	1·9695	1·5534	1·1457	·5721	·0078
·4	—	3·5995	3·0544	2·5610	1·9693	1·5521	1·1441	·5709	·0077
·6	—	3·6081	3·0593	2·5631	1·9691	1·5510	1·1425	·5697	·0076
·8	—	3·6163	3·0639	2·5651	1·9689	1·5499	1·1411	·5686	·0076
9·0	—	3·6240	3·0682	2·5670	1·9687	1·5488	1·1397	0·5676	0·0075
					$\sqrt{\beta_1}=0·2$				
1·8	1·4965	1·4946	1·4919	1·4857	1·4627	1·4163	1·3063	0·9007	0·0818
2·0	1·7065	1·6892	1·6756	1·6512	1·5869	1·4915	1·3179	0·8414	0·0649
·2	1·9644	1·8897	1·8531	1·7982	1·6806	1·5363	1·3127	·7965	·0542
·4	2·3018	2·0819	2·0127	1·9206	1·7483	1·5618	1·3012	·7620	·0467
·6	2·7890	2·2563	2·1499	2·0193	1·7967	1·5757	1·2877	·7351	·0414
·8	3·6335	2·4097	2·2655	2·0984	1·8317	1·5827	1·2743	·7136	·0373
3·0	6·1355	2·5425	2·3621	2·1619	1·8573	1·5857	1·2618	0·6961	0·0341
·2	∞	2·6570	2·4431	2·2132	1·8763	1·5863	1·2503	·6815	·0316
·4	—	2·7557	2·5114	2·2553	1·8907	1·5855	1·2399	·6693	·0295
·6	—	2·8411	2·5693	2·2901	1·9018	1·5838	1·2306	·6589	·0278
·8	—	2·9153	2·6189	2·3193	1·9103	1·5817	1·2222	·6499	·0264
4·0	—	2·9803	2·6616	2·3440	1·9171	1·5793	1·2145	0·6421	0·0251
·2	—	3·0375	2·6988	2·3650	1·9224	1·5768	1·2076	·6352	·0241
·4	—	3·0881	2·7314	2·3832	1·9267	1·5743	1·2014	·6292	·0231
·6	—	3·1332	2·7601	2·3990	1·9302	1·5718	1·1957	·6237	·0223
·8	—	3·1735	2·7855	2·4128	1·9330	1·5693	1·1905	·6189	·0216
5·0	—	3·2098	2·8082	2·4249	1·9353	1·5669	1·1857	0·6145	0·0209
·2	—	3·2425	2·8286	2·4357	1·9372	1·5647	1·1813	·6105	·0203

Table 32 (*continued*)

Table A (*cont.*). *Upper standardized percentage points (all signs positive)*

Percent	25·0	10·0	5·0	2·5	1·0	0·5	0·25	0·0	Type
β_2				$\sqrt{\beta_1} = 0\cdot1$					
1·6	0·9420	1·4169	1·5249	1·5631	1·5786	1·5820	1·5831	1·5838	I (U)
·8	·8563	1·4202	1·6151	1·7149	1·7764	1·7974	1·8081	1·8193	I (J)
2·0	0·7974	1·4008	1·6602	1·8233	1·9511	2·0079	2·0442	2·1084	
·2	·7555	1·3758	1·6793	1·8953	2·0918	2·1946	2·2701	2·4845	
·4	·7244	1·3513	1·6849	1·9422	2·2004	2·3506	2·4717	3·0175	
·6	·7004	1·3293	1·6837	1·9727	2·2833	2·4777	2·6447	3·8881	I (Ω)
·8	·6815	1·3099	1·6792	1·9928	2·3469	2·5805	2·7908	5·8156	
3·0	0·6661	1·2930	1·6733	2·0061	2·3964	2·6640	2·9135	32·3383	
·2	·6535	1·2782	1·6668	2·0150	2·4353	2·7325	3·0168	∞	IV
·4	·6428	1·2653	1·6602	2·0209	2·4665	2·7892	3·1044		
·6	·6337	1·2539	1·6538	2·0248	2·4918	2·8366	3·1792		↓
·8	·6259	1·2438	1·6477	2·0272	2·5126	2·8767	3·2436		
4·0	0·6191	1·2348	1·6420	2·0287	2·5299	2·9109	3·2994		
·2	·6131	1·2268	1·6366	2·0295	2·5444	2·9404	3·3481		
·4	·6079	1·2195	1·6315	2·0298	2·5567	2·9660	3·3910		
·6	·6031	1·2130	1·6269	2·0297	2·5673	2·9884	3·4290		
·8	·5989	1·2071	1·6225	2·0294	2·5764	3·0082	3·4627		
5·0	0·5951	1·2017	1·6184	2·0289	2·5844	3·0257	3·4930		
·2	·5916	1·1967	1·6146	2·0283	2·5913	3·0413	3·5202		
·4	·5885	1·1922	1·6111	2·0275	2·5974	3·0553	3·5448		
·6	·5856	1·1880	1·6078	2·0267	2·6028	3·0679	3·5671		
·8	·5829	1·1841	1·6046	2·0259	2·6076	3·0793	3·5875		
6·0	0·5805	1·1805	1·6017	2·0251	2·6120	3·0897	3·6061		
·2	·5782	1·1771	1·5990	2·0242	2·6158	3·0991	3·6232		
·4	·5761	1·1740	1·5964	2·0233	2·6193	3·1078	3·6389		
·6	·5742	1·1711	1·5940	2·0225	2·6225	3·1157	3·6535		
·8	·5724	1·1684	1·5917	2·0216	2·6254	3·1231	3·6670		
7·0	0·5707	1·1658	1·5895	2·0208	2·6280	3·1298	3·6795		
·2	·5691	1·1634	1·5874	2·0200	2·6304	3·1361	3·6911		
·4	·5676	1·1612	1·5855	2·0192	2·6326	3·1419	3·7020		
·6	·5662	1·1590	1·5836	2·0184	2·6346	3·1474	3·7122		
·8	·5649	1·1570	1·5819	2·0176	2·6365	3·1524	3·7217		
8·0	0·5636	1·1551	1·5802	2·0169	2·6382	3·1571	3·7307		
·2	·5625	1·1533	1·5786	2·0161	2·6398	3·1616	3·7391		
·4	·5614	1·1516	1·5771	2·0154	2·6413	3·1657	3·7470		
·6	·5603	1·1500	1·5757	2·0148	2·6426	3·1697	3·7545		
·8	·5593	1·1484	1·5743	2·0141	2·6439	3·1734	3·7616		
9·0	0·5583	1·1469	1·5730	2·0135	2·6451	3·1768	3·7683		
				$\sqrt{\beta_1} = 0\cdot2$					
1·8	0·8522	1·4561	1·6644	1·7700	1·8341	1·8557	1·8665	1·8774	I (J)
2·0	0·7910	1·4298	1·7063	1·8799	2·0152	2·0749	2·1127	2·1782	
·2	·7483	1·3996	1·7212	1·9505	2·1590	2·2677	2·3472	2·5690	
·4	·7169	1·3713	1·7227	1·9948	2·2682	2·4272	2·5551	3·1200	
·6	·6930	1·3463	1·7181	2·0224	2·3504	2·5557	2·7321	4·0064	I (Ω)
·8	·6743	1·3247	1·7107	2·0398	2·4125	2·6587	2·8802	5·8643	
3·0	0·6591	1·3061	1·7023	2·0506	2·4602	2·7415	3·0037	16·1355	
·2	·6466	1·2900	1·6937	2·0572	2·4973	2·8089	3·1073	∞	IV
·4	·6362	1·2760	1·6854	2·0611	2·5266	2·8643	3·1945		
·6	·6273	1·2637	1·6776	2·0632	2·5501	2·9103	3·2685		↓
·8	·6196	1·2529	1·6702	2·0641	2·5693	2·9490	3·3319		
4·0	0·6130	1·2433	1·6634	2·0641	2·5850	2·9818	3·3867		
·2	·6072	1·2348	1·6571	2·0637	2·5981	3·0100	3·4344		
·4	·6020	1·2271	1·6512	2·0628	2·6091	3·0343	3·4761		
·6	·5974	1·2202	1·6458	2·0618	2·6185	3·0555	3·5130		
·8	·5933	1·2139	1·6408	2·0605	2·6265	3·0741	3·5457		
5·0	0·5896	1·2082	1·6361	2·0592	2·6334	3·0905	3·5749		
·2	·5862	1·2029	1·6318	2·0578	2·6394	3·1051	3·6011		

Table 32 (continued). Pearson curves

Table A (cont.). Lower standardized percentage points (all signs negative)

Percent	0·0	0·25	0·5	1·0	2·5	5·0	10·0	25·0	50·0
β₂					$\sqrt{\beta_1} = 0\cdot2$ (cont.)				
5·4	∞	3·2723	2·8470	2·4453	1·9388	1·5625	1·1772	0·6069	0·0198
·6	—	3·2993	2·8636	2·4539	1·9401	1·5604	1·1735	·6036	·0193
·8	—	3·3241	2·8787	2·4617	1·9411	1·5584	1·1700	·6006	·0189
6·0	—	3·3468	2·8925	2·4687	1·9420	1·5565	1·1668	0·5978	0·0185
·2	—	3·3678	2·9051	2·4751	1·9428	1·5547	1·1638	·5952	·0181
·4	—	3·3871	2·9167	2·4809	1·9434	1·5530	1·1610	·5928	·0178
·6	—	3·4050	2·9274	2·4862	1·9439	1·5514	1·1583	·5906	·0175
·8	—	3·4216	2·9373	2·4911	1·9443	1·5498	1·1559	·5885	·0172
7·0	—	3·4370	2·9465	2·4956	1·9446	1·5483	1·1535	0·5866	0·0169
·2	—	3·4515	2·9550	2·4997	1·9449	1·5469	1·1514	·5848	·0167
·4	—	3·4649	2·9630	2·5036	1·9451	1·5456	1·1493	·5831	·0165
·6	—	3·4776	2·9704	2·5072	1·9453	1·5443	1·1474	·5815	·0162
·8	—	3·4894	2·9774	2·5105	1·9455	1·5430	1·1455	·5799	·0160
8·0	—	3·5006	2·9839	2·5136	1·9456	1·5418	1·1438	0·5785	0·0158
·2	—	3·5111	2·9900	2·5165	1·9456	1·5407	1·1421	·5772	·0157
·4	—	3·5210	2·9958	2·5192	1·9457	1·5396	1·1405	·5759	·0155
·6	—	3·5304	3·0012	2·5217	1·9457	1·5386	1·1390	·5747	·0153
·8	—	3·5392	3·0063	2·5241	1·9457	1·5376	1·1376	·5736	·0152
9·0	—	3·5477	3·0112	2·5263	1·9457	1·5366	1·1363	0·5725	0·0150
					$\sqrt{\beta_1} = 0\cdot3$				
1·8	1·3638	1·3634	1·3626	1·3603	1·3498	1·3243	1·2520	0·9233	0·1321
2·0	1·5443	1·5380	1·5317	1·5189	1·4801	1·4146	1·2813	0·8643	0·1034
·2	1·7590	1·7243	1·7028	1·6676	1·5848	1·4736	1·2873	·8173	·0855
·4	2·0278	1·9103	1·8634	1·7969	1·6638	1·5100	1·2826	·7807	·0732
·6	2·3904	2·0852	2·0060	1·9044	1·7221	1·5319	1·2734	·7518	·0644
·8	2·9441	2·2430	2·1288	1·9921	1·7651	1·5449	1·2628	·7287	·0579
3·0	4·0528	2·3820	2·2331	2·0634	1·7972	1·5523	1·2521	0·7098	0·0528
·2	∞	2·5032	2·3213	2·1216	1·8214	1·5563	1·2419	·6941	·0487
·4	—	2·6085	2·3961	2·1695	1·8401	1·5581	1·2325	·6810	·0454
·6	—	2·7001	2·4599	2·2094	1·8546	1·5585	1·2238	·6698	·0427
·8	—	2·7802	2·5147	2·2429	1·8660	1·5581	1·2159	·6602	·0404
4·0	—	2·8504	2·5620	2·2713	1·8752	1·5571	1·2087	0·6518	0·0384
·2	—	2·9123	2·6032	2·2956	1·8827	1·5558	1·2022	·6444	·0368
·4	—	2·9672	2·6394	2·3166	1·8887	1·5543	1·1962	·6379	·0353
·6	—	3·0161	2·6713	2·3349	1·8938	1·5526	1·1907	·6321	·0340
·8	—	3·0599	2·6996	2·3510	1·8980	1·5509	1·1857	·6269	·0329
5·0	—	3·0994	2·7249	2·3651	1·9015	1·5492	1·1811	0·6222	0·0319
·2	—	3·1350	2·7476	2·3777	1·9044	1·5475	1·1769	·6180	·0309
·4	—	3·1674	2·7681	2·3889	1·9069	1·5458	1·1729	·6141	·0301
·6	—	3·1969	2·7867	2·3989	1·9091	1·5442	1·1693	·6106	·0294
·8	—	3·2239	2·8035	2·4080	1·9109	1·5426	1·1659	·6074	·0287
6·0	—	3·2487	2·8189	2·4162	1·9125	1·5411	1·1628	0·6044	0·0281
·2	—	3·2715	2·8331	2·4237	1·9139	1·5397	1·1598	·6017	·0275
·4	—	3·2925	2·8460	2·4306	1·9151	1·5383	1·1571	·5991	·0270
·6	—	3·3120	2·8580	2·4368	1·9162	1·5369	1·1545	·5968	·0265
·8	—	3·3302	2·8691	2·4425	1·9171	1·5356	1·1521	·5946	·0261
7·0	—	3·3470	2·8794	2·4478	1·9179	1·5344	1·1499	0·5925	0·0257
·2	—	3·3628	2·8889	2·4527	1·9186	1·5332	1·1477	·5906	·0253
·4	—	3·3775	2·8978	2·4573	1·9192	1·5320	1·1457	·5888	·0249
·6	—	3·3913	2·9061	2·4615	1·9198	1·5309	1·1438	·5871	·0246
·8	—	3·4042	2·9139	2·4654	1·9203	1·5299	1·1420	·5855	·0243
8·0	—	3·4164	2·9212	2·4691	1·9207	1·5288	1·1403	0·5840	0·0240
·2	—	3·4278	2·9281	2·4725	1·9211	1·5279	1·1387	·5826	·0237
·4	—	3·4387	2·9345	2·4757	1·9214	1·5269	1·1371	·5812	·0234
·6	—	3·4489	2·9406	2·4788	1·9217	1·5260	1·1357	·5800	·0232
·8	—	3·4586	2·9464	2·4816	1·9220	1·5252	1·1343	·5787	·0229
9·0	—	3·4678	2·9518	2·4843	1·9222	1·5243	1·1329	0·5776	0·0227

Table 32 (*continued*)

Table A (*cont.*). *Upper standardized percentage points (all signs positive)*

Percent	25·0	10·0	5·0	2·5	1·0	0·5	0·25	0·0	Type
β_2				$\sqrt{\beta_1} = 0\cdot2$ (*cont.*)					
5·4	0·5831	1·1982	1·6278	2·0564	2·6446	3·1181	3·6248	∞	IV
·6	·5803	1·1937	1·6240	2·0550	2·6492	3·1298	3·6462		
·8	·5777	1·1897	1·6205	2·0536	2·6533	3·1404	3·6657		↓
6·0	0·5754	1·1859	1·6172	2·0522	2·6569	3·1499	3·6835		
·2	·5732	1·1824	1·6141	2·0508	2·6601	3·1586	3·6998		
·4	·5712	1·1791	1·6112	2·0495	2·6629	3·1666	3·7148		
·6	·5693	1·1761	1·6085	2·0482	2·6655	3·1739	3·7286		
·8	·5675	1·1732	1·6059	2·0470	2·6678	3·1806	3·7414		
7·0	0·5659	1·1706	1·6035	2·0457	2·6699	3·1867	3·7533		
·2	·5643	1·1680	1·6012	2·0446	2·6719	3·1925	3·7643		
·4	·5629	1·1657	1·5991	2·0434	2·6736	3·1977	3·7746		
·6	·5615	1·1635	1·5970	2·0424	2·6752	3·2027	3·7842		
·8	·5602	1·1614	1·5951	2·0413	2·6766	3·2072	3·7932		
8·0	0·5590	1·1594	1·5932	2·0403	2·6780	3·2115	3·8017		
·2	·5579	1·1575	1·5915	2·0393	2·6792	3·2155	3·8096		
·4	·5568	1·1557	1·5898	2·0384	2·6803	3·2192	3·8170		
·6	·5558	1·1540	1·5882	2·0374	2·6814	3·2228	3·8241		
·8	·5548	1·1524	1·5867	2·0366	2·6824	3·2261	3·8307		
9·0	0·5539	1·1508	1·5852	2·0357	2·6833	3·2292	3·8370		
				$\sqrt{\beta_1} = 0\cdot3$					
1·8	0·8546	1·4956	1·7075	1·8098	1·8682	1·8865	1·8953	1·9031	I (U)
2·0	0·7887	1·4634	1·7505	1·9266	2·0593	2·1158	2·1504	2·2051	I (J)
·2	·7439	1·4275	1·7633	1·9997	2·2107	2·3183	2·3954	2·5932	
·4	·7117	1·3948	1·7617	2·0439	2·3244	2·4852	2·6128	3·1299	
·6	·6874	1·3665	1·7539	2·0702	2·4086	2·6186	2·7973	3·9605	I (Ω)
·8	·6684	1·3423	1·7437	2·0856	2·4714	2·7245	2·9509	5·5411	
3·0	0·6532	1·3216	1·7329	2·0944	2·5187	2·8089	3·0782	10·7195	
·2	·6407	1·3039	1·7222	2·0991	2·5550	2·8769	3·1840	∞	IV
·4	·6303	1·2886	1·7121	2·1012	2·5833	2·9323	3·2726		
·6	·6215	1·2752	1·7027	2·1017	2·6057	2·9780	3·3474		↓
·8	·6140	1·2635	1·6940	2·1011	2·6236	3·0160	3·4112		
4·0	0·6074	1·2531	1·6860	2·0998	2·6382	3·0481	3·4659		
·2	·6017	1·2439	1·6786	2·0982	2·6502	3·0755	3·5134		
·4	·5966	1·2357	1·6719	2·0962	2·6601	3·0990	3·5548		
·6	·5921	1·2283	1·6656	2·0941	2·6684	3·1193	3·5911		
·8	·5880	1·2216	1·6599	2·0920	2·6755	3·1370	3·6233		
5·0	0·5844	1·2155	1·6546	2·0898	2·6815	3·1526	3·6519		
·2	·5811	1·2099	1·6497	2·0877	2·6866	3·1664	3·6775		
·4	·5781	1·2048	1·6451	2·0856	2·6910	3·1787	3·7006		
·6	·5753	1·2002	1·6409	2·0835	2·6949	3·1897	3·7214		
·8	·5728	1·1959	1·6369	2·0815	2·6982	3·1995	3·7403		
6·0	0·5705	1·1919	1·6332	2·0796	2·7011	3·2084	3·7575		
·2	·5683	1·1882	1·6298	2·0777	2·7037	3·2165	3·7732		
·4	·5664	1·1847	1·6266	2·0759	2·7060	3·2239	3·7876		
·6	·5645	1·1815	1·6235	2·0742	2·7080	3·2306	3·8009		
·8	·5628	1·1785	1·6207	2·0725	2·7099	3·2367	3·8132		
7·0	0·5612	1·1757	1·6180	2·0709	2·7115	3·2423	3·8245		
·2	·5597	1·1731	1·6154	2·0694	2·7129	3·2475	3·8351		
·4	·5583	1·1706	1·6130	2·0679	2·7142	3·2524	3·8449		
·6	·5570	1·1682	1·6108	2·0665	2·7154	3·2568	3·8540		
·8	·5557	1·1660	1·6086	2·0652	2·7165	3·2610	3·8626		
8·0	0·5546	1·1639	1·6066	2·0639	2·7174	3·2648	3·8706		
·2	·5534	1·1620	1·6046	2·0626	3·7183	3·2684	3·8781		
·4	·5524	1·1601	1·6028	2·0614	2·7191	3·2718	3·8852		
·6	·5514	1·1583	1·6010	2·0603	2·7198	3·2749	3·8918		
·8	·5505	1·1566	1·5994	2·0592	2·7205	3·2779	3·8981		
9·0	0·5496	1·1550	1·5978	2·0581	2·7211	3·2807	3·9040		

Table 32 (continued). Pearson curves

Table A (cont.). Lower standardized percentage points (all signs negative)

Percent	0·0	0·25	0·5	1·0	2·5	5·0	10·0	25·0	50·0
β_2					$\sqrt{\beta_1} = 0\cdot4$				
2·0	1·3842	1·3828	1·3808	1·3761	1·3582	1·3213	1·2320	0·8897	0·1506
·2	1·5616	1·5499	1·5401	1·5221	1·4727	1·3968	1·2539	·8418	·1226
·4	1·7741	1·7244	1·6977	1·6563	1·5643	1·4472	1·2590	·8029	·1040
·6	2·0432	1·8959	1·8439	1·7726	1·6346	1·4798	1·2560	·7717	·0908
·8	2·4127	2·0563	1·9739	1·8702	1·6877	1·5006	1·2493	·7465	·0810
3·0	3·0000	2·2012	2·0866	1·9508	1·7281	1·5139	1·2412	0·7259	0·0735
·2	4·3557	2·3298	2·1833	2·0175	1·7590	1·5223	1·2328	·7089	·0675
·4	∞	2·4429	2·2661	2·0727	1·7830	1·5275	1·2246	·6945	·0628
·6	—	2·5420	2·3370	2·1188	1·8019	1·5306	1·2168	·6823	·0588
·8	—	2·6291	2·3982	2·1577	1·8170	1·5323	1·2096	·6718	·0555
4·0	—	2·7057	2·4512	2·1908	1·8292	1·5331	1·2029	0·6627	0·0527
·2	—	2·7734	2·4975	2·2191	1·8392	1·5332	1·1967	·6547	·0503
·4	—	2·8336	2·5381	2·2436	1·8475	1·5329	1·1911	·6477	·0482
·6	—	2·8873	2·5739	2·2650	1·8544	1·5323	1·1859	·6414	·0464
·8	—	2·9354	2·6058	2·2837	1·8602	1·5315	1·1811	·6358	·0448
5·0	—	2·9788	2·6343	2·3003	1·8652	1·5305	1·1766	0·6308	0·0433
·2	—	3·0179	2·6598	2·3150	1·8694	1·5295	1·1725	·6262	·0421
·4	—	3·0535	2·6829	2·3282	1·8731	1·5284	1·1687	·6221	·0409
·6	—	3·0860	2·7037	2·3400	1·8762	1·5273	1·1652	·6183	·0399
·8	—	3·1157	2·7227	2·3506	1·8790	1·5262	1·1619	·6148	·0389
6·0		3·1429	2·7401	2·3603	1·8814	1·5251	1·1589	0·6116	0·0381
·2	—	3·1680	2·7560	2·3690	1·8835	1·5240	1·1560	·6087	·0373
·4	—	3·1912	2·7706	2·3771	1·8854	1·5229	1·1533	·6060	·0365
·6	—	3·2126	2·7841	2·3844	1·8871	1·5219	1·1508	·6034	·0359
·8	—	3·2325	2·7965	2·3912	1·8886	1·5209	1·1485	·6011	·0352
7·0	—	3·2511	2·8081	2·3974	1·8899	1·5199	1·1462	0·5989	0·0347
·2	—	3·2684	2·8188	2·4032	1·8911	1·5190	1·1442	·5968	·0341
·4	—	3·2846	2·8289	2·4085	1·8922	1·5180	1·1422	·5949	·0336
·6	—	3·2997	2·8382	2·4135	1·8931	1·5171	1·1403	·5931	·0332
·8	—	3·3139	2·8470	2·4181	1·8940	1·5163	1·1385	·5914	·0327
8·0	—	3·3273	2·8552	2·4225	1·8948	1·5155	1·1369	0·5898	0·0323
·2	—	3·3399	2·8629	2·4265	1·8956	1·5147	1·1353	·5883	·0319
·4	—	3·3518	2·8702	2·4303	1·8962	1·5139	1·1338	·5868	·0315
·6	—	3·3631	2·8771	2·4339	1·8968	1·5131	1·1323	·5855	·0312
·8	—	3·3737	2·8836	2·4372	1·8974	1·5124	1·1310	·5842	·0309
9·0	—	3·3838	2·8897	2·4404	1·8979	1·5117	1·1297	0·5830	0·0306
					$\sqrt{\beta_1} = 0\cdot5$				
2·0	1·2316	1·2314	1·2311	1·2301	1·2248	1·2101	1·1631	0·9138	0·2120
·2	1·3785	1·3761	1·3732	1·3666	1·3442	1·3018	1·2064	·8684	·1693
·4	1·5477	1·5326	1·5211	1·5006	1·4473	1·3688	1·2262	·8282	·1415
·6	1·7504	1·6943	1·6661	1·6234	1·5307	1·4152	1·2325	·7948	·1222
·8	2·0067	1·8526	1·8008	1·7306	1·5961	1·4466	1·2318	·7673	·1081
3·0	2·3589	2·0011	1·9215	1·8216	1·6468	1·4679	1·2276	0·7447	0·0973
·2	2·9227	2·1364	2·0272	1·8981	1·6862	1·4823	1·2218	·7260	·0890
·4	4·3052	2·2574	2·1190	1·9621	1·7171	1·4920	1·2154	·7102	·0823
·6	∞	2·3649	2·1984	2·0160	1·7417	1·4987	1·2089	·6967	·0768
·8	—	2·4600	2·2673	2·0615	1·7615	1·5032	1·2026	·6852	·0722
4·0	—	2·5442	2·3271	2·1003	1·7775	1·5062	1·1966	0·6752	0·0684
·2	—	2·6188	2·3795	2·1337	1·7908	1·5082	1·1909	·6664	·0651
·4	—	2·6853	2·4255	2·1625	1·8018	1·5094	1·1857	·6587	·0622
·6	—	2·7448	2·4662	2·1877	1·8110	1·5100	1·1808	·6519	·0598
·8	—	2·7981	2·5024	2·2098	1·8189	1·5103	1·1762	·6458	·0576
5·0	—	2·8462	2·5347	2·2293	1·8256	1·5103	1·1720	0·6403	0·0557
·2	—	2·8896	2·5637	2·2466	1·8314	1·5101	1·1681	·6353	·0539
·4	—	2·9291	2·5899	2·2621	1·8364	1·5097	1·1645	·6308	·0524
·6	—–	2·9651	2·6136	2·2760	1·8408	1·5092	1·1611	·6267	·0510
·8	—	2·9981	2·6351	2·2885	1·8447	1·5087	1·1579	·6229	·0497

Table 32 (*continued*)

Table A (*cont.*). *Upper standardized percentage points (all signs positive)*

Percent	25·0	10·0	5·0	2·5	1·0	0·5	0·25	0·0	Type
β_2				$\sqrt{\beta_1} = 0\cdot4$					
2·0	0·7910	1·5036	1·7934	1·9619	2·0807	2·1275	2·1544	2·1906	I (J)
·2	·7425	1·4615	1·8067	2·0428	2·2450	2·3436	2·4114	2·5616	
·4	·7084	1·4234	1·8031	2·0900	2·3679	2·5227	2·6422	3·0598	
·6	·6831	1·3908	1·7924	2·1167	2·4578	2·6653	2·8385	3·7932	
·8	·6637	1·3633	1·7794	2·1313	2·5236	2·7775	3·0014	5·0491	I (Ω)
3·0	0·6482	1·3401	1·7659	2·1387	2·5724	2·8661	3·1357	8·0000	
·2	·6356	1·3203	1·7530	2·1418	2·6092	2·9366	3·2466	35·3557	
·4	·6251	1·3033	1·7409	2·1422	2·6373	2·9935	3·3388	∞	IV
·6	·6163	1·2886	1·7297	2·1411	2·6591	3·0400	3·4161		
·8	·6088	1·2758	1·7195	2·1391	2·6764	3·0784	3·4816		$\downarrow$
4·0	0·6022	1·2645	1·7102	2·1365	2·6901	3·1105	3·5375		
·2	·5965	1·2545	1·7017	2·1335	2·7012	3·1376	2·5856		
·4	·5915	1·2455	1·6939	2·1305	2·7103	3·1606	3·6273		
·6	·5870	1·2375	1·6867	2·1274	2·7177	3·1805	3·6639		
·8	·5830	1·2303	1·6802	2·1243	2·7239	3·1977	3·6960		
5·0	0·5794	1·2238	1·6741	2·1212	2·7291	3·2128	3·7245		
·2	·5761	1·2178	1·6686	2·1183	2·7334	3·2260	3·7499		
·4	·5732	1·2123	1·6634	2·1154	2·7371	3·2377	3·7727		
·6	·5705	1·2073	1·6586	2·1127	2·7403	3·2480	3·7932		
·8	·5680	1·2027	1·6542	2·1101	2·7430	3·2573	3·8117		
6·0	0·5657	1·1985	1·6500	2·1076	2·7453	3·2657	3·8285		
·2	·5636	1·1945	1·6462	2·1052	2·7473	3·2732	3·8439		
·4	·5617	1·1909	1·6426	2·1029	2·7490	3·2800	3·8579		
·6	·5599	1·1875	1·6392	2·1007	2·7505	3·2862	3·8708		
·8	·5582	1·1843	1·6360	2·0986	2·7518	3·2919	3·8827		
7·0	0·5566	1·1813	1·6330	2·0966	2·7529	3·2971	3·8937		
·2	·5552	1·1785	1·6302	2·0947	2·7539	3·3018	3·9038		
·4	·5538	1·1759	1·6275	2·0928	2·7548	3·3062	3·9132		
·6	·5525	1·1734	1·6250	2·0911	2·7555	3·3102	3·9220		
·8	·5513	1·1711	1·6226	2·0894	2·7562	3·3140	3·9302		
8·0	0·5501	1·1689	1·6204	2·0878	2·7568	3·3174	3·9379		
·2	·5490	1·1668	1·6182	2·0863	2·7573	3·3207	3·9451		
·4	·5480	1·1648	1·6162	2·0848	2·7578	3·3237	3·9518		
·6	·5471	1·1629	1·6142	2·0834	2·7582	3·3265	3·9581		
·8	·5461	1·1612	1·6124	2·0821	2·7585	3·3291	3·9641		
9·0	0·5453	1·1595	1·6106	2·0808	2·7589	3·3316	3·9697		
				$\sqrt{\beta_1} = 0\cdot5$					
2·0	0·7987	1·5529	1·8335	1·9816	2·0745	2·1066	2·1232	2·1407	I (J)
·2	·7441	1·5036	1·8521	2·0777	2·2580	2·3392	2·3914	2·4849	
·4	·7070	1·4587	1·8480	2·1325	2·3962	2·5358	2·6389	2·9323	
·6	·6802	1·4207	1·8349	2·1622	2·4965	2·6929	2·8519	3·5568	
·8	·6599	1·3889	1·8188	2·1773	2·5687	2·8158	3·0290	4·5284	I (Ω)
3·0	0·6439	1·3624	1·8025	2·1840	2·6212	2·9119	3·1744	6·3589	
·2	·6310	1·3400	1·7870	2·1858	2·6599	2·9876	3·2937	11·7798	
·4	·6204	1·3209	1·7725	2·1848	2·6889	3·0478	3·3921	∞	VI
·6	·6115	1·3044	1·7594	2·1822	2·7110	3·0965	3·4740		IV
·8	·6039	1·2902	1·7474	2·1787	2·7280	3·1362	3·5428		
4·0	0·5973	1·2777	1·7365	2·1747	2·7413	3·1691	3·6012		$\downarrow$
·2	·5916	1·2667	1·7267	2·1704	2·7518	3·1966	3·6511		
·4	·5866	1·2569	1·7177	2·1662	2·7602	3·2198	3·6941		
·6	·5821	1·2481	1·7095	2·1619	2·7669	3·2396	3·7315		
·8	·5781	1·2403	1·7020	2·1578	2·7723	3·2566	3·7642		
5·0	0·5746	1·2331	1·6951	2·1539	2·7768	3·2713	3·7931		
·2	·5713	1·2267	1·6888	2·1500	2·7804	3·2841	3·8187		
·4	·5684	1·2208	1·6829	2·1464	2·7834	3·2954	3·8415		
·6	·5658	1·2154	1·6775	2·1429	2·7859	3·3054	3·8620		
·8	·5633	1·2104	1·6725	2·1396	2·7879	3·3142	3·8804		

Table 32 (*continued*). *Pearson curves*

Table A (*cont.*). *Lower standardized percentage points (all signs negative)*

Percent	0·0	0·25	0·5	1·0	2·5	5·0	10·0	25·0	50·0
β₂				$\sqrt{\beta_1} = 0.5$ (*cont.*)					
6·0	∞	3·0283	2·6548	2·2999	1·8480	1·5081	1·1549	0·6195	0·0486
·2	—	3·0561	2·6728	2·3103	1·8511	1·5075	1·1521	·6163	·0475
·4	—	3·0818	2·6894	2·3197	1·8538	1·5068	1·1495	·6134	·0466
·6	—	3·1056	2·7047	2·3284	1·8562	1·5061	1·1471	·6106	·0457
·8	—	3·1277	2·7188	2·3363	1·8583	1·5055	1·1448	·6081	·0448
7·0	—	3·1482	2·7319	2·3437	1·8603	1·5048	1·1426	0·6057	0·0441
·2	—	3·1674	2·7441	2·3505	1·8620	1·5041	1·1406	·6035	·0434
·4	—	3·1853	2·7554	2·3568	1·8636	1·5034	1·1386	·6014	·0427
·6	—	3·2021	2·7660	2·3626	1·8651	1·5028	1·1368	·5995	·0421
·8	—	3·2178	2·7759	2·3681	1·8664	1·5022	1·1351	·5977	·0415
8·0	—	3·2327	2·7852	2·3732	1·8677	1·5015	1·1334	0·5959	0·0410
·2	—	3·2466	2·7940	2·3780	1·8688	1·5009	1·1319	·5943	·0405
·4	—	3·2598	2·8022	2·3825	1·8698	1·5003	1·1304	·5928	·0400
·6	—	3·2722	2·8100	2·3867	1·8708	1·4997	1·1290	·5913	·0395
·8	—	3·2840	2·8173	2·3906	1·8717	1·4992	1·1276	·5899	·0391
9·0	—	3·2951	2·8242	2·3943	1·8725	1·4986	1·1264	0·5886	0·0387
				$\sqrt{\beta_1} = 0.6$					
2·2	1·2122	1·2120	1·2115	1·2102	1·2038	1·1871	1·1375	0·8928	0·2311
·4	1·3490	1·3463	1·3431	1·3361	1·3130	1·2707	1·1776	·8549	·1895
·6	1·5055	1·4905	1·4792	1·4594	1·4083	1·3335	1·1981	·8205	·1613
·8	1·6914	1·6393	1·6131	1·5733	1·4868	1·3786	1·2067	·7911	·1410
3·0	1·9234	1·7857	1·7385	1·6741	1·5498	1·4105	1·2087	0·7664	0·1258
·2	2·2363	1·9244	1·8522	1·7610	1·5998	1·4331	1·2070	·7457	·1141
·4	2·7207	2·0520	1·9531	1·8351	1·6395	1·4492	1·2034	·7282	·1049
·6	3·8016	2·1676	2·0418	1·8981	1·6714	1·4607	1·1989	·7133	·0974
·8	∞	2·2712	2·1194	1·9518	1·6971	1·4690	1·1940	·7005	·0912
4·0	—	2·3638	2·1874	1·9976	1·7182	1·4751	1·1890	0·6894	0·0860
·2	—	2·4464	2·2470	2·0371	1·7356	1·4795	1·1842	·6797	·0816
·4	—	2·5203	2·2996	2·0713	1·7501	1·4827	1·1795	·6712	·0778
·6	—	2·5865	2·3461	2·1012	1·7623	1·4850	1·1751	·6636	·0745
·8	—	2·6460	2·3875	2·1274	1·7727	1·4867	1·1709	·6569	·0716
5·0	—	2·6997	2·4245	2·1505	1·7817	1·4879	1·1670	0·6508	0·0691
·2	—	2·7483	2·4577	2·1710	1·7894	1·4887	1·1633	·6454	·0668
·4	—	2·7925	2·4876	2·1894	1·7961	1·4893	1·1599	·6405	·0648
·6	—	2·8327	2·5147	2·2059	1·8020	1·4896	1·1566	·6360	·0630
·8	—	2·8696	2·5394	2·2207	1·8072	1·4897	1·1536	·6319	·0613
6·0	—	2·9034	2·5618	2·2342	1·8118	1·4897	1·1508	0·6281	0·0599
·2	—	2·9345	2·5824	2·2464	1·8159	1·4896	1·1481	·6246	·0585
·4	—	2·9632	2·6014	2·2576	1·8196	1·4895	1·1456	·6214	·0572
·6	—	2·9897	2·6188	2·2678	1·8229	1·4892	1·1432	·6184	·0561
·8	—	3·0144	2·6349	2·2772	1·8258	1·4890	1·1410	·6157	·0550
7·0	—	3·0373	2·6498	2·2859	1·8285	1·4887	1·1389	0·6131	0·0540
·2	—	3·0587	2·6637	2·2939	1·8310	1·4883	1·1369	·6107	·0531
·4	—	3·0787	2·6766	2·3014	1·8332	1·4880	1·1350	·6085	·0523
·6	—	3·0974	2·6887	2·3083	1·8353	1·4876	1·1332	·6064	·0515
·8	—	3·1150	2·7000	2·3147	1·8371	1·4872	1·1315	·6044	·0508
8·0	—	3·1315	2·7106	2·3207	1·8388	1·4868	1·1299	0·6025	0·0501
·2	—	3·1470	2·7205	2·3264	1·8404	1·4864	1·1284	·6008	·0494
·4	—	3·1617	2·7299	2·3316	1·8419	1·4861	1·1269	·5991	·0488
·6	—	3·1755	2·7387	2·3366	1·8433	1·4857	1·1255	·5975	·0482
·8	—	3·1886	2·7470	2·3412	1·8445	1·4853	1·1242	·5961	·0477
9·0	—	3·2010	2·7548	2·3456	1·8457	1·4849	1·1230	0·5946	0·0472

Table 32 (*continued*)

Table A (*cont.*). *Upper standardized percentage points (all signs positive)*

Percent	25·0	10·0	5·0	2·5	1·0	0·5	0·25	0·0	Type
β_2				$\sqrt{\beta_1} = 0\cdot5$ (*cont.*)					
6·0	0·5611	1·2059	1·6678	2·1365	2·7896	3·3221	3·8971	∞	IV
·2	·5590	1·2016	1·6635	2·1335	2·7910	3·3292	3·9123		↓
·4	·5571	1·1977	1·6595	2·1307	2·7922	3·3355	3·9261		
·6	·5553	1·1940	1·6557	2·1280	2·7932	3·3413	3·9387		
·8	·5536	1·1906	1·6521	2·1254	2·7940	3·3465	3·9504		
7·0	0·5521	1·1875	1·6488	2·1229	2·7946	3·3513	3·9611		
·2	·5507	1·1845	1·6456	2·1206	2·7952	3·3556	3·9709		
·4	·5493	1·1817	1·6427	2·1184	2·7956	3·3596	3·9801		
·6	·5480	1·1790	1·6399	2·1163	2·7959	3·3633	3·9886		
·8	·5469	1·1766	1·6372	2·1143	2·7962	3·3666	3·9965		
8·0	0·5457	1·1742	1·6347	2·1123	2·7964	3·3697	4·0039		
·2	·5447	1·1720	1·6323	2·1105	2·7966	3·3726	4·0108		
·4	·5437	1·1699	1·6301	2·1087	2·7967	3·3753	4·0172		
·6	·5427	1·1679	1·6279	2·1071	2·7968	3·3778	4·0233		
·8	·5418	1·1660	1·6259	2·1054	2·7968	3·3801	4·0290		
9·0	0·5410	1·1642	1·6240	2·1039	2·7968	3·3823	4·0344		
β_2				$\sqrt{\beta_1} = 0\cdot6$					
2·2	0·7491	1·5569	1·8982	2·0996	2·2428	2·2996	2·3323	2·3764	} I (J)
·4	·7074	1·5033	1·8971	2·1693	2·4041	2·5187	2·5974	2·7701	
·6	·6783	1·4580	1·8824	2·2061	2·5212	2·6966	2·8318	3·2928	
·8	·6567	1·4205	1·8634	2·2239	2·6046	2·8360	3·0287	4·0427	} I (∩)
3·0	0·6400	1·3896	1·8438	2·2310	2·6640	2·9440	3·1904	5·2568	
·2	·6267	1·3637	1·8252	2·2320	2·7068	3·0281	3·3224	7·7069	
·4	·6158	1·3418	1·8081	2·2298	2·7382	3·0943	3·4305	16·4350	
·6	·6068	1·3232	1·7925	2·2257	2·7614	3·1469	3·5198	∞	VI
·8	·5991	1·3071	1·7784	2·2206	2·7789	3·1894	3·5940		IV
4·0	0·5925	1·2931	1·7657	2·2151	2·7922	3·2241	3·6565		↓
·2	·5867	1·2809	1·7542	2·2095	2·8024	3·2527	3·7095		
·4	·5817	1·2700	1·7438	2·2039	2·8103	3·2766	3·7548		
·6	·5773	1·2603	1·7343	2·1985	2·8165	3·2968	3·7939		
·8	·5733	1·2517	1·7257	2·1932	2·8213	3·3139	3·8280		
5·0	0·5697	1·2438	1·7178	2·1882	2·8251	3·3286	3·8578		
·2	·5665	1·2368	1·7106	2·1834	2·8280	3·3413	3·8840		
·4	·5636	1·2303	1·7040	2·1789	2·8304	3·3524	3·9074		
·6	·5610	1·2245	1·6978	2·1746	2·8322	3·3620	3·9281		
·8	·5586	1·2191	1·6922	2·1705	2·8336	3·3706	3·9468		
6·0	0·5564	1·2141	1·6869	2·1667	2·8347	3·3781	3·9635		
·2	·5543	1·2095	1·6820	2·1631	2·8355	3·3848	3·9787		
·4	·5524	1·2053	1·6774	2·1596	2·8361	3·3908	3·9925		
·6	·5507	1·2013	1·6732	2·1563	2·8365	3·3961	4·0051		
·8	·5491	1·1977	1·6692	2·1532	2·8368	3·4010	4·0165		
7·0	0·5475	1·1942	1·6655	2·1503	2·8370	3·4054	4·0271		
·2	·5461	1·1910	1·6620	2·1475	2·8370	3·4093	4·0368		
·4	·5448	1·1880	1·6586	2·1449	2·8370	3·4129	4·0458		
·6	·5436	1·1852	1·6555	2·1424	2·8369	3·4162	4·0541		
·8	·5424	1·1825	1·6526	2·1400	2·8368	3·4192	4·0618		
8·0	0·5413	1·1800	1·6498	2·1377	2·8366	3·4220	4·0689		
·2	·5402	1·1777	1·6472	2·1355	2·8364	3·4246	4·0756		
·4	·5393	1·1754	1·6446	2·1334	2·8361	3·4269	4·0818		
·6	·5383	1·1733	1·6423	2·1314	2·8359	3·4291	4·0877		
·8	·5374	1·1713	1·6400	2·1295	2·8356	3·4311	4·0931		
9·0	0·5366	1·1694	1·6378	2·1277	2·8353	3·4330	4·0983		

Percent	0·0	0·25	0·5	1·0	2·5	5·0	10·0	25·0	50·0
β_2					$\sqrt{\beta_1} = 0\cdot7$				
2·4	1·1752	1·1750	1·1746	1·1733	1·1673	1·1518	1·1056	0·8780	0·2538
·6	1·2998	1·2975	1·2947	1·2887	1·2683	1·2304	1·1458	·8467	·2120
·8	1·4406	1·4287	1·4193	1·4025	1·3580	1·2915	1·1687	·8169	·1826
3·0	1·6053	1·5647	1·5429	1·5091	1·4338	1·3372	1·1805	0·7906	0·1611
·2	1·8062	1·7000	1·6604	1·6052	1·4961	1·3709	1·1855	·7680	·1447
·4	2·0680	1·8299	1·7686	1·6896	1·5466	1·3956	1·1865	·7487	·1319
·6	2·4484	1·9512	1·8661	1·7627	1·5877	1·4138	1·1851	·7322	·1216
·8	3·1566	2·0625	1·9529	1·8257	1·6211	1·4275	1·1825	·7179	·1132
4·0	∞	2·1634	2·0298	1·8800	1·6486	1·4377	1·1792	0·7055	0·1063
·2	—	2·2545	2·0977	1·9269	1·6714	1·4455	1·1756	·6947	·1004
·4	—	2·3366	2·1579	1·9677	1·6905	1·4514	1·1719	·6852	·0954
·6	—	2·4105	2·2114	2·0033	1·7065	1·4560	1·1682	·6768	·0911
·8	—	2·4771	2·2590	2·0345	1·7203	1·4596	1·1646	·6694	·0873
5·0	—	2·5374	2·3016	2·0622	1·7320	1·4624	1·1611	0·6627	0·0840
·2	—	2·5920	2·3398	2·0867	1·7422	1·4646	1·1578	·6566	·0811
·4	—	2·6417	2·3743	2·1085	1·7511	1·4663	1·1546	·6512	·0785
·6	—	2·6870	2·4055	2·1282	1·7589	1·4676	1·1517	·6462	·0761
·8	—	2·7285	2·4339	2·1458	1·7657	1·4686	1·1488	·6417	·0740
6·0	—	2·7665	2·4598	2·1619	1·7718	1·4694	1·1462	0·6375	0·0721
·2	—	2·8015	2·4835	2·1764	1·7773	1·4700	1·1436	·6337	·0703
·4	—	2·8338	2·5052	2·1897	1·7822	1·4705	1·1413	·6302	·0688
·6	—	2·8637	2·5252	2·2018	1·7865	1·4708	1·1390	·6270	·0673
·8	—	2·8914	2·5437	2·2130	1·7905	1·4710	1·1369	·6239	·0660
7·0	—	2·9172	2·5609	2·2232	1·7941	1·4712	1·1348	0·6211	0·0647
·2	—	2·9412	2·5768	2·2327	1·7974	1·4713	1·1329	·6185	·0636
·4	—	2·9636	2·5916	2·2415	1·8004	1·4713	1·1311	·6161	·0625
·6	—	2·9846	2·6054	2·2497	1·8031	1·4713	1·1294	·6138	·0615
·8	—	3·0043	2·6183	2·2573	1·8056	1·4712	1·1277	·6166	·0606
8·0	—	3·0228	2·6304	2·2644	1·8079	1·4711	1·1262	0·6096	0·0597
·2	—	3·0402	2·6417	2·2710	1·8101	1·4710	1·1247	·6077	·0589
·4	—	3·0566	2·6524	2·2773	1·8121	1·4709	1·1233	·6059	·0581
·6	—	3·0721	2·6625	2·2831	1·8139	1·4707	1·1219	·6042	·0574
·8	—	3·0868	2·6720	2·2886	1·8156	1·4705	1·1206	·6026	·0567
9·0	—	3·1006	2·6809	2·2938	1·8172	1·4704	1·1194	0·6010	0·0561
					$\sqrt{\beta_1} = 0\cdot8$				
2·6	1·1248	1·1246	1·1243	1·1235	1·1189	1·1066	1·0680	0·8666	0·2804
·8	1·2361	1·2346	1·2327	1·2284	1·2128	1·1822	1·1104	·8414	·2373
3·0	1·3601	1·3524	1·3458	1·3332	1·2983	1·2432	1·1369	0·8158	0·2063
·2	1·5021	1·4755	1·4594	1·4334	1·3725	1·2907	1·1525	·7923	·1831
·4	1·6707	1·5998	1·5695	1·5256	1·4350	1·3269	1·1610	·7715	·1652
·6	1·8811	1·7212	1·6727	1·6082	1·4871	1·3544	1·1649	·7534	·1511
·8	2·1654	1·8366	1·7674	1·6810	1·5301	1·3753	1·1661	·7376	·1396
4·0	2·6117	1·9440	1·8530	1·7448	1·5658	1·3915	1·1655	0·7238	0·1303
·2	3·7639	2·0429	1·9298	1·8004	1·5955	1·4039	1·1639	·7117	·1224
·4	∞	2·1331	1·9984	1·8490	1·6204	1·4137	1·1617	·7011	·1158
·6	—	2·2151	2·0597	1·8915	1·6415	1·4214	1·1592	·6917	·1101
·8	—	2·2896	2·1146	1·9290	1·6595	1·4276	1·1565	·6834	·1052
5·0	—	2·3572	2·1638	1·9621	1·6749	1·4326	1·1538	0·6759	0·1009
·2	—	2·4187	2·2080	1·9915	1·6883	1·4366	1·1510	·6692	·0971
·4	—	2·4748	2·2480	2·0177	1·6999	1·4398	1·1483	·6631	·0937
·6	—	2·5260	2·2841	2·0412	1·7101	1·4425	1·1457	·6576	·0907
·8	—	2·5729	2·3170	2·0623	1·7191	1·4447	1·1432	·6526	·0880
6·0	—	2·6159	2·3469	2·0815	1·7271	1·4465	1·1408	0·6480	0·0856
·2	—	2·6555	2·3743	2·0988	1·7342	1·4480	1·1385	·6437	·0834
·4	—	2·6920	2·3994	2·1147	1·7406	1·4493	1·1363	·6399	·0814
·6	—	2·7258	2·4226	2·1291	1·7464	1·4503	1·1342	·6363	·0795
·8	—	2·7572	2·4439	2·1424	1·7516	1·4512	1·1322	·6329	·0778

Table 32 (*continued*)

Table A (*cont.*). *Upper standardized percentage points (all signs positive)*

Percent	25·0	10·0	5·0	2·5	1·0	0·5	0·25	0·0	Type
β_2				$\sqrt{\beta_1} = 0.7$					
2·4	0·7094	1·5608	1·9497	2·1948	2·3828	2·4633	2·5128	2·5910	} I (J)
·6	·6769	1·5055	1·9360	2·2460	2·5257	2·6687	2·7711	3·0266	
·8	·6536	1·4602	1·9144	2·2703	2·6271	2·8318	2·9936	3·6118	
3·0	0·6360	1·4232	1·8913	2·2797	2·6983	2·9579	3·1778	4·4624	} I (Ω)
·2	·6222	1·3927	1·8691	2·2809	2·7485	3·0552	3·3282	5·8623	
·4	·6111	1·3672	1·8486	2·2777	2·7843	3·1307	3·4505	8·7546	
·6	·6019	1·3457	1·8301	2·2723	2·8102	3·1899	3·5506	19·5595	
·8	·5941	1·3273	1·8134	2·2657	2·8291	3·2370	3·6332	∞	VI
4·0	0·5874	1·3113	1·7984	2·2586	2·8430	3·2748	3·7020		IV
·2	·5817	1·2975	1·7850	2·2514	2·8534	3·3057	3·7598		
·4	·5767	1·2852	1·7728	2·2443	2·8611	3·3311	3·8088		↓
·6	·5722	1·2744	1·7619	2·2375	2·8669	3·3522	3·8508		
·8	·5683	1·2647	1·7519	2·2310	2·8712	3·3700	3·8869		
5·0	0·5648	1·2561	1·7428	2·2248	2·8744	3·3850	3·9184		
·2	·5616	1·2482	1·7345	2·2189	2·8767	3·3978	3·9459		
·4	·5587	1·2411	1·7269	2·2134	2·8784	3·4089	3·9702		
·6	·5561	1·2347	1·7199	2·2082	2·8796	3·4184	3·9917		
·8	·5537	1·2288	1·7135	2·2032	2·8804	3·4267	4·0109		
6·0	0·5516	1·2233	1·7075	2·1986	2·8808	3·4340	4·0280		
·2	·5495	1·2183	1·7019	2·1942	2·8810	3·4404	4·0434		
·4	·5477	1·2137	1·6968	2·1901	2·8810	3·4461	4·0574		
·6	·5460	1·2094	1·6920	2·1862	2·8809	3·4511	4·0700		
·8	·5444	1·2054	1·6875	2·1825	2·8806	3·4556	4·0815		
7·0	0·5429	1·2017	1·6833	2·1790	2·8803	3·4597	4·0921		
·2	·5415	1·1982	1·6793	2·1757	2·8798	3·4633	4·1017		
·4	·5402	1·1950	1·6756	2·1725	2·8793	3·4665	4·1106		
·6	·5390	1·1919	1·6721	2·1695	2·8788	3·4695	4·1188		
·8	·5378	1·1890	1·6688	2·1667	2·8782	3·4722	4·1263		
8·0	0·5367	1·1863	1·6657	2·1640	2·8776	3·4746	4·1333		
·2	·5357	1·1838	1·6628	2·1614	2·8770	3·4768	4·1398		
·4	·5348	1·1814	1·6600	2·1590	2·8764	3·4789	4·1459		
·6	·5338	1·1791	1·6573	2·1566	2·8757	3·4807	4·1516		
·8	·5330	1·1769	1·6548	2·1544	2·8751	3·4824	4·1568		
9·0	0·5322	1·1749	1·6524	2·1523	2·8744	3·4840	4·1618		
				$\sqrt{\beta_1} = 0.8$					
2·6	0·6751	1·5676	1·9954	2·2755	2·4990	2·5989	2·6624	2·7718	} I (J)
·8	·6497	1·5112	1·9732	2·3137	2·6286	2·7937	2·9141	3·2361	
3·0	0·6312	1·4657	1·9465	2·3292	2·7192	2·9462	3·1279	3·8601	
·2	·6169	1·4287	1·9201	2·3325	2·7819	3·0634	3·3035	4·7653	
·4	·6055	1·3983	1·8956	2·3293	2·8257	3·1533	3·4463	6·2421	} I (Ω)
·6	·5962	1·3729	1·8734	2·3228	2·8564	3·2228	3·5623	9·2144	
·8	·5885	1·3514	1·8535	2·3146	2·8782	3·2772	3·6571	19·1654	
4·0	0·5818	1·3329	1·8358	2·3059	2·8937	3·3203	3·7352	∞	} VI
·2	·5761	1·3170	1·8199	2·2970	2·9049	3·3548	3·8002		
·4	·5712	1·3030	1·8056	2·2882	2·9128	3·3828	3·8548		IV
·6	·5668	1·2908	1·7927	2·2798	2·9185	3·4057	3·9010		
·8	·5629	1·2799	1·7811	2·2718	2·9225	3·4246	3·9405		↓
5·0	0·5594	1·2701	1·7706	2·2642	2·9252	3·4405	3·9745		
·2	·5563	1·2614	1·7610	2·2571	2·9270	3·4538	4·0041		
·4	·5535	1·2534	1·7522	2·2504	2·9280	3·4651	4·0299		
·6	·5509	1·2463	1·7441	2·2441	2·9286	3·4747	4·0526		
·8	·5486	1·2397	1·7367	2·2381	2·9287	3·4830	4·0727		
6·0	0·5465	1·2337	1·7299	2·2326	2·9285	3·4902	4·0906		
·2	·5445	1·2282	1·7236	2·2273	2·9280	3·4964	4·1066		
·4	·5427	1·2231	1·7177	2·2224	2·9274	3·5019	4·1209		
·6	·5410	1·2184	1·7123	2·2177	2·9267	3·5066	4·1338		
·8	·5394	1·2140	1·7072	2·2134	2·9258	3·5108	4·1455		

Percent	0·0	0·25	0·5	1·0	2·5	5·0	10·0	25·0	50·0
β_2					$\sqrt{\beta_1} = 0.8$ (*cont.*)				
7·0	∞	2·7863	2·4637	2·1546	1·7563	1·4519	1·1303	0·6298	0·0763
·2	—	2·8134	2·4820	2·1659	1·7606	1·4525	1·1285	·6270	·0748
·4	—	2·8388	2·4991	2·1763	1·7645	1·4530	1·1268	·6243	·0735
·6	—	2·8625	2·5150	2·1860	1·7681	1·4534	1·1252	·6218	·0722
·8	—	2·8847	2·5298	2·1950	1·7714	1·4538	1·1236	·6194	·0711
8·0	—	2·9055	2·5437	2·2035	1·7745	1·4540	1·1221	0·6172	0·0700
·2	—	2·9251	2·5568	2·2113	1·7773	1·4543	1·1207	·6151	·0690
·4	—	2·9436	2·5690	2·2187	1·7799	1·4544	1·1193	·6131	·0680
·6	—	2·9611	2·5805	2·2256	1·7823	1·4546	1·1180	·6113	·0672
·8	—	2·9775	2·5914	2·2320	1·7846	1·4547	1·1168	·6095	·0663
9·0	—	2·9931	2·6017	2·2381	1·7867	1·4548	1·1156	0·6078	0·0655
					$\sqrt{\beta_1} = 0.9$				
2·8	1·0651	1·0650	1·0649	1·0644	1·0617	1·0533	1·0247	0·8560	0·3114
3·0	1·1633	1·1626	1·1616	1·1590	1·1488	1·1266	1·0703	0·8372	0·2661
·2	1·2709	1·2670	1·2630	1·2549	1·2303	1·1883	1·1013	·8159	·2328
·4	1·3914	1·3769	1·3665	1·3486	1·3033	1·2382	1·1214	·7952	·2075
·6	1·5303	1·4897	1·4688	1·4369	1·3667	1·2776	1·1339	·7762	·1878
·8	1·6963	1·6021	1·5669	1·5179	1·4206	1·3085	1·1413	·7591	·1721
4·0	1·9060	1·7110	1·6587	1·5907	1·4661	1·3327	1·1453	0·7440	0·1593
·2	2·1953	1·8144	1·7432	1·6555	1·5045	1·3517	1·1471	·7307	·1488
·4	2·6754	1·9110	1·8201	1·7128	1·5369	1·3669	1·1474	·7189	·1399
·6	∞	2·0004	1·8896	1·7634	1·5644	1·3790	1·1468	·7084	·1324
·8	—	2·0826	1·9524	1·8082	1·5879	1·3887	1·1456	·6990	·1259
5·0	—	2·1580	2·0091	1·8479	1·6081	1·3967	1·1440	0·6907	0·1203
·2	—	2·2269	2·0602	1·8832	1·6256	1·4032	1·1422	·6831	·1154
·4	—	2·2900	2·1065	1·9147	1·6408	1·4086	1·1402	·6763	·1110
·6	—	2·3479	2·1484	1·9429	1·6541	1·4131	1·1382	·6702	·1072
·8	—	2·4009	2·1866	1·9683	1·6658	1·4169	1·1362	·6646	·1038
6·0	—	2·4497	2·2214	1·9913	1·6762	1·4201	1·1342	0·6595	0·1007
·2	—	2·4946	2·2532	2·0121	1·6855	1·4228	1·1323	·6548	·0979
·4	—	2·5361	2·2824	2·0311	1·6938	1·4251	1·1304	·6504	·0953
·6	—	2·5745	2·3092	2·0484	1·7013	1·4271	1·1285	·6465	·0930
·8	—	2·6101	2·3340	2·0643	1·7081	1·4288	1·1268	·6428	·0909
7·0	—	2·6431	2·3569	2·0789	1·7142	1·4303	1·1251	0·6393	0·0889
·2	—	2·6739	2·3782	2·0923	1·7198	1·4316	1·1234	·6362	·0871
·4	—	2·7027	2·3979	2·1047	1·7248	1·4327	1·1218	·6332	·0855
·6	—	2·7296	2·4163	2·1163	1·7295	1·4336	1·1203	·6304	·0839
·8	—	2·7547	2·4334	2·1270	1·7338	1·4345	1·1189	·6278	·0825
8·0	—	2·7784	2·4495	2·1370	1·7378	1·4352	1·1175	0·6254	0·0812
·2	—	2·8006	2·4645	2·1463	1·7414	1·4359	1·1162	·6231	·0799
·4	—	2·8215	2·4787	2·1550	1·7448	1·4365	1·1149	·6209	·0787
·6	—	2·8412	2·4919	2·1632	1·7479	1·4370	1·1136	·6189	·0776
·8	—	2·8598	2·5045	2·1709	1·7509	1·4374	1·1125	·6169	·0766
9·0	—	2·8775	2·5163	2·1781	1·7536	1·4378	1·1113	0·6151	0·0756
					$\sqrt{\beta_1} = 1.0$				
3·0	1·0000	1·0000	0·9999	0·9998	0·9985	0·9938	0·9753	0·8437	0·3472
·2	1·0860	1·0858	1·0854	1·0842	1·0786	1·0646	1·0245	·8323	·2990
·4	1·1787	1·1771	1·1752	1·1709	1·1558	1·1269	1·0606	·8159	·2628
·6	1·2803	1·2738	1·2682	1·2574	1·2272	1·1793	1·0858	·7983	·2350
·8	1·3940	1·3745	1·3619	1·3412	1·2911	1·2222	1·1029	·7813	·2131
4·0	1·5249	1·4768	1·4539	1·4199	1·3470	1·2569	1·1143	0·7655	0·1955
·2	1·6811	1·5782	1·5420	1·4923	1·3953	1·2848	1·1216	·7512	·1812
·4	1·8777	1·6765	1·6248	1·5580	1·4366	1·3073	1·1261	·7383	·1692
·6	2·1477	1·7701	1·7014	1·6171	1·4721	1·3255	1·1287	·7267	·1591
·8	2·5949	1·8582	1·7718	1·6700	1·5026	1·3403	1·1300	·7163	·1506

Table 32 (*continued*)

Table A (*cont.*). *Upper standardized percentage points* (*all signs positive*)

Percent	25·0	10·0	5·0	2·5	1·0	0·5	0·25	0·0	Type
β_2				$\sqrt{\beta_1} = 0\cdot 8$ (*cont.*)					
7·0	0·5380	1·2100	1·7024	2·2092	2·9249	3·5145	4·1562	∞	IV
·2	·5366	1·2062	1·6980	2·2053	2·9239	3·5178	4·1659		↓
·4	·5354	1·2026	1·6938	2·2016	2·9229	3·5208	4·1748		
·6	·5342	1·1993	1·6899	2·1981	2·9219	3·5234	4·1829		
·8	·5331	1·1962	1·6862	2·1948	2·9208	3·5257	4·1904		
8·0	0·5320	1·1932	1·6827	2·1916	2·9198	3·5278	4·1974		
·2	·5310	1·1905	1·6794	2·1886	2·9187	2·5297	4·2038		
·4	·5301	1·1879	1·6762	2·1857	2·9177	3·5314	4·2097		
·6	·5292	1·1854	1·6733	2·1830	2·9166	3·5330	4·2152		
·8	·5284	1·1831	1·6705	2·1804	2·9156	3·5344	4·2204		
9·0	0·5276	1·1809	1·6678	2·1779	2·9146	3·5356	4·2252		
				$\sqrt{\beta_1} = 0\cdot 9$					
2·8	0·6433	1·5786	2·0399	2·3470	2·5960	2·7089	2·7813	2·9096	
3·0	0·6240	1·5207	2·0112	2·3766	2·7174	2·8972	3·0290	3·3855	I (J)
·2	·6095	1·4745	1·9803	2·3859	2·8011	3·0436	3·2378	4·0196	
·4	·5982	1·4371	1·9510	2·3845	2·8584	3·1554	3·4089	4·9251	
·6	·5891	1·4063	1·9242	2·3777	2·8977	3·2410	3·5476	6·3595	
·8	·5815	1·3806	1·9002	2·3683	2·9248	3·3068	3·6601	9·0698	I (Ω)
4·0	0·5751	1·3588	1·8789	2·3578	2·9436	3·3581	3·7519	16·5572	
·2	·5695	1·3402	1·8599	2·3470	2·9566	3·3984	3·8275	218·1953	
·4	·5647	1·3240	1·8429	2·3364	2·9655	3·4306	3·8902	∞	VI
·6	·5605	1·3099	1·8277	2·3262	2·9715	3·4565	3·9428		IV
·8	·5568	1·2974	1·8141	2·3165	2·9754	3·4776	3·9873		↓
5·0	0·5534	1·2863	1·8017	2·3073	2·9778	3·4949	4·0252		
·2	·5504	1·2764	1·7905	2·2986	2·9791	3·5092	4·0578		
·4	·5477	1·2675	1·7803	2·2905	2·9796	3·5211	4·0860		
·6	·5452	1·2594	1·7710	2·2829	2·9795	3·5312	4·1106		
·8	·5430	1·2521	1·7624	2·2758	2·9790	3·5397	4·1321		
6·0	0·5409	1·2454	1·7546	2·2692	2·9781	3·5469	4·1512		
·2	·5390	1·2393	1·7473	2·2629	2·9770	3·5531	4·1680		
·4	·5373	1·2336	1·7406	2·2570	2·9757	3·5584	4·1831		
·6	·5357	1·2284	1·7344	2·2515	2·9743	3·5629	4·1966		
·8	·5342	1·2236	1·7286	2·2463	2·9728	3·5669	4·2087		
7·0	0·5328	1·2191	1·7232	2·2414	2·9713	3·5703	4·2196		
·2	·5315	1·2149	1·7181	2·2368	2·9697	3·5733	4·2296		
·4	·5302	1·2110	1·7134	2·2325	2·9681	3·5759	4·2386		
·6	·5291	1·2074	1·7089	2·2283	2·9665	3·5782	4·2468		
·8	·5280	1·2040	1·7048	2·2244	2·9650	3·5802	4·2543		
8·0	0·5270	1·2008	1·7008	2·2207	2·9634	3·5820	4·2613		
·2	·5261	1·1978	1·6971	2·2172	2·9619	3·5835	4·2676		
·4	·5252	1·1949	1·6936	2·2139	2·9603	3·5849	4·2735		
·6	·5243	1·1922	1·6903	2·2107	2·9588	3·5861	4·2789		
·8	·5235	1·1897	1·6871	2·2077	2·9574	3·5872	4·2840		
9·0	0·5227	1·1873	1·6841	2·2048	2·9560	3·5882	4·2887		
				$\sqrt{\beta_1} = 1\cdot 0$					
3·0	0·6114	1·5946	2·0859	2·4130	2·6767	2·7951	2·8704	3·0000	I (J)
·2	·5977	1·5344	2·0519	2·4372	2·7945	2·9815	3·1172	3·4706	
·4	·5873	1·4867	2·0171	2·4421	2·8750	3·1259	3·3253	4·0878	
·6	·5789	1·4482	1·9847	2·4371	2·9294	3·2360	3·4956	4·9469	
·8	·5720	1·4166	1·9555	2·4273	2·9662	3·3198	3·6336	6·2512	I (Ω)
4·0	0·5661	1·3903	1·9296	2·4153	2·9909	3·3840	3·7454	8·5249	
·2	·5611	1·3680	1·9066	2·4026	3·0076	3·4336	3·8365	13·6811	
·4	·5567	1·3490	1·8862	2·3899	3·0186	3·4725	3·9112	38·8777	
·6	·5528	1·3324	1·8680	2·3775	3·0257	3·5032	3·9732	∞	VI
·8	·5494	1·3179	1·8517	2·3658	3·0301	3·5278	4·0249		

Table 32 (*continued*). *Pearson curves*

Table A (*cont.*). *Lower standardized percentage points (all signs negative)*

Percent	0·0	0·25	0·5	1·0	2·5	5·0	10·0	25·0	50·0
β₂					$\sqrt{\beta_1} = 1\cdot0$ (*cont.*)				
5·0	∞	1·9403	1·8361	1·7172	1·5289	1·3524	1·1303	0·7070	0·1432
·2	—	2·0163	1·8947	1·7594	1·5516	1·3625	1·1300	·6986	·1368
·4	—	2·0866	1·9480	1·7972	1·5714	1·3709	1·1293	·6910	·1311
·6	—	2·1514	1·9965	1·8312	1·5888	1·3779	1·1283	·6841	·1262
·8	—	2·2112	2·0408	1·8617	1·6041	1·3839	1·1271	·6779	·1217
6·0	—	2·2663	2·0812	1·8894	1·6176	1·3889	1·1258	0·6721	0·1178
·2	—	2·3173	2·1182	1·9144	1·6297	1·3933	1·1244	·6669	·1142
·4	—	2·3644	2·1522	1·9372	1·6404	1·3970	1·1230	·6621	·1110
·6	—	2·4080	2·1835	1·9580	1·6501	1·4003	1·1215	·6576	·1081
·8	—	2·4485	2·2123	1·9770	1·6588	1·4031	1·1201	·6535	·1054
7·0	—	2·4861	2·2389	1·9945	1·6667	1·4056	1·1187	0·6497	0·1030
·2	—	2·5211	2·2636	2·0106	1·6739	1·4077	1·1173	·6462	·1007
·4	—	2·5539	2·2866	2·0255	1·6805	1·4096	1·1159	·6429	·0987
·6	—	2·5844	2·3079	2·0392	1·6865	1·4113	1·1146	·6398	·0968
·8	—	2·6131	2·3278	2·0520	1·6920	1·4128	1·1133	·6369	·0950
8·0	—	2·6399	2·3464	2·0639	1·6971	1·4142	1·1121	0·6342	0·0933
·2	—	2·6652	2·3639	2·0750	1·7018	1·4154	1·1109	·6317	·0918
·4	—	2·6889	2·3802	2·0854	1·7061	1·4165	1·1098	·6293	·0903
·6	—	2·7113	2·3956	2·0951	1·7102	1·4174	1·1086	·6271	·0890
·8	—	2·7325	2·4101	2·1042	1·7139	1·4183	1·1076	·6249	·0877
9·0	—	2·7525	2·4237	2·1127	1·7174	1·4191	1·1065	0·6229	0·0865
					$\sqrt{\beta_1} = 1\cdot1$				
3·2	0·9326	0·9326	0·9326	0·9326	0·9321	0·9301	0·9201	0·8270	0·3880
·4	1·0079	1·0078	1·0077	1·0073	1·0048	·9975	·9723	·8242	·3364
·6	1·0876	1·0871	1·0864	1·0845	1·0768	1·0594	1·0134	·8139	·2970
·8	1·1732	1·1710	1·1685	1·1631	1·1456	1·1138	1·0442	·8003	·2661
4·0	1·2668	1·2591	1·2528	1·2411	1·2092	1·1601	1·0666	0·7859	0·2417
·2	1·3710	1·3502	1·3373	1·3163	1·2665	1·1988	1·0826	·7717	·2218
·4	1·4899	1·4425	1·4203	1·3874	1·3173	1·2307	1·0938	·7584	·2055
·6	1·6301	1·5341	1·5001	1·4534	1·3617	1·2570	1·1016	·7462	·1919
·8	1·8033	1·6232	1·5756	1·5138	1·4004	1·2787	1·1069	·7349	·1805
5·0	2·0342	1·7087	1·6462	1·5687	1·4342	1·2967	1·1104	0·7247	0·1707
·2	2·3920	1·7898	1·7116	1·6184	1·4635	1·3116	1·1127	·7155	·1622
·4	3·4656	1·8660	1·7718	1·6632	1·4892	1·3242	1·1139	·7071	·1548
·6	∞	1·9372	1·8272	1·7037	1·5117	1·3347	1·1145	·6994	·1484
·8	—	2·0035	1·8781	1·7404	1·5316	1·3437	1·1147	·6924	·1427
6·0	—	2·0651	1·9248	1·7735	1·5491	1·3513	1·1144	0·6860	0·1376
·2	—	2·1224	1·9677	1·8036	1·5647	1·3579	1·1139	·6802	·1330
·4	—	2·1755	2·0071	1·8310	1·5786	1·3636	1·1133	·6748	·1289
·6	—	2·2249	2·0435	1·8560	1·5911	1·3686	1·1125	·6699	·1252
·8	—	2·2709	2·0770	1·8789	1·6024	1·3729	1·1116	·6653	·1219
7·0	—	2·3136	2·1081	1·8999	1·6126	1·3767	1·1106	0·6610	0·1188
·2	—	2·3535	2·1368	1·9192	1·6218	1·3801	1·1096	·6571	·1160
·4	—	2·3908	2·1635	1·9370	1·6303	1·3831	1·1086	·6534	·1134
·6	—	2·4256	2·1884	1·9535	1·6380	1·3857	1·1076	·6500	·1110
·8	—	2·4582	2·2116	1·9688	1·6450	1·3881	1·1066	·6468	·1088
8·0	—	2·4889	2·2332	1·9830	1·6515	1·3903	1·1056	0·6438	0·1068
·2	—	2·5176	2·2535	1·9963	1·6575	1·3922	1·1046	·6410	·1049
·4	—	2·5447	2·2724	2·0086	1·6631	1·3939	1·1037	·6384	·1031
·6	—	2·5702	2·2903	2·0202	1·6682	1·3955	1·1027	·6359	·1014
·8	—	2·5943	2·3071	2·0310	1·6730	1·3969	1·1018	·6335	·0999
9·0	—	2·6170	2·3229	2·0412	1·6774	1·3982	1·1009	0·6313	0·0984

Table 32 (*continued*)

Table A (*cont.*). *Upper standardized percentage points (all signs positive)*

Percent	25·0	10·0	5·0	2·5	1·0	0·5	0·25	0·0	Type
β_2				$\sqrt{\beta_1} = 1\cdot0$ (*cont.*)					
5·0	0·5463	1·3051	1·8371	2·3547	3·0325	3·5475	4·0685	∞	IV
·2	·5435	1·2938	1·8239	2·3443	3·0336	3·5636	4·1056		↓
·4	·5410	1·2836	1·8119	2·3345	3·0336	3·5768	4·1373		
·6	·5387	1·2744	1·8010	2·3254	3·0329	3·5877	4·1647		
·8	·5366	1·2661	1·7911	2·3169	3·0317	3·5967	4·1885		
6·0	0·5347	1·2586	1·7820	2·3089	3·0302	3·6042	4·2093		
·2	·5329	1·2517	1·7736	2·3015	3·0283	3·6105	4·2276		
·4	·5313	1·2454	1·7658	2·2945	3·0263	3·6158	4·2438		
·6	·5298	1·2396	1·7587	2·2880	3·0242	3·6203	4·2581		
·8	·5284	1·2342	1·7520	2·2818	3·0220	3·6240	4·2709		
7·0	0·5270	1·2293	1·7458	2·2760	3·0198	3·6273	4·2824		
·2	·5258	1·2246	1·7401	2·2706	3·0176	3·6300	4·2927		
·4	·5247	1·2203	1·7347	2·2655	3·0154	3·6323	4·3021		
·6	·5236	1·2163	1·7296	2·2606	3·0132	3·6343	4·3105		
·8	·5226	1·2126	1·7249	2·2560	3·0110	3·6360	4·3182		
8·0	0·5216	1·2091	1·7204	2·2517	3·0089	3·6374	4·3252		
·2	·5207	1·2057	1·7162	2·2476	3·0068	3·6386	4·3316		
·4	·5199	1·2026	1·7122	2·2437	3·0047	3·6397	4·3375		
·6	·5191	1·1997	1·7085	2·2400	3·0028	3·6405	4·3429		
·8	·5183	1·1969	1·7049	2·2365	3·0008	3·6413	4·3479		
9·0	0·5176	1·1943	1·7016	2·2331	2·9989	3·6419	4·3525		
β_2				$\sqrt{\beta_1} = 1\cdot1$					
3·2	0·5768	1·6161	2·1355	2·4755	2·7423	2·8583	2·9301	3·0441	
·4	·5693	1·5524	2·0965	2·4971	2·8614	3·0474	3·1795	3·4955	I (J)
·6	·5631	1·5024	2·0577	2·4991	2·9422	3·1942	3·3909	4·0752	
·8	·5579	1·4622	2·0220	2·4913	2·9962	3·3058	3·5643	4·8580	
4·0	0·5534	1·4294	1·9901	2·4789	3·0320	3·3905	3·7049	5·9907	
·2	·5495	1·4021	1·9619	2·4645	3·0556	3·4551	3·8187	7·8100	
·4	·5460	1·3790	1·9370	2·4496	3·0709	3·5047	3·9112	11·2971	I (Ω)
·6	·5428	1·3592	1·9150	2·4350	3·0805	3·5431	3·9869	21·0719	
·8	·5400	1·3421	1·8953	2·4209	3·0863	3·5733	4·0494	287·8033	
5·0	0·5374	1·3271	1·8778	2·4075	3·0893	3·5972	4·1015	∞	
·2	·5350	1·3139	1·8621	2·3950	3·0905	3·6162	4·1452		VI
·4	·5329	1·3022	1·8479	2·3833	3·0903	3·6315	4·1822		
·6	·5309	1·2916	1·8350	2·3723	3·0891	3·6438	4·2137		IV
·8	·5291	1·2822	1·8233	2·3621	3·0873	3·6538	4·2408		
6·0	0·5274	1·2736	1·8127	2·3526	3·0851	3·6620	4·2643		↓
·2	·5258	1·2658	1·8029	2·3437	3·0825	3·6688	4·2847		
·4	·5244	1·2587	1·7939	2·3354	3·0798	3·6743	4·3025		
·6	·5230	1·2521	1·7856	2·3276	3·0769	3·6788	4·3182		
·8	·5217	1·2461	1·7779	2·3203	3·0739	3·6825	4·3321		
7·0	0·5206	1·2406	1·7707	2·3135	3·0710	3·6856	4·3444		
·2	·5195	1·2354	1·7641	2·3071	3·0680	3·6881	4·3554		
·4	·5184	1·2306	1·7579	2·3010	3·0651	3·6902	4·3653		
·6	·5174	1·2262	1·7521	2·2953	3·0622	3·6919	4·3741		
·8	·5165	1·2220	1·7467	2·2900	3·0593	3·6933	4·3821		
8·0	0·5157	1·2181	1·7416	2·2849	3·0566	3·6944	4·3893		
·2	·5148	1·2145	1·7368	2·2801	3·0539	3·6953	4·3959		
·4	·5141	1·2110	1·7323	2·2755	3·0512	3·6959	4·4019		
·6	·5133	1·2078	1·7281	2·2712	3·0487	3·6965	4·4073		
·8	·5126	1·2048	1·7241	2·2671	3·0462	3·6968	4·4123		
9·0	0·5120	1·2019	1·7203	2·2632	3·0438	3·6971	4·4169		

Table 32 (*continued*). *Pearson curves*

Table A (*cont.*). *Lower standardized percentage points (all signs negative)*

Percent	0·0	0·25	0·5	1·0	2·5	5·0	10·0	25·0	50·0
β_2					$\sqrt{\beta_1} = 1\cdot2$				
3·6	0·9312	0·9312	0·9311	0·9310	0·9303	0·9272	0·9140	0·8104	0·3786
·8	1·0000	·9999	·9997	·9991	·9960	·9873	·9593	·8077	·3356
4·0	1·0727	1·0721	1·0713	1·0692	1·0607	1·0424	0·9956	0·7994	0·3014
·2	1·1504	1·1480	1·1455	1·1400	1·1226	1·0913	1·0236	·7886	·2739
·4	1·2346	1·2274	1·2213	1·2103	1·1801	1·1336	1·0448	·7768	·2515
·6	1·3275	1·3092	1·2975	1·2784	1·2326	1·1696	1·0606	·7650	·2330
·8	1·4320	1·3921	1·3726	1·3433	1·2797	1·2000	1·0723	·7537	·2174
5·0	1·5529	1·4748	1·4453	1·4040	1·3215	1·2256	1·0809	0·7431	0·2043
·2	1·6982	1·5559	1·5147	1·4603	1·3586	1·2471	1·0872	·7332	·1930
·4	1·8832	1·6343	1·5802	1·5120	1·3913	1·2653	1·0917	·7242	·1833
·6	2·1439	1·7093	1·6415	1·5594	1·4201	1·2807	1·0949	·7158	·1749
·8	2·6198	1·7805	1·6986	1·6026	1·4456	1·2939	1·0972	·7081	·1674
6·0	∞	1·8476	1·7516	1·6419	1·4682	1·3051	1·0987	0·7011	0·1608
·2	—	1·9106	1·8006	1·6778	1·4884	1·3148	1·0996	·6946	·1550
·4	—	1·9697	1·8459	1·7106	1·5064	1·3232	1·1002	·6886	·1497
·6	—	2·0249	1·8879	1·7406	1·5225	1·3305	1·1004	·6831	·1450
·8	—	2·0766	1·9267	1·7680	1·5370	1·3369	1·1004	·6780	·1407
7·0	—	2·1248	1·9628	1·7932	1·5501	1·3425	1·1001	0·6733	0·1369
·2	—	2·1700	1·9962	1·8164	1·5619	1·3475	1·0998	·6689	·1333
·4	—	2·2122	2·0272	1·8378	1·5727	1·3519	1·0993	·6649	·1301
·6	—	2·2518	2·0561	1·8576	1·5826	1·3559	1·0988	·6610	·1271
·8	—	2·2889	2·0831	1·8759	1·5916	1·3594	1·0982	·6575	·1243
8·0	—	2·3238	2·1083	1·8929	1·5999	1·3626	1·0976	0·6542	0·1218
·2	—	2·3565	2·1319	1·9087	1·6075	1·3655	1·0969	·6510	·1194
·4	—	2·3874	2·1540	1·9235	1·6146	1·3681	1·0962	·6481	·1173
·6	—	2·4164	2·1747	1·9373	1·6211	1·3704	1·0955	·6453	·1152
·8	—	2·4439	2·1942	1·9502	1·6272	1·3726	1·0949	·6427	·1133
9·0	—	2·4698	2·2125	1·9623	1·6328	1·3745	1·0942	0·6403	0·1115
					$\sqrt{\beta_1} = 1\cdot3$				
4·0	0·9173	0·9172	0·9172	0·9171	0·9162	0·9128	0·8987	0·7947	0·3788
·2	·9795	·9794	·9792	·9786	·9754	·9668	·9395	·7934	·3411
·4	1·0449	1·0444	1·0436	1·0416	1·0338	1·0168	·9729	·7875	·3104
·6	1·1142	1·1123	1·1101	1·1054	1·0899	1·0617	·9996	·7792	·2850
·8	1·1887	1·1830	1·1781	1·1688	1·1427	1·1013	1·0205	·7697	·2639
5·0	1·2697	1·2560	1·2466	1·2307	1·1914	1·1357	1·0368	0·7600	0·2462
·2	1·3595	1·3302	1·3145	1·2902	1·2357	1·1653	1·0493	·7504	·2311
·4	1·4610	1·4046	1·3809	1·3466	1·2758	1·1907	1·0589	·7412	·2181
·6	1·5791	1·4783	1·4449	1·3994	1·3117	1·2125	1·0663	·7326	·2069
·8	1·7222	1·5502	1·5059	1·4486	1·3438	1·2312	1·0720	·7244	·1971
6·0	1·9070	1·6197	1·5637	1·4941	1·3725	1·2473	1·0763	0·7169	0·1886
·2	2·1764	1·6863	1·6180	1·5360	1·3981	1·2612	1·0795	·7099	·1809
·4	2·7530	1·7497	1·6689	1·5746	1·4211	1·2733	1·0820	·7034	·1742
·6	∞	1·8098	1·7164	1·6100	1·4418	1·2838	1·0838	·6973	·1681
·8	—	1·8666	1·7607	1·6427	1·4604	1·2930	1·0851	·6917	·1627
7·0	—	1·9201	1·8020	1·6727	1·4771	1·3012	1·0861	0·6865	0·1577
·2	—	1·9705	1·8405	1·7004	1·4924	1·3084	1·0867	·6817	·1532
·4	—	2·0178	1·8764	1·7260	1·5062	1·3147	1·0871	·6771	·1491
·6	—	2·0624	1·9098	1·7497	1·5188	1·3204	1·0873	·6729	·1454
·8	—	2·1043	1·9411	1·7716	1·5303	1·3255	1·0874	·6690	·1420
8·0	—	2·1437	1·9703	1·7920	1·5408	1·3301	1·0873	0·6653	0·1388
·2	—	2·1809	1·9977	1·8109	1·5505	1·3343	1·0871	·6618	·1359
·4	—	2·2159	2·0234	1·8286	1·5595	1·3380	1·0869	·6586	·1331
·6	—	2·2489	2·0475	1·8450	1·5678	1·3414	1·0866	·6555	·1306
·8	—	2·2801	2·0701	1·8604	1·5754	1·3445	1·0863	·6526	·1283
9·0	—	2·3096	2·0915	1·8749	1·5826	1·3473	1·0859	0·6499	0·1261
·2	—	2·3376	2·1116	1·8885	1·5892	1·3499	1·0855	·6473	·1240
·4	—	2·3640	2·1306	1·9012	1·5954	1·3523	1·0850	·6449	·1221

Table 32 (*continued*)

Table A (*cont.*). *Upper standardized percentage points (all signs positive)*

Percent	25·0	10·0	5·0	2·5	1·0	0·5	0·25	0·0	Type
β_2				$\sqrt{\beta_1} = 1\cdot2$					
3·6	0·5366	1·5755	2·1465	2·5572	2·9178	3·0944	3·2152	3·4696	
·8	·5355	1·5219	2·1033	2·5580	3·0027	3·2478	3·4337	4·0000	
4·0	0·5341	1·4793	2·0638	2·5482	3·0589	3·3647	3·6142	4·6934	I (J)
·2	·5324	1·4446	2·0287	2·5334	3·0956	3·4531	3·7609	5·6504	
·4	·5307	1·4159	1·9979	2·5167	3·1192	3·5201	3·8796	7·0767	
·6	·5290	1·3917	1·9706	2·4996	3·1341	3·5713	3·9759	9·4703	
·8	·5273	1·3710	1·9466	2·4829	3·1429	3·6106	4·0545	14·4320	I (Ω)
5·0	0·5256	1·3531	1·9253	2·4669	3·1477	3·6412	4·1191	31·5529	
·2	·5240	1·3375	1·9063	2·4519	3·1497	3·6651	4·1727	∞	
·4	·5225	1·3237	1·8892	2·4378	3·1497	3·6839	4·2174		VI
·6	·5211	1·3115	1·8739	2·4246	3·1484	3·6988	4·2552		
·8	·5197	1·3005	1·8600	2·4124	3·1461	3·7106	4·2872		
6·0	0·5185	1·2907	1·8474	2·4010	3·1433	3·7201	4·3145		IV
·2	·5173	1·2817	1·8358	2·3903	3·1400	3·7277	4·3381		
·4	·5161	1·2736	1·8253	2·3804	3·1365	3·7337	4·3584		
·6	·5150	1·2662	1·8156	2·3711	3·1328	3·7386	4·3762	↓
·8	·5140	1·2594	1·8066	2·3625	3·1290	3·7425	4·3917		
7·0	0·5130	1·2532	1·7984	2·3544	3·1252	3·7456	4·4053		
·2	·5121	1·2474	1·7907	2·3468	3·1214	3·7480	4·4173		
·4	·5113	1·2420	1·7835	2·3397	3·1177	3·7499	4·4280		
·6	·5104	1·2370	1·7769	2·3330	3·1140	3·7513	4·4375		
·8	·5097	1·2324	1·7706	2·3266	3·1104	3·7524	4·4460		
8·0	0·5089	1·2281	1·7648	2·3207	3·1069	3·7532	4·4536		
·2	·5082	1·2240	1·7593	2·3151	3·1035	3·7537	4·4605		
·4	·5076	1·2202	1·7542	2·3097	3·1002	3·7541	4·4667		
·6	·5069	1·2166	1·7493	2·3047	3·0970	3·7542	4·4723		
·8	·5063	1·2133	1·7448	2·2999	3·0939	3·7542	4·4774		
9·0	0·5058	1·2101	1·7404	2·2954	3·0909	3·7541	4·4820		
β_2				$\sqrt{\beta_1} = 1\cdot3$					
4·0	0·5024	1·5457	2·1550	2·6192	3·0555	3·2851	3·4520	3·8814	
·2	·5057	1·4996	2·1111	2·6082	3·1171	3·4112	3·6435	4·4851	I (J)
·4	·5077	1·4625	2·0722	2·5915	3·1568	3·5065	3·7999	5·2828	
·6	·5087	1·4318	2·0380	2·5726	3·1820	3·5785	3·9267	6·3976	
·8	·5092	1·4062	2·0080	2·5532	3·1973	3·6331	4·0294	8·0866	
5·0	0·5093	1·3843	1·9816	2·5343	3·2060	3·6748	4·1130	10·9893	I (Ω)
·2	·5091	1·3654	1·9583	2·5163	3·2102	3·7067	4·1815	17·2699	
·4	·5088	1·3490	1·9375	2·4994	3·2114	3·7315	4·2380	41·9054	
·6	·5083	1·3345	1·9189	2·4835	3·2106	3·7507	4·2850	∞	
·8	·5078	1·3217	1·9022	2·4688	3·2083	3·7657	4·3244		
6·0	0·5072	1·3102	1·8871	2·4551	3·2050	3·7774	4·3576		VI
·2	·5065	1·2999	1·8733	2·4423	3·2011	3·7866	4·3858		
·4	·5059	1·2906	1·8608	2·4304	3·1969	3·7938	4·4100		
·6	·5053	1·2821	1·8494	2·4194	3·1923	3·7994	4·4307		IV
·8	·5046	1·2743	1·8389	2·4091	3·1877	3·8038	4·4487		
7·0	0·5040	1·2672	1·8292	2·3994	3·1830	3·8071	4·4643		↓
·2	·5034	1·2607	1·8202	2·3904	3·1783	3·8096	4·4779		
·4	·5028	1·2546	1·8119	2·3820	3·1737	3·8114	4·4899		
·6	·5023	1·2490	1·8042	2·3740	3·1691	3·8128	4·5004		
·8	·5017	1·2438	1·7970	2·3666	3·1647	3·8136	4·5097		
8·0	0·5012	1·2390	1·7903	2·3596	3·1604	3·8141	4·5180		
·2	·5006	1·2345	1·7840	2·3530	3·1561	3·8144	4·5253		
·4	·5001	1·2302	1·7781	2·3467	3·1521	3·8143	4·5319		
·6	·4997	1·2263	1·7725	2·3408	3·1481	3·8141	4·5378		
·8	·4992	1·2225	1·7673	2·3353	3·1443	3·8137	4·5431		
9·0	0·4988	1·2190	1·7623	2·3300	3·1406	3·8132	4·5478		
·2	·4983	1·2157	1·7577	2·3249	3·1371	3·8126	4·5521		
·4	·4979	1·2126	1·7533	2·3202	3·1336	3·8119	4·5560		

Table 32 (continued). *Pearson curves*

Table A (cont.). *Lower standardized percentage points (all signs negative)*

Percent	0·0	0·25	0·5	1·0	2·5	5·0	10·0	25·0	50·0
β_2					$\sqrt{\beta_1} = 1\cdot4$				
4·4	0·8938	0·8938	0·8937	0·8936	0·8928	0·8897	0·8767	0·7795	0·3852
·6	·9496	·9495	·9493	·9489	·9462	·9387	·9144	·7803	·3512
·8	1·0077	1·0074	1·0068	1·0053	·9990	·9846	·9463	·7769	·3227
5·0	1·0689	1·0676	1·0660	1·0625	1·0501	1·0266	0·9724	0·7709	0·2988
·2	1·1339	1·1302	1·1266	1·1196	1·0988	1·0642	·9937	·7637	·2785
·4	1·2037	1·1948	1·1880	1·1759	1·1444	1·0975	1·0107	·7558	·2612
·6	1·2796	1·2608	1·2492	1·2306	1·1865	1·1268	1·0243	·7478	·2463
·8	1·3636	1·3274	1·3097	1·2830	1·2251	1·1524	1·0352	·7400	·2334
6·0	1·4584	1·3939	1·3686	1·3328	1·2602	1·1746	1·0438	0·7324	0·2221
·2	1·5682	1·4596	1·4255	1·3796	1·2920	1·1941	1·0507	·7252	·2122
·4	1·7007	1·5237	1·4799	1·4234	1·3208	1·2110	1·0562	·7184	·2034
·6	1·8704	1·5859	1·5316	1·4643	1·3468	1·2259	1·0606	·7120	·1955
·8	2·1144	1·6457	1·5805	1·5022	1·3703	1·2389	1·0640	·7060	·1885
7·0	2·6174	1·7029	1·6267	1·5374	1·3916	1·2504	1·0668	0·7003	0·1822
·2	∞	1·7574	1·6700	1·5700	1·4109	1·2606	1·0690	·6951	·1764
·4	—	1·8092	1·7107	1·6003	1·4285	1·2696	1·0707	·6901	·1713
·6	—	1·8583	1·7489	1·6284	1·4445	1·2777	1·0720	·6855	·1665
·8	—	1·9049	1·7848	1·6545	1·4592	1·2849	1·0731	·6812	·1622
8·0	—	1·9489	1·8184	1·6787	1·4726	1·2914	1·0739	0·6771	0·1582
·2	—	1·9905	1·8500	1·7013	1·4849	1·2972	1·0745	·6733	·1545
·4	—	2·0299	1·8796	1·7223	1·4963	1·3025	1·0749	·6697	·1512
·6	—	2·0671	1·9075	1·7420	1·5068	1·3073	1·0752	·6663	·1480
·8	—	2·1024	1·9337	1·7604	1·5164	1·3117	1·0754	·6632	·1451
9·0	—	2·1358	1·9584	1·7776	1·5254	1·3157	1·0755	0·6602	0·1424
·2	—	2·1674	1·9817	1·7937	1·5338	1·3193	1·0755	·6573	·1399
·4	—	2·1975	2·0038	1·8089	1·5416	1·3227	1·0755	·6546	·1375
·6	—	2·2259	2·0246	1·8232	1·5488	1·3258	1·0754	·6521	·1353
·8	—	2·2530	2·0443	1·8367	1·5556	1·3286	1·0752	·6497	·1332
					$\sqrt{\beta_1} = 1\cdot5$				
4·8	0·8634	0·8634	0·8634	0·8633	0·8627	0·8603	0·8496	0·7640	0·3959
5·0	0·9131	0·9131	0·9130	0·9126	0·9107	0·9050	0·8852	0·7673	0·3646
·2	·9645	·9643	·9640	·9630	·9585	·9474	·9161	·7664	·3378
·4	1·0181	1·0174	1·0164	1·0141	1·0052	·9869	·9422	·7629	·3149
·6	1·0745	1·0724	1·0702	1·0654	1·0502	1·0230	·9641	·7578	·2951
·8	1·1341	1·1292	1·1248	1·1164	1·0930	1·0556	·9821	·7518	·2780
6·0	1·1980	1·1873	1·1797	1·1665	1·1331	1·0847	0·9970	0·7454	0·2631
·2	1·2672	1·2465	1·2344	1·2151	1·1703	1·1105	1·0092	·7388	·2501
·4	1·3433	1·3061	1·2884	1·2618	1·2047	1·1335	1·0193	·7323	·2386
·6	1·4283	1·3655	1·3410	1·3064	1·2363	1·1537	1·0275	·7260	·2284
·8	1·5258	1·4242	1·3920	1·3485	1·2652	1·1717	1·0342	·7199	·2193
7·0	1·6411	1·4817	1·4410	1·3882	1·2916	1·1876	1·0398	0·7141	0·2112
·2	1·7847	1·5377	1·4879	1·4255	1·3158	1·2017	1·0444	·7086	·2038
·4	1·9798	1·5918	1·5325	1·4604	1·3378	1·2143	1·0481	·7034	·1972
·6	2·3088	1·6439	1·5748	1·4931	1·3580	1·2255	1·0513	·6985	·1912
·8	∞	1·6938	1·6149	1·5236	1·3764	1·2355	1·0538	·6938	·1857
8·0	—	1·7416	·6528	1·5521	1·3934	1·2446	1·0560	0·6894	0·1807
·2	—	1·7871	1·6885	1·5787	1·4089	1·2527	1·0577	·6853	·1761
·4	—	1·8305	1·7223	1·6036	1·4232	1·2600	1·0592	·6814	·1718
·6	—	1·8717	1·7542	1·6268	1·4365	1·2667	1·0604	·6777	·1679
·8	—	1·9110	1·7842	1·6486	1·4487	1·2728	1·0614	·6742	·1643
9·0	—	1·9483	1·8126	1·6691	1·4600	1·2783	1·0622	0·6710	0·1609
·2	—	1·9838	1·8395	1·6882	1·4705	1·2834	1·0628	·6678	·1578
·4	—	2·0175	1·8648	1·7063	1·4803	1·2880	1·0633	·6649	·1548
·6	—	2·0496	1·8889	1·7232	1·4894	1·2923	1·0637	·6621	·1521
·8	—	2·0802	1·9116	1·7392	1·4979	1·2962	1·0641	·6594	·1495
10·0	—	2·1093	1·9332	1·7543	1·5059	1·2999	1·0643	0·6569	0·1471
·2	—	2·1370	1·9536	1·7685	1·5134	1·3032	1·0645	·6545	·1449
·4	—	2·1634	1·9731	1·7820	1·5204	1·3064	1·0646	·6522	·1427

Table 32 *(continued)*

Table A *(cont.).* *Upper standardized percentage points (all signs positive)*

Percent	25·0	10·0	5·0	2·5	1·0	0·5	0·25	0·0	Type
β_2				$\sqrt{\beta_1} = 1\cdot 4$					
4·4	0·4708	1·5238	2·1651	2·6719	3·1691	3·4425	3·6488	4·2574	
·6	·4775	1·4832	2·1214	2·6538	3·2148	3·5487	3·8191	4·9197	I (J)
·8	·4822	1·4501	2·0833	2·6328	3·2433	3·6287	3·9576	5·7972	
5·0	0·4856	1·4225	2·0499	2·6111	3·2604	3·6891	4·0699	7·0264	
·2	·4879	1·3991	2·0206	2·5898	3·2699	3·7348	4·1611	8·8907	
·4	·4896	1·3790	1·9948	2·5696	3·2742	3·7696	4·2355	12·0926	I (Ω)
·6	·4909	1·3616	1·9719	2·5505	3·2750	3·7962	4·2966	18·9855	
·8	·4917	1·3463	1·9514	2·5327	3·2734	3·8166	4·3472	45·3636	
6·0	0·4923	1·3328	1·9331	2·5162	3·2703	3·8323	4·3893	∞	
·2	·4926	1·3207	1·9165	2·5008	3·2661	3·8443	4·4246		
·4	·4928	1·3098	1·9015	2·4865	3·2612	3·8536	4·4545		
·6	·4929	1·3000	1·8879	2·4733	3·2560	3·8607	4·4798		VI
·8	·4929	1·2911	1·8754	2·4609	3·2505	3·8660	4·5014		
7·0	0·4929	1·2829	1·8639	2·4494	3·2448	3·8700	4·5200		
·2	·4927	1·2755	1·8534	2·4387	3·2392	3·8729	4·5361		IV
·4	·4926	1·2686	1·8436	2·4286	3·2336	3·8749	4·5500		
·6	·4924	1·2623	1·8346	2·4192	3·2281	3·8762	4·5621		↓
·8	·4922	1·2564	1·8262	2·4104	3·2227	3·8770	4·5727		
8·0	0·4919	1·2510	1·8184	2·4022	3·2174	3·8773	4·5820		
·2	·4917	1·2459	1·8111	2·3944	3·2123	3·8773	4·5901		
·4	·4914	1·2412	1·8043	2·3870	3·2073	3·8770	4·5974		
·6	·4912	1·2367	1·7979	2·3801	3·2025	3·8764	4·6037		
·8	·4909	1·2326	1·7919	2·3736	3·1979	3·8756	4·6094		
9·0	0·4907	1·2287	1·7862	2·3674	3·1934	3·8747	4·6145		
·2	·4904	1·2250	1·7809	2·3615	3·1891	3·8737	4·6190		
·4	·4902	1·2215	1·7758	2·3559	3·1849	3·8726	4·6230		
·6	·4899	1·2182	1·7710	2·3507	3·1809	3·8714	4·6266		
·8	·4897	1·2151	1·7665	2·3456	3·1770	3·8701	4·6298		
				$\sqrt{\beta_1} = 1\cdot 5$					
4·8	0·4397	1·5074	2·1779	2·7208	3·2674	3·5760	3·8141	4·5777	
5·0	0·4493	1·4709	2·1347	2·6980	3·3021	3·6680	3·9685	5·2767	
·2	·4565	1·4408	2·0971	2·6739	3·3229	3·7372	4·0941	6·1986	I (J)
·4	·4620	1·4155	2·0643	2·6501	3·3343	3·7893	4·1960	7·4797	
·6	·4661	1·3940	2·0354	2·6274	3·3394	3·8287	4·2790	9·3970	
·8	·4694	1·3753	2·0099	2·6060	3·3403	3·8584	4·3468	12·6124	
6·0	0·4719	1·3590	1·9872	2·5860	3·3384	3·8810	4·4027	19·1980	I (Ω)
·2	·4740	1·3446	1·9669	2·5674	3·3347	3·8982	4·4489	40·6958	
·4	·4755	1·3318	1·9487	2·5501	3·3297	3·9112	4·4875	∞	
·6	·4768	1·3203	1·9321	2·5341	3·3239	3·9209	4·5198		
·8	·4778	1·3099	1·9171	2·5193	3·3177	3·9282	4·5471		
7·0	0·4786	1·3005	1·9035	2·5054	3·3112	3·9336	4·5702		VI
·2	·4793	1·2920	1·8909	2·4926	3·3046	3·9374	4·5900		
·4	·4798	1·2841	1·8794	2·4806	3·2979	3·9400	4·6069		
·6	·4802	1·2769	1·8687	2·4694	3·2914	3·9417	4·6214		
·8	·4805	1·2703	1·8589	2·4589	3·2849	3·9426	4·6340		IV
8·0	0·4807	1·2641	1·8497	2·4491	3·2786	3·9429	4·6448		↓
·2	·4809	1·2584	1·8412	2·4399	3·2725	3·9427	4·6543		
·4	·4810	1·2531	1·8333	2·4312	3·2665	3·9421	4·6626		
·6	·4811	1·2481	1·8259	2·4231	3·2608	3·9413	4·6698		
·8	·4812	1·2435	1·8189	2·4154	3·2552	3·9402	4·6761		
9·0	0·4812	1·2391	1·8124	2·4081	3·2498	3·9389	4·6817		
·2	·4812	1·2350	1·8062	2·4013	3·2446	3·9374	4·6866		
·4	·4812	1·2311	1·8004	2·3947	3·2396	3·9359	4·6909		
·6	·4811	1·2275	1·7950	2·3886	3·2348	3·9342	4·6947		
·8	·4811	1·2241	1·7898	2·3827	3·2301	3·9325	4·6981		
10·0	0·4810	1·2208	1·7849	2·3771	3·2256	3·9307	4·7011		
·2	·4810	1·2177	1·7802	2·3718	3·2213	3·9289	4·7037		
·4	·4809	1·2148	1·7758	2·3668	3·2172	3·9271	4·7061		

Table 32 (*continued*). *Pearson curves*

Table A (*cont.*). *Lower standardized percentage points (all signs negative)*

Percent	0·0	0·25	0·5	1·0	2·5	5·0	10·0	25·0	50·0
β₂					$\sqrt{\beta_1} = 1\cdot6$				
5·2	0·8284	0·8284	0·8284	0·8284	0·8280	0·8264	0·8185	0·7474	0·4098
·4	·8726	·8725	·8725	·8723	·8712	·8673	·8524	·7533	·3806
·6	·9179	·9178	·9176	·9171	·9143	·9066	·8826	·7551	·3551
·8	·9648	·9645	·9639	·9626	·9568	·9438	·9089	·7541	·3328
6·0	1·0135	1·0125	1·0113	1·0085	0·9983	0·9784	0·9315	0·7512	0·3134
·2	1·0645	1·0621	1·0596	1·0544	1·0383	1·0102	·9507	·7471	·2964
·4	1·1183	1·1130	1·1085	1·1000	1·0763	1·0392	·9669	·7423	·2814
·6	1·1756	1·1650	1·1576	1·1447	1·1122	1·0654	·9806	·7371	·2682
·8	1·2371	1·2178	1·2065	1·1883	1·1458	1·0890	·9921	·7318	·2564
7·0	1·3040	1·2709	1·2547	1·2303	1·1771	1·1101	1·0018	0·7264	0·2459
·2	1·3779	1·3240	1·3020	1·2706	1·2061	1·1291	1·0099	·7211	·2365
·4	1·4610	1·3766	1·3481	1·3090	1·2329	1·1461	1·0168	·7160	·2280
·6	1·5568	1·4283	1·3926	1·3454	1·2576	1·1614	1·0226	·7110	·2203
·8	1·6716	1·4789	1·4354	1·3799	1·2804	1·1751	1·0275	·7063	·2133
8·0	1·8170	1·5282	1·4764	1·4124	1·3014	1·1874	1·0316	0·7017	0·2069
·2	2·0229	1·5758	1·5156	1·4431	1·3208	1·1986	1·0351	·6974	·2011
·4	2·4366	1·6218	1·5529	1·4719	1·3386	1·2086	1·0381	·6933	·1958
·6	∞	1·6661	1·5885	1·4990	1·3552	1·2178	1·0407	·6893	·1909
·8	—	1·7085	1·6222	1·5244	1·3705	1·2261	1·0429	·6856	·1863
9·0	—	1·7492	1·6543	1·5484	1·3846	1·2336	1·0447	0·6821	0·1821
·2	—	1·7881	1·6847	1·5710	1·3978	1·2406	1·0463	·6787	·1782
·4	—	1·8253	1·7135	1·5922	1·4100	1·2469	1·0477	·6755	·1746
·6	—	1·8609	1·7409	1·6122	1·4214	1·2527	1·0489	·6725	·1712
·8	—	1·8949	1·7670	1·6311	1·4321	1·2581	1·0499	·6696	·1680
10·0	—	1·9274	1·7917	1·6489	1·4420	1·2631	1·0507	0·6669	0·1651
·2	—	1·9584	1·8151	1·6657	1·4513	1·2676	1·0515	·6642	·1623
·4	—	1·9880	1·8375	1·6816	1·4601	1·2719	1·0521	·6617	·1597
·6	—	2·0163	1·8587	1·6967	1·4683	1·2758	1·0526	·6594	·1572
·8	—	2·0434	1·8790	1·7110	1·4760	1·2795	1·0531	·6571	·1549
11·0	—	2·0693	1·8982	1·7245	1·4833	1·2829	1·0534	0·6549	0·1527
·2	—	2·0941	1·9166	1·7374	1·4901	1·2861	1·0538	·6529	·1506
·4	—	2·1179	1·9342	1·7497	1·4966	1·2891	1·0540	·6509	·1487
					$\sqrt{\beta_1} = 1\cdot7$				
5·8	0·8299	0·8299	0·8299	0·8298	0·8292	0·8269	0·8168	0·7375	0·3984
6·0	0·8699	0·8699	0·8698	0·8695	0·8680	0·8632	0·8463	0·7421	0·3741
·2	·9109	·9108	·9106	·9099	·9066	·8981	·8727	·7437	·3524
·4	·9531	·9528	·9522	·9507	·9446	·9311	·8959	·7432	·3333
·6	·9969	·9959	·9947	·9918	·9817	·9621	·9162	·7411	·3163
·8	1·0425	1·0402	1·0378	1·0329	1·0176	·9908	·9338	·7381	·3011
7·0	1·0902	1·0855	1·0814	1·0737	1·0519	1·0171	0·9490	0·7344	0·2876
·2	1·1406	1·1318	1·1252	1·1138	1·0844	1·0413	·9620	·7303	·2755
·4	1·1943	1·1787	1·1689	1·1531	1·1151	1·0632	·9732	·7260	·2647
·6	1·2520	1·2259	1·2122	1·1911	1·1440	1·0832	·9828	·7216	·2549
·8	1·3147	1·2733	1·2549	1·2279	1·1710	1·1013	·9911	·7172	·2460
8·0	1·3838	1·3204	1·2965	1·2631	1·1961	1·1177	0·9982	0·7129	0·2379
·2	1·4614	1·3669	1·3371	1·2968	1·2195	1·1326	1·0043	·7086	·2305
·4	1·5507	1·4128	1·3764	1·3289	1·2413	1·1461	1·0096	·7045	·2238
·6	1·6570	1·4576	1·4143	1·3595	1·2616	1·1584	1·0142	·7006	·2176
·8	1·7911	1·5013	1·4507	1·3884	1·2804	1·1696	1·0181	·6967	·2119
9·0	1·9790	1·5437	1·4857	1·4158	1·2979	1·1798	1·0216	0·6931	0·2066
·2	2·3469	1·5848	1·5192	1·4418	1·3142	1·1892	1·0246	·6896	·2017
·4	∞	1·6245	1·5512	1·4663	1·3293	1·1977	1·0272	·6862	·1972
·6	—	1·6627	1·5817	1·4896	1·3435	1·2056	1·0295	·6830	·1930
·8	—	1·6995	1·6109	1·5116	1·3567	1·2128	1·0315	·6799	·1891

Table 32 (*continued*)

Table A (*cont.*). *Upper standardized percentage points (all signs positive)*

Percent	25·0	10·0	5·0	2·5	1·0	0·5	0·25	0·0	Type
β_2				$\sqrt{\beta_1} = 1\cdot6$					
5·2	0·4076	1·4947	2·1939	2·7687	3·3561	3·6922	3·9542	4·8284	
·4	·4201	1·4613	2·1510	2·7425	3·3832	3·7743	4·0974	5·5392	
·6	·4297	1·4336	2·1136	2·7161	3·3983	3·8359	4·2140	6·4663	
·8	·4372	1·4102	2·0810	2·6906	3·4055	3·8822	4·3088	7·7340	} I (J)
6·0	0·4432	1·3900	2·0523	2·6665	3·4073	3·9170	4·3861	9·5849	
·2	·4480	1·3725	2·0269	2·6440	3·4056	3·9432	4·4495	12·5645	
·4	·4519	1·3571	2·0042	2·6230	3·4016	3·9628	4·5017	18·2092	
·6	·4551	1·3435	1·9839	2·6036	3·3960	3·9775	4·5449	33·1756	} I (Ω)
·8	·4577	1·3313	1·9656	2·5856	3·3894	3·9884	4·5809	197·2371	}
7·0	0·4599	1·3203	1·9490	2·5689	3·3823	3·9963	4·6111	∞	
·2	·4618	1·3104	1·9339	2·5534	3·3748	4·0020	4·6365		
·4	·4633	1·3013	1·9201	2·5390	3·3672	4·0059	4·6580		
·6	·4647	1·2931	1·9074	2·5255	3·3595	4·0085	4·6763		
·8	·4658	1·2855	1·8957	2·5130	3·3520	4·0099	4·6919		} VI
8·0	0·4667	1·2785	1·8849	2·5013	3·3445	4·0105	4·7053		
·2	·4675	1·2720	1·8749	2·4904	3·3372	4·0105	4·7168		
·4	·4682	1·2660	1·8656	2·4801	3·3302	4·0099	4·7267		
·6	·4688	1·2604	1·8569	2·4704	3·3233	4·0088	4·7352		IV
·8	·4693	1·2552	1·8488	2·4614	3·3167	4·0074	4·7426		↓
9·0	0·4697	1·2503	1·8412	2·4528	3·3103	4·0058	4·7490		
·2	·4701	1·2458	1·8341	2·4447	3·3041	4·0040	4·7546		
·4	·4705	1·2415	1·8274	2·4371	3·2981	4·0020	4·7595		
·6	·4707	1·2374	1·8211	2·4299	3·2923	3·9999	4·7637		
·8	·4710	1·2336	1·8152	2·4230	3·2868	3·9977	4·7674		
10·0	0·4712	1·2300	1·8095	2·4165	3·2815	3·9955	4·7706		
·2	·4714	1·2266	1·8042	2·4103	3·2763	3·9932	4·7734		
·4	·4715	1·2234	1·7992	2·4044	3·2714	3·9909	4·7758		
·6	·4716	1·2203	1·7944	2·3988	3·2666	3·9886	4·7779		
·8	·4717	1·2174	1·7898	2·3935	3·2620	3·9863	4·7797		
11·0	0·4718	1·2146	1·7855	2·3884	3·2576	3·9840	4·7813		
·2	·4719	1·2120	1·7813	2·3835	3·2533	3·9817	4·7827		
·4	·4720	1·2095	1·7774	2·3789	3·2492	3·9794	4·7838		
				$\sqrt{\beta_1} = 1\cdot7$					
5·8	0·3889	1·4536	2·1701	2·7885	3·4603	3·8708	4·2097	5·7029	
6·0	0·4010	1·4278	2·1327	2·7600	3·4714	3·9274	4·3205	6·6002	
·2	·4107	1·4058	2·1000	2·7329	3·4754	3·9697	4·4108	7·8008	I (J)
·4	·4185	1·3868	2·0711	2·7075	3·4748	4·0014	4·4845	9·4986	
·6	·4249	1·3703	2·0456	2·6838	3·4710	4·0250	4·5450	12·0989	
·8	·4303	1·3557	2·0228	2·6619	3·4651	4·0425	4·5948	16·6125	}
7·0	0·4347	1·3426	2·0023	2·6415	3·4580	4·0553	4·6361	26·4633	} I (Ω)
·2	·4385	1·3310	1·9838	2·6227	3·4500	4·0646	4·6705	65·3629	}
·4	·4417	1·3205	1·9670	2·6052	3·4416	4·0711	4·6992	∞	
·6	·4444	1·3109	1·9517	2·5890	3·4330	4·0755	4·7234		
·8	·4468	1·3022	1·9376	2·5739	3·4243	4·0783	4·7437		
8·0	0·4488	1·2942	1·9248	2·5599	3·4157	4·0798	4·7610		
·2	·4506	1·2868	1·9129	2·5468	3·4072	4·0802	4·7756		
·4	·4521	1·2800	1·9019	2·5345	3·3989	4·0799	4·7881		VI
·6	·4535	1·2737	1·8917	2·5230	3·3908	4·0789	4·7988		
·8	·4547	1·2678	1·8821	2·5122	3·3830	4·0775	4·8079		}
9·0	0·4557	1·2624	1·8733	2·5021	3·3754	4·0757	4·8157		
·2	·4566	1·2572	1·8650	2·4926	3·3681	4·0735	4·8224		
·4	·4575	1·2525	1·8572	2·4836	3·3610	4·0712	4·8282		IV
·6	·4582	1·2480	1·8499	2·4751	3·3542	4·0687	4·8331		
·8	·4588	1·2437	1·8430	2·4670	3·3476	4·0661	4·8374		↓

Table 32 (*continued*). *Pearson curves*

Table A (*cont.*). *Lower standardized percentage points (all signs negative)*

Percent	0·0	0·25	0·5	1·0	2·5	5·0	10·0	25·0	50·0
β_2				$\sqrt{\beta_1} = 1\cdot7$ (*cont.*)					
10·0	∞	1·7349	1·6387	1·5324	1·3690	1·2195	1·0333	0·6770	0·1855
·2	—	1·7689	1·6653	1·5520	1·3806	1·2257	1·0348	·6742	·1820
·4	—	1·8015	1·6906	1·5707	1·3914	1·2314	1·0362	·6715	·1788
·6	—	1·8328	1·7148	1·5884	1·4016	1·2367	1·0374	·6689	·1758
·8	—	1·8629	1·7378	1·6052	1·4112	1·2416	1·0385	·6665	·1730
11·0	—	1·8917	1·7598	1·6211	1·4202	1·2462	1·0394	0·6642	0·1703
·2	—	1·9193	1·7808	1·6362	1·4287	1·2505	1·0402	·6619	·1678
·4	—	1·9459	1·8009	1·6506	1·4367	1·2545	1·0410	·6598	·1654
·6	—	1·9713	1·8201	1·6644	1·4443	1·2582	1·0416	·6577	·1631
·8	—	1·9958	1·8385	1·6774	1·4514	1·2617	1·0422	·6557	·1610
				$\sqrt{\beta_1} = 1\cdot8$					
6·4	0·8219	0·8219	0·8219	0·8218	0·8211	0·8184	0·8075	0·7266	0·3942
·6	·8579	·8579	·8578	·8575	·8559	·8509	·8338	·7309	·3733
·8	·8947	·8946	·8944	·8937	·8905	·8822	·8575	·7329	·3544
7·0	0·9325	0·9321	0·9316	0·9302	0·9246	0·9120	0·8788	0·7331	0·3374
·2	·9714	·9706	·9695	·9670	·9580	·9401	·8976	·7320	·3221
·4	1·0117	1·0099	1·0079	1·0037	·9903	·9664	·9142	·7300	·3084
·6	1·0536	1·0501	1·0467	1·0403	1·0215	·9908	·9287	·7273	·2959
·8	1·0975	1·0910	1·0858	1·0764	1·0513	1·0133	·9415	·7243	·2847
8·0	1·1438	1·1325	1·1248	1·1119	1·0797	1·0341	0·9526	0·7209	0·2744
·2	1·1928	1·1744	1·1636	1·1465	1·1066	1·0532	·9623	·7174	·2651
·4	1·2454	1·2165	1·2020	1·1801	1·1319	1·0707	·9708	·7138	·2566
·6	1·3022	1·2586	1·2398	1·2126	1·1558	1·0867	·9783	·7102	·2488
·8	1·3644	1·3004	1·2768	1·2439	1·1781	1·1014	·9848	·7066	·2417
9·0	1·4336	1·3418	1·3129	1·2739	1·1991	1·1149	0·9906	0·7031	0·2351
·2	1·5122	1·3825	1·3479	1·3026	1·2188	1·1273	·9956	·6996	·2290
·4	1·6042	1·4225	1·3818	1·3301	1·2372	1·1386	1·0001	·6963	·2234
·6	1·7168	1·4616	1·4146	1·3563	1·2544	1·1491	1·0040	·6930	·2182
·8	1·8657	1·4997	1·4462	1·3812	1·2706	1·1587	1·0075	·6899	·2133
10·0	2·1027	1·5367	1·4766	1·4050	1·2857	1·1676	1·0105	0·6869	0·2088
·2	∞	1·5726	1·5057	1·4276	1·2999	1·1758	1·0133	·6840	·2046
·4	—	1·6074	1·5338	1·4491	1·3132	1·1834	1·0157	·6812	·2006
·6	—	1·6410	1·5606	1·4695	1·3257	1·1904	1·0179	·6785	·1969
·8	—	1·6734	1·5864	1·4890	1·3375	1·1970	1·0199	·6759	·1934
11·0	—	1·7047	1·6110	1·5075	1·3486	1·2031	1·0216	0·6734	0·1901
·2	—	1·7349	1·6347	1·5251	1·3590	1·2087	1·0232	·6710	·1871
·4	—	1·7640	1·6573	1·5419	1·3689	1·2140	1·0246	·6687	·1841
·6	—	1·7921	1·6790	1·5579	1·3782	1·2190	1·0259	·6665	·1814
·8	—	1·8191	1·6999	1·5731	1·3870	1·2236	1·0270	·6644	·1788
12·0	—	1·8451	1·7198	1·5876	1·3954	1·2280	1·0280	0·6624	0·1763
·2	—	1·8701	1·7389	1·6015	1·4033	1·2321	1·0290	·6604	·1740
·4	—	1·8942	1·7573	1·6148	1·4108	1·2359	1·0298	·6586	·1717
·6	—	1·9175	1·7749	1·6275	1·4179	1·2396	1·0306	·6567	·1696
				$\sqrt{\beta_1} = 1\cdot9$					
7·0	0·8067	0·8067	0·8067	0·8066	0·8059	0·8034	0·7929	0·7151	0·3948
·2	·8390	·8390	·8389	·8386	·8372	·8326	·8168	·7197	·3763
·4	·8718	·8717	·8715	·8710	·8682	·8609	·8386	·7223	·3595
·6	·9054	·9051	·9047	·9036	·8989	·8880	·8584	·7234	·3441
·8	·9398	·9392	·9384	·9364	·9290	·9138	·8762	·7232	·3302
8·0	0·9752	0·9739	0·9725	0·9693	0·9584	0·9381	0·8921	0·7222	0·3174
·2	1·0117	1·0094	1·0070	1·0020	·9869	·9609	·9063	·7205	·3058
·4	1·0497	1·0454	1·0417	1·0345	1·0144	·9823	·9190	·7184	·2952
·6	1·0893	1·0820	1·0765	1·0666	1·0407	1·0021	·9302	·7159	·2855
·8	1·1309	1·1191	1·1112	1·0981	1·0659	1·0205	·9402	·7132	·2765
9·0	1·1748	1·1564	1·1457	1·1289	1·0898	1·0376	0·9490	0·7104	0·2683
·2	1·2214	1·1938	1·1799	1·1588	1·1125	1·0534	·9569	·7075	·2607
·4	1·2714	1·2312	1·2136	1·1879	1·1339	1·0680	·9639	·7045	·2537

Table 32 (*continued*)

Table A (*cont.*). *Upper standardized percentage points (all signs positive)*

Percent	25·0	10·0	5·0	2·5	1·0	0·5	0·25	0·0	Type
β_2				$\sqrt{\beta_1} = 1·7$ (*cont.*)					
10·0	0·4594	1·2397	1·8365	2·4594	3·3413	4·0633	4·8410	∞	IV
·2	·4600	1·2360	1·8304	2·4522	3·3352	4·0606	4·8441		
·4	·4604	1·2324	1·8246	2·4453	3·3293	4·0577	4·8468		↓
·6	·4609	1·2290	1·8191	2·4388	3·3237	4·0549	4·8491		
·8	·4612	1·2258	1·8139	2·4326	3·3182	4·0521	4·8510		
11·0	0·4616	1·2228	1·8089	2·4267	3·3130	4·0492	4·8526		
·2	·4619	1·2199	1·8042	2·4210	3·3079	4·0464	4·8539		
·4	·4622	1·2171	1·7997	2·4156	3·3031	4·0436	4·8551		
·6	·4624	1·2145	1·7954	2·4105	3·2984	4·0409	4·8560		
·8	·4627	1·2120	1·7914	2·4055	3·2938	4·0382	4·8567		
				$\sqrt{\beta_1} = 1·8$					
6·4	0·3696	1·4225	2·1542	2·8063	3·5435	4·0132	4·4154	6·6165	
·6	·3816	1·4018	2·1211	2·7776	3·5452	4·0531	4·5034	7·7151	
·8	·3915	1·3839	2·0919	2·7507	3·5425	4·0828	4·5754	9·2155	
									I (J)
7·0	0·3997	1·3681	2·0660	2·7258	3·5370	4·1047	4·6344	11·3976	
·2	·4066	1·3542	2·0428	2·7028	3·5296	4·1207	4·6830	14·8805	
·4	·4124	1·3418	2·0220	2·6814	3·5211	4·1323	4·7233	21·3595	
·6	·4174	1·3306	2·0032	2·6617	3·5118	4·1404	4·7567	37·7459	I (Ω)
·8	·4217	1·3205	1·9861	2·6433	3·5023	4·1458	4·7847	163·0975	
8·0	0·4254	1·3112	1·9705	2·6263	3·4925	4·1492	4·8081	∞	
·2	·4286	1·3028	1·9561	2·6105	3·4828	4·1510	4·8277		
·4	·4315	1·2951	1·9430	2·5957	3·4733	4·1515	4·8443		
·6	·4340	1·2879	1·9308	2·5820	3·4639	4·1511	4·8584		
·8	·4362	1·2813	1·9196	2·5691	3·4547	4·1500	4·8702		
9·0	0·4381	1·2751	1·9091	2·5570	3·4458	4·1482	4·8803		
·2	·4398	1·2694	1·8993	2·5457	3·4372	4·1460	4·8888		
·4	·4414	1·2641	1·8902	2·5350	3·4289	4·1435	4·8961		VI
·6	·4428	1·2591	1·8817	2·5250	3·4208	4·1406	4·9022		
·8	·4440	1·2544	1·8737	2·5155	3·4131	4·1376	4·9075		
10·0	0·4452	1·2499	1·8662	2·5065	3·4056	4·1345	4·9119		
·2	·4462	1·2458	1·8591	2·4980	3·3984	4·1312	4·9156		IV
·4	·4471	1·2418	1·8524	2·4900	3·3915	4·1279	4·9187		
·6	·4480	1·2381	1·8461	2·4824	3·3849	4·1245	4·9213		↓
·8	·4487	1·2346	1·8401	2·4751	3·3785	4·1211	4·9235		
11·0	0·4494	1·2312	1·8344	2·4682	3·3723	4·1177	4·9253		
·2	·4501	1·2281	1·8290	2·4617	3·3663	4·1144	4·9268		
·4	·4507	1·2250	1·8239	2·4554	3·3606	4·1110	4·9279		
·6	·4512	1·2222	1·8190	2·4494	3·3551	4·1077	4·9288		
·8	·4517	1·2194	1·8143	2·4437	3·3498	4·1044	4·9295		
12·0	0·4522	1·2168	1·8099	2·4382	3·3446	4·1012	4·9300		
·2	·4526	1·2143	1·8056	2·4330	3·3397	4·0980	4·9304		
·4	·4530	1·2119	1·8016	2·4280	3·3349	4·0949	4·9305		
·6	·4534	1·2096	1·7977	2·4232	3·3303	4·0919	4·9306		
				$\sqrt{\beta_2} = 1·9$					
7·0	0·3495	1·3977	2·1443	2·8249	3·6153	4·1331	4·5874	7·5205	
·2	·3616	1·3807	2·1145	2·7965	3·6111	4·1618	4·6592	8·8143	
·4	·3718	1·3657	2·0880	2·7703	3·6041	4·1829	4·7181	10·6058	
·6	·3804	1·3524	2·0643	2·7459	3·5954	4·1980	4·7666	13·2612	
·8	·3877	1·3405	2·0430	2·7234	3·5856	4·2087	4·8067	17·6227	I (J)
8·0	0·3941	1·3298	2·0237	2·7026	3·5752	4·2160	4·8400	26·1559	
·2	·3996	1·3201	2·0062	2·6833	3·5645	4·2206	4·8678	50·5001	
·4	·4044	1·3112	1·9902	2·6654	3·5538	4·2232	4·8909	723·0497	I (Ω)
·6	·4086	1·3030	1·9755	2·6488	3·5431	4·2243	4·9103	∞	
·8	·4123	1·2955	1·9620	2·6332	3·5325	4·2240	4·9266		
9·0	0·4156	1·2886	1·9495	2·6187	3·5222	4·2229	4·9403		VI
·2	·4185	1·2822	1·9379	2·6051	3·5122	4·2210	4·9518		
·4	·4212	1·2762	1·9272	2·5924	3·5024	4·2185	4·9614		

Table 32 *(continued)*. *Pearson curves*

Table A *(cont.)*. *Lower standardized percentage points (all signs negative)*

Percent	0·0	0·25	0·5	1·0	2·5	5·0	10·0	25·0	50·0
β_2					$\sqrt{\beta_1} = 1·9$ *(cont.)*				
9·6	1·3256	1·2684	1·2466	1·2160	1·1542	1·0815	0·9701	0·7015	0·2473
·8	1·3850	1·3052	1·2789	1·2430	1·1734	1·0940	·9757	·6986	·2412
10·0	1·4513	1·3417	1·3104	1·2691	1·1914	1·1056	0·9807	0·6957	0·2356
·2	1·5268	1·3775	1·3411	1·2941	1·2085	1·1163	·9851	·6929	·2304
·4	1·6155	1·4126	1·3708	1·3181	1·2245	1·1263	·9891	·6901	·2255
·6	1·7250	1·4470	1·3995	1·3411	1·2397	1·1355	·9926	·6874	·2210
·8	1·8722	1·4805	1·4273	1·3630	1·2539	1·1441	·9959	·6848	·2167
11·0	2·1230	1·5132	1·4542	1·3840	1·2674	1·1521	0·9988	0·6823	0·2127
·2	∞	1·5450	1·4800	1·4041	1·2801	1·1595	1·0014	·6799	·2089
·4	—	1·5759	1·5050	1·4233	1·2921	1·1665	1·0038	·6775	·2054
·6	—	1·6058	1·5290	1·4417	1·3035	1·1730	1·0059	·6752	·2020
·8	—	1·6348	1·5521	1·4593	1·3142	1·1791	1·0079	·6730	·1988
12·0	—	1·6629	1·5743	1·4760	1·3244	1·1848	1·0096	0·6709	0·1958
·2	—	1·6901	1·5957	1·4921	1·3341	1·1901	1·0113	·6688	·1930
·4	—	1·7164	1·6163	1·5074	1·3432	1·1951	1·0127	·6668	·1903
·6	—	1·7418	1·6361	1·5221	1·3519	1·1999	1·0141	·6649	·1877
·8	—	1·7664	1·6552	1·5362	1·3602	1·2043	1·0153	·6631	·1853
13·0	—	1·7902	1·6736	1·5497	1·3681	1·2086	1·0164	0·6613	0·1830
·2	—	1·8131	1·6912	1·5626	1·3755	1·2125	1·0175	·6596	·1808
·4	—	1·8353	1·7082	1·5750	1·3827	1·2163	1·0184	·6579	·1787
					$\sqrt{\beta_1} = 2·0$				
7·6	0·7863	0·7863	0·7862	0·7862	0·7856	0·7834	0·7742	0·7030	0·3986
·8	·8151	·8151	·8150	·8148	·8137	·8099	·7962	·7081	·3821
8·0	0·8443	0·8442	0·8441	0·8437	0·8416	0·8356	0·8166	0·7115	0·3669
·2	·8740	·8739	·8736	·8728	·8692	·8605	·8353	·7134	·3528
·4	·9043	·9040	·9034	·9021	·8965	·8843	·8524	·7143	·3398
·6	·9353	·9346	·9337	·9314	·9233	·9070	·8679	·7143	·3279
·8	·9672	·9658	·9642	·9608	·9494	·9284	·8820	·7135	·3170
9·0	1·0000	0·9975	0·9950	0·9899	0·9747	0·9487	0·8946	0·7123	0·3069
·2	1·0339	1·0297	1·0259	1·0189	·9992	·9678	·9061	·7107	·2975
·4	1·0691	1·0622	1·0569	1·0475	1·0227	·9856	·9163	·7088	·2889
·6	1·1059	1·0951	1·0879	1·0756	1·0453	1·0023	·9256	·7067	·2809
·8	1·1443	1·1282	1·1186	1·1032	1·0669	1·0179	·9339	·7045	·2735
10·0	1·1849	1·1614	1·1491	1·1301	1·0875	1·0325	0·9414	0·7021	0·2666
·2	1·2280	1·1947	1·1792	1·1563	1·1072	1·0461	·9481	·6997	·2601
·4	1·2741	1·2278	1·2088	1·1817	1·1258	1·0588	·9542	·6973	·2542
·6	1·3238	1·2607	1·2379	1·2063	1·1436	1·0706	·9597	·6949	·2486
·8	1·3782	1·2932	1·2664	1·2301	1·1604	1·0816	·9647	·6924	·2433
11·0	1·4384	1·3254	1·2942	1·2531	1·1763	1·0919	0·9692	0·6901	0·2384
·2	1·5066	1·3571	1·3213	1·2753	1·1915	1·1015	·9733	·6877	·2338
·4	1·5858	1·3882	1·3476	1·2966	1·2058	1·1104	·9770	·6854	·2294
·6	1·6817	1·4187	1·3732	1·3171	1·2194	1·1189	·9804	·6832	·2254
·8	1·8068	1·4485	1·3980	1·3368	1·2324	1·1267	·9835	·6810	·2215
12·0	2·0000	1·4777	1·4220	1·3557	1·2446	1·1341	0·9863	0·6788	0·2179
·2	∞	1·5061	1·4453	1·3739	1·2563	1·1410	·9889	·6768	·2144
·4	—	1·5338	1·4678	1·3913	1·2673	1·1475	·9913	·6747	·2111
·6	—	1·5607	1·4896	1·4081	1·2778	1·1537	·9934	·6728	·2080
·8	—	1·5869	1·5106	1·4241	1·2878	1·1595	·9954	·6709	·2051
13·0	—	1·6124	1·5309	1·4396	1·2973	1·1649	0·9973	0·6690	0·2023
·2	—	1·6371	1·5505	1·4544	1·3064	1·1700	·9990	·6672	·1996
·4	—	1·6611	1·5694	1·4687	1·3150	1·1749	1·0005	·6655	·1971
·6	—	1·6844	1·5877	1·4824	1·3233	1·1795	1·0020	·6638	·1947
·8	—	1·7070	1·6054	1·4955	1·3311	1·1839	1·0033	·6622	·1924
14·0	—	1·7289	1·6224	1·5082	1·3386	1·1880	1·0045	0·6606	0·1902
·2	—	1·7502	1·6389	1·5204	1·3458	1·1919	1·0057	·6591	·1881
·4	—	1·7708	1·6548	1·5321	1·3527	1·1956	1·0067	·6576	·1861

Table 32 (*continued*)

Table A (*cont.*). *Upper standardized percentage points (all signs positive)*

Percent	25·0	10·0	5·0	2·5	1·0	0·5	0·25	0·0	Type
β_2				$\sqrt{\beta_1} = 1\cdot9$ (*cont.*)					
9·6	0·4235	1·2706	1·9171	2·5805	3·4930	4·2156	4·9696	∞	
·8	·4256	1·2654	1·9077	2·5692	3·4840	4·2124	4·9764		
10·0	0·4276	1·2605	1·8989	2·5586	3·4752	4·2089	4·9822		
·2	·4293	1·2559	1·8907	2·5486	3·4667	4·2052	4·9870		
·4	·4309	1·2515	1·8829	2·5391	3·4586	4·2015	4·9910		VI
·6	·4323	1·2474	1·8756	2·5302	3·4508	4·1976	4·9943		
·8	·4336	1·2436	1·8687	2·5217	3·4432	4·1937	4·9970		
11·0	0·4348	1·2399	1·8621	2·5136	3·4360	4·1897	4·9992		
·2	·4359	1·2364	1·8559	2·5059	3·4290	4·1858	5·0009		IV
·4	·4370	1·2331	1·8501	2·4986	3·4223	4·1818	5·0023		
·6	·4379	1·2300	1·8445	2·4917	3·4158	4·1779	5·0033		↓
·8	·4388	1·2270	1·8392	2·4850	3·4096	4·1741	5·0041		
12·0	0·4396	1·2241	1·8341	2·4787	3·4035	4·1703	5·0046		
·2	·4403	1·2214	1·8293	2·4726	3·3977	4·1665	5·0049		
·4	·4410	1·2188	1·8246	2·4668	3·3921	4·1628	5·0050		
·6	·4417	1·2163	1·8202	2·4613	3·3867	4·1592	5·0049		
·8	·4423	1·2139	1·8160	2·4560	3·3815	4·1556	5·0047		
13·0	0·4428	1·2116	1·8120	2·4509	3·3765	4·1521	5·0044		
·2	·4433	1·2095	1·8081	2·4460	3·3716	4·1487	5·0039		
·4	·4438	1·2073	1·8044	2·4412	3·3669	4·1454	5·0034		
				$\sqrt{\beta_1} = 2\cdot0$					
7·6	0·3282	1·3768	2·1389	2·8452	3·6809	4·2387	4·7361	8·3577	
·8	·3406	1·3626	2·1116	2·8174	3·6728	4·2597	4·7962	9·8151	
8·0	0·3511	1·3499	2·0872	2·7916	3·6629	4·2746	4·8457	11·8443	
·2	·3602	1·3385	2·0653	2·7678	3·6520	4·2849	4·8865	14·8740	I (J)
·4	·3681	1·3283	2·0454	2·7458	3·6405	4·2918	4·9204	19·9043	
·6	·3749	1·3189	2·0274	2·7254	3·6287	4·2959	4·9485	29·9353	
·8	·3810	1·3104	2·0109	2·7065	3·6169	4·2979	4·9719	59·9672	
9·0	0·3863	1·3026	1·9957	2·6889	3·6052	4·2983	4·9915	∞	Exponen-tial
·2	·3910	1·2954	1·9818	2·6725	3·5937	4·2975	5·0078		
·4	·3952	1·2887	1·9689	2·6571	3·5824	4·2957	5·0214		
·6	·3990	1·2824	1·9570	2·6428	3·5715	4·2931	5·0328		
·8	·4024	1·2766	1·9458	2·6293	3·5609	4·2900	5·0423		
10·0	0·4054	1·2712	1·9355	2·6167	3·5507	4·2865	5·0503		
·2	·4082	1·2661	1·9258	2·6048	3·5408	4·2826	5·0569		
·4	·4107	1·2614	1·9167	2·5936	3·5313	4·2785	5·0624		
·6	·4130	1·2569	1·9081	2·5830	3·5221	4·2742	5·0669		VI
·8	·4151	1·2526	1·9001	2·5729	3·5132	4·2698	5·0705		
11·0	0·4170	1·2486	1·8925	2·5635	3·5047	4·2654	5·0735		
·2	·4188	1·2448	1·8854	2·5545	3·4966	4·2609	5·0758		
·4	·4204	1·2412	1·8786	2·5459	3·4887	4·2564	5·0777		
·6	·4219	1·2378	1·8722	2·5378	3·4811	4·2518	5·0791		
·8	·4232	1·2346	1·8661	2·5301	3·4738	4·2474	5·0801		
12·0	0·4245	1·2315	1·8603	2·5227	3·4667	4·2429	5·0807		
·2	·4257	1·2285	1·8548	2·5156	3·4599	4·2385	5·0811		IV
·4	·4268	1·2257	1·8495	2·5089	3·4534	4·2342	5·0813		
·6	·4278	1·2230	1·8445	2·5025	3·4471	4·2300	5·0812		↓
·8	·4288	1·2204	1·8397	2·4963	3·4410	4·2258	5·0809		
13·0	0·4297	1·2180	1·8351	2·4904	3·4351	4·2217	5·0805		
·2	·4305	1·2156	1·8307	2·4848	3·4295	4·2177	5·0799		
·4	·4313	1·2133	1·8265	2·4794	3·4240	4·2137	5·0792		
·6	·4320	1·2112	1·8225	2·4741	3·4187	4·2099	5·0784		
·8	·4327	1·2091	1·8186	2·4691	3·4136	4·2061	5·0775		
14·0	0·4334	1·2070	1·8149	2·4643	3·4086	4·2024	5·0766		
·2	·4340	1·2051	1·8113	2·4597	3·4039	4·1988	5·0756		
·4	·4346	1·2032	1·8079	2·4552	3·3992	4·1952	5·0745		

Lower standardized percentage points (all signs negative)

$\sqrt{\beta_1}$	β_2	a	b	0·0	1·0	2·5	5·0	10·0	25·0
0·2	1·6	0·5139	0·6368	1·31742	1·31675	1·31344	1·30210	1·25859	0·97582
0·4	1·8	0·5245	0·8088	1·23014	1·22951	1·22655	1·21671	1·17986	0·94450
0·5	1·8	0·3891	0·6586	1·09984	1·09980	1·09944	1·09747	1·08581	0·95361
0·6	2·0	0·4307	0·8160	1·08904	1·08894	1·08825	1·08512	1·06949	0·92600
0·7	2·2	0·4453	0·9423	1·06218	1·06207	1·06128	1·05791	1·04192	0·90384
0·8	2·2	0·2915	0·6631	0·92689	0·92689	0·92687	0·92670	0·92485	0·87980
	2·4	·4358	1·0258	1·02258	1·02249	1·02188	1·01914	1·00573	0·88455
0·9	2·4	0·2779	0·6973	0·88728	0·88728	0·88727	0·88717	0·88596	0·85158
	2·6	·4074	1·0601	·97372	·97368	·97334	·97164	·96229	·86527
1·0	2·6	0·2525	0·6949	0·84123	0·84123	0·84123	0·84119	0·84064	0·81898
	2·8	·3661	1·0457	·91886	·91885	·91872	·91792	·91266	·84304
1·1	3·0	0·3175	0·9883	0·86072	0·86072	0·86069	0·86043	0·85817	0·81504
1·2	3·2	0·2663	0·8970	0·80140	0·80140	0·80140	0·80135	0·80068	0·77904
	3·4	·3619	1·2745	·86522	·86521	·86511	·86449	·86028	·80283
1·3	3·4	0·2157	0·7819	0·74239	0·74239	0·74239	0·74238	0·74227	0·73438
	3·6	·2955	1·1153	·79927	·79927	·79926	·79914	·79791	·76900
	3·8	·3861	1·5332	·85738	·85736	·85720	·85631	·85095	·78795
1·4	3·8	0·2344	0·9432	0·73567	0·73567	0·73567	0·73566	0·73545	0·72482
	4·0	·3088	1·2995	·78727	·78727	·78725	·78709	·78559	·75457
	4·2	·3924	1·7456	·83983	·83981	·83964	·83872	·83331	·77193
1·5	4·0	0·1796	0·7678	0·67490	0·67490	0·67490	0·67490	0·67488	0·67253
	4·2	·2407	1·0696	·72111	·72111	·72111	·72110	·72086	·70983
	4·4	·3086	1·4382	·76773	·76773	·76771	·76757	·76617	·73730
	4·6	·3841	1·8976	·81506	·81504	·81491	·81415	·80955	·75479
1·6	4·4	0·1818	0·8510	0·65890	0·65890	0·65890	0·65890	0·65888	0·65658
	4·6	·2371	1·1557	·70069	·70069	·70069	·70068	·70049	·69095
	4·8	·2980	1·5255	·74273	·74273	·74272	·74262	·74157	·71758
	5·0	·3652	1·9827	·78523	·78522	·78514	·78464	·78126	·73607
1·7	4·8	0·1766	0·9003	0·63832	0·63832	0·63832	0·63832	0·63831	0·63655
	5·0	·2261	1·2000	·67612	·67612	·67612	·67611	·67599	·66891
	5·2	·2801	1·5607	·71400	·71400	·71400	·71394	· 71329	·69536
	5·4	·3390	2·0021	·75215	·75214	·75211	·75183	·74968	·71522
	5·6	·4035	2·5533	·79072	·79070	·79052	·78959	·78441	·72893
1·8	5·2	0·1662	0·9165	0·61455	0·61455	0·61455	0·61455	0·61455	0·61346
	5·4	·2100	1·2047	·64876	·64876	·64876	·64876	·64870	·64418
	5·6	·2574	1·5480	·68294	·68294	·68294	·68291	·68259	·67060
	5·8	·3087	1·9632	·71721	·71721	·71720	·71708	·71592	·69183
	6·0	·3643	2·4745	·75172	·75171	·75164	·75120	·74820	·70785
	6·2	·4247	3·1175	·78659	·78655	·78629	·78509	·77890	·71918
1·9	5·6	0·1522	0·9028	0·58868	0·58868	0·58868	0·58868	0·58868	0·58815
	5·8	·1907	1·1745	·61971	·61971	·61971	·61971	·61969	·61724
	6·0	·2320	1·4947	·65061	·65061	·65061	·65061	·65047	·64342
	6·2	·2764	1·8771	·68150	·68150	·68149	·68145	·68092	·66574
	6·4	·3242	2·3408	·71245	·71245	·71243	·71225	·71076	·68380
	6·6	·3756	2·9137	·74358	·74357	·74348	·74296	·73962	·69773
	6·8	·4310	3·6371	·77498	·77494	·77466	·77340	·76710	·70798
2·0	6·0	0·1362	0·8638	0·56155	0·56155	0·56155	0·56155	0·56155	0·56136
	6·2	·1698	1·1159	·58979	·58979	·58979	·58979	·58978	·58870
	6·4	·2057	1·4097	·61783	·61783	·61783	·61782	·61778	·61423
	6·6	·2441	1·7559	·64575	·64575	·64575	·64574	·64555	·63710
	6·8	·2850	2·1696	·67364	·67364	·67363	·67358	·67296	·65672
	7·0	·3287	2·6713	·70156	·70156	·70154	·70135	·69981	·67291
	7·2	·3754	3·2912	·72959	·72958	·72950	·72900	·72581	·68579
	7·4	·4254	4·0746	·75780	·75777	·75753	·75641	·75070	·69567

The Type I distribution is taken in the form $f(x|a, b) = \Gamma(a+b)/\{\Gamma(a)\,\Gamma(b)\}x^{a-1}(1-x)^{b-1}$.

Table 33 (*continued*)

Upper standardized percentage points (all signs positive, except for 50 per cent point)

β_2	50·0*	25·0	10·0	5·0	2·5	1·0	0·5	0·25	0·0	Type
1·6	0·1113	0·9445	1·4595	1·5736	1·6126	1·6278	1·6309	1·6320	1·6325	U
1·8	0·1962	0·8649	1·5409	1·7430	1·8310	1·8755	1·8878	1·8930	1·8968	U
1·8	0·2842	0·8865	1·5922	1·7655	1·8279	1·8533	1·8588	1·8607	1·8617	U
2·0	0·2970	0·8137	1·6133	1·8654	1·9776	2·0351	2·0511	2·0579	2·0631	U
2·2	0·3170	0·7582	1·6250	1·9401	2·0982	2·1908	2·2204	2·2347	2·2478	U
2·2	0·4391	0·7735	1·7103	1·9632	2·0569	2·0956	2·1041	2·1071	2·1087	U
2·4	·3432	·7124	1·6362	2·0013	2·1971	2·3203	2·3628	2·3846	2·4072	J
2·4	0·4680	0·7156	1·7349	2·0359	2·1546	2·2068	2·2189	2·2235	2·2261	U
2·6	·3753	·6712	1·6508	2·0563	2·2806	2·4260	2·4776	2·5047	2·5341	J
2·6	0·5035	0·6602	1·7636	2·1007	2·2344	2·2932	2·3069	2·3119	2·3149	U
2·8	·4131	·6305	1·6709	2·1100	2·3532	2·5101	2·5653	2·5941	2·6247	J
3·0	0·4558	0·5867	1·6981	2·1652	2·4173	2·5737	2·6265	2·6528	2·6789	U
3·2	0·5014	0·5353	1·7340	2·2237	2·4731	2·6165	2·6609	2·6816	2·6994	U
3·4	·4332	·5368	1·6443	2·1901	2·5351	2·7926	2·8981	2·9602	3·0470	J
3·4	0·5455	0·4705	1·7814	2·2862	2·5187	2·6367	2·6684	2·6816	2·6909	U
3·6	·4812	·4874	1·6805	2·2512	2·5912	2·8252	2·9129	2·9605	3·0163	J
3·8	·4250	·4968	1·6043	2·2031	2·6177	2·9622	3·1205	3·2228	3·4049	J
3·8	0·5274	0·4230	1·7271	2·3197	2·6410	2·8365	2·9004	2·9313	2·9600	U
4·0	·4737	·4463	1·6403	2·2679	2·6775	2·9910	3·1222	3·2004	3·3130	J
4·2	·4258	·4611	1·5747	2·2143	2·6826	3·0981	3·3026	3·4426	3·7364	J
4·0	0·5633	0·3348	1·7884	2·3953	2·6786	2·8215	2·8594	2·8748	2·8854	U
4·2	·5198	·3793	1·6858	2·3422	2·7336	2·9988	3·0956	3·1470	3·2039	J
4·4	·4742	·4074	1·6102	2·2829	2·7473	3·1262	3·2956	3·4022	3·5779	J
4·6	·4324	·4264	1·5526	2·2273	2·7392	3·2119	3·4543	3·6261	4·0263	J
4·4	0·5541	0·2868	1·7451	2·4269	2·7797	2·9785	3·0376	3·0640	3·0851	U
4·6	·5185	·3356	1·6544	2·3628	2·8102	3·1328	3·2583	3·3285	3·4150	J
4·8	·4798	·3681	1·5872	2·2999	2·8092	3·2404	3·4405	3·5704	3·8016	J
5·0	·4430	·3909	1·5356	2·2433	2·7924	3·3113	3·5833	3·7796	4·2635	J
4·8	0·5486	0·2362	1·7115	2·4560	2·8646	3·1090	3·1861	3·2223	3·2537	U
5·0	·5207	·2895	1·6300	2·3855	2·8788	3·2464	3·3939	3·4784	3·5883	J
5·2	·4882	·3265	1·5692	2·3203	2·8679	3·3402	3·5631	3·7096	3·9786	J
5·4	·4559	·3534	1·5220	2·2629	2·8451	3·4010	3·6949	3·9082	4·4421	J
5·6	·4257	·3734	1·4844	2·2131	2·8174	3·4386	3·7953	4·0738	5·0040	J
5·2	0·5442	0·1810	1·6849	2·4871	2·9407	3·2186	3·3082	3·3509	3·3890	U
5·4	·5239	·2395	1·6102	2·4120	2·9441	3·3447	3·5068	3·5999	3·7219	J
5·6	·4977	·2814	1·5542	2·3446	2·9263	3·4299	3·6676	3·8236	4·1077	J
5·8	·4698	·3125	1·5106	2·2861	2·8990	3·4843	3·7927	4·0155	4·5619	J
6·0	·4427	·3362	1·4756	2·2356	2·8681	3·5171	3·8879	4·1758	5·1066	J
6·2	·4174	·3548	1·4468	2·1920	2·8367	3·5352	3·9595	4·3077	5·7745	J
5·6	0·5386	0·1198	1·6626	2·5226	3·0125	3·3114	3·4068	3·4517	3·4910	U
5·8	·5261	·1842	1·5931	2·4433	3·0088	3·4314	3·5999	3·6955	3·8166	J
6·0	·5064	·2315	1·5409	2·3734	2·9862	3·5119	3·7565	3·9148	4·1910	J
6·2	·4835	·2673	1·5001	2·3131	2·9552	3·5628	3·8786	4·1036	4·6273	J
6·4	·4597	·2951	1·4673	2·2614	2·9215	3·5930	3·9717	4·2619	5·1442	J
6·6	·4367	·3171	1·4402	2·2168	2·8877	3·6089	4·0418	4·3926	5·7684	J
6·8	·4149	·3349	1·4173	2·1781	2·8554	3·6153	4·0942	4·4998	6·5397	J
6·0	0·5298	0·0517	1·6427	2·5640	3·0827	3·3896	3·4836	3·5264	3·5616	U
6·2	·5253	·1224	1·5771	2·4801	3·0749	3·5080	3·6749	3·7668	3·8755	J
6·4	·5127	·1757	1·5280	2·4069	3·0487	3·5875	3·8311	3·9846	4·2332	J
6·6	·4952	·2168	1·4896	2·3442	3·0147	3·6377	3·9535	4·1734	4·6458	J
6·8	·4755	·2491	1·4587	2·2906	2·9783	3·6670	4·0472	4·3327	5·1282	J
7·0	·4552	·2750	1·4331	2·2445	2·9422	3·6820	4·1179	4·4649	5·7016	J
7·2	·4353	·2961	1·4115	2·2046	2·9077	3·6873	4·1708	4·5737	6·3963	J
7·4	·4164	·3136	1·3930	2·1697	2·8753	3·6862	4·2099	4·6629	7·2578	J

* *N.B.* Signs in this column are negative.

Table 34. Johnson S_U system: parameter $-\gamma$ in terms of $\sqrt{\beta_1}$, β_2

β_2 \ $\sqrt{\beta_1}$	0.05	0.10	0.15	0.20	0.25	0.30	0.35	0.40	0.45	0.50
3·1	0·7008	1·5838	3·0386	6·7397						
3·2	·3479	0·7372	1·2278	1·9387	3·1875	6·3675				
3·3	·2332	·4843	0·7762	1·1455	1·6616	2·4876	4·1465	10·7437		
3·4	·1763	·3626	·5710	0·8184	1·1328	1·5666	2·2360	3·4723	6·9742	
3·5	·1424	·2911	·4536	·6397	0·8640	1·1508	1·5455	2·1458	3·2184	5·9700
3·6	0·1198	0·2440	0·3776	0·5270	0·7011	0·9136	1·1875	1·5653	2·1392	3·1567
3·7	·1036	·2106	·3243	·4495	·5919	·7602	0·9681	1·2382	1·6139	2·1883
3·8	·0916	·1856	·2849	·3928	·5134	·6528	·8197	1·0280	1·3018	1·6865
3·9	·0822	·1663	·2546	·3495	·4544	·5734	·7127	0·8814	1·0946	1·3782
4·0	·0746	·1509	·2305	·3155	·4083	·5122	·6317	·7733	0·9470	1·1691
4·1	0·0685	0·1383	0·2109	0·2879	0·3713	0·4637	0·5684	0·6902	0·8363	1·0178
4·2	·0633	·1278	·1946	·2651	·3409	·4241	·5174	·6243	·7503	0·9031
4·3	·0590	·1189	·1809	·2460	·3156	·3914	·4755	·5708	·6814	·8132
4·4	·0552	·1113	·1692	·2297	·2941	·3637	·4404	·5265	·6250	·7407
4·5	·0520	·1048	·1590	·2156	·2756	·3401	·4106	·4891	·5780	·6811
4·6	0·0492	0·0990	0·1501	0·2034	0·2595	0·3197	0·3850	0·4571	0·5382	0·6311
4·7	·0467	·0939	·1423	·1926	·2454	·3018	·3627	·4295	·5040	·5886
4·8	·0444	·0894	·1354	·1830	·2330	·2860	·3431	·4054	·4744	·5520
4·9	·0424	·0853	·1292	·1745	·2219	·2721	·3258	·3842	·4484	·5202
5·0	·0406	·0817	·1236	·1668	·2119	·2595	·3104	·3653	·4254	·4922
5·1	0·0390	0·0783	0·1185	0·1599	0·2029	0·2483	0·2965	0·3484	0·4050	0·4674
5·2	·0375	·0753	·1139	·1536	·1948	·2381	·2840	·3332	·3866	·4453
5·3	·0361	·0726	·1097	·1478	·1874	·2288	·2726	·3195	·3701	·4255
5·4	·0349	·0700	·1058	·1426	·1806	·2203	·2623	·3070	·3551	·4076
5·5	·0337	·0677	·1023	·1377	·1744	·2126	·2528	·2956	·3415	·3913
5·6	0·0326	0·0656	0·0990	0·1332	0·1686	0·2054	0·2441	0·2851	0·3290	0·3765
5·7	·0317	·0636	·0959	·1291	·1633	·1988	·2361	·2755	·3176	·3629
5·8	·0307	·0617	·0931	·1252	·1583	·1927	·2287	·2666	·3070	·3504
5·9	·0299	·0600	·0905	·1216	·1537	·1870	·2218	·2584	·2973	·3389
6·0	·0291	·0583	·0880	·1183	·1494	·1817	·2153	·2507	·2882	·3282
6·1	0·0283	0·0568	0·0857	0·1152	0·1454	0·1767	0·2093	0·2436	0·2798	0·3183
6·2	·0276	·0554	·0835	·1122	·1417	·1721	·2037	·2369	·2719	·3091
6·3	·0269	·0540	·0815	·1095	·1381	·1677	·1985	·2306	·2645	·3005
6·4	·0263	·0528	·0796	·1068	·1348	·1636	·1935	·2248	·2576	·2925
6·5	·0257	·0516	·0778	·1044	·1317	·1598	·1889	·2193	·2512	·2849
6·6	0·0252	0·0504	0·0760	0·1021	0·1287	0·1561	0·1845	0·2141	0·2451	0·2778
6·7	·0246	·0494	·0744	·0999	·1259	·1526	·1803	·2091	·2393	·2711
6·8	·0241	·0484	·0729	·0978	·1232	·1494	·1764	·2045	·2339	·2648
6·9	·0236	·0474	·0714	·0958	·1207	·1463	·1727	·2001	·2288	·2589
7·0	·0232	·0465	·0700	·0939	·1183	·1433	·1691	·1959	·2239	·2532
7·1	0·0227	0·0456	0·0687	0·0921	0·1160	0·1405	0·1658	0·1920	0·2193	0·2479
7·2	·0223	·0447	·0674	·0904	·1138	·1378	·1626	·1882	·2149	·2428
7·3	·0219	·0439	·0662	·0887	·1117	·1353	·1595	·1846	·2107	·2379
7·4	·0215	·0432	·0650	·0872	·1097	·1328	·1566	·1811	·2067	·2333
7·5	·0212	·0424	·0639	·0857	·1078	·1305	·1538	·1779	·2029	·2290
7·6	0·0208	0·0417	0·0628	0·0842	0·1060	0·1283	0·1511	0·1747	0·1992	0·2248
7·7	·0205	·0411	·0618	·0829	·1042	·1261	·1486	·1717	·1957	·2208
7·8	·0202	·0404	·0608	·0815	·1026	·1241	·1461	·1689	·1924	·2169
7·9	·0199	·0398	·0599	·0803	·1010	·1221	·1438	·1661	·1892	·2132
8·0	·0196	·0392	·0590	·0790	·0994	·1202	·1415	·1635	·1862	·2097
8·2	0·0190	0·0381	0·0573	0·0767	0·0965	0·1166	0·1373	0·1585	0·1804	0·2031
8·4	·0185	·0370	·0557	·0746	·0938	·1133	·1333	·1538	·1750	·1970
8·6	·0180	·0360	·0542	·0726	·0912	·1102	·1296	·1495	·1701	·1913
8·8	·0175	·0351	·0528	·0707	·0889	·1073	·1262	·1455	·1655	·1860
9·0	·0171	·0343	·0515	·0690	·0866	·1046	·1230	·1418	·1611	·1811
9·2	0·0167	0·0334	0·0503	0·0673	0·0846	0·1021	0·1200	0·1383	0·1571	0·1765
9·4	·0163	·0327	·0492	·0658	·0826	·0997	·1172	·1350	·1533	·1722

$X = \gamma + \delta \sinh^{-1} y = \gamma + \delta \sinh^{-1}\{(x - \xi)/\lambda\}$ is a $N(0,1)$ variate. For expressions for $E(y)$, $\sigma(y)$ and λ see pp. 81–2.

Table 34 (*continued*). *Values of* $-\gamma$

β_2 \ $\sqrt{\beta_1}$	0·55	0·60	0·65	0·70	0·75	0·80	0·85	0·90	0·95	1·00
3·6	5·7259									
3·7	3·2178	5·9298								
3·8	2·2838	3·3834	6·6379							
3·9	1·7831	2·4255	3·6643	8·6227						
4·0	1·4691	1·9057	2·6208	4·1054						
4·1	1·2532	1·5767	2·0596	2·8859	4·8282					
4·2	1·0955	1·3491	1·7051	2·2537	3·2533	6·2811				
4·3	0·9751	1·1820	1·4598	1·8599	2·5031	3·7922				
4·4	·8802	1·0539	1·2796	1·5893	2·0500	2·8347	4·6887			
4·5	·8033	0·9526	1·1415	1·3915	1·7436	2·2895	3·3012	6·9275		
4·6	0·7398	0·8704	1·0321	1·2402	1·5217	1·9314	2·6028	4·0314		
4·7	·6865	·8024	0·9434	1·1206	1·3531	1·6763	2·1664	3·0367	5·5267	
4·8	·6410	·7451	·8698	1·0237	1·2206	1·4847	1·8640	2·4723	3·7010	
4·9	·6017	·6961	·8079	0·9435	1·1135	1·3352	1·6410	2·0991	2·8945	4·9902
5·0	·5675	·6539	·7550	·8760	1·0251	1·2152	1·4691	1·8313	2·4057	3·5401
5·1	0·5374	0·6170	0·7092	0·8184	0·9509	1·1166	1·3324	1·6289	2·0706	2·8312
5·2	·5106	·5845	·6693	·7686	·8876	1·0342	1·2209	1·4699	1·8243	2·3848
5·3	·4868	·5556	·6341	·7252	·8331	0·9641	1·1281	1·3416	1·6348	2·0719
5·4	·4653	·5298	·6028	·6869	·7855	·9039	1·0497	1·2357	1·4841	1·8382
5·5	·4459	·5066	·5749	·6529	·7437	·8515	0·9825	1·1468	1·3610	1·6562
5·6	0·4283	0·4856	0·5497	0·6226	0·7066	0·8054	0·9242	1·0709	1·2586	1·5100
5·7	·4122	·4665	·5270	·5953	·6735	·7647	·8732	1·0055	1·1719	1·3898
5·8	·3975	·4491	·5063	·5706	·6437	·7283	·8281	0·9484	1·0975	1·2890
5·9	·3839	·4331	·4874	·5481	·6168	·6957	·7880	·8982	1·0330	1·2033
6·0	·3714	·4184	·4701	·5276	·5923	·6663	·7521	·8536	0·9764	1·1293
6·1	0·3598	0·4049	0·4542	0·5088	0·5700	0·6395	0·7197	0·8137	0·9264	1·0649
6·2	·3491	·3923	·4395	·4915	·5496	·6152	·6904	·7779	·8819	1·0083
6·3	·3390	·3806	·4258	·4755	·5308	·5929	·6636	·7455	·8420	0·9580
6·4	·3297	·3697	·4131	·4607	·5134	·5724	·6392	·7161	·8060	0·9132
6·5	·3209	·3595	·4013	·4469	·4973	·5534	·6168	·6892	·7733	·8728
6·6	0·3127	0·3500	0·3902	0·4341	0·4824	0·5359	0·5961	0·6645	0·7436	0·8364
6·7	·3049	·3410	·3799	·4221	·4684	·5197	·5770	·6418	·7163	·8032
6·8	·2976	·3326	·3702	·4109	·4554	·5045	·5592	·6209	·6913	·7730
6·9	·2907	·3247	·3611	·4004	·4433	·4904	·5427	·6015	·6683	·7453
7·0	·2842	·3172	·3524	·3905	·4318	·4772	·5273	·5834	·6469	·7197
7·1	0·2781	0·3101	0·3443	0·3812	0·4211	0·4648	0·5129	0·5666	0·6271	0·6962
7·2	·2722	·3034	·3366	·3723	·4110	·4531	·4994	·5509	·6087	·6743
7·3	·2666	·2970	·3293	·3640	·4014	·4421	·4868	·5362	·5915	·6541
7·4	·2614	·2910	·3224	·3561	·3924	·4318	·4748	·5224	·5754	·6352
7·5	·2563	·2852	·3159	·3486	·3838	·4220	·4636	·5094	·5603	·6175
7·6	0·2515	0·2797	0·3096	0·3415	0·3757	0·4127	0·4530	0·4972	0·5462	0·6010
7·7	·2469	·2745	·3037	·3347	·3680	·4039	·4429	·4856	·5328	·5855
7·8	·2426	·2695	·2980	·3283	·3607	·3956	·4334	·4747	·5202	·5709
7·9	·2384	·2647	·2926	·3221	·3537	·3876	·4243	·4644	·5084	·5571
8·0	·2343	·2602	·2874	·3163	·3470	·3801	·4157	·4546	·4971	·5441
8·1	0·2305	0·2558	0·2824	0·3106	0·3407	0·3729	0·4076	0·4452	0·4864	0·5319
8·2	·2268	·2516	·2777	·3053	·3346	·3660	·3998	·4364	·4763	·5202
8·3	·2232	·2476	·2731	·3001	·3288	·3594	·3923	·4279	·4667	·5092
8·4	·2198	·2437	·2687	·2952	·3232	·3531	·3852	·4198	·4575	·4987
8·5	·2165	·2400	·2645	·2904	·3179	·3471	·3784	·4121	·4488	·4888
8·6	0·2134	0·2364	0·2605	0·2859	0·3127	0·3413	0·3719	0·4048	0·4404	0·4793
8·7	·2103	·2329	·2566	·2815	·3078	·3358	·3657	·3977	·4324	·4702
8·8	·2074	·2296	·2528	·2773	·3031	·3305	·3597	·3910	·4248	·4616
8·9	·2045	·2264	·2492	·2732	·2985	·3253	·3539	·3845	·4175	·4533
9·0	·2018	·2233	·2457	·2693	·2941	·3204	·3484	·3783	·4105	·4454
9·2	0·1966	0·2174	0·2391	0·2619	0·2858	0·3111	0·3380	0·3666	0·3923	0·4305
9·4	·1917	·2119	·2329	·2550	·2781	·3024	·3283	·3558	·3852	·4168
9·6	·1871	·2067	·2271	·2485	·2708	·2944	·3193	·3457	·3739	·4042
9·8	·1828	·2019	·2217	·2424	·2641	·2868	·3108	·3363	·3634	·3925
10·0	·1787	·1973	·2166	·2367	·2577	·2798	·3030	·3275	·3537	·3816

β_2 \ $\sqrt{\beta_1}$	1·05	1·10	1·15	1·20	1·25	1·30	1·35	1·40	1·45	1·50
5·1	4·7951									
5·2	3·4900									
5·3	2·8265	4·8278								
5·4	2·4008	3·5289								
5·5	2·0985	2·8723	5·0999							
5·6	1·8706	2·4499	3·6557							
5·7	1·6917	2·1487	2·9684	5·8122						
5·8	1·5471	1·9207	2·5324	3·8918						
5·9	1·4275	1·7410	2·2230	3·1224						
6·0	1·3269	1·5953	1·9891	2·6525	4·3029					
6·1	1·2409	1·4744	1·8048	2·3241	3·3537					
6·2	1·1665	1·3724	1·6552	2·0779	2·8195	5·1295				
6·3	1·1015	1·2851	1·5311	1·8847	2·4577	3·7083				
6·4	1·0442	1·2094	1·4262	1·7283	2·1908	3·0520				
6·5	0·9933	1·1431	1·3364	1·5987	1·9834	2·6340	4·3176			
6·6	0·9476	1·0845	1·2584	1·4893	1·8166	2·3344	3·3901			
6·7	·9066	1·0323	1·1900	1·3956	1·6789	2·1056	2·8716	5·9718		
6·8	·8694	0·9856	1·1296	1·3143	1·5631	1·9235	2·5195	3·9390		
6·9	·8355	·9435	1·0758	1·2431	1·4640	1·7744	2·2582	3·2098		
7·0	·8046	·9052	1·0275	1·1801	1·3783	1·6496	2·0540	2·7662	5·2016	
7·1	0·7762	0·8704	0·9839	1·1240	1·3032	1·5433	1·8888	2·4535	3·7502	
7·2	·7500	·8385	·9443	1·0737	1·2369	1·4516	1·7518	2·2163	3·1159	
7·3	·7258	·8093	·9083	1·0282	1·1779	1·3716	1·6359	2·0281	2·7135	4·9683
7·4	·7033	·7823	·8752	0·9870	1·1249	1·3010	1·5363	1·8740	2·4239	3·6796
7·5	·6825	·7573	·8449	·9494	1·0772	1·2382	1·4498	1·7450	2·2014	3·0854
7·6	0·6630	0·7341	0·8169	0·9150	1·0339	1·1820	1·3737	1·6351	2·0230	2·7026
7·7	·6448	·7125	·7910	·8833	0·9944	1·1314	1·3063	1·5401	1·8758	2·4245
7·8	·6277	·6924	·7669	·8541	·9583	1·0856	1·2460	1·4570	1·7519	2·2094
7·9	·6117	·6736	·7445	·8271	·9250	1·0438	1·1919	1·3836	1·6456	2·0361
8·0	·5966	·6559	·7236	·8020	·8944	1·0056	1·1429	1·3183	1·5534	1·8925
8·1	0·5824	0·6393	0·7040	0·7786	0·8660	0·9705	1·0983	1·2597	1·4724	1·7710
8·2	·5690	·6237	·6856	·7567	·8397	·9381	1·0576	1·2069	1·4007	1·6666
8·3	·5563	·6089	·6683	·7363	·8151	·9082	1·0203	1·1589	1·3366	1·5757
8·4	·5443	·5950	·6521	·7171	·7922	·8804	0·9858	1·1152	1·2790	1·4956
8·5	·5328	·5818	·6367	·6991	·7708	·8545	0·9540	1·0751	1·2268	1·4245
8·6	0·5220	0·5693	0·6222	0·6821	0·7507	0·8304	0·9245	1·0383	1·1794	1·3609
8·7	·5116	·5574	·6085	·6661	·7318	·8078	·8971	1·0042	1·1360	1·3036
8·8	·5018	·5461	·5955	·6509	·7140	·7866	·8715	0·9727	1·0962	1·2516
8·9	·4924	·5354	·5831	·6366	·6972	·7667	·8476	·9435	1·0596	1·2042
9·0	·4834	·5251	·5713	·6230	·6813	·7479	·8252	·9162	1·0257	1·1608
9·1	0·4748	0·5153	0·5601	0·6100	0·6662	0·7302	0·8041	0·8907	0·9942	1·1210
9·2	·4666	·5060	·5494	·5977	·6520	·7135	·7843	·8668	·9649	1·0842
9·3	·4587	·4970	·5392	·5860	·6384	·6977	·7656	·8444	·9376	1·0501
9·4	·4511	·4885	·5295	·5749	·6255	·6827	·7479	·8233	·9121	1·0185
9·5	·4439	·4803	·5202	·5642	·6133	·6684	·7312	·8035	·8881	0·9890
9·6	0·4369	0·4724	0·5112	0·5540	0·6016	0·6549	0·7153	0·7847	0·8656	0·9615
9·7	·4302	·4648	·5027	·5443	·5904	·6420	·7003	·7670	·8444	·9357
9·8	·4237	·4576	·4944	·5349	·5797	·6297	·6860	·7502	·8244	·9115
9·9	·4175	·4506	·4865	·5260	·5695	·6179	·6724	·7343	·8055	·8888
10·0	·4115	·4438	·4790	·5174	·5597	·6067	·6594	·7191	·7876	·8673
10·2	0·4001	0·4311	0·4646	0·5012	0·5413	0·5857	0·6352	0·6910	0·7545	0·8280
10·4	·3895	·4192	·4513	·4862	·5243	·5663	·6130	·6653	·7246	·7926
10·6	·3796	·4081	·4389	·4723	·5086	·5485	·5927	·6419	·6974	·7607
10·8	·3703	·3978	·4273	·4593	·4940	·5320	·5739	·6204	·6726	·7317
11·0	·3615	·3880	·4165	·4472	·4804	·5167	·5565	·6006	·6498	·7053
11·2	0·3533	0·3789	0·4063	0·4358	0·4677	0·5024	0·5404	0·5823	0·6288	0·6811
11·4	·3455	·3703	·3968	·4252	·4559	·4891	·5254	·5653	·6095	·6588
11·6	·3381	·3621	·3878	·4152	·4447	·4766	·5114	·5495	·5915	·6382
11·8	·3311	·3544	·3792	·4058	·4342	·4649	·4983	·5347	·5748	·6192
12·0	·3245	·3472	·3712	·3968	·4243	·4539	·4860	·5209	·5592	·6015

Table 34 (*continued*). *Values of* $-\gamma$

β_2 \ $\sqrt{\beta_1}$	1·55	1·60	1·65	1·70	1·75	1·80	1·85	1·90	1·95	2·00
7·6	5·0364									
7·7	3·7042									
7·8	3·1096									
7·9	2·7288	5·5073								
8·0	2·4526	3·8279								
8·1	2·2388	3·1889								
8·2	2·0663	2·7921								
8·3	1·9233	2·5080	4·0904							
8·4	1·8021	2·2895	3·3342							
8·5	1·6977	2·1138	2·8977							
8·6	1·6068	1·9683	2·5938	4·6419						
8·7	1·5266	1·8452	2·3635	3·5758						
8·8	1·4552	1·7393	2·1799	3·0578						
8·9	1·3913	1·6469	2·0288	2·7167	7·6116					
9·0	1·3336	1·5654	1·9013	2·4650	4·0001					
9·1	1·2812	1·4929	1·7919	2·2677	3·3003					
9·2	1·2335	1·4279	1·6966	2·1068	2·8901					
9·3	1·1897	1·3693	1·6128	1·9721	2·6021	5·0330				
9·4	1·1495	1·3160	1·5382	1·8570	2·3823	3·6981				
9·5	1·1123	1·2675	1·4714	1·7572	2·2062	3·1427				
9·6	1·0778	1·2229	1·4111	1·6696	2·0604	2·7897				
9·7	1·0458	1·1819	1·3564	1·5919	1·9369	2·5330	4·5560			
9·8	1·0159	1·1440	1·3065	1·5223	1·8305	2·3332	3·5474			
9·9	0·9880	1·1088	1·2607	1·4597	1·7374	2·1708	3·0594			
10·0	·9618	1·0762	1·2186	1·4029	1·6552	2·0350	2·7372			
10·1	0·9372	1·0457	1·1797	1·3511	1·5819	1·9190	2·4986	4·4118		
10·2	·9141	1·0172	1·1436	1·3037	1·5160	1·8184	2·3106	3·4939		
10·3	·8923	0·9905	1·1100	1·2600	1·4563	1·7300	2·1566	3·0319		
10·4	·8717	·9654	1·0787	1·2197	1·4020	1·6516	2·0270	2·7233		
10·5	·8522	·9417	1·0494	1·1823	1·3524	1·5813	1·9159	2·4931	4·4843	
10·6	0·8337	0·9194	1·0219	1·1476	1·3067	1·5179	1·8190	2·3109	3·5214	
10·7	·8162	·8984	0·9961	1·1152	1·2646	1·4603	1·7335	2·1611	3·0537	
10·8	·7995	·8784	·9718	1·0849	1·2256	1·4078	1·6574	2·0347	2·7441	
10·9	·7836	·8595	·9489	1·0565	1·1894	1·3596	1·5891	1·9259	2·5141	4·8560
11·0	·7685	·8415	·9272	1·0298	1·1556	1·3152	1·5273	1·8310	2·3323	3·6370
11·1	0·7541	0·8245	0·9067	1·0047	1·1241	1·2741	1·4710	1·7470	2·1830	3·1264
11·2	·7403	·8082	·8873	0·9810	1·0945	1·2360	1·4195	1·6721	2·0571	2·8003
11·3	·7271	·7927	·8688	·9586	1·0667	1·2005	1·3723	1·6047	1·9487	2·5619
11·4	·7144	·7779	·8512	·9374	1·0406	1·1674	1·3286	1·5437	1·8540	2·3752
11·5	·7023	·7637	·8345	·9173	1·0160	1·1364	1·2882	1·4881	1·7702	2·2226
11·6	0·6907	0·7502	0·8185	0·8982	0·9927	1·1073	1·2506	1·4371	1·6954	2·0943
11·7	·6795	·7372	·8033	·8800	·9706	1·0800	1·2156	1·3902	1·6281	1·9842
11·8	·6688	·7248	·7887	·8627	·9497	1·0542	1·1828	1·3469	1·5671	1·8881
11·9	·6585	·7129	·7748	·8462	·9299	1·0298	1·1521	1·3067	1·5115	1·8032
12·0	·6485	·7014	·7614	·8305	·9110	1·0068	1·1233	1·2693	1·4604	1·7275
12·1	0·6389	0·6904	0·7486	0·8154	0·8931	0·9850	1·0961	1·2344	1·4135	1·6593
12·2	·6297	·6798	·7363	·8010	·8759	·9643	1·0705	1·2018	1·3700	1·5976
12·3	·6208	·6696	·7245	·7872	·8596	·9446	1·0463	1·1712	1·3297	1·5413
12·4	·6122	·6597	·7132	·7740	·8440	·9258	1·0234	1·1424	1·2922	1·4897
12·5	·6039	·6502	·7022	·7613	·8290	·9080	1·0016	1·1152	1·2572	1·4421
12·6	0·5958	0·6411	0·6917	0·7491	0·8147	0·8909	0·9809	1·0896	1·2244	1·3982
12·7	·5881	·6322	·6816	·7373	·8010	·8746	·9613	1·0653	1·1936	1·3574
12·8	·5805	·6237	·6718	·7260	·7878	·8590	·9426	1·0423	1·1646	1·3194
12·9	·5732	·6154	·6624	·7152	·7751	·8441	·9247	1·0205	1·1373	1·2839
13·0	·5662	·6074	·6532	·7047	·7630	·8298	·9076	0·9998	1·1114	1·2507
13·2	0·5527	0·5643	0·6359	0·6848	0·7400	0·8029	0·8757	0·9612	1·0638	1·1901
13·4	·5399	·5516	·6197	·6663	·7186	·7780	·8464	·9261	1·0209	1·1362
13·6	·5279	·5396	·6044	·6489	·6987	·7550	·8194	·8940	0·9820	1·0879
13·8	·5166	·5282	·5901	·6327	·6801	·7336	·7944	·8644	·9465	1·0444
14·0	·5058	·5174	·5766	·6174	·6627	·7136	·7712	·8372	·9140	1·0049
14·2	0·4956	0·5072	0·5638	0·6030	0·6464	0·6949	0·7496	0·8120	0·8841	0·9688
14·4	·4859	·4974	·5518	·5894	·6310	·6774	·7294	·7885	·8565	·9358
14·6	·4767	·4881	·5403	·5766	·6165	·6609	·7105	·7667	·8309	·9054
14·8	·4679	·4793	·5295	·5644	·6029	·6454	·6929	·7463	·8071	·8773
15·0	·4595	·4708	·5191	·5529	·5899	·6308	·6762	·7272	·7850	·8513

Table 35. *Johnson S_U system: parameter δ in terms of $\sqrt{\beta_1}$, β_2*

β_2 \ $\sqrt{\beta_1}$	0·05	0·10	0·15	0·20	0·25	0·30	0·35	0·40	0·45	0·50
3·1	6·548	6·904	7·662	9·351						
3·2	4·671	4·787	5·004	5·368	5·992	7·197				
3·3	3·866	3·927	4·037	4·209	4·472	4·880	5·566	6·944		
3·4	3·396	3·435	3·504	3·608	3·759	3·978	4·300	4·809	5·719	
3·5	3·081	3·108	3·156	3·228	3·329	3·468	3·663	3·943	4·369	5·090
3·6	2·852	2·872	2·908	2·960	3·034	3·133	3·266	3·448	3·705	4·087
3·7	2·676	2·692	2·720	2·760	2·816	2·891	2·989	3·120	3·295	3·539
3·8	2·535	2·548	2·571	2·604	2·648	2·707	2·783	2·882	3·011	3·184
3·9	2·420	2·431	2·450	2·477	2·514	2·561	2·623	2·701	2·801	2·931
4·0	2·324	2·333	2·349	2·372	2·403	2·442	2·493	2·556	2·637	2·739
4·1	2·242	2·250	2·264	2·283	2·309	2·343	2·385	2·439	2·505	2·588
4·2	2·171	2·178	2·190	2·207	2·229	2·258	2·295	2·340	2·396	2·465
4·3	2·109	2·115	2·126	2·141	2·160	2·186	2·217	2·256	2·304	2·363
4·4	2·054	2·060	2·069	2·082	2·100	2·122	2·150	2·184	2·226	2·276
4·5	2·005	2·010	2·018	2·030	2·046	2·066	2·090	2·121	2·157	2·202
4·6	1·961	1·966	1·973	1·984	1·998	2·016	2·038	2·065	2·097	2·136
4·7	1·921	1·925	1·932	1·942	1·955	1·971	1·991	2·015	2·044	2·079
4·8	1·885	1·889	1·895	1·904	1·916	1·930	1·948	1·970	1·997	2·028
4·9	1·852	1·855	1·861	1·869	1·880	1·893	1·910	1·930	1·954	1·982
5·0	1·822	1·825	1·830	1·837	1·847	1·860	1·875	1·893	1·915	1·941
5·1	1·793	1·796	1·801	1·808	1·817	1·829	1·843	1·859	1·880	1·903
5·2	1·767	1·770	1·775	1·781	1·790	1·800	1·813	1·829	1·847	1·869
5·3	1·743	1·746	1·750	1·756	1·764	1·774	1·786	1·800	1·817	1·837
5·4	1·721	1·723	1·727	1·732	1·740	1·749	1·760	1·774	1·789	1·808
5·5	1·699	1·702	1·705	1·711	1·718	1·726	1·737	1·749	1·764	1·781
5·6	1·680	1·682	1·685	1·690	1·697	1·705	1·715	1·726	1·740	1·756
5·7	1·661	1·663	1·666	1·671	1·677	1·685	1·694	1·705	1·718	1·733
5·8	1·643	1·645	1·648	1·653	1·658	1·666	1·674	1·685	1·697	1·711
5·9	1·627	1·628	1·631	1·636	1·641	1·648	1·656	1·666	1·677	1·691
6·0	1·611	1·613	1·615	1·619	1·625	1·631	1·639	1·648	1·659	1·672
6·1	1·596	1·598	1·600	1·604	1·609	1·615	1·623	1·631	1·642	1·653
6·2	1·582	1·583	1·586	1·590	1·594	1·600	1·607	1·615	1·625	1·636
6·3	1·568	1·570	1·572	1·576	1·580	1·586	1·593	1·600	1·610	1·620
6·4	1·556	1·557	1·559	1·563	1·567	1·572	1·579	1·586	1·595	1·605
6·5	1·543	1·545	1·547	1·550	1·554	1·559	1·565	1·573	1·581	1·591
6·6	1·532	1·533	1·535	1·538	1·542	1·547	1·553	1·560	1·568	1·577
6·7	1·520	1·522	1·524	1·527	1·530	1·535	1·541	1·547	1·555	1·564
6·8	1·510	1·511	1·513	1·516	1·519	1·524	1·529	1·535	1·543	1·551
6·9	1·499	1·501	1·502	1·505	1·509	1·513	1·518	1·524	1·531	1·539
7·0	1·490	1·491	1·492	1·495	1·498	1·502	1·507	1·513	1·520	1·528
7·1	1·480	1·481	1·483	1·485	1·489	1·492	1·497	1·503	1·509	1·517
7·2	1·471	1·472	1·474	1·476	1·479	1·483	1·487	1·493	1·499	1·506
7·3	1·462	1·463	1·465	1·467	1·470	1·474	1·478	1·483	1·489	1·496
7·4	1·454	1·455	1·456	1·458	1·461	1·465	1·469	1·474	1·480	1·487
7·5	1·445	1·446	1·448	1·450	1·453	1·456	1·460	1·465	1·471	1·477
7·6	1·438	1·438	1·440	1·442	1·445	1·448	1·452	1·457	1·462	1·468
7·7	1·430	1·431	1·432	1·434	1·437	1·440	1·444	1·448	1·454	1·460
7·8	1·423	1·423	1·425	1·427	1·429	1·432	1·436	1·440	1·445	1·451
7·9	1·415	1·416	1·418	1·419	1·422	1·425	1·428	1·433	1·438	1·443
8·0	1·408	1·409	1·411	1·412	1·415	1·418	1·421	1·425	1·430	1·435
8·2	1·395	1·396	1·397	1·399	1·401	1·404	1·407	1·411	1·416	1·421
8·4	1·383	1·383	1·385	1·386	1·388	1·391	1·394	1·398	1·402	1·407
8·6	1·371	1·372	1·373	1·374	1·376	1·379	1·382	1·385	1·389	1·394
8·8	1·360	1·361	1·362	1·363	1·365	1·367	1·370	1·373	1·377	1·381
9·0	1·349	1·350	1·351	1·352	1·354	1·356	1·359	1·362	1·366	1·370
9·2	1·339	1·340	1·341	1·342	1·344	1·346	1·349	1·352	1·355	1·359
9·4	1·330	1·330	1·331	1·333	1·334	1·336	1·339	1·342	1·345	1·348

$X = \gamma + \delta \sinh^{-1} y = \gamma + \delta \sinh^{-1}\{(x - \xi)/\lambda\}$ is a $N(0, 1)$ variate. For expressions for $E(y)$, $\sigma(y)$, ξ and λ see pp. 81-2

Table 35 (continued). Values of δ

β_2 \ $\sqrt{\beta_1}$	0.55	0.60	0.65	0.70	0.75	0.80	0.85	0.90	0.95	1.00
3.6	4.718									
3.7	3.900	4.487								
3.8	3.424	3.776	4.348							
3.9	3.104	3.344	3.699	4.278						
4.0	2.872	3.049	3.294	3.659						
4.1	2.694	2.830	3.013	3.269	3.654					
4.2	2.552	2.662	2.804	2.996	3.266	3.681				
4.3	2.435	2.526	2.641	2.791	2.994	3.286				
4.4	2.338	2.414	2.510	2.631	2.791	3.010	3.329			
4.5	2.255	2.320	2.401	2.502	2.631	2.803	3.042	3.400		
4.6	2.183	2.240	2.309	2.395	2.502	2.642	2.828	3.093		
4.7	2.120	2.170	2.231	2.304	2.395	2.511	2.662	2.868	3.167	
4.8	2.065	2.109	2.162	2.226	2.305	2.403	2.528	2.694	2.925	
4.9	2.015	2.055	2.100	2.159	2.227	2.312	2.418	2.555	2.739	3.001
5.0	1.971	2.007	2.049	2.099	2.160	2.233	2.325	2.440	2.592	2.799
5.1	1.931	1.963	2.001	2.045	2.100	2.165	2.245	2.344	2.471	2.641
5.2	1.894	1.924	1.958	1.999	2.048	2.105	2.176	2.262	2.371	2.512
5.3	1.860	1.888	1.919	1.957	2.000	2.052	2.115	2.191	2.285	2.405
5.4	1.830	1.855	1.884	1.918	1.958	2.005	2.061	2.128	2.211	2.315
5.5	1.801	1.824	1.851	1.883	1.918	1.962	2.012	2.073	2.146	2.237
5.6	1.775	1.796	1.821	1.850	1.884	1.923	1.969	2.023	2.089	2.170
5.7	1.750	1.770	1.794	1.820	1.851	1.887	1.929	1.979	2.038	2.110
5.8	1.728	1.746	1.768	1.793	1.821	1.855	1.893	1.939	1.992	2.057
5.9	1.706	1.724	1.744	1.767	1.794	1.824	1.860	1.902	1.951	2.009
6.0	1.686	1.703	1.722	1.743	1.768	1.797	1.830	1.868	1.913	1.967
6.1	1.667	1.683	1.701	1.721	1.744	1.771	1.802	1.837	1.879	1.928
6.2	1.649	1.664	1.681	1.700	1.722	1.747	1.776	1.809	1.847	1.892
6.3	1.633	1.647	1.663	1.681	1.701	1.725	1.752	1.782	1.818	1.860
6.4	1.617	1.630	1.645	1.662	1.682	1.704	1.729	1.758	1.791	1.830
6.5	1.602	1.614	1.629	1.645	1.663	1.684	1.707	1.735	1.766	1.802
6.6	1.587	1.599	1.613	1.628	1.646	1.666	1.688	1.713	1.742	1.776
6.7	1.574	1.585	1.598	1.613	1.629	1.648	1.669	1.693	1.721	1.752
6.8	1.561	1.572	1.584	1.598	1.614	1.632	1.652	1.674	1.700	1.730
6.9	1.548	1.559	1.571	1.584	1.599	1.616	1.635	1.656	1.681	1.708
7.0	1.537	1.547	1.558	1.571	1.585	1.601	1.619	1.639	1.663	1.689
7.1	1.525	1.535	1.546	1.558	1.572	1.587	1.604	1.623	1.645	1.670
7.2	1.514	1.524	1.534	1.546	1.559	1.573	1.590	1.608	1.629	1.653
7.3	1.504	1.513	1.523	1.534	1.547	1.561	1.576	1.594	1.614	1.636
7.4	1.494	1.503	1.512	1.523	1.535	1.548	1.563	1.580	1.599	1.620
7.5	1.484	1.493	1.502	1.512	1.524	1.537	1.551	1.567	1.585	1.605
7.6	1.475	1.483	1.492	1.502	1.513	1.525	1.539	1.555	1.572	1.591
7.7	1.466	1.474	1.483	1.492	1.503	1.515	1.528	1.543	1.559	1.578
7.8	1.458	1.465	1.473	1.483	1.493	1.504	1.517	1.531	1.547	1.565
7.9	1.450	1.457	1.465	1.474	1.483	1.494	1.507	1.520	1.536	1.552
8.0	1.442	1.448	1.456	1.465	1.474	1.485	1.497	1.510	1.524	1.541
8.1	1.434	1.440	1.448	1.456	1.466	1.476	1.487	1.500	1.514	1.529
8.2	1.426	1.433	1.440	1.448	1.457	1.467	1.478	1.490	1.504	1.519
8.3	1.419	1.425	1.432	1.440	1.449	1.458	1.469	1.481	1.494	1.508
8.4	1.412	1.418	1.425	1.433	1.441	1.450	1.460	1.472	1.484	1.498
8.5	1.405	1.411	1.418	1.425	1.433	1.442	1.452	1.463	1.475	1.489
8.6	1.399	1.405	1.411	1.418	1.426	1.435	1.444	1.455	1.467	1.479
8.7	1.392	1.398	1.404	1.411	1.419	1.427	1.437	1.447	1.458	1.471
8.8	1.386	1.392	1.398	1.404	1.412	1.420	1.429	1.439	1.450	1.462
8.9	1.380	1.386	1.391	1.398	1.405	1.413	1.422	1.431	1.442	1.454
9.0	1.374	1.380	1.385	1.392	1.399	1.406	1.415	1.424	1.434	1.446
9.2	1.363	1.368	1.373	1.379	1.386	1.393	1.401	1.410	1.420	1.431
9.4	1.353	1.357	1.362	1.368	1.374	1.381	1.389	1.397	1.406	1.416
9.6	1.343	1.347	1.352	1.357	1.363	1.370	1.377	1.385	1.394	1.403
9.8	1.333	1.337	1.342	1.347	1.353	1.359	1.366	1.373	1.381	1.390
10.0	1.324	1.328	1.332	1.337	1.343	1.349	1.355	1.362	1.370	1.379

Table 35(continued). *Johnson S_U system: parameter δ in terms of $\sqrt{\beta_1}$, β_2*

β_2 \ $\sqrt{\beta_1}$	1·05	1·10	1·15	1·20	1·25	1·30	1·35	1·40	1·45	1·50
5·1	2·878									
5·2	2·704									
5·3	2·564	2·785								
5·4	2·449	2·631								
5·5	2·353	2·505	2·714							
5·6	2·270	2·400	2·574							
5·7	2·199	2·311	2·458	2·661						
5·8	2·136	2·234	2·361	2·531						
5·9	2·080	2·167	2·278	2·423						
6·0	2·030	2·109	2·206	2·331	2·499					
6·1	1·986	2·056	2·143	2·252	2·396					
6·2	1·945	2·009	2·087	2·184	2·309	2·477				
6·3	1·908	1·966	2·037	2·124	2·234	2·378				
6·4	1·875	1·928	1·992	2·070	2·168	2·294				
6·5	1·843	1·893	1·951	2·022	2·109	2·220	2·367			
6·6	1·815	1·860	1·914	1·978	2·057	2·156	2·284			
6·7	1·788	1·830	1·880	1·939	2·011	2·099	2·213	2·362		
6·8	1·763	1·803	1·849	1·903	1·968	2·049	2·150	2·281		
6·9	1·740	1·777	1·820	1·870	1·930	2·003	2·094	2·210		
7·0	1·719	1·753	1·793	1·840	1·895	1·962	2·044	2·148	2·284	
7·1	1·698	1·731	1·768	1·811	1·863	1·924	1·999	2·092	2·213	
7·2	1·679	1·710	1·745	1·785	1·833	1·890	1·958	2·043	2·150	
7·3	1·661	1·690	1·723	1·761	1·806	1·858	1·921	1·998	2·095	2·220
7·4	1·644	1·671	1·703	1·738	1·780	1·829	1·887	1·958	2·045	2·157
7·5	1·628	1·654	1·683	1·717	1·756	1·802	1·856	1·921	2·001	2·101
7·6	1·613	1·637	1·665	1·697	1·734	1·776	1·827	1·887	1·960	2·051
7·7	1·598	1·622	1·648	1·678	1·713	1·753	1·800	1·856	1·923	2·006
7·8	1·584	1·607	1·632	1·660	1·693	1·731	1·775	1·827	1·889	1·965
7·9	1·571	1·593	1·616	1·644	1·675	1·710	1·751	1·800	1·858	1·928
8·0	1·559	1·579	1·602	1·628	1·657	1·691	1·730	1·775	1·829	1·894
8·1	1·547	1·566	1·588	1·613	1·640	1·672	1·709	1·752	1·802	1·862
8·2	1·535	1·554	1·575	1·598	1·625	1·655	1·690	1·730	1·777	1·833
8·3	1·524	1·542	1·562	1·585	1·610	1·639	1·671	1·709	1·754	1·806
8·4	1·514	1·531	1·550	1·571	1·596	1·623	1·654	1·690	1·732	1·781
8·5	1·504	1·520	1·538	1·559	1·582	1·608	1·638	1·672	1·711	1·758
8·6	1·494	1·510	1·527	1·547	1·569	1·594	1·623	1·655	1·692	1·736
8·7	1·484	1·500	1·517	1·536	1·557	1·581	1·608	1·639	1·674	1·715
8·8	1·475	1·490	1·507	1·525	1·545	1·568	1·594	1·623	1·657	1·695
8·9	1·467	1·481	1·497	1·514	1·534	1·556	1·580	1·608	1·640	1·677
9·0	1·458	1·472	1·487	1·504	1·523	1·544	1·568	1·594	1·625	1·660
9·1	1·450	1·463	1·478	1·495	1·513	1·533	1·556	1·581	1·610	1·643
9·2	1·442	1·455	1·469	1·485	1·503	1·522	1·544	1·568	1·596	1·628
9·3	1·435	1·447	1·461	1·476	1·493	1·512	1·533	1·556	1·583	1·613
9·4	1·427	1·440	1·453	1·468	1·484	1·502	1·522	1·545	1·570	1·599
9·5	1·420	1·432	1·445	1·459	1·475	1·492	1·512	1·534	1·558	1·586
9·6	1·413	1·425	1·437	1·451	1·466	1·483	1·502	1·523	1·546	1·573
9·7	1·407	1·418	1·430	1·443	1·458	1·474	1·492	1·513	1·535	1·560
9·8	1·400	1·411	1·423	1·436	1·450	1·466	1·483	1·503	1·524	1·549
9·9	1·394	1·404	1·416	1·428	1·442	1·458	1·474	1·493	1·514	1·538
10·0	1·388	1·398	1·409	1·421	1·435	1·450	1·466	1·484	1·504	1·527
10·1	1·382	1·392	1·403	1·414	1·428	1·442	1·458	1·475	1·495	1·516
10·2	1·376	1·386	1·396	1·408	1·420	1·434	1·450	1·467	1·485	1·506
10·3	1·371	1·380	1·390	1·401	1·414	1·427	1·442	1·458	1·477	1·497
10·4	1·365	1·374	1·384	1·395	1·407	1·420	1·435	1·450	1·468	1·488
10·5	1·360	1·369	1·378	1·389	1·401	1·413	1·427	1·443	1·460	1·479
10·6	1·355	1·363	1·373	1·383	1·394	1·407	1·420	1·435	1·452	1·470
10·7	1·349	1·358	1·367	1·377	1·388	1·400	1·414	1·428	1·444	1·462
10·8	1·345	1·353	1·362	1·372	1·382	1·394	1·407	1·421	1·437	1·454
10·9	1·340	1·348	1·357	1·366	1·377	1·388	1·401	1·414	1·429	1·446
11·0	1·335	1·343	1·352	1·361	1·371	1·382	1·394	1·408	1·422	1·439
11·2	1·326	1·334	1·342	1·351	1·360	1·371	1·383	1·395	1·409	1·424
11·4	1·317	1·325	1·332	1·341	1·350	1·360	1·371	1·383	1·396	1·411
11·6	1·309	1·316	1·323	1·332	1·340	1·350	1·361	1·372	1·384	1·398
11·8	1·301	1·308	1·315	1·323	1·331	1·340	1·350	1·361	1·373	1·386
12·0	1·293	1·300	1·307	1·314	1·322	1·331	1·341	1·351	1·363	1·375

Table 35 (*continued*). *Values of* δ

β_2 \ $\sqrt{\beta_1}$	1·55	1·60	1·65	1·70	1·75	1·80	1·85	1·90	1·95	2·00
7·6	2·169									
7·7	2·112									
7·8	2·061									
7·9	2·015	2·127								
8·0	1·974	2·075								
8·1	1·936	2·028								
8·2	1·901	1·985								
8·3	1·869	1·946	2·044							
8·4	1·840	1·911	2·000							
8·5	1·812	1·878	1·960							
8·6	1·787	1·848	1·924	2·019						
8·7	1·763	1·821	1·891	1·978						
8·8	1·741	1·795	1·860	1·940						
8·9	1·720	1·770	1·831	1·905	1·999					
9·0	1·700	1·748	1·805	1·874	1·960					
9·1	1·682	1·727	1·780	1·844	1·923					
9·2	1·664	1·707	1·757	1·817	1·890					
9·3	1·648	1·688	1·735	1·791	1·860	1·945				
9·4	1·632	1·670	1·715	1·768	1·831	1·910				
9·5	1·617	1·653	1·696	1·745	1·805	1·878				
9·6	1·603	1·637	1·678	1·725	1·781	1·849				
9·7	1·589	1·622	1·660	1·705	1·758	1·821	1·900			
9·8	1·576	1·608	1·644	1·686	1·736	1·796	1·869			
9·9	1·564	1·594	1·629	1·669	1·716	1·772	1·841			
10·0	1·552	1·581	1·614	1·652	1·697	1·750	1·814			
10·1	1·541	1·569	1·600	1·636	1·679	1·729	1·789	1·863		
10·2	1·530	1·557	1·587	1·621	1·662	1·709	1·766	1·835		
10·3	1·520	1·545	1·574	1·607	1·646	1·690	1·744	1·809		
10·4	1·509	1·534	1·562	1·594	1·630	1·673	1·723	1·784		
10·5	1·500	1·523	1·550	1·581	1·616	1·656	1·704	1·761	1·831	
10·6	1·491	1·513	1·539	1·568	1·602	1·640	1·686	1·740	1·805	
10·7	1·482	1·504	1·528	1·556	1·588	1·625	1·669	1·720	1·781	
10·8	1·473	1·494	1·518	1·545	1·576	1·611	1·652	1·701	1·759	
10·9	1·465	1·485	1·508	1·534	1·564	1·597	1·637	1·682	1·737	1·804
11·0	1·456	1·476	1·499	1·524	1·552	1·584	1·622	1·665	1·717	1·780
11·1	1·449	1·468	1·489	1·514	1·541	1·572	1·608	1·649	1·699	1·758
11·2	1·441	1·460	1·481	1·504	1·530	1·560	1·594	1·634	1·681	1·737
11·3	1·434	1·452	1·472	1·494	1·520	1·549	1·581	1·619	1·664	1·717
11·4	1·427	1·444	1·464	1·485	1·510	1·538	1·569	1·605	1·648	1·698
11·5	1·420	1·437	1·456	1·477	1·500	1·527	1·557	1·592	1·633	1·681
11·6	1·413	1·430	1·448	1·468	1·491	1·517	1·546	1·580	1·618	1·664
11·7	1·407	1·423	1·441	1·460	1·482	1·507	1·535	1·567	1·604	1·648
11·8	1·400	1·416	1·433	1·452	1·474	1·498	1·525	1·556	1·591	1·633
11·9	1·394	1·409	1·426	1·445	1·466	1·489	1·515	1·545	1·579	1·618
12·0	1·388	1·403	1·419	1·437	1·458	1·480	1·505	1·534	1·567	1·604
12·1	1·383	1·397	1·413	1·430	1·450	1·471	1·496	1·524	1·555	1·591
12·2	1·377	1·391	1·406	1·423	1·442	1·463	1·487	1·514	1·544	1·579
12·3	1·371	1·385	1·400	1·417	1·435	1·455	1·478	1·504	1·533	1·567
12·4	1·366	1·379	1·394	1·410	1·428	1·448	1·470	1·495	1·523	1·555
12·5	1·361	1·374	1·388	1·404	1·421	1·440	1·462	1·486	1·513	1·544
12·6	1·356	1·369	1·382	1·398	1·415	1·433	1·454	1·477	1·504	1·534
12·7	1·351	1·363	1·377	1·392	1·408	1·426	1·446	1·469	1·495	1·523
12·8	1·346	1·358	1·371	1·386	1·402	1·420	1·439	1·461	1·486	1·514
12·9	1·341	1·353	1·366	1·380	1·396	1·413	1·432	1·453	1·477	1·504
13·0	1·337	1·348	1·361	1·375	1·390	1·407	1·425	1·446	1·469	1·495
13·2	1·328	1·339	1·351	1·364	1·379	1·394	1·412	1·431	1·453	1·478
13·4	1·319	1·330	1·341	1·354	1·368	1·383	1·400	1·418	1·438	1·461
13·6	1·311	1·321	1·332	1·344	1·358	1·372	1·388	1·405	1·425	1·446
13·8	1·303	1·313	1·324	1·335	1·348	1·362	1·377	1·393	1·412	1·432
14·0	1·296	1·305	1·315	1·326	1·339	1·352	1·366	1·382	1·399	1·419
14·2	1·289	1·298	1·307	1·318	1·330	1·342	1·356	1·371	1·388	1·406
14·4	1·282	1·290	1·300	1·310	1·321	1·333	1·346	1·361	1·377	1·394
14·6	1·275	1·283	1·293	1·302	1·313	1·325	1·337	1·351	1·366	1·383
14·8	1·269	1·277	1·285	1·295	1·305	1·316	1·328	1·342	1·356	1·372
15·0	1·262	1·270	1·279	1·288	1·298	1·308	1·320	1·333	1·346	1·362

Table 36. Johnson S_B system: parameters in terms of $\sqrt{\beta_1}$, β_2

β_2	δ	$\sigma(y)$		γ	δ	$\mu_1'(y)$	$\sigma(y)$	γ	δ	$\mu_1'(y)$	$\sigma(y)$
	$\sqrt{\beta_1} = 0.00$				$\sqrt{\beta_1} = 0.05$				$\sqrt{\beta_1} = 0.10$		
1.1	0.0883	0.4639		0.0316	0.0862	0.4875	0.4646	0.0633	0.0796	0.4750	0.4669
1.2	0.1692	0.4306		0.0327	0.1671	0.4875	0.4313	0.0652	0.1608	0.4750	0.4334
1.3	0.2465	0.3999		0.0342	0.2444	0.4875	0.4006	0.0681	0.2382	0.4750	0.4025
1.4	0.3227	0.3714	For $\sqrt{\beta_1} = 0.00$	0.0361	0.3205	0.4874	0.3721	0.0719	0.3141	0.4749	0.3740
1.5	0.3994	0.3451		0.0385	0.3972	0.4874	0.3457	0.0765	0.3904	0.4748	0.3475
1.6	0.4780	0.3204	$\gamma = 0$,	0.0413	0.4757	0.4873	0.3210	0.0820	0.4685	0.4746	0.3227
1.7	0.5599	0.2973	$\mu_1'(y) = 0.5$	0.0447	0.5573	0.4871	0.2979	0.0887	0.5496	0.4742	0.2995
1.8	0.6465	0.2754		0.0487	0.6436	0.4868	0.2760	0.0966	0.6351	0.4737	0.2776
1.9	0.7393	0.2547		0.0536	0.7360	0.4865	0.2552	0.1061	0.7266	0.4732	0.2568
2.0	0.8403	0.2347		0.0594	0.8367	0.4862	0.2353	0.1174	0.8259	0.4725	0.2370
2.1	0.9522	0.2157		0.0666	0.9480	0.4857	0.2162	0.1315	0.9357	0.4716	0.2177
2.2	1.079	0.1971		0.0757	1.074	0.4851	0.1976	0.1491	1.059	0.4704	0.1992
2.3	1.225	0.1788		0.0873	1.219	0.4844	0.1794	0.1717	1.201	0.4691	0.1810
2.4	1.398	0.1608		0.1029	1.391	0.4834	0.1613	0.2014	1.369	0.4672	0.1631
2.5	1.613	0.1427		0.1244	1.603	0.4822	0.1433	0.2429	1.574	0.4648	0.1450
2.6	1.892	0.1241		0.1571	1.879	0.4804	0.1247	0.3043	1.839	0.4614	0.1266
2.7	2.286	0.1046		0.2111	2.266	0.4777	0.1053	0.4044	2.205	0.4564	0.1074
2.8	2.918	0.0833		0.3180	2.885	0.4733	0.0840	0.5957	2.776	0.4482	0.0864
2.9	4.241	0.0582		0.6295	4.195	0.4632	0.0584	1.109	3.916	0.4308	0.0617

β_2	γ	δ	$\mu_1'(y)$	$\sigma(y)$	γ	δ	$\mu_1'(y)$	$\sigma(y)$	γ	δ	$\mu_1'(y)$	$\sigma(y)$
		$\sqrt{\beta_1} = 0.15$				$\sqrt{\beta_1} = 0.20$				$\sqrt{\beta_1} = 0.25$		
1.7	0.1314	0.5368	0.4614	0.3024	0.1720	0.5193	0.4488	0.3064	0.2102	0.4977	0.4365	0.3114
1.8	0.1428	0.6211	0.4608	0.2804	0.1866	0.6020	0.4480	0.2843	0.2276	0.5783	0.4356	0.2892
1.9	0.1565	0.7111	0.4600	0.2595	0.2040	0.6899	0.4471	0.2633	0.2480	0.6636	0.4344	0.2682
2.0	0.1729	0.8084	0.4590	0.2396	0.2248	0.7846	0.4458	0.2433	0.2724	0.7552	0.4330	0.2481
2.1	0.1932	0.9154	0.4577	0.2204	0.2502	0.8883	0.4442	0.2241	0.3019	0.8550	0.4311	0.2289
2.2	0.2182	1.035	0.4561	0.2019	0.2816	1.004	0.4422	0.2056	0.3380	0.9650	0.4288	0.2103
2.3	0.2502	1.173	0.4541	0.1837	0.3211	1.135	0.4397	0.1875	0.3833	1.089	0.4260	0.1922
2.4	0.2922	1.334	0.4515	0.1658	0.3726	1.287	0.4365	0.1696	0.4414	1.232	0.4224	0.1745
2.5	0.3499	1.529	0.4481	0.1479	0.4423	1.470	0.4323	0.1519	0.5184	1.401	0.4177	0.1569
2.6	0.4338	1.777	0.4434	0.1297	0.5411	1.698	0.4267	0.1339	0.6253	1.607	0.4116	0.1392
2.7	0.5671	2.113	0.4366	0.1108	0.6932	1.999	0.4188	0.1154	0.7834	1.872	0.4031	0.1211
2.8	0.8098	2.619	0.4259	0.0903	0.9548	2.433	0.4068	0.0956	1.041	2.238	0.3908	0.1020
2.9	1.391	3.546	0.4050	0.0668	1.513	3.163	0.3853	0.0733	1.532	2.804	0.3705	0.0810
3.0									2.839	3.911	0.3285	0.0557
		$\sqrt{\beta_1} = 0.30$				$\sqrt{\beta_1} = 0.35$				$\sqrt{\beta_1} = 0.40$		
1.7	0.2458	0.4716	0.4243	0.3177	0.2785	0.4419	0.4124	0.3251	0.3084	0.4091	0.4007	0.3336
1.8	0.2652	0.5502	0.4234	0.2952	0.2993	0.5185	0.4114	0.3024	0.3301	0.4835	0.3998	0.3106
1.9	0.2880	0.6329	0.4221	0.2740	0.3239	0.5983	0.4101	0.2810	0.3558	0.5605	0.3985	0.2890
2.0	0.3151	0.7212	0.4205	0.2539	0.3529	0.6830	0.4085	0.2607	0.3859	0.6415	0.3969	0.2685
2.1	0.3477	0.8164	0.4185	0.2346	0.3875	0.7738	0.4065	0.2413	0.4215	0.7277	0.3948	0.2490
2.2	0.3873	0.9209	0.4161	0.2160	0.4291	0.8737	0.4039	0.2226	0.4640	0.8206	0.3923	0.2303
2.3	0.4362	1.037	0.4130	0.1980	0.4799	0.9814	0.4007	0.2046	0.5153	0.9221	0.3891	0.2122
2.4	0.4980	1.170	0.4091	0.1803	0.5433	1.104	0.3968	0.1871	0.5784	1.035	0.3852	0.1947
2.5	0.5786	1.324	0.4042	0.1629	0.6242	1.244	0.3918	0.1698	0.6574	1.162	0.3803	0.1776
2.6	0.6875	1.510	0.3978	0.1455	0.7309	1.409	0.3855	0.1526	0.7591	1.309	0.3742	0.1606
2.7	0.8431	1.741	0.3893	0.1277	0.8780	1.610	0.3772	0.1353	0.8946	1.483	0.3664	0.1437
2.8	1.082	2.046	0.3773	0.1094	1.093	1.865	0.3660	0.1176	1.084	1.697	0.3562	0.1265

$X = \gamma + \delta\log\{y/(1-y)\} = \gamma + \delta\log\{(x-\xi)/(\xi+\lambda-x)\}$ is a $N(0, 1)$ variate.
Since $\xi \leqslant x \leqslant \xi+\lambda$, $\lambda = \sigma(x)/\sigma(y)$, $\xi = \mu_1'(x) - \lambda\mu_1'(y)$.

Table 36 (*continued*)

β_2	γ	δ	$\mu_1'(y)$	$\sigma(y)$	γ	δ	$\mu_1'(y)$	$\sigma(y)$	γ	δ	$\mu_1'(y)$	$\sigma(y)$
	$\sqrt{\beta_1} = $ **0.30** (*cont.*)				$\sqrt{\beta_1} = $ **0.35** (*cont.*)				$\sqrt{\beta_1} = $ **0.40** (*cont.*)			
2.9	1.496	2.486	0.3590	0.0896	1.435	2.211	0.3498	0.0989	1.366	1.973	0.3421	0.1087
3.0	2.388	3.225	0.3265	0.0670	2.068	2.730	0.3241	0.0783	1.831	2.354	0.3215	0.0897
3.1	5.711	5.004	0.2439	0.0367	3.626	3.676	0.2749	0.0536	2.739	2.945	0.2878	0.0683
3.2									5.312	4.107	0.2180	0.0413
	$\sqrt{\beta_1} = $ **0.45**				$\sqrt{\beta_1} = $ **0.50**				$\sqrt{\beta_1} = $ **0.55**			
1.8	0.3576	0.4455	0.3885	0.3200	0.3822	0.4051	0.3773	0.3304	0.4040	0.3624	0.3664	0.3421
1.9	0.3837	0.5198	0.3872	0.2981	0.4081	0.4769	0.3762	0.3082	0.4294	0.4319	0.3655	0.3194
2.0	0.4142	0.5974	0.3857	0.2773	0.4385	0.5511	0.3748	0.2872	0.4590	0.5032	0.3642	0.2980
2.1	0.4501	0.6792	0.3837	0.2576	0.4739	0.6288	0.3729	0.2673	0.4934	0.5770	0.3626	0.2779
2.2	0.4925	0.7665	0.3812	0.2388	0.5154	0.7109	0.3706	0.2483	0.5336	0.6545	0.3603	0.2586
2.3	0.5432	0.8611	0.3781	0.2207	0.5646	0.7989	0.3677	0.2301	0.5807	0.7365	0.3577	0.2403
2.4	0.6045	0.9645	0.3743	0.2032	0.6234	0.8943	0.3641	9.2125	0.6362	0.8244	0.3544	0.2227
2.5	0.6801	1.080	0.3697	0.1862	0.6945	0.9988	0.3598	0.1956	0.7025	0.9198	0.3504	0.2057
2.6	0.7752	1.211	0.3639	0.1694	0.7823	1.116	0.3545	0.1790	0.7829	1.025	0.3456	0.1892
2.7	0.8982	1.362	0.3567	0.1528	0.8929	1.248	0.3479	0.1626	0.8818	1.141	0.3397	0.1730
2.8	1.063	1.543	0.3475	0.1361	1.036	1.402	0.3397	0.1463	1.006	1.274	0.3324	0.1570
2.9	1.296	1.766	0.3353	0.1191	1.229	1.586	0.3292	0.1298	1.168	1.428	0.3233	0.1410
3.0	1.647	2.056	0.3186	0.1013	1.502	1.814	0.3154	0.1130	1.384	1.611	0.3119	0.1249
3.1	2.239	2.461	0.2938	0.0821	1.917	2.109	0.2964	0.0953	1.690	1.837	0.2968	0.1083
3.2	3.447	3.104	0.2524	0.0600	2.622	2.524	0.2682	0.0760	2.152	2.130	0.2762	0.0909
3.3	7.310	4.425	0.1632	0.0308	4.088	3.181	0.2213	0.0536	2.935	2.536	0.2462	0.0718
3.4									4.551	3.170	0.1969	0.0495
	$\sqrt{\beta_1} = $ **0.60**				$\sqrt{\beta_1} = $ **0.65**				$\sqrt{\beta_1} = $ **0.70**			
2.0	0.4764	0.4539	0.3539	0.3099	0.4914	0.4034	0.3438	0.3228	0.5045	0.3518	0.3338	0.3369
2.1	0.5095	0.5243	0.3524	0.2894	0.5227	0.4711	0.3425	0.3019	0.5336	0.4170	0.3328	0.3155
2.2	0.5478	0.5975	0.3505	0.2699	0.5588	0.5404	0.3409	0.2821	0.5674	0.4834	0.3314	0.2953
2.3	0.5923	0.6744	0.3481	0.2514	0.6006	0.6127	0.3387	0.2633	0.6063	0.5516	0.3296	0.2761
2.4	0.6444	0.7557	0.3451	0.2337	0.6490	0.6885	0.3361	0.2454	0.6510	0.6225	0.3274	0.2580
2.5	0.7058	0.8432	0.3415	0.2165	0.7054	0.7687	0.3329	0.2282	0.7027	0.6967	0.3246	0.2406
2.6	0.7788	0.9375	0.3372	0.2001	0.7717	0.8545	0.3292	0.2117	0.7626	0.7754	0.3213	0.2239
2.7	0.8670	1.041	0.3319	0.1840	0.8504	0.9476	0.3245	0.1956	0.8328	0.8594	0.3172	0.2078
2.8	0.9754	1.157	0.3255	0.1682	0.9449	1.049	0.3189	0.1800	0.9156	0.9500	0.3124	0.1924
2.9	1.111	1.288	0.3178	0.1526	1.060	1.162	0.3122	0.1645	1.015	1.049	0.3067	0.1770
3.0	1.287	1.439	0.3081	0.1370	1.204	1.289	0.3040	0.1493	1.135	1.158	0.2998	0.1620
3.1	1.520	1.618	0.2959	0.1212	1.389	1.436	0.2941	0.1342	1.284	1.280	0.2915	0.1472
3.2	1.847	1.837	0.2801	0.1050	1.632	1.608	0.2816	0.1188	1.472	1.420	0.2814	0.1324
3.3	2.337	2.118	0.2588	0.0879	1.969	1.816	0.2656	0.1030	1.718	1.582	0.2690	0.1175
3.4	3.151	2.501	0.2284	0.0693	2.463	2.078	0.2444	0.0864	2.052	1.776	0.2533	0.1022
3.5	4.770	3.079	0.1800	0.0477	3.258	2.426	0.2149	0.0684	2.529	2.015	0.2329	0.0862
3.6					4.759	2.932	0.1700	0.0479	3.271	2.325	0.2052	0.0691
3.7									4.580	2.754	0.1652	0.0498
3.8									7.610	3.419	0.1005	0.0266
	$\sqrt{\beta_1} = $ **0.75**				$\sqrt{\beta_1} = $ **0.80**				$\sqrt{\beta_1} = $ **0.85**			
2.2	0.5743	0.4262	0.3222	0.3094	0.5802	0.3689	0.3129	0.3246	0.5858	0.3112	0.3037	0.3409
2.3	0.6101	0.4911	0.3207	0.2899	0.6129	0.4312	0.3118	0.3046	0.6152	0.3715	0.3030	0.3203
2.4	0.6512	0.5579	0.3189	0.2714	0.6503	0.4946	0.3103	0.2856	0.6490	0.4322	0.3018	0.3008
2.5	0.6983	0.6272	0.3164	0.2537	0.6931	0.5597	0.3084	0.2677	0.6877	0.4941	0.3003	0.2824
2.6	0.7525	0.6997	0.3136	0.2369	0.7420	0.6271	0.3060	0.2506	0.7316	0.5572	0.2983	0.2650
2.7	0.8150	0.7762	0.3101	0.2207	0.7979	0.6975	0.3030	0.2342	0.7816	0.6226	0.2959	0.2483

β_2	γ	δ	$\mu_1'(y)$	$\sigma(y)$	γ	δ	$\mu_1'(y)$	$\sigma(y)$	γ	δ	$\mu_1'(y)$	$\sigma(y)$
		$\sqrt{\beta_1} = $ **0·75** (cont.)				$\sqrt{\beta_1} = $ **0·80** (cont.)				$\sqrt{\beta_1} = $ **0·85** (cont.)		
2·8	0·8879	0·8577	0·3060	0·2050	0·8622	0·7717	0·2995	0·2184	0·8385	0·6907	0·2930	0·2324
2·9	0·9735	0·9453	0·3011	0·1898	0·9367	0·8503	0·2954	0·2032	0·9036	0·7621	0·2896	0·2171
3·0	1·075	1·040	0·2953	0·1751	1·024	0·9344	0·2904	0·1884	0·9786	0·8377	0·2854	0·2022
3·1	1·198	1·145	0·2883	0·1604	1·126	1·025	0·2847	0·1740	1·065	0·9180	0·2806	0·1879
3·2	1·348	1·261	0·2801	0·1461	1·248	1·125	0·2778	0·1599	1·167	1·004	0·2749	0·1738
3·3	1·535	1·393	0·2702	0·1318	1·397	1·234	0·2698	0·1459	1·287	1·098	0·2683	0·1601
3·4	1·777	1·544	0·2580	0·1173	1·580	1·357	0·2602	0·1320	1·431	1·201	0·2605	0·1465
3·5	2·098	1·722	0·2430	0·1025	1·811	1·496	0·2486	0·1180	1·606	1·314	0·2514	0·1331
3·6	2·545	1·937	0·2238	0·0872	2·112	1·657	0·2345	0·1039	1·824	1·442	0·2405	0·1196
3·7	3·210	2·207	0·1987	0·0710	2·520	1·849	0·2169	0·0893	2·102	1·587	0·2274	0·1060
3·8	4·309	2·565	0·1639	0·0531	3·102	2·082	0·1944	0·0739	2·467	1·756	0·2115	0·0921
3·9	6·510	3·080	0·1118	0·0324	4·003	2·379	0·1646	0·0574	2·968	1·957	0·1916	0·0777
4·0					5·602	2·780	0·1227	0·0389	3·701	2·204	0·1663	0·0624
4·1									4·876	2·519	0·1325	0·0457
4·2									7·146	2·948	0·0850	0·0266
		$\sqrt{\beta_1} = $ **0·90**				$\sqrt{\beta_1} = $ **0·95**				$\sqrt{\beta_1} = $ **1·00**		
1·9	0·5429	0·0644	0·2948	0·4311								
2·0	0·5538	0·1303	0·2949	0·4052	0·5708	0·0680	0·2855	0·4255				
2·1	0·5704	0·1925	0·2948	0·3810	0·5823	0·1322	0·2855	0·4004	0·5980	0·0681	0·2764	0·4212
2·2	0·5918	0·2527	0·2946	0·3583	0·5993	0·1928	0·2855	0·3769	0·6095	0·1307	0·2765	0·3968
2·3	0·6177	0·3118	0·2941	0·3370	0·6213	0·2515	0·2853	0·3549	0·6268	0·1900	0·2764	0·3740
2·4	0·6479	0·3706	0·2933	0·3170	0·6476	0·3091	0·2848	0·3342	0·6489	0·2472	0·2762	0·3526
2·5	0·6825	0·4296	0·2922	0·2981	0·6782	0·3662	0·2840	0·3148	0·6754	0·3032	0·2758	0·3324
2·6	0·7219	0·4896	0·2907	0·2802	0·7132	0·4237	0·2829	0·2964	0·7061	0·3589	0·2750	0·3135
2·7	0·7665	0·5510	0·2887	0·2632	0·7529	0·4818	0·2815	0·2790	0·7411	0·4146	0·2740	0·2955
2·8	0·8170	0·6142	0·2863	0·2470	0·7977	0·5412	0·2795	0·2623	0·7807	0·4710	0·2726	0·2785
2·9	0·8742	0·6799	0·2835	0·2315	0·8480	0·6020	0·2772	0·2465	0·8251	0·5283	0·2708	0·2622
3·0	0·9393	0·7483	0·2801	0·2165	0·9049	0·6651	0·2744	0·2313	0·8749	0·5869	0·2685	0·2468
3·1	1·014	0·8205	0·2760	0·2021	0·9693	0·7308	0·2712	0·2168	0·9309	0·6473	0·2659	0·2322
3·2	1·099	0·8969	0·2714	0·1881	1·042	0·7995	0·2673	0·2027	0·9939	0·7100	0·2628	0·2177
3·3	1·199	0·9785	0·2659	0·1745	1·126	0·8719	0·2628	0·1890	1·065	0·7753	0·2591	0·2040
3·4	1·315	1·067	0·2596	0·1611	1·222	0·9488	0·2577	0·1758	1·146	0·8438	0·2549	0·1907
3·5	1·413	1·162	0·2522	0·1480	1·333	1·031	0·2517	0·1628	1·238	0·9160	0·2500	0·1777
3·6	1·619	1·267	0·2436	0·1349	1·464	1·120	0·2448	0·1500	1·343	0·9929	0·2444	0·1651
3·7	1·821	1·383	0·2335	0·1220	1·619	1·216	0·2368	0·1374	1·466	1·075	0·2380	0·1527
3·8	2·073	1·513	0·2216	0·1089	1·804	1·321	0·2275	0·1249	1·609	1·163	0·2306	0·1405
3·9	2·396	1·662	0·2073	0·0957	2·032	1·438	0·2167	0·1124	1·779	1·259	0·2222	0·1285
4·0	2·824	1·835	0·1899	0·0821	2·315	1·570	0·2039	0·0998	1·982	1·364	0·2124	0·1164
4·1	3·417	2·041	0·1684	0·0679	2·679	1·719	0·1887	0·0870	2·230	1·480	0·2011	0·1044
4·2	4·298	2·293	0·1409	0·0527	3·162	1·892	0·1704	0·0737	2·540	1·609	0·1879	0·0922
4·3	5·764	2·615	0·1046	0·0361	3·835	2·097	0·1479	0·0599	2·935	1·756	0·1723	0·0798
4·4					4·846	2·346	0·1194	0·0450	3·459	1·925	0·1536	0·0670
4·5					6·574	2·661	0·0823	0·0287	4·192	2·124	0·1308	0·0536
4·6									5·292	2·363	0·1025	0·0393
4·7									7·201	2·659	0·0662	0·0236
		$\sqrt{\beta_1} = $ **1·05**				$\sqrt{\beta_1} = $ **1·10**				$\sqrt{\beta_1} = $ **1·15**		
2·7	0·7315	0·3488	0·2664	0·3130	0·7247	0·2838	0·2586	0·3314	0·7213	0·2181	0·2507	0·3510
2·8	0·7662	0·4029	0·2654	0·2954	0·7546	0·3361	0·2580	0·3133	0·7464	0·2702	0·2504	0·3321
2·9	0·8053	0·4574	0·2641	0·2787	0·7887	0·3887	0·2571	0·2961	0·7744	0·3214	0·2499	0·3143
3·0	0·8490	0·5125	0·2623	0·2629	0·8269	0·4414	0·2559	0·2797	0·8086	0·3723	0·2491	0·2974

$X = \gamma + \delta \log \{y/(1-y)\} = \gamma + \delta \log \{(x-\xi)/(\xi+\lambda-x)\}$ is a $N(0, 1)$ variate.
Since $\xi \leqslant x \leqslant \xi+\lambda$, $\lambda = \sigma(x)/\sigma(y)$, $\xi = \mu_1'(x) - \lambda\mu_1'(y)$.

Table 36 (*continued*)

β_2	γ	δ	$\mu'_1(y)$	$\sigma(y)$	γ	δ	$\mu'_1(y)$	$\sigma(y)$	γ	δ	$\mu'_1(y)$	$\sigma(y)$
	$\sqrt{\beta_1} = \mathbf{1 \cdot 05}$ (*cont.*)				$\sqrt{\beta_1} = \mathbf{1 \cdot 10}$ (*cont.*)				$\sqrt{\beta_1} = \mathbf{1 \cdot 15}$ (*cont.*)			
3·1	0·8979	0·5690	0·2603	0·2477	0·8696	0·4947	0·2543	0·2642	0·8458	0·4232	0·2480	0·2814
3·2	0·9525	0·6268	0·2577	0·2332	0·9171	0·5487	0·2523	0·2494	0·8871	0·4745	0·2466	0·2662
3·3	1·013	0·6865	0·2548	0·2193	0·9701	0·6041	0·2500	0·2352	0·9331	0·5265	0·2448	0·2516
3·4	1·082	0·7485	0·2514	0·2059	1·029	0·6609	0·2473	0·2215	0·9840	0·5795	0·2427	0·2376
3·5	1·160	0·8133	0·2474	0·1929	1·095	0·7198	0·2441	0·2084	1·040	0·6337	0·2402	0·2243
3·6	1·247	0·8811	0·2429	0·1802	1·168	0·7809	0·2404	0·1956	1·103	0·6894	0·2373	0·2114
3·7	1·346	0·9526	0·2377	0·1680	1·251	0·8445	0·2362	0·1833	1·173	0·7471	0·2339	0·1989
3·8	1·461	1·029	0·2318	0·1559	1·344	0·9113	0·2315	0·1713	1·250	0·8066	0·2301	0·1868
3·9	1·592	1·110	0·2251	0·1441	1·450	0·9816	0·2261	0·1596	1·337	0·8692	0·2257	0·1751
4·0	1·746	1·197	0·2174	0·1324	1·571	1·056	0·2200	0·1481	1·435	0·9344	0·2208	0·1637
4·1	1·928	1·291	0·2087	0·1209	1·710	1·135	0·2131	0·1368	1·545	1·003	0·2153	0·1526
4·2	2·145	1·394	0·1987	0·1093	1·872	1·220	0·2053	0·1257	1·671	1·075	0·2091	0·1416
4·3	2·409	1·507	0·1871	0·0978	2·062	1·312	0·1964	0·1146	1·816	1·152	0·2021	0·1308
4·4	2·736	1·633	0·1737	0·0861	2·288	1·411	0·1863	0·1036	1·982	1·234	0·1943	0·1201
4·5	3·153	1·775	0·1581	0·0741	2·562	1·521	0·1748	0·0924	2·177	1·323	0·1855	0·1095
4·6	3·702	1·936	0·1396	0·0619	2·898	1·641	0·1616	0·0813	2·408	1·418	0·1755	0·0990
4·7	4·462	2·124	0·1173	0·0490	3·323	1·775	0·1463	0·0699	2·684	1·521	0·1643	0·0884
4·8	5·597	2·346	0·0901	0·0354	3·877	1·927	0·1284	0·0582	3·021	1·635	0·1514	0·0777
4·9	7·559	2·616	0·0560	0·0206	4·634	2·100	0·1072	0·0460	3·442	1·760	0·1368	0·0669
5·0					5·745	2·303	0·0819	0·0332	3·983	1·900	0·1199	0·0558
5·1					7·622	2·543	0·0508	0·0194	4·709	2·058	0·1002	0·0443
5·2									5·748	2·240	0·0770	0·0323
5·3									7·431	2·450	0·0493	0·0196
	$\sqrt{\beta_1} = \mathbf{1 \cdot 20}$				$\sqrt{\beta_1} = \mathbf{1 \cdot 25}$				$\sqrt{\beta_1} = \mathbf{1 \cdot 30}$			
3·1	0·8263	0·3540	0·2414	0·2995	0·8114	0·2859	0·2346	0·3184	0·8015	0·2179	0·2275	0·3384
3·2	0·8621	0·4032	0·2405	0·2837	0·8419	0·3338	0·2340	0·3021	0·8268	0·2655	0·2273	0·3214
3·3	0·9020	0·4528	0·2392	0·2687	0·8763	0·3817	0·2332	0·2865	0·8559	0·3123	0·2268	0·3053
3·4	0·9461	0·5027	0·2376	0·2544	0·9144	0·4294	0·2321	0·2718	0·8885	0·3587	0·2261	0·2899
3·5	0·9948	0·5534	0·2357	0·2407	0·9566	0·4775	0·2306	0·2576	0·9248	0·4049	0·2252	0·2753
3·6	1·049	0·6051	0·2334	0·2275	1·003	0·5260	0·2289	0·2442	0·9648	0·4511	0·2239	0·2614
3·7	1·108	0·6580	0·2307	0·2148	1·054	0·5753	0·2269	0·2312	1·009	0·4977	0·2224	0·2481
3·8	1·173	0·7124	0·2277	0·2026	1·110	0·6256	0·2245	0·2187	1·057	0·5448	0·2206	0·2353
3·9	1·246	0·7686	0·2242	0·1908	1·172	0·6771	0·2217	0·2067	1·110	0·5927	0·2185	0·2230
4·0	1·327	0·8269	0·2202	0·1793	1·239	0·7301	0·2186	0·1952	1·167	0·6415	0·2160	0·2112
4·1	1·417	0·8874	0·2158	0·1682	1·314	0·7846	0·2150	0·1839	1·231	0·6914	0·2132	0·1998
4·2	1·518	0·9507	0·2108	0·1573	1·397	0·8410	0·2110	0·1729	1·300	0·7426	0·2100	0·1888
4·3	1·632	1·017	0·2053	0·1466	1·490	0·8996	0·2066	0·1623	1·376	0·7954	0·2064	0·1780
4·4	1·761	1·087	0·1991	0·1362	1·592	0·9607	0·2016	0·1519	1·460	0·8498	0·2025	0·1676
4·5	1·908	1·161	0·1921	0·1259	1·708	1·025	0·1961	0·1418	1·554	0·9062	0·1981	0·1575
4·6	2·076	1·240	0·1844	0·1157	1·837	1·092	0·1900	0·1318	1·657	0·9648	0·1932	0·1478
4·7	2·272	1·324	0·1758	0·1056	1·985	1·162	0·1832	0·1219	1·772	1·026	0·1878	0·1379
4·8	2·502	1·414	0·1661	0·0955	2·153	1·237	0·1757	0·1122	1·901	1·090	0·1818	0·1283
4·9	2·775	1·511	0·1553	0·0854	2·346	1·316	0·1674	0·1026	2·047	1·157	0·1753	0·1189
5·0	3·105	1·617	0·1431	0·0753	2·571	1·401	0·1582	0·0930	2·212	1·228	0·1681	0·1096
5·1	3·511	1·733	0·1293	0·0650	2·836	1·492	0·1479	0·0834	2·400	1·302	0·1602	0·1004
5·2	4·025	1·861	0·1136	0·0545	3·152	1·590	0·1365	0·0738	2·617	1·381	0·1515	0·0913
5·3	4·699	2·003	0·0956	0·0438	3·536	1·696	0·1236	0·0641	2·870	1·466	0·1418	0·0822
5·4	5·636	2·164	0·0748	0·0326	4·013	1·812	0·1092	0·0542	3·168	1·556	0·1312	0·0731
5·5	7·073	2·346	0·0505	0·0210	4·624	1·940	0·0929	0·0442	3·523	1·652	0·1194	0·0639
5·6					5·445	2·080	0·0744	0·0339	3·959	1·757	0·1063	0·0547
5·7					6·638	2·238	0·0533	0·0232	4·503	1·870	0·0917	0·0453
5·8									5·210	1·994	0·0753	0·0358

(*continued over page*)

β_2	γ	δ	$\mu_1'(y)$	$\sigma(y)$	γ	δ	$\mu_1'(y)$	$\sigma(y)$	γ	δ	$\mu_1'(y)$	$\sigma(y)$
									\multicolumn — $\sqrt{\beta_1} = 1.30$ (*cont.*)			
5.9									6.184	2.130	0.0570	0.0260
6.0									7.687	2.280	0.0362	0.0158
	$\sqrt{\beta_1} = 1.35$				$\sqrt{\beta_1} = 1.40$				$\sqrt{\beta_1} = 1.45$			
3.6	0.9335	0.3791	0.2185	0.2794	0.9085	0.3090	0.2126	0.2982	0.8902	0.2396	0.2065	0.3179
3.7	0.9713	0.4238	0.2175	0.2656	0.9408	0.3524	0.2120	0.2839	0.9170	0.2826	0.2062	0.3030
3.8	1.013	0.4686	0.2161	0.2525	0.9763	0.3956	0.2112	0.2703	0.9471	0.3250	0.2057	0.2888
3.9	1.058	0.5137	0.2145	0.2399	1.015	0.4389	0.2100	0.2572	0.9803	0.3668	0.2050	0.2753
4.0	1.108	0.5594	0.2126	0.2277	1.058	0.4821	0.2087	0.2448	1.017	0.4086	0.2041	0.2624
4.1	1.162	0.6058	0.2104	0.2160	1.104	0.5258	0.2070	0.2328	1.057	0.4502	0.2029	0.2500
4.2	1.220	0.6529	0.2080	0.2048	1.154	0.5700	0.2051	0.2213	1.100	0.4921	0.2015	0.2381
4.3	1.285	0.7011	0.2051	0.1939	1.209	0.6147	0.2029	0.2101	1.147	0.5343	0.1999	0.2267
4.4	1.355	0.7506	0.2020	0.1834	1.268	0.6602	0.2005	0.1994	1.197	0.5768	0.1980	0.2158
4.5	1.432	0.8014	0.1985	0.1732	1.333	0.7067	0.1977	0.1890	1.252	0.6200	0.1958	0.2051
4.6	1.516	0.8537	0.1946	0.1632	1.403	0.7543	0.1945	0.1790	1.311	0.6639	0.1934	0.1949
4.7	1.609	0.9078	0.1902	0.1535	1.480	0.8030	0.1911	0.1692	1.376	0.7085	0.1907	0.1850
4.8	1.712	0.9637	0.1855	0.1441	1.564	0.8532	0.1873	0.1597	1.446	0.7542	0.1876	0.1754
4.9	1.826	1.022	0.1803	0.1348	1.656	0.9048	0.1831	0.1504	1.521	0.8008	0.1843	0.1660
5.0	1.952	1.083	0.1746	0.1257	1.757	0.9581	0.1785	0.1413	1.604	0.8487	0.1806	0.1569
5.1	2.094	1.146	0.1683	0.1167	1.868	1.013	0.1735	0.1325	1.694	0.8979	0.1766	0.1480
5.2	2.254	1.212	0.1615	0.1078	1.992	1.071	0.1681	0.1237	1.792	0.9486	0.1722	0.1393
5.3	2.435	1.282	0.1540	0.0991	2.129	1.130	0.1621	0.1152	1.901	1.001	0.1674	0.1308
5.4	2.642	1.356	0.1458	0.0904	2.282	1.193	0.1557	0.1067	2.019	1.055	0.1623	0.1225
5.5	2.880	1.434	0 1368	0 0817	2.454	1.258	0.1487	0.0984	2.151	1.111	0.1567	0.1143
5.6	3.157	1.516	0.1270	0.0731	2.649	1.326	0.1411	0.0901	2.296	1.169	0.1507	0.1062
5.7	3.484	1.604	0.1163	0.0645	2.871	1.397	0.1328	0.0819	2.459	1.230	0.1442	0.0982
5.8	3.875	1.698	0.1044	0.0558	3.126	1.473	0.1238	0.0737	2.640	1.293	0.1371	0.0904
5.9	4.353	1.799	0.0914	0.0470	3.422	1.553	0.1140	0.0656	2.846	1.359	0.1295	0.0826
6.0	4.955	1.908	0.0770	0.0382	3.771	1.637	0.1034	0.0574	3.079	1.428	0.1213	0.0748
6.1	5.748	2.025	0.0611	0.0291	4.188	1.727	0.0918	0.0492	3.346	1.500	0.1125	0.0671
6.2	6.873	2.153	0.0433	0.0199	4.700	1.823	0.0791	0.0410	3.655	1.576	0.1029	0.0594
6.3					5.346	1.925	0.0653	0.0326	4.018	1.656	0.0926	0.0518
6.4					6.206	2.035	0.0501	0.0242	4.452	1.741	0.0814	0.0441
6.5					7.458	2.153	0.0334	0.0156	4.984	1.830	0.0694	0.0363
6.6									5.656	1.925	0.0563	0.0285
6.7									6.554	2.026	0.0421	0.0207
6.8									7.886	2.134	0.0268	0.0127
	$\sqrt{\beta_1} = 1.50$				$\sqrt{\beta_1} = 1.55$				$\sqrt{\beta_1} = 1.60$			
4.1	1.017	0.3778	0.1983	0.2679	0.9863	0.3074	0.1931	0.2865	0.9629	0.2377	0.1877	0.3060
4.2	1.054	0.4181	0.1973	0.2556	1.018	0.3467	0.1926	0.2738	0.9889	0.2767	0.1874	0.2927
4.3	1.095	0.4583	0.1962	0.2438	1.052	0.3856	0.1919	0.2616	1.018	0.3151	0.1870	0.2799
4.4	1.138	0.4988	0.1948	0.2325	1.089	0.4245	0.1909	0.2498	1.050	0.3531	0.1864	0.2677
4.5	1.185	0.5394	0.1932	0.2216	1.130	0.4633	0.1897	0.2386	1.084	0.3906	0.1857	0.2561
4.6	1.236	0.5804	0.1913	0.2111	1.173	0.5023	0.1883	0.2277	1.121	0.4281	0.1848	0.2449
4.7	1.291	0.6220	0.1891	0.2010	1.220	0.5415	0.1867	0.2173	1.161	0.4656	0.1836	0.2341
4.8	1.349	0.6641	0.1868	0.1912	1.270	0.5810	0.1849	0.2073	1.205	0.5032	0.1822	0.2238
4.9	1.413	0.7070	0.1841	0.1817	1.324	0.6209	0.1829	0.1976	1.251	0.5408	0.1807	0.2138
5.0	1.482	0.7507	0.1812	0.1724	1.382	0.6614	0.1805	0.1882	1.301	0.5789	0.1789	0.2041
5.1	1.556	0.7952	0.1779	0.1635	1.445	0.7024	0.1780	0.1791	1.354	0.6172	0.1770	0.1948
5.2	1.637	0.8408	0.1744	0.1548	1.512	0.7442	0.1752	0.1702	1.411	0.6560	0.1748	0.1858
5.3	1.724	0.8876	0.1706	0.1462	1.585	0.7867	0.1721	0.1618	1.472	0.6953	0.1723	0.1770
5.4	1.820	0.9356	0.1665	0.1379	1.663	0.8301	0.1688	0.1532	1.537	0.7351	0.1696	0.1685
5.5	1.924	0.9850	0.1620	0.1298	1.748	0.8745	0.1652	0.1450	1.607	0.7756	0.1668	0.1602

$X = \gamma + \delta \log\{y/(1-y)\} = \gamma + \delta \log\{(x-\xi)/(\xi+\lambda-x)\}$ is a $N(0, 1)$ variate.
Since $\xi \leqslant x \leqslant \xi+\lambda$, $\lambda = \sigma(x)/\sigma(y)$, $\xi = \mu_1'(x) - \lambda\mu_1'(y)$.

Table 36 (*continued*)

β_2	γ	δ	$\mu_1'(y)$	$\sigma(y)$	γ	δ	$\mu_1'(y)$	$\sigma(y)$	γ	δ	$\mu_1'(y)$	$\sigma(y)$
	$\sqrt{\beta_1} = \mathbf{1\cdot50}$ (*cont.*)				$\sqrt{\beta_1} = \mathbf{1\cdot55}$ (*cont.*)				$\sqrt{\beta_1} = \mathbf{1\cdot60}$ (*cont.*)			
5·6	2·037	1·036	0·1571	0·1218	1·839	0·9199	0·1613	0·1370	1·683	0·8169	0·1636	0·1522
5·7	2·162	1·088	0·1519	0·1139	1·938	0·9665	0·1571	0·1292	1·764	0·8590	0·1602	0·1443
5·8	2·300	1·143	0·1463	0·1062	2·047	1·014	0·1525	0·1215	1·852	0·9019	0·1565	0·1366
5·9	2·452	1·199	0·1403	0·0986	2·165	1·064	0·1477	0·1140	1·946	0·9459	0·1526	0·1291
6·0	2·621	1·257	0·1338	0·0911	2·294	1·114	0·1425	0·1066	2·049	0·9908	0·1484	0·1218
6·1	2·809	1·318	0·1268	0·0837	2·435	1·166	0·1369	0·0994	2·159	1·037	0·1439	0·1146
6·2	3·021	1·381	0·1194	0·0763	2·591	1·220	0·1310	0·0922	2·280	1·084	0·1391	0·1075
6·3	3·261	1·447	0·1114	0·0690	2·764	1·276	0·1246	0·0851	2·412	1·133	0·1340	0·1005
6·4	3·535	1·515	0·1028	0·0618	2·956	1·334	0·1173	0·0781	2·555	1·183	0·1285	0·0937
6·5	3·851	1·587	0·0936	0·0546	3·171	1·394	0·1106	0·0712	2·713	1·234	0·1227	0·0869
6·6	4·221	1·662	0·0838	0·0474	3·413	1·456	0·1029	0·0644	2·887	1·287	0·1166	0·0803
6·7	4·660	1·741	0·0732	0·0402	3·689	1·521	0·0947	0·0576	3·080	1·342	0·1101	0·0737
6·8	5·195	1·824	0·0619	0·0329	4·005	1·588	0·0860	0·0508	3·295	1·398	0·1032	0·0672
6·9	5·871	1·911	0·0498	0·0257	4·372	1·658	0·0767	0·0440	3·535	1·457	0·0959	0·0607
7·0	6·773	2·003	0·0367	0·0184	4·806	1·731	0·0669	0·0373	3·807	1·517	0·0881	0·0543
7·1	8·117	2·100	0·0228	0·0111	5·331	1·807	0·0564	0·0306	4·117	1·579	0·0800	0·0480
7·2					5·989	1·886	0·0453	0·0239	4·474	1·644	0·0713	0·0417
7·3					6·857	1·969	0·0335	0·0172	4·893	1·711	0·0622	0·0354
7·4									5·396	1·780	0·0526	0·0292
7·5									6·017	1·852	0·0424	0·0229
7·6									6·826	1·927	0·0318	0·0167
7·7									7·982	2·004	0·0205	0·0106
	$\sqrt{\beta_1} = \mathbf{1\cdot65}$				$\sqrt{\beta_1} = \mathbf{1\cdot70}$				$\sqrt{\beta_1} = \mathbf{1\cdot75}$			
4·6	1·079	0·3569	0·1805	0·2626	1·045	0·2872	0·1759	0·2811	1·020	0·2178	0·1709	0·3004
4·7	1·113	0·3932	0·1798	0·2515	1·074	0·3229	0·1755	0·2695	1·044	0·2537	0·1708	0·2882
4·8	1·150	0·4293	0·1789	0·2408	1·106	0·3582	0·1749	0·2583	1·070	0·2888	0·1705	0·2766
4·9	1·190	0·4654	0·1778	0·2304	1·140	0·3933	0·1742	0·2476	1·099	0·3233	0·1701	0·2654
5·0	1·233	0·5016	0·1765	0·2205	1·176	0·4281	0·1733	0·2373	1·130	0·3575	0·1696	0·2547
5·1	1·278	0·5378	0·1750	0·2190	1·215	0·4629	0·1723	0·2274	1·164	0·3913	0·1689	0·2444
5·2	1·327	0·5743	0·1733	0·2016	1·257	0·4977	0·1710	0·2179	1·200	0·4249	0·1680	0·2345
5·3	1·379	0·6111	0·1714	0·1927	1·302	0·5326	0·1696	0·2086	1·238	0·4585	0·1670	0·2250
5·4	1·434	0·6483	0·1693	0·1840	1·349	0·5677	0·1680	0·1997	1·279	0·4920	0·1658	0·2158
5·5	1·494	0·6858	0·1670	0·1755	1·400	0·6030	0·1662	0·1911	1·322	0·5255	0·1645	0·2069
5·6	1·557	0·7239	0·1645	0·1674	1·454	0·6385	0·1642	0·1827	1·369	0·5592	0·1630	0·1982
5·7	1·625	0·7625	0·1618	0·1594	1·511	0·6744	0·1621	0·1746	1·418	0·5931	0·1613	0·1899
5·8	1·697	0·8017	0·1588	0·1516	1·572	0·7107	0·1597	0·1666	1·470	0·6271	0·1595	0·1818
5·9	1·775	0·8415	0·1556	0·1441	1·637	0·7475	0·1572	0·1590	1·525	0·6614	0·1574	0·1740
6·0	1·858	0·8822	0·1522	0·1367	1·707	0·7847	0·1544	0·1515	1·583	0·6960	0·1552	0·1664
6·1	1·948	0·9235	0·1485	0·1294	1·781	0·8226	0·1514	0·1442	1·646	0·7310	0·1528	0·1589
6·2	2·044	0·9658	0·1447	0·1224	1·860	0·8609	0·1483	0·1371	1·712	0·7665	0·1503	0·1517
6·3	2·148	1·009	0·1405	0·1154	1·944	0·9000	0·1449	0·1301	1·782	0·8023	0·1475	0·1447
6·4	2·261	1·053	0·1361	0·1086	2·035	0·9398	0·1412	0·1233	1·857	0·8386	0·1446	0·1378
6·5	2·383	1·098	0·1314	0·1020	2·132	0·9803	0·1374	0·1166	1·937	0·8755	0·1414	0·1311
6·6	2·515	1·145	0·1264	0·0954	2·237	1·022	0·1333	0·1101	2·022	0·9129	0·1381	0·1245
6·7	2·659	1·192	0·1211	0·0889	2·350	1·064	0·1290	0·1037	2·113	0·9510	0·1346	0·1181
6·8	2·816	1·241	0·1156	0·0826	2·471	1·107	0·1245	0·0974	2·210	0·9897	0·1309	0·1118
6·9	2·990	1·291	0·1096	0·0763	2·603	1·151	0·1197	0·0912	2·314	1·029	0·1269	0·1056
7·0	3·180	1·343	0·1035	0·0701	2·745	1·196	0·1147	0·0851	2·426	1·069	0·1228	0·0995
7·1	3·391	1·396	0·0969	0·0640	2·900	1·242	0·1094	0·0791	2·546	1·110	0·1184	0·0936
7·2	3·626	1·450	0·0900	0·0579	3·070	1·289	0·1038	0·0732	2·675	1·152	0·1138	0·0878
7·3	3·890	1·506	0·0828	0·0519	3·256	1·337	0·0979	0·0673	2·815	1·194	0·1090	0·0820
7·4	4·188	1·564	0·0752	0·0460	3·461	1·387	0·0918	0·0616	2·966	1·237	0·1040	0·0763
7·5	4·530	1·623	0·0672	0·0401	3·687	1·437	0·0853	0·0559	3·130	1·282	0·0988	0·0708
7·6	4·927	1·685	0·0588	0·0343	3·940	1·489	0·0786	0·0503	3·310	1·327	0·0933	0·0653
7·7	5·397	1·748	0·0501	0·0284	4·223	1·543	0·0716	0·0447	3·506	1·373	0·0875	0·0598
7·8	5·970	1·813	0·0409	0·0227	4·545	1·597	0·0642	0·0392	3·722	1·420	0·0815	0·0545
7·9	6·699	1·880	0·0313	0·0170	4·915	1·653	0·0566	0·0337	3·961	1·468	0·0753	0·0492
8·0	7·702	1·948	0·0213	0·0113	5·347	1·710	0·0486	0·0283	4·227	1·517	0·0688	0·0440

Table 36 (continued). Johnson S_B system: parameters in terms of $\sqrt{\beta_1}, \beta_2$

β_2	γ	δ	$\mu_1'(y)$	$\sigma(y)$	γ	δ	$\mu_1'(y)$	$\sigma(y)$	γ	δ	$\mu_1'(y)$	$\sigma(y)$
					$\sqrt{\beta_1} = 1\cdot70$ (cont.)				$\sqrt{\beta_1} = 1\cdot75$ (cont.)			
8·1					5·865	1·769	0·0403	0·0230	4·527	1·567	0·0621	0·0388
8·2					6·508	1·829	0·0317	0·0177	4·867	1·618	0·0551	0·0337
8·3					7·355	1·891	0·0228	0·0125	5·259	1·670	0·0479	0·0287
8·4									5·720	1·723	0·0404	0·0237
8·5									6·278	1·777	0·0327	0·0188
8·6									6·986	1·832	0·0248	0·0140
8·7									7·957	1·888	0·0166	0·0092
	$\sqrt{\beta_1} = 1\cdot80$				$\sqrt{\beta_1} = 1\cdot85$				$\sqrt{\beta_1} = 1\cdot90$			
5·2	1·152	0·3547	0·1644	0·2518	1·114	0·2861	0·1603	0·2696	1·086	0·2178	0·1558	0·2883
5·3	1·185	0·3874	0·1637	0·2418	1·142	0·3184	0·1599	0·2593	1·109	0·2504	0·1557	0·2774
5·4	1·220	0·4199	0·1629	0·2323	1·172	0·3503	0·1595	0·2493	1·134	0·2822	0·1555	0·2671
5·5	1·258	0·4522	0·1620	0·2231	1·204	0·3819	0·1589	0·2398	1·161	0·3135	0·1552	0·2571
5·6	1·298	0·4846	0·1609	0·2142	1·238	0·4132	0·1581	0·2305	1·190	0·3443	0·1547	0·2475
5·7	1·340	0·5168	0·1597	0·2056	1·275	0·4444	0·1572	0·2216	1·221	0·3748	0·1542	0·2382
5·8	1·384	0·5491	0·1582	0·1973	1·313	0·4755	0·1562	0·2131	1·254	0·4051	0·1535	0·2293
5·9	1·432	0·5815	0·1567	0·1892	1·354	0·5066	0·1551	0·2047	1·290	0·4352	0·1527	0·2207
6·0	1·482	0·6142	0·1550	0·1814	1·397	0·5376	0·1538	0·1967	1·327	0·4652	0·1518	0·2123
6·1	1·535	0·6470	0·1531	0·1738	1·443	0·5688	0·1523	0·1889	1·366	0·4951	0·1507	0·2043
6·2	1·591	0·6801	0·1510	0·1664	1·491	0·6000	0·1507	0·1813	1·408	0·5249	0·1495	0·1965
6·3	1·650	0·7134	0·1488	0·1593	1·542	0·6314	0·1490	0·1740	1·451	0·5549	0·1482	0·1889
6·4	1·713	0·7471	0·1464	0·1523	1·595	0·6630	0·1471	0·1668	1·498	0·5849	0·1467	0·1816
6·5	1·780	0·7811	0·1439	0·1455	1·652	0·6948	0·1450	0·1599	1·546	0·6149	0·1451	0·1745
6·6	1·851	0·8155	0·1412	0·1388	1·712	0·7268	0·1428	0·1531	1·597	0·6451	0·1433	0·1675
6·7	1·926	0·8503	0·1383	0·1323	1·775	0·7592	0·1405	0·1465	1·651	0·6754	0·1415	0·1608
6·8	2·005	0·8855	0·1352	0·1260	1·842	0·7918	0·1380	0·1401	1·708	0·7060	0·1394	0·1542
6·9	2·090	0·9214	0·1320	0·1198	1·912	0·8248	0·1353	0·1338	1·767	0·7367	0·1373	0·1478
7·0	2·180	0·9577	0·1286	0·1137	1·987	0·8581	0·1325	0·1277	1·830	0·7676	0·1350	0·1416
7·1	2·277	0·9945	0·1250	0·1077	2·066	0·8918	0·1296	0·1216	1·896	0·7989	0·1325	0·1355
7·2	2·379	1·032	0·1212	0·1019	2·149	0·9259	0·1264	0·1158	1·966	0·8304	0·1300	0·1295
7·3	2·489	1·070	0·1172	0·0962	2·238	0·9604	0·1232	0·1100	2·040	0·8623	0·1273	0·1237
7·4	2·606	1·109	0·1131	0·0905	2·333	0·9955	0·1197	0·1044	2·117	0·8944	0·1244	0·1180
7·5	2·732	1·148	0·1088	0·0850	2·433	1·031	0·1161	0·0989	2·199	0·9268	0·1214	0·1125
7·6	2·868	1·188	0·1042	0·0796	2·540	1·067	0·1123	0·0934	2·286	0·9597	0·1183	0·1070
7·7	3·014	1·228	0·0995	0·0742	2·654	1·103	0·1084	0·0881	2·379	0·9929	0·1150	0·1016
7·8	3·172	1·270	0·0945	0·0690	2·776	1·140	0·1043	0·0829	2·476	1·027	0·1116	0·0964
7·9	3·344	1·312	0·0894	0·0638	2·906	1·178	0·1000	0·0777	2·580	1·060	0·1080	0·0912
8·0	3·530	1·355	0·0841	0·0587	3·046	1·216	0·0956	0·0727	2·690	1·095	0·1043	0·0862
8·1	3·734	1·398	0·0785	0·0536	3·197	1·255	0·0910	0·0677	2·807	1·130	0·1005	0·0812
8·2	3·958	1·443	0·0728	0·0487	3·360	1·294	0·0862	0·0628	2·932	1·165	0·0965	0·0764
8·3	4·205	1·488	0·0669	0·0438	3·535	1·334	0·0813	0·0580	3·065	1·201	0·0923	0·0716
8·4	4·481	1·534	0·0607	0·0389	3·726	1·374	0·0762	0·0532	3·208	1·237	0·0880	0·0669
8·5	4·791	1·581	0·0544	0·0342	3·935	1·415	0·0709	0·0485	3·361	1·273	0·0836	0·0622
8·6	5·143	1·628	0·0478	0·0295	4·163	1·457	0·0655	0·0439	3·526	1·311	0·0790	0·0577
8·7	5·550	1·676	0·0411	0·0248	4·415	1·499	0·0598	0·0394	3·703	1·348	0·0743	0·0532
8·8	6·032	1·725	0·0342	0·0203	4·695	1·542	0·0541	0·0349	3·896	1·386	0·0695	0·0488
8·9	6·620	1·774	0·0271	0·0158	5·010	1·585	0·0481	0·0305	4·106	1·424	0·0645	0·0444
9·0	7·380	1·824	0·0198	0·0113	5·368	1·629	0·0421	0·0262	4·335	1·463	0·0594	0·0402
9·1	8·466	1·875	0·0124	0·0070	5·782	1·673	0·0358	0·0219	4·587	1·502	0·0541	0·0360
9·2					6·273	1·718	0·0295	0·0177	4·868	1·542	0·0487	0·0318
9·3					6·877	1·763	0·0230	0·0136	5·182	1·582	0·0432	0·0277
9·4					7·666	1·808	0·0164	0·0095	5·538	1·622	0·0376	0·0237
9·5					8·830	1·853	0·0097	0·0056	5·950	1·662	0·0319	0·0198

$X = \gamma + \delta \log\{y/(1-y)\} = \gamma + \delta \log\{(x-\xi)/(\xi+\lambda-x)\}$ is a $N(0, 1)$ variate.
Since $\xi \leqslant x \leqslant \xi+\lambda$, $\lambda = \sigma(x)/\sigma(y)$, $\xi = \mu_1'(x) - \lambda\mu_1'(y)$.

Table 36 (*continued*)

β_2	γ	δ	$\mu'_1(y)$	$\sigma(y)$	γ	δ	$\mu'_1(y)$	$\sigma(y)$
		$\sqrt{\beta_1} = \mathbf{1\cdot90}$ (*cont.*)						
9·6	6·438	1·703	0·0261	0·0159				
9·7	7·039	1·744	0·0202	0·0122				
9·8	7·828	1·785	0·0143	0·0084				
9·9	9·006	1·826	0·0083	0·0048				
		$\sqrt{\beta_1} = \mathbf{1\cdot95}$			$\sqrt{\beta_1} = \mathbf{2\cdot00}$			
5·7	1·178	0·3070	0·1506	0·2553	1·144	0·2399	0·1466	0·2732
5·8	1·206	0·3369	0·1502	0·2460	1·167	0·2698	0·1465	0·2634
5·9	1·236	0·3664	0·1497	0·2371	1·193	0·2993	0·1462	0·2541
6·0	1·268	0·3957	0·1491	0·2284	1·220	0·3283	0·1459	0·2451
6·1	1·302	0·4248	0·1484	0·2201	1·249	0·3569	0·1454	0·2364
6·2	1·338	0·4537	0·1475	0·2120	1·280	0·3852	0·1449	0·2280
6·3	1·376	0·4825	0·1465	0·2042	1·313	0·4133	0·1442	0·2198
6·4	1·416	0·5113	0·1454	0·1966	1·347	0·4412	0·1434	0·2120
6·5	1·458	0·5400	0·1442	0·1893	1·384	0·4690	0·1425	0·2044
6·6	1·502	0·5688	0·1428	0·1821	1·422	0·4967	0·1415	0·1970
6·7	1·548	0·5976	0·1414	0·1752	1·462	0·5243	0·1404	0·1899
6·8	1·597	0·6264	0·1398	0·1684	1·504	0·5520	0·1392	0·1830
6·9	1·648	0·6554	0·1381	0·1619	1·548	0·5796	0·1379	0·1762
7·0	1·701	0·6846	0·1362	0·1555	1·594	0·6073	0·1364	0·1697
7·1	1·758	0·7138	0·1342	0·1493	1·643	0·6350	0·1348	0·1633
7·2	1·817	0·7433	0·1321	0·1433	1·693	0·6628	0·1331	0·1571
7·3	1·879	0·7730	0·1299	0·1373	1·746	0·6908	0·1313	0·1510
7·4	1·944	0·8028	0·1276	0·1316	1·802	0·7188	0·1294	0·1451
7·5	2·013	0·8329	0·1251	0·1259	1·860	0·7471	0·1274	0·1394
7·6	2·085	0·8633	0·1225	0·1204	1·921	0·7754	0·1252	0·1337
7·7	2·161	0·8939	0·1197	0·1150	1·985	0·8039	0·1230	0·1283
7·8	2·241	0·9248	0·1169	0·1097	2·053	0·8326	0·1206	0·1229
7·9	2·326	0·9559	0·1139	0·1045	2·123	0·8615	0·1181	0·1176
8·0	2·415	0·9874	0·1108	0·0994	2·197	0·8906	0·1155	0·1125
8·1	2·509	1·019	0·1076	0·0945	2·275	0·9200	0·1128	0·1075
8·2	2·609	1·051	0·1042	0·0896	2·357	0·9495	0·1100	0·1025
8·3	2·714	1·084	0·1007	0·0848	2·443	0·9794	0·1071	0·0977
8·4	2·826	1·116	0·0971	0·0801	2·533	1·009	0·1040	0·0930
8·5	2·945	1·150	0·0934	0·0754	2·629	1·040	0·1009	0·0883
8·6	3·071	1·183	0·0895	0·0709	2·729	1·070	0·0976	0·0838
8·7	3·206	1·217	0·0856	0·0664	2·836	1·101	0·0942	0·0793
8·8	3·349	1·251	0·0815	0·0620	2·948	1·132	0·0908	0·0749
8·9	3·503	1·285	0·0772	0·0577	3·067	1·164	0·0872	0·0706
9·0	3·668	1·320	0·0729	0·0535	3·194	1·195	0·0835	0·0663
9·1	3·846	1·355	0·0685	0·0493	3·328	1·227	0·0797	0·0622
9·2	4·037	1·391	0·0639	0·0452	3·471	1·259	0·0758	0·0581
9·3	4·246	1·427	0·0592	0·0412	3·623	1·291	0·0718	0·0540
9·4	4·472	1·463	0·0544	0·0372	3·787	1·324	0·0677	0·0501
9·5	4·721	1·499	0·0496	0·0333	3·962	1·357	0·0635	0·0462
9·6	4·997	1·535	0·0446	0·0295	4·150	1·390	0·0593	0·0424
9·7	5·305	1·572	0·0395	0·0257	4·354	1·423	0·0549	0·0386
9·8	5·653	1·609	0·0344	0·0220	4·576	1·457	0·0505	0·0349
9·9	6·054	1·646	0·0292	0·0184	4·818	1·490	0·0460	0·0313
10·0	6·527	1·683	0·0239	0·0148	5·085	1·524	0·0414	0·0278
10·1	7·107	1·720	0·0185	0·0113	5·381	1·558	0·0367	0·0243
10·2	7·863	1·757	0·0132	0·0079	5·715	1·591	0·0320	0·0209
10·3	8·978	1·794	0·0078	0·0046	6·098	1·625	0·0273	0·0175
10·4					6·546	1·659	0·0224	0·0142
10·5					7·090	1·693	0·0176	0·0110
10·6					7·787	1·726	0·0128	0·0079
10·7					8·780	1·760	0·0079	0·0048

Table 37. *Maximum likelihood estimator of p in the gamma (Type III) distribution, start assumed known*

v	$v\hat{p}$	v	$v\hat{p}$	v	$v\hat{p}$	v	$v\hat{p}$	v	$v\hat{p}$
0·00	0·500 000								
·01	·501 661	0·46	0·564 332	0·91	0·608 283	1·36	0·641 056	9·2	0·823 29
·02	·503 311	·47	·565 478	·92	·609 112	1·37	·641 694	9·4	·825 18
·03	·504 949	·48	·566 615	·93	·609 935	1·38	·642 329	9·6	·827 02
·04	·506 576	·49	·567 743	·94	·610 754	1·39	·642 960	9·8	·828 82
·05	·508 191	·50	·568 862	·95	·611 567	1·40	·643 589	10·0	·830 57
0·06	0·509 794	0·51	0·569 973	0·96	0·612 375			10·2	0·832 28
·07	·511 386	·52	·571 074	·97	·613 178	1·4	0·643 59	10·4	·833 94
·08	·512 965	·53	·572 167	·98	·613 976	1·6	·655 51	10·6	·835 57
·09	·514 532	·54	·573 252	·99	·614 769	1·8	·666 33	10·8	·837 16
·10	·516 088	·55	·574 328	1·00	·615 557	2·0	·676 23	11·0	·838 71
0·11	0·517 631	0·56	0·575 396	1·01	0·616 340	2·2	0·685 34	11·2	0·840 22
·12	·519 161	·57	·576 456	1·02	·617 118	2·4	·693 75	11·4	·841 70
·13	·520 680	·58	·577 508	1·03	·617 892	2·6	·701 57	11·6	·843 15
·14	·522 186	·59	·578 552	1·04	·618 661	2·8	·708 85	11·8	·844 56
·15	·523 681	·60	·579 588	1·05	·619 425	3·0	·715 66	12·0	·845 94
0·16	0·525 163	0·61	0·580 616	1·06	0·620 185	3·2	0·722 06	12·2	0·847 30
·17	·526 633	·62	·581 636	1·07	·620 940	3·4	·728 07	12·4	·848 62
·18	·528 091	·63	·582 649	1·08	·621 691	3·6	·733 75	12·6	·849 92
·19	·529 536	·64	·583 655	1·09	·622 437	3·8	·739 12	12·8	·851 19
·20	·530 970	·65	·584 653	1·10	·623 179	4·0	·744 20	13·0	·852 44
0·21	0·532 392	0·66	0·585 644	1·11	0·623 916	4·2	0·749 04	13·2	0·853 66
·22	·533 802	·67	·586 627	1·12	·624 650	4·4	·753 63	13·4	·854 85
·23	·535 200	·68	·587 604	1·13	·625 378	4·6	·758 01	13·6	·856 03
·24	·536 587	·69	·588 573	1·14	·626 103	4·8	·762 19	13·8	·857 18
·25	·537 962	·70	·589 536	1·15	·626 823	5·0	·766 19	14·0	·858 31
0·26	0·539 325	0·71	0·590 492	1·16	0·627 540	5·2	0·770 02	14·2	0·859 41
·27	·540 677	·72	·591 440	1·17	·628 252	5·4	·773 69	14·4	·860 50
·28	·542 017	·73	·592 383	1·18	·628 960	5·6	·777 21	14·6	·861 57
·29	·543 347	·74	·593 318	1·19	·629 664	5·8	·780 59	14·8	·862 61
·30	·544 665	·75	·594 247	1·20	·630 364	6·0	·783 84	15·0	·863 64
0·31	0·545 972	0·76	0·595 170	1·21	0·631 060	6·2	0·786 97	15·2	0·864 65
·32	·547 268	·77	·596 086	1·22	·631 753	6·4	·789 99	15·4	·865 64
·33	·548 554	·78	·596 996	1·23	·632 441	6·6	·792 90	15·6	·866 62
·34	·549 829	·79	·597 900	1·24	·633 126	6·8	·795 71	15·8	·867 57
·35	·551 093	·80	·598 797	1·25	·633 807	7·0	·798 43	16·0	·868 51
0·36	0·552 346	0·81	0·599 688	1·26	0·634 484	7·2	0·801 05	16·2	0·869 44
·37	·553 590	·82	·600 574	1·27	·635 157	7·4	·803 59	16·4	·870 35
·38	·554 823	·83	·601 453	1·28	·635 827	7·6	·806 05	16·6	·871 25
·39	·556 046	·84	·602 327	1·29	·636 493	7·8	·808 44	16·8	·872 13
·40	·557 259	·85	·603 195	1·30	·637 155	8·0	·810 75	17·0	·872 99
0·41	0·558 462	0·86	0·604 057	1·31	0·637 814	8·2	0·812 99	17·2	0·873 84
·42	·559 655	·87	·604 913	1·32	·638 469	8·4	·815 17	17·4	·874 68
·43	·560 838	·88	·605 764	1·33	·639 121	8·6	·817 29	17·6	·875 51
·44	·562 013	·89	·606 609	1·34	·639 770	8·8	·819 34	17·8	·876 32
·45	·563 177	·90	·607 449	1·35	·640 415	9·0	·821 34	18·0	·877 12

NOTE: $v = \log \bar{x} - \sum_i (\log x_i)/N$, where $\bar{x}$ is the mean of a sample of N observations, $x_1, x_2, \ldots, x_N$. The gamma distribution is taken in the form

$$f(x) = \left(\frac{p}{b}\right)^p \frac{1}{\Gamma(p)} x^{p-1} e^{-px/b} \quad (0 \leqslant x < \infty).$$

304

Table 38. *Coefficients in expansions for bias and variance of the maximum likelihood estimator $\hat{p}$ in a gamma distribution, derived from Table 37*

p	Bias of $\hat{p}$					Sampling variance of $\hat{p}$				
	a_0	a_1	a_2	a_3	a_4	b_0	b_1	b_2	b_3	b_4
0·1	1·6843	2·442	5·481	8·52	36·6	1·0937	6·620	34·26	160·8	738
·2	1·8396	2·460	6·372	17·70	56·2	1·1755	7·501	43·54	233·0	1219
·3	1·9698	2·579	7·213	21·63	67·8	1·2468	8·185	51·40	295·2	1632
·4	2·0790	2·684	7·810	23·85	73·3	1·3088	8·714	57·57	343·5	1943
·5	2·1709	2·764	8·207	25·07	75·7	1·3630	9·123	62·31	379·5	2166
0·6	2·2487	2·823	8·464	25·73	76·9	1·4104	9·441	65·92	406·1	2325
·7	2·3149	2·866	8·629	26·10	77·6	1·4520	9·690	68·69	425·9	2441
·8	2·3717	2·898	8·736	26·31	78·2	1·4888	9·886	70·82	440·8	2528
·9	2·4206	2·921	8·807	26·45	78·7	1·5215	10·043	72·47	452·2	2595
1·0	2·4632	2·938	8·854	26·55	79·2	1·5505	10·170	73·79	461·1	2648
2·0	2·6966	2·989	8·972	26·89	80·7	1·7249	10·697	78·97	496·4	2862
5·0	2·8712	2·999	8·996	26·99	81·0	1·8759	10·913	81·09	511·3	2953
10·0	2·9344	3·000	8·999	27·00	81·0	1·9356	10·962	81·59	515·0	2976
25·0	2·9735	3·000	9·000	27·00	81·0	1·9737	10·986	81·85	516·8	2988
50·0	2·9867	3·000	9·000	27·00	81·0	1·9868	10·993	81·93	517·4	2991

The Type III or gamma distribution is taken in the form

$$f(x) = \left(\frac{p}{b}\right)^p \frac{1}{\Gamma(p)} x^{p-1} e^{-px/b} \quad (0 \leqslant x < \infty),$$

the origin being at the lower terminal, assumed known. Then the maximum likelihood estimator of b is the sample mean, $\bar{x}$, and the estimator, $\hat{p}$, of p is given by the solution of equation (191), and may be found from Table 37.

The bias and sampling variance of $\hat{p}$ may be derived approximately from the following expansions:

$$E(\hat{p} - p)/p = a_0 N^{-1}(1 + a_1/N + a_2/N^2 + \ldots),$$

$$\text{Var } \hat{p}/p = b_0 N^{-1}(1 + b_1/N + b_2/N^2 + \ldots),$$

where the coefficients a, b are given in the table above for certain values of the parameter p and where N is the sample size.

Table 39. *Minimum normit χ^2 procedure: weights for arguments r and $n \leqslant 50$*

Upper figure in table is $w = Z^2/pq$; lower figure is wX

For $r < \tfrac{1}{2}n$, wX is negative. For $r > \tfrac{1}{2}n$, use $n-r$ as argument, and wX is positive

$r \backslash n$	2	3	4	5	6	7	8	9	10
0	0.53857	0.44951	0.38743	0.34222	0.30763	0.28031	0.25813	0.23974	0.22394
	·36326	·43480	·44569	·43858	·42551	·41078	·39601	·38187	·36834
1	·63662	·59490	·53857	·48987	·44951	·41588	·38743	·36317	·34222
	0	·25630	·36326	·41228	·43480	·44390	·44569	·44332	·43858
2	—	—	·63662	·62192	·59490	·56612	·53857	·51309	·48987
			0	·15756	·25630	·32042	·36326	·39240	·41228
3	—	—	—	—	·63662	·62917	·61350	·59490	·57567
					0	·11321	·19549	·25630	·30188
4	—	—	—	—	—	—	·63662	·63211	·62192
							0	·08838	·15756
5	—	—	—	—	—	—	—	—	0·63662
									0

$r \backslash n$	11	12	13	14	15	16	17	18	19	20
0	0.21059	0.19881	0.18850	0.17916	0.17090	0.16345	0.15689	0.15093	0.14520	0.14014
	·35592	·34420	·33335	·32302	·31348	·30458	·29648	·28890	·28143	·27466
1	·32386	·30763	·29324	·28031	·26880	·25813	·24841	·23974	·23138	·22394
	·43243	·42551	·41823	·41078	·40342	·39601	·38875	·38187	·37487	·36834
2	·46870	·44951	·43186	·41588	·40099	·38743	·37477	·36317	·35241	·34222
	·42582	·43480	·44062	·44390	·44547	·44569	·44488	·44332	·44119	·43858
3	·55672	·53857	·52138	·50513	·48987	·47555	·46214	·44951	·43758	·42638
	·33663	·36326	·38385	·39986	·41228	·42188	·42923	·43480	·43895	·44191
4	·60899	·59490	·58048	·56612	·55214	·53857	·52557	·51309	·50119	·48987
	·21245	·25630	·29162	·32042	·34389	·36326	·37920	·39240	·40330	·41228
5	0·63360	0·62645	0·61697	0·60623	0·59490	0·58337	0·57182	0·56049	0·54940	0·53857
	·07242	·13177	·18103	·22202	·25630	·28514	·30961	·33034	·34805	·36326
6	—	·63662	·63446	·62917	·62192	·61350	·60437	·59490	·58530	·57567
		0	·06132	·11321	·15756	·19549	·22815	·25630	·28064	·30188
7	—	—	—	·63662	·63501	·63092	·62521	·61843	·61094	·60306
				0	·05307	·09925	·13937	·17451	·20533	·23237
8	—	—	—	—	—	·63662	·63536	·63211	·62751	·62192
						0	·04687	·08838	·12492	·15756
9	—	—	—	—	—	—	—	·63662	·63561	·63298
								0	·04193	·07954
10	—	—	—	—	—	—	—	—	—	0·63662
										0

Table 39 (*continued*)

Upper figure in table is $w = Z^2/pq$; lower figure is wX

For $r < \frac{1}{2}n$, wX is negative. For $r > \frac{1}{2}n$, use $n-r$ as argument, and wX is positive

r \ n	21	22	23	24	25	26	27	28	29	30
0	0·13537 ·26815	0·13091 ·26194	0·12679 ·25609	0·12301 ·25064	0·11961 ·24564	0·11615 ·24050	0·11308 ·23587	0·11042 ·23179	0·10727 ·22692	0·10499 ·22335
1	·21689 ·36190	·21059 ·35592	·20445 ·34990	·19881 ·34420	·19338 ·33855	·18850 ·33335	·18354 ·32791	·17916 ·32302	·17506 ·31833	·17090 ·31348
2	·33268 ·43561	·32386 ·43243	·31564 ·42910	·30763 ·42551	·30029 ·42193	·29324 ·41821	·28673 ·41458	·28031 ·41078	·27449 ·40714	·26880 ·40342
3	·41588 ·44390	·40589 ·44511	·39633 ·44567	·38743 ·44569	·37894 ·44525	·37090 ·44445	·36317 ·44332	·35579 ·44193	·34880 ·44032	·34222 ·43858
4	·47907 ·41969	·46870 ·42582	·45885 ·43098	·44951 ·43480	·44048 ·43804	·43186 ·44062	·42361 ·44251	·41588 ·44390	·40822 ·44488	·40099 ·44547
5	0·52812 ·37625	0·51805 ·38738	0·50829 ·39698	0·49887 ·40525	0·48987 ·41228	0·48116 ·41834	0·47281 ·42350	0·46476 ·42791	0·45693 ·43168	0·44951 ·43480
6	·56612 ·32042	·55672 ·33663	·54757 ·35076	·53857 ·36326	·52984 ·37422	·52138 ·38385	·51309 ·39240	·50513 ·39986	·49738 ·40647	·48987 ·41228
7	·59490 ·25630	·58669 ·27735	·57838 ·29617	·57022 ·31272	·56208 ·32760	·55406 ·34088	·54628 ·35263	·53857 ·36326	·53109 ·37272	·52372 ·38128
8	·61570 ·18647	·60899 ·21245	·60204 ·23556	·59490 ·25630	·58771 ·27487	·58048 ·29162	·57327 ·30674	·56612 ·32042	·55909 ·33270	·55214 ·34389
9	·62917 ·11321	·62450 ·14355	·61921 ·17086	·61350 ·19549	·60748 ·21775	·60129 ·23787	·59490 ·25630	·58850 ·27294	·58206 ·28812	·57567 ·30188
10	0·63580 ·03795	0·63360 ·07242	0·63041 ·10349	0·62645 ·13177	0·62192 ·15756	0·61697 ·18103	0·61173 ·20236	0·60623 ·22202	0·60062 ·23989	0·59490 ·25630
11	—	·63662 0	·63593 ·03461	·63409 ·06640	·63137 ·09532	·62797 ·12181	·62403 ·14617	·61973 ·16842	·61509 ·18903	·61026 ·20786
12	—	—	—	·63662 0	·63604 ·03190	·63446 ·06132	·63211 ·08838	·62917 ·11321	·62573 ·13627	·62192 ·15756
13	—	—	—	—	—	·63662 0	·63612 ·02951	·63476 ·05688	·63272 ·08223	·63012 ·10585
14	—	—	—	—	—	—	—	·63662 0	·63619 ·02744	·63501 ·05307
15	—	—	—	—	—	—	—	—	—	0·63662 0

Table 39 (*continued*). *Minimum normit χ^2 procedure: weights for arguments r and $n \leqslant 50$*

Upper figure in table is $w = Z^2/pq$; lower figure is wX

For $r < \frac{1}{2}n$, wX is negative. For $r > \frac{1}{2}n$, use $n-r$ as argument, and wX is positive

r \ n	31	32	33	34	35	36	37	38	39	40
0	0·10223	0·09990	0·09802	0·09564	0·09371	0·09177	0·08981	0·08833	0·08634	0·08483
	·21897	·21523	·21219	·20830	·20514	·20191	·19862	·19612	·19272	·19013
1	·16737	·16381	·16019	·15689	·15393	·15093	·14789	·14520	·14249	·14014
	·30931	·30501	·30058	·29648	·29274	·28890	·28496	·28143	·27782	·27466
2	·26326	·25813	·25318	·24841	·24384	·23974	·23559	·23138	·22768	·22394
	·39964	·39601	·39237	·38875	·38517	·38187	·37844	·37487	·37166	·36834
3	·33589	·32984	·32386	·31820	·31285	·30763	·30276	·29781	·29324	·28884
	·43666	·43463	·43243	·43018	·42789	·42551	·42317	·42066	·41823	·41579
4	·39405	·38743	·38100	·37477	·36894	·36317	·35765	·35241	·34726	·34222
	·44572	·44569	·44540	·44488	·44419	·44332	·44231	·44119	·43994	·43857
5	0·44226	0·43535	0·42854	0·42214	0·41588	0·40977	0·40384	0·39827	0·39274	0·38743
	·43745	·43961	·44141	·44280	·44390	·44472	·44528	·44560	·44574	·44569
6	·48254	·47555	·46870	·46214	·45565	·44951	·44348	·43758	·43186	·42638
	·41743	·42188	·42582	·42923	·43225	·43480	·43703	·43895	·44062	·44191
7	·51660	·50970	·50286	·49631	·48987	·48357	·47755	·47161	·46587	·46025
	·38887	·39566	·40186	·40733	·41228	·41674	·42065	·42420	·42733	·43014
8	·54531	·53857	·53198	·52557	·51929	·51309	·50708	·50119	·49544	·48987
	·35402	·36326	·37164	·37920	·38608	·39240	·39810	·40330	·40802	·41228
9	·56928	·56301	·55672	·55058	·54449	·53857	·53268	·52694	·52138	·51583
	·31453	·32597	·33663	·34627	·35518	·36326	·37077	·37762	·38385	·38966
10	0·58917	0·58337	0·57757	0·57182	0·56612	0·56049	0·55490	0·54940	0·54392	0·53857
	·27128	·28514	·29791	·30961	·32042	·33034	·33955	·34805	·35599	·36326
11	·60522	·60014	·59490	·58966	·58443	·57919	·57393	·56873	·56358	·55843
	·22538	·24133	·25630	·27003	·28269	·29444	·30543	·31556	·32497	·33381
12	·61782	·61350	·60899	·60437	·59971	·59490	·59011	·58530	·58048	·57567
	·17724	·19549	·21245	·22815	·24262	·25630	·26892	·28064	·29162	·30188
13	·62711	·62370	·62005	·61620	·61212	·60795	·60370	·59932	·59490	·59049
	·12757	·14802	·16690	·18436	·20087	·21614	·23034	·24377	·25630	·26794
14	·63321	·63092	·62821	·62521	·62192	·61843	·61476	·61094	·60706	·60306
	·07701	·09925	·12009	·13937	·15756	·17451	·19038	·20533	·21923	·23237
15	0·63624	0·63520	0·63360	0·63157	0·62917	0·62645	0·62348	0·62030	0·61697	0·61350
	·02568	·04973	·07242	·09343	·11321	·13177	·14926	·16568	·18103	·19549
16	—	·63662	·63628	·63536	·63394	·63211	·62994	·62751	·62482	·62192
		0	·02425	·04687	·06830	·08838	·10726	·12492	·14169	·15756
17	—	—	—	·63662	·63632	·63550	·63423	·63259	·63062	·62839
				0	·02281	·04432	·06450	·08365	·10176	·11884
18	—	—	—	—	—	·63662	·63635	·63561	·63446	·63298
						0	·02154	·04193	·06132	·07954
19	—	—	—	—	—	—	—	·63662	·63638	·63571
								0	·02042	·03986
20	—	—	—	—	—	—	—	—	—	0·63662
										0

Table 39 (*continued*)

Upper figure in table is $w = Z^2/pq$; lower figure is wX
For $r < \frac{1}{2}n$, wX is negative. For $r > \frac{1}{2}n$, use $n-r$ as argument, and wX is positive

r \ n	41	42	43	44	45	46	47	48	49	50
0	0·08330 ·18750	0·08177 ·18483	0·08022 ·18212	0·07919 ·18029	0·07762 ·17751	0·07657 ·17563	0·07498 ·17277	0·07391 ·17084	0·07283 ·16889	0·07175 ·16692
1	·13776 ·27144	·13537 ·26815	·13335 ·26536	·13091 ·26194	·12886 ·25904	·12679 ·25609	·12512 ·25369	·12301 ·25064	·12132 ·24816	·11961 ·24564
2	·22044 ·36517	·21689 ·36190	·21361 ·35881	·21059 ·35592	·20723 ·35265	·20445 ·34990	·20164 ·34709	·19881 ·34420	·19595 ·34124	·19338 ·33855
3	·28460 ·41335	·28031 ·41078	·27644 ·40838	·27252 ·40587	·26880 ·40342	·26503 ·40087	·26148 ·39839	·25813 ·39601	·25475 ·39354	·25160 ·39118
4	·33749 ·43716	·33268 ·43561	·32820 ·43405	·32386 ·43243	·31968 ·43078	·31564 ·42910	·31155 ·42731	·30763 ·42551	·30387 ·42371	·30029 ·42193
5	0·38237 ·44548	0·37721 ·44511	0·37249 ·44464	0·36769 ·44402	0·36317 ·44332	0·35876 ·44252	0·35448 ·44165	0·35032 ·44070	0·34611 ·43964	0·34222 ·43857
6	·42096 ·44303	·41588 ·44390	·41070 ·44461	·40589 ·44511	·40099 ·44547	·39633 ·44567	·39192 ·44574	·38743 ·44569	·38305 ·44551	·37894 ·44525
7	·45474 ·43264	·44951 ·43480	·44429 ·43675	·43924 ·43844	·43437 ·43989	·42955 ·44116	·42478 ·44226	·42022 ·44317	·41588 ·44390	·41147 ·44451
8	·48437 ·41619	·47907 ·41969	·47376 ·42294	·46870 ·42582	·46376 ·42842	·45885 ·43080	·45409 ·43292	·44951 ·43480	·44497 ·43651	·44048 ·43804
9	·51041 ·39499	·50513 ·39986	·49993 ·40437	·49480 ·40853	·48987 ·41228	·48505 ·41572	·48023 ·41895	·47555 ·42188	·47100 ·42454	·46649 ·42701
10	0·53330 ·37001	0·52812 ·37625	0·52307 ·38200	0·51805 ·38738	0·51309 ·39240	0·50829 ·39698	0·50359 ·40123	0·49887 ·40525	0·49436 ·40887	0·48987 ·41228
11	·55337 ·34196	·54837 ·34958	·54342 ·35668	·53857 ·36326	·53374 ·36946	·52903 ·37519	·52437 ·38055	·51996 ·38554	·51534 ·39016	·51091 ·39452
12	·57089 ·31143	·56612 ·32042	·56143 ·32873	·55672 ·33663	·55214 ·34389	·54757 ·35076	·54301 ·35725	·53857 ·36326	·53417 ·36892	·52984 ·37422
13	·58606 ·27886	·58157 ·28920	·57713 ·29884	·57275 ·30779	·56819 ·31626	·56394 ·32434	·55961 ·33183	·55528 ·33894	·55105 ·34556	·54684 ·35181
14	·59903 ·24463	·59490 ·25630	·59082 ·26711	·58669 ·27735	·58254 ·28704	·57838 ·29617	·57431 ·30465	·57022 ·31272	·56612 ·32042	·56208 ·32760
15	0·60994 ·20905	0·60623 ·22202	0·60250 ·23411	0·59873 ·24549	0·59490 ·25630	0·59109 ·26641	0·58720 ·27611	0·58337 ·28514	0·57950 ·29377	0·57567 ·30188
16	·61885 ·17254	·61570 ·18647	·61239 ·19982	·60899 ·21245	·60558 ·22421	·60204 ·23556	·59849 ·24620	·59490 ·25630	·59131 ·26585	·58771 ·27487
17	·62593 ·13503	·62331 ·15018	·62049 ·16476	·61759 ·17831	·61454 ·19128	·61142 ·20355	·60820 ·21525	·60496 ·22626	·60162 ·23686	·59829 ·24677
18	·63119 ·09689	·62917 ·11321	·62692 ·12882	·62450 ·14355	·62192 ·15756	·61921 ·17086	·61641 ·18345	·61350 ·19549	·61050 ·20697	·60748 ·21775
19	·63467 ·05831	·63332 ·07574	·63169 ·09232	·62982 ·10820	·62776 ·12321	·62552 ·13751	·62317 ·15095	·62064 ·16399	·61806 ·17618	·61534 ·18798
20	0·63640 ·01946	0·63580 ·03795	0·63485 ·05561	0·63360 ·07242	0·63211 ·08838	0·63041 ·10349	0·62850 ·11806	0·62645 ·13177	0·62425 ·14494	0·62192 ·15756
21	—	·63662 0	·63642 ·01851	·63587 ·03620	·63501 ·05307	·63386 ·06925	·63249 ·08460	·63092 ·09925	·62917 ·11321	·62725 ·12664
22	—	—	—	·63662 0	·63644 ·01771	·63593 ·03461	·63514 ·05084	·63409 ·06640	·63283 ·08112	·63137 ·09532
23	—	—	—	—	·63662 0	·63646 ·01691	·63599 ·03317	·63526 ·04877	·63429 ·06370	
24	—	—	—	—	—	—	·63662 0	·63647 ·01627	·63604 ·03190	
25	—	—	—	—	—	—	—	—	—	0·63662 0

Table 40. *Minimum normit χ^2 procedure: weights for arguments $p = r/n$*

p	0	1	2	3	4	5	6	7	8	9		
						Thousandths, for p on left						
0·00	—	0·01135	0·02014	0·02799	0·03523	0·04203	0·04847	0·05463	0·06054	0·06624	0·07175	0·99
	—	·03507	·05796	·07690	·09343	·10825	·12177	·13424	·14584	·15670	·16692	
·01	0·07175	·07709	·08228	·08733	·09226	·09707	·10177	·10636	·11087	·11528	·11961	·98
	·16692	·17657	·18572	·19443	·20272	·21064	·21823	·22550	·23248	·23919	·24564	
·02	·11961	·12386	·12803	·13213	·13617	·14014	·14404	·14789	·15168	·15541	·15910	·97
	·24564	·25187	·25787	·26366	·26925	·27466	·27989	·28496	·28987	·29462	·29923	
·03	·15910	·16273	·16631	·16984	·17333	·17678	·18018	·18354	·18686	·19014	·19338	·96
	·29923	·30370	·30804	·31225	·31633	·32031	·32416	·32791	·33156	·33511	·33855	
·04	·19338	·19659	·19976	·20289	·20600	·20906	·21210	·21510	·21808	·22102	·22394	·95
	·33855	·34191	·34517	·34835	·35144	·35445	·35738	·36023	·36300	·36571	·36834	
0·05	0·22394	0·22682	0·22968	0·23251	0·23531	0·23809	0·24084	0·24357	0·24627	0·24895	0·25160	0·94
	·36834	·37091	·37340	·37584	·37821	·38051	·38276	·38495	·38708	·38916	·39118	
·06	·25160	·25423	·25684	·25942	·26199	·26453	·26705	·26955	·27203	·27449	·27693	·93
	·39118	·39315	·39507	·39694	·39875	·40052	·40225	·40392	·40555	·40714	·40868	
·07	·27693	·27935	·28175	·28413	·28649	·28884	·29116	·29347	·29576	·29804	·30029	·92
	·40868	·41019	·41165	·41307	·41445	·41579	·41709	·41836	·41958	·42078	·42193	
·08	·30029	·30253	·30476	·30697	·30916	·31134	·31350	·31564	·31777	·31989	·32199	·91
	·42193	·42306	·42415	·42520	·42622	·42722	·42817	·42910	·43000	·43087	·43171	
·09	·32199	·32407	·32614	·32820	·33024	·33227	·33429	·33629	·33828	·34026	·34222	·90
	·43171	·43251	·43330	·43405	·43477	·43547	·43614	·43679	·43741	·43800	·43857	
0·10	0·34222	0·34417	0·34611	0·34803	0·34994	0·35184	0·35373	0·35560	0·35747	0·35932	0·36116	0·89
	·43857	·43912	·43964	·44013	·44061	·44106	·44148	·44189	·44227	·44263	·44297	
·11	·36116	·36299	·36480	·36661	·36840	·37019	·37196	·37372	·37547	·37721	·37894	·88
	·44297	·44329	·44359	·44386	·44412	·44436	·44457	·44477	·44495	·44511	·44525	
·12	·37894	·38066	·38237	·38407	·38576	·38743	·38910	·39076	·39241	·39405	·39568	·87
	·44525	·44537	·44548	·44556	·44563	·44569	·44572	·44574	·44574	·44572	·44569	
·13	·39568	·39730	·39891	·40051	·40210	·40369	·40526	·40682	·40838	·40993	·41147	·86
	·44569	·44564	·44558	·44550	·44540	·44529	·44517	·44502	·44487	·44470	·44451	
·14	·41147	·41299	·41452	·41603	·41753	·41903	·42051	·42199	·42346	·42492	·42638	·85
	·44451	·44431	·44410	·44387	·44363	·44338	·44311	·44283	·44254	·44223	·44191	
0·15	0·42638	0·42782	0·42926	0·43069	0·43211	0·43353	0·43493	0·43633	0·43772	0·43910	0·44048	0·84
	·44191	·44158	·44123	·44088	·44051	·44012	·43973	·43933	·43891	·43848	·43804	
·16	·44048	·44185	·44321	·44456	·44591	·44725	·44858	·44990	·45122	·45253	·45383	·83
	·43804	·43759	·43713	·43665	·43617	·43567	·43516	·43465	·43412	·43358	·43303	
·17	·45383	·45513	·45642	·45770	·45898	·46025	·46151	·46276	·46401	·46525	·46649	·82
	·43303	·43247	·43191	·43133	·43074	·43014	·42953	·42892	·42829	·42765	·42701	
·18	·46649	·46772	·46894	·47016	·47136	·47257	·47376	·47495	·47614	·47732	·47849	·81
	·42701	·42635	·42569	·42502	·42433	·42364	·42294	·42224	·42152	·42080	·42006	
·19	·47849	·47965	·48081	·48196	·48311	·48425	·48539	·48652	·48764	·48876	·48987	·80
	·42006	·41932	·41857	·41781	·41705	·41627	·41549	·41470	·41390	·41310	·41228	
0·20	0·48987	0·49097	0·49207	0·49317	0·49425	0·49534	0·49641	0·49748	0·49855	0·49961	0·50066	0·79
	·41228	·41146	·41063	·40980	·40895	·40810	·40725	·40638	·40551	·40463	·40375	
·21	·50066	·50171	·50275	·50379	·50482	·50585	·50687	·50789	·50890	·50991	·51091	·78
	·40375	·40285	·40195	·40105	·40013	·39921	·39829	·39735	·39642	·39547	·39452	
·22	·51091	·51190	·51289	·51387	·51485	·51583	·51680	·51776	·51872	·51967	·52062	·77
	·39452	·39356	·39259	·39162	·39065	·38966	·38868	·38768	·38668	·38567	·38466	
·23	·52062	·52157	·52250	·52344	·52437	·52529	·52621	·52712	·52803	·52894	·52984	·76
	·38466	·38364	·38262	·38159	·38055	·37951	·37846	·37741	·37636	·37529	·37422	
·24	·52984	·53073	·53162	·53251	·53339	·53426	·53513	·53600	·53686	·53772	·53857	·75
	·37422	·37315	·37207	·37099	·36990	·36881	·36771	·36660	·36549	·36438	·36326	
	9	8	7	6	5	4	3	2	1	0		

Thousandths, for p on right

p

Table 40 (*continued*)

Upper figure in table is $w = Z^2/pq$; lower figure is wX
For $p < 0.50$ on left, wX is negative. For $p > 0.50$ on right, wX is positive

Thousandths, for p on left

p	0	1	2	3	4	5	6	7	8	9		
0.25	0.53857	0.53942	0.54026	0.54110	0.54193	0.54276	0.54359	0.54441	0.54523	0.54604	0.54684	0.74
	·36326	·36214	·36101	·35987	·35874	·35759	·35645	·35529	·35414	·35298	·35181	
·26	·54684	·54765	·54845	·54924	·55003	·55081	·55159	·55237	·55314	·55391	·55468	·73
	·35181	·35064	·34946	·34829	·34710	·34591	·34472	·34353	·34233	·34112	·33991	
·27	·55468	·55543	·55619	·55694	·55769	·55843	·55917	·55990	·56063	·56136	·56208	·72
	·33991	·33870	·33748	·33626	·33504	·33381	·33257	·33134	·33010	·32885	·32760	
·28	·56208	·56280	·56351	·56422	·56493	·56563	·56632	·56702	·56771	·56839	·56907	·71
	·32760	·32635	·32510	·32384	·32257	·32131	·32003	·31876	·31748	·31620	·31492	
·29	·56907	·56975	·57042	·57109	·57176	·57242	·57308	·57373	·57438	·57503	·57567	·70
	·31492	·31363	·31234	·31104	·30974	·30844	·30713	·30583	·30451	·30320	·30188	
0.30	0.57567	0.57631	0.57694	0.57757	0.57820	0.57882	0.57944	0.58005	0.58066	0.58127	0.58188	0.69
	·30188	·30056	·29923	·29791	·29657	·29524	·29390	·29256	·29122	·28987	·28852	
·31	·58188	·58248	·58307	·58366	·58425	·58484	·58542	·58600	·58657	·58714	·58771	·68
	·28852	·28717	·28582	·28446	·28310	·28173	·28037	·27900	·27762	·27625	·27487	
·32	·58771	·58827	·58883	·58939	·58994	·59049	·59103	·59158	·59211	·59265	·59318	·67
	·27487	·27349	·27211	·27072	·26933	·26794	·26655	·26515	·26375	·26235	·26095	
·33	·59318	·59371	·59423	·59475	·59527	·59578	·59629	·59679	·59730	·59780	·59829	·66
	·26095	·25954	·25813	·25672	·25531	·25389	·25247	·25105	·24963	·24820	·24677	
·34	·59829	·59878	·59927	·59976	·60024	·60072	·60119	·60166	·60213	·60260	·60306	·65
	·24677	·24534	·24391	·24248	·24104	·23960	·23816	·23671	·23527	·23382	·23237	
0.35	0.60306	0.60351	0.60397	0.60442	0.60487	0.60531	0.60575	0.60619	0.60662	0.60706	0.60748	0.64
	·23237	·23092	·22946	·22801	·22655	·22509	·22363	·22216	·22070	·21923	·21776	
·36	·60748	·60791	·60833	·60875	·60916	·60957	·60998	·61038	·61078	·61118	·61158	·63
	·21776	·21629	·21481	·21334	·21186	·21038	·20890	·20741	·20593	·20444	·20295	
·37	·61158	·61197	·61236	·61274	·61312	·61350	·61387	·61425	·61462	·61498	·61534	·62
	·20295	·20146	·19997	·19848	·19698	·19549	·19399	·19249	·19098	·18948	·18798	
·38	·61534	·61570	·61606	·61641	·61676	·61711	·61745	·61779	·61812	·61846	·61879	·61
	·18798	·18647	·18496	·18345	·18194	·18043	·17891	·17740	·17588	·17436	·17284	
·39	·61879	·61912	·61944	·61976	·62008	·62039	·62070	·62101	·62132	·62162	·62192	·60
	·17284	·17132	·16979	·16827	·16674	·16522	·16369	·16216	·16063	·15910	·15756	
0.40	0.62192	0.62221	0.62251	0.62280	0.62308	0.62337	0.62365	0.62392	0.62420	0.62447	0.62474	0.59
	·15756	·15603	·15449	·15295	·15141	·14987	·14833	·14679	·14525	·14370	·14216	
·41	·62474	·62500	·62526	·62552	·62578	·62603	·62628	·62653	·62677	·62701	·62725	·58
	·14216	·14061	·13906	·13751	·13596	·13441	·13286	·13130	·12975	·12819	·12664	
·42	·62725	62748	·62772	·62794	·62817	·62839	·62861	·62883	·62904	·62925	·62946	·57
	·12664	·12508	·12352	·12196	·12040	·11884	·11728	·11572	·11415	·11259	·11102	
·43	·62946	·62966	·62986	·63006	·63026	·63045	·63064	·63082	·63101	·63119	·63137	·56
	·11102	·10945	·10789	·10632	·10475	·10318	·10161	·10004	·09846	·09689	·09532	
·44	·63137	·63154	·63171	·63188	·63205	·63221	·63237	·63252	·63268	·63283	·63298	·55
	·09532	·09374	·09217	·09059	·08901	·08744	·08586	·08428	·08270	·08112	·07954	
0.45	0.63298	0.63312	0.63326	0.63340	0.63354	0.63367	0.63380	0.63393	0.63405	0.63417	0.63429	0.54
	·07954	·07796	·07638	·07480	·07321	·07163	·07005	·06846	·06688	·06529	·06370	
·46	·63429	·63441	·63452	·63463	·63473	·63484	·63494	·63503	·63513	·63522	·63531	·53
	·06370	·06212	·06053	·05894	·05736	·05577	·05418	·05259	·05100	·04941	·04782	
·47	·63531	·63540	·63548	·63556	·63564	·63571	·63578	·63585	·63592	·63598	·63604	·52
	·04782	·04623	·04464	·04305	·04146	·03986	·03827	·03668	·03509	·03349	·03190	
·48	·63604	·63609	·63615	·63620	·63625	·63629	·63633	·63637	·63641	·63644	·63647	·51
	·03190	·03031	·02871	·02712	·02552	·02393	·02234	·02074	·01915	·01755	·01596	
·49	·63647	·63650	·63653	·63655	·63657	·63658	·63660	·63661	·63661	·63662	·63662	·50
	·01596	·01436	·01277	·01117	·00957	·00798	·00638	·00479	·00319	·00160	·00000	
	9	8	7	6	5	4	3	2	1	0		p

Thousandths, for p on right

Table 41. *Logits, $l = \log[P/(1-P)]$ for argument P*

P	·000	·001	·002	·003	·004	·005	·006	·007	·008	·009
0·50	0·00000	0·00400	0·00800	0·01200	0·01600	0·02000	0·02400	0·02800	0·03200	0·03600
·51	·04001	·04401	·04801	·05201	·05601	·06002	·06402	·06803	·07203	·07604
·52	·08004	·08405	·08806	·09206	·09607	·10008	·10409	·10811	·11212	·11613
·53	·12014	·12416	·12818	·13219	·13621	·14023	·14425	·14827	·15229	·15632
·54	·16034	·16437	·16840	·17243	·17646	·18049	·18452	·18856	·19259	·19663
0·55	0·20067	0·20471	0·20875	0·21280	0·21685	0·22089	0·22494	0·22900	0·23305	0·23710
·56	·24116	·24522	·24928	·25335	·25741	·26148	·26555	·26962	·27370	·27777
·57	·28185	·28593	·29002	·29410	·29819	·30228	·30637	·31047	·31457	·31867
·58	·32277	·32688	·33099	·33510	·33922	·34333	·34745	·35158	·35570	·35983
·59	·36397	·36810	·37224	·37638	·38053	·38467	·38883	·39298	·39714	·40130
0·60	0·40547	0·40963	0·41381	0·41798	0·42216	0·42634	0·43053	0·43472	0·43891	0·44311
·61	·44731	·45152	·45573	·45994	·46416	·46838	·47260	·47683	·48107	·48531
·62	·48955	·49379	·49805	·50230	·50656	·51083	·51509	·51937	·52365	·52793
·63	·53222	·53651	·54081	·54511	·54942	·55373	·55804	·56237	·56669	·57103
·64	·57536	·57971	·58406	·58841	·59277	·59713	·60150	·60588	·61026	·61465
0·65	0·61904	0·62344	0·62784	0·63225	0·63667	0·64109	0·64552	0·64995	0·65439	0·65884
·66	·66329	·66775	·67222	·67669	·68117	·68566	·69015	·69465	·69915	·70367
·67	·70819	·71271	·71724	·72179	·72633	·73089	·73545	·74002	·74460	·74918
·68	·75377	·75837	·76298	·76759	·77222	·77685	·78148	·78613	·79079	·79545
·69	·80012	·80480	·80949	·81418	·81889	·82360	·82832	·83305	·83779	·84254
0·70	0·84730	0·85206	0·85684	0·86162	0·86642	0·87122	0·87604	0·88086	0·88569	0·89053
·71	·89538	·90025	·90512	·91000	·91489	·91979	·92471	·92963	·93456	·93951
·72	·94446	·94943	·95440	·95939	·96439	·96940	·97442	·97945	·98450	·98955
·73	·99462	·99970	1·00479	1·00990	1·01501	1·02014	1·02528	1·03043	1·03560	1·04078
·74	1·04597	1·05117	1·05639	1·06162	1·06686	1·07212	1·07739	1·08268	1·08797	1·09329
0·75	1·09861	1·10395	1·10931	1·11468	1·12006	1·12546	1·13087	1·13630	1·14175	1·14720
·76	1·15268	1·15817	1·16368	1·16920	1·17474	1·18029	1·18586	1·19145	1·19705	1·20267
·77	1·20831	1·21397	1·21964	1·22533	1·23104	1·23676	1·24251	1·24827	1·25405	1·25985
·78	1·26567	1·27150	1·27736	1·28324	1·28913	1·29505	1·30098	1·30694	1·31291	1·31891
·79	1·32493	1·33096	1·33702	1·34310	1·34921	1·35533	1·36148	1·36765	1·37384	1·38006
0·80	1·38629	1·39256	1·39884	1·40515	1·41148	1·41784	1·42423	1·43063	1·43707	1·44353
·81	1·45001	1·45652	1·46306	1·46962	1·47621	1·48283	1·48948	1·49615	1·50286	1·50959
·82	1·51635	1·52314	1·52996	1·53681	1·54369	1·55060	1·55754	1·56451	1·57152	1·57856
·83	1·58563	1·59273	1·59987	1·60704	1·61425	1·62149	1·62876	1·63607	1·64342	1·65081
·84	1·65823	1·66569	1·67318	1·68072	1·68830	1·69591	1·70357	1·71126	1·71900	1·72678
0·85	1·73460	1·74247	1·75037	1·75833	1·76632	1·77437	1·78246	1·79059	1·79878	1·80701
·86	1·81529	1·82362	1·83200	1·84043	1·84892	1·85745	1·86605	1·87469	1·88339	1·89215
·87	1·90096	1·90983	1·91876	1·92775	1·93680	1·94591	1·95508	1·96432	1·97363	1·98299
·88	1·99243	2·00193	2·01151	2·02115	2·03087	2·04066	2·05052	2·06046	2·07047	2·08057
·89	2·09074	2·10100	2·11133	2·12176	2·13227	2·14286	2·15355	2·16433	2·17520	2·18616
0·90	2·19722	2·20839	2·21965	2·23101	2·24248	2·25406	2·26574	2·27754	2·28946	2·30149
·91	2·31363	2·32591	2·33830	2·35083	2·36348	2·37627	2·38920	2·40227	2·41548	2·42884
·92	2·44235	2·45601	2·46984	2·48382	2·49798	2·51231	2·52681	2·54149	2·55637	2·57143
·93	2·58669	2·60215	2·61783	2·63371	2·64982	2·66616	2·68273	2·69955	2·71662	2·73394
·94	2·75154	2·76941	2·78756	2·80601	2·82477	2·84385	2·86326	2·88301	2·90311	2·92358
0·95	2·94444	2·96569	2·98736	3·00947	3·03202	3·05505	3·07857	3·10260	3·12718	3·15232
·96	3·17805	3·20441	3·23143	3·25914	3·28757	3·31678	3·34680	3·37769	3·40950	3·44228
·97	3·47610	3·51103	3·54715	3·58455	3·62331	3·66356	3·70541	3·74899	3·79447	3·84201
·98	3·89182	3·94413	3·99922	4·05740	4·11904	4·18459	4·25460	4·32972	4·41078	4·49880
·99	4·59512	4·70149	4·82028	4·95482	5·10998	5·29330	5·51745	5·80614	6·21261	6·90675
P	·000	·001	·002	·003	·004	·005	·006	·007	·008	·009

For values of $P < 0·50$ the logit is the negative value of the logit for $(1-P)$. For instance the logit of $0·236$ is $-1·17474$.

Table 42. *Antilogits: table giving P for argument l*

l	·00	·01	·02	·03	·04	·05	·06	·07	·08	·09
0·0	0·50000	0·50250	0·50500	0·50750	0·51000	0·51250	0·51500	0·51749	0·51999	0·52248
0·1	·52498	·52747	·52996	·53245	·53494	·53743	·53991	·54240	·54488	·54736
0·2	·54983	·55231	·55478	·55725	·55971	·56218	·56464	·56709	·56955	·57200
0·3	·57444	·57689	·57932	·58176	·58419	·58662	·58904	·59146	·59387	·59628
0·4	·59869	·60109	·60348	·60587	·60826	·61064	·61301	·61538	·61775	·62011
0·5	0·62246	0·62481	0·62715	0·62948	0·63181	0·63414	0·63645	0·63876	0·64107	0·64337
0·6	·64566	·64794	·65022	·65249	·65475	·65701	·65926	·66150	·66374	·66597
0·7	·66819	·67040	·67261	·67481	·67700	·67918	·68135	·68352	·68568	·68783
0·8	·68997	·69211	·69424	·69635	·69847	·70057	·70266	·70475	·70682	·70889
0·9	·71095	·71300	·71504	·71708	·71910	·72112	·72312	·72512	·72711	·72909
1·0	0·73106	0·73302	0·73497	0·73692	0·73885	0·74077	0·74269	0·74460	0·74649	0·74838
1·1	·75026	·75213	·75399	·75584	·75768	·75951	·76133	·76315	·76495	·76674
1·2	·76852	·77030	·77206	·77382	·77556	·77730	·77903	·78074	·78245	·78415
1·3	·78583	·78751	·78918	·79084	·79249	·79413	·79576	·79738	·79899	·80059
1·4	·80218	·80377	·80534	·80690	·80845	·81000	·81153	·81306	·81457	·81608
1·5	0·81757	0·81906	0·82054	0·82201	0·82346	0·82491	0·82635	0·82778	0·82920	0·83062
1·6	·83202	·83341	·83480	·83617	·83753	·83889	·84024	·84158	·84290	·84422
1·7	·84553	·84684	·84813	·84941	·85069	·85195	·85321	·85446	·85570	·85693
1·8	·85815	·85936	·86057	·86176	·86295	·86413	·86530	·86646	·86761	·86876
1·9	·86989	·87102	·87214	·87325	·87435	·87545	·87653	·87761	·87868	·87974
2·0	0·88080	0·88184	0·88288	0·88391	0·88493	0·88595	0·88695	0·88795	0·88894	0·88993
2·1	·89090	·89187	·89283	·89379	·89473	·89567	·89660	·89752	·89844	·89935
2·2	·90025	·90114	·90203	·90291	·90378	·90465	·90551	·90636	·90721	·90805
2·3	·90888	·90970	·91052	·91133	·91214	·91293	·91373	·91451	·91529	·91606
2·4	·91683	·91759	·91834	·91909	·91983	·92056	·92129	·92201	·92273	·92344
2·5	0·92414	0·92484	0·92553	0·92622	0·92690	0·92757	0·92824	0·92891	0·92956	0·93022
2·6	·93086	·93150	·93214	·93277	·93339	·93401	·93462	·93523	·93584	·93643
2·7	·93703	·93761	·93820	·93877	·93935	·93991	·94048	·94103	·94159	·94213
2·8	·94268	·94321	·94375	·94428	·94480	·94532	·94583	·94634	·94685	·94735
2·9	·94785	·94834	·94883	·94931	·94979	·95026	·95073	·95120	·95166	·95212
3·0	0·95257	0·95302	0·95347	0·95391	0·95435	0·95478	0·95521	0·95564	0·95606	0·95648
3·1	·95689	·95730	·95771	·95811	·95851	·95891	·95930	·95969	·96007	·96046
3·2	·96083	·96121	·96158	·96195	·96231	·96267	·96303	·96339	·96374	·96408
3·3	·96443	·96477	·96511	·96544	·96578	·96610	·96643	·96675	·96707	·96739
3·4	·96770	·96802	·96832	·96863	·96893	·96923	·96953	·96982	·97011	·97040
3·5	0·97069	0·97097	0·97125	0·97153	0·97180	0·97208	0·97235	0·97262	0·97288	0·97314
3·6	·97340	·97366	·97392	·97417	·97442	·97467	·97491	·97516	·97540	·97564
3·7	·97587	·97611	·97634	·97657	·97680	·97702	·97725	·97747	·97769	·97790
3·8	·97812	·97833	·97854	·97875	·97896	·97916	·97937	·97957	·97977	·97996
3·9	·98016	·98035	·98054	·98073	·98092	·98111	·98129	·98148	·98166	·98184
4·0	·098201	0·98219	0·98236	0·98254	0·98271	0·98288	0·98304	0·98321	0·98337	0·98354
4·1	·98370	·98386	·98402	·98417	·98433	·98448	·98463	·98478	·98493	·98508
4·2	·98523	·98537	·98551	·98566	·98580	·98594	·98607	·98621	·98635	·98648
4·3	·98661	·98674	·98687	·98700	·98713	·98726	·98738	·98751	·98763	·98775
4·4	·98787	·98799	·98811	·98823	·98834	·98846	·98857	·98868	·98879	·98890
4·5	0·98901	0·98912	0·98923	0·98933	0·98944	0·98954	0·98965	0·98975	0·98985	0·98995
4·6	·99005	·99015	·99024	·99034	·99043	·99053	·99062	·99071	·99081	·99090
4·7	·99099	·99108	·99116	·99125	·99134	·99142	·99151	·99159	·99167	·99176
4·8	·99184	·99192	·99200	·99208	·99215	·99223	·99231	·99239	·99246	·99253
4·9	·99261	·99268	·99275	·99283	·99290	·99297	·99304	·99310	·99317	·99324
l	·00	·01	·02	·03	·04	·05	·06	·07	·08	·09

If l is negative, P is $1-$tabled value.

Table 43. *Minimum logit χ² procedure: weights for argument P*

Upper figure in table is $w = PQ$; lower figure is $wl = PQl$.

P	Thousandths, for P on left											
---	0	1	2	3	4	5	6	7	8	9	—	
0·00	0·0000	0·0010	0·0020	0·0030	0·0040	0·0050	0·0060	0·0070	0·0079	0·0089	0·0099	**0·99**
	—	·0069	·0124	·0174	·0220	·0263	·0305	·0344	·0383	·0419	·0455	
·01	0·0099	·0109	·0119	·0128	·0138	·0148	·0157	·0167	·0177	·0186	·0196	·98
	·0455	·0489	·0523	·0556	·0587	·0618	·0649	·0678	·0707	·0735	·0763	
·02	·0196	·0206	·0215	·0225	·0234	·0244	·0253	·0263	·0272	·0282	·0291	·97
	·0763	·0790	·0816	·0842	·0868	·0893	·0918	·0942	·0965	·0989	·1012	
·03	·0291	·0300	·0310	·0319	·0328	·0338	·0347	·0356	·0366	·0375	·0384	·96
	·1012	·1034	·1056	·1078	·1099	·1120	·1141	·1161	·1181	·1201	·1220	
·04	·0384	·0393	·0402	·0412	·0421	·0430	·0439	·0448	·0457	·0466	·0475	·95
	·1220	·1239	·1258	·1277	·1295	·1313	·1331	·1348	·1365	·1382	·1399	
0·05	0·0475	0·0484	0·0493	0·0502	0·0511	0·0520	0·0529	0·0538	0·0546	0·0555	0·0564	**0·94**
	·1399	·1415	·1431	·1447	·1463	·1478	·1493	·1508	·1523	·1538	·1552	
·06	·0564	·0573	·0582	·0590	·0599	·0608	·0616	·0625	·0634	·0642	·0651	·93
	·1552	·1566	·1580	·1594	·1607	·1620	·1633	·1646	·1659	·1672	·1684	
·07	·0651	·0660	·0668	·0677	·0685	·0694	·0702	·0711	·0719	·0728	·0736	·92
	·1684	·1696	·1708	·1720	·1731	·1743	·1754	·1765	·1776	·1787	·1798	
·08	·0736	·0744	·0753	·0761	·0769	·0778	·0786	·0794	·0803	·0811	·0819	·91
	·1798	·1808	·1818	·1828	·1838	·1848	·1858	·1867	·1877	·1886	·1895	
·09	·0819	·0827	·0835	·0844	·0852	·0860	·0868	·0876	·0884	·0892	·0900	·90
	·1895	·1904	·1913	·1921	·1930	·1938	·1946	·1954	·1962	·1970	·1977	
0·10	0·0900	0·0908	0·0916	0·0924	0·0932	0·0940	0·0948	0·0956	0·0963	0·0971	0·0979	**0·89**
	·1977	·1985	·1992	·2000	·2007	·2014	·2021	·2027	·2034	·2040	·2047	
·11	·0979	·0987	·0995	·1002	·1010	·1018	·1025	·1033	·1041	·1048	·1056	·88
	·2047	·2053	·2059	·2065	·2071	·2077	·2083	·2088	·2093	·2099	·2104	
·12	·1056	·1064	·1071	·1079	·1086	·1094	·1101	·1109	·1116	·1124	·1131	·87
	·2104	2109	·2114	·2119	·2124	·2128	·2133	·2137	·2142	·2146	·2150	
·13	·1131	·1138	·1146	·1153	·1160	·1168	·1175	·1182	·1190	·1197	·1204	·86
	·2150	·2154	·2158	·2162	·2165	·2169	·2173	·2176	·2179	·2182	·2186	
·14	·1204	·1211	·1218	·1226	·1233	·1240	·1247	·1254	·1261	·1268	·1275	·85
	·2186	·2189	·2192	·2194	·2197	·2200	·2202	·2205	·2207	·2209	·2212	
0·15	0·1275	0·1282	0·1289	0·1296	0·1303	0·1310	0·1317	0·1324	0·1330	0·1337	0·1344	**0·84**
	·2212	·2214	·2216	·2218	·2219	·2221	·2223	·2224	·2226	·2227	·2229	
·16	·1344	·1351	·1358	·1364	·1371	·1378	·1384	·1391	·1398	·1404	·1411	·83
	·2229	·2230	·2231	·2232	·2233	·2234	·2235	·2236	·2236	·2237	·2237	
·17	·1411	·1418	·1424	·1431	·1437	·1444	·1450	·1457	·1463	·1470	·1476	·82
	·2237	·2238	·2238	·2238	·2239	·2239	·2239	·2239	·2239	·2238	·2238	
·18	·1476	·1482	·1489	·1495	·1501	·1508	·1514	·1520	·1527	·1533	·1539	·81
	·2238	·2238	·2237	·2237	·2236	·2236	·2235	·2234	·2233	·2233	·2232	
·19	·1539	·1545	·1551	·1558	·1564	·1570	·1576	·1582	·1588	·1594	·1600	·80
	·2232	·2231	·2229	·2228	·2227	·2226	·2224	·2223	·2221	·2220	·2218	
0·20	0·1600	0·1606	0·1612	0·1618	0·1624	0·1630	0·1636	0·1642	0·1647	0·1653	0·1659	**0·79**
	·2218	·2216	·2215	·2213	·2211	·2209	·2207	·2205	·2203	·2200	·2198	
·21	·1659	·1665	·1671	·1676	·1682	·1688	·1693	·1699	·1705	·1710	·1716	·78
	·2198	·2196	·2193	·2191	·2188	·2186	·2183	·2180	·2178	·2175	·2172	
·22	·1716	·1722	·1727	·1733	·1738	·1744	·1749	·1755	·1760	·1766	·1771	·77
	·2172	·2169	·2166	·2163	·2160	·2157	·2153	·2150	·2147	·2143	·2140	
·23	·1771	·1776	·1782	·1787	·1792	·1798	·1803	·1808	·1814	·1819	·1824	·76
	·2140	·2136	·2133	·2129	·2126	·2122	·2118	·2114	·2110	·2106	·2102	
·24	·1824	·1829	·1834	·1840	·1845	·1850	·1855	·1860	·1865	·1870	·1875	·75
	·2102	·2098	·2094	·2090	·2086	·2082	·2078	·2073	·2069	·2064	·2060	
	—	9	8	7	6	5	4	3	2	1	0	P

Thousandths, for P on right

For $P < 0.500$, wl is negative.

Table 43 (*continued*)

Upper figure in table is $w = PQ$; lower figure is $wl = PQl$.

P	0	1	2	3	4	5	6	7	8	9	—	
0·25	0·1875	0·1880	0·1885	·01890	0·1895	0·1900	0·1905	0·1910	0·1914	0·1919	0·1924	**0·74**
	·2060	·2055	·2051	·2046	·2041	·2037	·2032	·2027	·2022	·2017	·2012	
·26	·1924	·1929	·1934	·1938	·1943	·1948	·1952	·1957	·1962	·1966	·1971	**·73**
	·2012	·2007	·2002	·1997	·1992	·1987	·1982	·1976	·1971	·1966	·1960	
·27	·1971	·1976	·1980	·1985	·1989	·1994	·1998	·2003	·2007	·2012	·2016	**·72**
	·1960	·1955	·1949	·1944	·1938	·1933	·1927	·1921	·1916	·1910	·1904	
·28	·2016	·2020	·2025	·2029	·2033	·2038	·2042	·2046	·2051	·2055	·2059	**·71**
	·1904	·1898	·1892	·1886	·1880	·1874	·1868	·1862	·1856	·1850	·1844	
·29	·2059	·2063	·2067	·2072	·2076	·2080	·2084	·2088	·2092	·2096	·2100	**·70**
	·1844	·1837	·1831	·1825	·1818	·1812	·1805	·1799	·1792	·1786	·1779	
0·30	0·2100	0·2104	0·2108	0·2112	0·2116	0·2120	0·2124	0·2128	0·2131	0·2135	0·2139	**0·69**
	·1779	·1773	·1766	·1759	·1753	·1746	·1739	·1732	·1725	·1718	·1711	
·31	·2139	·2143	·2147	·2150	·2154	·2158	·2161	·2165	·2169	·2172	·2176	**·68**
	·1711	·1704	·1697	·1690	·1683	·1676	·1669	·1662	·1655	·1647	·1640	
·32	·2176	·2180	·2183	·2187	·2190	·2194	·2197	·2201	·2204	·2208	·2211	**·67**
	·1640	·1633	·1626	·1618	·1611	·1603	·1596	·1588	·1581	·1573	·1566	
·33	·2211	·2214	·2218	·2221	·2224	·2228	·2231	·2234	·2238	·2241	·2244	**·66**
	·1566	·1558	·1551	·1543	·1535	·1527	·1520	·1512	·1504	·1496	·1488	
·34	·2244	·2247	·2250	·2254	·2257	·2260	·2263	·2266	·2269	·2272	·2275	**·65**
	·1488	·1481	·1473	·1465	·1457	·1449	·1441	·1433	·1425	·1416	·1408	
0·35	0·2275	0·2278	0·2281	0·2284	0·2287	0·2290	0·2293	0·2296	0·2298	0·2301	0·2304	**0·64**
	·1408	·1400	·1392	·1384	·1376	·1367	·1359	·1351	·1342	·1334	·1326	
·36	·2304	·2307	·2310	·2312	·2315	·2318	·2320	·2323	·2326	·2328	·2331	**·63**
	·1326	·1317	·1309	·1300	·1292	·1283	·1275	·1266	·1258	·1249	·1241	
·37	·2331	·2334	·2336	·2339	·2341	·2344	·2346	·2349	·2351	·2354	·2356	**·62**
	·1241	·1232	·1223	·1215	·1206	·1197	·1189	·1180	·1171	·1162	·1153	
·38	·2356	·2358	·2361	·2363	·2365	·2368	·2370	·2372	·2375	·2377	·2379	**·61**
	·1153	·1145	·1136	·1127	·1118	·1109	·1100	·1091	·1082	·1073	·1064	
·39	·2379	·2381	·2383	·2386	·2388	·2390	·2392	·2394	·2396	·2398	·2400	**·60**
	·1064	·1055	·1046	·1037	·1028	·1019	·1010	·1001	·0991	·0982	·0973	
0·40	0·2400	0·2402	0·2404	0·2406	0·2408	0·2410	0·2412	0·2414	0·2415	0·2417	0·2419	**0·59**
	·0973	·0964	·0955	·0945	·0936	·0927	·0918	·0908	·0899	·0890	·0880	
·41	·2419	·2421	·2423	·2424	·2426	·2428	·2429	·2431	·2433	·2434	·2436	**·58**
	·0880	·0871	·0862	·0852	·0843	·0834	·0824	·0815	·0805	·0796	·0786	
·42	·2436	·2438	·2439	·2441	·2442	·2444	·2445	·2447	·2448	·2450	·2451	**·57**
	·0786	·0777	·0767	·0758	·0748	·0739	·0729	·0720	·0710	·0700	·0691	
·43	·2451	·2452	·2454	·2455	·2456	·2458	·2459	·2460	·2462	·2463	·2464	**·56**
	·0691	·0681	·0672	·0662	·0652	·0643	·0633	·0623	·0614	·0604	·0594	
·44	·2464	·2465	·2466	·2468	·2469	·2470	·2471	·2472	·2473	·2474	·2475	**·55**
	·0594	·0584	·0575	·0565	·0555	·0546	·0536	·0526	·0516	·0506	·0497	
0·45	0·2475	0·2476	0·2477	0·2478	0·2479	0·2480	0·2481	0·2482	0·2482	0·2483	0·2484	**0·54**
	·0497	·0487	·0477	·0467	·0457	·0448	·0438	·0428	·0418	·0408	·0398	
·46	·2484	·2485	·2486	·2486	·2487	·2488	·2488	·2489	·2490	·2490	·2491	**·53**
	·0398	·0388	·0379	·0369	·0359	·0349	·0339	·0329	·0319	·0309	·0299	
·47	·2491	·2492	·2492	·2493	·2493	·2494	·2494	·2495	·2495	·2496	·2496	**·52**
	·0299	·0289	·0279	·0269	·0260	·0250	·0240	·0230	·0220	·0210	·0200	
·48	·2496	·2496	·2497	·2497	·2497	·2498	·2498	·2498	·2499	·2499	·2499	**·51**
	·0200	·0190	·0180	·0170	·0160	·0150	·0140	·0130	·0120	·0110	·0100	
·49	·2499	·2499	·2499	·2500	·2500	·2500	·2500	·2500	·2500	·2500	·2500	**·50**
	·0100	·0090	·0080	·0070	·0060	·0050	·0040	·0030	·0020	·0010	·0000	
	—	9	8	7	6	5	4	3	2	1	0	P

Thousandths, for P on right

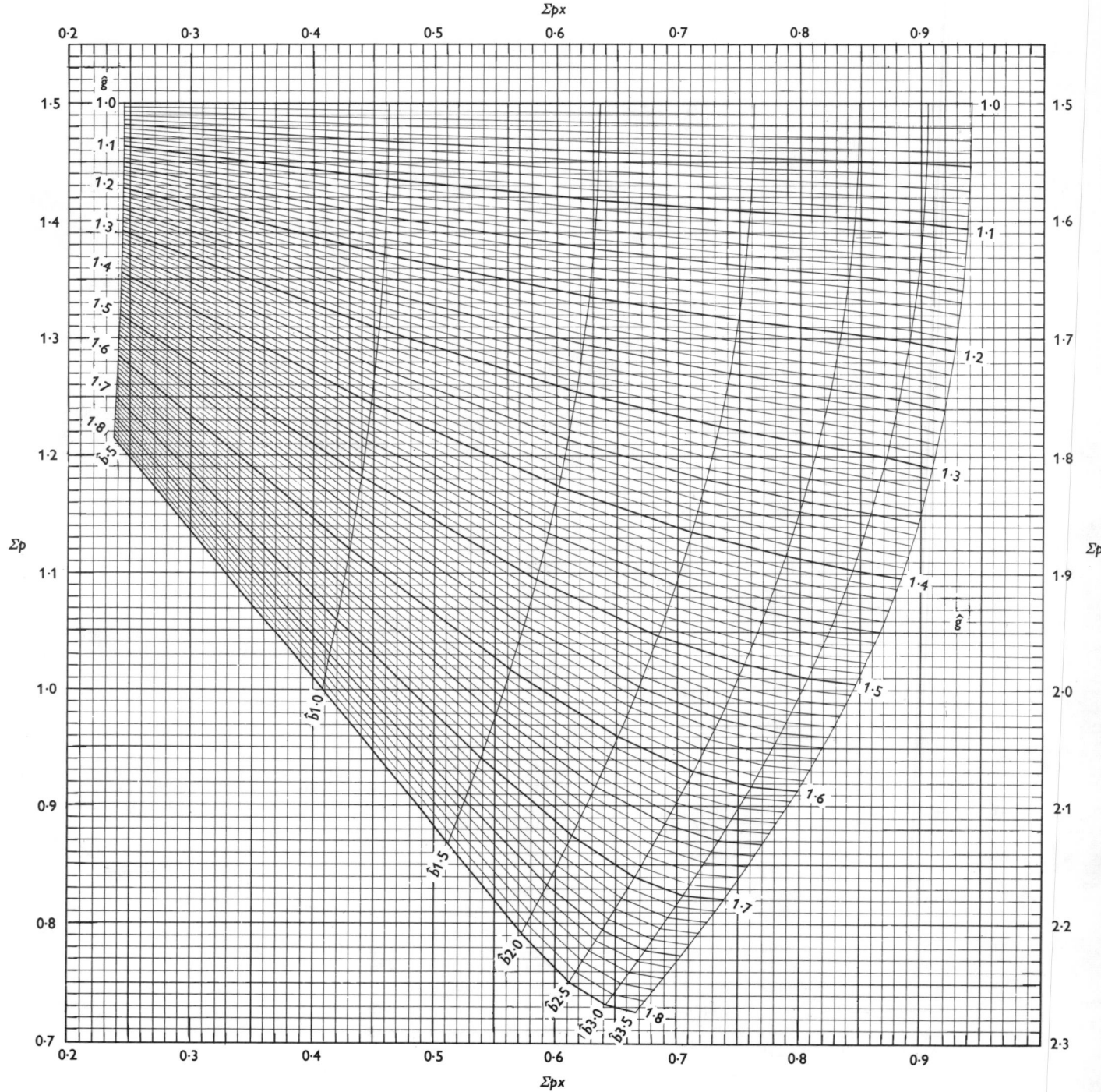

316

Table 44 (*continued*). $\hat{b}$ = estimate of β, 3 doses

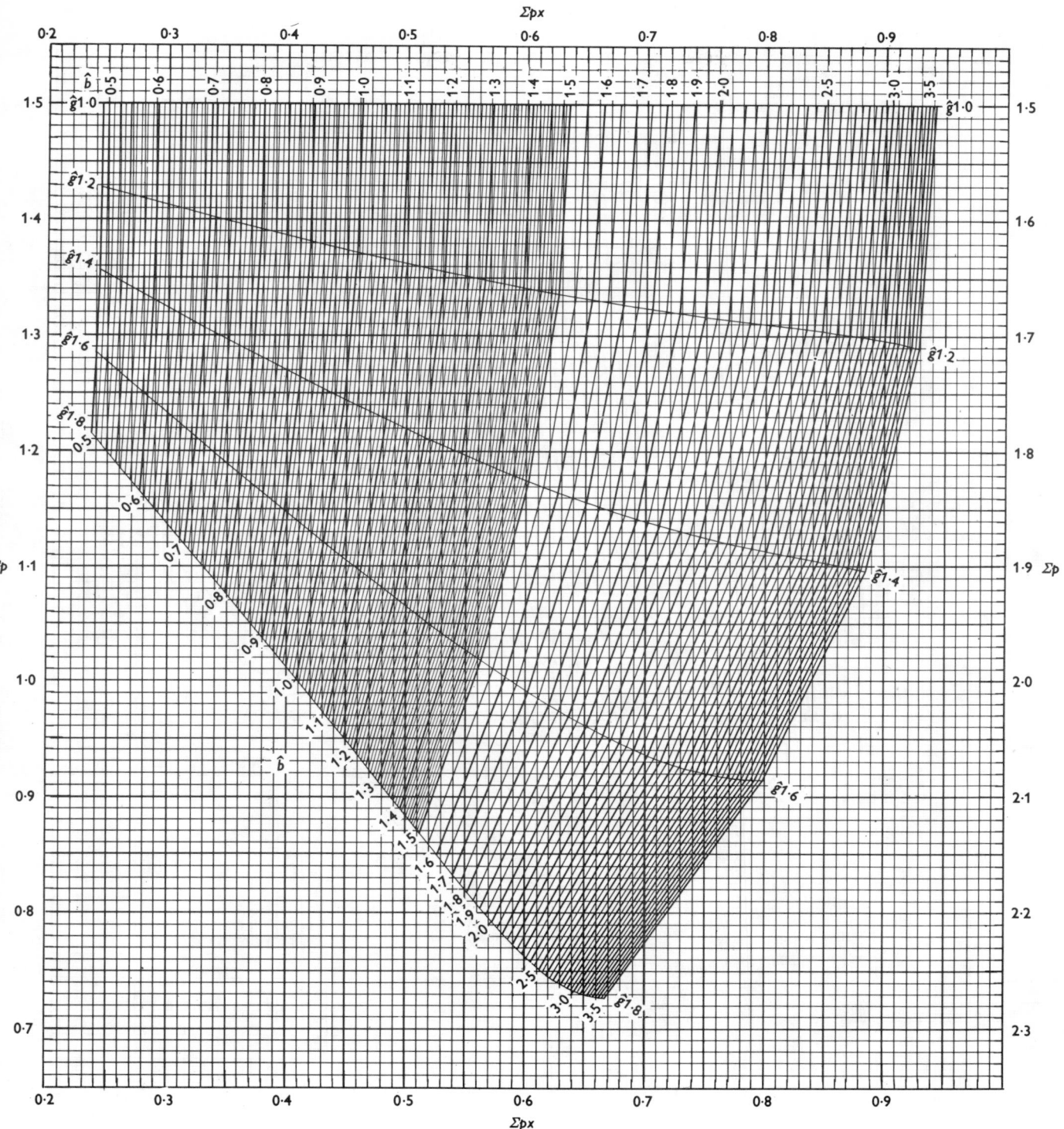

Table 44 (*continued*). *Nomograms to assist in fitting the logistic function* $\hat{g}$ = estimate of γ, (ED 50), 4 doses

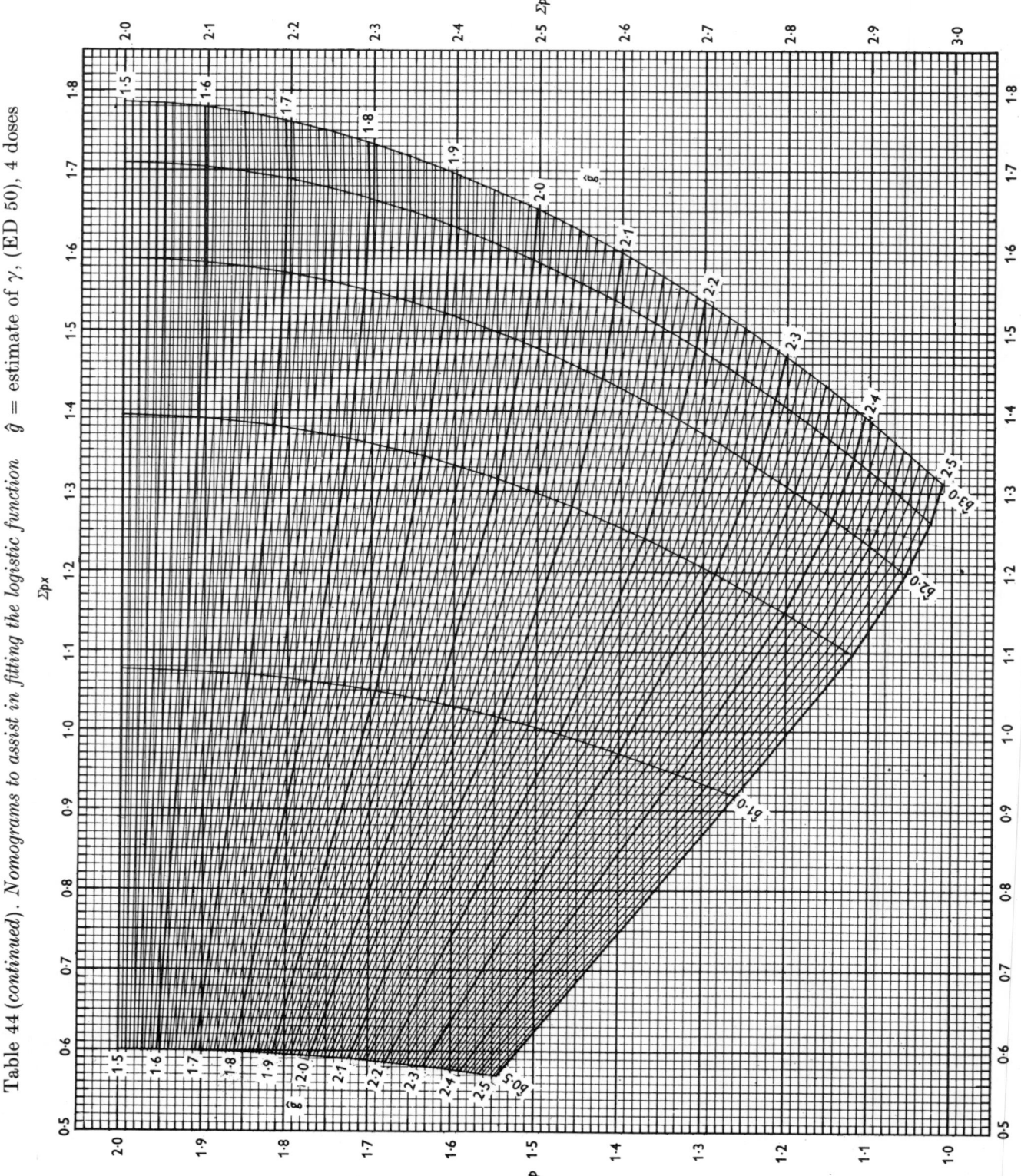

Table 44 (*continued*). $\hat{b} = \dfrac{\text{estimate of } \beta, \text{ 4 doses}}{\Sigma px}$

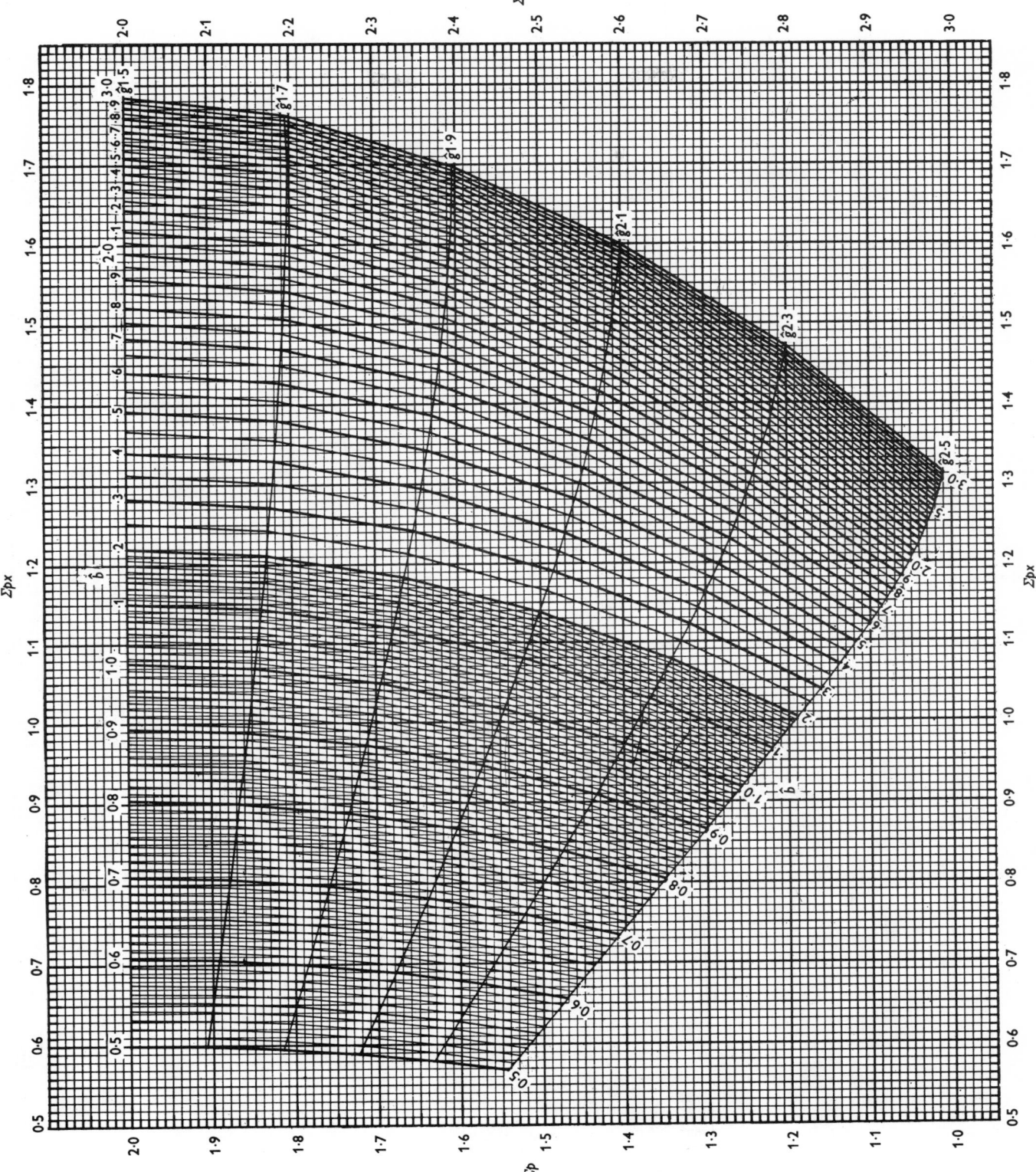

319

Table 44 (*continued*). *Nomograms to assist in fitting the logistic function* $\hat{g}$ = *estimate of* γ, (ED 50), 5 *doses*

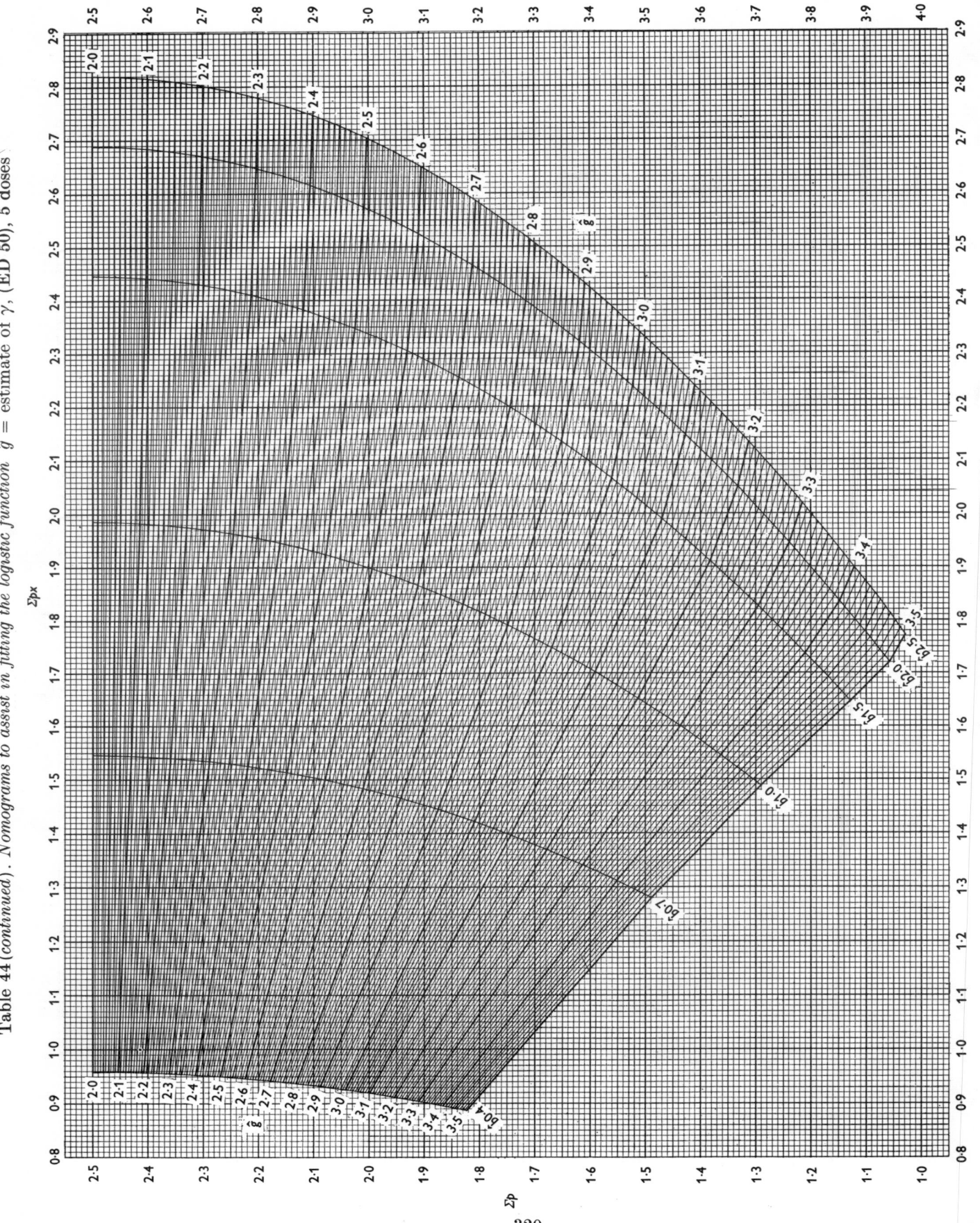

Table 44 (*continued*). $\hat{b}$ = estimate of β, $\hat{g}$ doses

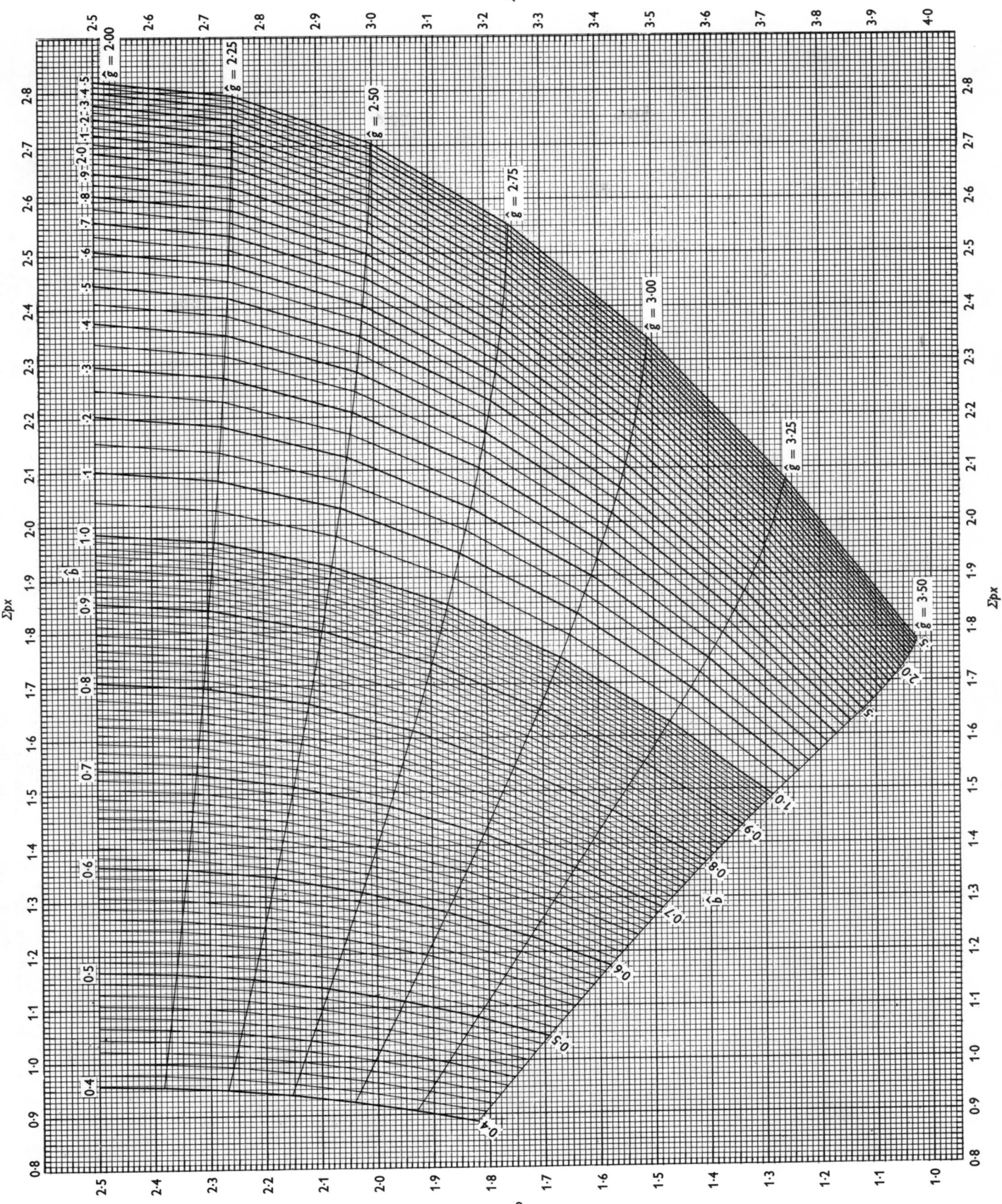

Table 44 (continued). *Nomograms to assist in fitting the logistic funtion* $\hat{g}$ = estimate of γ, (ED 50), 6 doses

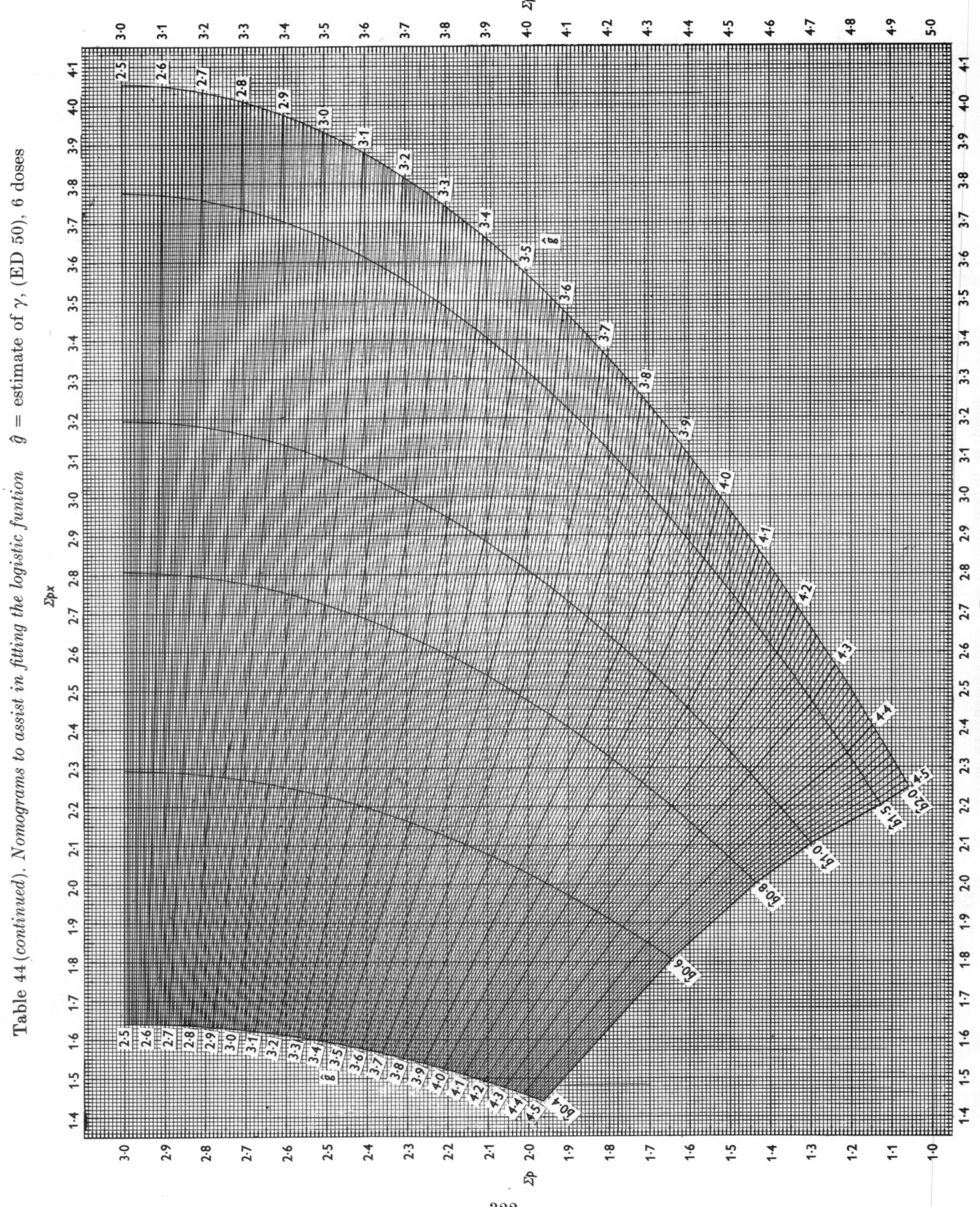

Table 44 (*continued*). b = estimate of β, 6 doses

Table 45. Logistic function fitted by maximum likelihood: standard errors of estimators derived using charts of Table 44

Three doses. Entries are standard errors × $\sqrt{n}$

β	1·0 s(ĝ)	1·0 s(b̂)	1·1 s(ĝ)	1·1 s(b̂)	1·2 s(ĝ)	1·2 s(b̂)	1·3 s(ĝ)	1·3 s(b̂)	1·4 s(ĝ)	1·4 s(b̂)	1·45 s(ĝ)	1·45 s(b̂)	1·5 s(ĝ)	1·5 s(b̂)	1·55 s(ĝ)	1·55 s(b̂)	1·6 s(ĝ)	1·6 s(b̂)	1·65 s(ĝ)	1·65 s(b̂)	1·7 s(ĝ)	1·7 s(b̂)	1·75 s(ĝ)	1·75 s(b̂)	1·8 s(ĝ)	1·8 s(b̂)
0·50	2·4	1·5	2·4	1·5	2·4	1·5	2·5	1·5	2·6	1·5	2·7	1·5	2·7	1·5	2·8	1·5	2·9	1·5	3·0	1·5	3·1	1·5	3·2	1·5	3·2	1·5
·52	2·3	1·5	2·3	1·5	2·3	1·5	2·4	1·5	2·5	1·5	2·6	1·5	2·6	1·5	2·7	1·5	2·8	1·5	2·9	1·5	3·0	1·5	3·0	1·5	3·1	1·5
·54	2·2	1·5	2·2	1·5	2·2	1·5	2·3	1·5	2·4	1·5	2·5	1·5	2·5	1·5	2·6	1·5	2·7	1·5	2·8	1·5	2·9	1·5	2·9	1·5	3·0	1·5
·56	2·1	1·5	2·1	1·5	2·2	1·5	2·2	1·5	2·3	1·5	2·4	1·5	2·5	1·5	2·5	1·5	2·6	1·5	2·7	1·5	2·8	1·5	2·8	1·5	2·9	1·5
·58	2·0	1·5	2·0	1·5	2·1	1·5	2·2	1·5	2·3	1·5	2·3	1·5	2·4	1·5	2·4	1·5	2·5	1·5	2·6	1·5	2·7	1·5	2·7	1·5	2·8	1·5
0·60	2·0	1·5	2·0	1·5	2·0	1·5	2·1	1·5	2·2	1·5	2·2	1·5	2·3	1·5	2·3	1·5	2·4	1·5	2·5	1·5	2·6	1·5	2·6	1·5	2·7	1·5
·62	1·9	1·5	1·9	1·5	2·0	1·5	2·0	1·5	2·1	1·5	2·1	1·5	2·2	1·5	2·2	1·5	2·3	1·5	2·4	1·5	2·5	1·5	2·5	1·5	2·6	1·5
·64	1·9	1·5	1·9	1·5	1·9	1·5	2·0	1·5	2·0	1·5	2·1	1·5	2·1	1·5	2·2	1·5	2·3	1·5	2·3	1·5	2·4	1·5	2·4	1·5	2·5	1·5
·66	1·8	1·5	1·8	1·5	1·9	1·5	1·9	1·5	2·0	1·5	2·0	1·5	2·1	1·5	2·1	1·5	2·2	1·5	2·3	1·5	2·3	1·5	2·4	1·5	2·5	1·5
·68	1·8	1·5	1·8	1·5	1·8	1·5	1·9	1·5	1·9	1·5	2·0	1·5	2·0	1·5	2·1	1·5	2·1	1·5	2·2	1·5	2·3	1·5	2·3	1·5	2·4	1·5
0·70	1·7	1·5	1·7	1·5	1·8	1·5	1·8	1·5	1·9	1·5	1·9	1·5	2·0	1·5	2·0	1·5	2·1	1·5	2·1	1·5	2·2	1·5	2·3	1·6	2·3	1·6
·72	1·7	1·5	1·7	1·5	1·7	1·5	1·8	1·5	1·8	1·5	1·9	1·5	1·9	1·5	2·0	1·5	2·0	1·5	2·1	1·5	2·1	1·6	2·2	1·6	2·3	1·6
·74	1·6	1·5	1·6	1·5	1·7	1·5	1·7	1·5	1·7	1·5	1·8	1·5	1·9	1·5	1·9	1·5	2·0	1·6	2·0	1·6	2·0	1·6	2·1	1·6	2·2	1·6
·76	1·6	1·5	1·6	1·5	1·6	1·5	1·7	1·5	1·7	1·5	1·8	1·5	1·8	1·5	1·9	1·5	1·9	1·6	2·0	1·6	2·0	1·6	2·1	1·6	2·2	1·6
·78	1·6	1·5	1·6	1·5	1·6	1·5	1·6	1·5	1·7	1·5	1·7	1·5	1·8	1·6	1·8	1·6	1·9	1·6	1·9	1·6	2·0	1·6	2·0	1·6	2·1	1·6
0·80	1·5	1·5	1·5	1·5	1·6	1·5	1·6	1·5	1·7	1·5	1·7	1·6	1·7	1·6	1·8	1·6	1·8	1·6	1·9	1·6	1·9	1·6	2·0	1·6	2·0	1·6
·85	1·4	1·6	1·5	1·6	1·5	1·6	1·5	1·6	1·6	1·6	1·6	1·6	1·6	1·6	1·7	1·6	1·7	1·6	1·8	1·6	1·8	1·6	1·9	1·6	1·9	1·6
·90	1·4	1·6	1·4	1·6	1·4	1·6	1·4	1·6	1·5	1·6	1·5	1·6	1·5	1·6	1·6	1·6	1·6	1·6	1·7	1·6	1·7	1·6	1·8	1·7	1·8	1·7
·95	1·3	1·6	1·3	1·6	1·3	1·6	1·4	1·6	1·4	1·6	1·4	1·6	1·4	1·6	1·5	1·6	1·5	1·7	1·6	1·7	1·6	1·7	1·7	1·7	1·7	1·7
1·00	1·2	1·6	1·2	1·6	1·3	1·6	1·3	1·6	1·4	1·6	1·4	1·6	1·4	1·7	1·4	1·7	1·4	1·7	1·5	1·7	1·5	1·7	1·6	1·7	1·6	1·7
1·05	1·2	1·6	1·2	1·6	1·2	1·6	1·3	1·7	1·3	1·7	1·3	1·7	1·3	1·7	1·4	1·7	1·4	1·7	1·4	1·7	1·4	1·7	1·5	1·7	1·5	1·7
1·10	1·2	1·6	1·2	1·6	1·2	1·6	1·2	1·7	1·2	1·7	1·3	1·7	1·2	1·7	1·3	1·7	1·3	1·8	1·4	1·8	1·4	1·7	1·4	1·8	1·5	1·8
1·15	1·1	1·7	1·1	1·7	1·1	1·7	1·2	1·7	1·2	1·7	1·2	1·7	1·2	1·7	1·3	1·8	1·3	1·8	1·3	1·8	1·3	1·8	1·4	1·8	1·4	1·8
1·20	1·1	1·7	1·1	1·7	1·1	1·7	1·1	1·7	1·1	1·7	1·2	1·7	1·1	1·8	1·2	1·8	1·2	1·8	1·3	1·8	1·3	1·8	1·3	1·8	1·4	1·8
1·25	1·0	1·7	1·0	1·7	1·1	1·7	1·1	1·7	1·1	1·7	1·1	1·8	1·1	1·8	1·2	1·8	1·2	1·8	1·2	1·8	1·2	1·8	1·3	1·9	1·3	1·9
1·30	1·0	1·7	1·0	1·7	1·0	1·7	1·0	1·7	1·1	1·8	1·1	1·8	1·1	1·8	1·1	1·8	1·2	1·8	1·2	1·8	1·2	1·9	1·2	1·9	1·3	1·9
1·32	0·99	1·7	0·99	1·7	1·0	1·7	1·0	1·8	1·1	1·8	1·1	1·8	1·1	1·8	1·1	1·8	1·1	1·9	1·2	1·9	1·2	1·9	1·2	1·9	1·2	1·9
1·34	·98	1·7	·98	1·7	0·99	1·8	1·0	1·8	1·0	1·8	1·1	1·8	1·1	1·8	1·1	1·8	1·1	1·9	1·1	1·9	1·2	1·9	1·2	1·9	1·2	1·9
1·36	·97	1·8	·97	1·8	·98	1·8	0·99	1·8	1·0	1·8	1·0	1·8	1·0	1·8	1·1	1·9	1·1	1·9	1·1	1·9	1·1	1·9	1·2	1·9	1·2	2·0
1·38	·96	1·8	·97	1·8	·97	1·8	·99	1·8	1·0	1·8	1·0	1·8	1·0	1·8	1·1	1·9	1·1	1·9	1·1	1·9	1·1	1·9	1·2	1·9	1·2	2·0
1·40	0·95	1·8	0·95	1·8	0·96	1·8	0·98	1·8	1·0	1·8	1·0	1·8	1·0	1·9	1·1	1·9	1·1	2·0	1·1	1·9	1·1	1·9	1·2	2·0	1·2	2·0
1·42	·94	1·8	·94	1·8	·95	1·8	·97	1·8	0·99	1·9	1·0	1·9	1·0	1·9	1·0	1·9	1·0	2·0	1·1	1·9	1·1	2·0	1·1	2·0	1·1	2·0
1·44	·93	1·8	·93	1·8	·94	1·8	·96	1·8	·98	1·9	·99	1·9	1·0	1·9	1·0	1·9	1·0	2·0	1·1	2·0	1·1	2·0	1·1	2·0	1·1	2·0
1·46	·92	1·8	·92	1·8	·93	1·8	·95	1·9	·97	1·9	·98	1·9	0·99	1·9	1·0	2·0	1·0	2·0	1·0	2·0	1·1	2·0	1·1	2·0	1·1	2·0
1·48	·91	1·8	·91	1·8	·92	1·8	·94	1·9	·96	2·0	·97	2·0	1·0	1·9	1·0	2·0	1·0	2·0	1·0	2·0	1·0	2·0	1·1	2·0	1·1	2·1
1·50	0·90	1·8	0·90	1·8	0·91	1·8	0·93	1·9	0·95	1·9	0·96	1·9	0·98	1·9	0·99	1·9	1·0	2·0	1·0	2·0	1·1	2·0	1·1	2·0	1·1	2·1
1·52	·89	1·8	·89	1·8	·90	1·9	·92	1·9	·94	1·9	·95	1·9	·97	1·9	·98	2·0	1·0	2·0	1·0	2·0	1·0	2·0	1·1	2·0	1·1	2·1
1·54	·88	1·9	·89	1·9	·89	1·9	·91	1·9	·93	1·9	·94	1·9	·96	2·0	·97	2·0	0·99	2·0	1·0	2·0	1·0	2·0	1·0	2·0	1·1	2·1
1·56	·87	1·9	·88	1·9	·89	1·9	·90	1·9	·92	2·0	·93	2·0	·95	2·0	·96	2·0	·98	2·0	1·0	2·0	1·0	2·0	1·0	2·1	1·1	2·1
1·58	·87	1·9	·87	1·9	·88	1·9	·89	1·9	·91	2·0	·92	2·0	·93	2·0	·95	2·0	·97	2·0	1·0	2·0	1·0	2·1	1·0	2·1	1·0	2·1
1·60	0·86	1·9	0·86	1·9	0·87	1·9	0·88	1·9	0·90	2·0	0·91	2·0	0·92	2·0	0·94	2·0	0·96	2·1	0·98	2·1	1·0	2·1	1·0	2·1	1·1	2·2
1·62	·85	1·9	·85	1·9	·86	1·9	·87	2·0	·89	2·0	·90	2·1	·92	2·1	·93	2·1	·95	2·1	·97	2·1	0·99	2·1	1·0	2·1	1·0	2·2
1·64	·84	1·9	·85	1·9	·85	1·9	·86	2·0	·88	2·0	·90	2·1	·91	2·1	·92	2·1	·94	2·1	·96	2·1	·98	2·1	1·0	2·2	1·0	2·2
1·66	·84	1·9	·84	1·9	·85	2·0	·86	2·0	·87	2·0	·89	2·1	·90	2·1	·91	2·1	·93	2·1	·95	2·1	·97	2·1	0·99	2·2	1·0	2·2
1·68	·83	1·9	·83	1·9	·84	2·0	·85	2·0	·87	2·0	·88	2·1	·89	2·1	·90	2·1	·92	2·1	·94	2·1	·96	2·2	·98	2·2	1·0	2·2

Table 45 (continued)

Three doses (continued)

γ

	1·0		1·1		1·2		1·3		1·4		1·45		1·5		1·55		1·6		1·65		1·7		1·75		1·8	
	$s(\phi)$	$s(\hat{b})$	$s(\phi)$	$s(\hat{b})$	$s(\phi)$	$s(\hat{b})$	$s(\phi)$	$s(\hat{b})$	$s(\phi)$	$s(\hat{b})$	$s(\phi)$	$s(\hat{b})$	$s(\phi)$	$s(\hat{b})$	$s(\phi)$	$s(\hat{b})$	$s(\phi)$	$s(\hat{b})$	$s(\phi)$	$s(\hat{b})$	$s(\phi)$	$s(\hat{b})$	$s(\phi)$	$s(\hat{b})$	$s(\phi)$	$s(\hat{b})$
1·70	0·82	2·0	0·82	2·0	0·83	2·0	0·84	2·0	0·86	2·0	0·87	2·0	0·88	2·1	0·89	2·1	0·91	2·1	0·93	2·1	0·95	2·2	0·97	2·2	0·99	2·3
1·72	·82	2·0	·82	2·0	·82	2·0	·83	2·0	·85	2·0	·86	2·1	·87	2·1	·88	2·1	·90	2·1	·92	2·2	·94	2·2	·96	2·2	·98	2·3
1·74	·81	2·0	·81	2·0	·82	2·0	·83	2·0	·84	2·0	·85	2·1	·86	2·1	·88	2·1	·89	2·1	·91	2·2	·93	2·2	·95	2·2	·97	2·3
1·76	·80	2·0	·81	2·0	·81	2·0	·82	2·0	·83	2·1	·84	2·1	·86	2·1	·87	2·1	·88	2·2	·90	2·2	·92	2·2	·94	2·3	·96	2·3
1·78	·80	2·0	·80	2·0	·80	2·0	·82	2·0	·83	2·1	·84	2·1	·85	2·1	·86	2·1	·87	2·2	·89	2·2	·91	2·2	·93	2·3	·95	2·3
1·80	0·79	2·0	0·79	2·0	0·80	2·0	0·81	2·1	0·82	2·1	0·83	2·1	0·84	2·1	0·85	2·2	0·87	2·2	0·88	2·2	0·90	2·3	0·92	2·3	0·94	2·4
1·82	·78	2·0	·79	2·0	·79	2·1	·80	2·1	·81	2·1	·82	2·1	·83	2·2	·85	2·2	·86	2·2	·87	2·2	·89	2·3	·91	2·4	·93	2·4
1·84	·78	2·1	·78	2·1	·79	2·1	·80	2·1	·81	2·1	·82	2·1	·83	2·2	·84	2·2	·85	2·2	·87	2·3	·88	2·3	·91	2·3	·93	2·4
1·86	·77	2·1	·78	2·1	·78	2·1	·79	2·1	·80	2·1	·81	2·2	·82	2·2	·83	2·2	·84	2·2	·86	2·3	·88	2·3	·90	2·4	·92	2·4
1·88	·77	2·1	·77	2·1	·77	2·1	·79	2·1	·80	2·2	·80	2·2	·81	2·2	·82	2·2	·84	2·3	·85	2·3	·87	2·3	·89	2·4	·91	2·4
1·90	0·76	2·1	0·76	2·1	0·77	2·1	0·78	2·1	0·79	2·1	0·80	2·2	0·81	2·2	0·82	2·2	0·83	2·3	0·84	2·3	0·86	2·4	0·88	2·4	0·90	2·5
1·92	·76	2·1	·76	2·1	·76	2·1	·77	2·2	·78	2·2	·79	2·2	·80	2·2	·81	2·3	·82	2·3	·84	2·3	·85	2·4	·87	2·4	·89	2·5
1·94	·75	2·1	·75	2·2	·76	2·1	·77	2·2	·78	2·2	·79	2·2	·79	2·3	·80	2·3	·81	2·3	·83	2·3	·84	2·4	·86	2·5	·88	2·5
1·96	·75	2·1	·75	2·2	·75	2·2	·76	2·2	·77	2·2	·78	2·2	·79	2·3	·80	2·3	·81	2·3	·82	2·4	·84	2·4	·86	2·5	·87	2·5
1·98	·74	2·2	·74	2·2	·75	2·2	·76	2·2	·77	2·2	·77	2·3	·78	2·3	·79	2·3	·80	2·3	·81	2·4	·83	2·4	·85	2·5	·87	2·5
2·00	0·74	2·2	0·74	2·2	0·74	2·2	0·75	2·2	0·76	2·3	0·77	2·3	0·78	2·3	0·79	2·3	0·80	2·4	0·81	2·4	0·82	2·4	0·84	2·5	0·86	2·6
2·02	·73	2·2	·73	2·2	·74	2·2	·75	2·2	·76	2·3	·76	2·3	·77	2·3	·78	2·3	·79	2·4	·80	2·4	·81	2·5	·83	2·5	·85	2·6
2·04	·73	2·2	·73	2·2	·73	2·2	·74	2·3	·75	2·3	·76	2·3	·76	2·3	·77	2·4	·78	2·4	·79	2·4	·81	2·5	·82	2·6	·84	2·6
2·06	·72	2·2	·72	2·3	·73	2·3	·74	2·3	·75	2·3	·75	2·3	·76	2·4	·77	2·4	·78	2·4	·79	2·5	·80	2·6	·82	2·6	·84	2·6
2·08	·72	2·3	·72	2·3	·72	2·3	·73	2·3	·74	2·4	·75	2·3	·75	2·4	·76	2·4	·77	2·4	·78	2·5	·79	2·6	·81	2·6	·83	2·7
2·10	0·71	2·3	0·72	2·3	0·72	2·3	0·73	2·3	0·74	2·3	0·74	2·3	0·75	2·4	0·76	2·4	0·77	2·5	0·78	2·5	0·79	2·5	0·80	2·6	0·82	2·7
2·12	·71	2·3	·71	2·3	·72	2·3	·72	2·3	·73	2·3	·74	2·4	·74	2·4	·75	2·4	·76	2·6	·77	2·6	·78	2·6	·80	2·6	·81	2·7
2·14	·70	2·3	·71	2·3	·71	2·3	·72	2·4	·73	2·4	·73	2·4	·74	2·4	·75	2·4	·75	2·6	·76	2·6	·78	2·6	·79	2·7	·81	2·7
2·16	·70	2·3	·70	2·3	·71	2·4	·71	2·4	·72	2·4	·73	2·4	·73	2·4	·74	2·5	·75	2·6	·76	2·6	·77	2·7	·78	2·7	·80	2·8
2·18	·70	2·3	·70	2·4	·70	2·4	·71	2·4	·72	2·4	·72	2·4	·73	2·5	·74	2·5	·74	2·6	·75	2·6	·76	2·7	·78	2·7	·79	2·8
2·20	0·69	2·4	0·69	2·4	0·70	2·4	0·71	2·4	0·71	2·5	0·72	2·4	0·72	2·5	0·73	2·5	0·74	2·6	0·75	2·6	0·76	2·7	0·77	2·8	0·79	2·8
2·22	·69	2·4	·69	2·4	·69	2·4	·70	2·4	·71	2·5	·71	2·5	·72	2·5	·72	2·6	·73	2·6	·74	2·6	·75	2·8	·76	2·9	·78	2·8
2·24	·69	2·4	·69	2·4	·69	2·4	·70	2·5	·70	2·5	·71	2·5	·72	2·5	·72	2·6	·73	2·6	·74	2·7	·75	2·8	·76	2·9	·78	2·8
2·26	·68	2·4	·68	2·5	·69	2·5	·69	2·5	·70	2·5	·71	2·5	·71	2·5	·72	2·6	·73	2·6	·74	2·7	·74	2·9	·76	3·0	·77	2·8
2·28	·68	2·4	·68	2·5	·68	2·5	·69	2·5	·70	2·5	·70	2·5	·71	2·6	·71	2·6	·72	2·6	·73	2·7	·74	2·9	·75	3·0	·76	2·9
2·30	0·67	2·5	0·68	2·5	0·68	2·5	0·69	2·5	0·69	2·5	0·70	2·5	0·70	2·6	0·71	2·6	0·72	2·6	0·72	2·7	0·73	2·8	0·74	2·8	0·76	2·9
2·35	·67	2·5	·67	2·6	·67	2·5	·68	2·6	·69	2·6	·69	2·6	·69	2·6	·70	2·7	·71	2·7	·71	2·8	·72	2·8	·73	2·9	·75	3·0
2·40	·66	2·6	·66	2·6	·66	2·6	·67	2·6	·68	2·6	·68	2·6	·68	2·7	·69	2·7	·69	2·7	·70	2·8	·71	2·9	·72	3·0	·73	3·1
2·45	·65	2·7	·65	2·7	·65	2·6	·66	2·7	·67	2·7	·67	2·7	·67	2·7	·68	2·8	·68	2·8	·69	2·9	·70	2·9	·71	3·0	·72	3·1
2·50	·64	2·7	·64	2·8	·65	2·7	·65	2·7	·66	2·7	·66	2·7	·66	2·8	·67	2·8	·67	2·9	·68	2·9	·69	3·0	·69	3·1	·70	3·2
2·55	·63	2·8	·63	2·8	·64	2·7	·64	2·8	·66	2·8	·65	2·8	·66	2·8	·66	2·9	·67	2·9	·67	3·0	·68	3·1	·68	3·2	·69	3·3
2·60	·63	2·8	·63	2·9	·63	2·8	·64	2·8	·64	2·8	·65	2·8	·65	2·9	·65	2·9	·66	3·0	·66	3·0	·67	3·1	·67	3·3	·68	3·3
2·65	·62	2·9	·62	3·0	·62	2·9	·63	2·9	·64	2·9	·64	2·9	·64	2·9	·65	3·0	·65	3·0	·65	3·1	·66	3·2	·66	3·3	·67	3·4
2·70	·61	2·9	·61	3·0	·62	2·9	·62	2·9	·63	2·9	·63	2·9	·64	3·0	·64	3·0	·64	3·1	·65	3·1	·65	3·2	·65	3·4	·66	3·4
2·75	·61	3·0	·60	3·1	·61	3·0	·62	3·0	·62	3·0	·62	3·0	·63	3·0	·63	3·0	·63	3·1	·64	3·2	·65	3·3	·65	3·4	·65	3·5
2·80	·60	3·0	·60	3·2	·60	3·1	·61	3·0	·62	3·0	·61	3·0	·62	3·1	·62	3·1	·63	3·1	·63	3·2	·64	3·3	·64	3·5	·64	3·5
2·85	·60	3·1	·60	3·3	·60	3·1	·60	3·1	·61	3·1	·61	3·1	·61	3·1	·61	3·1	·62	3·2	·62	3·3	·63	3·4	·63	3·5	·63	3·6
2·90	·59	3·2	·59	3·3	·59	3·2	·60	3·2	·61	3·1	·61	3·1	·61	3·2	·61	3·2	·61	3·2	·61	3·3	·62	3·5	·62	3·6	·62	3·6
2·95	·58	3·3	·58	3·4	·59	3·3	·60	3·2	·60	3·2	·60	3·2	·61	3·2	·61	3·2	·61	3·2	·61	3·3	·61	3·5	·61	3·6	·61	3·7
3·0	0·57	3·3	0·57	3·3	0·58	3·2	0·59	3·2	0·60	3·2	0·60	3·2	0·60	3·2	0·60	3·2	0·60	3·3	0·60	3·4	0·60	3·5	0·60	3·6	0·61	3·8
3·1	·56	3·5	·56	3·5	·57	3·4	·58	3·3	·59	3·3	·59	3·3	·59	3·3	·59	3·3	·59	3·4	·59	3·5	·59	3·6	·59	3·7	·59	3·9
3·2	·55	3·6	·55	3·6	·56	3·5	·57	3·4	·58	3·4	·58	3·4	·58	3·4	·58	3·4	·58	3·5	·58	3·6	·58	3·7	·58	3·9	·58	4·0
3·3	·54	3·8	·54	3·8	·55	3·7	·56	3·6	·57	3·5	·57	3·5	·58	3·6	·58	3·5	·57	3·6	·57	3·7	·57	3·8	·57	4·0	·56	4·2
3·4	·53	4·0	·53	3·9	·54	3·8	·55	3·7	·56	3·6	·57	3·6	·57	3·7	·57	3·6	·57	3·7	·56	3·8	·56	3·9	·56	4·1	·55	4·3
3·5	·52	4·2	·52	4·1	·53	4·0	·54	3·8	·56	3·7	·56	3·7	·56	3·7	·56	3·7	·56	3·8	·56	3·9	·55	4·1	·55	4·3	·54	4·5

Table 45 (continued). *Logistic function fitted by maximum likelihood: standard errors of estimates*

Four doses. Entries are standard errors × √n

γ

β	1·5 s(β̂)	1·5 s(b̂)	1·6 s(β̂)	1·6 s(b̂)	1·7 s(β̂)	1·7 s(b̂)	1·8 s(β̂)	1·8 s(b̂)	1·9 s(β̂)	1·9 s(b̂)	2·0 s(β̂)	2·0 s(b̂)	2·1 s(β̂)	2·1 s(b̂)	2·2 s(β̂)	2·2 s(b̂)	2·25 s(β̂)	2·25 s(b̂)	2·3 s(β̂)	2·3 s(b̂)	2·35 s(β̂)	2·35 s(b̂)	2·4 s(β̂)	2·4 s(b̂)	2·45 s(β̂)	2·45 s(b̂)	2·5 s(β̂)	2·5 s(b̂)
0·50	2·1	0·95	2·1	0·95	2·1	0·95	2·1	0·95	2·2	0·96	2·2	0·96	2·3	0·96	2·4	0·97	2·4	0·97	2·5	0·97	2·5	0·97	2·6	0·97	2·7	0·98	2·7	0·98
·52	2·0	·96	2·0	·96	2·0	·96	2·1	·96	2·1	·96	2·2	·96	2·2	·97	2·3	·97	2·4	·97	2·4	·98	2·5	·98	2·5	·98	2·6	·98	2·6	·99
·54	1·9	·96	1·9	·96	2·0	·96	2·0	·96	2·0	·96	2·1	·97	2·2	·97	2·2	·98	2·3	·98	2·3	·98	2·4	·99	2·4	·99	2·5	·99	2·5	1·0
·56	1·9	·97	1·9	·97	1·9	·97	1·9	·97	2·0	·97	2·0	·97	2·1	·98	2·2	·98	2·2	·99	2·2	·99	2·3	·99	2·3	·99	2·4	1·0	2·4	1·0
·58	1·8	·97	1·8	·97	1·8	·97	1·9	·98	1·9	·98	2·0	·98	2·0	·99	2·1	·99	2·1	·99	2·2	1·0	2·2	1·0	2·3	1·0	2·3	1·0	2·3	1·0
0·60	1·8	0·98	1·8	0·98	1·8	0·98	1·8	0·98	1·8	0·98	1·9	0·99	1·9	0·99	2·0	0·99	2·1	1·0	2·1	1·0	2·1	1·0	2·2	1·0	2·2	1·0	2·3	1·0
·62	1·7	·98	1·7	·98	1·7	·98	1·8	·99	1·8	·99	1·8	·99	1·9	1·0	2·0	1·0	2·0	1·0	2·0	1·0	2·1	1·0	2·1	1·0	2·2	1·0	2·2	1·0
·64	1·7	·99	1·7	·99	1·7	·99	1·7	·99	1·7	1·0	1·8	1·0	1·8	1·0	1·9	1·0	1·9	1·0	2·0	1·0	2·0	1·0	2·0	1·0	2·1	1·0	2·1	1·0
·66	1·6	1·0	1·6	1·0	1·6	1·0	1·7	1·0	1·7	1·0	1·7	1·0	1·8	1·0	1·8	1·0	1·9	1·0	1·9	1·0	1·9	1·1	2·0	1·0	2·0	1·0	2·1	1·0
·68	1·6	1·0	1·6	1·0	1·6	1·0	1·6	1·0	1·6	1·0	1·7	1·0	1·7	1·0	1·8	1·0	1·8	1·1	1·9	1·1	1·9	1·1	1·9	1·1	2·0	1·1	2·0	1·1
0·70	1·5	1·0	1·5	1·0	1·6	1·0	1·6	1·0	1·6	1·0	1·6	1·1	1·7	1·0	1·8	1·0	1·8	1·0	1·8	1·0	1·8	1·0	1·9	1·1	1·9	1·1	2·0	1·1
·72	1·5	1·0	1·5	1·0	1·5	1·0	1·5	1·1	1·6	1·1	1·6	1·1	1·6	1·1	1·7	1·1	1·7	1·1	1·8	1·1	1·8	1·1	1·8	1·1	1·9	1·1	1·9	1·1
·74	1·5	1·0	1·5	1·0	1·5	1·1	1·5	1·1	1·5	1·1	1·6	1·1	1·6	1·1	1·6	1·1	1·6	1·1	1·7	1·1	1·7	1·1	1·8	1·1	1·8	1·1	1·9	1·1
·76	1·4	1·0	1·4	1·0	1·4	1·1	1·5	1·1	1·5	1·1	1·5	1·1	1·6	1·1	1·6	1·1	1·6	1·1	1·6	1·1	1·7	1·1	1·7	1·1	1·8	1·1	1·8	1·1
·78	1·4	1·0	1·4	1·0	1·4	1·1	1·4	1·1	1·5	1·1	1·5	1·1	1·5	1·1	1·6	1·1	1·6	1·1	1·6	1·1	1·7	1·1	1·7	1·1	1·7	1·1	1·8	1·2
0·80	1·4	1·0	1·4	1·0	1·4	1·1	1·4	1·2	1·4	1·1	1·5	1·1	1·5	1·1	1·5	1·1	1·6	1·2	1·6	1·2	1·6	1·1	1·7	1·1	1·7	1·1	1·7	1·1
·82	1·3	1·1	1·3	1·1	1·4	1·1	1·3	1·3	1·4	1·3	1·4	1·3	1·5	1·3	1·5	1·3	1·5	1·3	1·5	1·2	1·6	1·2	1·6	1·2	1·7	1·2	1·7	1·2
·84	1·3	1·1	1·3	1·1	1·3	1·2	1·3	1·3	1·3	1·3	1·4	1·3	1·4	1·3	1·4	1·3	1·5	1·2	1·5	1·3	1·6	1·3	1·5	1·3	1·6	1·3	1·6	1·3
·86	1·3	1·1	1·3	1·1	1·3	1·2	1·3	1·3	1·3	1·3	1·4	1·3	1·4	1·3	1·4	1·3	1·4	1·2	1·5	1·4	1·5	1·4	1·5	1·4	1·6	1·4	1·6	1·4
·88	1·3	1·1	1·3	1·1	1·3	1·2	1·3	1·3	1·3	1·3	1·3	1·3	1·4	1·3	1·4	1·4	1·4	1·4	1·4	1·4	1·5	1·4	1·5	1·4	1·5	1·4	1·6	1·4
0·90	1·2	1·1	1·2	1·1	1·3	1·2	1·3	1·3	1·3	1·3	1·3	1·3	1·3	1·3	1·4	1·4	1·4	1·4	1·4	1·5	1·4	1·5	1·5	1·5	1·5	1·5	1·5	1·4
1·00	1·1	1·1	1·1	1·2	1·2	1·2	1·2	1·3	1·2	1·3	1·2	1·3	1·2	1·4	1·3	1·5	1·3	1·5	1·3	1·5	1·3	1·5	1·3	1·5	1·4	1·5	1·4	1·4
1·10	1·1	1·2	1·1	1·2	1·1	1·2	1·1	1·3	1·1	1·4	1·1	1·4	1·1	1·4	1·2	1·5	1·2	1·5	1·2	1·5	1·2	1·5	1·2	1·5	1·3	1·5	1·3	1·4
1·20	1·0	1·2	1·0	1·2	1·0	1·3	1·0	1·3	1·0	1·3	1·0	1·3	1·1	1·3	1·1	1·4	1·1	1·4	1·1	1·5	1·1	1·3	1·1	1·3	1·2	1·4	1·2	1·4
1·22	0·98	1·2	0·99	1·2	0·99	1·3	1·0	1·3	1·0	1·3	1·0	1·3	1·0	1·3	1·0	1·4	1·1	1·4	1·1	1·5	1·1	1·4	1·1	1·4	1·1	1·4	1·2	1·4
1·24	·97	1·3	·97	1·3	·98	1·3	0·99	1·3	0·99	1·3	1·0	1·4	1·0	1·4	1·0	1·4	1·0	1·4	1·1	1·4	1·1	1·4	1·1	1·4	1·1	1·4	1·1	1·4
1·26	·96	1·3	·96	1·3	·97	1·3	·98	1·3	·99	1·3	0·99	1·4	1·0	1·4	1·0	1·4	1·0	1·4	1·0	1·4	1·1	1·4	1·1	1·4	1·1	1·4	1·1	1·4
1·28	·95	1·3	·95	1·3	·96	1·3	·97	1·3	·98	1·3	·99	1·5	1·0	1·4	1·0	1·4	1·0	1·4	1·0	1·4	1·1	1·4	1·1	1·4	1·1	1·4	1·1	1·4
1·30	0·94	1·3	0·94	1·3	0·95	1·3	0·95	1·3	0·96	1·3	0·98	1·3	0·99	1·4	1·0	1·4	1·0	1·4	1·0	1·5	1·0	1·5	1·1	1·4	1·1	1·4	1·1	1·5
1·32	·93	1·3	·93	1·3	·94	1·3	·94	1·3	·95	1·3	·96	1·3	·98	1·4	0·99	1·4	1·0	1·4	1·0	1·5	1·0	1·5	1·0	1·4	1·1	1·5	1·1	1·5
1·34	·92	1·3	·92	1·3	·93	1·3	·93	1·3	·94	1·3	·95	1·4	·97	1·4	·98	1·5	0·99	1·4	1·0	1·5	1·0	1·5	1·0	1·5	1·0	1·5	1·0	1·5
1·36	·91	1·3	·91	1·3	·92	1·3	·92	1·3	·93	1·3	·94	1·4	·96	1·5	·97	1·5	·99	1·5	0·99	1·5	1·0	1·5	1·0	1·5	1·0	1·5	1·0	1·5
1·38	·90	1·3	·90	1·3	·91	1·3	·91	1·3	·92	1·4	·93	1·5	·95	1·5	·96	1·5	·98	1·5	·99	1·5	1·0	1·5	1·0	1·5	1·0	1·5	1·0	1·5
1·40	0·89	1·4	0·90	1·4	0·90	1·4	0·90	1·4	0·91	1·4	0·92	1·4	0·93	1·4	0·95	1·4	0·96	1·4	0·98	1·5	0·99	1·5	1·0	1·5	1·0	1·5	1·0	1·5
1·42	·89	1·4	·89	1·4	·90	1·4	·90	1·4	·90	1·4	·91	1·4	·93	1·4	·94	1·5	·95	1·5	·96	1·6	·98	1·6	0·99	1·5	0·99	1·5	1·0	1·6
1·44	·88	1·4	·88	1·4	·88	1·4	·89	1·4	·89	1·4	·90	1·4	·92	1·5	·93	1·5	·94	1·5	·95	1·6	·97	1·6	·98	1·5	·98	1·6	1·0	1·6
1·46	·87	1·4	·87	1·4	·87	1·4	·88	1·4	·89	1·5	·90	1·5	·91	1·5	·92	1·6	·93	1·6	·94	1·6	·96	1·6	·97	1·6	·98	1·6	0·99	1·6
1·48	·86	1·4	·86	1·4	·87	1·4	·87	1·4	·88	1·5	·89	1·5	·90	1·5	·91	1·6	·92	1·6	·93	1·6	·94	1·6	·96	1·6	·96	1·6	·98	1·6
1·50	0·86	1·4	0·86	1·4	0·86	1·4	0·86	1·4	0·87	1·4	0·88	1·5	0·89	1·5	0·90	1·5	0·91	1·5	0·92	1·5	0·93	1·6	0·95	1·6	0·96	1·6	0·98	1·6
1·52	·85	1·4	·85	1·4	·85	1·4	·85	1·4	·86	1·5	·87	1·5	·88	1·5	·89	1·5	·90	1·6	·91	1·6	·92	1·6	·94	1·6	·95	1·6	·97	1·6
1·54	·84	1·4	·84	1·4	·84	1·5	·85	1·5	·85	1·5	·86	1·5	·87	1·5	·88	1·6	·89	1·6	·90	1·6	·91	1·6	·93	1·6	·94	1·6	·95	1·7
1·56	·83	1·5	·84	1·5	·84	1·5	·84	1·5	·85	1·5	·86	1·5	·86	1·5	·87	1·6	·88	1·6	·90	1·6	·91	1·6	·92	1·7	·93	1·7	·94	1·7
1·58	·83	1·5	·83	1·5	·83	1·5	·83	1·5	·84	1·5	·85	1·5	·86	1·6	·87	1·6	·88	1·6	·89	1·6	·90	1·6	·91	1·6	·92	1·7	·93	1·7

Table 45 (*continued*)

Four doses (*continued*)

γ

β	1·5 s(θ)	1·5 s(b)	1·6 s(θ)	1·6 s(b)	1·7 s(θ)	1·7 s(b)	1·8 s(θ)	1·8 s(b)	1·9 s(θ)	1·9 s(b)	2·0 s(θ)	2·0 s(b)	2·1 s(θ)	2·1 s(b)	2·2 s(θ)	2·2 s(b)	2·25 s(θ)	2·25 s(b)	2·3 s(θ)	2·3 s(b)	2·35 s(θ)	2·35 s(b)	2·4 s(θ)	2·4 s(b)	2·45 s(θ)	2·45 s(b)	2·5 s(θ)	2·5 s(b)
1·60	0·82	1·5	0·82	1·5	0·82	1·5	0·83	1·5	0·83	1·5	0·84	1·5	0·85	1·6	0·86	1·6	0·87	1·6	0·88	1·6	0·89	1·6	0·90	1·7	0·91	1·7	0·92	1·7
1·62	·81	1·5	·81	1·5	·82	1·5	·82	1·5	·83	1·5	·83	1·6	·84	1·6	·85	1·6	·86	1·6	·87	1·6	·88	1·7	·89	1·7	·90	1·7	·91	1·7
1·64	·81	1·5	·81	1·5	·81	1·5	·81	1·5	·82	1·6	·83	1·6	·83	1·6	·84	1·6	·85	1·6	·86	1·6	·87	1·7	·88	1·7	·89	1·7	·91	1·8
1·66	·80	1·5	·80	1·5	·81	1·5	·81	1·6	·81	1·6	·82	1·6	·83	1·7	·84	1·6	·85	1·7	·85	1·7	·86	1·7	·87	1·7	·88	1·7	·90	1·8
1·68	·80	1·6	·80	1·6	·80	1·6	·80	1·6	·81	1·6	·81	1·6	·82	1·6	·83	1·7	·84	1·7	·85	1·7	·86	1·7	·87	1·7	·88	1·8	·89	1·8
1·70	0·79	1·6	0·79	1·6	0·80	1·6	0·80	1·6	0·80	1·6	0·81	1·6	0·82	1·6	0·83	1·7	0·83	1·7	0·84	1·7	0·85	1·7	0·86	1·8	0·87	1·8	0·88	1·8
1·72	·78	1·6	·79	1·6	·79	1·6	·79	1·6	·79	1·6	·80	1·6	·81	1·7	·82	1·7	·83	1·7	·83	1·7	·84	1·8	·85	1·8	·86	1·8	·87	1·8
1·74	·78	1·6	·78	1·6	·78	1·7	·78	1·6	·79	1·6	·80	1·7	·80	1·7	·81	1·7	·82	1·7	·83	1·8	·83	1·8	·84	1·8	·85	1·8	·86	1·8
1·76	·77	1·6	·78	1·6	·78	1·7	·78	1·6	·78	1·7	·79	1·7	·80	1·7	·81	1·7	·81	1·8	·82	1·8	·83	1·8	·84	1·8	·85	1·8	·86	1·9
1·78	·77	1·6	·77	1·6	·77	1·7	·77	1·7	·78	1·7	·78	1·7	·79	1·7	·80	1·8	·81	1·8	·81	1·8	·82	1·8	·83	1·8	·84	1·9	·85	1·9
1·80	0·76	1·6	0·76	1·7	0·77	1·7	0·77	1·7	0·77	1·7	0·78	1·7	0·78	1·7	0·79	1·8	0·80	1·8	0·81	1·8	0·81	1·8	0·82	1·8	0·83	1·9	0·84	1·9
1·82	·76	1·7	·76	1·7	·76	1·7	·76	1·7	·77	1·7	·77	1·7	·78	1·8	·78	1·8	·79	1·8	·80	1·8	·81	1·9	·81	1·8	·82	1·9	·83	1·9
1·84	·75	1·7	·75	1·7	·76	1·7	·76	1·7	·76	1·7	·77	1·7	·77	1·8	·78	1·8	·79	1·8	·79	1·9	·80	1·9	·81	1·9	·81	1·9	·83	1·9
1·86	·75	1·7	·75	1·7	·76	1·7	·75	1·7	·76	1·7	·76	1·8	·77	1·8	·77	1·8	·78	1·9	·79	1·9	·79	1·9	·80	1·9	·81	1·9	·82	2·0
1·88	·74	1·7	·74	1·7	·75	1·7	·75	1·7	·75	1·8	·76	1·8	·76	1·8	·77	1·8	·78	1·9	·78	1·9	·79	1·9	·79	1·9	·80	2·0	·81	2·0
1·90	0·74	1·7	0·74	1·7	0·74	1·7	0·74	1·8	0·75	1·8	0·75	1·8	0·76	1·8	0·77	1·9	0·77	1·9	0·78	1·9	0·78	1·9	0·79	1·9	0·80	2·0	0·80	2·0
1·92	·74	1·7	·74	1·8	·74	1·8	·74	1·8	·74	1·8	·75	1·8	·75	1·9	·76	1·9	·76	1·9	·77	1·9	·78	2·0	·78	2·0	·79	2·0	·80	2·0
1·94	·73	1·8	·73	1·8	·73	1·8	·73	1·8	·74	1·8	·74	1·9	·75	1·9	·76	1·9	·76	1·9	·76	2·0	·77	2·0	·78	2·0	·78	2·0	·79	2·1
1·96	·73	1·8	·73	1·8	·73	1·8	·73	1·8	·73	1·8	·74	1·9	·74	1·9	·75	1·9	·75	2·0	·76	2·0	·77	2·0	·77	2·0	·77	2·1	·78	2·1
1·98	·72	1·8	·72	1·8	·72	1·8	·72	1·8	·73	1·9	·73	1·9	·74	1·9	·75	1·9	·75	2·0	·75	2·0	·76	2·0	·77	2·0	·77	2·1	·78	2·1
2·00	0·72	1·8	0·72	1·8	0·72	1·9	0·72	1·9	0·72	1·9	0·73	1·9	0·73	2·0	0·74	2·0	0·74	2·0	0·75	2·0	0·75	2·0	0·76	2·0	0·77	2·1	0·78	2·1
2·02	·72	1·8	·72	1·9	·72	1·9	·72	1·9	·72	1·9	·72	2·0	·73	2·0	·73	2·0	·74	2·0	·74	2·1	·75	2·1	·76	2·1	·76	2·1	·77	2·1
2·04	·71	1·9	·71	1·9	·71	1·9	·71	1·9	·72	2·0	·72	2·0	·72	2·0	·73	2·1	·73	2·1	·74	2·1	·74	2·1	·75	2·1	·76	2·2	·76	2·2
2·06	·71	1·9	·71	1·9	·71	2·0	·71	2·0	·71	2·0	·72	2·0	·72	2·1	·73	2·1	·73	2·1	·73	2·1	·74	2·1	·75	2·2	·75	2·2	·76	2·2
2·08	·70	1·9	·70	2·0	·70	2·0	·70	2·0	·71	2·0	·71	2·1	·71	2·1	·72	2·1	·73	2·2	·73	2·2	·73	2·2	·74	2·2	·75	2·2	·75	2·2
2·10	0·70	1·9	0·70	2·0	0·70	2·0	0·70	2·0	0·70	2·0	0·71	2·1	0·71	2·1	0·72	2·2	0·72	2·2	0·73	2·2	0·73	2·2	0·74	2·2	0·74	2·3	0·75	2·3
2·12	·70	1·9	·70	2·1	·70	2·1	·70	2·1	·70	2·1	·70	2·2	·71	2·2	·71	2·2	·72	2·2	·72	2·3	·73	2·3	·73	2·3	·73	2·3	·74	2·4
2·14	·69	2·0	·70	2·1	·69	2·2	·69	2·2	·70	2·2	·70	2·2	·70	2·3	·71	2·3	·71	2·3	·72	2·3	·72	2·3	·73	2·3	·73	2·4	·74	2·5
2·16	·69	2·0	·69	2·2	·69	2·2	·69	2·2	·69	2·2	·70	2·3	·70	2·4	·71	2·3	·71	2·4	·71	2·4	·72	2·4	·72	2·4	·72	2·5	·73	2·6
2·18	·69	2·0	·69	2·2	·69	2·3	·69	2·3	·69	2·3	·69	2·4	·69	2·4	·70	2·4	·70	2·4	·71	2·4	·71	2·4	·72	2·4	·72	2·5	·73	2·6
2·20	0·68	2·0	0·68	2·1	0·68	2·0	0·68	2·0	0·68	2·1	0·68	2·1	0·69	2·1	0·70	2·2	0·70	2·2	0·70	2·2	0·71	2·3	0·71	2·3	0·72	2·3	0·72	2·3
2·25	·67	2·1	·67	2·1	·67	2·1	·67	2·1	·68	2·1	·68	2·2	·68	2·2	·69	2·2	·69	2·2	·69	2·3	·69	2·3	·69	2·3	·71	2·3	·71	2·4
2·30	·67	2·1	·67	2·2	·67	2·1	·67	2·2	·67	2·2	·67	2·2	·67	2·3	·68	2·3	·68	2·3	·69	2·3	·68	2·3	·69	2·3	·70	2·4	·70	2·4
2·35	·66	2·2	·66	2·2	·66	2·2	·66	2·2	·66	2·2	·66	2·3	·66	2·4	·67	2·3	·67	2·3	·68	2·4	·68	2·3	·69	2·4	·70	2·4	·70	2·5
2·40	·65	2·2	·65	2·3	·65	2·3	·65	2·3	·65	2·3	·65	2·3	·65	2·4	·66	2·4	·66	2·4	·67	2·4	·67	2·4	·68	2·4	·69	2·4	·69	2·5
2·45	·65	2·3	·64	2·3	·64	2·4	·64	2·4	·64	2·4	·64	2·4	·65	2·4	·65	2·5	·66	2·5	·66	2·5	·66	2·5	·67	2·5	·68	2·5	·68	2·6
2·50	·64	2·3	·64	2·3	·64	2·4	·64	2·4	·64	2·4	·64	2·5	·64	2·5	·65	2·5	·65	2·5	·65	2·5	·66	2·5	·67	2·5	·67	2·5	·67	2·6
2·55	·63	2·4	·63	2·4	·64	2·5	·63	2·5	·63	2·5	·63	2·5	·63	2·6	·64	2·6	·64	2·6	·65	2·6	·65	2·6	·66	2·6	·66	2·6	·67	2·7
2·60	·63	2·4	·63	2·5	·63	2·5	·62	2·6	·62	2·6	·63	2·6	·62	2·6	·63	2·6	·64	2·6	·64	2·6	·64	2·6	·65	2·6	·66	2·6	·66	2·7
2·65	·62	2·5	·62	2·5	·62	2·6	·61	2·6	·61	2·6	·61	2·7	·61	2·7	·62	2·7	·63	2·7	·63	2·7	·63	2·7	·64	2·7	·65	2·7	·65	2·8
2·70	·62	2·5	·62	2·6	·61	2·6	·61	2·6	·61	2·7	·61	2·7	·61	2·7	·62	2·7	·62	2·7	·62	2·7	·63	2·7	·63	2·7	·64	2·8	·64	2·8
2·75	·61	2·6	·61	2·6	·61	2·6	·61	2·7	·60	2·7	·60	2·8	·60	2·8	·61	2·8	·61	2·8	·62	2·8	·62	2·8	·62	2·8	·63	2·9	·63	2·9
2·8	0·61	2·6	0·60	2·6	0·60	2·7	0·60	2·7	0·59	2·8	0·60	2·9	0·60	2·9	0·60	2·9	0·61	2·9	0·61	2·9	0·61	2·9	0·62	2·9	0·62	2·9	0·62	2·9
2·9	·60	2·7	·59	2·8	·59	2·8	·59	2·9	·58	3·1	·58	3·2	·59	3·0	·59	3·0	·60	3·0	·60	3·0	·60	3·0	·61	3·0	·61	3·0	·61	3·0
3·0	·59	2·8	·59	2·9	·58	2·9	·58	3·0	·57	3·1	·57	3·2	·57	3·2	·58	3·2	·59	3·1	·59	3·1	·59	3·1	·60	3·1	·60	3·1	·60	3·1

Table 45 (continued). *Logistic function fitted by maximum likelihood: standard errors of estimators*

Five doses. Entries are standard errors $\times \sqrt{n}$

β	2·0 $s(\hat{g})$	2·0 $s(\hat{b})$	2·1 $s(\hat{g})$	2·1 $s(\hat{b})$	2·2 $s(\hat{g})$	2·2 $s(\hat{b})$	2·3 $s(\hat{g})$	2·3 $s(\hat{b})$	2·4 $s(\hat{g})$	2·4 $s(\hat{b})$	2·5 $s(\hat{g})$	2·5 $s(\hat{b})$	2·6 $s(\hat{g})$	2·6 $s(\hat{b})$	2·7 $s(\hat{g})$	2·7 $s(\hat{b})$	2·8 $s(\hat{g})$	2·8 $s(\hat{b})$	2·9 $s(\hat{g})$	2·9 $s(\hat{b})$
0·40	2·3	0·68	2·3	0·68	2·3	0·68	2·4	0·68	2·4	0·68	2·4	0·68	2·5	0·68	2·6	0·68	2·6	0·68	2·7	0·69
·42	2·2	·68	2·2	·68	2·2	·68	2·3	·68	2·3	·68	2·3	·68	2·4	·68	2·4	·69	2·5	·69	2·6	·69
·44	2·1	·68	2·1	·68	2·1	·68	2·2	·69	2·2	·69	2·2	·69	2·3	·69	2·3	·69	2·4	·69	2·5	·70
·46	2·0	·69	2·0	·69	2·1	·69	2·1	·69	2·1	·69	2·1	·69	2·2	·70	2·2	·70	2·3	·70	2·4	·70
·48	2·0	·69	2·0	·69	2·0	·70	2·0	·70	2·0	·70	2·1	·70	2·1	·70	2·2	·70	2·2	·71	2·3	·71
0·50	1·9	0·70	1·9	0·70	1·9	0·70	1·9	0·70	2·0	0·70	2·0	0·70	2·0	0·71	2·1	0·71	2·1	0·71	2·2	0·72
·52	1·8	·71	1·8	·71	1·8	·71	1·9	·71	1·9	·71	1·9	·71	2·0	·71	2·0	·72	2·0	·72	2·1	·72
·54	1·8	·71	1·8	·71	1·8	·71	1·8	·71	1·8	·71	1·8	·72	1·9	·72	1·9	·72	2·0	·72	2·0	·73
·56	1·7	·72	1·7	·72	1·7	·72	1·7	·72	1·8	·72	1·8	·72	1·8	·73	1·9	·73	1·9	·73	2·0	·74
·58	1·7	·72	1·7	·72	1·7	·72	1·7	·73	1·7	·73	1·7	·73	1·8	·73	1·8	·74	1·8	·74	1·9	·74
0·60	1·6	0·73	1·6	0·73	1·6	0·73	1·6	0·73	1·7	0·73	1·7	0·74	1·7	0·74	1·8	0·74	1·8	0·75	1·8	0·75
·62	1·6	·74	1·6	·74	1·6	·74	1·6	·74	1·6	·74	1·6	·74	1·7	·75	1·7	·75	1·7	·75	1·8	·76
·64	1·5	·74	1·5	·74	1·5	·74	1·6	·75	1·6	·75	1·6	·75	1·6	·75	1·7	·76	1·7	·76	1·7	·77
·66	1·5	·75	1·5	·75	1·5	·75	1·5	·75	1·5	·75	1·5	·76	1·6	·76	1·6	·77	1·6	·77	1·7	·78
·68	1·5	·76	1·5	·76	1·5	·76	1·5	·76	1·5	·76	1·5	·77	1·5	·77	1·6	·77	1·6	·78	1·6	·78
0·70	1·4	0·76	1·4	0·76	1·4	0·77	1·4	0·77	1·5	0·77	1·5	0·77	1·5	0·78	1·5	0·78	1·6	0·79	1·6	0·79
·75	1·3	·78	1·3	·78	1·3	·79	1·4	·79	1·4	·79	1·4	·79	1·4	·80	1·5	·80	1·5	·81	1·5	·82
·80	1·3	·80	1·3	·80	1·3	·81	1·3	·81	1·3	·81	1·3	·82	1·3	·82	1·4	·83	1·4	·83	1·4	·84
·85	1·2	·83	1·2	·83	1·2	·83	1·2	·83	1·2	·83	1·3	·84	1·3	·84	1·3	·85	1·3	·86	1·3	·87
·90	1·2	·85	1·2	·85	1·2	·85	1·2	·85	1·2	·86	1·2	·86	1·2	·87	1·2	·88	1·3	·89	1·3	·89
·95	1·1	·87	1·1	·88	1·1	·88	1·1	·88	1·1	·88	1·1	·89	1·2	·90	1·2	·90	1·2	·91	1·2	·92
1·00	1·1	·90	1·0	·90	1·1	·90	1·1	·91	1·1	·91	1·1	·92	1·1	·92	1·1	·93	1·2	·94	1·2	·95
1·05	1·0	·93	1·0	·93	1·1	·93	1·1	·93	1·1	·94	1·1	·95	1·1	·95	1·1	·97	1·1	·97	1·1	·99
1·10	1·0	0·96	1·0	0·96	1·0	0·96	1·0	0·96	1·0	0·97	1·0	0·97	1·0	0·98	1·1	0·99	1·1	1·0	1·1	1·0
1·12	1·0	·97	1·0	·97	1·0	·97	1·0	·98	1·0	·98	1·0	·99	1·0	·99	1·0	1·0	1·1	1·0	1·1	1·0
1·14	0·99	·98	0·99	·98	0·99	·98	1·0	·99	1·0	·99	1·0	1·0	1·0	1·0	1·0	1·0	1·0	1·0	1·1	1·0
1·16	·98	·99	·98	·99	·98	·99	0·98	1·0	0·99	1·0	0·99	1·0	1·0	1·0	1·0	1·0	1·0	1·0	1·0	1·0
1·18	·97	1·0	·97	1·0	·97	1·0	·97	1·0	·98	1·0	·98	1·0	0·99	1·0	1·0	1·0	1·0	1·1	1·0	1·1
1·20	0·96	1·0	0·96	1·0	0·96	1·0	0·96	1·0	0·97	1·0	0·97	1·0	0·98	1·0	0·99	1·1	1·0	1·1	1·0	1·1
1·22	·95	1·0	·95	1·0	·95	1·0	·95	1·0	·96	1·0	·96	1·1	·97	1·1	·98	1·1	0·99	1·1	1·0	1·1
1·24	·94	1·0	·94	1·0	·94	1·0	·94	1·1	·95	1·1	·95	1·1	·96	1·1	·97	1·1	·98	1·1	0·99	1·1
1·26	·93	1·1	·93	1·1	·93	1·1	·93	1·1	·94	1·1	·94	1·1	·95	1·1	·96	1·1	·97	1·1	·98	1·1
1·28	·92	1·1	·92	1·1	·92	1·1	·92	1·1	·93	1·1	·93	1·1	·94	1·1	·95	1·1	·96	1·1	·97	1·1
1·30	0·91	1·1	0·91	1·1	0·91	1·1	0·91	1·1	0·92	1·1	0·92	1·1	0·93	1·1	0·94	1·1	0·95	1·1	0·96	1·2
1·32	·90	1·1	·90	1·1	·90	1·1	·90	1·1	·91	1·1	·91	1·1	·92	1·1	·93	1·1	·94	1·2	·95	1·2
1·34	·89	1·1	·89	1·1	·89	1·1	·90	1·1	·90	1·1	·90	1·1	·91	1·1	·92	1·2	·93	1·2	·94	1·2
1·36	·88	1·1	·88	1·1	·89	1·1	·89	1·1	·89	1·1	·90	1·1	·90	1·2	·91	1·2	·92	1·2	·93	1·2
1·38	·88	1·1	·88	1·1	·88	1·1	·88	1·1	·88	1·2	·89	1·2	·89	1·2	·90	1·2	·91	1·2	·92	1·2
1·40	0·87	1·2	0·87	1·2	0·87	1·2	0·87	1·2	0·88	1·2	0·88	1·2	0·88	1·2	0·89	1·2	0·90	1·2	0·91	1·2
1·42	·86	1·2	·86	1·2	·86	1·2	·86	1·2	·87	1·2	·87	1·2	·88	1·2	·88	1·2	·89	1·2	·90	1·3
1·44	·85	1·2	·85	1·2	·85	1·2	·86	1·2	·86	1·2	·86	1·2	·87	1·2	·87	1·2	·88	1·3	·89	1·3
1·46	·84	1·2	·84	1·2	·85	1·2	·85	1·2	·85	1·2	·86	1·2	·86	1·2	·87	1·3	·87	1·3	·88	1·3
1·48	·83	1·2	·83	1·2	·84	1·2	·84	1·2	·84	1·2	·85	1·2	·85	1·3	·86	1·3	·86	1·3	·87	1·3
1·50	0·83	1·2	0·83	1·2	0·84	1·2	0·84	1·2	0·84	1·2	0·84	1·3	0·85	1·3	0·85	1·3	0·86	1·3	0·87	1·3
1·52	·83	1·2	·83	1·2	·83	1·3	·83	1·3	·83	1·3	·84	1·3	·84	1·3	·85	1·3	·85	1·3	·86	1·3
1·54	·82	1·3	·82	1·3	·82	1·3	·82	1·3	·83	1·3	·83	1·3	·83	1·3	·84	1·3	·84	1·3	·85	1·4
1·56	·81	1·3	·82	1·3	·82	1·3	·82	1·3	·82	1·3	·82	1·3	·83	1·3	·83	1·3	·84	1·4	·85	1·4
1·58	·81	1·3	·81	1·3	·81	1·3	·81	1·3	·81	1·3	·81	1·3	·82	1·3	·82	1·4	·83	1·4	·84	1·4
1·60	0·80	1·3	0·80	1·3	0·80	1·3	0·81	1·3	0·81	1·3	0·81	1·3	0·81	1·4	0·82	1·4	0·82	1·4	0·83	1·4
1·62	·80	1·3	·80	1·3	·80	1·3	·80	1·3	·80	1·3	·80	1·4	·81	1·4	·81	1·4	·82	1·4	·82	1·4
1·64	·79	1·3	·79	1·3	·79	1·4	·79	1·4	·80	1·4	·80	1·4	·80	1·4	·81	1·4	·81	1·4	·82	1·4
1·66	·79	1·4	·79	1·4	·79	1·4	·79	1·4	·79	1·4	·79	1·4	·80	1·4	·80	1·4	·80	1·4	·81	1·5
1·68	·78	1·4	·78	1·4	·78	1·4	·78	1·4	·79	1·4	·79	1·4	·79	1·4	·79	1·4	·80	1·5	·80	1·5
1·70	0·78	1·4	0·78	1·4	0·78	1·4	0·78	1·4	0·78	1·4	0·78	1·4	0·78	1·4	0·79	1·5	0·79	1·5	0·80	1·5
1·72	·77	1·4	·77	1·4	·77	1·4	·77	1·4	·77	1·4	·78	1·4	·78	1·5	·78	1·5	·79	1·5	·79	1·5
1·74	·77	1·4	·77	1·4	·77	1·5	·77	1·5	·77	1·5	·77	1·5	·77	1·5	·78	1·5	·78	1·5	·79	1·5
1·76	·77	1·5	·77	1·5	·77	1·5	·77	1·5	·77	1·5	·77	1·5	·77	1·5	·78	1·5	·78	1·5	·78	1·6
1·78	·76	1·5	·76	1·5	·76	1·5	·76	1·5	·76	1·5	·76	1·5	·76	1·5	·77	1·5	·77	1·6	·77	1·6
1·80	0·75	1·5	0·75	1·5	0·75	1·5	0·75	1·5	0·76	1·5	0·76	1·5	0·76	1·5	0·76	1·5	0·77	1·6	0·77	1·6
1·82	·75	1·5	·75	1·5	·75	1·5	·75	1·5	·75	1·5	·75	1·5	·76	1·5	·76	1·6	·76	1·6	·77	1·6
1·84	·74	1·5	·74	1·5	·74	1·5	·74	1·5	·75	1·5	·75	1·6	·75	1·6	·75	1·6	·76	1·6	·76	1·7
1·86	·74	1·5	·74	1·5	·74	1·6	·74	1·6	·74	1·6	·75	1·6	·75	1·6	·75	1·6	·75	1·6	·76	1·7
1·88	·73	1·6	·73	1·6	·73	1·6	·73	1·6	·73	1·6	·74	1·6	·74	1·6	·74	1·6	·75	1·6	·75	1·7
1·90	0·73	1·6	0·73	1·6	0·73	1·6	0·73	1·6	0·73	1·6	0·73	1·6	0·74	1·6	0·74	1·6	0·74	1·7	0·74	1·7
1·95	·72	1·6	·72	1·6	·72	1·6	·72	1·6	·72	1·6	·72	1·7	·73	1·7	·73	1·7	·73	1·7	·73	1·7
2·00	·71	1·7	·71	1·7	·71	1·7	·71	1·7	·71	1·7	·71	1·7	·72	1·7	·72	1·7	·72	1·8	·72	1·8
2·05	·70	1·7	·70	1·7	·70	1·7	·70	1·7	·70	1·7	·70	1·8	·71	1·8	·71	1·8	·71	1·8	·71	1·8
2·10	·69	1·8	·69	1·8	·69	1·8	·69	1·8	·70	1·8	·70	1·8	·70	1·8	·70	1·8	·70	1·9	·70	1·9
2·15	·68	1·8	·68	1·8	·68	1·8	·69	1·8	·69	1·9	·69	1·9	·69	1·9	·69	1·9	·69	1·9	·69	2·0
2·20	0·67	1·9	0·68	1·9	0·68	1·9	0·68	1·9	0·68	1·9	0·68	1·9	0·68	1·9	0·68	2·0	0·68	2·0	0·68	2·0
2·25	·67	2·0	·67	2·0	·67	2·0	·67	2·0	·67	2·0	·67	2·0	·67	2·0	·67	2·0	·67	2·0	·67	2·1
2·30	·66	2·0	·66	2·0	·66	2·0	·66	2·0	·66	2·0	·66	2·0	·66	2·0	·66	2·1	·66	2·1	·67	2·1
2·35	·65	2·1	·65	2·1	·65	2·1	·65	2·1	·65	2·1	·66	2·1	·66	2·1	·66	2·1	·66	2·2	·66	2·2
2·40	·64	2·1	·64	2·1	·65	2·1	·65	2·1	·65	2·1	·65	2·1	·65	2·1	·65	2·2	·65	2·2	·65	2·3
2·45	·64	2·2	·64	2·2	·64	2·2	·64	2·2	·64	2·2	·64	2·2	·64	2·2	·64	2·2	·64	2·3	·64	2·3
2·50	·63	2·3	·63	2·3	·63	2·3	·64	2·2	·64	2·2	·64	2·2	·64	2·3	·64	2·3	·63	2·3	·63	2·4
$\gamma \rightarrow$	2·0		2·1		2·2		2·3		2·4		2·5		2·6		2·7		2·8		2·9	

Table 45 (*continued*)

Five doses (*continued*)

	γ																	
	3·0		3·1		3·2		3·25		3·3		3·35		3·4		3·45		3·5	
β	s(ĝ)	s(b̂)	s(ĝ)	s(b̂)	s(ĝ)	s(b̂)	s(ĝ)	s(b̂)	s(ĝ)	s(b̂)	s(ĝ)	s(b̂)	s(ĝ)	s(b̂)	s(ĝ)	s(b̂)	s(ĝ)	s(b̂)
0·40	2·8	0·69	2·9	0·69	3·0	0·69	3·0	0·69	3·1	0·70	3·1	0·70	3·2	0·70	3·2	0·70	3·3	0·70
·42	2·6	·69	2·7	·70	2·8	·70	2·9	·70	2·9	·70	3·0	·70	3·0	·71	3·1	·71	3·1	·71
·44	2·5	·70	2·6	·70	2·7	·71	2·8	·71	2·8	·71	2·9	·71	2·9	·71	3·0	·72	3·0	·72
·46	2·4	·71	2·5	·71	2·6	·71	2·6	·71	2·7	·72	2·7	·72	2·8	·72	2·8	·72	2·9	·73
·48	2·3	·71	2·4	·72	2·5	·72	2·5	·72	2·6	·72	2·6	·73	2·7	·73	2·7	·73	2·8	·73
0·50	2·2	0·72	2·3	0·72	2·4	0·73	2·4	0·73	2·5	0·73	2·5	0·73	2·6	0·74	2·6	0·74	2·7	0·74
·52	2·2	·73	2·2	·73	2·3	·73	2·4	·74	2·4	·74	2·5	·74	2·5	·75	2·5	·75	2·6	·75
·54	2·1	·73	2·2	·74	2·2	·74	2·3	·75	2·3	·75	2·3	·75	2·4	·75	2·4	·76	2·5	·76
·56	2·0	·74	2·1	·75	2·1	·75	2·2	·75	2·2	·76	2·3	·76	2·3	·76	2·3	·77	2·4	·77
·58	2·0	·75	2·0	·75	2·1	·76	2·1	·76	2·1	·77	2·2	·77	2·2	·77	2·3	·78	2·3	·78
0·60	1·9	0·76	1·9	0·76	2·0	0·77	2·0	0·77	2·1	0·78	2·1	0·78	2·2	0·78	2·2	0·79	2·2	0·79
·62	1·8	·76	1·9	·77	1·9	·78	2·0	·78	2·0	·78	2·0	·79	2·1	·79	2·1	·80	2·2	·80
·64	1·8	·77	1·8	·78	1·9	·79	1·9	·79	2·0	·79	2·0	·80	2·0	·80	2·1	·81	2·1	·81
·66	1·7	·78	1·8	·79	1·8	·80	1·9	·80	1·9	·80	1·9	·81	2·0	·81	2·0	·82	2·0	·82
·68	1·7	·79	1·7	·80	1·8	·81	1·8	·81	1·8	·81	1·9	·82	1·9	·82	1·9	·83	2·0	·83
0·70	1·6	0·80	1·7	0·81	1·7	0·82	1·8	0·82	1·8	0·83	1·8	0·83	1·9	0·84	1·9	0·84	1·9	0·85
·75	1·5	·82	1·6	·83	1·6	·84	1·7	·85	1·7	·85	1·7	·86	1·7	·86	1·8	·87	1·8	·88
·80	1·5	·85	1·5	·86	1·5	·87	1·6	·88	1·6	·88	1·6	·89	1·6	·90	1·7	·90	1·7	·91
·85	1·4	·88	1·4	·89	1·5	·90	1·5	·91	1·5	·91	1·5	·92	1·6	·93	1·6	·94	1·6	·94
·90	1·3	·91	1·3	·92	1·4	·93	1·4	·94	1·4	·95	1·5	·95	1·5	·96	1·5	·97	1·5	·98
·95	1·3	·94	1·3	·95	1·3	·96	1·3	·97	1·4	·98	1·4	·99	1·4	1·0	1·4	1·0	1·5	1·0
1·00	1·2	·97	1·2	·98	1·3	1·0	1·3	1·0	1·3	1·0	1·4	1·0	1·3	1·0	1·4	1·0	1·4	1·1
1·05	1·1	1·0	1·2	1·0	1·2	1·0	1·2	1·0	1·2	1·1	1·3	1·1	1·3	1·1	1·3	1·1	1·3	1·1
1·10	1·1	1·0	1·1	1·1	1·2	1·1	1·2	1·1	1·2	1·1	1·2	1·1	1·2	1·1	1·3	1·1	1·3	1·1
1·12	1·1	1·0	1·1	1·1	1·1	1·1	1·2	1·1	1·2	1·1	1·2	1·1	1·2	1·1	1·2	1·1	1·3	1·2
1·14	1·1	1·1	1·1	1·1	1·1	1·1	1·1	1·1	1·2	1·1	1·2	1·1	1·2	1·1	1·2	1·2	1·2	1·2
1·16	1·0	1·1	1·1	1·1	1·1	1·1	1·1	1·1	1·1	1·1	1·2	1·2	1·2	1·2	1·2	1·2	1·2	1·2
1·18	1·0	1·1	1·1	1·1	1·1	1·1	1·1	1·1	1·1	1·2	1·1	1·2	1·2	1·2	1·2	1·2	1·2	1·2
1·20	1·0	1·1	1·1	1·1	1·1	1·1	1·1	1·2	1·1	1·2	1·1	1·2	1·1	1·2	1·2	1·2	1·2	1·2
1·22	1·0	1·1	1·0	1·1	1·1	1·2	1·1	1·2	1·1	1·2	1·1	1·2	1·1	1·2	1·1	1·2	1·2	1·2
1·24	1·0	1·1	1·0	1·2	1·1	1·2	1·1	1·2	1·1	1·2	1·1	1·2	1·1	1·2	1·1	1·3	1·1	1·3
1·26	0·99	1·2	1·0	1·2	1·0	1·2	1·0	1·2	1·1	1·2	1·1	1·2	1·1	1·3	1·1	1·3	1·1	1·3
1·28	·98	1·2	1·0	1·2	1·0	1·2	1·0	1·2	1·0	1·2	1·1	1·2	1·1	1·3	1·1	1·3	1·1	1·3
1·30	0·97	1·2	0·99	1·2	1·0	1·2	1·0	1·2	1·0	1·3	1·1	1·3	1·1	1·3	1·1	1·3	1·1	1·3
1·32	·96	1·2	·98	1·2	0·99	1·2	1·0	1·3	1·0	1·3	1·0	1·3	1·0	1·3	1·1	1·3	1·1	1·3
1·34	·95	1·2	·97	1·2	·99	1·3	1·0	1·3	1·0	1·3	1·0	1·3	1·0	1·3	1·1	1·3	1·1	1·4
1·36	·94	1·2	·96	1·3	·98	1·3	0·99	1·3	1·0	1·3	1·0	1·3	1·0	1·3	1·0	1·4	1·1	1·4
1·38	·93	1·2	·95	1·3	·96	1·3	·98	1·3	0·99	1·3	1·0	1·3	1·0	1·4	1·0	1·4	1·0	1·4
1·40	0·92	1·3	0·94	1·3	0·95	1·3	0·96	1·3	0·98	1·3	0·99	1·4	1·0	1·4	1·0	1·4	1·0	1·4
1·42	·91	1·3	·93	1·3	·94	1·3	·95	1·3	·96	1·4	·98	1·4	0·99	1·4	1·0	1·4	1·0	1·4
1·44	·90	1·3	·92	1·3	·93	1·3	·94	1·4	·95	1·4	·97	1·4	·98	1·4	0·99	1·4	1·0	1·5
1·46	·90	1·3	·91	1·3	·92	1·4	·93	1·4	·94	1·4	·95	1·4	·97	1·4	·98	1·5	0·99	1·5
1·48	·89	1·3	·90	1·4	·91	1·4	·92	1·4	·93	1·4	·94	1·4	·96	1·5	·97	1·5	·98	1·5
1·50	0·88	1·3	0·89	1·4	0·90	1·4	0·91	1·4	0·92	1·4	0·93	1·5	0·95	1·5	0·96	1·5	0·97	1·5
1·52	·87	1·4	·88	1·4	·90	1·4	·90	1·4	·91	1·5	·92	1·5	·94	1·5	·95	1·5	·96	1·5
1·54	·86	1·4	·87	1·4	·89	1·4	·90	1·5	·90	1·5	·92	1·5	·93	1·5	·94	1·5	·95	1·6
1·56	·86	1·4	·87	1·4	·88	1·5	·89	1·5	·90	1·5	·91	1·5	·92	1·5	·93	1·6	·94	1·6
1·58	·85	1·4	·86	1·4	·87	1·5	·88	1·5	·89	1·5	·90	1·5	·91	1·6	·92	1·6	·93	1·6
1·60	0·84	1·4	0·85	1·5	0·86	1·5	0·87	1·5	0·88	1·5	0·89	1·6	0·90	1·6	0·91	1·6	0·92	1·6
1·62	·83	1·5	·84	1·5	·85	1·5	·86	1·5	·87	1·6	·88	1·6	·89	1·6	·90	1·6	·91	1·6
1·64	·82	1·5	·83	1·5	·85	1·5	·85	1·6	·86	1·6	·87	1·6	·88	1·6	·89	1·7	·91	1·7
1·66	·82	1·5	·83	1·5	·84	1·6	·84	1·6	·85	1·6	·86	1·6	·87	1·6	·88	1·7	·90	1·7
1·68	·81	1·5	·82	1·5	·83	1·6	·84	1·6	·85	1·6	·86	1·6	·87	1·7	·88	1·7	·89	1·7
1·70	0·81	1·5	0·81	1·6	0·83	1·6	0·83	1·6	0·84	1·6	0·85	1·7	0·86	1·7	0·87	1·7	0·88	1·7
1·72	·80	1·5	·81	1·6	·82	1·6	·82	1·6	·83	1·7	·84	1·7	·85	1·7	·86	1·7	·87	1·8
1·74	·79	1·6	·80	1·6	·81	1·6	·82	1·7	·83	1·7	·83	1·7	·84	1·7	·85	1·7	·86	1·8
1·76	·79	1·6	·80	1·6	·80	1·7	·81	1·7	·82	1·7	·82	1·7	·83	1·7	·84	1·8	·85	1·8
1·78	·78	1·6	·79	1·6	·79	1·7	·80	1·7	·81	1·7	·81	1·7	·82	1·8	·83	1·8	·84	1·8
1·80	0·78	1·6	0·78	1·7	0·79	1·7	0·80	1·7	0·81	1·7	0·81	1·8	0·82	1·8	0·83	1·8	0·84	1·8
1·82	·77	1·6	·78	1·7	·79	1·7	·79	1·7	·80	1·8	·80	1·8	·81	1·8	·82	1·8	·83	1·9
1·84	·76	1·7	·77	1·7	·78	1·7	·79	1·8	·79	1·8	·80	1·8	·81	1·8	·82	1·9	·83	1·9
1·86	·76	1·7	·76	1·7	·78	1·8	·78	1·8	·78	1·8	·79	1·8	·80	1·8	·81	1·9	·82	1·9
1·88	·75	1·7	·76	1·7	·77	1·8	·77	1·8	·78	1·8	·79	1·8	·80	1·9	·80	1·9	·81	1·9
1·90	0·75	1·7	0·76	1·8	0·76	1·8	0·77	1·8	0·78	1·8	0·78	1·9	0·79	1·9	0·80	1·9	0·81	1·9
1·95	·74	1·8	·74	1·8	·75	1·9	·75	1·9	·76	1·9	·77	1·9	·77	1·9	·78	2·0	·79	2·0
2·00	·73	1·8	·73	1·9	·74	1·9	·74	1·9	·75	1·9	·75	2·0	·76	2·0	·77	2·0	·78	2·0
2·05	·72	1·9	·72	1·9	·73	2·0	·73	2·0	·73	2·0	·74	2·0	·75	2·1	·75	2·1	·76	2·1
2·10	·70	1·9	·70	2·0	·72	2·0	·72	2·0	·72	2·0	·73	2·1	·74	2·1	·74	2·1	·75	2·2
2·15	·70	2·0	·70	2·0	·71	2·1	·71	2·1	·71	2·1	·72	2·1	·72	2·2	·73	2·2	·74	2·2
2·20	0·69	2·0	0·69	2·1	0·70	2·1	0·70	2·1	0·70	2·2	0·71	2·2	0·71	2·2	0·72	2·2	0·72	2·3
2·25	·68	2·1	·68	2·1	·69	2·2	·69	2·2	·69	2·2	·70	2·2	·70	2·3	·71	2·3	·71	2·3
2·30	·67	2·2	·67	2·2	·68	2·2	·68	2·3	·68	2·3	·69	2·3	·69	2·3	·70	2·4	·70	2·4
2·35	·66	2·2	·66	2·3	·67	2·3	·67	2·3	·67	2·3	·68	2·4	·68	2·4	·69	2·4	·69	2·4
2·40	·65	2·3	·65	2·3	·66	2·4	·66	2·4	·67	2·4	·67	2·4	·67	2·4	·68	2·5	·68	2·5
2·45	·64	2·4	·65	2·4	·65	2·4	·66	2·4	·66	2·4	·66	2·5	·66	2·5	·67	2·5	·68	2·6
2·50	·64	2·4	·64	2·5	·64	2·5	·65	2·5	·65	2·5	·65	2·5	·66	2·5	·66	2·6	·67	2·6
γ →	3·0		3·1		3·2		3·25		3·3		3·35		3·4		3·45		3·5	

Table 45 (*continued*). *Logistic function fitted by maximum likelihood: standard errors of estimators*

Six doses. Entries are standard errors $\times \sqrt{n}$

	γ																							
	2·5		2·6		2·7		2·8		2·9		3·0		3·1		3·2		3·3		3·4		3·5		3·6	
β	s(g)	s(b)	s(g)	s(b)	s(g)	s(b)	s(g)	s(b)	s(g)	s(b)	s(g)	s(b)	s(g)	s(b)	s(g)	s(b)	s(g)	s(b)	s(g)	s(b)	s(g)	s(b)	s(g)	s(b)
0·40	2·2	0·53	2·2	0·53	2·2	0·53	2·2	0·53	2·2	0·53	2·2	0·53	2·3	0·53	2·3	0·53	2·3	0·53	2·4	0·53	2·4	0·54	2·5	0·54
·42	2·1	·53	2·1	·53	2·1	·53	2·1	·53	2·1	·53	2·1	·53	2·2	·53	2·2	·54	2·2	·54	2·3	·54	2·3	·54	2·4	·54
·44	2·0	·53	2·0	·54	2·0	·54	2·0	·54	2·0	·54	2·0	·54	2·1	·54	2·1	·54	2·1	·54	2·2	·55	2·2	·55	2·3	·55
·46	1·9	·54	1·9	·54	1·9	·54	1·9	·54	1·9	·54	2·0	·54	2·0	·55	2·0	·55	2·0	·55	2·1	·55	2·1	·55	2·2	·56
·48	1·8	·55	1·8	·55	1·9	·55	1·9	·55	1·9	·55	1·9	·55	1·9	·55	1·9	·55	2·0	·55	2·0	·56	2·1	·56	2·1	·56
0·50	1·8	0·55	1·8	0·55	1·8	0·55	1·8	0·55	1·8	0·56	1·8	0·56	1·8	0·56	1·8	0·56	1·9	0·56	1·9	0·56	2·0	0·57	2·0	0·57
·52	1·7	·56	1·7	·56	1·7	·56	1·7	·56	1·7	·56	1·8	·56	1·8	·56	1·8	·57	1·8	·57	1·9	·57	1·9	·58	1·9	·58
·54	1·7	·57	1·7	·57	1·7	·57	1·7	·57	1·7	·57	1·7	·57	1·7	·57	1·7	·58	1·8	·58	1·8	·58	1·8	·58	1·9	·59
·56	1·6	·57	1·6	·57	1·6	·57	1·6	·57	1·6	·57	1·7	·58	1·7	·58	1·7	·59	1·7	·59	1·7	·59	1·8	·59	1·8	·59
·58	1·6	·58	1·6	·58	1·6	·58	1·6	·58	1·6	·58	1·6	·58	1·6	·59	1·7	·59	1·7	·59	1·7	·59	1·7	·60	1·8	·60
0·60	1·5	0·59	1·5	0·59	1·5	0·59	1·5	0·59	1·5	0·59	1·6	0·59	1·6	0·60	1·6	0·60	1·6	0·60	1·6	0·61	1·6	0·61	1·7	0·61
·62	1·5	·59	1·5	·59	1·5	·59	1·5	·60	1·5	·60	1·5	·60	1·5	·60	1·5	·61	1·6	·61	1·6	·61	1·6	·62	1·6	·62
·64	1·4	·60	1·4	·60	1·5	·60	1·5	·60	1·5	·60	1·5	·61	1·5	·61	1·5	·61	1·5	·61	1·5	·62	1·6	·62	1·6	·63
·66	1·4	·61	1·4	·61	1·4	·61	1·4	·61	1·4	·61	1·4	·61	1·5	·62	1·5	·62	1·5	·62	1·5	·63	1·6	·63	1·6	·64
·68	1·4	·62	1·4	·62	1·4	·62	1·4	·62	1·4	·62	1·4	·62	1·4	·62	1·4	·63	1·4	·63	1·5	·64	1·5	·64	1·5	·65
0·70	1·3	0·62	1·4	0·63	1·4	0·63	1·4	0·63	1·4	0·63	1·4	0·63	1·4	0·63	1·4	0·64	1·4	0·64	1·4	0·65	1·5	0·65	1·5	0·66
·75	1·3	·65	1·3	·65	1·3	·65	1·3	·65	1·3	·65	1·3	·65	1·3	·66	1·3	·66	1·3	·66	1·4	·67	1·4	·68	1·4	·68
·80	1·2	·67	1·2	·67	1·2	·67	1·2	·67	1·2	·67	1·2	·68	1·2	·68	1·2	·68	1·2	·69	1·3	·69	1·3	·70	1·3	·71
·85	1·2	·69	1·2	·69	1·2	·69	1·2	·69	1·2	·70	1·2	·70	1·2	·71	1·2	·71	1·2	·72	1·2	·72	1·3	·73	1·3	·74
·90	1·1	·72	1·1	·72	1·1	·72	1·1	·72	1·1	·73	1·1	·73	1·1	·73	1·2	·74	1·2	·74	1·2	·75	1·2	·76	1·2	·77
·95	1·1	·75	1·1	·75	1·1	·75	1·1	·75	1·1	·75	1·1	·76	1·1	·76	1·1	·77	1·1	·77	1·1	·78	1·1	·79	1·1	·80
1·00	1·0	·77	1·0	·78	1·1	·78	1·1	·78	1·1	·78	1·1	·78	1·1	·79	1·1	·80	1·1	·80	1·1	·81	1·1	·82	1·1	·83
1·05	1·0	·80	1·0	·81	1·0	·81	1·0	·81	1·0	·81	1·0	·82	1·0	·82	1·0	·83	1·0	·83	1·1	·84	1·1	·85	1·1	·86
1·10	0·99	0·84	0·99	0·84	0·99	0·84	0·99	0·84	0·99	0·84	1·0	0·85	1·0	0·85	1·0	0·86	1·0	0·87	1·0	0·88	1·0	0·89	1·0	0·90
1·12	·98	·85	·98	·85	·98	·85	·98	·85	·98	·85	0·98	·86	0·99	·87	0·99	·87	1·0	·88	1·0	·89	1·0	·90	1·0	·91
1·14	·97	·86	·97	·86	·97	·86	·97	·87	·97	·87	·97	·87	·98	·88	·98	·89	0·99	·90	1·0	·91	1·0	·92	1·0	·93
1·16	·96	·88	·96	·88	·96	·88	·96	·88	·96	·89	·96	·89	·97	·89	·97	·90	·98	·91	0·98	·92	0·99	·93	1·0	·94
1·18	·95	·89	·95	·89	·95	·89	·95	·89	·95	·90	·95	·90	·96	·91	·96	·92	·97	·92	·97	·93	·98	·94	0·99	·96
1·20	0·94	0·90	0·94	0·91	0·94	0·91	0·94	0·91	0·94	0·91	0·94	0·92	0·95	0·92	0·95	0·93	0·96	0·94	0·96	0·95	0·97	0·96	0·98	0·97
1·22	·93	·92	·93	·92	·93	·92	·93	·92	·93	·93	·93	·93	·94	·94	·94	·94	·95	·95	·96	·96	·96	·97	·96	·99
1·24	·92	·93	·92	·93	·92	·93	·92	·93	·92	·94	·92	·94	·93	·95	·93	·96	·94	·97	·94	·98	·95	·99	·96	1·0
1·26	·91	·95	·91	·95	·91	·95	·91	·95	·91	·95	·91	·96	·92	·97	·92	·97	·93	·98	·93	·99	·94	1·0	·95	1·0
1·28	·90	·96	·90	·96	·90	·96	·90	·97	·90	·97	·91	·97	·91	·98	·91	·99	·92	1·0	·92	1·0	·93	1·0	·94	1·0
1·30	0·89	0·97	0·89	0·98	0·89	0·98	0·90	0·98	0·90	0·98	0·90	0·99	0·90	1·0	0·91	1·0	0·91	1·0	0·91	1·0	0·92	1·0	0·93	1·0
1·32	·88	·99	·88	·99	·89	·99	·89	·99	·89	·99	·89	1·0	·89	1·0	·90	1·0	·90	1·0	·90	1·0	·91	1·1	·92	1·1
1·34	·88	1·0	·88	1·0	·88	1·0	·88	1·0	·88	1·0	·88	1·0	·88	1·0	·89	1·0	·89	1·1	·90	1·1	·90	1·1	·91	1·1
1·36	·87	1·0	·87	1·0	·87	1·0	·87	1·0	·87	1·0	·87	1·0	·88	1·0	·88	1·0	·88	1·1	·89	1·1	·89	1·1	·90	1·1
1·38	·86	1·0	·86	1·0	·86	1·0	·86	1·0	·86	1·0	·86	1·0	·87	1·1	·87	1·1	·87	1·1	·88	1·1	·88	1·1	·89	1·1
1·40	0·86	1·1	0·86	1·1	0·86	1·1	0·86	1·1	0·86	1·1	0·86	1·1	0·86	1·1	0·87	1·1	0·87	1·1	0·87	1·1	0·88	1·1	0·88	1·1
1·42	·85	1·1	·85	1·1	·85	1·1	·85	1·1	·85	1·1	·85	1·1	·86	1·1	·86	1·1	·86	1·1	·86	1·1	·87	1·1	·87	1·2
1·44	·84	1·1	·84	1·1	·84	1·1	·84	1·1	·85	1·1	·85	1·1	·85	1·1	·85	1·1	·85	1·1	·86	1·1	·86	1·1	·87	1·2
1·46	·84	1·1	·84	1·1	·84	1·1	·84	1·1	·84	1·1	·83	1·1	·84	1·1	·84	1·1	·84	1·1	·85	1·2	·85	1·2	·86	1·2
1·48	·83	1·1	·83	1·1	·83	1·1	·83	1·1	·83	1·1	·83	1·1	·83	1·1	·83	1·1	·84	1·1	·84	1·2	·85	1·2	·85	1·2
1·50	0·82	1·1	0·83	1·1	0·83	1·1	0·83	1·1	0·83	1·1	0·83	1·2	0·83	1·2	0·83	1·2	0·83	1·2	0·84	1·2	0·84	1·2	0·85	1·2
1·52	·82	1·2	·82	1·2	·82	1·2	·82	1·2	·82	1·2	·82	1·2	·82	1·2	·83	1·2	·83	1·2	·83	1·2	·83	1·2	·84	1·2
1·54	·81	1·2	·81	1·2	·81	1·2	·81	1·2	·82	1·2	·82	1·2	·82	1·2	·82	1·2	·82	1·2	·82	1·2	·83	1·3	·83	1·3
1·56	·81	1·2	·81	1·2	·81	1·2	·81	1·2	·81	1·2	·81	1·2	·81	1·2	·81	1·2	·81	1·2	·82	1·2	·83	1·3	·83	1·3
1·58	·80	1·2	·80	1·2	·80	1·2	·80	1·2	·80	1·2	·80	1·2	·81	1·2	·81	1·2	·81	1·2	·81	1·3	·81	1·3	·82	1·3
1·60	0·80	1·2	0·80	1·2	0·80	1·2	0·80	1·2	0·80	1·2	0·80	1·2	0·80	1·2	0·80	1·3	0·80	1·3	0·81	1·3	0·81	1·3	0·81	1·3
1·62	·79	1·2	·79	1·2	·79	1·2	·79	1·3	·80	1·3	·80	1·3	·80	1·3	·80	1·3	·80	1·3	·80	1·3	·80	1·3	·80	1·3
1·64	·78	1·3	·79	1·3	·79	1·3	·79	1·3	·79	1·3	·79	1·3	·79	1·3	·79	1·3	·79	1·3	·79	1·3	·80	1·3	·80	1·3
1·66	·78	1·3	·78	1·3	·78	1·3	·78	1·3	·78	1·3	·78	1·3	·78	1·3	·79	1·3	·79	1·3	·79	1·3	·79	1·3	·80	1·4
1·68	·78	1·3	·78	1·3	·78	1·3	·78	1·3	·78	1·3	·78	1·3	·78	1·3	·78	1·3	·78	1·3	·78	1·4	·79	1·4	·79	1·4
1·70	0·77	1·3	0·77	1·3	0·77	1·3	0·77	1·3	0·77	1·3	0·77	1·3	0·77	1·3	0·78	1·3	0·78	1·4	0·78	1·4	0·78	1·4	0·78	1·4
1·72	·77	1·3	·77	1·3	·77	1·3	·77	1·3	·77	1·3	·77	1·3	·77	1·4	·77	1·4	·77	1·4	·78	1·4	·78	1·4	·78	1·4
1·74	·76	1·4	·76	1·4	·76	1·4	·77	1·4	·77	1·4	·77	1·4	·77	1·4	·77	1·4	·77	1·4	·77	1·4	·77	1·4	·77	1·5
1·76	·76	1·4	·76	1·4	·76	1·4	·76	1·4	·76	1·4	·76	1·4	·76	1·4	·76	1·4	·77	1·4	·77	1·4	·77	1·4	·77	1·5
1·78	·75	1·4	·75	1·4	·75	1·4	·75	1·4	·75	1·4	·75	1·4	·75	1·4	·75	1·4	·76	1·4	·76	1·4	·76	1·5	·76	1·5
1·80	0·75	1·4	0·75	1·4	0·75	1·4	0·75	1·4	0·75	1·4	0·75	1·4	0·75	1·4	0·75	1·4	0·75	1·4	0·75	1·4	0·76	1·5	0·76	1·5
1·82	·74	1·4	·74	1·4	·74	1·4	·74	1·4	·74	1·4	·74	1·4	·74	1·5	·74	1·5	·75	1·5	·75	1·5	·75	1·5	·75	1·5
1·84	·74	1·4	·74	1·4	·74	1·5	·74	1·5	·74	1·5	·74	1·5	·74	1·5	·74	1·5	·74	1·5	·75	1·5	·75	1·5	·75	1·5
1·86	·74	1·5	·74	1·5	·74	1·5	·74	1·5	·74	1·5	·74	1·5	·74	1·5	·74	1·5	·74	1·5	·74	1·5	·74	1·5	·74	1·6
1·88	·73	1·5	·73	1·5	·73	1·5	·73	1·5	·73	1·5	·73	1·5	·73	1·5	·73	1·5	·74	1·5	·74	1·5	·74	1·6	·74	1·6
1·90	0·73	1·5	0·73	1·5	0·73	1·5	0·73	1·5	0·73	1·5	0·73	1·5	0·73	1·5	0·73	1·6	0·73	1·6	0·73	1·6	0·73	1·6	0·74	1·6
1·92	·72	1·5	·72	1·5	·73	1·5	·73	1·5	·73	1·6	·73	1·6	·73	1·6	·73	1·6	·73	1·6	·73	1·6	·73	1·6	·73	1·6
1·94	·72	1·5	·72	1·6	·72	1·6	·72	1·6	·72	1·6	·72	1·6	·72	1·6	·72	1·6	·72	1·6	·72	1·6	·73	1·6	·73	1·6
1·96	·72	1·6	·72	1·6	·72	1·6	·72	1·6	·72	1·6	·72	1·6	·72	1·6	·72	1·6	·72	1·6	·72	1·6	·72	1·6	·73	1·7
1·98	·71	1·6	·71	1·6	·71	1·6	·71	1·6	·71	1·6	·71	1·6	·71	1·6	·71	1·6	·72	1·6	·72	1·6	·72	1·7	·72	1·7
2·00	0·71	1·6	0·71	1·6	0·71	1·6	0·71	1·6	0·71	1·6	0·71	1·6	0·71	1·6	0·71	1·6	0·71	1·7	0·71	1·7	0·71	1·7	0·72	1·7
γ →	2·5		2·6		2·7		2·8		2·9		3·0		3·1		3·2		3·3		3·4		3·5		3·6	

Table 45 (*continued*)

Six doses (*continued*)

γ

β	3.7 $s(\hat{g})$	3.7 $s(\hat{b})$	3.8 $s(\hat{g})$	3.8 $s(\hat{b})$	3.9 $s(\hat{g})$	3.9 $s(\hat{b})$	4.0 $s(\hat{g})$	4.0 $s(\hat{b})$	4.1 $s(\hat{g})$	4.1 $s(\hat{b})$	4.2 $s(\hat{g})$	4.2 $s(\hat{b})$	4.25 $s(\hat{g})$	4.25 $s(\hat{b})$	4.3 $s(\hat{g})$	4.3 $s(\hat{b})$	4.35 $s(\hat{g})$	4.35 $s(\hat{b})$	4.4 $s(\hat{g})$	4.4 $s(\hat{b})$	4.45 $s(\hat{g})$	4.45 $s(\hat{b})$	4.5 $s(\hat{g})$	4.5 $s(\hat{b})$
0·40	2·6	0·54	2·6	0·54	2·7	0·54	2·8	0·55	2·9	0·55	2·9	0·55	3·0	0·55	3·0	0·56	3·1	0·56	3·1	0·56	3·2	0·56	3·2	0·56
·42	2·4	·55	2·5	·55	2·6	·55	2·6	·55	2·7	·56	2·8	·56	2·8	·56	2·9	·56	2·9	·57	3·0	·57	3·0	·57	3·1	·57
·44	2·3	·55	2·4	·56	2·5	·56	2·5	·56	2·6	·56	2·7	·57	2·7	·57	2·8	·57	2·8	·57	2·8	·58	2·9	·58	2·9	·58
·46	2·2	·56	2·3	·56	2·4	·57	2·4	·57	2·5	·57	2·6	·58	2·6	·58	2·6	·58	2·7	·58	2·7	·59	2·8	·59	2·8	·59
·48	2·1	·57	2·2	·57	2·3	·57	2·3	·58	2·4	·59	2·5	·59	2·5	·59	2·5	·59	2·6	·59	2·6	·60	2·7	·60	2·7	·60
0·50	2·1	0·57	2·1	0·58	2·2	0·58	2·2	0·59	2·3	0·59	2·4	0·59	2·4	0·60	2·4	0·60	2·5	0·60	2·5	0·60	2·6	0·61	2·6	0·61
·52	2·0	·58	2·0	·58	2·1	·59	2·2	·59	2·2	·60	2·3	·60	2·3	·61	2·3	·61	2·4	·61	2·4	·61	2·5	·62	2·5	·62
·54	1·9	·59	2·0	·59	2·1	·60	2·1	·60	2·1	·61	2·2	·61	2·2	·62	2·3	·62	2·3	·62	2·3	·63	2·4	·63	2·4	·63
·56	1·9	·60	1·9	·60	2·0	·61	2·0	·61	2·1	·62	2·1	·62	2·2	·63	2·2	·63	2·3	·63	2·3	·64	2·3	·64	2·4	·64
·58	1·8	·61	1·8	·61	1·9	·62	1·9	·62	2·0	·63	2·1	·63	2·1	·64	2·1	·64	2·2	·64	2·2	·65	2·2	·65	2·3	·66
0·60	1·7	0·61	1·8	0·62	1·8	0·62	1·9	0·63	1·9	0·64	2·0	0·64	2·0	0·65	2·1	0·65	2·1	0·66	2·1	0·66	2·2	0·66	2·2	0·67
·62	1·7	·62	1·7	·63	1·8	·63	1·8	·64	1·9	·65	1·9	·65	2·0	·66	2·0	·66	2·0	·67	2·1	·67	2·1	·68	2·1	·68
·64	1·6	·63	1·7	·64	1·7	·64	1·7	·65	1·8	·66	1·8	·66	1·9	·67	1·9	·67	2·0	·68	2·0	·68	2·0	·69	2·0	·69
·66	1·6	·64	1·6	·65	1·7	·65	1·7	·66	1·8	·67	1·8	·67	1·9	·68	1·9	·68	1·9	·69	1·9	·69	2·0	·70	2·0	·71
·68	1·6	·65	1·6	·66	1·6	·67	1·7	·67	1·7	·68	1·8	·69	1·8	·69	1·8	·70	1·9	·70	1·9	·71	1·9	·71	2·0	·72
0·70	1·5	0·66	1·6	0·67	1·6	0·68	1·6	0·68	1·7	0·69	1·7	0·70	1·8	0·71	1·8	0·71	1·8	0·71	1·8	0·72	1·9	0·72	1·9	0·73
·75	1·4	·69	1·5	·70	1·5	·70	1·5	·71	1·6	·72	1·6	·73	1·7	·74	1·7	·74	1·7	·75	1·7	·76	1·8	·76	1·8	·77
·80	1·4	·72	1·4	·72	1·4	·73	1·5	·74	1·5	·75	1·5	·77	1·5	·77	1·6	·78	1·6	·79	1·6	·79	1·7	·80	1·7	·81
·85	1·3	·74	1·3	·75	1·3	·76	1·4	·77	1·4	·79	1·4	·80	1·5	·81	1·5	·82	1·5	·82	1·5	·83	1·6	·84	1·6	·85
·90	1·2	·78	1·3	·79	1·3	·80	1·3	·81	1·3	·82	1·4	·84	1·4	·84	1·4	·85	1·4	·86	1·5	·87	1·5	·88	1·5	·89
·95	1·2	·81	1·2	·82	1·2	·83	1·3	·84	1·3	·86	1·3	·88	1·3	·88	1·3	·89	1·4	·90	1·4	·91	1·4	·92	1·4	·93
1·00	1·1	·84	1·2	·85	1·2	·87	1·2	·88	1·2	·90	1·3	·91	1·3	·92	1·3	·93	1·3	·94	1·3	·95	1·4	·97	1·4	·98
1·05	1·1	·88	1·1	·89	1·1	·90	1·2	·92	1·2	·94	1·2	·96	1·2	·97	1·2	·98	1·3	·99	1·3	1·0	1·3	1·0	1·3	1·0
1·10	1·1	0·91	1·1	0·92	1·1	0·94	1·1	0·96	1·1	0·98	1·2	1·0	1·2	1·0	1·2	1·0	1·2	1·0	1·2	1·0	1·2	1·0	1·3	1·0
1·12	1·0	·93	1·0	·94	1·1	·96	1·1	·97	1·1	·99	1·1	1·0	1·2	1·0	1·2	1·0	1·2	1·0	1·2	1·1	1·2	1·1	1·2	1·1
1·14	1·0	·94	1·0	·95	1·1	·97	1·1	·99	1·1	1·0	1·1	1·0	1·1	1·0	1·2	1·0	1·2	1·1	1·2	1·1	1·2	1·1	1·2	1·1
1·16	1·0	·96	1·0	·97	1·0	·99	1·1	1·0	1·1	1·0	1·1	1·0	1·1	1·1	1·1	1·1	1·2	1·1	1·2	1·1	1·2	1·1	1·2	1·1
1·18	1·0	·97	1·0	·99	1·0	1·0	1·0	1·0	1·1	1·0	1·1	1·1	1·1	1·1	1·1	1·1	1·1	1·1	1·2	1·1	1·2	1·1	1·2	1·1
1·20	0·99	0·99	1·0	1·0	1·0	1·0	1·0	1·0	1·0	1·1	1·1	1·1	1·1	1·1	1·1	1·1	1·1	1·1	1·1	1·1	1·1	1·2	1·2	1·2
1·22	·98	1·0	0·99	1·0	1·0	1·0	1·0	1·1	1·0	1·1	1·0	1·1	1·1	1·1	1·1	1·1	1·1	1·1	1·1	1·2	1·1	1·2	1·2	1·2
1·24	·97	1·0	·98	1·0	0·99	1·1	1·0	1·1	1·0	1·1	1·0	1·1	1·1	1·1	1·1	1·1	1·1	1·1	1·1	1·2	1·1	1·2	1·1	1·2
1·26	·96	1·0	·97	1·0	·98	1·1	0·99	1·1	1·0	1·1	1·0	1·1	1·0	1·2	1·0	1·2	1·1	1·2	1·1	1·2	1·1	1·2	1·1	1·2
1·28	·95	1·0	·96	1·1	·97	1·1	·98	1·1	1·0	1·1	1·0	1·2	1·0	1·2	1·0	1·2	1·1	1·2	1·1	1·2	1·1	1·2	1·1	1·3
1·30	0·94	1·1	0·95	1·1	0·96	1·1	0·97	1·1	0·99	1·1	1·0	1·2	1·0	1·2	1·0	1·2	1·0	1·2	1·1	1·2	1·1	1·3	1·1	1·3
1·32	·93	1·1	·94	1·1	·95	1·1	·96	1·1	·98	1·2	1·0	1·2	1·0	1·2	1·0	1·2	1·0	1·2	1·1	1·3	1·1	1·3	1·1	1·3
1·34	·92	1·1	·93	1·1	·94	1·1	·95	1·2	·97	1·2	0·99	1·2	1·0	1·2	1·0	1·2	1·0	1·3	1·0	1·3	1·1	1·3	1·1	1·3
1·36	·91	1·1	·92	1·1	·93	1·2	·94	1·2	·96	1·2	·98	1·2	0·98	1·2	1·0	1·3	1·0	1·3	1·0	1·3	1·0	1·3	1·1	1·4
1·38	·90	1·1	·91	1·1	·92	1·2	·93	1·2	·95	1·2	·96	1·2	·97	1·3	0·99	1·3	1·0	1·3	1·0	1·3	1·0	1·3	1·0	1·4
1·40	0·89	1·1	0·90	1·2	0·91	1·2	0·92	1·2	0·94	1·2	0·95	1·3	0·96	1·3	0·98	1·3	0·99	1·3	1·0	1·3	1·0	1·4	1·0	1·4
1·42	·88	1·2	·89	1·2	·90	1·2	·91	1·2	·93	1·3	·94	1·3	·95	1·3	·96	1·3	·97	1·3	0·99	1·4	1·0	1·4	1·0	1·4
1·44	·87	1·2	·88	1·2	·89	1·2	·90	1·2	·92	1·3	·93	1·3	·94	1·3	·95	1·3	·96	1·4	·98	1·4	0·99	1·4	1·0	1·4
1·46	·86	1·2	·87	1·2	·88	1·2	·89	1·3	·91	1·3	·92	1·3	·93	1·3	·94	1·4	·95	1·4	·97	1·4	·98	1·4	0·99	1·4
1·48	·86	1·2	·87	1·2	·87	1·3	·88	1·3	·90	1·3	·91	1·3	·92	1·4	·93	1·4	·94	1·4	·96	1·4	·97	1·4	·98	1·5
1·50	0·85	1·2	0·86	1·3	0·87	1·3	0·88	1·3	0·89	1·3	0·90	1·4	0·91	1·4	0·92	1·4	0·93	1·4	0·95	1·4	0·96	1·5	0·97	1·5
1·52	·84	1·3	·85	1·3	·86	1·3	·87	1·3	·88	1·3	·90	1·4	·90	1·4	·91	1·4	·93	1·4	·94	1·5	·95	1·5	·96	1·5
1·54	·84	1·3	·84	1·3	·85	1·3	·86	1·3	·87	1·4	·89	1·4	·90	1·4	·90	1·4	·91	1·5	·93	1·5	·94	1·5	·95	1·5
1·56	·83	1·3	·84	1·3	·85	1·3	·85	1·4	·86	1·4	·88	1·4	·89	1·4	·90	1·5	·91	1·5	·92	1·5	·93	1·5	·94	1·6
1·58	·82	1·3	·83	1·3	·84	1·4	·85	1·4	·85	1·4	·87	1·4	·88	1·5	·89	1·5	·90	1·5	·91	1·5	·92	1·6	·93	1·6
1·60	0·82	1·3	0·82	1·3	0·83	1·4	0·84	1·4	0·85	1·4	0·86	1·5	0·87	1·5	0·88	1·5	0·89	1·5	0·90	1·5	0·91	1·6	0·92	1·6
1·62	·81	1·3	·81	1·4	·82	1·4	·83	1·4	·84	1·4	·85	1·5	·85	1·5	·87	1·5	·88	1·5	·89	1·6	·90	1·6	·91	1·6
1·64	·81	1·4	·81	1·4	·82	1·4	·83	1·4	·84	1·5	·85	1·5	·85	1·5	·86	1·5	·87	1·6	·88	1·6	·89	1·6	·90	1·6
1·66	·80	1·4	·80	1·4	·81	1·4	·82	1·5	·83	1·5	·84	1·5	·85	1·5	·85	1·6	·86	1·6	·87	1·6	·88	1·6	·90	1·7
1·68	·79	1·4	·80	1·4	·80	1·4	·81	1·5	·82	1·5	·83	1·5	·84	1·6	·84	1·6	·85	1·6	·86	1·6	·87	1·7	·89	1·7
1·70	0·79	1·4	0·79	1·4	0·80	1·5	0·81	1·5	0·81	1·5	0·83	1·6	0·83	1·6	0·84	1·6	0·85	1·6	0·86	1·7	0·87	1·7	0·88	1·7
1·72	·78	1·4	·79	1·5	·79	1·5	·80	1·5	·81	1·6	·82	1·6	·83	1·6	·83	1·6	·84	1·7	·85	1·7	·86	1·7	·87	1·7
1·74	·78	1·5	·78	1·5	·79	1·5	·79	1·5	·80	1·6	·81	1·6	·82	1·6	·82	1·7	·83	1·7	·84	1·7	·85	1·7	·86	1·8
1·76	·77	1·5	·77	1·5	·78	1·5	·78	1·6	·79	1·6	·81	1·6	·81	1·7	·82	1·7	·83	1·7	·84	1·7	·85	1·7	·86	1·8
1·78	·76	1·5	·77	1·5	·77	1·5	·78	1·6	·79	1·6	·80	1·7	·81	1·7	·81	1·7	·82	1·7	·83	1·7	·84	1·8	·85	1·8
1·80	0·76	1·5	0·77	1·5	0·77	1·6	0·78	1·6	0·78	1·6	0·79	1·7	0·80	1·7	0·81	1·7	0·81	1·7	0·82	1·8	0·83	1·8	0·84	1·8
1·82	·75	1·5	·76	1·6	·76	1·6	·77	1·6	·78	1·7	·78	1·7	·79	1·7	·79	1·7	·80	1·8	·81	1·8	·82	1·8	·83	1·9
1·84	·75	1·6	·76	1·6	·76	1·6	·77	1·7	·77	1·7	·78	1·7	·79	1·7	·79	1·8	·80	1·8	·81	1·8	·82	1·8	·83	1·9
1·86	·75	1·6	·75	1·6	·75	1·6	·76	1·7	·77	1·7	·78	1·7	·78	1·8	·79	1·8	·79	1·8	·80	1·9	·81	1·9	·82	1·9
1·88	·74	1·6	·74	1·6	·75	1·7	·75	1·7	·76	1·7	·77	1·8	·77	1·8	·78	1·8	·79	1·8	·79	1·9	·80	1·9	·81	1·9
1·90	0·74	1·6	0·74	1·6	0·74	1·7	0·75	1·7	0·76	1·7	0·76	1·8	0·77	1·8	0·78	1·8	0·78	1·8	0·79	1·9	0·80	1·9	0·81	1·9
1·92	·73	1·6	·74	1·7	·74	1·7	·75	1·7	·75	1·8	·76	1·8	·77	1·8	·77	1·8	·78	1·9	·78	1·9	·79	1·9	·80	2·0
1·94	·73	1·7	·73	1·7	·74	1·7	·74	1·7	·75	1·8	·75	1·8	·76	1·8	·76	1·9	·77	1·9	·78	1·9	·79	2·0	·79	2·0
1·96	·73	1·7	·73	1·7	·73	1·7	·74	1·7	·74	1·8	·75	1·8	·75	1·9	·76	1·9	·77	1·9	·78	1·9	·78	2·0	·79	2·0
1·98	·72	1·7	·72	1·7	·73	1·8	·73	1·8	·73	1·8	·74	1·9	·75	1·9	·75	1·9	·76	1·9	·77	2·0	·77	2·0	·78	2·0
2·00	0·72	1·7	0·72	1·7	0·72	1·8	0·73	1·8	0·73	1·8	0·74	1·9	0·74	1·9	0·75	1·9	0·75	2·0	0·76	2·0	0·77	2·0	0·78	2·1
γ →	3·7		3·8		3·9		4·0		4·1		4·2		4·25		4·3		4·35		4·4		4·45		4·5	

Table 46. *Maximum likelihood solution for the logistic (general case): weights w = PQ for argument l*

l	0·00	0·01	0·02	0·03	0·04	0·05	0·06	0·07	0·08	0·09
0·0	0·25000	0·24999	0·24998	0·24994	0·24990	0·24984	0·24978	0·24969	0·24960	0·24949
·1	·24938	·24925	·24910	·24895	·24878	·24860	·24841	·24820	·24799	·24776
·2	·24752	·24726	·24700	·24672	·24643	·24613	·24582	·24550	·24516	·24482
·3	·24446	·24409	·24371	·24332	·24291	·24250	·24207	·24164	·24119	·24073
·4	·24026	·23978	·23929	·23879	·23828	·23776	·23723	·23669	·23613	·23557
0·5	0·23500	0·23442	0·23383	0·23323	0·23263	0·23201	0·23138	0·23075	0·23010	0·22945
·6	·22878	·22811	·22743	·22675	·22605	·22535	·22464	·22392	·22319	·22245
·7	·22171	·22096	·22021	·21944	·21867	·21789	·21711	·21632	·21552	·21472
·8	·21391	·21309	·21227	·21145	·21061	·20977	·20893	·20808	·20723	·20636
·9	·20550	·20463	·20376	·20288	·20200	·20111	·20022	·19932	·19842	·19752
1·0	0·19661	0·19570	0·19479	0·19387	0·19295	0·19203	0·19110	0·19017	0·18924	0·18831
1·1	·18737	·18643	·18549	·18455	·18360	·18265	·18171	·18075	·17980	·17885
1·2	·17790	·17694	·17598	·17502	·17407	·17310	·17214	·17119	·17022	·16926
1·3	·16830	·16734	·16637	·16541	·16445	·16349	·16253	·16157	·16060	·15965
1·4	·15869	·15772	·15677	·15581	·15486	·15390	·15295	·15199	·15105	·15009
1·5	0·14915	0·14820	0·14725	·014631	0·14537	0·14443	0·14350	0·14256	0·14163	0·14069
1·6	·13976	·13884	·13791	·13699	·13607	·13515	·13424	·13332	·13242	·13151
1·7	·13061	·12970	·12881	·12791	·12702	·12613	·12524	·12436	·12348	·12260
1·8	·12173	·12086	·11999	·11913	·11827	·11741	·11656	·11571	·11486	·11402
1·9	·11318	·11234	·11151	·11068	·10986	·10904	·10823	·10741	·10660	·10580
2·0	0·10499	0·10420	0·10340	0·10261	0·10183	0·10104	0·10027	0·09949	0·09873	0·09795
2·1	·09720	·09644	·09568	·09493	·09419	·09345	·09271	·09198	·09125	·09052
2·2	·08980	·08909	·08837	·08766	·08696	·08626	·08556	·08487	·08418	·08350
2·3	·08282	·08215	·08147	·08081	·08014	·07949	·07883	·07817	·07753	·07689
2·4	·07625	·07562	·07499	·07436	·07374	·07313	·07251	·07191	·07130	·07070
2·5	0·07011	0·06951	0·06892	0·06834	0·06776	0·06718	0·06661	0·06604	0·06548	0·06491
2·6	·06436	·06381	·06326	·06271	·06217	·06164	·06111	·06057	·06004	·05953
2·7	·05900	·05850	·05798	·05748	·05697	·05648	·05598	·05549	·05500	·05452
2·8	·05403	·05356	·05309	·05262	·05215	·05169	·05124	·05078	·05033	·04988
2·9	·04943	·04899	·04855	·04812	·04769	·04727	·04684	·04642	·04600	·04559
3·0	0·04518	0·04477	0·04436	0·04397	0·04357	0·04318	0·04278	0·04239	0·04201	0·04163
3·1	·04125	·04088	·04050	·04014	·03977	·03940	·03904	·03869	·03834	·03798
3·2	·03764	·03729	·03694	·03660	·03627	·03594	·03560	·03527	·03495	·03463
3·3	·03430	·03399	·03367	·03337	·03305	·03275	·03244	·03214	·03185	·03155
3·4	·03126	·03096	·03068	·03039	·03010	·02982	·02954	·02927	·02900	·02872
3·5	0·02845	0·02819	0·02792	0·02766	0·02740	0·02714	0·02689	0·02663	0·02638	0·02614
3·6	·02589	·02565	·02540	·02516	·02493	·02469	·02446	·02422	·02399	·02377
3·7	·02355	·02332	·02310	·02288	·02266	·02245	·02223	·02202	·02181	·02161
3·8	·02140	·02120	·02100	·02080	·02060	·02041	·02020	·02001	·01982	·01964
3·9	·01945	·01926	·01908	·01890	·01872	·01853	·01836	·01818	·01800	·01783
4·0	0·01767	0·01749	0·01733	0·01716	0·01699	0·01683	0·01667	0·01651	0·01635	0·01619
4·1	·01603	·01588	·01572	·01558	·01542	·01528	·01513	·01499	·01484	·01470
4·2	·01455	·01442	·01428	·01413	·01400	·01386	·01374	·01360	·01346	·01334
4·3	·01321	·01308	·01296	·01283	·01270	·01258	·01246	·01233	·01222	·01210
4·4	·01198	·01187	·01175	·01163	·01152	·01141	·01130	·01119	·01108	·01098
4·5	0·01087	0·01076	0·01065	0·01056	0·01045	0·01034	0·01024	0·01014	0·01005	0·00995
4·6	·00985	·00975	·00966	·00957	·00947	·00938	·00929	·00920	·00911	·00902
4·7	·00893	·00884	·00876	·00867	·00859	·00851	·00842	·00834	·00826	·00817
4·8	·00809	·00801	·00794	·00786	·00779	·00771	·00763	·00755	·00748	·00741
4·9	·00734	·00727	·00720	·00712	·00705	·00698	·00691	·00685	·00678	·00671

Table 47. *Wilks' likelihood criterion, $W = |\mathbf{A}|/|\mathbf{A}+\mathbf{B}|$. Factors $C(p, \nu_2, M)$ to adjust to $\chi^2_{p\nu_2}$*

α \\ M	0·05	0·01	0·05	0·01	0·05	0·01	0·05	0·01	0·05	0·01
	$p=3,\ \nu_2=2$		$p=3,\ \nu_2=4$		$p=3,\ \nu_2=6$		$p=3,\ \nu_2=8$		$p=3,\ \nu_2=10$	
1	1·295	1·356	1·422	1·514	1·535	1·649	1·632	1·763	1·716	1·862
2	1·109	1·131	1·174	1·207	1·241	1·282	1·302	1·350	1·359	1·413
3	1·058	1·070	1·099	1·116	1·145	1·167	1·190	1·216	1·232	1·262
4	1·036	1·043	1·065	1·076	1·099	1·113	1·133	1·150	1·167	1·187
5	1·025	1·030	1·046	1·054	1·072	1·082	1·100	1·112	1·127	1·141
6	1·018	1·022	1·035	1·040	1·056	1·063	1·078	1·087	1·101	1·112
7	1·014	1·016	1·027	1·031	1·044	1·050	1·063	1·070	1·082	1·091
8	1·011	1·013	1·022	1·025	1·036	1·041	1·052·	1·058	1·068	1·075
9	1·009	1·010	1·018	1·021	1·030	1·034	1·043	1·048	1·058	1·064
10	1·007	1·009	1·015	1·017	1·025	1·028	1·037	1·041	1·050	1·055
12	1·005	1·006	1·011	1·012	1·019	1·021	1·028	1·031	1·038	1·042
15	1·003	1·004	1·008	1·009	1·013	1·014	1·020	1·021	1·027	1·030
20	1·002	1·002	1·004	1·005	1·008	1·009	1·012	1·013	1·017	1·019
30	1·001	1·001	1·002	1·002	1·004	1·004	1·006	1·007	1·009	1·009
60	1·000	1·000	1·001	1·001	1·001	1·001	1·002	1·002	1·002	1·003
∞	1·000	1·000	1·000	1·000	1·000	1·000	1·000	1·000	1·000	1·000
$\chi^2_{p\nu_2}$	12·5916	16·8119	21·0261	26·2170	28·8693	34·8053	36·4150	42·9798	43·7730	50·8922
	$p=3,\ \nu_2=12$		$p=3,\ \nu_2=14$		$p=3,\ \nu_2=16$		$p=3,\ \nu_2=18$		$p=3,\ \nu_2=20$	
1	1·791	1·949	1·857	2·026	1·916	2·095	1·971	2·158	2·021	2·216
2	1·410	1·470	1·458	1·523	1·501	1·571	1·542	1·616	1·580	1·657
3	1·272	1·306	1·309	1·346	1·344	1·384	1·377	1·420	1·408	1·453
4	1·199	1·221	1·229	1·254	1·258	1·285	1·286	1·315	1·313	1·344
5	1·154	1·170	1·179	1·198	1·204	1·224	1·228	1·249	1·251	1·274
6	1·123	1·136	1·145	1·159	1·167	1·182	1·188	1·204	1·208	1·226
7	1·101	1·111	1·121	1·132	1·139	1·152	1·158	1·171	1·176	1·190
8	1·085	1·093	1·102	1·111	1·119	1·129	1·135	1·146	1·151	1·163
9	1·073	1·080	1·088	1·095	1·102	1·111	1·117	1·127	1·132	1·142
10	1·063	1·069	1·076	1·082	1·089	1·097	1·103	1·111	1·116	1·125
12	1·048	1·053	1·059	1·064	1·070	1·076	1·081	1·087	1·092	1·099
15	1·035	1·038	1·043	1·047	1·052	1·056	1·060	1·065	1·069	1·074
20	1·022	1·024	1·028	1·030	1·034	1·036	1·040	1·043	1·046	1·049
30	1·011	1·012	1·015	1·016	1·018	1·019	1·021	1·023	1·025	1·027
60	1·003	1·004	1·004	1·005	1·006	1·006	1·007	1·007	1·008	1·009
∞	1·000	1·000	1·000	1·000	1·000	1·000	1·000	1·000	1·000	1·000
$\chi^2_{p\nu_2}$	50·9985	58·6192	58·1240	66·2062	65·1708	73·6826	72·1532	81·0688	79·0819	88·3794
	$p=3,\ \nu_2=22$		$p=4,\ \nu_2=2$		$p=4,\ \nu_2=4$		$p=4,\ \nu_2=6$		$p=4,\ \nu_2=8$	
1	2·067	2·269	1·407	1·490	1·451	1·550	1·517	1·628	1·583	1·704
2	1·616	1·696	1·161	1·192	1·194	1·229	1·240	1·279	1·286	1·330
3	1·438	1·485	1·089	1·106	1·114	1·132	1·148	1·168	1·183	1·207
4	1·338	1·371	1·057	1·068	1·076	1·088	1·102	1·115	1·130	1·146
5	1·273	1·297	1·040	1·047	1·055	1·063	1·076	1·085	1·099	1·109
6	1·227	1·246	1·030	1·035	1·042	1·048	1·059	1·066	1·078	1·086
7	1·193	1·209	1·023	1·027	1·033	1·037	1·047	1·052	1·063	1·070
8	1·167	1·180	1·018	1·021	1·027	1·030	1·038	1·043	1·052	1·058
9	1·147	1·157	1·015	1·017	1·022	1·025	1·032	1·036	1·044	1·048
10	1·129	1·139	1·012	1·014	1·018	1·021	1·027	1·030	1·038	1·041
12	1·103	1·110	1·009	1·010	1·014	1·015	1·020	1·023	1·029	1·031
15	1·078	1·083	1·006	1·007	1·009	1·010	1·014	1·016	1·020	1·022
20	1·052	1·056	1·003	1·004	1·006	1·006	1·009	1·010	1·013	1·014
30	1·029	1·031	1·002	1·002	1·003	1·003	1·004	1·005	1·006	1·007
60	1·009	1·010	1·000	1·000	1·001	1·001	1·001	1·001	1·002	1·002
∞	1·000	1·000	1·000	1·000	1·000	1·000	1·000	1·000	1·000	1·000
$\chi^2_{p\nu_2}$	85·9649	95·6257	15·5073	20·0902	26·2962	31·9999	36·4150	42·9798	46·1943	53·4858

p = number of variates; ν_2 = hypothesis degrees of freedom; ν_1 = error degrees of freedom; $M = \nu_1 - p + 1$.
Level for $-\{\nu_1 - \tfrac{1}{2}(p - \nu_2 + 1)\}\log W = C(p, \nu_2, M) \times$ level for χ^2 on $p\nu_2$ degrees of freedom.
For the derivation of critical values for $\alpha = 0\cdot10$, $0\cdot025$ and $0\cdot005$, see p. 102.

Table 47 (continued). Wilks' likelihood criterion, $W = |\mathbf{A}|/|\mathbf{A}+\mathbf{B}|$. Factors $C(p, \nu_2, M)$ to adjust to $\chi^2_{p\nu_2}$

M $\backslash$ α	0·05	0·01	0·05	0·01	0·05	0·01	0·05	0·01	0·05	0·01
	$p=4,$	$\nu_2=10$	$p=4,$	$\nu_2=12$	$p=4,$	$\nu_2=14$	$p=4,$	$\nu_2=16$	$p=4,$	$\nu_2=18$
1	1·644	1·774	1·700	1·838	1·751	1·896	1·799	1·949	1·843	1·999
2	1·331	1·379	1·373	1·424	1·413	1·467	1·450	1·507	1·485	1·545
3	1·218	1·244	1·252	1·280	1·284	1·314	1·314	1·347	1·343	1·378
4	1·159	1·176	1·186	1·205	1·213	1·234	1·239	1·261	1·264	1·287
5	1·122	1·134	1·145	1·159	1·168	1·183	1·190	1·207	1·212	1·230
6	1·097	1·107	1·118	1·128	1·137	1·149	1·157	1·169	1·176	1·189
7	1·080	1·088	1·097	1·106	1·115	1·124	1·132	1·142	1·149	1·160
8	1·067	1·073	1·082	1·089	1·097	1·105	1·113	1·121	1·128	1·137
9	1·057	1·062	1·070	1·076	1·084	1·091	1·098	1·105	1·111	1·119
10	1·049	1·054	1·061	1·066	1·073	1·079	1·086	1·092	1·098	1·105
12	1·038	1·041	1·047	1·051	1·058	1·062	1·068	1·073	1·078	1·083
15	1·027	1·029	1·035	1·037	1·042	1·045	1·050	1·053	1·058	1·062
20	1·017	1·019	1·022	1·024	1·027	1·029	1·033	1·035	1·039	1·041
30	1·009	1·009	1·011	1·012	1·014	1·015	1·018	1·019	1·021	1·022
60	1·003	1·003	1·003	1·004	1·004	1·005	1·005	1·006	1·007	1·007
∞	1·000	1·000	1·000	1·000	1·000	1·000	1·000	1·000	1·000	1·000
$\chi^2_{p\nu_2}$	55·7585	63·6907	65·1708	73·6826	74·4683	83·5134	83·6753	93·2168	92·8083	102·816

M	0·05	0·01	0·05	0·01	0·05	0·01	0·05	0·01	0·05	0·01
	$p=4,$	$\nu_2=20$	$p=5,$	$\nu_2=2$	$p=5,$	$\nu_2=4$	$p=5,$	$\nu_2=6$	$p=5,$	$\nu_2=8$
1	1·884	2·045	1·503	1·606	1·483	1·589	1·514	1·625	1·556	1·672
2	1·518	1·580	1·209	1·248	1·216	1·253	1·245	1·284	1·280	1·321
3	1·371	1·408	1·120	1·141	1·130	1·150	1·154	1·175	1·182	1·204
4	1·288	1·313	1·079	1·092	1·089	1·101	1·108	1·121	1·131	1·145
5	1·233	1·252	1·056	1·065	1·065	1·074	1·081	1·090	1·100	1·110
6	1·194	1·208	1·042	1·049	1·050	1·056	1·063	1·070	1·079	1·087
7	1·165	1·177	1·033	1·038	1·040	1·044	1·051	1·056	1·065	1·071
8	1·143	1·153	1·026	1·031	1·032	1·036	1·042	1·046	1·054	1·059
9	1·125	1·133	1·022	1·025	1·027	1·030	1·035	1·039	1·046	1·050
10	1·110	1·118	1·018	1·021	1·023	1·025	1·030	1·033	1·039	1·043
12	1·088	1·094	1·013	1·015	1·017	1·019	1·023	1·025	1·030	1·033
15	1·066	1·071	1·009	1·010	1·011	1·013	1·016	1·017	1·021	1·023
20	1·045	1·047	1·005	1·006	1·007	1·008	1·010	1·011	1·013	1·015
30	1·024	1·026	1·002	1·003	1·003	1·004	1·005	1·005	1·007	1·007
60	1·008	1·008	1·001	1·001	1·001	1·001	1·001	1·001	1·002	1·002
∞	1·000	1·000	1·000	1·000	1·000	1·000	1·000	1·000	1·000	1·000
$\chi^2_{p\nu_2}$	101·879	112·329	18·3070	23·2093	31·4104	37·5662	43·7730	50·8922	55·7585	63·6907

M	0·05	0·01	0·05	0·01	0·05	0·01	0·05	0·01	0·05	0·01
	$p=5,$	$\nu_2=10$	$p=5,$	$\nu_2=12$	$p=5,$	$\nu_2=14$	$p=5,$	$\nu_2=16$	$p=6,$	$\nu_2=2$
1	1·600	1·721	1·643	1·768	1·683	1·813	1·722	1·855	1·587	1·707
2	1·315	1·359	1·350	1·396	1·383	1·431	1·415	1·465	1·254	1·300
3	1·211	1·235	1·240	1·265	1·267	1·294	1·294	1·323	1·150	1·175
4	1·155	1·171	1·179	1·196	1·203	1·221	1·226	1·245	1·100	1·116
5	1·120	1·131	1·141	1·153	1·161	1·174	1·181	1·196	1·072	1·084
6	1·097	1·105	1·114	1·124	1·132	1·143	1·150	1·161	1·055	1·063
7	1·080	1·087	1·095	1·103	1·111	1·119	1·127	1·136	1·043	1·050
8	1·067	1·073	1·081	1·087	1·095	1·102	1·109	1·116	1·035	1·040
9	1·057	1·062	1·070	1·075	1·082	1·088	1·095	1·101	1·029	1·033
10	1·050	1·054	1·061	1·065	1·072	1·077	1·083	1·089	1·024	1·028
12	1·038	1·041	1·047	1·051	1·057	1·060	1·066	1·070	1·018	1·021
15	1·028	1·030	1·034	1·037	1·042	1·044	1·049	1·052	1·012	1·014
20	1·018	1·019	1·022	1·024	1·027	1·029	1·033	1·034	1·007	1·008
30	1·009	1·010	1·012	1·012	1·014	1·015	1·018	1·019	1·003	1·004
60	1·003	1·003	1·004	1·004	1·004	1·005	1·006	1·006	1·001	1·001
∞	1·000	1·000	1·000	1·000	1·000	1·000	1·000	1·000	1·000	1·000
$\chi^2_{p\nu_2}$	67·5048	76·1539	79·0819	88·3794	90·5312	100·425	101·879	112·329	21·0261	26·2170

When both p and ν_2 are odd, obtain C by interpolation between values for ν_2 even. Other gaps may be filled by noting that $C(p, \nu_2, \nu_1-p+1) = C(\nu_2, p, \nu_1-p+1)$. For the derivation of critical values for $\alpha = 0\cdot10$, $0\cdot025$ and $0\cdot005$, see p. 102.

Table 47 (*continued*)

M \ α	0·05	0·01	0·05	0·01	0·05	0·01	0·05	0·01	0·05	0·01
	$p = 6,$	$\nu_2 = 6$	$p = 6,$	$\nu_2 = 8$	$p = 6,$	$\nu_2 = 10$	$p = 6,$	$\nu_2 = 12$	$p = 7,$	$\nu_2 = 2$
1	1·520	1·631	1·543	1·656	1·573	1·687	1·605	1·722	1·662	1·797
2	1·255	1·294	1·279	1·319	1·307	1·348	1·335	1·378	1·297	1·348
3	1·163	1·183	1·184	1·205	1·208	1·230	1·232	1·255	1·178	1·207
4	1·116	1·129	1·134	1·148	1·154	1·169	1·175	1·191	1·121	1·140
5	1·088	1·097	1·103	1·113	1·120	1·131	1·138	1·150	1·089	1·102
6	1·069	1·076	1·082	1·090	1·097	1·106	1·113	1·122	1·068	1·078
7	1·056	1·061	1·068	1·074	1·081	1·087	1·095	1·102	1·054	1·062
8	1·046	1·051	1·057	1·062	1·068	1·074	1·081	1·086	1·044	1·050
9	1·039	1·043	1·048	1·052	1·059	1·063	1·070	1·075	1·036	1·042
10	1·034	1·037	1·042	1·045	1·051	1·055	1·061	1·065	1·031	1·035
12	1·025	1·028	1·032	1·035	1·040	1·042	1·048	1·051	1·023	1·026
15	1·018	1·020	1·023	1·024	1·029	1·030	1·035	1·037	1·016	1·018
20	1·011	1·012	1·014	1·015	1·018	1·019	1·023	1·024	1·010	1·011
30	1·006	1·006	1·007	1·008	1·010	1·010	1·012	1·013	1·005	1·005
60	1·002	1·002	1·002	1·002	1·003	1·003	1·004	1·004	1·001	1·001
∞	1·000	1·000	1·000	1·000	1·000	1·000	1·000	1·000	1·000	1·000
$\chi^2_{p\nu_2}$	50·9985	58·6192	65·1708	73·6826	79·0819	88·3794	92·8083	102·816	23·6848	29·1412
	$p = 7,$	$\nu_2 = 4$	$p = 7,$	$\nu_2 = 6$	$p = 7,$	$\nu_2 = 8$	$p = 7,$	$\nu_2 = 10$	$p = 8,$	$\nu_2 = 2$
1	1·550	1·667	1·530	1·642	1·538	1·648	1·557	1·666	1·729	1·879
2	1·263	1·305	1·266	1·306	1·282	1·321	1·303	1·342	1·336	1·394
3	1·165	1·188	1·173	1·194	1·189	1·210	1·208	1·229	1·206	1·238
4	1·116	1·130	1·124	1·138	1·139	1·152	1·155	1·169	1·142	1·163
5	1·087	1·097	1·095	1·105	1·108	1·117	1·122	1·132	1·105	1·120
6	1·068	1·076	1·075	1·083	1·086	1·094	1·099	1·107	1·081	1·092
7	1·055	1·061	1·062	1·067	1·071	1·077	1·083	1·089	1·065	1·074
8	1·045	1·050	1·051	1·056	1·060	1·065	1·070	1·075	1·053	1·060
9	1·038	1·042	1·043	1·047	1·051	1·055	1·060	1·065	1·044	1·050
10	1·032	1·036	1·037	1·041	1·044	1·048	1·053	1·056	1·038	1·043
12	1·024	1·027	1·029	1·031	1·034	1·037	1·042	1·044	1·028	1·032
15	1·017	1·019	1·020	1·022	1·024	1·025	1·031	1·032	1·019	1·022
20	1·011	1·012	1·013	1·014	1·016	1·017	1·019	1·020	1·012	1·013
30	1·005	1·006	1·006	1·007	1·008	1·009	1·010	1·011	1·006	1·007
60	1·001	1·002	1·002	1·002	1·002	1·003	1·003	1·003	1·001	1·002
∞	1·000	1·000	1·000	1·000	1·000	1·000	1·000	1·000	1·000	1·000
$\chi^2_{p\nu_2}$	41·3371	48·2782	58·1240	66·2062	74·4683	83·5134	90·5312	100·425	26·2962	31·9999
	$p = 8,$	$\nu_2 = 8$	$p = 9,$	$\nu_2 = 2$	$p = 9,$	$\nu_2 = 4$	$p = 9,$	$\nu_2 = 6$	$p = 10,$	$\nu_2 = 2$
1	1·538	1·646	1·791	1·953	1·614	1·740	1·558	1·671	1·847	2·021
2	1·288	1·326	1·373	1·436	1·309	1·355	1·293	1·333	1·408	1·476
3	1·195	1·215	1·232	1·267	1·201	1·226	1·196	1·218	1·257	1·296
4	1·144	1·158	1·162	1·185	1·144	1·161	1·144	1·158	1·182	1·207
5	1·113	1·123	1·121	1·138	1·110	1·122	1·112	1·122	1·137	1·155
6	1·091	1·099	1·094	1·107	1·088	1·096	1·090	1·098	1·107	1·121
7	1·076	1·082	1·076	1·086	1·071	1·078	1·074	1·080	1·087	1·098
8	1·064	1·069	1·062	1·070	1·060	1·065	1·062	1·067	1·072	1·081
9	1·055	1·059	1·052	1·059	1·050	1·055	1·053	1·058	1·061	1·068
10	1·048	1·051	1·045	1·050	1·043	1·047	1·046	1·050	1·052	1·058
12	1·038	1·040	1·034	1·038	1·033	1·036	1·035	1·037	1·039	1·044
15	1·027	1·028	1·023	1·026	1·023	1·026	1·025	1·027	1·028	1·031
20	1·017	1·018	1·014	1·016	1·015	1·016	1·016	1·017	1·017	1·019
30	1·009	1·009	1·007	1·008	1·007	1·008	1·008	1·009	1·009	1·010
60	1·003	1·003	1·002	1·002	1·002	1·002	1·002	1·003	1·002	1·003
∞	1·000	1·000	1·000	1·000	1·000	1·000	1·000	1·000	1·000	1·000
$\chi^2_{p\nu_2}$	83·6753	93·2168	28·8693	34·8053	50·9985	58·6192	72·1532	81·0688	31·4104	37·5662

p = number of variates; ν_2 = hypothesis degrees of freedom; ν_1 = error degrees of freedom; $M = \nu_1 - p + 1$.
Level for $-\{\nu_1 - \frac{1}{2}(p - \nu_2 + 1)\}\log W = C(p, \nu_2, M) \times$ level for χ^2 on $p\nu_2$ degrees of freedom.

Table 48. *Percentage points of the largest characteristic root of the determinantal equation* $|\mathbf{B} - t(\mathbf{A}+\mathbf{B})| = 0$ *(after Pillai et al.)*

Upper 5 per cent points

n \ m	0	1	2	3	4	5	7	10	15
					$p = 2$				
5	0·5646	0·6507	0·7063	0·7459	0·7758	0·7992	0·8337	0·8676	0·9011
10	·3737	·4550	·5143	·5605	·5981	·6293	·6786	·7316	·7889
15	·2780	·3477	·4015	·4455	·4826	·5145	·5670	·6266	·6955
20	·2211	·2809	·3287	·3688	·4034	·4339	·4855	·5462	·6198
25	·1835	·2355	·2780	·3143	·3463	·3748	·4239	·4835	·5580
30	0·1568	0·2027	0·2408	0·2738	0·3031	0·3296	0·3760	0·4333	0·5071
35	·1369	·1780	·2124	·2425	·2696	·2942	·3377	·3924	·4644
40	·1214	·1585	·1898	·2175	·2425	·2655	·3064	·3585	·4282
45	·1093	·1431	·1718	·1974	·2206	·2420	·2805	·3300	·3973
50	·0993	·1304	·1569	·1807	·2023	·2224	·2586	·3057	·3704
48	0·1031	0·1352	0·1626	0·1870	0·2093	0·2299	0·2670	0·3150	0·3807
60	·0836	·1103	·1333	·1540	·1731	·1909	·2233	·2661	·3260
80	·0638	·0846	·1027	·1192	·1346	·1490	·1756	·2114	·2630
120	·0433	·0577	·0704	·0821	·0931	·1035	·1230	·1498	·1896
240	·0220	·0295	·0362	·0424	·0483	·0540	·0647	·0798	·1030
∞	·0000	·0000	·0000	·0000	·0000	·0000	·0000	·0000	·0000
					$p = 3$				
5	0·6689	0·7292	0·7698	0·7994	0·8221	0·8400	0·8668	0·8933	0·9199
10	·4718	·5373	·5862	·6249	·6564	·6828	·7246	·7696	·8185
15	·3620	·4219	·4690	·5079	·5407	·5691	·6157	·6687	·7298
20	·2931	·3465	·3898	·4265	·4582	·4861	·5334	·5889	·6559
25	·2461	·2937	·3332	·3671	·3970	·4237	·4697	·5252	·5944
30	0·2120	0·2548	0·2907	0·3221	0·3500	0·3752	0·4192	0·4734	0·5429
35	·1863	·2250	·2579	·2869	·3129	·3366	·3784	·4308	·4993
40	·1660	·2013	·2316	·2584	·2828	·3050	·3447	·3950	·4620
45	·1499	·1823	·2103	·2353	·2581	·2790	·3165	·3647	·4298
50	·1367	·1666	·1926	·2160	·2373	·2570	·2926	·3387	·4017
48	0·1417	0·1726	0·1994	0·2234	0·2452	0·2654	0·3018	0·3486	0·4125
60	·1157	·1417	·1644	·1850	·2040	·2217	·2538	·2961	·3550
80	·0888	·1093	·1274	·1441	·1595	·1740	·2008	·2366	·2880
120	·0606	·0750	·0879	·0999	·1111	·1217	·1415	·1687	·2089
240	·0310	·0386	·0455	·0519	·0580	·0639	·0750	·0905	·1143
∞	·0000	·0000	·0000	·0000	·0000	·0000	·0000	·0000	·0000
					$p = 4$				
5	0·7387	0·7825	0·8131	0·8360	0·8537	0·8679	0·8892	0·9108	0·9326
10	·5472	·6004	·6412	·6737	·7004	·7229	·7588	·7976	·8401
15	·4307	·4822	·5235	·5578	·5869	·6121	·6538	·7012	·7561
20	·3543	·4017	·4409	·4742	·5031	·5286	·5719	·6228	·6843
25	·3006	·3439	·3802	·4117	·4395	·4644	·5072	·5590	·6235
30	0·2609	0·3004	0·3341	0·3636	0·3899	0·4137	0·4552	0·5064	0·5720
35	·2306	·2667	·2978	·3254	·3502	·3728	·4127	·4626	·5279
40	·2063	·2396	·2685	·2943	·3177	·3391	·3773	·4256	·4899
45	·1870	·2178	·2447	·2688	·2908	·3111	·3475	·3941	·4569
50	·1709	·1995	·2247	·2473	·2681	·2873	·3220	·3668	·4279
48	0·1770	0·2065	0·2323	0·2555	0·2768	0·2964	0·3317	0·3772	0·4391
60	1454	·1704	·1927	·2129	·2315	·2488	·2805	·3219	·3796
80	·1122	·1322	·1501	·1666	·1820	·1964	·2230	·2586	·3094
120	·0770	·0913	·1042	·1162	·1274	·1381	·1581	·1854	·2257
240	·0397	·0473	·0542	·0608	·0670	·0730	·0843	·1002	·1243
∞	·0000	·0000	·0000	·0000	·0000	·0000	·0000	·0000	·0000

p = number of variates; $m = \frac{1}{2}(|\nu_2 - p| - 1)$; $n = \frac{1}{2}(\nu_1 - p - 1)$, where ν_1 and ν_2 are error and hypothesis degrees of freedom, respectively.

Table 48 (*continued*)

Upper 1 per cent points

n \ m	0	1	2	3	4	5	7	10	15
					p = 2				
5	0·6770	0·7446	0·7872	0·8171	0·8394	0·8568	0·8820	0·9066	0·9306
10	·4701	·5443	·5971	·6377	·6703	·6971	·7391	·7834	·8309
15	·3573	·4247	·4757	·5168	·5511	·5803	·6279	·6812	·7418
20	·2875	·3473	·3941	·4329	·4661	·4951	·5435	·5998	·6670
25	·2404	·2935	·3360	·3719	·4032	·4309	·4782	·5347	·6045
30	0·2065	0·2540	0·2926	0·3258	0·3550	0·3812	0·4265	0·4819	0·5521
35	·1811	·2239	·2592	·2898	·3171	·3417	·3847	·4383	·5077
40	·1610	·2000	·2325	·2608	·2863	·3094	·3503	·4017	·4697
45	·1452	·1810	·2110	·2373	·2611	·2828	·3215	·3708	·4369
50	·1322	·1652	·1931	·2177	·2399	·2604	·2971	·3443	·4083
48	0·1372	0·1712	0·1999	0·2251	0·2480	0·2689	0·3064	0·3544	0·4193
60	·1117	·1403	·1646	·1863	·2061	·2244	·2576	·3008	·3607
80	·0855	·1080	·1273	·1448	·1609	·1759	·2035	·2402	·2925
120	·0582	·0740	·0877	·1002	·1118	·1228	·1433	·1711	·2120
240	·0297	·0380	·0453	·0520	·0583	·0644	·0758	·0917	·1160
∞	·0000	·0000	·0000	·0000	·0000	·0000	·0000	·0000	·0000
					p = 3				
5	0·7582	0·8040	0·8344	0·8564	0·8730	0·8862	0·9056	0·9247	0·9437
10	·5586	·6164	·6590	·6923	·7192	·7416	·7767	·8141	·8544
15	·4375	·4937	·5374	·5730	·6029	·6285	·6703	·7172	·7708
20	·3586	·4104	·4519	·4867	·5166	·5428	·5866	·6376	·6985
25	·3034	·3506	·3893	·4223	·4511	·4767	·5203	·5726	·6370
30	0·2629	0·3058	0·3416	0·3726	0·3999	0·4245	0·4670	0·5189	0·5846
35	·2319	·2712	·3043	·3332	·3591	·3824	·4233	·4741	·5397
40	·2073	·2434	·2742	·3012	·3256	·3477	·3869	·4361	·5010
45	·1876	·2211	·2497	·2750	·2979	·3189	·3563	·4038	·4673
50	·1714	·2024	·2291	·2529	·2746	·2944	·3301	·3758	·4378
48	0·1776	0·2095	0·2369	0·2613	0·2835	0·3038	0·3401	0·3865	0·4491
60	·1456	·1727	·1963	·2175	·2369	·2549	·2874	·3298	·3883
80	·1121	·1338	·1528	·1701	·1861	·2010	·2284	·2648	·3166
120	·0769	·0922	·1059	·1185	·1302	·1413	·1619	·1899	·2309
240	·0395	·0477	·0551	·0619	·0684	·0746	·0863	·1025	·1272
∞	·0000	·0000	·0000	·0000	·0000	·0000	·0000	·0000	·0000
					p = 4				
5	0·8110	0·8436	0·8662	0·8830	0·8959	0·9062	0·9216	0·9370	0·9526
10	·6247	·6708	·7057	·7334	·7560	·7748	·8047	·8369	·8717
15	·5016	·5490	·5867	·6177	·6439	·6664	·7034	·7452	·7930
20	·4175	·4627	·4997	·5309	·5579	·5815	·6213	·6678	·7233
25	·3570	·3992	·4343	·4645	·4910	·5146	·5550	·6033	·6631
30	0·3117	0·3507	0·3837	0·4125	0·4380	0·4609	0·5007	0·5494	0·6111
35	·2765	·3126	·3435	·3707	·3951	·4171	·4558	·5039	·5661
40	·2483	·2819	·3108	·3365	·3596	·3807	·4181	·4651	·5270
45	·2255	·2568	·2839	·3081	·3301	·3502	·3861	·4318	·4928
50	·2066	·2358	·2612	·2841	·3049	·3241	·3586	·4028	·4626
48	0·2138	0·2438	0·2699	0·2933	0·3145	0·3341	0·3691	0·4139	0·4742
60	·1763	·2021	·2249	·2454	·2643	·2818	·3135	·3548	·4118
80	·1367	·1575	·1760	·1930	·2087	·2234	·2505	·2864	·3373
120	·0943	·1092	·1227	·1352	·1469	·1579	·1785	·2065	·2474
240	·0488	·0568	·0642	·0711	·0777	·0839	·0957	·1122	·1371
∞	·0000	·0000	·0000	·0000	·0000	·0000	·0000	·0000	·0000

For $n > 50$, $240/n$ may be used as argument in harmonic interpolation.

Upper 5 per cent points (continued)

n \ m	0	1	2	3	4	5	7	10	15
					$p = 5$				
5	0·7882	0·8210	0·8447	0·8627	0·8768	0·8883	0·9058	0·9236	0·9419
10	·6069	·6507	·6849	·7125	·7354	·7547	·7858	·8197	·8570
15	·4883	·5328	·5690	·5993	·6252	·6477	·6850	·7277	·7773
20	·4072	·4495	·4847	·5150	·5414	·5647	·6043	·6511	·7077
25	·3488	·3881	·4215	·4507	·4764	·4995	·5394	·5877	·6480
30	0·3049	0·3413	0·3726	0·4003	0·4250	0·4474	0·4865	0·5349	0·5967
35	·2708	·3045	·3338	·3599	·3834	·4049	·4428	·4904	·5525
40	·2434	·2746	·3021	·3267	·3490	·3696	·4061	·4525	·5141
45	·2212	·2503	·2761	·2992	·3204	·3400	·3750	·4200	·4806
50	·2027	·2299	·2541	·2760	·2961	·3147	·3483	·3918	·4510
48	0·2097	0·2377	0·2625	0·2849	0·3054	0·3244	0·3585	0·4026	0·4624
60	·1732	·1973	·2188	·2385	·2567	·2736	·3045	·3450	·4013
80	·1344	·1539	·1714	·1877	·2028	·2171	·2433	·2785	·3286
120	·0928	·1068	·1196	·1316	·1428	·1535	·1735	·2008	·2409
240	·0481	·0557	·0627	·0693	·0756	·0816	·0931	·1091	·1335
∞	·0000	·0000	·0000	·0000	·0000	·0000	·0000	·0000	·0000
					$p = 6$				
5	0·8247	0·8499	0·8686	0·8830	0·8945	0·9039	0·9185	0·9335	0·9491
10	·6552	·6917	·7206	·7442	·7640	·7808	·8079	·8377	·8708
15	·5372	·5759	·6077	·6346	·6577	·6779	·7115	·7500	·7951
20	·4535	·4913	·5231	·5506	·5747	·5960	·6324	·6754	·7278
25	·3919	·4276	·4583	·4852	·5091	·5306	·5677	·6128	·6692
30	0·3447	0·3782	0·4074	0·4333	0·4565	0·4775	0·5144	0·5600	0·6184
35	·3076	·3390	·3665	·3912	·4135	·4338	·4699	·5151	·5743
40	·2775	·3069	·3329	·3563	·3777	·3973	·4322	·4767	·5357
45	·2530	·2806	·3051	·3273	·3476	·3664	·4001	·4434	·5017
50	·2324	·2583	·2815	·3025	·3219	·3399	·3724	·4144	·4717
48	0·2403	0·2668	0·2905	0·3120	0·3317	0·3500	0·3830	0·4256	0·4833
60	·1995	·2226	·2434	·2624	·2801	·2966	·3267	·3662	·4210
80	·1556	·1745	·1916	·2075	·2224	·2364	·2623	·2969	·3462
120	·1081	·1218	·1344	·1463	·1574	·1681	·1880	·2151	·2551
240	·0563	·0638	·0708	·0775	·0838	·0899	·1014	·1176	·1422
∞	·0000	·0000	·0000	·0000	·0000	·0000	·0000	·0000	·0000
					$p = 7$				
5	0·8523	0·8722	0·8872	0·8990	0·9085	0·9163	0·9286	0·9413	0·9548
10	·6950	·7257	·7503	·7707	·7878	·8025	·8263	·8527	·8823
15	·5792	·6130	·6412	·6651	·6858	·7039	·7342	·7692	·8104
20	·4944	·5282	·5570	·5820	·6040	·6236	·6570	·6968	·7453
25	·4305	·4631	·4914	·5162	·5384	·5583	·5930	·6351	·6879
30	0·3809	0·4119	0·4390	0·4632	0·4850	0·5048	0·5395	0·5825	0·6378
35	·3415	·3707	·3965	·4198	·4409	·4603	·4944	·5374	·5939
40	·3093	·3369	·3615	·3837	·4040	·4227	·4561	·4986	·5552
45	·2828	·3088	·3322	·3533	·3728	·3908	·4232	·4648	·5210
50	·2604	·2850	·3072	·3273	·3459	·3632	·3946	·4352	·4907
48	0·2690	0·2941	0·3167	0·3373	0·3562	0·3738	0·4056	0·4466	0·5024
60	·2244	·2465	·2665	·2850	·3021	·3181	·3474	·3858	·4392
80	·1759	·1942	·2109	·2264	·2410	·2547	·2801	·3141	·3626
120	·1229	·1363	·1487	·1605	·1715	·1820	·2018	·2287	·2684
240	·0644	·0718	·0788	·0854	·0918	·0979	·1095	·1257	·1504
∞	·0000	·0000	·0000	·0000	·0000	·0000	·0000	·0000	·0000

p = number of variates; $m = \frac{1}{2}(|\nu_2 - p| - 1)$; $n = \frac{1}{2}(\nu_1 - p - 1)$, where ν_1 and ν_2 are error and hypothesis degrees of freedom, respectively.

Table 48 (*continued*)

Upper 1 per cent points

n＼m	0	1	2	3	4	5	7	10	15
					$p = 5$				
5	0·8477	0·8719	0·8892	0·9023	0·9125	0·9208	0·9334	0·9461	0·9591
10	·6762	·7136	·7425	·7658	·7850	·8011	·8268	·8548	·8853
15	·5544	·5948	·6274	·6546	·6777	·6977	·7306	·7680	·8111
20	·4677	·5074	·5404	·5684	·5928	·6143	·6505	·6930	·7440
25	·4038	·4415	·4735	·5011	·5255	·5473	·5846	·6295	·6851
30	0·3549	0·3904	0·4208	0·4475	0·4713	0·4927	0·5301	0·5757	0·6337
35	·3165	·3498	·3786	·4041	·4270	·4478	·4844	·5299	·5889
40	·2854	·3166	·3438	·3681	·3900	·4101	·4457	·4906	·5497
45	·2601	·2893	·3150	·3380	·3590	·3783	·4127	·4565	·5151
50	·2388	·2663	·2906	·3124	·3324	·3509	·3841	·4267	·4844
48	0·2469	0·2751	0·2999	0·3222	0·3426	0·3614	0·3950	0·4382	0·4962
60	·2048	·2293	·2512	·2710	·2893	·3063	·3371	·3772	·4326
80	·1596	·1796	·1977	·2142	·2296	·2441	·2706	·3059	·3559
120	·1108	·1253	·1386	·1509	·1625	·1735	·1940	·2217	·2624
240	·0577	·0656	·0730	·0799	·0865	·0927	·1047	·1212	·1464
∞	·0000	·0000	·0000	·0000	·0000	·0000	·0000	·0000	·0000
					$p = 6$				
5	0·8745	0·8929	0·9065	0·9169	0·9252	0·9320	0·9424	0·9531	0·9642
10	·7173	·7482	·7724	·7922	·8086	·8225	·8449	·8694	·8964
15	·5986	·6334	·6619	·6858	·7063	·7240	·7535	·7872	·8262
20	·5111	·5462	·5757	·6010	·6231	·6426	·6757	·7147	·7616
25	·4450	·4790	·5081	·5335	·5559	·5760	·6106	·6524	·7042
30	0·3936	0·4261	0·4542	0·4789	0·5011	0·5211	0·5561	0·5990	0·6536
35	·3527	·3835	·4103	·4342	·4557	·4754	·5100	·5531	·6090
40	·3194	·3484	·3740	·3969	·4177	·4367	·4706	·5134	·5698
45	·2919	·3193	·3436	·3655	·3854	·4038	·4368	·4788	·5350
50	·2687	·2946	·3177	·3386	·3577	·3755	·4074	·4485	·5041
48	0·2775	0·3040	0·3276	0·3488	0·3683	0·3863	0·4187	0·4602	0·5160
60	·2315	·2548	·2757	·2948	·3125	·3289	·3588	·3977	·4515
80	·1814	·2006	·2181	·2342	·2493	·2634	·2894	·3240	·3730
120	·1266	·1407	·1538	·1659	·1774	·1882	·2085	·2360	·2763
240	·0663	·0741	·0814	·0883	·0949	·1012	·1132	·1298	·1550
∞	·0000	·0000	·0000	·0000	·0000	·0000	·0000	·0000	·0000
					$p = 7$				
5	0·8947	0·9091	0·9199	0·9284	0·9352	0·9408	0·9496	0·9587	0·9682
10	·7508	·7766	·7971	·8140	·8282	·8403	·8599	·8815	·9056
15	·6363	·6665	·6914	·7126	·7308	·7467	·7732	·8037	·8392
20	·5490	·5803	·6068	·6297	·6497	·6675	·6978	·7336	·7770
25	·4817	·5125	·5391	·5624	·5831	·6016	·6338	·6726	·7210
30	0·4286	0·4583	0·4843	0·5073	0·5280	0·5467	0·5795	0·6198	0·6713
35	·3858	·4142	·4393	·4617	·4820	·5005	·5332	·5740	·6272
40	·3506	·3777	·4017	·4233	·4431	·4612	·4934	·5342	·5881
45	·3213	·3471	·3700	·3908	·4099	·4275	·4590	·4993	·5532
50	·2965	·3210	·3429	·3629	·3812	·3982	·4289	·4685	·5221
48	0·3060	0·3309	0·3533	0·3736	0·3922	0·4094	0·4405	0·4803	0·5341
60	·2565	·2787	·2987	·3171	·3341	·3500	·3789	·4167	·4689
80	·2020	·2205	·2375	·2532	·2678	·2816	·3070	·3409	·3889
120	·1418	·1556	·1683	·1803	·1916	·2023	·2223	·2496	·2894
240	·0747	·0824	·0897	·0966	·1031	·1094	·1214	·1380	·1633
∞	·0000	·0000	·0000	·0000	·0000	·0000	·0000	·0000	·0000

For $n > 50$, $240/n$ may be used as argument in harmonic interpolation.

Upper 5 per cent points

n \ m	0	1	2	3	4	5	7	10	15
					p = 8				
5	0·8739	0·8898	0·9020	0·9118	0·9197	0·9263	0·9367	0·9478	0·9595
10	·7281	·7542	·7754	·7931	·8080	·8209	·8419	·8655	·8921
15	·6156	·6453	·6703	·6917	·7103	·7266	·7541	·7859	·8236
20	·5307	·5611	·5872	·6100	·6302	·6481	·6789	·7157	·7607
25	·4655	·4953	·5213	·5443	·5648	·5834	·6157	·6551	·7047
30	0·4141	0·4428	0·4680	0·4906	0·5110	0·5296	0·5623	0·6029	0·6552
35	·3728	·4001	·4243	·4462	·4662	·4845	·5170	·5578	·6115
40	·3388	·3648	·3880	·4091	·4284	·4463	·4782	·5188	·5730
45	·3106	·3352	·3574	·3776	·3962	·4136	·4447	·4846	·5387
50	·2867	·3101	·3312	·3506	·3685	·3852	·4154	·4546	·5081
48	0·2958	0·3197	0·3412	0·3609	0·3791	0·3961	0·4267	0·4662	0·5200
60	·2480	·2692	·2885	·3063	·3229	·3384	·3668	·4041	·4560
80	·1954	·2131	·2293	·2445	·2587	·2722	·2971	·3304	·3779
120	·1372	·1503	·1626	·1741	·1850	·1954	·2149	·2417	·2810
240	·0723	·0797	·0866	·0932	·0996	·1057	·1173	·1335	·1583
∞	·0000	·0000	·0000	·0000	·0000	·0000	·0000	·0000	·0000
					p = 9				
5	0·8910	0·9039	0·9141	0·9222	0·9289	0·9346	0·9435	0·9531	0·9635
10	·7560	·7784	·7968	·8122	·8253	·8367	·8554	·8765	·9006
15	·6473	·6736	·6959	·7151	·7318	·7466	·7716	·8007	·8353
20	·5631	·5906	·6143	·6351	·6536	·6701	·6985	·7326	·7745
25	·4972	·5245	·5485	·5697	·5888	·6061	·6363	·6732	·7198
30	0·4446	0·4712	0·4947	0·5158	0·5350	0·5524	0·5832	0·6216	0·6711
35	·4018	·4274	·4502	·4709	·4897	·5070	·5378	·5767	·6278
40	·3664	·3908	·4128	·4329	·4512	·4682	·4987	·5376	·5894
45	·3367	·3600	·3811	·4005	·4182	·4348	·4647	·5032	·5551
50	·3115	·3336	·3539	·3725	·3896	·4057	·4349	·4727	·5244
48	0·3211	0·3437	0·3643	0·3833	0·4006	0·4169	0·4464	0·4845	0·5362
60	·2704	·2907	·3093	·3265	·3426	·3576	·3852	·4214	·4718
80	·2141	·2312	·2470	·2618	·2757	·2888	·3132	·3458	·3924
120	·1511	·1639	·1760	·1873	·1981	·2083	·2277	·2542	·2931
240	·0801	·0874	·0943	·1009	·1072	·1133	·1249	·1412	·1660
∞	·0000	·0000	·0000	·0000	·0000	·0000	·0000	·0000	·0000
					p = 10				
5	0·9049	0·9155	0·9240	0·9309	0·9366	0·9414	0·9492	0·9576	0·9672
10	·7798	·7991	·8151	·8287	·8403	·8504	·8671	·8861	·9079
15	·6752	·6986	·7185	·7358	·7510	·7644	·7871	·8138	·8457
20	·5922	·6171	·6387	·6578	·6747	·6900	·7162	·7479	·7870
25	·5261	·5512	·5733	·5930	·6108	·6269	·6551	·6897	·7336
30	0·4726	0·4973	0·5193	0·5391	0·5570	0·5734	0·6025	0·6388	0·6857
35	·4287	·4527	·4742	·4937	·5114	·5278	·5571	·5942	·6429
40	·3922	·4152	·4360	·4550	·4725	·4887	·5178	·5550	·6047
45	·3614	·3834	·4035	·4218	·4389	·4548	·4834	·5204	·5704
50	·3350	·3561	·3753	·3931	·4097	·4252	·4532	·4897	·5396
48	0·3451	0·3665	0·3861	0·4041	0·4209	0·4366	0·4648	0·5015	0·5516
60	·2918	·3113	·3292	·3458	·3613	·3758	·4025	·4377	·4867
80	·2321	·2487	·2640	·2784	·2920	·3048	·3286	·3605	·4062
120	·1646	·1772	·1890	·2002	·2108	·2209	·2400	·2662	·3045
240	·0878	·0950	·1019	·1084	·1147	·1208	·1323	·1486	·1734
∞	·0000	·0000	·0000	·0000	·0000	·0000	·0000	·0000	·0000

p = number of variates; $m = \frac{1}{2}(|\nu_2-p|-1)$; $n = \frac{1}{2}(\nu_1-p-1)$, where ν_1 and ν_2 are error and hypothesis degrees of freedom, respectively.

Table 48 (*continued*)

Upper 1 per cent points

n \ m	0	1	2	3	4	5	7	10	15
					p = 8				
5	0·9103	0·9218	0·9305	0·9375	0·9432	0·9480	0·9554	0·9632	0·9715
10	·7785	·8003	·8179	·8325	·8448	·8554	·8727	·8919	·9135
15	·6687	·6950	·7171	·7359	·7522	·7665	·7904	·8180	·8505
20	·5825	·6104	·6343	·6550	·6733	·6896	·7174	·7504	·7907
25	·5147	·5427	·5670	·5884	·6075	·6247	·6546	·6908	·7361
30	0·4604	0·4877	0·5118	0·5332	0·5524	0·5700	0·6007	0·6387	0·6873
35	·4162	·4425	·4659	·4870	·5060	·5235	·5544	·5932	·6436
40	·3795	·4048	·4274	·4479	·4665	·4837	·5144	·5533	·6047
45	·3488	·3730	·3947	·4145	·4326	·4494	·4795	·5181	·5699
50	·3226	·3457	·3665	·3856	·4032	·4195	·4489	·4870	·5387
48	0·3326	0·3561	0·3773	0·3967	0·4145	0·4310	0·4607	0·4990	0·5508
60	·2801	·3012	·3205	·3381	·3546	·3699	·3979	·4345	·4851
80	·2217	·2396	·2560	·2712	·2855	·2989	·3237	·3569	·4039
120	·1564	·1699	·1824	·1941	·2052	·2158	·2355	·2625	·3019
240	·0829	·0906	·0977	·1046	·1111	·1174	·1293	·1459	·1712
∞	·0000	·0000	·0000	·0000	·0000	·0000	·0000	·0000	·0000
					p = 9				
5	0·9226	0·9319	0·9392	0·9450	0·9498	0·9538	0·9602	0·9670	0·9743
10	·8018	·8203	·8355	·8482	·8590	·8683	·8836	·9008	·9203
15	·6968	·7199	·7395	·7563	·7709	·7838	·8055	·8307	·8605
20	·6122	·6373	·6589	·6777	·6944	·7094	·7349	·7655	·8028
25	·5444	·5699	·5922	·6120	·6296	·6456	·6734	·7072	·7498
30	0·4894	0·5146	0·5369	0·5568	0·5749	0·5913	0·6201	0·6559	0·7018
35	·4441	·4687	·4906	·5103	·5283	·5447	·5740	·6107	·6587
40	·4063	·4300	·4513	·4706	·4883	·5046	·5338	·5709	·6201
45	·3744	·3972	·4178	·4365	·4538	·4698	·4987	·5357	·5854
50	·3471	·3689	·3887	·4069	·4237	·4394	·4677	·5043	·5541
48	0·3575	0·3797	0·3999	0·4183	0·4353	0·4511	0·4796	0·5164	0·5662
60	·3025	·3226	·3410	·3580	·3739	·3887	·4157	·4511	·5002
80	·2406	·2578	·2736	·2884	·3023	·3154	·3396	·3720	·4180
120	·1706	·1837	·1959	·2075	·2184	·2288	·2482	·2748	·3138
240	·0910	·0985	·1056	·1124	·1189	·1251	·1370	·1536	·1789
∞	·0000	·0000	·0000	·0000	·0000	·0000	·0000	·0000	·0000
					p = 10				
5	0·9326	0·9402	0·9462	0·9512	0·9552	0·9587	0·9642	0·9702	0·9768
10	·8215	·8374	·8506	·8617	·8712	·8795	·8931	·9085	·9262
15	·7213	·7418	·7593	·7743	·7875	·7992	·8189	·8419	·8693
20	·6387	·6613	·6809	·6981	·7134	·7271	·7507	·7790	·8138
25	·5714	·5947	·6152	·6334	·6498	·6646	·6905	·7222	·7622
30	0·5160	0·5393	0·5600	0·5786	0·5955	0·6108	0·6380	0·6717	0·7152
35	·4700	·4929	·5134	·5319	·5489	·5644	·5921	·6270	·6727
40	·4313	·4536	·4736	·4919	·5087	·5242	·5519	·5873	·6344
45	·3984	·4199	·4394	·4573	·4737	·4890	·5166	·5520	·5998
50	·3701	·3908	·4097	·4270	·4431	·4581	·4853	·5205	·5685
48	0·3809	0·4020	0·4211	0·4387	0·4549	0·4700	0·4974	0·5327	0·5807
60	·3237	·3429	·3606	·3769	·3922	·4064	·4326	·4669	·5144
80	·2587	·2752	·2906	·3049	·3184	·3312	·3548	·3864	·4313
120	·1844	·1971	·2091	·2204	·2311	·2413	·2605	·2867	·3251
240	·0989	·1063	·1133	·1200	·1265	·1327	·1446	·1611	·1863
∞	·0000	·0000	·0000	·0000	·0000	·0000	·0000	·0000	·0000

For $n > 50$, $240/n$ may be used as argument in harmonic interpolation.

Table 49. *Percentage points of the largest characteristic root of the determinantal equation* $|\mathbf{B}-t(\mathbf{A}+\mathbf{B})| = 0$ *(after Foster & Rees)*

Case $p = 2$

ν_1	P	ν_2 = 2	3	5	7	9	11	13	15	17	19	21
5	0·80	0·7011	0·7728	0·8454	0·8825	0·9052	0·9205	0·9315	0·9398	0·9464	0·9516	0·9559
	·85	·7449	·8075	·8696	·9013	·9205	·9334	·9427	·9497	·9552	·9596	·9632
	·90	·7950	·8463	·8968	·9221	·9374	·9476	·9550	·9605	·9649	·9683	·9712
	·95	·8577	·8943	·9296	·9471	·9576	·9645	·9696	·9733	·9763	·9787	·9806
	·99	·9377	·9542	·9698	·9774	·9819	·9850	·9872	·9888	·9900	·9910	·9918
7	0·80	0·5638	0·6469	0·7416	0·7954	0·8303	0·8550	0·8734	0·8876	0·8989	0·9082	0·9158
	·85	·6085	·6851	·7712	·8194	·8507	·8726	·8889	·9014	·9114	·9196	·9264
	·90	·6628	·7307	·8058	·8474	·8741	·8928	·9066	·9173	·9257	·9326	·9383
	·95	·7370	·7919	·8514	·8839	·9045	·9189	·9295	·9376	·9440	·9493	·9536
	·99	·8498	·8826	·9173	·9358	·9475	·9556	·9615	·9660	·9695	·9724	·9748
9	0·80	0·4688	0·5526	0·6558	0·7189	0·7619	0·7933	0·8173	0·8363	0·8517	0·8644	0·8751
	·85	·5108	·5903	·6869	·7452	·7848	·8136	·8354	·8527	·8666	·8782	·8878
	·90	·5632	·6366	·7244	·7768	·8120	·8374	·8567	·8720	·8842	·8943	·9027
	·95	·6383	·7017	·7761	·8197	·8487	·8696	·8853	·8976	·9076	·9157	·9225
	·99	·7635	·8074	·8575	·8862	·9051	·9185	·9286	·9364	·9427	·9478	·9521
11	0·80	0·4003	0·4810	0·5859	0·6536	0·7016	0·7376	0·7657	0·7884	0·8069	0·8225	0·8357
	·85	·4389	·5169	·6169	·6808	·7257	·7592	·7854	·8063	·8235	·8378	·8500
	·90	·4880	·5617	·6551	·7138	·7548	·7854	·8089	·8278	·8433	·8561	·8670
	·95	·5603	·6267	·7091	·7600	·7952	·8212	·8413	·8573	·8702	·8810	·8902
	·99	·6878	·7381	·7989	·8357	·8607	·8790	·8929	·9039	·9128	·9202	·9265
13	0·80	0·3490	0·4253	0·5286	0·5982	0·6489	0·6880	0·7190	0·7443	0·7654	0·7832	0·7984
	·85	·3843	·4590	·5589	·6252	·6735	·7103	·7395	·7632	·7829	·7996	·8138
	·90	·4298	·5016	·5965	·6587	·7035	·7375	·7644	·7862	·8042	·8194	·8324
	·95	·4981	·5646	·6507	·7063	·7459	·7757	·7992	·8181	·8337	·8468	·8580
	·99	·6233	·6770	·7446	·7872	·8171	·8394	·8568	·8706	·8821	·8915	·8997
15	0·80	0·3091	0·3809	0·4812	0·5508	0·6030	0·6439	0·6769	0·7042	0·7271	0·7467	0·7636
	·85	·3415	·4124	·5102	·5775	·6275	·6664	·6978	·7236	·7453	·7638	·7798
	·90	·3837	·4527	·5468	·6106	·6577	·6942	·7235	·7475	·7675	·7847	·7993
	·95	·4478	·5130	·6003	·6584	·7011	·7338	·7598	·7810	·7989	·8138	·8268
	·99	·5687	·6237	·6954	·7422	·7758	·8013	·8216	·8378	·8512	·8629	·8726
17	0·80	0·2774	0·3447	0·4412	0·5101	0·5628	0·6047	0·6389	0·6676	0·6919	0·7129	0·7312
	·85	·3072	·3741	·4690	·5360	·5869	·6272	·6600	·6874	·7105	·7304	·7478
	·90	·3463	·4122	·5043	·5685	·6169	·6550	·6860	·7116	·7334	·7519	·7681
	·95	·4065	·4697	·5564	·6160	·6605	·6951	·7232	·7464	·7659	·7825	·7969
	·99	·5222	·5773	·6512	·7008	·7373	·7652	·7875	·8061	·8212	·8346	·8458
19	0·80	0·2515	0·3148	0·4073	0·4748	0·5273	0·5697	0·6047	0·6344	0·6597	0·6817	0·7010
	·85	·2791	·3424	·4338	·4999	·5509	·5919	·6257	·6541	·6785	·6995	·7179
	·90	·3155	·3782	·4677	·5315	·5805	·6196	·6517	·6786	·7016	·7214	·7387
	·95	·3719	·4327	·5182	·5782	·6238	·6599	·6894	·7139	·7349	·7528	·7684
	·99	·4823	·5369	·6116	·6630	·7014	·7313	·7555	·7756	·7926	·8071	·8198
21	0·80	0·2300	0·2895	0·3782	0·4439	0·4959	0·5383	0·5738	0·6040	0·6301	0·6529	0·6729
	·85	·2557	·3155	·4034	·4682	·5189	·5602	·5946	·6237	·6489	·6707	·6900
	·90	·2897	·3493	·4358	·4988	·5479	·5875	·6204	·6482	·6721	·6929	·7112
	·95	·3427	·4012	·4847	·5445	·5906	·6277	·6581	·6838	·7058	·7248	·7415
	·99	·4479	·5014	·5762	·6285	·6685	·6997	·7254	·7469	·7652	·7810	·7946

p = number of variates; ν_2 = hypothesis degrees of freedom; ν_1 = error degrees of freedom.

Table 49 (*continued*)

Case $p = 2$ (*continued*)

ν_1	ν_2	2	3	5	7	9	11	13	15	17	19	21
	P											
23	0·80	0·2119	0·2680	0·3528	0·4167	0·4678	0·5101	0·5457	0·5763	0·6028	0·6262	0·6469
	·85	·2359	·2924	·3769	·4401	·4903	·5315	·5661	·5958	·6215	·6441	·6640
	·90	·2677	·3244	·4080	·4699	·5185	·5584	·5918	·6202	·6448	·6663	·6853
	·95	·3177	·3737	·4551	·5143	·5606	·5981	·6294	·6558	·6787	·6986	·7160
	·99	·4179	·4701	·5443	·5971	·6380	·6703	·6970	·7197	·7391	·7558	·7705
25	0·80	0·1964	0·2494	0·3306	0·3926	0·4428	0·4846	0·5202	0·5509	0·5777	0·6015	0·6226
	·85	·2189	·2725	·3536	·4151	·4645	·5055	·5402	·5702	·5963	·6193	·6397
	·90	·2488	·3027	·3834	·4439	·4921	·5319	·5655	·5944	·6194	·6415	·6610
	·95	·2960	·3498	·4287	·4872	·5333	·5710	·6027	·6298	·6533	·6738	·6920
	·99	·3915	·4424	·5155	·5685	·6096	·6429	·6708	·6941	·7143	·7319	·7474
27	0·80	0·1830	0·2333	0·3110	0·3711	0·4202	0·4615	0·4968	0·5275	0·5546	0·5785	0·6000
	·85	·2042	·2551	·3331	·3928	·4413	·4818	·5165	·5465	·5728	·5962	·6170
	·90	·2324	·2839	·3616	·4206	·4682	·5077	·5413	·5704	·5958	·6183	·6383
	·95	·2771	·3286	·4052	·4626	·5084	·5462	·5781	·6056	·6296	·6506	·6693
	·99	·3682	·4176	·4895	·5422	·5837	·6175	·6458	·6700	·6909	·7092	·7254
29	0·80	0·1713	0·2191	0·2936	0·3518	0·3998	0·4404	0·4754	0·5060	0·5331	0·5572	0·5789
	·85	·1913	·2398	·3147	·3727	·4202	·4603	·4947	·5247	·5512	·5747	·5958
	·90	·2180	·2672	·3420	·3996	·4463	·4855	·5191	·5482	·5738	·5966	·6170
	·95	·2604	·3099	·3840	·4404	·4855	·5232	·5553	·5830	·6074	·6288	·6480
	·99	·3475	·3954	·4659	·5182	·5597	·5938	·6225	·6472	·6687	·6876	·7043
31	0·80	0·1611	0·2065	0·2780	0·3344	0·3812	0·4211	0·4557	0·4861	0·5131	0·5373	0·5591
	·85	·1800	·2262	·2982	·3546	·4010	·4405	·4746	·5045	·5309	·5546	·5759
	·90	·2053	·2523	·3246	·3805	·4264	·4651	·4985	·5277	·5534	·5763	·5969
	·95	·2457	·2931	·3650	·4200	·4647	·5022	·5342	·5620	·5866	·6082	·6278
	·99	·3290	·3754	·4444	·4961	·5374	·5717	·6008	·6258	·6477	·6671	·6843
33	0·80	0·1519	0·1953	0·2639	0·3186	0·3643	0·4034	0·4375	0·4677	0·4946	0·5187	0·5406
	·85	·1699	·2141	·2834	·3381	·3835	·4223	·4560	·4857	·5121	·5358	·5572
	·90	·1940	·2389	·3087	·3632	·4081	·4464	·4794	·5084	·5342	·5572	·5781
	·95	·2324	·2781	·3478	·4015	·4455	·4825	·5145	·5424	·5671	·5890	·6088
	·99	·3123	·3573	·4247	·4757	·5168	·5511	·5803	·6057	·6279	·6476	·6653
35	0·80	0·1438	0·1852	0·2512	0·3042	0·3487	0·3871	0·4208	0·4506	0·4773	0·5014	0·5233
	·85	·1609	·2032	·2699	·3230	·3674	·4055	·4388	·4682	·4945	·5181	·5396
	·90	·1838	·2270	·2943	·3473	·3913	·4290	·4617	·4906	·5163	·5394	·5603
	·95	·2206	·2645	·3320	·3845	·4277	·4644	·4962	·5240	·5487	·5708	·5907
	·99	·2972	·3408	·4066	·4569	·4974	·5318	·5612	·5867	·6091	·6292	·6471
37	0·80	0·1365	0·1762	0·2397	0·2910	0·3344	0·3721	0·4052	0·4347	0·4612	0·4852	0·5070
	·85	·1528	·1933	·2577	·3092	·3526	·3900	·4228	·4519	·4781	·5017	·5231
	·90	·1747	·2161	·2812	·3328	·3759	·4129	·4453	·4739	·4995	·5226	·5434
	·95	·2098	·2521	·3175	·3689	·4113	·4475	·4791	·5068	·5315	·5536	·5737
	·99	·2834	·3257	·3900	·4394	·4797	·5138	·5430	·5688	·5915	·6117	·6299
39	0·80	0·1299	0·1679	0·2292	0·2790	0·3213	0·3582	0·3907	0·4198	0·4460	0·4699	0·4916
	·85	·1455	·1844	·2465	·2965	·3389	·3756	·4079	·4367	·4627	·4861	·5076
	·90	·1664	·2062	·2691	·3194	·3616	·3980	·4299	·4583	·4837	·5067	·5277
	·95	·2001	·2408	·3044	·3544	·3961	·4319	·4631	·4906	·5152	·5375	·5576
	·99	·2709	·3119	·3747	·4232	·4631	·4969	·5260	·5517	·5747	·5950	·6134

This table gives the values of x for which $\Pr(t_{\text{max.}} < x) = I_x(2; p, q) = P$, where $p = \frac{1}{2}(\nu_2 - 1)$, $q = \frac{1}{2}(\nu_1 - 1)$.

Table 49 (continued). *Percentage points of the largest characteristic root of the determinantal equation* $|\mathbf{B} - t(\mathbf{A}+\mathbf{B})| = 0$ *(after Foster & Rees)*

Case $p = 2$ (cont.)

ν_1	P	2	3	5	7	9	11	13	15	17	19	21
41	0·80	0·1239	0·1604	0·2195	0·2679	0·3091	0·3452	0·3772	0·4059	0·4319	0·4555	0·4771
	·85	·1388	·1762	·2362	·2849	·3262	·3622	·3940	·4225	·4482	·4715	·4928
	·90	·1589	·1972	·2582	·3070	·3483	·3840	·4155	·4436	·4689	·4918	·5127
	·95	·1912	·2306	·2922	·3411	·3819	·4172	·4480	·4754	·4999	·5221	·5423
	·99	·2594	·2993	·3605	·4079	·4472	·4812	·5100	·5358	·5585	·5792	·5977
51	0·80	0·1006	0·1311	0·1814	0·2233	0·2598	0·2923	0·3216	0·3482	0·3725	0·3950	0·4157
	·85	·1129	·1443	·1955	·2380	·2748	·3073	·3366	·3631	·3874	·4097	·4303
	·90	·1295	·1619	·2142	·2571	·2941	·3267	·3559	·3823	·4063	·4284	·4487
	·95	·1565	·1900	·2434	·2868	·3239	·3564	·3853	·4114	·4350	·4566	·4765
	·99	·2140	·2486	·3029	·3462	·3828	·4144	·4424	·4675	·4900	·5106	·5295
61	0·80	0·0846	0·1109	0·1545	0·1914	0·2240	0·2534	0·2801	0·3047	0·3274	0·3485	0·3682
	·85	·0951	·1221	·1667	·2043	·2372	·2668	·2936	·3182	·3409	·3620	·3816
	·90	·1093	·1373	·1830	·2211	·2544	·2842	·3111	·3357	·3583	·3792	·3987
	·95	·1324	·1615	·2086	·2474	·2810	·3109	·3378	·3622	·3847	·4054	·4246
	·99	·1821	·2126	·2610	·3004	·3341	·3637	·3903	·4142	·4361	·4561	·4743
71	0·80	0·0730	0·0960	0·1345	0·1675	0·1969	0·2236	0·2481	0·2708	0·2919	0·3117	0·3303
	·85	·0822	·1059	·1454	·1789	·2087	·2357	·2604	·2832	·3043	·3241	·3427
	·90	·0946	·1191	·1597	·1939	·2242	·2514	·2762	·2991	·3203	·3401	·3586
	·95	·1148	·1404	·1824	·2175	·2481	·2756	·3006	·3236	·3447	·3644	·3828
	·99	·1584	·1855	·2293	·2651	·2963	·3239	·3488	·3715	·3924	·4118	·4298
81	0·80	0·0643	0·0847	0·1191	0·1489	0·1756	0·2000	0·2226	0·2437	0·2634	0·2819	0·2994
	·85	·0723	·0934	·1288	·1592	·1863	·2110	·2338	·2550	·2748	·2934	·3109
	·90	·0833	·1052	·1417	·1727	·2003	·2253	·2483	·2697	·2896	·3082	·3257
	·95	·1013	·1242	·1620	·1939	·2221	·2475	·2707	·2922	·3122	·3308	·3483
	·99	·1402	·1646	·2044	·2374	·2662	·2919	·3153	·3368	·3567	·3751	·3924
91	0·80	0·0574	0·0757	0·1069	0·1340	0·1585	0·1810	0·2019	0·2215	0·2399	0·2573	0·2738
	·85	·0646	·0836	·1156	·1433	·1682	·1910	·2122	·2319	·2505	·2680	·2845
	·90	·0745	·0942	·1273	·1556	·1810	·2042	·2255	·2455	·2642	·2818	·2984
	·95	·0906	·1114	·1457	·1750	·2010	·2245	·2462	·2664	·2852	·3029	·3195
	·99	·1257	·1479	·1844	·2149	·2416	·2657	·2874	·3081	·3270	·3444	·3608
101	0·80	0·0518	0·0685	0·0969	0·1218	0·1444	0·1652	0·1847	0·2029	0·2202	0·2366	0·2522
	·85	·0584	·0756	·1049	·1304	·1533	·1745	·1942	·2127	·2301	·2466	·2622
	·90	·0673	·0853	·1155	·1416	·1651	·1866	·2066	·2253	·2428	·2595	·2752
	·95	·0820	·1009	·1325	·1594	·1835	·2055	·2258	·2447	·2625	·2792	·2951
	·99	·1140	·1343	·1678	·1961	·2211	·2436	·2644	·2836	·3015	·3184	·3342
121	0·80	0·0434	0·0575	0·0817	0·1030	0·1225	0·1407	0·1577	0·1739	0·1892	0·2038	0·2178
	·85	·0489	·0635	·0885	·1104	·1303	·1487	·1660	·1824	·1978	·2126	·2267
	·90	·0565	·0717	·0976	·1200	·1404	·1593	·1768	·1934	·2091	·2240	·2382
	·95	·0688	·0849	·1120	·1353	·1563	·1756	·1936	·2105	·2264	·2415	·2559
	·99	·0960	·1133	·1423	·1670	·1891	·2090	·2274	·2447	·2610	·2763	·2907
161	0·80	0·0328	0·0435	0·0622	0·0788	0·0941	0·1085	0·1221	0·1351	0·1476	0·1596	0·1711
	·85	·0370	·0481	·0674	·0844	·1001	·1148	·1287	·1419	·1545	·1666	·1783
	·90	·0427	·0544	·0744	·0920	·1081	·1231	·1372	·1507	·1635	·1758	·1876
	·95	·0521	·0645	·0856	·1039	·1206	·1361	·1506	·1644	·1775	·1900	·2020
	·99	·0730	·0864	·1092	·1288	·1464	·1627	·1778	·1921	·2056	·2185	·2309

This table gives the values of x for which $\Pr(t_{\mathrm{max.}} < x) = I_x(2; p, q) = P$, where $p = \frac{1}{2}(\nu_2 - 1)$, $q = \frac{1}{2}(\nu_1 - 1)$.

Table 49 (*continued*)

Case $p = 3$

ν_1	ν_2	3	4	5	6	7	8	9	10
	P								
4	0·80	0·9516	0·9635	0·9707	0·9755	0·9790	0·9816	0·9836	0·9852
	·85	·9645	·9733	·9786	·9821	·9846	·9865	·9880	·9892
	·90	·9769	·9826	·9861	·9884	·9900	·9913	·9922	·9930
	·95	·9887	·9915	·9932	·9943	·9951	·9957	·9962	·9966
	·99	·9978	·9983	·9987	·9989	·9990	·9992	·9993	·9993
6	0·80	0·8294	0·8629	0·8852	0·9012	0·9132	0·9226	0·9302	0·9364
	·85	·8561	·8846	·9036	·9171	·9273	·9352	·9416	·9468
	·90	·8857	·9087	·9238	·9346	·9427	·9490	·9540	·9582
	·95	·9218	·9378	·9482	·9556	·9612	·9655	·9689	·9717
	·99	·9664	·9734	·9779	·9811	·9835	·9853	·9868	·9880
8	0·80	0·7180	0·7639	0·7965	0·8210	0·8400	0·8554	0·8680	0·8786
	·85	·7497	·7911	·8203	·8421	·8591	·8728	·8840	·8933
	·90	·7871	·8229	·8480	·8667	·8812	·8929	·9024	·9103
	·95	·8365	·8646	·8842	·8986	·9098	·9188	·9261	·9322
	·99	·9086	·9247	·9359	·9441	·9504	·9554	·9595	·9628
10	0·80	0·6281	0·6798	0·7181	0·7478	0·7717	0·7913	0·8077	0·8217
	·85	·6610	·7090	·7443	·7716	·7935	·8114	·8264	·8392
	·90	·7008	·7440	·7757	·8000	·8195	·8353	·8486	·8598
	·95	·7560	·7922	·8185	·8386	·8546	·8676	·8784	·8876
	·99	·8439	·8679	·8852	·8983	·9086	·9170	·9239	·9298
12	0·80	0·5564	0·6102	0·6513	0·6840	0·7108	0·7332	0·7523	0·7688
	·85	·5887	·6396	·6783	·7089	·7340	·7549	·7726	·7879
	·90	·6287	·6757	·7112	·7392	·7620	·7810	·7971	·8109
	·95	·6857	·7266	·7574	·7815	·8010	·8172	·8309	·8426
	·99	·7816	·8113	·8334	·8505	·8643	·8757	·8853	·8934
14	0·80	0·4986	0·5525	0·5946	0·6289	0·6574	0·6816	0·7025	0·7207
	·85	·5297	·5813	·6215	·6541	·6811	·7039	·7236	·7407
	·90	·5687	·6172	·6548	·6851	·7101	·7313	·7494	·7652
	·95	·6254	·6689	·7024	·7292	·7512	·7698	·7857	·7994
	·99	·7245	·7582	·7837	·8040	·8206	·8344	·8462	·8564
16	0·80	0·4512	0·5042	0·5464	0·5812	0·6106	0·6359	0·6579	0·6773
	·85	·4809	·5321	·5728	·6062	·6343	·6584	·6794	·6978
	·90	·5185	·5672	·6057	·6372	·6637	·6863	·7058	·7230
	·95	·5739	·6185	·6535	·6820	·7058	·7261	·7436	·7589
	·99	·6735	·7096	·7376	·7601	·7788	·7947	·8083	·8201
18	0·80	0·4118	0·4633	0·5050	0·5398	0·5696	0·5954	0·6181	0·6383
	·85	·4401	·4902	·5307	·5643	·5930	·6179	·6396	·6589
	·90	·4760	·5242	·5629	·5950	·6222	·6457	·6663	·6845
	·95	·5296	·5745	·6103	·6398	·6647	·6861	·7048	·7212
	·99	·6282	·6657	·6953	·7195	·7398	·7571	·7721	·7853
20	0·80	0·3787	0·4284	0·4692	0·5037	0·5334	0·5595	0·5825	0·6031
	·85	·4054	·4542	·4940	·5276	·5564	·5816	·6038	·6237
	·90	·4397	·4870	·5254	·5576	·5852	·6093	·6304	·6493
	·95	·4914	·5359	·5719	·6019	·6275	·6497	·6692	·6864
	·99	·5879	·6262	·6568	·6821	·7035	·7220	·7381	·7523
22	0·80	0·3504	0·3983	0·4380	0·4719	0·5014	0·5274	0·5505	0·5714
	·85	·3758	·4230	·4619	·4951	·5238	·5491	·5715	·5917
	·90	·4085	·4545	·4924	·5244	·5521	·5764	·5979	·6172
	·95	·4580	·5019	·5377	·5679	·5938	·6165	·6365	·6544
	·99	·5521	·5906	·6218	·6478	·6700	·6893	·7063	·7214

This table gives the values x for which $\Pr(t_{\max.} < x) = I_x(3; p, q) = P$, where $p = \frac{1}{2}(\nu_2 - 2)$, $q = \frac{1}{2}(\nu_1 - 2)$.

Table 49 (*continued*). *Percentage points of the largest characteristic root of the determinantal equation* $|\mathbf{B} - t(\mathbf{A}+\mathbf{B})| = 0$ *(after Foster & Rees)*

Case $p = 3$ (*continued*)

ν_1	ν_2	3	4	5	6	7	8	9	10
	P								
24	0·80	0·3259	0·3720	0·4106	0·4438	0·4728	0·4986	0·5217	0·5426
	·85	·3501	·3957	·4337	·4662	·4947	·5198	·5423	·5626
	·90	·3813	·4260	·4631	·4947	·5223	·5466	·5683	·5878
	·95	·4288	·4718	·5072	·5373	·5633	·5862	·6066	·6249
	·99	·5201	·5586	·5900	·6164	·6392	·6590	·6766	·6923
26	0·80	0·3046	0·3490	0·3864	0·4187	0·4473	0·4727	0·4957	0·5165
	·85	·3276	·3716	·4086	·4404	·4685	·4934	·5158	·5361
	·90	·3574	·4007	·4370	·4681	·4954	·5196	·5413	·5610
	·95	·4030	·4450	·4798	·5096	·5356	·5586	·5792	·5977
	·99	·4914	·5296	·5610	·5876	·6107	·6309	·6490	·6651
28	0·80	0·2859	0·3286	0·3648	0·3963	0·4243	0·4493	0·4720	0·4926
	·85	·3078	·3503	·3861	·4173	·4448	·4694	·4917	·5119
	·90	·3363	·3783	·4136	·4441	·4710	·4951	·5167	·5363
	·95	·3801	·4210	·4552	·4846	·5104	·5333	·5539	·5726
	·99	·4656	·5033	·5345	·5612	·5844	·6049	·6232	·6398
30	0·80	0·2694	0·3104	0·3455	0·3761	0·4035	0·4280	0·4504	0·4708
	·85	·2903	·3312	·3660	·3964	·4234	·4476	·4696	·4897
	·90	·3175	·3581	·3925	·4224	·4489	·4726	·4941	·5136
	·95	·3595	·3993	·4328	·4618	·4873	·5101	·5307	·5493
	·99	·4423	·4794	·5103	·5369	·5601	·5808	·5993	·6160
32	0·80	0·2546	0·2941	0·3280	0·3579	0·3845	0·4087	0·4307	0·4508
	·85	·2746	·3141	·3479	·3775	·4039	·4277	·4494	·4693
	·90	·3007	·3400	·3734	·4027	·4287	·4521	·4733	·4927
	·95	·3411	·3798	·4125	·4410	·4661	·4887	·5092	·5278
	·99	·4211	·4575	·4881	·5144	·5376	·5583	·5769	·5938
34	0·80	0·2414	0·2795	0·3123	0·3413	0·3673	0·3909	0·4125	0·4324
	·85	·2605	·2986	·3314	·3602	·3861	·4095	·4308	·4504
	·90	·2855	·3236	·3561	·3847	·4102	·4332	·4542	·4734
	·95	·3244	·3620	·3940	·4219	·4467	·4690	·4893	·5079
	·99	·4018	·4375	·4676	·4937	·5168	·5374	·5561	·5730
36	0·80	0·2295	0·2662	0·2980	0·3261	0·3515	0·3746	0·3958	0·4154
	·85	·2478	·2846	·3164	·3445	·3697	·3927	·4137	·4330
	·90	·2718	·3087	·3403	·3682	·3932	·4158	·4364	·4555
	·95	·3093	·3458	·3770	·4043	·4287	·4508	·4709	·4893
	·99	·3842	·4191	·4488	·4746	·4974	·5180	·5366	·5536
38	0·80	0·2187	0·2541	0·2849	0·3123	0·3370	0·3596	0·3804	0·3997
	·85	·2363	·2719	·3027	·3300	·3547	·3772	·3978	·4169
	·90	·2594	·2951	·3258	·3530	·3775	·3997	·4200	·4388
	·95	·2955	·3309	·3614	·3882	·4122	·4339	·4537	·4720
	·99	·3680	·4022	·4313	·4568	·4794	·4998	·5183	·5353
40	0·80	0·2088	0·2430	0·2729	0·2995	0·3237	0·3458	0·3662	0·3851
	·85	·2258	·2602	·2901	·3167	·3408	·3628	·3831	·4018
	·90	·2480	·2826	·3125	·3390	·3630	·3848	·4048	·4233
	·95	·2828	·3173	·3470	·3732	·3968	·4182	·4377	·4558
	·99	·3531	·3865	·4151	·4402	·4626	·4828	·5012	·5181
42	0·80	0·1998	0·2329	0·2619	0·2878	0·3113	0·3329	0·3529	0·3715
	·85	·2161	·2495	·2785	·3045	·3280	·3495	·3694	·3878
	·90	·2376	·2711	·3002	·3261	·3495	·3709	·3906	·4088
	·95	·2712	·3048	·3337	·3594	·3825	·4035	·4228	·4407
	·99	·3393	·3720	·4001	·4248	·4469	·4669	·4851	·5020

Table 49 (*continued*)

Case $p = 3$ (*continued*)

ν_1	ν_2	3	4	5	6	7	8	9	10
	P								
44	0·80	0·1916	0·2236	0·2517	0·2769	0·2999	0·3210	0·3406	0·3588
	·85	·2073	·2396	·2678	·2931	·3161	·3371	·3566	·3748
	·90	·2280	·2605	·2888	·3141	·3370	·3580	·3773	·3953
	·95	·2605	·2931	·3241	·3465	·3692	·3898	·4089	·4265
	·99	·3266	·3586	·3861	·4104	·4321	·4519	·4700	·4867
46	0·80	0·1840	0·2150	0·2423	0·2668	0·2892	0·3099	0·3290	0·3469
	·85	·1991	·2304	·2579	·2825	·3050	·3256	·3447	·3625
	·90	·2192	·2507	·2783	·3030	·3254	·3459	·3649	·3826
	·95	·2506	·2824	·3099	·3345	·3567	·3770	·3958	·4132
	·99	·3147	·3460	·3730	·3969	·4183	·4379	·4558	·4724
50	0·80	0·1704	0·1996	0·2254	0·2487	0·2700	0·2898	0·3082	0·3254
(4)*	·85	·1846	·2141	·2401	·2635	·2849	·3047	·3231	·3403
	·90	·2034	·2332	·2594	·2829	·3043	·3241	·3424	·3595
	·95	·2329	·2630	·2893	·3128	·3342	·3538	·3719	·3888
	·99	·2934	·3233	·3493	·3723	·3932	·4122	·4297	·4460
54	0·80	0·1588	0·1863	0·2107	0·2328	0·2532	0·2721	0·2898	0·3064
	·85	·1721	·1999	·2246	·2469	·2674	·2863	·3040	·3206
	·90	·1897	·2179	·2428	·2653	·2858	·3048	·3225	·3390
	·95	·2175	·2461	·2712	·2937	·3142	·3332	·3507	·3671
	·99	·2748	·3034	·3284	·3506	·3708	·3893	·4064	·4223
58	0·80	0·1486	0·1746	0·1978	0·2189	0·2383	0·2565	0·2734	0·2894
	·85	·1611	·1875	·2110	·2322	·2518	·2700	·2870	·3030
	·90	·1777	·2045	·2282	·2497	·2694	·2876	·3047	·3207
	·95	·2041	·2313	·2552	·2768	·2966	·3148	·3318	·3477
	·99	·2584	·2858	·3098	·3312	·3508	·3687	·3854	·4009
62	0·80	0·1396	0·1643	0·1864	0·2065	0·2251	0·2425	0·2588	0·2742
	·85	·1515	·1765	·1989	·2192	·2380	·2555	·2718	·2873
	·90	·1672	·1927	·2153	·2358	·2547	·2723	·2887	·3042
	·95	·1921	·2181	·2410	·2617	·2807	·2983	·3148	·3302
	·99	·2438	·2701	·2932	·3139	·3328	·3502	·3664	·3816
66	0·80	0·1317	0·1552	0·1762	0·1955	0·2133	0·2300	0·2457	0·2605
(3)*	·85	·1429	·1668	·1881	·2076	·2256	·2424	·2582	·2731
	·90	·1578	·1821	·2038	·2234	·2416	·2585	·2744	·2893
	·95	·1815	·2063	·2283	·2482	·2665	·2835	·2994	·3144
	·99	·2308	·2560	·2782	·2982	·3165	·3335	·3492	·3640
70	0·80	0·1246	0·1470	0·1671	0·1855	0·2026	0·2187	0·2338	0·2482
	·85	·1353	·1580	·1784	·1971	·2144	·2306	·2458	·2602
	·90	·1495	·1727	·1934	·2123	·2297	·2461	·2614	·2758
	·95	·1720	·1958	·2168	·2360	·2536	·2701	·2855	·3000
	·99	·2191	·2433	·2647	·2840	·3018	·3182	·3335	·3479
98	0·80	0·0905	0·1073	0·1226	0·1368	0·1501	0·1627	0·1747	0·1861
(2)*	·85	·0984	·1156	·1312	·1456	·1591	·1719	·1840	·1955
	·90	·1090	·1266	·1425	·1572	·1709	·1839	·1962	·2079
	·95	·1259	·1441	·1604	·1755	·1895	·2026	·2151	·2270
	·99	·1616	·1805	·1975	·2130	·2273	·2408	·2535	·2655
194	0·80	0·0467	0·0557	0·0641	0·0719	0·0794	0·0866	0·0935	0·1001
(1)*	·85	·0508	·0602	·0687	·0768	·0844	·0917	·0987	·1055
	·90	·0565	·0661	·0749	·0831	·0910	·0984	·1056	·1125
	·95	·0655	·0756	·0847	·0933	·1013	·1090	·1164	·1235
	·99	·0849	·0956	·1054	·1144	·1229	·1310	·1388	·1462

* Values of $192/(\nu_1 - 2)$ to be used as argument in harmonic interpolation. When $\nu_1 = \infty$, the entry is zero.

Case $p = 4$

ν_1	ν_2	4	5	6	7	8	9	10	11
	P								
5	0·80	0·9725	0·9779	0·9816	0·9842	0·9862	0·9877	0·9889	0·9899
	·85	·9799	·9839	·9865	·9885	·9899	·9910	·9919	·9926
	·90	·9869	·9895	·9913	·9925	·9934	·9942	·9947	·9952
	·95	·9936	·9949	·9957	·9963	·9968	·9972	·9974	·9977
	·99	·9987	·9990	·9992	·9993	·9994	·9994	·9995	·9995
7	0·80	0·8902	0·9083	0·9212	0·9309	0·9385	0·9445	0·9495	0·9536
	·85	·9078	·9231	·9340	·9422	·9485	·9536	·9578	·9613
	·90	·9272	·9394	·9480	·9545	·9595	·9636	·9668	·9696
	·95	·9505	·9589	·9648	·9692	·9726	·9754	·9776	·9795
	·99	·9789	·9825	·9850	·9869	·9884	·9895	·9905	·9913
9	0·80	0·8034	0·8311	0·8518	0·8678	0·8807	0·8913	0·9001	0·9075
	·85	·8264	·8512	·8695	·8838	·8952	·9045	·9123	·9189
	·90	·8532	·8744	·8900	·9022	·9118	·9197	·9263	·9319
	·95	·8882	·9045	·9166	·9259	·9333	·9393	·9443	·9486
	·99	·9381	·9473	·9541	·9593	·9634	·9668	·9696	·9719
11	0·80	0·7259	0·7596	0·7856	0·8063	0·8233	0·8374	0·8494	0·8598
	·85	·7514	·7824	·8062	·8251	·8405	·8534	·8643	·8737
	·90	·7820	·8095	·8306	·8473	·8610	·8723	·8819	·8901
	·95	·8236	·8463	·8636	·8773	·8884	·8976	·9054	·9121
	·99	·8885	·9032	·9144	·9231	·9302	·9361	·9410	·9453
13	0·80	0·6594	0·6965	0·7259	0·7498	0·7697	0·7865	0·8010	0·8136
	·85	·6858	·7206	·7479	·7701	·7886	·8042	·8176	·8293
	·90	·7180	·7497	·7746	·7947	·8114	·8255	·8376	·8481
	·95	·7632	·7904	·8116	·8287	·8429	·8548	·8650	·8738
	·99	·8374	·8567	·8716	·8836	·8934	·9017	·9088	·9149
15	0·80	0·6028	0·6417	0·6730	0·6989	0·7208	0·7396	0·7559	0·7703
	·85	·6292	·6661	·6957	·7201	·7407	·7584	·7737	·7871
	·90	·6619	·6961	·7235	·7460	·7650	·7812	·7952	·8075
	·95	·7085	·7387	·7628	·7825	·7991	·8131	·8253	·8360
	·99	·7882	·8110	·8290	·8436	·8559	·8663	·8752	·8830
17	0·80	0·5544	0·5940	0·6264	0·6536	0·6768	0·6969	0·7146	0·7302
	·85	·5804	·6183	·6492	·6751	·6971	·7162	·7329	·7477
	·90	·6128	·6485	·6774	·7016	·7222	·7399	·7554	·7691
	·95	·6599	·6920	·7180	·7396	·7579	·7737	·7874	·7995
	·99	·7424	·7677	·7881	·8049	·8190	·8312	·8417	·8510
19	0·80	0·5128	0·5524	0·5853	0·6131	0·6372	0·6582	0·6768	0·6933
	·85	·5381	·5763	·6079	·6346	·6576	·6777	·6955	·7112
	·90	·5700	·6063	·6361	·6614	·6830	·7019	·7185	·7333
	·95	·6166	·6499	·6771	·7000	·7197	·7367	·7517	·7649
	·99	·7003	·7275	·7495	·7680	·7837	·7973	·8092	·8197
21	0·80	0·4768	0·5160	0·5489	0·5770	0·6015	0·6231	0·6423	0·6595
	·85	·5013	·5394	·5712	·5983	·6219	·6427	·6611	·6776
	·90	·5323	·5688	·5991	·6250	·6474	·6670	·6845	·7000
	·95	·5782	·6120	·6400	·6638	·6844	·7024	·7183	·7325
	·99	·6619	·6903	·7136	·7333	·7502	·7650	·7780	·7895
23	0·80	0·4453	0·4839	0·5165	0·5447	0·5693	0·5912	0·6108	0·6285
	·85	·4690	·5066	·5383	·5656	·5895	·6107	·6296	·6466
	·90	·4991	·5353	·5658	·5920	·6148	·6350	·6530	·6692
	·95	·5439	·5779	·6064	·6307	·6519	·6706	·6872	·7021
	·99	·6270	·6561	·6803	·7010	·7188	·7345	·7483	·7607

This table gives the values of x for which $\Pr(t_{\max} < x) = I_x(4; p, q) = P$, where $p = \frac{1}{2}(\nu_2 - 3)$, $q = \frac{1}{2}(\nu_1 - 3)$.

Table 49 (*continued*)

Case $p = 4$ (*continued*)

ν_1	P	4	5	6	7	8	9	10	11
25	0·80	0·4177	0·4554	0·4876	0·5155	0·5402	0·5622	0·5820	0·6000
	·85	·4405	·4774	·5089	·5361	·5601	·5815	·6007	·6180
	·90	·4696	·5054	·5358	·5621	·5851	·6056	·6240	·6406
	·95	·5133	·5472	·5758	·6004	·6220	·6412	·6583	·6737
	·99	·5951	·6247	·6495	·6708	·6894	·7057	·7203	·7334
27	0·80	0·3932	0·4300	0·4616	0·4893	0·5138	0·5358	0·5557	0·5738
	·85	·4152	·4513	·4823	·5094	·5333	·5548	·5741	·5917
	·90	·4433	·4786	·5086	·5348	·5580	·5786	·5973	·6141
	·95	·4858	·5194	·5479	·5727	·5945	·6139	·6314	·6472
	·99	·5661	·5959	·6211	·6428	·6619	·6787	·6938	·7075
29	0·80	0·3713	0·4072	0·4382	0·4655	0·4898	0·5116	0·5315	0·5496
	·85	·3925	·4279	·4583	·4851	·5089	·5303	·5496	·5673
	·90	·4197	·4543	·4840	·5100	·5331	·5538	·5725	·5896
	·95	·4609	·4941	·5225	·5472	·5691	·5887	·6064	·6225
	·99	·5395	·5694	·5948	·6168	·6362	·6534	·6690	·6830
31	0·80	0·3518	0·3867	0·4170	0·4438	0·4678	0·4895	0·5092	0·5274
	·85	·3722	·4067	·4365	·4629	·4865	·5077	·5271	·5448
	·90	·3985	·4323	·4615	·4873	·5102	·5309	·5496	·5668
	·95	·4384	·4711	·4992	·5238	·5457	·5654	·5832	·5995
	·99	·5152	·5450	·5704	·5926	·6122	·6297	·6456	·6600
33	0·80	0·3341	0·3681	0·3977	0·4240	0·4476	0·4691	0·4887	0·5067
	·85	·3538	·3874	·4167	·4426	·4659	·4870	·5062	·5239
	·90	·3792	·4123	·4410	·4664	·4891	·5097	·5284	·5456
	·95	·4180	·4500	·4778	·5022	·5240	·5437	·5616	·5779
	·99	·4929	·5224	·5478	·5700	·5898	·6075	·6236	·6382
35	0·80	0·3181	0·3511	0·3801	0·4058	0·4291	0·4503	0·4697	0·4876
	·85	·3371	·3699	·3985	·4240	·4469	·4678	·4869	·5044
	·90	·3617	·3940	·4222	·4472	·4697	·4901	·5087	·5258
	·95	·3993	·4307	·4581	·4822	·5039	·5235	·5414	·5578
	·99	·4724	·5016	·5268	·5490	·5688	·5867	·6029	·6177
37	0·80	0·3036	0·3357	0·3639	0·3891	0·4120	0·4329	0·4521	0·4698
	·85	·3220	·3538	·3818	·4068	·4294	·4500	·4689	·4863
	·90	·3457	·3773	·4049	·4295	·4516	·4718	·4903	·5074
	·95	·3822	·4130	·4399	·4637	·4852	·5047	·5225	·5389
	·99	·4534	·4823	·5073	·5294	·5492	·5671	·5834	·5983
39	0·80	0·2903	0·3215	0·3490	0·3738	0·3962	0·4167	0·4357	0·4532
	·85	·3081	·3391	·3665	·3910	·4132	·4335	·4522	·4695
	·90	·3311	·3618	·3889	·4131	·4349	·4549	·4732	·4901
	·95	·3664	·3966	·4230	·4466	·4678	·4871	·5048	·5212
	·99	·4359	·4644	·4891	·5111	·5308	·5487	·5650	·5800
41	0·80	0·2782	0·3085	0·3353	0·3595	0·3815	0·4017	0·4204	0·4377
	·85	·2953	·3255	·3523	·3763	·3981	·4181	·4365	·4537
	·90	·3176	·3476	·3741	·3978	·4193	·4390	·4572	·4740
	·95	·3519	·3814	·4074	·4306	·4516	·4707	·4883	·5046
	·99	·4196	·4476	·4722	·4939	·5135	·5314	·5477	·5627
43	0·80	0·2670	0·2965	0·3227	0·3463	0·3679	0·3878	0·4061	0·4233
	·85	·2836	·3130	·3391	·3626	·3841	·4037	·4219	·4389
	·90	·3051	·3345	·3604	·3837	·4048	·4242	·4422	·4588
	·95	·3385	·3674	·3929	·4157	·4364	·4553	·4727	·4889
	·99	·4044	·4321	·4563	·4778	·4973	·5151	·5313	·5464

Table 49 (*continued*). *Percentage points of the largest characteristic root of the determinantal*
equation $|\mathbf{B} - t(\mathbf{A} + \mathbf{B})| = 0$ (*after Foster & Rees*)

Case $p = 4$ (*continued*)

ν_1	P	4	5	6	7	8	9	10	11
45	0·80	0·2566	0·2853	0·3109	0·3340	0·3552	0·3747	0·3928	0·4097
	·85	·2727	·3014	·3269	·3499	·3710	·3903	·4083	·4250
	·90	·2936	·3222	·3476	·3704	·3913	·4104	·4281	·4446
	·95	·3260	·3543	·3793	·4017	·4221	·4409	·4581	·4742
	·99	·3903	·4175	·4414	·4627	·4820	·4997	·5159	·5309
47	0·80	0·2471	0·2750	0·2999	0·3226	0·3433	0·3625	0·3803	0·3969
	·85	·2626	·2906	·3155	·3381	·3587	·3778	·3954	·4119
	·90	·2830	·3109	·3357	·3581	·3786	·3974	·4149	·4312
	·95	·3144	·3421	·3666	·3887	·4088	·4273	·4444	·4603
	·99	·3772	·4039	·4274	·4485	·4676	·4851	·5013	·5162
51	0·80	0·2299	0·2564	0·2802	0·3018	0·3218	0·3403	0·3575	0·3737
(4)*	·85	·2446	·2712	·2950	·3166	·3365	·3549	·3720	·3881
	·90	·2638	·2904	·3141	·3357	·3554	·3737	·3907	·4066
	·95	·2936	·3200	·3436	·3649	·3844	·4024	·4191	·4347
	·99	·3533	·3791	·4019	·4224	·4412	·4584	·4743	·4891
55	0·80	0·2149	0·2402	0·2629	0·2836	0·3028	0·3206	0·3372	0·3529
	·85	·2288	·2542	·2769	·2977	·3168	·3346	·3512	·3668
	·90	·2470	·2724	·2951	·3159	·3349	·3526	·3691	·3846
	·95	·2752	·3006	·3233	·3439	·3628	·3802	·3965	·4117
	·99	·3322	·3571	·3792	·3992	·4175	·4343	·4499	·4645
59	0·80	0·2018	0·2258	0·2475	0·2674	0·2858	0·3030	0·3191	0·3343
	·85	·2150	·2391	·2609	·2808	·2993	·3164	·3325	·3476
	·90	·2322	·2565	·2783	·2983	·3167	·3338	·3498	·3648
	·95	·2591	·2834	·3052	·3251	·3434	·3603	·3762	·3910
	·99	·3134	·3374	·3589	·3783	·3961	·4126	·4279	·4422
63	0·80	0·1902	0·2131	0·2339	0·2530	0·2707	0·2873	0·3029	0·3176
	·85	·2027	·2258	·2467	·2658	·2836	·3001	·3157	·3304
	·90	·2191	·2423	·2633	·2825	·3002	·3168	·3323	·3470
	·95	·2447	·2680	·2890	·3082	·3259	·3424	·3578	·3723
	·99	·2966	·3198	·3406	·3594	·3768	·3929	·4079	·4219
67	0·80	0·1798	0·2018	0·2217	0·2400	0·2571	0·2731	0·2881	0·3024
(3)*	·85	·1917	·2138	·2339	·2523	·2694	·2854	·3005	·3148
	·90	·2074	·2296	·2498	·2683	·2854	·3015	·3165	·3307
	·95	·2318	·2542	·2745	·2930	·3101	·3261	·3411	·3552
	·99	·2816	·3039	·3240	·3424	·3592	·3749	·3896	·4034
71	0·80	0·1706	0·1915	0·2107	0·2283	0·2448	0·2602	0·2748	0·2886
	·85	·1819	·2031	·2223	·2401	·2566	·2721	·2867	·3005
	·90	·1968	·2182	·2376	·2554	·2720	·2875	·3021	·3160
	·95	·2202	·2418	·2613	·2792	·2958	·3113	·3259	·3396
	·99	·2679	·2896	·3090	·3268	·3432	·3585	·3729	·3864
99	0·80	0·1252	0·1414	0·1562	0·1701	0·1832	0·1956	0·2074	0·2186
(2)*	·85	·1338	·1502	·1652	·1792	·1924	·2049	·2168	·2281
	·90	·1451	·1618	·1770	·1912	·2045	·2171	·2291	·2405
	·95	·1630	·1800	·1955	·2098	·2233	·2360	·2481	·2596
	·99	·2000	·2173	·2331	·2477	·2614	·2742	·2863	·2979
195	0·80	0·0655	0·0744	0·0828	0·0907	0·0982	0·1055	0·1125	0·1192
(1)*	·85	·0701	·0793	·0878	·0958	·1035	·1108	·1179	·1247
	·90	·0763	·0857	·0943	·1025	·1104	·1178	·1250	·1320
	·95	·0862	·0958	·1047	·1132	·1212	·1288	·1362	·1433
	·99	·1068	·1169	·1263	·1351	·1434	·1514	·1590	·1663

* Values of $192/(\nu_1 - 3)$ to be used as argument in harmonic interpolation. When $\nu_1 = \infty$, the entry is zero.

Table 50. *Test for equality of k covariance matrices*
5 per cent points of M

ν_0 \ k	2	3	4	5	6	7	8	9	10
				$p = 2$					
3	12·18	18·70	24·55	30·09	35·45	40·68	45·81	50·87	55·87
4	10·70	16·65	22·00	27·07	31·97	36·76	41·45	46·07	50·64
5	9·97	15·63	20·73	25·56	30·23	34·79	39·26	43·67	48·02
6	9·53	15·02	19·97	24·66	29·19	33·61	37·95	42·22	46·45
7	9·24	14·62	19·46	24·05	28·49	32·82	37·07	41·26	45·40
8	9·04	14·33	19·10	23·62	27·99	32·26	36·45	40·57	44·65
9	8·88	14·11	18·83	23·30	27·62	31·84	35·98	40·06	44·08
10	8·76	13·94	18·61	23·05	27·33	31·51	35·61	36·65	43·64
				$p = 3$					
5	19·2	30·5	41·0	51·0	60·7	70·3	79·7	89·0	98·3
6	17·57	28·24	38·06	47·49	56·68	65·69	74·58	83·37	92·09
7	16·59	26·84	36·29	45·37	54·21	62·89	71·45	79·91	88·29
8	15·93	25·90	35·10	43·93	52·54	60·99	69·33	77·56	85·72
9	15·46	25·22	34·24	42·90	51·34	59·62	67·79	75·86	83·86
10	15·11	24·71	33·59	42·11	50·42	58·58	66·62	74·57	82·45
11	14·83	24·31	33·08	41·50	49·71	57·76	65·71	73·56	81·35
12	14·61	23·99	32·67	41·01	49·13	57·11	64·97	72·75	80·46
13	14·43	23·73	32·33	40·60	48·66	56·57	64·37	72·08	79·72
				$p = 4$					
6	30·07	48·63	65·91	82·6	98·9	115·0	131·0	—	—
7	27·31	44·69	60·90	76·56	91·89	107·0	121·9	137·0	152·0
8	25·61	42·24	57·77	72·78	87·46	101·9	116·2	130·4	144·6
9	24·46	40·56	55·62	70·17	84·42	98·45	112·3	126·1	139·8
10	23·62	39·34	54·05	68·27	82·19	95·91	109·5	122·9	136·3
11	22·98	38·41	52·85	66·81	80·49	93·95	107·3	120·5	133·6
12	22·48	37·67	51·90	65·66	79·14	92·41	105·5	118·5	131·5
13	22·08	37·08	51·13	64·73	78·04	91·16	104·1	117·0	129·7
14	21·75	36·59	50·50	63·96	77·14	90·12	103·0	115·7	128·3
15	21·47	36·17	49·97	63·31	76·38	89·25	102·0	114·6	127·1

ν_0 \ k	2	3	4	5	6	7
			$p = 5$			
8	39·29	65·15	89·46	113·0	—	—
9	36·70	61·40	84·63	107·2	129·3	151·5
10	34·92	58·79	81·25	103·1	124·5	145·7
11	33·62	56·86	78·76	100·0	120·9	141·6
12	32·62	55·37	76·83	97·68	118·2	138·4
13	31·83	54·19	75·30	95·81	116·0	135·9
14	31·19	53·24	74·06	94·29	114·2	133·8
15	30·66	52·44	73·02	93·03	112·7	132·1
16	30·21	51·77	72·14	91·95	111·4	130·6

ν_0 \ k	2	3	4	5
		$p = 6$		
10	49·95	84·43	117·0	—
11	47·43	80·69	112·2	142·9
12	45·56	77·90	108·6	138·4
13	44·11	75·74	105·7	135·0
14	42·96	74·01	103·5	132·2
15	42·03	72·59	101·6	129·9
16	41·25	71·41	100·1	128·0
17	40·59	70·41	98·75	126·4
18	40·02	69·55	97·63	125·0
19	39·53	68·80	96·64	123·8
20	39·11	68·14	95·78	122·7

p = number of variates; k = number of samples, each of equal size $n_t = n_0$; $\nu_t = \nu_0 = n_0 - 1$; $N = k\nu_0$:

$$M = N \log |s_{uv}| - \sum_{t=1}^{k} (\nu_0 \log |s_{uvt}|).$$

s_{uvt} and s_{uv} are defined in equations (240) and (241).

Table 51. *Percentage points of the extreme roots of* $|\mathbf{S\Sigma^{-1}}-c\mathbf{I}| = 0$

Upper percentage points, $C(\alpha)$, of largest root.

ν \ α	$p=2$ 0·05	0·01	$p=3$ 0·05	0·01	$p=4$ 0·05	0·01	$p=5$ 0·05	0·01	$p=6$ 0·05	0·01
2	8·594	12·16	10·74	14·57	12·68	16·73	14·49	18·73	16·21	20·64
3	10·74	14·57	13·11	17·18	15·24	19·50	17·21	21·65	19·09	23·69
4	12·68	16·73	15·24	19·50	17·52	21·96	19·63	24·24	21·62	26·38
5	14·49	18·73	17·21	21·65	19·63	24·24	21·85	26·62	23·95	28·86
6	16·21	20·64	19·09	23·69	21·62	26·38	23·95	28·86	26·14	31·19
7	17·88	22·47	20·88	25·64	23·53	28·43	25·96	31·00	28·23	33·40
8	19·49	24·23	22·62	27·52	25·37	30·41	27·88	33·05	30·24	35·53
9	21·06	25·95	24·31	29·34	27·15	32·32	29·75	35·04	32·18	37·59
10	22·61	27·63	25·96	31·12	28·90	34·18	31·57	36·97	34·08	39·59
11	24·12	29·28	27·58	32·86	30·60	36·00	33·35	38·86	35·93	41·54
12	25·61	30·89	29·17	34·56	32·27	37·78	35·09	40·71	37·73	43·45
15	29·96	35·59	33·80	39·52	37·13	42·94	40·15	46·05	42·96	48·96
20	36·94	43·08	41·18	47·37	44·84	51·10	48·14	54·49	51·21	57·63
25	43·67	50·27	48·27	54·89	52·22	58·88	55·78	62·51	59·07	65·87
30	50·24	57·24	55·15	62·15	59·37	66·40	63·16	70·23	66·66	73·79
40	63·02	70·75	68·50	76·18	73·18	80·86	77·37	85·08	81·24	88·98
50	75·46	83·84	81·44	89·73	86·53	94·79	91·08	99·34	95·27	103·6
60	87·66	96·72	94·09	102·9	99·55	108·3	104·4	113·2	108·9	117·7
70	99·70	109·2	106·5	115·9	112·3	121·6	117·5	126·8	122·3	131·5
80	111·6	121·6	118·8	128·6	124·9	134·7	130·4	140·1	135·4	145·0
90	123·4	133·8	130·9	141·2	137·4	147·5	143·1	153·2	148·3	158·3
100	135·0	145·9	143·0	153·6	149·7	160·2	155·6	166·1	161·1	171·5
120	158·1	169·9	166·7	178·2	173·9	185·2	180·4	191·5	186·2	197·3
140	181·0	193·5	190·1	202·3	197·8	209·8	204·7	216·5	211·0	222·7
160	2·037	216·9	213·3	226·2	221·5	234·1	228·8	241·2	235·4	247·7
180	226·2	240·0	236·3	249·8	244·9	258·1	252·6	265·6	259·5	272·4
200	248·6	263·0	259·2	273·3	268·2	282·0	276·2	289·7	283·4	296·8

Lower percentage points, $c(\alpha)$, of smallest root.

ν \ α	$p=2$ 0·05	0·01	$p=3$ 0·05	0·01	$p=4$ 0·05	0·01	$p=5$ 0·05	0·01	$p=6$ 0·05	0·01
2	0·0015	0.0^463								
3	·0513	·0010	0.0^398	0.0^439						
4	·1980	·0648	·0342	·0067	0.0^371	0.0^428				
5	·4314	·1812	·1390	·0455	·0256	·0050	0.0^355	0.0^422		
6	·7333	·3573	·3142	·1322	·1073	·0351	·0205	·0040	0.0^346	0.0^418
7	1·090	·5858	·5492	·2682	·2481	·1045	·0875	·0286	·0171	·0033
8	1·489	·8595	·8339	·4497	·4414	·2158	·2054	·0865	·0739	·0242
9	1·926	1·172	1·160	·6719	·6798	·3671	·3698	·1809	·1753	·0738
10	2·392	1·518	1·522	0·9300	0·9574	0·5552	0·5754	0·3110	0·3185	0·1558
15	5·059	3·629	3·724	2·638	2·781	1·935	2·073	1·411	1·529	1·012
20	8·094	6·177	6·364	4·833	5·096	3·839	4·109	3·063	3·313	2·440
25	11·37	9·009	9·285	7·350	7·730	6·095	6·493	5·092	5·475	4·264
30	14·80	12·05	12·41	10·10	10·59	8·607	9·128	7·394	7·907	6·379
40	22·03	18·56	19·07	16·10	16·79	14·18	14·93	12·59	13·25	11·24
50	29·60	25·48	26·14	22·57	23·45	20·27	21·23	18·35	19·33	16·69
60	37·39	32·70	33·48	29·37	30·43	26·73	27·88	24·51	25·69	22·58
70	45·37	40·14	41·04	36·43	37·65	33·47	34·81	30·97	32·35	28·79
80	53·48	47·76	48·77	43·69	45·06	40·44	41·94	37·68	39·24	35·27
90	61·71	55·52	56·64	51·12	52·63	47·59	49·25	44·58	46·32	41·95
100	70·04	63·40	64·63	58·69	60·33	54·89	56·71	51·66	53·56	48·82

Table 51 (*continued*)

Upper percentage points, $C(\alpha)$, of largest root.

ν	α 0.05	0.01	0.05	0.01	0.05	0.01	0.05	0.01
	$p = 7$		$p = 8$		$p = 9$		$p = 10$	
2	17·88	22·47	19·49	24·23	21·06	25·95	22·61	27·63
3	20·88	25·64	22·62	27·52	24·31	29·34	25·96	31·12
4	23·53	28·43	25·37	30·41	27·15	32·32	28·90	34·18
5	25·96	31·00	27·88	33·05	29·75	35·04	31·57	36·97
6	28·23	33·40	30·24	35·53	32·18	37·59	34·08	39·59
7	30·40	35·69	32·48	37·89	34·50	40·01	36·45	42·07
8	32·48	37·89	34·63	40·15	36·70	42·33	38·72	44·45
9	34·50	40·01	36·70	42·33	38·84	44·57	40·91	46·74
10	36·45	42·07	38·72	44·45	40·91	46·74	43·04	48·95
11	38·36	44·08	40·69	46·51	42·93	48·85	45·10	51·11
12	40·22	46·04	42·60	48·52	44·90	50·91	47·12	53·22
15	45·61	51·70	48·15	54·32	50·58	56·85	52·94	59·28
20	54·10	60·60	56·86	63·43	59·50	66·14	62·05	68·77
25	62·17	69·03	65·12	72·04	67·94	74·93	70·67	77·72
30	69·95	77·13	73·07	80·31	76·05	83·35	78·93	86·29
40	84·86	92·64	88·29	96·11	91·57	99·43	94·72	102·6
50	99·18	107·5	102·9	111·2	106·4	114·8	109·8	118·2
60	113·1	121·9	117·0	125·8	120·8	129·6	124·4	133·3
70	126·7	135·9	130·9	140·1	134·8	144·1	138·7	147·9
80	140·0	149·7	144·4	154·0	148·6	158·2	152·6	162·2
90	153·2	163·2	157·8	167·8	162·1	172·1	166·3	176·3
100	166·1	176·5	170·9	181·3	175·4	185·8	179·8	190·1
120	191·6	202·7	196·8	207·8	201·6	212·7	206·3	217·3
140	216·7	228·4	222·2	233·8	227·3	239·0	232·3	243·9
160	241·4	253·7	247·2	259·4	252·6	264·8	257·8	270·0
180	265·8	278·7	271·9	284·6	277·6	290·3	283·0	295·7
200	290·0	303·4	296·4	309·6	302·4	315·5	308·0	321·2

Lower percentage points, $c(\alpha)$, of smallest root.

ν	α 0.05	0.01	0.05	0.01	0.05	0.01	0.05	0.01
	$p = 7$		$p = 8$		$p = 9$		$p = 10$	
7	0·0³38	0·0⁴15						
8	·0147	·0029	0·0³33	0·0⁴13				
9	·0639	·0209	·0128	·0025	0·0³29	0·0⁴12		
10	0·1530	0·0644	0·0564	0·0185	0·0114	0·0022	0·0³26	0·0⁴11
15	1·105	·7071	·7744	·4753	·5202	·3024	·3284	·1777
20	2·662	1·931	2·122	1·513	1·672	1·169	1·298	·8863
25	4·620	3·569	3·892	2·979	3·267	2·475	2·728	2·042
30	6·867	5·513	5·968	4·764	5·183	4·111	4·493	3·538
40	11·98	10·06	10·77	9·026	9·698	8·104	8·738	7·278
50	17·66	15·24	16·19	13·95	14·86	12·79	13·66	11·74
60	23·77	20·88	22·04	19·36	20·49	17·98	19·07	16·72
70	30·18	26·36	28·23	25·12	26·47	23·54	24·85	22·09
80	36·84	33·12	34·69	31·18	32·72	29·41	30·92	27·78
90	43·71	39·60	41·35	37·48	39·20	35·53	37·23	33·74
100	50·74	46·28	48·20	43·97	45·88	41·86	43·74	39·90

If $20 \leqslant \nu \leqslant 200$, approximate percentage points, $C(\alpha)$, for $\alpha = 0.10, 0.025, 0.005$, may be found as follows:

$$C(0.10) = 1.50C(0.05) - 0.50C(0.01), \quad C(0.025) = 0.55C(0.05) + 0.45C(0.01),$$

$$C(0.005) = -0.39C(0.05) + 1.39C(0.01).$$

For corresponding lower percentage points of smallest root, $c(\alpha)$, see Introduction, p. 113.

Table 52. *Percentage points of the multiple correlation coefficient R*

Lower 5 per cent points

ν_2	ν_1	R 0·0	0·1	0·2	0·3	0·4	0·5	0·6	0·7	0·8	0·9
10	2	0·101	0·104	0·114	0·133	0·167	0·224	0·314	0·441	0·599	0·785
	4	·251	·255	·268	·291	·328	·382	·457	·555	·679	·827
	6	·359	·363	·376	·399	·433	·481	·546	·629	·731	·855
	8	·439	·443	·455	·477	·508	·552	·608	·681	·769	·875
	10	·501	·505	·517	·536	·565	·605	·656	·719	·798	·891
	12	·551	·554	·565	·584	·610	·646	·692	·750	·820	·903
	16	0·625	0·628	0·638	0·654	0·677	0·707	0·746	0·794	0·852	0·920
	20	·678	·681	·689	·703	·724	·750	·784	·825	·875	·933
	24	·718	·721	·728	·741	·759	·782	·812	·848	·891	·942
	30	·762	·764	·771	·782	·797	·817	·842	·873	·909	·951
	34	·785	·787	·792	·802	·816	·835	·858	·885	·918	·956
	40	·811	·813	·818	·827	·839	·856	·876	·900	·929	·962
20	2	0·072	0·076	0·089	0·118	0·172	0·260	0·374	0·507	0·656	0·820
	4	·183	·188	·205	·237	·287	·359	·452	·565	·694	·839
	6	·268	·274	·290	·321	·366	·430	·511	·609	·724	·854
	8	·336	·341	·357	·385	·427	·484	·557	·645	·749	·867
	10	·391	·396	·411	·437	·476	·528	·594	·675	·770	·878
	12	·437	·442	·456	·481	·517	·565	·626	·700	·787	·887
	16	0·510	0·514	0·527	0·549	0·581	0·623	0·676	0·740	0·815	0·902
	20	·566	·570	·581	·601	·629	·667	·713	·770	·836	·913
	24	·610	·613	·624	·642	·668	·701	·743	·794	·853	·922
	30	·661	·664	·674	·689	·712	·741	·778	·822	·873	·933
	34	·688	·691	·700	·715	·735	·762	·796	·836	·884	·938
	40	·722	·724	·732	·745	·764	·788	·818	·854	·896	·945
30	2	0·058	0·063	0·081	0·119	0·191	0·292	0·410	0·541	0·683	0·836
	4	·151	·157	·178	·216	·278	·361	·462	·578	·707	·848
	6	·223	·230	·250	·286	·341	·414	·504	·609	·727	·858
	8	·282	·289	·308	·342	·391	·458	·540	·636	·745	·867
	10	·332	·337	·356	·387	·433	·494	·570	·659	·761	·875
	12	·374	·379	·396	·426	·469	·526	·596	·679	·775	·882
	16	0·442	0·447	0·463	0·489	0·527	0·577	0·639	0·713	0·798	0·894
	20	·496	·501	·515	·539	·574	·618	·674	·740	·817	·904
	24	·540	·545	·558	·580	·611	·652	·702	·763	·833	·912
	30	·593	·597	·609	·628	·656	·692	·737	·790	·852	·922
	34	·622	·626	·637	·655	·680	·714	·755	·805	·862	·927
	40	·658	·661	·671	·688	·711	·741	·779	·823	·875	·934
40	2	0·051	0·056	0·077	0·125	0·210	0·316	0·434	0·562	0·699	0·845
	4	·131	·138	·162	·208	·277	·367	·472	·589	·716	·853
	6	·196	·203	·226	·267	·329	·409	·504	·613	·732	·861
	8	·248	·255	·277	·316	·372	·445	·533	·634	·746	·868
	10	·293	·300	·321	·356	·408	·476	·558	·652	·758	·874
	12	·332	·338	·358	·392	·440	·503	·580	·669	·769	·880
	16	0·396	0·402	0·420	0·450	0·493	0·549	0·618	0·698	0·789	0·890
	20	·448	·453	·469	·497	·536	·587	·649	·722	·805	·898
	24	·491	·496	·511	·536	·572	·618	·676	·743	·819	·905
	30	·543	·548	·561	·584	·616	·657	·708	·768	·837	·914
	34	·572	·577	·589	·610	·640	·679	·726	·783	·847	·920
	40	·609	·613	·625	·644	·671	·707	·750	·801	·860	·926
50	2	0·045	0·052	0·076	0·133	0·225	0·333	0·451	0·576	0·710	0·851
	4	·118	·126	·153	·204	·279	·373	·480	·598	·723	·858
	6	·176	·184	·210	·256	·323	·408	·507	·616	·736	·864
	8	·224	·232	·256	·299	·360	·438	·530	·634	·747	·869
	10	·266	·273	·296	·336	·392	·465	·551	·649	·757	·874
	12	·301	·309	·330	·368	·421	·489	·570	·663	·767	·879
	16	0·362	0·368	0·388	0·422	0·469	0·530	0·604	0·689	0·783	0·887
	20	·411	·417	·435	·466	·509	·565	·632	·710	·798	·895
	24	·453	·458	·475	·503	·543	·594	·656	·729	·811	·901
	30	·504	·509	·524	·550	·585	·631	·687	·753	·827	·910
	34	·533	·538	·552	·576	·609	·652	·705	·766	·836	·914
	40	·570	·575	·588	·609	·640	·680	·728	·784	·849	·921

R = population coefficient; p = number of variates; N = sample size; $\nu_1 = p - 1$, $\nu_2 = N - p$.

Table 52 (*continued*)

Upper 5 per cent points

ν_2	ν_1	R 0·0	0·1	0·2	0·3	0·4	0·5	0·6	0·7	0·8	0·9
10	2	0·671	0·682	0·710	0·748	0·789	0·829	0·868	0·904	0·939	0·970
	4	·763	·768	·784	·806	·833	·862	·891	·920	·948	·974
	6	·812	·815	·826	·842	·861	·884	·907	·931	·954	·978
	8	·843	·846	·854	·866	·881	·899	·919	·939	·960	·980
	10	·865	·867	·874	·884	·896	·912	·928	·946	·964	·982
	12	·882	·884	·889	·897	·908	·921	·935	·951	·967	·983
	16	0·905	0·906	0·910	0·916	0·925	0·935	0·946	0·959	0·972	0·986
	20	·920	·922	·925	·930	·936	·945	·954	·965	·976	·988
	24	·932	·932	·935	·939	·945	·952	·960	·969	·979	·989
	30	·943	·944	·946	·950	·954	·960	·966	·974	·982	·991
	34	·949	·950	·952	·955	·959	·964	·970	·976	·984	·992
	40	·956	·957	·958	·961	·964	·968	·973	·979	·986	·993
20	2	0·509	0·528	0·576	0·634	0·693	0·751	0·806	0·859	0·908	0·955
	4	·604	·615	·645	·685	·731	·778	·826	·872	·916	·959
	6	·662	·670	·692	·723	·760	·801	·842	·883	·923	·962
	8	·703	·709	·727	·752	·784	·819	·855	·892	·929	·965
	10	·735	·740	·754	·776	·803	·834	·866	·900	·933	·967
	12	·760	·764	·776	·795	·819	·846	·876	·906	·938	·969
	16	0·797	0·801	0·810	0·825	0·844	0·867	0·891	0·918	0·945	0·972
	20	·825	·827	·835	·847	·863	·882	·903	·926	·950	·975
	24	·845	·847	·854	·864	·878	·894	·913	·933	·955	·977
	30	·868	·870	·875	·884	·895	·909	·924	·942	·960	·980
	34	·880	·882	·886	·894	·904	·916	·930	·946	·963	·981
	40	·895	·896	·899	·906	·915	·925	·938	·952	·967	·983
30	2	0·425	0·451	0·510	0·577	0·645	0·710	0·774	0·834	0·892	0·947
	4	·514	·529	·569	·620	·676	·733	·790	·845	·899	·950
	6	·571	·582	·612	·654	·702	·753	·804	·855	·905	·953
	8	·614	·623	·647	·683	·724	·770	·816	·863	·910	·956
	10	·647	·655	·675	·706	·743	·784	·827	·871	·914	·958
	12	·675	·681	·699	·726	·760	·797	·837	·878	·919	·960
	16	0·718	0·723	0·737	0·759	0·787	0·819	0·853	0·889	0·926	0·963
	20	·750	·754	·766	·785	·808	·836	·866	·899	·932	·966
	24	·776	·779	·789	·805	·826	·850	·877	·907	·937	·968
	30	·805	·808	·816	·829	·847	·868	·891	·917	·944	·971
	34	·821	·823	·830	·842	·858	·877	·899	·922	·947	·973
	40	·840	·842	·848	·858	·872	·889	·908	·929	·952	·975
40	2	0·373	0·403	0·469	0·541	0·614	0·685	0·753	0·819	0·882	0·942
	4	·455	·473	·520	·578	·641	·704	·767	·828	·888	·945
	6	·509	·523	·560	·609	·664	·722	·779	·837	·893	·947
	8	·551	·562	·592	·635	·684	·737	·790	·844	·897	·949
	10	·585	·594	·620	·657	·702	·750	·800	·851	·901	·951
	12	·613	·621	·644	·677	·718	·762	·809	·857	·905	·953
	16	0·657	0·664	0·682	0·710	0·745	0·784	0·825	0·868	0·912	0·956
	20	·692	·697	·713	·737	·767	·801	·839	·878	·918	·959
	24	·720	·724	·738	·758	·785	·816	·850	·886	·924	·962
	30	·753	·757	·768	·785	·808	·835	·865	·897	·930	·965
	34	·771	·774	·784	·800	·820	·845	·873	·903	·934	·967
	40	·793	·796	·804	·818	·836	·858	·883	·910	·939	·969
50	2	0·336	0·370	0·440	0·517	0·593	0·667	0·739	0·808	0·874	0·938
	4	·412	·434	·485	·549	·616	·684	·751	·816	·879	·941
	6	·464	·480	·522	·576	·637	·699	·762	·823	·884	·943
	8	·504	·517	·552	·600	·655	·713	·771	·830	·888	·945
	10	·537	·548	·578	·621	·671	·725	·781	·836	·892	·946
	12	·565	·575	·601	·640	·686	·737	·789	·842	·896	·948
	16	0·610	0·618	0·639	0·672	0·712	0·757	0·804	0·853	0·902	0·951
	20	·645	·652	·670	·699	·734	·774	·817	·862	·908	·954
	24	·674	·680	·696	·721	·753	·789	·828	·870	·913	·956
	30	·709	·714	·727	·749	·776	·808	·843	·881	·920	·960
	34	·728	·733	·745	·764	·789	·819	·852	·887	·924	·962
	40	·753	·756	·767	·784	·806	·833	·863	·895	·929	·964

Table 52 (*continued*). *Percentage points of the multiple correlation coefficient R*

Lower 1 per cent points

ν_2	ν_1	R 0·0	0·1	0·2	0·3	0·4	0·5	0·6	0·7	0·8	0·9
10	2	0·045	0·046	0·051	0·059	0·075	0·105	0·161	0·269	0·444	0·685
	4	·164	·166	·175	·192	·218	·260	·325	·422	·562	·752
	6	·266	·269	·280	·298	·327	·370	·432	·519	·637	·795
	8	·348	·351	·362	·381	·410	·451	·508	·586	·691	·826
	10	·413	·417	·428	·446	·474	·513	·566	·637	·730	·849
	12	·467	·471	·481	·499	·525	·562	·612	·677	·761	·867
	16	0·550	0·553	0·563	0·579	0·603	0·636	0·679	0·735	0·805	0·892
	20	·610	·613	·622	·637	·659	·688	·727	·775	·835	·910
	24	·657	·659	·667	·681	·701	·727	·762	·805	·858	·922
	30	·708	·711	·718	·730	·747	·771	·800	·837	·882	·936
	34	·735	·737	·744	·755	·771	·792	·820	·853	·894	·942
	40	·767	·769	·775	·785	·799	·818	·843	·872	·908	·950
20	2	0·032	0·033	0·040	0·053	0·081	0·140	0·244	0·386	0·559	0·762
	4	·119	·122	·134	·156	·193	·254	·343	·462	·611	·789
	6	·197	·202	·215	·239	·277	·334	·414	·520	·651	·811
	8	·264	·268	·281	·306	·343	·397	·470	·565	·684	·829
	10	·319	·324	·337	·361	·397	·447	·515	·602	·711	·843
	12	·367	·371	·384	·407	·441	·489	·553	·634	·734	·856
	16	0·444	0·448	0·460	0·482	0·513	0·556	0·612	0·683	0·770	0·875
	20	·504	·508	·519	·539	·568	·607	·657	·720	·798	·890
	24	·552	·556	·566	·585	·611	·647	·693	·750	·819	·902
	30	·609	·612	·622	·638	·662	·694	·734	·784	·844	·916
	34	·639	·642	·651	·667	·689	·718	·756	·802	·857	·923
	40	·677	·679	·688	·702	·722	·749	·782	·824	·873	·932
30	2	0·026	0·028	0·036	0·055	0·098	0·184	0·304	0·447	0·610	0·793
	4	·098	·102	·116	·143	·192	·267	·369	·494	·641	·809
	6	·164	·169	·184	·213	·260	·328	·420	·533	·667	·823
	8	·221	·226	·242	·270	·315	·378	·462	·566	·690	·835
	10	·270	·275	·291	·318	·361	·420	·498	·594	·710	·845
	12	·312	·317	·333	·360	·400	·456	·529	·619	·727	·854
	16	0·383	0·388	0·402	0·427	0·464	0·515	0·580	0·660	0·757	0·870
	20	·440	·444	·458	·481	·515	·561	·620	·693	·780	·882
	24	·487	·491	·504	·525	·557	·599	·653	·720	·799	·893
	30	·543	·547	·559	·579	·607	·645	·693	·752	·823	·905
	34	·575	·578	·589	·608	·635	·670	·715	·770	·835	·912
	40	·614	·617	·627	·645	·669	·702	·743	·792	·851	·921
40	2	0·022	0·025	0·034	0·059	0·119	0·220	0·343	0·483	0·639	0·811
	4	·085	·090	·106	·139	·196	·282	·390	·517	·661	·822
	6	·143	·149	·167	·200	·254	·331	·429	·546	·680	·831
	8	·194	·200	·218	·250	·301	·372	·462	·571	·697	·840
	10	·238	·244	·261	·293	·341	·407	·492	·594	·713	·848
	12	·277	·282	·300	·330	·376	·438	·518	·614	·727	·855
	16	0·342	0·347	0·364	0·392	0·434	0·490	0·562	0·648	0·751	0·868
	20	·396	·401	·416	·442	·481	·533	·598	·677	·771	·878
	24	·440	·445	·460	·484	·520	·568	·628	·701	·788	·887
	30	·496	·500	·514	·536	·569	·612	·666	·732	·809	·898
	34	·527	·531	·544	·565	·596	·636	·687	·748	·821	·905
	40	·567	·571	·582	·602	·630	·667	·714	·770	·836	·913
50	2	0·020	0·023	0·034	0·066	0·139	0·247	0·371	0·508	0·658	0·822
	4	·075	·082	·100	·138	·204	·295	·407	·534	·675	·830
	6	·129	·135	·155	·193	·253	·336	·438	·557	·690	·838
	8	·175	·181	·201	·238	·294	·370	·466	·577	·704	·845
	10	·215	·222	·241	·276	·329	·401	·490	·596	·716	·851
	12	·251	·257	·276	·310	·360	·428	·512	·613	·728	·857
	16	0·312	0·318	0·336	0·367	0·413	0·474	0·551	0·642	0·748	0·867
	20	·363	·368	·385	·414	·457	·513	·583	·667	·765	·876
	24	·405	·411	·427	·454	·493	·546	·611	·689	·780	·884
	30	·459	·464	·479	·504	·540	·587	·646	·717	·800	·894
	34	·490	·494	·508	·532	·566	·610	·666	·733	·811	·900
	40	·529	·533	·545	·568	·600	·641	·692	·754	·825	·907

R = population coefficient; p = number of variates; N = sample size; $\nu_1 = p-1$; $\nu_2 = N-p$.

Table 52 (*continued*)

Upper 1 per cent points

ν_2	ν_1	R 0·0	0·1	0·2	0·3	0·4	0·5	0·6	0·7	0·8	0·9
10	2	0·776	0·785	0·807	0·835	0·863	0·890	0·916	0·940	0·961	0·982
	4	·840	·844	·856	·872	·891	·911	·930	·949	·967	·984
	6	·874	·877	·884	·896	·909	·925	·940	·956	·971	·986
	8	·895	·897	·903	·912	·923	·935	·948	·961	·974	·987
	10	·911	·912	·917	·923	·932	·943	·954	·965	·977	·989
	12	·922	·923	·927	·932	·940	·949	·958	·969	·979	·990
	16	0·937	0·938	0·941	0·945	0·951	0·958	0·965	0·974	0·982	0·991
	20	·948	·948	·951	·954	·959	·964	·970	·977	·985	·992
	24	·955	·956	·957	·960	·964	·969	·974	·980	·986	·993
	30	·963	·963	·965	·967	·970	·974	·978	·983	·988	·994
	34	·967	·967	·968	·970	·973	·976	·980	·985	·990	·995
	40	·971	·972	·973	·974	·977	·979	·983	·987	·991	·995
20	2	0·607	0·627	0·670	0·719	0·767	·0·812	0·855	0·895	0·933	0·968
	4	·685	·696	·723	·757	·795	·833	·869	·905	·938	·970
	6	·733	·740	·759	·786	·817	·849	·881	·913	·943	·972
	8	·767	·772	·787	·809	·835	·862	·891	·919	·947	·974
	10	·792	·797	·809	·827	·849	·874	·899	·925	·951	·976
	12	·812	·816	·826	·842	·861	·883	·906	·930	·954	·977
	16	0·842	0·845	0·853	0·865	0·881	0·898	0·918	0·938	0·959	0·979
	20	·864	·866	·872	·882	·895	·910	·927	·945	·963	·981
	24	·880	·882	·887	·896	·907	·920	·934	·950	·966	·983
	30	·898	·900	·904	·911	·920	·930	·943	·956	·970	·985
	34	·907	·909	·912	·918	·926	·936	·947	·959	·972	·986
	40	·918	·920	·923	·928	·935	·943	·953	·964	·975	·987
30	2	0·514	0·541	0·596	0·655	0·713	0·768	0·820	0·870	0·916	0·959
	4	·591	·606	·643	·689	·738	·786	·833	·878	·921	·961
	6	·640	·651	·679	·717	·759	·801	·844	·885	·925	·963
	8	·677	·685	·708	·740	·776	·815	·853	·892	·929	·965
	10	·706	·713	·732	·759	·791	·826	·862	·897	·933	·967
	12	·729	·735	·752	·776	·805	·836	·869	·903	·936	·968
	16	0·766	0·771	0·783	0·803	0·827	0·854	0·882	0·912	0·941	0·971
	20	·793	·797	·808	·824	·844	·867	·893	·919	·946	·973
	24	·815	·818	·827	·841	·858	·879	·902	·925	·950	·975
	30	·839	·842	·849	·861	·875	·893	·912	·933	·955	·977
	34	·852	·855	·861	·871	·885	·900	·918	·938	·958	·979
	40	·868	·870	·876	·884	·896	·910	·926	·943	·961	·981
40	2	0·454	0·486	0·548	0·614	0·678	0·739	0·797	0·852	0·904	0·953
	4	·526	·545	·590	·644	·700	·755	·808	·859	·909	·955
	6	·575	·589	·624	·669	·718	·769	·818	·866	·913	·957
	8	·612	·623	·652	·691	·735	·781	·827	·872	·916	·959
	10	·642	·651	·676	·710	·750	·792	·835	·878	·920	·960
	12	·667	·674	·696	·727	·763	·802	·842	·883	·923	·962
	16	0·706	0·712	0·729	0·755	0·785	0·819	0·855	0·892	0·928	0·964
	20	·736	·741	·756	·777	·804	·834	·866	·899	·933	·967
	24	·761	·765	·777	·796	·819	·846	·876	·906	·937	·969
	30	·789	·793	·803	·818	·838	·862	·887	·915	·943	·971
	34	·805	·808	·817	·831	·849	·870	·894	·919	·946	·973
	40	·824	·827	·834	·846	·863	·882	·903	·926	·950	·975
50	2	0·410	0·447	0·514	0·584	0·652	0·718	0·780	0·839	0·896	0·949
	4	·479	·502	·552	·611	·672	·732	·790	·846	·900	·951
	6	·526	·543	·583	·634	·689	·744	·799	·852	·903	·953
	8	·562	·576	·610	·655	·704	·756	·807	·858	·907	·954
	10	·592	·603	·633	·673	·718	·766	·815	·863	·910	·956
	12	·617	·627	·653	·689	·731	·776	·822	·867	·913	·957
	16	0·658	0·665	0·686	0·716	0·753	0·793	0·834	0·876	0·918	0·959
	20	·689	·696	·713	·739	·772	·807	·845	·884	·923	·962
	24	·715	·721	·736	·759	·787	·820	·854	·890	·927	·964
	30	·746	·751	·763	·783	·808	·836	·867	·899	·933	·966
	34	·764	·767	·779	·796	·819	·845	·874	·904	·936	·968
	40	·785	·788	·798	·814	·834	·857	·883	·911	·940	·970

Table 53. *Test of the hypothesis that a covariance matrix* $\Sigma = \Sigma_0$. *Percentage points of L*

$p = 2$

ν	5%	1%
2	13·50	19·95
3	10·64	15·56
4	9·69	14·13
5	9·22	13·42
6	8·94	13·00
7	8·75	12·73
8	8·62	12·53
9	8·52	12·38
10	8·44	12·26

$p = 4$

ν	5%	1%
6	25·8	30·8
7	24·06	29·33
8	23·00	28·36
9	22·28	27·66
10	21·75	27·13
11	21·35	26·71
12	21·03	26·38
13	20·77	26·10
14	20·56	25·87

$p = 7$

ν	5%	1%
18	48·6	56·9
19	48·2	56·3
20	47·7	55·8
21	47·34	55·36
22	47·00	54·96
24	46·43	54·28
26	45·97	53·73
28	45·58	53·27
30	45·25	52·88
32	44·97	52·55
34	44·73	52·27

$p = 3$

ν	5%	1%
4	18·8	25·6
5	16·82	22·68
6	15·81	21·23
7	15·19	20·36
8	14·77	19·78
9	14·47	19·36
10	14·24	19·04
11	14·06	18·80
12	13·92	18·61
13	13·80	18·45
14	13·70	18·31
15	13·62	18·20

$p = 8$

ν	5%	1%
24	58·4	67·1
26	57·7	66·3
28	57·09	65·68
30	56·61	65·12
32	56·20	64·64
34	55·84	64·23
36	55·54	63·87
38	55·26	63·55
40	55·03	63·28

$p = 5$

ν	5%	1%
9	32·5	40·0
10	31·4	38·6
11	30·55	37·51
12	29·92	36·72
13	29·42	36·09
14	29·02	35·57
15	28·68	35·15
16	28·40	34·79
17	28·15	34·49
18	27·94	34·23
19	27·76	34·00
20	27·60	33·79

$p = 9$

ν	5%	1%
28	70·1	79·6
30	69·4	78·8
32	68·8	78·17
34	68·34	77·60
36	(67·91)	(77·08)
38	(67·53)	(76·65)
40	67·21	76·29
45	66·54	75·51
50	66·02	74·92
55	65·61	74·44
60	65·28	74·06

$p = 6$

ν	5%	1%
12	40·9	49·0
13	40·0	47·8
14	39·3	47·0
15	38·7	46·2
16	38·22	45·65
17	37·81	45·13
18	37·45	44·70
19	37·14	44·32
20	36·87	43·99
21	36·63	43·69
22	36·41	43·43
24	36·05	42·99
26	35·75	42·63
28	35·49	42·32
30	35·28	42·07

$p = 10$

ν	5%	1%
34	(82·3)	(92·4)
36	81·7	91·8
38	81·2	91·2
40	80·7	90·7
45	79·83	89·63
50	79·13	88·83
55	78·57	88·20
60	78·13	87·68
65	77·75	87·26
70	77·44	86·89
75	77·18	86·59

Entries in parentheses have been interpolated or extrapolated into Korin's table.

p = number of variates; N = number of observations; $\nu = N - 1$.

$L = \nu \log|\Sigma_0| - \nu p - \nu \log|S| + \nu \, \mathrm{tr}\,(S\,\Sigma_0^{-1})$, where S is the sample covariance matrix.

Table 54. *Modifications yielding approximate percentage points for the statistics D, V, W², U² and A in finite samples of n observations*

Case 1: Modifications for the test when $F(x)$ completely known

Statistic	Modified forms $T(D^+)$, $T(D)$, $T(V)$, etc.	Upper percentage points for modified T				
		15·0	**10·0**	**5·0**	**2·5**	**1·0**
D^+ (D^-)	$D^+(\sqrt{n}+0{\cdot}12+0{\cdot}11/\sqrt{n})$	0·973	1·073	1·224	1·358	1·518
D	$D(\sqrt{n}+0{\cdot}12+0{\cdot}11/\sqrt{n})$	1·138	1·224	1·358	1·480	1·628
V	$V(\sqrt{n}+0{\cdot}155+0{\cdot}24/\sqrt{n})$	1·537	1·620	1·747	1·862	2·001
W^2	$(W^2-0{\cdot}4/n+0{\cdot}6/n^2)\,(1{\cdot}0+1{\cdot}0/n)$	0·284	0·347	0·461	0·581	0·743
U^2	$(U^2-0{\cdot}1/n+0{\cdot}1/n^2)\,(1{\cdot}0+0{\cdot}8/n)$	0·131	0·152	0·187	0·221	0·267
A	For all $n \geqslant 5$:*	1·61	1·933	2·492	3·020	3·857

* Marshall (1958) showed that the distribution of A for $n = 1$ gives results remarkably close to the asymptotic ones, at least in the upper tail. To fill the gap Stephens carried out a Monte Carlo study for $n = 5$ and found the upper tail asymptotic points to be very close to the corresponding Monte Carlo points.

Case 2: Modifications for a test for Normality, μ and σ unspecified

Statistic	Modified forms $T(D)$, $T(V)$, $T(W^2)$, etc.	Upper percentage points for modified T				
		15·0	**10·0**	**5·0**	**2·5**	**1·0**
D	$D(\sqrt{n}-0{\cdot}01+0{\cdot}85/\sqrt{n})$	0·775	0·819	0·895	0·955	1·035
V	$V(\sqrt{n}+0{\cdot}05+0{\cdot}82/\sqrt{n})$	1·320	1·386	1·489	1·585	1·693
W^2	$W^2(1+0{\cdot}5/n)$	0·091	0·104	0·126	0·148	0·178
U^2	$U^2(1+0{\cdot}5/n)$	0·085	0·096	0·117	0·136	0·163
A	$(A-0{\cdot}7/n)\,(1+3{\cdot}6/n-8{\cdot}0/n^2)$	0·576	0·656	0·787	0·918	1·092

Case 3: Modifications for a test for Exponentality, a unspecified

Statistic	Modified forms $T(D)$, $T(V)$, $T(W^2)$, etc.	Upper percentage points for modified T				
		15·0	**10·0**	**5·0**	**2·5**	**1·0**
D	$(D-0{\cdot}2/n)\,(\sqrt{n}+0{\cdot}26+0{\cdot}5/\sqrt{n})$	0·926	0·990	1·094	1·190	1·308
V	$(V-0{\cdot}2/n)\,(\sqrt{n}+0{\cdot}24+0{\cdot}35/\sqrt{n})$	1·445	1·527	1·655	1·774	1·910
W^2	$W^2(1+0{\cdot}16/n)$	0·149	0·177	0·224	0·273	0·337
U^2	$U^2(1+0{\cdot}16/n)$	0·112	0·129	0·159	0·189	0·229
A	$A(1+1{\cdot}5/n-5/n^2)$	0·922	1·078	1·341	1·606	1·957

Table 55. *The Kolmogorov two-sample test. Upper critical values of* $c = mnD_{m,n}$

n	$m=1$ ·100	·050	·025	·010	·005	·001	$m=2$ ·100	·050	·025	·010	·005	·001	n
2													2
3													3
4							—						4
5							10						5
6							12						6
7							14	—					7
8							(16)	16					8
9							(18)	18					9
10							18	20					10
11							20	22	—				11
12							22	(24)	24				12
13							24	(26)	26				13
14							24	26	28				14
15							26	28	30				15
16							28	30	32				16
17							30	32	34				17
18	—						32	34	36	—			18
19	19						32	36	(38)	38			19
20	20						34	38	(40)	40			20
21	21						36	38	40	42			21
22	22						38	40	42	44			22
23	23						38	42	44	46			23
24	24						40	44	46	48			24
25	25		—				42	46	48	50	—		25

n	$m=3$ ·100	·050	·025	·010	·005	·001	$m=4$ ·100	·050	·025	·010	·005	·001	n
3	9												
4	12	—					(16)	16	—				4
5	(15)	15	—				16	(20)	20	—			5
6	15	(18)	18				18	20	(24)	24	—		6
7	18	(21)	21				21	24	(28)	28	—		7
8	(21)	21	24	—			24	(28)	28	(32)	32		8
9	21	24	(27)	27			27	28	32	(36)	36		9
10	24	27	(30)	30			28	30	(36)	36	40		10
11	27	(30)	30	33	—		29	33	36	40	44	—	11
12	27	30	33	(36)	36		(36)	36	40	44	48	—	12
13	30	33	36	(39)	39		35	39	44	(48)	48	52	13
14	33	36	39	(42)	42		38	42	44	48	52	56	14
15	33	36	39	42	45		40	44	45	52	56	60	15
16	36	39	42	45	48		44	48	52	56	60	64	16
17	36	42	45	48	51		44	48	52	60	64	68	17
18	39	45	48	51	54		46	50	54	60	64	72	18
19	42	45	51	54	57		49	53	57	64	68	76	19
20	42	48	51	57	57	—	52	60	64	68	72	76	20
21	45	51	54	57	60	63	52	59	63	72	76	80	21
22	48	51	57	60	63	66	56	62	66	72	76	84	22
23	48	54	60	63	66	69	57	64	69	76	80	88	23
24	51	57	60	66	69	72	60	68	72	80	84	92	24
25	54	60	63	69	72	75	63	68	75	84	88	96	25

The entries are the smallest value of c for which $\Pr\{D_{m,n} \geqslant c/(mn)\} \leqslant \alpha$, where α is shown at the head of each column. A blank space indicates that for this particular combination of m, n no value of c is significant at that level. Owing to the discontinuous nature of the distribution cases occur where the same value of c corresponds to two α-levels; in such cases the value corresponding to the larger α is repeated within parentheses.

Table 55 (*continued*)

n	m = 5 ·100	·050	·025	·010	·005	·001	m = 6 ·100	·050	·025	·010	·005	·001	n
5	20	(25)	(25)	25	—								
6	(24)	24	(30)	(30)	30		(30)	30	(36)	(36)	36		6
7	25	28	30	(35)	35		28	30	35	36	42	—	7
8	27	30	32	35	40	—	30	34	36	40	42	48	8
9	30	35	36	40	(45)	45	33	39	42	45	48	54	9
10	35	(40)	40	(45)	45	50	36	40	44	48	50	60	10
11	35	39	44	45	50	55	38	43	48	54	55	66	11
12	36	43	45	50	55	60	(48)	48	54	(60)	60	66	12
13	40	45	47	52	55	65	46	52	54	60	65	72	13
14	42	46	51	56	60	70	48	54	58	64	66	78	14
15	50	(55)	55	60	65	70	51	57	63	69	72	84	15
16	48	54	59	64	70	75	54	60	64	72	74	84	16
17	50	55	60	68	70	80	56	62	67	73	79	85	17
18	52	60	65	70	72	85	66	72	78	(84)	84	96	18
19	56	61	66	71	76	85	64	70	76	83	89	96	19
20	60	65	75	80	85	90	66	72	78	88	90	100	20
21	60	69	74	80	84	95	69	75	81	90	96	105	21
22	63	70	78	83	88	100	70	78	86	92	98	110	22
23	65	72	80	87	92	105	73	80	86	97	103	114	23
24	67	76	81	90	95	105	78	90	96	102	108	120	24
25	75	80	90	95	100	110	78	88	96	107	113	125	25

n	m = 7 ·100	·050	·025	·010	·005	·001	m = 8 ·100	·050	·025	·010	·005	·001	n
7	35	(42)	(42)	42	(49)	49							7
8	34	40	41	(48)	48	56	40	(48)	48	(56)	56	64	8
9	36	42	45	49	54	63	40	46	48	55	56	64	9
10	40	46	49	53	56	63	44	48	54	60	62	70	10
11	44	48	52	59	63	70	48	53	58	64	66	77	11
12	46	53	56	60	65	72	52	60	64	68	72	80	12
13	50	56	58	65	70	78	54	62	65	72	78	88	13
14	56	63	70	(77)	77	84	58	64	70	76	82	90	14
15	56	62	68	75	77	90	60	67	74	81	88	97	15
16	59	64	73	77	84	96	72	(80)	80	88	96	104	16
17	61	68	77	84	85	98	68	77	80	88	96	111	17
18	65	72	80	87	91	101	72	80	86	94	100	112	18
19	69	76	84	91	95	107	74	82	90	98	104	117	19
20	72	79	86	93	99	112	80	88	96	104	112	124	20
21	77	91	98	105	112	119	81	89	97	107	115	126	21
22	77	84	96	103	110	125	84	94	102	112	120	132	22
23	80	89	98	108	112	126	89	98	106	115	122	137	23
24	84	92	102	112	119	133	96	104	112	128	136	152	24
25	86	97	105	115	122	136	95	104	112	125	134	150	25

n	m = 9 ·100	·050	·025	·010	·005	·001	m = 10 ·100	·050	·025	·010	·005	·001	n
9	(54)	54	(63)	63	(72)	72							9
10	50	53	60	63	70	80	60	(70)	70	(80)	80	90	10
11	52	59	63	70	72	81	57	60	68	77	79	89	11
12	57	63	69	75	78	87	60	66	72	80	84	96	12
13	59	65	72	78	82	91	64	70	77	84	90	100	13
14	63	70	76	84	89	98	68	74	82	90	96	106	14
15	69	75	81	90	93	105	75	80	90	100	105	115	15
16	69	78	85	94	99	110	76	84	90	100	108	118	16
17	74	82	90	99	102	117	79	89	96	106	110	126	17
18	81	90	99	108	117	126	82	92	100	108	116	132	18
19	80	89	98	107	114	126	85	94	103	113	122	133	19
20	84	93	100	111	117	133	100	110	120	(130)	130	150	20
21	90	99	108	117	123	138	95	105	116	126	130	149	21
22	91	101	110	122	127	144	98	108	118	130	138	154	22
23	94	106	115	126	134	152	101	114	124	137	144	160	23
24	99	111	120	132	138	156	106	118	128	140	148	166	24
25	101	114	123	135	144	162	110	125	135	150	155	175	25

Table 55 (*continued*). *The Kolmogorov two-sample test. Upper critical values of* $c = mnD_{m,n}$

α / n	m = 11 ·100	·050	·025	·010	·005	·001	m = 12 ·100	·050	·025	·010	·005	·001	n
11	66	(77)	77	(88)	88	99							
12	64	72	76	86	88	99	72	84	(96)	96	108	120	12
13	67	75	84	91	97	108	71	81	84	95	104	117	13
14	73	82	87	96	101	115	78	86	94	104	108	120	14
15	76	84	94	102	109	120	84	93	99	108	117	129	15
16	80	89	96	106	112	127	88	96	104	116	124	136	16
17	85	93	102	110	119	132	90	100	108	119	127	141	17
18	88	97	107	118	125	140	96	108	120	126	138	150	18
19	92	102	111	122	130	146	99	108	120	130	140	156	19
20	96	107	116	127	136	154	104	116	124	140	148	164	20
21	101	112	123	134	143	157	108	120	129	141	150	168	21
22	110	121	132	143	154	176	110	124	134	148	154	174	22
23	108	119	131	142	153	173	113	125	137	149	160	182	23
24	111	124	137	150	159	176	132	144	156	168	180	192	24
25	117	129	140	154	164	184	120	138	150	165	175	192	25

α / n	m = 13 ·100	·050	·025	·010	·005	·001	m = 14 ·100	·050	·025	·010	·005	·001	n
13	(91)	91	104	(117)	117	130							
14	78	89	100	104	115	129	98	(112)	112	(126)	126	154	14
15	87	96	104	115	122	137	92	98	110	123	125	140	15
16	91	101	111	121	128	143	96	106	116	126	136	152	16
17	96	105	114	127	135	152	100	111	122	134	140	159	17
18	99	110	120	131	141	156	104	116	126	140	148	166	18
19	104	114	126	138	145	164	110	121	133	148	154	176	19
20	108	120	130	143	154	169	114	126	138	152	160	180	20
21	113	126	137	150	161	179	126	140	147	161	175	189	21
22	117	130	141	156	168	185	124	138	148	164	174	196	22
23	120	135	146	161	171	191	127	142	154	170	179	202	23
24	125	140	151	166	177	199	132	146	160	176	186	210	24
25	131	145	158	172	184	200	136	150	166	182	194	219	25

α / n	m = 15 ·100	·050	·025	·010	·005	·001	m = 16 ·100	·050	·025	·010	·005	·001	n
15	105	120	(135)	135	150	165							
16	101	114	119	133	144	162	112	128	144	(160)	160	176	16
17	105	116	129	142	148	165	109	124	136	143	157	174	17
18	111	123	135	147	156	174	116	128	140	154	162	186	18
19	114	127	141	152	161	180	120	133	145	160	170	192	19
20	125	135	150	160	170	195	128	140	156	168	180	200	20
21	126	138	153	168	177	198	130	145	157	173	183	208	21
22	130	144	154	173	182	205	136	150	164	180	192	216	22
23	134	149	163	179	187	210	141	157	169	187	198	221	23
24	141	156	168	186	198	222	152	168	184	200	208	232	24
25	145	160	175	195	205	230	149	167	181	199	213	238	25

The entries are the smallest value of c for which $\Pr\{D_{m,n} \geqslant c/(mn)\} \leqslant \alpha$, where α is shown at the head of each column. A blank space indicates that for this particular combination of m, n no value of c is significant at that level. Owing to the discontinuous nature of the distribution cases occur where the same value of c corresponds to two α-levels; in such cases the value corresponding to the larger α is repeated within parentheses.

Table 55 (*continued*)

n \ α	m = 17 .100	.050	.025	.010	.005	.001	m = 18 .100	.050	.025	.010	.005	.001	n
17	(136)	136	153	(170)	170	204							
18	118	133	148	164	168	187	144	(162)	162	180	198	216	18
19	126	141	151	166	179	200	133	142	159	176	180	212	19
20	132	146	160	175	186	209	136	152	166	182	194	214	20
21	136	151	166	180	193	217	144	159	174	189	201	225	21
22	142	157	170	187	199	225	148	164	178	196	208	234	22
23	146	163	179	196	207	232	152	170	184	204	216	242	23
24	151	168	183	203	214	240	162	180	198	216	228	252	24
25	156	173	190	207	222	249	162	180	196	216	231	257	25

n \ α	m = 19 .100	.050	.025	.010	.005	.001	m = 20 .100	.050	.025	.010	.005	.001	n
19	152	171	(190)	190	209	228							
20	144	160	169	187	204	225	160	180	200	(220)	220	260	20
21	147	163	180	199	207	237	154	173	180	199	217	239	21
22	152	169	185	204	219	242	160	176	192	212	226	254	22
23	159	177	190	209	224	253	164	184	199	219	233	262	23
24	164	183	199	218	232	261	172	192	208	228	244	272	24
25	168	187	205	224	241	268	180	200	215	235	250	280	25

n \ α	m = 21 .100	.050	.025	.010	.005	.001	m = 22 .100	.050	.025	.010	.005	.001	n
21	168	189	210	231	252	273							
22	163	183	203	223	229	267	(198)	198	220	242	264	286	22
23	171	189	206	227	242	269	173	194	214	237	253	282	23
24	177	198	213	237	252	282	182	204	222	242	258	292	24
25	182	202	220	244	258	290	189	209	228	250	268	299	25

n \ α	m = 23 .100	.050	.025	.010	.005	.001	m = 24 .100	.050	.025	.010	.005	.001	n
23	207	(230)	230	253	276	299							
24	183	205	226	249	270	296	216	240	264	(288)	288	336	24
25	195	216	237	262	274	312	204	225	238	262	283	312	25

n \ α	m = 25 .100	.050	.025	.010	.005	.001
25	225	250	275	300	325	350

Table 56. *Percentage points of R/N (on circle), for given N and κ*

N \ κ	0·0	0·5	1·0	1·5	2·0	2·5	3·0	3·5	4·0	4·5	5·0
5	—	0·922	0·961	0·973	0·977	0·980	0·984	0·987	0·990	0·992	0·993
	—	·815	·864	·937	·956	·965	·972	·976	·980	·983	·985
	—	·145	·197	·306	·432	·537	·625	·688	·733	·767	·794
	—	—	—	·170	·274	·386	·484	·563	·625	·672	·710
6	0·825	0·877	0·936	0·960	0·969	0·974	0·979	0·983	0·986	0·988	0·990
	·690	·764	·844	·915	·941	·955	·963	·969	·973	·977	·979
	—	·127	·194	·321	·450	·571	·638	·698	·742	·775	·800
	—	—	—	·181	·304	·419	·514	·588	·646	·691	·726
7	0·771	0·838	0·912	0·946	0·961	0·968	0·974	0·978	0·982	0·984	0·986
	·642	·724	·828	·896	·928	·945	·956	·963	·968	·972	·975
	—	·116	·195	·334	·465	·600	·649	·706	·749	·781	·805
	—	—	—	·196	·330	·445	·537	·608	·663	·705	·739
8	0·725	0·804	0·890	0·933	0·952	0·962	0·969	0·974	0·978	0·981	0·983
	·602	·691	·809	·879	·917	·937	·949	·957	·963	·967	·971
	—	·107	·199	·345	·478	·601	·657	·714	·755	·786	·810
	—	—	—	·212	·351	·466	·555	·624	·677	·717	·749
9	0·687	0·775	0·870	0·920	0·944	0·956	0·964	0·970	0·974	0·978	0·980
	·569	·665	·789	·865	·906	·929	·943	·952	·959	·964	·968
	—	·102	·204	·356	·489	·599	·665	·720	·760	·790	·814
	—	—	—	·228	·369	·483	·571	·637	·688	·727	·758
10	0·655	0·750	0·853	0·909	0·936	0·950	0·959	0·966	0·971	0·975	0·978
	·540	·642	·772	·852	·897	·922	·937	·947	·955	·960	·965
	—	·097	·209	·365	·498	·601	·679	·726	·765	·794	·817
	—	—	—	·242	·385	·498	·584	·649	·698	·736	·765
12	0·602	0·709	0·823	0·888	0·922	0·940	0·951	0·959	0·965	0·969	0·973
	·494	·605	·742	·831	·882	·911	·928	·940	·948	·954	·959
	—	·092	·220	·382	·514	·612	·696	·735	·773	·801	·823
	—	—	—	·268	·412	·522	·605	·667	·713	·749	·777
16	0·525	0·649	0·778	0·857	0·900	0·924	0·938	0·948	0·955	0·961	0·965
	·429	·554	·694	·801	·859	·894	·915	·928	·938	·946	·952
	—	·088	·240	·406	·537	·632	·703	·748	·783	·811	·832
	—	—	—	·307	·450	·556	·634	·692	·735	·768	·794
20	0·472	0·607	0·746	0·833	0·883	0·911	0·928	0·940	0·948	0·954	0·959
	·385	·519	·663	·780	·843	·881	·905	·920	·931	·940	·946
	—	·088	·256	·424	·553	·645	·711	·759	·791	·817	·838
	—	—	·157	·336	·476	·579	·654	·709	·749	·781	·805
30	0·387	0·540	0·694	0·794	0·854	0·889	0·910	0·925	0·935	0·943	0·949
	·315	·466	·626	·747	·818	·861	·888	·907	·920	·930	·937
	—	·097	·285	·453	·578	·667	·728	·772	·805	·829	·848
	—	—	·204	·382	·517	·615	·684	·735	·772	·800	·822
40	0·336	0·500	0·662	0·770	0·835	0·874	0·899	0·916	0·927	0·936	0·943
	·273	·434	·606	·727	·802	·849	·879	·898	·913	·923	·932
	—	·107	·303	·471	·594	·680	·739	·782	·812	·836	·854
	—	—	·234	·411	·542	·636	·702	·750	·785	·812	·832
60	0·276	0·452	0·623	0·740	0·812	0·856	0·885	0·903	0·917	0·927	0·935
	·223	·397	·577	·703	·783	·834	·866	·888	·904	·916	·925
	—	·123	·327	·493	·613	·695	·752	·792	·822	·844	·861
	—	·060	·271	·445	·571	·660	·723	·767	·800	·825	·844
100	0·214	0·404	0·584	0·709	0·788	0·837	0·869	0·891	0·906	0·917	0·926
	·173	·361	·547	·679	·764	·819	·854	·878	·895	·908	·918
	—	·144	·353	·516	·632	·711	·765	·803	·831	·852	·868
	—	·097	·310	·479	·600	·685	·743	·785	·815	·838	·856
200	0·152	0·356	0·544	0·676	0·762	0·817	0·853	0·877	0·894	0·907	0·917
	·122	·326	·517	·654	·745	·803	·841	·867	·886	·900	·911
	—	·170	·379	·539	·651	·727	·778	·814	·841	·860	·876
	—	·137	·349	·513	·630	·709	·764	·802	·830	·851	·867
∞	0·000	0·243	0·446	0·596	0·698	0·765	0·810	0·841	0·864	0·880	0·893

Table 57. *Charts to determine percentage points of R (on circle), for given N and X*

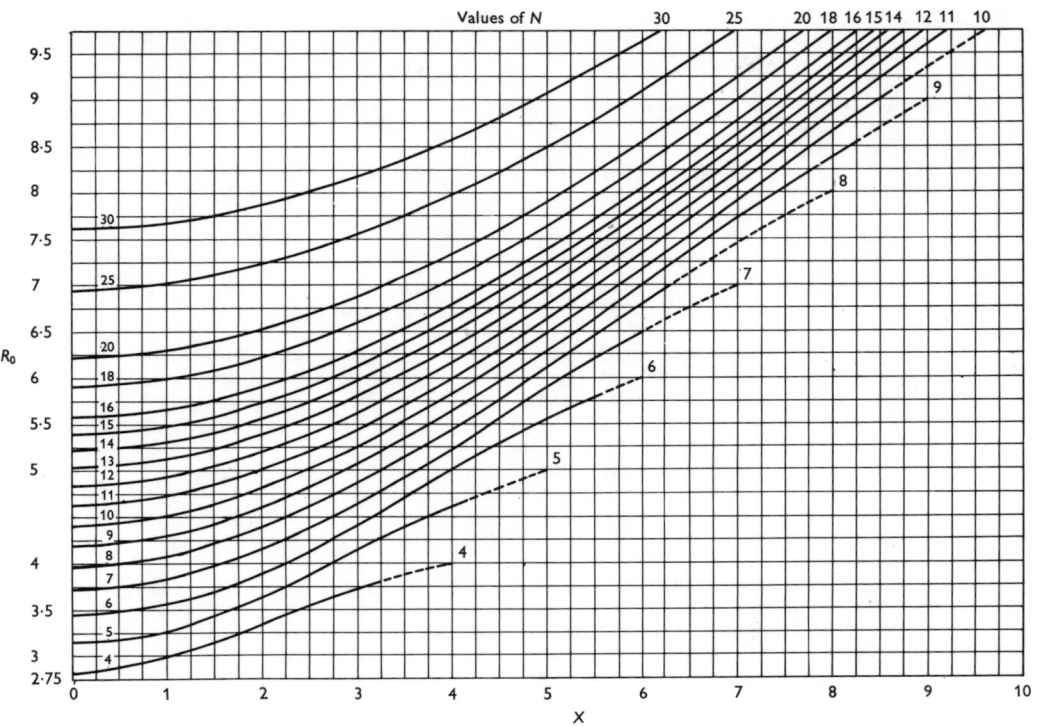

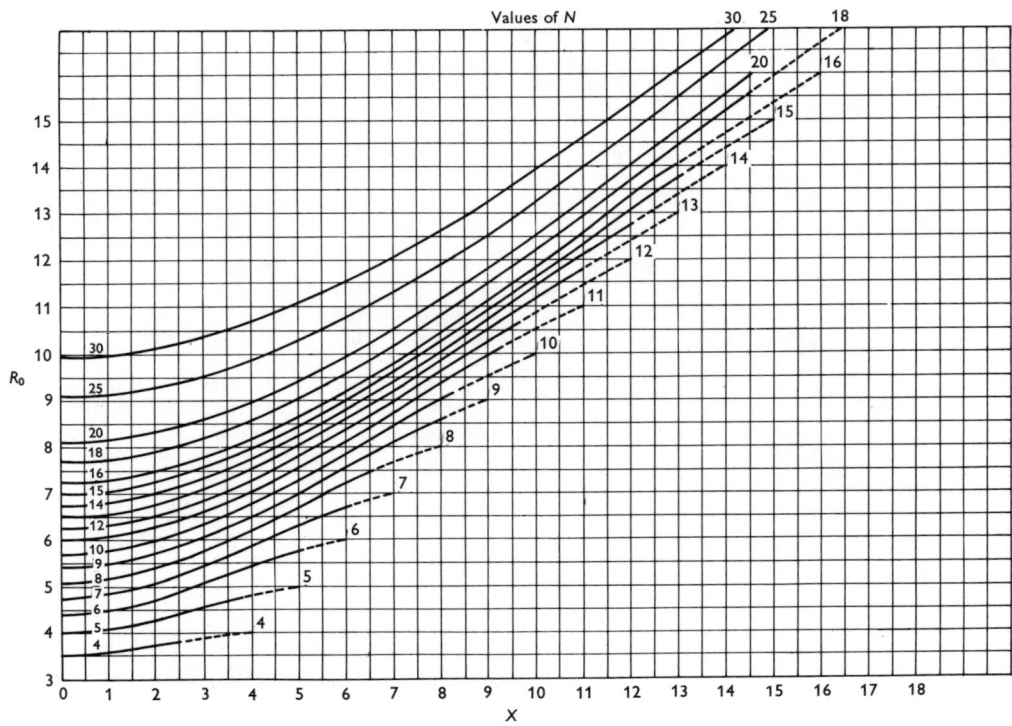

365

Table 58A. *Critical values of Z for test of equality of two modal vectors (on circle):*
equal sample sizes, $N_1 = N_2 = \frac{1}{2}N$

N (N_1, N_2) \ W	0·05	0·10	0·15	0·20	0·25	0·30	0·35	0·40	0·45	0·50	0·55	0·60	0·65	0·70
12	630	630	631	633	637	644	655	671	692	717	744	772	797	822
(6, 6)	569	570	572	576	582	592	606	624	648	676	706	738	769	801
	517	519	522	527	536	547	564	585	612	642	675	710	746	782
	457	460	464	471	482	497	517	542	572	606	643	681	721	761
16	543	545	547	552	560	572	589	611	638	667	698	731	755	797
(8, 8)	490	492	496	502	513	527	547	572	601	633	668	704	736	778
	444	447	452	460	472	489	512	539	571	606	643	682	719	761
	392	396	402	412	427	448	474	505	540	578	618	660	701	745
20	485	487	491	498	509	525	547	573	603	635	669	705	742	780
(10, 10)	437	440	445	454	467	486	510	539	572	607	644	683	722	762
	396	399	406	416	432	453	480	511	547	585	624	665	707	749
	349	353	361	374	393	417	448	483	521	562	604	647	691	735
24	442	445	450	459	473	492	517	546	579	614	650	688	727	766
(12, 12)	398	402	408	419	435	457	485	517	552	589	629	669	710	752
	360	365	372	385	403	428	458	493	531	570	612	654	697	740
	318	323	332	347	369	397	431	468	509	551	595	639	684	729
30	395	399	406	417	434	458	486	519	554	592	631	671	713	756
(15, 15)	355	360	368	381	401	428	459	494	532	572	613	655	699	743
	321	327	336	351	374	403	437	475	514	556	599	643	688	734
	283	290	301	319	344	377	414	454	497	540	585	631	677	724
40	342	347	356	371	393	421	454	491	529	570	611	654	697	740
(20, 20)	308	313	324	341	366	397	432	471	512	554	597	642	686	731
	278	285	297	316	343	377	415	456	498	542	587	632	678	724
	245	253	267	290	320	357	397	440	485	530	576	623	670	717
60	280	286	299	320	349	383	421	461	504	547	590	636	681	727
(30, 30)	251	259	274	297	329	365	405	448	491	536	581	628	674	721
	227	236	253	279	312	351	393	437	482	528	574	621	669	716
	200	211	230	259	296	337	381	426	473	520	567	615	663	711
120	199	210	232	264	301	343	386	431	479	526	573	621	668	716
(60, 60)	179	192	216	250	290	333	378	424	472	520	568	616	664	712
	162	176	203	239	281	326	372	418	467	515	564	612	661	709
	144	160	189	229	272	318	365	413	462	511	560	609	658	707
240	142	161	193	233	276	322	369	418	466	516	564	611	661	709
(120, 120)	130	149	183	225	270	317	364	413	463	512	562	609	658	707
	118	140	177	220	266	312	361	411	460	509	558	607	656	705
	105	130	169	214	260	309	358	407	457	506	555	606	654	703
∞	0·05	0·10	0·15	0·20	0·25	0·30	0·35	0·40	0·45	0·05	0·55	0·60	0·65	0·70

$N = N_1 + N_2$, $W = R/N$, $Z = (R_1 + R_2)/N$. The table entries, preceded by a decimal point, give values of z such that $\mathrm{Pr}\{Z > z \mid W, N_1, N_2\} = \alpha$, for values of $\alpha = 0.01$, 0.025, 0.05, 0.10, in descending order. For $W > 0.70$, see § 33.3.

Table 58B. *Critical values of Z for test of equality of two modal vectors (on circle): unequal sample sizes, $N_1 \neq N_2$*

	N	W 0.05	0.10	0.15	0.20	0.25	0.30	0.35	0.40
	20	454	462	471	487	514	532	561	577
		410	417	430	447	464	487	509	540
		375	378	392	410	427	455	492	513
		335	340	345	369	390	424	453	484
	24	416	424	437	454	474	496	520	549
		375	383	397	414	435	460	487	519
		340	349	362	381	403	430	461	495
		301	309	323	343	369	399	432	470
Case $r = N_1/N_2 = 2$	30	373	382	397	415	436	461	488	521
$N = N_1 + N_2$		336	345	360	379	403	430	460	496
$R = R_1 + R_2$		304	314	329	350	375	405	437	476
		268	278	295	317	346	378	414	455
$W = R/N$	40	324	334	351	371	396	424	453	492
$Z = (R_1 + R_2)/N$		291	302	319	341	368	398	432	472
		264	274	292	317	345	379	416	456
For $W > 0.40$ use Table 58A.		232	244	263	290	322	358	397	440
	60	267	279	298	322	351	384	413	462
		239	252	273	299	330	366	406	448
		217	230	252	280	314	352	394	437
		191	205	229	260	297	338	381	427
	120	191	208	233	265	302	343	386	431
		172	190	217	251	290	333	378	424
		156	175	204	240	282	326	372	418
		138	159	190	229	273	318	365	413

	N	W 0.05	0.10	0.15	0.20	0.25	0.30	0.35	0.40
	20	397	407	443	479	513	531	561	575
		351	384	404	438	493	479	531	538
		329	336	365	386	438	448	510	499
		298	311	325	356	418	408	475	499
	24	345	372	402	433	463	492	524	553
		318	340	367	397	430	457	492	523
		292	309	336	366	398	429	466	497
		259	277	302	333	367	398	438	474
Case $r = N_1/N_2 = 4$	30	313	339	367	396	425	458	491	526
$N = N_1 + N_2$		286	306	335	364	392	431	462	501
$R = R_1 + R_2$		260	282	309	341	369	407	437	483
		229	249	279	310	338	381	414	456
$W = R/N$	40	276	302	331	360	391	424	459	496
$Z = (R_1 + R_2)/N$		251	273	303	333	364	401	436	476
		228	251	280	312	344	381	417	461
For $W > 0.40$ use Table 58A.		201	223	254	286	319	361	399	441
	60	232	257	288	320	352	388	425	464
		209	235	265	298	333	369	409	449
		190	215	246	279	316	354	396	438
		168	193	225	260	299	339	384	428
	120	171	199	232	266	304	345	387	431
		155	183	216	253	291	334	378	424
		140	170	204	242	282	326	371	419
		125	155	191	230	273	319	365	413

Table 59. *Percentage points for R/N (on sphere), for given N and* κ

For each cell of the Table, the four entries are (respectively) the upper 1 per cent, upper 5 per cent, lower 5 per cent and lower 1 per cent points for R/N.

N \ κ	0·0	0·5	1·0	1·5	2·0	2·5	3·0	3·5	4·0	4·5	5·0
4	0·8725	0·8863	0·9117	0·9325	0·9469	0·9568	0·9638	0·9689	0·9728	0·9758	0·9782
	·7758	·7969	·8383	·8747	·9008	·9191	·9321	·9417	·9489	·9546	·9591
	·1805	·1908	·2228	·2779	·3498	·4253	·4951	·5569	·6087	·6509	·6854
	·1020	·1079	·1270	·1620	·2165	·2859	·3584	·4254	·4845	·5364	·5811
5	0·8046	0·8275	0·8668	0·8982	0·9197	0·9347	0·9453	0·9530	0·9588	0·9634	0·9670
	·7002	·7288	·7843	·8327	·8675	·8919	·9093	·9220	·9317	·9393	·9454
	·1609	·1721	·2074	·2693	·3496	·4310	·5031	·5640	·6147	·6562	·6901
	·0924	·0990	·1202	·1610	·2240	·3016	·3790	·4480	·5071	·5571	·5995
6	0·7467	0·7767	0·8278	0·8683	0·8963	0·9156	0·9291	0·9391	0·9467	0·9526	0·9574
	·6422	·6764	·7241	·7994	·8410	·8702	·8910	·9063	·9179	·9270	·9343
	·1454	·1577	·1974	·2667	·3531	·4375	·5106	·5713	·6211	·6618	·6952
	·0832	·0905	·1142	·1616	·2341	·3178	·3973	·4665	·5248	·5736	·6145
7	0·6986	0·7346	0·7949	0·8426	0·8760	0·8990	0·9153	0·9271	0·9362	0·9433	0·9490
	·5969	·6355	·7084	·7725	·8194	·8525	·8761	·8935	·9067	·9170	·9253
	·1339	·1472	·1907	·2667	·3579	·4440	·5176	·5780	·6271	·6671	·6999
	·0766	·0843	·1108	·1644	·2447	·3326	·4131	·4819	·5393	·5870	·6267
8	0·6579	0·6990	0·7667	0·8207	0·8585	0·8847	0·9033	0·9169	0·9271	0·9352	0·9417
	·5600	·6024	·6813	·7504	·8015	·8378	·8637	·8829	·8974	·9087	·9179
	·1247	·1389	·1863	·2682	·3630	·4503	·5239	·5839	·6325	·6720	·7043
	·0713	·0796	·1087	·1685	·2553	·3459	·4267	·4950	·5513	·5982	·6369
9	0·6236	0·6691	0·7425	0·8016	0·8431	0·8722	0·8928	0·9079	0·9193	0·9282	0·9353
	·5291	·5751	·6587	·7320	·7865	·8253	·8533	·8736	·8895	·9017	·9115
	·1172	·1323	·1834	·2705	·3680	·4561	·5296	·5892	·6373	·6763	·7081
	·0670	·0758	·1075	·1734	·2654	·3577	·4385	·5061	·5618	·6076	·6456
10	0·5940	0·6432	0·7217	0·7849	0·8299	0·8612	0·8835	0·8999	0·9124	0·9221	0·9298
	·5028	·5518	·6396	·7163	·7735	·8147	·8443	·8661	·8827	·8957	·9061
	·1109	·1269	·1815	·2732	·3729	·4614	·5347	·5940	·6416	·6802	·7116
	·0636	·0727	·1070	·1781	·2742	·3682	·4489	·5158	·5708	·6158	·6530
12	0·5457	0·6012	0·6872	0·7572	0·8075	0·8428	0·8680	0·8866	0·9007	0·9117	0·9205
	·4603	·5147	·6090	·6909	·7526	·7972	·8295	·8534	·8716	·8858	·8972
	·1008	·1185	·1799	·2791	·3817	·4708	·5437	·6021	·6490	·6868	·7177
	·0577	·0680	·1071	·1888	·2907	·3856	·4662	·5319	·5855	·6292	·6652
16	0·476	0·541	0·638	0·717	0·774	0·815	0·845	0·867	0·883	0·896	0·906
	·400	·463	·567	·655	·723	·773	·809	·835	·856	·872	·884
	·087	·107	·182	·291	·397	·486	·557	·615	·660	·697	·727
	·050	·055	·109	·210	·317	·412	·491	·555	·607	·648	·683
20	0·428	0·500	0·604	0·688	0·751	0·796	0·828	0·852	0·871	0·885	0·897
	·358	·428	·538	·631	·703	·755	·794	·823	·845	·862	·876
	·078	·100	·186	·301	·408	·496	·567	·624	·668	·704	·733
	·044	·049	·111	·225	·337	·432	·509	·571	·621	·662	·695
30	0·355	0·436	0·550	0·643	0·713	0·764	0·802	0·829	0·850	0·867	0·880
	·295	·374	·493	·594	·671	·729	·771	·803	·827	·846	·862
	·063	·093	·197	·319	·427	·515	·584	·639	·682	·716	·744
	·036	·043	·133	·257	·369	·463	·538	·597	·645	·683	·714
40	0·307	0·398	0·517	0·616	0·690	0·745	0·785	0·815	0·838	0·856	0·870
	·255	·343	·467	·572	·653	·713	·758	·791	·817	·837	·853
	·054	·090	·206	·332	·440	·527	·595	·648	·690	·724	·751
	·031	·043	·150	·278	·390	·482	·555	·613	·659	·696	·726
60	0·251	0·353	0·479	0·583	0·663	0·722	0·765	0·798	0·823	0·842	0·858
	·208	·307	·437	·546	·631	·694	·742	·777	·805	·826	·844
	·044	·092	·221	·348	·456	·541	·608	·660	·701	·733	·760
	·025	·048	·174	·304	·416	·506	·576	·632	·676	·711	·739
100	0·194	0·308	0·441	0·550	0·635	0·698	0·745	0·780	0·807	0·828	0·845
	·161	·272	·407	·521	·609	·676	·725	·763	·792	·815	·834
	·034	·098	·237	·366	·472	·556	·621	·672	·711	·743	·768
	·020	·062	·201	·333	·442	·529	·598	·651	·693	·726	·753
∞	0·000	0·164	0·313	0·438	0·537	0·613	0·672	0·716	0·751	0·778	0·800

For interpolation for N, note that R/N, when plotted against $1/\sqrt{N}$, is closely linear.

Table 60. *Charts to determine percentage points of R (on sphere), for given N and X*

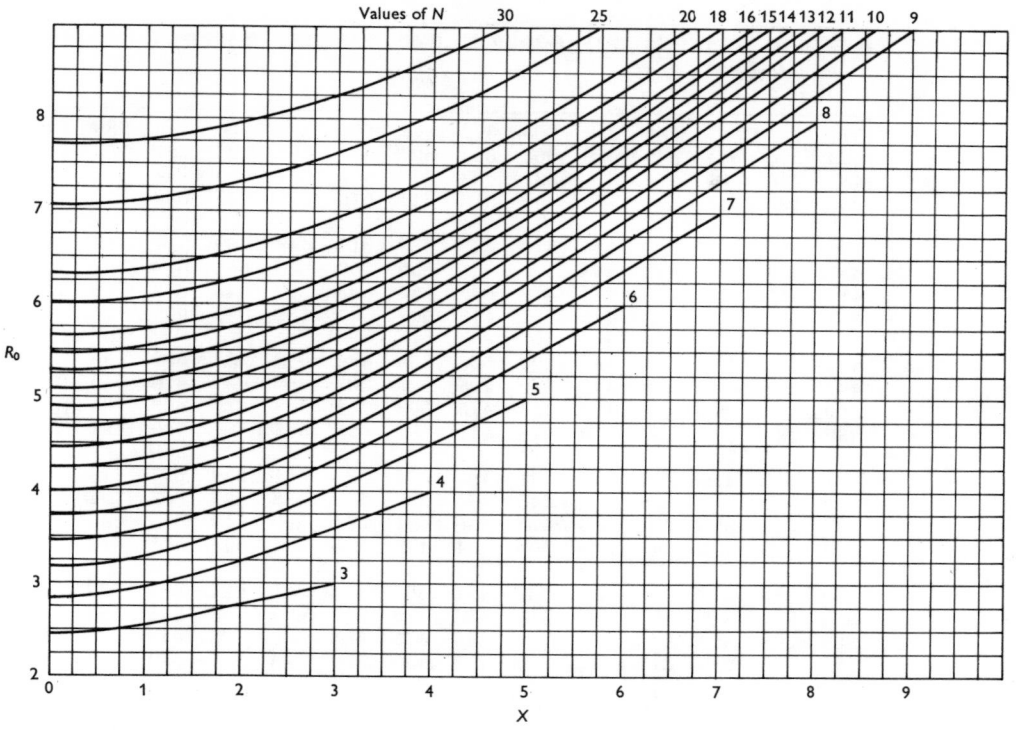

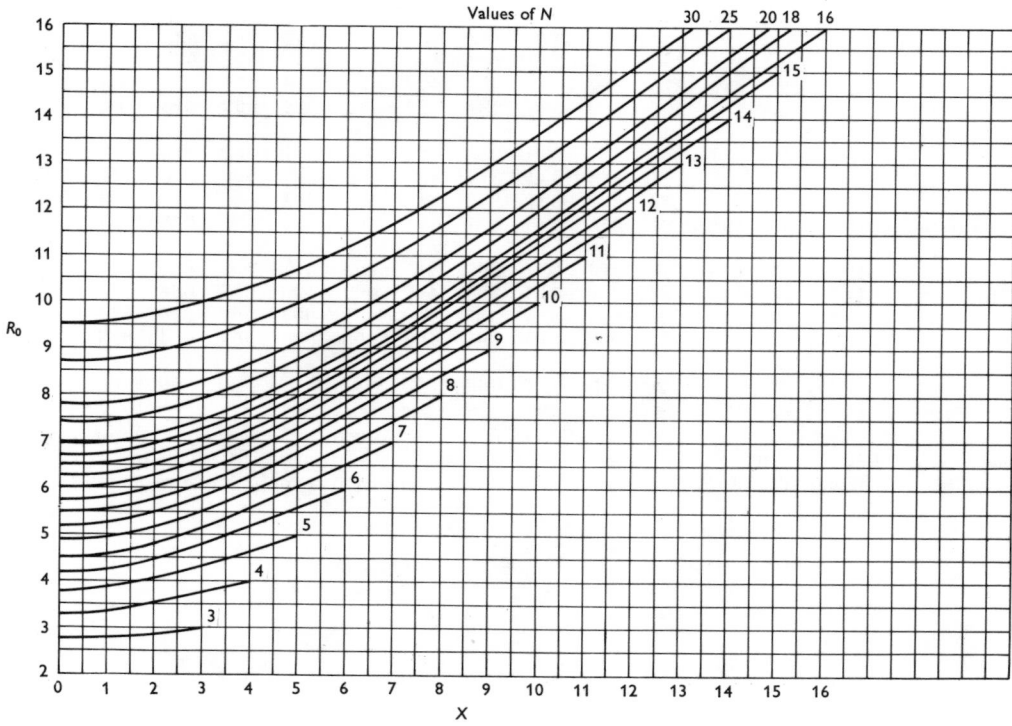

Table 61A. *Critical values of Z for test of equality of two modal vectors (on sphere): equal sample sizes, $N_1 = N_2 = \frac{1}{2}N$*

N (N_1, N_2) \ W	0·05	0·10	0·15	0·20	0·25	0·30	0·35	0·40	0·45	0·50	0·55	0·60	0·65	0·70
12 (6, 6)	571	573	577	583	592	605	622	642	666	692	720	749	780	811
	523	526	531	539	550	565	584	607	633	662	692	724	758	793
	482	486	492	501	514	531	552	577	606	637	670	704	741	778
	435	439	446	457	473	492	516	544	576	610	646	684	722	762
16 (8, 8)	493	496	502	511	524	542	563	589	617	648	680	714	749	784
	451	455	462	473	488	507	531	559	590	623	658	694	731	769
	415	419	427	440	457	478	505	535	568	603	640	679	718	758
	373	379	328	403	422	447	476	508	544	582	622	662	704	746
20 (10, 10)	440	444	452	464	480	500	525	555	586	620	655	692	730	768
	402	407	416	429	447	470	498	529	563	599	637	676	715	756
	369	375	385	400	420	446	475	509	545	583	622	663	704	746
	332	339	350	368	390	418	451	487	525	565	607	649	693	736
24 (12, 12)	401	407	416	429	448	471	499	531	565	601	639	677	716	757
	366	372	383	398	419	445	475	509	545	583	623	663	704	746
	337	343	355	372	395	423	455	491	529	569	610	652	695	738
	303	310	323	343	368	399	434	472	513	554	597	641	685	730
30 (15, 15)	359	365	376	392	414	441	474	507	544	581	621	662	703	746
	327	334	346	364	389	417	453	488	527	567	608	651	693	737
	300	308	322	341	368	400	435	473	514	555	598	642	686	731
	271	279	295	317	346	380	417	458	500	543	587	632	678	723
40 (20, 20)	311	319	332	352	378	409	444	481	521	562	604	647	691	734
	284	292	307	329	357	390	427	467	508	551	594	638	683	728
	260	270	286	310	340	376	414	455	492	542	586	631	677	723
	234	245	263	290	322	360	401	443	487	532	578	624	671	718
60 (30, 30)	255	265	282	307	339	375	414	455	498	542	586	632	677	723
	232	243	263	290	324	362	402	445	489	534	579	625	672	718
	213	225	247	276	312	351	393	437	482	528	574	621	668	715
	192	206	229	261	299	340	384	429	475	522	569	616	664	712
120 (60, 60)	182	197	223	258	297	339	383	428	474	521	568	616	664	711
	167	183	211	247	288	332	377	423	470	517	565	613	661	709
	153	171	201	239	281	326	372	419	466	514	562	610	659	708
	139	159	191	231	275	320	367	414	462	511	559	608	657	706
240 (120, 120)	133	155	189	230	274	320	367	415	463	511	559	608	657	706
	122	144	182	224	269	316	364	412	460	509	557	606	655	705
	113	139	177	220	267	314	363	410	458	507	556	605	654	704
	103	131	171	216	262	310	360	408	456	505	554	604	653	703
∞	0·05	0·10	0·15	0·20	0·25	0·30	0·35	0·40	0·45	0·50	0·55	0·60	0·65	0·70

$N = N_1 + N_2$, $W = R/N$, $Z = (R_1 + R_2)/N$. The table entries, preceded by a decimal point, give values of z such that $\Pr(Z > z \mid W, N_1, N_2) = \alpha$, for values of $\alpha = 0.01, 0.025, 0.05, 0.10$, in descending order. For $W > 0.70$, see p. 132. For intermediate N-values, linear interpolation with argument $1/N$ is adequate.

Table 61 B. *Critical values of Z for test of equality of two modal vectors (on sphere): unequal sample sizes, $N_1 \neq N_2$*

N \ W	$r = N_1/N_2 = 2$						$r = N_1/N_2 = 4$		
	0·10	0·15	0·20	0·25	0·30	0·35	0·10	0·20	0·30
20	420	436	454	474	497	525	367	423	478
	382	400	421	438	468	498	334	396	457
	355	371	392	414	444	475	313	370	433
	320	341	361	385	417	451	285	338	406
24	385	403	422	445	469	499	340	400	457
	350	370	392	416	443	475	312	372	436
	325	345	366	392	422	455	291	350	416
	295	315	338	366	398	434	265	323	394
30	350	366	387	412	441	472	310	368	435
	321	338	361	387	416	451	285	345	414
	296	314	338	367	399	435	265	328	396
	268	288	314	345	379	417	240	305	378
40	307	325	350	378	409	—	277	337	408
	283	302	327	359	391	—	255	317	387
	261	281	309	340	376	—	237	302	375
	237	258	288	322	360	—	216	283	360
60	257	278	307	339	375	—	238	302	374
	237	260	289	324	361	—	220	285	361
	220	244	275	312	351	—	204	271	350
	200	226	260	299	340	—	187	258	340
120	195	223	258	—	—	—	186	257	339
	181	211	247	—	—	—	173	247	331
	169	201	239	—	—	—	163	240	326
	157	191	231	—	—	—	152	230	320
∞	0·10	0·15	0·20	0·25	0·30	0·35	0·10	0·20	0·30

For W beyond range of tables, use Table 61 A.

Table 62. *Estimation of κ for dispersion on circle*

Solution of $I_0'(\hat{\kappa})/I_0(\hat{\kappa}) = a$

a	$\hat{\kappa}$	a	$\hat{\kappa}$
0·10	0·2010	**0·60**	1·516
·15	·3034	·65	1·739
·20	·4083		
·25	·5165	**0·70**	2·014
·30	·6292	·72	2·144
		·74	2·289
0·35	0·7478	·76	2·455
·40	·8741	·78	2·646
·45	1·0102		
·50	1·1593	**0·80**	2·871
·55	1·3257	·82	3·143
		·84	3·479
		·86	3·911

For $a < 0.10$, $\hat{\kappa} \simeq 2a$.
For $a > 0.80$, $1/\hat{\kappa} \simeq 2(1-a) - (1-a)^2$.

Table 63. *Estimation of κ for dispersion on sphere*

Solution of $\coth \hat{\kappa} - 1/\hat{\kappa} = a$

a	$\hat{\kappa}$	a	$\hat{\kappa}$
0·10	0·3018	**0·60**	2·401
·15	·4562	·62	2·549
·20	·6149	·64	2·711
·25	·7799	·66	2·888
·30	·9531	·68	3·085
0·35	1·137	**0·70**	3·304
·40	1·336	·72	3·551
·45	1·554	·74	3·832
·50	1·797	·76	4·158
·55	2·074	·78	4·541
		·80	4·998

For $a < 0.10$, $\hat{\kappa} \simeq 3a$.
For $a > 0.80$, $\hat{\kappa} \simeq 1/(1-a)$.

Table 64. *Percentage points of $S = \sum_i (\cos^2 \theta_i)/N$ (on sphere)*

Sample size N	Lower tail (per cent) 0·5	1·0	2·5	5·0	10·0	Upper tail (per cent) 10·0	5·0	2·5	1·0	0·5
3	0·015	0·024	0·044	0·070	0·111	0·569	0·639	0·697	0·761	0·801
4	·032	·045	·071	·101	·142	·534	·594	·641	·703	·740
5	·049	·065	·094	·124	·164	·512	·565	·611	·663	·697
6	0·066	0·083	0·113	0·142	0·180	0·495	0·544	0·585	0·633	0·665
7	·081	·098	·128	·156	·190	·483	·527	·566	·610	·640
8	·094	·111	·140	·168	·200	·472	·514	·550	·592	·620
9	·105	·123	·150	·176	·207	·464	·503	·537	·577	·603
10	·115	·133	·159	·184	·214	·457	·494	·526	·564	·589
12	0·132	0·148	0·173	0·196	0·224	0·446	0·480	0·509	0·543	0·566
14	·145	·160	·185	·206	·232	·438	·468	·495	·527	·548
16	·155	·171	·194	·214	·239	·431	·459	·485	·514	·534
18	·165	·179	·201	·221	·244	·425	·452	·476	·503	·522
20	·173	·187	·208	·226	·249	·420	·446	·468	·494	·512
25	0·188	0·201	0·220	0·237	0·258	0·411	0·434	0·454	0·477	0·493
30	·200	·212	·230	·246	·264	·404	·425	·443	·464	·479
35	·210	·221	·237	·252	·269	·399	·418	·435	·454	·467
40	·217	·228	·243	·257	·273	·394	·412	·428	·446	·459
45	·223	·232	·248	·261	·277	·391	·408	·422	·440	·451
50	0·229	0·238	0·253	0·265	0·280	0·388	0·404	0·418	0·434	0·445
60	·238	·246	·259	·271	·284	·383	·398	·410	·425	·435
70	·244	·253	·265	·275	·288	·379	·393	·404	·418	·427
80	·250	·258	·269	·279	·291	·376	·389	·400	·412	·421
90	·255	·262	·273	·282	·293	·374	·386	·396	·408	·416
100	·258	·265	·276	·285	·295	·372	·383	·393	·404	·412

Table 65. *Lower tail percentage points for $S_{\min}$ and upper tail for $S_{\max}$ (on sphere)*

(For $N > 100$, use the approximation $0.3333 + b/\sqrt{N}$, where b is given in the last row)

N	$S_{\min}$: lower tail (per cent) 1·0	2·5	5·0	10·0	$S_{\max}$: upper tail (per cent) 10·0	5·0	2·5	1·0
5	0·007	0·011	0·019	0·031	0·714	0·751	0·784	0·821
6	·016	·024	·034	·050	·678	·712	·743	·779
7	·026	·038	·050	·067	·651	·685	·712	·746
8	·037	·051	·064	·081	·630	·662	·687	·718
9	·048	·062	·075	·093	·610	·641	·667	·694
10	·058	·073	·087	·105	·596	·625	·650	·677
12	0·076	0·091	0·106	0·123	0·574	0·598	0·621	0·648
14	·091	·107	·120	·137	·554	·578	·599	·623
16	·103	·120	·133	·150	·538	·559	·581	·604
18	·114	·131	·144	·158	·526	·544	·566	·587
20	·124	·140	·152	·167	·515	·535	·553	·575
25	·144	·158	·170	·184	·496	·512	·530	·550
30	0·160	0·172	0·184	0·196	0·479	0·495	0·510	0·528
40	·183	·192	·203	·214	·459	·473	·487	·501
50	·198	·207	·216	·227	·447	·460	·471	·484
60	·208	·217	·226	·235	·438	·449	·458	·470
70	·216	·226	·234	·243	·429	·439	·448	·461
80	·223	·231	·239	·248	·423	·432	·441	·452
100	·233	·242	·248	·257	·413	·422	·430	·440
b	−1·038	−0·948	−0·874	−0·788	0·788	0·874	0·948	1·038

Table 66. Coefficients B_2, B_3, B_4 for Bessel interpolation formula

p	B_2 −		B_3 ±	B_4 +	p	p	B_2 −		B_3 ±	B_4 +	p
0.000	0.000000		0.00000	0.0000	1.000	0.050	0.011875		0.00356	0.0020	0.950
.001	250	250	08	0	0.999	.051	12100	225	362	21	.949
.002	499	249	17	1	.998	.052	12324	224	368	21	.948
.003	748	249	25	1	.997	.053	12548	224	374	21	.947
.004	996	248	33	2	.996	.054	12771	223	380	22	.946
		248						223			
0.005	0.001244		0.00041	0.0002	0.995	0.055	0.012994		0.00385	0.0022	0.945
.006	1491	247	49	2	.994	.056	13216	222	391	23	.944
.007	1738	247	57	3	.993	.057	13438	222	397	23	.943
.008	1984	246	65	3	.992	.058	13659	221	402	23	.942
.009	2230	246	73	4	.991	.059	13880	221	408	24	.941
		245						220			
0.010	0.002475		0.00081	0.0004	0.990	0.060	0.014100		0.00414	0.0024	0.940
.011	2720	245	089	5	.989	.061	14320	220	419	25	.939
.012	2964	244	096	5	.988	.062	14539	219	425	25	.938
.013	3208	244	104	5	.987	.063	14758	219	430	25	.937
.014	3451	243	112	6	.986	.064	14976	218	435	26	.936
		243						218			
0.015	0.003694		0.00119	0.0006	0.985	0.065	0.015194		0.00441	0.0026	0.935
.016	3936	242	127	7	.984	.066	15411	217	446	26	.934
.017	4178	242	135	7	.983	.067	15628	217	451	27	.933
.018	4419	241	142	7	.982	.068	15844	216	456	27	.932
019	4660	241	149	8	.981	.069	16060	216	461	28	.931
		240						215			
0.020	0.004900		0.00157	0.0008	0.980	0.070	0.016275		0.00467	0.0028	0.930
.021	5140	240	164	09	.979	.071	16490	215	472	28	.929
.022	5379	239	171	09	.978	.072	16704	214	477	29	.928
.023	5618	239	179	09	.977	.073	16918	214	482	29	.927
.024	5856	238	186	10	.976	.074	17131	213	487	30	.926
		238						213			
0.025	0.006094		0.00193	0.0010	0.975	0.075	0.017344		0.00491	0.0030	0.925
.026	6331	237	200	11	.974	.076	17556	212	496	30	.924
.027	6568	237	207	11	.973	.077	17768	212	501	31	.923
.028	6804	236	214	11	.972	.078	17979	211	506	31	.922
.029	7040	236	221	12	.971	.079	18190	211	511	31	.921
		235						210			
0.030	0.007275		0.00228	0.0012	0.970	0.080	0.018400		0.00515	0.0032	0.920
.031	7510	235	235	13	.969	.081	18610	210	520	32	.919
.032	7744	234	242	13	.968	.082	18819	209	524	33	.918
.033	7978	234	248	14	.967	.083	19028	209	529	33	.917
.034	8211	233	255	14	.966	.084	19236	208	533	33	.916
		233						208			
0.035	0.008444		0.00262	0.0014	0.965	0.085	0.019444		0.00538	0.0034	0.915
.036	8676	232	268	15	.964	.086	19651	207	542	34	.914
.037	8908	232	275	15	.963	.087	19858	207	547	34	.913
.038	9139	231	281	16	.962	.088	20064	206	551	35	.912
.039	9370	231	288	16	.961	.089	20270	206	555	35	.911
		230						205			
0.040	0.009600		0.00294	0.0016	0.960	0.090	0.020475		0.00560	0.0036	0.910
.041	09830	230	301	17	.959	.091	20680	205	564	36	.909
.042	10059	229	307	17	.958	.092	20884	204	568	36	.908
.043	10288	229	313	17	.957	.093	21088	204	572	37	.907
.044	10516	228	320	18	.956	.094	21291	203	576	37	.906
		228						203			
0.045	0.010744		0.00326	0.0018	0.955	0.095	0.021494		0.00580	0.0037	0.905
.046	10971	227	332	19	.954	.096	21696	202	584	38	.904
.047	11198	227	338	19	.953	.097	21898	202	588	38	.903
.048	11424	226	344	19	.952	.098	22099	201	592	38	.902
.049	11650	226	350	20	.951	.099	22300	201	596	39	.901
		225						200			
0.050	0.011875		0.00356	0.0020	0.950	0.100	0.022500		0.00600	0.0039	0.900

Table 66 (continued). Coefficients B_2, B_3, B_4 for Bessel interpolation formula

p	B_2 (−)	B_3 (±)	B_4 (+)	p	p	B_2 (−)	B_3 (±)	B_4 (+)	p
0.100	0.022500	0.00600	0.0039	0.900	0.150	0.031875	0.00744	0.0057	0.850
.101	22700 _200_	604	40	.899	.151	32050 _175_	746	57	.849
.102	22899 _199_	608	40	.898	.152	32224 _174_	748	57	.848
.103	23098 _199_	611	40	.897	.153	32398 _174_	749	57	.847
.104	23296 _198_	615	41	.896	.154	32571 _173_	751	58	.846
0.105	0.023494 _198_	0.00619	0.0041	0.895	0.155	0.032744 _173_	0.00753	0.0058	0.845
.106	23691 _197_	622	41	.894	.156	32916 _172_	755	58	.844
.107	23888 _197_	626	42	.893	.157	33088 _172_	757	59	.843
.108	24084 _196_	629	42	.892	.158	33259 _171_	758	59	.842
.109	24280 _196_	633	42	.891	.159	33430 _171_	760	59	.841
0.110	0.024475 _195_	0.00636	0.0043	0.890	0.160	0.033600 _170_	0.00762	0.0060	0.840
.111	24670 _195_	640	43	.889	.161	33770 _170_	763	60	.839
.112	24864 _194_	643	44	.888	.162	33939 _169_	765	60	.838
.113	25058 _194_	646	44	.887	.163	34108 _169_	766	61	.837
.114	25251 _193_	650	44	.886	.164	34276 _168_	768	61	.836
0.115	0.025444 _193_	0.00653	0.0045	0.885	0.165	0.034444 _168_	0.00769	0.0061	0.835
.116	25636 _192_	656	45	.884	.166	34611 _167_	771	62	.834
.117	25828 _192_	659	45	.883	.167	34778 _167_	772	62	.833
.118	26019 _191_	663	46	.882	.168	34944 _166_	773	62	.832
.119	26210 _191_	666	46	.881	.169	35110 _166_	775	63	.831
0.120	0.026400 _190_	0.00669	0.0046	0.880	0.170	0.035275 _165_	0.00776	0.0063	0.830
.121	26590 _190_	672	47	.879	.171	35440 _165_	777	63	.829
.122	26779 _189_	675	47	.878	.172	35604 _164_	779	64	.828
.123	26968 _189_	678	47	.877	.173	35768 _164_	780	64	.827
.124	27156 _188_	681	48	.876	.174	35931 _163_	781	64	.826
0.125	0.027344 _188_	0.00684	0.0048	0.875	0.175	0.036094 _163_	0.00782	0.0064	0.825
.126	27531 _187_	686	48	.874	.176	36256 _162_	783	65	.824
.127	27718 _187_	689	49	.873	.177	36418 _162_	784	65	.823
.128	27904 _186_	692	49	.872	.178	36579 _161_	785	65	.822
.129	28090 _186_	695	49	.871	.179	36740 _161_	786	66	.821
0.130	0.028275 _185_	0.00697	0.0050	0.870	0.180	0.036900 _160_	0.00787	0.0066	0.820
.131	28460 _185_	700	50	.869	.181	37060 _160_	788	66	.819
.132	28644 _184_	703	50	.868	.182	37219 _159_	789	67	.818
.133	28828 _184_	705	51	.867	.183	37378 _159_	790	67	.817
.134	29011 _183_	708	51	.866	.184	37536 _158_	791	67	.816
0.135	0.029194 _183_	0.00710	0.0051	0.865	0.185	0.037694 _158_	0.00792	0.0068	0.815
.136	29376 _182_	713	52	.864	.186	37851 _157_	792	68	.814
.137	29558 _182_	715	52	.863	.187	38008 _157_	793	68	.813
.138	29739 _181_	718	53	.862	.188	38164 _156_	794	68	.812
.139	29920 _181_	720	53	.861	.189	38320 _156_	794	69	.811
0.140	0.030100 _180_	0.00722	0.0053	0.860	0.190	0.038475 _155_	0.00795	0.0069	0.810
.141	30280 _180_	725	54	.859	.191	38630 _155_	796	69	.809
.142	30459 _179_	727	54	.858	.192	38784 _154_	796	70	.808
.143	30638 _179_	729	54	.857	.193	38938 _154_	797	70	.807
.144	30816 _178_	731	55	.856	.194	39091 _153_	797	70	.806
0.145	0.030994 _178_	0.00734	0.0055	0.855	0.195	0.039244 _153_	0.00798	0.0071	.305
.146	31171 _177_	736	55	.854	.196	39396 _152_	798	71	.804
.147	31348 _177_	738	56	.853	.197	39548 _152_	799	71	.803
.148	31524 _176_	740	56	.852	.198	39699 _151_	799	71	.802
.149	31700 _176_	742	56	.851	.199	39850 _151_	800	72	.801
0.150	0.031875 _175_	0.00744	0.0057	0.850	0.200	0.040000 _150_	0.00800	0.0072	0.800

Table 66 (*continued*)

p	B_2 −		B_3 ±	B_4 +	p	p	B_2 −		B_3 ±	B_4 +	p
0·200	0·040000	150	0·00800	0·0072	0·800	0·250	0·046875	125	0·00781	0·0085	0·750
·201	40150	149	800	72	·799	·251	47000	124	780	86	·749
·202	40299	149	801	73	·798	·252	47124	124	779	86	·748
·203	40448	148	801	73	·797	·253	47248	123	778	86	·747
·204	40596	148	801	73	·796	·254	47371	123	777	86	·746
0·205	0·040744	147	0·00801	0·0073	0·795	0·255	0·047494	122	0·00776	0·0087	0·745
·206	40891	147	801	74	·794	·256	47616	122	775	87	·744
·207	41038	146	802	74	·793	·257	47738	121	773	87	·743
·208	41184	146	802	74	·792	·258	47859	121	772	87	·742
·209	41330	145	802	75	·791	·259	47980	120	771	88	·741
0·210	0·041475	145	0·00802	0·0075	0·790	0·260	0·048100	120	0·00770	0·0088	0·740
·211	41620	144	802	75	·789	·261	48220	119	768	88	·739
·212	41764	144	802	75	·788	·262	48339	119	767	88	·738
·213	41908	143	802	76	·787	·263	48458	118	766	89	·737
·214	42051	143	802	76	·786	·264	48576	118	764	89	·736
0·215	0·042194	142	0·00802	0·0076	0·785	0·265	0·048694	117	0·00763	0·0089	0·735
·216	42336	142	802	77	·784	·266	48811	117	761	89	·734
·217	42478	141	801	77	·783	·267	48928	116	760	90	·733
·218	42619	141	801	77	·782	·268	49044	116	759	90	·732
·219	42760	140	801	77	·781	·269	49160	115	757	90	·731
0·220	0·042900	140	0·00801	0·0078	0·780	0·270	0·049275	115	0·00756	0·0090	0·730
·221	43040	139	801	78	·779	·271	49390	114	754	90	·729
·222	43179	139	800	78	·778	·272	49504	114	752	91	·728
·223	43318	138	800	78	·777	·273	49618	113	751	91	·727
·224	43456	138	800	79	·776	·274	49731	113	749	91	·726
0·225	0·043594	137	0·00799	0·0079	0·775	0·275	0·049844	112	0·00748	0·0091	0·725
·226	43731	137	799	79	·774	·276	49956	112	746	92	·724
·227	43868	136	798	80	·773	·277	50068	111	744	92	·723
·228	44004	136	798	80	·772	·278	50179	111	743	92	·722
·229	44140	135	797	80	·771	·279	50290	110	741	92	·721
0·230	0·044275	135	0·00797	0·0080	0·770	0·280	0·050400	110	0·00739	0·0092	0·720
·231	44410	134	796	81	·769	·281	50510	109	737	93	·719
·232	44544	134	796	81	·768	·282	50619	109	736	93	·718
·233	44678	133	795	81	·767	·283	50728	108	734	93	·717
·234	44811	133	795	81	·766	·284	50836	108	732	93	·716
0·235	0·044944	132	0·00794	0·0082	0·765	0·285	0·050944	107	0·00730	0·0094	0·715
·236	45076	132	793	82	·764	·286	51051	107	728	94	·714
·237	45208	131	793	82	·763	·287	51158	106	726	94	·713
·238	45339	131	792	82	·762	·288	51264	106	725	94	·712
·239	45470	130	791	83	·761	·289	51370	105	723	94	·711
0·240	0·045600	130	0·00790	0·0083	0·760	0·290	0·051475	105	0·00721	0·0095	0·710
·241	45730	129	790	83	·759	·291	51580	104	719	95	·709
·242	45859	129	789	83	·758	·292	51684	104	717	95	·708
·243	45988	128	788	84	·757	·293	51788	103	715	95	·707
·244	46116	128	787	84	·756	·294	51891	103	713	95	·706
0·245	0·046244	127	0·00786	0·0084	0·755	0·295	0·051994	102	0·00711	0·0096	0·705
·246	46371	127	785	84	·754	·296	52096	102	709	96	·704
·247	46498	126	784	85	·753	·297	52198	101	706	96	·703
·248	46624	126	783	85	·752	·298	52299	101	704	96	·702
·249	46750	125	782	85	·751	·299	52400	100	702	96	·701
0·250	0·046875		0·00781	0·0085	0·750	0·300	0·052500		0·00700	0·0097	0·700

Table 66 (continued). Coefficients B_2, B_3, B_4 for Bessel interpolation formula

p	B_2 (−)		B_3 (±)	B_4 (+)	p
0·300	0·052500		0·00700	0·0097	0·700
·301	52600	100	698	97	·699
·302	52699	99	696	97	·698
·303	52798	99	693	97	·697
·304	52896	98	691	97	·696
0·305	0·052994	98	0·00689	0·0098	0·695
·306	53091	97	687	98	·694
·307	53188	97	684	98	·693
·308	53284	96	682	98	·692
·309	53380	96	680	98	·691
0·310	0·053475	95	0·00677	0·0099	0·690
·311	53570	95	675	99	·689
·312	53664	94	673	99	·688
·313	53758	94	670	99	·687
·314	53851	93	668	99	·686
0·315	0·053944	93	0·00665	0·0100	0·685
·316	54036	92	663	100	·684
·317	54128	92	660	100	·683
·318	54219	91	658	100	·682
·319	54310	91	655	100	·681
0·320	0·054400	90	0·00653	0·0101	0·680
·321	54490	90	650	101	·679
·322	54579	89	648	101	·678
·323	54668	89	645	101	·677
·324	54756	88	642	101	·676
0·325	0·054844	88	0·00640	0·0101	0·675
·326	54931	87	637	102	·674
·327	55018	87	635	102	·673
·328	55104	86	632	102	·672
·329	55190	86	629	102	·671
0·330	0·055275	85	0·00626	0·0102	0·670
·331	55360	85	624	102	·669
·332	55444	84	621	103	·668
·333	55528	84	618	103	·667
·334	55611	83	615	103	·666
0·335	0·055694	83	0·00613	0·0103	0·665
·336	55776	82	610	103	·664
·337	55858	82	607	103	·663
·338	55939	81	604	104	·662
·339	56020	81	601	104	·661
0·340	0·056100	80	0·00598	0·0104	0·660
·341	56180	80	596	104	·659
·342	56259	79	593	104	·658
·343	56338	79	590	104	·657
·344	56416	78	587	105	·656
0·345	0·056494	78	0·00584	0·0105	0·655
·346	56571	77	581	105	·654
·347	56648	77	578	105	·653
·348	56724	76	575	105	·652
·349	56800	76	572	105	·651
0·350	0·056875	75	0·00569	0·0106	0·650

p	B_2 (−)		B_3 (±)	B_4 (+)	p
0·350	0·056875		0·00569	0·0106	0·650
·351	56950	75	566	106	·649
·352	57024	74	563	106	·648
·353	57098	74	560	106	·647
·354	57171	73	556	106	·646
0·355	0·057244	73	0·00553	0·0106	0·645
·356	57316	72	550	106	·644
·357	57388	72	547	107	·643
·358	57459	71	544	107	·642
·359	57530	71	541	107	·641
0·360	0·057600	70	0·00538	0·0107	0·640
·361	57670	70	534	107	·639
·362	57739	69	531	107	·638
·363	57808	69	528	107	·637
·364	57876	68	525	108	·636
0·365	0·057944	68	0·00521	0·0108	0·635
·366	58011	67	518	108	·634
·367	58078	67	515	108	·633
·368	58144	66	512	108	·632
·369	58210	66	508	108	·631
0·370	0·058275	65	0·00505	0·0108	0·630
·371	58340	65	502	109	·629
·372	58404	64	498	109	·628
·373	58468	64	495	109	·627
·374	58531	63	492	109	·626
0·375	0·058594	63	0·00488	0·0109	0·625
·376	58656	62	485	109	·624
·377	58718	62	481	109	·623
·378	58779	61	478	109	·622
·379	58840	61	475	110	·621
0·380	0·058900	60	0·00471	0·0110	0·620
·381	58960	60	468	110	·619
·382	59019	59	464	110	·618
·383	59078	59	461	110	·617
·384	59136	58	457	110	·616
0·385	0·059194	58	0·00454	0·0110	0·615
·386	59251	57	450	110	·614
·387	59308	57	447	111	·613
·388	59364	56	443	111	·612
·389	59420	56	440	111	·611
0·390	0·059475	55	0·00436	0·0111	0·610
·391	59530	55	433	111	·609
·392	59584	54	429	111	·608
·393	59638	54	425	111	·607
·394	59691	53	422	111	·606
0·395	0·059744	53	0·00418	0·0111	0·605
·396	59796	52	415	112	·604
·397	59848	52	411	112	·603
·398	59899	51	407	112	·602
·399	59950	51	404	112	·601
0·400	0·060000	50	0·00400	0·0112	0·600

Table 66 (continued)

p	B_2 −		B_3 ±	B_4 +	p	p	B_2 −		B_3 ±	B_4 +	p
0·400	0·060000		0·00400	0·0112	0·600	0·450	0·061875		0·00206	0·0116	0·550
		50						25			
·401	60050	49	396	112	·599	·451	61900	24	202	116	·549
·402	60099	49	393	112	·598	·452	61924	24	198	116	·548
·403	60148	48	389	112	·597	·453	61948	23	194	116	·547
·404	60196	48	385	112	·596	·454	61971	23	190	116	·546
0·405	0·060244	47	0·00382	0·0113	0·595	0·455	0·061994	22	0·00186	0·0116	0·545
·406	60291	47	378	113	·594	·456	62016	22	182	116	·544
·407	60338	46	374	113	·593	·457	62038	21	178	116	·543
·408	60384	46	370	113	·592	·458	62059	21	174	116	·542
·409	60430	45	367	113	·591	·459	62080	20	170	116	·541
0·410	0·060475	45	0·00363	0·0113	0·590	0·460	0·062100	20	0·00166	0·0116	0·540
·411	60520	44	359	113	·589	·461	62120	19	162	116	·539
·412	60564	44	355	113	·588	·462	62139	19	157	116	·538
·413	60608	43	352	113	·587	·463	62158	18	153	116	·537
·414	60651	43	348	113	·586	·464	62176	18	149	117	·536
0·415	0·060694	42	0·00344	0·0113	0·585	0·465	0·062194	17	0·00145	0·0117	0·535
·416	60736	42	340	114	·584	·466	62211	17	141	117	·534
·417	60778	41	336	114	·583	·467	62228	16	137	117	·533
·418	60819	41	332	114	·582	·468	62244	16	133	117	·532
·419	60860	40	329	114	·581	·469	62260	15	129	117	·531
0·420	0·060900	40	0·00325	0·0114	0·580	0·470	0·062275	15	0·00125	0·0117	0·530
·421	60940	39	321	114	·579	·471	62290	14	120	117	·529
·422	60979	39	317	114	·578	·472	62304	14	116	117	·528
·423	61018	38	313	114	·577	·473	62318	13	112	117	·527
·424	61056	38	309	114	·576	·474	62331	13	108	117	·526
0·425	0·061094	37	0·00305	0·0114	0·575	0·475	0·062344	12	0·00104	0·0117	0·525
·426	61131	37	302	114	·574	·476	62356	12	100	117	·524
·427	61168	36	298	114	·573	·477	62368	11	096	117	·523
·428	61204	36	294	114	·572	·478	62379	11	091	117	·522
·429	61240	35	290	115	·571	·479	62390	10	087	117	·521
0·430	0·061275	35	0·00286	0·0115	0·570	0·480	0·062400	10	0·00083	0·0117	0·520
·431	61310	34	282	115	·569	·481	62410	9	79	117	·519
·432	61344	34	278	115	·568	·482	62419	9	75	117	·518
·433	61378	33	274	115	·567	·483	62428	8	71	117	·517
·434	61411	33	270	115	·566	·484	62436	8	67	117	·516
0·435	0·061444	32	0·00266	0·0115	0·565	0·485	0·062444	7	0·00062	0·0117	0·515
·436	61476	32	262	115	·564	·486	62451	7	58	117	·514
·437	61508	31	258	115	·563	·487	62458	6	54	117	·513
·438	61539	31	254	115	·562	·488	62464	6	50	117	·512
·439	61570	30	250	115	·561	·489	62470	5	46	117	·511
0·440	0·061600	30	0·00246	0·0115	0·560	0·490	0·062475	5	0·00042	0·0117	0·510
·441	61630	29	242	115	·559	·491	62480	4	37	117	·509
·442	61659	29	238	115	·558	·492	62484	4	33	117	·508
·443	61688	28	234	115	·557	·493	62488	3	29	117	·507
·444	61716	28	230	116	·556	·494	62491	3	25	117	·506
0·445	0·061744	27	0·00226	0·0116	0·555	0·495	0·062494	2	0·00021	0·0117	0·505
·446	61771	27	222	116	·554	·496	62496	2	17	117	·504
·447	61798	26	218	116	·553	·497	62498	1	12	117	·503
·448	61824	26	214	116	·552	·498	62499	1	08	117	·502
·449	61850	25	210	116	·551	·499	62500	0	04	117	·501
0·450	0·061875		0·00206	0·0116	0·550	0·500	0·062500		0·00000	0·0117	0·500

377

Table 67. *Miscellaneous four-point Lagrangian interpolation coefficients*

A. *Coefficients L_{-1}, L_0, L_1, L_2 and common divisor L, for use when the arguments of tabular values are equally spaced*

$\downarrow \rightarrow$	L_{-1}	L_0	L_1	L_2	θ	Divisor L
0·05	-247	15561	819	-133	**0·95**	16000
·10	-57	1881	209	-33	**·90**	2000
·15	-629	14467	2553	-391	**·85**	16000
·20	-12	216	54	-8	**·80**	250
·25	-7	105	35	-5	**·75**	128
0·30	-119	1547	663	-91	**0·70**	2000
·35	-1001	11583	6237	-819	**·65**	16000
·40	-8	84	56	-7	**·60**	125
·45	-1023	9889	8091	-957	**·55**	16000
·50	-1	9	9	-1	**·50**	16
θ	L_2	L_1	L_0	L_{-1}	$\leftarrow \uparrow$	L

f_θ, $(0 < \theta < 1)$, is obtained by multiplying the tabular values f_{-1}, f_0, f_1 and f_2 by the factors L_{-1}, L_0, L_1 and L_2, summing and dividing by L.

B. *Coefficients for use as in Table 67 A, to obtain f_θ, $(1 < \theta < 2)$, in an end panel*

θ	L_{-1}	L_0	L_1	L_2	θ	Divisor L
1·1	33	-189	2079	77	**1·1**	2000
1·2	4	-22	132	11	**1·2**	125
1·3	91	-483	2093	299	**1·3**	2000
1·4	7	-36	126	28	**1·4**	125
1·5	1	-5	15	5	**1·5**	16
1·6	8	-39	104	52	**1·6**	125
1·7	119	-567	1377	1071	**1·7**	2000
1·8	6	-28	63	84	**1·8**	125
1·9	57	-261	551	1653	**1·9**	2000

C. *For use with Tables 24 and 51, where argument values are unequally spaced*

ν	**11**	**12**	**15**	**20**	Divisor L
13	-35	105	21	-1	90
14	-20	45	36	-1	60
16	8	-15	24	1	18
17	5	-9	9	1	6
18	20	-35	28	7	20
19	35	-60	42	28	45

The table gives the coefficients L_{-1}, L_0, L_1, L_2 and the common divisor L to be used in the formula

$$f(\nu = i) = \{L_{-1} f(\nu = 11) + L_0 f(\nu = 12) + L_1 f(\nu = 15) + L_2 f(\nu = 20)\}/L.$$

Column headings are the degrees of freedom of the four tabled values $f(\nu)$; row headings are the degrees of freedom of the interpolate at $\nu = i$.

D. *For use with Table 48, where argument values are unequally spaced*

m	**4**	**5**	**7**	**10**	Divisor L
6	-10	36	20	-1	45

m	**5**	**7**	**10**	**15**	Divisor L
8	-28	175	56	-3	200
9	-6	25	32	-1	50
11	8	-25	64	3	50
12	60	-175	280	35	200
13	9	-25	32	9	25
14	28	-75	84	63	100

This table is to be used in the same way as Table 67 C, except that the argument is now m, not ν. To determine $t_{\max}$ at $m = 6$, tabular values for $m = 4, 5, 7$ and 10 are used; for values at $m \geq 8$, the tabular values are those for $m = 5, 7, 10$ and 15.

Table 68. *Lagrangian coefficients for use with harmonic arguments in certain tables of percentage points (see p. 138 of introduction)*

Ordinary

	7 −	8 +	9 −	10 +	12 +	15 −	20 +
11	0·069 231	0·428 571	1·090 909	1·440 000	0·300 000	0·008 571	0·000 140

	8 −	9 +	10	12 +	15 +	20 −	24 +
13	0·171 875	0·777 778	1·100 000	1·336 805	0·162 963	0·006 250	0·000 579
14	0·223 214	0·969 697	1·285 714	1·041 667	0·507 936	0·011 364	0·000 992

	9 −	10 +	12 −	15 +	20 −	24 −	30 +
16	0·172 391	0·448 000	0·604 938	1·238 914	0·106 909	0·017 284	0·000 790
17	0·306 397	0·780 000	0·983 025	1·258 272	0·289 546	0·040 124	0·001 728
18	0·332 468	0·833 143	1·000 000	1·024 000	0·530 182	0·057 143	0·002 286
19	0·222 222	0·550 000	0·636 574	0·570 370	0·787 500	0·050 926	0·001 852

Harmonic

	10 +	12 −	15 +	20 +	24 −	30 +	40 −
16	0·003 052	0·039 551	0·692 139	0·769 043	0·632 813	0·247 192	0·039 062
17	0·003 097	0·037 459	0·409 711	1·213 958	0·856 212	0·315 162	0·048 257
18	0·001 996	0·022 993	0·201 189	1·341 259	0·735 777	0·251 486	0·037 160
19	0·000 818	0·009 091	0·069 601	1·237 345	0·407 263	0·126 547	0·017 957

(*Continued over page.*)

Table 68 (*continued*). *Lagrangian coefficients for use with harmonic arguments in certain tables of percentage points*

	Harmonic						
	12	15	20	24	30	40	60
	+	−	+	+	−	+	−
21	0·000 600	0·010 497	0·629 840	0·537 463	0·209 947	0·060 616	0·008 075
22	0·000 579	0·009 653	0·337 838	0·864 864	0·253 378	0·068 640	0·008 890
23	0·000 306	0·004 908	0·130 868	1·005 068	0·168 259	0·042 230	0·005 305

	15	20	24	30	40	60	120
	+	+	+	+	−	+	−
25	0·000 730	0·040 858	0·817 152	0·306 432	0·108 954	0·029 184	0·003 686
26	0·000 993	0·050 984	0·611 813	0·573 575	0·174 804	0·044 986	0·005 579
27	0·000 927	0·044 488	0·415 220	0·778 537	0·191 640	0·047 184	0·005 740
28	0·000 670	0·030 498	0·243 980	0·914 925	0·162 653	0·038 122	0·004 546
29	0·000 335	0·014 607	0·105 172	0·985 984	0·095 611	0·021 204	0·002 477

	20 (10)	24 (12)	30 (15)	40 (20)	60 (30)	120 (60)	∞ (∞)
	+	−	+	+	−	+	−
31 (15·5)	0·003 664	0·041 459	0·906 909	0·179 142	0·062 545	0·016 304	0·002 015
32 (16·0)	0·005 875	0·063 446	0·793 076	0·352 478	0·113 297	0·028 839	0·003 525
33 (16·5)	0·006 875	0·071 503	0·670 341	0·510 736	0·148 964	0·036 984	0·004 469
34 (17·0)	0·006 948	0·070 033	0·547 129	0·648 450	0·168 348	0·040 717	0·004 863
35 (17·5)	0·006 358	0·062 423	0·429 158	0·762 947	0·171 663	0·040 391	0·004 768
36 (18·0)	0·005 335	0·051 212	0·320 073	0·853 529	0·160 037	0·036 580	0·004 268
37 (18·5)	0·004 062	0·038 250	0·221 984	0·920 823	0·135 121	0·029 955	0·003 453
38 (19·0)	0·002 684	0·024 848	0·135 887	0·966 308	0·098 827	0·021 212	0·002 416
39 (19·5)	0·001 305	0·011 904	0·061 998	0·991 960	0·053 141	0·011 022	0·001 240
	−	+	−	+	+	−	+
41 (20·5)	0·001 182	0·010 511	0·050 764	0·992 724	0·058 780	0·011 310	0·001 241
42 (21·0)	0·002 210	0·019 448	0·091 161	0·972 384	0·121 548	0·022 440	0·002 431
43 (21·5)	0·003 069	0·026 748	0·122 164	0·941 117	0·186 839	0·033 000	0·003 529
44 (22·0)	0·003 754	0·032 432	0·144 787	0·900 900	0·253 378	0·042 674	0·004 505
45 (22·5)	0·004 268	0·036 580	0·160 037	0·853 529	0·320 073	0·051 212	0·005 335
46 (23·0)	0·004 619	0·039 302	0·168 878	0·800 606	0·386 006	0·058 422	0·006 005
47 (23·5)	0·004 819	0·040 733	0·172 219	0·743 549	0·450 419	0·064 169	0·006 506
48 (24·0)	0·004 883	0·041 016	0·170 899	0·683 594	0·512 695	0·068 359	0·006 836
49 (24·5)	0·004 824	0·040 293	0·165 679	0·621 808	0·572 346	0·070 939	0·006 995
50 (25·0)	0·004 659	0·038 707	0·157 248	0·559 104	0·628 992	0·071 885	0·006 989
51 (25·5)	0·004 402	0·036 392	0·146 218	0·496 255	0·682 351	0·071 202	0·006 824
52 (26·0)	0·004 068	0·033 473	0·133 132	0·433 910	0·732 223	0·068 915	0·006 509
53 (26·5)	0·003 669	0·030 065	0·118 464	0·372 604	0·778 476	0·065 067	0·006 055
54 (27·0)	0·003 220	0·026 273	0·102 630	0·312 777	0·821 038	0·059 712	0·005 474
55 (27·5)	0·002 730	0·022 191	0·085 989	0·254 781	0·859 886	0·052 916	0·004 777
56 (28·0)	0·002 210	0·017 901	0·068 849	0·198 897	0·895 035	0·044 752	0·003 978
57 (28·5)	0·001 669	0·013 477	0·051 474	0·145 339	0·926 536	0·035 297	0·003 088
58 (29·0)	0·001 116	0·008 983	0·034 088	0·094 268	0·954 463	0·024 631	0·002 121
59 (29·5)	0·000 558	0·004 475	0·016 878	0·045 797	0·978 914	0·012 838	0·001 088
	+	−	+	−	+	+	−
61 (30·5)	0·000 552	0·004 402	0·016 417	0·043 083	1·017 846	0·013 801	0·001 131
62 (31·0)	0·001 093	0·008 695	0·032 268	0·083 441	1·032 585	0·028 485	0·002 295
63 (31·5)	0·001 619	0·012 854	0·047 471	0·121 085	1·044 357	0·043 973	0·003 481
64 (32·0)	0·002 128	0·016 853	0·061 959	0·156 045	1·053 303	0·060 189	0·004 681
65 (32·5)	0·002 616	0·020 675	0·075 683	0·188 368	1·059 570	0·077 060	0·005 886
66 (33·0)	0·003 082	0·024 304	0·088 608	0·218 113	1·063 300	0·094 516	0·007 089
67 (33·5)	0·003 524	0·027 730	0·100 709	0·245 348	1·064 636	0·112 490	0·008 281
68 (34·0)	0·003 940	0·030 945	0·111 971	0·270 151	1·063 721	0·130 919	0·009 455
69 (34·5)	0·004 329	0·033 942	0·122 388	0·292 605	1·060 692	0·149 745	0·010 607

Table 68 (*continued*)

	Harmonic						
	20 (10) +	24 (12) −	30 (15) +	40 (20) −	60 (30) +	120 (60) +	∞ (∞) −
70 (35·0)	0·004 692	0·036 719	0·131 960	0·312 795	1·055 683	0·168 909	0·011 730
71 (35·5)	0·005 027	0·039 275	0·140 696	0·330 812	1·048 823	0·188 360	0·012 819
72 (36·0)	0·005 335	0·041 610	0·148 605	0·346 746	1·040 238	0·208 048	0·013 870
73 (36·5)	0·005 615	0·043 725	0·155 705	0·360 690	1·030 048	0·227 925	0·014 878
74 (37·0)	0·005 867	0·045 623	0·162 013	0·372 737	1·018 370	0·247 951	0·015 841
75 (37·5)	0·006 093	0·047 309	0·167 552	0·382 976	1·005 312	0·268 083	0·016 755
76 (38·0)	0·006 292	0·048 787	0·172 345	0·391 499	0·990 981	0·288 285	0·017 617
77 (38·5)	0·006 465	0·050 062	0·176 416	0·398 393	0·975 477	0·308 523	0·018 426
78 (39·0)	0·006 613	0·051 141	0·179 793	0·403 745	0·958 894	0·328 764	0·019 178
79 (39·5)	0·006 736	0·052 030	0·182 502	0·407 639	0·941 324	0·348 979	0·019 872
80 (40·0)	0·006 836	0·052 734	0·184 570	0·410 156	0·922 851	0·369 141	0·020 508
81 (40·5)	0·006 912	0·053 262	0·186 027	0·411 376	0·903 557	0·389 225	0·021 083
82 (41·0)	0·006 967	0·053 621	0·186 898	0·411 373	0·883 518	0·409 208	0·021 597
83 (41·5)	0·007 000	0·053 816	0·187 212	0·410 223	0·862 805	0·429 071	0·022 049
84 (42·0)	0·007 012	0·053 855	0·186 997	0·407 993	0·841 486	0·448 793	0·022 440
85 (42·5)	0·007 005	0·053 746	0·186 279	0·404 753	0·819 625	0·468 357	0·022 767
86 (43·0)	0·006 980	0·053 495	0·185 083	0·400 567	0·797 283	0·487 749	0·023 033
87 (43·5)	0·006 936	0·053 110	0·183 437	0·395 496	0·774 514	0·506 954	0·023 235
88 (44·0)	0·006 875	0·052 596	0·181 366	0·389 600	0·751 371	0·525 960	0·023 376
89 (44·5)	0·006 798	0·051 961	0·178 892	0·382 934	0·727 905	0·544 755	0·023 455
90 (45·0)	0·006 706	0·051 212	0·176 040	0·375 552	0·704 161	0·563 329	0·023 472
91 (45·5)	0·006 600	0·050 354	0·172 833	0·367 506	0·680 182	0·581 673	0·023 428
92 (46·0)	0·006 479	0·049 393	0·169 293	0·358 843	0·656 009	0·599 780	0·023 325
93 (46·5)	0·006 346	0·048 337	0·165 440	0·349 609	0·631 680	0·617 642	0·023 162
94 (47·0)	0·006 200	0·047 190	0·161 295	0·339 848	0·607 229	0·635 254	0·022 940
95 (47·5)	0·006 043	0·045 959	0·156 878	0·329 602	0·582 689	0·652 611	0·022 660
96 (48·0)	0·005 875	0·044 647	0·152 207	0·318 909	0·558 090	0·669 708	0·022 324
97 (48·5)	0·005 696	0·043 262	0·147 299	0·307 806	0·533 462	0·686 542	0·021 931
98 (49·0)	0·005 509	0·041 806	0·142 173	0·296 330	0·508 829	0·703 109	0·021 484
99 (49·5)	0·005 312	0·040 287	0·136 844	0·284 511	0·484 217	0·719 408	0·020 983
100 (50·0)	0·005 107	0·038 707	0·131 328	0·272 384	0·459 648	0·735 437	0·020 429
101 (50·5)	0·004 894	0·037 072	0·125 640	0·259 976	0·435 143	0·751 194	0·019 823
102 (51·0)	0·004 675	0·035 385	0·119 793	0·247 316	0·410 721	0·766 679	0·019 167
103 (51·5)	0·004 448	0·033 651	0·113 802	0·234 429	0·386 400	0·781 891	0·018 461
104 (52·0)	0·004 216	0·031 873	0·107 680	0·221 342	0·362 196	0·796 831	0·017 708
105 (52·5)	0·003 978	0·030 056	0·101 437	0·208 077	0·338 125	0·811 499	0·016 906
106 (53·0)	0·003 735	0·028 201	0·095 087	0·194 656	0·314 199	0·825 895	0·016 059
107 (53·5)	0·003 486	0·026 314	0·088 639	0·181 099	0·290 433	0·840 022	0·015 167
108 (54·0)	0·003 234	0·024 397	0·082 104	0·167 427	0·266 837	0·853 880	0·014 231
109 (54·5)	0·002 978	0·022 452	0·075 492	0·153 658	0·243 423	0·867 470	0·013 253
110 (55·0)	0·002 719	0·020 484	0·068 812	0·139 809	0·220 199	0·880 796	0·012 233
111 (55·5)	0·002 456	0·018 494	0·062 074	0·125 896	0·197 175	0·893 858	0·011 173
112 (56·0)	0·002 190	0·016 485	0·055 284	0·111 933	0·174 358	0·906 660	0·010 074
113 (56·5)	0·001 922	0·014 459	0·048 452	0·097 936	0·151 755	0·919 203	0·008 937
114 (57·0)	0·001 651	0·012 420	0·041 584	0·083 918	0·129 374	0·931 491	0·007 762
115 (57·5)	0·001 379	0·010 368	0·034 688	0·069 891	0·107 219	0·943 525	0·006 552
116 (58·0)	0·001 106	0·008 307	0·027 770	0·055 866	0·085 295	0·955 309	0·005 307
177 (58·5)	0·000 831	0·006 238	0·020 837	0·041 854	0·063 608	0·966 845	0·004 029
118 (59·0)	0·000 554	0·004 162	0·013 894	0·027 867	0·042 161	0·978 137	0·002 717
119 (59·5)	0·000 278	0·002 083	0·006 947	0·013 913	0·020 957	0·989 188	0·001 374

Table 69. *Five-point Lagrangian coefficients, L_i ($i = 1, 2, ..., 5$) for interpolation between tabled percentage points*

Standard P-values for which x is tabled

→ ↓	·001	·0025	·005	·01	·025	Grid 1
·0015	0·300992	1·280742	− 0·879660	0·339684	− 0·041758	·9985
·002	0·076356	1·271386	− 0·501175	0·173593	− 0·020161	·998
·003	− 0·021913	0·707699	0·408803	− 0·105503	0·010914	·997
·004	− 0·016278	0·257308	0·877037	− 0·129895	0·011828	·996
						↑
Grid 1	·999	·9975	·995	·99	·975	←

→ ↓	·001	·005	·01	·025	·05	Grid 1 A
·0015	0·484430	1·810223	− 1·992997	0·938249	− 0·239905	·9985
·002	0·258454	2·169059	− 2·142048	0·952678	− 0·238152	·998
·003	0·079449	1·895151	− 1·394473	0·552436	− 0·132564	·997
·004	0·020576	1·417449	− 0·598543	0·208716	−0·048198	·996
						↑
Grid 1 A	·999	·995	·99	·975	·95	←

→ ↓	·0025	·005	·01	·025	·05	Grid 2
·003	0·554706	0·730128	− 0·384159	0·127983	− 0·028658	·997
·004	0·143656	1·115735	− 0·336894	0·098793	− 0·021289	·996
·006	− 0·043067	0·762403	0·337295	− 0·070767	0·014137	·994
·007	− 0·046041	0·519362	0·607230	− 0·099703	0·019153	·993
·008	− 0·033665	0·307094	0·801578	− 0·091969	0·016961	·992
·009	− 0·016724	0·134328	0·928578	− 0·056092	0·009910	·991
						↑
Grid 2	·9975	·995	·99	·975	·95	←

→ ↓	·005	·01	·025	·05	·10	Grid 3
·006	0·567662	0·649704	− 0·371893	0·190872	− 0·036346	·994
·007	0·311174	0·941211	− 0·421622	0·208091	− 0·038855	·993
·008	0·154870	1·045782	− 0·327352	0·155111	− 0·028411	·992
·009	0·058707	1·049891	− 0·173023	0·078539	− 0·014114	·991
·011	− 0·034781	0·922168	0·171012	− 0·070613	0·012114	·989
·012	− 0·054030	0·831426	0·329849	− 0·129158	0·021914	·988
·013	− 0·063117	0·736580	0·471900	− 0·174376	0·029012	·987
·014	− 0·065560	0·642793	0·595536	− 0·206441	0·033671	·986
						↑
Grid 3	·995	·99	·975	·95	·90	←

Interpolated value: $x_P = \sum\limits_{i=1}^{5} L_i x_{Pi}$

P-values for which *x* is required

382

Table 69 (*continued*)

Standard P-values for which x is tabled

$\rightarrow$ $\downarrow$	·005	·01	·025	·05	·10	Grid 3 (*cont.*)
·015	− 0·063709	0·553046	0·700728	− 0·226221	0·036156	·985
·016	− 0·059154	0·468985	0·788286	− 0·234885	0·036769	·984
·017	− 0·052984	0·391433	0·859431	− 0·233691	0·035811	·983
·018	− 0·045944	0·320702	0·915559	− 0·223881	0·033564	·982
·019	− 0·038547	0·256788	0·958099	− 0·206625	0·030285	·981
·020	− 0·031146	0·199495	0·988448	− 0·183001	0·026203	·980
·021	− 0·023977	0·148515	1·007920	− 0·153980	0·021521	·979
·022	− 0·017197	0·103477	1·017740	− 0·120437	0·016416	·978
·023	− 0·010906	0·063982	1·019029	− 0·083146	0·011041	·977
·024	− 0·005164	0·029623	1·012807	− 0·042798	0·005531	·976
·026	0·004576	− 0·025276	0·981441	0·044710	− 0·005451	·974
·027	0·008569	− 0·046574	0·957884	0·090858	− 0·010737	·973
·028	0·011995	− 0·064242	0·930004	0·138027	− 0·015784	·972
·029	0·014875	− 0·078607	0·898411	0·185849	− 0·020528	·971
·030	0·017237	− 0·089972	0·863651	0·234000	− 0·024916	·970
·031	0·019109	− 0·098620	0·826215	0·282196	− 0·028900	·969
·032	0·020523	− 0·104813	0·786546	0·330187	− 0·032442	·968
·033	0·021510	− 0·108792	0·745040	0·377751	− 0·035509	·967
·034	0·022103	− 0·110781	0·702056	0·424695	− 0·038072	·966
·035	0·022332	− 0·110987	0·657914	0·470848	− 0·040107	·965
·036	0·022228	− 0·109598	0·612904	0·516061	− 0·041596	·964
·037	0·021820	− 0·106790	0·567287	0·560204	− 0·042520	·963
·038	0·021137	− 0·102726	0·521296	0·603161	− 0·042869	·962
·039	0·020205	− 0·097552	0·475145	0·644832	− 0·042630	·961
·040	0·019051	− 0·091407	0·429022	0·685129	− 0·041795	·960
·041	0·017698	− 0·084416	0·383101	0·723976	− 0·040359	·959
·042	0·016170	− 0·076697	0·337536	0·761307	− 0·038316	·958
·043	0·014489	− 0·068356	0·292466	0·797065	− 0·035663	·957
·044	0·012674	− 0·059493	0·248017	0·831201	− 0·032399	·956
·045	0·010746	− 0·050199	0·204304	0·863672	− 0·028523	·955
·046	0·008722	− 0·040559	0·161427	0·894444	− 0·024035	·954
·047	0·006620	− 0·030649	0·119480	0·923485	− 0·018936	·953
·048	0·004456	− 0·020543	0·078545	0·950771	− 0·013229	·952
·049	0·002245	− 0·010306	0·038696	0·976282	− 0·006916	·951
·055	− 0·011284	0·050729	− 0·174282	1·091356	0·043481	·945
·060	− 0·021727	0·096286	− 0·312988	1·137078	0·101350	·940
·065	− 0·030341	0·132823	− 0·413081	1·137682	0·172917	·935
·070	− 0·036417	0·157748	− 0·473113	1·094325	0·257457	·930
·075	− 0·039455	0·169332	− 0·492635	1·008500	0·354258	·925
·080	− 0·039102	0·166447	− 0·471834	0·881850	0·462640	·920
·085	− 0·035115	0·148385	− 0·411290	0·716053	0·581967	·915
·090	− 0·027331	0·114734	− 0·311821	0·512765	0·711654	·910
·095	− 0·015646	0·065291	− 0·174384	0·273577	0·851162	·905
Grid 3	·995	·99	·975	·95	·90	$\uparrow$ $\leftarrow$

P-values for which *x* is required

Standard *P*-values for which *x* is tabled

P-values for which *x* is required

→ ↓	·05	·10	·20	·30	·40	Grid 4
·11	− 0·025356	0·859866	0·285176	− 0·160075	0·040390	·89
·12	− 0·036389	0·715509	0·530410	− 0·278173	0·068643	·88
·13	− 0·038757	0·577398	0·729257	− 0·352933	0·085036	·87
·14	− 0·036069	0·451048	0·881062	− 0·386880	0·090840	·86
·15	− 0·030654	0·339088	0·988157	− 0·384330	0·087740	·85
·16	− 0·024019	0·242443	1·054338	− 0·350307	0·077545	·84
·17	− 0·017136	0·161032	1·084042	− 0·289977	0·062039	·83
·18	− 0·010616	0·094186	1·081884	− 0·208368	0·042916	·82
·19	− 0·004835	0·040902	1·052415	− 0·110233	0·021751	·81
·21	0·003792	− 0·029781	0·928756	0·118236	− 0·021004	·79
·22	0·006523	− 0·049726	0·842540	0·240696	− 0·040033	·78
·23	0·008229	− 0·061108	0·744946	0·363889	− 0·055957	·77
·24	0·008982	− 0·065170	0·639329	0·484586	− 0·067727	·76
·25	0·008881	− 0·063114	0·528820	0·599780	− 0·074366	·75
·26	0·008042	− 0·056096	0·416352	0·706660	− 0·074958	·74
·27	0·006595	− 0·045228	0·304686	0·802579	− 0·068632	·73
·28	0·004676	− 0·031576	0·196433	0·885026	− 0·054559	·72
·29	0·002429	− 0·016169	0·094077	0·951604	− 0·031941	·71
Grid 4	·95	·90	·80	·70	·60	↑ ←

→ ↓	·025	·05	·10	·25	·50	Grid 4 A
·11	0·019030	− 0·118956	1·053062	0·052313	− 0·005448	·89
·12	0·035041	− 0·208698	1·071238	0·113604	− 0·011184	·88
·13	0·047586	− 0·272728	1·060658	0·181273	− 0·016790	·87
·14	0·056623	− 0·314473	1·026571	0·253217	− 0·021938	·86
·15	0·062314	− 0·337100	0·973423	0·327732	− 0·026370	·85
·16	0·064925	− 0·343451	0·904972	0·403432	− 0·029878	·84
·17	0·064766	− 0·336046	0·824397	0·479181	− 0·032298	·83
·18	0·062159	− 0·317104	0·734401	0·554039	− 0·033495	·82
·19	0·057421	− 0·288578	0·637290	0·627224	− 0·033357	·81
·20	0·050856	− 0·252188	0·535047	0·698075	− 0·031790	·80
·21	0·042750	− 0·209453	0·429389	0·766030	− 0·028714	·79
·22	0·033370	− 0·161724	0·321811	0·830601	− 0·024058	·78
·23	0·022967	− 0·110203	0·213629	0·891366	− 0·017759	·77
·24	0·011771	− 0·055970	0·106011	0·947945	− 0·009758	·76
Grid 4 A	·975	·95	·90	·75	·50	↑ ←

Interpolated value: $x_P = \sum\limits_{i=1}^{5} L_i x_{P_i}$

Table 69 (*continued*)

Standard P-values for which x is tabled

$\rightarrow$ $\downarrow$	·20	·30	·40	·50	·60	Grid 5
·31	− 0·013677	0·882770	0·187213	− 0·068138	0·011832	·69
·32	− 0·021677	0·761555	0·362771	− 0·123693	0·021044	·68
·33	− 0·025292	0·640453	0·522124	− 0·164686	0·027401	·67
·34	− 0·025611	0·522766	0·661855	− 0·189836	0·030826	·66
·35	− 0·023545	0·411123	0·779490	− 0·198441	0·031372	·65
·36	− 0·019855	0·307583	0·873362	− 0·190297	0·029207	·64
·37	− 0·015178	0·213721	0·942487	− 0·165627	0·024597	·63
·38	− 0·010037	0·130694	0·986474	− 0·125022	0·017892	·62
·39	− 0·004862	0·059295	1·005449	− 0·069407	0·009526	·61
·41	0·004278	− 0·047002	0·971131	0·081706	− 0·010112	·59
·42	0·007764	− 0·081777	0·920227	0·173960	− 0·020174	·58
·43	0·010311	− 0·104626	0·849030	0·274764	− 0·029481	·57
·44	0·011827	− 0·116069	0·759627	0·381880	− 0·037264	·56
·45	0·012266	− 0·116834	0·654435	0·492822	− 0·042689	·55
·46	0·011634	− 0·107851	0·536206	0·604861	− 0·044849	·54
·47	0·009977	− 0·090248	0·408027	0·715005	− 0·042762	·53
·48	0·007389	− 0·065350	0·273336	0·819996	− 0·035371	·52
·49	0·004004	− 0·034687	0·135931	0·916282	− 0·021530	·51

Grid 5	·80	·70	·60	·50	·40	$\uparrow$ $\leftarrow$

$\rightarrow$ $\downarrow$	·10	·25	·50	·75	·90	Grid 5A
·26	− 0·010954	0·958245	0·072343	− 0·023522	0·003889	·74
·27	− 0·019766	0·914347	0·143395	− 0·045424	0·007447	·73
·28	− 0·026729	0·868902	0·212727	− 0·065559	0·010658	·72
·29	− 0·032096	0·822408	0·279997	− 0·083820	0·013511	·71
·30	− 0·036083	0·775281	0·344931	− 0·100128	0·015999	·70
·31	− 0·038878	0·727872	0·407310	− 0·114426	0·018121	·69
·32	− 0·040641	0·680476	0·466963	− 0·126678	0·019879	·68
·33	− 0·041516	0·633346	0·523752	− 0·136858	0·021277	·67
·34	− 0·041625	0·586692	0·577567	− 0·144955	0·022321	·66
·35	− 0·041076	0·540699	0·628324	− 0·150965	0·023018	·65
·36	− 0·039967	0·495521	0·675956	− 0·154889	0·023379	·64
·37	− 0·038380	0·451292	0·720411	− 0·156736	0·023412	·63
·38	− 0·036391	0·408129	0·761651	− 0·156519	0·023130	·62
·39	− 0·034068	0·366130	0·799646	− 0·154251	0·022543	·61
·40	− 0·031469	0·325384	0·834372	− 0·149952	0·021664	·60
·41	− 0·028649	0·285967	0·865816	− 0·143640	0·020507	·59
·42	− 0·025656	0·247945	0·893964	− 0·135336	0·019084	·58
·43	− 0·022534	0·211378	0·918809	− 0·125063	0·017410	·57
·44	− 0·019322	0·176318	0·940347	− 0·112843	0·015500	·56
·45	− 0·016057	0·142814	0·958573	− 0·098699	0·013370	·55
·46	− 0·012772	0·110907	0·973487	− 0·082657	0·011035	·54
·47	− 0·009497	0·080638	0·985086	− 0·064739	0·008512	·53
·48	− 0·006259	0·052042	0·993372	− 0·004973	0·005819	·52
·49	− 0·003086	0·025152	0·998343	− 0·023385	0·002975	·51

Grid 5A	·90	·75	·50	·25	·10	$\uparrow$ $\leftarrow$

P-values for which *x* is required

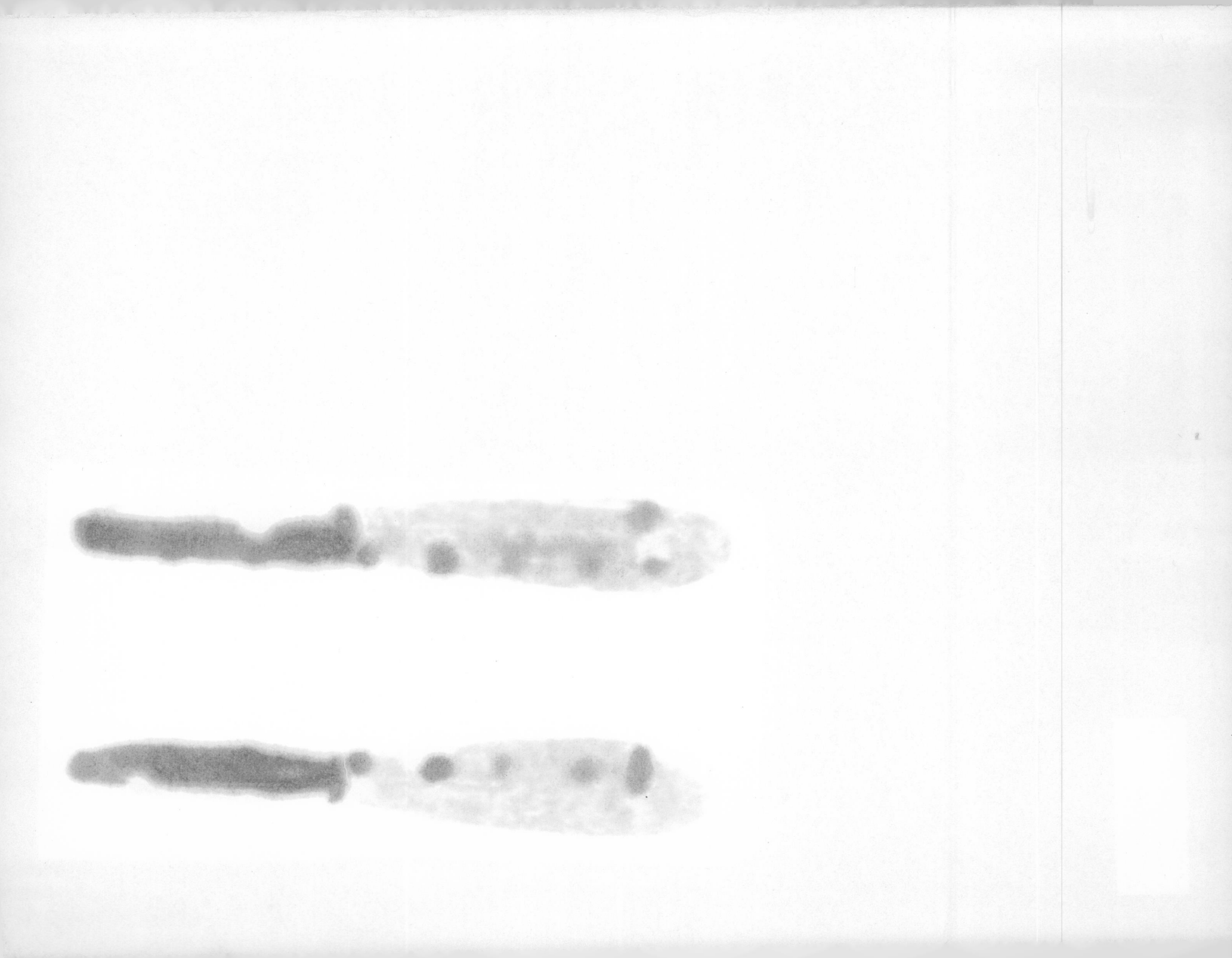